Revised Second Edition

Masterplots

1,801 Plot Stories and Critical Evaluations
of the World's Finest Literature

Revised Second Edition

Volume 5
Gcn – Hyp
2491 – 3110

Edited by
FRANK N. MAGILL

Story Editor, Revised Edition
DAYTON KOHLER

Consulting Editor, Revised Second Edition
LAURENCE W. MAZZENO

SALEM PRESS
Pasadena, California   Englewood Cliffs, New Jersey

Editor in Chief: Dawn P. Dawson

Consulting Editor: Laurence W. Mazzeno   *Managing Editor:* Christina J. Moose

Project Editors: Eric Howard   *Research Supervisor:* Jeffry Jensen

Juliane Brand   *Research:* Irene McDermott

Acquisitions Editor: Mark Rehn   *Proofreading Supervisor:* Yasmine A. Cordoba

Production Editor: Cynthia Breslin Beres   *Layout:* William Zimmerman

Library of Congress Cataloging-in-Publication Data

Masterplots / edited by Frank N. Magill; consulting editor, Laurence W. Mazzeno. — Rev. 2nd ed.

    p.   cm.

Expanded and updated version of the 1976 rev. ed.

Includes bibliographical references and indexes.

1. Literature—Stories, plots, etc. 2. Literature—History and criticism. I. Magill, Frank Northen, 1907-   . II. Mazzeno, Laurence W.

PN44.M33   1996

809—dc20   96-23382

ISBN 0-89356-084-7 (set)   CIP

ISBN 0-89356-089-8 (volume 5)

Revised Second Edition

First Printing

LIST OF TITLES IN VOLUME 5

MASTERPLOTS

LIST OF TITLES IN VOLUME 5

MASTERPLOTS

Revised Second Edition

THE "GENIUS"

Type of work: Novel
Author: Theodore Dreiser (1871-1945)
Type of plot: Naturalism
Time of plot: 1889-1914
Locale: Alexandria and Chicago, Illinois, and New York
First published: 1915

Principal characters:
> EUGENE WITLA, the "genius"
> THOMAS WITLA, his father, a sewing machine agent
> SYLVIA and
> MYRTLE, his sisters
> STELLA APPLETON, Eugene's first love
> ANGELA BLUE, a schoolteacher and later Eugene's wife
> MARGARET DUFF, a laundry worker and Eugene's first lover
> RUBY KENNY, an artist's model
> MIRIAM FINCH, a sculptor in New York
> CHRISTINA CHANNING, a singer in New York
> ANATOLE CHARLES, an art dealer
> FRIEDA ROTH, a young woman in Alexandria
> CARLOTTA WILSON, a gambler's wife
> DANIEL SUMMERFIELD, the head of an advertising agency
> OBADIAH KALVIN, the head of a publishing company
> MARSHALL P. COLFAX, a publisher
> FLORENCE J. WHITE, Eugene's associate and enemy
> MRS. EMILY DALE, a wealthy socialite friend of Eugene
> SUZANNE, her daughter
> MRS. JOHNS, a Christian Science practitioner

The Story:

Eugene Witla, a sensitive seventeen-year-old boy, lived with his parents and two sisters in Alexandria, Illinois. Eugene had little idea of what he wanted to do, although his aspirations were vaguely artistic. His father, a sewing machine agent and a respectable member of the middle class, got him a job setting type for the local newspaper. He fell in love with a local girl named Stella Appleton, but even this did not keep him from leaving the small town and going to Chicago to seek his fortune.

In Chicago, Eugene at first supported himself by moving stoves, driving a laundry wagon, and collecting for a furniture company. While at the laundry, he met the passionate young Margaret Duff and entered into his first real love affair. About this time, he also met a schoolteacher named Angela Blue, a fair-haired, beautiful young woman who represented everything fine and elegant to impressionable young Eugene.

Eugene began attending art classes at night at the Chicago Art Institute. He showed some talent, particularly in life drawing, for he seemed to have a special sensitivity in conveying the beauty of the human form. He met a model there, Ruby Kenny, who soon became his mistress. Ruby, like Margaret, was from the lower classes and made her charms easily available to men.

Eugene finally left them both, preferring the finer and more fragile beauty of Angela, to whom he became engaged before he left Chicago to seek his artistic fortune in New York.

There, Eugene painted powerful and realistic pictures of what he saw in the city. From time to time, he sold a few of his paintings, and after several years, he had become moderately successful. Some of the women he met, like Miriam Finch and Christina Channing, began to educate him in the well-read and knowledgeable polish of the New York art world. For a short time, he had a sophisticated affair with Christina that somewhat baffled him; despite his new polish and elegance, he still thought of Angela. Returning to the Middle West to visit her, he seduced her and then, feeling his responsibility, married her and took her back to New York. Angela felt that all her dreams of happiness had been fulfilled.

Eugene's work impressed Anatole Charles, the manager of a distinguished firm of art dealers in New York. Monsieur Charles held an exhibit which was a great success and gave Eugene a reputation as a rising young artist. Full of enthusiasm, he and Angela went to Paris. The works he showed when he returned were not as successful and were judged less fresh and unusual. While in Paris, Eugene had begun to suffer from a vague malaise and lack of energy and purpose. He did not realize at the time that his marriage was causing him to feel uneasy and restless.

Eugene and Angela returned to Alexandria for an inexpensive rest. While there, Eugene met eighteen-year-old Frieda Roth, whom he found all the more attractive because he was twenty-nine by this time, and Frieda represented a connection to youth and beauty. Angela was able to stop this relationship before it advanced further than a few kisses. Eugene and Angela left Alexandria and stayed at several resorts until their money ran out. Angela then returned to her parents, while Eugene returned to New York to reestablish his reputation as an artist.

Eugene was still restless, however, and found himself unable to paint. He took a job doing manual labor for the railroad in a town near New York. There he met and had a passionate affair with his landlady's married daughter, Carlotta Wilson. Angela heard of the affair and again reclaimed Eugene. They decided to try to start again in New York.

Eugene worked for a newspaper and then as art director for an advertising agency. When his superior there, Daniel Summerfield, broke his promises and failed to pay him adequately, Eugene left for another job with the advertising department of the *North American Weekly*, under the directorship of Obadiah Kalvin. Successful there, he moved to Philadelphia to accept a higher paying job as head of advertising for all books and publications directed by Marshall P. Colfax. When Eugene was made a vice president, the other vice president, Florence J. White, became jealous of Eugene.

Eugene became very successful, both financially and socially. His marriage was hollow, but both he and Angela accepted the situation and coped fairly well. Although Eugene had money enough to retire and go back to painting, he had been instilled with the desire for greater financial success and had lost the will to paint. His artistic lassitude was matched by the emotional emptiness of his marriage.

About this time, Eugene met Mrs. Emily Dale, a rich socialite. They exchanged visits and became friendly. One day, Mrs. Dale brought Suzanne, her eighteen-year-old daughter, to tea, and Eugene fell in love with her at first sight. All his yearning for beauty returned, and soon Eugene and Suzanne were meeting secretly. Although she was a cultured and sophisticated young woman, Suzanne was willing to enter into an affair with Eugene. Filled with romantic ideas about being an artist's mistress, she insisted on telling her mother of her plans, for she was sure that her mother would approve. However, Mrs. Dale did not approve, and Angela, when she learned of the affair, decided that the only way to hold Eugene was to have a baby, despite the fact that doctors had warned her against having children. Angela, who had become a

Christian Scientist, believed that her firm faith and will power would allow her to have a healthy child. Mrs. Dale took her daughter to Canada to take her away from Eugene. When he tried to follow Suzanne to Canada, Mrs. Dale put pressure on Florence J. White and threatened the firm with scandal, whereupon Eugene was fired from his job. Having lost both his job and Suzanne, Eugene returned to comfort Angela during her ordeal.

Angela died giving birth to a daughter, who was also named Angela. Eugene asked his sister Myrtle to come east to help him make a home for the child. In his desolation, Eugene began to read about Christian Science, but he failed to find comfort or salvation in its message.

When Eugene and Suzanne met by accident on the street two years later, they were both too self-conscious to acknowledge the other's presence. Living sanely with his daughter and Myrtle and her husband, Eugene began to paint again. He had several shows, was sponsored again by M. Charles, and again became a popular and fairly successful artist. He began to weave romantic dreams around his daughter, Angela, thinking of the time when she would grow up and they could search for beauty together. In spite of his new awareness of human beings' inability to control their fate, and of the delusions that belief in beauty or belief in Christian Science represented, Eugene's emotional impulse toward beauty remained strong, and he continued to dream impossible dreams for himself and his daughter.

Critical Evaluation:

The "Genius" is generally conceded to be the weakest of Theodore Dreiser's major novels, but critical opinion differs as to whether it is a magnificent failure or simply a failure. Its weaknesses are generally seen to derive from the fact that Dreiser was too subjectively involved with his artistic protagonist to clarify his ideas. Although all of Dreiser's writings contain many transcriptions of direct experience, *The "Genius"* chronicles traumatic events that were recent personal history. In many aspects, Witla's artistic career closely parallels Dreiser's own— impoverished youth, odd jobs, modest artistic success, nervous breakdown, restoration, financial success, monetary and professional collapse, and, finally, serious artistic endeavors. More important, in terms of Dreiser's emotional identification with the story, is the fact that Witla's marriage to Angela Blue—with all of its consequent disappointments, frustrations, hostilities, and psychic damage—is a thinly disguised rendering of his own drawn-out, agonized marriage to Sallie White.

If the extreme subjectivity of *The "Genius"* weakens the book artistically, however, it also makes it however a vital document to anyone interested in Dreiser's life and works. The novel focuses on the tensions among three fundamental human elements: the urge to artistic creation, the sexual drive, and the corrupting influence of material success. For all of its complexity, inconsistency, redundancy, and confusion, at the center of *The "Genius"*—and what gives the novel its redeeming strength—is Eugene Witla's prolonged and agonized attempt to reconcile those three forces.

In the opening segment of the book, Eugene is introduced to creative activity and sexuality almost simultaneously. His artistic impulse, like Dreiser's, is to portray life as realistically and graphically as possible. His vision of women, however, is idealistic: The perfect woman is beautiful, sensual, and "always eighteen." His sexual impulses are intensified by the fact that he seeks an impossibility and becomes increasingly frustrated in his effort to find that ideal— which recedes even further as he ages.

His situation is made more complicated and painful by his foolish marriage to Angela Blue, the one woman for whom he feels, at best, a lukewarm sexual attraction. Initially, Angela represents America's small-town, conservative, hypocritical morality, especially in sexual matters.

Her narrowness, provinciality, possessiveness, and domineering attitude toward Eugene frustrate both his artistic development and his personal fulfillment. When he begins to drift to other women, Angela becomes sexually aggressive in an attempt to save the marriage. In the novel's most absurd hypothesis, Dreiser ascribes Eugene's nervous breakdown to the excessive sexual activity Angela instigates.

Dreiser also blames Angela for Eugene's turn from artistic creativity to crass commercialism. It is at her prompting that Eugene puts his painting aside and becomes an advertising executive. It is suggested, therefore, that a curious alliance of sex, materialism, and middle-class morality have combined temporarily to suppress Eugene's creativity; his return to serious painting does not result from a repudiation of materialism but is the consequence, once again, of his sexual adventuring. Eugene's affair with the daughter of a rich and powerful socialite costs him his job, his fortune, and his social standing, but it also forces him back to the easel where he apparently regains all of his creative powers very quickly.

Dreiser demonstrates that even the strong-willed and talented are ultimately buffeted by forces over which they have little control. Despite his remarkable abilities and powerful drive, Eugene allows major decisions—whether to be an artist, to marry, to become a businessman, to return to painting—to be made for him by outside circumstances and internal impulses over which he chooses to exercise little conscious control. At the end of the book, there are hopeful hints—his painting, his "forgiveness" of Angela, his feelings for his daughter—but the final image is that of an aged and unreconciled artist who feels neither personal satisfaction nor social identification nor even a conviction that his own life and art have real value and meaning.

Bibliography:
Gerber, Philip L. *Theodore Dreiser Revisited*. New York: Twayne, 1992. Concludes that Dreiser while writing *The "Genius"* was too close to the work's autobiographical elements (his own failing marriage and frustrating editorial work during the years 1898-1910) to shape a convincing story about his hero's conflicting artistic, materialistic, and sexual desires.
Lundquist, James. *Theodore Dreiser*. New York: Frederick Ungar, 1974. Posits that in *The "Genius"* Dreiser begins to show an increased sympathy toward his characters, especially Witla, an artist struggling in a world that overvalues both material success and marital fidelity. Notes resemblances between Dreiser's cityscapes and Everett Shinn's paintings of the so-called Ashcan School.
Mencken, H. L. "A Literary Behemoth." In *Critical Essays on Theodore Dreiser*, edited by Donald Pizer. Boston: G. K. Hall, 1981. Reprint of Mencken's 1915 article, in which he rebukes Dreiser for piling on details in numbingly dull prose, but praises him for showing that spiritual corruption follows Witla's financial successes and that his inner conflicts add to his bitterness.
Swanberg, W. A. *Dreiser*. New York: Charles Scribner's Sons, 1965. Shows how thoroughly Dreiser based his main characters and episodes on his own acquaintances and experiences. Details efforts of the New York Society for the Suppression of Vice to censor Dreiser's alleged blasphemy and obscenity.
Warren, Robert Penn. *Homage to Theodore Dreiser*. New York: Random House, 1971. Castigates Dreiser for self-indulgence and self-vindication in *The "Genius"* and for naïvely believing that a collection of supposedly true details of his life would take on artistic form.

GEORGICS

Type of work: Poetry
Author: Vergil (Publius Vergilius Maro, 70-19 B.C.E.)
First transcribed: 37-29 B.C.E. (English translation, 1589)

Vergil's *Georgics*, a long poetic work in four sections, was written at the request of the poet's patron, Maecenas, to bolster the Emperor Augustus' agricultural policy. It was essential to the progress of the Roman nation that farming be seen as a worthy and patriotic occupation for soldiers returning from military campaigns, and Vergil's work glorifies many aspects of country life. His poem is quite remarkable, for in it he has managed to provide a considerable amount of what was, in his day, accurate information on the cultivation of crops and the care of animals, while maintaining a lofty tone that is far from the prosaic quality of the subject matter.

Vergil uses mythology extremely effectively, invoking the gods traditionally associated with agriculture at the beginning of each section and describing such ordinary phenomena as spring rains in metaphorical terms; the rain is Aether, the atmosphere's embrace of his wife, the earth. By referring to familiar deities, Vergil lifts details of the weather and conditions of the soil far above the realm of the mundane. His metaphorical language, his use of epic similes, and his references to the greatness of his country also contribute to making the *Georgics* fine poetry.

Each of the four sections deals with a specific problem of farming, but each also has a number of digressions that add interest and grandeur to the work as a whole. The first Georgic begins with a long invocation to the deities who control the growth of grain, vines, and olives, and a special prayer to Julius Caesar, who has become a new divinity, with his own place among the constellations. The body of this section is devoted to the plowing, planting, and harvesting of crops and to the helpful knowledge that can be gained by study of the stars. Practical advice on the best time to plow and sow, on crop rotation, fertilizing the soil, and the tools needed by the farmer is enlivened by a majestic description of a storm, brief vignettes of farm life, and a description of the worship of the goddess Ceres at harvest time. A discussion of the changing appearance of the sun under different weather conditions leads to a description of the eclipse that was one of the disastrous omens that appeared at the time of the assassination of Julius Caesar. The conclusion of this section is a prayer that Augustus, Rome's new champion, may bring peace to the nation and allow farmers to return from the battlefield to their own lands.

The cultivation of the vine and the olive, staples of the Italian economy, is the central theme of the second Georgic, and Vergil makes the appropriate invocation to Bacchus, the wine god, as well as to the poet's patron, as this part of the poem opens. Perhaps the most memorable passages here are the poet's lines in praise of Italy, in which he cites the special virtues of each part of the country and evokes patriotic sentiments as he alludes to famous ruling families of past ages. Also notable is the restatement of the pastoral ideal, Vergil's picture of the happy state of the farmers who live at peace on their own lands, far from the battlefield, the rule of law courts, and the frenzy of politics.

Even subjects like the grafting of trees and the preparation of soil for the planting of seedlings are treated in majestic language, and the catalog of the virtues of the various wines of the country is equally poetic. John Milton learned much from his classical master about the evocative effect of place names.

Vergil's praise of country life at the end of this section is tied to his political aims; he asserts that it was through the efforts of the sturdy farmers of the past that Etruria and Rome won their first greatness, and he suggests that much of the fate of the new empire will rest on those who cultivate the Italian fields.

The third Georgic opens with a general statement on poetry. Vergil realizes that he is opening new doors in writing about fields and flocks; he also knows that the old myths have been repeated so often that they no longer lend lustre to the poet. He hopes eventually to win fame for himself and for his homeland, Mantua, by describing the heroic exploits of Augustus Caesar and his army; but meanwhile, he must follow Maecenas' request that he chronicle the domain of the wood nymphs, and he turns to a new topic, the breeding of horses and cattle. He pictures vividly the strength and grace of the thoroughbred horse, alert and eager for action as the mount of a great soldier. Vergil elevates the tone of his subject by alluding to the magnificent horsemen and charioteers among the Homeric heroes.

The nurture of sheep and goats forms another part of this section. The poet even suggests remedies for diseases that strike these animals, and he gives a moving and realistic description of a devastating plague among them, picturing their death agonies as the result of the avenging force of the fury Tisiphone, who drives slaughter and terror before her.

The fourth Georgic probably has provided the greatest pleasure for modern readers, who can share Vergil's fascination with the habits of bees more readily than his interest in various kinds of soil and methods of grafting. The poet relates the popular belief that the highly complex society of the bees results from a special blessing bestowed on them by Jupiter after they aided him when he was imprisoned in a cave; they alone of all the creatures live under law.

The poet has observed colonies of bees closely, and he describes with great accuracy their characteristic swarms and the battles between the "king" bees for supremacy. He suggests the best sweet-smelling plants for attracting the swarms to new hives and recommends the playing of cymbals to aid in drawing them toward their new homes. He also offers helpful hints about the flowers that make the best honey and mourns regretfully that he lacks time and space to speak of gardens.

The last half of this Georgic deals with the curious subject of spontaneous generation from corruption, a belief that has fascinated humankind as recently as the seventeenth century, when Sir Francis Bacon discussed it in his *New Atlantis* (1627). There was a tradition, apparently quite widespread, that, should a whole colony of bees perish, a new swarm could be born from the corruption of the blood of a slaughtered bullock. Vergil explains this phenomenon by relating a mythological tale about a shepherd, Aristaeus, the son of Apollo and a sea nymph, who goes to the sea god Proteus to learn why his bees have died. He finds that the nymphs who mourn the deaths of Orpheus and Eurydice have brought about this misfortune, and he sacrifices four bulls to placate the spirits of the singer and his bride. A great cloud of bees arises from the carcasses of these animals, signifying the acceptability of the sacrifice; from that time on, hives were believed to be replenished in the same way.

The concluding lines of the fourth Georgic summarize the poet's achievement in this poem; he speaks a little apologetically about singing of the cultivation of fields, flocks, and trees while Caesar is winning great victories, and he identifies himself as the same writer who formerly sang of the shepherd Tityrus, in his *Eclogues*.

While the *Aeneid* is unquestionably Vergil's masterpiece, the *Georgics* perhaps reveals his remarkable poetic imagination even more fully. There are few successful didactic poems in Western literature, only a small number of which achieve the majestic tone of Vergil's work. Like all great practitioners of the genre, Vergil pays careful attention to the specifics of his subject, in this case farming, and his clear affection for the simple, unsullied lifestyle of the rural inhabitants of Italy shines forth in a work that allows him to transform the commonplace into the materials of great art. No doubt his patrons (including the emperor Augustus) would have been exceedingly pleased to find such a compelling argument for the continuance of the agrarian lifestyle expressed in mellifluous language. The work stands with Lucretius' *De rerum natura* (c. 60 B.C.E.) as one of the finest transformations of technical materials into poetry produced during the classical period in literature.

Were the work only a technical treatise, however, its appeal to succeeding generations would have long since faded. As numerous critics have pointed out, in the *Georgics*, Vergil transcends his subject to present to readers a more universal theme about humankind and the relationship of humanity to the natural world. Working as he often does on the principle of analogy, Vergil draws constant, if subtle, parallels between the farmer's life and that of all people: The cycle of life parallels the yearly cycle that the farmer repeats, working sometimes in cooperation with the world around him and sometimes against it, to forge a meaningful life and achieve a sense of happiness and accomplishment.

The work highlights the theme of regeneration and the symbiotic relationship between humans and the natural world. The work is also visionary in that it rises above the details of farming life to present a vision of "the function and value of human art." Seen in this light, the many details of the work, including the curious inclusion of the story of Aristaeus at the conclusion of the fourth book, become important keys to understanding the classical view of the art of living. More properly, perhaps, the *Georgics* suggests ways that one can make an art out of living.

Vergil's indirect method of presenting his theme is effective precisely because it is evocative rather than directive. The method has been practiced by many since that time but never with greater subtlety or technical skill.

Updated by Laurence W. Mazzeno

Bibliography:

Griffin, Jasper. *Virgil*. Oxford, England: Oxford University Press, 1986. A general introduction to Vergil. The third chapter examines the *Georgics* in detail and provides a good explanation of the important themes of labor and duty. Bibliography and index.

Perret, Jacques. "The *Georgics*." In *Virgil: A Collection of Critical Essays*, edited by Steele Commager. Englewood Cliffs, N.J.: Prentice-Hall, 1966. A concise examination of the *Georgics*. Discusses changes in Vergil's life and his poetry in the period of the composition of the *Georgics*. Provides a useful chronology of Vergil's life and relevant Roman history. Bibliography.

Slavitt, David R. *Virgil*. New Haven, Conn.: Yale University Press, 1991. A superior overview of Vergil's poetry. The second chapter discusses the *Georgics* and offers a rewarding analysis of the societal influences in the composition of the work, and its influence on ancient and modern literature. Index and bibliography.

Wilkinson, L. P. *The Georgics of Virgil: A Critical Survey*. London: Cambridge University Press, 1969. The standard work of criticism for the *Georgics*. Places the poems within their literary and historical context and provides an exhaustive scholarly analysis.

_____, trans. *Virgil: The Georgics*. Harmondsworth, Middlesex, England: Penguin Books, 1982. Excellent translation of the four books. The introduction is a rewarding source for beginners; summarizes Vergil's life and the political situation of the time, and discusses the *Georgics*' place in literary tradition. Bibliography and copious notes.

GERMINAL

Type of work: Novel
Author: Émile Zola (1840-1902)
Type of plot: Naturalism
Time of plot: Nineteenth century
Locale: France
First published: 1885 (English translation, 1885)

Principal characters:
ÉTIENNE LANTIER, a socialist laborer
VINCENT MAHEU or "BONNEMORT," a miner
MAHEUDE, his wife
CATHERINE,
ZACHARIE,
JEANLIN, and
ALZIRE, the Maheus' children
CHAVAL, another workman

The Story:

Étienne Lantier set out to walk from Marchiennes to Montsou looking for work. On the way, he met Vincent Maheu, another workman, called Bonnemort because of successive escapes from death in the mines. Nearing sixty years old, Bonnemort suffered a bad cough because of particles of dust from the mine pits. Bonnemort had a son whose family consisted of seven children. Zacharie, the eldest son, twenty-one years old, Catherine, sixteen years old, and Jeanlin, eleven years old, worked in the mines. In the morning, as they were dressing, they listened to the sounds of Levaque leaving the next door apartment. Soon afterward, Bouteloup joined the Levaque woman. Philomène Levaque, the eldest daughter and Zacharie's mistress, coughed from her lung ailment. Such was the life of those who worked in the mine pits.

Étienne was given a job in the mine. He descended the mine shaft along with Maheu, Zacharie, Chaval, Levaque, and Catherine. At first Étienne mistook the latter for a boy. During lunchtime, Chaval roughly forced the girl to kiss him. This act angered Étienne; the girl insisted that the brute was not her lover. The head captain, Dansaert, came with Monsieur Négrel, Monsieur Hennebeau's nephew, to inspect Étienne, the new worker. There was bitterness among the workers, danger lurking in the shafts, and so little pay that it was hardly worth working. Étienne, however, decided to stay in the mine.

M. Grégoire had inherited from his grandfather a share in the Montsou mines. He lived in peace and luxury with his wife and only daughter, Cecile. A marriage had been arranged between Cecile and Négrel. One morning Maheude, Maheu's wife, and two of her small children went to the Grégoires to seek help. They were given warm clothing but no money, since the Grégoires believed working people would only spend money in drinking and nonsense. Maheude had to beg for some groceries and money from Maigrat, who kept a shop and who would lend money if he received a woman's caresses in return. He had Catherine in mind. Catherine, however, escaped him, met Chaval that night, and allowed him to seduce her. Étienne witnessed the seduction and was disillusioned by the young girl.

Étienne so quickly and expertly adapted himself to the mine that he earned the respect of Maheu. He made friends with the other workers. Only toward Chaval was he clandestinely hostile, for Catherine now openly showed herself as the man's mistress. At the place where

Étienne lived, he would chat with Souvarine, a friendly man who thought that true social change could only be achieved through violent social revolution. Étienne discussed a new movement he had heard about from his friend Pluchart, a Lille mechanic. It was a Marxist movement to free the workers. Étienne had come to loathe the working conditions and the lives of the miners and their families, and he hoped to collect a fund to sustain the forthcoming strike. He discussed his plan with Rasseneur, with whom he boarded.

After Zacharie married his mistress Philomène, the mother of two of his children, Étienne came to the Maheu household as a boarder. Night after night he urged them to accept his socialistic point of view. As the summer wore on, he gained prestige among the neighbors, and his fund grew. As the secretary, he drew a small fee and was able to put aside money for himself. He began to take on airs.

The threat of a strike was provoked when the company changed the structure of the wages of the workers, essentially lowering wages. As a final blow to the Maheus, a cave-in struck Jeanlin, leaving him a cripple. Catherine went to live with Chaval, who had been accusing her of sleeping with Étienne. In December, the miners struck. While the Grégoires and the Hennebeaus were at lunch, arranging the plans for the marriage between Cecile and Négrel, the miners' delegation came to see M. Hennebeau, but he refused to give any concessions. The strike wore on through the weeks, while the workers slowly starved. Étienne preached social-ism, and the strikers listened; as their misery increased, they became more adamant in their resistance to M. Hennebeau. The endless weeks of strike at the Montsou mines ended in a riot when the people advanced to other pits to force the workers to quit their labors and join the strike. The mob destroyed property throughout the day and raged against their starvation. Catherine had remained faithful to Chaval, but when, during the riot, he turned renegade and ran to get the gendarmes, she deserted him to warn her comrades, especially Étienne.

Étienne went into hiding, assisted by Jeanlin, who had become a street urchin and a thief. The Maheu family fared poorly. Crippled Alzire, one of the younger children, was dying of starvation. Everywhere neighbors quarreled fretfully over trifles. Étienne frequently slipped into Maheu's house for a visit. For the most part, he wandered alone at night. After the strike had been in force for two months, there was a rumor that the company was bringing strikebreak-ers to the pits. Étienne began to despair. He suggested to the Maheus that the strikers bargain with M. Hennebeau, but Maheude, who once had been so sensible and had resisted violence, shouted that they should not give in to the pressure of their demands.

One night at Rasseneur's, while Étienne was discussing matters with Souvarine, Chaval and Catherine entered. The animosity between Étienne and Chaval flared up, and they fought. Chaval was overpowered and ordered Catherine not to follow him but to stay with Étienne. Left alone, Catherine and Étienne were embarrassed and confused. Étienne had no place to take the girl. It was not possible for her to go home, since Maheude could not forgive her for having deserted the family and for working during the strike. Resignedly, Catherine went back to her lover.

After Catherine had gone, Étienne walked by the pits, where he was a witness to the murder of a guard by little Jeanlin. Étienne dragged the body away and hid it. When the strikebreakers began to work, the strikers stormed the entrance to the pit and threatened the soldiers on guard. After a while, the soldiers fired into the mob. Maheu was among those killed. Twenty-five workers had been wounded, and fourteen were dead. Company officials came to Montsou to settle the strike. The strikebreakers were sent away. Étienne's popularity ended. He brought Catherine home and began to stay at Maheu's house again. The bleak house of mourning filled Étienne with remorse.

Souvarine resolved to leave Montsou. Before he went, he sneaked into the pit and caused enough damage to cause a breakdown in the shafts. That same morning, Étienne and Catherine decided that they must go back to work. Chaval managed to be placed on the same work crew with Étienne and Catherine. Repeatedly the two men clashed; Chaval still wanted Catherine. Water began rushing into the shaft. Chaval, Étienne, and the rest were trapped below when the cage made its last trip up and did not come down again. The people above waited and watched the mine slowly become flooded. Négrel set about to rescue the entombed workers; as long as they were below, they must be assumed to be still alive. At last, he and a rescue party heard faint thumpings from the trapped workers. The men began to dig. An explosion injured several of them and killed Zacharie.

Meanwhile, the trapped workers had scattered, trying to find a place of safety. Étienne and Catherine came upon Chaval in the gallery to which he had climbed. There the animosity between the two men led to a fight which ended when Étienne killed Chaval. Alone, the two lovers heard the rescuers' tapping. For days they continued to answer the tapping. Catherine died before the men outside reached them. Étienne was still alive when help came.

After six weeks in a hospital, Étienne prepared to go to Paris, where more revolutionary work awaited him.

Critical Evaluation:

From the opening sentence through the final words of *Germinal*, Émile Zola sets a tone that is as relentless as it is bleak. His naturalism is clearly signaled by his opening paragraph, which depicts a solitary man trudging across a lifeless plain, buffeted by March winds that cut like ice and, subsequently, seem to echo with cries of famine and suffering. From this beginning, Zola propels the reader into a metaphorical abyss and devotes the first two (of seven) parts of the novel to a single day, during which the reader is given a panoramic view of the living and working conditions of Montsou.

The Voreux (voracious) mine is introduced. It is a ghoulish monster capable of devouring all who come in contact with it. Its awesomeness, first suggested by Bonnemort, who speaks of the mine as if it were a higher power to which all have surrendered, is reinforced by Étienne's observation that it appears to swallow men in large mouthfuls without taking the slightest notice. Then, once Étienne descends into its bowels, details accumulate and the mine emerges as an elaborate maze that deprives man and beast alike of air, light, and meaningful communication. Its ravenous appetite, no less than its inhospitable nature, makes it a force to be reckoned with even during its destruction following Souvarine's sabotage.

It quickly becomes clear, however, that the mine is not the enemy. The enemies are the board of directors (safely ensconced in Paris, who siphon off the mine's profits with little or no regard for the workers who have generated them), and the lack of class consciousness among the workers. The directors are worse than indifferent. They are calculating in their every move, restructuring wages just after learning that a strikers' contingency fund has been started and bringing in soldiers and Belgian workers with the clear intent of escalating the crisis brought about by the strike. Their heartlessness is not, however, aimed solely at the workers. They also take aim at M. Deneulin, the owner of the Jean-Bart mine, which they hope to add to their acquisitions. When, toward the end of the novel, Deneulin is forced to capitulate, Zola treats it as a death knell for independent entrepreneurs, destined to be picked off one by one by the "maw of capital."

Despite his obvious indignation regarding the aggregation of wealth, Zola tempers his view of the bourgeoisie when depicting its local representatives, which include the Grégoires, Deneulins, Hennebeaus, and Paul Négrel. They are not perpetrators of evil so much as they are flawed humans which they also must answer to the soulless board of directors. They, like Étienne and his coworkers, are shown to be victims of social, psychological, historical, and economic forces which they have a "tormenting desire to see and yet a fear of seeing." In part, their reluctance to see is an unwillingness to confront their own powerlessness. On another level their reluctance is a function of their own complicity in the maintenance of the status quo. This complicity, however, is not limited to the upper class. The workers, too, have resigned themselves to their situation and actively compete against one another rather than working together to challenge those in authority.

To emphasize this point, Zola gives Étienne center stage for much of the novel. Being an outsider, he is not accustomed to things that the other miners take for granted. As a result, he not only has the capacity to feel outrage and horror but also the capacity to begin asking questions and seeking answers. His is not, as Zola repeatedly reminds the reader, an ideological campaign so much as it is a quest for understanding and justice. He reads constantly and seems, on occasion, to be testing out ideas. When he galvanizes the workers during the forest meeting, for example, he has no idea that he is essentially giving them license to embark on a rampage of wanton and purposeless destruction. Accordingly, he tries vainly to regain control or, at the very least, to redirect the miners' energies. This failing, he begins to doubt his own words and wonders whether the untutored masses can contribute to meaningful social change.

He cannot embrace Souvarine's advocacy of violent destruction of the existing system. He clearly believes that education and experience will lead individuals to truth. He detests violence, be it Souvarine's calculated sabotage or Jeanlin's capricious killing of the young soldier. It is for this reason that he maintains his resolve to promote socialism through trade unions and legislative initiatives.

His departure from Montsou marks the end of one part of his education. He has learned and taught as much as he can and must seek a new channel. The miners too have learned a great deal and are better prepared to work for social justice. The objective circumstances of their lives do not appear to have changed, and in many instances have clearly worsened, but one comes away with the feeling that the excesses and violence were necessary parts of their collective education. Significantly, the image of the miners germinating like good seeds with which Zola concludes the novel has already been introduced at two other critical junctures in the book. Its first occurrence comes in the third chapter of part 3, soon after Étienne moves in with the Maheus and begins trying to convert them. The second occurrence comes at the end of part 4, just prior to their storming of the neighboring mines. Each of these episodes has taught important lessons, as Maheude's prophesy of future vindication, just prior to the end of the novel, indicates. Maheude, who has suffered the most, has also grown. She emerges at the end of the novel as clear-headed and pragmatic. Catherine and Lydie, by contrast, symbolize the compliant, abused female; they can only be liberated through death. Maheude survives and, even though she is forced to return to the mines, has a much better understanding of her responsibilities.

The book is not, therefore, simply a protest against the subjugation of the working class. It is also a direct appeal to the workers to band together, to stop killing one another on behalf of the rich, and to take responsible action in order to improve their lives. The conclusion is intentionally left ambiguous; a ray of hope emerges as Étienne leaves Montsou.

"Critical Evaluation" by C. Lynn Munro

Bibliography:
Berg, William J., and Laurey K. Martin. *Émile Zola Revisited*. Boston: Twayne, 1992. Textual analysis of Zola's twenty-volume series *Les Rougon-Macquart* and discusses naturalism's debt to positivism. Devotes a major part of chapter 3 to a study of the ideological ambiguity of *Germinal* and explores Zola's functional use of imagery.

Grant, Elliot M. *Émile Zola*. Boston: Twayne, 1966. Examines the historical context as well as the literary devices (color, symbolism, and anthropomorphism) used in *Germinal*. Detailed critique of the major characters.

King, Graham. *Garden of Zola: Émile Zola and His Novels for English Readers*. London: Barrie & Jenkins, 1978. Explains some of the choices Zola made while writing *Germinal*. Concludes that there are no villains, only victims, and that the main character of *Germinal* is the community.

Nichols, Brian. *Zola and the Bourgeoisie*. London: Macmillan, 1983. Offers a structural analysis of Zola's treatment of the values of the capitalist class. *Germinal* figures prominently in the first part of the book's analysis.

Walker, Philip. *Zola*. London: Routledge & Kegan Paul, 1985. Compares *Germinal* to an intricately crafted fresco teeming with mythic imagery. Argues that Zola's blend of archetypal and historic forms is responsible for the book's epic grandeur and universality.

GERMINIE LACERTEUX

Type of work: Novel
Author: Edmond de Goncourt (1822-1896) and Jules de Goncourt (1830-1870)
Type of plot: Naturalism
Time of plot: Nineteenth century
Locale: Paris
First published: 1865 (English translation, 1887)

Principal characters:
GERMINIE LACERTEUX, a maidservant
MADEMOISELLE DE VARANDEUIL, Germinie's employer
MADAME JUPILLON, Germinie's friend
MONSIEUR JUPILLON, Madame Jupillon's son and Germinie's lover
MONSIEUR GAUTRUCHE, an artist

The Story:

When Germinie Lacerteux was left an orphan at the age of four, her sisters took care of her. At the age of fourteen, she was sent to Paris to live with an older sister who had settled with her husband in the city. Not wishing to pay for all the expenses of the child from their own meager income, the sister and her husband found Germinie a job as a waitress in a café. She had been working in the café for several months when she became pregnant. Germinie suffered many indignities at the hands of her relatives because she would not tell them that she had literally been raped by one of the waiters; they thought she must have invited seduction. Her child was born dead, and giving birth almost killed Germinie. Finally, a retired actor took pity on her and hired her as a maid and companion. For Germinie, this was a step up in the world, but the old actor died within a few months. Germinie then filled a host of positions as maid to kept women and boarding school mistresses.

One day, Mademoiselle de Varandeuil's maid died suddenly. Through the influence of her sister, Germinie was given the position. Mademoiselle de Varandeuil was an old maid whose father had prevented her from being anything but a servant to him until his death, so that she now had few friends and acquaintances. Other members of her family had died, and she herself was an old woman. She had a sufficient income to live fairly comfortably, but she could not afford many extravagances. In her old age, she needed someone to look after her, as much a companion as a maidservant.

For a time after her entry into Mademoiselle de Varandeuil's service, Germinie was a devoted Christian. She spent a great deal of time at church and went to confession regularly. Through her devotions, she fell in love with a young priest, but he, sensing her state of mind, sent her to another confessor and refused to speak to her. With that, Germinie's devotions ceased.

Germinie's next devotion was to her sister's niece, who had been left in her care when the mother died. Germinie's happiness, however, was short-lived, for another sister took the child to Africa. When word came by letter that the child was ill and the sister's husband out of work, Germinie sent everything she could spare to aid the stricken child and the family that was taking care of her. After depriving herself of necessities for two years, Germinie learned that the child had died shortly after leaving Paris and that the letters from her sister and her husband had been a ruse to get Germinie's hard-earned money.

About that time, a dairy store was opened very close to the house in which Germinie lived with Mademoiselle de Varandeuil. In her dealings with the store, Germinie found a friend in

Madame Jupillon, the proprietress. Madame Jupillon had a son, who was at a trade school learning to become a glove maker. Germinie was quite impressed by the youngster and often went with his mother to see him on visiting days. One day, when Madame Jupillon was ill, Germinie went to the school by herself. Upon arriving, she learned that the young man was in trouble because some questionable books had been found in his possession. Germinie helped him out of his difficulty, but when she tried to lecture him, she found herself unable to do so.

Soon Germinie realized that she had a great deal of affection for the young man, who was ten years her junior. In order to be near him and to have company, she spent a great deal of time with the Jupillons, who took advantage of her willingness to help in the store. She was exceedingly jealous when the young man was attracted to a woman of notoriety, and she did everything she could to keep the two apart. By her actions, she left herself open to his advances.

Germinie was extremely happy as the lover of young Jupillon. She soon discovered, however, that Jupillon spent much time in the company of other women. To help keep him for herself, Germinie spent all of her money to buy him a place in which to open his own business, meanwhile providing him with an apartment of his own. Shortly after she had done so much for him, Germinie was turned away from Jupillon's door by another woman who had become his mistress. In the meantime, Germinie had become pregnant and gave birth to a baby daughter. Because it was impossible to keep the child at home while acting as Mademoiselle de Varandeuil's maidservant, Germinie farmed out the child. The death of the baby a few months later brought Germinie great sorrow.

Some time after she had been turned out by Jupillon, the young man was unfortunate enough to be called for military service. He had no money to secure his release, but he knew that he could get the money from Germinie, who still loved him. After some trepidation, Germinie went into debt to keep her false lover near her. She was compelled to borrow so much money that the bare interest on it took everything she could spare from her small income.

As the years passed, Jupillon took less and less interest in Germinie, so that she finally gave him up and turned to liquor for comfort. Drunkenness became her one joy, although she managed to keep the secret of her vice to herself; old Mademoiselle de Varandeuil never even guessed the truth. Everyone noticed, however, that she had become slovenly in her appearance and in her work. Mademoiselle de Varandeuil kept her on only because the old woman could not stand the thought of a new servant in the house. Germinie had two grave problems: She had no one to love, and she was miserably in debt because of a man who cared nothing for her.

When Germinie was approaching the age of forty, she met a man in his fifties, a painter, and took him as a lover. She did not love Gautruche except as an object upon which to lavish her pent-up affections. Before long, she felt much better, behaved much better, and was a better servant to her mistress. Gautruche, however, saw her only as a servant for himself, and he believed that she would be only too happy to leave her job and marry him. Much to his surprise, she refused his offer of marriage, and the two parted forever. Once again, Germinie was left with no one who cared for her or upon whom she could lavish her affections. In desperation, she began picking up any man she could find on the streets. One night, as she roamed Paris looking for a lover, she saw Jupillon. She followed him to a house and spent the night outside in the rain, while waiting for a chance to see him again. The next morning, she was desperately ill with pleurisy. She kept on working in spite of her illness, but Mademoiselle de Varandeuil finally sent her to a hospital, where Germinie died. After her death, all of her secrets became known, for everyone to whom she owed money attempted to collect from her employer. At first, Mademoiselle de Varandeuil was outraged; then she came to realize the agony and frustration of Germinie's life and felt only pity for the wretched woman.

Critical Evaluation:

The Brothers Goncourt, who are associated with the naturalist school in nineteenth century French fiction, were the first to create the documentary novel. Naturalist plots are frequently based on newspaper scandals and take place in brothels, hospitals, slums, and oppressive bourgeois interiors. Certain characters recur, among them hysterical women or prostitutes brought to ruin, disenchanted intellectuals, bachelors or unhappily married men, and hypocritical merchants. Typically, there is a wide range of discourse to ensure resemblance to reality. Naturalist novels are characterized by themes of disintegration and confusion, as well as by ironic treatment of political and social institutions.

Germinie Lacerteux became a paradigm of naturalist texts. The novel documents the Goncourts' own interaction with the working class, recording the life of their maid, who had served them faithfully for years. They were shocked to learn of her life of debauchery and of her death in a workhouse. Creditors had tried to collect money she owed for liquor, and through those creditors and other townspeople the Goncourts discovered that she had squandered her money on young men. In addition to interviewing friends and coworkers, they read studies on hysteria, a diagnosis that became a blanket term for a number of symptoms in the nineteenth century. They also visited ragpickers' huts on the edge of the city and explored the dance-halls while collecting material for *Germinie Lacerteux*.

In earlier novels, the Brothers Goncourt had presented life as a series of discontinuous tableaux, and their characters had lacked personal history and been unattached to family or society. Because the Goncourts knew their maid, Rose, well, they were able to maintain continuity of character and story line in *Germinie Lacerteux*. The novel begins with an exposition of Germinie's childhood and describes the death of her parents and the hardship of poverty. A series of episodes follows, showing Germinie as a passive victim in society; the episodes include neglect by a sister, rape at fifteen, the stillbirth of a child, and her drifting from job to job before finally settling at the residence of Mademoiselle de Varandeuil. During the course of her education in life's miseries, Germinie leans to accept hard work and to expect exploitation.

The story also traces Germinie's quest for love. Her first love centers on religion. Catholicism provides a temporary outlet for her emotional needs, but her devotion is ultimately disappointed by her displaced and unrequited love for a priest. Germinie informally adopts her sister's niece, only to experience that loss as well. She acts as a foster mother to Monsieur Jupillon, but motherly love eventually turns to obsessive, romantic love, exacerbated by jealousy. Pregnancy brings only temporary joy, since she must hide her physical state from her mistress and give away her child. The decline of Germinie's personal circumstances is attributed to her consistently foiled attempts at love. Fate becomes a physiological imperative. Germinie's temperament is described as lymphatic, sluggish in thought and action; she is sensitive and anxious and has a need for love and maternity.

Rather than representing the simple opposition of illusion and reality, multiple realities coexist in the character of the protagonist. Germinie embodies the victim, the ideal servant, the obsessive lover, the alcoholic, and the thief. Although the novel appears to depict a simple psychological decline, on closer examination, the positive traits typical of her younger years continue to be revealed even as she lapses into despair. The concept of a multiple personality is demonstrated by the use of mirrors: Germinie is frequently confronted with her own image in the mirror and, in the end, recoils from her own reflection.

The story depicts class issues as well as individual psychology. The Goncourts do not limit misery to the lower classes. Mademoiselle de Varandeuil, who had been tormented by a tyrannical father, shares similar experiences—but not sympathy—with Germinie. The difference in social class makes a friendship between the two women impossible. Germinie learns that class distinctions form insurmountable barriers. The Goncourts demonstrate how poverty not only makes everyday survival difficult but also limits possibilities.

Germinie's psychological development, while played out in the artificial and corrupt atmosphere of Paris, is set against a natural backdrop. Nature's beauty heightens her bitterness, but nature also grows more ominous. The narrator emphasizes the sameness of the road of life and the gathering night of oblivion. At the end of the novel, funereal winter reigns. There are images of enclosure and there is absence of communication. The Goncourts are conscious of the stylistic possibilities of exhausting a place through detailed description. Both painters themselves, they likened the technique of description to that of mimetic painting.

Like many naturalist novels, *Germinie Lacerteux* does not contain documents such as newspaper articles or court records. Instead, dialogue and thought are transcribed, with little narrative or interpretive intervention. Free indirect discourse approximates the collective voice of the audience rather than the voice of an individual narrator. The language of the novel stresses corruption and depicts a society in its death throes. At the end of society, there are no more doctrines, and there one can find unusual, prodigious, free adventurers who risk everything in art and life.

Germinie Lacerteux is recognized as one of the first novels in the naturalist tradition; the novel draws a documentary portrait based on authentic observation and a record of existing conditions. In the preface, the Goncourts repudiate any desire to titillate with the graphic subject matter. Contemporaries were, however, shocked by the clinical descriptions of Germinie's sexuality and the realistic detail of lower class squalor. While the novel was condemned as pornography and only experienced mild popularity, *Germinie Lacerteux* became a model for Émile Zola and other great writers of the period.

"Critical Evaluation" by Pamela Pavliscak

Bibliography:
Auerbach, Erich. *Mimesis: The Representation of Reality in Western Literature.* Translated by Willard Trask. New York: Doubleday, 1953. Discusses the Goncourts as representatives of the naturalist school.
Baldick, Robert. *The Goncourts.* London: Bowes, 1960. A brief but excellent survey of the Goncourts' novels. Concentrates on biographical background to the novels. Also explores major themes and aspects of the Goncourts' literary style. Cites *Germinie Lacerteux* as the precursor to the naturalist movement because the work concentrates on the lower classes. Asserts that the work served as a model for the Goncourts' own later novels.
Billy, Andre. *The Goncourt Brothers.* Translated by Margaret Shaw. New York: Horizon Press, 1960. The standard biography of the Goncourts. Elucidates events from which the novels emerged. Also furnishes contemporary reaction to their novels.
Grant, Richard B. *The Goncourt Brothers.* New York: Twayne, 1972. Survey of the life and works of Jules and Edmond de Goncourt. Ordered chronologically, the book carefully integrates the lives of the authors with detailed stylistic and thematic analysis of all of their novels.
Nelson, Brian, ed. *Naturalism in the European Novel: New Critical Perspectives.* New York: Berg, 1992. Essays on the naturalist school in England, France, Germany, and Spain. Includes important discussions of the Goncourts' role in the literary development of social documentary.

THE GHOST SONATA

Type of work: Drama
Author: August Strindberg (1849-1912)
Type of plot: Expressionism
Time of plot: c. 1900
Locale: An apartment house somewhere in Sweden
First published: Spöksonaten, 1907 (English translation, 1916); first performed, 1908

Principal characters:
>THE OLD MAN, the eighty-year-old Jacob Hummel
>THE STUDENT, a young man named Arkenholz
>THE MILKMAID, an apparition who appears to the student
>THE COLONEL
>THE MUMMY, the Colonel's wife
>THE YOUNG LADY, the Colonel's daughter, but really Hummel's daughter
>JOHANSSON, Hummel's servant
>BENGTSSON, the Colonel's footman

The Story:

The building superintendent's wife was sweeping and polishing brass while the Old Man, Director Hummel, sat in a wheelchair reading a newspaper. As a Milkmaid came in and drank from the fountain in front of the apartment building, a Student, "sleepless and unshaven," approached and asked for the dipper. The Milkmaid reacted in terror, for she was an apparition and unaccustomed to being seen, and the Old Man stared at the Student in amazement because he could not see the Milkmaid. Neither of them knew that the Student was a child born on a Sunday, which gave him special perceptions.

This puzzling tableau yielded to a conversation between the Old Man and the Student. The Student, Arkenholz, was exhausted from having treated people who had been injured that night in a collapsing house. The Old Man's questions disclosed that the Student was the son of a man who—so the Old Man said—had swindled him out of his life savings many years before. The Old Man, whose behavior and casual remarks suggest some mythic, timeless quality, had apparently contrived the Student's occasion for heroism as a ruse to meet him so that he could manipulate the Student into friendship and ultimately marriage with the daughter of a Colonel, who is actually the Old Man's daughter. To this end, the Old Man instructed the Student to attend a performance of Richard Wagner's opera *The Valkyrie* that evening and to sit in a certain seat.

The Student agreed to these arrangements, all of which seemed like the manipulations of an eighty-year-old man who admitted that "I take an interest in people's destinies." The Old Man took the Student by the hand, claimed exhaustion from an "infinitely long life," and proclaimed that their destinies were "intertwined through your father." The Student, repulsed by this intimacy, withdrew his hand, and protested, "You're draining my strength, you're freezing me. What do you want of me?" What the Old Man wanted, was to perpetuate himself through the Student, who is young, vital, and a fit mate for the Old Man's daughter. The Student worried about these arrangements, wondering if they meant "some kind of pact," but the Old Man assured him that his motive was simply that all his life he had taken and that now, poised for an uncertain eternity, he wanted to give.

The Old Man rather gleefully recited several bits of gossip. He revealed that a mysterious lady in black standing on the steps was the daughter of the superintendent's wife by a dead man, a former consul, whose body lay upstairs; this adulterous liaison was explained as the occasion by which the superintendent had been given his job. Furthermore, divulged the Old Man, the lady in black was having an affair with an aristocrat whose wife was not only giving him a divorce but throwing in an estate to be rid of him. The Old Man concluded by noting that the aristocrat pursuing the lady in black was a son-in-law of the dead man upstairs. After the Old Man's servant, Johansson, pushed him around the corner in his wheelchair, the Student learned from Johansson that the Old Man had always wanted power and was afraid of only one thing: the Milkmaid.

Bengtsson, the Colonel's footman, gave Johansson his orders for the evening as they entered the Round Room on the ground floor. They were to serve the Colonel and his wife, the Mummy, a "ghost supper," so called because they have looked like ghosts for years. The Mummy, secluded in a closet, spoke childish parrot talk to Bengtsson when he opened her door. Bengtsson then pointed out to Johansson the "death screen" put up around a dying person. At this point, the Old Man arrived and the Mummy emerged to speak to him of their daughter, who sat next door in the Hyacinth Room, reading.

In the conversation that followed, the Old Man humiliated the Colonel by exposing all the pretensions in his life and revealing that he had bought up the Colonel's promissory notes. But the Old Man was humiliated in turn by Bengtsson, who declared that years before in Hamburg the Old Man had "lured a girl out onto the ice to drown her, because she had witnessed a crime he was afraid would be discovered." At this disclosure, the Mummy demanded all the notes and by stroking him on the back transformed Hummel into a parrot-speaker; she switched places with him in the closet and placed the death screen before the closet door.

In the Hyacinth Room, the Student elaborated to the Young Lady on his love for hyacinths, finding in this flower "a replica of the universe" as its star flowers shoot up to become a veritable "globe of heaven." The Young Lady responded by criticizing her cook, a vampire like Hummel, and her maid, whose carelessness demanded the Young Lady's regular attention. When the Young Man recounted an episode when his father had criticized all of his friends at the dinner table, "strip[ping] everybody naked, one after another, exposing all their falseness," he harangued the Young Lady with his own devotion to perfection and ended with the plea, "Alas! Alas for us all! Savior of the world, save us, we are perishing!" This unexpected verbal assault destroyed the Young Lady, who crumpled and died as harp music accompanied the Student's tender elegy for her. The room then disappeared and Arnold Böcklin's painting "The Island of the Dead" emerged in the background.

Critical Evaluation:

In a life charged with personal and spiritual obsessions, August Strindberg wrote three dozen plays, seven novels, six volumes of essays and three of short stories, and a volume of poems. Most of these works reflect his extensive reading of the Bible, mythology, theosophy, Friedrich Nietzsche, and Emanuel Swedenborg, as well as much else that stimulated his creative impulses. *The Ghost Sonata* can be grouped with *Stormy Weather*, *The House That Burned*, *The Pelican* (all written in 1907), and *The Black Glove* (1909) as the third in a quintet of what Strindberg called chamber plays. The term "chamber play" was a reference to their analogies to musical forms, and they were written for Strindberg's Intimate Theater in Stockholm. He initially thought *The Ghost Supper* an appropriate title to evoke the central event of the play, but switched to *The Ghost Sonata* as proper for a play built around three scenes.

Strindberg preceded and influenced such playwrights as Eugene O'Neill, Samuel Beckett, and Edward Albee in his exploitation of expressionist techniques and in the use of settings, sound effects, and other devices to suggest states of mind. The apparition of the Milkmaid, for instance, prompts a reaction in Hummel that expresses his guilt over the events in Hamburg. For Hummel, the Milkmaid functions much as the Furies do in Greek tragedy, guilty consciences that drive their victims toward expiation. Other examples include the Mummy and the Colonel. The Mummy hides in her closet, dehumanized and reduced by the manipulative Old Man to a mere parrot of a person; the Colonel, with his spurious military title, his wig, and his mustache, collapses as a hollow man under Hummel's ruthless attack on his puffed-up self. When the Old Man himself is exposed, he succumbs to the Mummy's parrot speech as a sign of his own spiritual emptiness.

Vampirism and exploitation constitute the main theme of *The Ghost Sonata*. Johansson says of the Old Man that "he's like a horse thief, only with people. He steals them, in all kinds of ways." Hummel rides around, Johansson says, "like the great god Thor," destroying houses, killing his enemies, and forgiving nothing. In his younger days, he had been a Don Juan who was so clever that he got his women to leave when he had used them up. Hummel knows everyone's dark secrets, and his corrosive cynicism shows up in his talk about them, as when he reveals the identity of the lady in black.

The Old Man explains at the ghost supper that "Nature itself plants in human beings an instinct for hiding that which should be hidden" but that "sometimes the opportunity presents itself to reveal the deepest of secrets, to tear the mask off the imposter." That is what he has chosen to do at the ghost supper, "to pull up the weeds" and "settle the accounts" so that the Student and the Young Lady can start afresh. It is too late, however, for the Old Man Hummel himself: The Mummy charms him into her parrot role and puts the death screen around him.

Ironically, it was the folly of the Student's father, to expose everyone's pretensions at a dinner party, that led to his incarceration in a madhouse. The Student has clearly inherited his father's inverted idealism and his disgust for a world that cannot live up to his standards of honesty and goodness. His tirade in the last minutes of the play condemns creation: "Why is it that the most beautiful flowers are so poisonous, the most poisonous? Damnation hangs over the whole of creation." Students of Strindberg's life see autobiographical elements in the Student's bitterness. Whatever its source in the author's creative impulses, *The Ghost Sonata* dramatizes with great power the dark and apocalyptic side of existence.

Frank Day

Bibliography:

Haugen, Einar. "Strindberg the Regenerated." *Journal of English and Germanic Philology* 29 (1930): 257-270. Discusses *The Ghost Sonata* as one of several late plays by Strindberg in which Christian virtues triumph over the bleak vision of the earlier plays.

Johnson, Walter. *August Strindberg*. Boston: Twayne, 1976. One of the Twayne series' standard overviews of life and works, with a useful bibliography for beginning readers. A chapter entitled "Dramatist of Penetration and Representation" is helpful on the chamber plays.

Mays, Milton A. "Strindberg's *Ghost Sonata*: Parodied Fairy Tale on Original Sin." *Modern Drama* 10, no. 2 (September, 1967): 189-194. An excellent explication of the manner in which Strindberg turns folkloric elements into allegories.

Meyer, Michael. *Strindberg*. New York: Random House, 1985. A long, well-written biography with excellent illustrations. One entire chapter is devoted to the chamber plays.

Williams, Raymond. "August Strindberg." In *Drama, from Ibsen to Eliot*. London: Chatto & Windus, 1952. Williams chooses five plays—*The Father* (1887), *Miss Julie* (1888), *To Damascus* (1898), *Easter* (1901), and *The Ghost Sonata*—to trace the evolution of Strindberg's dramatic style and technique. An excellent commentary on Strindberg the artist.

GHOSTS

Type of work: Drama
Author: Henrik Ibsen (1828-1906)
Type of plot: Social realism
Time of plot: Nineteenth century
Locale: Rosenvold, Norway
First published: Gengangere, 1881 (English translation, 1885); first performed, 1882

Principal characters:
MRS. HELEN ALVING, a widow
OSWALD ALVING, her son, an artist
MANDERS, pastor of the parish
JACOB ENGSTRAND, a carpenter
REGINA ENGSTRAND, his daughter, in Mrs. Alving's service

The Story:

Pastor Manders called on Mrs. Helen Alving on the eve of the tenth anniversary of her husband's death to discuss certain details concerning the opening of an orphanage in memory of her late husband. The pastor found Mrs. Alving in the best of spirits, for her son Oswald, an artist, had returned from Paris to attend the dedication of the memorial to his father. Oswald, now twenty-six, had lived away from his parents since he was seven, and Mrs. Alving was delighted at the prospect of having her son spend the entire winter with her.

Oswald had idealized his father, for in her letters his mother had portrayed Captain Alving as a sort of hero. The boy's own memories of his father were confined to one incident in his childhood when his father had taken him on his knee and encouraged him to smoke a large meerschaum pipe. Upon his return home, Oswald took a certain pride in lighting up his father's old pipe and parading in front of his mother and Pastor Manders.

Pastor Manders did not approve of smoking; in fact, he did not approve of anything that could even loosely be interpreted as sin. He did not approve of Oswald's bohemian way of life in Paris and blamed Mrs. Alving for her son's ideas. He reminded Mrs. Alving that she had come to him scarcely one year after having married, wanting to leave her husband, and that he had sent her back to her duty. Manders considered this act the greatest moral victory of his life.

Mrs. Alving thought it high time that the pastor know the truth about her late husband. Years before, when he had advised her to return to Captain Alving, the minister had been aware of her husband's profligacy, but he had not known that the profligacy continued after his wife's return. Her relationship with her husband consisted principally of helping him into bed when he came home from one of his drinking bouts; on one occasion she had come across him making love to her own maidservant. The most abominable aspect of her situation, and what she had discovered soon after her marriage, was that her husband had contracted syphilis and that her son might have inherited the disease. Manders' religious influence and her own cowardice had led Mrs. Alving to keep silent.

While Mrs. Alving and the minister talked, Oswald flirted in the adjoining dining room with the maid, Regina. To Mrs. Alving it sounded like the ghost of the flirtation she had overheard years earlier between her husband and Regina's mother. Regina, ostensibly the daughter of a drunken carpenter named Jacob Engstrand, was actually the daughter of Captain Alving and the maidservant. It was that discovery that had sent Mrs. Alving flying to Pastor Manders for solace and help. Engstrand had been willing to turn Regina over to Mrs. Alving for her education and care, but now he planned to enlist her aid in the establishment of a seamen's home. Regina had other plans for herself, and saw no reason why she should throw herself away on worthless and irresponsible sailors when she might, as she thought, have the heir of a wealthy family.

Oswald, who was unaware of the blood relationship, wanted to marry Regina. He confided to his mother that before he left Paris he had gone to a doctor because he felt listless and had lost his ambition to paint. The doctor had commented on the sins of fathers. Oswald, knowing only the picture of his father that his mother's letters had given him, had been furious and thought he must have contracted venereal disease himself. He told his mother that he wanted to marry Regina and be happy for what remained of his life. Mrs. Alving realized that at last she must tell the two young people the truth. Before she had a chance to do so, however, news came that the orphanage that was to have been Captain Alving's memorial was on fire.

At the time the orphanage had caught fire, Manders and Engstrand had been in the carpenter shop nearby. After the fire, Engstrand accused the pastor of dropping a lighted candle wick into some shavings. Although he was probably not guilty, Manders was anxious not to endanger his position in the community. When Engstrand offered to take the blame for the fire in return for money from the remainder of Captain Alving's fortune, with which he could build his sailors' home, the self-righteous Manders agreed to the blackmail and promised to help Engstrand.

Mrs. Alving told Oswald and Regina about their father, explaining the nature of his illness and that his children might have inherited it. When she heard that she was really Alving's daughter, Regina was angry, feeling that she should have been reared and educated as a lady. Now, preferring to cast her lot with Engstrand, she left. Alone with his mother, Oswald revealed that symptoms of his inherited venereal disease had already become evident, and that he was doomed to paretic insanity. Mrs. Alving assured her son that she would always be by his side to take care of him. Oswald begged his mother to kill him and showed her the morphium he had brought with him, but Mrs. Alving was shocked. Mother and son were still talking at daybreak. When Mrs. Alving blew out the light, she was horrified to see Oswald begin to cry childishly for the sun.

Critical Evaluation:

Ghosts is Henrik Ibsen's effort to substitute the modern scientific concept of heredity for the Greek idea of fate. More important, it is a mordant attack on society and societal standards. In explicitly stating that these standards were responsible for Mrs. Alving's tragedy, Ibsen inflamed even the liberal sensibilities of his day. The play can still be read as a study in what has come to be known as the science of semantics—the disruptive effect caused when words or concepts are, in society, divorced from the realities for which they are supposed to stand.

Frequently called the "father of modern drama," Henrik Ibsen, like Pablo Picasso in painting and Igor Stravinsky in music, was a dynamic innovator whose far-ranging experiments had a continuing influence on Western theater and culture. *Ghosts*, Ibsen's most celebrated, at one time even notorious, play, was the key document in his "social-realistic" period during the 1870's and 1880's. To some extent, the play obscured the fact that he was a protean writer whose social-realistic phase occupied only two decades of a career that spanned half a century, from 1849 to 1899, during which he explored many social, psychological, and metaphysical problems in a wide range of theatrical styles.

In the 1880's, however, *Ghosts* was a red flag to the conventional theater audience and a defiant banner for the avant garde. Ibsen's earlier social play, *A Doll's House* (1879), in which a woman leaves her husband to achieve maturity, found stout defenders but also excited denunciation (in fact, the playwright was forced to produce a happy end, in which Nora stays home, for German consumption). The controversy was in large part responsible for the play's commercial success on stage and, even more emphatically, in book form. *Ghosts*, which deals with a woman who does stay home, was another matter, for this time the public concluded that the play was entirely too shocking, especially for its open treatment of venereal disease and its defense of unmarried cohabitation. Even the sales of Ibsen's earlier plays dropped off. One newspaper critic summed up the general opinion when he wrote, "The book has no place on the Christmas table of any Christian home." Eventually, the play became one of the pillars of literature.

One aspect of *Ghosts* is its attack on conventional morality. Pastor Manders embodies everything Ibsen hated in those conventions—the "ghosts" of the title. Manders is an unconscious hypocrite. Though he sees himself as a moral and ethical leader, he is motivated almost exclusively by fear of what others think of him. When he discusses the question of insuring the new orphanage, he states that he is not opposed to the principle of insurance—he himself is insured, and his parishioners insure themselves and their businesses—but he fears that by insuring the orphanage, his wealthier patrons may insist he is showing less reliance than he should on divine Providence. The decision not to insure the orphanage is based neither on an interpretation of God's will nor out of concern for the orphans but for fear of public opinion. To Ibsen, the conventional moral code is itself hypocritical, and those who adhere to it are neither morally nor spiritually motivated.

In the closing act, fear of what others may think proves to be Manders' undoing. After the orphanage has burned to the ground, the unscrupulous, consciously hypocritical Engstrand convinces the pastor that he, Manders, caused the fire. Since Manders' sole concern is his reputation, when Engstrand "accepts" the blame for the fire (and it is clear that he set it), the greatly relieved Manders agrees to provide financial support for Engstrand's "Sailors' Home"— a "home" that will clearly be little more than a brothel. To save his own skin, the spiritual mentor agrees to underwrite immorality.

Hypocrisy and opportunism pervade the moral landscape of the play. Engstrand is an obvious and open hypocrite, a confidence man who has persuaded Manders that he is a worthy soul. Regina sets her cap for Oswald not because she loves him but because she wants to be taken to Paris; as a second string to her bow, she makes advances to Pastor Manders. Although Mrs. Alving is a thoroughly sympathetic character, she too has played the hypocrite in the past, hiding the lifelong philanderings of her husband behind a wall of public respectability: The last stone in that wall was to have been the orphanage named in Captain Alving's honor; ironically, his real and more fitting memorial will be Engstrand's "Sailors' Home."

Ibsen believed that the moral code enforces hypocrisy, and that it ranges far beyond the reach of Mrs. Alving's house. When Manders suggests that men of means might object to insuring the orphanage, he suggests also (without himself understanding the implications of his statement) that these men, while speaking in spiritual terms, are interested in the orphanage solely for financial reasons; it will reduce the taxes they pay for charitable purposes. In an intense confrontation with Oswald (one of the scenes the audience of Ibsen's time found objectionable because Oswald defends unmarried cohabitation), Manders accuses Oswald of having moved in openly immoral circles in Paris, only to be told that Oswald has indeed seen a good deal of immorality abroad—when some of Manders' respectable parishioners have come to Paris to have their fling: "Then we had a chance of learning something, I can tell you."

The exposure of the conventional code in itself might have created a comedy, for Engstrand and Manders are in many ways comic figures, or it might have led to a serious problem play.

There is, however, a second, more subtly stated theme, and in it lies the play's tragic momentum. According to Ibsen, understanding and exposing the conventions do not destroy them or their power to harm; the truth does not make one free in Ibsen's worlds.

Mrs. Alving is quite contemptuous of the conventional code. She sees herself as an emancipated woman who has freed herself of her past and, by recalling Oswald from Paris, ensured her future happiness. In Act I, she seems in complete control of the situation; she is tranquil, confident, certain of herself. "And from tomorrow on," she tells Manders at the conclusion of the act, "I shall be free at last. . . . I shall forget that such a person as Alving ever lived in this house—there'll be no one here but my son and me." Yet at that point, she and Manders hear Oswald running after the maid (unbeknown to him, his half sister) in an echo of the affair between Captain Alving and the maid who was Regina's mother. In the sad and bitter discussion that opens Act II, Mrs. Alving, no longer certain that the past can be put aside, states the second theme of the play explicitly: "We're all haunted in this world . . . by the ghosts of innumerable old prejudices and beliefs—half-forgotten cruelties and betrayals . . . and we can't get rid of them."

She does make several efforts to "get rid of them." When Oswald, guiltily confessing to her that he has acquired a venereal disease, speaks of the "joy of life" and the "joy of work," Mrs. Alving sees a pattern in the past that she had not discerned before. When she tells Oswald and Regina the truth about Captain Alving—that he was a drunkard and a philanderer all his life—she at long last has come to understand and excuse him, insisting that he had a "joy of life" in him for which his conventional environment could provide no outlet. The Captain's wasted life, she goes on to declare, was her own responsibility, because, instead of offering him "joy," she judged him by society's standards, thus driving him elsewhere—to one of the servants, among others. Yet Mrs. Alving's final effort to face and thereby perhaps undo the past fails. Regina reacts with bitterness and leaves. Oswald, facing mental oblivion, is more alone than ever. As the curtain comes down, Captain Alving's legacy to Oswald, the last stage of venereal disease, strikes the boy as Mrs. Alving stares at the horror that is her life. Physically and spiritually, the past has destroyed both present and future.

Ghosts is a richly orchestrated play and remains one of the most complex and significant realistic dramas of the century. Its symbols—the rain that beats darkly on the large parlor window and represents the moral ghosts of the play, the sun that rises at the close to shine on Oswald's darkness—mesh closely with the action and with the themes of the play. Its structure, a gradual revelation of the past that is fully disclosed only at the final catastrophe, is clearly and firmly joined to the idea that the past enters into and destroys the present. This form, developed and perfected by Ibsen, was to be employed over and over again as his influence merged with other developments of the twentieth century.

"Critical Evaluation" by Max Halperen

Bibliography:
Clurman, Harold. *Ibsen*. New York: Collier Books, 1977. This introductory study provides the general reader with a good starting place for reading about Ibsen. Clurman, a renowned stage director, discusses the plays as theater as well as literature. His discussion of *Ghosts* clarifies a misunderstanding about the play's title and explores at some length the motivations of the characters.
Fjelde, Rolf, ed. *Ibsen: A Collection of Critical Essays*. Englewood Cliffs, N.J.: Prentice-Hall, 1965. Sixteen essays that cover Ibsen's conception of truth, realism, and stage craftsmanship,

among other topics. Francis Fergusson discusses the realism, suspense, and tragic nature of *Ghosts*.

Lyons, Charles R., comp. *Critical Essays on Henrik Ibsen*. Boston: G. K. Hall, 1987. A thorough and useful volume of essays that includes discussions that address topics like realism and dramatic form in Ibsen's works. The remarks on *Ghosts* explore the use of asides, disease, and dramatic language.

McFarlane, James, ed. *The Cambridge Companion to Ibsen*. Cambridge, England: Cambridge University Press, 1994. Sixteen newly written essays on Ibsen's life and work provide a good resource. Chapters 9-13 discuss Ibsen's working methods and the stage history of the plays up through the age of film and television.

Valency, Maurice. *The Flower and the Castle: An Introduction to Modern Drama*. New York: Schocken Books, 1982. Readers interested in Ibsen as the founder of twentieth century drama will find rewarding material in this study, the first in Valency's modern drama series. The author devotes more than 100 pages to Ibsen, and his comments on *Ghosts* are a good introduction to the play.

GIANTS IN THE EARTH
A Saga of the Prairie

Type of work: Novel
Author: O. E. Rölvaag (1876-1931)
Type of plot: Regional
Time of plot: Late nineteenth century
Locale: The Dakotas
First published: I de dage, 1924 and *Riket grundlægges*, 1925 (English translation, 1927)

> *Principal characters:*
> PER HANSA, a Norwegian settler
> BERET, his wife
> OLE,
> ANNA MARIE,
> HANS KRISTIAN, and
> PEDER VICTORIOUS, their children

The Story:

Per Hansa moved all his family and his possessions from Minnesota into the Dakota Territory. His family consisted of his wife, Beret, and three children, Ole, Anna Marie, and Hans Kristian. Beret was fearful and sad, for she had been uprooted too often and the prairie country through which they traveled seemed bleak, lonely, and savage.

Per Hansa staked out his claim near the family of Hans Olsa at Spring Creek. Then Beret announced that she was carrying another child. Money was scarce. Per Hansa faced overwhelming odds, and thoughts of the great risks he was taking kept him awake long after Beret and the children slept. Being something of a poet, Per Hansa thought at times that the land spoke to him, and he often watched and listened and forgot to keep to his work as he cleared his land and built his house. He labored from before dawn until after dark during those long, northern summer days.

When Indians came and drove away the settlers' cows, only Per Hansa had the courage to follow them. Only he had the sense to doctor a sick Indian. Beret mistrusted his wisdom and there were harsh words between them. The grateful Indian gave Per Hansa a pony. Then Per Hansa went on a buying expedition and returned with many needed supplies and, what was more, news of coming settlers.

The next summer, Per Hansa discovered claim stakes that bore Irish names. The stakes were on his neighbor's land; the homesteaders had settled where others had already filed claim. Secretly he removed the stakes and burned them, but not before Beret realized what he was doing. She began to worry over her husband's deed. Per Hansa sold some potatoes to people traveling through and awoke the slumbering jealousy of his neighbors.

In midsummer, more people arrived, the settlers who had set out the stakes that Per Hansa had burned. They called the Norwegians claim jumpers, but after a fight, they took up other land nearby. Per Hansa managed to sell some of his goods to them. That fall, more Norwegians came. The little community was thriving. Beret, however, depressed by the open spaces and her fear that her husband had done a bad thing, brewed a dark remorse within herself. Day by day, she brooded over her lonely life, and she covered her window at night because of her nameless fears. At least Per Hansa, on his infrequent trips around to different settlements, met other people.

When winter came, Per Hansa rested. He could sleep long hours while the winds blew outside, but his wife worried and fretted. He began to quarrel with her. Soon, however, he noticed that his neighbors were suffering hardship and privation. The unmarried young men who had settled near the Hansas were planning to desert the settlement. It required all his ability to convince them to stay and to face the desolate, bitter winter to its end. The settlers began to talk of a school that would move from house to house so that the parents might learn English along with the children.

During the winter, Per Hansa became lost in a blizzard, and only his tremendous strength and courage saw him and his oxen safely through the storm to the Tronders' settlement. The following day, forgetting how Beret must be worrying about him, he stayed on and cut a load of wood to take back home with him. His next expedition was to bargain with the Indians for furs. He suffered greatly from exposure and lost two toes through frostbite.

When spring came, Per Hansa could not wait to get into his fields to plant his wheat. His friends thought he was planting too early, and so it seemed, for snow fell the next day and freezing weather set in. Determined not to lose heart, Per Hansa decided to plant potatoes in place of the wheat. Beret took to her Bible, convinced that evil was working its way into their lives. Then, unexpectedly, their wheat came up.

Another couple arrived. They were exhausted with travel, the wife saddened by the death of her son on the prairie. Per Hansa and Beret took them in. When they moved on, greater despondency seized Beret. She felt some doom was working its way closer and closer to her life.

That summer, grasshoppers destroyed much of the grain. Most of Per Hansa's crop was saved, but Beret took his good fortune only as a sign that the underground trolls, or evil spirits, were planning greater ruin for her and her husband.

In the following years, the scourge of the grasshoppers returned. Many of the settlers were ruined. Some starved. Some went mad. One summer, a traveling Norwegian minister took up residence with them to plan a religious service for the whole community. His coming worked a change in Per Hansa's household. Per Hansa took courage from it and consolation, but the reveries in Beret's mind grew deeper and stranger. Because it was the largest house in the district, the minister held a communion service in Per Hansa's cabin. Disconnected parts of the service floated all that week in Beret's head. Her mind was filled with strange fancies. She began to think of Peder Victorious, her youngest child, who was born on the prairie, as a savior who would work their salvation. As the autumn came on, the great plains seemed hungry for the blood and strength of those who had come to conquer them.

That winter, Hans Olsa froze his legs and one hand. In spite of all that Per Hansa and the others did for their neighbor, Hans Olsa grew weaker. Beret stood beside him, predicting that he had not long to live. She put into the sick man's mind the idea to send for the minister. Per Hansa thought that Hans Olsa was weak in calling for a minister and that the way to throw off illness was to get out of bed and go to work. He had never spared himself nor had he spared his sons. He was the man able to go for the minister, but this time, he was unwilling to set out on a long winter journey. Hans Olsa was a good man; he did not need a minister to help him die. The weather itself was threatening. However, Per Hansa reconsidered. His sons were digging a tunnel through snow to the pigsty. Inside, his wife was preparing a meal for him. They watched as he took down his skis and prepared to make the journey for the sake of his dying friend. He did not look back at his house or speak farewell to Beret as he started out. So Per Hansa, on his errand of mercy, walked into the snowstorm. There death overtook him.

Critical Evaluation:

Ole Rölvaag was born in the Helgoland district of Norway and lived there until he was twenty years of age. He attended school irregularly; his ambition to become a poet, once broached in the family circle, brought a discouraging barrage of ridicule. At age fourteen, he left school entirely and went out with the Lofoten fishing fleet. He seemed destined to pursue this hard vocation all his life, and the prospect brought him little contentment. Although considered by his family as too stupid to learn, he read voraciously, both Norwegian and foreign authors. His reading gave him a view of the possibilities of life that made the existence to which he was bound seem intolerably circumscribed. When he had been a fisherman for five years, something occurred that forced him to a decision. The master of his boat, whom he greatly admired, offered to stake him to a boat of his own. Rölvaag realized that if he accepted the offer, he would never be anything but a fisherman, so he declined it and emigrated to America.

For three years he farmed for an uncle in South Dakota; then at the age of twenty-three, with great trepidation, he entered a preparatory school in Canton, South Dakota. Six years later, he was graduated *cum laude* from St. Olaf College. After a year of postgraduate study in Oslo, he took the chair of Norwegian literature at St. Olaf, which he held until his death.

By the time Rölvaag began work on *Giants in the Earth*, at age forty-seven, he had already written five novels, of which four had been published. All were written in Norwegian, published in Minneapolis, and read exclusively by the Norwegian-speaking population of the Midwest. All the works deal with aspects of the Norwegian settlement and appealed strongly to an audience of immigrants. *Giants in the Earth* is actually an English translation of two novels previously written in Norwegian: *I de dage* and *Riket grundlægges*. This novel and its sequel, *Peder Victorious* (1928), spring from a European artistic tradition but treat matters utterly American. They are perhaps unique in both American and foreign literature.

The European and specifically Norwegian elements that distinguish *Giants in the Earth* are its orientation toward the psychology rather than the adventures of its characters, and its strain of Nordic pessimism. The characters of Beret and Per Hansa illustrate two complementary facets in the psychology of the Norwegian settlers. In Per Hansa, the desire to own and work his own land, to "found a new kingdom," seems to feed on the hazards he encounters. The brute resistance of the soil, the violence of the weather, the plagues of grasshoppers, the danger from Indians, the dispute over the claimstakes only spur him on to greater feats of daring, endurance, and ingenuity. Every victory over misfortune makes him feel more lucky and fuels his dream of a prosperous life for himself and his children. Freed from the cramped spaces and conventions of an old culture, he embraces the necessities of the new life joyfully, trusting in his instinct for the fitness of things to help him establish a new order. Beret, on the other hand, takes no joy in pioneer life and is instead deeply disturbed at having to leave an established way of life to confront the vast, unpeopled plains. Uprooted, she feels morally cast adrift, as if her ethical sense and her identity were attached to some physical place. Beret sees Per Hansa's exultant adaptability to pioneer life as evidence of the family's reversion to savagery. For a man to shelter with his livestock, to change his name or give his child a strange name, to parley with Indians, or to christen in the absence of a minister indicate to her a failure of conscience, a giving up of the hallmarks of civilization.

Yet, Beret, like Per, has brought her worst troubles with her from home. Her growing despondency about Per and her neighbor's spiritual condition springs from her own sense of sin in having borne Ole out of wedlock. She sees herself as the deserving object of divine retribution; in her deranged state, she takes every escape from disaster as a sign that God has marked her for some still more awful punishment. The very openness that thrills Per Hansa with its endless potentialities fills her with dread: "Here, far off in the great stillness, where there was nothing to hide behind—here the punishment would fall!" Per, bearing her in his heart, is drawn down into her despair.

Ironically, it is only after Beret regains her courage and her faith through religious ministration and ceases to expect calamity from minute to minute, that Per Hansa dies. It even seems as if she sends him out to die. From an aesthetic point of view, however, his death is necessary to the work itself. For all of its realism and modernity of tone, *Giants in the Earth* is a saga, and as sagas must, it ends with the death of heroes. Per Hansa and Hans Olsa are heroes of epic stature, and like the heroes of old legend, they complement each other's virtues. They have loved each other from their youth, and in their prime, their strength and wit combine to carve a new home out of the wilderness. Like Beowulf braving Grendel, they sacrifice themselves in a last great struggle with the prairie before it succumbs to the plow and the fence. Thus "the great plain drinks the blood of Christian men and is satisfied." The deaths of Hans Olsa and Per Hansa signal the passing of the time of legend, when giants walked the earth, and one man could do the work of ten; they signal as well the beginning of a more comfortable time of clapboard houses and hot coffee and of heroes of a wholly different kind.

"Critical Evaluation" by Jan Kennedy Foster

Bibliography:
Gross, David S. *No Place to Hide: Gothic Naturalism in O. E. Rölvaag.* Madison, N.J.: Fairleigh Dickinson University Press, 1993. Relates traditional gothic tradition to Rölvaag's use of the frontier as a gothic setting of terror and wonder, which is especially a problem for Beret. Includes treatment of frontier and immigrant life.
Reigstad, Paul. *Rölvaag: His Life and Art.* Lincoln: University of Nebraska Press, 1972. Examines Rölvaag's novels in a biographical context, revealing the forces and influences that shaped Rölvaag's work. Relates the treatment of folklore, myth, and Norwegian religious beliefs and values to Rölvaag's early life and experiences in Norway, and the plot incidents to his father-in-law's stories of Dakota frontier life. Analyzes where in the plot reminiscences are superseded by imagination.
Schultz, April. "To Lose the Unspeakable: Folklore and Landscape in O. E. Rölvaag's *Giants in the Earth.*" In *Mapping American Culture,* edited by Wayne Franklin and Michael Steiner. Iowa City: University of Iowa Press, 1992. Treats Rölvaag's use of landscape and its relationship to folk myths of the Norwegian immigrant community, and how these shape plot events.
Simonson, Harold P. *Prairies Within: The Tragic Trilogy of Ole Rölvaag.* Seattle: University of Washington Press, 1987. A good look at Beret, the central character, especially how her religious values and her fearful attitude toward frontier space affect all three novels.
Sledge, Martha. "Truth and Fact: The Rhetoric of Fiction and History in Immigrant Literature." *South Dakota Review* 29, no. 2 (Summer, 1991): 159-169. Compares Rölvaag's treatment of immigrant life to that of other Scandinavian writers.

THE GIFT OF THE MAGI

Type of work: Short fiction
Author: O. Henry (William Sydney Porter, 1862-1910)
Type of plot: Moral
Time of plot: Early twentieth century
Locale: New York City
First published: 1905

Principal characters:
DELLA, a young housewife
JIM, her husband
MME SOFRONIE, proprietress of a hair goods shop

The Story:

Tomorrow would be Christmas Day, and Della was distraught. The meager savings she had managed to put aside to purchase a gift for her beloved husband was a mere $1.87. It was simply not enough for a present worthy of her Jim.

There had been brighter days for this young, loving couple. Earlier, Jim had managed to bring home thirty dollars a week. Now, with their income reduced to twenty dollars a week, there was nothing left after basic living expenses had been met. Della had only managed to save her $1.87 by doggedly bullying the grocer, the vegetable man, and the butcher into giving her better prices. Lean living, however, had not dimmed the couple's devotion to one another. Jim returned home from his job punctually every evening to be greeted by Della's loving embrace.

Della simply could not bear the thought of giving her husband a shabby gift, or no gift at all. She collapsed in tears of frustration, but then inspiration struck. After taking a long look at herself in a mirror, Della was reminded that her assets extended beyond the pittance she had been hoarding. She caught sight of her long, flowing hair, the one worldly possession she took pride in, and realized that there was a way to accomplish her goal.

Della shed a few tears for what would be her lost glory. Just as quickly, however, she repressed her emotions, scooped up her old jacket and hat, and left the flat. Arriving at a shop whose sign read MME SOFRONIE. HAIR GOODS OF ALL KINDS, Della inquired what the proprietress would pay for her hair. Coldly, Madame Sonofrie appraised Della's tresses with an experienced eye and hand and offered twenty dollars. Without hesitation, Della submitted to the shearing and walked out with money in hand. After two hours of joyful searching, Della found the perfect gift for Jim.

If Della had had one possession that meant the world to her, Jim had one, too, a beautiful gold watch that had belonged to his father and his grandfather before him. Jim did not display the watch willingly, however, for it hung on an old leather strap, instead of a suitable gold chain.

Jim would not have to be circumspect any longer about his watch; Della had found a platinum fob chain, simple in design and of exquisite quality, which would do justice to Jim's treasure. Thrilled that she had procured a gift worthy of her husband, Della hurried home to repair the damage the shearing had done.

After styling her short hair into curls that resembled those of a "truant schoolboy" or a "Coney Island chorus girl," Della readied the dinner things and sat down near the door. As she waited expectantly, gift in hand, she prayed that he would still find her pretty.

Punctual as always, Jim arrived. As he stepped inside the door, he froze, his eyes on Della. Della could not read his reaction. It did not seem to be anger, disapproval, surprise, or anything she might have expected. He simply stared. She ran up to him and pleaded with him not to be upset; she had had to sell her hair so that she could give him a present for Christmas.

When Jim finally came out of his stupor of disbelief, he took Della into his arms. He admitted that nothing could make him love her any less, but that if she would have a look at what he had bought her for Christmas, she would understand his shock. He drew a package out of his overcoat pocket and handed it to her. Della quickly unwrapped the parcel and let out a shriek of joy which soon turned to tears, for Jim's gift to her was a pair of combs, side and back, tortoise shell with jeweled rims, which she had long admired in a shop window. She had never dreamed that she would actually be able to have them.

Once her tears subsided, she reminded Jim, weakly, that her hair grew very fast. She brightened when she recalled that Jim had not yet seen his present. She held the fob out to him expectantly, reminding him that now he could look at the time a hundred times a day. Upon seeing Della's gift, Jim collapsed on the couch and smiled at her. He suggested that they put their lovely Christmas gifts away for a while; he had sold his watch to buy Della the combs.

Critical Evaluation:

When, in 1919, the O. Henry Memorial Award Prize Stories was inaugurated, the work of O. Henry was the standard by which other short stories were evaluated. In the space of about a decade, William Sidney Porter, writing under the pseudonym O. Henry, produced almost three hundred short stories. Wildly popular, his stories were both commercially successful and critically acclaimed from 1908 until 1930. Sadly, O. Henry's death in 1910 prevented him from enjoying the fruits of his labor and its attendant praise. Mercifully, perhaps, it also prevented him from witnessing the critical crucifixion his work endured from 1930 until around 1960.

O. Henry's stories were noted for their thoroughly American spirit. His stories were always sympathetic to the underdog, and his characters, rooted in the grind of making a living, managed to transcend their humdrum existence by dint of love, loyalty, and self-sacrifice. A smart-alecky, brash humor, which is also typically American, also fills his stories.

O. Henry's stories were once lauded as the highest form of short story, but his mechanized plot structure was considered contrived after 1930. Fraught with sentimentality, the stories rely heavily on the use of irony in their paradoxically predictable surprise endings. While there may have been a strong commercial and critical appetite for this work in pre-Depression America, after 1930 the critics' taste for it soured. A new era in literature was emerging; it was an era which had no use for the previous generation's moralism. Critically acclaimed short stories now embraced subtlety, indirectness, and the symbolic. Next to them, O. Henry's stories' overstatement, predictable plots, and clear moral messages were deemed shallow and non-intellectual.

"The Gift of the Magi" has endured as one of O. Henry's best-known stories. A tribute to the transcendent power of sacrificial love, the story extols the foolish impulsiveness of the two lovers as being rooted in a deeper wisdom, sacrificial giving.

Della and Jim are typical O. Henry characters; they are hard-working and poor, and their existence is full of struggle. They manage to transcend it, however, and they experience joy through the power of their love for one another. When the lovers, unbeknown to each other, sell the possessions most dear to their hearts because they hope to make each other happy, they unwittingly undercut the effectiveness of their gifts. Beyond the minor tragedy of the situation, however, is the larger gift underlying it. The joy and sustaining power of self-sacrificial love is the greatest gift of all, and that, ultimately, is the gift these two share together.

Kim Dickson Rogers

Bibliography:
Current-Garcia, Eugene. *O. Henry (William Sydney Porter)*. New York: Twayne, 1965. Includes a biography of O. Henry and a critical analysis of his work's structure and its technical characteristics. Analyzes his popularity and the subsequent decline of his reputation. Discusses his influence on the development of the American short story.
Langford, Gerald. *Alias O. Henry: A Biography of William Sydney Porter*. New York: Macmillan, 1957. Analyzes the work as well as the life of the writer. Asserts that O. Henry's rightful place in American literature is that of a minor but classic writer.
Long, E. Hudson. *O. Henry: The Man and His Work*. Philadelphia: University of Pennsylvania Press, 1949. This biography makes a case for O. Henry as a "humorist, craftsman, and social historian." Long claims that O. Henry is properly understood and appreciated in the context of the times in which he lived and the audience for which he wrote.
O'Connor Richard. *O. Henry: The Legendary Life of William Porter*. Garden City, New York: Doubleday, 1970. Traces the life of O. Henry from his boyhood in North Carolina through his Texas and Ohio prison years, and, finally, to New York. Vividly portrays the early twentieth century New York City evoked in his work.
Smith, C. Alphonso. *O. Henry*. Edgemont, Pa.: Chelsea House, 1980. Reprint. Garden City, N.Y.: Doubleday Page, 1916. A biography and analysis of O. Henry's work written by a professor who knew O. Henry. Most interesting because, having been written in 1916, during the height of his popularity, it reveals a great deal about late Victorian culture and literary tastes.

GIL BLAS

Type of work: Novel
Author: Alain-René Lesage (1668-1747)
Type of plot: Picaresque
Time of plot: Seventeenth century
Locale: Spain
First published: Histoire de Gil Blas de Santillane, 4 volumes; 1715, 1724, 1735; (*The History of Gil Blas of Santillane,* 1716, 1735)

> *Principal characters:*
> GIL BLAS, a rogue
> SCIPIO, his servant
> DON ALPHONSO, his patron
> DUKE OF LERMA, his employer and prime minister of Spain

The Story:

Blas of Santillane retired from the wars and married a chambermaid no longer young. After the birth of Gil, the parents settled in Oviedo, where the father became a minor squire and the mother went into service. Happily, Gil Perez, Gil Blas's uncle, was a canon in the town. He was three and a half feet high and enormously overweight. Without his aid, Gil Blas would never have received an education. Perez provided a tutor for his nephew, and at the age of seventeen, Gil Blas had studied the classics and some logic.

When the time came for him to seek his fortune, the family sent Gil Blas to Salamanca to study. The uncle provided him with forty pistoles and a mule. Shortly after setting out, Gil Blas was foolish enough to join the train of a muleteer who concocted a story that he had been robbed of a hundred pistoles and threatened all of his passengers with arrest and torture. His purpose was to frighten the men away so that he could seduce the wife of one of the travelers. Gil Blas had some thought of helping the woman, but he fled upon the arrival of a police patrol.

Gil Blas was found in the woods by a band of ruffians who had an underground hideout nearby. Under Captain Rolando, they made Gil their serving boy. After an unsuccessful escape attempt, he set out to ingratiate himself with the captain. At the end of six months, he became a member of the gang and embarked on a career of robbery and murder. One day the robbers attacked a coach, killed all the men, and captured a beautiful woman. She was well-born and modest, and Gil Blas resolved to rescue her. Waiting until the robbers were asleep, he tied up the cook and escaped with the woman, whose name, he learned, was Doña Mencia. Grateful for her rescue, she dressed Gil Blas in fine clothes and presented him with a bag of money. So he went on his way, comparatively rich and comfortable.

On his travels, he met Fabricio, a former schoolmate who had become a barber. Scornful of Gil's intention to study, Fabricio soon persuaded him to go into service as a lackey. Gil turned out to be well adapted to flattery and intrigue, and he soon became proficient by serving a variety of masters, among them Doctor Sangrado, a physician. The doctor's one remedy for all maladies was forced drinking of water and frequent bleeding. Gil Blas won the doctor's esteem and was permitted to attend poor patients in his master's place. During an epidemic, he had a record as good as that of Sangrado; all of their patients died.

Another master was Don Matthias, a fashionable man about town. By means of a little judicious thievery and daring, Gil Blas found his new life highly satisfying. Each day was spent in eating and polite conversation and every night in carousing. During this service, Gil dressed

2523

in his master's clothes and tried to get a mistress among the titled ladies of the town. An old lady who arranged these affairs introduced him to a grand lady who was pining for a lover. Gil was disillusioned when he went with Don Matthias to the house of Arsenia, an actress, and found that his grand lady was really a serving maid.

After Don Matthias was killed in a duel, Gil attended Arsenia for a time. Later he went into service in the household of Aurora, a virtuous young woman who grieved because a student named Lewis paid no attention to her charms. At Gil's suggestion, Aurora disguised herself as a man and took an apartment in the same house with Lewis. Striking up a friendship with him, Aurora skillfully led him on. Then she received him in her own house in her proper person, and soon Lewis and Aurora were married. Gil Blas left their service content with his part in the romance.

On the road again, Gil was able to frustrate a band of robbers who had planned to kill Don Alphonso. Thus, Gil and the don began a lasting friendship.

After losing a situation because he learned that the dueña had an ulcer on her back, Gil next took service with an archbishop. His work was to write out the homilies composed by the archbishop. After he had won his master's confidence, the churchman made Gil promise to tell him when his homilies showed signs of degenerating in quality. After a stroke, the archbishop failed mentally, and Gil told him his homilies were not up to the usual standard. In his rage, the archbishop dismissed Gil, who learned in this manner the folly of being too truthful.

Engaged as secretary by the duke of Lerma, prime minister of Spain, Gil soon became the duke's confidential agent. Gil was now in a position to sell favors, and his avarice grew apace with his success in court intrigue. During this successful period, he engaged Scipio as his servant. Gil's high position enabled him to secure the governorship of Valencia for Don Alphonso.

Gil became involved in a high court scandal. At the request of the prime minister, he acted as panderer for the prince of Spain, the heir apparent. About the same time, Scipio arranged a wealthy marriage for Gil with the daughter of a rich goldsmith. One night, however, the king's spies caught Gil conducting the prince to a house of pleasure, and Gil was confined to prison. Faithful Scipio shared his imprisonment. After months of sickness, Gil was released and exiled from Madrid. Fortunately, Don Alphonso gave Gil a country estate at Lirias, and there he and Scipio settled to lead the simple lives of country gentlemen. Attracted by Antonia, the daughter of one of his farmers, Gil married, but his happiness was brief. After Antonia and his baby daughter died, Gil became restless for new adventures. The prince was now king, and Gil resolved to try court life again. He became an intimate of the new prime minister, Count Olivarez. Once again, he was employed to arrange a liaison for the king, a mission that turned out badly. Forced to resign, Gil returned for good to Lirias. There, he married again, to a girl named Dorothea. Now content, Gil Blas hoped for children whose education would provide amusement for his old age.

Critical Evaluation:

The history of the picaresque novel has been cyclical; the genre has appeared, disappeared, and reappeared sporadically throughout its history but traditionally reappears during periods when there is economic upheaval and marked social inequality. The picaresque novel addresses these inequities in a satiric, pseudoautobiographical mode, teaching not by moralizing but by offering the protagonist—the picaro—as a negative example.

The actual historical origin of the form is uncertain. Some critics believe it sprang initially from ancient mythologies, primarily the myth of Odysseus, while others pinpoint its beginnings in Spanish picaresque novels of the 1500's. Regardless of when the genre began, it remains characterized, if not defined, by a collection of elements. Often any novel that is constructed in an episodic format, features a first-person narrator, and is satiric may be considered picaresque. Also, the true picaresque novel combines elements of realism and idealism as the picaro moves from ignorance to knowledge as a student in the school of hard knocks. He or she may be a rogue, a scoundrel, and even a criminal, but the true picaro is no more than an initiated but still innocent youth trapped in a situation in which a choice must be made between survival and integrity. The picaro chooses the former.

The picaresque novel is a Spanish tradition. Writers in other countries have emulated the picaresque novel, however. The hallmark of the French picaresque novel is *Gil Blas*, which is modeled on its Spanish predecessors. In honor of the novel's sources and to maintain credibility, Alain-René Lesage set his work in Spain; however, he wrote the novel in his native French. The novel's formality of language sets it apart from the tradition of the colloquial charm of the typical picaresque novel, with its lower-class cast of characters and its high-flown parody of the language of the rich and educated. Additionally, the work is tediously long, something many picaresque novels are not; *Gil Blas* is constructed in two volumes of incessant repetition of events and types.

Gil Blas may also be considered different from the typical picaresque novel in that its protagonist is not a poverty-stricken creature who will survive and maintain at all costs. Obviously influenced by his contemporary, Jean-Jacques Rousseau, Lesage develops his character into a semi-respectable courtier, modifying the picaresque model of a lowly reprobate who must use his wits to live. Lesage's character thus "transcends" picarism and is endowed with the gifts of middle-class respectability. The protagonist also develops his native abilities, his patience, and his ability to choose his words carefully.

Although the work is a reaction to social inequality and is set in Spain within a picaresque framework, it cannot be considered pure picaresque. The ideas and tone are French and the protagonist is little more than the prototype of Rousseau's "natural man," who is also imbued with middle-class morality. From the initial separation instructions of his parents to "go honestly through the world" and "not to lay [his] hands on other people's property" to his pious reversal in prison, Gil Blas is not a typical picaro. The true picaro, while he or she may pretend to be redeemed, is not destined for sainthood or aristocracy in any form. He or she is only waiting for the next sucker to wander by.

The basic picaresque quality missing in *Gil Blas* is longing. The protagonist begins his journey not from need but with money for school and the good wishes of his family. Although the protagonist's subsequent adventures are tainted with misfortune, the reader feels little empathy with the plight of Gil Blas. It is assumed he could return to his native village and be welcomed with open arms. Alienation, stemming from a life begun in poverty, is pervasive in the picaresque tradition. Such alienation is absent in *Gil Blas*.

One quality that Gil Blas shares with the typical picaro is his skill at manipulation. Although it gives him no joy, Gil Blas is an adept role player. His is a world of disguises, and his troubles begin whenever he fails to see the person behind each mask, for few people in his world are what they seem to be. He rationalizes his roguish behavior as a means of coping, but, in non-picaresque fashion, he suffers from guilt and remorse at every turn. When the situation threatens his moral code or the work to be done becomes too dirty, he delegates it to his servant and alter ego, Scipio.

Gil Blas's divergence from a moral course happens only once, when he is aligned with the duke of Lerma. The character has difficulty acknowledging his dark side, and the tale grows complex as Gil Blas the character debates with Gil Blas the narrator. His personality assumes the duality of an existence within the plot simultaneous to a satiric detachment from it.

In service to the duke, Gil Blas's morality is threatened by his greed. He is lured by avarice into a world of bribery and solicitation until he becomes a different person and is eventually required to compensate for his digression. The salvation for the character and boredom for the reader is an ethical reversal during his political imprisonment. There, the character undergoes a symbolic moral rebirth and vows that he prefers exile in a hermitage to a life of amoral prosperity. Thus, Gil Blas is whisked, a changed man, away to the throne of a Rousseauistic natural aristocracy.

According to Alexander Blackburn, renowned critic of the picaresque, Lesage, in this novel, has converted the picaresque into a novel of manners. The novel may be considered an accurate history of prerevolutionary France and the fall of the feudal plutocracy, but it should not be considered picaresque. Although many of the characters are rogues and scoundrels, Gil Blas is too inherently moral to be a picaro.

"Critical Evaluation" by Joyce Duncan

Bibliography:
Alter, Robert. *Rogue's Progress: Studies in the Picaresque Novel.*Cambridge, Mass.: Harvard University Press, 1964. One of the better-known works on the picaresque novel. Discusses the variety of the genre. Contains an extended discussion of *Gil Blas.*
Bjornson, Richard. *The Picaresque Hero in European Fiction.* Madison: University of Wisconsin Press, 1977. Includes a thorough treatment of *Gil Blas* as the epitome of the genre in French. Traces the history of the picaresque from its conception in Spain to the books of Tobias Smollett.
Blackburn, Alexander. *The Myth of the Picaro.* Chapel Hill: University of North Carolina Press, 1979. Considered the one of two definitive experts on the picaresque, Blackburn traces the recurrence of the genre from 1554 to 1954.
Chandler, Frank Wadleigh. *The Literature of Roguery.* New York: Burt Franklin, 1958. Although dated, this work is a thorough examination of the picaresque genre.
Monteser, Frederick. *The Picaresque Element in Western Literature.* Tuscaloosa: University of Alabama Press, 1975. A study of the history and evolution of the picaresque. Through examination of a variety of examples, the author attempts to locate important elements.

THE GILDED AGE
A Tale of Today

Type of work: Novel
Author: Mark Twain (Samuel Langhorne Clemens, 1835-1910) and Charles Dudley Warner (1829-1900)
Type of plot: Satire
Time of plot: Late 1840's to early 1870's
Locale: United States
First published: 1873

> *Principal characters:*
> WASHINGTON HAWKINS, a young Westerner
> LAURA HAWKINS, his adopted sister
> COLONEL BERIAH SELLERS, an improvident optimist
> PHILIP STERLING, a young engineer
> HARRY BRIERLY, his friend
> SENATOR DILWORTHY, a member of Congress
> RUTH BOLTON, a Quaker

The Story:

Squire Hawkins of Obedstown, Tennessee, received a letter from Colonel Beriah Sellers asking Hawkins to come to Missouri with his wife Nancy and their two children, Emily and George Washington. Moved by the Colonel's eloquent account of opportunities to be found in the new territory, the family traveled west. On the journey, they stopped at a house where a young child was mourning the death of his mother. Feeling compassion for the orphan, Hawkins offered to adopt him. His name was Henry Clay.

The travelers boarded the *Boreas*, a steamboat headed up the Mississippi. The *Boreas* began to race with another, rival steamboat, the *Amaranth*. The boiler on the *Amaranth* exploded, causing a fire on board and killing or injuring scores of passengers. As the *Boreas* rescued survivors, Hawkins found a stray child, Laura, whose parents apparently had died. The Hawkinses, although now burdened with four children, found hope in the promise of Tennessee lands that they still owned.

After a tiresome journey, they reached their new home, a log cabin surrounded by a dozen or so other ramshackle dwellings. There Colonel Sellers helped the Hawkinses start their new life. Yet Squire Hawkins did not prosper as he had hoped; rather, he made and lost several fortunes.

Ten years later, Colonel Sellers was living in Hawkeye, a town some distance away. Squire Hawkins, by that time, was impoverished. Clay had gone off to find work, and Laura, now a beautiful young girl, volunteered to do so. Washington and Emily could not decide what to do. Clay brought money to the destitute family and paid Washington's stagecoach fare to Hawkeye, where he found Colonel Sellers as poorly off as the Hawkins family. Colonel Sellers, however, was a magnificent talker. His fireless stove became a secret invention, his meager dinner a feast, his barren house a mansion, and under the spell of his words, Washington's dismal prospects were changed to expectations of a glowing future. Colonel Sellers spoke confidentially of private deals with New York bankers and the Rothschilds. He confided that he was working on a patent medicine that would bring him a fortune.

Colonel Sellers took Washington to the real estate office of General Boswell. It was arranged that the young man should live with the Boswells while working for the General. Before long, he fell in love with Boswell's daughter Louise.

Squire Hawkins died, leaving his family only the lands in Tennessee. Among his papers, Laura found some letters from a Major Lackland, who apparently had come across a man believed to be Laura's father. Before Hawkins could get in touch with the man, he had disappeared. Laura's doubtful parentage made her an object of scorn in the region.

Two young New Yorkers, Philip Sterling and Harry Brierly, set out for Missouri to work as construction engineers for a railroad company. In St. Louis, they met Colonel Sellers, who entertained them with boasts about his investments and treated them to drinks and cigars. When he showed embarrassment, pretending to have lost his money, Philip relieved him by paying the bill.

In Philadelphia, Ruth Bolton, the daughter of Eli and Margaret Bolton, both Quakers, received a letter from Philip. Rebelling against the rules of the Friends, Ruth told her parents that she wanted to do something different, perhaps study medicine.

Colonel Sellers continued to befriend the two young men in St. Louis. He went so far as to suggest that the railroad should be built through Stone's Landing, a small village not along the route planned for the road. Like the Colonel, Harry was a man of imagination. When their money ran out, Harry and Philip went to an engineer's camp near Hawkeye, and the Colonel joined them to plan the city to be built there.

Philip and Harry arrived in Hawkeye eight years after the death of Squire Hawkins. The Civil War had been fought; the Hawkinses were still supported by Clay, and Laura had become a beauty. During the war, she had married a Colonel Selby, who, already married, had deserted her when his regiment was transferred. After that calamity, she turned her eye upon Harry Brierly, who fell in love with her.

When Senator Dilworthy went to Hawkeye to investigate Colonel Sellers' petition for funds to improve the area, the Senator met Washington Hawkins. Thinking Washington a fine young man, the Senator took him on as an unpaid secretary. Laura charmed Senator Dilworthy to such an extent that he invited her to visit his family in Washington.

Ruth Bolton was in school at Fallkill, where she stayed with a family named Montague. On their way to New York, Philip and Harry stopped to see her. Philip was disappointed with the manner in which Ruth accepted him. Alice Montague was kinder to him; Ruth seemed too attentive to Harry. In Washington, Harry saw the appropriation for Stone's Landing passed by Congress. When the New York office sent no money with which to pay the workers at Stone's Landing, Harry went to New York to investigate. Speculation was everywhere; even Mr. Bolton decided to buy some land near the railroad in Pennsylvania. Unfortunately, Harry learned that the bribes to obtain the Congressional appropriation had been so costly that there was no money left to pay for the work at Stone's Landing.

Hired by Mr. Bolton, Philip went to develop the natural resources of a tract of land in Ilium, Pennsylvania. He became a frequent visitor at the Boltons'.

Senator Dilworthy invited Laura to come to Washington, where she immediately became a belle—much to Harry Brierly's consternation. Many people believed her an heiress. The Senator attempted to use her influence in getting congressmen to vote in favor of a bill in which he was interested. At a party, Laura saw Colonel Selby, who had come to Washington to claim reimbursement for some cotton destroyed during the war. When the former lovers met, Laura knew that she still loved Selby and the two began to be seen together. When he left Washington and Laura, she followed him to a New York hotel, where she shot him.

The opening of the Ilium coal mine found Philip and Harry hard at work. Before they had located the main vein, however, Mr. Bolton went bankrupt and surrendered all his property to his creditors. Philip was able to buy the Ilium tract. Ruth, graduated from medical school, had gone to work in a Philadelphia hospital. Harry was in New York, a witness at Laura's murder trial. Philip, hoping to read law in the squire's office, visited the Montagues in Fallkill. Mr. Montague, seeing value in Philip's mine, offered to finance a further excavation.

Laura's trial attracted much attention. Claiming that she was insane, her lawyer tried to show that her mind had been deranged from the time she lost her parents in the riverboat fire.

Senator Dilworthy's bill, a measure to establish a university for blacks on the Hawkins land in Tennessee, had been for some time in committee. Washington Hawkins and Colonel Sellers expected to make a fortune when the bill passed. Then Dilworthy, up for reelection, attempted to buy votes and was exposed, and his bill was defeated on the floor of the Senate. Washington and Sellers were crestfallen.

Laura was acquitted of the murder charge. Penniless, she tried to begin a lecture tour, but on her first appearance, she found only an empty auditorium. On the streets, she was attacked by angry citizens and driven home to a cold room, where she died of a broken heart.

Philip finally found coal in his shaft, but his elation subsided when a telegram from the Boltons told him that Ruth was gravely ill. He hurried to her bedside, where his loving presence brought her back to life and him.

Critical Evaluation:

The Gilded Age, as opposed to a golden age, is an excellent portrait of the American post-Civil War years, a period for which Mark Twain's title has become a name. Lacking a cohesive plot, the novel derives its unity from its satiric purpose and ironic tone. These begin with the preface, which lampoons contemporary fictional practices, and continue by satirizing formulaic fiction, economic speculation, political corruption, fraudulent piety, visionaries, exploiters, confidence men, and the get-rich-quick mentality. The book is considered one of the best sources for an understanding of the economic boom years during the administration of President Ulysses S. Grant.

Reportedly, when Mark Twain and Charles Dudley Warner, essayist and editor of the *Hartford Courant*, were ridiculing the contemporary sentimental novels their wives were reading, the women taunted them to write something better. Although both were seasoned writers, neither had attempted a novel before. Twain turned out the first eleven chapters and Warner the next twelve. For the remaining forty, they alternated small and larger units, then patched them together to make the book, completing it in about three months. Of the total, Twain claimed thirty-three chapters and parts of three others. He contributed most of the frontier episodes and Warner most of those concerning the East, the two parts interwoven by the theme of speculation, by Senator Dilworthy's moves between the West and the East, by the trip to Missouri of Philip Sterling and Harry Brierly, by travels to Washington, D.C., and by Laura Hawkins. Mark Twain's portion was reworked into a successful play. The numerous stock sitautions—the adopted child searching for a father hinted to be aristocratic, the villainous seducer, the false marriage, the steamboat disaster, the adopted child becoming more helpful to his parents than the natural child, the reliable Philip contrasted with the foppish Harry, a heroine saved from grave illness, the beautiful wronged woman turned vengeful, the industrious young man finally earning wealth—were intended to burlesque the fiction that was then popular. Similarly, the obscure mottoes, contributed by the Hartford philologist James Hammond Trumbull, parody the contemporary practice of heading chapters with erudite quotations suggestive of moral profundity. Adding the mottoes' translations in 1899 provided a basis for extending the copyright.

Many reviewers have judged Twain's opening chapters, drawn almost completely from his own family history, to be the best part of the book. Squire Silas Hawkins and his wife Nancy, with their children Washington and Emily, move from Tennessee to Missouri as had John and Jane Clemens with Samuel's older siblings, Orion, Pamela, Margaret, and Benjamin. The Tennessee land that represents false expectations to Hawkins had held the same meaning for Twain's father. The delightful but unreliable Colonel Beriah Sellers was, Twain said, a close portrayal of his mother's cousin, James Lampton. Beyond making use of the family history, the authors drew many characters and episodes in the novel as clear parodies of contemporary well-known persons and events. Laura's story is based on the historical Laura D. Fair, whose insanity plea in 1870 extended the notoriety of her having shot her lover. Senator Dilworthy's escapades reenact the vote-buying scandal of Senator Samuel C. Pomeroy of Kansas, which made news in January, 1873. William M. Weed and Mr. Fairoaks were readily recognized by the contemporary audience as "Boss Tweed" of Tammany Hall and Representative Oakes Ames, scandalously exposed for bribing congressmen to fund and then control watered railroad stock. The many topical allusions recognizable to readers of 1873 make the novel a *roman à clef*. Land development speculation and other ambitious schemes were so widespread, however, as were religious cant and hypocrisy motivated by an ethics of greed, that the satire is effective even without identification of all the allusions to actual chicanery.

Social satire gives the novel its dominant theme. The displacement of democratic ideals—those of Thomas Jefferson, Benjamin Franklin, and Thomas Paine—stressing integrity of character and virtuous industry, by dreams of bonanzas that would repeat the robber barons' leaps to luxury represented to Twain and Warner the national evil that supported the Old World idea that one's worth could be measured by one's birth and wealth instead of by one's values and honest achievement. Thus, only the honest work of Philip Sterling and Clay Hawkins is rewarded with material success. Their education for useful work and their genuinely humanitarian motives contrast with the illusory ambitions toward wealth and station that corrupt Washington and Laura into becoming tools of the scoundrels. Laura's expectations from reading sentimental novels, especially those concerning an aristocratic father and a dashing lover, prime her for the seduction and betrayal by Colonel Selby, who embodies the authors' bitter distaste for the myth of Southern chivalry. This theme of appearance contrasted with reality is captured in Colonel Sellers' insistence, as his family and guest suffer from the chill, that one needs only the appearance of heat, not the actual heat itself. The contrast plays out in the perversions of the legal system at Laura's trial: the self-serving bases for choosing jurors, the manipulations of the defense attorney, the corrupt politician-judge, and the misuse of the insanity plea. The preference for appearance over reality also governs the absurdities of Washington, D.C.'s social caste system. The book's title emphasizes the difference between the truly golden and what only appears to be. The book helped establish Twain as a satirist of corrupted American political and religious institutions. It sold 35,000 copies before the panic of 1873 reduced sales—a panic caused by the speculation it burlesqued.

"Critical Evaluation" by Carolyn F. Dickinson

Bibliography:
French, Bryant Morey. *Mark Twain and "The Gilded Age."* Dallas, Tex.: Southern Methodist University Press, 1965. A definitive study of *The Gilded Age*. Identifies the events, persons,

and practices that the novel satirizes. A bibliography and illustrations.

Gerber, John. *Mark Twain*. Boston: Twayne, 1988. Offers a full account of the background for the novel and an evaluation of its significance in the development of Twain as a writer of fiction. Bibliography.

Goldner, Ellen J. "Tangled Web: Lies, Capitalist Expansion, and the Dissolution of the Subject in *The Gilded Age*." *Arizona Quarterly* 49, no. 3 (Autumn, 1993): 59-92. Details the threat to American individualism from the expanding global economy in 1873, allegorized in some of Colonel Sellers' tall tales. Bibliography of economic studies.

Harris, Susan K. "Four Ways to Inscribe a Mackerel: Mark Twain and Laura Hawkins." *Studies in the Novel* 21 (1989): 138-153. Interprets the character of Laura as not only a parody of the sentimental heroine, but also evidence of the authors' antifeminist attitudes.

Rasmussen, R. Kent. *Mark Twain A to Z*. New York: Facts On File, 1995. Contains a chapter-by-chapter synopsis of *The Gilded Age*, identifying which author wrote each part, with cross-references to individual essays on major characters, places, and other topics appearing in the novel.

Sewall, David. *Mark Twain's Languages: Discourse, Dialogue, and Linguistic Variety*. Berkeley: University of California Press, 1987. Explores the corruption of language that accompanies the corruption of institutions. Bibliography.

GILES GOAT-BOY
Or, The Revised New Syllabus

Type of work: Novel
Author: John Barth (1930-   )
Type of plot: Fantasy
Time of plot: A time like the 1960's
Locale: New Tammany College
First published: 1966

Principal characters:
>GEORGE GILES, also called Billy Bocksfuss
>MAXIMILIAN SPIELMAN, his tutor
>VIRGINIA HECTOR, his mother
>GEORGE HERROLD, a person who saved George's life when he was an infant
>ANASTASIA STOKER, loved by George
>MAURICE STOKER, the husband of Anastasia
>PETER GREENE, a friend of George
>CROAKER, a brutish exchange student and football hero
>EBLIS EIERKOPF, former Bonifacist scientist who lives with Croaker and rides on his shoulders
>HAROLD BRAY, who claims to be a Grand Tutor

The Story:

Billy Bocksfuss lived contentedly in the goat barns of New Tammany College, thinking he was a goat and the child of Maximilian "Max" Spielman, his keeper and tutor, and a goat named Mary V. Appenzeller. One day, after killing his best friend, a goat named Redfern's Tommy, Billy learned that he was human. For his human name, he chose George, after George Herrold, the man who found him as an infant on a booklift leading into the belly of WESCAC (West Campus Automatic Computer), the giant computer that ran New Tammany College. In a way, George's father was WESCAC, for George resulted from an experiment in which WESCAC collected samples of human sperm to produce the GILES, Grand-Tutorial Ideal, Laboratory Eugenical Specimen.

In rescuing the baby, George Herrold was partly EATen by WESCAC. EAT stood for Electo-encephalic Amplification and Transmission, a means of disrupting brain waves and thus killing people; its first test was against the Amaterasus, against whom New Tammany College still fought after it had defeated Siegfrieder College in Campus Riot II. Max and Eblis Eierkopf pushed the EAT button, killing thousands of Amaterasus, something for which Max felt great remorse. Only partially EATen when he rescued the infant, George Herrold still lived but acted like a child.

George learned about sex from watching students make love around the goat barns. He learned about love from Max and from a woman he called Lady Creamhair, who fed him peanut butter sandwiches and told him stories such as "The Three Billy Goats Gruff." Later, he discovered she was Virginia Hector, his mother, but first he decided that her concern for him was sexual and acted accordingly, to his later shame.

At the age of twenty-two, George set out to achieve what he felt was his destiny and to fulfill his assignment, "Pass All Fail All." Only a Grand Tutor could enter WESCAC's belly un-

EATen. Since he had come from WESCAC's belly by means of the booklift, he thought he must be destined to be a Grand Tutor. As Grand Tutor, he intended to enter WESCAC's belly, destroy its AIM (Automatic Implementation Mechanism), and thus prevent Campus Riot III. One night, awakening to the sound of Max blowing the shofar, he left the goat barns, walking toward the central campus of New Tammany College. When George reached a fork in the road and Max tried to get him to return to the barns, he plunged through the woods, determined to continue. George Herrold and Max accompanied George. They reached a river with a washed-out bridge. There, George Herrold drowned trying to cross to Anastasia Stoker, who stood on the other side displaying her nude body and shouting, "Croaker," attempting to lure Croaker, a gigantic, primitive exchange student who had run amuck. Anastasia had been brought up as Virginia Hector's daughter. Anastasia, however, was not Virginia's biological child. After George Herrold drowned, Croaker came, took George on his back, crossed the river, and raped Anastasia. George then recrossed the river on Croaker's back, got Max, and brought him to the other side.

Maurice Stoker, Anastasia's husband, then came with his troopers on motorcycles and took Anastasia, George, and George Herrold's body to the Power House, which Stoker ran. The Power House supplied the power for WESCAC and New Tammany College, which was engaged in the Quiet Riot with the Nikolayans and EASCAC, the Nikolayan equivalent of WESCAC. George enjoyed the chaos in the Power House. He attended a party that Stoker threw at which, during George Herrold's funeral service, George "serviced" Anastasia.

The next morning, George, riding Croaker, found Max near a wrecked motorcycle. George put Max on Croaker, and George started riding the motorcycle toward the main campus of New Tammany College, when they met Peter Greene, owner of many industries and businesses, including Greene Timber and Plastics, a company that was destroying the forests of New Tammany College. Greene, who was hitchhiking, accompanied the travelers to the main campus.

Arriving the last day of Carnival, they attended a performance of *The Tragedy of Taliped Decanus*, about the dean who killed his father and married his mother. Toward the performance's end, Max disappeared, having been arrested for the murder of Herman Hermann, the Siegfrieder leader of the Bonifacists during Campus Riot II, who had been working as one of Stoker's troopers. At the performance's end, Harold Bray flew from the sky and announced that he was the new Grand Tutor. George protested that Bray was an imposter.

After spending the night with Eblis Eierkopf, who felt that WESCAC was the real Grand Tutor, George successfully endured the Trial by Turnstile and went successfully through Scrapegoat Grate. Then, he received his assignment, *"To Be Done At Once, In No Time,"* to *"Fix the Clock," "End the Boundary Dispute," "Overcome Your Infirmity," "See Through Your Ladyship," "Re-Place the Founder's Scroll," "Pass the Finals,"* and *"Present Your ID-Card, Appropriately Signed, to the Proper Authority."* In the course of trying to complete his assignment, George created chaos on the New Tammany campus and brought his college and the Nikolayans to the verge of Campus Riot III. He then entered WESCAC's belly, along with Harold Bray, and when he emerged, he saw that all was ruined.

Arrested, George spent forty weeks imprisoned in the Nether Campus. When he emerged, he tried to correct the problems he had caused earlier. He entered WESCAC's belly a second time. When he emerged, he was almost lynched. Later, George entered the belly for a third time, now locked in a sexual embrace with Anastasia. When they emerged, Virginia Hector, who had gone insane, greeted them with the word, "A-*plus.*" George pronounced her his first graduate.

Briefly going to the goat barns with Anastasia, George returned to campus with a goat, Tom's

Tommy's Tom, who attacked Bray, driving him from New Tammany College at the exact time that Max was being shafted for the murder to which he had confessed. In a "Posttape," George said that at the age of thirty-three and one-third, again in the Nether Campus, he dictated his story to WESCAC and the book about his adventures resulted. He felt that he would eventually be shafted and that it did not matter whether people believed his story.

Critical Evaluation:

Giles Goat-Boy came from what John Barth called the Ur-Myth, or the myth of the hero, that he read about in *The Hero: A Study in Tradition, Drama, and Myth* by Fitzroy Richard Somerset, Fourth Baron Raglan and *The Hero With a Thousand Faces* by Joseph Campbell. *Giles Goat-Boy* follows Campbell's description of the pattern of the mythic hero. Giles's journey parallels those of the heroes Campbell treats, including Odysseus, Aeneas, and Jesus. The mythic hero's adventure includes a humble birth or infancy that belies the hero's great origins, a journey to the underworld, and a triumphant return.

George's comic adventures parody the hero's quest and satirize many prominent people and events of the twentieth century. Max, for example, is partially modeled on Albert Einstein and J. Robert Oppenheimer. A character called Lucius "Lucky" Rexford is largely modeled on John F. Kennedy; Campus Riot II is modeled on World War II; the Quiet Riot, on the Cold War; and New Tammany College, on the United States. Barth combines topical satire and allusion with perhaps the most universal story known to humanity—the hero's journey—to produce a book of epic proportions.

In addition to the story itself, *Giles Goat-Boy* employs metafictional devices reminiscent of earlier works by Barth. A "Publisher's Disclaimer" by the "Editor-in-Chief," for example, contains statements by four editors arguing whether the book should be published. Also included are a "Cover-Letter to the Editors and publisher" by "This regenerate Seeker after Answers, J.B.," a "Posttape," a "Postscript to the Posttape," and a "footnote to the Postscript to the Posttape"—all by Barth himself, in which he creates the fiction that Barth is an editor of a manuscript given to him by one Giles [,] Stoker, son of George Giles and Anastasia, but that parts of the manuscript got mixed with one of Barth's own. The manuscript caused him, the frame story goes, to give up his career as a writer to pursue the truths in it. The manuscript itself may or may not have been put on tape by WESCAC. The Posttape tends to contradict everything toward which the manuscript points, the Postscript to the Posttape questions all that the Posttape says, and the Footnote casts doubt on the authenticity of the Postscript. The art of fiction humbly emulates the life of academe.

Barth plays numerous other jokes on the reader. For example, the play about Taliped Decanus is a highly comical retelling of the story of Oedipus. Taliped, like Oedipus, means swollen- or club-footed, and decanus means dean, the university-world equivalent of rex (king). George Giles's life in many ways parallels and parodies Oedipus' life. Barth often uses names jokingly. Giles is the name of the seventh-century patron saint of cripples; George Giles limps because his foot was damaged when, as an infant, he was put in the booklift. Bocksfuss means goat's foot, again referring to George's limp. Eblis Eierkopf means devilish egghead. He eats eggs, is bald, and is thoroughly committed to science, to the exclusion of human values. Unlike Max, he feels no remorse at having pushed the EAT button. Peter Greene becomes the Gilesian parody of Saint Peter; he is the anything-but-saintly founder of the Gilesian church. Maurice Stoker, as his last name implies, is a Satan figure. Once, when George enters the library, he finds a woman reading a book that probably is *Giles Goat-Boy*; she seems to be up to the exact place at which George finds her reading.

In addition to the book's humor, there is an element of seriousness: George Giles is a definite hero. When faced with a dilemma, such as the one he encounters at the fork in the road, he unhesitatingly creates a third choice by making his own path between the two forks. He achieves his destiny to "Pass All Fail All." Like the typical hero, he snatches victory from the jaws of defeat, but the victory is ambiguous and may not be a victory at all. Like Jesus and other saviors, he descends into the nether regions, achieves a victory there, rises from the land of the dead, and works what at least seem to be miracles. Critics interpret his three descents into WESCAC's belly as involving George's visions, first of diversity (a Western concept), second of unity (an Eastern view), and, finally, of the interdependence of opposites (a synthesis). In the end, George leaves a disputed legacy further complicated by disputes between his disciples. Thus, *Giles Goat-Boy* is a parody of the New Testament, recounting the life of what may or may not be the Grand Tutor of New Tammany College who came to campus to show students the way to Commencement Gate.

Richard Tuerk

Bibliography:

Harris, Charles B. *Passionate Virtuosity: The Fiction of John Barth*. Champaign: University of Illinois Press, 1983. Sees the book as a search for unity, in which Barth speaks the unspeakable.

Safer, Elaine B. *The Contemporary American Comic Epic: The Novels of Barth, Pynchon, Gaddis, and Kesey*. Detroit: Wayne State University Press, 1988. Treats elements of the absurd and the parody of Emersonian ideas of education in the novel.

Scholes, Robert. *Fabulation and Metafiction*. Champaign: University of Illinois Press, 1979. Contains a pioneering treatment of the novel. Sees the book as a combination of philosophy and myth.

Tobin, Patricia. *John Barth and the Anxiety of Continuance*. Philadelphia: University of Pennsylvania Press, 1992. Sees George Giles as poet-as-hero. Focuses on the Oedipus story as source.

Walkiewicz, E. P. *John Barth*. Boston: Twayne, 1986. Treats the novel in terms of myth, satire, and parody and the idea of repetition within it.

THE GILGAMESH EPIC

Type of work: Poetry
Author: Unknown
Type of plot: Adventure
Time of plot: Antiquity
Locale: The ancient world
First published: c. 2000 B.C.E. (English translation, 1917)

Principal characters:
 GILGAMESH, the ruler of Uruk
 ENGIDU, his companion
 ANU, the chief god
 ISHTAR, the divinity of fertility
 UTNAPISHTIM, a man who found the secret of life
 UR-SHANABI, the boatman on the waters of death
 NINSUN, a goddess
 SIDURI, the divine cup-bearer
 KHUMBABA, a dragon

The Story:

Gilgamesh was the wisest, strongest, and most handsome of mortals, for he was two-thirds god and one-third man. As king of the city-state of Uruk he built a monumental wall around the city, but in doing so he overworked the city's inhabitants unmercifully, to the point where they prayed to the gods for relief.

The god Anu listened to their plea and called the goddess Aruru to fashion another demigod like Gilgamesh in order that the two heroes might fight, and thus give Uruk peace. Aruru created the warrior Engidu out of clay and sent him to live among the animals of the hills. A hunter of Uruk found Engidu and in terror reported his existence to Gilgamesh. Gilgamesh advised the hunter to take a priestess to Engidu's watering place to lure Engidu to the joys of civilization and away from his animal life. The priestess initiated Engidu into civilization with her body, her bread, and her wine. Having forsaken his animal existence, Engidu and the priestess started for Uruk. On their arrival she told him of the strength and wisdom of Gilgamesh and of how Gilgamesh had told the goddess Ninsun about his dreams of meeting Engidu, his equal, in combat.

Engidu challenged Gilgamesh by barring his way to the temple. An earth-shaking fight ensued in which Gilgamesh stopped Engidu's onslaught. Engidu praised Gilgamesh's strength and the two enemies became inseparable friends. Gilgamesh informed Engidu of his wish to conquer the terrible monster, Khumbaba, and challenged him to go along. Engidu replied that the undertaking was full of peril for both. Gilgamesh answered that Engidu's fear of death deprived him of his might. At last Engidu agreed to go with his friend. Gilgamesh then went to the elders and they, like Engidu, warned him of the perils he would encounter. Seeing his determination, the elders gave him their blessing. Gilgamesh then went to Ninsun and she also warned him of the great dangers, but to no avail. Then she took Engidu aside and told him to give Gilgamesh special protection.

Upon climbing the cedar mountain to reach Khumbaba, Gilgamesh related three terrible dreams to Engidu, who shored up Gilgamesh's spirit by placing a favorable interpretation on them. On reaching the gate to the cedar wood where Khumbaba resided, the pair were stopped by the watchman, who possessed seven magic mantles. The two heroes succeeded in overcoming him. Accidentally, Engidu touched the magic portal of the gate; immediately he felt faint and weak, as if afraid of death. The champions entered the cedar wood and, with the aid of the sun god, slew Khumbaba.

Upon their return to Uruk after their victory, the goddess Ishtar fell in love with Gilgamesh and asked him to be her consort. Gilgamesh, being wiser than her previous consorts, recalled all of the evil things she had done to her earlier lovers. Ishtar then angrily ascended to heaven and reported his scornful refusal to Anu. Threatening to destroy humanity, she forced Anu to create a monster bull that would kill Gilgamesh.

Anu formed the bull and sent it to Uruk. After it had slain five hundred warriors in two snorts, Engidu jumped on its back while Gilgamesh drove his sword into its neck. Engidu then threw the bull's thighbone in Ishtar's face, and Gilgamesh held a feast of victory in his palace.

Engidu, still ailing from touching the portal to the cedar wood, cursed those who had showed him civilization. He related his nightmares to Gilgamesh, grew faint-hearted, and feared death. Since Engidu had been cursed by touching the gate, he died. Gilgamesh mourned his friend six days and nights; on the seventh he left Uruk to cross the steppes in search of Utnapishtim, the mortal who had discovered the secret of life.

Upon reaching the mountain named Mashu, he found scorpion men guarding the entrance to the underground passage. They received him cordially when they learned he was seeking Utnapishtim, but they warned him that no one had ever found a way through the mountain.

Gilgamesh traveled the twelve miles through the mountain in pitch darkness, and at last he entered a garden. There he found Siduri, the cup-bearing goddess, who remarked on his haggard condition. Gilgamesh explained that his woeful appearance had been caused by the loss of Engidu, and that he sought Utnapishtim. The goddess advised him to live in pleasure at home and warned him of the dangers ahead.

Gilgamesh continued ahead, seeking the boatman Ur-Shanabi, who might possibly take him across the waters of death. On finding Ur-Shanabi's stone coffers, Gilgamesh broke them in anger, but he made up for them by presenting the boatman with huge poles. Ur-Shanabi then ferried Gilgamesh across the waters of death.

Utnapishtim, meeting Gilgamesh on the shore, also spoke of his haggard condition. Gilgamesh told him about the loss of Engidu and his own search for the secret of life. Utnapishtim replied that nothing was made to last forever, that life was transient, and that death was part of the inevitable process.

Gilgamesh then asked how Utnapishtim had found the secret of eternal life, and Utnapishtim told him the story of the Great Flood. Utnapishtim had been told in a dream of the gods' plans to flood the land. So he built an ark and put his family and all kinds of animals on it. When the flood came, he and those on the ark survived, and when the flood subsided he found himself on Mount Nisser. After the waters had returned to their normal level, he gave thanks to the gods, and in return the god Ea blessed him and his wife with the secret of life everlasting.

After finishing his story Utnapishtim advised Gilgamesh to return home, but before he had Ur-Shanabi bathe Gilgamesh and clothe him in a robe that remained clean as long as he lived. As Gilgamesh was leaving, Utnapishtim gave him the secret of life, a magic plant that grew at the bottom of the waters of death. However, as Gilgamesh bathed in a pool on his way home, an evil serpent ate the plant.

On arriving home Gilgamesh went to Ninsun to inquire how he could reach Engidu in the land of the dead. Although Ninsun directed him, he failed in his attempt because he broke some of the taboos that she had laid out for him. Deeply disappointed, he made one final appeal to the god Ea, the lord of the depths of the waters, and Engidu was brought forth. Gilgamesh asked Engidu what happened to one after death, and Engidu laid bare the full terrors of the afterworld. Worms, neglect, and disrespect were the lot of the dead.

Critical Evaluation:

The Sumerian tale of *Gilgamesh* is the oldest to have survived into the modern era. Thus the greatest value of *Gilgamesh* is that it opens a window for modern readers into their collective past. The tale's content reveals much about humanity's earliest social and religious concerns, while its form reveals equivalent insights about the relationship between instruction and entertainment in an oral culture.

The story of *Gilgamesh* reveals both a desire to commemorate the hero's greatness and an obligation to learn from his flaws. The first thing the audience learns from the story is that Gilgamesh built protective walls around the city, a great gift to his society. When the audience next learns that the king has been abusive to the young men of the city and has deflowered young maidens, their disapproval of these acts is tempered by their initial approval of his great accomplishment. Overall, the early portions of the story demonstrate that the abiding criterion for judgment is not the happiness of the individual, even if that individual is the king, but the good of society as a whole. When Gilgamesh exercises the kingly privilege in deflowering maidens, his actions may be legal, but they fail to provide any benefit for Uruk, and are therefore condemned. Thus does the audience learn that greatness entails responsibility, not just strength.

Crucial to the lesson of the story is Gilgamesh's status as two-thirds god, one-third human. Kings are more than human, and therefore are revered; yet at the same time kings are imperfect, so that as they learn, their growth will serve as a model for the improvement of their subjects. One special feature of *Gilgamesh* is its introduction of an additional intermediary between the king and his people, Engidu. Precisely because the hero is so far above his subjects, he needs to befriend someone who is thoroughly human, though possessing heroic strength; only in this way can the audience achieve an emotional identification, or at least a profound empathy, with the hero. They can never quite see themselves as Gilgamesh, but they can see themselves as Engidu, standing by the hero's side, supporting him, making possible his glorious triumphs. Thus when the pair are confronted by the Bull of Heaven, it is Engidu who leaps upon him, allowing Gilgamesh to make the killing blow. Gilgamesh gains a triumph, but Engidu shares in the moment—and the audience shares in both.

Nevertheless, Engidu is mortal. His death motivates the greatest feat of *Gilgamesh*, the hero's quest for the secret of immortality. In his desperation, in his willingness to commit all of his strength to his search, and most of all in his willingness to share the secret of renewed youth with the people of Uruk once he has obtained it, Gilgamesh displays the true nobility of the heroic character. It is his failure in this final quest, not his ability to triumph over Khumbaba or the Bull of Heaven, that stays with the audience and teaches the final lesson of the story. If even the greatest hero of them all cannot escape his destiny, if every man and woman is doomed someday to die, then perhaps each member of the audience who hears the Gilgamesh story has done the right thing, simply by choosing life. For if the city is to thrive, its citizens must accept the will of the gods, obey the will of the king, and strive not for more than can be granted but for such happiness as is their lot. In a society such as Uruk's, whose religion offers no travel after death to some promised land of gardens and fountains, such a lesson is the only one that can lead to success.

Nevertheless, Gilgamesh's desire for immortality is not totally denigrated. It is what separates the long series of forgotten kings in Uruk from the heroic figure who earns the title role in his own story. When Gilgamesh expresses the desire to set his name in brick where no man's name has ever appeared, he is articulating a yearning shared by many. This approval is clear in the large proportion of the story that is given over to the campaign against Khumbaba. This is Gilgamesh's great triumph, the fulfillment of his desire to do what no man has ever done. Modern speculation is that this section of the tale is based on an actual expedition—perhaps one led by the historical king Gilgamesh—across the desert, into the mountains, which brought tons of precious wood back to the city and perhaps even enabled the building of the walls and temples so proudly referred to at the beginning and end of the tale.

Finally, the form of the Gilgamesh story also reveals much about the special demands of oral composition and performance. Speeches with vital plot or thematic content are repeated, to ensure that the audience gets the message or to underscore the importance of the event. In a world without written communication, messengers typically repeated back what they had been told in order to make sure they had heard correctly; when this feature is incorporated into the world of the story, it provides additional connection between the tale and its audience. Formulaic phrases are also repeated, often accumulating great power. The best example of this feature of oral composition occurs during Gilgamesh's trip through the darkness of the mountain tunnel between his world and the world of the gods, when the hero travels many leagues with "darkness ahead of him and darkness behind him."

"Critical Evaluation" by Hartley S. Spatt

Bibliography:

Gardner, John, and John Maier, trans. *Gilgamesh*. New York: Vintage Books, 1985. Each column of the actual tablets is translated, then supplemented by numerous parallel texts. An appendix analyzes the tablets in more detail, demonstrating the extreme difficulty of establishing any single version of *Gilgamesh*.

Heidel, Alexander. *The Gilgamesh Epic and Old Testament Parallels*. 2d ed. Chicago: University of Chicago Press, 1963. The first, and still the clearest, study of the close links between Sumerian and Hebrew tales of natural heroism and supernatural disaster. The parallels will be striking to the reader.

Kovacs, Maureen G., trans. *The Epic of Gilgamesh*. Stanford, Calif.: Stanford University Press, 1989. This translation attempts to serve as a readable text for the student reader, including substantial notes on parallel and supplementary texts. Although Kovacs manages to create a continuous story, she achieves neither the readability of Sandars' translation, nor the precision of Gardner and Maier's work.

Sandars, N. K., trans. *The Epic of Gilgamesh*. Harmondsworth, Middlesex, England: Penguin, 1960. This is the standard text version of the epic, rendered as a continuous, compelling story. Although its exact readings have been superseded in many cases by discoveries made during recent decades, it remains the best attempt at recapturing the original audience's experience of the epic.

Tigay, Jeffrey H. *The Evolution of the Gilgamesh Epic*. Philadelphia: University of Pennsylvania Press, 1982. Tigay demonstrates that numerous differences among the various redactions of the Gilgamesh saga resulted in significantly different versions of the story. Translations that combine passages from separate versions in order to achieve a more readable story therefore distort the saga.

THE GLASS KEY

Type of work: Novel
Author: Dashiell Hammett (1894-1961)
Type of plot: Detective and mystery
Time of plot: 1930's
Locale: New York City area
First published: serial, 1930; book, 1931

> *Principal characters:*
> NED BEAUMONT, a gambler and amateur detective
> PAUL MADVIG, his friend and the city's political boss
> SENATOR HENRY, Madvig's candidate for reelection
> JANET HENRY, his daughter
> SHAD O'RORY, Madvig's rival
> OPAL MADVIG, Madvig's daughter
> BERNIE DESPAIN, a gambler who owes Ned money

The Story:

Ned Beaumont reported to his friend, Paul Madvig, the political boss of a town in the New York City area that he had found the dead body of Taylor Henry, the son of Senator Henry, Madvig's candidate for reelection. When Madvig failed to show much interest, Ned told his story to the police. The next day, he went to Bernie Despain to collect $3,250 that he had won betting on a horse race. He found that Bernie had vanished, leaving behind IOU's made out by Taylor Henry to the worth of $1,200. Ned asked to be appointed special investigator in the district attorney's office so that he could work on the Taylor Henry case. What he really wanted to do was to find Bernie and get his money.

His first step was to get the help of Madvig's daughter, Opal, who had been meeting Taylor secretly. Ned had not found a hat on Taylor the night of the murder. Opal gave him one from the room she and Taylor had rented. Then Ned went to a speakeasy in New York that Bernie frequented. Bernie came in accompanied by a burly bodyguard who, when Ned demanded his money, struck Ned a terrific blow. With the help of Jack Rumsen, a private detective, Ned trailed Bernie from the hotel where he was staying to a brownstone house on Forty-ninth Street. There he told Bernie that he had planted Taylor's hat behind a sofa cushion in Bernie's hotel room and would leave it there for the police to find if Bernie did not pay him what he owed him. Bernie paid.

Back in town, Ned went to see Farr, the district attorney, who showed him an envelope enclosing paper on which were typed three questions that implicated Madvig in Taylor's murder. Meanwhile, Madvig had decided to have the police close down several speakeasies belonging to the gangster and ward boss Shad O'Rory. O'Rory had reopened the Dog House, and when Ned went there for information, O'Rory had him tortured for several days. Ned finally escaped and was taken to a hospital.

There he had many callers, including Madvig and Taylor's sister, Janet Henry. Opal Madvig went to tell Ned she was sure her father had killed Taylor. Ned assured her that he did not believe Madvig had committed the murder. Partly recovered, he left the hospital against orders.

Shortly afterward, Ned and Madvig dined with Senator Henry and his daughter Janet. Ned made Janet admit that she secretly hated Madvig, who was in love with her. Ned went to see

Madvig and told him that even his henchmen were beginning to betray him because they thought he had committed the murder. Madvig admitted that Taylor had followed him out of the Henry house that night, that they had quarreled, and that he had killed Taylor with a brown, knobby cane that Taylor had been carrying. Madvig claimed he had then carried the cane away under his coat and burned it. When Ned later asked Janet to look for the cane, she told him it was with others in the hall of their home. She also told him of a dream in which she and Ned had found a house with a banquet spread inside; they had to unlock the door and let out a great many snakes before they could go in to enjoy the food.

Ned went to Farr's office and signed an affidavit account of Madvig's confession. Then he went to a bar where he found Jeff, O'Rory's bodyguard. In a private room upstairs, he accused Jeff of being involved in a killing planned by O'Rory. O'Rory walked in on them, and in the ensuing quarrel, Jeff strangled O'Rory. Ned had a waiter call the police to the scene.

Ned went to the Madvig home, where Madvig's mother said that her son was nowhere to be found and that Opal had unsuccessfully attempted to commit suicide. The next morning, Ned went to Senator Henry's house and told the senator that Madvig had confessed. It was all Janet and Ned could do to keep the senator from rushing out to kill Madvig. The senator asked Janet to leave him alone with Ned. Ned told him that Janet hated Madvig. The senator insisted he was not going to permit the murderer of his son to go unpunished. Then Ned accused Senator Henry of killing Taylor, of wanting to kill Madvig so that he would not testify against him, and of caring more for his own reelection than for the life of his son. The senator confessed that he had interfered in a street quarrel between Taylor and Madvig and had asked the political boss to leave him with his son. Madvig had done so after giving him the cane that Madvig had taken away from Taylor. The senator, angry with his son for the quarrel he had forced on Madvig, had angrily struck Taylor with the cane and killed him. He had then carried home the cane. After hearing the old man's confession, Ned refused to leave him alone because he feared he would kill himself before the police arrived.

The next day, Janet begged Ned to let her go with him to New York. She said the key to the house in her dream had been of glass and had shattered just as they opened the door because they had had to force the lock. When Madvig came in, he learned that he had lost Janet and that she was going away with Ned Beaumont.

Critical Evaluation:

The Glass Key was Dashiell Hammett's favorite among his novels and may well be, in the words of critic-novelist Julian Symons, "the peak of Hammett's achievement, which is to say, the peak of the crime writer's art in the twentieth century."

Although Ned Beaumont has much in common with Hammett's other "hard-boiled" heroes, Sam Spade and Continental Op, he is not only a professional detective hired to solve a crime but also a man involuntarily thrust into the center of a violent and puzzling situation. The fate of his employer and best friend, Paul Madvig—and ultimately his own—depends on his ability to solve the murder of Taylor Henry. Beaumont's search for the murderer becomes, moreover, not only a problem in detection but also an exploration of the social mores and political forces operative in the America of 1931. As Ned pursues his quest, he comes to understand his own relationship to that social and political system.

Hammett's picture of big-city politics has little to do with electoral niceties. Favors are bought and sold. Survival and power go to the fittest, that is, to those most willing and able to manipulate the power factions as they vie to maintain and expand their own self-interests. Paul Madvig is no more honest than his rival Shad O'Rory, only a bit more adroit and likeable.

Holding on to power is a matter of keeping a delicate balance between contending factions; the slightest mistake can topple anyone from the pinnacle. Those not at the center of the struggle, from District Attorney Farr down to the bartender at the speakeasy where O'Rory is murdered, are loyal only to themselves and switch sides at the slightest indication that power relationships are changing. Thus, to everyone except his sister Janet, the murder of Taylor Henry represents only a dangerous variable in the struggle for political dominance. The most "respectable" member of the establishment, old Senator Henry, turns out to be the most corrupt. He kills his own son in a fit of temper and is willing to kill again to keep the truth concealed.

Ned Beaumont accepts and even participates in this system of institutionalized corruption. His loyalty to Paul, Janet, and the "job" he has to do, however, suggests another morality, one based on personal relationships rather than on adherence to particular institutions or abstract principles. Although Beaumont fights with Madvig, leaves him at one point, and finally goes off with his girl, he maintains a dogged loyalty to his boss and friend throughout the book, even in the face of nearly fatal tortures and beatings. If the system is corrupt, Hammett seems to be saying, it is still possible for a man to retain his moral integrity by holding fast to his own sense of self, his personal code, and those commitments, to self and others, that are the product of that code.

The book ends on an optimistic note, with Ned and Janet about to leave together. Paul accepts the new arrangement with equanimity and promises to use his expertise and power to do a "housecleaning." This final optimism is unconvincing, and the image of the American Dream that remains in the mind of the reader is Janet's dream, which gives the book its title: a delicious banquet apparently free for the taking, but guarded by hidden snakes that swarm over the unwary who dare to unlock the door with a glass key.

Bibliography:
Dooley, Dennis. *Dashiell Hammett*. New York: Frederick Ungar, 1984. A basic survey of Hammett's work and life specifically aimed at the general reader, as well as discussions of the five novels. Dooley considers *The Glass Key* less intense and suspenseful than the earlier novels.
Gregory, Sinda. *Private Investigations: The Novels of Dashiell Hammett*. Carbondale: Southern Illinois University Press, 1985. A full-length study of the five major novels. Chapter 5, "*The Glass Key:* A Psychological Detective Novel," argues that the work is an ultimately unsuccessful attempt to move beyond the genre of the detective novel into the realm of the serious psychological novel.
Layman, Richard. *Shadow Man: The Life of Dashiell Hammett*. New York: Harcourt Brace Jovanovich, 1981. An objective, readable, and carefully researched and documented biography. Provides valuable historical and biographical context for *The Glass Key*.
Marling, William. *Dashiell Hammett*. Boston: Twayne, 1983. A concise introductory survey specifically aimed at the general reader. The brief discussion of *The Glass Key* focuses on the relationship of the three main characters.
Metress, Christopher, ed. *The Critical Response to Dashiell Hammett*. Westport, Conn.: Greenwood, 1994. Includes an introduction, which surveys the history of Hammett criticism, as well as excerpts from reviews, commentaries, and critical discussions of his novels. The section on *The Glass Key* includes a revised version of a complete essay on the novel by Jon Thompson.

THE GLASS MENAGERIE

Type of work: Drama
Author: Tennessee Williams (Thomas Lanier Williams, 1911-1983)
Type of plot: Psychological realism
Time of plot: 1940's, following World War II
Locale: St. Louis, Missouri
First Performed: 1944; first published, 1945

Principal characters:
TOM WINGFIELD, the play's narrator
AMANDA WINGFIELD, his mother
LAURA WINGFIELD, his sister
JIM O'CONNOR, Laura's gentleman caller

The Story:

Tom and Laura's father—Amanda Wingfield's husband—had abandoned his family some years ago, and Tom tells the audience that he is about to relate a "memory play," "truth in the pleasant guise of illusion." The time Tom recalls is shortly after World War II, when he lived with his mother and sister in a St. Louis apartment building described as "one of those vast hive-like conglomerations of cellular living-units." Amanda dominated the household as an aging Southern belle who retained her girlish charm as well as an eternal optimism and a fierce determination that she and her children would overcome what she insisted on viewing as temporary obstacles. Laura, who had lived at home since high school, spent her days listening to her father's record collection and playing with the glass animals she collected and called her "menagerie." Tom worked in a shoe factory, a job he loathed and therefore barely tended to, instead focusing his passion on writing poetry and his leisure on going to films.

Tom's recollection of the family's interactions began with an occasion when Amanda told Tom precisely how to eat his dinner. Tom could not stomach his mother's remarks and responded to his mother's lecture with anger. Amanda then turned to Laura, who was upset by the scene, and coddled her while she also cajoled her to remain "fresh and pretty" for the gentleman callers that Laura knew would never arrive. Amanda ignored both her adult children's frustration and embarrassment, and she proceeded to recall aloud her many beaux who sought her company when she was a girl.

Tom remembered that on another day his mother decided to stop in at the business college Laura was supposedly attending, only to find that Laura had quit school early in the semester. Amanda went home and confronted Laura, accusing her of deception. Laura, crippled from a teenage bout with pleurosis, suffered even greater paralysis from shyness and confessed to her mother that she had spent her hours scheduled for class wandering about the city, taking refuge in the museum, the zoo, and the Jewel Box, a hothouse for exotic plants. Amanda's hurt at the thought that Laura had deceived her turned to anguish at the notion that Laura had forfeited her future, until Laura admitted to having once liked a boy in high school. Immediately, Amanda perked up and launched a plan to ensure Laura's welfare by snaring her daughter an eligible man.

Amanda plotted a liaison for Laura while she also attempted to supplement the family income by soliciting magazine subscriptions. She chided Tom for his lack of ambition, and her actions and words resulted in repeated, escalating arguments between them. More and more often, Tom fled to the movies for respite. One day while Amanda and Tom fought, Laura fell, causing mother and son to temporarily halt their hostilities. The separate nature of their care for

Laura caused further angst, as Tom insisted that his mother recognize Laura's personality and physical impairment in order to accept her as she was, and Amanda recoiled at Tom's words, declaring that Laura's crippled state was but a slight "defect."

Amanda nagged Tom to bring home a "gentleman caller" for Laura, and one evening Tom announced to Amanda that he had invited a man from work to come to dinner the following evening. Amanda's initial excitement turned to panic when she realized that she lacked the time necessary to completely transform the Wingfield apartment in honor of the rare guest. Amanda performed her magic, however, and when the gentleman caller arrived she had restored not only the Wingfield apartment but also herself to a semblance of former glory.

Prior to the arrival of Jim O'Connor, the gentleman caller, Laura discovered that in all probability the man her brother would be bringing home was the same one on whom she had had a crush in high school. When Jim arrived and Laura realized that he was indeed the boy she once knew, shyness and embarrassment overcame her to the extent that she found herself incapable of sharing the meal Amanda pretended her daughter cooked. During dinner, the lights went out, and although Amanda carried forth gaily, noting the romance of dining by candlelight, she knew that Tom had failed to pay the electric bill. What she did not know was what Tom had confessed to Jim—the fact that he had sent the money to the Union of Merchant Seamen as a first step toward leaving home.

After dinner, Jim sought out Laura and engaged her in conversation. Laura learned that Jim was not married, as she had first thought. Jim told Laura that her singular traits made her special instead of defective. They danced, and Laura's self-consciousness turned to romantic hope. Laura's dream shattered when Jim accidentally broke the horn off her favorite glass animal, a unicorn, and as he told her he was engaged to another woman. Laura gave Jim the broken unicorn as a "souvenir." After Jim left, Amanda railed against Tom, first accusing him of having known Jim was engaged and then calling him irresponsible for not having realized the truth.

In the end, Tom again addressed the audience alone. Years and miles separated him from the mother he could not live with and the sister he could not forget. In the darkness, Tom cried out his anguish that "nowadays the world is lit by lightning!" and that his memory of Laura was but a candle that he must blow out to free himself of her haunting, dreamlike presence.

Critical Evaluation:

Winner of the Drama Critics Circle Award when it opened on Broadway in 1945, *The Glass Menagerie* has become a classic of the American theater. *The Glass Menagerie* is rich in themes. One of the play's primary interests lies in exploring illusion versus reality. From the beginning, Tennessee Williams, through his narrator, Tom, explains to the audience that his is a memory play, and he emphasizes the irony that truth is often cloaked by illusion.

Amanda represents the past, the pre-World War II era of the South, where she once reigned supreme in a culture that taught her to confuse appearance with substance. Amanda expends her ingenuity in manipulating others to care for her and for themselves, a seemingly selfish but also naïvely altruistic stance that ironically alienates and defeats those she most wants to encourage. Instead of acknowledging her children as individuals both gifted and flawed, she subconsciously denies them their humanity by insisting on their perfection. Tom and Laura retreat—Tom to the movies and eventually to distant lands, and Laura to the world of her imagination, peopled by music and glass animals. Tom and Laura react subconsciously to their mother's demands by avoiding any possibility of success, a stance that ensures their psychological and social defeat.

Tom is every bit the romantic his mother is, despite the fact that he does not realize it. He sees himself as a poet, as an artist whose very soul is stifled by his warehouse existence. In much the same way as Amanda is stuck in the past, Tom survives only on dreams of the future, ironically failing to realize his goals and the satisfaction he covets by dismissing his relationships and work obligations. He and Amanda both love Laura, but Tom believes that Amanda's refusal to recognize Laura's limitations is now what most demeans her daughter. Amanda believes that Tom's failure to treat his sister as the prize Amanda would have her be will seal Laura's sad fate.

Laura, the character who at first appears most divorced from reality, emerges as the only member of the Wingfield family who is in touch with the truth about herself. She understands her limitations, and even as she escapes the business school that does not fit her psychological needs, she seeks refuge in places designed to showcase precious and exotic specimens. Like her mother and brother, Laura takes comfort in illusion, as her preoccupation with her glass menagerie proves. When Jim, who provides Laura with hope, destroys her illusion, Laura realizes that she is indeed ordinary, like her unicorn-turned-horse. She understands the irony of the unicorn's accident and accepts her own altered psychological circumstances. Thus, in spite of the illusion that Laura is the weakest Wingfield, she emerges as the emotionally strongest family member. Laura is also the family peacemaker, the single person who understands the others so well that she refuses to challenge their fantasies, knowing that they, as has she, depend on their illusions to survive.

In the end, Tom leaves St. Louis, but as he so eloquently states, he cannot escape his memory of Laura. "[Time] is the longest distance between two places," he notes. Tom realizes that he cannot start life anew without coming to terms with the past. The audience understands that he is a metaphor for the post-World War II future.

Williams himself stated the play's essential significance best in his 1945 article "How to Stage *The Glass Menagerie*." He wrote "Everyone should know nowadays the unimportance of the photographic in art: that truth, life, or reality is an organic thing which the poetic imagination can represent or suggest, in essence, only through transformation, through changing into other forms than those which were merely present in appearance." That one must look beyond the facts to find the truth is Williams' loudest message, an early and significant literary manifestation of the psychological implications of human behavior first noted by Sigmund Freud. The playwright also observes that truth itself is subjective, its delineation ironically depending on a character's and an audience's always-illusory perspective.

L. Elisabeth Beattie

Bibliography:
Donahue, Francis. *The Dramatic World of Tennessee Williams*. New York: Frederick Ungar, 1964. A discussion of Williams' plays, with a focus on *The Glass Menagerie*.
Leavitt, Richard F., ed. *The World of Tennessee Williams*. New York: G. P. Putnam's Sons, 1978. A competent introduction to the playwright and his plays, focusing on his themes.
Nelson, Benjamin. *Tennessee Williams: The Man and His Work*. New York: Obolensky, 1961. The first comprehensive study of the playwright and his work.
Spoto, Donald. *The Kindness of Strangers: The Life of Tennessee Williams*. Boston: Little, Brown, 1985. The first complete critical biography of Williams. Delineates the connections between the playwright's work and life.
Stanton, Stephen S., ed. *Tennessee Williams: A Collection of Critical Essays*. Englewood Cliffs, N.J.: Prentice-Hall, 1977. Cogent, in-depth analysis of Williams' plays, including *The Glass Menagerie*.

GLENGARRY GLEN ROSS

Type of work: Drama
Author: David Mamet (1947-   )
Type of plot: Psychological realism
Time of plot: 1982
Locale: Chicago
First performed: 1983; first published, 1983

> *Principal characters:*
> SHELLY LEVENE, a real estate salesman
> JOHN WILLIAMSON, the office manager
> DAVE MOSS, a real estate salesman
> GEORGE AARONOW, a real estate salesman
> RICHARD ROMA, a real estate salesman
> JAMES LINGK, a prospective buyer
> BAYLEN, a police detective

The Story:

Levene, Moss, Aaronow, and Roma were competing in yet another sales promotion contest to sell plots of overpriced, vacant land in a subdivision in Florida. The ruthless bosses Mitch and Murray had decreed that the winner would get a new Cadillac, the runner-up a set of steak knives, and the other two would be fired. All four salesmen were unhappy with the leads (the names, addresses, and phone numbers of supposedly interested prospects) the company was providing and were voicing their complaints to one another as well as to the office manager, Williamson, a company man who was only obeying orders. Levene was desperate because he had no sales on the board and was having a streak of bad luck. He pleaded with Williamson for better leads but got nowhere with the inflexible office manager, who regarded Levene as an over-the-hill loser on his way out.

In a confidential conversation at the Chinese restaurant, Moss suggested to Aaronow that they stage a fake break-in at the office and steal the premium leads, which were considered valuable because they came from good sources and had not yet been worked over. He claimed he could sell them to a competitor named Graff and that they could both go to work for him. Moss said Aaronow would receive $2,500 as his share of Graff's payment for the stolen leads. Aaronow was tempted but afraid of getting caught. In the same Chinese restaurant, Richard Roma, a younger, more successful salesman who seemed destined to win the Cadillac, began to display his sales skills by nearly hypnotizing a gullible prospect named James Lingk with a line of double-talk that insidiously introduced the subject of Glengarry Highlands, the wildly inappropriate name for the Florida swampland the company was currently promoting.

The next morning when Roma came in to claim the Cadillac because he had made a big sale to Lingk, he discovered that the office had been burglarized. There was broken glass all over the floor and a detective named Baylen was questioning the salesmen one by one. Roma was outraged when he learned that some of the recently executed sales contracts had been stolen, along with some office equipment and the premium leads. To add to his problems, Lingk appeared and announced that his wife had demanded that he back out of the land deal. While Roma was trying to stall his balky client by telling him that it would take several days for the paperwork to clear, Williamson blurted out that the contract and Lingk's check had been sent in to the main office. The frightened Lingk rushed off to get legal help to cancel the deal, while Roma turned on Williamson and cursed him roundly for butting into a situation he knew nothing about.

Levene, who was feeling euphoric and rejuvenated because he had made a big sale the night before, heaped his own profane abuse on Williamson for killing Roma's deal. Inadvertently, however, he revealed guilty knowledge about the break-in. His incriminating statement was to call Williamson a liar. Levene was the only one (besides Williamson himself) who knew that Williamson was lying about the contract and the check. Williamson thought by lying that he was helping Roma. Lingk's contract and check had not been sent in but rather had been laying on Williamson's desk where Levene must have seen it when he was stealing the premium leads.

Levene confessed, pulling out the $2,500 in cash and offering to give all of it to Williamson if he would only keep quiet. Williamson, however, reported Levene to the detective. It was evident that Levene would go to prison along with Moss, on whom he informed, while the two surviving salesmen would continue to pray for better leads and worry about their uncertain futures in their dog-eat-dog business.

Critical Evaluation:

Fortunately for the public, the salesmen depicted in David Mamet's play are not typical of the real estate business as a whole, although they use many of the sales techniques taught by big real estate brokerage firms at motivational seminars. Mamet's salesmen are "hard sell" con artists selling land for far more than it is worth. Typically they obtain prospects from coupons mailed in by people responding to glowing advertisements in newspapers and magazines. The leads are requesting a brochure but do not realize that the brochure will be attached to the end of a high-pressure salesman's arm. Prospects rarely see the land itself but are shown maps and photographs designed to create the illusion that these subdivisions in far-off Florida, Arizona, Hawaii, or some other sunny place will be turned into a vacation and retirement paradise with golf courses, tennis courts, swimming pools, clubhouses, and other amenities. The buyers are buying a dream and an illusion. Most make only a small down payment and continue to pay monthly installments for years, looking forward to the day when they can leave the noisy, dangerous city and move to their patch of paradise. If any actually visit their property, they are likely to be so disillusioned that they will stop making payments, forfeiting everything they have invested, and the land will revert to the developers who will sell it to somebody else. The victims are likely to find that their land is located in the middle of an alligator-infested swamp or on the side of a smoking volcano or in the middle of a desert inhabited only by coyotes and rattlesnakes. They are likely to find that streets and roads shown on the maps are nothing but tracks scraped out by bulldozers and that the amenities depicted in the brochures are nothing but cardboard signs and scraps of faded cloth fluttering on wooden stakes.

While Mamet was struggling to become a successful writer, he worked at a variety of part-time and temporary jobs. In one he did clerical work for a company of "land sharks" such as those he depicted in *Glengarry Glen Ross*. He liked and admired the salesmen, although he could see they were little better than crooks. What he liked about them was their histrionics and poetry. They had to have vivid imaginations as well as a raw eloquence in order to create the illusions that would make their prospects sign on the line. Salesmen make good stage characters because they are articulate. Mamet's reputation as a playwright is based on his ability to reproduce the poetry of the American vernacular. He is a successor to writers such as Mark Twain, Sherwood Anderson, Ernest Hemingway, and others who have reproduced the beauty in the cadences, humor, and imagery of ordinary American speech.

Glengarry Glen Ross is an example of minimalism, a highly popular school of American literature since the 1960's. The minimalist writer provides a minimum of information and forces the reader or audience member to make guesses, inferences, and assumptions. This effective technique is challenging and involving. None of the characters in *Glengarry Glen Ross* is described as to physical appearance. The name of their company is not even mentioned. Their employers are not given last names. The audience must infer that there are other salesmen who do not appear on stage, since it seems unlikely that Mitch and Murray would fire two salesmen if they only had a total of four. Audience members who might be unfamiliar with real estate jargon get no explanation of terms such as "leads," "sits," "shot," and that most holy of holy words, "closing."

Levene refers to his daughter with emotion, and the audience, without any information, must assume that this girl or woman is sick or handicapped and totally dependent upon her father. Mamet's salesmen are all such liars it is conceivable that Levene invented a sick daughter for the purpose of eliciting sympathy. No information is given about the salesmen's personal lives; they may not have any lives outside of their work. They seem to spend most of their free time in a Chinese restaurant. With all the information that is not given, it is amazing what a multi-dimensional world the audience can visualize from guesses, inferences, and assumptions based on rapid-fire dialogue full of slang, insults, and outrageous profanity.

The play is well plotted. After both Roma and Levene, in a rhapsody of profanity, vent their rage at the system on the stooge Williamson, there is a surprise ending worthy of Guy de Maupassant or O. Henry. The audience has been led to believe that Aaronow committed the burglary but suddenly realizes that Moss must have given up on the weak-willed Aaronow and persuaded Levene to become his accomplice.

Glengarry Glen Ross, like Arthur Miller's *Death of a Salesman* (1949), is an indictment of laissez-faire capitalism. Both plays demonstrate how capitalism promotes greed, competition, and envy, causing people to wear themselves out, wasting their lives in pursuit of an illusion. The contest in *Glengarry Glen Ross* resembles the dance marathon in Horace McCoy's bitter novel of the Great Depression era, *They Shoot Horses, Don't They?* (1935), which describes dance marathons in which there are no winners but in which exhausted dancers who fall behind are eliminated. Mamet has been quoted as saying that capitalism is "obviously an idea whose time has come and gone." He has also pointed out that *Glengarry Glen Ross* "is about a society based on business . . . a society with only one bottom line: How much money you make." Arthur Miller believed that socialism would solve most social problems. Mamet, like many modern writers, does not believe there are easy solutions. Like many other modern writers, he has seen in the histories of the Soviet Union and the People's Republic of China that socialism only transfers power from one group of imperfect human beings to another. Mamet seems content, like many other minimalists, to dramatize the human condition without trying to explain how that condition might be improved. Writers are not obligated to provide solutions to the problems they illuminate.

Mamet has at least one thing in common with some of the world's greatest writers: He likes people in spite of their faults and perhaps even because of their faults. He appreciates his boastful, unscrupulous, nervy, frightened salesmen as colorful specimens of humanity. He makes his audience identify with these characters and suffer along with them, pitying them for their empty lives and forgiving them for their faults. By sharing their feelings, the audience experiences a sense of unity with the characters on the stage.

Bill Delaney

Bibliography:

Bigsby, C. W. E. *David Mamet*. New York: Methuen, 1985. A study of the life and work of David Mamet, with one chapter devoted to a detailed discussion of *Glengarry Glen Ross*. This first book-length study of Mamet presents an interesting portrait of Mamet that is based partly on personal interviews.

Carroll, Dennis. *David Mamet*. New York: Macmillan, 1987. An in-depth study of Mamet's plays, grouping them thematically, with chapters on business, sex, learning, and communion. The chapter on "Business" compares *Glengarry Glen Ross* with another popular Mamet play, *American Buffalo* (1975).

Dean, Anne. *David Mamet: Language as Dramatic Action*. London: Associated University Presses, 1990. Focuses on Mamet's poetic use of the American vernacular. Contains many quotes from five of Mamet's plays and devotes a chapter to *Glengarry Glen Ross*.

Jones, Nesta, and Steven Dykes, comps. *File on Mamet*. London: Methuen, 1991. This small book is packed with useful information about David Mamet, including excerpts from reviews of various performances of *Glengarry Glen Ross*. Detailed chronology and a bibliography.

Mamet, David. *Writing in Restaurants*. New York: Viking Penguin, 1986. A collection of thirty essays in which Mamet expresses his thoughts about a number of subjects, including the theater and film making in Hollywood.

GO DOWN, MOSES

Type of work: Novel
Author: William Faulkner (1897-1962)
Type of plot: Psychological realism
Time of plot: 1859-1941
Locale: Mississippi
First published: 1942

Principal characters:

ISAAC MCCASLIN (UNCLE IKE), heir to the McCaslin plantation, who
relinquishes his birthright upon reaching twenty-one

CAROTHERS MCCASLIN EDMONDS (CASS), Isaac's elder cousin

THEOPHILUS MCCASLIN (UNCLE BUCK), Isaac's father

LUCAS BEAUCHAMP, lives and farms on the McCaslin land, a great
grandson of Isaac's grandfather, descended from slaves

CAROTHERS EDMONDS (ROTH), Cass's grandson

SAM FATHERS, of Indian, black, and white ancestry; sold to the founder
of the McCaslin plantation; mentor to Isaac

The Story:

In "Was," set in the pre-Civil War South, Uncle Buck and Cass set off after Turl, who regularly fled the McCaslin plantation to court Tennie at the neighboring Beauchamp plantation. Uncle Buck wanted to catch Turl before he reached the Beauchamp plantation because Sophonsiba, who lived there, was husband hunting. Uncle Buck failed to do so but bet Hubert Beauchamp that he would be off the plantation before nightfall. Uncle Buck failed at this resolution too and at night mistakenly lay down in bed with Sophonsiba. Caught, Buck played a card game with Hubert to get out of the marriage. Buck lost again and Cass rode home to get Uncle Buddy. In a poker game between Hubert and Buddy, with Turl dealing, Buddy won Buck's freedom. Cass, Buck, Buddy, Turl, and, by the complicated bet of the card game, Tennie, returned to the McCaslin land.

In "The Fire and the Hearth," Lucas Beauchamp, while hiding his still, discovered what he thought was part of a fortune hidden on McCaslin land almost a century ago. Lucas told Roth Edmonds that George Wilkins was making whiskey on McCaslin land. Roth alerted the police, but Wilkins and Lucas' daughter Nat placed the evidence on Lucas' porch. Although Wilkins and Lucas were arrested, Lucas kept them both out of jail by hurriedly marrying Nat and Wilkens so that, as relatives, none of the three could testify against another. A flashback presented Lucas' memory of Roth's mother dying in childbirth and Zack, Roth's father, keeping Mollie, Lucas' wife, at his house to care for the infant. After six months, Lucas demanded that Zack return Mollie and implied that Zack had been using her sexually as well as domestically. The morning after Mollie returned, Lucas went to Zack's bedroom to kill him; the gun misfired. A few months after Lucas' and George Wilkens' arrest, Lucas asked Roth for $300 to rent a gold-finding machine. When Roth refused, Lucas talked a salesman into accepting Roth's mule as collateral. After Roth discovered his mule had been used as collateral, Lucas tricked the salesman into returning the bill of sale for the mule and the machine. Lucas continued to search for gold, so Mollie asked Roth to arrange a divorce between her and Lucas. Another flashback revealed Lucas demanding his patrimony at age twenty-one and Roth's repudiation of kinship with Lucas' son Henry when they were seven. Just before Mollie's divorce was finalized, Lucas gave up the machine and his search.

In "Pantaloon in Black," Rider, a millworker who rented a house on McCaslin land, put himself in a number of suicidal positions after burying his wife of only six months. His killing a night watchman who regularly cheated the mill workers at dice brought about his death: He was found hanging two miles from the mill. Before being killed by the lynch mob, Rider had been arrested. In prison, Rider tore the cot out of the floor and the bars out of his cell door. He said, "Hit look lack Ah just cant quit thinking." The deputy, telling his wife about Rider's last few days, asked what she thought of such behavior. She replied that she wanted him to finish dinner quickly so she could go to the movies.

In "The Old People," Sam Fathers guided Isaac in the shooting of his first deer and marked him with the blood. When leaving the Big Bottom, Boon reported seeing a huge fourteen-point buck. The hunters waited while Boon, Walter Ewell, and Isaac, with Sam Fathers, tried to corner the deer. Walter Ewell killed a young buck, but noted the huge footprints it left. Meanwhile, Isaac and Sam Fathers watched the huge buck walk near them and neither shot it. That night, Isaac told Cass about seeing the big buck and Cass treated it as if it were a phantom deer. Isaac insisted, "But I saw it," and Cass replied, "Steady. I know you did. So did I. Sam took me in there once after I killed my first deer."

In "The Bear," Isaac was at the Big Bottom, age sixteen. He narrated his memory of his first hunt and of the ritual of hunting the bear, Ben. Isaac remembered first seeing the bear tracks and leaving behind his gun to get a look at the bear. Eventually Lion, a wild dog, was trained to track Ben. When Isaac was sixteen, the ritual bear hunt left Lion, Ben, and Sam Fathers dead. The setting of part 4 of "The Bear" changed from the wilderness to the commissary of the McCaslin land. At twenty-one, arguing with Cass, Isaac relinquished his patrimony. At sixteen, Isaac read the family ledgers that revealed the miscegenation, incest, and refusal to recognize black family members. Isaac wanted to be free of such an inheritance. He also felt no one should own land. Much of the McCaslin family history was revealed in this section, including Isaac's inheritance of IOUs from Hubert Beauchamp and Isaac's move to Jefferson and his unsuccessful marriage. In part 5 of "The Bear," Isaac, still a teenager, went back to hunt at the Big Bottom one last time before the lumber company moved in.

In "Delta Autumn," Isaac, Roth, and Legate drove to the annual hunt. In the morning as the hunters were leaving camp and Isaac was still in his cot, Roth left an envelope with him saying a messenger would come. Isaac was to give her the money in the envelope and say, Roth indicated, "No." A woman came holding Roth's infant son. Isaac gave her the money, and she revealed her relationship to Isaac—she was James Beauchamp's granddaughter. Isaac gave her his hunting horn for her son and advised her to marry a man of her own race. She replied, "Old man . . . have you lived so long and forgotten so much that you don't remember anything you even knew or felt or even heard about love?" Legate returned for a knife for a deer shot by Roth. Isaac surmised the deer was a doe.

In "Go Down, Moses," Mollie Beauchamp came to Jefferson to ask Gavin Stevens, a lawyer, to find her grandson, Samuel Worsham Beauchamp, whom she had not seen in five years. She felt he was in trouble and blamed Roth for ordering him off the McCaslin land after he broke into the commissary. Stevens discovered Beauchamp was to be executed the next day in Illinois. With other members of the community, Stevens arranged for the body to be brought back for a proper burial and to keep the circumstances of his death from Mollie. Mollie asked the newspaper editor to print the news of the death.

Critical Evaluation:

Perhaps America's greatest fiction writer, William Faulkner was awarded the 1949 Nobel Prize in Literature, receiving the award in 1950. *Go Down, Moses* addresses an important theme in American literature—the relationships between blacks and whites in the South through several generations. The novel narrates events between 1859 and 1941, but also presents in retrospect events dealing with the McCaslin plantation from its founding by Lucius Quintus Carothers McCaslin near the beginning of the nineteenth century. The seven stories that compose the novel are linked geographically and thematically. All the events take place on or near the McCaslin land in Mississippi and all but one deal with members of the McCaslin family. The family includes the McCaslins, descendants from the male line, the Edmondses, descendants from the female line, and the Beauchamps, descendants through Lucius Quintus Carothers McCaslin's relations with his slaves. Themes that link the stories are family, love, and race relationships, and the ritual of the hunt. Stylistic devices such as repetition with variations and a complicated chronology also link the stories. By repeating with variations many events of the novel, Faulkner provides for multiple views and voices. By avoiding a strict chronology of events and by reiterating events already narrated, Faulkner leaves the impression of oral history, of a family history being recovered or discovered by different members at different times.

Each of the seven stories includes a hunt, but the type of hunt and its connotations vary widely. Treated humorously are Sophonsiba's husband-hunting in "Was" and Lucas' hunt for buried treasure in "The Fire and the Hearth." Most of the hunts in the novel are more serious. Manhunts occur in "Was," "Pantaloon in Black," and "Go Down, Moses." "Was" treats the pursuit of Turl humorously, but the reader discovers in "The Bear" that Buck is hunting his half brother. "Pantaloon in Black" relates Rider's death by a white lynch mob, and "Go Down, Moses" shows Gavin Stevens' search for Samuel Worsham Beauchamp, who has already been hunted down by the law and sentenced to be executed. These manhunts suggest both repetition and variation. Turl is hunted down and brought back to the McCaslin plantation in 1859, while about eighty years later the same is done to his great-grandson. Turl returns with his goal, Tennie, and together they raise a family on the McCaslin land. Samuel returns only as a corpse. "The Old People," "The Bear," and "Delta Autumn," appearing side by side in the novel, focus around the annual November trips to the woods to hunt game and participate in male comradeship and mentoring. Even in these wilderness stories, Faulkner presents repetition with a difference. The action in "Delta Autumn," unlike in the other two stories, takes place in the new South, that of 1940, when the men drive in cars instead of riding in a wagon to travel to woods that are two hundred miles away instead of thirty. The land for hunting is more scarce; train tracks now appear where once were bear tracks. Faulkner foreshadows the dwindling of the wilderness in the last section of "The Bear," as Isaac goes to hunt at General Compson's camp one more time before the lumber company takes over.

Family, love, and race relationships also permeate the novel. Similarities and differences between characters and generations are emphasized by the stylistic devices of repetition with variation and a complicated chronology. The successful marriages in *Go Down, Moses* are those between Lucas and Mollie and between Rider and Mannie. In fact, Rider patterns his marriage after Lucas' by placing a fire in his hearth as Lucas did in his to symbolize the warmth and continuity of the marriage. Lucas and Mollie's union lasts forty-five years, but Rider loses Mannie to death after only six months. The only marriage of significant length depicted on the Edmonds or McCaslin branch is the unsuccessful, barren marriage of Issac McCaslin. The McCaslin and Edmonds families wear out as Isaac, the last one to bear the McCaslin name, leaves no children. Roth, the last member of the Edmonds family, a bachelor at forty, refuses to recognize his infant son. Roth's child by James Beauchamp's granddaughter repeats the legally unrecognized births of Tomasina and Turl, both fathered by the founder of the McCaslin dynasty. Of the three branches, the Beauchamp branch is the most fruitful. As the novel ends, the McCaslin name belongs to a man near eighty who is a "father to no one" and the Edmonds name belongs to a bachelor of forty who refuses to give it to his son. The Beauchamp family has the infant who will not bear Roth's name and another child expected in the next spring, a grandchild of Lucas.

Other repetitions with variations deal with inheritances, spiritual or material. A family ritual enacted through generations is the recognition, first by Zack and then a generation later by his son Roth, that, as white males, they see themselves as superior to the black children they have been living with almost as brothers. A more uplifting parallel is the vision both Isaac and Cass have after shooting their first deer; Sam Fathers leads them both to an understanding of the ideal buck, a kind of God of the wilderness. The McCaslin blood provokes conflicting feelings: Lucas is proud of his McCaslin blood and, upon reaching twenty-one, demands not only his inheritance but also that portion not collected by his brother James. Isaac is devastated by his heritage and relinquishes his inheritance, leaving the Edmonds family to accept it. Isaac's relinquishment, key to the novel, prompts many comments. Isaac, his wife, Cass, Lucas, and General Compson all hold different views concerning Issac's refusal to accept the McCaslin land. All the variations and variety of voices work to develop Faulkner's subject—the complicated history of the South.

Marion Boyle Petrillo

Bibliography:
Beck, Warren. *Faulkner: Essays.* Madison: University of Wisconsin Press, 1976. Contains a 248-page essay that discusses each story in the novel.
Brooks, Cleanth. *William Faulkner: The Yoknapatawpha Country.* New Haven, Conn.: Yale University Press, 1963. Deals with Faulkner's novels set in the fictional Yoknapatawpha County; chapter on *Go Down, Moses* discusses each of the seven stories in the novel.
Early, James. *The Making of "Go Down, Moses."* Dallas: Southern Methodist University Press, 1972. Book length study of how the novel was made from a series of stories; discusses Faulkner's themes, characterization, and narrative techniques; includes the words of the spiritual "Go Down, Moses" and a McCaslin genealogy.
Kinney, Arthur F., ed. *Critical Essays on William Faulkner: The McCaslin Family.* Boston: G. K. Hall, 1990. Provides a McCaslin genealogy, a chronology for the action of *Go Down, Moses*, character descriptions, and a number of essays on *Go Down, Moses* and on Southern history and culture.
Muste, John M. "The Failure of Love in *Go Down, Moses*." *Modern Fiction Studies* 10, no. 4 (Winter, 1964-1965): 366-378. Theme of the white characters' inability to love unifies the novel.

GO TELL IT ON THE MOUNTAIN

Type of work: Novel
Author: James Baldwin (1924-1987)
Type of plot: Social realism
Time of plot: 1880-1935
Locale: Harlem
First published: 1953

Principal characters:
>JOHN GRIMES, a fourteen-year-old adolescent who attempts self-understanding as he experiences manhood and a religious peak awareness
>GABRIEL GRIMES, John's stepfather, who is both rigid morally and oppressive toward John
>ELIZABETH GRIMES, John's mother and Gabriel's second wife, proud and gentle
>ROY GRIMES, John's younger brother, whose future is interpreted as troubling
>FLORENCE GRIMES, Gabriel Grimes's sister, who mocks him, evidencing her bitterness toward him
>BROTHER ELISHA, a young minister to whom John is attracted

The Story:

It was John's fourteenth birthday, but he did not feel pleased. He was worried that no one would remember his birthday or help him to celebrate it in any way. He was surprised when his mother, Elizabeth, recognized the special day and offered him two different kinds of gifts. The first was money; the second was the opportunity to spend the day without interference from the rest of the family. He could be alone if he chose.

John had already accomplished the chores to which he was assigned, so he was free to experience uninterrupted adult events. He decided to go to the theater in Harlem, across Sixth Avenue, which he felt was an adventure. For John, it was a mature and independent thing to do. Even this decision, however, was not made without reflection; for him, it represented a kind of release from the protectiveness of his mother, in whom he found a sense of security. It also represented, however, a release from the tyranny that he experienced from his stepfather, Gabriel, in whom he no longer had any confidence or trust. He had always felt that Gabriel favored his own children, such as John's stepbrother, Roy.

When John returned home from the theater, he encountered a family tragedy. Roy had been injured in a race-oriented gang war. Stepfather Gabriel, as usual, did not blame Roy and, when he focused his anger on Elizabeth, Roy defended her. Although John realized that he was not the cause of this event, he was also not surprised when Gabriel took out his anger on him as well, repeating his frequent criticisms of John. It was time for church, and John left the house to meet with the young preacher, Elisha.

Elisha was seventeen, and John was drawn to him, not only spiritually but also physically and emotionally. Elisha seemed to provide many havens and refuges for John. During the church service this day, John was prayed for by other members and had a "peak experience," a religious conversion or redirection. He then formally offered himself to God.

John's church experience also included the prayers of his family members. Each prayer revealed much about its speaker, as well as implying reasons for each speaker's different relationship with John. During the service, John turned away from Gabriel, and Elisha gave him a kiss on his forehead. Since his stepfather did not seem to affirm his conversion, John looked increasingly to both Elisha and Elizabeth for the affirmations he needed. He felt self-esteem from his good relationships with the preacher and with Elizabeth. Other elders showed in their prayers that day why he was not in such good relationships with them. John realized during the service that others in the family were attempting to find the salvation he had found, but they had not yet succeeded.

John's step-aunt, Florence, revealed in her prayers that she was far too embittered to find salvation. She desperately wanted to leave her Southern home and did so, but she walked out just as her mother became seriously ill. Florence had experienced only torment by leaving the south. She had grown to hate her brother Gabriel, John's stepfather, but stayed in an uneasy relationship with him. It had been difficult for both, since Florence knew all of Gabriel's past and considered him a religious hypocrite. Gabriel, by contrast, was a preacher and had had considerable success as a church leader. However, Gabriel married a friend of Florence, and his choice was based on the expectations of his church community, expectations that did not satisfy him as a man. He did not remain faithful to his wife and had a son by another woman. When the illegitimate son and his wife died, Gabriel felt tremendous guilt about his lifestyle. This guilt was expressed partly through his tyranny over John. John realized how much his stepfather hated him, a hatred that really emerged because of the love he had for his illegitimate son. Gabriel could not accept the sinfulness that produced this son, so he acted out his disgust by abusing his wife's son.

John's mother, Elizabeth, said a sad "prayer" that did not acknowledge Gabriel's or Florence's hostilities but did admit to a life of torment. Elizabeth had grown up with family conflicts as well, but she had found love in a passionate man named Richard. Elizabeth's dilemma was that this passion was not blessed by the church, and its power made it even more reprehensible religiously. Elizabeth escaped the experiences of a childhood without love by finding love as an adult, but her religion forced her to make a choice between the love of Richard and the love of God. Elizabeth became pregnant by Richard, and, during her pregnancy with John, Richard committed suicide. Elizabeth agreed to marry Gabriel, who also agreed to accept John as his own son. Gabriel did not keep his agreement; John was too much of a reminder of his own infidelity and of his own revered dead son.

John's religious experience during the church service was an acceptance from a religious community in the midst of his world of secular rejection. He fell to the floor with others surrounding him and encouraging him. He prayed that Jesus would save him in many of the ways in which his family members had not been saved, including salvation from the hatred that dominated so many of his family relations. He also prayed that Jesus would lead him to overcome his indecisiveness. All of his prayers and those of his family members included all of their histories, their beings, and their relationships, no matter how difficult. This fourteenth birthday occasion was their time to recount and to attempt to regenerate. For John, his peak experience, his salvation event, was climactic. It suggested the possibility of a happier, less ambiguous relationship to the world around him.

Critical Evaluation:

In *Go Tell It on the Mountain*, James Baldwin writes in the tradition of the African American male authors before him, including W. E. B. Du Bois, Langston Hughes, and Richard Wright.

Each of these authors wrote autobiographical works while communicating the rich experience of African American social life. Since the publication of *Go Tell It on the Mountain*, succeeding writers such as Eldridge Cleaver, Claude Brown, Nikki Giovanni, and Alice Walker have also emphasized personal perspectives and events while detailing the African American community's social conditions, hopes, and difficulties. Each considers his or her own story to be a story of a community rather than an isolated event or an aberration. Each identifies himself or herself as a communal person.

James Baldwin's works are often termed "psychological realism." *Go Tell It on the Mountain* successfully explores the emotional depths of all of its main characters. However, these explored emotions are surrounded by social aspects. People are seen as emotionally functional or dysfunctional as a result of the community to which they belong, the larger society in which it is placed, and the institutions to which they attempt to give allegiance or attempt to reject. The realism in Baldwin is never merely an apt description of the character's feelings; it is always a detailed description of these feelings within a social context. That social context is a primary rationale for why people think, feel, behave, and live as they do. The psychological realism of the author is encompassed in a larger "social realism."

There are two predominating social institutions in *Go Tell It on the Mountain*. The first is the African American church. The impact of distinctively African American religion is more than explicitly expressed in the Pentecostal rituals described by Baldwin. The event of salvation and attempted salvation through public confession is only an indicator of how important the religious institution is in people's lives. It is through the teachings of the church that one gets an idea of how a father, for example, should be. John evaluates his stepfather as unforgiving, unmerciful, hateful, and biased. These are not the descriptors, however, that are used for God the Father and should not be present in human fathers. Conversely, Elizabeth's tenderness toward John is more reflective of the nurturing acts of God toward people. The African American church is the channel through which one gets ultimate values; it is the institution that shows religious people how life should be on earth. Its God and prophets exemplify and admonish what human relations should be. As the source for final meaning, the African American church is, along with the family, the social institution that has the most impact on the African American community. A family's dysfunctions are somewhat counteracted by the church's functionalism. John does find love and a role model in his young preacher friend.

The second predominating social institution in Baldwin's novel is racism. By implication, Baldwin is claiming that racism is institutionalized, a part of society's ongoing functioning. This goes beyond the inability of characters to adjust to a hostile society or their being involved in race-oriented confrontations. It emphasizes that the uniqueness of African American experience in America is in their sense of community as they rely on one another in order to survive oppression. They identify with each other because they share a common historical and contemporary experience of rejection by the larger society. Baldwin uses words and phrases such as "melancholy," "bitterest patience," and "humility most wretched" to reveal how painful this institutionalization of race prejudice is for African Americans. Their lives are lived in specific ways because the external society oppresses; their options are limited because of this oppression. Individual and family dysfunctionalism is a symptom of this situation. The psychological realities of Baldwin's characters are, again, the product of social realities.

While the author described *Go Tell It on the Mountain* as a kind of love song, it is neither sentimental nor romantic in its expression of love. Instead, it is a song about love and its absence. The primary character, John, does succeed in finding love in two other characters, his mother and the young preacher. Most of the other characters, however, experience either love that is denied to them or love that cannot be acted out in acceptable, religious ways. Even John realizes that his hostile stepfather, Gabriel, is the man for whom he should feel the most affection and admiration. John's potential love for Gabriel, however, is rejected, indicating that a love song does not guarantee loving relations; it includes defeats as well as victories. Baldwin's own life has sometimes been compared to that of the character John. Although he rejected the idea that this novel was autobiographical, Baldwin did acknowledge that it paralleled his attempts to experience love as a writer, a homosexual, and an African American man.

William Osborne
Max Orezzoli

Bibliography:
Baldwin, James. *Conversations with James Baldwin.* Edited by Fred Standley and Louis H. Pratt. Jackson: University Press of Mississippi, 1989. The conversations are the widest-ranging collection in one book. Their subject areas are broad, including race, hatred, sex, the new South, and the role of the writer. The interviewers include a similarly broad array of writers, philosophers, and people in political and social movements, such as Studs Terkel, David Frost, Nat Hentoff, and Josephine Baker.
Campbell, James. *Talking at the Gates: A Life of James Baldwin.* New York: Viking Press, 1991. This biography had the cooperation of James Baldwin, who suggested the title. It relies heavily on documentary evidence and on the perceptions of James Baldwin's friends for its perspectives on him as a person and a writer.
Gibson, Donald B., ed. *Five Black Writers: Essays on Wright, Ellison, Baldwin, Hughes, and LeRoi Jones.* New York: New York University Press, 1970. There are four excellent chapters on Baldwin's work, including his philosophy of being, his interpretation of the African American community in relation to the larger American society, and defenses of his work in response to critics.
Inge, M. Thomas, Maurice Duke, and Jackson Bryer, eds. *Black American Writers: Bibliographical Essays.* New York: St. Martin's Press, 1978. The long segment on Baldwin not only reviews his major works, including *Go Tell It on the Mountain,* but also includes his additional manuscripts and interviews that he granted about his writings.
Weatherby, W. J. *James Baldwin: Artist on Fire.* New York: Donald Fine, 1989. This biographical interpretation is based on the author's and other friends' views of Baldwin's major themes. It emphasizes the debated perspective of Baldwin as mystical in interpreting his own life and work. *Go Tell It on the Mountain* becomes the focus as the author questions the ways in which that novel is really an autobiography.

GOBLIN MARKET

Type of work: Poetry
Author: Christina Rossetti (1830-1894)
First published: 1862, in *Goblin Market and Other Poems*

"Goblin Market," which appeared in Christina Rossetti's first published collection of poetry, is unquestionably her most original poem and stands out as a masterwork of aesthetic taste. Rosetti's ties with her brother Dante's Pre-Raphaelite Brotherhood (she contributed verses to their short-lived magazine, *Germ*) also explain why the anthology has been labeled the movement's first literary success. It was Dante, furthermore, who suggested the title, having written a poem himself about the market of fallen girls. "Goblin Market," however, differs notably from her other poetic work, which possesses a depth and a Victorian pathos all its own, principally in its alluring singsong quality and pervasive sexuality.

That Christina Rosetti could have been unaware of the intense sexual imagery of "Goblin Market" seems unlikely, although in a note to the poem, her brother William Michael (who edited most of her poetry) speaks of her insistence that nothing "profound" had been intended. It is far more feasible to see her apparent obsession with certain images in the poem as suggestive of a more religious interpretation, one in which the goblins may be seen as maliciously evil creatures who have set out to beguile—and then seduce—the two girls. In this respect, the poem does bear a resemblance to Rosetti's major poetic themes, which are so heavily laden with introspection, suffering, and otherworldly love.

Dedicated to Rosetti's sister Maria, "Goblin Market" deals with two sisters, Laura and Lizzie, who, while on their usual way to a brook to fetch water, hear goblins hawking their wares, the goblin fruits. Lizzie warns Laura not to listen to them and flees, knowing that their sister Jeanie, who had eaten of the goblin fruit, had languished on to her death. Laura, however, is thoroughly enticed by the goblins and buys their luscious fruit, paying them with a lock of her golden hair, as she has no coins. Shortly afterward, she begins to undergo the same transformation that Jeanie did, her hair growing thin and gray, and, almost inexplicably, she can no longer hear the goblin men's cries, though she yearns passionately for their figs and plums.

The strong-willed Lizzie, in a desperate attempt to save her sister, returns to the goblin men that only she can now hear and offers to buy their fruit, although she adamantly refuses to join them at their feast. After bravely resisting the evil creatures' attacks, during which her mouth and face are smeared with fruit juices, Lizzie makes her way home. Greeted by Laura, she invites her sister to partake of the restorative juices she knows will cure her:

> Hug me, kiss me, suck my juices
> Squeezed from goblin fruits for you,
> Goblin pulp and goblin dew.
> Eat me, drink me, love me;
> Laura, make much of me.

After Laura does as she is asked, Lizzie spends the night tending to her, holding water to her lips and cooling her face. When dawn comes, Laura has been restored to her former self, her hair once again gleaming and golden. Later, when the grown girls have become wives and mothers, they tell the story to their own children, exhorting them to cling together: "For there is no friend like a sister,/ In calm or stormy weather. . . ." Quite clearly, the main themes of the poem revolve around temptation and seduction as well as individual sacrifice and its saving grace. In a moral sense, which is perhaps the best of interpretive modes, the poem is very similar to those of Samuel Taylor Coleridge (and those of the French poet Paul Verlaine, in its nuances and musical cadence), evoking in the mind of the reader a wealth of pictorial images, a strong sense of the magical, and an almost spellbinding musical quality. There is no doubt that the language is captivatingly sensuous, almost shamelessly so, as can readily be seen from such lines as "She sucked and sucked and sucked the more/ Fruits which that unknown orchard bore."

It is a unique trait of the poem that, even beyond its moral apologue, one can truly appreciate the richness of the language and the exquisite delight of the rhythm, as it jaunts on its way to the almost cloying climax. Clearly, in "Goblin Market," it is not the buying of the fruit that presents a danger to the soul, but the actual consuming of it. Ironically, even though Lizzie "tossed them her penny," holding out her apron to be filled with the delectable fruits, the goblins seek to entice her to sit and eat with them. Indeed, when Lizzie tells them she cannot join them in their repast, for she has one who "waits at home alone for me," the creatures begin grunting and snarling, viciously attacking her. In essence, it is the "sharing" of the fruit in the physical presence of the goblins that holds the key to this particular type of damnation. Laura is in the thrall of their bewitchment, for this is precisely the "sin" she has committed, as Jeanie did. The goblin men have no need of money and take both pennies and curls alike, but the fruit they deliver must be consumed in their presence, in what could almost be described as a copulatory ritual. When Lizzie indicates to her tormentors that, if they will not sell her their fruits, she will want her money back and will very likely be on her way, their chattering turns to violence, and they begin trying to force the forbidden fruits into her unwilling mouth. Lizzie knows, however, that if she keeps the fruit from entering her mouth, she will be safe. Once she has returned home to her sister and explained the "sacrifice" she has endured for Laura's sake, only the sucking of the juices from Lizzie's face and mouth can truly restore Laura's health. By kissing her sister "with a hungry mouth," Laura is now allowed to taste the bitterness of the sacrifice itself, a sacrifice which was "wormwood to her tongue," but which brought solace to her aching soul and healed its lost innocence. The juices on Lizzie's mouth no longer harbor the sickly sweet taste of the original fruit/sin but have now been transformed into the chrism of salvation.

Rosetti's basic message is a strong one: There is no love like that of a sister. It is interesting to speculate how the suggestive intimacy of the two girls, Laura and Lizzie, emphasized as it is throughout the poem, bears a resemblance to the close relationship between Christina (who never married) and Maria (who became an Anglican nun). It would indeed seem that, while avoiding forbidden pleasure will certainly keep Laura safe and chaste, physical intimacy with Lizzie (though not sexual in nature) is to be encouraged. It should be recalled that Christina originally wanted to call the poem "A Peep at the Goblins," as if the two girls, totally unfamiliar with men and the seductions of the mundane world, had for one brief moment been allowed a glimpse of sexual pleasure outside the bonds of matrimony. Although the reader may wonder what physical pleasures, if any, were eventually reserved for Laura and Lizzie when they became "wives with children of their own," Rosetti reminds us that, after all, Jeanie was in her grave because of "joys brides hope to have." As unmarried maidens, Lizzie and Laura cannot taste the fruit of the tree of sexual knowledge, a joy granted to them only after marriage.

Proposed to by two different suitors during her lifetime (the first, James Collinson, was a friend and fellow art student of Dante and the second, Charles Cayley, was a scholar and linguist), Rosetti saw both of these relationships come to an abrupt end. Although it is presumed that Collinson left her (and that her family merely kept up appearances by saying she had broken off the engagement), she turned Cayley down of her own volition. It appears that, in both cases, religion played a part in the difficulties, as Collinson wavered between Catholicism and Anglicanism and Cayley seemed an agnostic. Rosetti's devout Anglican upbringing, in which her mother and her sister played such intrinsic roles, probably made her shrink from the idea of the fulfillment of love. To the quiet and often clinically depressed Rosetti, this may have been a way of reconciling her love of man with her love of God. It is unlikely, in fact, that she really would have married either man, perhaps more from a sense of honoring her own Victorian conviction that she would not give to man what was reserved for Christ than for any other reason.

In this regard, then, "Goblin Market" becomes the ultimate vehicle for Rosetti's matrimonial convictions, and it is perhaps more revelatory than her other poems since it so fittingly weds the theme of unbridled sensuality—and its inherent dangers—with the salvation that can only be offered through family ties. The latter were especially strong for Rosetti and were assuredly a source of consolation in her later years. Though her later poems reveal a desolatory kind of suffering and an almost ethereal desire to transcend death in search of a more perfect love, "Goblin Market" seems to lightly foreshadow such yearnings, especially in her descriptions of Jeanie's death and of Lizzie's sufferings at the hands of the goblins. Until Laura and Lizzie do become the wives and mothers they were meant to be, thus eligible to eat the "goblin fruit," they can only lie "cheek to cheek and breast to breast" in sisterly—but irreproachable—intimacy.

It should further be suggested, to emphasize the recently developed theory of child eroticism, that the poem is also a unique interpretation of how the Victorian mind imagined children within the spectrum of human sexuality. In retrospect, to identify the two girls as representatives of the erotic life of children and to see their misadventures as typical of a Victorian nightmare nursery world in which cruelty and sexuality are revealed in all their forcefulness would seem almost overemphatic. Yet, there is something musically childlike in the repetitious lilt Rosetti lends to the poem as well as in the girlish relationship between the two sisters, the infantile sucking of the fruit and the odd aloofness between the two sisters and the goblin "brothers"—the latter quite possibly suggesting a latent sibling animosity (although to all appearances the Rossettis had a serene and lifelong relationship).

In a perhaps equally disturbing analysis based on the transmigration of the personality or, more appropriately, on the metamorphosis of woman into grotesque creature—a theme dear to Victorian mythos—the reader can see how Laura, in her desire to eat more of the fruit she can no longer have, begins gnashing her teeth and weeping uncontrollably, revealing her own potential to become one of the goblins herself. This curious vampirish quality, at which Rosetti hints only subtly throughout the poem, makes "Goblin Market" all the more remarkable because the reader senses, and rightly so, that its enduring quality lies in both the fleeting elusiveness of its images and in the fact that Laura is, in actuality, waging a war with her own self.

From the moment she stretches her gleaming neck to the instant she sucks the fair fruit globes, Laura is destined to suffer a lasting change. She does not know whether it is night or day and, her mouth constantly watering, she begins exhibiting the signs of a hunger-crazed creature who longs for the night, the time she will be able to return to the brook and seek out the goblins. The fruit merchant goblins, however, whose seduction of Laura is by now complete, have no desire to pursue their intercourse with her and abandon her to her fate. Laura, cold as stone and in the throes of exceeding pain, dwindles in listless apathy, no longer tending to her chores and unable to get her seeds to bear the tiniest of shoots. Even her physical appearance coincides with her inner decay as her sunken eyes and fading mouth become the mark of the vampire's victim. The only hope for Laura is the redeeming ruby juices on her sister's face, whose cleansing properties work a miracle on Laura's soul, restoring her wholesomeness and purifying her virtue, much like the blood of a sacrificial lamb. Lizzie's steadfastness, like the cradling arms of an angelic savior, has ultimately broken the goblins' witchery.

Kathryn Dorothy Marocchino

Bibliography:
Bellas, Ralph A. *Christina Rossetti*. Boston: Twayne, 1977. A straightforward look at both Rossetti's life and works. Suitable for beginning students of Rossetti. Useful notes, bibliography and index.
Campbell, Elizabeth. "Of Mothers and Merchants: Female Economics in Christina Rossetti's *Goblin Market*." In *Victorian Studies: A Journal of the Humanities, Arts, and Sciences* 33, no. 3 (Spring, 1990): 393-410. A scholarly journal article that deals with the treatment of capitalism and economics in "Goblin Market" and their relationship to Victorian women.
Morrill, David F. "'Twilight Is Not Good for Maidens': Uncle Polidori and the Psychodynamics of Vampirism in *Goblin Market*." *Victorian Poetry* 28, no. 1 (Spring, 1990): 1-16. A fascinating journal article that deals with the theme of vampirism in "Goblin Market," tracing its origins back to John William Polidori's "The Vampyre."
Spivack, Charlotte. "'The Hidden World Below': Victorian Women Fantasy Poets." In *The Poetic Fantastic: Studies in an Evolving Genre*, edited by Patrick Murphy and Vernon Ross Hyles. Westport, Conn.: Greenwood, 1989. This book article examines the theme of the fantastic as it was used by Victorian women poets (such as Christina Rossetti) and makes specific reference to "Goblin Market." Among other things, it applies the theories of Joseph Campbell to the genre.
Thompson, Deborah Ann. "Anorexia as a Lived Trope: Christina Rossetti's *Goblin Market*." In *Mosaic: A Journal for the Interdisciplinary Study of Literature* 24, nos. 3/4 (Summer/Fall, 1991): 89-106. This scholarly journal article presents an unusual, yet exceptionally well-written interpretation of "Goblin Market," by viewing anorexia nervosa as the underlying theme of the poem.

GOD'S LITTLE ACRE

Type of work: Novel
Author: Erskine Caldwell (1903-1987)
Type of plot: Naturalism
Time of plot: Late 1920's
Locale: Georgia and South Carolina
First published: 1933

Principal characters:
TY TY WALDEN, patriarch of the family
BUCK,
JIM LESLIE, and
SHAW, his sons
DARLING JILL and
ROSAMOND, his daughters
WILL THOMPSON, Rosamond's husband
GRISELDA, Buck's wife

The Story:

Ty Ty Walden and his sons, Shaw and Buck, had been digging holes on their Georgia farm for fifteen years in search of gold, without success. Ty Ty decided to bring back an albino to find the gold, ignoring a plea for food from the two black men who farmed his land. Ty Ty was a man with gold fever and did not have time for anything else. The father had set aside "God's little acre" to give the church whatever money it produced, but he moved the acre with each new hole to avoid giving the gold to a preacher. Pluto Swint, a sheriff's candidate, and Darling Jill, who rejected his offers of marriage, went to Carolina to bring her sister Rosamond and her millworker husband, Will Thompson, back to help dig, because he was out on strike.

At Rosamond's, her husband Will, drunk, announced he was going to have Buck's wife, Griselda, whom Ty Ty had said was a perfect female. Will told his protesting wife it was all in the family. Rosamond apologized for her husband and forgave his remark. Later, Will said he would soon turn on the power at the mill and the workers would run it. In the morning, with Rosamond gone, Darling Jill got in bed with Will. Rosamond caught them and blistered both with a hair brush. Rosamond grabbed a pistol and fired between Will's legs. He jumped out the window and ran naked down the street. Rosamond and Darling Jill wept and consoled each other. Back in borrowed pants, Will, forgiven by his wife, agreed to go dig.

They passed through the city where Jim Leslie, Ty Ty's son, gone from home fifteen years, lived in luxury with his society wife. Ty Ty had taken his dying wife to see the son, and he had turned them away. Back at the farm, Ty Ty showed Dave Dawson, the albino forced to be the gold diviner, off to the others. Ty Ty and Will caught Darling Jill and Dave together on the ground that night. Rosamond and Griselda made the men leave the lovers alone. Buck and Shaw had a fight with Will because he called them "clodhoppers," and Buck accused the "lint-head" of looking at Griselda. Ty Ty stopped the fight and asked for family peace. At Will's suggestion, Ty Ty and his entire family drove to see Jim Leslie in the city to borrow money. Ty Ty, Darling Jill, and Griselda slipped into Jim Leslie's house and surprised him. Jim Leslie stared at Griselda as Ty Ty ridiculed him for marrying a less pretty wife who had gonorrhea. Jim Leslie protested that his money was tied up in real estate, and his evicted tenants' furniture was still unsold, but he finally gave his father some money and told him to start raising crops instead of searching for gold. Jim Leslie followed them to the car and jumped on the running board. Darling Jill had to swerve the car and hurl him off as he tore at Griselda's dress. He was not badly hurt.

At the farm, Ty Ty decided that Dave wanted to stay, even though Darling Jill was through with him. No longer guarded, the albino was put in the hole to help dig. Ty Ty asked Will, who understood the secrets of the mind and body as he did, to stay and manage the crops, but he refused. Will agreed with Darling Jill that she should be worried about their brief affair, because when he drove a nail, it stayed nailed. Darling Jill decided she loved Pluto and agreed to marry him later. Griselda rode with Pluto and Darling Jill to take Rosamond and Will back home. Buck was angry, but Ty Ty led him off to dig. When the group reached the mill town, Will disappeared. He returned later and said he was "strong as God Almighty Himself," and would turn the power on the next morning. In front of the others, Will told Griselda to stand up, it was time. Rosamond and Darling Jill warned him that Buck would kill him, but Will was not scared. Will tore Griselda's clothes into shreds and lint. He dragged her, unprotesting, to another part of the house. Rosamond and Darling Jill gathered the lint from the floor. The next morning the three women served Will's breakfast. At the mill, the three women joined a crowd watching Will and the other workers occupy the structure. Will turned on the power, but then gunfire was heard. A man told them Will had been killed by company guards waiting inside. With their leader gone, the workers gave in. At the farm, Ty Ty felt guilty about Will's death and wished God's little acre was closer to the house. Griselda said Ty Ty and Will were the only two real men she had known, and had been born that way. If Will had lived, she would have stayed with him. Jill said Will was a real man, because he felt things inside, but Buck could not. Ty Ty interrupted Buck's accusation of Griselda and talked of having not the God heard about in churches but the God inside who helped a man live. For that reason he had set aside God's little acre, even though the Lord had not gotten a penny yet.

Ty Ty concluded it was best that Will was dead; the three women could not have stayed with him, because it would have made a mess the law did not allow. Jim Leslie drove up and said he had come for Griselda. Called from digging, Buck twisted Jim Leslie's arm, but Jim Leslie got away and ran in the house. He ordered Griselda into his car. Buck grabbed a shotgun and chased his brother outside. Jim Leslie turned at the car and shook his fist. Buck shot him twice. He died shortly after. Ty Ty sent Shaw for the sheriff. The three women hugged Buck. Then Buck walked away across the fields, carrying the shotgun. Ty Ty willed that God's little acre would follow and be with Buck. Then Ty Ty crawled in the hole and began shoveling, wondering when Shaw would be back to help.

Critical Evaluation:

Although Erskine Caldwell's principal works include twenty-seven novels and numerous collections of stories, his reputation in American fiction rests on two novels, *Tobacco Road* (1932) and *God's Little Acre*. Both were made into successful films, and a dramatization of *Tobacco Road* ran for seven years on Broadway. A minister's son from Georgia, Caldwell became a world traveler as a writer and newspaperman. His best works, however, were about his home, about back-country Georgia families. *God's Little Acre* is a naturalistic novel, in which victimized characters are less individuals than they are members of groups that are typical of a given place and time. In *God's Little Acre*, the characters are archetypal residents of Southern farms and mill towns during the first years of the Depression. The Walden family members are victims of larger forces: economic (hard times for farmers and labor disputes in the mills), biological (strong sexual drives disturbing marriages), social (class struggles), and cosmic (the proper relationship to God). The novel is made more than a sociological study by the human and individual dignity achieved by Ty Ty and his son-in-law Will, who choose to struggle against the odds. Ty Ty struggles against the unyielding earth and Will against the mill owners who lock out their workers. Ironically, neither succeeds; they trust in goals that are romantic and unrealistic. Ty Ty never finds gold, and his involvement of his family in the search tears the family apart. Will is killed by company guards after heroically turning on the power at the mill. Perversity of actions and outcomes becomes a motif that adds to the grotesque humor, something unusual in naturalistic works. The myth of the farmer's closeness to the land and crops is exploded by Ty Ty, who refuses to farm and craters the land looking for gold, until the house itself teeters on the edge of a hole. The father fights for family unity and peace, but stimulates the sexual desire that ultimately ruins the family with his public promotion of Griselda's physical charms. Will represents the life force that is the desire of all the women in the story, but becomes the object of slapstick humor as he runs naked down the street to escape his wife's gunfire. Ty Ty, being religious, dedicates the proceeds of God's little acre to the Lord, but moves the acre constantly to avoid giving any gold to the church. The humor turns to tragedy when he wills the acre to follow Buck, on his way to take his own life after killing his brother. Romance and poetic description are often attached to the naturalistic situations of the family saga. Will, driven to lead the workers, sees "girls with eyes like morning glories and breasts so erect, running into the ivy-covered mills." His wife and two sisters-in-law are ready to follow—and share—this superman the rest of their lives.

Opposed dualities contend in the working out of family destiny: dream and reality, science and superstition, head and heart, flesh and spirit, power and impotence, fate and free will, and the forces of life and death. The final duality resides in the family-member-become-outsider, Jim Leslie, who symbolizes the larger world, corrupting to the family with its materialism, selfishness, and class divisions. He comes to take what success has denied him, a perfect woman, and his death at the hands of the brother whose wife he seeks destroys Ty Ty's dream of joining his clan in peaceful labor and love.

Ty Ty voices the novel's themes at the end. People must accept what God has given God's creations, even though the Lord has played a "mean trick" by putting human souls in the bodies of animals and then trying to make people act like people. A man can live by inner feeling, or he can live like preachers tell him, and be dead on the inside. Women understand this, and live like God created them to live. The life force, the God-in-man which is strongly sexual, liberates a man's will, but it releases an energy that is almost uncontrollable. When one tries to keep someone of the opposite sex for oneself, there will be trouble and sorrow the rest of one's life. Ty Ty also discovers that God's little acre is not a place to be hypocritically moved and manipulated, but is an abiding spirit. Ironically, Ty Ty returns to his obsession because he does not know what else to do. He begins digging in the empty hole, anticipating the return of his remaining son.

M. E. Gandy

Bibliography:
Burke, Kenneth. *The Philosophy of Literary Form.* 3d ed. Berkeley: University of California Press, 1973. Contains an article by the author that investigates the symbolic landscape, sexual taboos, fertility rites, caricatures, and grotesques in Caldwell's two major novels.
Cantwell, Robert, ed. *The Humorous Side of Erskine Caldwell.* New York: Duell, Sloan and Pearce, 1951. An introduction to Caldwell's humorous imagination, which makes the works more impressive and entertaining.

Devlin, James. *Erskine Caldwell*. Boston: Twayne, 1984. Contains a chapter on the major themes in *God's Little Acre*. Extensive annotated list of criticism.

Klevar, Harvey L. *Erskine Caldwell: A Biography*. Knoxville: University of Tennessee Press, 1993. A detailed biography. Includes discussion of the Caldwell canon, including background, notoriety, dramatization, and key reviews of *God's Little Acre*.

Korges, James. *Erskine Caldwell*. Minneapolis: University of Minnesota Press, 1969. An excellent condensed discussion of Caldwell's works.

THE GOLD-BUG

Type of work: Short fiction
Author: Edgar Allan Poe (1809-1849)
Type of plot: Detective and mystery
Time of plot: Early nineteenth century
Locale: South Carolina
First published: 1843

Principal characters:
THE NARRATOR
WILLIAM LEGRAND, discoverer of the gold bug
JUPITER, Legrand's black servant

The Story:

William Legrand has been reduced to poverty by a series of misfortunes. In order to avoid the embarrassment of meeting friends from his more prosperous days, he left New Orleans and went to live on Sullivan's Island, near Charleston, South Carolina. It was a small island, usually uninhabited except for Legrand and his black servant, Jupiter. Jupiter would not leave his master, even though he was a free man and could have found work to support himself in comfort.

Winters on the island were mild and fires were usually unnecessary, but on a night in October when a friend from Charleston visited Legrand, he found Legrand and Jupiter away from the house and a fire blazing in the fireplace. The two soon returned from a quest for entomological specimens. Legrand was in rare good humor. He had stumbled upon an entirely new specimen, a bug of gold. On his way home, he met Lieutenant G——, who took the bug to examine it. Because the friend could not examine it before morning, Legrand took an old piece of parchment from his pocket and drew a picture of the specimen.

As the friend took the drawing, Legrand's dog entered, jumped upon the guest, and licked his face in joy. When the friend finally looked at the paper, he found that the drawing resembled a human skull. Legrand, somewhat disgruntled at this slur on his drawing, took the paper back and prepared to throw it into the fire. After one last glance, however, he paled visibly, rose, and seated himself at the table. Then he carefully placed the paper in his wallet. As Legrand appeared distracted and a little sulky, the friend canceled his plans for spending the night and returned to Charleston.

About a month later, the friend received a visit from old Jupiter. The servant reported that his master was not well. Going around as if in a daze, Legrand worked constantly at a cipher. Once he had eluded Jupiter and stayed away the whole day. Jupiter knew that the gold bug was to blame, for it had bitten Legrand on the day he captured it. Jupiter knew that the bug was the reason for Legrand's talk about gold in his sleep. He produced a letter from his master begging the friend to return to the island with Jupiter.

At the island, the friend found Legrand in a state of great excitement. Filled with plans for an expedition to the mainland, he asked the friend to accompany him. After getting Legrand's promise that he would consult a doctor before long, for the man was obviously deranged, the friend joined Legrand and Jupiter in their adventure. Taking the dog with them, they left that evening. Jupiter carried picks and shovels for the three. Legrand took with him the gold bug, attached to a long cord.

After traveling about two hours, they stopped at the foot of a huge tulip tree situated near an almost inaccessible hill. There Legrand commanded Jupiter to take the bug and climb the tree to the seventh limb. Jupiter obeyed, climbing out to the very tip of the limb. On the outer edge, he found a human skull, nailed to the wood. Then Legrand told him to drop the bug through the left eye of the skull. After this strange act, Jupiter climbed down. Legrand, working in feverish anxiety, then began a series of measurements. By the light of lanterns, the men, following Legrand's lead, dug out a hole four feet wide and seven feet deep. When they failed to unearth the treasure Legrand obviously thought he would find, he questioned Jupiter again about the eye through which he had dropped the gold bug. The old man, they learned, had mistakenly dropped the bug through the right eye. Again, Legrand measured and drew circles. By that time the friend shared Legrand's excitement. Again they dug, and at last they came upon an old chest, too heavy to move. Prying open the lid, their eyes fell upon gold and jewels of unbelievable value. They later computed that the total worth was over a million and a half dollars. Leaving Jupiter and the dog to guard what they could not carry, Legrand and his friend took one load home. Then they returned and, with Jupiter's help, carried the rest of the treasure back to the island.

Legrand told his friend in detail how he had solved the riddle of the treasure. The piece of parchment upon which he had drawn the picture of the gold bug had been found near the bug, on the beach. Although the paper had been blank on both sides when he drew the picture, the friend had seen the shape of a skull. He remembered then that the dog had leaped on the friend, causing the paper to come near the fire. Heat from the fire had brought out the outline of a skull. Legrand, seeing the skull when he took the parchment, had begun a feverish attempt to solve its meaning. By dipping the paper in warm water, he had found a numerical code. Deciphering had long been a hobby of his, and thus after a month, he had found the secret of the parchment. It was his belief that the treasure was a fabulous one believed to have been buried by Captain Kidd. Even after he had deciphered the numbering, transposing the figures into words, he had had trouble finding the location of the landmarks revealed in the writing. On the day he had slipped away from Jupiter, however, he had discovered the hill and the tree. On the day of their search, Jupiter's mistake about the left eye had caused an error, but the rectifying of that error had brought the treasure to light. The deciphered code had instructed that a bullet was to be dropped through the left eye of the death's head. Legrand, using the gold bug, wished only to punish his friend for suspecting his sanity.

Critical Evaluation:

"The Gold-Bug" belongs to the small group of stories that Poe called "tales of ratiocination," that is, tales in which logical reasoning is employed to solve a puzzle. Other Poe stories of this type are *The Murders in the Rue Morgue*, *The Mystery of Marie Roget*, and *The Purloined Letter*—a series of three in which the protagonist is Monsieur C. Auguste Dupin, an amateur detective, whose unnamed friend tells the stories. Arthur Conan Doyle's Sherlock Holmes stories were admittedly inspired by the Dupin tales, and Poe has often been called the father of the modern detective story.

Poe's ratiocinative tales differ from his others in several ways. The vocabulary of several of his tales of terror not only reveals a nervous or fearful state of mind on the part of the narrator, but it is also intended to arouse an emotional response in the reader. The vocabulary of the ratiocinative tales, however, is consciously unemotional to stress the analytical nature of the tales. The structure of these tales also differs from that found in the tales of terror. A representative terror tale builds up to a climax of action, often violent, as in *The Fall of the House of*

Usher or *The Pit and the Pendulum*. The limited action of a ratiocinative tale occurs mainly in the first half of the story; most of the latter half is devoted to the explication of the mystery or puzzle given earlier. In "The Gold-Bug," the action centers upon locating, digging up, and transporting the treasure, and this action is completed almost exactly halfway through the story. Nearly all of the remaining half is made up of the narrator's questions and Legrand's detailed answers or explanations concerning the parchment map and the translation of the cryptic message contained in the numbers and other characters or symbols on it.

In "The Gold-Bug," then, Poe has combined the romance of finding buried treasure with the mental excitement of unraveling a mystery. Critics have pointed out inaccuracies in geography and topography, defects in character portrayal, and weak attempts at humor in Jupiter's speech; but one forgets or ignores these as Poe carries one along in the search first for immense wealth and then for a meaning in an enigma.

Bibliography:
Davidson, Edward H. *Poe: A Critical Study*. Cambridge, Mass.: The Belknap Press of Harvard University Press, 1966. One of the most important philosophic studies of Poe's work. Presents Poe as basically a religious writer in that he becomes his own god, his own supreme maker of prophecies and parables.
Hassell, J. Woodrow, Jr. "The Problem of Realism in 'The Gold-Bug.'" *American Literature* 25 (May, 1953): 179-192. Includes a discussion of how fantasy and realism are blended and sometimes in conflict in "The Gold-Bug." Shows how Poe was able to give an appearance of reality to the fanciful elements in the story.
Kempton, Daniel. "The Gold/Goole/Ghoul Bug." *Emerson Society Quarterly* 33 (1987): 1-19. Interesting study of the basic logical/aesthetic pattern of "The Gold-Bug"; notes that the protagonist of the story looks on the world as if it were an encoded message written for the elect by the hand of God.
Kennedy, J. Gerald. *Poe, Death, and the Life of Writing*. New Haven, Conn.: Yale University Press, 1987. A useful study of the nature of writing in Poe's stories and the relationship of writing to death. Important for understanding pattern and interpretation in "The Gold-Bug."
Williams, Michael. "The Language of the Cipher: Interpretation in 'The Gold-Bug.'" In *Edgar Allan Poe: A Study of the Short Fiction*, edited by Charles May. New York: Twayne, 1991. Excellent study of Poe's philosophic interest in the power of language and his tactic of embedding interpretative strategies within his stories.

THE GOLDEN APPLES

Type of work: Short fiction
Author: Eudora Welty (1909-   )
First published: 1949

>*Principal characters:*
>KING MACLAIN, the wandering patriarch of the town
>MRS. SNOWDIE HUDSON MACLAIN, his wife and an albino
>RANDALL MACLAIN and
>EUGENE MACLAIN, the twin sons of King and Snowdie
>MRS. FATE RAINEY, the town gossip
>VIRGIE RAINEY, her daughter and the protégée of Miss Eckhart
>MISS ECKHART, a half-crazed music teacher
>LOCH MORRISON, a boy who saves a drowning girl
>CASSIE MORRISON, his sister
>EASTER, a girl saved from drowning by Loch

The Golden Apples is a collection of seven short stories, interrelated and held together by their characters, a common setting in Morgana, Mississippi, and their common theme of the wanderer's search for happiness. The stories, which were initially published separately, cover about forty years in the lives of the inhabitants of Morgana and outline the complete drama of their lives. The list of a dramatis personae on the first page of the book indicates that readers are to consider the work as a unified whole. The book is in some ways Eudora Welty's attempt to create a regional world like William Faulkner's, but her focus is on comfortable members of the upper middle class and such everyday activities as piano recitals, camping trips for the young girls, gossip between neighbors, and funerals. This world is examined from all sides and points of view. Thus the first story, "Shower of Gold," is narrated by the gossipy Mrs. Rainey, whose matter-of-factness contrasts with the mystery of what she reveals about King MacLain and his influence on the community. "June Recital" is described through the eyes of Loch Morrison, the young boy who sees everything wrong yet peculiarly right, and older Cassie, his sister, who sees correctly but does not share the insights or life force of her brother. "The Whole World Knows," revealed through the eyes of Randall MacLain, is a somewhat blurred vision that discovers a certain truth in reenacting what has been observed. Whatever the point of view, Welty is able to get beneath the veneer of middle-class comfort to get at the hidden springs and mysteries of her characters.

Beyond the common setting in MacLain County, the stories are held together by William Butler Yeats's poem, "The Song of the Wandering Aengus," from which the title of the collection is taken. This poem breaks into Cassie's mind as she tells her narrative, and in a very real way it provides the key to the meaning of the entire work. The poem itself is about a search for golden apples that represent beauty, poetry, ultimate meaning. The search is marked by the pursuit of a vision in which a silver trout becomes a "glimmering girl" before the eyes of Aengus. Eudora Welty's people are also wanderers in search of meaning to transform the commonness of their lives and make the name of the town, Morgana, as magical as the name from which it is derived, Morgan le Fay. Their search reveals the mysterious beauty beneath the surfaces of their lives, which Welty brings out as part of the process of transformation that is typical of most of her work.

The tone of the stories, on the other hand, is rather unlike Welty's earlier fiction. There is not as much variety of mood here as in her early work but rather a pervasive feeling of solemnity and sadness. This is true even in such works as "Moon Lake," in which a "silver trout," this time a girl named Easter, is presumably drowned and brought back to shore but then resurrected by Loch Morrison. Here the trout does not become a "glimmering girl" but remains a choking twelve-year-old with mud and blood coming from her mouth. The mystery of life is here, but the beauty is somewhat harder to perceive. Welty accepts the symbols of Yeats but is unwilling to accept the direction in which the symbols point. Only the search is there, accompanied by the sadness of the knowledge that there will be no glimmering girl.

Despite a measure of solemnity and sadness, there is affirmation of human life and values in *The Golden Apples*. The journey from innocence to experience and meaning is painful, and often the wanderers' knowledge is only of their predicament, not of its solution, but it is knowledge won from experience. This affirmation is tied to the region but becomes symbolic of the universality of the human condition, as is so often the case with Southern writers. Welty's manner of achieving this universality is, however, unique, for, invoking the mythic and the magical, she takes a real world, Mississippi, and makes it legendary Morgana.

The title of the book is the first hint of the pervasive use of myth and symbol. The poem from which the title is taken sets the mythical mood, and the character and events are consonant with it. The figure of King MacLain—who seems to grow out of the character of Don McInnis in Welty's early story "Asphodel," a story that also makes use of myth for its mood of gentle fantasy—first appears in "Shower of Gold" and thereafter reappears throughout most of the other stories, flitting in and out of the action. Morgana is in MacLain County, in fact, and thus even geographically the king's presence is felt. King finally comes to rest in the last story, "The Wanderers," but even there his vitality at the funeral of Mrs. Rainey is a source of amazement and admiration for Virgie Rainey. MacLain is not only king but also Zeus, and there are many conscious allusions to him in this role. As a sort of wandering pagan god, he lies in wait for unsuspecting girls in the woods and populates the town with his progeny—"Sir Rabbit" is a story of such a seduction. There is something beautiful as well as slyly humorous in his comings and goings, as can be seen in all the children who have inherited their golden hair from his golden touch upon their mothers. Mrs. Rainey states in "Shower of Gold" that King has run away to the gold fields, and whenever he returns, he brings some of it with him.

There are thus many people in the town who are related to him, and Randall and Eugene MacLain are not his only children. There are broad hints that Loch Morrison might be his child, as well as Easter, the resurrected orphan girl in "Moon Lake." They both share his preoccupation with the vital forces of life and are wanderers like himself. Because each of the seven stories has a character related to him, he is consequently intimately connected with the golden apples as a unifying symbol; indeed, he is more symbol than human and connected with the wandering search that the quest for the golden apples entails. All of his fellow seekers and roamers are brought together in the final story, "The Wanderers," in which each of these wanderers, like Aengus in Yeats's poem, has his own "song."

Perhaps the most attractive and memorable of the wanderers is Virgie Rainey, whose name connects her with King in "Shower of Gold." Virgie, whose father's name is Fate and who is the best musician in Morgana, is the protégée of Miss Eckhart, the outsider who is the music teacher for all Morgana and remains one of the most pathetic characters in the book. Miss Eckhart belongs to the large group of Welty grotesques, lonely and isolated characters who have been warped by their lack of love. In "June Recital," Miss Eckhart escapes from a mental institution to try to burn down the house in which she had taught her many lessons and had given the town music without getting anything in return.

Virgie is Miss Eckhart's pupil but not her disciple. Music has set her free, and she moves toward freedom by leaving Miss Eckhart and becoming the pianist at the silent motion picture cinema; she makes her final escape after her mother's death in "The Wanderers." She is joined as a wanderer with Randall MacLain, inheritor of his father's domain when he becomes mayor of Morgana; in "The Whole World Knows," he creates tragedy by involving another in his quest. Maideen Sumrall commits suicide because he does not seem able to see beyond his own problems and realize that others too are seekers. Eugene MacLain discovers what it means to be a wanderer on a beach in California, where he has gone in company with a Spanish musician he met by chance. Loch Morrison is the blower of the golden horn, the Boy Scout in charge of reveille at Moon Lake. Easter is the orphan who wants to be a singer. All the wanderers have their song.

The one constant in all of these songs is that they are sung in silence by solitary singers. Virgie accepts the gift of Beethoven from Miss Eckhart, but the gift does not bind her to the giver. That is the tragic and perhaps ennobling aspect of the wanderers. They give the gift of love, but love truly given separates and does not create a recognizable union. Those who truly know the value of the golden apples realize that the search is never over. What union there is remains a union in search of the unattainable. This is the community that is felt by some of the wanderers, notably Virgie. They are all victims of the search, and that is the reason for the pervasive sadness. Yet in their common circumstance as victims, they are also all heroes. Welty expressed this idea well and characteristically at the end of "The Wanderers" by referring to the myth of Medusa and Perseus. To cut off the Medusa's head was heroic but it revealed a horror about life that is life's separateness. Life is a condition in which both the Medusa and Perseus are ever present. The glory is in the struggle; the tragedy is in the lack of that struggle's completion. The golden apples are more beautiful because they will always be on the tree.

Bibliography:

Devlin, Albert J., ed. *Welty: A Life in Literature*. Jackson: University Press of Mississippi, 1987. Includes Yaeger's essay, "Because a Fire Was in My Head: Eudora Welty and the Dialogic Imagination," which analyzes the importance of gender and sexuality in *The Golden Apples* and explores the work's dialogue with Yeats's poetry. Also includes general articles on Welty and an annotated checklist of Welty criticism.

Kreyling, Michael. *Eudora Welty's Achievement of Order*. Baton Rouge: Louisiana State University Press, 1980. One of the best book-length studies of Welty's fiction. Focuses on the development of Welty's fictional technique and the growth of her aesthetic sensibility and unique voice.

Prenshaw, Peggy W., ed. *Eudora Welty: Thirteen Essays*. Jackson: University Press of Mississippi, 1983. Includes two excellent essays on Greek and Celtic mythology in *The Golden Apples:* "Golden Apples and Silver Apples" and "Technique as Myth: The Structure of *The Golden Apples*." Also includes general essays on Welty's fiction.

Schmidt, Peter. *The Heart of the Story: Eudora Welty's Short Fiction*. Jackson: University Press of Mississippi, 1991. A clearly written and accessible feminist and historicist study of Welty's stories. Explores the mixture of comedy and tragedy and the patterns of gender difference in *The Golden Apples*. An excellent starting point for serious study.

Vande Kieft, Ruth M. *Eudora Welty*. Rev. ed. Boston, Mass.: Twayne, 1987. The best beginner's source on Welty, despite more recent scholarship. Analyzes the structure, themes, and characters with a focus on the mystery and duality at the heart of Welty's fiction.

THE GOLDEN ASS

Type of work: Folklore
Author: Lucius Apuleius (c. 124-probably after 170 C.E.)
Type of plot: Picaresque
Time of plot: Early second century
Locale: Greece
First transcribed: Metamorphoses, second century (English translation, 1566)

Principal characters:
    LUCIUS, a traveler
    CHARITES, a Greek lady
    LEPOLEMUS, her husband
    THRASILLUS, a man in love with Charites
    MILO, a rich usurer
    PAMPHILE, his wife
    FOTIS, her maid

The Story:
When Lucius set out on his travels in Thessaly, he happened to fall in with two strangers who were telling unusual stories of the mysterious life of the region. At the urging of Lucius, one of the strangers, a merchant named Aristomenes, told of his strange adventure in Hippata, the chief city of Thessaly.

Aristomenes had gone to the market to buy honey and cheese, but he found that a rival merchant had been there before him and had bought up the supply. As he sadly turned away, he spied his friend Socrates, clad in rags, sitting on the ground. Socrates had fallen among thieves, who beat him and robbed him even of his clothes. Touched by his friend's plight, Aristomenes led him to an inn, bathed and clothed him, and took him to his own chamber to sleep.

Socrates warned of the woman who kept the inn, a carnal woman possessed of magical powers. When she saw a comely man, she wanted him for a lover; if he refused, he was changed into a beast or bird. Aristomenes was a little frightened; he barred the door securely and moved his bed against it for safety. Socrates was already sleeping soundly.

About midnight two hags came to the door, which fell away at their approach. One bore a torch and the other a sponge and sword. While the landlady stood over Socrates and accused him of trying to get away from her, the two hags seized his head, thrust the sword into his throat, and reached in and took out his heart. They caught all of his blood in a bladder. Then they put the sponge in the gaping throat wound.

In the morning, Socrates looked like a whole man. The two friends crept away quietly, without arousing the landlady. A few miles out of town, they stopped to eat. Socrates, after eating a whole cheese, leaned over to drink from the stream. As he did so, the wound in his throat opened, the sponge fell out, and Socrates fell dead.

Warned by this story of what he might expect in Thessaly, Lucius presented his letter of introduction to Milo, a rich usurer. He was well received in Milo's house. Attracted by Fotis, a buxom maid, Lucius hung around the kitchen admiring her hair and hips. She agreed quickly to come to his room that night as soon as she had put her mistress, Pamphile, to bed. Fotis was as good as her word, and several nights were passed agreeably.

In the city, Lucius met a cousin, Byrrhaena, a rich gentlewoman. She invited him to dine and at dinner warned him of the witch Pamphile. On his way home and full of wine, Lucius saw three thugs trying to get into Milo's house. He rushed on them and slew them with his sword. The next day was the Feast of Laughter. As an elaborate hoax, Lucius was arrested and tried for murder in the public place. At the last minute, the three "corpses" were revealed to be three bladders, blown up and given temporary life by Pamphile.

One night Fotis let Lucius look through the keyhole of Pamphile's bedroom. To his amazement, Lucius saw the witch smear herself with ointment and turn into an eagle that flew away in majestic flight. Filled with envy, Lucius demanded of Fotis that she smear him with ointment and turn him into an eagle. Fotis reluctantly consented.

At a propitious time, Fotis stole a box of ointment and smeared Lucius, but to his horror he found himself turned into an ass instead of an eagle. He looked around at the mocking Fotis, who professed to have made a mistake and promised to get him some roses in the morning. If he would only eat roses, he would turn into a man again. So Lucius resigned himself to being an ass for the night.

During the darkness, thieves broke into Milo's house, loaded much of Milo's gold on Lucius' back, and drove him out on the road. That morning, Lucius saw some roses along the way, but as he was about to eat them he suddenly thought that if he turned into a man in the company of thieves they would surely kill him. He trotted on until they came to the thieves' lair, which was governed by an old woman.

On another night the thieves took captive the gentle Charites, whom they had abducted from her wedding with Lepolemus. Charites wept bitterly. To console her, the old hag told the story of Cupid and Psyche.

There was a merchant who had three daughters. The two older girls, well-favored, were soon married off. The youngest, a true beauty, was admired by all who saw her. No man came to woo her, however, for Venus had become jealous of her beauty and had put a spell upon her. In despair, the parents consulted an oracle, who told them to expose their daughter on a rocky cliff, where she would become the bride of a loathsome beast. The sorrowing couple obeyed, and the lovely virgin was exposed one night on a cliff. After she had been left alone, a gentle wind whisked her down into a rich castle.

That night, a man with a lovely, gentle voice, but whose face she never saw, made her his wife. For a while she was content not to see her husband, but at last her jealous sisters persuaded her to light a lamp in order to see his face. When she did, she learned her husband was Cupid, who had succumbed to her charms when Venus had sent him to make her fall in love with a monster.

Although the young woman was pregnant, Venus refused to recognize her son's marriage with a mortal. Then Jupiter took pity on her and brought her to heaven. There he conferred immortality on her and named her Psyche. Cupid and Psyche became the epitome of faithful love.

Lepolemus, the resourceful bridegroom, rescued Charites by ingratiating himself with the robbers and becoming one of their band. Watching his chance, he made them all drunk and chained them. Setting Charites on the back of Lucius, Lepolemus took his bride home and returned with a band of citizens, who killed all the thieves of the den.

Lucius was given over to a herdsman of Charites, and for a time he lived a hard life as a mill ass. One day, news came of the death of Lepolemus, who was killed on a hunting trip with his friend, Thrasillus. In a dream, Lepolemus told Charites that Thrasillus had killed him. When Thrasillus came wooing Charites soon afterward, she pretended to listen to his proposals. He came to her chamber late one night, and there the old nurse of Charites gave him wine. When he was drunk, Charites took a pin and pricked out both of his eyes.

These irregularities of their owners made the shepherds uneasy. As a group, they left Charites' estate and struck out on their own. Lucius passed through several hands, some good owners, some bad. He bore his lot as best he could, but he could never be a proper ass because he still longed to eat bread and meat. One of his owners discovered this peculiarity and exhibited Lucius as a performing ass.

As a performer, Lucius led an easier life. Now that spring was approaching, he hoped to find some roses. In the meantime, he enjoyed himself; he even had a rich matron as his mistress for a few nights, but when his master proposed to exhibit him in a cage, making love to a harlot, Lucius decided to rebel. He escaped and sought the aid of Queen Isis. Taking pity on Lucius, she caused a priest to carry a garland of roses in a parade. The priest offered the flowers to Lucius, who ate them eagerly. Once again, Lucius became a man.

Critical Evaluation:

The Transformation of Lucius Apuleius of Madaura is another title of the picaresque story typically known, through William Adlington's celebrated sixteenth century English translation, as *The Golden Ass*. From antiquity, the word "golden" has been added to the title, because a common custom for Roman storytellers was to demand payment for a "golden" story. In his "Address to the Reader," Lucius Apuleius describes the literary conventions of his tale as Egyptian, but the major sources for the book—which may be called a prototype of the novel—are Lucius of Patra's *The Ass*, of which no copy survives, or Lucian of Samosata's (c. 120-after 180) *Lucius, Or The Ass*, a bawdy and comparatively crude tale that is still extant. Apuleius' novel is much longer, richer in invention, and more fully detailed than Lucian's. Moreover, it contains many stories left out of the source, including the splendid ironical tale, "Cupid and Psyche"; the stories of Aristomenes, Thelyphron, and others; the episode concerning the Festival of Laughter; and the conclusion, written in an elevated, religious manner, instead of the farcical version of the original. The tone of Apuleius' Latin, for the most part intentionally archaic and odd, has been reproduced for generations of English readers in Adlington's translation; among modern English translations, Robert Graves's version has effectively captured the vigor, sly humor, and spontaneity of the author's language.

The Golden Ass, taken as a whole, is robustly comical and satirical, so many readers may not fully appreciate the serious, religious parts of the novel. Yet the troubles of Lucius spring from his carelessness—if not impiety—toward the gods. He is guilty of two crimes: meddling with the powers of the supernatural and associating with people who have bad luck. Through his dangerous curiosity about witchcraft, he brings upon himself the troubles resulting from his transformation; through his sexual dalliance with the household slave Fotis, he invites all sorts of disasters, not the least of which is falling from the respectable class of well-born freeman to a level even beneath that of a slave, to the subhuman condition of the ass. Moreover, his extreme punishment is, from the standpoint of the cult of Isis and Osiris, fully deserved. The ass, which to the cultists represents lust, wickedness, and cruelty rather than stubbornness or indolence, is the perfect agent of Lucius' metamorphosis. He must endure twelve months of suffering in the ass's skin, until he is redeemed at last—through the benevolent intercession of the goddess Isis—as a human being. Thus, his transformation is a spiritual autobiography, in which the hero's conversion from ass to man is shown symbolically as a religious rebirth.

In his condition as an ass, however, Lucius is powerless either to help himself or others. Indeed, the bad luck that plagues him passes over to those who merely come to possess him.

Even those who befriend the ass or are otherwise guiltless in their association with him, such as the innocent Charites and her intrepid lover Thrasillus, come to a tragic end. As for the wicked tormenters of the ass—the bandits, the bailiff, the boy at the stud farm, the eunuch priests, the baker and his Christian wife—all suffer terrible fates. Ill-luck, Apuleius implies, is catching, and he does not spare the reader's sensibilities in his grisly accounts of cruelty. The author skillfully counterpoints scenes of mirth with others of terror, and his effects often resemble those of modern black comedy. The comedy verges upon the horrific; the horrors—for example, the robbers' plan to sew up Charites in the skin of the flayed ass—are so outrageous that they become comic. Above all, however, Apuleius keeps sight of his religious message. Erring humanity must be chastened, whether through terror or folly, until each penitent discovers the true path of salvation, as does the transformed ass. By the end of the tale, Lucius has not only redeemed himself from the indignity of his subhuman condition but has also become a prosperous lawyer, a priest in the cult of Isis, and is once again a freeborn citizen of Rome.

Bibliography:
Anderson, Graham. *Ancient Fiction: The Novel in the Graeco-Roman World.* New York: Barnes & Noble Books, 1984. A ground-breaking but accessible work that places *The Golden Ass* in the wider context of ancient prose fiction and that traces the form's origins "to the earliest known Near Eastern civilisation." Excellent bibliography.
Apuleius. *The Golden Ass.* Translated by Jack Lindsay. Bloomington: Indiana University Press, 1962. The translator's 24-page introduction is the best starting point. Also helpful explanatory notes in the text.
Haight, Elizabeth Hazelton. *Essays on the Greek Romances.* Port Washington, N.Y.: Kennikat, 1965. Haight's final essay compares and contrasts *The Golden Ass* (which was written in Latin) with its predecessors in Greek. Rates the work as "the greatest ancient novel extant."
Tatum, James. *Apuleius and "The Golden Ass."* Ithaca, N.Y.: Cornell University Press, 1979. Detailed but highly readable study. Supplemented with useful maps and illustrations, a good bibliography, and an appendix.
Walsh, P. G. *The Roman Novel: The "Satyricon" of Petronius and the "Metamorphoses" of Apuleius.* Cambridge, England: Cambridge University Press, 1970. Considers the story of Cupid and Psyche, embedded in *The Golden Ass,* in a separate chapter, and includes an appendix discussing the career of Apuleius and the date of the composition of his best-known work.

THE GOLDEN BOUGH
A Study in Magic and Religion

Type of work: Anthropology
Author: Sir James George Frazer (1854-1941)
First published: 1890-1915

The Golden Bough, perhaps the most famous work in anthropology, began appearing in 1890. Originally intended as a two-volume work, Sir James George Frazer eventually expanded it to twelve volumes, the last of which appeared in 1915. In 1936, he added a supplementary volume, *Aftermath*. The work is undoubtedly best known in the one-volume abridgment that Frazer published in 1922, which was subsequently revised by Theodore Gaster in 1959.

Although many of Frazer's ideas have been superseded in the intervening years, his overall thesis has stood the test of time well; certainly its influence outside the field of anthropology—for example, in twentieth century poetry, fiction, and drama—was unprecedented.

Starting in the dramatic opening scene, in which the doomed priest of Nemi stalks the grove of Diana at Aricia on the Italian coast, sword in hand, waiting for the unknown rival who will assail him, murder him, and in turn become the priest, Frazer investigates one basic theme, the meaning in myth and ritual of the sacrifice of the heroic leader whose people are renewed through his death. Frazer industriously ransacked accounts of missionaries and travelers and transferred his data into huge notebooks from which he synthesized his parallel myths of the Middle East and Europe and composed his theories about the relations of myth to ritual, magic to religion, hero to god, and leader to people. Frazer's power to synthesize is undoubtedly the key to his impact on his intellectual contemporaries and those who followed. He never left his Cambridge study to investigate anything at first hand, choosing rather to examine his data, taken from correspondents and diarists, for its symbolic meaning. In the course of that examination, he traced the connections between myths and religious rituals with both the cultures that had produced them and the cultures that came later. At the same time Sigmund Freud was theorizing about the profoundly significant world of human unconsciousness, Frazer uncovered the elements and meanings of human group behavior, which, though generally buried in the past, often remained alive in folk customs and beliefs.

Frazer's quest for the meaning of the life and death of the priest of Nemi took him through the mythology of the Mediterranean area and Europe. He first discussed magic and religion, suggesting that religion is the civilized offspring of primitive magic and arose out of what he called a "homeopathic" or sympathetic magic that associates acts through similarity. When a tribe or clan desired rain, the magician commanded it through pouring water on the parched soil; priests later invoked it by the same act. Frazer also postulated "contagious" magic, in which primitive humans believed that things once associated can never be separated in the ideal sense. Here he cites the practice, known widely through voodoo, of endeavoring to harm a real person by mistreating a symbolic representation containing the intended victim's real hair or nail parings.

Frazer suggested that the primitive magician became first the tribal priest or medicine man (known to today's anthropologist as the shaman, from the name for this vocation among the Manchurians), then, as civilization developed, the sacred king of his people. Retaining his original religious significance, this king in the highly developed ancient civilizations of the Middle East became divine. The myths of sacrificial death and spiritual rebirth are actually stories describing the regimen of the king's rule. On the basis of his examination of a wealth of totem and taboo customs that saturated the ritualized existence of a divine king, Frazer drew a portrait of a being whose life was set apart from the rest of the people by their need to solve cultural problems through his life and death. Because the physical and spiritual well-being of the tribe was actually dependent on the well-being of the priest-king, an extraordinary number of rules (totem and taboo) governed his existence. Frazer also collected a number of stories of primitive people who either deposed or killed their shaman-king when his health or potency failed. Frazer considered this ritual death the explanation for why the old priest at Nemi expected attack from a mysterious stranger, for that stranger had actually been chosen to succeed him.

To show how a king's life and death are related to myth, Frazer compiled parallel incidents from the tales of such pagan deities as Adonis, Attis, Osiris, Dionysus, Demeter, and Virbius. Adonis was said to be born of tree bark; his life was linked with fruition and his death was celebrated in the early spring. Killed by a boar on Mount Lebanon, his body was said to join the land, for the red mud that washed down the rivers in the spring rains was said to be his blood. Thus the god was thought literally to fertilize the land; his resurrection, and that of the land, are celebrated shortly after. By trying to influence, even coerce, nature through homeopathic magic, Frazer maintains, primitive humans in their ignorant simplicity confused the human with the earth and wish with fulfillment. Frazer associated the death of Osiris with the flooding of the Nile, upon whose waters the fertility of Egyptian civilization depended. Osiris, like Orpheus, was said to have been torn apart by his sacred murderers and his body scattered to ensure fecundity of land, animals, and people. Other myths tell of eating the slain god for his power and holiness, and Frazer traces this obvious forerunner of transubstantiation in Christian communion through numerous cults. Cannibalism and the eating of sacred bread and wine are similar patterns of sympathetic magic.

Along with rites designed to bring health and prosperity, some primitive rituals were thought to ward off danger and evil. In many rites, a sacrificial victim or scapegoat served as the representative of an entire people's atonement. Frazer suggested that the sacrificed god frequently served as a scapegoat, thus introducing the idea of sacrifice to later cultures and to literature. He linked this phenomenon with later festivals of saturnalia and carnival, with their kings of misrule who are allowed free conduct and then deposed.

Frazer linked fire festivals throughout Europe both to seasonal religious ritual and to human and animal sacrifices. He suggested that the life-giving property of the sun is invoked, and the destructive power of fire appeased, through such complex ritual, especially at midsummer, which Frazer found to be the time of most widespread religious rites known to Aryans.

Using the legend of the Norse god Balder, Frazer drew the threads of his theme together. Balder is alleged to have been slain by a branch of mistletoe and burned in a great funeral fire. The parasitical mistletoe is strange and magical because it is rootless, and it grows on oaks, which makes both mistletoe and oak sacred. Returning to the sacred oak grove on the shore of Lake Nemi, Frazer described the priest of the sacred wood as a representative of the divine king, the doomed god of organic life who must die that his spirit and power may be propagated throughout the world. The yellow, waxy mistletoe represents the spirit of the oak, the sacred tree, and is the golden bough carried by Vergil's Aeneas through the world of the dead in order to show the power of life available to the hero of myth and epic that enables him to triumph over death.

Later anthropologists and linguists revised many of Frazer's speculations about the material he had accumulated. Ironically, some of the principal revisions involved his primary concern. The sacred grove at Nemi was not of oak, and the famous bough was probably generalized greenery carried by suppliants in religious ceremony everywhere. The shrine at Nemi, most scholars later agreed, seems to have been a sanctuary for escaped slaves, not a temple of a seasonal god of death and resurrection. Later scholars also criticized Frazer for being too simplistic and logical when he interpreted his material according to the tenets of his orderly Darwinian mind. Frazer had called almost all humans living in cultures before the birth of the city-state "primitive," but, gradually, knowledge accumulated as to the stratification that existed in so-called primitive cultures. Religious ritual did not grow out of magical practice, for magic is a separate cultural phenomenon. Most of Frazer's deities are not merely seasonal or vegetable gods; they are also embodiments of divine force and heroic human qualities. Osiris, for example, is more the avatar of the sacredness of the Pharaoh than he is a vegetable deity. Frazer tended to oversimplify and often to denigrate his subjects, and he tended to trace too mechanically human movement toward the Victorian world. He was also handicapped by having to rely on second-hand accounts compiled by amateur travelers, many of whom did not really know the cultures about which they reported and rarely knew the languages and dialects spoken in the regions they had visited.

Given all these qualifications, T. H. Gaster, Frazer's contemporary editor, claimed that *The Golden Bough* contributed more to the intellectual and artistic climate of the twentieth century than any other anthropological work. In Frazer's vast compilation, he turns up materials of myth and ritual that lie at the root of twentieth century customs and literature, many of which continue to survive in folk customs associated with festivities such as Christmas, Easter, and May Day. Frazer's work remains the most influential anthropological study known to well-educated general readers. Despite the voluminous number of examples cited by Frazer, the work possesses distinctive clarity and great dramatic drive. Its drama still moves because Frazer's primary plot—the quest for the secret of the life and death of the haunted priest in the grove at Nemi—is analogous to myth.

Bibliography:
Douglas, Mary. "Judgements on James Frazer." *Daedalus* 107, no. 4 (Fall, 1978): 151-164. A masterful assessment of Frazer's critics and work by a leading anthropologist. Addresses the intellectual and cultural problems involved in criticizing works produced by earlier generations.
Downie, R. Angus. *Frazer and "The Golden Bough."* London: Victor Gollancz, 1970. A clearly written introduction by Frazer's biographer and amanuensis. Outlines the comparative approach, narrative, and critical impact of *The Golden Bough* and examines the work in the context of Frazer's other scholarly and literary efforts.
Fraser, Robert. *The Making of "The Golden Bough": The Origins and Growth of an Argumet.* New York: St. Martin's Press, 1990. Traces the genesis and evolution of Frazer's ideas from the original 1890 two-volume edition of *The Golden Bough* through the massive 1911-1915 third edition and to the 1936 addendum.
Manganaro, Marc. *Myth, Rhetoric, and the Voice of Authority: A Critique of Frazer, Eliot, Frye, and Campbell.* New Haven, Conn.: Yale University Press, 1992. Applies the language of postmodern literary scrutiny and rhetorical analysis to *The Golden Bough.* Argues that Frazer moved strategically from being an anthropological fact-finder to claiming authority as a literary author during the twenty-five years that he revised and expanded *The Golden Bough.*
Vickery, John B. *The Literary Impact of "The Golden Bough."* Princeton, N.J.: Princeton University Press, 1973. Outlines the ideas and intellectual importance of *The Golden Bough* and discusses in depth the literary uses of *The Golden Bough* by William Butler Yeats, T. S. Eliot, D. H. Lawrence, and James Joyce.

THE GOLDEN BOWL

Type of work: Novel
Author: Henry James (1843-1916)
Type of plot: Psychological realism
Time of plot: c. 1900
Locale: England and the Continent
First published: 1904

Principal characters:
    MR. VERVER, a wealthy American living in England
    MAGGIE VERVER, his daughter
    PRINCE AMERIGO, an Italian nobleman
    CHARLOTTE STANT, a school friend of Maggie Verver
    MRS. ASSINGHAM, a friend of the Ververs and the prince

The Story:

Maggie Verver was the daughter of a wealthy American widower who had devoted all of his life to his daughter. The Ververs lived a lazy life. Their time was spent in collecting items with which to decorate their own existence and to fill a museum that Mr. Verver was giving to his native city in the United States. They had few friends, and Maggie's only confidante was Mrs. Assingham, the American-born wife of a retired British Army officer. It was Mrs. Assingham who introduced the Ververs to Prince Amerigo, a handsome, quiet young Italian nobleman who struck Maggie's fancy. When she informed her father that she would like to marry the prince, Mr. Verver provided a handsome dowry so that the wedding might take place.

A few days before the wedding, a painful scene occurred in Mrs. Assingham's home, where the prince and Charlotte Stant, deeply in love with each other, met to say good-bye. They were both penniless, and marriage between them had been out of the question. As a farewell lark, they spent their last afternoon together in searching for Charlotte's wedding present for Maggie. In a tiny shop, they discovered a golden bowl that Charlotte wished to purchase as a remembrance for the prince from her. He refused it because of a superstitious fear that a crack in a golden bowl might bring bad luck.

After the prince and Maggie were married, their life coincided with the life the Ververs had been living for years. Maggie and her father spent much of their time together. After a year and a half, a baby was born to the prince and Maggie, but the child made no apparent difference in the relationships between Maggie and her father and between Maggie and her husband. Maggie decided that her father also needed a wife, and that Charlotte Stant would be the right sort of person; she would be thankful to marry a wealthy man and she would cause little trouble.

Mr. Verver, anxious to please his daughter in this as in everything else, married Charlotte a short time later. Maggie and her father both took houses in London where they could be together a great deal of the time. The association of father and daughter left the prince and Charlotte together much of the time. Maggie encouraged them to go out and to represent her and her father at balls and dinners. Several years went by in this manner, but slowly the fact that there was something strange in the relationships dawned on Maggie. She eventually went to Mrs. Assingham and poured out her suspicions. Mrs. Assingham, who knew the full circumstances, decided to keep silent.

Maggie resolved to say nothing of her suspicions to anyone else. Yet her attitude of indifference and her insistence in throwing the prince and Charlotte together, aroused their suspicions that she knew they had been sweethearts and that she suspected them of being lovers now. Each of the four speculated at length as to what the other three knew or suspected. Yet their mutual confidence and love prevented them from asking anything of the others.

One day, Maggie went shopping for some unusual art object to present to her father on his birthday. She accidentally happened into the same shop where the prince and Charlotte had gone several years before, and she purchased the golden bowl that they had passed over because of its flaw. The following day, the shopkeeper visited her. The name and address had told him that she was the wife of the prince who had passed up the bowl years before. He knew that the existence of the crack would quickly come to the attention of the prince, and so he had hastened to inform Maggie of the flaw and to return part of the purchase price. He also told her of the prince's first visit to the shop and of the young woman who had been with him. Maggie thereby knew that the prince and Charlotte had known each other before her marriage and that they had spent an afternoon together the day before she was married. Again, she confided in Mrs. Assingham.

Having learned that there was no present serious relationship between the prince and Charlotte, Mrs. Assingham informed Maggie that she was making a great ado over nothing at all. To back up her remark, she raised the bowl above her head and smashed it to the floor, where it broke into several pieces. As she did so, the prince entered the room and saw the fragments of the bowl. After Mrs. Assingham's departure, he tried to learn how much Maggie knew. He and Maggie agreed to say nothing to either Maggie's father or to Charlotte.

Charlotte, too, had begun to sense that something was disturbing Maggie, and she guessed what it was. Maggie tried to realign the relationships between the four of them by proposing that she and Charlotte stay together for a while and that the prince and her father go to the Continent to buy art objects. She made the proposal gently, and it was as gently rebuffed by the other three.

Maggie and her father began to realize that their selfishness in continuing their father-daughter relationship had been wrong. Soon after, Charlotte told Maggie that she wished to return to America and to take her husband with her. She bluntly informed Maggie that she was afraid that if Mr. Verver continued to live so close to his daughter, he would lose interest in his wife. Mr. Verver agreed to return to the United States with Charlotte, although he realized that once he was away, Charlotte would never agree to his coming back to Europe to live.

On an autumn afternoon, Mr. Verver and Charlotte went to have tea with Maggie and the prince before leaving England. It was almost heartbreaking to Maggie to see her father's carriage take him out of sight and to know that her old way of life had really ended. The only thing that kept her from breaking down completely was the look on the prince's face as he turned her face away from the direction her father's carriage had taken. At that moment, seeing his eyes, Maggie knew she had won her husband for herself and not for her money.

Critical Evaluation:

With *The Golden Bowl*, as well as with *The Wings of the Dove* (1902) and *The Ambassadors* (1903), Henry James definitively established his reputation. In these novels, James's already complex style reaches new levels of sophistication. Increasingly, the writing becomes more and more intricate and convoluted and it tends toward increasingly subtle levels of analysis of character and event. Gradually the "center of consciousness" in the mind of a character, which had been essential to James's earlier works, gives way to an omniscient narrative point of view that is James's own. Though it hardly appears so to the eye, James's style of this period is essentially oral—he had developed the habit of dictating his material to a secretary—and reflects his characteristically ponderous manner of speech. James's language and technique in these late novels seems endlessly to circle or enfold a subject or an idea without ever touching it directly.

With *The Golden Bowl*, James continues the "international theme" of Americans in Europe that had characterized his work from the beginning. Adam Verver, in particular, can be seen as an avatar of the American Adam, who recurs in James's fiction, in search of European culture, which he then takes back to his culturally barren homeland. Prince Amerigo, linked through his name to the historic connection between America and Europe, might be seen as dramatizing a new dependence of the Old World upon the New. Yet *The Golden Bowl* differs from the kind of international novel represented by such works as *The American* (1876-1877), *Daisy Miller* (1878), or *The Ambassadors* by being ultimately concerned more with individuals than with cultures. Though the Ververs begin in America and Adam returns there at the novel's end, neither his experience nor that of Maggie or Charlotte is essentially contingent upon the sort of conflict of cultural values that is at the heart of James's international novels and stories. The problems of love and marriage at the heart of *The Golden Bowl* are universal; neither their nature nor their solution depends upon an American perspective.

Like many of James's works, *The Golden Bowl* began in his notebooks with the recording of an anecdote he had heard concerning a young woman and her widower father, each of whom had taken a spouse and then learned the partners were engaged in an affair. From this scant beginning, James crafted his longest and most elaborate novel. He did so not by greatly complicating the plot but by scrupulously elaborating the conflicts and resolutions resulting from the complex relations among the four central characters. By making his characters members of the wealthy leisure class, James frees them from the mundane worries of the world. He is thus able to focus his, and their, entire attention on one particular problem without regard to external complications. Ultimately, the novel poses moral and philosophical questions that transcend both the psychological and social levels of the work to confront the basic question of Maggie's adjustment to a less-than-perfect world.

The golden bowl is James's metaphor for the marriage between Amerigo and Maggie, and perhaps, in its larger implications, for life itself. The bowl, not really "golden" at all, but crystal gilded with gold leaf, has the superficial appearance of perfection, but is, in fact, cracked. As a symbol of Maggie's "perfect" marriage, the bowl very clearly illustrates the flaw at the heart of the relationship—a flaw that no doubt existed even before the prince and Charlotte resumed their old love affair and that represents a potential threat to the marriage. Both Maggie and her father are guilty of treating the prince as nothing more than one of the valuable objects they have come to Europe to purchase—they have bought the perfect marriage for Maggie. Unlike art, however, human relationships are not subject to purchase, nor can they, as in the case of Adam's marriage to Charlotte, be arranged for convenience without regard to the human factors concerned. In fact, both Maggie and her father tend to live in a small, supremely selfish world. Insulated by their money from the actuality of life, they isolate themselves from the real complexities of daily existence. Their world is, in effect, more "art" than "life."

The resolution of the novel turns around Maggie's positive act, but in the earlier parts of the novel, she is more passive than active. The marriage itself, for example, seems more of an arrangement between the prince and Adam Verver than a particular choice made by Maggie: Adam wants the perfect marriage for his daughter, and Prince Amerigo wants access to the Verver millions, so they come to an agreement. Maggie apparently has little to say about it, and even, judging from her relationship to the prince throughout most of the novel, no very great interest in the marriage. Her real desire seems to be to continue life with her father as always, rather than to begin an independent life with her husband. Only when confronted with the prince's infidelity does Maggie recognize that she must confront reality for the sake of everyone concerned. In choosing to separate from her father in order to begin making the best of her imperfect marriage, Maggie discovers a latent ability to confront the world as it really is and to rise above the romantic idealism that had characterized her life with Adam Verver.

"Critical Evaluation" by William E. Grant

Bibliography:
Edel, Leon. *Henry James: A Life.* 1st ed. New York: Harper & Row, 1985. Abridged version of Edel's standard biography of James. Comments on the genesis of *The Golden Bowl* and explains its subtle relationship to the author's life. Briefly sketches portraits of major characters.
Gard, Roger, ed. *Henry James: The Critical Heritage.* London: Routledge & Kegan Paul, 1968. Excerpts from reviews by British and American writers that provide an overview of the reception given to *The Golden Bowl* by James's contemporaries. Most cite James's skill in storytelling, though some note the complexities of style that make reading difficult.
Jones, Granville H. *Henry James's Psychology of Experience: Innocence, Responsibility, and Renunciation in the Fiction of Henry James.* The Hague: Mouton, 1975. Focuses on James's portrait of the heroine of *The Golden Bowl*, Maggie Verver. Discusses several important scenes in which she gradually learns the nature of the relationship between Prince Amerigo and Charlotte and explains how she achieves a moral victory.
Macnaughton, William R. *Henry James: The Later Novels.* Boston: Twayne, 1987. In a chapter analyzing *The Golden Bowl*, Macnaughton comments on the genesis of the work and the influences that shaped James's tale. Characterizes the novel as a study in the folly of goodness and offers a careful explication of key scenes.
Sicker, Philip. *Love and the Quest for Identity in the Fiction of Henry James.* Princeton, N.J.: Princeton University Press, 1980. Includes a chapter on *The Golden Bowl* that explores James's ability to create "multipersonal love relationships." Describes parallels between the novel and the traditional fairy tale, which provides a symbolic framework for the story.

GOLDEN BOY

Type of work: Drama
Author: Clifford Odets (1906-1963)
Type of plot: Social realism
Time of plot: 1930's
Locale: New York
First performed: 1937; first published, 1937

Principal characters:
  JOE BONAPARTE, a prizefighter
  TOM MOODY, a fight manager
  LORNA MOON, his mistress
  MR. BONAPARTE, Joe's father
  EDDIE FUSELI, a gunman
  TOKIO, Joe's trainer

The Story:

Tom Moody, a fight manager, and Lorna Moon, his mistress who wanted to marry him, were having an argument about Tom's wife, who would not give him a divorce. Tom, wanting money for the divorce, needed to find a winning fighter. While they were talking, Joe Bonaparte arrived to tell them that Moody's fighter had broken his hand and could not fight that night. Joe, whom nobody knew, persuaded them to let him substitute, and he won.

Joe, a musician, had always wanted a good violin, and his father had bought him one for his twenty-first birthday. When Joe returned home, his father, who had not been told of the fight, had read of it in the papers and was very much distressed. He tried to persuade Joe to give up fighting and continue his study of music, but Joe wanted to fight. His father, hurt, did not give him the violin.

Joe fought well after that, but there was a serious conflict between the sensitive musician that he truly was and the brutal fighter he had to be. He held back in the ring, fearing that he would ruin his hands for the violin. When Moody tried to persuade him that fame and money would be more important than music, he succeeded only in antagonizing Joe, who threatened to quit. Lorna agreed to try to persuade Joe to reconsider. Joe was basically a musician, but he had been ridiculed and hurt by people. Fighting was not a part of his nature, but he wanted to fight back and music could not do that for him. While he was explaining all this to Lorna, he had already decided to remain in the ring. When Joe was preparing for a fight tour, Mr. Bonaparte asked Lorna to help the young man find himself. When he tried to give Joe the violin, the boy refused it. Then he asked for a blessing, which his father refused to give.

Joe's tour was a great success except for one fight. He had not fought well on that occasion because he had seen a man with a violin and was reminded of his music and his own past. Moody realized that Joe had to be prevented from having any contact with his family and his past.

The fight world changed Joe's personality. He liked the money and the notoriety. He bought an expensive sports car, which he drove recklessly, and he became difficult to manage. Eddie Fuseli, a gambler and a gunman, wanted to buy a piece of Joe, and Joe agreed, to Moody's dislike. He told Lorna to take care of Joe in her own way. Joe fell in love with Lorna and asked her to give up Moody. She denied loving Joe and said that she could not leave Moody because she felt sorry for him. Joe knew that she was not telling the truth when she began to cry. They talked about their love, and Joe demanded that she tell Moody at once. She said that she would, but when she went to tell him she learned that his wife had agreed to a divorce and that they could be married in a few months. Because of this, she was unable to tell him about her love for Joe. Later Joe had an argument with Moody and demanded that Lorna tell Moody about their love. Although Lorna denied that there was anything between them, she confessed the truth to Moody when they were alone again.

One night Mr. Bonaparte came to see Joe fight. Fuseli was disturbed because he did not want Joe to see his father, but Joe saw him anyway. He also saw Moody and Lorna together. Mr. Bonaparte, seeing that Joe had completely changed, finally gave his blessing to Joe's career. Joe cried after his father left. During the fight, Mr. Bonaparte went back into the dressing room rather than see the fighters hurt each other. Joe returned after he had won the fight, but when his trainer attempted to remove the gloves, Joe told him that he would have to cut one of them off. His hand was broken.

Now that he could never be a musician, Joe was all fighter. Moody and Lorna announced that they were getting married in a few days. Joe was still in love with Lorna, and it was obvious that his unhappiness was hurting his career. While Joe was fighting badly in his most important match, Fuseli blamed Lorna and threatened to kill her. Joe, however, returned to the dressing room a victor. A few moments later they were all told that the other fighter had died after being floored by Joe's knockout punch. Everyone left the dressing room except Lorna and Joe. She told him that she loved him and asked him to go back to his music. He showed her his mutilated hands. However, he decided to give up fighting, and he and Lorna went for a wild ride in order to celebrate.

Fuseli, Moody, and the others, not knowing where Joe and Lorna had gone, went to Joe's home and drank and talked while they waited for his return. The telephone rang in the middle of an argument to decide who would own Joe in the future. Joe and Lorna had been killed in an automobile accident. Mr. Bonaparte left to claim Joe's body and bring him home where he belonged.

Critical Evaluation:

Clifford Odets is generally regarded as one of the most talented playwrights to emerge from the Depression generation. In his mid-twenties he became one of the founders of the Group Theatre, the most exciting and innovative American theater group of the period, and its dominant playwright. In the spirit of the times, Odets quickly established himself as a volatile political dramatist with such intense theatrical statements as *Waiting for Lefty* (1935), *Till the Day I Die* (1935), *Awake and Sing!* (1935), and *Paradise Lost* (1935). Although admitting that *Golden Boy* was consciously written "to be a hit" and shore up the sagging finances of the Group Theatre, Odets insisted that it, too, was an anticapitalist social play. To a modern audience, however, the personal tragedy of Joe Bonaparte is the most important concern of the drama.

In essence, *Golden Boy* is a variation on the theme of the man who sells himself for success and discovers, too late, that he has made a bad bargain. A poor Italian youth coming of age in the middle of the Depression, Joe knows that he can find personal satisfaction playing the violin, but the bitterness in his feelings of poverty, coupled with a desire for revenge against people who have scorned him for years, drives him into opting for fighting instead of music.

At first, he boxes gingerly, trying to protect his hands for his music, but by the end of the first act he no longer cares. The remainder of the play is devoted to showing how this decision corrupts and destroys him. The question of whether it is a social or a personal play probably depends on whether one interprets Joe's decision as resulting from individual weakness or social pressure. Once he makes it, however, there is no doubt that the ethics of success which he embraces is totally self-destructive.

In the earliest version of the play Odets subtitled it an allegory, and, as such, it almost resembles a morality play. Embodiments of good and evil contend for Joe's "soul," although these other characters are, for the most part, also the victims of conflicting needs and values.

The positive moral forces in the story are represented by old Mr. Bonaparte, a fruit peddler, who encourages Joe's violin playing and is horrified by what he sees in the boxing business; Joe's brother, Frank, a labor organizer, who represents the right kind of militant, one who fights for the things he believes in; and Joe's trainer, Tokio, who, although a part of the fighting business, is a sensitive man who understands Joe's needs and tries to help him find himself.

Joe, however, cannot take good advice. He must find things out for himself and, when he does, he has gone too far, and it is too late. He rejects his real father and accepts Eddie Fuseli, the gangster-gambler, as his model. Joe emulates Fuseli's taste in clothing, goals, and values, and only at the end of the play realizes that Fuseli owns him, literally as well as professionally.

Success has done nothing to soften the hatred in Joe, and it is this unleashed hostility that destroys him. He hits his last opponent, the Chocolate Drop, with all his might and kills him. In doing so, Joe finally realizes that he has killed himself too. No longer able to fight, ruined for the violin, he commits suicide, either consciously or unconsciously, in the most appropriate way, by crashing his sports car, symbol of materialism and speed, in the company of Lorna Moon, the good-bad girl who shares his confusion of values.

Bibliography:

Brenman-Gibson, Margaret. *Clifford Odets, American Playwright: The Years from 1906 to 1940.* New York: Atheneum, 1981. This thorough psychoanalytical study of Odets discusses the origins and psychological significance of *Golden Boy.*

Clurman, Harold. *The Fervent Years: The Story of the Group Theatre and the Thirties.* New York: Alfred A. Knopf, 1945. Clurman tells how Odets wrote *Golden Boy* to rescue the Group Theatre from insolvency. He offers worthwhile artistic insights into the play.

Miller, Gabriel, ed. *Critical Essays on Clifford Odets.* Boston: G. K. Hall, 1991. This useful collection contains essays on most of Odets' plays, including *Golden Boy*, which is also referred to in many of the essays.

Shuman, R. Baird. *Clifford Odets.* New York: Twayne, 1962. Shuman devotes one nine-page section to *Golden Boy* and refers to the play frequently throughout his critical biography.

Strouse, Charles. *"Golden Boy": The Book of a Musical.* New York: Bantam Books, 1966. The musical version of *Golden Boy* is presented in its entirety, accompanied by a revealing foreword by William Gibson, who completed the musical version after Odets' death in 1963.

Weales, Gerald. *Odets: The Playwright.* New York: Methuen, 1985. A sensible starting point for beginners, this lucid, concise overview of Clifford Odets includes a six-page section devoted to *Golden Boy*, along with frequent other references to the play.

THE GOLDEN NOTEBOOK

Type of work: Novel
Author: Doris Lessing (1919-   )
Type of plot: Social realism
Time of plot: 1940's-1950's
Locale: London, England
First published: 1962

Principal characters:

ANNA WULF, a writer (Ella in the Yellow Notebook)
MOLLY JACOBS, Anna's friend (Julia in the Yellow Notebook)
RICHARD PORTMAIN, Molly's former husband (George in the Yellow Notebook)
TOMMY JACOBS, Molly and Richard's son
MARION JACOBS, Richard's present wife (Muriel in the Yellow Notebook)

The Story:

Book One. In the "Free Women" section, Anna visited her old friend Molly, feeling distant and cynical about their personal talks. Richard and Molly fought about their son, his new wife, and his choice of career. Tommy, sarcastic, watched his parents, and Anna went home depressed to write. Beginning as a parody of a novel synopsis, the Black Notebook then continues with Anna's reminiscences about her experiences with a group of communist intellectuals in World War II Rhodesia. The group discovered a resort hotel in the veld, where they spent their weekends drinking and discussing political ideas. An older member of the group, George Hounslow, had an affair and a child with an African woman, the hotel cook's wife. When the hotel owner discovered this, she dismissed the cook, ruining his family. Anna had a sexual encounter with her lover's friend, and these two incidents ended the group's association.

In the Red Notebook, Anna was cynical about the British Communist Party but joined anyway. She decided she did this because she, like others, could not give up hope for a better world. Anna worked for the party canvassing neighborhoods and discovered her real interest was the life of the average housewife, who was home going "quietly mad," a subject for study not considered serious by the party leaders.

Anna wrote the Yellow Notebook as a novel. Ella, a women's magazine writer, became involved with Paul Tanner, a married psychologist with two children. They began to behave more like the stereotypical man and woman. In a plot sketch of the novel, Ella and Paul were involved for five years. He refused to leave his wife, then got a job in Africa to escape Ella. Anna was frustrated that the novel, like her first book, did not capture her actual lived experience.

In the Blue Notebook, a diary, Anna went to a psychotherapist and immediately began dreaming. She cut out articles from the newspapers that examined the violence in the world, trying to understand it. In her dreams, a menacing dwarf who represented chaos appeared.

Book Two. In "Free Women," Tommy visited Anna to tell her he had turned down his father's job offer and read her private notebooks. Marion, Richard's new wife, arrived, drunk, and in the middle of their conversation, Molly called to say Tommy had shot himself. In the Black Notebook, Anna had dinner with television agents who wanted to buy the rights to her novel. Both wanted to change the novel beyond recognition to be socially acceptable. In the Red Notebook, Anna toyed with quitting the Communist Party. In a dream, she saw a tapestry that stretched over the earth. Someone pulled a string and it dissolved into chaos. She attended a writing group in which everyone was afraid to criticize a badly written pamphlet because it was politically correct. In the Yellow Notebook, on a rough plane trip home, Ella realized she wanted to die. She met an American on the plane and had a physically unsatisfying affair with him. In the Blue Notebook, Anna wrote a long, detailed description of one day hoping to capture reality in writing. She rewrote the scene in short, terse language the next morning, trying to be objective.

Book Three. Tommy was blinded by his suicide attempt, and Marion began spending all her time with him. Richard tried to bully Anna into doing something about this situation, and Ivar, Anna's gay roommate, and his new lover were rude to Anna. She dreamed she must cross a desert. On waking, she confronted Ivar.

In the Black Notebook, Anna reminisced about a pigeon-hunting episode with her Rhodesian group during which Paul, an aristocratic sort, bullied Jimmy, the working class member of the group. They discussed how communist philosophy did not consider the possibility of a destructive element in the world. Anna wrote parodies that revealed how decadent writing had become. Then she examined various Soviet reviews of her novel, which revealed to her that the various writers were responding to the social climate of their country rather than to the book. In the Red Notebook, Anna noticed a growth of enthusiasm in her communist group, then another return of cynicism, which confirmed for her that this sort of political activity was meaningless. Tommy became involved in a young socialist group which repeated the same self-righteous polemics that Anna was involved with in her youth.

In the Yellow Notebook, Ella became more disturbed by her dependency. She visited her father and discovered that her intuition that he wrote poetry was correct. In the Blue Notebook, Ella began to experience a loss of meaning in words. She dreamed about the dwarf again and had two affairs with very destructive men, noticing how they seemed split into two personalities, reminding her of Paul.

Book Four. In "Free Women," Marion left Richard and moved in with Tommy, and the two were arrested at a political demonstration. Anna tried to calm everyone, but noticed that she was beginning to crack up herself. Marion refused to return to Richard, and Anna returned home to kick Ivar out.

In the Black Notebook, in Anna's dream a "director" appeared and began changing the memories of the resort hotel. She realized what she remembered was colored by her own point of view. The Red Notebook told the story of Harry Mathews, an insignificant Communist Party member. He cherished the illusion that one day his correct analysis of the political situation would be appreciated in Russia. When he was invited to Russia, he imagined his time had come, but was only able to talk with a lowly interpreter. He realized his mistake and, on returning home, married and began a new life.

The Yellow Notebook listed a series of story ideas, exploring a whole variety of possible scenarios between men and women. The Blue Notebook told the story of Anna's affair with Saul Green. In this affair, they enact all the plot lines written in the Yellow Notebook. Anna understood that she was not in control of herself, but acted out cultural ideas of relationships and that she and Saul were psychically connected.

The Golden Notebook. Anna and Saul finally acted out all their insanity with each other. They both recognized this by saying, "Well, we'll never have to say that again." The film projectionist began to show Anna in her dreams the story of the resort hotel weekends as perceived by the characters whom Anna least understood. She felt that something new had now emerged in her life. She and Saul gave each other the first sentence of their next novels.

Free Women. Anna moved to a smaller flat and got a job as a social worker. Molly married a progressive businessman. Marion and Tommy took Molly's house. Tommy was to follow in his father's footsteps as a business tycoon. Marion bought a dress shop.

Critical Evaluation:

The structure of *The Golden Notebook* is its most important feature and was the most overlooked aspect of the novel when it was first released. Critics immediately pronounced the novel to be simply about the "sex war," a notion which provoked Doris Lessing into adding a preface directing the reader's attention to the shape of the novel and the theme of breakdown that is reflected in that shape. Anna Wulf cannot write about her world as a whole, because it no longer fits together for her, so she breaks it down into parts in the hope that she can discover an underlying meaning which will bring a new order. Anna understands that she is herself internally divided when she examines the discrepancies between her belief system or sense of self and her actual behavior. By allowing herself to move into these contradictions and live them rather than suppress them, Anna is eventually able to break through into a new paradigm.

One theme of this novel is considering the function of language as ideology (belief system), a way to stop or control the thinking process. The Black Notebook looks at the relationship between Anna's memories and the novel she wrote out of them, and how literature is controlled by cultural ideology. The Red Notebook examines the ideology of political life. Anna discovers how she is manipulated, how her identity is shaped, by the surrounding cultural belief systems. She knows that the Communist Party has become corrupt, that members (including herself) will say one thing when alone or with one another, and adopt or be taken over by another "viewpoint" while functioning in an official Party capacity. This does not stop Anna from participating in all this activity even while she is ironically aware of its irrationality. The Red Notebook also ends with clippings and a story about a man whose whole life was built on the delusion that the Russians would one day send for him to set the history of the Party straight.

The Yellow Notebook separates out sexual politics and examines the "woman in love" figure who emerges in the psyche of Ella. She is dismayed at her own conventional responses to her lover and realizes that she cannot stop herself from acting out cultural stereotypes. Paul is as internally divided as Ella is, and acts the part of the irresponsible husband, the jealous lover, seemingly against his will as well. Ella escapes the social formulas by writing out plot summaries in which she discovers these preplanned scenarios encapsulated in her head, thus purging herself of their influence.

In the Blue Notebook Anna experiences language becoming inadequate to reflect reality. Try as she might, she cannot stop social ideology from contaminating her attempts to capture "pure reality" in her diary. Anna comes to understand slogans and ideology as substitutes for self-knowledge and independent action. This notebook ends with the purchase of the Golden Notebook, which contains the dreams which bring Anna out of the grip of the cultural image of woman and the mind-containing slogans of politics and psychoanalysis.

Anna escapes the disintegration of her personality, which is intricately related to the social disintegration around her, by playing out all the possibilities of the male-female role with Saul Green, another man whose personality is fractured. By exploring each other's psychoses, by having both sides of the formula of gender available, they are able to break through their entrapment in the ideology of male-female relationships. Anna discovers in this process that individual consciousness is not isolated and discrete as society would have her believe, but rather is connected to culture and to other people in an intimate way.

The "Free Women" section shows how a traditional novel cannot capture the rich complexity of life that is revealed in the journals. Lessing states that she felt the shape of the book would "make its own comment about the conventional novel," which would amount to "how little I have caught of all that complexity." Readers understand that the conventional novel in *The Golden Notebook* fails; the source of the failure is the notebooks, the sources from which she wrote the novel, which are much richer, complex, and interesting, but Anna Wulf has succeeded in creating a new definition of the nature of human consciousness and identity.

In writing this book, Lessing was interested in capturing the feeling and culture of mid-twentieth century Britain, and in so doing, chooses a female narrator. For a woman's consciousness to serve as the center of a work of such scope was unusual even late into the twentieth century. *The Golden Notebook* expresses many women's experiences. The novel explores issues of intimate relationships, sexuality, and identity that had not previously been discussed in such detail or from a woman's perspective.

Theresa L. Crater

Bibliography:

Greene, Gayle. *Changing the Story: Feminist Fiction and the Tradition.* Bloomington: Indiana University Press, 1991. Feminist criticism of Lessing, among others. Examines how language plays an important role in *The Golden Notebook.*

Kaplan, Carey, and Ellen Cronan Rose, eds. *Approaches to Teaching Lessing's "The Golden Notebook."* New York: Modern Language Association of America, 1989. An excellent close look at *The Golden Notebook*, from several perspectives.

Pickering, Jean. *Understanding Doris Lessing.* Columbia: University of South Carolina Press, 1990. Excellent summaries of the novels, with helpful commentary.

Pratt, Annis, and L. S. Dembo, eds. *Doris Lessing: Critical Studies.* Madison: University of Wisconsin Press, 1973. A collection of essays on Lessing's work, containing an excellent interview with Lessing by Florence Howe.

Rubenstein, Roberta. *The Novelistic Vision of Doris Lessing: Breaking the Forms of Consciousness.* Champaign: University of Illinois Press, 1979. This book gives special attention to Lessing's focus on human consciousness, what the theme means in her work, and how she challenges the limits of consciousness in her prose.

GONE WITH THE WIND

Type of work: Novel
Author: Margaret Mitchell (1900-1949)
Type of plot: Historical
Time of plot: 1861-1873
Locale: Atlanta and Tara Plantation, Georgia
First published: 1936

Principal characters:

> SCARLETT O'HARA, a Southern belle who maintains her family through the Civil War and Reconstruction
> ELLEN and GERALD O'HARA, her parents
> ASHLEY WILKES, the neighbor Scarlett loves
> MELANIE HAMILTON, the woman Ashley marries, his cousin
> INDIA, Ashley's sister
> CHARLES HAMILTON, Melanie's brother, Scarlett's first husband
> FRANK KENNEDY, Scarlett's second husband
> RHETT BUTLER, a blockade runner, Scarlett's third husband
> BONNIE BLUE, the child of Scarlett and Rhett
> MISS PITTYPAT, Melanie's maiden aunt
> MAMMY, Scarlett's nurse, a slave, then a servant
> WADE HAMPTON HAMILTON and
> ELLA KENNEDY, Scarlett's other children

The Story:

Scarlett O'Hara, sixteen, was the most popular belle in Clayton County, Georgia, where her family's plantation, Tara, was located. The daughter of fiery Gerald O'Hara and Ellen Robillard O'Hara, Scarlett had her father's courage and temper, which her genteel mother and her slave Mammy tried to "refine."

The best families in the county were invited to nearby Twelve Oaks plantation for Ashley Wilkes's birthday party in April, 1861, when talk concerned whether the South would secede from the Union. Ashley announced his engagement to his cousin, Melanie Hamilton. When Scarlett told Ashley she loved him, he said that Wilkeses always married cousins. Scarlett later realized that Rhett Butler, a scoundrel from Charleston, had been eavesdropping.

Upset by Ashley's rejection, Scarlett accepted the proposal of Melanie's brother, Charles. The party dissolved in chaos at the announcement that Union troops had fired on Fort Sumter. Both weddings occurred immediately, so that the men could go fight for the Confederacy. Charles became ill and died in the army leaving Scarlett pregnant with their son, Wade Hampton. Scarlett then went to stay with Melanie at her Aunt Pittypat's in Atlanta, where the two young women nursed sick and wounded soldiers, a task Scarlett hated. Rhett Butler, now a blockade runner, frequently visited the women.

As Union soldiers shelled Atlanta, Melanie went into labor, and Scarlett had to deliver the baby. Then she, Melanie, the baby, and their slave Prissy escaped the burning city, aided by Rhett Butler, who left them to join the Confederate army. Scarlett went to Tara, where she found her mother dead, her sisters sick, her father insane (he was later killed in a fall from his horse), most of the slaves gone, and the food and money stolen by Union soldiers. Most of the neighboring plantations had been burned.

Scarlett's family, with the help of Mammy, Pork, and Dilcey, their former slaves, scrounged for food and farmed. When a Yankee soldier came into the house to pillage, Scarlett killed him. Other Union soldiers tried to burn Tara, but Scarlett and Melanie extinguished the fire.

The war ended, and Ashley returned from a Northern prison camp. He helped farm, as did a wounded soldier the O'Haras had nursed back to health. The Yankees had burned their cotton, however, and their work did not yield enough to pay the high taxes.

Scarlett learned that Rhett Butler was in jail because the Yankees thought he had illicit money from blockade running. She had Mammy make her a dress from the drapes and went to Atlanta to try to persuade him to give her the money. He said he could not get to it. She ran into Frank Kennedy, her sister Suellen's fiancé. Realizing that if Suellen married him she would send none of his money to Tara, Scarlett got him to marry her instead by lying about Suellen's engagement to someone else. Frank and Scarlett had a daughter, Ella.

Scarlett bought a sawmill with money secretly borrowed from Rhett Butler, and managed her own affairs. Frank and other citizens of Atlanta were appalled that a lady would transact business. Scarlett had even picked cotton to save Tara, however, and was determined never to be poor again. She also brought Ashley to Atlanta to run a second mill.

One night as Scarlett drove her buggy to check on her mills, she was attacked by freed slaves. One of her family's former slaves saved her, but that night, Frank and his friends went to avenge her. Frank was killed and Ashley injured. The Union occupation troops came to find Frank and the others, but Rhett Butler lied, saying they had been with him at a brothel and that Frank had been killed in a duel. Belle Watling, the madam, vouched for the men, saving them from hanging.

Rhett Butler proposed to Scarlett; they married, honeymooned in New Orleans, and built an enormous house. Rhett treated Scarlett like a spoiled child. When she became pregnant and contemplated an abortion, however, he was furious. So Scarlett had the baby. Rhett adored his daughter, Bonnie Blue, and began to behave more respectably so that she would later be received into society.

One day, as Melanie planned a birthday party for Ashley, Scarlett went to the sawmill to discuss business. They began reminiscing about the way things were before the war. As they commiserated, Ashley's sister and two other people came in and saw them embracing. Melanie refused to believe the gossip and asked Scarlett to receive guests with her at the party.

Scarlett and Rhett had a miserable marriage. Scarlett used a separate bedroom because she did not want more children. Rhett often visited Belle Watling. The night after Scarlett was caught in Ashley's arms, Rhett forced her to have sex with him, although she was ready to reconcile with him the following morning. Scarlett became pregnant again, but miscarried during a fight with Rhett. She almost died, and Rhett was overcome with guilt and worry.

After Scarlett recovered, she and Rhett returned to their bickering. They argued over the raising of Bonnie, whom Rhett indulged. When the pony he bought the child threw her and killed her, Scarlett blamed Rhett, and he blamed himself. His grief almost destroyed him, and their marriage lost its only tie.

Melanie, who had never been healthy, died after a miscarriage. On her deathbed, she asked Scarlett to take care of Ashley and their son, Beau. She also said, "Captain Butler—be kind to him. He—loves you so." Finally, Scarlett realized that her love for Ashley was just an old habit, and that she loved her own husband. When she got home, however, Rhett was leaving her. As he left, she repeated her response to almost every crisis: "I'll think of it all tomorrow, at Tara."

"The Story" by M. Katherine Grimes

Critical Evaluation:

Gone with the Wind, one of the best-selling novels of all time, is the story of the beautiful, headstrong daughter of a wealthy plantation owner who, when reduced to poverty and hardship in the wake of Sherman's destruction of the countryside, uses her feminine wiles to regain her lost wealth. Having at last attained this goal, she is unable to hold the one man she really loves.

A historical romance of prodigious proportions, this first novel by an unknown author went through twelve printings within two months of publication. Its 1,037 pages have enthralled millions, and the sales in a single year exceeded two million copies. The novel has been translated into more than two dozen languages and, even after many years, sales have continued at a pace brisk enough to please any publisher. The motion picture version lives up to Hollywood's superlatives.

The unprecedented success of Margaret Mitchell's only novel may be attributed to a combination of the author's style—a sustained narrative power combined with remarkable character delineation—and the universality of her subject: the struggle for survival when the life to which one is accustomed is abruptly swept away. In spite of the fast-moving narrative, one is aware of this underlying thread.

Perhaps the most lasting impression one gets from the novel, however, is the skill with which Mitchell handles her characterizations. Scarlett O'Hara is, without question, one of the most memorable characters in fiction. So lifelike did she become in the public mind that the producers of the motion picture preferred not to risk an established actress in the role and thus be accused of miscasting. For this reason, among others (including the reaping of enormous publicity in the "search for Scarlett"), Vivien Leigh was chosen.

The story of Scarlett O'Hara alone would be reason enough for a best-seller; many books have achieved such fame on far less. This daughter of Irish temper and French sensibilities displays emotions, many of them unladylike, that grip the reader. One follows her intense, futile love for Ashley Wilkes, her spiteful marriage to Charles Hamilton, her opportunistic stealing of her sister's fiancé, Frank Kennedy, and her grasping arrangement of convenience with Rhett Butler. One is sometimes appalled at her callous use of her sex to gain her ends; one looks in vain for some sign of lofty ideals in this woman; and yet, in spite of all of this, one finds laudable her will to survive and her contempt for her conquerors. She is a feminist and a romantic heroine at the same time. Those who would disparage her do so at the risk of belittling themselves, as envious schoolchildren might in making fun of the most popular girl in the school.

Three other characters stand out, admirably drawn but not quite inspiring the amount of interest created by Scarlett. Rhett Butler, dissolute son of Charleston blue bloods, is a cynical, materialistic blockade runner who consorts openly with the enemy and scoffs at patriotic ideals. Forceful and masculine, he is accustomed to taking what he wants. His one unfulfilled desire is the love of Scarlett, and this frustration finally breaks his spirit. When at last, after several years of unhappy marriage, he gains her love as Ashley fails her, Rhett, a bitter, fleshy drinker, has already reached his decision to leave her.

Ashley Wilkes, the weak-willed object of Scarlett's misguided passion, depicts the impractical idealist dependent on a stronger will to solve life's problems for him. When Scarlett observes his unstable reaction to his wife's death, she is finally able to see him as he really is. Shorn of his cavalier manners and the aura of courtly romance she had bestowed upon him, he becomes an ineffectual weakling in her eyes, and the sterility of her love for him is at last apparent.

Melanie, in a way a winner despite her death at the end of the novel, finds happiness and tranquillity in her devotion to her insecure husband. Reticent, ladylike, saccharine, but intellectually attuned to Ashley, there is never any question that she, not Scarlett, should be Ashley's wife.

High-spirited Scarlett is sixteen years old when the Civil War begins. She fancies herself in love with Ashley Wilkes, the sensitive, sophisticated son at a neighboring plantation, but he does not acknowledge her love. Upon the announcement of his engagement to his soft-spoken cousin Melanie Hamilton, Scarlett impetuously marries Melanie's brother Charles, to that surprised young man's pride and delight. Less than a year later, Scarlett is a war widow and an unwilling mother. Leaving her father's plantation, Tara, in the middle of a war, Scarlett travels to Atlanta to stay with her dead husband's relatives. Later, as Atlanta is besieged by Sherman's troops, Scarlett returns home to Tara, crossing the battle lines at night in a wagon provided by Rhett. With her are Melanie and Ashley's day-old son, whom Scarlett delivered as guns sounded in the distance. She returns to find her home destroyed and her family nearly destroyed. These events shape the character of Scarlett O'Hara, and they explain the hardness and avarice that prompt many of her actions. For example, she is determined to hold on to Tara, and when the carpetbaggers arbitrarily levy an extra three-hundred-dollar tax, with the expectation of taking over the property for unpaid taxes, Scarlett unhesitatingly marries store owner Frank Kennedy, who is engaged to her sister Suellen. He dutifully pays the three-hundred-dollar tax.

Mitchell's art makes such reprehensible acts seem normal under the circumstances, for the author brings readers along the same harsh road Scarlett has traveled. Once Scarlett learns the law of war, her native abilities come into their own. Borrowing money from Rhett, she buys and successfully operates a sawmill and soon is financially secure. When Frank is killed by occupation troops, she marries Rhett, who has amassed half a million dollars during the war as a blockade runner. Even the birth of a child, Bonnie Blue, does not bring happiness to this union, however, because of the love for Ashley to which Scarlett absurdly clings. Rhett, always jealous of her contrary emotion, is unable to cope. Ironically, Rhett overcomes his love for Scarlett just as she discovers that it is he, not Ashley, whom she loves. When she tries to tell him this, Rhett announces brusquely that she is too late, that he is leaving her forever. There was no mistaking the finality of his words but, characteristically, Scarlett, the self-confident schemer, does not accept them as such. *Gone with the Wind* is not a happy book. There are flicks of humor but, for the most part, a deadly seriousness pervades the novel, and in the end the callous, grasping cynicism of the leading characters mocks them and, properly, leaves them with an empty loneliness. *Gone with the Wind* will remain a memorable work of literature not only because Scarlett O'Hara embodies some of the most admirable, if not respectable, qualities of human behavior but also because it chronicles a period and culture of American history that have become mythic in their proportions.

Bibliography:

Gailliard, Dawson. "*Gone with the Wind* as *Bildungsroman*: Or, Why Did Rhett Butler Really Leave Scarlett O'Hara?" *Georgia Review* 28 (1974): 9-18. Argues that the work is a female maturation novel. Scarlett moves from being a "Southern Lady" to becoming a "New Woman," but not with impunity, for she loses Rhett. Sees her as a child, and when she grows up, he leaves.

May, Robert E. "*Gone with the Wind* as Southern History: A Reappraisal." *Southern Quarterly* 17 (1978): 51-64. Asserts that the novel is not really romantic, but rather propaganda that exaggerates the horrors of Reconstruction. Footnotes lead to sources about *Gone with the Wind*, Southern history, slavery, and the Confederacy.

Pyron, Darden Asbury, ed. *Recasting: "Gone with the Wind" in American Culture.* Miami:

University Press of Florida, 1983. Examines the novel from a variety of angles, including mythic elements and America's obsession with the book and the movie.

_____. *Southern Daughter: The Life of Margaret Mitchell*. New York: Oxford University Press, 1991. Devotes a considerable number of pages to the composition of the novel, including problems, inspirations, and reactions.

Rubin, Louis D., Jr. "Scarlett O'Hara and the Two Quentin Compsons." In *The South and Faulkner's Yoknapatawpha: The Actual and the Apocryphal*, edited by Evans Harrington and Ann J. Abadie. Jackson: University Press of Mississippi, 1977. One of the greatest scholars of Southern literature argues that the death of Scarlett's mother frees her from the rules of the Old South to become an entrepreneur in the New South.

THE GOOD COMPANIONS

Type of work: Novel
Author: J. B. Priestley (1894-1984)
Type of plot: Social realism
Time of plot: 1920's
Locale: England
First published: 1929

> *Principal characters:*
> MISS TRANT, a British woman who has come into an inheritance
> INIGO JOLLIFANT, a former teacher at a boys' school
> JESS OAKROYD, a workman
> SUSIE DEAN, a musical comedy singer
> JERRY JERNINGHAM, a dancer

The Story:

Jess Oakroyd, a stolid Yorkshireman who was burdened with a nagging wife and sarcastic son, finally decided to pack a small basket of clothes and set off to travel about England. His adventures began when he got a ride in a large van loaded with stolen goods. The driver of the van and the driver's helper left Jess at an inn in a small hamlet after having robbed him while he was asleep. Rudely awakened by the innkeeper, Jess had no money to buy his breakfast. Setting off afoot, he came upon another van, in which a man was attempting to repair a battered peddler's stall. In return for his help, the peddler, who sold fancy balloons, gave Jess breakfast and a ride.

Jess stayed with him for three days, and then set out walking again. Within the hour, he came upon a stalled car and helped the driver, Miss Trant, start the motor. Miss Trant, who had recently inherited several hundred pounds from her father, was thirty-five years old. Since all of her previous adventures had been limited to those in historical novels, she had decided to travel across England. While Jess worked on the car, it began to rain, so they headed for a tearoom nearby. There they met Inigo Jollifant and his odd-looking companion, who was carrying a banjo. Just like Jess and Miss Trant, Inigo had begun his adventures on the previous Monday evening.

Inigo had been unhappy as an instructor at a boys' school because of the headmaster's petty tyranny. He had been dismissed after he became drunk and played the piano in celebration of his twenty-sixth birthday. Inigo, too drunk to do the prudent thing and wait for morning, had packed a knapsack and immediately set out on his travels. In the railroad station of a small town, he had met his banjo-carrying companion, Morton Mitcham, a professional entertainer.

In the tearoom, the shrewish proprietress was berating a group of customers who were unable to pay their bill. The banjo player recognized them as members of a theatrical troupe who were stranded, as they explained, after their manager absconded with their funds and a young woman. On impulse, Miss Trant decided to take over the stranded company. That night, they made plans for taking the show back on the road, and they decided on the name The Good Companions. The troupe was made up of an elderly comedian, a young and pretty musical comedy singer named Susie Dean, Morton Mitcham, a dancer named Jerry Jerningham, a girl singer, and an older couple who sang duets. Miss Trant became the manager, Inigo the accompanist, and Jess, at Miss Trant's insistence, the handyman.

The troupe's first appearance was in the little town where Miss Trant had found them. The show was not a success, but their second engagement, at a seaside hotel, met with obvious favor. The most appreciated actors were Jerry Jerningham and Susie Dean, for whose acts Inigo wrote catchy tunes. For several weeks, the company's routine was one of rehearsals and performances, with train rides between the two- or three-night engagements in each town.

As the weeks passed, Inigo Jollifant fell in love with Susie Dean; she laughed at him and said that she could not fall in love and marry until she had become a star and had played in London. Miss Trant was enjoying herself thoroughly. All of her life had been spent in the sleepy village of Hitherton in southern England, where her father had settled upon his retirement from the army. She considered her theater associates far more interesting than the small sedate group of her father's village friends.

When The Good Companions played in an almost deserted mill town in the Midlands, where the mills had been shut down for some months and the townspeople had little money or interest in a traveling vaudeville troupe, the troupe became dispirited and almost broke up. It was Jess Oakroyd who persuaded the others to stick with Miss Trant, since she would lose the money she had invested in them if they did not carry on with their engagements. The fortunes of the troupe gradually took a turn for the better. Inigo Jollifant composed new tunes for the acts that met with great success, but his love affair did not fare as well. Susie Dean could not understand why he did not take his music as seriously as he did his writing for literary periodicals. She felt sure that he was making a mistake in trying to be a second-rate essayist when he could be a first-rate songwriter.

The Good Companions finally had a long engagement in a series of prosperous manufacturing towns. They drew large audiences and Miss Trant finally began to see a return on her investment. The troupe became daring and engaged a large hall for a stand of several nights. Inigo had in the meantime gone to London, where a famous producer listened to his new songs. Inigo, determined to help Susie become a star, refused to sell his songs unless the producer agreed to hear Susie Dean perform.

The first night in the large auditorium was disastrous. The operator of the local motion picture houses had hired toughs, who started a riot and set fire to the hall during the performance. In the mêlée, the producer from London was punched in the nose, whereupon he refused to hear any more about either Inigo's music or Susie Dean. Miss Trant too was injured during the riot.

The future looked dark indeed, when an elderly woman took a fancy to Jerry Jerningham, married him, and put her money and influence at his disposal. As a result an even more important producer than the first one gave Susie Dean her chance at musical comedy in London and bought Inigo's music.

The troupe disbanded, but at Jerningham's request, the other performers found excellent places with the same producer. In the hospital, Miss Trant met a doctor with whom she had been in love for many years; they intended to marry as soon as she was well. With the help of his old friend the balloon peddler, Jess Oakroyd did some detective work in connection with the riot and discovered the identity of the men who had hired the thugs. They were made responsible for the disturbance and had to take over Miss Trant's debts for the damages.

After solving the mystery of the riot, Jess went back to his home in Yorkshire because he had received a telegram from his son, telling him that Mrs. Oakroyd was seriously ill. When she died shortly after, Jess prepared to continue traveling, having discovered that even a man as old and settled as he could become addicted to adventuring away from home. He decided to visit his married daughter in Canada.

Critical Evaluation:

The Good Companions is best described as a comic or romantic picaresque novel, although some commentators complain that, technically, it is not. J. B. Priestley's characters are not rogues, vagabonds, or rascals but simply an unlikely collection of individuals who join together to fight life's battles while wandering, trying make a success of a Pierrot troupe called The Good Companions. In this, his fourth novel, Priestley perfected one of his favorite devices, that of uniting a disparate group through a common goal. In describing the struggles of his characters, Priestley develops his theme that individual fulfillment results from helping others. They learn the importance of community, the individual's responsibility to others, and the lesson that happiness can be found only in the heart.

As a novelist, Priestley is difficult to categorize because he never became identified with any particular literary movement. He enjoyed the technical challenge of writing in various genres and styles. In *The Good Companions,* he succeeded in writing an old-fashioned novel that most closely resembles the Victorian style, including such outward trappings as humorous chapter subtitles such as "In Which Colonel Trant's Daughter Goes into Action, Sticks to Her Guns, and May Be Considered Victorious." The novel's style and popular success placed Priestley in the company of such masters of the traditional long English novel as Henry Fielding, Charles Dickens, and William Makepeace Thackeray.

In order successfully to negotiate the challenges of writing a novel twice the length of the usual British novel of its day, Priestley hit upon the device of constructing *The Good Companions* like a three-act play. In book 1, strangers meet and band together. In book 2, they set out to tour the provinces together, and there follows the chronicle of their dreams, frustrations, hard work, joys, and sorrows. In book 3, the inevitable demise of The Good Companions occurs and members of the troupe disperse. An epilogue concludes the novel, addressing "Those Who Insist Upon Having All the Latest News."

In *The Good Companions,* Priestley perfected another stylistic aspect that became a trademark in his novels and plays: He developed a remarkable ability to capture the mood, personality, rhythm, and dialect of particular locales and characters. His ear for language became a distinguishing feature of his characterizations. In fact, his ability to describe locale sometimes led to the criticism that his novels were no more than "reporting." These detailed descriptions are, however, at the heart of the storytelling in *The Good Companions.* Priestley's early readers recognized their own experiences in his descriptions, while in later years his readers relied upon these works to bring to life English society of the late 1920's.

Priestley begins this novel from a vantage point high above the Pennine Mountains, from where the camera moves down to the towns of West Riding and on to Bruddersford (a thinly disguised Bradford, the town of Priestley's own youth). There the reader is introduced to Jess Oakroyd in the crowd leaving the football grounds. The descriptions of locale and character merge to become one, each helping to define the other. This same technique of merging the individuals and their environs is used to introduce the other main characters as well. The novel comes full circle at the end, with the sequence reversed. Jess Oakroyd is again described leaving the football grounds in Bruddersford, after which the narrative soars over the Pennines, symbolizing the author's view, that the story was not limited to its characters but extends to and includes all of England. This is not merely a tidy literary device in an otherwise tidy literary structure. Rather, it establishes Jess Oakroyd as the backbone of the novel. Miss Trant is the central character, but nothing could happen without Jess Oakroyd.

Throughout the novel, but especially in book 2, no character, major or minor, appears without being given a detailed description. The details become a mosaic through which Priestley accomplishes a social analysis of the society and culture of the time. It is the great accomplishment of the novel that this analysis is delivered subtly and without extraneous comment. Priestley's England between the wars is as clearly presented as the England of Dickens' time is presented in that author's novels. Indirectly, Priestley depicts how hard life was at the time, how hard people had to work, and how close many of them lived to ruin, yet how much joy some were able to find in life. The theatrical world of The Good Companions becomes a supporting metaphor for the illusion and romance of their lives.

Priestley valued clarity. He wanted to tell a story, to cause his reader to laugh, to cry, and even to think, but he always started writing from the belief that people read primarily to be entertained. Priestley's own enthusiasm for life and his tendency toward sentimentality are reflected in the romantic view of life in *The Good Companions*, his seventeenth book, which became a best-selling phenomenon and catapulted Priestley into the role of celebrity. For almost three decades after that, his novels were more widely read and his plays more often produced than those of any of his English contemporaries. Although some of his more than thirty other novels achieved immediate success, none of them enjoyed the lasting popularity of *The Good Companions*.

"Critical Evaluation" by Gerald S. Argetsinger

Bibliography:
Atkins, John. *J. B. Priestley: The Last of the Sages*. New York: Riverrun Press, 1981. In chapter 22, "The Craft of Fiction," Atkins admires the book's vigor, observation, humor, and pace, but he finds fault with *The Good Companions* where others find strength and labels the book a literary phenomenon rather than a masterpiece.
Braine, John. *J. B. Priestley*. London: Weidenfeld and Nicolson, 1978. Chapter 3, "The Crowded Page," provides an excellent introduction to *The Good Companions*. Shows how this novel established Priestley's literary persona, why it did not become dated, and how Priestley combines objective narrative with subjective themes.
Cooper, Susan. *J. B. Priestley: Portrait of an Author*. London: Heinemann, 1970. Chapter 2, "Professional," examines Priestley's ability to delineate character and demonstrate keen insight in even his minor character portraits. Points out Priestley's ability to weave a seemingly effortless tale while concealing his brilliant craft. Concludes that it is a great escapist romance of character and situation that does not wallow in false emotion or sentimentality.
DeVitis, A. A., and Albert Kalson. *J. B. Priestley*. Boston: Twayne, 1980. In chapters 2, "The Novels: Themes and Directions," and 3, "First Efforts," the authors assert that *The Good Companions*' greatest achievement is its social analysis.
Hughes, David. *J. B. Priestley: An Informal Study of His Work*. London: Rupert Hart-Davis, 1958. Chapter 4, "A Promising Young Novelist," discusses Priestley's ability to describe locale and character. Examines how *The Good Companions* captured and interpreted the mood of its time.

THE GOOD EARTH

Type of work: Novel
Author: Pearl S. Buck (1892-1973)
Type of plot: Social realism
Time of plot: Early twentieth century
Locale: Northern China
First published: 1931

Principal characters:
    WANG LUNG, a Chinese farmer
    O-LAN, his wife
    LOTUS BLOSSOM, his concubine
    PEAR BLOSSOM, his slave
    NUNG EN, his oldest son
    NUNG WEN, his second son
    THE FOOL, his first daughter

The Story:

Wang Lung's father had chosen for his son's bride a slave girl from the house of Hwang, a girl who would keep the house clean, prepare the food, and not waste her time thinking about clothes. In the morning, Wang Lung led her out through the gate of the big house, and they stopped at a temple and burned incense. That was their marriage. O-lan was a good wife. She thriftily gathered twigs and wood so they would not have to buy fuel. She mended Wang Lung's and his father's winter clothes and scoured the house. She worked in the fields beside her husband, even on the day she bore their first son.

The harvest was a good one that year. Wang Lung had a handful of silver dollars from the sale of his wheat and rice. He and O-lan bought new coats for themselves and new clothes for the baby. Together with their child, they went to pay their respects to the Hwangs, where O-lan had once been a slave. With some of the silver dollars, Wang Lung bought a small field of rich land from the Hwangs.

The second child was born a year later, and again it was a year of good harvest. Wang Lung's third baby was a girl. On the day of her birth, crows flew about the house, mocking Wang Lung with their cries. The farmer did not rejoice when his little daughter was born, for poor farmers reared their daughters only to serve the rich. The crows were an evil omen, for the child was born feebleminded.

That summer was dry, and for months no rain fell. The harvest was poor. After the little rice and wheat had been eaten and the ox killed for food, there was nothing for the poor peasants to do but die or go south to find work and food in a province of plenty. Wang Lung sold the furniture for a few pieces of silver, and after O-lan had borne their fourth child, which was dead with bruises on its neck when he saw it for the first time, the family began their journey. They were lucky to fall in with a crowd of refugees who led them to a railroad. With the money Wang Lung had received for his furniture, they traveled on a train to their new home.

In the city, they constructed a hut of mats against a wall, and while O-lan and the two older children begged, Wang Lung pulled a ricksha. In that way, they spent the winter, each day earning enough to buy rice for the next day. One day, there was to be a battle in the town between the soldiers and an approaching enemy. When the wealthy people in the town fled, the poor broke into their houses. By threatening one fat fellow who had been left behind, Wang Lung obtained enough money to take his family home.

O-lan soon repaired the damage to their house caused by the weather during their absence; then, with jewels O-lan had plundered during the looting in the city, Wang Lung bought more land from the house of Hwang. He allowed O-lan to keep two small pearls that she liked. Wang Lung now had more land than one man could handle, and he hired one of his neighbors, Ching, as overseer. Several years later, he had six men working for him. O-lan had borne him twins, a boy and a girl, after their return from the south. She no longer went out into the fields to work but kept the new house he had built. Wang Lung's two oldest sons were sent to school in the town.

When his land was flooded and work was impossible until the water receded, Wang Lung began to go regularly to a tea shop in town. There he fell in love with Lotus Blossom and brought her home to his farm to be his concubine. O-lan would have nothing to do with the girl, and Wang Lung was forced to set up a separate establishment for Lotus in order to keep the peace.

When he found that his oldest son visited Lotus often while he was away, Wang Lung arranged to have the boy marry the daughter of Liu, a grain merchant in the town. The wedding took place shortly before O-lan, still in the prime of life, died of a chronic stomach illness. To cement the bond between himself and Liu, Wang Lung apprenticed his second son to the grain merchant, and his youngest daughter was betrothed to Liu's young son. Soon after O-lan's death, Wang Lung's father died, and they were buried near each other on a hill.

When Wang Lung grew wealthy, an uncle, his wife, and his shiftless son came to live with him. One year, there was a great flood, but although his neighbors' houses were pillaged by robbers during the confusion, Wang Lung was not bothered. Then he learned that his uncle was second to the chief of the robbers. From that time on, he had to give way to his uncle's family, who were his insurance against robbery and possibly murder.

One day, Wang Lung succeeded in coaxing his uncle and aunt to smoke opium, and they became too involved in their dreams to bother him. He did not succeed, however, in curbing their son. When the boy began to annoy the wife of his oldest son, Wang Lung rented the deserted house of Hwang and moved to town with his immediate family. The cousin left to join the soldiers, and the uncle and aunt were left in the country with their pipes to console them.

After Wang Lung's overseer died, he did no more farming himself. From that time on, he rented his land, hoping that his youngest son would work it after his death. When Wang Lung took a slave young enough to be his granddaughter, however, the boy, who was in love with the girl, ran away from home and became a soldier.

When he felt that his death was near, Wang Lung went back to live on his land, taking with him only his slave, young Pear Blossom, his feebleminded first daughter, and some servants. One day, as he accompanied his sons across the fields, he overheard them planning what they would do with their inheritance, with the money they would get from selling their father's property. Wang Lung cried out, protesting that they must never sell the land because only from it could they be sure of earning a living. He did not notice them looking at each other over his head and smiling.

Critical Evaluation:

Pearl Sydenstricker Buck referred to herself as "mentally bifocal" with respect to her American and Chinese ways of looking at things. The daughter of American missionaries in China, Buck came to know that country better than any other, for she spent her early formative years there, and during that extremely significant time many of her ideas, viewpoints, and philosophy developed. She attended schools both in China and in the United States and made several trips back and forth, some unwillingly, as when she and her parents were expelled from China during the Boxer Rebellion of 1900.

As a girl in China, Buck began to write articles and short stories. There is no doubt that she had a gift for making the strange, unknown, and distant appear familiar. Until the time of her first published success, *East Wind, West Wind* (1930), very little had been written about the life of the simple Chinese, although China was of increasing interest to businessmen, diplomats, and missionaries. Nevertheless, the general public did not think of the Chinese as people with whom they could easily identify. Buck's feeling for the fundamental truths of life transcended the preconceived notions of the reading public about China because she portrayed her characters as understandable human beings struggling for happiness and success.

The Good Earth was published in 1931 and became Buck's most popular and widely read novel. It depicts a life cycle from a man's early years until his death. Some Chinese felt that the portrayal of their people was inaccurate and incomplete, and many Chinese intellectuals objected to the choice of a peasant farmer as the subject of a novel, preferring that the Western world see the intellectual and philosophical Chinese, even though that group was a minority. Buck's only answer to such criticism was that she wrote about what she knew best, and these were the people whom she had seen and come to know and love during her years in the interior of China.

The theme of *The Good Earth* is an uncomplicated one with universal appeal, and the author shows a man rising from poverty and relative insignificance to a position of importance and wealth. In some ways, the story is the proverbial Horatio Alger tale that so many Americans know and admire. The difference here, and what makes it unique, is the setting. Wang Lung, the main character around whom the action in the novel revolves, is a poor man who knows very little apart from the fact that land is valuable, solid, and worth owning. Therefore, he spends his entire life trying to acquire as much land as he can to ensure both his own security and that of his family and descendants for generations to come. Ironically, he eventually becomes like the rich whom he at first held in awe when he allows himself to follow in their path and separate himself from the land to live above toil and dirt. The earth theme appears repeatedly throughout the book. Wang Lung's greatest joy is to look out over his land, to hold it in his fingers, and to work it for his survival. At the end of the novel, he returns to the old quarters he occupied on his first plot of land so that he can find the peace he knows the land can bring him.

The Good Earth is a simple, direct narrative. There are no complicated literary techniques, no involved subplots to detract from the main story line. Wang Lung is the central character, and all the other characters and their actions relate in some way to him. The book depends on characterization, and its dramatic episodes are projected through the sensitivities and experiences of its characters. It may be said that a strength of the author's characterization is her consistency, for all of her characters act and react in keeping with their personalities. None is a stereotype, for their motives are complex. O-lan is a sympathetic portrait, but there are aspects of her personality that give her depth, dimension, and originality. Such actions as stealing the jewels from the plundered rich or killing the small baby girl born to her when she is in ill health are consistent with her character. She is realistic and sees her acts as producing more good than evil. Throughout the novel O-lan is courageous and faithful, and she maintains a dignity that gives her a special identity of her own.

One of the most obvious and significant Chinese customs that appears repeatedly in the novel is the submission of the wife in all things to the will of the man. Girl children were born only to be reared for someone else's house as slaves, whereas boys were born to carry on family names, traditions, and property. This situation is based on the Chinese position that women are inferior to men. The reader cannot help but be struck by this attitude as it manifests itself in the lives of the men and women in *The Good Earth*.

The novel has no high point or climax, no point of great and significant decision. There is no one who causes Wang Lung any serious struggle. His only antagonists are the adversity of the elements and the occasional arguments he has with his lazy uncle and his worthless nephew. Dramatic interest is sustained in the novel by well-placed turning points in the narrative. The first is Wang Lung's marriage to O-lan and their early, satisfying years together. When, in the face of poverty, destitution, and hopelessness, Wang Lung demands the handful of gold from the rich man that enables him to get back to his land, Buck makes clear how much Wang Lung's land means to him and what he is willing to do to have it back. In the closing pages of the novel, the quiet servitude and devotion of Pear Blossom, a simple slave girl in a house full of discord, afford him the only peace and contentment of his late years, though Buck refrains from moralizing on the fact that this is the extent of Wang Lung's years of hard labor and sacrifice.

Buck won the Pulitzer Prize for *The Good Earth*, which, in addition to being widely read in many languages, was also dramatized and made into a motion picture. Its universal appeal undoubtedly derives from its clear and precise portrayal of one man's struggle for survival, success, and happiness.

"Critical Evaluation" by Constance A. Cutler

Bibliography:
Buck, Pearl S. *The Good Earth*. New York: Washington Square Press, 1994. Provides a lengthy introduction about Pearl Buck and *The Good Earth* by Peter Conn. Also includes commentary from the time of the novel's publication and sources for further research.
Cowley, Malcolm. "Wang Lung's Children." *The New Republic* 99, no. 1275 (May 10, 1939): 24-25. Contains information about the style of *The Good Earth* as well as the other two novels in the trilogy: *Sons* (1932) and *A House Divided* (1935). Includes a short explanation for Buck's unfavorable reputation in some literary circles.
Doyle, Paul A. *"The Good Earth."* In *Pearl S. Buck*. Rev. ed. Boston: Twayne, 1980. Presents information about the development and portrayal of the main characters, the novel's style, and Buck's writing style. The chapter that follows includes a short section about the controversy regarding Buck's portrayal of Chinese life (especially in *The Good Earth*) and Buck's response.
Harris, Theodore F. *Pearl S. Buck: A Biography*. 2 vols. New York: John Day, 1969-1971. Because of its importance, *The Good Earth* is discussed at various points in both volumes. Indicates the effect of the Wang Lung and O-lan characters on Buck's formulation of *The Good Earth*.
Spencer, Cornelia. *The Exile's Daughter: A Biography of Pearl S. Buck*. New York: Coward-McCann, 1944. Cornelia Spencer is the pseudonym for Grace Sydenstricker Yaukey, Pearl Buck's sister. Includes an interesting passage on why Buck's publishers accepted *The Good Earth* for publication.

THE GOOD SOLDIER

Type of work: Novel
Author: Ford Madox Ford (Ford Madox Hueffer, 1873-1939)
Type of plot: Psychological realism
Time of plot: Early twentieth century
Locale: England, Germany, and the United States
First published: 1915

Principal characters:
JOHN DOWELL, a rich American
FLORENCE, his wife
EDWARD ASHBURNHAM, a British landowner
LEONORA, his wife
NANCY, a young woman cared for by the Ashburnhams

The Story:

Florence Dowell and Edward Ashburnham were dead, both having committed suicide, and Nancy, the Ashburnhams' charge, was insane. Leonora remarried, and John Dowell, caring for Nancy, was now the owner of the Ashburnham estate in England. He was in love with Nancy, but her mental state prohibited him from marrying her. He considered the tragic history of the Dowells and the Ashburnhams, which led to the unhappy situation in which he found himself.

It had begun innocently enough with the meeting several years before of the Dowells and the Ashburnhams at the German spa town of Nauheim, where Dowell had taken Florence directly after their marriage in America. Florence was suffering from a heart condition, and they came to the spa for her to rest. Edward Ashburnham was supposedly there for the same reason. The two couples got along, and spent most of their time together. Leonora came from a penniless, Irish Roman Catholic family; Edward owned an estate in England, and a substantial fortune. So it seemed at the outset of their association. Both couples were in their thirties, and they remained in close association over a period of several years. Then the disaster struck.

What Dowell learned, after the deaths of his wife and Edward, was that his own peculiar relationship with his wife had a part in the sudden tragedy. Dowell, a decent, naïve gentleman, had married Florence, who came from a socially prominent family, without knowing much about her, except that she had a serious heart condition. He took her for an innocent girl, determined to get away from a stifling family, but she was, in fact, a problem to herself and especially to young men, given her enthusiasm for very questionable liaisons. She was not a virgin, as Dowell believed (he, however, was), and she was not particularly attracted to Dowell, although he was besotted with her. As a result of her illness, there was no chance of consummating their marriage, and she informed him that her doctors had forbidden her to chance a further sea voyage, once they reached Europe. They were, therefore, to remain in the pricy European hotels and spas permanently. Dowell was to care for his wife without any hope of a normal married life.

The truth, which Dowell only learned after her death, was that not only had Florence lied to him about her sexual state, but also about her health. She was not ill, and was perfectly able to have sex, but she had no desire to do so with Dowell, who was a pleasant, normal young man, but without sex appeal. Florence began an affair with Edward Ashburnham. He and his wife, who seemed happy with each other, were living a lie as well. The Ashburnhams were also not sexually compatible. This state had perhaps been caused in part by the innocence of both parties at the time of their marriage, and the rigorous Roman Catholic upbringing of Leonora, which had left her with some distaste for sexual encounter. They started out in love but gradually drifted apart. They were also at odds because Leanora considered Edward too generous and too indulgent with his estate workers. Leonora continued to love Edward, but by the time she had come to terms with her sexuality, Edward had drifted off into a series of affairs. He was not a simple philanderer, but a man who needed love and was easily enchanted by women, some who adored him and some who took advantage of him. Two women cost him a large amount of money, and his family fortune was severely affected. Leonora stood by him, but only on the condition that she be allowed to deal with the estate, and keep him from additional expensive, romantic adventures. They were at Nauheim to save money, having rented out the English estate in an attempt to recoup losses. He disliked her penny-pinching and her harshness in dealing with his estate staff.

Leonora's vigilance, however, was no match for Florence's seductive ways, and soon Florence and Edward were sexually involved. Leonora learned of it but grudgingly accepted it, realizing that Florence, at least, had no interest in Edward's money or in any scandal. John Dowell suspected nothing, although there were occasions when he might well have been suspicious, had he not been such an unusually innocent and trusting man, with a great admiration for Edward. Dowell would have liked to have a more meaningful relationship with his wife, but believed that he must not touch her. Leonora had some limited control of the situation, since she knew that Florence was terrified of Dowell's learning of her conduct. Florence thought that despite the mildness of Dowell's temperament, he might kill her if he ever discovered the truth. After several years, things changed regarding the death of Florence. Dowell thought that the death was natural; it was, in fact, a suicide, which he only learned much later. It may have been caused by the arrival at the spa of a man who knew of Florence's sordid past, and who, she thought, had told Dowell; he had not. It may have been caused by the fact that Florence, who was in love with Edward Ashburnham, discovered, by chance, that he was in love with his ward, Nancy. He had no intention of revealing this to Nancy, who looked upon the Ashburnhams as her foster parents. Ultimately, Leonora, despairing of ever reviving her husband's love for her, lost control and told Nancy of Edward's feelings for her. Vindictively, she urged the girl to give herself sexually to Edward. The girl, shattered, offered herself to Edward, and he, appalled by what his wife had done, rejected Nancy. The situation was so bad that Nancy was sent back to her family, but on the way to the Far East to join them, she had a serious mental breakdown, and was returned to England. Ashburnham, distressed by this and the battle that had broken out with his wife, committed suicide. Leonora, seemingly unaffected by the tragedy, married a rather seedy man, who she knew cheated on her but not in any way that might have caused financial difficulties. Dowell bought the Ashburnham estate, where he took care of the hopelessly insane Nancy and contemplated the past, which began to make some sense in the light of information supplied, in the main, by Leonora. Incidents that had seemed innocent he mentally reviewed in the context of the betrayals and lies. He was once again a nursemaid for a woman who could not satisfy his desire for love, but this time it was real.

Critical Evaluation:

Graham Greene has called *The Good Soldier* the finest French novel ever written in English, and it has often been considered one of the best novels written in English in the twentieth century. What Greene probably meant is that the novel is remarkable for the subtlety with which it gets into the nuance and detail of male-female relations. What saves the novel from being simply a tale of sexual obsession is John Dowell. He is the key to understanding the work. Most narrators are, at best, only part of a story. He is, despite his inaction, the most interesting person in it.

John Dowell is telling the story some time after it has happened, but seems uncertain how to absorb it. Modest, decent, and in all things a gentleman, he cannot imagine his wife's and others' conduct, particularly in society as he thinks he knows it. The novel is, therefore, more than simply a telling of the tale. Dowell is using the narration to attempt to understand what happened, and that attempt is severely hampered by his character. He is not a man prone to sexual passion, and he takes people as he finds them. He is, for instance, telling this story as if he is speaking to a gentleman, someone like himself, and he is trying to tell it fairly, delicately, and with concern for all involved. He often does not see things that a reader sees immediately. Occasionally, however, his placid, patient manner is breached by odd phrases that suggest a hidden, deeper turmoil behind his blandness. His description, for instance, of the threesome in the afterlife, standing on the hand of God, is disturbingly gothic, and once in a while imprecations against Florence break through his attempt to be fair to everyone.

Dowell is intelligent, sensible, sensitive, restrained, and gentlemanly, but not always so, although he tends to react to his sudden, colorful outbreaks of feeling very quickly and with considerable fastidiousness. He is also a marvelous storyteller, although he seems not to know it, just as he seems not quite to know when he has stumbled on a truth that he clearly should have realized long before. The narrative, as a result, is a kind of disorganized accumulation of facts, some of which he remarks upon, and some of which he either does not understand or cannot face. The facts do not necessarily come to him in the right order. This discontinuity is an example of a theory that Ford Madox Ford had about the relationship between life and novels. He believed that in life, people do not get facts, necessarily, in logical sequence, and in the novel Ford is attempting to re-create the way in which, realistically, Dowell, given his character and given the way he has been deceived, comes upon the truth more by accident than design. If the story of marital betrayal is something of a comment upon the hypocrisies of the upper-middle classes, somewhat reminiscent of the work of Henry James, it goes beyond that in its scarifying exploration of an innocent, betrayed man, who for all his decency leaves one with mixed feelings about his refusal to face facts and with a sense that he, for all his obvious virtue, is out of his time and place in a world that no longer is bound by ideas of honor and gentlemanly conduct.

Technically the novel is a great success. Narrators are usually chosen to tell a story as clearly and succinctly as possible. Ford has chosen a narrator who is possessed of a fine capacity for language, and an occasional inclination for bizarre imagery, but who is also often unreliable, and as much a problem for the reader as the story he tells.

Charles Pullen

Bibliography:
Hoffmann, Charles G. *Ford Madox Ford.* Boston: Twayne, 1967. Short, concise, for students, with sensible analysis of *The Good Soldier.*
Lid, R. W. *Ford Madox Ford: The Essence of His Art.* Berkeley: University of California Press, 1964. Definitive study, with emphasis placed on technique.
MacShane, Frank, ed. *Ford Madox Ford: The Critical Heritage.* London: Routledge & Kegan Paul, 1972. Collection of essays by several Ford scholars on several topics, including *The Good Soldier.*

Mizener, Arthur. *The Saddest Story: A Biography of Ford Madox Ford*. New York: World Publishing, 1971. There is a close relationship between Ford's personal life and the themes in his novels, and this is the best critical biography. There is substantial discussion of *The Good Soldier*.

Stang, Sondra J. *Ford Madox Ford*. New York: Frederick Ungar, 1977. One of Ford's best critics discusses the novel in terms of method of construction, point of view, and experimentation.

THE GOOD SOLDIER ŠVEJK

Type of work: Novel
Author: Jaroslav Hašek (1883-1923)
Type of plot: Satire
Time of plot: World War I
Locale: Bohemia and Austria
First published: Osudy dobreho vojáka Švejka ve světove války, 1921-1923 (English
  translation, 1930; unabridged translation, 1973)

Principal characters:
> JOSEF ŠVEJK, a soldier
> JINDRICH LUKÁŠ, a lieutenant and Švejk's superior
> OTTO KATZ, a chaplain
> COLONEL KRAUS, Lieutenant Lukáš' superior
> LIEUTENANT DUB, a former schoolteacher

The Story:

Josef Švejk, by profession a dog trader, was discharged from his military service saddled with the classification of "feebleminded." The shots in Sarajevo, however, which signaled the beginning of World War I, brought Švejk back into the army. A careless remark soon led to his arrest, but he convinced the police of his feebleminded condition and was sent to a lunatic asylum. Medical authorities were so irritated by Švejk's cheerfulness that they classified him as a malingerer of weak intellect and sent him back to the police. Švejk's habit of giving the most innocent and confusing replies to all bureaucratic inquiries caused the police to send him home again.

When the Austrian Army suffered its first major losses, however, the war ministry decided that Švejk should be conscripted into military service once more. Švejk came to the medical examination in a wheelchair, with crutches by his side to indicate the bad state of his rheumatism. The army doctor, who was in the habit of finding everybody fit for service, was incensed by Švejk's performance. The good soldier Švejk's first station became the military prison. Treatment in the infirmary of the military prison was aimed at intensifying each patient's desire to serve his fatherland away from the infirmary.

The main diversion in the prison was the Mass celebrated by the chaplain, Otto Katz, a priest whose love for alcohol surpassed by far his dedication to priestly duties. Otto Katz, impressed by Švejk, requested that the soldier be assigned to him as an orderly. In this capacity, Švejk became indispensable as an altar boy during Mass, as a helper at various drinking bouts, and as a stimulating partner during unorthodox religious debates.

Švejk's good fortune did not last long. Chaplain Katz was as fond of gambling as he was of wine. During a poker game, he lost Švejk to Lieutenant Lukáš, who was beloved by his subordinates but disliked by his superiors. Švejk was now expected to handle many delicate situations in connection with Lieutenant Lukáš' love for the opposite sex. Frequently, the lieutenant despaired over the embarrassing predicaments that developed each time Švejk was handling a project.

One day Švejk procured a dog, which he gave to Lieutenant Lukáš. The animal actually belonged to Colonel Kraus, one of Lukáš' superiors. When the lieutenant took an evening stroll with the dog, he had a most unpleasant encounter with Colonel Kraus, who recognized his missing pet. The colonel promptly arranged a transfer for the lieutenant and his orderly to a battalion destined for frontline duty.

On the train, Švejk managed to insult a fellow passenger who turned out to be an inspector general. When he inadvertently released the emergency brake and was unable to pay the requested fine, he was taken from the train, much to the delight of Lieutenant Lukáš, who had not yet recovered from the incident of the dog. The train moved on without Švejk, who found himself considered a mistreated war hero by the people at the railroad station. A collection was taken up to pay his fine, and he was entertained with free beer. Later, military police arrested Švejk when they discovered that he was without identification papers. A cross-examination, conducted at headquarters, frustrated the investigating officer, and he ordered Švejk to proceed on foot to the destination point he was supposed to have reached by train.

Švejk marched off in the wrong direction and was arrested as a suspected spy. An ambitious sergeant, interpreting Švejk's confusing way of answering questions as highly intelligent evasions, considered him a prize catch. Švejk was transferred to higher authorities, but the captain in charge preferred to believe Švejk's implausible explanation to the more implausible report that the sergeant had prepared. Švejk was returned to his regiment and to the surprised Lieutenant Lukáš. The lieutenant, determined that Švejk should not cause him any further embarrassment, ordered Švejk transferred to the regimental dungeon for unauthorized absence from duty. After three days, however, Lieutenant Lukáš' superior officer, who nourished a grudge against him, sent Švejk back to the lieutenant to resume his old position, and Lieutenant Lukáš was forced to accept the situation.

Before long, Lieutenant Lukáš discovered a lady whom he considered a good prospect for another amorous adventure. Švejk was assigned to deliver a letter to the lady, but the letter reached her husband instead. The delivery of the letter turned into a street fight, which in turn resulted in Švejk's arrest and a great deal of unfavorable publicity around the garrison.

Lieutenant Lukáš was now appointed company commander of a unit on its way to the Russian front; he also had strict orders to take Švejk along as a company orderly. In his new duty post, Švejk's first assignment was that of telephone operator, a duty that gave him ample opportunity to confuse the preparations for the transfer to the front. His next contribution to the war effort occurred as the result of exercising his commonsense judgment: When a coding system based on the second volume of a novel was to be installed for the regiment, Švejk distributed the first volume because he was of the opinion that everybody should start reading a book at the beginning.

The most disliked officer of the regiment was Lieutenant Dub, a former schoolteacher who considered it his duty to transplant barracks drill discipline to the front line. Several episodes with Švejk convinced Lieutenant Dub that he had enough material to proceed with a court-martial against Švejk. During a short stay in a small village, however, Švejk, having been ordered to look for Lieutenant Dub, discovered his superior drunk in a brothel. This discovery gave Švejk an opportunity to ridicule the lieutenant in front of all the soldiers. Švejk was also valuable in assisting the quartermaster to find billets and supplies.

Švejk's last assignment was an order from Lieutenant Lukáš to find the road to the next village. Švejk, trusting his common sense, disregarded the map and lost his way. When he approached a pond, he found a Russian prisoner of war taking a bath. The sight of Švejk caused the Russian to flee stark naked. Švejk could not resist the temptation to try on the Russian's uniform. At this moment soldiers arrived to recapture the escaped "enemy." Švejk was assigned to a gang of Russian prisoners repairing the railroad leading to the Russian front.

Critical Evaluation:

Jaroslav Hašek, creator of the best-known character in Czech literature, was, like his character, a troublemaker. Hašek's penchant for participating in radical politics and for instigating public hoaxes rendered him nearly unemployable. For that reason, he turned to freelance writing to earn a living and produced hundreds of articles and short stories, including several about Josef Švejk, an early version of the title character of the later novel.

After being drafted to serve in the Austrian army during World War I, Hašek was sent to the front, where he was quickly taken prisoner by the Russians. He volunteered to serve in a Czech-Slovak unit of the Russian army, became a supporter of the Bolshevik movement, and returned to Prague in 1920 to help establish and party in the newly formed Republic of Czechoslovakia. The Russians eventually abandoned their efforts. Hašek began work on *The Good Soldier Švejk* in 1921, basing the book largely on his war experiences.

Although the novel was well received by German critics such as Max Brod, who had helped to establish Franz Kafka's literary reputation, Czech critics were much less enthusiastic, a reaction, in part, to Hašek's reputation as an irresponsible drunkard and a Russian sympathizer. Throughout the twentieth century, critical response reflected changing political conditions in Europe, and the novel, while soon regarded as a classic, remained controversial. The book was burned by the Nazis, who found in Švejk's disruptive nature a threat to the conformity and discipline demanded by the fascist state. Their censorship drew international attention to the novel, however, and redeemed its reputation with earlier detractors. When the Communists gained control of Czechoslovakia following World War II, the government officially declared Švejk a national folk hero and a member of the proletariat and potential revolutionary for the Communist cause. At the same time, political dissidents embraced the novel because of Švejk's ability to undermine authority. By the mid-twentieth century, *The Good Soldier Švejk* had gained an international reputation as a powerful antiwar novel, and by the latter part of the century, Hašek was recognized as a major Czech writer who worked in the tradition of Czech satire, used elements of national folk tales, and influenced the development of Czech theater and such writers as Václav Havel. Hašek is also often compared with Franz Kafka, a Prague contemporary whose writings explore the theme of conflict between the individual and society.

Although the book achieved popularity for its humor and acclaim for its political significance, *The Good Soldier Švejk* has been criticized as "unliterary" because of its language and structure. The novel is written in common Czech, the everyday language of the people, rather than in the formal Czech of literature. For some native speakers, this use of the vernacular disqualifies the novel from classification as art; however, since the distinction between common and formal dialects does not translate, English speakers have not been troubled by debates over language. A more common concern is structure. *The Good Soldier Švejk* does not employ traditional narrative structure; instead, the work is episodic, at times almost rambling. Hašek's defenders claim that the novel's form mirrors the characterization and reinforces the book's themes. Indeed, it can be stated that just as Švejk continually thwarts the military system that would send him directly to the front, so the structure of the novel repeatedly loops back on itself. Some critics argue that any thematic significance of structure was unintentional, but the fact remains that the novel exhibits a formal pattern of advance and retreat. It is important to note that the work is incomplete, Hašek having died before finishing the final two volumes. It is therefore difficult to draw conclusions about structure since the novel's intended ending may have provided more closure and unity.

The major point of contention lies in the character of Švejk. For those who view him as a blundering fool, he seems an unlikely candidate for literary immortality as a universal representation of humankind, and some Czechs have been incensed that the typical Czech has been portrayed as an idiot. Others, however, regard Švejk as an ingenious survivor who represents the triumph of the individual over impersonal and oppressive systems of power. Whether the character is a fool or a genius is difficult to determine, for Hašek provides little psychological insight into Švejk's motives. The character is presented almost entirely through his actions and his speech, and he repeatedly fails to explain himself to the reader.

Perhaps Švejk is best understood through his adaptability. He possesses an uncanny ability to assess his situation and respond in the manner that will produce the desired result. For example, when arrested for treason, he confounds his accusers by agreeing with them, accepting their authority without question, and offering his full cooperation; as a result, he is dismissed as a lunatic and avoids imprisonment, possibly even execution. At other times, he exasperates superior officers with rambling monologues that digress to the point of absurdity; that predicament is resolved when the officer becomes sufficiently frustrated with Švejk's diversionary tales to dismiss the matter and get rid of him. Through such improvisational skills, Švejk is able to extract himself from difficult situations and delay his progress toward the front.

Unlike Kafka's characters, who react against power structures and are crushed by them, Švejk works within systems, turning hierarchy and bureaucracy to his own advantage. Although a troublemaker, he is not a rebel. When he breaks rules and creates havoc, he does so by following the orders of a superior officer, often by carrying out these orders to the letter. It is those officers most representative of blind obedience to authority, like Lieutenant Dub, who fail to recognize that it is Švejk's obedience rather than disobedience that produces chaos. Dub and those like him believe Švejk to be a dodger, that is, one attempting to avoid military duty. Yet while Švejk successfully dodges combat he remains a loyal soldier and refuses opportunities to desert. He is, literally, the good soldier Švejk. Hašek has created a fictitious world in which the individual must act the fool in order to meet the demands of the government; it is the system, not the person, that suffers from patent lunacy.

"Critical Evaluation" by K Edgington

Bibliography:
Doležel, Lubomír. "The Road of History and the Detours of the Good Soldier." In *Language and Literary Theory: In Honor of Ladislav Matejko*, edited by Benjamin A. Stoltz. Ann Arbor: University of Michigan Press, 1984. An accessible example of postmodernist scholarship, which discusses the character Švejk as inhabiting "ludic" space between obligation and punishment. Although the article employs a few complex literary terms, it is a highly readable and astute analysis of the character.
Goetz-Stankiewicz, Marketa. "Kafka and Hašek—Reflections on a Meeting in the House of Fiction." In *Language and Literary Theory: In Honor of Ladislav Matejko*, edited by Benjamin A. Stoltz. Ann Arbor: University of Michigan Press, 1984. A comparison of the two authors, focusing on the differences in their literary themes. The essay also provides a valuable discussion of Hašek's influences on later writers.
Parrott, Cecil. *The Bad Bohemian: A Life of Jaroslav Hašek.* London: Bodley Head, 1978. A biography by the English translator of the 1973 edition that examines parallels between Hašek's life and *The Good Soldier Švejk.*
_____. *Jaroslav Hašek.* Cambridge, England: Cambridge University Press, 1982. A comprehensive survey of the historical background of the work, Hašek's political activities and literary career, and the continuing critical controversy about the novel. Includes a

character analysis and discussion of structure and themes.

Součková, Milada. *A Literary Satellite: Czechoslovak-Russian Literary Relations.* Chicago: University of Chicago Press, 1970. Examines Russian and Czechoslovakian responses to the novel as literary propaganda and the debate over whether Švejk is a suitable character to represent the Czech military.

GOOD-BYE, MR. CHIPS

Type of work: Novel
Author: James Hilton (1900-1954)
Type of plot: Sentimental
Time of plot: 1870-1933
Locale: An English boys' school
First published: 1934

Principal characters:
MR. CHIPS, an old schoolmaster
MRS. WICKETT, his landlady
BROOKFIELD BOYS

The Story:

Mr. Chips was eighty-five years old, but he thought himself far from ill. Dr. Merivale had told him he should not venture out on this cold November day, but he also added that Mr. Chips was fitter than the doctor himself. What Mr. Chips did not know was that the doctor had told the landlady, Mrs. Wickett, to look after him; Mr. Chips's chest clouded in bad weather.

Mr. Chips sank into his armchair by the fire, happy in the peace and warmth. The first thing about his remembered career set him laughing. He had come to teach at Brookfield in 1870, and in a kindly talk, old Wetherby, the acting headmaster, had advised him to watch his disciplinary measures. Mr. Wetherby had heard that discipline was not one of Mr. Chips's strong points. When one of the boys dropped his desktop too loudly on the first day of class, Mr. Chips assigned him a hundred lines and had no trouble after that. The boy's name was Colley—Mr. Chips seldom forgot a name or a face—and he remembered that years later he had taught Colley's son, and then his grandson, who, he used to say pleasantly, was the biggest young nitwit of them all. Mr. Chips was fond of making little jokes about the boys, who took his jibes well and grew to love him for his honesty and friendliness. Indeed, Mr. Chips's jokes were regarded as the funniest anywhere, and the boys had great sport telling of his latest.

Remembering these things, Mr. Chips thought growing old was a great joke, although a little sad; when Mrs. Wickett came in with his tea, she could not tell whether Mr. Chips was laughing or crying. Tears were spilling down his withered cheeks.

Brookfield had known periods of grandeur as well as of decay. When Mr. Chips arrived there, the school was already a century old and regarded as a place for boys whose lineage was respectable but seldom distinguished. Mr. Chips's own background was not distinguished either, but it had been hard for him to realize that his mind was not the type to assume leadership. He had longed to work his way into the position of headmaster. After many failures, however, he knew that his role was that of a teacher, and he gave up his administrative ambitions. He loved his students, and they often came to chat with him over tea and crumpets. Sometimes they remarked, as they left, what a typical bachelor old Mr. Chips was.

It was painful to Mr. Chips that no one at Brookfield remembered his wife. When he was forty-eight years old, he had married Kathy Bridges, and even now he wondered how that miracle had come about. He had seen a girl waving from the top of a rocky ledge one day when he was out walking, and thinking her in trouble, he set out to rescue her. On the way, he sprained his ankle, and Kathy had ended up assisting him. It was a remarkable love, for she was years younger than he. Kathy, however, left an enduring mark upon Mr. Chips. He grew more lenient with the boys, more understanding of their problems, and more courageous in his teaching. Ironically, Kathy died on the first day of April in childbirth; that day, not realizing the tragedy that had befallen Mr. Chips, the boys played April Fool jokes on the stricken teacher.

Mr. Chips began to remember the war years. Names of boys whose faces he could still visualize had been read out in chapel from the casualty lists. When the headmaster died and no one could be found to fill his place, Mr. Chips was asked to head Brookfield. Standing in his tattered gown, which newcomers often considered disgraceful, tears filled his eyes as he read out the names. Even now, sitting in front of the fire, he could recall that roll, and he read it over to himself, remembering the faces that had looked so hopefully at him in the classroom.

One day, he met a Latin class while German bombs were crashing nearby. The boys squirmed in their seats as the explosions came nearer and nearer, but Mr. Chips quietly told them that they should never judge the importance of anything by the noise it made. Then, asking one of the more courageous lads to translate, Mr. Chips chose a passage from Caesar that was particularly apt because it dealt with German methods of fighting. Later, the boys told how Mr. Chips stood steady and calm, and they remarked that while Latin might be a dead language, it was nevertheless valuable at times.

After the war, Mr. Chips gave up the headmastership and returned to his room at Mrs. Wickett's. Now, fifteen years later, he was always asked to greet visiting dignitaries who came to Brookfield. He was amused to find that many of the barons, members of Parliament, and war heroes had been his former pupils, and he remembered their faces, although, to his chagrin, he now often forgot their names. He would make amusing, appropriate remarks, not always complimentary, and the visitors would shake with laughter. Sometimes during those postwar years, he was asked to make little speeches at school banquets, and because of his reputation for funny sayings, his audience would laugh uproariously, often before Mr. Chips reached the point of his jokes. Mr. Chips was privileged now, and his eccentricities only made him more loved at Brookfield. Indeed, Mr. Chips was Brookfield.

Mr. Chips thought of the rich life he had led. There were so many memories. As he sat by the fire, he heard a timid knock at the door, and a youngster, much abashed, came in. He had been told that Mr. Chips had sent for him. The old man laughed, knowing that this was a prank the old boys often played on a newcomer, and he saved the boy from embarrassment by telling him that he had sent for him. After conversation and tea, Mr. Chips dismissed the boy in his abrupt but kindly fashion. The boy waved as he went down the walk.

Later, the boy told his comrades that he had been the last to tell Mr. Chips good-bye; Mr. Chips died quietly in his sleep that cold November night.

Critical Evaluation:

It was not until the American publication of *Good-bye, Mr. Chips* in June, 1934, that James Hilton became a popular, successful, and critically admired author. Before that, he had written eight full-length novels, as well as a large body of topical commentary and literary criticism, but he had remained relatively unknown and unappreciated. Even *Lost Horizon* (1933), which was later to become one of the best-selling books of its time, was largely ignored when it first appeared. The spectacular success of *Good-bye, Mr. Chips* surprised the author as well as all the critics.

Because *Good-bye, Mr. Chips* is presented as the reminiscence of an old man, the dominant mood is that of sentimental, nostalgic reverie. Hilton adroitly maintains a fine balance between the gentle humor characteristic of Mr. Chips's everyday life and the pathos of several sad incidents, including the death of Mr. Chips's wife in childbirth and the many deaths among his students in war. Basing Mr. Chips on a synthesis of his own father and his favorite Latin teacher, Hilton created a character many readers recognized in their own experience. It is doubtful, however, that simple reader identification or the fact that Mr. Chips (a fond nickname for Chipping) is a clearly defined, amiable, slightly eccentric, modestly humorous man is enough to account for the novel's enormous popularity. There is something in this figure of a man with unexceptional ability, living an ordinary life, that struck a deeply responsive chord in the mid-1930's and has continued to do so since.

Mr. Chips's life covers the second half of the nineteenth century and the first third of the twentieth. The historically crucial events in the book are World War I and, somewhat more vaguely in the background, the Great Depression. Mr. Chips's appeal can be fully understood only by seeing his uneventful life in the context of the very eventful historical epoch in which it passed and by remembering the significance of 1934, the time of its publication.

Mr. Chips is, above all, a "common man." He admits to being an ordinary teacher at a good but essentially second-class preparatory school. He gives up his early headmaster ambitions because he decides that he is not suited for the job. When he courts and marries Kathy Bridges, he cannot understand what she sees in him.

Nevertheless, this ordinary man in moments of crisis demonstrates an essential strength and resourcefulness. The outstanding example of that is the Latin lesson he conducts in the midst of an air raid. However frantic and chaotic the modern world becomes, Hilton assures readers, the common man can find the needed inner strength and will to survive with dignity.

Mr. Chips is not just an ordinary man, however; he is also the embodiment of a tradition. Brookfield is not a great school, but it is a school rooted in the British tradition of greatness. As its exemplar, Mr. Chips stands for honor, dignity, continuity, and a strong organic connection to the past. Yet, primarily because of his marriage to Kathy, he also has a sense of social movement and a compassion for the disadvantaged.

Mr. Chips balances the best of the old and the new, though he has a bias toward the old. At one point, he clashes with a progressive headmaster, and it almost costs him his job. During World War I, he defies popular prejudice publicly to commemorate a former German teacher who died fighting for the enemy.

Accurately labeled prewar by his students, Mr. Chips represents the traditional values and disciplined lifestyle that existed prior to World War I; through him, Hilton suggests that those values remain valid and can survive even in a more fast-paced, frenetic era.

Bibliography:
Bellman, Samuel Irving. "The Apocalypse in Literature." *Costerus* 7 (1973): 13-25. Describes the episode in which the boys play an April Fools' Day joke on Mr. Chips, who, distraught over the deaths of his wife and child, does not understand the prank. Uses this incident to discuss human estrangement.
Mathews, T. S. "A Gallery of Novels." *The New Republic* 19, no. 1024 (July 18, 1934): 271-272. Calls *Good-bye, Mr. Chips* a little tale that "gives us the soft English character in a hard nutshell." Notes that the real world is not as tender and gentle as the one portrayed in the book.
Mott, Frank Luther. *Golden Multitudes: The Story of Best Sellers in the United States.* New York: Macmillan, 1947. Tells how Hilton's bicycle ride through the English countryside inspired him to write a novel based on the recollections of his own school days.
Scott, Patrick. "James Hilton's *Good-bye, Mr. Chips* and the Strange Death of Liberal England." *South Atlantic Quarterly* 85, no 4 (Autumn, 1986): 319-328. Calls for a reassessment of the

novel, pointing to the importance of Hilton's commentary on the historical and cultural significance of the old schoolmaster and the school.

Weeks, Edward. Foreword to *Good-bye, Mr. Chips*. Boston: Little, Brown, 1962. Hails *Good-bye Mr. Chips* as Hilton's most successful novel and "the most endearing portrait of a schoolteacher in our time."

GORBODUC

Type of work: Drama
Authors: Thomas Norton (1532-1584) and Thomas Sackville (1536-1608)
Type of plot: Tragedy
Time of plot: Before the Saxon invasion of England
Locale: England
First performed: 1561; first published, 1565; authorized publication, 1570

> *Principal characters:*
> GORBODUC, the aged king of England
> VIDENA, his queen
> FERREX and
> PORREX, their sons
> AROSTUS,
> PHILANDER, and
> EUBULUS, Gorboduc's counselors
> DORDAN, counselor to Ferrex
> HERMON, parasite and confidant of Ferrex

The Story:

Gorboduc, king of Britain and last of the line beginning with the legendary Brute, decided that he would not wait until his death before handing over the rule of his kingdom. In addition, he decided that he would set aside the rule of primogeniture and divide Britain between his two sons, Ferrex and Porrex. To Ferrex, the older, he planned to give all lands south of the Humber River; to Porrex, the younger, he intended to give those lands north of the Humber.

Calling in his chief advisers, Gorboduc told them what was in his mind. Arostus was in complete agreement with the king's wishes, but Philander and Eubulus warned of the dangers of the plan. Although they admitted that the king would be able to aid his sons in the early years of their reigns, they felt that the sons might not be willing to take advice from their father after he had placed power in their hands. The advisers also warned that when the authority of the kingdom was divided, the allegiance of the people might be divided, and they pointed out that Ferrex might very well resent having to share the kingdom with a younger brother, since custom made it the rule that the firstborn son inherited the entire kingdom. Last of all, they warned Gorboduc that history had proved a kingdom divided was easier prey to foreign conquest.

Gorboduc listened to his counselors. When they had finished speaking, however, he told them his mind was made up, that he felt the advantages to be gained by dividing the kingdom during his lifetime outweighed the disadvantages. Accordingly, he set his plan in operation, not knowing that his queen, Videna, was extremely jealous of her older son's prerogatives and hated the younger son for receiving a part of the kingdom which she felt rightfully belonged in its entirety to Ferrex.

Gorboduc sent trusted advisers of his own with each of the princes when they took over their separate domains, but before long both sons began to disregard their father's counselors. Instead, they listened to young men who preyed upon their vanities. Ferrex began to seek the advice of a parasite named Hermon, a man who flattered the young ruler's ego. Hermon told Ferrex that as the older son he should not have been given such a meager part of Britain and that, according to custom and his own ability, Ferrex should have been made ruler of the entire domain.

More than flattering Ferrex, Hermon told him that the younger king beyond the Humber was jealous of the older brother and was plotting to invade the kingdom of Ferrex. Dordan, the elderly counselor sent to Ferrex by Gorboduc, prevailed enough on the young man so that Ferrex made only secret preparations against a possible attack by his brother.

Meanwhile, north of the Humber, the same situation had developed. Porrex, the younger son, scorned the wise advice of his father's counselor and turned to a flattering parasite, who told Porrex about the secret plans being made for war by Ferrex. Porrex, who distrusted his brother, decided that a preventive war was the best solution to the problem, and he set out to invade the kingdom south of the Humber. Dordan sent a letter to Gorboduc advising him of the state of affairs between the two brothers. The aged father-king called his trusted men about him to ask their advice. While the council met to seek a solution, word came that Porrex had invaded the older brother's kingdom and had murdered Ferrex with his own hand.

Queen Videna, when she heard what had happened to her beloved older son, swore she would be avenged on Porrex. She vowed that he was no longer a son of hers but a criminal to be punished for his evil deeds. Porrex, sent for by his father, appeared at Gorboduc's court and readily admitted invading his brother's kingdom and murdering his brother. Porrex said that he was genuinely sorry that the deed had been committed, but that he still felt the murder justified. He swore that Ferrex had tried to have him poisoned and that he had killed Ferrex in order to save his own life. Gorboduc, not knowing what to do until he had investigated the situation further, sent Porrex from his sight until he should send word that he wanted the young man's presence.

Scarcely had the young man left his father when he was killed by his mother, who thereby avenged the murder of Ferrex. The Britons, outraged at such conduct on the part of their rulers, then rose up in arms and murdered both Gorboduc and Queen Videna.

The nobles of Britain, left without a leader, tried to put down the uprising of the common people. They feared that if they did not quell the revolt at once, the country would be weakened and left prey to some invading power. The nobles saw themselves, their families, their lands, and the whole country threatened by the horrible mistake that had destroyed the royal house. The nobles, however, could not agree on a course of action.

When a number of them met in a solemn conclave to organize against the uprisen rabble, they learned that the duke of Albany, filled with ambition to become ruler, had raised an army and set out on a campaign to make himself master of Britain. King Gorboduc's counselors advised the other nobles to join together to put down the duke, since he wished to usurp the throne. Faced by a common danger, they at last chose a new king for Britain, the old line having become extinct with the deaths of Gorboduc and his two sons.

Critical Evaluation:

Gorboduc, written by Thomas Norton and Thomas Sackville soon after their entry into law and public life, and first presented before Queen Elizabeth I during Christmas of 1561, is a landmark in English literature for several reasons, most notably because it is the first English drama written in blank verse—that is, largely unrhyming iambic pentameter, the form used by later writers such as Christopher Marlowe, Ben Jonson, and William Shakespeare. For this reason alone, the play has a place in the English literary canon. *Gorboduc* is important for further reasons as well.

In addition to establishing blank verse as a language for the stage, *Gorboduc* set the basic pattern for the structure of English Renaissance drama. For the structure of *Gorboduc* Sackville and Norton turned to classical models, most notably those of closet plays of the Roman author Lucius Annaeus Seneca (closet plays are dramas which are meant to be read rather than acted) and the comedies of Titus Maccius Plautus, another Roman playwright, and so based their own drama on a five-act division, with each act subdivided into a varying number of scenes.

This simple device proved extremely important for the development of English Renaissance drama, since it provided a vehicle equally suitable for all major genres—tragedy, comedy, and history. Additionally, as Norton and Sackville demonstrated, the flexible act and scene structure allows playwrights to shift rapidly but logically from large, public settings to small, intimate ones, thus extending the range and scope of their dramas.

Perhaps *Gorboduc*'s most telling use of this flexibility is the dumb shows that punctuate the play and comment on its actions. These plays within plays developed from native English mystery and miracle plays, such as *Everyman* (1508), and are allegorical representations of *Gorboduc*'s plot. They emphasize and offer silent comment upon the moral of the story being enacted. The dumb shows are a highly effective combination of morality and theater.

As an example, *Gorboduc* opens with six wild men, characteristically dressed in leaves, who appear on stage, trying and failing to break a bundle of sticks; taking the bundle apart, each wild man easily snaps an isolated branch. This symbolic representation of the disastrous effects of disunity in a kingdom is acted out in the following scenes, as King Gorboduc divides his kingdom. The division brings disorder and anarchy, a point which is later emphasized in another dumb show in which armed men march about the stage discharging their firearms in a stylized representation of civil war.

Another way in which *Gorboduc* is precedent setting is in its use of English history as the basis for a dramatic plot. The play, loosely based on supposed events in ancient British history, is the first of the long series of history plays that re-created for Elizabethan and Jacobean audiences the glories and sorrows of the nation's past. This series would reach its ultimate culmination in William Shakespeare's history cycles of the English medieval monarchy.

The Gorboduc story is found in Geoffrey of Monmouth's *History of the Kings of Britain* (c. 1135-1139), a collection of loosely related accounts that chronicle the supposed development of England after Brute, the great-grandson of Aeneas, founded New Troy, or London. King Gorboduc, or Gorbogudo in Geoffrey's version, supposedly lived in the seventh century before Christ. The Gorboduc tale is taken up in later chronicles also.

Gorboduc also set precedent in that it established the tradition of English stage productions being vehicles for commentary, discussion, and even polemics on political issues. The central political theme of *Gorboduc* is its intention to warn Queen Elizabeth of the dangers of leaving her realm without a single, definite heir. At the time the drama was written and produced, Elizabeth was unmarried, and although she was to remain so throughout her reign, there was constant pressure on her to contract a suitable marriage and produce an heir. Many Englishmen, Sackville and Norton clearly among them, felt that this was the only way the kingdom could escape the ravages of civil war, remembered from the Wars of the Roses, which had pitted the rival houses of York and Lancaster against one another for several generations.

Sackville and Norton had been members of Elizabeth's first Parliament of 1558, which had petitioned the Queen either to marry and produce an heir, or at least to name a successor. *Gorboduc* articulates in dramatic form the Tudor ideal of a unified and peaceful kingdom by demonstrating, in graphic and vivid fashion, the consequences of divided power and uncertain succession. In this, it is specifically geared to the political concerns of the moment. The drama also has wider implications, demonstrating what can occur in any realm when power is dispersed instead of being concentrated in the hands of a wise prince and the prince's trusted advisers—in the case of England, Elizabeth and Parliament. The tradition of the drama as a political vehicle would continue throughout the period.

These conventions and devices, which rapidly became an integral part of English Renaissance drama, are key elements of *Gorboduc*, and are handled with considerable skill. Critics and scholars have sometimes noted the static nature of the play, pointing out that the true actions—such as the multiple killings that mark the progression of the plot—take place offstage, and are merely recounted, rather than shown. It should be remembered, however, that the device of offstage violence was part of the Senecan tradition and, in recompense, the dumb shows that punctuate and comment upon the acts provide symbolic representation of the more violent actions.

In the end, the success of *Gorboduc* can be divided into two parts: its own success as an individual work of dramatic art, which offers a historical story, a political commentary, and an artistic presentation; and its triumphant role as a precursor and template for later English drama. *Gorboduc* succeeds for what it is and for what it prefigures.

"Critical Evaluation" by Michael Witkoski

Bibliography:
Baugh, Albert. *A Literary History of England.* 2d ed. East Norwalk, Conn.: Appleton-Century-Crofts, 1967. A discussion of the play and its authors, setting them within the contemporary artistic world and reflecting on later developments of the dramatic form they introduced.
Berlin, Normand. *Thomas Sackville.* New York: Twayne, 1974. An excellent introductory volume that places Sackville the author and *Gorboduc* the drama within the context of their times, as well as identifying their continued importance for English literature.
Brooke, C. F. Tucker. *The Tudor Drama.* Hamden, Conn.: Archon Books, 1964. Discusses the play's historical and literary sources, the impact of the blank verse upon contemporary writers, and the overall effects the play had on the development of English drama.
Ousby, Ian. *The Cambridge Guide to Literature in English.* Cambridge, England: Cambridge University Press, 1993. A good starting point for the first-time reader or student of the play. Briefly explains its plot, its stage and stylistic innovations, and the influence it had on English drama.

A GRAIN OF WHEAT

Type of work: Novel
Author: Ngugi wa Thiong'o (James Ngugi, 1938-   )
Type of plot: Social realism
Time of plot: Mid-twentieth century
Locale: Kenya
First published: 1967

> *Principal characters:*
> MUGO, a young farmer
> GIKONYO, a young carpenter
> KIHIKA, a young revolutionary
> KARANJA, a young librarian
> MUMBI, Gikonyo's wife
> THOMAS ROBSON, the colonial District Officer, murdered by Kihika
> JOHN THOMPSON, the colonial District Officer after Robson's murder

The Story:

When the British colonizers came to Kenya, they strengthened their hold on the territory by building a great railroad. Waiyaki and other warrior leaders had taken up arms against this imposition, but they had been defeated. Most Kenyans gradually learned to make accommodations with the new regime, though the seeds of revolution spread underground in "the Movement," known to the British as Mau Mau.

Among the younger generation were Gikonyo, a well-known carpenter in the village of Thabai, and Mumbi, his wife and one of the most beautiful women in the area. They listened as one of their peers, Kihika, spoke before a large crowd and encouraged guerrilla warfare against the British. Mugo also listened, but, unlike Gikonyo and Mumbi, he hated what Kihika said. Mugo thought native Kenyans had no chance of successfully opposing the British, and he had decided to do his job quietly and succeed in the new order of things. Karanja, who had unsuccessfully sought the hand of Mumbi, felt even more strongly that the best policy was to accept the British as invincible.

Before long, Kihika disappeared into the forest with many other young men who had armed themselves. A year later, their most successful raid was the capture of the Mahee police post; this infuriated the British. They declared a state of emergency and imprisoned many of the young men of Thabai, including Gikonyo. Even Mugo was arrested for intervening when a woman was being beaten. Despite the efforts by the British to quell the Kenyan resistance, the violence continued, and District Officer Thomas Robson was assassinated.

Mugo was taken to Rira camp, where John Thompson was the warden. Though Mugo respected the British, in these circumstances he felt unjustly accused and refused to cooperate. He began to get a reputation among the other detainees as an inspiration to courage. Mugo did nothing to justify their hopes, but he did feel vague and grandiose religious impulses and began to see himself as a possible messiah for his people. Finally, there was an uprising in which Mugo played no part, and twenty-one prisoners were killed. This episode placed a blot on Thompson's career, the British believing he had overreacted; nevertheless, he was named as Robson's replacement as District Officer.

Before long, Mugo was released. After his return to the village, he received an unexpected— and unwelcome—visit from Kihika, a hunted man. Kihika revealed that he, disguised as an old man, had killed Thomas Robson, the District Officer. This news terrified Mugo. Oblivious to Mugo's cowardice, Kihika encouraged him to lead an underground movement in the village and asked him to think about it and to meet him the next evening. Mugo resented the ethical choice that Kihika had thrust upon him. He decided to betray him and secretly told Thompson where Kihika would be the next night. The soldiers arrested Kihika and murdered him.

Gikonyo was moved from one detention camp to another—seven in all—and finally, after six years, had most of his revolutionary zeal drained from him. He thought only of Mumbi. He signed a confession and was released. There were rumors that freedom was coming to the country. When Gikonyo returned to the village, however, he received two unwelcome surprises. The first was that Karanja, whom he had never respected, had risen from leader of the homeguards (who reported to the British) to village chief. The second was that his wife, Mumbi, had given birth to a son in his absence, and the father was Karanja. Gikonyo became embittered and disillusioned.

Kenya regained its independence (*uhuru*) on December 12, 1963. Thabai, like the other towns, celebrated with a large rally that all villagers attended. Warui, Wambui, General R., and Lieutenant Koina, who had worked in the Movement for many years, were planning to use the occasion to unmask Kihika's betrayer. All their suspicions fell upon Karanja, who was the most notorious collaborator in the village. When independence was approaching, Karanja resigned as chief and went to work in the library. He also served, however, as a messenger for John Thompson, his mistress, and his wife.

Their plan was to have Mugo, whose reputation as a hero had by now grown by leaps and bounds, present a speech that would climax with the naming of Karanja. Mugo, burdened with guilt, refused and asked to be left alone. Mumbi tried to change his mind, so he told her the truth. She warned Karanja not to attend the rally, but he ignored her advice. Then the people dispatched a delegation that dragged Mugo into their midst, where they awaited his triumphant speech. They called him "Kihika-born-again." Instead, he stood before them all and revealed himself as the traitor.

Mugo's aged aunt died, and he was left totally alone in the world. Wambui, General R., and Lieutenant Koina visited him, confirmed his guilt, and executed him. Karanja, who had placed all his hopes on the British, recognized how dangerous his situation was when John Thompson left the country. Karanja fled, but he knew he had nowhere to go. Warui and Wambui, who had been with the Movement for such a long time, now felt empty, wondering whether things had improved or whether they had simply exchanged one corrupt government for another. Gikonyo and Mumbi, on the other hand, reconciled and looked forward to the future.

Critical Evaluation:

Ngugi wa Thiong'o is among the most prominent East African writers, and *A Grain of Wheat* is generally considered the masterpiece of the first half of his career. In the second half of his career, he dropped his Christian name (James), and his novels became more overtly political. *Petals of Blood* (1977) is considered the high point of this second period. In 1977, he decided to write no longer in English but in Gikuyu, the principal language of Kenya, or in Swahili. He thereafter become one of the preeminent spokespersons not only for Kenyan culture but also for the anticolonial voices throughout Africa and, indeed, throughout the world.

Within Kenya, however, he would remain a controversial figure. His fiction attacks not only the European colonizers but also the native Kenyans who took up the reins of power from the British. In Ngugi's view, the latter rulers continue, as "neocolonials," to oppress their own people. His eloquent and internationally recognized condemnation of corruption led, in 1977, to his imprisonment in Kenya without a trial and to the loss of his teaching position at the University of Nairobi. In 1982, he went into self-imposed exile in London and the United States.

A Grain of Wheat displays the themes to which Ngugi returns in much of his writing: betrayal, the difficulties of self-definition after years of colonization, and marital tensions. He frequently casts his novels with four to six principal figures who together embody prevalent reactions to the problems of the emerging nation. Much of his international appeal depends not only on his courageous denunciation of political oppression of various sorts but also on these complex characters. They share the ambiguities and mixed motivations of real human beings and are not simply flat characters used to give voice to a particular political philosphy.

Another aspect of Ngugi's writing has garnered praise: his technique of gradually revealing, through the use of flashbacks, the past experiences that have shaped his characters. His narration is seldom simplistically chronological. In *A Grain of Wheat*, for example, the story begins near the end of the novel's events (preparations for the freedom celebrations and the revelation to the crowds of the betrayer of Kihika) and then moves backward in time to reveal how the major characters reached this point in the story. By the time Ngugi returns to the present in his narration, the reader knows the characters completely. This device allows the author to surprise his reader when a character takes a step that, given his or her previously revealed personality, is courageous. In this way Ngugi suggests that, despite one's past failings, there may still be hope for the future.

Ngugi's talent for balancing complex characters stands out in *A Grain of Wheat*. When, for example, one eventually learns that Mugo has betrayed Kihika, the knowledge comes long after one has been led to believe (along with the villagers) that the culprit was Karanja. Ngugi has portrayed Karanja in such a negative light that the reader instinctively feels a greater sense of sympathy for Mugo when he finally confesses. Conversely, despite his many other horrible crimes, Karanja's innocence of this especially notorious one encourages the reader to empathize with this collaborator's ultimate alienation from his people.

Some critics have charted Ngugi's developing sense of female characterization. Mumbi's lapse in fidelity may surprise the reader, and her explanation for it may not be especially convincing. Nevertheless, Gikonyo's harsh and self-pitying response raises Mumbi's comparative nobility in the reader's eyes. In later novels, Ngugi's women characters assume roles of greater importance in the revolutionary struggle (roles foreseen in *A Grain of Wheat* in Njeri's fleeting heroism and Wambui's long-suffering dedication to the cause).

Though reared as a Christian, Ngugi gradually concluded that the colonizers had used the missionaries to undermine whatever sense of rebellion the Kenyans might have felt. Kihika, educated in a missionary school, becomes imbued with the spirit of biblical prophecy but finds in Mau Mau a more immediately satisfying expression of that call for justice. Mugo, too, is greatly influenced by missionaries, but his understanding of the Bible seems to enable him to rationalize his betrayal of his people as a messianic act on their behalf. The book is filled with biblical references, and each of the four sections is preceded by a biblical quotation. The title refers to St. John's injunction to self-sacrifice. Kihika reads it in strictly political terms.

John C. Hawley

Bibliography:
Dramé, Kandioura. *The Novel as Transformation Myth: A Study of the Novels of Mongo Beti and Ngugi wa Thiong'o.* Foreign and Comparative Studies African Series 43. Syracuse, N.Y.: Maxwell School of Citizenship and Public Affairs, Syracuse University, 1990. Situates

the novel as the second in Ngugi's Mau Mau trilogy. Discusses use of Ngugi's popular myths and his use of the novel to present a fictionalized history of Kenya and of the transformation of the people's consciousness of their responsibilities as citizens.

Harrow, Kenneth. "Ngugi wa Thiong'o's *A Grain of Wheat:* Season of Irony." *Research in African Literatures* 16, no. 2 (1985): 243-263. Describes the novel as the highest achievement in East African literature and notes that its irony is the final expression of the anarchy that has followed independence. Shows how the author utilizes techniques in a specifically non-European manner.

Jabbi, Bu-Buakei. "The Structure of Symbolism in *A Grain of Wheat*." *Research in African Literatures* 16, no. 2 (1985): 210-242. Acknowledges the influence of D. H. Lawrence and Joseph Conrad on Ngugi's novel and shows how he brings together various symbols almost as if they were voices in a chorus. Discusses African ritual as a dynamic influence in Ngugi's symbol system.

Mugesera, Leon. "Guilt and Redemption in Ngugi wa Thiong'o's *A Grain of Wheat*." *Présence Africaine: Cultural Review of the Negro World* 125 (1983): 214-232. Argues that guilt and betrayal, followed by redemption, is the theme not only of this novel but of all of postindependence African literature. Ngugi typically uses the situations of marriage to weave variations on this theme. Sees this as Ngugi's most successful novel.

Sicherman, Carol M. "Ngugi wa Thiong'o and the Writing of Kenyan History." *Research in African Literatures* 20, no. 3 (1989): 347-370. Points out that in the second edition of the novel the author made certain revisions that show his increasing condemnation of the neocolonialism he sees among his fellow Kenyans, and his clear decision to use fiction to show citizens their history as a movement away from enslavement.

THE GRANDISSIMES
A Story of Creole Life

Type of work: Novel
Author: George Washington Cable (1844-1925)
Type of plot: Regional
Time of plot: 1804
Locale: New Orleans
First published: 1880

Principal characters:
> HONORÉ GRANDISSIME, head of the Grandissime family
> THE DARKER HONORÉ GRANDISSIME, his quadroon half-brother
> AGRICOLA FUSILIER, Honoré's uncle
> AURORA NANCANOU, a young widow
> CLOTILDE NANCANOU, her daughter
> JOSEPH FROWENFELD, a young American
> DR. KEENE, Joseph's physician and friend
> PALMYRE, a freed slave
> BRAS COUPÉ, a rebellious slave

The Story:

Honoré Grandissime and Aurora Nancanou, both members of the Creole aristocracy though they were unaware of one another's identity, met at a masked ball and fell in love at first sight. Honoré was a young merchant and the head of the Grandissime family. Aurora, a young widow, was from the De Grapion family. Aurora's husband had accused Honoré's uncle, Agricola Fusilier, of cheating at cards, which had led to a duel in which Agricola killed him. With that, Agricola had cleared his honor, and he also collected the gambling debt of Aurora's husband, his entire estate. Aurora and her daughter Clotilde were left penniless. Agricola had given the estate to Honoré, making him a wealthy man.

Joseph Frowenfeld, a young American immigrant, arrived in New Orleans with his parents and sisters. All were stricken with fever, and only Joseph survived. The lonely young man formed a friendship with his physician, Dr. Keene. Joseph and Honoré met by chance one day and found a common interest in their concern over the injustice of slavery and the caste system of New Orleans society. Honoré's life, however, depended upon these institutions. Joseph wished them to be wiped out at once.

Deciding to earn his living as a druggist, Joseph opened a small shop and soon became friendly with his aristocratic landlord. The landlord was Honoré's half-brother, who bore the same name but was not acknowledged as a member of the family because he was a quadroon. He was called the darker Honoré. Joseph found another new friend in Agricola, and he was also struck by the charm of Aurora and Clotilde when they called to make purchases. He learned more about Aurora from Dr. Keene. The physician told him about Palmyre, a freed slave who had once been Aurora's maid and who hated Agricola in part because of his role in the capture and punishment of her husband, the rebellious slave Bras Coupé. One night, Joseph was awakened by pistol shots nearby. A few minutes later, Dr. Keene and several others entered the shop with Agricola, who had been stabbed; his companions had fired on his assailant.

Several days later, Aurora called upon her landlord in order to make some arrangements about the rent she could not pay. She knew her landlord's name was Honoré Grandissime, but she did not connect this name with the man she loved until learning that they were half-brothers.

When Dr. Keene fell sick, he asked Joseph to attend to one of his patients. The patient was Palmyre, who had been wounded after stabbing Agricola. Joseph promised Dr. Keene to keep her trouble a secret and went to dress the wound. When Joseph paid his last visit to Palmyre, now almost recovered, she begged him to help her make the white Honoré love her. Palmyre's maid, however, misunderstanding the conversation, thought that Joseph had wronged her mistress. She struck him over the head, and Joseph reeled groggily into the street. Some passing pedestrians, seeing him emerge bleeding from Palmyre's house, drew a natural inference, and soon everyone knew about Joseph's misfortune. Only Clotilde and Honoré believed him innocent. Public feeling among the Creoles was running high against Americans, and Joseph found that both his liberal views and his trouble at Palmyre's house were held against him.

Honoré's conscience bothered him. He felt that he held Aurora's property unjustly, but he also knew if he returned it to her he would ruin his family. He made his choice, however, and called upon Aurora and Clotilde to present them with their property and the income from it. Now he could not declare his love for Aurora, for if he did so, his family would think he had returned the property out of love instead of a sense of justice.

On his return from Aurora's house, Honoré met the darker Honoré with Dr. Keene. The physician had risen from his sickbed because he had heard of Honoré's call at Aurora's house. Dr. Keene, also in love with Aurora, was jealous. His exertion caused a hemorrhage of the lungs, and the two Honorés carried him home and watched over him. While they attended the sick man, the darker Honoré proposed to his brother that they go into partnership, so that the darker Honoré's money could save the family from ruin. His brother accepted the offer. The decision turned Honoré's family against him, however, and Agricola led an unsuccessful lynching party to find the darker Honoré. Not finding him, the mob broke the windows of Joseph's shop as a gesture against liberal views in general.

Aurora set Joseph up in business again on the ground floor of her house and made Clotilde a partner in the store. Brought together in this manner, the two young people fell in love. At the same time, the darker Honoré lay wasting away for love of Palmyre, who was trying to revenge herself upon Agricola by voodoo spells. When Agricola could no longer sleep at night, his family determined to catch Palmyre in her acts of witchcraft. They caught her accomplice, but Palmyre escaped.

When the darker Honoré went to Joseph's store to get medicine for himself, he met Agricola, who insulted him. The darker Honoré stabbed Agricola and escaped. The wounded man was carried upstairs to Aurora's house to die; there the two families were united at his deathbed. Agricola revealed that he had once promised Aurora's father to promote a marriage between Aurora and Honoré.

The darker Honoré and Palmyre escaped together to France. There he committed suicide because she still would not accept his love. Joseph finally declared his love for Clotilde. Aurora refused to accept Honoré's offer of marriage because she thought he had made it out of obligation to Agricola. Then Honoré made his offer again as a man in love. In a last gesture of family pride, Aurora refused him, but at the same time, she threw herself into her lover's arms.

Critical Evaluation:

For many years relegated to obscurity as a regional writer, George Washington Cable eventually became recognized as one of the most significant Southern writers in the period between the Civil War and the early twentieth century. Unlike racial apologists such as Thomas Nelson Page, who sought to romanticize and sentimentalize the institution of slavery and its effects, Cable was a penetrating social critic whose novels and short stories interrogate the political and ideological structures of Southern society. The acute political and social analysis in his fiction led Mark Twain to call him "the South's finest literary genius."

The Grandissimes, considered by many to be Cable's most successful work, was the first Southern novel to treat the complexity of race in the South. In his representation of the South's divided heritage and his refusal to simplify or resolve the tensions and contradictions of race, Cable was the forerunner of William Faulkner's differentiated treatment of race in works such as *Absalom, Absalom!* (1936) and *Go Down Moses* (1942).

At the physical and moral center of the novel is the tragic tale of Bras Coupé, an African prince captured by slavers and transported to Louisiana. Bras Coupé possesses as much dignity and courage as his Spanish Creole master, and his enslavement is portrayed as a violation of natural and divine orders. Bras Coupé's punishment for violating the Code Noir (Black Code)—he is lashed, his ears cut off, and tendons behind his knees slashed—destroys the myth of Southern slavery as a paternalistic system. Cable tried to publish this tale as his first short story, "Bibi," but it was rejected by the editor of *Scribner's Monthly* as being too "distressful" and by the editor of *The Atlantic Monthly* as having an "unmitigatedly distressful effect."

By embedding Bras Coupé's story in a romantic plot with a rich social setting, Cable effectively positioned slavery at the start of the South's social structure. The story of Bras Coupé becomes the moral measure of the characters and of the Creole society. Honoré Grandissime's attempts to intervene and prevent Bras Coupé's punishment are contrasted to Agricola Fusilier's role in the conquest and humiliation of the proud African. The story is repeated several times in the novel, revealing the moral corruption at the foundation of the sensuous and beautiful Creole society. Bras Coupé's curse on his master and the plantation represents the curse of slavery on the Southern economic and social system. Cable's use of the name Bras Coupé, meaning "the arm cut off," makes the point that "all Slavery is Maiming."

Cable's treatment of race results in a double vision that runs throughout the novel. The charm and sensuousness of New Orleans are qualified by signs of decadence and disintegration. Feuds divide the Creole aristocracy and individual families into opposing camps. Cable contrasts the refined social setting of New Orleans with the primal swamp in which Bras Coupé hides. Running parallel to the love story of Honoré Grandissime and Aurora Nancanou is the story of miscegenation as depicted in the Grandissime family's dual racial heritage. The two half-brothers, both named Honoré Grandissime, one white and one of mixed blood, serve as a metaphor for the interconnectedness of the races; through their shared name and shared education in Paris, Cable demonstrates the arbitrary harm of a system that privileges racial purity over the ties of brotherhood. That the quadroon Honoré Grandissime is a free man of color (f. m. c.) does not, for Cable, resolve the issue. Joseph Frowenfeld argues that the "slavery of caste . . . like all slaveries on earth, is a double bondage. And what a bondage it is which compels a community, in order to preserve its established tyrannies, to walk behind the rest of the intelligent world."

Caught between Joseph Frowenfeld and Agricola Fusiler, two passionate and engaging characters who represent extreme and opposing positions, the white Honoré Grandissime is the character in the novel who seeks to mediate the multiple dualities of the novel. Frowenfeld, the American pharmacist and outsider to New Orleans and Creole society, represents an ideal and absolute moral position that ignores the claims of historical, social, and personal contexts. On the other side is Agricola, Honoré's uncle, the champion of family and community, and spokesperson for the Creole social structure. Honoré, who "looks at both sides of a question," perceives the injustice, division, and tragedy resulting from Agricola's absolute loyalty to the family and caste systems of Creole society; at the same time, he realizes that Frowenfeld's moral imperative of absolute honor and justice would destroy the society he wishes to reform.

Honoré's decision to restore Aurora Nancanou's plantation and to enter into a business partnership with his half-brother can satisfy neither position fully. The differences that run throughout the narrative cannot be fully reconciled or resolved. Many of the Grandissimes are outraged by his public recognition of his quadroon half-brother. Agricola's attempt to lynch Honoré Grandissime, f. m. c., their public quarrel, and Agricola's resulting death qualify the success of Honoré's moral stance. Honoré's success is further qualified by his half-brother's suicide out of despair because the woman he loves is in love with the white Honoré.

While two of the love stories end happily, with an engagement between Frowenfeld and Clotilde Nancanou and an understanding between Honoré and Aurora, the racial story ends in ambivalence and limited success. This reflects Cable's conviction that an end to the slavery of caste would require a lengthy process of committed social restructuring and education. Cable wanted his writing to speak to "the conscience of the South"; his novel *The Grandissimes* speaks today as eloquently as it did in 1880 through Cable's vividly textured portrait of Creole culture, its pioneering use of dialect, and its deep moral conviction.

"Critical Evaluation" by Suzan Harrison

Bibliography:

Butcher, Philip. *George W. Cable*. New York: Twayne, 1962. An excellent beginner's source for discussions of Cable's fiction. Analyzes the themes, structure, and characters of *The Grandissimes* and discusses the novel's importance in Cable's development as a writer.

Elfenbein, Anna Shannon. *Women on the Color Line: Evolving Stereotypes and the Writings of George Washington Cable, Grace King, Kate Chopin*. Charlottesville: University Press of Virginia, 1989. Compares Cable's female characters with those of two other turn-of-the-century New Orleans writers. Places special emphasis on Cable's treatment of women of color.

Rubin, Louis D., Jr. *George W. Cable: The Life and Times of a Southern Heretic*. New York: Pegasus, 1969. An excellent study of Cable in the context of Southern fiction and culture. Calls *The Grandissimes* "the first 'modern' Southern novel" and explores Cable's treatment of race. Compares Cable to later Southern writers such as William Faulkner. A good starting point for serious study.

Turner, Arlin. *George W. Cable: A Biography*. Durham, N.C.: Duke University Press, 1956. An excellent biographical study with a detailed chapter on *The Grandissimes* that analyzes the novel's place in Cable's artistic and political development. Analyzes Cable's philosophy of fiction and his pioneering use of dialect in fiction.

Wilson, Edmund. *Patriotic Gore: Studies in the Literature of the American Civil War*. New York: Oxford University Press, 1962. Examines the political dimensions of *The Grandissimes*, including a discussion of the historical setting of the novel in comparison to the historical period in which it was written.

THE GRANDMOTHERS
A Family Portrait

Type of work: Novel
Author: Glenway Wescott (1901-1987)
Type of plot: Family
Time of plot: 1830-1925
Locale: Wisconsin
First published: 1927

Principal characters:
ALWYN TOWER, a young boy
HENRY TOWER, his grandfather
ROSE TOWER, his grandmother
JIM TOWER, his uncle
EVAN TOWER, another uncle
FLORA TOWER, his aunt
RALPH TOWER, his father
MARIANNE TOWER, his mother

The Story:

During his childhood, Alwyn Tower spent many hours poring over the family albums: everything his ancestors or relatives had done was interesting to the boy. He begged his Grandmother Tower to tell him stories of her childhood and stories about her children and other relatives. Often, the old lady could not remember what he wanted to know, and sometimes she seemed reluctant to talk about the past. Yet, piece by piece, from his Grandmother Tower, his parents, his aunts and uncles, and from the albums, Alwyn learned something of what he wanted to know.

Alwyn's Grandfather Tower died when the boy was twelve years old, and so his memories of that old man were rather vague. Grandfather Tower's chief interest during his old age was his garden, where he never allowed his grandchildren to go without his permission. He had failed at farming, but he was the best gardener in that part of Wisconsin.

Grandfather Tower had come to Wisconsin from New York. Like so many others, he had planned to get rich in the new West; like so many others, he had failed. He had been a young boy full of dreams when he first cleared the wilderness for his farm. He fell in love with and married Serena Cannon and, shortly afterward, went off to the Civil War. When he returned, Serena was ill with a fever and died soon after, leaving a baby boy. Grandfather Tower could never love another as he had loved Serena. Because the boy needed a mother, however, he married Rose Hamilton, who had been jilted by his brother Leander. Serena's boy died a week before Rose bore Henry's first child. After that, life seemed unimportant to Henry Tower. There were more children, some a small pleasure to him, some a disgrace; but they seemed to be Rose's children, not his. Part of Grandfather Tower had died with Serena, and although he lived to be eighty-two years old, he had never seemed to be completely alive as far as Alwyn was concerned.

Grandmother Tower, too, had come to Wisconsin when she was a child. Growing up in the wilderness, she suffered all the hardships of the pioneers—hunger and cold and fear of Indians. When she was in her early teens, she met and fell in love with Leander Tower. When the Civil

War came, Leander enlisted, and the girl went to stay with Serena Tower. While Serena lay ill with fever, the young girl cared for her and the baby. Leander returned, but he had changed. Although he could not explain himself clearly, Rose knew that he no longer wanted to marry her. After Serena's husband came home and Serena had died, Leander went to California. Rose married Serena's widower and bore his children, but like him, she was only partly alive. She never ceased to love Leander, but she was faithful to Grandfather Tower, even after Leander returned to Wisconsin. To Alwyn, she was a quiet, serene woman, resigned to life, but not unhappy with her lot.

Alwyn learned about many of his more distant relatives as he studied the albums and listened to the stories of his elders. There was his Great-Aunt Nancy Tower, who had been insane for part of her life. There was his Great-Aunt Mary Harris, who had been married three times and had traveled all over the world. Grandmother Tower said that Great-Aunt Mary was a real pioneer. She had seen her first husband killed by Southerners because he sympathized with the Union. Her second husband was a drunken sot who beat her, and often she had to beg for food to stay alive. After her second husband divorced her, she married one of the Tower men, and for the first time, she knew happiness and prosperity.

Old Leander Tower seemed to be happy only when he was helping a young boy. His younger brother Hilary had disappeared in the war, and it seemed almost as if Leander were trying to find a substitute for his brother.

Alwyn knew his father's brothers and sisters quite well. His Uncle Jim was a minister who had married a rich woman, and they took Alwyn to live with them in Chicago, giving the boy his only chance for a good education. Uncle Jim's wife persuaded her husband to give up preaching. After her death, he continued to live with her mother and sisters and to humor their whims. Alwyn liked his Uncle Jim, but he could not admire him.

Uncle Evan, a deserter in the Spanish-American War, had gone West to live after taking a new name. Once or twice he came home to visit his father, but both men seemed embarrassed during those meetings. Grandfather Tower had always been ashamed of Evan, and during the last visit Evan made, the old man refused to enter the house while his son was there.

Aunt Flora was an old maid, although she still thought of herself as a young girl. She had had many chances to marry, but she was afraid of the force of love, afraid that something hidden in her would be roused and not satisfied. It was a mysterious thing she could not understand. She turned to Alwyn, giving him her love and accepting his, for she could love the young boy wholeheartedly, having nothing to fear from him. When she was twenty-nine years old, she fell ill and died. Alwyn thought she looked happy as she took her last breath.

Alwyn's father, Ralph Tower, had always wanted to be a veterinarian, for he had a way with animals. Yet Uncle Jim had been the one chosen for an education, and after Uncle Evan deserted and went West, Ralph had to take over the farm for his father. He was never bitter, merely resigned. Perhaps he would have envied Jim if it had not been for Alwyn's mother.

His parents had one of the few really happy marriages in the family Alwyn realized as he watched them together. Alwyn knew something of the girlhood of his mother. Her parents had hated each other fiercely and had taken pleasure in showing that hatred. Alwyn's mother was a lonely child until she met Ralph Tower. Sometimes it embarrassed Alwyn to see his parents together because they revealed so much of their feeling for each other.

Alwyn realized that the Towers were one of the last pioneer families in America. He knew that in his heritage there was a deep religious feeling, a willingness to accept poverty and hardship as the will of God. His heritage was a disordered one; a deserter, an insane woman, a man and a wife who hated each other, and an uncle who lived on the wealth of his wife's mother.

These people were just as much a part of him as were the others. Alwyn knew that his life would be a rearrangement of the characters of the others. He knew that he could understand himself once he understood his people.

Critical Evaluation:

The Grandmothers is the kind of novel that is usually damned with faint praise as a minor classic. Wescott's novel, however, is more than a curiosity. This lyrical mixture of memory and desire gives meaning and resonance to a time, a place, and a sensibility, all the while remaining aware of the highest standards of novelistic craft.

Most of the U.S. literature that is usually called regionalist was written in the latter half of the nineteenth century. Authors wrote primarily a realist, local-color mode. By the time Wescott came of age as a writer, regionalism was in disrepute in U.S. literary circles; indeed, the most renowned U.S. writers, such as F. Scott Fitzgerald and Ernest Hemingway, wrote substantially of life abroad. Writers who wrote about the United States, such as Sinclair Lewis, were uniformly perceived as satirical and negative. The rise of literary modernism and of a more artistically self-conscious approach to fiction made regionalist realism seem behind the times. Wescott's achievement in *The Grandmothers* is to have pioneered a form of modernist region-alism that recounts the history of a particular part of the land while keeping the psychological and literary complexity of ambitious art.

In *The Grandmothers*, there is a conflict between the young, sensitive artist, represented by Alwyn in Wescott's novel, and the ingrown and provincial atmosphere that has produced him. Wescott uses a mixture of narrative modes, combining third-person point-of-view narration, stream of consciousness, and documents—such as the 1911 memoir of Grandfather Tower—to make up a rich fictional tableau. In Wescott's works, however, unlike those of many other writers of his time, what predominates is not the urge to break free and find a new, more liberated life (as Alwyn does when he goes to Europe) but rather the sweet regret about what has been left behind. Alwyn feels superior to his parents, grandparents, and other relatives because he has a fuller perspective on life than they do; but their experience is what his acquired perspective permits him to interpret.

As an adult in Europe, Alwyn finds that he cannot leave the United States (meaning, for him, Wisconsin) behind. Taunted by an Austrian that the United States has no sense of sin and therefore no history, Alwyn responds by immersing himself in his family history, which he had an opportunity to observe and learn about as a youth. The Tower family represents the U.S. past and the creativity of the American spirit. Particularly in remembering the religiosity of his mother, Marianne, Alwyn exalts ordinary U.S. piety even as he perceives what, for him, are its limitations. His mother's faith is a distinctly American kind of religiosity, because of its social concern and combination of emotional passion with a public identity in the church and in the community. As much as Alwyn believes his family represents the American soul, the United States has not rewarded them in kind. The Towers seem to perceive themselves as losers and failures, their dreaminess always at odds with the more materially oriented people among whom they live. When Evan Tower deserts the U.S. Army during the Spanish-American War (of which Wescott provides the best evocation in extant American fiction), goes to London to marry Suzanne Orfeo, and returns to the United States to forge a new identity as John Craig, he is acting out in literal terms the sense of being at odds with the rest of the country that is felt by all the Towers. Another demonstration of the Towers' sense of uniqueness and vulnerability is in the marriage of Alwyn's Uncle Jim, deemed the brightest and most talented of all the Towers. Jim marries into the bourgeois and complacent Fielding family and fritters his talents away in order to please them, becoming a run-of-the-mill local minister, lacking the genuine emotion of his sister-in-law Marianne's piety. Jim was a talented singer and could have pursued his talent in that direction, but was forced to renounce this ambition and pursue a more conventional path. Alwyn's decision to become a writer and leave Wisconsin can be seen as a fulfillment of Jim's thwarted desires.

Despite Alwyn's physical escape from Wisconsin, it still seems to psychologically captivate him. Alwyn brings tenderness and empathy to his observation of his family's past, making sensitive observations about the lives of older people. There also might be something slightly pathological about Alwyn's obsession with his family's past, at the cost of fashioning the independent identity he has externally achieved. The surname "Tower" may symbolize, in Alwyn's case, the self-conscious artist: witness the towers always used as symbols for poetic isolation in French symbolist poetry. In the context of the entire family, the surname may well symbolize their enclosure and isolation from the rest of U.S. society. Alwyn plunges into his family's past to avoid this isolation, but sometimes his feelings for his family tell us as much about himself as about others. His grandparents had a loveless marriage, due to Serena Tower's early death and Uncle Leander's escape westward, leaving Henry Tower and Rose Hamilton to marry each other. Alwyn's great interest in these events may give readers clues about Alwyn's own confusion about matters of love, including his possible homosexuality.

In the United States, where literature has often celebrated the promise of the future, *The Grandmothers* is saturated with the bittersweet memories of the past. This may make it minor in the eyes of some critics, but it does not diminish the novel's emotional power and resonance.

"Critical Evaluation" by Nicholas Birns

Bibliography:
Aldridge, John. Introduction to *The Grandmothers, A Family Portrait* by Glenway Wescott. New York: Arbor House, 1986. Sensitive overview of the novel by a respected veteran U.S. critic. Comprehends what is unique about the novel and those qualities that give it a permanent place in the reader's memory; discusses how it partakes of an experience specific to the United States.
Bawer, Bruce. "Glenway Wescott 1901-1987." *The New Criterion* 5 (May, 1987): 36-45. The most cogent general overview of Wescott's career and significance. Stresses the aesthetic side of *The Grandmothers*; especially good on Alwyn's psychological dilemmas and how his tangled relationship with his family affects his conflicts over his own identity.
Johnson, Ira. *Glenway Wescott: The Paradox of Voice.* Port Washington, N.Y.: Kennikat, 1971. Stresses the poetic qualities in Wescott's novelistic method and the extent of his identification with Alwyn. Explores issues of emotional involvement, emotional distance, and authorial perspective in the book.
Rueckert, William H. *Glenway Wescott.* New York: Twayne, 1965. General overview of Wescott's career. Devotes a long chapter to *The Grandmothers*. Gives a good summary of the novel's often complicated and crowded plot, and acknowledges the book's symbolic dimension.
Wescott, Glenway. *Continual Lessons: The Journals of Glenway Wescott, 1937-1955.* Edited by Robert Phelps with Jerry Rosco. New York: Farrar, Straus & Giroux, 1990. Provides a crucial picture of Wescott's sympathies, prejudices, and concerns during the major years of his writing career. Contains impressions from Wescott's childhood that are interesting to compare to the novel.

THE GRAPES OF WRATH

Type of work: Novel
Author: John Steinbeck (1902-1968)
Type of plot: Social realism
Time of plot: 1930's
Locale: Midwestern United States and California
First published: 1939

> *Principal characters:*
> TOM JOAD, JR., a former convict
> PA JOAD, an Okie
> MA JOAD, his wife
> ROSE OF SHARON (ROSASHARN), Tom's sister
> JIM CASY, a labor agitator

The Story:

Tom Joad, Jr. was released from the Oklahoma state penitentiary where he had served a sentence for killing a man in self-defense. He traveled homeward through a region made barren by drought and dust storms. On the way, he met Jim Casy, a former preacher; the pair went together to the home of Tom's family. They found the Joad place deserted. While Tom and Casy were wondering what had happened, Muley Graves, a die-hard tenant farmer, came by and disclosed that all the families in the neighborhood had gone to California or were going. Tom's folks, Muley said, had gone to a relative's place to prepare for going west. Muley was the only sharecropper to stay behind. All over the southern Midwest states, farmers, no longer able to make a living because of land banks, weather, and machine farming, had sold or were forced out of the farms they had tenanted. Junk dealers and used-car salesmen profiteered on them. Thousands of families took to the roads leading to the promised land: California.

Tom and Casy found the Joads at Uncle John's place, all busy with preparations for their trip to California. Assembled for the trip were Pa and Ma Joad; Noah, their mentally retarded son; Al, the adolescent younger brother of Tom and Noah; Rose of Sharon, Tom's sister, and her husband, Connie; the Joad children, Ruthie and Winfield; and Granma and Grampa Joad. Al had bought an ancient truck to take them West. The family asked Jim Casy to go with them. The night before they started, they killed the pigs they had left and salted down the meat so that they would have food on the way.

Spurred by handbills which stated that agricultural workers were badly needed in California, the Joads, along with thousands of others, made their tortuous way, in a worn-out vehicle, across the plains toward the mountains. Grampa died of a stroke during their first overnight stop. Later, there was a long delay when the truck broke down. Small business people along the way treated the migrants as enemies, and, to add to their misery, returning migrants told the Joads that there was no work to be had in California, that conditions were even worse than they were in Oklahoma. The dream of a bountiful West Coast, however, urged the Joads onward.

Close to the California line, where the group stopped to bathe in a river, Noah, feeling he was a hindrance to the others, wandered away. It was there that the Joads first heard themselves addressed as Okies, another word for tramps. Granma died during the night trip across the desert. After burying her, the group went into a Hooverville, as the migrants' camps were called. There they learned that work was all but impossible to find. A contractor came to the camp to sign up men to pick fruit in another county. When the Okies asked to see his license, the contractor turned the leaders over to a police deputy who had accompanied him to camp. Tom was involved in the fight that followed. He escaped, and Casy surrendered himself in Tom's place. Connie, husband of the pregnant Rose of Sharon, suddenly disappeared from the group. The family was breaking up in the face of its hardships. Ma Joad did everything in her power to keep the group together.

Fearing recrimination after the fight, the Joads left the Hooverville and went to a government camp maintained for transient agricultural workers. The camp had sanitary facilities, a local government made up of the transients themselves, and simple organized entertainment. During the Joads' stay at the camp, the Okies successfully defeated an attempt of the local citizens to give the camp a bad name and thus to have it closed to the migrants. For the first time since they had arrived in California, the Joads found themselves treated as human beings.

Circumstances eventually forced them to leave the camp, however, for there was no work in the district. They drove to a large farm where work was being offered. There they found agitators attempting to keep the migrants from taking the work because of the unfair wages offered. The Joads, however, thinking only of food, were escorted by motorcycle police to the farm. The entire family picked peaches for five cents a box and earned in a day just enough money to buy food for one meal. Tom, remembering the pickets outside the camp, went out at night to investigate. He found Casy, who was the leader of the agitators. While Tom and Casy were talking, deputies, who had been searching for Casy, closed in on them. The pair fled but were caught. Casy was killed. Tom received a cut on his head, but not before he had felled a deputy with an ax handle. The family concealed Tom in their shack. The rate for a box of peaches dropped, meanwhile, to two-and-a-half cents. Tom's danger and the futility of picking peaches drove the Joads on their way. They hid the injured Tom under the mattresses in the back of the truck, and then they told the suspicious guard at the entrance to the farm that the extra man they had had with them when they came was a hitchhiker who had stayed behind to pick.

The family found at last a migrant crowd encamped in abandoned boxcars along a stream. They joined the camp and soon found temporary jobs picking cotton. Tom, meanwhile, hid in a culvert near the camp. Ruthie innocently disclosed Tom's presence to another little girl. Ma, realizing that Tom was no longer safe, sent him away. Tom promised to carry on Casy's work in trying to improve the lot of the downtrodden everywhere.

The autumn rains began. Soon the stream that ran beside the camp overflowed and water entered the boxcars. Under these all but impossible conditions, Rose of Sharon gave birth to a dead baby. When the rising water made their position no longer bearable, the family moved from the camp on foot. The rains had made their old truck useless. They came to a barn, which they shared with a boy and his starving father. Rose of Sharon, bereft of her baby, nourished the famished man with the milk from her breasts. So the poor kept each other alive in the years of the Great Depression.

Critical Evaluation:

The publication of John Steinbeck's *The Grapes of Wrath* caused a nationwide stir in 1939. This account of the predicament of migrant workers was taken more as a social document than as fiction. Some saw it as an exposé of capitalist excesses; others, as a distorted call to revolution. Frequently compared to Harriet Beecher Stowe's *Uncle Tom's Cabin: Or, Life Among the Lowly* (1852), it was awarded the Pulitzer Prize for Literature in 1940.

Recent literary critics, taking a second look at the novel, have often lumped it with a number of other dated books of the 1930's as "proletarian fiction." A careful reader, however, recognizes that beneath this outraged account of an outrageous social situation lies a dynamic, carefully structured story that applies not only to one era or society but also to the universal human predicament.

As a social document, the novel presents such a vivid picture of oppression and misery that one tends to doubt its authenticity. Steinbeck, however, had done more than academic research. He had journeyed from Oklahoma to California, lived in a migrant camp, and worked alongside the migrants. (According to one report, after the novel appeared, the workers sent Steinbeck a patchwork dog sewn from scraps of their clothing and wearing a tag labeled "Migrant John.") Before making the motion picture, which still stands as one of the great films of the era, Darryl F. Zanuck hired private detectives to verify Steinbeck's story; they reported that conditions were even worse than those depicted in the book. The political situation was a powder keg.

Social injustice was depicted so sharply that Steinbeck himself was accused of being a revolutionary. Certainly, he painted the oppressive economic system in bleak colors. Many critics note, however, that Steinbeck was basically a reformer, not a revolutionary. He wanted to change the attitudes and behavior of people—both migrants and economic barons—not overturn the private enterprise system. Indeed, Steinbeck observes that ownership of land is morally edifying to humankind.

Steinbeck once declared that the writer must "set down his time as nearly as he can understand it" and that he should "serve as the watchdog of society . . . to satirize its silliness, to attack its injustices, to stigmatize its faults." In *The Grapes of Wrath*, he does all these things, then goes further to interpret events from a distinctly American point of view. Like Walt Whitman, he expresses love for all men and respect for manual labor. Like Thomas Jefferson, he asserts a preference for agrarian society in which people retain a close, nourishing tie to the soil. His farmers dwindle psychologically as they are separated from their land, and the California owners become oppressors as they substitute ledgers for direct contact with the soil. Like Ralph Waldo Emerson, Steinbeck demonstrates faith in the common people and in the ideal of self-reliance. He also develops the Emersonian religious concept of an oversoul. The preacher Jim Casy muses ". . . maybe that's the Holy Sperit—the human sperit—the whole shebang. Maybe all men got one big soul ever'body's a part of it." Later, Tom Joad reassures Ma that even if he isn't physically with her, "Wherever they's a fight so hungry people can eat, I'll be there. Wherever they's a cop beatin' up a guy, I'll be there. . . . I'll be in the way kids laugh when they're hungry an' they know supper's ready. . . ."

This theme, that all people essentially belong together and are a part of one another and of a greater whole that transcends momentary reality, is what removes *The Grapes of Wrath* from the genre of timely proletarian fiction and makes it an allegory for all people in all circumstances. Warren French notes that the real story of this novel is not the Joads' search for economic security but their education, which transforms them from self-concern to a recognition of their bond with the whole human race. At first, Tom Joad is intensely individualistic, interested mainly in making his own way; Pa's primary concern is keeping bread on his table; Rose of Sharon dreams only of traditional middle-class success; and Ma, an earth mother with a spine of steel, concentrates fiercely upon keeping the "fambly" together. At the end, Tom follows Casy's example in fighting for human rights; Pa, in building the dike, sees the necessity for all people to work together; Rose of Sharon forgets her grief over her stillborn child and unhesitatingly lifts a starving man to her milk-filled breast; and Ma can say "Use' ta be the fambly was fust. It ain't so now. It's anybody. Worse off we get, the more we got to do." Thus the Joads have overcome that separation that one may equate with sin, the alienation from others that existentialists are so fond of describing as the inescapable human condition.

It is interesting to note how much *The Grapes of Wrath*, which sometimes satirizes, sometimes attacks organized Christian religion, reflects the Bible. In structure, as critics have been quick to notice, it parallels the story of the Exodus to a "promised land." Symbolically, as has been noted by critics, the initials of Jim Casy are those of Jesus Christ, another itinerant preacher who rebelled against traditional religion, went into the wilderness, discovered his own gospel, and eventually gave his life in service to others. Language, too, is frequently biblical, especially in those chapters which, like a Greek chorus, restate, reinforce, and generalize from the specific happenings of the narrative. The cadences, repetitions, and parallel lines all echo the patterns of the Psalms—Ma Joad's favorite book. Even the title of the novel is biblical; the exact phrase is from the American reformer Julia Ward Howe, but the reference is to Jeremiah and Revelation. The grapes have been a central symbol throughout the book—first of promise, representing the fertile California valleys, but finally of bitter rage as the Midwesterners realize that they have been lured West with false bait and that they will not partake of this fertility. The wrath grows, a fearsome, terrible wrath, but, as several chapters make clear, better wrath than despair, because wrath moves to action. Steinbeck would have his people act, in concert and in concern for one another, and finally prevail over all forms of injustice.

"Critical Evaluation" by Sally Buckner

Bibliography:
Ditsky, John, ed. *Critical Essays on Steinbeck's "The Grapes of Wrath."* Boston: G. K. Hall, 1989. In addition to important essays on the novel's composition, critical reception, and other topics, this collection provides contemporary reviews of the novel and useful maps of the 1936 Dust Bowl, westward migration in the 1930's, Route 66, and a government camp.
Donohue, Agnes McNeill. *A Casebook on "The Grapes of Wrath."* New York: Thomas Y. Crowell, 1968. Contains thirty-seven discussions of the novel as both a social document and as literature. Also reprints Steinbeck's 1962 Nobel Prize acceptance speech and suggests topics for studying or writing about the novel.
Gladstein, Mimi Reisel. *The Indestructible Woman in Faulkner, Hemingway, and Steinbeck.* Ann Arbor: University of Michigan Research Press, 1986. A fresh and intelligent discussion of Ma Joad, Granma Joad, and Rose of Sharon as "indestructible women" who hold the family together. This study opens ground for feminist consideration of Steinbeck's works.
Steinbeck, John. *Working Days: The Journals of "The Grapes of Wrath," 1938-1941.* Edited by Robert DeMott. New York: Viking, 1989. Steinbeck's journals and correspondence while writing the novel are valuable resources for studying the cultural, historical, and literary origins of the book, as well as the author's creative process. DeMott provides an insightful introduction to these materials.
Wyatt, David, ed. *New Essays on "The Grapes of Wrath."* New York: Cambridge University Press, 1990. Five essays covering Steinbeck's portrayal of human history as an organic process, Ma Joad's character, the novel's relationship to journalism, and the propagandistic aspects of John Ford's 1940 film version of the novel.

GRAVITY'S RAINBOW

Type of work: Novel
Author: Thomas Pynchon (1937-   )
Type of plot: Historical realism
Time of plot: 1944-1945
Locale: Europe
First published: 1973

Principal characters:

TYRONE SLOTHROP, protagonist, American lieutenant, experimental
   subject, and rake
DR. EDWARD W. A. POINTSMAN, Pavlovian researcher
ROGER MEXICO, statistician employed by Pointsman
VASLAV TCHITCHERINE, Russian intelligence officer
MAJOR WEISMANN/CAPTAIN BLICERO, German rocket scientist
OBERST ENZIAN, African protégé of Weismann and leader of the
   Schwarzkommando
KATJE BORGESIUS, Dutch triple agent
GELI TRIPPING, girlfriend of Tchitcherine and apprentice witch
JESSICA SWANLAKE, companion of Roger Mexico and secret employee
   of Pointsman

The Story:
   World War II was winding down, and in London, Tyrone Slothrop had been assigned to a
new post under the command of the Firm. The location known as the White Visitation had
formerly been a mental hospital exclusively but was now occupied in part by Pavlovian
scientists, among them Dr. Edward Pointsman, who were conducting a series of experiments
on conditioned response. The scientists worked under the code name PISCES, an acronym for
Psychological Intelligence Schemes for Expediting Surrender, and the section experimenting
on dogs as subjects was subcoded Abreaction Research Facility or ARF. Slothrop was of
particular interest to Pointsman because it was a known fact that within minutes of each German
rocket launch, Slothrop became involved in a sexual liaison and it was assumed that he had the
foreknowledge to predict such attacks.
   As the experiments intensified in nature and threatened imminent bodily harm, Slothrop
grew increasingly paranoid and was allowed to take a holiday, of sorts. With companions, he
traveled to a resort in the south of France where he had a strange encounter with Katje
Borgesius, who at the moment of their meeting was under attack by a giant octopus. It was not
until after his best friend mysteriously disappeared, however, that Slothrop realized the encounter with Katje—trained octopus and all—had been staged by Pointsman and that Katje had been
placed in his path to keep him in line.
   At this point Slothrop made a run for his life and vanished into the Zone, the inner recesses
of mainland Europe. It was his misguided assumption that if he could trace the source of the
rocket, specifically the German A-4, he could then trade that information for his freedom.
During his circular attempt at seeking the rocket, which came to be his Grail, Slothrop
encountered a cross-section of humanity and a multiplicity of situations. His natural inclinations
led to many of his encounters being sexual conquests, drug deals, hallucinations, and devil-

may-care heroics. His paranoia increased constantly, with reason. While he was in the Zone, Slothrop was forced to live off the land and the kindness of strangers, usually female, and by his wits.

Through various changes in his identity and costume, Slothrop slipped into and out of potentially dangerous, possibly fatal, situations. With a falsified identification card, he went across border checkpoints as the actor Max Schlepzig. He cohabited in a bombed-out building with an apprentice witch Geli Tripping. He escaped in a cream-pie-laden hot air balloon. He stowed away on an orgiastic ship of fools going nowhere. He donned a cape and a Viking helmet without horns to become Rocketman and smuggled hashish out of the occupied Zone. He accepted the role of a liberator pig god in an ancient village ritual and escaped in the pig's costume. Appropriately, he spent the majority of his time as Rocketman, the merger of the rocket and the man, and as the pig, having started his peripatetic quest as a guinea pig. In the process of altering himself with these aliases and disguises, however, Slothrop's true self ceased to exist and essentially disintegrated, along with any interest he may have had in locating the rocket and in returning home. His final escape was into the mountains, where he discovered an aging harp, which he learned to play, and the wonders of nature, which he learned to appreciate, and he was heard of no more.

While Slothrop looked for the rocket, others raced around seeking various goals. Oberst Enzian, the leader of the Swartzkommando, a displaced band of militant Africans brought to Germany to act as Nazi soldiers, searched for the parts to construct an identical rocket, assuming that with the information of how to build it he could gain revenge for the group's forced relocation. Pointsman and others continued to search for Slothrop. Roger Mexico searched for a means of making Jessica Swanlake his permanently. Vaslav Tchitcherine pretended to search for information while he really sought his half-brother Enzian. Geli Tripping searched for a spell to make Tchitcherine fall in love with her. Only one character searched for nothing because he already had the answers and the rocket. Methodically, Captain Blicero placed his lover on board the weapon, began the countdown, aimed the rocket, and incinerated himself in the rocket's afterburn.

Critical Evaluation:

To reduce a novel as complex as *Gravity's Rainbow* to its skeletal bones is a travesty that omits, for the reader of the summary, Thomas Pynchon's circuitous plot contrivances, his undeniable wit, his interweaving of story within story, and his obvious love for manipulating language. This is a work to be read, to be devoured, to be mulled over; it is a treatise to make the reader think, and that cannot be reduced. It must be experienced.

Gravity's Rainbow is a big book, not only in length but in style, vision, and ideology. It incorporates a multitude of literary styles, devices, and types. The work is an archetypal hero cycle, a Grail quest, a picaresque, a satire, an apocalyptic vision, a social criticism, a historical encyclopedia, a work of magic realism, and an engaging narrative. It is replete with literary and cinematic allusion, word play, puns, name symbolism, mythology, dark comedy, cataloguing, and adoration of The Word. Additionally, there are references to the occult, psychics, sexual deviants, Masons, war, politics, money, cartels, drugs, psychology, and philosophy. Consequently, the novel embodies much of the twentieth century and the artist's response to it.

Critical reception is polarized. It seems one either loves the book or hates it; few claim to understand it completely. For example, although many on the Pulitzer Prize committee felt *Gravity's Rainbow* was the best offering of the year, it was rejected for a Pulitzer as being "obscure and obscene." The scope of Pynchon's knowledge appears boundless and, in part, beyond the grasp of the typical reader. It is unlikely that one will comprehend the novel in its entirety, but this fact is irrelevant because the work is like a fictional smorgasbord, offering something for each appetite.

The frame story involves the escapades of Tyrone Slothrop. Thus, he is regarded as the protagonist. It is his connection to the German rocket, the A-4, however, that ties together the disjointed parts of the story and the multitude of characters within its pages. The rocket can be regarded as a phallic, creative symbol as well as a symbol of destruction; it meshes the corresponding themes of sex and death, and each of the characters is in some way enslaved to the production or acquisition of the rocket. By the end of the work, the reader knows more about the rocket than about any of the characters.

In a novel featuring thirteen main characters, fourteen important minor characters, and a cast of thousands more, the plot, if indeed it can be called a plot, is complex and convoluted. Each player in the story looks for something without much apparent success, and paths are crossed and recrossed as subplots develop and disappear. Even the main story line, that of Slothrop himself, moves in increasingly wider circles until it simply vanishes without warning. There is chaos and fragmentation in the plot that is at first disorienting until one realizes that the book's pages unfold as life does. Then the reader slows down, stops attempting complete understanding, and begins to enjoy the individual episodes. Only then can one realize that the tale is a labyrinth adventure and one never knows what surprising tidbit may wait around the next corner.

In addition to the Slothrop story and the rocket quest, the narrative point of view lends cohesion to the book. The narrator slips out of third-person omniscience at will to form a relationship with the reader and to interject elements of foreshadowing, use of a conversational "you," and wry humor. Although the work is certainly not comedy, humor brings it to life. The book's humor is more than comic relief, however; it is thematic, a cosmic understanding of the absurdity of the human condition. The humor, too, is apocalyptic in the implicit warning that humankind must not ever, for even a second in the most extreme of circumstances, take itself too seriously.

Although critical evaluations are mixed, there are several threads of shared opinion. First is that Pynchon is predicting the ultimate demise of modern culture and advocating that a new world be built on its remains. Although it addresses such issues as war, genocide, mental illness, and sexual depravity, the work is not entirely pessimistic. Pynchon admits glimmers of light through the dark curtains of the tale.

Another common critical response is that the main focus of the novel is entropy. A theory of entropy argues that the world is winding down, burning itself out, and running out of energy. Based on Sir Isaac Newton's second law of thermodynamics, entropy is personified by Slothrop. In fact, the first five letters of his last name are an acronym for the theory, and the letters *r*, *o*, and *p* may suggest rites of passage. Slothrop never succeeds in his mission because he is lazy, easily distracted, and too slow to grasp the sometimes painfully obvious clues that are strewn in his path. He is entropy at work. The dissemination and utilization of information, so important during World War II and after, is a secondary theme. Information (or data) is also subject to the laws of entropy; it too becomes less useful over time. For Slothrop, seeking information is like looking for a "needle in a haaay-stack" and entirely too much trouble. Slothrop is a microcosm of the war, of bureaucratic nonsense, of entropic theory, and of historic repetition.

The reader may also note Pynchon's consistent reference to film and filmmakers. Several of the minor characters are involved in filmmaking, and it is discussed so often that one finally questions, as Pynchon intends, whether the work itself is merely a Hollywood version of reality. In fact, in the novel's final scene, the narrator instructs the audience in a movie theater on proper behavior as the rocket begins its descent toward the building where they sit.

Gravity's Rainbow is more than a novel, it is a literary feast. It is a work to be savored slowly, page by page and word by word, until reaching the final apocalyptic and high-spirited: "now, everybody."

Joyce Duncan

Bibliography:

Clerc, Charles, ed. *Approaches to "Gravity's Rainbow."* Columbus: Ohio State University Press, 1983. The work features a series of collected critical essays that address the novel from a variety of perspectives, including history, comedy, and psychology.

Hume, Kathryn. "Repetition and the Construction of Character in *Gravity's Rainbow.*" *Studies in Contemporary Fiction* 33 (Summer, 1992): 243-255. Discusses Pynchon's forcing his characters to deal with a recurring set of pressures as an implication that he prefers to deal with humanity at large rather than individual characters in detail.

Safer, Elaine B. *The Contemporary American Comic Epic.* Detroit: Wayne State University Press, 1988. Critical essays on the works of John Barth, Pynchon, William Gaddis, and Ken Kesey are included. The work addresses Pynchon's dark humor.

Scholes, Robert. *Fabulation and Metafiction.* Champaign: University of Illinois Press, 1979. Discusses the twentieth century tendency toward allegory and the grotesque and makes multiple references to the work of Pynchon.

Siegel, Mark Richard. *Pynchon: Creative Paranoia in "Gravity's Rainbow."* Port Washington, N.Y.: Kennikat Press, 1978. Discusses the work of Pynchon according to point of view, narrative structure, and metaphor.

GREAT EXPECTATIONS

Type of work: Novel
Author: Charles Dickens (1812-1870)
Type of plot: Bildungsroman
Time of plot: Nineteenth century
Locale: England
First published: 1860-1861

Principal characters:
  PIP, an orphan
  JOE GARGERY, Pip's brother-in-law
  MISS HAVISHAM, an eccentric recluse
  ESTELLA, Miss Havisham's ward
  HERBERT POCKET, Pip's roommate
  MR. JAGGERS, a solicitor
  ABEL MAGWITCH (MR. PROVIS), a convict
  COMPEYSON, a villain

The Story:

Little Pip had been left an orphan when he was a small boy, and his much older sister had grudgingly reared him in her cottage. Pip's brother-in-law, Joe Gargery, on the other hand, was kind and loving to the boy. Pip often wandered alone in the marsh country where he lived with his sister and Joe. One day, he was accosted by a wild-looking stranger who was an escaped prisoner. He frightened Pip and demanded that the boy secretly bring him food and a file to cut the iron chain that bound his leg. When Pip brought him a pork pie and file, he saw another mysterious figure on the marsh. This man engaged in a desperate struggle with the escaped prisoner, then escaped into the fog. The man whom Pip had aided promised that he would somehow repay the boy for helping him. He was later apprehended.

Mrs. Joe sent Pip to the large mansion of strange Miss Havisham upon that lady's request. Miss Havisham lived in a gloomy, locked house where all the clocks had been stopped on the day her bridegroom failed to appear for the wedding ceremony. She often dressed in her bridal robes; a wedding breakfast molded on the table in an unused room. Pip went there every day to visit the old lady and a beautiful young girl, named Estella, who delighted in tormenting the shy boy. Miss Havisham enjoyed watching the two children together, and she encouraged Estella in her haughty teasing of Pip.

Living in the grim atmosphere of Joe's blacksmith shop and the uneducated poverty of his sister's home, Pip was eager to learn. One day, a London solicitor named Jaggers presented him with the opportunity to go to London and become a gentleman. Both Pip and Joe accepted the proposal. Pip imagined that his kind backer was Miss Havisham and that perhaps she wanted to make a gentleman out of him so that he would be fit someday to marry Estella.

In London, Pip found a small apartment set up for him. Herbert Pocket, a young relative of Miss Havisham, was his living companion. When Pip needed money, he was instructed to go to Mr. Jaggers. Although Pip pleaded with the lawyer to disclose the name of his benefactor, Jaggers advised the eager young man not to make inquiries; when the proper time arrived, Pip's benefactor would make himself known.

Soon Pip became one of a small group of London dandies, among them a disagreeable chap named Bentley Drummle. To Pip's dismay, Joe Gargery came to visit; Pip, who had outgrown his rural background, was ashamed of Joe's simple manners, but Herbert Pocket cheerfully helped Pip to entertain Joe in their apartment. After he had left for the evening, Pip felt ashamed of himself. Joe had brought word that Miss Havisham wanted to see the young man, so Pip returned to his old home with his brother-in-law. Miss Havisham and Estella noted the changes in Pip, and when Estella left Pip alone with the old lady, she told him he must fall in love with the beautiful girl. She also said it was time for Estella to come to London, and that she wished Pip to meet her adopted daughter when she arrived. This request made Pip feel even more certain that he had been sent to London by Miss Havisham to be groomed to marry Estella.

Estella had not been in London long before she had many suitors. Of all the men who courted her, she seemed to favor Bentley Drummle. Pip saw Estella frequently. Although she treated him kindly and with friendship, he knew she did not return his love.

On his twenty-first birthday, Pip received a caller. It was Abel Magwitch, the man whom Pip had helped in the marsh many years earlier. He told Pip that it was he who had been financing him ever since he had come to London. At first, the boy was horrified to discover he owed so much to this crude, coarse man, a former criminal. Magwitch told Pip that he had been sent to the Colonies, where he had grown rich. Now he wanted Pip to enjoy all the privileges that he himself had been denied in life. He had returned to England to see the boy to whom he had tried to be a second father. He warned Pip that he was in danger should his presence be discovered, for it was death for a prisoner to return to England once he had been sent to a convict colony. Pip detested his plight. He realized that Miss Havisham had had nothing to do with his great expectations in life, but he was too conscious of his debt to consider abandoning the man whose person he disliked. He determined to do all in his power to please his benefactor. Magwitch, who was using the name Provis to hide his identity, told Pip that the man with whom Pip had seen him struggling long ago in the marsh was his enemy, Compeyson, who had vowed to destroy him. Herbert Pocket, a distant cousin of Miss Havisham, informed Pip that the lover who had betrayed her on her wedding day had been named Arthur Compeyson.

Pip went to see Miss Havisham to denounce her for having allowed him to believe that she was helping him. On his arrival, he was informed that Estella was to marry Bentley Drummle. Since Miss Havisham had suffered at the hands of one faithless man, she had reared Estella to inflict as much hurt as possible upon the many men who would fall in love with her. Estella reminded Pip that she had warned him not to fall in love with her, since she had no compassion for any human being. Pip returned once more to visit Miss Havisham after Estella was married. An accident started a fire in the old, dust-filled mansion; although Pip tried to save the old woman, she died in the blaze, which also badly damaged the gloomy house.

From Provis' story of his association with Compeyson and from other evidence, Pip had learned that Provis was Estella's father; he did not reveal his discovery to anyone but Jaggers, whose housekeeper was Estella's mother. Pip had also learned that Compeyson was in London and plotting to kill Provis. In order to protect the man who had tried to befriend him, Pip arranged to smuggle Provis across the channel to France with the help of Herbert Pocket. Pip intended to join the old man there. Elaborate and secretive as their plans were, Compeyson managed to overtake them as they were putting Provis on the boat. The two enemies fought one last battle in the water, and Provis killed his enemy. He was then taken to jail, where he died before he could be brought to trial.

When Pip fell ill shortly afterward, it was Joe Gargery who came to nurse him. Older and wiser from his many experiences, Pip realized that he no longer needed to be ashamed of the kind man who had given so much love to him when he was a boy. His sister, Mrs. Joe, had died and Joe had married again, this time very happily. Pip, still desolate and unhappy because of his lost Estella, returned to the blacksmith's home to recuperate. Later, Herbert Pocket and Pip set up business together in London.

Eleven years passed before Pip went to see Joe Gargery again. Curiosity led him to the site of Miss Havisham's former mansion. There he found Estella, now a widow, wandering over the grounds. During the intervening years, she had lost her cool aloofness and had softened a great deal. She told Pip she had thought of him often. Pip was able to foresee that perhaps he and Estella would never have to part again. The childhood friends walked hand in hand from the place that had once played such an enormous part in both of their lives.

Critical Evaluation:

G. K. Chesterton once observed that all of Charles Dickens' novels could be titled "Great Expectations," for they are full of an unsubstantial yet ardent expectation of everything. Nevertheless, as Chesterton pointed out with irony, the only book to which Dickens actually gave the title was one in which most of the expectations were never realized. To the Victorians, the word "expectations" meant legacy as well as anticipations. In that closed society, one of the few means by which a person born of the lower or lower-middle class could rise to wealth and high status was through inheritance. A major theme of the Victorian social novel involved a hero's passage through the class structure, and a major vehicle of that passage was money bestowed upon him, acquired through marriage, or inherited. Unlike many nineteenth century novels that rely upon the stale plot device of a surprise legacy to enrich the fortunate protagonists, *Great Expectations* probes deeply into the ethical and psychological dangers of advancing through the class system by means of wealth acquired from the toil of others.

Although the story of Pip's expectations dominates the novel, he is not the only person who waits to benefit from the money of another. His beloved Estella, the ward of Miss Havisham, is wholly dependent upon the caprices of the unstable old woman. Moreover, other characters are the mysterious instrumentalities of legacies. The solicitor Jaggers, who acts as the legal agent for both Miss Havisham and Abel Magwitch, richly benefits from his services. Even his lackey Mr. Wemmick, a mild soul who changes his personality from lamb to wolf to please his employer, earns his living from the legal machinery of the courts. Just as the source of Pip's money is revealed at last to be socially corrupted, so the uses of tainted wealth inevitably bring about corruption.

In *Bleak House* (1852-1853), Dickens had already explored with great skill the ruthless precincts of the law courts. His next three novels—*Hard Times* (1854), *Little Dorrit* (1855-1857), and *A Tale of Two Cities* (1859)—were not so well sustained and were, despite memorable scenes, less popular with the critics and public alike. *Great Expectations* (1860-1861, first published serially in *All the Year Round*) restored Dickens' supremacy with his vast reading audience. Serious, controlled, and nearly as complex structurally as *Bleak House*, the novel also reminded Victorian readers of *David Copperfield* (1849-1850). Both are apprenticeship novels that treat the life education of a hero. *Great Expectations* is somewhat less autobiographical than *David Copperfield*, but it repeats the basic formula of the genre: that of an honest, rather ingenuous but surely likeable young man who, through a series of often painful experiences, learns important lessons about life and himself. These lessons are always designed to reveal the hero's limitations. As he casts off his own weaknesses and better understands the dangers of the world, he succeeds by advancing through the class system and ends up less brash, a chastened but wiser man.

Great Expectations differs from *David Copperfield*, however, in the ways that the hero matures to self-knowledge. In the beginning, both David and Pip are young snobs (Pip more than David). Both suffer the traumas of a shattered childhood and troubled adolescence, but David's childhood suffering is fully motivated on the basis of his separation from loved ones. An innocent, he is the victim of evil that he does not cause. Pip, on the other hand, suffers from a childhood nightmare that forms a pattern of his later experience. An orphan like David, he lives with his brutal sister and her husband, the gentle blacksmith Joe Gargery. The abuse he endures from Mrs. Joe is more than compensated for by the brotherly affection of this simple, generous man. He also wins the loving sympathy of Biddy, another loyal friend. Nevertheless, he is not satisfied, and when he comes upon the convicts in the fog and is terrified, he feels a sense of guilt—misplaced but psychologically necessary—as much for his crimes against his protectors as for the theft of a pork pie. Thereafter, his motives, cloudy as the scene of his childhood terror, are weighted with secret apprehension and guilt. To regain his lost innocence, he must purge himself of the causes of this guilt.

Pip's life apprenticeship, therefore, involves his gaining a full understanding of his "crimes" against loved ones and of the ways to redeem himself. The causes of his guilt are, in order of severity, snobbish pride, his betrayal of friends and protectors, and finally his participation in the machinery of corruption.

As a snob, he not only breaks the social mold into which he has been cast but lords it over the underlings and unfortunates of the class system. Because of his presumed great expectations, he believes himself to be superior to the humbler Joe and Biddy. He makes such a pompous fool of himself that Trabb's boy—that brilliant comic invention, at once naughty boy and honest philosopher—parodies his absurd airs and pretensions. His snobbery, however, costs him a dearer price than humiliation by an urchin. He falls in love with Estella, like himself a pretender to high social class, only to be rejected in favor of a worthless cad, Bentley Drummle. His fanciful dreams of social distinction are shattered forever when he learns the bitter truth about his benefactor, who is not the highborn Miss Havisham but the escaped convict Magwitch, the wretched stranger of his terror in the fog.

As Pip comes to understand the rotten foundations for his social position, he also learns terrible truths about his own weaknesses. Out of foolish pride, he has betrayed his most loyal friends, Joe and Biddy. In a sense, he has even betrayed Miss Havisham. He has mistaken her insanity for mere eccentricity and allowed her to act out her fantasies of romantic revenge. When he tries to confront her with the reality of her life, he is too late, for she expires in flames. He is almost too late to come to the service of his real benefactor, Magwitch. He is so disturbed with the realization of the convict's sacrifice that he nearly flees from the old man when he is in danger. At best, he can repay Magwitch with gratitude, not love, and his sense of guilt grows from his understanding that he cannot ever repay his debt to a man he secretly loathes.

Pip's final lesson is that, no matter how pure might be his motives, he has been one of the instruments of social corruption. In a sense, he is the counterpart to the malcontent Dolge Orlick. Like Orlick, he had as a youth been an apprentice at the forge, but whereas he was fortunate in having moved upward into society, Orlick, consumed by hatred, failed in every enterprise. In chapter 53, a climactic scene of the novel, Orlick confronts his enemy and blames Pip for all of his failures. He even accuses Pip of responsibility for the death of Mrs. Joe. The charge is paranoiac and false: Orlick is the murderer. In his almost hallucinatory terror, however, Pip can psychologically accept Orlick's reasoning. As a child, Pip had hated his sister. If he had not been the active instrument of her death, he nevertheless profited from it. Similarly, Pip profited from the hard-earned toil of Magwitch. Indeed, most of the success he had enjoyed, thanks to the astute protection of Mr. Jaggers, had come not as his due but for a price, the payment of corrupted money. Since he had been the ignorant recipient of the fruits of corruption, his psychological guilt is all the greater.

Nevertheless, Pip, though chastened, is not destroyed by guilt. During the course of his apprenticeship to life, he learns valuable truths about himself and about his limitations. By the end of his career, when his apprenticeship is over and he is a responsible, mature being, he has cast off petty pride, snobbery, and the vexations of corrupted wealth. Although he has lost his innocence forever, he can truly appreciate Herbert Pocket, Joe, and Biddy, all of whom had retained their integrity. When he turns to Estella, also chastened by her wretched marriage to the sadistic Drummle, he has at least the hope of beginning a new life with her, one founded on an accurate understanding of himself and the dangers of the world.

"Critical Evaluation" by Leslie B. Mittleman

Bibliography:
Hornback, Bert G. *"Great Expectations": A Novel of Friendship.* Boston: Twayne, 1987. Helpful introduction to the novel's historical context, guilt theme, point of view, and symbols and images. Includes chapters on Pip and Magwitch that focus on Pip's moral education. Argues that the novel's significance lies in its thesis that evil in society can be fought only by confronting it in the self. Includes an annotated bibliography.

Johnson, Edgar. *Charles Dickens: His Tragedy and Triumph.* 2 vols. New York: Simon & Schuster, 1952. A standard biography that includes a chapter on *Great Expectations*, which provides a succinct discussion of characters and of Dickens' opinion that money and materialism are corrupting forces. Pip's fortunes are related to key events in Dickens' own life.

Miller, J. Hillis. *Charles Dickens: The World of His Novels.* Cambridge, Mass.: Harvard University Press, 1958. Includes an essay that explores the themes of identity and self-discovery in *Great Expectations* and traces Pip's development from childhood isolation and alienation to moral descent and eventual transformation through love.

Sadrin, Anny. *"Great Expectations."* Boston: Unwin Hyman, 1988. A comprehensive handbook with good chapters on the composition, historical background, setting, and biographical elements in the story. Presents a psychological interpretation of characters that mainly conforms to standard views while drawing on some critical perspectives and language. Includes an extensive bibliography.

Van Ghent, Dorothy. "On *Great Expectations*." In *The English Novel: Form and Function.* New York: Holt, Rinehart, and Winston, 1953. A groundbreaking essay that studies the themes of guilt and atonement in the context of a dehumanizing society.

THE GREAT GALEOTO

Type of work: Drama
Author: José Echegaray y Eizaguirre (1833-1916)
Type of plot: Social satire
Time of plot: Nineteenth century
Locale: Madrid, Spain
First performed: 1881; first published, 1881 as *El Gran Galeoto* (English translation, 1895)

Principal characters:
DON JULIÁN, a rich Spanish businessman
TEODORA, his young and beautiful wife
ERNESTO, a young dramatist befriended by Don Julián
SEVERO, Don Julián's brother
MERCEDES, Severo's wife

The Story:

Ernesto, a young playwright, was taken into the home of Don Julián, a rich businessman who had been a close friend of Ernesto's father. Ernesto was working on a great play, but he had difficulty in putting down on paper what was in his mind. As he told Don Julián, his play was to include everyone and to reflect the whole world, not simply a part of it, but the laws of the drama made it impossible for him to put down what he wished to say within the space of a play. Don Julián, a practical man, told Ernesto to go get some sleep and be ready to go partridge shooting the next day. After Don Julián left, Ernesto's eye fell on a work by Dante Alighieri. From it he took the title for his play, *The Great Galeoto*, after a character in the love story of Paolo and Francesca.

The following evening Don Julián and his wife Teodora sat watching the sunset. Don Julián told Teodora that he was afraid Ernesto was unhappy because they had done so much for him, that Ernesto felt he owed them much that could never be repaid. Ernesto joined them and in the ensuing conversation readily admitted his belief that he was living on charity and that people were talking about him. Don Julián said the situation could be remedied and suggested that Ernesto become his secretary, thus repaying, in the eyes of the world, what Julián gave him. Ernesto was pleased by the proposal and accepted.

Don Julián left the room. As the sun went down and Teodora and Ernesto continued to talk, Severo, Don Julián's brother, entered with Mercedes, his wife. Severo and Mercedes, speaking to each other, said that the whole city of Madrid was speaking of the affair going on in Don Julián's house between his young wife and the young man he had befriended. After the men left the room, Mercedes told Teodora about the slander that was being voiced in the city. Severo went to pass on the same information to Don Julián.

When Don Julián rejoined his wife, he expressed his anger that Severo should dare to insult his honor and Teodora's by bringing such slander into his home. Don Julián insisted that Ernesto remain in his house as he had before. Ernesto, told of the slander by Severo's son, left Don Julián's fine home to live in a garret. At first Don Julián was glad, thinking that there might have been some truth in the town's gossip. Later he arrived at a different conclusion and went to invite Ernesto to return. While he and his brother waited in Ernesto's garret, Severo's son appeared with word that Ernesto was to fight a duel with the Viscount Nebreda, who had openly aired his malicious gossip in Ernesto's presence at a café.

Don Julián immediately left to find Nebreda to force him to a duel in defense of his own honor. The boy, left behind, was searching the apartment when Ernesto returned. In the angry conversation that followed, Ernesto told the boy that he and all society, with their slanders, were no better than Galeoto, who had been the go-between for Lancelot and Guinevere in their infamous affair, as told in Dante's story of Paolo and Francesca.

After the boy had gone, Teodora came to Ernesto's quarters to see him. She had just learned that Ernesto was leaving Spain the following day and had come to tell him good-bye. Learning of the duel that Ernesto was to fight with Nebreda, she was disturbed that he should possibly humiliate her husband by dueling in his place, when Ernesto was the one, according to gossip, who had laid Don Julián's honor open to question.

While they argued, Severo's son returned to tell them that Don Julián had found Nebreda, fought with him, and had been wounded severely. He added that Don Julián had first returned to Ernesto's quarters to see him, but that a servant had told Don Julián he could not disturb Ernesto, who was with a lady. Severo and a servant appeared, carrying the wounded Don Julián. Teodora hid in the bedroom, but her presence was discovered when Don Julián asked to be placed on the bed.

After a dreadful scene Ernesto rushed out to find the Viscount Nebreda. He discovered him, fought a duel, and killed Nebreda. In the meantime Severo removed the wounded man to his home. After the duel, Ernesto went to Don Julián's house to tell what he had done and to say good-bye to Don Julián and Teodora. Mercedes and her son refused to let him see the sick man. Ernesto told them how Teodora happened to be in his garret and added that she had been trying to prevent the duel between her husband and Nebreda.

After his departure Mercedes brutally questioned Teodora in an effort to make the young woman confess she was in love with Ernesto. She failed, but Teodora promised that Ernesto could never enter the house again. When Ernesto returned, he was ordered to leave, but he agreed to do so only after Teodora had repeated the request. As he was leaving, Severo laid hands on Teodora. Ernesto returned and compelled Severo on his knees to beg Teodora's pardon. He assured Severo that she was innocent of any infidelity.

Don Julián, hearing the commotion, left his sickroom. Infuriated, he slapped Ernesto's face and threatened to kill him in a duel. Severo and Mercedes helped Don Julián, his strength exhausted, back to his room, where he died a few minutes later. Severo, refusing to let Teodora enter her husband's room, claimed the house was his, and after his brother's death he tried to put Teodora out of it because the scandal and shame that gossip had associated with her.

Teodora fainted. Ernesto picked her up and told Severo that he would take her away. He denounced Severo and society, who had forced him and Teodora into scandalous behavior. Society, he insisted, was no better than a pimp, a Galeoto.

Critical Evaluation:

Of the fifty-odd plays by José Echegaray y Eizaguirre, *The Great Galeoto* perhaps has gained a reputation above the others because its prologue claims to be an intellectual discussion of a new dramatic form. The newness does not manifest itself in the play, however, and in the final analysis *The Great Galeoto* is as formulaic as all the Spanish plays of the era.

Spanish drama gets its formula from the Golden Age of Lope de Vega Carpio, Tirso de Molina, and, above all, Pedro Calderón de la Barca. These playwrights in turn took as their criteria for perfect dramaturgy not so much the Greek models as the ideals of their times: honor above life, devotion to the monarchy above self-service, family reputation above expediency. In a world where El Cid can be both praised and damned, where defending one's name includes deadly fights over imagined slights, and where a lady's shame begins even with the appearance of impropriety, the playwright need only set the great moral machine in motion with some misunderstanding, and the machine will run itself into destruction.

Echegaray's particular approach to this formula is to turn on the phrase "he is with a lady." In fact, Ernesto is talking with Teodora, and their discussion is pure. When Teodora's husband discovers her in Ernesto's room, the entire drama would dissipate if Don Julián would simply ask questions and trust Ernesto and Teodora's answers. Echegaray's talent, however, is to suggest that the relationship is not pure in heart—Ernesto and Teodora love each other, without even admitting it to themselves. The underlying passions, held in by self-discipline and by subtle ambiguities, do not come to fruition. Ernesto especially feels that his emotions may not be pure, and he cannot forgive himself or clear his name in good faith because he secretly doubts the purity of his affection for Teodora. When in the final scene Ernesto carries Teodora away, the audience (and all of Madrid) breathe a collective "I told you so."

Another complication, not new with Echegaray, is the greed of the inheriting brother, disguised as moral outrage against Ernesto. With his wife Mercedes at his side, Severo demands that honor be served. His insistence that Don Julián be brought to Severo's home for his last breaths, his fretful wife, and small-minded son, and his knowledge that his own fortunes will be improved considerably if Ernesto is driven from Don Julian's favor, all drive the plot in the direction of tragedy. If Severo realizes his own weakness, he does not choose to admit his motives to those in whose power reputation resides: the people of Madrid.

Madrid is represented, as is usually the case in Spanish drama, by the servant class, whose ability to gossip and exaggerate can be relied on in this genre. The reputation of the household is also in the hands of Pepito, Severo's son, a vicious counterpart to the poetic Ernesto (their names suggest their differences). Finally, the offstage recipient of Don Julián's angry challenges, the Viscount Nebreda, transforms mere rumor into assertion and accusation, thus precipitating the consequences of the plot.

In a way, Madrid is a character is this lachrymose story. Like the town of Fuenteovejuna, in Lope's play of that name, the entire city shares certain characteristics that allow it to be treated as a whole, living, organism. Madrid's "personality" is one that believes in rumor, that becomes excited by the possibility of the fall of a great man, that publicly doubts the "purity" of Ernesto and Teodora but that secretly and privately delights in the possibility.

The list of borrowed, formulaic, or generic elements of this drama must include the jealous husband, the innocent wife in control of her passions because of her purity of mind, and the old ladies of the town, guardians and oracles of the moral codes of the civilization. Also, the language of the play, full of protestations, exaggerated disclaimers, either-or logic, and hyperbolic declarations of all the virtues—love, honor, obedience, innocence, righteousness—echoes the voices of other playwrights in other centuries. The plot follows the Aristotelian rules of action, place, and (with some allowances) time.

In other words, despite Echegaray's announcement in the prologue, *The Great Galeoto* explores no new ground in character, dialogue, or structure. Echegaray, a Nobel laureate, is turning out an excellent product, but tastes have changed since his day. He currently stands as a representative of a dramatic age waiting for the genius of Federico García Lorca.

"Critical Evaluation" by Tom Taylor

Bibliography:
Chandler, Frank W. "The Peninsular Tradition." In *Modern Continental Playwrights.* New

York: Harper & Row, 1931. Shows the passage of tradition from Calderón. Insightful regarding the power of self-examination and self-fulfilling gossip.

Clark, Barnett H., ed. *Masterpieces of Modern Spanish Drama*. New York: Duffield, 1917. A preface on the period, with a review of Spanish drama of the Golden Age. A biography of Echegaray, as a mathematics professor and government minister. Chronological list of his plays.

Hartnoll, Phyllis, ed. *Oxford Companion to the Theatre*. London: Oxford University Press, 1967. Pages 906-907 put Echegaray in the company of other writers of Spanish Romanticism, "essentially an alien growth, nurtured in France and England by the Liberal exiles of the 1820's and brought back to Spain with the return to power of the Liberals in 1835."

Newberry, Wilma. "Echegaray and Pirandello." *PMLA* 81, no. 1 (March, 1966): 123-129. Echegaray, here given credit for philosophical and aesthetic innovations not normally recognized in his work, aspired "to communicate a certain intellectual content in his plays" and dealt with the history of ideas. His plays remain relevant because they dramatize "the position of honesty for its own sake in our modern corrupt society."

Shank, Theodore J., ed. *A Digest of 500 Plays*. New York: Crowell-Collier, 1963. A summary, with staging problems, cast size, and other information helpful to produce the play. Points out the inadvertent humor of taking the play too seriously, but sees as the center of the play "violent situations violently portrayed."

Shaw, Bernard. *Dramatic Opinions and Essays*. Vol. 1. New York: Brentanos, 1925. Contains a discussion of Echegaray's talents in general. Acknowledges Echegaray's indebtedness to Henrik Ibsen.

_____. *Dramatic Opinions and Essays*. Vol. 2. New York: Brentanos, 1925. Argues in a review that Echegaray was "a man who comprehends his world and knows society not as any diner-out or Mayfair butler knows it, but as a capable statesman knows it."

THE GREAT GATSBY

Type of work: Novel
Author: F. Scott Fitzgerald (1896-1940)
Type of plot: Social realism
Time of plot: 1922
Locale: New York City and Long Island
First published: 1925

Principal characters:
NICK CARRAWAY, a young bond salesman
DAISY BUCHANAN, his cousin
TOM BUCHANAN, her husband
MYRTLE WILSON, Tom's mistress
JAY GATSBY, a racketeer of the 1920's

The Story:

Young Nick Carraway decided to forsake the hardware business of his family in the Midwest in order to sell bonds in New York City. He took a small house in West Egg on Long Island and there became involved in the lives of his neighbors. At a dinner party at the home of Tom Buchanan, he renewed his acquaintance with Tom's wife, Daisy, a distant cousin, and he met an attractive young woman, Jordan Baker. Almost at once he learned that Tom and Daisy were not happily married. It appeared that Daisy knew her husband was deliberately unfaithful.

Nick soon learned to despise the drive to the city through unkempt slums; particularly, he hated the ash heaps and the huge commercial signs. He was far more interested in the activities of his wealthy neighbors. Near his house lived Jay Gatsby, a mysterious man of great wealth. Gatsby entertained lavishly, but his past was unknown to his neighbors.

One day, Tom Buchanan took Nick to call on his mistress, a dowdy, plump, married woman named Myrtle Wilson, whose husband, George Wilson, operated a second-rate automobile repair shop. Myrtle, Tom, and Nick went to the apartment that Tom kept, and there the three were joined by Myrtle's sister Catherine and Mr. and Mrs. McKee. The party settled down to an afternoon of drinking, Nick unsuccessfully doing his best to escape.

A few days later, Nick attended another party, one given by Gatsby for a large number of people famous in speakeasy society. Food and liquor were dispensed lavishly. Most of the guests had never seen their host before. At the party, Nick met Gatsby for the first time. Gatsby, in his early thirties, looked like a healthy young roughneck. He was offhand, casual, and eager to entertain his guests as extravagantly as possible. Frequently he was called away by long-distance telephone calls. Some of the guests laughed and said that he was trying to impress them with his importance.

That summer, Gatsby gave many parties. Nick went to all of them, enjoying each time the society of people from all walks of life who appeared to take advantage of Gatsby's bounty. From time to time, Nick met Jordan Baker there and when he heard that she had cheated in an amateur golf match, his interest in her grew.

Gatsby took Nick to lunch one day and introduced him to a man named Wolfshiem, who seemed to be Gatsby's business partner. Wolfshiem hinted at some dubious business deals that betrayed Gatsby's racketeering activities, and Nick began to identify the sources of some of Gatsby's wealth.

Later, Jordan Baker told Nick the strange story of Daisy's wedding. Before the bridal dinner,

Daisy, who seldom drank, became wildly intoxicated and kept reading a letter that she had just received and crying that she had changed her mind. After she had become sober, however, she went through with her wedding to Tom without a murmur. The letter was from Jay Gatsby. At the time, Gatsby was poor and unknown; Tom was rich and influential. Gatsby was still in love with Daisy, however, and he wanted Jordan and Nick to bring Daisy and him together again. It was arranged that Nick should invite Daisy to tea the same day he invited Gatsby. Gatsby awaited the invitation nervously.

On the eventful day, it rained. Determined that Nick's house should be presentable, Gatsby sent a man to mow the wet grass; he also sent flowers for decoration. The tea was a strained affair at first, and both Gatsby and Daisy were shy and awkward in their reunion. Afterward, they went over to Gatsby's mansion, where he showed them his furniture, clothes, swimming pool, and gardens. Daisy promised to attend his next party. When Daisy disapproved of his guests, Gatsby stopped entertaining. The house was shut up and the usual crowd turned away.

Gatsby eventually informed Nick of his origin. His true name was Gatz, and he had been born in the Midwest. His parents were poor. When he was a boy, he had become the protégé of a wealthy old gold miner and had accompanied him on his travels until the old man died. He had changed his name to Gatsby and daydreamed of acquiring wealth and position. In the war, he distinguished himself. After the war, he had returned penniless to the States, too poor to marry Daisy, whom he had met during the war. Later, he became a partner in a drug business. He had been lucky and had accumulated money rapidly. He told Nick that he had acquired the money for his Long Island residence after three years of hard work.

The Buchanans gave a quiet party for Jordan, Gatsby, and Nick. The group drove into the city and took a room in a hotel. The day was hot, and the guests were uncomfortable. On the way, Tom, driving Gatsby's new yellow car, stopped at Wilson's garage. Wilson complained because Tom had not helped him in a projected car deal. He said he needed money because he was selling out and taking his wife, whom he knew to be unfaithful, away from the city.

At the hotel, Tom accused Gatsby of trying to steal his wife and also of being dishonest. He seemed to regard Gatsby's low origin with more disfavor than his interest in Daisy. During the argument, Daisy sided with both men by turns. On the ride back to the suburbs, Gatsby drove his own car, accompanied by Daisy, who temporarily would not speak to her husband.

Following them, Nick, Jordan, and Tom stopped to investigate an accident in front of Wilson's garage. They discovered an ambulance picking up the dead body of Myrtle Wilson, struck by a hit-and-run driver in a yellow car. They tried in vain to help Wilson and then went on to Tom's house, convinced that Gatsby had struck Myrtle Wilson.

Nick learned that night from Gatsby that Daisy had been driving when the woman was hit. Gatsby, however, was willing to take the blame if the death should be traced to his car. He explained that a woman had rushed out as though she wanted to speak to someone in the yellow car and Daisy, an inexpert driver, had run her down and then collapsed. Gatsby had driven on.

In the meantime, George Wilson, having traced the yellow car to Gatsby, appeared on the Gatsby estate. A few hours later, both he and Gatsby were discovered dead. He had shot Gatsby and then killed himself. Nick tried to make Gatsby's funeral respectable, but only one among all of Gatsby's former guests attended along with Gatsby's father, who thought his son had been a great man. None of Gatsby's racketeering associates appeared.

Shortly afterward, Nick learned of Tom's part in Gatsby's death. Wilson had visited Tom and, with the help of a revolver, forced him to reveal the name of the owner of the hit-and-run car. Nick vowed that his friendship with Tom and Daisy was ended. He decided to return to his people in the Midwest.

Critical Evaluation:

Born on September 24, 1896, in St. Paul, Minnesota, to the daughter of a self-made Irish immigrant and an unsuccessful furniture salesmen, F. Scott Fitzgerald was indoctrinated early with a belief in the American dream. Later he was to pursue it with a ferocity that would take a devastating toll upon his life.

Published in 1925, Fitzgerald's *The Great Gatsby* was to become his definitive work. In 1922, Fitzgerald declared, "I want to write something new—something extraordinary and beautiful and simple and intricately patterned." With the publication of *The Great Gatsby* he achieved just that. Set in America's Jazz Age, Fitzgerald creates a world of money, power, corruption, and murder.

Critics often assert that *The Great Gatsby* is a uniquely American novel that depicts American characters and themes. Indeed, Gatsby is the archetypal American character; he is self-made. A man who literally invents or reinvents himself. He believes in the American dream "in the green light, the orgiastic future." He believes that, in America, one can become anything. Like a young Benjamin Franklin, he maps out his resolves for future success and never wavers from his teenage conception of self. A seventeen-year-old James Gatz invents Jay Gatsby, and it is to this vision that he remains true. Ultimately, it is this vision that betrays him.

Gatsby represents the world of the ostentatious newly rich; however, he remains a romantic idealist. Right from the beginning, the reader learns of Gatsby's "extraordinary gift for hope [and] a romantic readiness" which Nick has never before witnessed in another human being. He is a paradox; the innocent bootlegger.

Nick Carraway, the narrator, is an idealistic Midwestern salesman of stocks and bonds, trying to make a go of it on Wall Street. The entire story is filtered through Nick and his vision of Gatsby. It is significant that Fitzgerald chooses to write *The Great Gatsby* in the past tense; indeed, the story is relayed entirely through memory which is, of course, selective. The lines between truth and fiction are blurred, and, essentially, the reader must become a participant within the text; he or she must separate the lies from the truth in order to glean the true meaning. Illusion versus reality is a central theme throughout the novel.

Without a "past," Gatsby himself becomes a "text" to be written, revised, and rewritten with each new "reader." He reflects the fears, fantasies, and desires of his audience, "Somebody told me they thought he killed a man once." Gatsby is a metaphor for the American experience; he is the product of a country without a past.

It is the past that Gatsby struggles to reinvent and reclaim. When Nick Carraway suggests that "you can't repeat the past." Gatsby maintains, "Why of course you can!" He remains unchanged, an innocent within a corrupt, disillusioned world. He fails to realize that the past is gone. In the end, it is this romantic idealism which destroys Gatsby; he refuses to relinquish the illusion that has propelled his life.

On one level, *The Great Gatsby* is about money: old, established wealth versus new currency. Gatsby can never hope to obtain Daisy because he doesn't have the "right" kind of money. *The Great Gatsby* is Fitzgerald's indictment of the American dream. For Nick, Gatsby's death represents the debasement of the dream. On another level, it employs American mythology based upon East and West. The East epitomizes the sophisticated realm of established wealth and privilege, while the West is the new frontier, the place of the pioneer without a past or identity. Nick becomes disillusioned with the East and returns to the Midwest, "the warm, center of the world."

Fitzgerald clearly delineates class difference through his employment of setting. The valley of ashes is "nowhere," a place to be driven through on the way to the "somewhere" by characters from both East and West Egg. It is here that Myrtle Wilson is "run down like a dog" by Daisy Buchanan.

Careless drivers become a metaphor for the demoralized world of wealth and privilege inhabited by people like the Buchanans. Early on, Nick accuses Jordan of being a "rotten driver," two drunks get into an accident at one of Gatsby's parties, and, finally, Daisy kills Myrtle with an automobile and leaves the scene of the crime.

Though *The Great Gatsby* is obviously a product of a post-World War I era, the novel still retains thematic significance. *the Great Gatsby* might be interpreted as a warning not only to Fitzgerald's generation but to future generations as well. Beware of pursuing that "orgiastic future" with too much fervor, one might well be destroyed by it just as Gatsby was.

"Critical Evaluation" by Angela D. Hickey

Bibliography:
Brucoli, Matthew J. *Some Sort of Epic Grandeur: The Life of F. Scott Fitzgerald.* New York: Carroll & Graf, 1993. Commonly regarded as the definitive Fitzgerald biography. Shows how the author became a kind of romantic archetype of the intoxicated, tragic genius. Includes an afterword by Scottie Fitzgerald Smith. See especially the section on *The Great Gatsby* entitled "Early Success, 1920-1925."
Bryer, Jackson R., ed. *"The Great Gatsby* (1925)." In *F. Scott Fitzgerald: The Critical Reception.* New York: Burt Franklin, 1978. Provides an extensive, representative sampling of *The Great Gatsby*'s critical reception and shows how most critics did not recognize the novel's remarkable mythic and symbolic dimensions.
Eble, Kenneth. *F. Scott Fitzgerald.* Rev. ed. Boston: Twayne, 1977. The section on *The Great Gatsby* traces the novel's literary genesis, explores the sources and consequences of Fitzgerald's provincial moral posture, and discusses the use of structure, mood, and action in the development of Gatsby's romantic vision.
Lockridge, Ernest, ed. *Twentieth Century Interpretations of "The Great Gatsby": A Collection of Critical Essays.* Englewood Cliffs, N.J.: Prentice-Hall, 1968. An impressive collection of critical interpretations and viewpoints on the novel. Includes commentary by Edith Wharton, Conrad Aiken, Lionel Trilling, Maxwell Perkins, and Fitzgerald himself.
Stern, Milton R. *The Golden Moment: The Novels of F. Scott Fitzgerald.* Urbana: University of Illinois Press, 1971. A very readable and fascinating analysis. The section on *The Great Gatsby* focuses on the biographical and mythical aspects of Fitzgerald's adolescent moral perspective.

THE GREAT TESTAMENT

Type of work: Poetry
Author: François Villon (1431-1463?)
First published: La Grand Testament, 1489 (English translation, 1878)

François Villon was a poet of the first order. In his themes and poetic forms, his poetry is characteristically medieval, although many critics consider that the personal element in his poetry gives it a timeless quality. In *The Great Testament,* Villon's art reaches its full maturity. His mastery of conventional medieval versification is evident in the use of complex rhyme schemes and verse forms that include the ballade, the rondeau, and the octave (an eight-line stanza). Octaves form the central body of the poem. The ballade, which demands considerable skill in the use of both rhyme and meter, consists of eight to ten lines grouped into three stanzas, each ending with a refrain and followed by a closing stanza (an envoy) of four to seven lines that concludes with the same refrain. Most of Villon's ballades contain twenty-eight lines, and he uses the same three rhymes in the ballades and the octaves.

In structure, *The Great Testament* follows the plan of a testamentary will of the period. A brief preamble is followed by a declaration of the poet's mental and physical state, a statement of his religious faith, the details of how his property is to be distributed to friends, relatives, acquaintances, and even strangers, and instructions as to how and where he is to be buried. This formal device establishes the framework, within which Villon provides a rich body of material interspersed with frequent displays of technical virtuosity.

Villon ranges through a wide variety of moods and subjects without losing the thread of his discourse or the personal focus of his poem. Whatever the subject under discussion, whether harlot, prelate, or profligate, the reader never loses sight of the poem's central figure, the poet himself, who refers throughout the poem to his own poverty, premature aging, and skirmishes with the law. Much of what is known of Villon's life, in fact, is taken from these personal references. His poem evokes pity because he is a self-confessed sinner, and because he is remorseful and presently suffering the consequences of his former follies. His subject is also universal because he is preoccupied with death throughout the poem. When he is most intensely personal, his appeal is most intense, touching the feelings and sentiments of readers across language barriers and across the ages.

Throughout the poem, a playful, mocking spirit mingles with serious reflection, self-pity, remorse, crude jokes, jibes, and satirical attacks on civil servants, figures of authority, and the clergy. There is also a shift from one subject to another, and the shift is sometimes abrupt. The poet's mood is always mercurial, but the poem's unity is sustained by the poet's ever-present voice and his continual references to himself. In the poem, for example, he offers a justification for his criminal activities by relating a story from antiquity in which a pirate explains to Alexander the Great that bad luck, not his own nature, has made him a thief, whereupon Alexander improves the thief's fortune, and the man is reformed. Villon sees reflected in this tale his own ill-spent life, and he regrets not having an Alexander of his own to help him reform.

Transitions in mood and subject can be seen in the way Villon follows this tale with references to his lost youth and his current poverty, the result, in part, of too little studying and too much pleasure-seeking. A sense of loss runs through the poem, with allusions to great lords and masters, beggars and mendicants; this sense of loss culminates in the ballade whose poignant refrain, "Where are the snows of yesteryear?" is both particular and also universal. Two ballades which follow this one continue the theme of the uncertainty of fortune and the brevity of life, both subjects often found in medieval literature. In one of the ballades, Villon lists the names of famous rulers who have been carried away by "the wind"—time, death. The fate of these rulers, he continues, serves as a reminder that the exalted and the powerful and those who have "stuffed their faces well" die. His thoughts turn to the plight of women who lose their former beauty to old age. Another ballade portrays these creatures as nothing more than devalued coins.

The thought of female beauty shifts the poet's attention to the dangers of loving women, for he thinks that they prefer many men to one, and his personal experience with a certain woman is painful proof of this. His ill-treatment at the hands of other people is enlarged to include the Bishop of Orleans, who is responsible for much of his suffering.

Wishing, he says, ironically, to speak to defame no one, the poet returns to his main business, the writing of his will. He commences with a serious ballade, bequeathed to his mother, in which he again declares his religious faith. This section of the poem, including the ballade, returns to one of the poem's major themes, the poet's relationship with women. At the same time, the tone shifts from the seriousness of Villon's reference to his "poor mother" to the jocular and to the bawdy. In high spirits, he achieves one of the more impressive technical feats in the poem, a ballade to love in which he not only ends each line with the letter *r*, but also forms an acrostic of the names Francois and Marthe in the first two stanzas (the acrostic of "Villon" is included in the envoy of the previous ballade). The subject of love continues to inspire his technical skills—and his sarcastic playfulness—as he bequeaths to an acquaintance a "lay" (actually, a rondeau), in which he complains that death has deprived him of his beloved.

The mood becomes harsher and the subjects coarser as Villon continues to dispose of his earthly belongings, real or imaginary. He gives to the wife of a wealthy official a "red ass," he gives wine to someone else, and to others he gives a cheese tart, dice, and a deck of cards. Each item reflects Villon's feelings of respect or disrespect. The emphasis on food in the bequests— cloves, hams, and milk, for example—befits the portrait of Villon as a poor, starving sinner making peace with the world, and the emphasis sustains the poem's principal undercurrent, the poet's pathetic condition. At the same time, many of these items have been given a symbolic meaning that pokes fun at the legatees. The more degraded the bequest, the greater the insult, playful or not. In his bequest to the Keeper of the Seals, Villon turns hostile and ironic, and he gives the "worthy man" an official seal that has been "spat upon."

Perhaps thinking of his own upbringing, the poet expresses a fatherly regard for "his" three orphans—they are to be well schooled, taught manners, and not harshly punished. The poet's thoughts continue to run in the direction of family as he offers to a newlywed a ballade on the subject of procreation, graciously including an acrostic of the bride's name. This graceful ballade is counterpointed by a ballade on "spiteful tongues," which are to be fried in the most repugnant things imaginable, among them feces, blood, ulcers, and sores. In a later ballade, the poet argues that it is better to live at one's ease than like the fat canon who gorges himself on food and lives sumptuously with "a naked woman." In another ballade, he praises the ability of Parisian women to speak well. After bequeathing a nearby hill to Montmartre, he is reminded of the chambermaids and the other women of Paris, including Fat Margot, to whom he offers a ballade celebrating the events in a brothel.

In the bequests that follow, Villon returns again to the pleasures to be found where women, food, and drink are plentiful; however, he remains preoccupied with death. He reminds his "comrades in pleasure" that one day they will all die. A ballade emphasizes his point that everything one has will go to the taverns and the girls. Those in power will one day be heaped together in death, which levels everyone, high and low alike. Thinking of his own death, the poet offers a song in which he speaks of returning from prison, and he asks whether Fortune is right or wrong if she bears him ill will.

Turning to the disposition of his remains, the poet directs that he be buried in Saint Avoye. The mood, again, is not entirely serious, for the name refers to a convent of nuns, and, there is a play on the word *avoier*, which means "to put on the right road." The rondeau that follows these lines contains the words that the poet wishes to be written and to be spoken over his grave. The words are a plea for eternal rest, and the tone remains playful, thereby undercutting the sincerity of Villon's final peacemaking gesture, expressed in one of the poem's final ballades; the ballade contains a roll call of the people from whom the poet asks for a pardon. These are, for the most part, people from the poet's world of the brothel, the jail, and the tavern. He excludes from this group those who have caused him suffering; instead, he wishes them harsh punishment. The final ballade dwells on his difficulties with love. He dies a martyr to it, having been an active participant in love's battles. His final gesture of raising a glass of dark red wine can be seen as a gesture of defiance or as a salute to the final victor, love.

The fact that Villon disappeared from historical view soon after composing *The Great Testament* may color the reading of it. Whether or not Villon was actually on the verge of dying while composing the poem will probably never be known. The references to his suffering, ill-spent youth, troubles with the law, and periods of imprisonment, take on greater poignancy if the reader believes that they reflect the poet's actual condition. *The Great Testament* gains in emotional power and significance if the reader believes it expresses the thoughts of a poet who is about to die.

The Great Testament may be considered from several perspectives: as a lyric poem of considerable power; as a mock will which the poet offers with both irony and sincerity to his audience; and/or as a masterful display of technical virtuosity in a variety of verse forms. Villon combines all of these strains into a poem that is serious, mocking, rebellious, ribald, self-pitying, sardonic, accusatory, and, for many, unforgettable.

Bernard E. Morris

Bibliography:
Fein, David A. *François Villon and His Reader*. Detroit, Mich.: Wayne State University Press, 1989. Approaches *The Great Testament* as a reader-oriented work, and seeks to identify the work's original audience and to compare that audience with later audiences. Focuses on those aspects of *The Great Testament* that call for reader interaction.
Peckham, Robert D. *François Villon: A Bibliography*. New York: Garland, 1990. A thorough listing of the manuscripts of Villon's poetry from as early as 1489; identifies those editions that offer the best, most detailed, and complete commentaries on Villon's poetry, including works that examine specific lines.
Villon, François. *Complete Poems of François Villon*. Translated by Beram Saklatvala. New York: E. P. Dutton, 1968. Attempts to render Villon's poetry in rhyme and meter. Saklatvala gives a literal, line-by-line translation of the French, following Villon's rhyme schemes and even using true and slant rhymes when Villon does. Also provides a useful introduction and explanatory index by John Fox.
_____. *François Villon: Complete Poems*. Edited and translated by Barbara N. Sargent-Baur. Toronto: University of Toronto Press, 1994. Original French text alongside the translation, which employs unrhymed stanzas. Provides variant readings of the original text at the bottom of each page. Excellent commentary, as well as extensive notes that not only

explain Villon's meanings and allusions but connect lines and passages to other critical studies.

_____. *The Poems of François Villon*. Translated by Galway Kinnell. Boston: Houghton Mifflin, 1977. The original text alongside Kinnell's translation. Includes textual notes and a critical introduction. Bibliography lists editions, translations, and critical studies of Villon's poetry.

THE GREEK PASSION

Type of work: Novel
Author: Nikos Kazantzakis (1883-1957)
Type of plot: Allegory
Time of plot: c. 1920
Locale: Lycovrissi, Anatolia
First published: Ho Christos xanastauronetai, 1954 (English translation, 1953)

> *Principal characters:*
> PRIEST GRIGORIS,
> ARCHON PATRIARCHEAS,
> OLD LADAS,
> CAPTAIN FORTOUNAS, and
> HADJI NIKOLIS, the elders of Lycovrissi
> MANOLIOS, the shepherd chosen to portray Christ in the Passion Play
> YANNAKOS, the merchant-peddler chosen to portray the Apostle Peter
> MICHELIS, the archon's son, portraying the Apostle John, betrothed to
>   Mariori
> MARIORI, the daughter of Priest Grigoris
> KOSTANDIS, an innkeeper, portraying the Apostle James
> PANAYOTAROS, nicknamed "Plaster-eater," portraying Judas
> KATERINA, a widow, portraying Mary Magdalene
> THE AGHA, Lord of Lycovrissi, living for the pleasures of raki and pretty
>   boys
> YOUSSOUFAKI, a dimpled, pretty boy
> LENIO, the handsome, rosy love child of old Patriarcheas
> FOTIS, a priest and the leader of a refugee band

The Story:

On Easter Tuesday of an unspecified year, apparently close to 1920, the Greek elders of Lycovrissi gathered to select the principals of the Passion Play that was given every seven years, at Easter time, under the portico of the church. Lycovrissi was a remote village in the mountains of Anatolia. Its poor, illiterate, superstitious peasants, although they had dim memories of the greatness of their Hellenic past, had lived under harsh Turkish rule for centuries.

Only two men in the town knew anything about the outside world. One was Captain Fortounas, a drunken old sailor retired from his rough seafaring life. The other was the Turkish agha, overlord of the village, a gross, sensual man who spent his days drinking raki and his nights amusing himself with pretty boys.

The elders revealed themselves as an avaricious, corrupt lot as they discussed possible candidates for the Passion Play. Eventually Manolios, a handsome young shepherd betrothed to the archon's illegitimate daughter, Lenio, was selected as the Christ; Michelis, the archon's son, as John; Yannakos, a rascally peddler, as Peter; Kostandis, the innkeeper, as James; Panayotaros, a red-bearded, sly man nicknamed "Plaster-eater," as Judas; and the widow Katerina, a woman of warm heart and easy virtue, as Mary Magdalene. The principals had to be selected a year in advance so that they could prepare themselves for the responsibilities of their roles in reenacting the story of the Passion and the Crucifixion.

On the same day, a party of miserable refugees arrived in the village. Driven from their homes by their Turkish masters, they were sick and starving after their long search for a place where they might settle. One ancient man carried the bones of his ancestors on his back. Their leader was an ascetic priest named Fotis, who asked for food for his people and land on which they might build their homes. Many of the villagers were sympathetic, but Priest Grigoris, a selfish, domineering man, wanted no religious rival in the neighborhood. Unfeelingly, he ordered the refugees to move on. When one woman collapsed and died from hunger, he shouted that she had died of cholera in his efforts to arouse the credulous villagers against the refugees.

Manolios, already feeling himself to be a changed man because he was chosen to suffer the five wounds and the burden of the cross, persuaded Michelis, Yannakos, and others to help the distressed people. Fotis' band was allowed to take refuge in the caves on the summit of Mount Sarakina nearby. Grigoris was enraged when Manolios and Michelis took from the archon's cellar four baskets filled with food to feed the famished women and children. Michelis was betrothed to Grigoris' daughter Mariori, so Grigoris claimed that the gift was actually a theft of goods that partly belonged to him.

Manolios withdrew to his mountain hut to battle with his weaknesses of the flesh, for he felt that if he was to act the part of Christ, he must struggle to become Christlike. Much to her distress, he denied Lenio. When his face broke out in strange sores, he believed that God was punishing him because his dreams at night were filled with visions of Katerina. Disappointed in her wedding plans, Lenio gave herself to Nikolio, a lusty young pagan who was Manolios' assistant in herding the archon's flocks.

As the summer passed, the other characters in the Passion Play also changed and began to act more in accordance with their roles in the biblical story. Michelis gave up Mariori, defied his father, and eventually went off to live with Manolios in his retreat. Yannakos foiled the scheme of Ladas, an elder and the village miser, to cheat the refugees of the few valuables they had left. Kostandis gave them alms. Katerina no longer opened her door to her midnight callers. Panayotaros, eaten by jealousy, planned to revenge himself on Manolios, whom he blamed for the widow's newfound virtue.

One morning, the agha's favorite young boy, Youssoufaki, was found dead in his bed. Wild with rage and grief, the agha arrested the village elders and threatened to hang one man each day until the murderer was discovered. As a result of a strange dream he had, Manolios believed that he must offer himself as a sacrifice, and he confessed to the slaying. When another jealous servant of the agha's household was revealed as the killer, the people of Lycovrissi showed no gratitude to the shepherd for his offer to die to save other innocent people. He further infuriated Grigoris when he tried to preach a sermon on charity and compassion at the Feast of St. Elijah.

As winter drew on, the plight of Fotis and his band grew more desperate. Manolios, who had been carving the wooden mask of a gentle Christ, carved a new mask of savagery: not the kind, compassionate Christ, but a warrior who came to bring, not peace, but a sword. It was as a Christ of burning and destruction that Manolios led the refugees in a raid on Lycovrissi on Christmas Eve. Panayotaros, however, had already played the part of Judas, and the attack failed. Grigoris became Caiaphas, and the agha Pontius Pilate, to Manolios' Christ. The shepherd died of his wounds. Fotis and his band began their wanderings once more.

Critical Evaluation:

Two world figures as dissimilar as Thomas Mann and Albert Schweitzer spoke up in public praise of Nikos Kazantzakis, the Greek novelist introduced to U.S. readers by *Zorba the Greek* in 1953. One wonders, however, whether their admiration sprang from his earlier picaresque novel, the lively account of a pantheistic and pagan spirit adrift in the modern world, or from the quite different story of savage emotions and primitive religious feeling that he told in *The Greek Passion*, which was also published in 1954 as *Christ Recrucified*. These two novels make it clear that Kazantzakis is capable of widely varied effects in his fiction, although each creates a haunting, poetic atmosphere and a depth of serious insight into human necessities and motives.

After Greece was liberated from the Turks in 1919, Kazantzakis was appointed director general of the ministry of public welfare. His task was to rescue the Greek minorities of the Caucasus and Transcaucasus from persecution by Kurds and Bolsheviks, who replaced Turks in massacring Greeks. During one year of his tenure, Kazantzakis rescued more than 100,000 Greeks. This experience provided material for *The Greek Passion*. Between 1942 and 1951, he was absorbed with Jesus as a literary subject. *The Greek Passion* was written in two months in 1948.

The story is simple and traditional. One who knows the New Testament can follow the plot easily. On the level of symbolism, Kazantzakis has kept fairly close to the spirit, if not the actual events, of the New Testament story. His one great departure is the scene of violence that gives the novel its grim climax. Perhaps the author is implying that in a disordered world, there is no place for a Christ of compassion and love.

The Passion Play is one of the most colorful and spiritually uplifting events of each year in Lycovrissi. Before, during, and after the Passion Play, there is always mass catharsis. Many miracles take place and many sinners repent. The selection process is straightforward. The characters of the biblical personages usually match those of the respective actors. The widow Katerina, a kindhearted prostitute, plays the role of Mary Magdalene. Panayotaros, a bearded, gorilla-like man spotted from smallpox, is selected to play Judas. Manolios, the handsome shepherd, is chosen to play Christ.

Dreams play a vital role in *The Greek Passion*, as they do in most of Kazantzakis' major works. Fantasy, dream, and reality become interchangeable. Christianity as an elaborate dream-motif runs throughout the novel. Reality and dream become fluid.

The little boy Youssoufaki sings the agha's favorite "Amane," a melancholy song. He sings, "World and dream are but one, *aman, aman.*" Agha, bloated by rich Oriental food and raki, secure in his inherited position, surrounded by servants and pretty boys, has difficulty distinguishing "dream" from "world." The agonizing truth about his beloved Youssoufaki, who was butchered in his bed, gives him but a glimmer of a nightmare, the agonizing vision of reality.

Once the suffering is over, the agha goes back to the good dream again. Phrases such as "It is written" or "It is willed" fill the air like the smoke of opium, giving the world a hazy, impressionist quality. When the actor who is to play Christ falsely confesses that the devil urged him to murder Youssoufaki, the agha knows the shepherd is innocent but follows the dreamlike rituals and hands the actor over to the crucifiers.

The notion of dream-world fluidity and interchangeability is demonstrated by most of the novel's characters. The quintessential example of this phenomenon is Manolios. He matches the role well, because, it is said, he suffers from a paranoid inability to distinguish between hallucination and reality. Perhaps that is why he is one of the most intense and endearing characters in this novel. The dynamism of the story begins to show itself when Manolios decides to purify himself by remaining chaste, leaving behind his fiancée, rejecting all the sensuality of life. The Manolios who leads the attack on the village is no longer the meek shepherd he was at the beginning of the novel. Yet the change has been accounted for in the visions that came to him in his solitary retreat. In a dream, he had seen Christ descending the mountain, his sad, angry face turned toward Lycovrissi, and carrying a can of petrol instead of a cross.

Kazantzakis pays close attention to Manolios' obsessions, mental predicaments, and other traits. Manolios was brought up with the monks from early childhood, and his teachers recalled that he was "a wee bit crazy." Since early childhood, he has wanted this role in the Passion Play. His destiny is finally fulfilled. Kazantzakis here examines the psyche of a person wanting to become a Christ. Having gone through similar experiences, he was interested in the process of transformation from a mere man to a Christlike figure.

Twenty years before Kazantzakis wrote *The Greek Passion*, he broke out with a strange affliction. His face puffed up, his swollen lips drooped, oozing yellowish fluid. No physician could diagnose it. One of Freud's great prodigies, Wilhelm Stekel, examined Kazantzakis and told him that his affliction resulted from sex-related guilt feelings. Manolios' face was similarly afflicted with disfiguring pustules, because he felt miserably guilty about dreaming of Katerina, the kindhearted prostitute.

The novel concerns the hero's four transformations. The first is his acceptance of the role and the beginning of piety and chastity. In this period, he simply wants to be worthy of the role. The second transformation begins when, despite his efforts, he still dreams about the prostitute. Because of this lapse, his face is swollen and disfigured. This transformation occurs when Manolios decides to give his life and be a martyr.

The third transformation occurs when he realizes that Christ, who appears in his dreams every night, no longer carries a cross. Instead, he carries guns and a can of gasoline. The new Christ preaches revolution. The last transformation occurs when Manolios realizes that any injustice has to be met with force. Thus, he leads Father Fotis' refugee band in the raid.

The first two transformations are spiritual. The later two are sociopolitical. All, in one way or another, parallel Kazantzakis' own intellectual and spiritual journey.

Manolios knows about the injustice in Lycovrissi. The town is full of people who devote their lives to the senses. The novel details the lives of these licentious and gluttonous people—the agha, Priest Grigoris, Captain Fortunas, and others. Kazantzakis presents these Turkish and Greek men as brothers-in-pleasure. Just as the historic Christ lost his battle with the Pharisees and the scribes, the actor-Christ struggles for power but loses it to Father Grigoris, who represents the institutional church. Kazantzakis ensures that the underdogs of any religious group, Islam or Christian, always lose to the malevolent church hierarchy.

Kazantzakis struggles to discover the primitive Christian values of love, brotherhood, humility, and self-abnegation. He painstakingly points out these missing qualities in the church of his day. Whether he is advocating reformation or renouncing the church altogether is not clear. What is clear is that he believes that Christianity has lost its original purpose and is no longer Christ's church.

Kazantzakis melded together the old and new, sacred and profane, mythology and theology. He imbued Manolios with a primitive martyr's passion, seeking Christianity side by side with his Marxist revolutionary desires. He was aware of man's power of myth-making and self-delusion. Mircea Iliade's *Sacred and the Profane* (1959) and Rudolf Otto's *The Idea of the Holy* (1950) point out this urge to divide the world into neat, manageable theological-mythological parts. Kazantzakis demonstrated that humankind would give its all for the illusion of certitude.

"Critical Evaluation" by Chogollah Maroufi

Bibliography:
Bien, Peter. *Nicos Kazantzakis, Novelist.* Bristol, England: Bristol Classical Press, 1989. Gives personal and philosophical background for Kazantzakis' novels. Helpful for tracing the historical and social motivations for most of his works, including *The Greek Passion.*
Dombrowski, Daniel. "Kazantzakis and the New Middle Ages." *Religion & Literature* 26, no. 3 (Fall, 1994): 19-32. Helpful background on Kazantzakis' basic sources and the motivations for creating his elaborately rich novels and characterizations. Describes his varied interests and studies to explain his ability to create an epic such as *The Greek Passion,* with more than forty diverse and colorful characters.
Levitt, Morton. *The Cretan Glance: The World and Art of Nikos Kazantzakis.* Columbus: Ohio State University Press, 1980. One chapter explains the historical, social, and political contexts for the novel. Describes Kazantzakis' own history as it relates to the creation of many characters. Identifies the locations where he worked as minister of public welfare.
_____. "Homer, Joyce, Kazantzakis: Modernism and the Epic Tradition." *Journal of the Hellenic Diaspora* 10, no. 4 (Winter, 1983): 41-45. A thorough comparison of the works of Homer, James Joyce, and Kazantzakis. Shows many of the subtleties of Kazantzakis' works, and his indebtedness to both the modern and ancient authors.
Raizis, M. Byron. "Symbolism and Meaning in Kazantzakis' *The Greek Passion.*" *Ball State University Forum* 11, no. 3 (Summer, 1970): 57-66. Clear, thorough analysis of the varied symbols and motifs found in the novel from both Christian and ancient Greek mythological perspectives.

GREEN GROW THE LILACS

Type of work: Drama
Author: Lynn Riggs (1899-1954)
Type of plot: Regional
Time of plot: 1900
Locale: Indian Territory (later Oklahoma)
First performed: 1931; first published, 1931

Principal characters:

CURLY McCLAIN, a cowboy
LAUREY WILLIAMS, a young farm owner
AUNT ELLER MURPHY, an elderly homesteader
JEETER FRY, a hired man
ADO ANNIE CARNES, Laurey's friend
A PEDDLER
OLD MAN PECK, a neighbor
CORD ELAM, another neighbor

The Story:

Curly McClain, a tall, curly-haired young cowboy, called at the home of Laurey Williams and Aunt Eller Murphy to ask if Laurey would go with him to a play-party at Old Man Peck's. Laurey, pretending indifference and even scorn for Curly, turned down the invitation and went back to her bedroom, reappearing later to say that she was going to the party but that Jeeter Fry, her hired man, was taking her. At first angry, Curly sat down at the small organ in the living-room and played and sang the old song "Green Grow the Lilacs," which tells of a rejected lover. Then, quickly recovered from Laurey's rebuff, he asked Aunt Eller to go to the party with him in his hired fringe-top surrey. He left, saying he would pay a little call at the smokehouse where Jeeter lived.

In Laurey's bedroom, a little later, Aunt Eller announced that she was going to the party with Curly. Laurey showed no great interest. Instead, musing on how much she loved her place, she confided her fear that Jeeter might sometime burn it down. This fear of him was what made her accept his attentions and go to parties with him. Aunt Eller belittled her fears.

Ado Annie Carnes arrived with a peddler, from whom Laurey bought for Ado Annie a pair of garters and some liquid powder to hide her freckles. They were startled when they heard a shot from the direction of the smokehouse, and then another.

Meanwhile, before and during a card game in the gloom and dirt of the smokehouse, Curly had learned that Jeeter's mind was obsessed by two things: lurid crime, which he liked to read about, and sex, which dominated his thinking and his talk much of the time. As they played cards, Jeeter's two pistols lay on the table. Curly's persistent needling of him about his dirty, dark thoughts and his filthy personal habits so angered Jeeter that he suddenly picked up one pistol and fired at random, splintering the opposite wall. Curly picked up the other pistol and fired neatly through a knothole. Aunt Eller, Laurey, Ado Annie, and the peddler, hurrying in to learn what the shooting was about, were relieved to learn that no harm had been done. After the women left, the peddler remained to bring forth his wares of special interest to men. He praised the efficiency of a long-bladed knife for Jeeter. Curly considered the possible advantage of buying a pair of brass knuckles—just in case.

At Old Man Peck's the party was already in progress when Aunt Eller arrived with Curly, followed a little later by Laurey, Ado Annie, and Jeeter, who complained to Laurey because she had invited Ado Annie to go with them. Keeping Laurey from entering the house, he asked why she tried so hard to keep from being alone with him. When, tormented by desire, he caught Laurey, she slapped him hard, then told him that he was no longer her hired hand and that he was to leave her place forever. He slunk away with a dark look. Laurey asked Ado Annie, who had come back to complain about her tight garters, to send Curly out.

When Laurey was finally able to tell Curly her fear of Jeeter, he promised to get her a new hired hand, suddenly asked her to marry him, and as quickly found himself accepted. Jokingly, he asked if she would give him, a penniless cowboy, a new saddle blanket for a wedding present.

When the party crowd came out on the porch, they joked about the two lovebirds. Jeeter, a bottle in his hand, looked broodingly at Laurey and Curly, started to drink a mocking toast to them, and then hurled the bottle across the yard, where it crashed. The crowd, keeping Curly and Jeeter apart, began to sing "Skip to My Lou."

One evening, a month later, Laurey and Curly stole quietly across a hayfield toward the Williams house. They were whispering that they had given the crowd the slip after going to town and getting married. They headed for the house, followed, unknown to them, by a group of men bent on shivareeing the new couple. Their rude jokes were interrupted when Curly, angry and with his shirt ripped, was dragged from the house by several men. Laurey in her nightgown, frightened and ashamed, followed, surrounded by a wide circle of other men. To the accompaniment of bawdy taunts, Curly and Laurey were made to climb the ladder of a tall haystack; then the ladder was thrown down.

Suddenly, amid the obscene jesting, there was the cry of "Fire!" and Jeeter came up with a flaming torch. As he sprang to light the stack, Curly leaped down and knocked the torch from his hand. The fire was quickly doused, but the drunken Jeeter, his knife out, attacked Curly. In the struggle Jeeter tripped, fell on his knife, and lay still. Cord Elam suggested that Curly go and explain the fight to the law.

A few nights later Aunt Eller and Ado Annie sat in the Williams living-room wondering when Curly would be let out of the Claremore jail. Laurey, coming from her room looking pale and much older, spoke of her fears for Curly, the shock of hearing the bawdy things the men had said at the shivaree, and the troubles that life brings people. Aunt Eller, citing many troubles, explained that one simply had to have the strength to endure such things. The lesson sank in, and Laurey apologized for being such a baby.

The dog Shep began barking outside, then suddenly stopped. A moment later Curly came in; he had broken out of jail the night before his trial in order to see Laurey. His pursuers would be after him in a little while, he said, but he had to know that she would wait for him, whatever might happen at the trial. When they let him free he would forget herding cows and learn to farm Laurey's beautiful acres.

Old Man Peck and several other deputies arrived to return Curly to jail, but Aunt Eller refused to let them have him before morning. When the others showed sympathy for Curly and Laurey, who had still not had their wedding night, Peck agreed, promising to return bright and early in the morning. Not too early, said Aunt Eller. From the bedroom came Curly's voice singing "Green Grow the Lilacs."

Critical Evaluation:

The great success and popularity of *Oklahoma!* (1943) has probably obscured the quality of the play upon which it is based, Lynn Riggs's *Green Grow the Lilacs*. Without slighting the creative and musical abilities of either Richard Rodgers or Oscar Hammerstein II, it is only fair to state that *Oklahoma!*, in essence, is *Green Grow the Lilacs*; the color, vitality, charm, and even many of the musical ideas are present in the original, as Hammerstein himself was the first to admit in the *New York Times* (September 5, 1943): "Mr. Riggs's play is the wellspring of almost all that is good in *Oklahoma!* . . . Lynn Riggs and *Green Grow the Lilacs* are the very soul of *Oklahoma!*"

While *Oklahoma!* made fortunes for most of those connected with the production, Riggs, a U.S. Army draftee at the time, collected a royalty of $250 per week. That fact is perhaps symbolic of Riggs's whole career. From his first play, *Knives from Syria* (1925), to his last, *Toward the Western Sky* (1951), Riggs was a prolific playwright who spent a lifetime on the brink of success in New York theater. Riggs was never able to establish himself as a Broadway playwright. Out of the twenty-seven plays he authored during his lifetime, only four were ever produced on Broadway, and of those, only two, *Green Grow the Lilacs* and *Russet Mantle* (1936), could be called even modest commercial successes. One of the final ironies of Riggs's career is that this authentic regional artist did his most profitable work in Hollywood, that most artificial of American environments, writing forgettable screenplays.

Green Grow the Lilacs is a kind of rollicking, larger-than-life folktale with some serious undertones. From Curly's singing entrance to the final curtain, the play moves with unflagging zest and color, punctuated by much music and dancing, extravagant gestures and speeches, and rowdy humor, with occasional moments of suspense and violence. The plot is simple and functional: boy meets girl, overcomes rival, defies the law for the sake of love, and wins out. The characters are broad and simple, but also quite energetic and colorful. Curly McClain is the cowboy braggart, a staple type in frontier humor, who is intelligent and sensitive beneath the braggadocio. Laurey Williams is the spoiled, spunky woman who flirts with all the men, but commits her affections freely at the right time, and who, for all of her apparent flightiness, demonstrates real strength and courage in moments of crisis. Jeeter Fry is the villain, a chronic misfit whose violence is only barely under control. Aunt Eller is the solid mother figure who appears to be the crusty, comical widowed aunt in the early scenes, but whose strong personality and common sense rescue the lovers at the play's climax.

Much of the play's charm and exuberance comes from Riggs's accurate and colorful use of the frontier milieu. Having grown up in the Indian Territory, Riggs could portray the customs, manners, and daily activities of these settlers with a sympathy and realism only slightly colored by nostalgic idealization. Two of the crucial scenes of the play occur as the result of popular local customs: the "hoe-down" where Curly proposes to Laurey, and the wedding night shivaree that leads to Jeeter's death and Curly's imprisonment.

No small part of the atmosphere is due to Riggs's command of the local vernacular. The language goes from the homey, slangy diction of the farmers to the highly charged folk rhetoric of the principals. The playwright insisted that there was no poetic exaggeration in his dialects. Riggs was probably the finest playwright to come out of the American Southwest and one of the very few authentic "folk dramatists" that the United States has produced. That so few of his works have received the attention they deserve is not so much a commentary on the plays as it is a judgment on the vagaries of the American commercial theater.

Bibliography:
Braunlich, Phyllis Cole. *Haunted by Home: The Life and Letters of Lynn Riggs.* Norman: University of Oklahoma Press, 1988. Written before a major acquisition of Riggs's papers was made available by Yale University Library. Good on Riggs's life in the 1930's; discusses important themes in Riggs's plays. Index and appendix.

_____. "The Oklahoma Plays of R. Lynn Riggs." *World Literature Today* 64, no. 3 (Summer, 1990): 390-395. Offers criticism and interpretation. Presents Riggs's serious artistic intentions in his Oklahoma plays. Describes the contemporary critical reception of the plays.

Erhard, Thomas. *Lynn Riggs: Southwest Playwright.* Austin, Tex.: Steck-Vaughn, 1970. An excellent introduction to research of Riggs's work. Comments on the playwright's use of the territorial Oklahoma dialect.

Sper, Felix. *From Native Roots: A Panorama of Our Regional Drama.* Caldwell, Idaho: The Caxton Printers, 1948. Describes the plots of nine plays by Riggs. Concludes that Riggs's use of violence, fury, incest, and murder seem to give the plays an unreal air. Bibliography and index.

GREEN HENRY

Type of work: Novel
Author: Gottfried Keller (1819-1890)
Type of plot: Autobiographical
Time of plot: Mid-nineteenth century
Locale: Switzerland and Bavaria
First published: Der grüne Heinrich, 1854-1855; revised, 1879-1880 (English translation, 1960)

Principal characters:
HEINRICH LEE, the son of an architect
FRAU LEE, Heinrich's mother
ANNA, Heinrich's first love
JUDITH, a well-to-do widow, who loved Heinrich
RÖMER, a painter and Heinrich's teacher
ERICSON, Heinrich's first friend among Munich painters
LYS, a Dutch painter, prominent among Munich painters
SCHMALHÖFER, a secondhand dealer
GRAF DIETRICH ZU W——BERG, an admirer of Heinrich's art
DOROTHEA, the adopted daughter of Count W——berg

The Story:
Heinrich Lee lost his father in early childhood. Thereafter, Frau Lee devoted her life to the happiness of her son. She had a boundless faith in the boy's future, and methodically she used her small inherited fortune for his education. A large supply of green cloth, left by the father, was used for Heinrich's clothing, which earned him the nickname "Grüner Heinrich," or Green Henry.

When fifteen-year-old Heinrich was dismissed from school for his part in a student prank, he visited relatives in the country and fell in love with his cousin Anna, a beautiful but frail girl. In the same village, he met Judith, a well-to-do widow, who loved Heinrich. She knew about his love for Anna but assured him that there was enough room in his heart for both. Judith did not intend to leave their relationship on a platonic basis only, and as a result Heinrich was torn between his deep love for the frail Anna and his attraction to the sensual Judith.

Because it was impossible for Heinrich to complete his course of studies, his mother agreed to help him fulfill his dream of becoming a painter. All of Frau Lee's friends opposed this idea, for it was unthinkable that the child of a respected citizen should embark on so insecure and uncertain a career. In spite of these objections, Frau Lee arranged Heinrich's apprenticeship in an etcher's studio. Thereafter, when he visited the village in which Anna and Judith lived, he enjoyed being called a painter.

After spending some time in a school in Switzerland, Anna became ill and died. Heinrich guarded her body during the night before her funeral.

Before long, Heinrich had exhausted the knowledge he could gain in the etcher's studio. His luck changed when he met a professional painter named Römer. From the start, Römer showed great interest in Heinrich's work and agreed to be his tutor for a reasonable fee. As usual, Frau Lee was willing to help her son, even though Herr Römer was regarded as completely unreliable, and his talk about connections with members of the aristocracy made him unpopular among her liberal-minded friends. Furthermore, Römer's financial situation seemed not to be as favorable as he tried to have it appear. Proof of this came when Heinrich, wanting to discontinue his lessons, was approached by Römer for a loan. Heinrich received more lessons in return for money regarded as a loan.

One day Römer sold a painting. He decided to use the money for a trip to Paris because life in the town had become unbearable for him. Frau Lee wrote a polite note in regard to the loan, and Heinrich tried to appeal to Römer's aristocratic code of honor in order to get the money. Surprisingly, Römer paid without hesitation. Weeks later, Heinrich received a letter, telling him that Römer was dying in an insane asylum in Paris; the payment to Heinrich had left him without a single franc after his arrival there. Heinrich felt guilty because he believed that he had destroyed Römer's only chance for a new life. He went to Judith to discuss his moral guilt. She declared bluntly that Heinrich had murdered Römer and that he would be forced to live with his crime. Heinrich told Judith that he could no longer meet her because he wanted to remain faithful to Anna. Disappointed, Judith decided to emigrate to America, taking Heinrich's diary with her.

Heinrich decided to go to Munich. Once more, Frau Lee had difficulty persuading the trustees of Heinrich's inheritance to release what remained of the money for his study in Munich, and pessimistic predictions were made about Frau Lee's folly. In Munich, Heinrich met Ericson, a painter with a realistic attitude toward his art. Attracted to young and idealistic Heinrich, he introduced the young man to a respected Dutch painter, Lys, who saw promise in Heinrich's drawings. Ericson and Lys gave Heinrich the contact he desired with the artistic world. Ericson married a wealthy widow and left Munich. On one occasion, Lys's irresponsible behavior toward a girl irked Heinrich, and a heated discussion followed. The Dutch painter was also an avowed atheist. Though Heinrich never attended church services, he defended his belief that there was a God so vehemently that Lys felt insulted and challenged him to a duel. The duel was never fought, however, for Lys left Munich.

Having now lost his most valuable connections with artistic circles, Heinrich decided to attend lectures at the university. Living a carefree and cheerful student life, he soon exhausted his credit. Realization of his financial situation caused him to resume painting. When he approached a well-known painter for help, the artist looked at his work and suggested that he show his paintings in a gallery. There Heinrich noticed that his work was placed in an obscure corner, but a canvas by the other painter, based on one of his own landscapes, hung in a prominent place. Heinrich realized that any other attempt to exhibit his works would stamp him as a plagiarist.

Discouraged, he tried without success to sell his work to small dealers. For days he did not eat; each night, he had apocalyptical nightmares. Money from Frau Lee brought temporary relief. After paying his debts, Heinrich had little left, and he tried to sell drawings he had made before leaving home. A secondhand dealer, Schmalhöfer, took a few of them. When Heinrich returned to the dealer, he was told that his drawings had been sold, and Schmalhöfer asked for more. Later, Schmalhöfer offered him work as a flagpole painter, and he accepted, working steadily from morning to night. After this work came to an end, he was able to pay all of his debts, with some money left over to make a trip home.

On the way, he accidentally found shelter at Count W——berg's estate. To his surprise, he learned that the count was the unknown patron who had bought his drawings. Delighted when he learned the identity of his guest, the count offered Heinrich a chance to paint undisturbed. Soon Heinrich forgot his intention to return to his mother. Count W——berg had an adopted daughter, Dorothea, with whom Heinrich had fallen deeply in love. It was impossible for him to declare his love openly, however, because he felt that to do so would abuse the count's hospitality.

Having found a sponsor in Count W——berg, Heinrich successfully exhibited a painting in Munich. His old friend Ericson, after reading an account of the exhibit, wrote asking to buy the painting, regardless of price. While in Munich, Heinrich experienced another great surprise when he was informed that Schmalhöfer had died, leaving him a large amount of money. The dealer had been impressed by a painter who was, despite his artistic ideals, ready to paint flagpoles all day to pay his debts. The sale of the painting, Schmalhöfer's bequest, and additional payments by the count for the drawings Schmalhöfer had sold to him made Heinrich a fairly rich man. In spite of his good fortunes, however, Heinrich was still not ready to declare his love to Dorothea. Heinrich, who had not written to his mother for many months, decided at last to complete his journey home. When he arrived, he found his mother dying. The neighbors informed him that a short time before, the police, trying to contact him in connection with Schmalhöfer's bequest, had asked Frau Lee to appear at police headquarters to give information as to her son's whereabouts. Because the police did not reveal the reason for their questions, his mother had believed rumors that a criminal investigation was the cause for the inquiries; her fears and Heinrich's silence had broken her spirit. After some time, Heinrich was able to regain the confidence of the townspeople and was elected a county official. Then a letter from the count informed him that Dorothea, uncertain of his love, had married another. Peace came into his life when Judith returned from America to be near him. A realistic woman, she convinced Heinrich that marriage would not be advisable, but she promised to be with him whenever he needed her. After twenty years, Judith died, and he recovered his diary, which he used to write the story of his life.

Critical Evaluation:

Gottfried Keller's *Green Henry*, a great German *Bildungsroman*, is frequently compared to Johann Wolfgang von Goethe's two Wilhelm Meister novels, *Wilhelm Meister's Apprenticeship* (1795-1796) and *Wilhelm Meister's Travels* (1821, 1829). The autobiographical content of *Green Henry* is unmistakable, for the book is almost entirely an authentic description of Keller's life in Switzerland, his struggles in Munich, and his disillusioned return home. The first version of the novel ends with Heinrich's death, but after Keller became a respected county official in his native country, a second, much revised, version appeared. This version, which became the standard one and reflects the author's newfound security, ends on a fatalistic but not destructive note. Keller, as enthusiastic about description of nature as were his Romantic contemporary writers, loved his native surroundings; however, he added strong realism to his stories, which was quite shocking to his audience. The value of the novel is increased by a dry sense of humor, which fills the basically tragic book with contrasts.

The novel, like the revised version of Goethe's *Wilhelm Meister's Travels*, rejects the youthful desire for irresponsible self-fulfillment typical of the Romantic personality in favor of individuals finding their place in society. The young Heinrich, an orphan with an indulgent mother and no father to guide him in the direction of responsibility, lives a life colored by fantasy; he is unable to perceive reality as it is and to measure himself against it. He paints from imagination rather than knowledge, and his painting, like his life, has no ties to the fabric of the natural world. In this sense, his art, rather than being a calling, is a symptom of his false relationship to the world, and his life is one long process of disillusionment.

It is only at the end that Heinrich sees his proper calling in the life of his town and in a career of service. This wisdom comes too late to spare him guilt and suffering, and his education in life has been gained at a terrible cost. In the end, however, the patient, loving humanity with which he tells his own story convinces the reader that his life is not, ultimately, a tragedy.

Bibliography:

Hart, Gail K. *Readers and Their Fictions in the Novels and Novellas of Gottfried Keller.* Chapel Hill: University of North Carolina Press, 1989. Insightful discussion of the changing image of literary fictions within the tradition of literary heroes who are led astray by books. Also discusses Paul Johann Anselm Feuerbach's influence on Keller's only novel, *Green Henry.*

Hauch, Edward Franklin. *Gottfried Keller as a Democratic Idealist.* New York: Columbia University Press, 1916.

Lindsay, James Martin. *Gottfried Keller: Life and Works.* London: Wolff, 1968. A thorough biographic study that incorporates discussions of Keller's works. Includes illustrations and a bibliography.

Richert, Herbert William. *Basic Concepts in the Philosophy of Gottfried Keller.* Chapel Hill: University of North Carolina Press, 1949. Remains a useful source on the belief system underlying Keller's works.

Ruppel, Richard R. *Gottfried Keller: Poet, Pedagogue and Humanist.* Munich: Peter Lang, 1988.

GREEN HILLS OF AFRICA

Type of work: Memoir
Author: Ernest Hemingway (1899-1961)
First published: 1935

In his foreword to *Green Hills of Africa*, Ernest Hemingway said that he was attempting "to write an absolutely true book to see whether the shape of a country and the pattern of a month's action can, if truly presented, compete with a work of the imagination." The result is a novelized account of a safari he joined in East Africa from December 8, 1933, to February 17, 1934.

Accompanying Hemingway were his wife Pauline Pfeiffer Hemingway (called P.O.M., meaning Poor Old Mama), a friend from Key West, Florida, named Charles Thompson (Karl Kabor in the book), a well-respected professional British hunter Philip Percival (called Pop, Jackson Phillips, and Mr. J. P.), and a visitor named Kandisky (really Hans Koritschoner, an Austrian-born businessman in Africa). Hemingway also hired many natives for various chores. The real names of several are given, including M'Cola (his gun-bearer), Kamau (his driver), and the trackers Abdullah, Charo, and Molo; some of the less important natives are nicknamed Droopy, David Garrick, and the Roman. One heroic Masai is simply called "the old man." In mid-January, Hemingway suffered an attack of dysentery and was rushed for medical treatment to Arusha in northeast Tanganyika and to Nairobi, Kenya, after which he rejoined the safari. In his book, which begins after his return from Nairobi, he incorporates a few events that occurred while he was hunting in the Serengeti Plain of northwest Tanganyika in December, 1933, and early January, 1934. Interrupting his narration are many insights concerning writers and the art of writing. *Green Hills of Africa* thus combines a report about hunters in competitive quest of big game, subjective thoughts on literature, and Hemingway's conscious and unconscious self-revelations.

The structure of *Green Hills of Africa* is complex, perhaps unnecessarily so. It is in four parts: "Pursuit and Conversation," "Pursuit Remembered," "Pursuit and Failure," and "Pursuit as Happiness." Hemingway thus is in pursuit of big game, knowledge of literature, and his own identity. The part about failure is the shortest; the part about remembrance, the longest. The section about conversation, mostly literary in nature, is shorter than that about happiness, which mainly concerns a successful hunt in an unspoiled area. However, Hemingway complicates matters. Parts 1 and 3 are mostly in dialogue and mainly concern past action. Parts 2 and 4 stress action and feature the competition of Hemingway and Karl. Furthermore, in part 2, Hemingway recalls events that occurred earlier than the "present," while part 4 begins abruptly in that present, retrogresses, and concludes later in Haifa, far to the north. Since the action, whether past or present, is exciting, the reader is not distressed by time shifts, which actually increase the suspense.

The story starts when Kandisky's truck splutters along a nearby road, sends potential animal targets skittering away, stalls, and must be fixed on the spot. Learning Hemingway's identity, Kandisky, who bravely calls hunting "silly," encourages his host to discuss writers instead. Hemingway opines that all American literature begins with Mark Twain and his *Adventures of Huckleberry Finn* (1884). He also avers that Edgar Allan Poe's works are skillfully constructed but are "dead," waxes negative about Ralph Waldo Emerson, Nathaniel Hawthorne, Henry David Thoreau (who he claims cannot read), and John Greenleaf Whittier, but praises Henry James and Stephen Crane. He complains that American writers are regularly destroyed by economics, politics, critics, drink, women, money, and ambition. Hemingway says that wartime experiences can help writers, praises Gustave Flaubert and Rudyard Kipling, and suggests that hunting and writing are equally valid artistic endeavors. He recalls drinking heavily with James Joyce in Paris, just before setting out for Africa. He gratuitously criticizes Gertrude Stein, though without naming her, for copying his dialogue writing technique and for being "jealous and malicious." He says that a great writer must have talent, discipline, intelligence, disinterestedness, and a firm conscience. He must also be fortunate enough to survive, and he must accept loneliness and ignore criticism.

Interest mounts when Hemingway astutely prepares the reader for the hunt, kudu and sable being the main targets, by reminiscing about past hunts. He immodestly recalls having killed a rhinoceros at three hundred yards but then adds that Karl, repeatedly labeled "lucky," killed a larger one. Hemingway got over an admittedly idiotic fit of jealousy by reading Leo Tolstoy. The group entered the Rift Valley, shot a few zebras for hides as gifts for friends at home, killed some teal for food, and penetrated a new region, which reminded Hemingway of Spain. His free-associating mind skips from topic to topic: the pain flies can inflict on horses, his own pain when he broke his right arm, the pain he has caused animals when wounding them instead of killing them "cleanly," and the expectation that he himself will die violently in due time.

Then, in the exact middle of the book, Hemingway offers the most graphic figure of speech he ever created. It concerns the Gulf Stream (a metaphor for nature), into which garbage is dumped by humans from a "high-piled scow" (civilization). The "ill-smelling . . . load"—disgustingly specified as palm fronds, corks and bottles, dead cats and rats and dogs, deflated condoms, and light bulbs among other things—pollutes, but only temporarily, the "one single, lasting thing—the stream." Significantly, he says that a true work of art is almost as lasting as that stream.

Chapter 10 returns the reader to the present, with these introductory words: "That all seemed a year ago. Now, this afternoon in the car . . . " The final shoot begins miserably, with time growing perilously short. Rain has spoiled a salt lick where they might have ambushed some game. Furthermore, a native, ridiculed in Swahili as *shenzi* (crazy), has also spooked a herd of kudu with ineffective bow-and-arrow hunting. Hemingway is furious with M'Cola for neglecting a direct order to clean and oil his Springfield rifle but is soon ecstatic when a strange and aged native reports a kudu herd, though it is at some distance from them. Hemingway quickly gathers a team of his natives, loads the car with petrol cans, drafts more help at an intriguing Masai village along the way, and in time enters an unhunted, uniquely lovely region more than fifty miles from camp. There, at last, in the climax of the book, he encounters success, shooting an enormous kudu, but he also experiences failure, killing a proscribed female sable but only wounding an elusive sable bull, whose spoor Hemingway and M'Cola follow under a murderously hot sun without seeing the pain-racked creature again.

A month later, Hemingway, Karl, Karl's wife, and P.O.M. are eating lunch and drinking wine in Haifa as they idly look at loons on the Sea of Galilee. When P.O.M. laments that her memories of the trip are already dimming, Hemingway valiantly promises to write about it all "some time."

Green Hills of Africa is an exemplary book in a tradition of "true" narratives as exciting as fiction. Examples include Richard Henry Dana, Jr.'s *Two Years Before the Mast* (1840), Francis Parkman's *The Oregon Trail* (1849), Henry David Thoreau's *Walden* (1854), and Mark Twain's *Roughing It* (1872). In each, the writer's self-revelations are as interesting as the sometimes ephemeral items along the story line. In *Green Hills of Africa*, Hemingway exposes himself more than he usually does when he describes urinating under the Southern Cross one long alcoholic night. He boasts about his marksmanship, his ability to track animals whether wounded or otherwise, his indifference to pains caused by long treks and little sleep (on occasion he reads while his companions nap), his drinking prowess, his ranging knowledge of literature, and his facile handling of Swahili. He undercuts this immense braggadocio rather too little by calling himself names every so often. He demeans his wife Pauline by calling her "girl" when he does not refer to her as P.O.M., by ostentatiously letting her shoot first at a lion and then asserting that she killed it when everyone knows she missed, by ordering her to stay behind to avoid dangers the men stalwartly confront, and by only recording her comments on one book. He praises a pretty native woman for being "very wifely" but then undresses her with his lecherous eyes. More general disrespect for women surfaces when he labels male American writers Old Mother Hubbards and female ones "Joan of Arc without the fighting."

Hemingway had the professional writer's recording eye and ear. He could remember every detail of sights seen. His verbal pictures of ranges of hills resemble multiplaned, subtly-colored impressionistic paintings. He is swept up in an almost orgasmic love for the virginal aspects of the final hunting locale, is sad to realize that humankind soon exploits every new "country," but conveniently rationalizes his orgy of killing on the grounds that he is only hastening the work of rampant death in these teeming jungles. If so, he does not explain his manifest delight in watching a hyena that has been shot in the belly chew out and eat its own intestines in agony. In his lengthy description of the event, he calls the hyena "a dirty joke." While stalking a variety of animals, he took note of their alertness, colors, markings, gaits, and "electric speed." In addition to describing nonhuman sounds, notably the lion's low-pitched cough, he could also repeat conversations with friends verbatim. (Percival later affirmed that Hemingway accurately quoted him word for word.)

Although *Green Hills of Africa* is a significant record of an important episode in the career of a world-famous author, it is not great art. It does not inculcate an admirable way of life, nor does it hold up a steady mirror to its times. Several contemporary reviewers criticized Hemingway for ignoring the ominous economic conditions of his own country in the 1930's, for his self-indulgence, and for writing about gory slaughter on a remote continent. The book does, however, have aesthetic balance and reveals much about its author. Furthermore, Hemingway's safari inspired two of his finest short stories: "The Snows of Kilimanjaro" and "The Short Happy Life of Francis Macomber" (both 1936). The former resulted from his dysentery and his plane flight to Nairobi for treatment. The latter takes place on a safari resembling Hemingway's own, and its three central characters are distorted echoes of Hemingway, his wife, and their British guide. The events related in *Green Hills of Africa* made both stories possible.

Robert L. Gale

Bibliography:
Baker, Carlos. *Ernest Hemingway: A Life Story.* New York: Charles Scribner's Sons, 1969. The authorized biography, with details of Hemingway's safari, his companions, itinerary, illness, successes and failures in hunting, and the literary uses he made of the adventure.
Bredahl, A. Carl, Jr., and Susan Lynn Drake, with William R. Robinson. *Hemingway's "Green Hills of Africa" as Evolutionary Narrative: Helix and Scimitar.* Lewiston, N.Y.: Edwin Mellen Press, 1990. The only book-length study of *Green Hills of Africa.* Combines farfetched commentary with fine insights concerning Hemingway's journeys in Africa (both inward and outward) and symbolism in the book (notably the kudu's spiral horn as life and the sable's scimitar horn as death).
Grebstein, Sheldon Norman. *Hemingway's Craft.* Carbondale: Southern Illinois University

Press, 1973. Includes well-supported analyses of structure, language, and narrative techniques in Hemingway's *Green Hills of Africa*.

Hays, Peter L. *Ernest Hemingway*. New York: Continuum, 1990. A compressed but useful study, with excellent comments on style and themes as evidenced in *Green Hills of Africa*.

Weber, Ronald. *Hemingway's Art of Non-fiction*. New York: St. Martin's Press, 1990. Of value for relating *Green Hills of Africa* to Hemingway's posthumously serialized *African Journal*.

THE GREEN HOUSE

Type of work: Novel
Author: Mario Vargas Llosa (1936-   )
Type of plot: Social realism
Time of plot: Forty years that include World War II
Locale: Piura and the Amazon jungle, Peru
First published: La casa verde, 1965 (English translation, 1968)

Principal characters:
    DON ANSELMO, builds the Green House
    FUSHÍA, a smuggler
    LALITA, Fushía's wife
    AQUILINO, a vendor
    NIEVES, a river pilot
    JULIO REÁTEGUI, the governor and a smuggler
    JUM, an Indian employee of Fushía
    BONIFACIA or WILDFLOWER, a prostitute, wife of Lituma
    LITUMA, a Sergeant in the Civil Guard

The Story:

Nuns and soldiers snatched two Indian girls out of the jungle to civilize them. They were taken to the mission school. There, Bonifacia took pity on them. Corporal Roberto Delgado went to Bagua, taking Adrian Nieves for a pilot. The Leons told Josefino that Lituma was out of jail and wanted to celebrate. Bonifacia felt sorry for the two new girls because they wanted to leave. When they left, the other girls followed them. Bonifacia would be blamed, expelled, and left homeless. A trader with the Indians, Fushía needed a partner, so he made friends with Aquilino, a water vendor. When the other three "champs"—the Leons and Josefino—arrived, they and Lituma began drinking.

Bonifacia found the two new girls in the pantry, spoke to them in Indian, and fed them. Bonifacia loved the sisters and did not want to be considered a heathen, but the children did not seem evil to her. Don Anselmo bought some desert land on which to build a house. Against Nieves' advice, Delgado ordered the men to loot an Indian village and to camp there for the night. Josefino told Lituma that Bonifacia had become a prostitute.

Don Anselmo built the Green House, a bordello named after its color, on his land. The Aguarunas, led by Jum, attacked Delgado and the porter. Nieves, eager to leave the military, swam to an island, where Fushía and Lalita promised him work and safety from the authorities. Don Julio Reátegui planned to take a nursemaid and a servant from among the orphans at the mission. One of the girls offered was Bonifacia. She cried, however, and Don Julio would not take her against her will. The soldiers could not find the missing students. Nieves invited the Sergeant to dine with his family and meet Bonifacia, who had been expelled from the mission.

A baby girl, left for dead when her guardians were murdered, was attacked by buzzards that devoured her eyes and tongue. Juana Baura, a washerwoman, raised the girl, Antonia.

Corporal Roberto Delgado and the Captain found Jum and the Urukusas. A little girl clung to Jum's legs. At Chunga's, the new Green House, Lituma looked for Bonifacia. At Nieves' house, Bonifacia was too frightened to come out until Fats announced that the students had been found. Lalita insisted that Bonifacia greet the Sergeant. Fushía's disease made him impotent. He was abusive to Lalita, and she fled to Nieves for comfort.

One day, when Juana left Antonia at the town square as usual, the girl disappeared. Jum told Reátegui that the Corporal had tried to steal from him, so he beat him and then gave him a canoe. Delgado contradicted the story. The girl with Jum was Bonifacia. Josefino reunited Wildflower and Lituma; the couple danced. While Lalita and Nieves were away, Lituma visited Bonifacia. She ran; he cornered her and ripped off her clothes, but she resisted him. She did, however, return his embrace before he left.

Don Anselmo told Juana Baura that Antonia, who had been living with him, was dead. Corporal Delgado lashed the Indians with a whip for their actions. Jum would be punished in Santa María de Nieva. Don Julio protected the little girl. The Leons staged a distraction in the bar; Lituma and Bonifacia slipped out. Josefino looked for them, and when he found Lituma outside, Lituma and the Leons savagely beat him for lying about why Bonifacia became a prostitute. When a new Lieutenant came to Santa Maria de Nieva, Jum, like many times before, asked that all his property taken by Reátegui be returned. The Lieutenant would have given Jum back his possessions, but they could not be retrieved.

The new Minister ordered a search for the bandits who stole rubber and hides from the Indians. When Lituma went to get Nieves for the trip, the pilot feigned illness to avoid going and being recognized. The Sergeant proposed marriage to Bonifacia while he was there. After Antonia's funeral, Father García and some women set the Green House on fire. Don Anselmo was distraught until Angelica Mercedes, the cook, appeared with his infant, Chunga.

Don Anselmo told Wildflower why Lituma had been sent to prison. The Leons and Josefino were drinking and singing when Seminario insulted them. They placated him because he had a gun. Then Lituma and two other patrolmen came into the bar. After Juana Baura saw Chunga for the first time, she started bringing the child dresses, shoes, and food. Finally, she took Chunga to raise. When the other two patrolmen left, Lituma joined the champs. Seminario kept insulting them and threatened to throw them out.

The soldiers hunting for bandits found an intoxicated man and took him to Borjas to see if any of the Aguarunas recognized him as a bandit. Lituma challenged Seminario to a round of Russian roulette. The Lieutenant learned that Fushía was the bandit and Nieves was his pilot. Drunk, Lituma prepared his gun for the game. The Sergeant survived his round, but Seminario did not. The Sergeant returned from the bandit search and married Bonifacia at the mission. The sisters had forgiven her. Don Anselmo fell in love with Antonia.

Lituma slapped Bonifacia for removing her shoes in public. When Lituma went to sleep, Josefino tried to seduce Bonifacia. Although Lituma had secretly told Nieves to escape, the pilot refused and the Sergeant had to arrest him for piloting Fushía's boat. Anselmo stole Antonia and took her to the Green House and kept her there as his wife. He longed to know how she felt about him. Josefino persuaded Bonifacia to stay in Piura while Lituma was imprisoned in Lima, and he tried to convince her to abort Lituma's child.

Lituma and Bonifacia moved from Santa Maria de Nieva to Piura. Lituma was excited, but Bonifacia was sad to leave Lalita and the sisters.

Upon learning that Antonia was pregnant, Anselmo was excited but later wondered if he had acted morally. Julio Reátegui took the girl found with Jum to the mission. The Mother Superior was angry about Jum hanging in the square, his body whipped and his head shaven, but Reátegui said Jum was an example to the other Indians.

Fushía screamed that Aquilino had not visited him in a year. Both men were old, and Fushía's teeth had fallen out. Aquilino, sickened by the smell and irritated by Fushía's screaming, reported only news of Lalita. Fushía became sad, and Aquilino promised to visit again next year. Father García grudgingly heard Anselmo's confession. Don Anselmo, however, died peacefully.

Critical Evaluation:

The Green House is a multilayered work filled with overlapping dreams and memories that bring to mind William Faulkner's belief that the past remains in the present. The action in the novel occurs over a forty-year span during which there is an allusion to World War II. The structure, however, is not linear. Present, past, and dream worlds intermingle, changing time and place, leaving the reader uncertain about some actions.

This discontinuous structure is Mario Vargas Llosa's attempt to present the separate worlds of each character as a combined whole, or totality. The seeming lack of structure prevents the omniscience that is often granted to a reader of a conventionally structured story. The purpose of this blending of past, present, and different points of view is to underscore the relative nature of reality. Just as one cannot know all the details and effects of causes, or situations, in life, one cannot know these things in *The Green House*.

The connective bonds in the novel are the five lines of narrative that tell the stories of Bonifacia, Fushía, Don Anselmo, Jum, and the slum. The story lines are presented in a predictable order within each chapter, creating a circular structure. Common to all of Vargas Llosa's novels is the idea that there are no "closed and autocratic orders" in society. In *The Green House*, for example, Don Julio Reátegui, governor of Santa Maria de Nieva, is a smuggler who abuses the Indians and his employees while at the same time supporting the mission and seriously striving to maintain good rapport with the sisters. Vargas Llosa highlights this idea when he compares the nuns to buzzards and death angels, showing the evil embodied in the good as the nuns destroy lives in the name of Christianity.

The theme of the novel, broadly stated, is exploitation. Throughout the work, the strong oppress the weak, the educated oppress the illiterate, and the wealthy oppress the poor. Bonifacia is forced into prostitution by Josefino, one of the champs, to support him and later Lituma. The champs' theme song expresses the men's desire to live well and carefree while others supply their needs.

Fushía exploits his own wife when he trades her for a boat, knowing she will have to give sexual favors, at least temporarily, to Julio Reátegui in return. The children whom the nuns "civilize" are also the victims of exploitation. The young women who grow up in the mission cannot go back to the jungle, so they are hired out as servants to the wealthy and to members of the military. The Indian women are sexually exploited. The soldiers, patrolmen, and smugglers rape the women frequently and without remorse, reducing them from humans to mere conveniences, and leaving them with illegitimate children. This type of exploitation is not new to South America. As one critic points out, women received the same treatment from the Spanish conquistadores.

The Indian men, with their superstitions and lack of business knowledge, are cheated by the smugglers. Jum knows he has been cheated, but he cannot prove it. His inability to speak the language of the businessmen prevents him from being treated fairly.

The novel also touches on the theme of predestination. This theme is evident when Fushía and Lituma bemoan their bad luck. Neither man has the ability to see that he has caused his condition.

The Green House presents a radical departure from traditional organization. With the novel's complex structure, the author is able to reveal more to the reader than simple story lines. The reader is forced to think about reality and totality. Vargas Llosa's successful experiment delves into philosophy and offers insight into Latin American history and culture.

Wilma J. Shires

Bibliography:

Beason, Gary. *"The Green House* Effect: A Study of Latin American Sex Roles." *RE: Artes Liberales* 13 (1986): 11-19. Offers insight into Latin American gender roles. It aids in the understanding of characters' actions and relationships.

Diez, Luys A. "The Sources of *The Green House:* The Mythical Background of a Fabulous Novel." *Texas Studies in Literature and Language* 19 (1977): 429-444. Shows the relationship among the novel, an interview with Vargas Llosa, Vargas Llosa's log book, and Diez's own responses to personal experiences at the locations of the novel.

Harss, Luis. "Green House Mirrors." *World Literature Today* 52 (1978): 34-38. Deals with archetypes found in literature and shows a relationship among similar images in various novels. Presents an interesting discussion of theme based on the color green.

Moody, Michael. "Landscapes of the Damned: Natural Setting in *La Casa Verde." Kentucky Romance Quarterly* 27 (1988): 495-508. Examines the use of setting to convey meaning and to express Vargas Llosa's view of reality. It shows how one literary element is vital to the whole novel.

_____. "A Small Whirlpool: Narrative Structure in *The Green House." Texas Studies in Literature and Language* 19 (1977): 408-428. Discusses the synthesis of the five story lines presented in *The Green House.* Moody asserts that the seemingly formless novel is unified by the chronological sequence of narrative episodes and that the various events make up one experience.

GREEN MANSIONS

Type of work: Novel
Author: W. H. Hudson (1841-1922)
Type of plot: Fantasy
Time of plot: Nineteenth century
Locale: South American jungles
First published: 1904

Principal characters:
MR. ABEL, an old man
RIMA, a creature of the forest
NUFLO, an old hunter

The Story:

No one in Georgetown could remember his full name, and so he was known only as Mr. Abel. He told a strange story one evening as he sat talking to a friend, a tale of his youth.

While he was living among the native people of the jungle, a nearby savannah caught his fancy. The natives claimed it was haunted and would not go near it. One day, he set out to explore the savannah for himself. For a long while he sat on a log trying to identify the calls of the birds. One particularly engaging sound seemed almost human, and it followed him as he returned to the village. Soon he bribed one of the natives to enter the haunted savannah. The guide became frightened, however, and ran away, leaving Abel alone with the weird sound. The man had said that the daughter of the spirit Didi inhabited the forest. Abel felt sure that the nearly intelligible language of the birdlike sounds was associated with the one to whom the man referred. Again and again, Abel returned to the forest in his search for the source of the warbling sound, but it always eluded him. Then, one day, he saw a girl playing with a bird. The girl disappeared among the trees, but not before Abel had decided that she must be connected in some way with the warbling sounds he had heard.

The native tribe had been encouraging him to continue his quests into the area of mystery. He decided at last that they were hoping he would try to kill the creature who seemed to be haunting their forest. He was stricken with horror at the idea. One day, he came face to face with the elusive being. He had been menaced by a small venomous snake, and he was about to kill it with a rock when the girl appeared before him to protest vigorously in her odd, birdlike, warbling language. She was not like any human he had ever seen. Her coloring was her most striking characteristic; it was luminescent and changed with her every mood. As he stood looking at her, fascinated by her loveliness, the snake bit him on the leg.

He started back toward the village for help, but a blinding rainstorm overtook him on the way. After falling unconscious while running through the trees, he awakened in a hut with a bearded old man named Nuflo. The man expressed fear and hatred of the natives who, he said, were afraid of his grandchild, Rima. It was she who had saved Abel from dying of the snake's venom, and it was she who had been following him in the forest. Abel could not believe that the listless, colorless girl standing in a corner of the hut was the lovely birdlike creature he had met. On closer examination, he could detect a likeness of figure and features, but her luminous radiance was missing. When Rima addressed him in Spanish, he questioned her about the musical language that she emitted in the trees. She gave no explanation and ran away.

In a few days, Abel learned that Rima would harm no living creature, not even for her own food. Abel grew to love the strange, beautiful, untamed girl of the green forest. When he questioned her, she spoke willingly, but her speech was strangely poetic and difficult to understand. She expressed deep, spiritual longings and made him understand that in the forest she communed with her mother, who had died long ago.

Rima began to sense that since Abel, the only person she had known except her grandfather, could not understand her language and did not understand her longings, she must be unlike other human beings in the world. In her desire to meet other people and to return to the place of her birth where her mother had died, Rima revealed to Abel the name of her birthplace, a mountain he knew well. Rima demanded that her grandfather guide her to Riolama Mountain. Old Nuflo consented and requested that Abel come also.

Before he took the long journey with Rima and Nuflo, Abel returned to the village. There, greeted with quiet suspicion and awe because of where he had been, Abel was held a prisoner. After six days' absence, he returned to Rima's forest. Nuflo and Abel made preparations for their journey. When they started, Rima followed them, only showing herself when they needed directions.

Nuflo began Rima's story. He had been wandering about with a band of outlaws when an ethereal woman appeared among them. After she had fallen and broken her ankle, Nuflo, who thought she must be a saint, nursed her back to health. Observing that she was to have a baby, he took her to a native village. Rima was born soon after. The woman could learn neither Spanish nor the language of the native people, and the soft melodious sounds that fell from her lips were unintelligible to everyone. Gradually, the woman faded. As she lay dying, she made the rough hunter understand that Rima could not live unless she were taken to the dry, cool mountains.

Knowing their search for her mother's people to be in vain, Abel sought to dissuade Rima from the journey. He explained to her that they must have disappeared or have been wiped out by natives. Rima believed him, but at the thought of her own continued loneliness, she fell fainting at his feet. When she had recovered, she spoke of being alone, of never finding anyone who could understand her sweet, warbling language. Abel promised to stay with her always in the forest. Rima insisted on making the journey back alone so that she could prepare herself for Abel's return.

The return to the savannah was not easy for Abel and the old man. They were nearly starving when they came to their own forest and saw, to their horror, that the hut was gone. Rima could not be found. As Abel ran through the forest searching for her, he came upon a lurking native tribesman. Then he realized that she must be gone, for the man would not have dared to enter the savannah if the daughter of Didi were still there. He went back to the village for food and learned from them that Rima had returned to her forest. Finding her in a tree, the chief, Runi, had ordered his men to burn the tree in order to destroy the daughter of Didi.

Half mad with sorrow, Abel fled to the village of an enemy tribe. There he made a pact with the villagers for the slaughter of the tribe of Runi. He then went to the forest, where he found Nuflo dead. He also found Rima's bones lying among the ashes of the fire-consumed tree. He placed her remains in an urn that he carried with him back to civilization.

Living in Georgetown, Abel at last understood Rima's sorrowful loneliness. Having known and lost her, he was suffering the same longings she had felt when she was searching for her people.

Critical Evaluation:

The story concerns the developing love between Abel and the birdlike Rima. Rima is associated with birds as a part of the natural order of the forest. Abel hears a birdlike warble, but one with some hint of intelligence in it. Following the warble, he searches until, looking through some foliage to an open space, he sees a girl reclining near a tree with one arm outstretched toward a bird, while the bird flirted with its wings and tail, just ready to hop onto the girl's pointing finger. Abel describes the girl as small, with a slim figure and with delicately shaped little hands and feet. Her dress and hair suggest a number of colors, something like the colored plumage of a bird. Elsewhere she is compared to a hummingbird. She eats no meat, only seeds and berries. In a tall tree, she walks along the branches with no fear of falling. Finally, at her murder, she falls from a high tree like a great white bird killed with a hunter's arrow. Rima is not only in tune with nature, she is a part of it.

An important charm of Rima lies in this closeness to nature. Rima prevents the native people from hunting in this area, thus protecting the animals. When Abel raises a stone to crush a venomous serpent, Rima appears, forbidding such a killing, and the snake gratefully winds itself about Rima's ankle. She wears a dress whose fabric has been spun from a spider's web; a priest has baptized her, not with a saint's name, but with a natural place name, Riolama, shortened to Rima. She travels without fear of being lost in this rain forest, or of being attacked by beasts, or of being found by hostile tribesmen. The color of her hair, of her skin, of her eyes, of her blush changes with the shades of light and foliage, reminding a reader of a chameleon's change or of birds in their many colors. Rima is of nature.

Rima knows a language of nature learned from her now deceased mother. She eventually impels Abel and Nuflo, her adopted grandfather, to walk eighteen days to Riolama, searching for the spot where Nuflo found her mother. Once there, Abel convinces Rima that her people of nature no longer exist. No one knows the language of nature but Rima. This is a turning point in the novel. Rima swoons, figuratively dying to her life as a forest sprite. She awakes to Abel's kiss, as though he were Prince Charming. She comes now into human love, becomes a person with new human recognition. In this scene, the world of nature gives way to the human world. The novel exemplifies the romantic theme of rebirth through love. Rima is reborn into a new way of being.

In contrast with the lovely, ethereal Rima, Abel must deal with the neighboring native people whom he describes as savages. These natives provide a striking contrast to Rima. Rima is in union with nature, seen in the way her coloring changes depending on the foliage around her. The natives, however, are at odds with the natural world. To satisfy their hunger for meat, they hunt birds with blowpipes and slay the coatimundi with arrows. They appear grotesque in drinking to intoxication, in lusting for the death of their enemy, Managa, and in coveting Abel's ornamental matchbox and pistol. As they eagerly destroy life in the world around them, so they also seek to destroy Rima, who is linked with this natural world.

This novel is also a romance. Its prologue and first chapter suggest the realistic frame so common in nineteenth century romances. Its setting in Guiana appeals to the love of the distant, of the exotic, of nature in unaltered state. Rima is a symbol of this vision of nature, a fantasy of love, chaste, a wisp of the imagination, too good to live for very long, symbolized by the legendary Hata flower, a single plant with a single bloom that lives only for one lunar cycle. When the native people burn Rima to death, Abel's fury brings murder on every villager, an emotional frenzy which we expect in romantic novels. On his march toward Georgetown, delirious Abel feels that he is always accompanied by a snake symbolizing Rima. The novel, while perhaps refraining from the impossible, draws the reader's imagination to the limits of the plausible.

This novel opened one area of the British Empire to readers. British Guiana seemed a place where romantic events might occur. Wonders existed not only along the Nile or in India but also in the mysterious rain forest of the New World. Indeed, eight years after this novel, Sir Arthur Conan Doyle placed *The Lost World* (1912) on Mount Riolama, a site seen by Abel in his final trek. In 1925, Sir Jacob Epstein created a memorial sculpture in London's Hyde Park to Rima, the ethereal girl embodying the spirit of the forest and of romantic love.

"Critical Evaluation" by Emmett H. Carroll

Bibliography:
Frederick, John T. *William Henry Hudson.* New York: Twayne, 1972. Explores the plausibility of the character Rima in relation to the humanity of the other characters.
Haymaker, Richard E. *From Pampas to Hedgerows and Downs: A Study of W. H. Hudson.* New York: Bookman Associates, 1954. Presents Rima as more of a passion than an actual individual. Explores Hudson's tragic vision in the context of Rima's death.
Miller, David. *W. H. Hudson and the Elusive Paradise.* London: Macmillan, 1990. Contains a chapter discussing the symbolic/mythopoetic elements such as landscape, snake and bird, darkness, and the character Rima.
Ronner, Amy D. *W. H. Hudson: The Man, the Novelist, the Naturalist.* New York: AMS Press, 1986. Explores the concept of humanity fusing with spirit as seen in Abel's relationship with Rima.
Shrubsall, Dennis. *W. H. Hudson, Writer and Naturalist.* Tisbury, England: Compton Press, 1978. Contains an exploration of the origins of *Green Mansions.*

GREENE'S GROATS-WORTH OF WITTE BOUGHT WITH A MILLION OF REPENTANCE

Type of work: Short fiction
Author: Robert Greene (1558-1592)
Type of plot: Satire
Time of plot: Late sixteenth century
Locale: A city resembling London
First published: 1592

Principal characters:
    ROBERTO, a scholar, turned playwright and rogue
    LUCANIO, his gullible brother
    LAMILIA, a courtesan

The Story:

Gorinius, an old usurer who lived in a city with strong resemblances to London, addressed his sons from his deathbed. He counseled the younger, Lucanio, his heir, to follow his example and "heap treasure upon treasure" in every way possible, moral or immoral, advising him above all to disregard conscience where profit is involved. He disinherited his older son, Roberto, who had dared to condemn his father and others of his profession for their unscrupulous dealings. Gorinius left Roberto with only "an old groat wherewith I wish him to buy a groatsworth of wit: for he in my life hath reproved my manner of life, and therefore at my death shall not be contaminated with corrupt gain."

Roberto forsook the path of right when he saw his brother's good fortune, and he devoted all his energies to securing Lucanio's wealth. He gave up his studies and plotted with a courtesan, Lamilia, to ensnare his innocent, malleable brother. According to the plan, Roberto was to induce Lucanio to wed Lamilia in return for half the wealth she would gain in the alliance.

Lamilia entertained Lucanio with a seductive song of pleasure and quickly made an ardent suitor of him. Then the three settled down to dinner together. Roberto proposed to tell a tale about the hazards of love, but Lamilia interrupted him with a fable about a crafty fox who makes a match between a badger and a ewe. On the eve of the wedding the fox kills the ewe and escapes, leaving the badger to the mercy of passing shepherds, who believe him guilty of the sheep's death. Lamilia concluded by telling Roberto, "Go forward with your tale, seek not by sly insinuation to turn our mirth to sorrow."

Roberto launched into a complicated story about the daughter of an old squire, who chose from all her suitors a farmer's son. A young gentleman who wanted her for himself schemed to betray the couple. With the help of an old country woman and her daughter he made the farmer unfaithful to his bride on their wedding night and won her for himself. The moral of this tale, he stated, was "the effects of sudden love."

Afterward, Lamilia and Lucanio settled down to play cards. Lucanio, unsuspecting, lost large sums to the lady, but his ardor was not dampened. Roberto was the first to suffer, for Lamilia simply laughed at him when he asked for half her winnings. She told Lucanio enough of their plot to make him cut all ties with Roberto but not enough to spoil her plans for marriage.

Roberto, penniless, was heard by an actor as he bemoaned his fate and cursed false women.

2682

The prosperous player told Roberto of the material advantages of working in the theater, described some of his own successful parts, and suggested that Roberto join his company as a playwright.

As Roberto took up his new career, Lucanio's fortunes plummeted. Lamilia took all his money and his property, then turned him out on the street, penniless, in rags. He worked for Roberto for a time, then turned to vice and ended his life as "a notorious Pandar." Roberto, in turn, fared little better than his brother. Alternately well-to-do and penniless, he became expert in all kinds of crimes, regularly cheating his landladies, failing to produce any work for which he was paid in advance, and leaving his virtuous wife to amuse himself with women of the streets. At last he found himself despised by his acquaintances, ill, and down to that single groat left him by his father. Repenting, he addressed it: "O now it is too late, too late to buy wit with thee: and therefore will I see if I can sell to careless youth what I negligently forgot to buy."

Critical Evaluation:

Little in the narrative of *Greene's Groats-Worth of Witte Bought with a Million of Repentance* distinguishes it from dozens of other Elizabethan tales of rogues and courtesans. Yet the pamphlet has attracted attention far beyond that merited by its intrinsic literary worth for its comments on the actors and dramatists of Robert Greene's day, and in particular for one of the earliest allusions to William Shakespeare. Greene composed the little book in 1592 when he was on his deathbed, telling of his own misadventures. He ends the work with an extensive list of morals to be drawn from his experiences and issues a special warning "to those Gentlemen his Quondam acquaintance, that spend their wits in making plays." Greene tells his tale in a plain, unadorned style, showing some of his dramatic skill in the dialogue. He concentrates his attention on only a few significant episodes and summarizes other experiences in a sentence or two.

The story at first follows the stock plot of the good child who prospers in virtue and the evil one who suffers the consequences of sin and folly. Greene adds a twist to the tale, however, when both brothers turn out bad. The morals, expressed first in a poem, then in ten rules for virtuous living, have to do with the deceptive pleasures of the world. Greene concludes the pamphlet with specific counsel to his playwright friends. His first remarks are addressed to a famous tragedian, probably Christopher Marlowe, who had died an atheist: "Why should thy excellent wit, [God's] gift, be so blinded, that thou shouldst give no glory to the giver?" This man's example, Greene argues, must be avoided at all costs.

He next speaks to "young Juvenal, that biting Satirist, that lastly with me together writ a Comedy," warning him to direct his criticism to general faults, not to specific individuals, for the latter course makes bitter enemies. Finally, he warns all his friends against the ingratitude of actors, "those Puppets that spake from our mouths, those Antics garnished in our colors." They have forsaken him and left him to starve; they may do the same thing to his friends.

He is especially bitter about one player, "an upstart Crow, beautified with our feathers, that with his *Tiger's heart wrapped in a Player's hide*, supposes he is as well able to bombast out a blank verse as the best of you: and being an absolute *Johannes fac totum*, is in his own conceit the only Shake-scene in a country." The allusion here is certainly to Shakespeare, who was both actor and dramatist and wrote in one of his early plays of a "tiger's heart wrapped in a woman's hide."

Greene ends his pamphlet by retelling Aesop's fable of the grasshopper and the ant. Greene is the grasshopper who spends the summer in revelry and starves in winter, while the provident ant feasts on the food he has stored up. Greene's book has almost no literary unity; it combines prose and verse, narrative and morality, fiction and personal reminiscence. It is, however, typical of the vast body of pamphlet literature of Elizabethan England, and it is a valuable document for the study of the history of the English drama.

Bibliography:
Berek, Peter. "The 'Upstart Crow,' Aesop's Crow, and Shakespeare as a Reviser." *Shakespeare Quarterly* 35, no. 2 (Summer, 1984): 205-207. Reviews interpretations of famous "upstart crow" reference to Shakespeare as either a boorish actor or plagiarist. Supports the plagiarist interpretation, noting that it was a charge based on Shakespeare's early career as a play reviser.
Carroll, D. Allen. "The Player-Patron in *Greene's Groatsworth of Wit.*" *Studies in Philology* 91, no. 3 (Summer, 1994): 301-312. Argues that the player-patron cannot be identified as an actual actor, that it is more likely that he is a "fictional caricature" created to facilitate the work's critique of the Elizabethan theater.

GRIMM'S FAIRY TALES

Type of work: Short fiction
Author: Jacob Grimm (1785-1863) and Wilhelm Grimm (1786-1859)
First published: Kinder- und Hausmärchen, 1812, 1815, revised 1819-1822 (English translation, 1823-1826)

Jacob and Wilhelm Grimm, commonly known as the Brothers Grimm, were not primarily writers but philologists whose names are still as well known in the field of linguistics as they are to readers of fairy tales. "Grimm's Law" is a basic rule in the study of Indo-European languages, and the dictionary of the German language is largely their work. Although the fairy tales were always intended to be read by children, they were also meant to represent German culture at its most fundamental level. The Grimms thought that culture at the level of the common people would be in its purest form and the least influenced by foreign traditions.

During the late eighteenth century, after centuries of cultural stagnation, Germany experienced a cultural renaissance, which brought with it a pride in all things German. The fairy tales were the Grimms' contribution to that flowering. Theirs remains one of the largest, and certainly the most famous, of national collections. Among the best-known stories are "Hansel and Gretel," "Snow White," "The Golden Goose," "The Goose Girl," "Rumplestiltskin," "The Frog Prince," "The Juniper Tree," and "Snow White and Rose Red," and these and many others have become the unquestioned property of childhood in the Western world. In many instances, popular children's books quickly become dated or are crowded into the background by more recent books, but *Grimm's Fairy Tales* remains as popular as when it was first published. New editions of single stories or of the whole collection continue to appear every year.

The term fairy tale is used both for children's stories that have been created and transmitted orally and for literary stories such as those by Hans Christian Andersen, which imitate the folktale form. The stories of the Brothers Grimm are genuine folktales and as such have certain characteristics. They are inevitably short, they involve obvious parallels and repetitions in structure and language, descriptions are brief and stylized, characters are obvious stereotypes, the setting in place and time is usually vague and generalized, animals can talk, and magic is commonplace. Because they are so stylized, very little practice is needed to learn to tell any folktale effectively. The Grimms refined the language of the stories extensively in the course of the seven editions that were published in their lifetimes, but the fact that the stories remain highly tellable shows their essentially oral nature.

The tales reveal little about the external world, history, culture, class, or politics. They are, however, close to the human unconscious, and they have much to say in symbolic terms about sibling rivalry, intergenerational hostility, human sexuality, ambivalence about the opposite sex, fear of parental desertion, and much else. Because fairy tales usually end happily, the term "fairy tale romance," came into being, but even the prettiest fairy tales touch on the darker sides of human nature. Snow White is menaced by her mother's murderous sexual jealousy, and her triumphant marriage coincides with the mother's death. It takes no great depth of psychological sophistication to see in the wicked witch, with her pretense of maternal concern covering treacherous intentions and her welcome house that proves to be a death trap, the malign image of the mother, or to see in the noisy, brutal, and stupid giant who seems always to be coming in from outdoors, the malign image of the father. It is this quality of psychological tension that gives the tales their power, not the quaint trappings of the story—castles, beautiful princesses, and talking frogs. It is this quality that also makes them a little uncomfortable. Literary imitations nearly always emphasize the quaintness and avoid the dangerous quality that underlies the stories, thereby producing fairy stories that are pretty but lifeless.

The Grimms were meticulous scholars and obeyed exacting standards for the collection and transmission of folktales. They have been very generally credited with being the creators of folktale studies, and they have been held up as the model of what a folktale collector should be. There is, however, increasing evidence that their practice was not quite as meticulous as they themselves had implied. Part of the problem was their mixed motives. A work cannot be a scholarly piece of field research, a socially acceptable and appealing children's book, and a patriotic monument to German culture all at the same time. As a result, there came to be increasingly critical views in the course of the twentieth century.

No two people tell a folktale in exactly the same words, and any collection that remains faithful to its sources will vary greatly in language. The Grimms, however, gave their whole collection a smooth, cohesive style. They also significantly lengthened most of the stories by adding small details, snatches of dialogue, and smooth transitions. The result is more satisfying as literature but no longer the pure voice of the people.

An examination of the Grimms' sources has shown that the stories were not after all discovered through extensive fieldwork among the peasantry. In fact, the sources for most of the stories were thoroughly educated, middle-class friends and relatives of the Grimms. If, as the Grimms implied, the ideal storyteller is an old and illiterate peasant woman sitting before her humble hearth telling the old stories to children and grandchildren, this is a person the Grimms never encountered.

From a patriotic viewpoint, too, the Grimms' sources are somewhat dubious. Their prime example of an ideal storyteller, Dorthea Viehman, not only came of a prominent middle-class family, she was found to have been of French extraction and fluent in that language. Other sources were also French, and clearly several of the stories derive at no very distant date from French written sources rather than from ancient Germanic tradition. It would be difficult in any case to show a clearly national character in a collection of folktales, for in their plots, motifs, and mannerisms folktales are international. Most of the stories in Grimm have close parallels in other European languages, and many show similarities with cultures as far away as India and Japan. Poor woodcutters, handsome princes, wicked witches, animal brides, miniature children, and all the other characters of folktales are a universal currency. Gradually it came to be seen that it is only the high literary quality of the Grimms' retelling of these stories, not their national character, that has made them a monument of German literature.

The tales have frequently been criticized for being violent and bloody, and the more gruesome scenes could be considered as evidence that the Grimms were faithful to their sources. In fact, however, they made a number of changes in detail. They carefully sidestepped suggestions of incest and softened hostility or violence within the family by such devices as making at least one of a pair of cruel parents well-intentioned, or by substituting a stepmother for a biological one. On the other hand, in several cases the Grimms added cruel punishments for the wicked that did not exist in the original sources. It is not clear whether those changes reflect the Grimms' sense of justice or whether the purpose was that of creating a neat antithesis between the contrasting fates of the good and evil characters. Certainly, however, the Grimms in a number of cases made the stories more obviously and conventionally moral than their original sources had been. Overall, the Grimms tended to make the fairy tales even more fairy tale-like and more stylized through repetition and parallelism that had not existed in the original source.

Between the first edition in 1812 and the seventh in 1857, the Grimms often discovered variants of the same tale, or what they and others have called "better" versions. As a result, some stories were replaced with other versions, and some tales were revised with elements taken from other versions. This procedure is not uncommon in editing folktales for publication, but the intention is obviously literary rather than scholarly. There is no more reason to believe that any tale once existed in a state of perfection and has been corrupted in the telling than there is to believe that an originally feeble tale has improved in the telling. What the Grimms accomplished is not what they are usually credited with: They did not transmit the actual tales in the actual words of the peasantry, but instead fashioned versions of the tales corresponding to what the Grimms conceived to be the ideal stories.

The earlier French stories of Charles Perrault are generally classed as literary fairy tales, whereas those of the Grimms are thought of as authentic folktales. Both collections, however, are based on folk material, and the Grimms apparently reworked their stories as extensively as Perrault had his. The difference is that Perrault's stories are filled with the atmosphere of the eighteenth century and of the French court, while the Grimms' stories seem timeless. The Grimms did modify their stories to suit their own attitudes and those of their age, but never in an obvious way. Although stories from an oral tradition do have a collective and impersonal quality, any given telling is usually noticeably colored by the personality and educational level of the teller. Perrault's "Cinderella," for example, is marked by its courtly and aristocratic tone, whereas "The Snow Queen" by Hans Christian Andersen reflects nineteenth century sentimentality and an idiosyncratic whimsicality. The Grimms' tales, by contrast, achieve a collective and impersonal voice that represents a great accomplishment in the history of the folktale.

Jack Hart

Bibliography:
Bottigheimer, Ruth B. *Grimm's Bad Girls and Bold Boys*. New Haven, Conn.: Yale University Press, 1987. Attempts to explain the tales in terms of their nineteenth century context.
Ellis, John M. *One Fairy Story Too Many*. Chicago: University of Chicago Press, 1983. A needed but perhaps overly harsh reappraisal of the Grimms' methods and intentions.
Mallet, Carl-Heinz. *Fairy Tales and Children*. Translated by Joachim Neugroschel. 1st American ed. New York: Schocken Books, 1984. A psychological approach to several of the tales, with special emphasis on the interaction between children and parents.
Sexton, Anne. *Transformations*. Boston: Houghton Mifflin, 1971. A verse adaption of a number of the tales in modern idiom. Sexton brings the tales into the twentieth century idiom without losing any of the Grimms' magic or wonder.
Zipes, Jack. *The Brothers Grimm: From Enchanted Forests to the Modern World*. New York: Routledge, 1989. A traditional discussion of the Brothers Grimm and their tales.

GROUP PORTRAIT WITH LADY

Type of work: Novel
Author: Heinrich Böll (1917-1985)
Type of plot: Social realism
Time of plot: 1922-1970
Locale: Rhineland, Germany
First published: Gruppenbild mit Dame, 1971 (English translation, 1973)

Principal characters:
> LENI PFEIFFER, née Gruyton, the lady
> HUBERT GRUYTON, Leni's father
> HEINRICH GRUYTON, Leni's brother
> LEV BORISOVICH GRUYTON, Leni's son
> ALOIS PFEIFFER, Leni's husband
> OTTO HOYSER, Hubert Gruyton's head bookkeeper
> LOTTE HOYSER, his daughter-in-law
> ERHART SCHWEIGERT, Leni's cousin and lover
> WALTER PELZER, Leni's boss
> RAPHEL, a nun
> MARGRET SCHLOMER, Leni's best friend
> BORIS LVOVICH, Leni's lover and Lev's Father
> AU, the author

The Story:

Leni Pfeiffer, at the age of forty-eight, seemed in serious financial and personal difficulty. Her son was in jail, she was unemployed, and bailiffs had seized many of her possessions. In addition, she was harassed daily by neighbors who called her bitch, slut, or Communist whore. The author learned this while writing a "portrait" of Leni. Because she was both taciturn and reticent, however, he was forced to obtain his information from interviews with as many informants as possible. These ranged from her loyal friends, such as Margret Schlomer and Lotte Hoyser, to a nun in Rome who knew of Leni only through gossip and records.

Leni's educational career had been disastrous, primarily because most subjects were presented in a way that neglected a sensual dimension. Her only successes came when, from the age of fourteen to sixteen, she attended a convent boarding school and met Sister Rahel, who understood Leni's type of intelligence and respected her instinctive appreciation of nature and of the entire body, including its waste, secretions, and internal organs.

In 1939, her brother, Heinrich, returned from school. The homecoming was troubled because Heinrich scorned his father's attempts to keep him out of the military and he refused to be spared when others were not. In defiance, Heinrich joined the army, together with his cousin Erhard. Leni loved Erhard, but he was too shy to consummate their relationship, sublimating his feelings in passionate poetry. In 1940, Heinrich and Erhard were sent to Denmark, where they offered an anti-aircraft cannon to the Danes for its value as scrap metal. At the trial, Erhard said, "We are dying for an honorable profession, for the arms trade." Just before they were executed, Heinrich cried "Shit on Germany."

A period of mourning fell on the Gruytons. Then in June, 1941, Leni attended an office party and met Alois Pfeiffer, the son of one of her father's friends. She danced with him fourteen times and spent the next three days with him, only to find him insensitive both as a lover and a man. At his insistence, they married the same day that Alois was called to join his division. After his son's death, Hubert Gruyton had lost interest in his own company and created a totally fictitious business staffed by characters from Russian literature. The deception was discovered and Gruyton was jailed for life. Shortly after, at the end of 1942, Leni's mother died.

To support herself, Leni got a job working as a wreath maker for Walter Pelzer. There she met Boris, a Russian prisoner under the secret protection of an unnamed important personage. When they met, Leni infuriated her patriotic colleagues by offering him a cup of coffee. In spite of the danger, Leni and Boris began an affair. Leni became radiantly happy at last, since this relationship provided her with the transcendent spiritual and physical experience she had been seeking.

Chaos engulfed the city in 1945 as the war neared its end, but Leni ignored this, selling her property in order to provide simple pleasures for herself and her lover. Freed from prison, her father returned. Boris got the papers of a dead German soldier, which enabled him to move about openly. The now pregnant Leni, Boris, Hubert, Lotte Hoyser and her sons, and Margret moved into vaults under the tombs in the cemetery. However, Boris was picked up by the Americans; believing he was a German, they gave him to the French. Leni sought him frantically and crossed military lines on her bicycle, only to discover his grave.

By 1970, Leni had left her job. Lotte Hoyser's father-in-law and sons planned to evict Leni from her apartment in the house she had once owned because they believed she was totally irresponsible when she sublet her apartment to foreigners and garbage collectors and refused to profit on the rent she charged. Discovering this, the author immediately contacted Leni's friends, who established a "Help Leni" committee, collecting money and using garbage trucks to create a huge traffic jam so that her debts could be paid before the bailiffs arrived.

Leni was content now. She was pregnant, her apartment was saved, and Lev was soon to be released from prison. The author and other members of the Help Leni committee were also secure in their lives and relationships, at least for the present.

Critical Evaluation:

Heinrich Böll, one of the most famous German writers of the post- World War II period, won the Nobel Prize in Literature in 1972, a year after the publication of *Group Portrait with Lady*. Described by many critics as the conscience of his nation because of his political and social views, he attempts in this novel to examine World War II and its aftermath. Böll once said that he placed the entire burden of German history from 1922 to 1970 on Leni's shoulders. The work shows a culmination of Böll's themes and stylistic devices. Using the story of the Gruytons, Böll presents the political and social climate in the Rhineland before, during, and after the war. He probes the relationship between government, business, and religious establishments and the individual, concentrating on the physical, emotional, and economic survival of ordinary citizens whose needs are often neglected when they conflict with the desires of the institution.

Since the focal point of the novel is World War II, the havoc that government can create for its citizens permeates the novel. However, the novel focuses not on the evil that the Nazi government unleashed but on the effects of those policies on the individual. Leni, for example, loses her family, her lovers, her mentor, and her home because of war.

For Böll, the economic establishment is as destructive as any government, since the two join together in a terrible alliance of war for profit. All of the fortunes in the novel are created through war: Hubert Gruyton built fortifications; Walter Pelzer began his career collecting gold from corpses after World War I; the Hoysers started their empire through "Anti-Aryanization," buying property that the Nazis had stolen and were now forced by to sell. Erhard's cry about dying for a noble profession is an ironic comment on the guilt of the business world. The evils of materialism are not just a product of war, however; peacetime also allows profiteers to flourish at the expense of the common people. The Hoysers represent the inhuman quality of capitalism. Leni does not wish to acquire wealth, and they condemn her for it. Although they had lived free in Leni's house for years, they charge her rent as soon as they own it. When she sublets to people they do not approve of—foreigners and refuse workers—lowering the value of the neighborhood, Werner Hoyser calls her monstrous. He notes that the state, the Church, and even the Marxists support his view that striving after profit is the only acceptable way to live. Love, kindness, and humanity are threatened by an economic system that places a greater value on profit than on the human spirit.

The last of these institutions is the Catholic church. Böll believed that the Church betrayed itself, first by signing a pact with Hitler and then by ignoring the plight of the poor after the war. The Church fails Leni and Rahel, both truly good individuals. Rahel is abandoned and eventually starves to death on church grounds. Church authority refuses to bless or recognize the love and humanity that falls outside of its rigid guidelines; the contrast between the sanctioned marriage between Alois and Leni, where he uses his conjugal rights to rape her, and the sinful relationship between Boris and Leni, which mirrors the holy family, reveals this.

Böll frequently uses religious symbolism. Both Leni and Rahel are connected to the Virgin Mary: Rahel through Leni's painting, "Part of the Retina of the Left Eye of the Virgin Mary alias Rahel" and Leni in multiple circumstances. Leni sees the Madonna regularly on television. When Klementina also sees the Madonna, she comments, "It is . . . Leni . . . appearing to herself." Leni, Boris, and Lev are compared to the Holy Family. Leni has many saintlike qualities. Her patience, generosity, and stoicism are almost unnatural. A common criticism of *Group Portrait with Lady* is that Leni is too unrealistic. Indeed, Leni miraculously ignores the unpleasantness around her. When she tries to find a book by Kafka in a library in January, 1945, she is totally unaware of the danger of requesting books by Jewish writers.

This symbolism reveals that Leni is more than an ordinary woman. She represents Böll's vision of the ideal, of utopian behavior. The establishment, which has proved itself corrupt, shallow, and avaricious, ignores the needs of the ordinary citizen. It is contrasted with the members of the Help Leni committee, a varied group of outsiders, intellectuals, and laborers, misfits of all sorts and "deliberate underachievers." What they have in common is a willingness to sacrifice themselves to help Leni, who herself provided a model for such generous behavior. Kurt Hoyser even calls her apartment a breeding ground for utopian ideals.

The main plot revolves about Leni. However, a secondary plot line introduces the Author, a professional writer who searches for Leni through extensive interviews. The novel is structured around the author's summation of his research, which is corroborated by statements from his informants. In the beginning of the story, he attempts to remain impartial and to provide an unbiased account of Leni. Before the last chapter, he has only seen her twice very briefly. He finds himself drawn to Leni, however, and in chapter 9, he describes his dilemma: how much should he report and what should he conceal to protect her. Eventually he loses all impartiality and becomes an active member of the Help Leni committee. This involvement reinforces Böll's vision. Once the author chooses sides, he discovers his own happiness. There is both a happy ending and no ending. Böll himself said that he stopped in mid story, but that he could have continued with Leni's saga forever.

Mary Mahony

Bibliography:
Butler, Michael, ed. *The Narrative Fiction of Heinrich Böll: Social Conscience and Literary Achievement.* Cambridge, England: Cambridge University Press, 1994. Analyzes Böll's recurring themes of love, morality, economic pressures, and organized religion and his emphasis on renewal and utopianism. Discusses Leni's influence on other characters and the role of the narrator.
Conrad, Robert C. *Heinrich Böll.* Boston: Twayne, 1981. Excellent introductory source. Provides a helpful chronological summary of the novel's complex development and identifies key actions, ideas, and symbols.
Reid, J. H. *Heinrich Böll: A German for His Time.* Oxford, England: Berg Publishers, 1988. Provides informative biographical information and evaluates historical and literary influences on the writer. Discusses symbolism and defines the refusal to participate in evils of society as Böll's central theme.
Vogt, Jochen. "Böll's Utopia: Great Refusal, Small Pleasures." In *From the Greeks to the Greens: Images of the Simple Life,* edited by Reinhold Grimm and Jost Hermand. Madison: University of Wisconsin Press, 1989. Examines historical and political influences on Böll's themes and discusses the effects of materialism and capitalism on the common man. Traces these themes through earlier novels, finding a culmination in the character of Leni.
Zachau, Reinhard K. *Heinrich Böll: Forty Years of Criticism.* Columbia, S.C.: Camden House, 1994. Discusses critical approaches to Böll's work. Provides a clear overview of theme, characterization, and symbolism and evaluates Böll's influence on subsequent German literature.

GROWTH OF THE SOIL

Type of work: Novel
Author: Knut Hamsun (Knut Pedersen, 1859-1952)
Type of plot: Social realism
Time of plot: Late nineteenth century
Locale: Norway
First published: Markens grøde, 1917 (English translation, 1920)

Principal characters:

ISAK, a Norwegian peasant
INGER, his wife
ELESEUS,
SIVERT,
LEOPOLDINE, and
REBECCA, their children
OLINE, Inger's relative
GEISSLER, Isak's friend
AXEL STRÖM, a neighbor
BARBRO, Axel's wife

The Story:

Isak left a small Norwegian village and set out into the wilds to claim a homestead. Carrying some food and a few rude implements, he wandered until he found a stretch of grass and woodland, with a stream nearby. There he cleared the land. He had to carry everything he brought out from the village on his back. He built a sod house, procured several goats, and prepared for winter.

He sent word by traveling Lapps that he needed a woman to help in the fields. One day, Inger appeared with her belongings. She had a harelip and was not beautiful, but she was a good worker and shared Isak's bed. She brought things from her home, including a cow.

That winter, Inger bore her first child, Eleseus. He was a fine boy, with no harelip. In the spring, Inger's relative Oline came to see the new family. She promised to return to take care of the farming in the fall, when Inger and Isak planned to go to town to be married and have the child baptized. The farm prospered through the summer.

The harvest was not good, but potatoes carried Isak's family through the winter without hunger. Inger bore a second son, Sivert. Then Geissler, the sheriff's officer, came to tell Isak that he would have to pay the government for his land. He promised to make the terms as easy as possible. Geissler lost his position, however, and a new officer came to look at the land with his assistant, Brede Olsen. He too promised to do what he could for Isak.

One day, Inger sent her husband to town. While he was gone, she bore her third child, a girl with a harelip. Knowing what the deformed child would suffer, Inger strangled the infant and buried the body in the woods. Later she convinced Isak she had not really been pregnant.

Oline, who had known that Inger was pregnant, found the grave in the woods when she came to the farm. Inger explained her deed as well as she could to Isak, and he was satisfied. When Lapp beggars told the story of the hidden grave, the sheriff's officer heard of it and there was an investigation and a trial. Inger was sent to prison at Bergen for eight years. Needing someone to help with the farm and the children, Isak hired Oline.

2692

Isak got the deed for his land and paid the first installment, but there was no joy in his farming now that Inger was gone. He worked only from habit and necessity. Geissler came to tell Isak that he had seen Inger in Bergen and that she had borne a girl in prison, a child without a blemish.

The old life was changing. Men came through to put up a telegraph line. Between Isak's place and the village, Brede started a farm. Other settlers appeared as the years passed. Oline was unbearable. She stole livestock from Isak and spent his money for trifles. Speculating on copper mining, Geissler bought some of Isak's land. With Geissler's help, Inger, whose harelip had been operated on in Bergen, was finally released from prison. At first she was happy to return to the farm with little Leopoldine, but she had learned city ways and now farm life seemed rough and lonely. She no longer helped Isak with his work. Eleseus was sent to town, where he got a job in an office. Sivert, who was much like his father, remained at home. Axel Ström now had a farm near Isak's. Brede's daughter, Barbro, came to stay with Axel and help him with his work.

Inger bore another daughter, Rebecca, and Isak hired a girl to help with the housework. Eleseus returned from town to help on the farm. Geissler sold the copper mine property, and Isak received a large sum for the rights he had retained on the property. He was able to buy the first mowing machine in the district. Eleseus took an interest in Barbro, but when he discovered that she was pregnant, he went back to the city. Axel bought Brede's farm when Brede moved back to town. One day, he found Barbro down by the brook with her drowned baby. She said she had fallen, and the baby had been born in the water. Axel did not quarrel with her, for fear she would leave him.

That winter, after Barbro went to Bergen, Axel had to manage the farm himself. One day, he was pinned to the ground by a falling tree during a snowstorm. Brede, who was angry with Axel, passed by without offering to help. Quite by chance, Oline heard Axel's cries for help and released him. Afterward, she stayed to manage his house for him, but she never let him forget his debt to her for saving his life. Little by little, she learned the story of Barbro and the baby.

A man named Aronsen built a big store in the new neighborhood. Miners soon moved in to begin working the land Geissler and Isak had sold. Then the mine played out. Geissler owned the additional land needed to keep the mine working, but he asked more than the mine owners would pay. The mine remained idle.

When the rumor about Barbro's baby at last came to the attention of the authorities, Axel and Barbro had to appear for trial in the town. Because there was so little evidence, Axel went free. Barbro went to work for the wife of the sheriff's officer, who promised to see that Barbro behaved herself.

There seemed little hope that the mine would reopen, for Geissler would not sell his land. After Aronsen sold his store to Isak, Eleseus was persuaded to return from the city and take over the store property. Isak was now a rich man. In the spring, Geissler sold his land and work resumed at the mine. The miners, however, lived on the far side of the property in another district. The village was no better off than before.

Barbro could no longer stand being watched by the wife of the sheriff's officer. When she returned to Axel, he took her in after she convinced him that she meant to stay and marry him. Old Oline would not leave Axel's farm, but she soon grew ill and died, leaving the young people by themselves.

Eleseus did not manage the store well. At last, when he saw failure staring him in the face, he borrowed more money from his father and set out for America. He never returned. Sivert and two other men carried some of the goods from the store to the new mine, but the mine had shut down again. They found Geissler wandering about the deserted mine; he said that he was thinking of buying back the property. When the three men returned, Isak was sowing corn. The copper mine and the store, good times and bad, had come and gone, but the soil was still there. For Isak and Inger, the first sowers in the wilds, the corn still grew.

Critical Evaluation:

Widely regarded as Norway's foremost novelist and one of the greatest prose writers of Scandinavia, Knut Hamsun won the Nobel Prize in Literature in 1920, after a career that had already spanned thirty years and was to last for almost thirty more. *Growth of the Soil* was preceded by twenty-eight earlier books, including fourteen novels and six plays; seven more volumes were to come. A man of scant formal education, Hamsun nevertheless read widely, particularly in the literature of his homeland, and he traveled a great deal, including two extended stays in America when he was a young man.

At first a practitioner (and, according to many literary historians, a chief innovator) of the psychological novel, Hamsun turned his attention to issues of recent history and contemporary society shortly after the turn of the century. In such books as *Children of the Age* (1913) and *Segelfoss Town* (1915), he voiced merciless criticism of the modern age for allowing industrial production to replace craftsmanship and democracy to substitute for the leadership of exceptional individuals. These concerns are also found in *Growth of the Soil*, but instead of simply criticizing modernity, Hamsun here attempted to prescribe a positive remedy for the problems he saw. He did so by presenting his readers with an example worthy of emulation and by pointing to nature's power to eliminate corruption and strengthen true humanity.

Hamsun's main theme is the salutary influence of a rural life and a close relationship with the soil. The protagonist of the book, Isak Sellanraa, is presented as a man without a personal history, but it is hinted that he may have had a dark past. He comes to an isolated area of northern Norway in search of a place to homestead and finds a spot far away from human society. He is presented as a simple but noble man. Not unlike the settlers on the American frontier, he builds a good farm and a fine life for himself and his family through hard work.

Like Isak, his wife Inger is also able to rebuild her life by working to establish the farm. Because she was born with a harelip, Inger has had a difficult time as a child and young woman. In contrast to her peers, who looked only at her outward appearance, however, Isak is able to appreciate Inger's essential qualities: her potential for becoming a help to him in his work and good mother for his children. Life on the wilderness farm allows Inger to flourish in a manner that would have been impossible for her in an established community.

Hamsun couples his emphasis on the simple values of hard work, cooperation with nature, and the natural attraction between a man and a woman with great simplicity of style and characterization. Inger and Isak, both very simple human beings, address each other without rhetorical flourish. Hamsun tells the story of an idealized enterprise almost in the style of a folktale. He focuses on the simple narration of events and adds few philosophical asides.

Like a folktale, however, *Growth of the Soil* describes challenges and tests to which a protagonist is subjected, and it is through his description of such trials that Hamsun voices his social criticism. Isak's first challenge comes form the Norwegian government. Having settled on public land, Isak is in danger of being deprived of the results of his hard work because he has neglected to secure legal title to his farm. Through the assistance of the local bailiff, a man named Geissler, Isak is allowed to purchase the land on quite favorable terms, but society has intruded into Isak's paradise with its insistence that the concept of ownership be acknowledged, and Isak must yield to the authority of the state. The law also makes itself felt when it is discovered that Inger has strangled one of her babies to death. Remembering her own suffering as a child and young woman, Inger could not bear to think that her daughter might meet with the same fate.

When as a result of her crime Inger is sent to prison, she is educated, learns to sew, and has an operation for her harelip. By the time she returns to Isak, she has changed both literally and figuratively. She has been profoundly affected by civilization and brings its contagion with her into Isak's family. Hamsun voices his social criticism by showing what becomes of the oldest son as a result of his mother's influence. Ill at ease with farm life, Eleseus first gets a position as a clerk in a local store and then moves to the city. After squandering much money, he finally emigrates to America and is never heard from again. Hamsun shows that the life of the city, with its emphasis on commerce and industry, has a destructive effect on human character. In contrast to Eleseus, his brother Sivert, who stays with the farm, avoids spiritual corruption.

Hamsun also develops his theme of social and spiritual degeneration by showing what happens to a community when it moves away from cultivating the soil. A small settlement is formed when Isak is joined by other homesteaders. When copper ore is discovered in a nearby mountain, however, industry comes to the area in the shape of a mining operation, and with it comes the establishment of a general store. People begin to rely increasingly on a monetary economy. Only when the mining enterprise collapses, do they discover that they should have stayed with the land.

The book's worst example of corruption is found in the character Barbro, who, motivated by the selfishness and lack of natural affection that Hamsun associates with city life, kills two healthy babies. Hamsun, nevertheless, allows even her to be rehabilitated through marriage to a hard-working homesteader. The final lesson of *Growth of the Soil* is that nature has an almost unlimited power to heal.

"Critical Evaluation" by Jan Sjåvik

Bibliography:

Ferguson, Robert. *Enigma: The Life of Knut Hamsun.* New York: Farrar, Straus & Giroux, 1987. The best biography of Humsun in any language. Presents a balanced and detailed overview of Humsun's life and places *Growth of the Soil* in the context of the author's life and works. Ferguson stresses the mythic aspects of the novel.

Ford, Jesse Hill. "On Knut Hamsun's *Growth of the Soil.*" In *Rediscoveries: Informal Essays in Which Well-Known Novelists Rediscover Neglected Works of Fiction by One of Their Favorite Authors,* edited by David Madden. New York: Crown Publishers, 1971. Emphasizes the ethical concerns underlying *Growth of the Soil,* particularly Hamsun's sense of the benefits of honest stewardship of the land.

Næss, Harald. *Knut Hamsun.* Boston: Twayne, 1984. A survey of Hamsun's works written by one of the world's foremost Hamsun scholars. Includes a section devoted to *Growth of the Soil* as well as additional references throughout the text. Næss emphasizes Geissler's role as a spokesperson for the author.

_____. "Knut Hamsun and *Growth of the Soil.*" *Scandinavica* 25, no. 1 (May, 1986): 5-17. A general discussion of the novel and Hamsun's ideas at the time when he was working on it.

GUARD OF HONOR

Type of work: Novel
Author: James Gould Cozzens (1903-1978)
Type of plot: Psychological realism
Time of plot: Three days during World War II
Locale: Air Force base in Florida
First published: 1948

Principal characters:

MAJOR GENERAL IRA N. "BUS" BEAL, the commanding general of the
  Ocanara Base
SAL BEAL, his wife
COLONEL NORMAN ROSS, the Air Inspector on General Beal's staff
CORA ROSS, his wife
CAPTAIN NATHANIEL HICKS, an officer in Special Projects and an editor
  in civilian life
SECOND LIEUTENANT AMANDA TURCK, a member of the Women's Army
  Corps (WAC)
LIEUTENANT COLONEL BENNY CARRICKER, General Beal's copilot
BRIGADIER GENERAL NICHOLS, the assistant to the commanding general
  of the Air Force
LIEUTENANT EDSELL, a writer assigned to Special Projects
LIEUTENANT LIPPA, a member of WAC who is in love with Edsell
LIEUTENANT WILLIS, a black pilot
MR. WILLIS, his father

The Story:

The huge and sprawling Air Force base at Ocanara, Florida, was almost a world in itself. At
its head was Major General "Bus" Beal, who had been a hero in the Pacific theater in the early
days of the war and was still at the age of forty-one an energetic and skillful flyer. To keep the
operation of the base running smoothly, the general relied heavily on his Air Inspector, Colonel
Norman Ross, who brought to his military duties the same resourcefulness that had characterized his career as a judge in peacetime; Judge Ross needed all of his acumen to do the job.

Landing his AT-7 one night at the Ocanara airstrip, the general came close to colliding with
a B-17 piloted by Lieutenant Willis, one of the black fliers recently assigned to Ocanara, who
had violated the right of way. Lieutenant Colonel Benny Carricker, General Beal's copilot,
struck Lieutenant Willis, who had to be hospitalized, whereupon General Beal confined
Carricker to his quarters. The incident, while small, triggered a series of problems that, in the
next two days, threatened to destroy the normal operations of the base. Several of the black
fliers, incensed by what had happened to Lieutenant Willis and further outraged because a
separate service club had been set up for them, attempted to enter the white officers' recreation
building, an action that came close to starting a riot.

To complicate the situation, tension had developed between the Air Force base and some
leading citizens of the town. Colonel Ross was the only member of General Beal's staff who
recognized the hazards of the situation. For the others—in particular Colonel Mowbray and his
assistant, Chief Warrant Officer Botwinick—the difficulties seemed routine. Even General Beal

was of little aid to Colonel Ross, for he was brooding unhappily over the arrest of Colonel Carricker and over the recent suicide of an old friend.

Other forces were compounding the difficulties among the members of the Air Force base. For Lieutenant Edsell, Willis' hospitalization was the springboard for agitation, and he helped arrange a visit from Lieutenant Willis' father to the base hospital. Only a few of the base personnel understood the difficulties Colonel Ross faced and the skill with which he operated. Those who did, like Captain Nathaniel Hicks, were too concerned with their own problems to be of much assistance.

On the day Mr. Willis was to visit his son, the Ocanara base was host to another unexpected visitor, Brigadier General Nichols, the personal representative of the commanding general of the Air Force. To the embarrassment of all concerned, General Nichols' purpose in coming to Ocanara was to award Lieutenant Willis a medal for bravery.

Whatever Colonel Ross may have dreaded from the visit, he was relieved to find General Nichols a not unsympathetic man, for the general had trained himself to be stoic and tolerant. He understood the situation at a glance, and at the awarding of the medal at the hospital, conducted himself so that Willis himself was charmed.

On the following day, the base prepared for a celebration in honor of General Beal's forty-first birthday. Colonel Mowbray had organized a military parade that was to include not only marching men and WACs but also planes flying in formation and parachute drops. General Nichols shared the reviewing stand with General Beal and his staff. In the nearby field, near a lake, Captain Hicks and his friend from the WAC detachment, Lieutenant Turck, were posted as observers.

The parade began, and from their observation post, Captain Hicks and Lieutenant Turck saw hundreds of parachutists begin the slow descent into a simulated conflict. Then tragedy struck. A group of parachutists, having timed their leap badly, dropped into the lake instead of hitting the field. In horror, Captain Hicks saw them struggle briefly in the water and then sink.

When knowledge of the disaster reached General Beal's office, there was a moment of furious commotion. Charges and countercharges were flung without restraint. To Colonel Ross, it seemed that fate had ordained nothing but problems for him and the base. General Beal finally took command and began directing rescue operations with precision and skill, revealing that throughout the past few days he had not been unaware of the conflicts going on.

That night, Colonel Ross accompanied General Nichols to the plane that was to return him to Washington. Reviewing the difficulties of the past three days, the Colonel saw that General Nichols was right: One could do no more than one's best and, for the rest, trust the situation to right itself.

Critical Evaluation:

Although *Guard of Honor* is one of the best military novels published shortly after the end of World War II, the war itself seems almost incidental to the action. The central problem of the book is how to manage a huge, complex, necessary institution in which a large number of men and women from all social, economic, and ethnic backgrounds reflecting the full spectrum of cultural, political, and racial attitudes must cooperate. The war only exacerbates preexistent social problems and underscores the severe dangers that can result if the system fails to function as it should.

James Gould Cozzens sees two likely problems in any institution: Incompetent or inadequate individuals will inevitably be placed in positions of authority, and the impersonal necessities of the organization will conflict with the justified personal needs of its functionaries. Reconciling these problems is the test to which Cozzens puts his characters. The "heroes" are those who recognize both the system's fallibility and its necessity, those who try to compensate for the weaknesses by accepting more than their share of responsibilities. The villains are those who cannot or will not accept their responsibilities within the system, as well as those who try to "solve" the problems outside the system.

Cozzens introduces the reader to a number of authority figures who fail for a variety of reasons to do their jobs adequately: old Colonel Mowbray, who simply lacks the requisite intelligence to perform in the job that seniority has given him; his superior, Major General "Bus" Beal, who is a strong leader in times of active crisis but cannot handle the kind of problem that demands a slow, patient untangling of complex attitudes and relationships under continuing pressure; and Beal's copilot, Lieutenant Colonel Benny Carricker, whose youthful, impulsive courage predisposes him to recklessness. Nevertheless, Cozzens suggests, such human weakness can be overcome if wiser and more dispassionate men are willing to accept additional responsibilities without thought of recognition or recompense.

The major action of the novel revolves around the racial tensions that surface at Ocanara when black Lieutenant Stanley Willis is struck by Carricker in a dispute over Willis' violation of the right of way. Subsequently, a confrontation ensues when the blacks are banned from the white Officer's Club. Willis, the potential black leader, is hospitalized, removing him from the situation, and Beal, the base commander, issues hasty and extreme orders and then escapes by going on solo airplane rides.

The brunt of the crisis falls on the shoulders of Colonel Ross, who is a typical Cozzens hero. Although old and in precarious health, Ross accepts the responsibility for Beal's job as well as his own, because he knows how quickly such incidents can get out of control. Ross acknowledges that the blacks have a basic right to equal treatment, but he is more afraid of disrupting the morale of the much larger group of white officers. In other words, the immediate practicality of the situation demands a moderate approach to the rights of the offended minority. A "parachutist," he thinks to himself, "cannot climb back. . . . Gravity is a condition, not a theory. In our trouble with the colored officers we also have a condition, not a theory."

Accepting this "condition," Ross slowly works it out, devoting more energy to it than is good for his health and aware that nobody understands or appreciates what he is doing. He knows that "these are tough times. . . . We have a job; and a man who's given part of it has to do it right—or else." He also knows that, since some are not going to "do it right," those others who see the difficulties as they arise must correct them immediately before they snowball into major disasters. Near the end of the book, a practice parachute jump ends in many deaths precisely because, in the early planning stages, small details were not worked out and small responsibilities not assumed.

Ross is not the only one to do more than his share. His problems are paralleled in those of several junior officers who take responsibility for the shortcomings of their men. The crisis is finally resolved when Lieutenant Willis returns to duty, takes over the leadership of the black officers, and moderates their demands.

Although Cozzens accepts well-intentioned failure with equanimity, he is less tolerant of overt challenges to authority. Lieutenant James Edsell represents the most destructive element in any organization, the individual who, acting out of a distorted moral sense, tries to force his own kind of solution to the problem. Edsell's kind of liberalism refuses to see the complexities of the problem, and he agitates for a solution in accordance with his personal moralistic judgments. Edsell interprets all events in terms of his own assumptions and makes no attempt to learn the real facts.

Instead of helping the blacks to secure their demands, he intensifies the problem and sharpens the racial antagonisms by importing a black newspaperman to publicize the problem and Willis' father to embarrass the Air Force. He not only attacks military policy, which he does not understand, but also competes with it. When the authorities attempt to move in the direction of his liberal views, he consciously avoids their help.

It is evident that Edsell is dedicated not to the betterment of the blacks at Ocanara but to the aggrandizement of his own self-righteous ego. Through the character of Edsell, Cozzens makes clear his attitude toward reformers and radicals who would force easy solutions to complex problems in accordance with their own abstract moral prejudices.

Cozzens makes no blanket approval of the system, but he demonstrates that its problems can be solved only within the institutional framework. There is, in *Guard of Honor*, no sudden revelation in time of crisis, only a painful awareness of the problems and of the methods necessary to solve them. At the center of those "solutions," which are usually temporary, inefficient compromises—the only kind available to men in the real, everyday world—are men like Colonel Ross: rational, moderate, sensitive individuals willing to do whatever needs to be done, even at the sacrifice of self. The success or failure of human beings, Cozzens seems to suggest, depends on whether or not, in times of continuing crisis, individuals of reason can rise to the occasion.

"Critical Evaluation" by Keith Neilson

Bibliography:
Bracher, Frederick. *The Novels of James Gould Cozzens*. New York: Harcourt, Brace, 1959. Points out that the flashback-filled opening episode introduces the themes of possession, power delegation, racial antagonisms, and personal and psychological tangles. Identifies Cozzens' skillful patterning of apparently random incidents and defines the novel's underlying message that inevitable concessions to circumstance should not invalidate an individual's moral, honorable ideals.

Bruccoli, Matthew J. *James Gould Cozzens: A Life Apart*. New York: Harcourt Brace Jovanovich, 1983. In one chapter, the author narrates Cozzens' military career and identifies military personnel used as models for characters in *Guard of Honor*. Another chapter discusses the novel's composition and contents and explains its popular and critical reception.

Dillard, R. H. W. "*Guard of Honor:* Providential Luck in a Hard-Luck World." In *James Gould Cozzens: New Acquist of True Experience*, edited by Matthew J. Bruccoli. Carbondale: Southern Illinois University Press, 1979. Sees *Guard of Honor* as a novel of freedom and values though in a context of seeming enclosure, restriction, and ruin.

Michel, Pierre. *James Gould Cozzens*. Boston: Twayne, 1974. Analyzes Cozzens' conclusions in *Guard of Honor* that war, like life, disrupts harmonies, that heroism is limited, that reality countermands principles, and that duty requires responsbile compromising, even the bending of rules. The center of the novel's intricate narrative is an observant, contemplative consciousness.

Mooney, Harry John, Jr. *James Gould Cozzens: Novelist of Intellect*. Pittsburgh, Pa.: University of Pittsburgh Press, 1963. Asserts that in *Guard of Honor*, Cozzens uses intelligent narrative points of view, pauses to dissect motives and principles, traces causes and effects, and dramatizes the acceptable consequences of intellectual limitations.

GUEST THE ONE-EYED

Type of work: Novel
Author: Gunnar Gunnarsson (1889-1975)
Type of plot: Domestic
Time of plot: c. 1900
Locale: Iceland
First published: Borgslægtens historie, 1912-1914 (4 volumes; abridged in translation as
Guest the One-Eyed, 1920)

Principal characters:

ØRLYGUR À BORG, a well-to-do landowner
ORMARR ØRLYGSSON, his son
KETILL ØRLYGSSON, Ormarr's brother
GUDRUN or RUNA, Pall à Seyru's daughter
ALMA, the daughter of Vivild, a Danish banker
ØRLYGUR THE YOUNGER, the son of Ketill and Runa
"BAGGA" SNEBIORG, an illegitimate woman

The Story:

The Borg farm, something of a refuge for anyone who needed help, was the home of Ørlygur the Rich, an energetic and compassionate Icelandic farmer sometimes spoken of as "the King" because of the vast number of servants he retained and the hundreds of cattle, horses, and sheep he owned. Ørlygur hoped that one of his sons, either Ormarr or Ketill, would become the master of Borg. Ormarr, however, was interested in playing the violin, and Ketill decided to become a priest.

The two brothers represented extremes of character. Ormarr was sensitive, intelligent, perceptive, creative, and honest, while Ketill was devious, jealous, destructive, blasphemous, and dishonest. Ormarr unselfishly married Runa, daughter of a poor farmer. Once Ketill, who was secretly eager to seize control of the property at Borg, had become the parish priest, he preached a series of sermons that incrementally encouraged the peasants to believe that a great sin had been committed by one of the community leaders. Finally, Ketill charged his own father with being the father of a child born to Runa, the daughter of a poor farmer, Pall à Seyru. The charge was coupled with the suggestion that Ørlygur also had persuaded Ormarr to marry Runa in order to hide his crime of lust. The depth of Ketill's depravity finally became evident to the citizens of the community when Ørlygur, with convincing simplicity and wrath, revealed that the priest who was condemning his own father was himself the father of Runa's child. The terrible accusation and its aftermath proved too much for Ørlygur; he died as a result. Ketill's wife went mad.

Repenting his sins, Ketill left Borg and, having rejected the idea of suicide, became a wanderer, dependent for his board and lodging on the Icelandic farmers to whom he brought simple, soul-restoring messages of love and compassion. He regarded himself as a guest on earth, and "Guest" became his name. He lost his eye in saving a child from a burning farm; hence, in the Icelandic tradition of using nicknames he became "Guest the One-Eyed."

Ormarr, after throwing away an opportunity to become a world famous concert violinist and after achieving a remarkable financial success as a shipping magnate, returned to Borg in search of a new challenge.

Later, Guest the One-Eyed returned to Borg. He carried with him the memory of the curses that everyone had put on Ketill, whom all believed dead. His reconciliation with his family—something almost beyond hope, since Ketill's lying charge from the pulpit had both killed his father and driven Ketill's wife mad—was partly the result of his having destroyed the old Ketill by his life as a wanderer, but it was also a result of the readiness of the Icelanders to forgive for the sake of the family, that union that makes life in inhospitable Iceland possible. Old wounds showed signs of healing in the prospective marriage of Ørlygur the younger, Ketill's son, and Bagga, the beautiful illegitimate daughter of the woman of Bolli who, like Ketill, had known the fire and ice of passion and repentance.

Critical Evaluation:

The history of the family at Borg—a more literal translation of *Borgslægtens historie*—is a four-part novel that tells the story of the family at Borg, of a father and his two sons, and of the illegitimate child of one of his sons. *Guest the One-Eyed*, is an abridged English translation.

Gunnar Gunnarsson is concerned with humanity's lot on earth, with struggle, and, ultimately, death. Iceland may be stony, misty, and barren, and sin may be a fact of life, but ultimately, his book makes clear, there is reason to hope and to expect humanity to prevail. Gunnar Gunnarsson's novel is of traditional form, made particularly fascinating by its Icelandic setting. The atmosphere of the ancient sagas pervades *Guest the One-Eyed*, putting its characters into association with the past while making the present nonetheless convincing. The drama of the novel is essentially moral, and the ethical dilemmas into which the characters fall are neither gross nor abnormal. Gunnarsson is adept at capturing the Icelandic character and the Icelandic atmosphere; the human beings about whom he writes move with dignity and passion across barren, stony, but beautiful northern plains.

Although Gunnarsson retains a tragic view of life, regarding human beings as helpless before forces more powerful than themselves, he never loses sight of the alleviating influences of love, humor, and tradition. Generation succeeds generation in his novels, and although individuals fall, families persevere, so that Icelandic traditions are strengthened and, in turn, strengthen those who share them. There are elements of melodrama in *Guest the One-Eyed*, but the effect is that of tragedy. To have been able to portray such extremes of character—Ormarr sacrifices his own concerns to marry Runa, while Ketill sacrifices his own family to win power and wealth—without making the characters mere devices for the development of plot is evidence of Gunnarsson's skill as a novelist.

The author's audacity also leads him to create a complete reversal in the character of Ketill. Ketill, the cold, scheming Icelandic Judas, becomes someone very much like Christ. There is perhaps no more difficult task in literature than the portrayal of a saintlike character. Readers are ready to accept the fact of evil, and there is no act so base that one cannot readily believe someone capable of it. Extreme selflessness and Christlike love, however, is an ideal, hinted at in the scriptures, and hardly to be found in the community. The novelist presuming to create a character who, having been in the depths of sin, becomes a lovable, living incarnation of virtue, is a writer confronting himself with the final challenge of his craft. Gunnarsson took up that challenge with the character Guest the One-Eyed. The novel has at once the characteristics of a myth and the characteristics of a modern saga.

Guest the One-Eyed ends affirmatively with the prospective marriage. Iceland may be stony, misty, barren, and demanding, but it is also a land of sunshine and changing moods, like the characters about whom Gunnarsson writes. In the end, the family continues to hope.

Bibliography:

Beck, Richard. "Gunnar Gunnarsson: Some Observations." In *Scandinavian Studies*, edited by Carl F. Bayerschmidt and Erik J. Friis. Seattle: University of Washington Press, 1965. A good starting place for further research on Gunnarsson.

Hallberg, Peter. "Gunnar Gunnarsson." In *Dictionary of Scandinavian Literature*, edited by Virpi Zuck. Westport, Conn.: Greenwood Press, 1990. Concise factual background on Gunnarsson and his major work, *Guest the One-Eyed*. Bibliography.

Rossel, Sven Hakon. *A History of Scandinavian Literature, 1870-1980*. Minneapolis: University of Minnesota Press, 1982. Pages 247-248 discuss Gunnarsson's major themes and his place in Icelandic literature.

THE GUIDE

Type of work: Novel
Author: R. K. Narayan (1907-   )
Type of plot: Social realism
Time of plot: Mid-twentieth century
Locale: India
First published: 1958

> *Principal characters:*
> RAILWAY RAJU, a tourist guide and later a swami
> RAJU'S MOTHER
> MARCO, an Indian art historian
> ROSIE, later NALINI, Marco's wife and a dancer
> VELAN, Swami Raju's disciple
> GAFFUR, a chauffeur and taxi driver

The Story:

When Raju was released from prison after serving two years for forgery, he went to the temple located on the Sarayu River in his hometown of Malgudi. He had thought prison was not too bad a place, and he was wondering what to do next with his life. Then a villager named Velan showed up and, taking Raju for a holy wise man or guru, consulted him about his sister, who refused to marry as the family wished. Well aware that he was not a guru, Raju was evasive, but Velan brought his sister anyway, and after their meeting she conformed to her family's wishes. So began Raju's life as a holy man.

He recalled his boyhood in a poor family; his father, who kept a very small shop; and his mother, who often complained of their life. Meanwhile, Velan returned with others from his village after work. No matter what Raju had to say, or even if he said nothing at all, they brought him food and begged him for words of wisdom. They felt the need for a spiritual adviser, so they made one out of a very unlikely prospect.

Raju then reflected on his father's small stall at the railroad station and on how he had built up the business himself after his father's death. His memories were interrupted periodically when other villagers came to seek his advice. Almost by accident, Raju found himself appointing an old man to run a school at the temple for the village children. This increased his fame, and Raju began to bask in the light of his own glory.

Later, Raju recalled, he became known as "Railway Raju," and people began to ask for him when their trains stopped at Malgudi. Before long, he had become a guide, even though he knew relatively little about the historic and scenic sites in the area. He simply learned from what he heard others say. He called on old Gaffur, who had a car, to act as chauffeur, and soon he was prospering.

One day he met a beautiful traditional dancer named Rosie—an odd name for an Indian— and when he took her to see a cobra and watched her do a snake dance he was charmed himself. Rosie's husband was a cold, distant art historian named Marco, and it was obvious to Raju that she had married him only for social status and financial security. Marco refused to allow Rosie to dance, and he ignored her for his scholarly research. Raju remembered the day he became romantically involved with her.

Back at the temple, Raju began to grow a long beard, and people referred to him as "swami." He was just beginning to enjoy the advantages of the position when a great drought hit the region. As the drought worsened, disease spread and the villagers resorted to violence against shopkeepers and one another. A feeble-minded villager misinterpreted Raju and told the others that the swami would undertake a fast in order to bring rain. When Velan turned to Raju as a "saint" who could bring rainfall, Raju felt obliged to tell him his life story. He wanted Velan and the others to see that he was just an ordinary man, perhaps even a worse sinner than most.

Indifferent to his wife, Marco had accepted Raju and, apparently unaware of their love affair, kept on paying Raju for his services as a guide. When he discovered the truth, Marco deserted Rosie, and she had nowhere to go but to the modest home of Raju and his mother. Raju's mother was scandalized, but she liked Rosie and endured the disgraceful situation as long as she could. Then Raju discovered that his business had been ruined while he was carrying on with Rosie, and his creditors took him to court. Finally, his stern, patriarchal uncle appeared to reprimand Raju and to take his mother back.

After several months, Raju decided to encourage Rosie to dance professionally, and he gave her the poetical name "Nalini." She was a great success, and both of them became very wealthy. From the first, Raju, who acted as her business manager, showed that he was extravagant and unable to deal with economic realities. Ironically, Rosie had a master's degree in economics, but she had devoted her life to her art. Marco sent Raju a copy of his book, but Raju concealed the fact from Rosie. When she read about the book in the newspapers, she was angry, but Raju avoided a confrontation over the matter.

One day a registered letter arrived for Rosie, requiring her signature for a box of jewels. Fearing that Rosie, who had gotten increasingly bored and dissatisfied with their relationship, would return to her husband, Raju forged her name. When he was caught, he was ruined financially and sent to prison. Rosie had to continue dancing to pay his court costs, and by the time he was released, she had settled down elsewhere. Raju spent his two-year prison term in relative ease, tending the superintendent's vegetable garden, and emerged feeling no resentment.

As he ended his story, a rooster crowed and Raju assumed he had convinced Velan that he was neither a saint nor a true swami, but this did not prove to be the case. Raju considered leaving town, but he felt compelled to go on with his fast. It was the first time he had done something in which he had no personal profit or interest. Much weakened by his abstinence from food, Raju had himself carried to the nearly dry river. On the twelfth day of the fast, he died, proclaiming in his last words that he could feel the water rising up his legs from rains high in the mountains.

"The Story" by Ron McFarland

Critical Evaluation:

Raju, the protagonist and, at times, the narrator, is the son of a poor shopkeeper from Malgudi (R. K. Narayan's imaginary village). His character undergoes various transformations as he goes from shopkeeper to guide ("Railway Raju"); to lover; to impresario, managing Rosie's career as a dancer; to prisoner; to imposter (fake guru); to, perhaps, genuine swami or mahatma (the highest of the Hindu spiritual leaders). Raju is clever, and although he succumbs to the temptations of luxury when Rosie succeeds as a dancer, he does offer her the chance to do what she has always wanted, and his love for her appears to be genuine. On the other hand, his forgery of her name, even if it is not for profit but to sustain their relationship, is unwise, and his initial willingness to assume the role of a guru simply in order to be fed suggests he may be just another confidence man. Readers must decide for themselves about the reality and depth of Raju's transformation by the end of the novel.

Raju's mother, a traditional Indian woman who defines herself in terms of her domestic role, is developed more fully as a character than her husband, about whom she complains frequently. Her initial, although reluctant, acceptance of the low-caste Rosie into her house and Rosie's affection for her indicate that she is a positive character, so Raju's failure to heal their relationship or to build her a new home when he becomes wealthy tends to undercut his character. When his mother calls in her imperious brother to deal with Rosie, she reveals the weakness of the traditional Indian woman, who relies on domineering males to resolve problems.

Rosie, a traditional, temple dancer—therefore of a lower caste—has received a master's degree in economics and been married off in order to improve her status. Still, she has the ambitions, dreams, and passion of a genuine artist. Her unusual name may suggest that she is something of a nonconformist, which would make her love of traditional dance ironic. She is a great dancer, and she shows her strength of character when she resists Raju's demands that she avoid the company of other artists and when she dances to raise money for his defense. Unlike Raju, she has little interest in wealth. On the other hand, she feels guilty about having deceived her husband, despite his ill treatment of her, and she is all too easily manipulated by Raju, who goes so far as to change her name. By the time of his imprisonment, their relationship has cooled. Significantly, she does not return to Raju or to her estranged husband at the end, but apparently is doing quite well for herself.

Marco, the name by which Raju identifies Rosie's husband with Marco Polo, is an archaeologist and art historian who is deeply devoted to his work and has little time for his wife. He also has no tolerance of her desire to dance. A cold man, as he is seen by Raju, Marco appears to be a dry scholar, and his icy treatment of Rosie before, during, and after her affair causes him to emerge as the least sympathetic character in the novel. That he should be so obsessed with the art and culture of southern India (the subject of his research and book) is ironic in light of his lack of interest in his wife's art, and of his failure to recognize her dancing as art.

Gaffur, the taxi driver who assists Raju with the tours, functions as a social conscience for Raju. He is usually seen winking knowingly, often through the rear-view mirror. Gaffur does not simply sneer, however. He attempts to dissuade Raju from continuing with the dangerous relationship, but his conventional views are of no avail.

Velan, a simple villager from Mangal, on the outskirts of Malgudi, reveres Raju for no particular reason other than the fact that he is at the temple and is willing to listen to him. He may be said to embody the universal need for spiritual leadership; that is, he may represent humanity in search of a guide. Both Rosie and Raju undergo profound transformations of character, but Velan (along with Gaffur, Marco, and Raju's mother) remains essentially unchanged. He retains faith in Raju until the end, and, depending on how one reads the last chapter (and perhaps the last paragraph in particular), one could say that his faith is rewarded, because Raju does become a holy man, or that it is mocked, because Raju goes from deceiving Marco to deceiving everyone.

Bibliography:
Holmstrom, Lakshmi. *The Novels of R. K. Narayan*. Calcutta: Writers Workshop, 1973. Notes the mythic theme of progress toward realizing one's true nature, in which Raju finds his true role in providing for people's needs, thus releasing himself from the wheel of existence.

Kirpal, Viney. "Moksha for Raju: The Archetypal Four-Stage Journey." *World Literature Written in English* 28 (1988): 356-363. Argues that the novel must be read in the Hindu metaphysical tradition, whereby Raju overcomes the "gross violation of dharma" in his relationship with Rosie to be reborn as a swami. Novel follows the pattern of excessive involvement with the worldly, renunciation of it, and self-realization.

Mukherjee, Meenakshi. *The Twice Born Fiction.* London: Heinemann, 1971. Argues that Raju's drift into the role of a guru follows the pattern of his life, because he is not so much a man who does things as one to whom things happen (except the forgery). At the end, he loses the feeling of being an actor, and "the mask becomes the man."

Walsh, William. *R. K. Narayan: A Critical Perspective.* Chicago: University of Chicago Press, 1982. The most readily available and accessible study, Walsh sees the novel as a serious comedy in which Raju's personality is defined by others, so his search for an independent identity is futile. Transformation of the personality by forces outside the relatively passive self is common in Eastern tales.

THE GULAG ARCHIPELAGO, 1918-1956
An Experiment in Literary Investigation

Type of work: Memoir
Author: Aleksandr Solzhenitsyn (1918-   )
Type of plot: Historical
Time of plot: Twentieth century
Locale: Soviet Union
First published: Arkhipelag GULag, 1918-1956; Opyt khudozhestvennogo issledovaniya,
parts 1-2, 1973; parts 3-4, 1974; parts 5-7, 1975 (English translation, 1974-1978)

> *Principal personages:*
> ALEKSANDR SOLZHENITSYN, a prisoner
> JOSEPH STALIN, the Soviet dictator
> G. I. GRIGORYEV, a soil scientist
> V. M. YAKOVENKO, a freed prisoner

The Story:

A string of prisons and labor camps scattered throughout the Soviet Union was called the gulag archipelago because its administrative title, the Chief Administration of Corrective Labor Camps, formed the acronym "gulag" in Russian and because its far-flung prisons and camps, with their own laws and their oppressed population of *zeks* (prisoners), resembled a separate country made up of hundreds, perhaps thousands, of islands. Vladimir Ilich Lenin, the leader of the Bolshevik revolution of 1917 and the first head of the Soviet state, established this extensive prison system in 1918, ostensibly to detain and "rehabilitate" Soviet citizens suspected of anti-Soviet or counterrevolutionary activity. The system was greatly expanded by Lenin's successor, Joseph Stalin, the ironfisted ruler of the Soviet Union from 1924 until his death in 1953. Under Stalin, the secret police arrested millions of people, nearly all of whom received either the death sentence or lengthy prison terms in the gulag archipelago.

A decorated captain of artillery in the Soviet Red Army during World War II, Aleksandr Solzhenitsyn was arrested for anti-Soviet activity in 1945 because he had criticized Stalin in letters to a friend. Solzhenitsyn's "guilt" had been already established in his letters, so the secret police interrogators tried to persuade Solzhenitsyn to implicate other anti-Soviet "conspirators" rather than to confess. The interrogators used only sleep deprivation, the mildest of their thirty-one documented methods of torture. He refused to sign the fabricated "confession" but relented when investigators threatened to begin the interrogation all over again. Sent to Butyrki prison in Moscow, he began his eight years as a *zek*.

At Butyrki, Solzhenitsyn watched in horror and sadness as thousands of repatriated Soviet soldiers, liberated from German prisoner of war camps, were imprisoned as traitors by their own country. In need of scapegoats, Stalin blamed them for his own enormous wartime blunders, including surrenders at Kerch (120,000 prisoners) and Kharkov (150,000 prisoners). Stalin also feared that returning prisoners of war might sow unrest among their countrymen by describing the relatively high standard of living they had seen in Europe and the greater degree of personal freedom enjoyed by the Germans, even under the wartime rule of the dictator Adolf Hitler. Reasoning that anyone who could survive a German prisoner of war camp must have collaborated with his captors, Stalin had many of the returning prisoners charged with "aiding and abetting the enemy" and given "tenners" (ten-year sentences).

In 1945, Solzhenitsyn was sent to a hard labor camp, from which he was miraculously saved in 1946 when he lied on a camp registration form; he listed his civilian occupation as nuclear physicist. He was removed to a special prison, a scientific research institute, or *sharashka*, near Moscow, one of the gulag archipelago's "paradise" islands, legendary among the *zek*s, where prisoners were well treated because of their value to the state.

Successfully impersonating a scientist, Solzhenitsyn remained there until 1950. From this special prison, he was taken to a camp for political prisoners in Ekibastuz, Kazakhstan. At Ekibastuz, Solzhenitsyn became part of a team of laborers building a new disciplinary barracks, a prison within a prison. He also witnessed a number of failed escape attempts. Some of the escapees were shot, and many were imprisoned in the unfinished disciplinary barracks even while Solzhenitsyn and other prisoners were still building it.

When his sentence had been completed, Solzhenitsyn was released from Ekibastuz in March, 1953; he was sent into permanent exile in the Kolk-Terek district, a desert region in central Kazakhstan. There he sought work as a teacher of mathematics and physics, but he was rebuffed by the district education department, even though he was the only available teacher in the district with a university degree. On March 6, his second day in Kolk-Terek, he heard the news that Stalin—the man who had murdered millions of Soviet citizens and imprisoned millions more—was dead. Astonished by the grief of the free people around him, Solzhenitsyn realized the extraordinary success of Stalin and his minions in keeping their barbarism secret. He began editing what little he had managed to write in the camps, and he wrote what he could remember, burying his work every evening in order to hide it from the secret police. In the spring of 1956, he applied for a review of his case. The sentence of exile was lifted in 1957, and Solzhenitsyn returned to Russia as a teacher.

Critical Evaluation:

The Gulag Archipelago is a modern epic. It is not a scholarly history and it is not fiction, though it is to an extent fictionalized. Denied the tools of the historian (he was forbidden paper and pencil during his entire sentence, and he had no access to libraries or government archives), Aleksandr Solzhenitsyn was forced to rely on his memory to store nearly all the material that makes up this massive, eighteen-hundred-page work. Accepting Solzhenitsyn's metaphor of the gulag as its own nation of islands within the Soviet Union, one might say that he single-handedly constructed the literature of the gulag.

Using his own experiences as a narrative thread tying together the stories he heard from other *zek*s, he manages to weave a tapestry depicting the cruelty and sorrow of the Soviet penal system. That tapestry is vast and filled with horrors. Few people in the West realize that Stalin's victims, perhaps as many as thirty million, far outnumbered Hitler's. In addition to the innocent millions murdered in the camps and in the prisons, fifteen million peasants died as a result of a single national program, the brutal resettlement that established the Soviet Union's network of collective farms. Solzhenitsyn's own story, briefly described in the plot summary above, seems innocuous by comparison. He was but lightly tortured during interrogation; other prisoners were starved, beaten, or shot. Many women prisoners were raped. He served a single eight-year sentence; other prisoners had extra "tenners" given them for minor infractions of camp rules. He hoodwinked his captors and so spent half his sentence in the relative comfort of a *sharashka*; other prisoners served ten, fifteen, or even twenty years—though few survived that long—in Siberian hard labor camps. Yet his story is the thread by which the others are bound. All the political prisoners in the gulag suffered under a penal code that was administrative rather than legislative. The People's Commissariat of Internal Affairs established three-person Special Boards throughout the Soviet Union, with the power to imprison and execute "socially dangerous" people without trial. These Special Boards, abolished after Stalin's death in 1953, applied their own criminal code containing eleven indictable offenses ranging from "anti-Soviet agitation" to "nurturing anti-Soviet feelings" to merely being a "member of the family" of an indicted person. Under such a code, no one was safe.

The evil of such a system is Solzhenitsyn's target. Through the testimony of 227 fellow prisoners, he pieces together a comprehensive history of the gulag, explaining various methods of arrest and interrogation, the often incongruous modes of transport between prisons—*zeks* sometimes traveled on the public railways with unarmed escorts, mixing with free citizens who frequently had no inkling that there were "enemies of the state" among them. Solzhenitsyn describes the character of his interrogators (the blue-caps), the endless variety of brutality practiced by the guards, and the seemingly inadvertent psychological torture built into the system. The banality of evil reveals itself in the details involved in running such a far-flung empire of prisons and labor camps. For example, arrests and interrogations nearly always took place at night, partly to heighten the terror of the victims and partly to exploit the vulnerability of arrestees deprived of sleep. Another reason for night arrests: The police and interrogators were paid extra for night work. Mixed among the horrifying statistics of death—forty thousand prisoners died from overwork, exposure, and disease at a single camp during the winter of 1941-1942—are the depressing statistics of life. Throughout the gulag, women prisoners were routinely forced into prostitution by the guards, and their tens of thousands of children were sent to state orphanages.

Solzhenitsyn observes all these horrors and more, expressing outrage at the unfeeling brutality of the system, wonder at the strength and courage of the *zeks*, and immense sadness for the tragedy that had befallen his country. A Marxist, Solzhenitsyn revered Lenin, although he hated Stalin. Still, rather than blame Stalin alone for the inhuman gulag, Solzhenitsyn explores his idol's part in its creation. Rather than make scapegoats of the thousands of policemen, interrogators, guards, and bureaucrats responsible for the day-to-day running of the gulag, Solzhenitsyn recognizes that they were not monsters; instead, they were Soviet citizens molded by his beloved Soviet state. In their arrogance and conviction, he can recognize traits he had himself developed as an officer in the Red Army. Despite the pain and humiliation suffered at the hands of his captors, he retains the humanity that allows him to admit that in different circumstances he himself—or anyone—might have become one of them.

There are stories of courage, as well. Some *zeks* were never defeated by the system. G. I. Grigoryev, a soil scientist, was captured by the Germans during World War II, and he was imprisoned by the Soviets immediately upon being repatriated. Despite being offered comparatively easy camp jobs, such as supervising other workers, Grigoryev refused to cooperate with his captors, choosing, instead, the hardest of manual labor. Another *zek*, V. M. Yakovenko, was released after twenty years; he was exiled to Vorkuta. In 1949, the authorities in Vorkuta began arresting former *zeks* and handing out new sentences. Yakovenko, though he himself could be arrested again at any moment, fearlessly delivered packages of food to friends already in custody. Following the 1953 execution of Lavrenty Beria, head of Stalin's secret police and of the gulag since 1938, the *zeks* began to rebel. In 1954, over a thousand *zeks* at Kengir prison camp in Kazakhstan went on strike against armed guards with a well-deserved reputation as murderers of prisoners; the strike paralyzed the camp for forty days. Solzhenitsyn recounts numerous examples of *zeks* fighting back. *The Gulag Archipelago* is a sprawling record of inhumanity; it is also a monument to human courage and determination.

Craig A. Milliman

Bibliography:

Bond, Anatole. *A Study of the English and the German Translations of Alexander I. Solzhenitsyn's "The Gulag Archipelago."* Vol. 1. New York: Peter Lang, 1983. In a work chiefly of value to the student interested in languages, Bond explains numerous inadequacies in translations available in 1982.

Dunlop, John B., Richard S. Haugh, and Michael Nicholson, eds. *Solzhenitsyn in Exile: Critical Essays and Documentary Materials.* Stanford, Calif.: Hoover Institution, 1985. Includes three critical essays on *The Gulag Archipelago.* Susan Richards' *"The Gulag Archipelago* as Literary Documentary" argues that the work transcends the genre of history by means of the voice of Solzhenitsyn the narrator. John B. Dunlop's *"The Gulag Archipelago*: Alternative to Ideology" discusses the positive social implications of the many examples of Soviet citizens rebelling against the system. Elisabeth Markstein's "Observations on the Narrative Structure of *The Gulag Archipelago*" argues that the interweaving of different *zeks'* narratives and styles gives the work a highly complex narrative structure.

Feuer, Kathryn, ed. *Solzhenitsyn: A Collection of Critical Essays.* Englewood Cliffs, N.J.: Prentice-Hall, 1976. Includes "On Solzhenitsyn's *The Gulag Archipelago,*" a historian's assessment of Solzhenitsyn's factual accuracy by Marxist writer Roy Medvedev. "On Reading *The Gulag Archipelago*" is an argument for Solzhenitsyn's literary skill, by Victor Erlich.

Kennan, George. "Between Earth and Hell." *The New York Review of Books,* March 21, 1974, 3. Insightful review of *The Gulag Archipelago* (parts 1 and 2) with commentary on Solzhenitsyn's politics and philosophy.

Kodjak, Andrej. *Alexander Solzhenitsyn.* Boston: G. K. Hall, 1978. Commentary on *The Gulag Archipelago.* Kodjak argues that Solzhenitsyn's narrative style transforms the work from mere documentation to artistic investigation.

GULLIVER'S TRAVELS

Type of work: Novel
Author: Jonathan Swift (1667-1745)
Type of plot: Satire
Time of plot: 1699-1713
Locale: England and various fictional lands
First published: 1726

Principal character:
LEMUEL GULLIVER, a surgeon, sea captain, and traveler

The Story:

Lemuel Gulliver, a physician, took the post of ship's doctor on the *Antelope*, which set sail from Bristol for the South Seas in May, 1699. When the ship was wrecked in a storm somewhere near Tasmania, Gulliver had to swim for his life. Wind and tide helped to carry him close to a low-lying shore, where he fell, exhausted, into a deep sleep. Upon awakening, he found himself held to the ground by hundreds of small ropes. He soon discovered that he was the prisoner of humans six inches tall. Still tied, Gulliver was fed by his captors; then he was placed on a special wagon built for the purpose and drawn by fifteen hundred small horses. Carried in this manner to the capital city of the small humans, he was exhibited as a great curiosity to the people of Lilliput, as the land of the diminutive people was called. He was kept chained to a huge Lilliputian building into which he crawled at night to sleep.

Gulliver soon learned the Lilliputian language, and through his personal charm and natural curiosity, he came into good graces at the royal court. At length, he was given his freedom, contingent upon his obeying many rules devised by the emperor prescribing his deportment in Lilliput. Now free, Gulliver toured Mildendo, the capital city, and found it to be similar, except in size, to European cities of the time.

Learning that Lilliput was in danger of an invasion by the forces of the neighboring empire, Blefuscu, he offered his services to the emperor of Lilliput. While the enemy fleet awaited favorable winds to carry their ships the eight hundred yards between Blefuscu and Lilliput, Gulliver took some Lilliputian cable, waded to Blefuscu, and brought back the entire fleet by means of hooks attached to the cables. He was greeted with great acclaim, and the emperor made him a nobleman. Soon, however, the emperor and Gulliver quarreled over differences concerning the fate of the now helpless Blefuscu. The emperor wanted to reduce the enemy to the status of slaves; Gulliver championed their liberty. The pro-Gulliver forces prevailed in the Lilliputian parliament; the peace settlement was favorable to Blefuscu. Gulliver, however, was now in disfavor at court.

He visited Blefuscu, where he was received graciously by the emperor and the people. One day, while exploring the empire, he found a ship's boat washed ashore from a wreck. With the help of thousands of Blefuscu artisans, he repaired the boat for his projected voyage back to his own civilization. Taking some cattle and sheep with him, he sailed away and was eventually picked up by an English vessel.

Back in England, Gulliver spent a short time with his family before he shipped aboard the *Adventure*, bound for India. The ship was blown off course by fierce winds. Somewhere on the coast of Great Tartary a landing party went ashore to forage for supplies. Gulliver, who had wandered away from the party, was left behind when a gigantic human figure pursued the sailors back to the ship. Gulliver was caught in a field by giants threshing grain that grew forty feet high. Becoming the pet of a farmer and his family, he amused them with his humanlike behavior. The farmer's nine-year-old daughter, who was not yet over forty feet high, took special charge of Gulliver.

The farmer displayed Gulliver first at a local market town. Then he took his little pet to the metropolis, where Gulliver was put on show repeatedly, to the great detriment of his health. The farmer, seeing that Gulliver was near death from overwork, sold him to the queen, who took a great fancy to the little curiosity. The court doctors and philosophers studied Gulliver as a quaint trick of nature. He subsequently had adventures with giant rats the size of lions, with a dwarf thirty feet high, with wasps as large as partridges, with apples the size of Bristol barrels, and with hailstones the size of tennis balls.

He and the king discussed the institutions of their respective countries, the king asking Gulliver many questions about Great Britain that Gulliver found impossible to answer truthfully without embarrassment. After two years in Brobdingnag, the land of the giants, Gulliver miraculously escaped when a large bird carried his portable quarters out over the sea. The bird dropped the box containing Gulliver, and he was rescued by a ship that was on its way to England. Back home, it took Gulliver some time to accustom himself once more to a world of normal size.

Soon afterward, Gulliver went to sea again. Pirates from a Chinese port attacked the ship. Set adrift in a small sailboat, Gulliver was cast away upon a rocky island. One day, he saw a large floating mass descending from the sky. Taken aboard the flying island of Laputa, he soon found it to be inhabited by intellectuals who thought only in the realm of the abstract and the exceedingly impractical. The people of the island, including the king, were so absentminded that they had to have servants following them to remind them even of their trends of conversation. When the floating island arrived above the continent of Balnibari, Gulliver received permission to visit that realm. There he inspected the Grand Academy, where hundreds of highly impractical projects for the improvement of agriculture and building were under way.

Next, Gulliver journeyed by boat to Glubbdubdrib, the island of sorcerers. By means of magic, the governor of the island showed Gulliver such great historical figures as Alexander the Great, Hannibal, Julius Caesar, Pompey, and Sir Thomas More. Gulliver talked to the apparitions and learned from them that history books were inaccurate.

From Glubbdubdrib, Gulliver ventured to Luggnagg. There he was welcomed by the king, who showed him the Luggnaggian immortals, or Struldbrugs—beings who would never die. Gulliver traveled on to Japan, where he took a ship back to England. He had been away for more than three years.

Gulliver became restless after a brief stay at his home, and he signed as captain of a ship that sailed from Portsmouth in August, 1710, destined for the South Seas. The crew mutinied, keeping Captain Gulliver prisoner in his cabin for months. At length, he was cast adrift in a longboat off a strange coast. Ashore, he came upon and was nearly overwhelmed by disgusting half-human, half-ape creatures who fled in terror at the approach of a horse. Gulliver soon discovered, to his amazement, that he was in a land where rational horses, the Houyhnhnms, were masters of irrational human creatures, the Yahoos. He stayed in the stable house of a Houyhnhnm family and learned to subsist on oaten cake and milk. The Houyhnhnms were horrified to learn from Gulliver that horses in England were used by Yahoolike creatures as beasts of burden. Gulliver described England to his host, much to the candid and straightforward Houyhnhnm's mystification. Such things as wars and courts of law were unknown to this race of intelligent horses. As he did in the other lands he visited, Gulliver attempted to explain the institutions of his native land, but the friendly and benevolent Houyhnhnms were appalled by many of the things Gulliver told them.

Gulliver lived in almost perfect contentment among the horses, until one day his host told him that the Houyhnhnm Grand Assembly had decreed Gulliver either be treated as an ordinary Yahoo or be released to swim back to the land from which he had come. Gulliver built a canoe and sailed away. At length, he was picked up by a Portuguese vessel. Remembering the Yahoos, he became a recluse on the ship and began to hate all humankind. Landing at Lisbon, he sailed from there to England; on his arrival, however, the sight of his own family repulsed him. He fainted when his wife kissed him. His horses became his only friends on earth.

Critical Evaluation:

It has been said that Dean Jonathan Swift hated humanity but loved the individual. His hatred is brought out in this caustic political and social satire aimed at the English people, humanity in general, and the Whigs in particular. By means of a disarming simplicity of style and of careful attention to detail in order to heighten the effect of the narrative, Swift produced one of the outstanding pieces of satire in world literature. Swift himself attempted to conceal his authorship of the book under its original title: *Travels into Several Remote Nations of the World, in Four Parts, by Lemuel Gulliver, First a Surgeon, and then a Captain of Several Ships.*

When Swift created the character of Lemuel Gulliver as his narrator for *Gulliver's Travels*, he developed a personality with many qualities admired by an eighteenth century audience and still admired by many readers. Gulliver is a decent sort of person: hopeful, simple, fairly direct, and full of good will. He is a scientist, a trained doctor, and, as any good scientist should, he loves detail. His literal-minded attitude makes him a keen observer of the world around him. Furthermore, he is, like another famous novel character of the eighteenth century—Robinson Crusoe—encouragingly resourceful in emergencies. Why is it, then, that such a seemingly admirable, even heroic character, should become, in the end, an embittered misanthrope, hating the world and turning against everyone, including people who show him kindness?

The answer lies in what Swift meant for his character to be, and Gulliver was certainly not intended to be heroic. Readers often confuse Gulliver the character and Swift the author, but to do so is to miss the point of *Gulliver's Travels*. The novel is a satire, and Gulliver is a mask for Swift the satirist. In fact, Swift does not share Gulliver's rationalistic, scientific responses to the world or Gulliver's beliefs in progress and in the perfectibility of humanity. Swift, on the contrary, believed that such values were dangerous, and that to put such complete faith in the material world, as scientific Gulliver did, was folly. Gulliver is a product of his age, and he is intended as a character to demonstrate the weakness underlying the values of the Enlightenment—the failure to recognize the power of the irrational.

Despite Gulliver's apparent congeniality in the opening chapters of the novel, Swift makes it clear that Gulliver has serious shortcomings, including blind spots about human nature, his own included. Book 3, the least readable section of *Gulliver's Travels*, is in some ways the most revealing part of the book. In it Gulliver complains, for example, that the wives of the scientists he is observing run away with the servants. The fact is that Gulliver—himself a scientist—gives little thought to the well-being of his own wife. In the eleven years covered in Gulliver's travel book, Swift's narrator spends a total of seven months and ten days with his wife.

Gulliver, too, is caught up in Swift's web of satire in *Gulliver's Travels*. Satire as a literary form tends to be ironic; the author says one thing but means another. Consequently, readers can assume that much of what Gulliver observes as good and much of what he thinks and does are not what Swift thinks.

As a type of the eighteenth century, Gulliver exhibits its major values: belief in rationality, in the perfectibility of humanity, in the idea of progress, and in the Lockean philosophy of the human mind as a *tabula rasa*, or blank slate, at the time of birth, controlled and developed entirely by the differing strokes and impressions made on it by the environment. Swift, in contrast to Gulliver, hated the abstraction that accompanied rational thinking; he abhorred the rejection of the past that resulted from a rationalistic faith in the new and improved; and he cast strong doubts on humanity's ability to gain knowledge through reason and logic.

The world Gulliver discovers during his travels is significant in Swift's satire. The Lilliputians, averaging not quite six inches in height, display the pettiness and the smallness Swift detects in much that motivates human institutions such as church and state. It is petty religious problems that lead to continual war in Lilliput. The Brobdingnagians continue the satire in part 2 by exaggerating human grossness through their enlarged size. (Swift divided human measurements by a twelfth for the Lilliputians and multiplied the same for the Brobdingnagians.)

The tiny people of part 1 and the giants of part 2 establish a pattern of contrasts that Swift follows in part 4 with the Houyhnhnms and the Yahoos. The Yahoos, "their heads and breasts covered with a thick hair, some frizzled and others lank," naked otherwise and scampering up trees like nimble squirrels, represent the animal aspect of humanity when that animality is viewed as separate from the rational. The Houyhnhnms, completing the other half of the split, know no lust, pain, or pleasure. Their rational temperaments totally rule what passions they have. The land of the Houyhnhnms is a utopia to Gulliver, and he tells the horse-people that his homeland is unfortunately governed by Yahoos.

The reader who takes all of this at face value misses much of the satire. What is the land of the Houyhnhnms really like, how much is it a Utopia? Friendship, benevolence, honesty, and equality are the principal virtues there. Decency and civility guide every action. As a result, each pair of horses mates to have one colt of each sex; after that, they no longer stay together. The marriages are exacted to ensure nice color combinations in the offspring. To the young, marriage is "one of the necessary actions of a reasonable being." After the function of the marriage has been fulfilled—after the race has been propagated—the two members of the couple are no closer to each other than to anybody else in the whole country. It is this kind of "equality" that Swift satirizes. As a product of the rational attitude, such a value strips life of its fullness, denies the power of emotion and instinct, subjugates all to logic, reason, the intellect, and makes life dull and uninteresting—as predictable as a scientific experiment.

Looking upon the Houyhnhnms as the perfect creatures, Gulliver makes his own life back in England intolerable:

> I . . . return to enjoy my own speculations in my little garden at Redriff; to apply those excellent lessons of virtue which I learned among the Houyhnhnms; to instruct the Yahoos of my own family as far as I shall find them docible animals; to behold my figure often in a glass, and thus if possible habituate myself by time to tolerate the sight of a human creature.

When Gulliver holds up the rational as perfect and when he cannot find a rational man to meet his ideal, he concludes in disillusionment that humanity is totally animalistic, like the ugly Yahoos. In addition to being a satire and a parody of travel books, *Gulliver's Travels* is an initiation novel. As Gulliver develops, he changes, but he fails to learn an important lesson of life, or he learns it wrong. His naïve optimism about progress and rationality leads him to bitter disillusionment.

It is tragically ironic that Swift died at the age of seventy-eight after three years of living without his reason, a victim of Ménière's disease, dying "like a rat in a hole." For many years, he had struggled against fits of deafness and giddiness, symptoms of the disease. As a master of the language of satire, Swift remains unequaled, despite his suffering and ill health. He gathered in *Gulliver's Travels*, written late in his life, all the experience he had culled from both courts and streets. For Swift knew people, and, as individuals, he loved them; but when they changed into groups, he hated them, satirized them, and stung them into realizing the dangers of the herd. Gulliver never understood this.

"Critical Evaluation" by Jean G. Marlowe

Bibliography:
Bloom, Harold, ed. *Jonathan Swift's "Gulliver's Travels."* New York: Chelsea House, 1986. A collection of criticism from the second half of the twentieth century, arranged in chronological order. Essays range from investigations of philosophical context and literary genre to psychoanalytic and deconstructionist approaches.
Brady, Frank, ed. *Twentieth Century Interpretations of "Gulliver's Travels": A Collection of Critical Essays.* Englewood Cliffs, N.J.: Prentice-Hall, 1968. A selection of essays examining the philosophical, religious, and scientific background of the work. Examines the literary sources and traditions the book reflects.
Carnochan, W. B. *Lemuel Gulliver's Mirror for Man.* Berkeley: University of California Press, 1968. Relates Swift's satiric intention to the epistemology of John Locke to illustrate his theory of Augustan satire. An epilogue examines how *Gulliver's Travels* anticipates later satirists Lewis Carroll, James Joyce, and Vladimir Nabokov.
Erskine-Hill, Howard. *Jonathan Swift: "Gulliver's Travels."* Cambridge, England: Cambridge University Press, 1993. A concise, accessible introduction. Final chapter surveys the work's influence on fiction from Herman Melville to Nathaniel West.
Smith, Frederik N., ed. *The Genres of "Gulliver's Travels."* Newark, N.J.: University of Delaware Press, 1990. A collection of previously unpublished essays, each taking the standpoint of a different literary genre. An afterword suggests how the reader might navigate the work, given the multiplicity of genres it represents. Assumed is the basic indeterminacy of texts.

GUY MANNERING
Or, The Astrologer

Type of work: Novel
Author: Sir Walter Scott (1771-1832)
Type of plot: Historical
Time of plot: Eighteenth century
Locale: Scotland
First published: 1815

Principal characters:
  COLONEL GUY MANNERING, a retired army officer
  JULIA MANNERING, his daughter
  CAPTAIN BROWN, a soldier
  LUCY BERTRAM, an orphan
  CHARLES HAZLEWOOD, Lucy's suitor
  SIR ROBERT HAZLEWOOD, Guy Mannering's father
  GILBERT GLOSSIN, the holder of the Bertram property
  DIRK HATTERAICK, a smuggler
  MEG MERRILIES, a gypsy
  DOMINIE SAMPSON, the tutor to the Bertram children

The Story:

Guy Mannering, a young English gentleman traveling in Scotland, stopped at the home of Godfrey Bertram, Laird of Ellangowan, on the night the first Bertram child, a boy, was born. Mannering, a student of astrology, cast the horoscope of the newborn babe and was distressed to find that the child's fifth, tenth, and twenty-first years would be hazardous. The young Englishman puzzled over the fact that the boy's twenty-first year would correspond with the thirty-ninth year of the woman Mannering loved, which was the year the stars said would bring her death or imprisonment. An old gypsy, Meg Merrilies, also predicted danger for the new baby. Not wishing to worry the parents, Mannering wrote down his finds and presented them to Mr. Bertram, first cautioning him not to open the packet until the child had passed by one day his fifth birthday. Then he departed.

Young Harry Bertram grew steadily and well. He was tutored and supervised by Dominie Sampson, a teacher and preacher retained by his father; at times, the child was also watched over by the gypsy Meg, who had great love for the boy. The child was four years old when the laird became a justice of the peace and promised to rid the countryside of gypsies and poachers. After he had ordered all gypsies to leave the district, old Meg put a curse on him, saying that his own house was in danger of being as empty as were now the homes of the gypsies. On Harry's fifth birthday, the prediction came true: The boy disappeared while on a ride with a revenue officer hunting smugglers. The man was killed and his body found, but there was no trace of the child. All search proving futile, he was at last given up for dead. In her grief, his mother, prematurely delivered of a daughter, died soon afterward.

Seventeen years passed. Old Mr. Bertram, cheated by his lawyer, Gilbert Glossin, was to have his estate sold to pay his debts. Glossin planned to buy the property without much outlay of money, for the law said that when an heir was missing a purchaser need not put up the full price, in case the heir should return and claim his inheritance. Before the sale, Guy Mannering returned and tried to buy the property to save it for the Bertram family, but a delay in the mail prevented his effort, and Glossin got possession of the estate. Old Mr. Bertram died before the transaction was completed, leaving his daughter Lucy homeless and penniless.

During these transactions, Mannering's past history came to light. Years before, he had gone as a soldier to India and married there. Through a misunderstanding, he had accused his wife of faithlessness with Captain Brown, who was in reality in love with Mannering's daughter, Julia. The two men fought a duel, and Brown was wounded. Later he was captured by bandits, and Mannering assumed that he was dead. When Mannering's wife died eight months later, the unhappy man, having learned she had not been unfaithful, resigned his commission and returned with his daughter to England.

When Mannering learned that he could not buy the Bertram estate and allow Lucy to remain there with the faithful Dominie Sampson, he leased a nearby house for them. He also brought his daughter Julia to the house after he learned from friends with whom she was staying that she had been secretly meeting an unknown young man. What Mannering did not know was that the man was Captain Brown, who had escaped from his bandit captors and followed Julia to England and later to Scotland. Julia and Lucy were unhappy in their love affairs. Lucy loved Charles Hazlewood, but since Lucy had no money, Charles's father would not permit their marriage.

Captain Brown, loitering near the house, met old Meg Merrilies, who took a great interest in him. Once she saved his life, and for his thanks, she made him promise to come to her whenever she sent for him. A short time later, Brown encountered Julia, Lucy, and Charles Hazlewood. Charles, thinking Brown a bandit, pulled a firearm from his clothing. In his attempt to disarm Charles, Brown accidentally discharged the weapon and wounded Charles. Brown fled.

Charles would have made little of the incident, but Glossin, desiring to gain favor with the gentry by whom he had been snubbed since he had bought the Bertram property, went to Sir Robert Hazlewood and offered to apprehend the man who had shot his son. Glossin, finding some papers marked with the name of Brown, used them in his search. He was momentarily deterred, however, when he was called to interview a prisoner named Dirk Hatteraick. Dirk, a Dutch smuggler, was the killer of the revenue officer found dead when the Bertram heir disappeared. Dirk told Glossin that the boy was alive and in Scotland. Glossin had planned the kidnapping many years before; it was to his advantage to have the young man disappear again. He was even more anxious to get rid of the Bertram heir forever when he learned from Dirk that the man was Captain Brown. Brown—or Harry Bertram—would claim his estate, and Glossin would lose the rich property he had acquired for almost nothing. Glossin finally captured Brown and had him imprisoned, after arranging with Dirk to storm the prison and carry Brown off to sea to be killed or lost.

Old Meg, learning of the plot in some mysterious way, foiled it when she had Harry Bertram rescued. She also secured Mannering's aid in behalf of the young man, whom she had loved from the day of his birth. Bertram was taken by his rescuers to Mannering's home. There his story was pieced together from what he remembered and from the memory of old Dominie Sampson. Bertram could hardly believe that he was the heir to Ellangowan and Lucy's brother. His sister was overjoyed at the reunion, but it would take more than the proof of circumstances to win back his inheritance from Glossin. Mannering, Sampson, and Sir Robert Hazlewood, who heard the story, tried to trace old papers to secure the needed proof.

In the meantime, old Meg sent Bertram a message reminding him of Brown's promise to come should she need him. She led him into a cave where Dirk was hiding out and there told him her story. She had kidnapped him for Dirk on the day the revenue officer was murdered.

She had promised Dirk and Glossin, also one of the gang, not to reveal her secret until the boy was twenty-one years old. Now she felt released from her promise, since that period had passed. She told Bertram to capture Dirk for the hangman, but before the smuggler could be taken, he shot the old gypsy in the heart.

Dirk was taken to prison and would not verify the gypsy's story; his sullenness was taken as proof of Bertram's right to his inheritance. Glossin's part in the plot was also revealed, and he, too, was put into prison to await trial. When the two plotters fought in the cell, Dirk killed Glossin. Then Dirk wrote a full confession and cheated the hangman by killing himself. His confession, added to other evidence, proved Bertram's claim, and he was restored to his rightful position. Successful at last in his suit for Julia Mannering, he settled part of his estate on his sister Lucy and so paved the way for her marriage with Charles Hazlewood. The predictions had come true; Mannering's work was done.

Critical Evaluation:

Guy Mannering was Sir Walter Scott's second novel, begun immediately after *Waverley* (1814) and completed in six weeks. On its publication it was compared somewhat unfavorably to his first novel mainly because of its uneven qualities. Certainly, the development and climax of the novel appears to shift from Scott's initial ideas. Scott quickly downplays the initial astrology, but criticism still fastened onto it as a major demerit.

In recent criticism, the novel's unevenness has been recognized as proceeding more fundamentally from ambivalences within Scott. He was a conventional middle-class conservative, with a legal background and sense of a class-based society. He was also a romantic visionary whose natural artistic inclination was to the feudal past and to the supernatural. It could be maintained that three different accounts could be given of *Guy Mannering*: as a romance (or adventure story), as a love-centered, or romantic fiction, and as a realistic novel.

In terms of the romance, Scott follows closely many of the typical features of the genre. Patterns and motifs are centered around the Romance hero, Harry Bertram. He is the lost heir, orphaned and kidnapped from the earth into the lower regions of the smugglers, but supposed dead. He forgets his noble past, is given an alter ego (Brown), and seeks to rise again, through gaining favor, trade, and soldiering. The army gives him the means to rise, but his rise is thwarted by the recurring failure of the father figure (Mannering), and a further kidnapping. Such cyclic, repeating structures are common in romance, where rise is interleaved with fall. Such patterns may be found in stories as varied as the Passion and the film *Star Wars* (1977).

Love typically produces the motivation to quest. Brown's entry from England into Scotland parallels exactly Mannering's twenty-one years before at the beginning of novel. His journeying is helped by the wisdom of the lower world, particularly Meg Merrilies, but also Dandy Dinmont, a border farmer, to overcome further obstacles. Finally, memory is restored, inheritance and name recovered, and the prophecy fulfilled.

Unlike in the realistic novel, in romance fate is the overall structuring device, and so the plot becomes more important than the moral choices of the main characters. In fact, usually things happen to characters, rather than actions stemming from their choices. The astrological predictions and Meg's prophecies are more significant than any moral choice made (not that there are many). Mannering's attempts to circumvent the weird (fate, prophecy) are futile.

Scott's popularity, however, was not simply due to his being a romancer, closely in touch with the folk literature of Scotland. It was also because of the Romantic revolution in literature. Scott quite consciously echoes those features of Romanticism that had most vividly caught the popular imagination. For example, the opening of the novel contains rich descriptions of the dreary Scots landscape in the border area of the Solway, as winter night falls. The ancient ruins of the castle are seen first by night, with the sea and the cliffs creating a dramatic backcloth. The Englishman is caught up in a strange world. Later, there are descriptions of the English Lake District, home of the most famous Romantic poets. Its sublimity is stressed. The common country people, such as Dinmont, are held to be sources of wisdom and morality, a typical Wordsworthian theme. The use of verse reminds readers that Scott was a poet and ballad writer before becoming a novelist. He tries hard to make the separated lovers romantic, though much of the time the tone is too artificial to convince. Hence the work may be considered a romance and a Romantic fiction.

Last, there are strong elements of the realistic. Scott's portrayal of country people, the exact representation of their dialect and customs, his descriptions of Edinburgh, and his precise knowledge of the law paint a real society at a real point in history in the second half of the eighteenth century. Guy Mannering is meant to anchor such realism in his own character.

What is perhaps most significant is that Scott anticipates the typical way that the great nineteenth century novels to come were to incorporate romance into realism: through the use of the detective. The mysterious fate of the Bertrams is finally "solved" by legal detective work. The eccentric Edinburgh attorney, Playdell, evolves form comic character to sleuth, cooperating with the local forces of the law to reestablish justice. Bertram's restoration is a forensic one, not a magical one. His estate and future fortune are assured because his right has been proved as much as his character.

At the conclusion, therefore, the typical romance structures of loss, retrieval, and reconciliation can be seen as moral and legal in a sound, realistic way. The villains receive their due punishments, and Meg is killed off, Mannering having long since renounced his astrology. What Scott anticipates, as he does in other novels, is a renewing of the feudal class structures. First, the landowners need renewing. Bertram has been renewed through ordeal, proved worthy of Mannering's approval and therefore of his daughter's love, and so will manage his estates properly. Scott's disordered novel yields a message of order.

What, however, gives continued interest in the novel is not any sort of political message, nor its exciting story, nor its rather two-dimensional lovers. It is a sense of Scott's humanity, seen best in Meg, Dandy, and the tutor Dominie. Such outsiders, eccentrics even, demand their humanity to be recognized, their sympathies allowed expression, and their loyalties honored. The true aristocracy is those with nobility of the moral sentiments, and it is in this that Scott is most truly Romantic.

"Critical Evaluation" by David Barratt

Bibliography:
Alexander, J. H., and David Hewitt, eds. *Scott and His Influence*. Aberdeen, Scotland: Association for Scottish Literary Studies, 1983. These papers are from the Scottish Literary Studies Conference of 1982, and contain two significant papers on *Guy Mannering* by Jana Davies and Jane Millgate, on landscape and chronology, respectively.

Bold, Alan, ed. *Sir Walter Scott: The Long-Forgotten Melody*. New York: Barnes & Noble Books, 1983. A collection of essays mainly concerned with the background to Scott's fiction. Index.

Cockshut, A. O. J. *The Achievement of Walter Scott*. New York: New York University Press, 1969. The first part of this study focuses particularly on Scott's two voices, the romantic and the social. *Guy Mannering* is discussed at some length in this light. Cockshut sees Scott as torn between the conventional and the romantic artist: It is a deeper dichotomy than mere literary technique. Index.

Garside, Peter. "Meg Merrilies and Gypsies." In *The Politics of the Picturesque: Literary Landscape and Aesthetics Since 1770*, edited by Stephen Copley and Peter Garside. Cambridge, England: Cambridge University Press, 1994. Helps place Scott's novels in the Romantic tradition.

Millgate, Jane. *Walter Scott: The Making of the Novelist*. Toronto: University of Toronto Press, 1984. One of the more penetrating and sophisticated studies of Scott and his techniques. Deals with *Guy Mannering* in one of its chapters, focusing on its structures, particularly on parallelism and Shakespearian allusions.

GUY OF WARWICK

Type of work: Poetry
Author: Unknown
Type of plot: Romance
Time of plot: Tenth century
Locale: England, Europe, and the Middle East
First transcribed: Gui de Warewic, c. 1240 (English translation, 1300)

Principal characters:
GUY, a knight of Warwick
FELICE LA BELLE, Guy's mistress
HERHAUD OF ARDERN, Guy's mentor and friend
ROHAUD, Earl of Warwick
OTOUS, Duke of Pavia
MORGADOUR, a German knight
REIGNIER, Emperor of Germany
SEGYN, Duke of Louvain
ERNIS, Emperor of Greece
LORET, Ernis' daughter
THE SOUDAN OF THE SARACENS
TIRRI, a knight of Gurmoise
ATHELSTAN, King of England
COLBRAND, a giant

The Story:

Love for a woman prompted Guy to inaugurate his long series of remarkable exploits. Guy, son of the steward to Rohaud, Earl of Warwick, was a very popular and handsome young squire. As the earl's principal cupbearer, he was instructed, on one fateful occasion, to superintend the service of the ladies during dinner. Gazing on Felice la Belle, Rohaud's beautiful and talented daughter, he fell desperately in love with the fair maiden. When he first declared himself to her, he was rejected because of his lowly birth and lack of attainments. Later, however, when from love-sickness he was close to death, Felice, following the advice of an angel, offered him some encouragement. If he became a knight and proved his valor, she would reward him with her hand in marriage.

After receiving knighthood, Sir Guy set out to prove his valor. Accompanied by his mentor, Herhaud of Ardern, he spent an entire year attending tournaments throughout Europe. Pitted against some of the most renowned knights of Christendom, Guy was indomitable; in every encounter he took the prize. His reputation established, he returned to Warwick to claim his reward from Felice. This fair lady, however, had decided to raise her standards. After acknowledging his accomplishments, she notified him that he must become the foremost knight in the world before she would marry him.

True to the laws of chivalric love, Guy returned to Europe to satisfy the fancy of his mistress. Again visiting the tournaments, again he was, without exception, victorious. Misfortune awaited him, however, in Italy. His high merit having excited their envy, seventeen knights, led by Otous, Duke of Pavia, laid an ambush for the English champion. Before Guy won the skirmish, two of his closest companions were dead, and his best friend, Herhaud, appeared to be slain. As Guy, himself grievously wounded, began his return journey to England, he was filled with remorse for having allowed the wishes of a haughty lady to lead him to this sad result. In Burgundy, where he was performing his customary deeds of valor, his spirits were considerably improved by his discovery of Herhaud, alive and disguised as a palmer.

As the two friends continued their journey homeward, they learned that Segyn, Duke of Louvain, was being attacked by Reignier, Emperor of Germany, who wrongfully claimed the duke's lands. Assembling a small army, Guy defeated two armies that were sent against Segyn. With a larger force, the emperor then encircled the city in which Guy, Segyn, and their followers were quartered. During this blockade Reignier, on a hunting trip, was surprised by Guy, who led the unarmed emperor into the city. There, in the true spirit of chivalry, a rapprochement was brought about between the ruler, Reignier, and his vassal, Segyn.

Soon after rendering these good services to Segyn, Guy found another occasion for the exercise of his talents. Learning that Ernis, Emperor of Greece, was besieged by the mighty forces of the Saracen Soudan, Guy levied an army of a thousand German knights and marched to Constantinople. Received with joy, he was promised for his efforts the hand of Princess Loret, the emperor's daughter. After repelling one Saracen attack, Guy took the offensive and left on the field fifteen acres covered with the corpses of his enemies. His greatest threat, however, came from one of his own knights, Morgadour, who had become enamored of Loret. Knowing that the Soudan had sworn to kill every Christian who should fall within his power, Morgadour duped Guy into entering the enemy camp and challenging the Saracen monarch to single combat. Ordered to be executed, the resourceful Guy cut off the Soudan's head, repelled his attackers, and made his escape.

The emperor, because of his great admiration for the English knight, hastened arrangements for the wedding of Guy and Loret. Guy, somehow having forgotten Felice, was agreeable to the plan, until, seeing the wedding ring, he was suddenly reminded of his first love. A true knight, he resolved to be faithful to Felice and to find some excuse for breaking his engagement to Loret. Another altercation with Morgadour ended with Guy's slaying of the treacherous German. Using the pretext that his continued presence in the court might lead to trouble between the Greeks and Germans, Guy took his leave.

Guy planned an immediate return to England, but he was destined to perform further deeds of knight errantry before being reunited with his beloved Felice. While traveling through Lorraine, he met an old friend, Sir Tirri, who was being persecuted by their mutual enemy, Duke Otous. The duke had abducted Tirri's fiancée. Guy wasted no time in rescuing the woman, but Otous did not give up easily. After attempting and failing to defeat Guy on the battlefield, he resorted to foul means and succeeded in capturing both Tirri and his fiancée. Guy, combining trickery with valor, killed the felon duke and freed the lovers.

One more incident delayed Guy's return to England. Unintentionally entering the game preserve of the King of Flanders, he was confronted by the king's son and found himself compelled to kill the dissenting prince. In an ensuing encounter with the wrathful father, Guy was forced to slaughter fourteen knights before he could make his escape. Arriving in his native country, Guy, in accordance with chivalric practice, repaired to the court of King Athelstan. He was honorably received, and almost immediately the king enlisted his services to kill a troublesome dragon. After a long and fierce battle, Guy in triumph carried the monster's head to the king.

Guy's homecoming was the less joyous upon his learning of the death of his parents, but this sorrow was compensated for by his immediate marriage to Felice. They were married only forty days, barely time to conceive a son, when Guy's conscience, troubled over the mischief he had done for the love of a lady, forced him on a penitential pilgrimage. His bereaved wife placed on his finger a gold remembrance ring and sorrowfully watched him depart for the Holy Land.

So great a warrior, however, could not escape his reputation or his duty. He interrupted his devotions to kill an Ethiopian giant and to assist Tirri again, this time by slaying a false accuser.

When the pious warrior returned to England he found King Athelstan besieged by King Anlaf of Denmark. It had been agreed that the outcome of the war should be determined by single combat between Colbrand, a Danish giant, and an English champion. In a dream King Athelstan was advised to ask the help of the first pilgrim he met at the entrance of the palace, and the aging Guy of Warwick was that pilgrim. In this last and most famous of his fights, Guy, shorn of his weapons, appeared certain of defeat. In his extremity he snatched up a convenient ax, fiercely assailed the giant, cut him to pieces, and thereby saved the English kingdom.

Guy paid one last visit to his own castle, where he discovered Felice engaged in acts of devotion and charity. Without having revealed his identity to her, he went off to the forests of Ardennes. When death was near, he dispatched the gold remembrance to his wife and begged her to supervise his burial. Arriving in time to receive his last breath, the faithful Felice survived him by only fifteen days. She was buried in the same grave as her warrior husband.

Critical Evaluation:

There have been numerous transformations of the story of Guy of Warwick since the thirteenth century to suit changing tastes or commercial necessity. What has remained constant is the hero's development from a self-absorbed, worldly person, to a mature individual, to near-sainthood. Clearly a patchwork composition, with diverse romance motifs following each other in loose sequence, *Guy of Warwick* has many themes that could easily be eliminated or transposed. This patchwork character, according to some critics, actually contributed to the epic's popularity.

Inventive poets who worked on versions of *Guy of Warwick* throughout the centuries put the work through many transformations in response to audience taste. For instance, the battle descriptions, long established in French romance, are modified to harmonize with English tradition. Elizabethans found their greatest interest was in the English history. In the nineteenth and twentieth centuries, children happily read it as a fairy tale, with Guy's fantastic accomplishments receiving emphasis.

Perhaps in actual life many a war-weary hero must have similarly renounced the world. Some critics believe, however, that the larger-than-life legend of Guy of Warwick was initially the product of monastic imagination at work to suit the religious orientation of the clergy. Many editorial changes can be observed in the second half of the epic poem, which tells of Guy's spiritual journey. In the second half, the change in the meter and tail-rhyme stanzas indicate that the new section is quite independent of the first. It would seem that, in content and form, English authors saw no objection to hybrid stories if they served nationalistic or religious purposes.

The Middle English romances and legends, from the period of their great flourishing between 1280 and 1380, are marked with common themes such as rejection, exile, constancy, and reward. This homogeneity in observing literary conventions is the "grammar" of Middle Ages romance. The same plot pattern, situations, and phrases recur insistently. The reason for this homogeneity is to be found in the social context of Middle English romance.

In this sense, *Guy of Warwick* is like other romances of legendary English heroes such as King Horn, Havelok the Dane, Bevis of Hampton, and Richard the Lionhearted. They have in common their indomitable chivalric knights, disdainful fair ladies, adventures in distant lands, brave and numerous enemies, and finally, success in love. There are supernatural elements such as dragons and giants. Angels give warnings against vicious animals and hostile humans. When the story threatens to get dull, gigantic champions appear, such as the Saracen Amoraunt or the Ethiopian giant.

In order to enhance exoticism, the author of *Guy of Warwick* includes fanciful Eastern elements. The hero goes to the relief of Constantinople when it is besieged by the Sultan. Inevitably, he defeats the heathens and demolishes their idols.

Aside from its entertainment value, the story is rooted in the need of the Anglo-Norman nobility to establish a native ancestry with a strong sense of history. Early printers treated it as serious history. William Shakespeare used it as a historical guide to appeal to patriotism.

Until the end of the Renaissance, *Guy of Warwick* had strong appeal to all English people, for Guy was thought to have saved his country from the Danes. By the middle of the thirteenth century, he was one of the most celebrated heroes of English legend. The story was well chosen to appeal to the new audience. *Guy of Warwick* is also an early example of bourgeois narratives in which the hero breaks into a higher social milieu through merit.

Guy, a hero of humble birth and a secular careerist, follows a familiar romance pattern. He is scorned by the lady he loves until he has proved himself worthy of knighthood in a series of increasingly hazardous tournaments. Felice is slow to yield. Her fears are not neurotic but socially valid expectations of courtly love. Guy is a model of behavior. Guy's dedication to his friend Tirri, for instance, is exemplary. Guy's adventures were supposed to teach the true virtues of worldly and spiritual chivalry and the value of struggle for equity and justice within and beyond the law.

The story effectively shows spiritual development from his victories in tournaments, to victory in battle, to dedication of his life to God. The motivations for his adventures evolve from simple desire to win tournaments to hatred of injustice. In this sense, the two disparate parts of the story gain a unifying purpose: The courtly romance leads to the sainthood legend. Glory of God wins in the end—but this could not be achieved without learning spiritual lessons in worldly contexts.

When Guy reaches a new spiritual level, he has many opportunities to display it. For example, Guy becomes the instrument by which God saves England from the Danes. This victory, and Guy's death, are announced by an angel, certifying him as a saint. Miracles take place near him and because of him. Some critics assume the poem was originally written by a cleric or monk who wished to glorify the family of the Earl of Warwick. To appeal to the masses, the anonymous author made the moral explicit through dramatization. The epic sustained its popularity throughout centuries because of its action-packed plot.

Moral and social lessons are skillfully embedded in wild adventures. Guy's seemingly improbable epiphany captures the imagination. Despite its weaknesses, *Guy of Warwick* has remained a popular work of literature for centuries.

"Critical Evaluation" by Chogollah Maroufi

Bibliography:
Barron, W. R. J. *English Medieval Romance.* New York: Longman, 1987. Barron's authoritative work on English romance of the medieval period contains a chapter titled "Ancestral Romances: *Guy of Warwick*," which analyzes the adventures of Guy of Warwick in terms of their narrative structure.

Burton, Julie. "Narrative Patterning and *Guy of Warwick.*" *Yearbook of English Studies* 22 (1992): 105-116. This article analyzes the techniques used in composing *Guy of Warwick* in their relation to traditional techniques of English romances of the Middle Ages.

Dannenbaum, Susan C. "*Guy of Warwick* and the Question of Exemplary Romance." *Genre* 17, no. 4 (Winter, 1984): 351-374. Deals with the notions of sainthood and piety in *Guy of Warwick* and explains how the complicated process by which biographies of venerated laymen and saints became an enduring genre and medium of romances during the Middle Ages.

Mehl, Dieter. *The Middle English Romances of the Thirteenth and Fourteenth Centuries.* New York: Barnes & Noble Books, 1969. Clear and astute analysis of thirteenth and fourteenth century English romances. Devotes a chapter to a discussion of the social context and related aspects of *Guy of Warwick.*

Menocal, Maria R. *Shards of Love: Exile and the Origins of the Lyric.* Durham, N.C.: Duke University Press, 1994. An excellent treatment of the history and philosophy of romance writing in medieval Europe and its relation to the notion of exile.

THE HAIRY APE

Type of work: Drama
Author: Eugene O'Neill (1888-1953)
Type of plot: Expressionism
Time of plot: Early twentieth century
Locale: At sea and on land
First performed: 1922; first published, 1922

> *Principal characters:*
> ROBERT SMITH (YANK), a stoker on a transatlantic liner
> PADDY, an old Irishman, also a stoker
> LONG, a shipmate
> MILDRED DOUGLAS, a passenger on the ship

The Story:

Below the decks of an ocean liner one hour out from its New York port, the firemen who powered the ship by stoking coal drank, cursed, and sang, creating a defiant uproar like beasts in a cage. The strongest and most respected of the group was Robert Smith, known as Yank, who took pride in his strength and in the ability of the crew to produce the speed of the engines. They belonged; they were men; they were steel. Yank's shipmate Paddy, a wizened old Irishman, yearned for the days of the graceful clipper ships that plowed the Atlantic silently, when men were in harmony with nature. Long, a socialist agitator, cursed the capitalist class that forced them to slave for wages in the bowels of the ship. Rejecting these views, Yank confidently believed that he was the mover of the world.

On the promenade deck, rich young heiress Mildred Douglas and her over-rouged aunt reclined in deck chairs. Mildred, the spoiled daughter of the president of a steel company and chairman of the liner's board of directors, defended her desire to visit the stokehold to discover how the other half lived. Although her aunt considered Mildred's interest in social service superficial and called her a poser, Mildred declared that she was sincere and that she wanted to help. Dressed in white, she insisted that the ship's officers take her below. When they revealed the stokers in all their brutality to her, she was repulsed and frightened. At the sight of Yank, who was caught unaware by her presence, she cried out and fainted. Later, Paddy remarked to Yank that she looked as though she had seen a hairy ape. His identity and sense of belonging shattered, Yank vowed to get even.

When the ship returned to New York, Long attempted to channel Yank's hurt and fury against Mildred into rage against the ruling class. He showed Yank goods displayed in Fifth Avenue store windows, goods that would never be available to Yank, and he railed against the callous behavior of the rich Sunday churchgoers. Unmoved at first, Yank was excited by a coat made of monkey fur in a store window. It reminded him of Mildred's insult. He became further irritated when the men and women of Fifth Avenue ignored his hostile advances and seemed not to see him. Maddened by the crowd's delighted cries at the sight of the monkey fur coat, he tried in vain to pull up a lamppost to use as a club. Not even punching a gentleman in the face brought him recognition: His arrest occurred only after the gentleman's accusation that Yank had caused him to miss his bus.

Jailed for thirty days on Blackwell's Island, Yank at first thought he might be caged at the zoo. His fellow inmates, learning of Yank's anger at Mildred, suggested that if he wanted revenge, he should join the Wobblies, the Industrial Workers of the World (IWW). According to the newspaper, the IWW was a tough gang whose members liked to dynamite buildings and sought to destroy American society. Yank realized that as president of the Steel Trust, Mildred's father made the steel of the ship where he thought he had belonged, as well as the steel that imprisoned him in jail.

Freed from jail, Yank entered the IWW office, believing that with his strength and purpose he would be useful to the group in its supposedly violent activities. After a welcome from the IWW secretary, Yank assured the men that he was a regular guy and indicated that he was "wise" to them. The secretary tried to explain that their activities were legal and aboveboard. When Yank boasted that he alone could and would blow up all the steel factories of the world, the members viewed him as a spy from the Secret Service. They wasted no time in throwing him out; he did not belong with them.

Despondent and unsure, Yank did not know where next to turn. The ship no longer represented home, society ignored him, and even the Wobblies had rejected him. He traveled to the monkey house at the zoo to encounter his animal counterpart. At least the gorilla could dream of the past and of the jungle where he belonged, he thought; he, Yank, was homeless. Jimmying the lock, Yank freed the gorilla. The two confronted each other outside the cage. Yank offered a hand to his "brother," but instead of shaking it, the beast enveloped him in its arms, crushing him in a murderous hug. Throwing the mortally injured man into the cage, the ape shuffled off. With a final ironic effort to stand as a human being, Yank mockingly acknowledged the cage and died.

Critical Evaluation:

Considered America's greatest twentieth century dramatist by scholars and critics alike, Eugene Gladstone O'Neill was awarded four Pulitzer Prizes as well as the Nobel Prize in Literature in 1936. The son of actor James O'Neill, he was educated at private schools and briefly at Princeton; after six months of illness in a tuberculosis sanatorium, he enrolled in George Pierce Baker's playwriting course at Harvard, an experience that solidified his determination to be a playwright.

The Hairy Ape, a long one-act play containing eight scenes, was written in 1921 and performed in March of 1922. Its background lies in O'Neill's sojourn at sea, and its burly central figure Yank is patterned after Robert Driscoll, a stoker acquaintance who was similarly proud of his physical strength and whose suicide at sea prompted O'Neill to imagine the factors that might have led him to it.

The major theme O'Neill explores in the play is the question of the place of human beings in the universe. In the increasingly dehumanized society of the modern world, the individual no longer is in harmony with nature, the forces that Paddy speaks poetically about in the first scene, the days when "a ship was part of the sea, and a man was part of a ship, and the sea joined all together and made it one."

Does the individual then belong in the mechanistic, industrial society that has been created? O'Neill seems also to reject this idea. Yank's animal nature, dramatized through his strength and physical appearance, is contrasted with the fragility of the would-be social worker, Mildred. Representing an affluent but insensitive society, Mildred makes a pitiful effort to reach out to those of a lower class, but her ancestral line has rendered her weak and lethargic, and she is unable even to stay conscious in Yank's presence.

The contrast between the individual and society is repeated with the unfeeling, churchgoing marionettes of Fifth Avenue who infuriate Yank with their materialistic delight in the monkey fur coat and their blindness to his existence. In his encounter with the Wobblies, Yank continues his quest to find an identity, but his motives are suspect and he is misunderstood. In his last misguided effort, at the zoo, he seeks acceptance in the animal world. He is again rejected and is killed by the gorilla. Although he is an outcast from various segments of society and no longer in harmony with the natural world, his death underscores the fact that he cannot return to a simian past because he is human.

O'Neill cautions in his stage directions against treating the play naturalistically, but he has created a central figure whose life is determined by his heredity and environment, thus fulfilling the definition of a naturalistic character. Yank's heredity is weak. He tells the audience in the first scene that home meant beatings to him. He is not very bright; he has difficulty reading the newspaper and his frequent sitting in the posture of Auguste Rodin's *Thinker* emphasizes his inability to reason. He is controlled by his environment: The ship is home until Mildred intrudes; thereafter, he desperately seeks a place, an environment, where he can feel comfortable. Yank is a victim of forces beyond his control; he simply does not belong.

What does "belonging" mean? In O'Neill's lexicon, to belong means to have an identity, to possess self-confidence, and to be a recognized member of a group and worthy of its respect. Yank lost his sense of belonging with Mildred's horrified cry. His quest to reconcile his humanity with society is unsuccessful, as is his attempt to find his identity in the gorilla. He is a modern alienated Everyman.

Although the character may be naturalistic, much of O'Neill's stylistic method is expressionistic, revealing the influence of August Strindberg's *The Dream Play* (1902) and *The Ghost Sonata* (1907). The psychological realism of Yank's behavior is contrasted with a number of deliberate nonrealistic visual and auditory devices associated with animal life and imprisonment. In the stage directions for the first scene, O'Neill indicates that the setting is not to be naturalistic. The rows of metal bunks and the uprights crossing them in the forecastle are meant to suggest the steel framework of a cage. The ceiling crushes down, and the men are cramped into an animal stance. At times the men respond in chorus to Yank's speeches with barking, mechanical laughter. When the bell rings, the men form a "prisoners' lockstep"; they shovel coal rhythmically, like "chained gorillas." Bells and furnace doors clang, flames roar, engines throb, and monkeys chatter. The cage motif is repeated in the jail on Blackwell's Island and in the cage at the zoo, indicating how individuals are imprisoned by forces beyond their control.

One of O'Neill's early plays, *The Hairy Ape* is a powerful drama that verges on tragedy. From his confident first appearance to the lonely, broken figure at his death, Yank is a larger-than-life human being whose struggle against his fate is compelling and heroic. With his attack upon materialism and his portrayal of alienation, O'Neill has defined major themes of American drama and foreshadowed the social and political dimensions of playwrights such as Arthur Miller, Sam Shepard, and Emily Mann.

Joyce E. Henry

Bibliography:
Berlin, Normand. *Eugene O'Neill*. New York: Grove Press, 1982. A succinct work of 178 pages that provides an introduction to O'Neill's works by decades. Includes a helpful explanation of expressionistic techniques in *The Hairy Ape*.
Egri, Peter. " 'Belonging' Lost: Alienation and Dramatic Form in Eugene O'Neill's *The Hairy Ape*." In *Critical Essays on Eugene O'Neill*, edited by James J. Martine. Boston: G. K. Hall, 1984. An excellent analysis of the alienation theme and how it is woven into the structure of the play. Considers the play dramatically significant and with universal appeal.

Floyd, Virginia. *The Plays of Eugene O'Neill: A New Assessment*. New York: Frederick Ungar, 1985. A critical discussion of the O'Neill canon, with one chapter devoted to *The Hairy Ape*. Contains several production photographs.

O'Neill, Eugene. *Selected Letters of Eugene O'Neill*. Edited by Travis Bogard and Jackson R. Bryer. New Haven, Conn.: Yale University Press, 1988. An engrossing collection of letters, revealing O'Neill in interpersonal and business relationships. Discusses details of creation and production of *The Hairy Ape*.

Sheaffer, Louis. *O'Neill*. 2 vols. Boston: Little, Brown, 1968-1973. An impressive biography, more than fifteen hundred pages long, with many photographs, and a bibliography. Its wealth of information includes analyses of plays, themes, and characters; reviews; and quotations from O'Neill. The first volume concludes with the production of *Beyond the Horizon* in 1920, the second with O'Neill's death.

HAKLUYT'S VOYAGES

Type of work: Travel writing
Author: Richard Hakluyt (c. 1552-1616)
First published: 1589; enlarged edition, 1598-1600

Richard Hakluyt, regarded as the first professor of modern geography at Oxford, made a point of getting to know the "chiefest Captains at sea, the greatest merchants, and the best Mariners of our nation." As a boy, he watched the ships come to port from distant journeys, and early lessons in geography fired him with an eagerness to know more. Studies at Oxford and a five-year period in Paris further set his resolution to collect the scattered records of English maritime discovery. The result of his interests was *Hakluyt's Voyages,* an invaluable sourcebook for those who wish to study the Age of Discovery and to determine the place of England in it. This work is an anthology of the explorations and travels of British adventurers down to the author's own time. The accounts are bold and vigorous, usually giving only the main events of the journeys, many of them written by those who made the voyages.

Published by Hakluyt in refutation of a French accusation that the English were insular and spiritless, the book is of value in several capacities. It gives faithful accounts of many sixteenth century exploratory journeys, it is an index to the temper of Elizabethan England, and it reflects the enthusiasm for travel literature which was so prevalent at the time of the original publication. It may have been begun as a piece of propaganda, but it soon became more than that. The second edition grew to three volumes issued over as many years. Hakluyt also translated narratives by Spanish explorers, but *Hakluyt's Voyages* remains his memorial, a true "prose epic" of the English people and nation.

The massive work is more than a documentary history of exploration, for in it, alongside tales of adventure, are mingled historical and economic papers intended to establish British sovereignty at sea. The purpose of the huge undertaking was to encourage overseas settlement and foreign trade. (It was asserted that the income of the East India Company was greatly increased through *Hakluyt's Voyages.*)

The first group of accounts gives thirty-eight tales of travel and exploration made by Britons up to the end of the sixteenth century. The first stories go back to the medieval ages, for the narrative which begins the work is that of what is probably a mythical voyage by King Arthur of Britain to Iceland and the most northern parts of Europe in 517.

The first ten narratives deal with voyages made before 1066, the year of the Norman Conquest of Britain. They include such journeys as the conquest of the isles of Man and Anglesey by Edwin, King of Northumberland in 624, the trips of Octher into Norway and Denmark in 890 and 891, the voyage of Wolstan into Danish waters in the tenth century, the voyage of King Edgar, with four thousand ships, about the island of Britain, and the journey of Edmund Ironside from England to Hungary in 1017. Another voyage which took place before the Norman Conquest was that of a man named Erigena, who was sent by Alfred, King of the West Saxons, to Greece. Alfred was one of the most cultured of British kings in premedieval times and very much interested in classical civilizations. His emissary, Erigena, went as far as Athens in 885, a long voyage for those ancient times.

The other voyages described are those taken after the Norman Conquest. The first of these is an account of a marvelous journey made by a company of English noblemen to escort the daughter of King Harold to Russia for her marriage to the Duke of Russia in 1067. The next account is of the surprising journey of an unknown Englishman who travels as far into Asia as

Tartaria in the first half of the thirteenth century. One notable voyage describes the adventures of Nicolaus de Linna, a Franciscan friar, to the northern parts of Scandinavia. The twenty-second voyage is that of Anthony Jenkinson, who travels to Russia from England in order to return Osep Napea, the first ambassador from Muscovia to Queen Mary of England, to his own country in 1557. Surprisingly, almost half of the journeys described in this first collection are those made to Russia by way of the Arctic Ocean, around northern Scandinavia. It is not ordinarily realized that there was any traffic at all between England and Russia at that time, because of the difficulty of both water and land transportation between the two countries. The final narrative of the first group tells of the greatest event of Elizabethan England, the meeting of the British naval fleet with the great Armada which Philip II of Spain had sent to subdue England and win for Spain the supremacy of the seas.

The second group of accounts describes trips taken to the region of the Straits of Gibraltar and the countries surrounding the Mediterranean Sea. Eleven of these accounts describe trips made before the Norman Conquest in 1066 and fifty-two describe trips made after that date. The earliest story is that of Helena, the wife of a Roman emperor and a daughter of Coelus, one of the early kings of Britain. Helena, famous as the mother of Constantine the Great, who made Christianity the official religion of Rome, traveled to Jerusalem in 337 because of her interest in the early Christian church. She built several churches there and brought back to Europe a collection of holy relics. One of the relics was a nail reputed to be from the True Cross. It was incorporated some time later into the so-called Iron Crown of Lombardy.

Several of the post-Conquest voyages were trips made by Englishmen to help in the recovery of Jerusalem from the Saracens during the Crusades. Among the best known are those of Richard I, often called the Lion-Hearted, and of Prince Edward, son of Henry III, who went to Syria in the last half of the thirteenth century. Another story is a narrative of the voyage of the English ship *Susan*, which took William Hareborne to Turkey in 1582. Hareborne was the first ambassador sent by a British monarch to the ruler of Turkey, who was at that time Murad Khan. Another interesting voyage was that of Ralph Fitch, a London merchant. Between the years 1583 and 1591 he traveled to Syria, to Ormuz, to Goa in the East Indies, to Cambia, to the River Ganges, to Bengala, to Chonderi, to Siam, and thence back to his homeland. It was rare for people to travel, even in the spice trade, as far as did merchant Fitch during the sixteenth century.

A third group of accounts connects with the exploration and discovery of America. The first account is of a voyage supposedly made to the West Indies in 1170 by Madoc, the son of Owen Guined, a prince of North Wales. It is also recorded that, in February, 1488, Columbus offered his services to Henry VII of England and petitioned that monarch to sponsor a voyage to the westward seas for the purpose of discovering a new route to the East Indies. Bartholomew, brother of Columbus, repeated the request a year later but was refused a second time by the English king.

Several voyages described are those made to America for the purpose of discovering a northwest passage to the Orient. The early voyage of Cabot is among them, as well as the voyages of Martin Frobisher and John Davis. Frobisher made three voyages in search of a passage, in the three successive years between 1576 and 1578. John Davis also made three fruitless efforts to find a passage in the years from 1585 to 1587. All of these were an important part of the colonial effort in Hakluyt's own time.

Several exploratory trips to Newfoundland and the Gulf of the St. Lawrence River are also related, the earliest being the voyage of Sir Humphrey Gilbert to Newfoundland. The ship *Grace of Bristol, England*, also made a trip up the Gulf of St. Lawrence, as far as Assumption

Island. There are also accounts of trips made by explorers of other European nations in the New World, such as the journeys made in Canada as far as Hudson's Bay by Jacques Cartier in 1534 and 1535. There are full accounts of all the voyages made to Virginia in the sixteenth century and of the two unsuccessful attempts by Sir Walter Raleigh to found a colony there in 1585 and in 1587. Another group of stories tells of both English and Spanish explorations of the Gulf of California. The voyage around the world undertaken by Sir Francis Drake is given, particularly the part during which he sailed up the western coast of America to a point forty-three degrees north of the equator and landed to take possession of what he called Nova Albion, in the name of his monarch, Queen Elizabeth I, thus giving the British a claim to that part of the New World.

Also described is a voyage taken under orders of the viceroy of New Spain by Francis Gualle. Gualle crossed the Pacific Ocean to the Philippine Islands, where he visited Manila. From there he went to Macao in the East Indies and to Japan and returned from the Orient to Acapulco, Mexico, in the 1580's.

Another group of stories contains short accounts of trips by Englishmen to various parts of Spanish America. Among these were trips to Mexico City as early as 1555, barely a quarter of a century after it had been conquered by Hernán Cortés, as well as to the Antilles Islands in the West Indies, to Guiana, to the coast of Portuguese Brazil, to the delta of the Rio Plata, and to the Straits of Magellan.

Hakluyt also tells the stories of the first two voyages made to the Straits of Magellan and thence around the world, first by Magellan—the trip completed by the survivors of the expedition—and then by Sir Francis Drake. The third man to sail through the strait and then to proceed around the world is one of the forgotten men of history. Hakluyt gave the credit for this trip to Thomas Cavendish, an Englishman who circled the globe in the years 1586 to 1588.

To the modern reader, *Hakluyt's Voyages* is alive with the Elizabethan spirit of adventure and reflects the suddenly expanding world of the Tudors. Although the work is basically an anthology, the stamp of Hakluyt's personality is on the entire book; his idealism, his admiration for brave men and noble deeds, and his ambitions for his nation are evident throughout the narrative.

As much as anything else, *Hakluyt's Voyages* should be read as economic history; some of the pieces included might be considered real estate promoters' descriptions of lands to be developed. Merchants found the book invaluable, and the queen and her ministers saw it as a worthy psychological push toward the readiness of the nation to embrace an empire. The accounts of the voyages are told with a simplicity and a directness that is far more effective than self-conscious artistry or literary pretension; the tales are the matter-of-fact reporting of people of action.

Bibliography:
Hakluyt, Richard. *The Principal Navigations, Voyages, Traffiques, and Discoveries of the English Nation, Made by Sea or Overland to the Remote and Farthest Distant Quarters of the Earth at Any Time Within the Compasse of These 1600 Yeares.* 8 vols. London: J. M. Dent, 1926. Hakluyt's major work. Includes detailed introduction to contents.
Lynam, Edward, ed. *Richard Hakluyt and His Successors: A Volume Issued to Commemorate the Centenary of the Hakluyt Society.* Nendeln, Liechtenstein: Kraus Reprint, 1967. Essays discuss Richard Hakluyt's activities as a publicist for sea ventures and describe other English collections of voyage and travel documents.
Parks, George Bruner. *Richard Hakluyt and the English Voyages.* Edited by James A. William-son. 2d ed. New York: Frederick Ungar, 1961. Parks describes Hakluyt's life as an active

scholar, government consultant, and a man of letters. Includes discussion of Hakluyt's contributions to oceanic voyages of trade and discovery. Features a full chronology.

Quinn, David B., ed. *The Hakluyt Handbook*. 2 vols. London: The Hakluyt Society, 1974. A comprehensive handbook with an updated chronology. In addition to numerous illustrations and maps, the handbook contains a collection of modern views concerning the significance of Hakluyt's work and presents an analysis of the efficiency and accuracy of Hakluyt's use of his source materials.

Wrench, Sir Evelyn. "Founders of Virginia." *National Geographic Magazine* 93, no. 4 (April, 1948): 433-462. This article places Richard Hakluyt's publications in the context of the Elizabethan spirit of discovery and expansion. Wrench describes Hakluyt's contributions, along with those of Sir Francis Drake and Sir Walter Raleigh, to the birth of the state of Virginia. Contains many relevant photographs.

THE HAMLET

Type of work: Novel
Author: William Faulkner (1897-1962)
Type of plot: Psychological realism
Time of plot: Late nineteenth century
Locale: Mississippi
First published: 1940

> *Principal characters:*
> WILL VARNER, the chief property owner in Frenchman's Bend
> JODY, his son
> EULA, his daughter
> V. K. RATLIFF, a sewing-machine salesman
> AB SNOPES, a newcomer to Frenchman's Bend
> FLEM SNOPES, his son
> ISAAC SNOPES, an idiot relative
> MINK SNOPES, another relative
> LABOVE, the schoolteacher at Frenchmen's Bend
> HENRY ARMSTID, a farmer

The Story:

In his later years, Will Varner, owner of the Old Frenchman place and almost everything else in Frenchman's Bend, began to turn many of his affairs over to his thirty-year-old son, Jody. One day, while Jody sat in the Varner store, he met Ab Snopes, a newcomer to town, and Ab arranged to rent one of the farms owned by the Varners. Jody then found out from Ratliff, a salesman, that Ab had been suspected of burning barns on other farms where he had been a tenant. Jody and his father concluded that Ab's unsavory reputation would do them no harm. Jody became afraid, however, that Ab might burn some of the Varner property; as a sort of bribe, he hired Ab's son, Flem, to clerk in the store.

From Ratliff came the explanation for Ab's grievance against the world. He had once struck a horse-trading deal with Pat Stamper, an almost legendary trader. Ab drove a mule and an old horse to Jefferson and, before showing them to Stamper, he skillfully doctored up the old nag. Stamper swapped Ab a team of mules that looked fine, but when Ab tried to drive them out of Jefferson, the mules collapsed. To get back his own mule, Ab spent the money his wife had given him to buy a milk separator. Stamper also forced him to purchase a dark, fat horse that looked healthy but rather peculiar. On the way home, Ab ran into a thunderstorm, and the horse changed from dark to light and from fat to lean. It was Ab's old horse, which Stamper had painted and then fattened up with a bicycle pump.

Will Varner's daughter, Eula, was a plump, sensuous girl who matured early. The new schoolteacher, Labove, fell in love with her the first day she came to the schoolhouse. An ambitious young man, Labove rode back and forth between Frenchman's Bend and the university, where he studied law and played on the football team. One day, he attempted to seduce Eula after school had been dismissed; he failed and later was horrified to discover that Eula did not even mention the attempt to Jody. Labove left Frenchman's Bend forever.

As she grew older, Eula had many suitors, the principal one being Hoake McCarron, who literally fought off the competition. When the Varners found out that Eula was pregnant,

McCarron and two other suitors left for Texas. Flem Snopes then stepped in, married Eula, and went off on a long honeymoon.

The Snopes clan, which had gathered in the wake of Ab and Flem, began to have troubles within the family. The idiot boy, Isaac, was neglected and mistreated; when he fell in love with a cow, his behavior become a town scandal. Mink Snopes, another relative, was charged with murdering Jack Houston, who had impounded Mink's wandering cattle. Flem stayed away from town throughout this trouble. When Mink was brought to trial, Flem, who might have helped him, ignored the whole case. Mink was sent to jail for life.

Flem came back from his honeymoon accompanied by Buck Hipps, a Texan, and a string of wild, spotted horses. The Texan arranged to auction these horses to farmers who had gathered from miles around. To start things off, the Texan gave one horse to Eck Snopes, provided that Eck would make the first bid on the next one. At this point, Henry Armstid and his wife drove up. Henry, in spite of his wife's protests, bought a horse for five dollars. By dark, all but three of the horses had been sold, and Henry was anxious to claim his purchase. He and his wife were almost killed in trying to rope their pony. Hipps wanted to return the Armstids' money. He gave the five dollars to Henry's wife, but Henry took the bill from her and gave it to Flem Snopes. Hipps told Mrs. Armstid that Flem would return it to her the next day.

When the other purchasers tried to rope their horses, the spotted devils ran through an open gate and escaped into the countryside. Henry Armstid broke his leg and almost died. Eck Snopes chased the horse that had been given him and ran it into a boardinghouse. The horse escaped from the house and ran down the road. At a bridge, it piled into a wagon driven by Vernon Tull and occupied by Tull's wife and family. The mules pulling the wagon became excited, and Tull was jerked out of the wagon onto his face.

The Tulls sued Eck Snopes for the damages done to Vernon and to their wagon; the Armstids sued Flem for damages to Henry and for the recovery of their five dollars. The justice of the peace was forced to rule in favor of the defendants. Flem could not be established as the owner of the horses, and Eck was not the legal owner of a horse that had been given to him.

One day, Henry Armstid told Ratliff that Flem was digging every night in the garden of the Old Frenchman place, which Flem had acquired from Will Varner. Since the Civil War, there had been rumors that the builder of the house had buried money and jewels in the garden. Henry and Ratliff took a man named Bookwright into their confidence and, with the aid of another man who could use a divining rod, they slipped into the garden after Flem had quit digging. After locating the position of buried metal, they began digging, and each unearthed a bag of silver coins. They decided to pool their resources and buy the land in a hurry. Ratliff agreed to pay Flem an exorbitant price. At night they kept on shoveling, but they unearthed no more treasure. Ratliff finally realized that no bag could remain intact in the ground for thirty years. When he and Bookwright examined the silver coins, they found that the money had been minted after the Civil War.

Armstid, now totally out of his mind, refused to believe there was no treasure. He kept on digging, day and night. People from all over the county came to watch his frantic shoveling. Passing by on his way to Jefferson, Flem Snopes paused only a moment to watch Henry; then with a flip of the reins, he drove his horses on.

Critical Evaluation:

The Hamlet, along with the subsequent volumes *The Town* and *The Mansion*, is William Faulkner's exploration of the life—social, cultural, economic, and moral—of Frenchman's Bend, a small portion of his fictional landscape of Yoknapatawpha County, Mississippi.

Frenchman's Bend is a microcosm within a microcosm, a tiny but representative cross-section of human life and the human condition. To achieve this broadness of scope and vision, Faulkner constructs the work loosely, making it more a collection of interwoven stories than a tightly knit novel.

Faulkner employs three techniques to establish coherence within *The Hamlet*: relations among characters, repeated patterns, and common themes. In *The Hamlet*, Faulkner makes good use of characters who resurface from story to story or, in many cases, who relate the stories in the book. Much of the action in *The Hamlet* is presented after the fact, often recounted by V. K. Ratliff, the sewing machine salesman who is a central character in the book. In this sense, *The Hamlet* is a "spoken" rather than "written" novel. It owes much of its character to the American tall tale tradition. The second technique employed by Faulkner to establish unity is repetition and variation in the stories within *The Hamlet*. Often the same underlying theme or basic event will be repeated, with different characters adopting differing attitudes and getting different results. For example, the unseemly and inappropriate lust felt by the schoolteacher Labove for Eula Varner is repeated, in ironic and grotesque variation, as the true but equally inappropriate love Ike Snopes has for a cow. This pattern of theme and variation is found throughout the novel. Flem Snopes, undertaking his usurpation of Will Varner's dominant economic and political role in Frenchman's Bend, adopts Varner's dress style (becoming the only other man in town, besides Varner, to own and wear a tie), imitates his mannerisms (Snopes begins speaking to the men on the gallery in front of the store in the same self-assured, oblivious fashion), and finally even moves into Varner's house (The Old Frenchman's Place). Thus, ironically, the repetition of Will Varner is accomplished not through his son Jody, but by his successor, Flem Snopes. In a similar fashion, practically every member of the Snopes clan apes Flem's attitudes and actions, trying to emulate his rise in the world. Their less spectacular results are caused by lack of innate ability, not from failure to imitate their more financially successful relative. The parents of little Wallstreet Panic Snopes are clear in their intentions, even if their choice of name is slightly off. The final way in which Faulkner weaves together the strands of stories in the book is by reducing his thematic concerns to simple opposition: economic enterprise contrasted with emotional life, or, in most cases, trading versus sex. While the stories are never so simply presented, the underlying foundation of *The Hamlet* is the contrast and conflict between the rational, social sphere of economics and the irrational, private realm of sex.

Flem Snopes is the economic man incarnate, obsessed with material and financial gain. He is often described in discussions of Faulkner's work as a scheming and unscrupulous villain, but this description is inaccurate. Flem Snopes is the most consistently and precisely honest character in the trilogy, if honesty is narrowly defined as abiding by the letter, rather than the spirit, of an agreement. Unlike the Varners, Flem does not cheat customers in small ways, such as by shortchanging them. He never allows himself to be "cheated" by acts of kindness or generosity. His schemes and machinations are carried out for purely rational ends and through legally correct, if ethically questionable, means. No emotional considerations intrude into Flem Snopes' calculations.

By contrast, Eula Varner is portrayed as the embodiment of pure female sexuality, capable, even before puberty, of arousing men to an irrational and uncontrollable degree of lust. Flem is described in precise and unemotional fashion, but the narrative, in Eula's presence, becomes lush and unbridled, its imagery more animalistic, even bestial. Eula's suitors are compared first to stampeding herds of cattle, later, to dogs aroused by a bitch in heat. Her primal sexuality is humorous in its power and in the intensity of feeling it evokes in the opposite sex. It is an ironic touch that in *The Hamlet*, Eula is indifferent, almost unaware of her power, unwilling or perhaps incapable of the self-consciousness necessary to understand what she does to males. That Flem Snopes, of all men, should become Eula's husband is perhaps the novel's most ironic touch. One reason that Flem is so detached from human feelings is that he seems to have almost none of his own. He is not, unlike every other man, physically attracted to Eula. He has no desire for her body and may, the novel broadly hints, not even have sexual relations with her. The child she is carrying when they marry is not Flem's. The marriage is a matter of material gain and advantage for Flem. The symbol of a union of the rational and the emotional, the marriage is unsatisfactory since Flem denies the importance of Eula and therefore the emotional and sexual facets of human life.

Consistent with the novel's pattern, this theme is repeated in other stories, most notably the relationship between Zack Houston and Lucy Pate, where there is true passion on both sides and where this passion is transmuted, after years of suffering and tempering, into a real relationship. The marriage ends tragically, however, with Lucy's accidental death, and it may be Faulkner's suggestion that such a combination, while desirable, is unstable.

In *The Hamlet*, the rational is in the ascendant, and trading comes to dominate sex. The book is filled with stories and accounts of bargains, deals, barters, and exchanges that take on an almost ritualistic quality. What specific goods or money change hands is less important than which party in the trade "got the better" of the other. Flem Snopes thrives in such a situation, though he can hardly be blamed for having caused it; such conditions existed in Frenchman's Bend before Flem's arrival, and the Varners profited from them prior to the Snopes. The Varners' weakness, and the weakness of all Flem Snopes' victims, is that they mix the emotional and the rational, while he does not. In this sense, the story of Flem Snopes' rise, which is the central motif of *The Hamlet*, is the novel's largest example of repetition and variation of themes.

"Critical Evaluation" by Michael Witkoski

Bibliography:
Blotner, Joseph. *Faulkner: A Biography*. 2 vols. New York: Random House, 1974. More of a vast collection of facts than a finely shaped biography, this study of Faulkner's life and work contains perceptive observations on *The Hamlet* and its place in the Faulkner canon.

Greet, T. Y. "The Theme and Structure of Faulkner's *The Hamlet*." In *William Faulkner: Three Decades of Criticism*. Edited by Frederick J. Hoffman and Olga W. Vickery. East Lansing: Michigan State University Press, 1960. A relatively brief but still useful overview of how Faulkner combined meanings and form in the novel.

Kenner, Hugh. *A Homemade World: The American Modernist Writers*. New York: Alfred A. Knopf, 1974. The section on Faulkner places *The Hamlet* within the context of Faulkner's own development as a writer and the range of modern American fiction.

Vickery, Olga W. *The Novels of William Faulkner*. Baton Rouge: Louisiana State University Press, 1959. Its chapter on *The Hamlet* is a close reading of the intertwined themes of sex and economics as primal forces in human action and how they determine the actions of the characters in the novel.

Watson, James Gray. *The Snopes Dilemma: Faulkner's Trilogy*. Coral Gables, Fla.: University of Miami Press, 1970. Argues persuasively that the heart of the Snopes trilogy (*The Hamlet*, *The Town*, and *The Mansion*) is a conflict between moral verities and "amoral Snopesism."

HAMLET, PRINCE OF DENMARK

Type of work: Drama
Author: William Shakespeare (1564-1616)
Type of plot: Tragedy
Time of plot: c. 1200
Locale: Elsinore, Denmark
First performed: c. 1600-1601; first published, 1603

> *Principal characters:*
> HAMLET, the prince of Denmark
> THE GHOST, Hamlet's father, the former king of Denmark
> CLAUDIUS, the present king
> GERTRUDE, Hamlet's mother
> POLONIUS, a courtier
> OPHELIA, his daughter
> LAERTES, his son
> HORATIO, Hamlet's friend

The Story:

Three times the ghost of Denmark's dead king had stalked the battlements of Elsinore Castle. On the fourth night Horatio, Hamlet's friend, brought the young prince to see the specter of his father. Since his father's untimely death two months earlier, Hamlet had been grief-stricken and exceedingly melancholy. The mysterious circumstances surrounding the death of his father perplexed him, and his mother had married Claudius, the dead king's brother, much too hurriedly to suit Hamlet's sense of decency.

That night, Hamlet saw his father's ghost and listened in horror when it told him that his father had not died from the sting of a serpent, as had been reported, but that he had been murdered by his own brother, Claudius, the present king. The ghost added that Claudius was guilty not only of murder but also of incest and adultery. The spirit cautioned Hamlet to spare Queen Gertrude, his mother, and leave her punishment to heaven.

The ghost's disclosures should have left no doubt in Hamlet's mind that Claudius must be killed, but the introspective prince was not quite sure that the ghost was his father's spirit and he feared it might have been a devil sent to torment him. Debating with himself the problem of whether or not to carry out the spirit's commands, Hamlet swore his friends, including Horatio, to secrecy concerning the appearance of the ghost. He also told them not to consider him mad if from then on he were to act strangely.

Claudius was facing not only the possibility of war with Norway, but also, much worse, his own conscience, which had been much troubled since his hasty marriage to Gertrude. It worried him that the prince was so melancholy, for he knew that he resented the marriage and he feared that Hamlet might try to take his throne away from him. The prince's strange behavior and wild talk made the king think that perhaps Hamlet was mad, but he was not sure. To learn whether Hamlet's manner and actions were caused by madness or ambition, Claudius commissioned two of Hamlet's friends, Rosencrantz and Guildenstern, to spy on the prince. Hamlet saw through their clumsy efforts, however, and confused them with his answers to their questions.

Polonius, the garrulous old chamberlain, believed that Hamlet's behavior resulted from lovesickness for his daughter, Ophelia. Hamlet, meanwhile, became increasingly melancholy.

Rosencrantz and Guildenstern, as well as Polonius, were constantly spying on him. Even Ophelia, he thought, had turned against him. The thought of deliberate murder was revolting to him, and he was plagued by uncertainty as to whether the ghost represented good or evil. When a troupe of actors visited Elsinore, Hamlet saw in them a chance to discover whether Claudius was guilty. He planned to have the players enact before the king and the court a scene resembling the one that, according to the ghost, had taken place the day the old king died. By watching Claudius during the performance, Hamlet hoped to discover the truth for himself.

His plan worked. Claudius became so unnerved during the performance that he walked out before the end of the scene. Convinced by the king's actions that the ghost was right, Hamlet had no reason to delay in carrying out the wishes of his dead father. Even so, he failed to take advantage of the first chance to kill Claudius when, coming upon the king in an attitude of prayer, he could have stabbed him in the back. Hamlet refrained because he did not want the king to die in a state of grace.

When the queen summoned Hamlet to her chamber to reprimand him for his insolence to Claudius, Hamlet, remembering what the ghost had told him, spoke to her so violently that she screamed for help. A noise behind a curtain followed her cries, and Hamlet, suspecting that Claudius was eavesdropping, plunged his sword through the curtain, killing old Polonius. Fearing an attack on his own life, the king hastily ordered Hamlet to England in company with Rosencrantz and Guildenstern, who carried a warrant for Hamlet's death. The prince discovered the orders and altered them so that the bearers should be killed on their arrival in England. Hamlet then returned to Denmark.

Much had happened in that unhappy land during Hamlet's absence. Ophelia, rejected by Hamlet, her former lover, had gone mad and later drowned herself. Laertes, Polonius' hot-tempered son, had returned from France and collected a band of malcontents to avenge the death of his father. He thought that Claudius had killed Polonius, but the king told him that Hamlet was the murderer and persuaded Laertes to take part in a plot to murder the prince.

Claudius arranged for a duel between Hamlet and Laertes. To allay suspicion of foul play, the king placed bets on Hamlet, who was an expert swordsman. At the same time, he had poison placed on the tip of Laertes' weapon and put a cup of poison within Hamlet's reach in the event that the prince became thirsty during the duel. Gertrude, who knew nothing of the king's treachery, drank from the poisoned cup and died. During the contest, Hamlet was mortally wounded with the poisoned rapier, but the two contestants exchanged foils in a scuffle, and Laertes himself received a fatal wound. Before he died, Laertes was filled with remorse and told Hamlet that Claudius was responsible for the poisoned sword. Hesitating no longer, Hamlet seized his opportunity to act, and fatally stabbed the king before himself dying.

Critical Evaluation:

Hamlet, Prince of Denmark has remained the most perplexing, as well as the most popular, of Shakespeare's tragedies. Whether considered as literature, philosophy, or drama, its artistic stature is universally admitted. To explain the reasons for its excellence in a few words, however, is a daunting task. Apart from the matchless artistry of its language, the play's appeal rests in large measure on the character of Hamlet himself. Called upon to avenge his father's murder, he is compelled to face problems of duty, morality, and ethics, which have been human concerns through the ages. Yet the play has tantalized critics with what has become known as the Hamlet mystery, that of Hamlet's complex behavior, most notably his indecision and his reluctance to act.

Freudian critics have located his motivation in the psychodynamic triad of the father-mother-son relationship. According to this view, Hamlet is disturbed and eventually deranged by his Oedipal jealousy of the uncle who has done what, we are to believe, all sons long to do themselves. Other critics have taken the more conventional tack of identifying as Hamlet's tragic flaw the lack of courage or moral resolution. In this view, Hamlet's indecision is a sign of moral ambivalence that he overcomes too late.

Both of these views presuppose a precise discovery of Hamlet's motivation. However, Renaissance drama is not generally a drama of motivation either by psychological set or moral predetermination. Rather, the tendency is to present characters with well-delineated moral and ethical dispositions who are faced with dilemmas. It is the outcome of these conflicts, the consequences, that normally hold center stage. What Shakespeare presents in *Hamlet, Prince of Denmark* is an agonizing confrontation between the will of a good and intelligent man and the uncongenial role—that of avenger—that fate calls upon him to play.

The role of avenger is a familiar one in Renaissance drama. In the opening description of Hamlet as bereft by the death of his father and distressed by his mother's hasty marriage, Shakespeare creates the ideal candidate to assume such a role. Hamlet's despondency need not be Oedipal to explain the extremity of his grief. His father, whom he deeply loved and admired, is recently deceased and he himself seems to have been robbed of his birthright. Shakespeare points to Hamlet's shock at Gertrude's disrespect to the memory of his father rather than his love for his mother as the source of his distress. Hamlet's suspicion is reinforced by the ghostly visitation and the revelation of murder.

If Hamlet had simply proceeded to act out the avenger role assigned to him, the play would have lacked the moral and theological complexity that provides its special fascination. Hamlet has, after all, been a student of theology at Wittenberg, and his knowledge complicates the situation. His accusation of incest is not an adolescent excess but an accurate theological description of a marriage between a widow and her dead husband's brother. Moreover, Hamlet's theological accomplishments do more than exacerbate his feelings. For the ordinary avenger, the commission from the ghost of a murdered father would be more than enough, but Hamlet is aware of the unreliability of otherworldly apparitions and consequently reluctant to heed its injunction to perform an action that is objectively evil. In addition, the fear that his father was murdered in a state of sin and is condemned to hell not only increases Hamlet's sense of injustice but also, paradoxically, casts further doubt on the reliability of the ghost's exhortation, for perhaps the ghost is merely an infernal spirit goading him to sin.

Hamlet's indecision is therefore not an indication of weakness but the result of his complex understanding of the moral dilemma with which he is faced. He is unwilling to act unjustly, yet he is afraid that he is failing to exact a deserved retribution. He debates the murky issue and himself becomes unsure whether his behavior is caused by moral scruple or cowardice. His ruminations are in sharp contrast with the cynicism of Claudius and the verbose moral platitudes of Polonius, just as the play is in sharp contrast with the moral simplicity of the ordinary revenge tragedy. Through Hamlet's intelligence, Shakespeare transformed a stock situation into a unique internal conflict.

Hamlet believes that he must have greater certitude of Claudius' guilt if he is to take action. The device of the play within a play provides greater assurance that Claudius is suffering from a guilty conscience, but it simultaneously sharpens Hamlet's anguish. Seeing a re-creation of his father's death and Claudius' response stiffens Hamlet's resolve to act, but once again he hesitates when he sees Claudius in prayer. Here Hamlet's inaction is not the result of cowardice or even perception of moral ambiguity but rather of the very thoroughness of his commitment, for, having once decided on revenge, he wants to destroy his uncle body and soul. It is ironic that Hamlet is thwarted this time by the combination of theological insight with the extreme ferocity of his vengeful intention.

That Hamlet loses his mental stability is clear in his behavior toward Ophelia and in his subsequent meanderings. Circumstance has enforced a role whose enormity has overwhelmed the fine emotional and intellectual balance of a sensitive, well-educated young man. Gradually, he is shown regaining control of himself and arming himself with a cold determination to do what he has decided is the just thing. Yet, even then, it is only in the carnage of the concluding scenes that Hamlet finally carries out his intention. Having concluded that "the readiness is all," he strikes his uncle only after he has discovered Claudius' final scheme to kill him and Laertes.

The arrival of Fortinbras, who has been lurking in the background throughout the play, superficially seems to indicate that a new, more direct and courageous order will prevail in the place of the evil of Claudius and the weakness of Hamlet. Yet Fortinbras' superiority is only superficial. He brings stasis and stability back to a disordered kingdom but does not have the self-consciousness and moral sensitivity that destroy and redeem Hamlet.

Gerald Else has interpreted Aristotle's notion of *katharsis* to be not a purging of the emotions but a purging of the moral horror, pity, and fear ordinarily associated with them. If that is so, then Hamlet, by the conflict of his ethical will with his role, has purged the avenger of his bloodthirstiness and turned the stock figure into a self-conscious hero in moral conflict.

"Critical Evaluation" by Edward E. Foster

Bibliography:

Bowers, Fredson Thayer. *Elizabethan Revenge Tragedy, 1587-1642.* Reprint. Princeton, N.J.: Princeton University Press, 1966. A full discussion of revenge tragedy and its connections to the central action of *Hamlet.* Bowers' historical account of the conventions of revenge tragedy provides an illuminating context for the play.

Grene, Nicholas. *Shakespeare's Tragic Imagination.* New York: St. Martin's Press, 1992. The chapter on *Hamlet* attempts to revise and question some of the Christian interpretations of the play. Also of value is Grene's connecting *Hamlet* to the play that preceded it in Shakespeare's oeuvre, *Julius Caesar* (c. 1599-1600).

Prosser, Eleanor. *"Hamlet" and Revenge.* Stanford, Calif.: Stanford University Press, 1967. Prosser uses an historical approach to try to answer such central questions as the Elizabethans' attitude toward revenge, the nature of the father's ghost, and regicide.

Shakespeare, William. *Hamlet.* Edited by Harold Jenkins. London: Methuen, 1982. Considered by many to be the best edition of the play, its notes are clear and thorough, and Jenkins includes a number of longer notes that discuss such controversies as those surrounding Hamlet's "To be, or not to be" speech. Also includes an excellent discussion of the sources for the play and earlier criticism on it.

Watts, Cedric. *Hamlet.* Boston: Twayne, 1988. Includes a stage history and a critical history that provide some of the contexts for *Hamlet.* The discussion is intended to preserve the play's mystery rather than offering another solution to the so-called Hamlet problem.

Wilson, John Dover. *What Happens in Hamlet.* 3d ed. Cambridge, England: Cambridge University Press, 1951. Wilson attempts to resolve all of the unsolved questions in the play by a close analysis of the text. Suggests plausible answers for some of the problems but fails to resolve the most important ones.

A HANDFUL OF DUST

Type of work: Novel
Author: Evelyn Waugh (1903-1966)
Type of plot: Social satire
Time of plot: Twentieth century
Locale: England
First published: 1934

> *Principal characters:*
> TONY LAST, the owner of Hetton Abbey
> BRENDA LAST, his wife
> JOHN, their son
> MRS. BEAVER, an interior decorator
> JOHN BEAVER, her son
> JOCK GRANT-MENZIES, Tony's friend
> DR. MESSINGER, an explorer
> TODD, a half-caste trader who loved Dickens

The Story:

John Beaver lived in London with his mother, an interior decorator. Beaver was a worthless young man of twenty-five years who moved in the social circles of his mother's wealthy customers. He was not well liked, but he was often invited to parties and weekends to fill a space made vacant at the last moment.

One weekend, Beaver was invited to Hetton Abbey by its young owner, Tony Last. Tony lived in the old Gothic abbey with his wife, Brenda, and his young son, John. It was Tony's dream that someday he would restore his mansion to its former feudal glory. Brenda, however, was bored with her husband's attachment to the past; she found relief in her weekly trips to London. Beaver's stay at Hetton Abbey was rather dull, but Brenda liked him and did her best to entertain him. On her next trip to London, she saw him again and asked him to take her to a party. At first, Beaver seemed reluctant; then he agreed to escort her.

Beaver and Brenda left the party early, creating some idle gossip. In a way, the gossipers were correct, for Brenda had definitely decided to have an affair with Beaver. She returned home to the unsuspecting Tony and told him that she was bored with life in the country. She said that she wanted to take some courses in economics at the university in London. Tony, feeling sorry for her, allowed her to rent a one-room flat in a building owned by Mrs. Beaver. Brenda moved to London and returned to Hetton Abbey only on weekends.

One day, when Tony went to London on impulse, he found that his wife already had engagements. He was forced to spend the evening getting drunk with his bachelor friend, Jock Grant-Menzies. Tony's escapade bothered his conscience so much that when Brenda returned for the weekend she was able to persuade him to let Mrs. Beaver redecorate in modern style one of the rooms of the old house.

Brenda's conscience also bothered her. She tried to interest Tony in a girl she brought down for a weekend, but it was no use. He only wanted to have his wife back home. He still, however, trusted her and suspected nothing of her affair in London.

Things might have remained the same indefinitely if young John Last had not been killed by a horse while he was fox hunting. Tony sent Jock up to London to break the news to Brenda.

At first, Brenda thought that Jock was speaking of John Beaver's death, for he was out of town. When she learned the truth, she was relieved, realizing for the first time how much she cared for Beaver.

With young John dead, she felt that nothing held her to Tony any longer. She wrote, telling him everything, and asked for a divorce. Stunned, Tony could not believe that Brenda had been unfaithful to him. At last, he consented to spend a weekend at Brighton with another woman to give her grounds for divorce.

Brenda's family was against the divorce and attempted to prevent it. Then, when they saw that the divorce was inevitable, they tried to force Tony to give Brenda more alimony than he had planned. He refused, for he could raise more money only by selling Hetton Abbey. The proposal angered him so much that he changed his mind about the divorce. He would not set Brenda free.

Wishing to get away from familiar faces, Tony accompanied an explorer, Dr. Messinger, on an expedition to find a lost city in the South American jungles. During the voyage across the Atlantic Ocean, Tony had a short affair with a young French girl from Trinidad, but when she learned that he was married, she would have nothing more to do with him.

Once the explorers had left civilization behind them, Tony found himself thinking of what was going on in London. He did not enjoy jungle life at all; insect bites, vermin, and vampire bats made sleep almost impossible. When black boatmen had taken Tony and Dr. Messinger far up the Demarara River, they left the explorers in the hands of Indian guides. Then the expedition struck out into unmapped territory.

In London, Brenda no longer found Beaver to be an ardent lover. He had counted strongly on getting a considerable amount of money when he married Brenda; now Brenda could get neither the money nor a divorce. Brenda began to grow desperate for money. She asked Mrs. Beaver for a job, but Mrs. Beaver thought that it would not look well for her to employ Brenda. A short time later, Beaver decided to accompany his mother on a trip to California.

Tony and Dr. Messinger at last came to a river they believed must flow into the Amazon, and they ordered the Indians to build canoes. The Indians obeyed, but they refused to venture down the river. There was nothing for the white men to do but to continue the journey without guides. Soon after they set out, Tony came down with a fever. Dr. Messinger left him on shore and went on alone to find help, but the explorer drowned when his boat capsized. Delirious, Tony struggled through the jungle and came by chance to the hut of a trader named Todd, who nursed him back to health but kept him a prisoner and forced him to read the novels of Dickens aloud to him. When some Englishmen came in search of Tony, the trader made them believe that his captive had died of fever. Tony faced the prospect of lifelong captivity spent reading Dickens' novels to the illiterate half-caste over and over.

When Beaver left for California, Brenda knew their affair was over. No news came from Tony in South America. Without his permission, Brenda could not draw upon the family funds. Then Tony was officially declared dead, and Hetton Abbey became the property of another branch of the Last family. The new owner of Hetton Abbey bred silver fox. Although he had even fewer servants than his predecessor and had shut off most of the house, he dreamed that Hetton Abbey would some day be as glorious as it was in the days of Cousin Tony. He erected a memorial to Tony at Hetton Abbey, but Brenda was unable to attend its dedication. She was engaged elsewhere with her new husband, Jock Grant-Menzies.

Critical Evaluation:
In his fourth novel, *A Handful of Dust*, Evelyn Waugh introduced a new style. He showed

that, in addition to the satiric romp, he could write a "straight" novel that was realistic rather than stylized. Despite the differences between *A Handful of Dust* and its three predecessors, the story goes back to Waugh's recurrent theme of the victim as hero. This theme of the civilized man's helpless plight among savages had previously been developed through a tone of wry indifference. However, while *A Handful of Dust* is on the surface a comedy of manners, it is a very dark comedy in which, for the first time, Waugh forces his reader to identify with the victim as hero.

The protagonists of Waugh's earlier novels are cardboard figures, whose passivity is thoroughly appropriate to the world of the novels—a world in which there is a crazy inconsequence to everything, even including infidelity, financial ruin, and violent death. Tony Last of *A Handful of Dust* has much in common with the earlier protagonists, and the things that happen to him will not be unfamiliar to the reader of Waugh's first three novels. Yet whereas these earlier protagonists are farcical figures, Tony is a tragic one.

The novel's motifs are familiar as well, the first that is readily apparent being the great house. In the earlier novels the once proud houses are being either thoughtlessly debased or consciously demolished. Tony Last loves his ancestral home, Hetton, which was once one of the notable houses of the county. It was entirely rebuilt in 1864 in the Gothic style, and the county Guide Book now declares it "devoid of interest." Yet Tony delights in every aspect of Hetton. Each bedroom features a brass bedstead and a frieze of Gothic text. Each is named from Sir Thomas Malory's *Le Morte d'Arthur* (1485). Tony has slept in Morgan le Fay since leaving the night nursery, and his wife Brenda sleeps in Guinevere (a fitting bedchamber for the adulteress she is to become).

In each of the early novels, the protagonist loses the woman he really wants (indeed, it can be asserted that this occurs in almost all of Waugh's novels). Tony's cuckolding by the despicable John Beaver, however, is comparable only in the most superficial way to earlier romantic misadventures. His loss of Brenda is not amusing but poignant, because he is neither merely witness to an unusual series of events nor merely the narrator's point of reference; he is a man. Tony engages the reader in a way that his predecessors never do.

Precisely because Tony (the metaphorical "last" remnant of Merrie England) engages the reader's sympathy, the motif of lost religious faith that adheres to him throughout the novel symbolizes no less than the doom of Western civilization. Waugh's early novels certainly suggest something is amiss in the contemporary practice of Christianity. Tony Last's predicament is another matter entirely; he is the first literally lost soul in Waugh's fiction.

Tony loves churchgoing. Every Sunday he sits in the family pew, and he reads the lessons on Christmas Day and Harvest Thanksgiving. Yet his religious practice, though not a sham, is merely part of the venerable Hetton tradition, a refuge within a refuge from the modern world. He is humane, not Christian. The liturgy is simply one part of the ambiance of gentle living to which Tony alone, of all the characters in the novel, instinctively responds. As he performs the familiar motions of the ritual, his thoughts drift from subject to subject, returning usually to the question of how more bathrooms and lavatories could be introduced at Hetton without disturbing the character of the house.

The Reverend Tendril adds his own eccentric touch of fantasy to the services. He had composed his sermons during his many years in India. They were addressed to the congregation at the garrison chapel, and he has made no attempt to accommodate them to his altered circumstances. They are therefore studded with references to the Gracious Queen Empress "in whose services we are here" and to "homes and dear ones far away." This in no way troubles his parishioners, who seldom associate things said in church with their own lives.

The vicar attempts to act as spiritual counselor on the day Tony's son, John Andrew, is kicked to death by a horse. Tony remarks that the vicar tried to be comforting, but "the last thing one wants to talk about at a time like this is religion." Still later, when the mad Mr. Todd contemplates putting up a cross to commemorate the death of a former captive and the arrival of a new one, he asks if Tony believes in God. Tony replies that he supposes so; he has never really thought about it much. Tony is secular man at his best: kindly, loving, selfless. Yet none of these qualities can save him (in fact, they make the task of the predator much easier), and he has no faith with which to save himself.

The reader's identification with Tony Last provides a basis for understanding Waugh's intent. Earlier, Waugh had led the reader merrily through a chaotic world in which sudden violent death is just another absurdity. Prior to *A Handful of Dust*, he had been accused of writing satire without a moral center. Because Tony is a real man in the real world, however, he may not walk away from the disasters of his life as do his predecessors. He must be called to account. In fact, Tony's weaknesses incur the most awful punishment Waugh ever meted out to any of his characters.

The action in *A Handful of Dust* is much less broad and much more realistic than in any of the three preceding novels. In truth, it could be argued that the novel is really naturalistic, for Tony and his way of life are doomed. From the outset, Waugh shows him being drawn inexorably toward disaster.

"Critical Evaluation" by Patrick Adcock

Bibliography:
Greenblatt, Stephen J. *Three Modern Satirists: Waugh, Orwell, and Huxley.* New Haven, Conn.: Yale University Press, 1965. Includes an extended discussion of *A Handful of Dust* in the Waugh section of the book. Greenblatt declares the novel to be "the culmination of [Waugh's] art."

Nardin, Jane. "The Myth of Decline in *A Handful of Dust.*" *Midwest Quarterly* 18 (1977): 119-130. Offers an interpretation that runs counter to most other criticism, in which the author sympathizes with the adulterous wife and casts most of the blame on the victim-hero. One of the few examples of feminist criticism applied to Waugh's fiction.

Phillips, Gene D. *Evelyn Waugh's Officers, Gentlemen, and Rogues: The Fact Behind His Fiction.* Chicago: Nelson-Hall, 1975. Documents some of the sources for much of Waugh's fictional worlds. Chapter 3, "Change and Decay: Further Satires," discusses *A Handful of Dust, Scoop* (1938), and *Put Out More Flags* (1942). Reveals that the faithless wife and tawdry divorce proceedings of the novel mirror details of Waugh's own painful first marriage.

Sykes, Christopher. *Evelyn Waugh: A Biography.* Boston: Little, Brown, 1975. This critical study by a personal friend and the official biographer of Waugh includes a discussion of *A Handful of Dust.*

Wasson, Richard. "*A Handful of Dust:* Critique of Victorianism." *Modern Fiction Studies* 7 (1961-1962): 327-337. Emphasizes Waugh's use of Victorian art and artifacts in the novel and discusses his critical stand toward many aspects of the era.

THE HANDMAID'S TALE

Type of work: Novel
Author: Margaret Atwood (1939-   )
Type of plot: Psychological realism
Time of plot: The future
Locale: The fictional Gilead
First published: 1985

Principal characters:
OFFRED, a Handmaid or legal concubine
THE COMMANDER, Offred's master
SERENA JOY, the Commander's wife
NICK, Offred's lover, the Commander's chauffeur
LUKE, Offred's husband (present in flashbacks)
MOIRA, Offred's best friend
OFGLEN, another Handmaid

The Story:

Sometime in the past, Protestant fundamentalists assassinated the president and the Congress and set up a theocratic regime called the Republic of Gilead. In this totalitarian state, women were under the domination of men. They could not hold jobs, own property, or have bank accounts in their own names. Nor were they allowed to read or write. Forced into the role of Handmaid, Offred was stripped of her own name and called by her master's name, preceded by "of."

Pollution and nuclear accidents made sterility a problem in Gilead (though officially only women could be sterile). Fertile women who were political dissidents or who were in marriages viewed as outside the law of the church, such as second marriages after divorce, were conscripted to serve as concubines to the political leaders of Gilead, whose wives were often sterile or past the age of childbearing.

Offred was obliged to endure an act of copulation with the Commander once a month in the hope that she would bear him a child. During the act, she rested between the legs of the Commander's wife in a ritual believed to be sanctioned by biblical precedent. In the Old Testament, Rachel commanded Jacob to sleep with her maid Billah: "Go in unto her, and she shall bear upon my knees, that I may have children by her." Offred hoped to conceive since that was her only safeguard against being sent to the "colonies," where women viewed as expendable were sent to clean up battlefields or nuclear waste sites.

Besides her monthly sexual obligations to the Commander, Offred's only duty was to walk out once a day to do the shopping for the household. She had to wear a prescribed costume consisting of a bright red ankle-length dress that concealed her body and a white headdress with wide wings that constricted her vision. In her shopping excursions, Offred had a partner, another Handmaid named Ofglen. After making their purchases, Ofglen and Offred almost always walked to the "the wall." On the wall, the hooded bodies of recently executed traitors to the regime were displayed. On these occasions, Offred looked for the body of her husband, Luke. Although Offred hoped that Luke was still alive, the most likely possibility was that he had been killed when the family made an escape attempt to Canada. It was during this attempt that Offred was captured, along with her daughter, who was taken away from her and given to a family with high connections in Gilead.

In her daily life, Offred had little to do, but she had ample time for reminiscence and reflection on her past and present life. She thought about her upbringing by her mother, a single parent by choice and a feminist of the 1970's, and her friendship with Moira, a strong individual who had the courage to defy authority. She thought about her life with Luke and her daughter and wished she could bring back the freedom she took for granted.

Although the Commander was not supposed to have any personal relationship with his Handmaid, he sent a message to her to arrange a clandestine meeting in his study. In a series of subsequent visits, Offred and the Commander played Scrabble and talked, and the Commander allowed her to read books and magazines officially forbidden in Gilead. The Commander wanted Offred to like him since he felt misunderstood by his wife, and on several occasions he asked her to kiss him.

The Commander's wife, Serena Joy, disliked Offred because she felt that Offred was encroaching on her role. In spite of her jealousy, however, Serena Joy wanted Offred to have a child, which she could then raise. Because she feared that her husband might be sterile, Serena Joy arranged secret meetings between Offred and Nick, an employee of the household. Offred cooperated in this scheme, in spite of the danger involved in unsanctioned sexual acts, because she needed to bear a child to save her own life. As time passed, however, Offred became deeply attracted to Nick and their meetings became the central focus of her life.

On their walks, Offred and Ofglen revealed to each other their hatred of the regime. Ofglen was a member of an underground organization working to overthrow the regime. Offred and Ofglen were required to take part in a public ritual called a "Salvaging," in which several women were hanged as traitors. On the same occasion they were expected to participate in a "Particicution," in which an alleged rapist was torn limb from limb by Handmaids. Ofglen recognized the man as a member of the underground and struck him on the head with her shoe to render him unconscious and spare him further pain. Knowing that she had been observed and was about to be arrested, Ofglen killed herself so that she would not confess and name others under torture.

Because of her association with Ofglen, Offred expected to be arrested. However, Nick, acting on behalf of the underground resistance, arranged for a mock arrest, which he told her would ensure her safety. Unsure of the truth of the matter, she felt she had no choice but to trust Nick. In an epilogue set almost two hundred years further in the future, it was revealed that tapes were discovered containing the narrative just read. Offred must certainly have made it to freedom, but it was unclear whether she lived her subsequent life in freedom or was recaptured.

Critical Evaluation:

Margaret Atwood suggests that the freedoms women enjoy in the late twentieth century may not be as secure as modern women would like to think. In interviews given around the time of the publication of the novel, Atwood pointed out that all the oppressive social practices she describes in the novel have historical precedents. Clearly she is suggesting that people must be on their guard to make sure that we do not allow these retrograde practices to gain a foothold again.

In *The Handmaid's Tale* an ultraconservative religious movement has obliterated women's rights, but Atwood is troubled by threats to freedom from any group, even feminists. Offred's mother fought for a society in which women would be safe from male violence, but had no qualms about taking part in book burnings of pornographic books and magazines. Although no supporter of pornography, Atwood finds troubling any attempt to enforce a rigid ideology of any kind. Atwood also notes that the citizens of the pre-Gilead state—a society much like that of the United States at the time of the novel's publication, in which Offred was a "liberated" woman with an equal relationship with her husband, her own interests, and financial independence—were passive in the face of threats to freedom, not fully comprehending what was happening until it was too late.

Although the rulers of Gilead have established a theocracy and claim to have based their laws on biblical decrees, it is clear that they are motivated more by the desire for power than by religious fervor. They claim to have made society better—indeed Offred's Commander seeks assurance to this effect from Offred—but they routinely flout the rules they establish for others. Taking Offred with him, Offred's Commander visits a nightclub maintained for the governmental elite in which women who have rebelled against their prescribed roles are forced to serve as prostitutes.

The Commanders rule over a rigidly hierarchical society. Men can be "Angels," or soldiers, who fight the regime's enemies—Baptists, Quakers, Catholics, and so forth—or they can be assigned to groups that provide other necessary functions. However, they have no personal freedom, and Gilead is, in effect, a police state with an elaborate spy system and complete censorship of information. The novel presents a terrifying picture of a repressive society in which attempts to learn and speak freely or to love as one chooses are punishable by death.

Women are particularly victimized by the regime. According to the ideology of Gilead, women exist only to fulfill gender-related functions. First and foremost, their function is to bear children. They also serve men as wives and household servants, or "Marthas." The lives of Handmaids, especially, are so regimented and so lacking in human contact that elaborate measures must be taken to prevent suicide attempts.

However, Atwood is careful not to portray women simply as victims. First of all, many women in Gilead support the regime and help to keep other women in line. Wives control Handmaids, and female government officials, called "Aunts," enforce discipline on other women. Atwood may be reminding her readers that women have traditionally served to enforce the rules of a patriarchal society, from bearing responsibility for the socialization of young girls to the policing of adult nonconformists through ridicule or ostracism. In a way, *The Handmaid's Tale* is about the present as well as the future, suggesting that until there are significant changes in women's and men's understandings and social practices, society will continue to be in danger of this kind of repression.

While Offred has admirable traits, including a deep love for her daughter and a powerful will to survive, she can also be seen to exhibit some weaknesses. She herself often points out that she wishes she appeared in a better light in her story. Unlike her friend Moira and her shopping partner Ofglen, she makes no efforts to overthrow the regime. After she begins her affair with Nick, her existence is totally ruled by her romantic feelings. Even the romantic notion that sexual love can justify one's existence is called into question in the novel. Offred is living in a dream or a fantasy, lulled into a passive state, not just by her biological drives but also by a romantic ideology that women are taught by society.

Atwood's compelling and horrifying picture of a possible future, her suspense-filled narrative, and her penetrating analysis of the psychology of women have made *The Handmaid's Tale* one of Atwood's most admired works. The recognition the novel received solidified her position as one of North America's foremost novelists.

Charlotte Templin

Bibliography:
Greene, Gayle. *Changing the Story: Feminist Fiction and the Tradition.* Bloomington: Indiana University Press, 1991. The author discusses Atwood and other contemporary women writers who employ narrative strategies that incorporate women's perspectives and challenge traditional modes of storytelling. She sees *The Handmaid's Tale* as less feminist in vision than Atwood's previous novels.
Hammar, Stephanie Barbe. "The World As It Will Be? Female Satire and the Technology of Power in *The Handmaid's Tale.*" *Modern Language Studies* 22, no. 2 (Spring, 1990): 39-49. The article discusses *The Handmaid's Tale* as a work with satiric intent. Atwood warns of the abuses of technology, the domination of women by men, and the propensity to allow oneself to be trapped in a rigid role.
McCombs, Judith, ed. *Critical Essays on Margaret Atwood.* Boston: G. K. Hall, 1988. This valuable volume contains thirty-two reviews, articles, and essays on Atwood's prose and poetry. The essays are arranged in chronological order. The volume contains a primary bibliography to 1986.
Mendez-Engle, Beatrice, ed. *Margaret Atwood: Reflections and Reality.* Edinburg, Tex.: Pan American University Press, 1987. This selection of critical essays on Atwood's work includes an interview with Atwood. The essays trace Atwood's development as a writer and include a discussion of her use of fables.
Van Spanckeren, Kathryn, and Jan Garden Castro, eds. *Margaret Atwood: Vision and Forms.* Carbondale: Southern Illinois University Press, 1988. This useful collection contains essays on Atwood's works that are of uniformly high quality. Several essays deal with *The Handmaid's Tale.*

HARD TIMES

Type of work: Novel
Author: Charles Dickens (1812-1870)
Type of plot: Social realism
Time of plot: Mid-nineteenth century
Locale: England
First published: 1854

Principal characters:

THOMAS GRADGRIND, a schoolmaster and a believer in "facts"
LOUISA GRADGRIND, his oldest daughter
TOM GRADGRIND, Louisa's brother
MR. JOSIAH BOUNDERBY, Louisa's husband and a manufacturer and banker
SISSY JUPE, a waif befriended by the Gradgrinds
MRS. SPARSIT, Bounderby's housekeeper
JAMES HARTHOUSE, a political aspirant
STEPHEN BLACKPOOL, Bounderby's employee
MRS. PEGLER, an old woman

The Story:

Thomas Gradgrind, proprietor of an experimental private school in Coketown, insisted that the children under him learn only facts. He believed that the world had no place for fancy or imagination. His own five children were models of a factual education. Never having been permitted to learn anything of the humanities, they were ignorant of literature and any conception of human beings as individuals. Even fairy tales and nursery rhymes had been excluded from their education.

One day, as he walked from the school to his home, Gradgrind was immensely displeased and hurt to find his two oldest children, Louisa and Tom, trying to peek through the canvas walls of a circus tent. Nor did it ease his mind to discover that the two youngsters were not at all sorry for acting against the principles under which they had been reared and educated. Later, Gradgrind and his industrialist friend, Mr. Josiah Bounderby, discussed possible means by which the children might have been misled from the study of facts. They concluded that another pupil, Sissy Jupe, whose father was a clown in the circus, had influenced the young Gradgrinds.

Having decided to remove Sissy Jupe from the school, Bounderby and Gradgrind set out immediately to tell the girl's father. When they arrived at the inn where the Jupes were staying, they found that the father had deserted his daughter. Moved by sentiment, Gradgrind decided to keep the girl in his home and let her be educated at his school, all against the advice of Bounderby, who thought Sissy Jupe would only be a bad influence on the Gradgrind children.

Years passed, and Louisa and young Tom matured. Gradgrind knew that Bounderby, who was thirty years his daughter's elder, had long wished to marry Louisa. Educated away from sentiment, she agreed to marry Bounderby. Tom, an employee in Bounderby's bank, was very glad to have his sister marry Bounderby; he wanted a friend to help him if he got into trouble there. In fact, he advised his sister to marry Bounderby for that reason, and she, loving her brother, agreed to help him by marrying the wealthy banker.

Bounderby was very happy to have Louisa as his wife. After his marriage, he placed his elderly housekeeper in a room at the bank. Mrs. Sparsit disliked Louisa and was determined to keep an eye on her for her employer's sake. After the marriage, all seemed peaceful at the bank, at the Gradgrind home, and at the Bounderby residence.

In the meantime, Gradgrind had been elected to Parliament from his district. He sent out from London an aspiring young politician, James Harthouse, who was to gather facts about the industrial city of Coketown, facts that were to be used in a survey of economic and social life in Britain. In order to facilitate the young man's labors, Gradgrind had given him a letter of introduction to Bounderby, who immediately told Harthouse the story of his career from street ragamuffin to industrialist and banker. Harthouse thought Bounderby was a fool, but he was greatly interested in the pretty Louisa.

Through his friendship with Bounderby, Harthouse met Tom Gradgrind, who lived with the Bounderbys. Harthouse took advantage of Tom's drinking problem to learn more about Louisa. He had heard that she had been subjected to a dehumanizing education and felt that she would be easy prey for seduction because of her loveless marriage to the pompous Bounderby. For these reasons, Harthouse decided to test Louisa's virtue. Before long, Harthouse gained favor in her eyes. Neither realized, however, that Mrs. Sparsit, jealous and resenting her removal from the comfortable Bounderby house, spied on them constantly.

Everyone was amazed to learn one day that the Bounderby bank had been robbed. The main suspect was Stephen Blackpool, an employee whom Bounderby had mistreated. Blackpool, who had been seen loitering in front of the bank, had disappeared on the night of the robbery. Suspicion also fell on Mrs. Pegler, an old woman known to have been in Blackpool's company. A search for Blackpool and Mrs. Pegler proved fruitless. Bounderby seemed content to wait; he said that the culprits would turn up sooner or later.

The affair between Louisa and Harthouse reached a climax when Louisa agreed to elope with the young man. Her better judgment, however, caused her to return to her father instead of running away with her lover. Gradgrind was horrified to see what his education had done to Louisa's character, and he tried to make amends to her. The situation was complicated by Mrs. Sparsit, who had learned of the proposed elopement and had told Bounderby. He angrily insisted that Louisa return to his home. Realizing that his daughter had never loved Bounderby, Gradgrind insisted that she be allowed to make her own choice. Harthouse disappeared, giving up all hope of winning Louisa.

Mrs. Sparsit returned to act as Bounderby's housekeeper during Louisa's absence and tried to reinstate herself in Bounderby's confidence by tracing down Mrs. Pegler. To her chagrin, Mrs. Pegler turned out to be Bounderby's mother. Bounderby was furious, for his mother disproved his boasts about being a self-made man. Meanwhile, Louisa and Sissy Jupe accidentally found Blackpool, who had fallen into a mine shaft while returning to Coketown to prove his innocence in the robbery. After his rescue, he told them that Tom Gradgrind was the real culprit. When the young man disappeared, his sister and father found him with the help of Sissy Jupe. They placed him, disguised, in a circus until arrangements could be made to spirit him out of the country. Before he could escape, however, Bounderby's agents found Tom and arrested him. With the aid of the circus roustabouts, he was rescued and put on a steamer that carried him away from the police and Bounderby's vengeance.

Mrs. Sparsit, who had caused Bounderby great embarrassment by producing Mrs. Pegler, was discharged from his patronage, much to her chagrin. Bounderby himself died unhappily in a fit a few years later. The Gradgrinds, all of them victims of an education of facts, continued to live unhappily, unable to see the human side of life.

Critical Evaluation:

Dedicated to social critic Thomas Carlyle, *Hard Times* represents Charles Dickens' first work of overt social criticism and reflects his contempt for utilitarian ideals of progress that valued over all other results that which produced the "greatest good for the greatest number." Coketown, the setting for *Hard Times*, is a mill city that represents the worst aspects of what the Industrial Revolution was doing to British people in the nineteenth century. In *Hard Times*, it is this "revolution" that Dickens blames for England's moral, legal, spiritual, and intellectual decay.

While all of the characters in this novel are flawed or damaged because of the changes brought about by the Industrial Revolution, Dickens holds Josiah Bounderby in the greatest contempt. In him, Dickens embodies the worst characteristics of the middle class: self-absorption, arrogance, and a lack of compassion for others in need of help. A self-made man, Bounderby demeans his family, claiming to have escaped a very abusive childhood through his wits alone. While it makes for a heartrending story, Dickens eventually exposes Bounderby as a fraud. Rather than having been abandoned as a child, Bounderby actually grew up in a loving, comfortable home. The reason he presented his family as villains was that, in Bounderby's eyes, they were not successful people because they did not prize self-reliance above all else, even love. In fact, Bounderby seems to think that love is just another acquisition, something he can have if he has the money to buy it. This is his attitude as he pursues Louisa Gradgrind to be his wife.

The Gradgrind children—Louisa, her younger brother Tom, and their siblings—are raised and educated by a father who prizes the utilitarian values of reason at the expense of the imagination, a system that encouraged the fostering of intellect but not the nurturing of the human heart. By some standards, it could be argued that Mr. Gradgrind has provided well for his family; however, when it comes to love, compassion, and supportive understanding—those things that Dickens sees as essential—the Gradgrind family appears much less blessed than either the mill workers or the economically disadvantaged, but loving, group of circus people, who provide Sissy Jupe with her extended family. In fact, throughout Louisa's troubles with her husband and during her infatuation with James Harthouse, it is Sissy, not her father or brother, who recognizes the depth of Louisa's unhappiness. Dickens clearly reviles a system such as the one practiced in Mr. Gradgrind's home and private school, a system that inculcates only cold hard fact at the expense of compassion and imagination. Despite her rearing and education, Dickens makes it clear that Louisa feels things deeply and needs someone to love, not only because she is attracted to the spoiled, idle dilettante James Harthouse but also because she cannot contain her hungry imagination during her quiet musings before the fire. Sadly, Louisa can no more tell her father, her husband, or Sissy what is troubling her, for Louisa really does not have the language to give a name to her need for tenderness, playfulness, and companionship—none of which is extolled in her father's school or exemplified in the behavior of her parents to each other or toward their children.

Dickens begins his story of Coketown with a scene depicting the visit of a government inspector to Mr. Gradgrind's school to make sure that these children are learning "facts" and not being overburdened with useless activities that involve their imaginations. When Sissy Jupe, a child from the local circus, defines a horse in an imaginative way, Mr. Gradgrind rebukes her. In this simple scene, Dickens sets the stage for the key issue he explores in this novel: the price that is paid when reason is sought at the expense of emotion. Even more so than Mr. Gradgrind, Mr. Bounderby is a strong proponent of the importance of reason over emotion, and he offers himself as an example to his apprentice, young Tom Gradgrind. Unfortunately, Tom has neither the necessary imagination nor the integrity derived from seeing one's connection and obligation to the community at large to withstand the temptation to gain easy wealth by stealing from his employer's safe.

Yet it is not Tom Gradgrind whom Bounderby and others blame for the theft, but Stephen Blackpool, an honest but poor mill hand. This aspect of *Hard Times* is Dickens' way of condemning the social inequalities of the capitalist system, such as the ones that Coketown, Bounderby's bank, Gradgrind's school, and the mill represent. Dickens makes it clear that he believes that facts alone will not enable Bounderby or the other town officials to get beyond their class prejudices and identify the real thief: Tom Gradgrind.

Hard Times offers ironic commentary at every turn, as, for example, in the deep regard for each other shared by Stephen Blackpool and another mill hand, Rachel. When Stephen momentarily has a chance to free himself from the burden of his half-mad, estranged, alcoholic wife by overdosing her on some medication, it is Rachel who unselfishly stays his hand, even though doing so prevents the two of them from marrying. In brutal contrast stands the wealthy, selfish young man James Harthouse, whose very name is loaded with irony. When he grows attracted to the now married Louisa Bounderby, Harthouse thinks nothing of pursuing her, nor does he mind losing her after his plot is discovered. For him, unlike Stephen and Rachel, "love" is only a game, one of the many in a world that concerns itself only with material possessions and wealth.

The book's conclusion is bitter. All of the principal characters are broken, isolated within themselves, or dead. Mr. Gradgrind is chastened to realize that he and his theories of family and education have brought about not only his daughter's breakdown and ruined marriage but also, indirectly, his son's disgrace, deportation, and later death. In contrast, Mr. Bounderby—the model businessman—has learned nothing, unaffected by his wife's desertion. Mr. Gradgrind's knowledge is dearly bought, for, although he has come to see the importance of love, his prior insistence on "fact" cost him his son and the respect of his peers. Worse, however, is that he must live with the knowledge that his wrongheadedness has denied Louisa a loving husband and children.

"Critical Evaluation" by Melissa E. Barth

Bibliography:
Leavis, F. R. *The Great Tradition.* London: Chatto and Windus, 1948. Provides an excellent introduction to the idea of class in Dickens' writing. Compares Dickens as a social critic to twentieth century writers such as D. H. Lawrence.
Miller, J. Hillis. *Charles Dickens: The World of His Novels.* Cambridge, Mass.: Harvard University Press, 1958. Explores Dickens' art in creating such rich worlds of characters and well-realized places. Very useful in its discussion of the themes and setting of *Hard Times.*
Morris, Pam. *Dickens's Class Consciousness: A Marginal View.* New York: St. Martin's Press, 1991. Helpful study of Dickens' attacks on the British class system. Applies contemporary critical theories to Dickens' polemical style of social criticism.
Newcomb, Mildred. *The Imagined World of Charles Dickens.* Columbus: Ohio State University Press, 1989. Informative discussion of the loss of childhood. Very interesting consideration of the role of children in Dickens' fiction as well as of the British educational system.
Watkins, Gwen. *Dickens in Search of Himself: Recurrent Themes and Characters in the Work of Charles Dickens.* Totowa, N.J.: Barnes & Noble Books, 1987. Good treatment of Dickens' interest in children, parenting, and love. Also helpful in its study of Dickens' attitudes toward imagination.

HARMONIUM

Type of work: Poetry
Author: Wallace Stevens (1879-1955)
First published: 1923

In 1923, when Wallace Stevens' *Harmonium* was published, the French Symbolists—Charles Baudelaire, Stéphane Mallarmé, Paul Verlaine, Arthur Rimbaud, and Jules Laforgue—were being assimilated as influences and models in English poetry as well, and the imagist movement had not yet run its course. Because Stevens exhibited the tangential imagery, elisions, and regard for symbolic order of the first group and the concentrated exactness of the second, most readers found little in his poetry to link it with the native tradition. Instead, they seized on the exotic and ornate qualities of his verse as if these were its final effect rather than a means to an end. Stevens appeared to be, at first reading, a poet whose purity of vision and absolute integrity insulated him from the material concerns of his society. In thus assuming a position of isolation and authority he resembled T. S. Eliot in England and James Joyce in Paris. The author of "Le Monocle de Mon Oncle," "The Comedian as the Letter C," and "Peter Quince at the Clavier" seemed to provide a similar image of the dedicated artist.

As it later developed, Stevens was neither a master of decor for decoration's sake—the literary dandy and Whistler in words, as some called him—nor the alienated poet the period demanded. An aesthetic-moral writer of the highest order, he had already in *Harmonium* charted those areas of experience and precept that were to form the whole body of his work: the re-creation of the physical world in bold and brilliant imagery, the relation of imagination to reality, the nature and function of art, the poet's place in modern society, and problems of structure and style.

Stevens was not a poet of growth but of clarification, and his later books merely ordered and refined his vision and techniques. Unlike most poets, who achieve only a temporary balance between temperament and environment, he created a total world for his imagination and his belief in the nourishing power of art. Perhaps the greatest service he provided was to show the possible in poetry if humans are to find a source of imaginative faith in an age of disbelief or to establish once more a sustaining relationship with the world about them. *Harmonium* "makes a constant sacrament of praise" to poetry—the imaginative ordering of experience—as the supreme fiction.

The unmistakable signature of these poems is the richness of their diction, the use of words not common (at least in those plain-speaking times) to English poetry, and a parade of brightly colored images and startling turns of phrase. Such words as fubbed, coquelicot, barque, phosphor, gobbet, fiscs, clavier, pannicles, girandoles, rapey, carked, diaphanes, unburgherly, minuscule, ructive, shebang, cantilene, pipping, curlicues, and funest reveal the poet's delight in the unusual and the rare. As R. P. Blackmur pointed out long ago, however, Stevens' poetic vocabulary was not chosen for affected elegance, coyness, or calculated obscurity. These words give an air of rightness and inevitability within what frames them. It is not the word itself but its relationship to other words in the poem that gives to Stevens' poetry its striking qualities of style. The same is true of his images, the strategic effectiveness of "barbaric glass," "poems of plums," "venereal soil," "golden quirks and Paphian caricatures," "rosy chocolate and gilt umbrellas," "oozing cantankerous gum," "women of primrose and purl," and "the emperor of ice cream," which convey a luxuriance of sense impressions. This diction of odd angles of vision and strange surfaces gives the impression of language revitalized as if it were the invention of the poet himself. It becomes a part of what Stevens once called "the essential gaudiness of poetry," and it is capable of a variety of effects, as the following examples show.

> The mules that angels ride come slowly down
> The blazing passes from beyond the sun.
> ("Le Monocle de Mon Oncle")

or

> Chieftain Iffucan of Azcan in caftan
> Of tan with henna hackles, halt!
> ("Bantams in Pine-Woods")

or

> . . . and not to think
> Of any misery in the sound of the wind,
> In the sound of the leaves,
> Which is the sound of the land
> Full of the same wind
> That is blowing in the same bare place
> For the listener, who listens in the snow,
> And, nothing himself, beholds
> Nothing that is not there and the nothing that is.
> ("The Snow Man")

Stevens' diction and imagery are not so much the verbalization of a mode of thought but in themselves a way of thinking. His poetry belongs to the order of solipsism, that philosophical theory that holds that the self is the only object of verifiable knowledge and that all things are re-created in the image of the human act of perceiving the world. This is the effect toward which Stevens' floating images tend, so that the reader emerges from the world of his verse with an altered perspective. There is in it a different way of seeing, a rearrangement of the familiar pattern of experience; poetry is no longer a way of looking at life but a form of life itself. Thus his images point to a passionate drive toward material comfort and rich living, as opposed to spiritual sterility in a world of waste and excess. In *Harmonium* the poles of his world become "our bawdiness unpurged by epitaph" and "the strict austerity of one vast, subjugating, final tone." Stevens is aware of tradition corrupted and a world fallen into disorder, a realization of humans dispossessed of unity between themselves and their universe, of nature violated, of old faiths gone. Out of his knowledge he writes these lines on a Prufrock theme:

> In the high west there burns a furious star.
> It is for fiery boys that star was set
> And for sweet-smelling virgins close to them.
> The measure of the intensity of love
> Is measure, also, of the verve of earth.
> For me, the firefly's quick, electric stroke
> Ticks tediously the time of one more year.
> And you? Remember how the crickets came
> Out of their mother grass, like little kin,
> In the pale nights, when your first imagery
> Found inklings of your bond to all that dust.

For a secular poet like Stevens, poetry was to become the "supreme fiction" and the imagination "the one reality in this imagined world," a way of imposing order on the chaos of experience. This is the theme of "Anecdote of the Jar," one of the simplest but most meaningful of the poems in *Harmonium*:

> I placed a jar in Tennessee,
> And round it was, upon a hill.
> It made the slovenly wilderness
> Surround that hill.

Here is the desire to impose order on the wildness of nature and, indirectly, on that of the world. It is not the image of the jar that is of first importance in the poem, but the act of placing the jar on such an eminence that it commands the landscape, so that

> It took dominion everywhere.
> The jar was gray and bare.
> It did not give of bird or bush,
> Like nothing else in Tennessee.

Stevens puts Keats's Grecian urn to other uses than those of contemplation or revelation.

This "rage for order" is worked out in more elaborate detail in "The Comedian as the Letter C." A fable in six parts, the poem is Stevens' most ambitious work before "Notes Toward a Supreme Fiction" on the relation of imagination to reality and the poet's place and function in society. It is characteristic of his self-satire that he should picture the poet as a picaresque mountebank trying to reconcile imagination to actuality. In part 1, "The World Without Imagination," Crispin the subjectivist sets sail upon the sea of life, to discover that the romantic imagination that has given him eminence within his own limited milieu is a world preoccupied with things and therefore lacking in imagination. Romanticism being equated with egotism, Crispin in the second section, "Concerning the Thunderstorms of Yucatan," decides that the only reality lies in the senses. His love for the exotic ends when he is brought to a realization of the overwhelming and destructive powers of nature. The third section, "Approaching Carolina," follows Crispin through a realm of the imagination symbolized by moonlight that is the antithesis of the sun, which lights up reality. Turning from the moon as a mere reflection of reality, Crispin in part 4, "The Idea of a Colony," enters a new phase of art based on the community and regional ties. Disillusioned, he turns in part 5, "A Nice Shady Home," to domesticity and, like Candide, digs in his own garden; he will become a philosopher. Part 6, "A Daughter with Curls," deals with the final wisdom Crispin found in his return to earth:

> Crispin concocted doctrine from the rout.
> The world, a turnip once so readily plucked,
> Sacked up and carried overseas, daubed out
> Of its ancient purple, pruned to the fertile main,
> And sown again by the stiffest realist,
> Came reproduced in purple, family font,
> The same insoluble lump.

Art, Stevens implies, cannot be made this or that, cannot be pursued like a chimera; it exists, separate and complete, in its own substance and shape.

There are times when Stevens' search for some standard of ultimate reality and the forms that it may take in poetry leads him away from concrete particularities into the realm of abstract speculation. If he appears at times more concerned with meaning than with being, the reader may also recognize in his work the power of a contemplative writer who insists on the need of discipline in life as in art. He sees the gap between the potential and the actual; consequently, he must try to uncover causes and create a way of seeing that his readers may share.

Stevens himself achieves the supreme, fictive mood of contemplation and understanding in "Sunday Morning," his best poem and one of the great poems of the century. In the image of a woman eating her late breakfast on a Sunday morning, we have a picture of modern boredom and uncertainty. The woman sits in external sunlight but also in the moral darkness of an age that has lost faith in the spiritual nature of human beings: "Why should she give her bounty to the dead?" The poet's answer is that happiness lies in the perception of nature, which in its recurrent changes and seasons creates an immortality in which humans may share.

> We live in an old chaos of the sun,
> Or old dependency of day and night,
> Or island solitude, unsponsored, free,
> Of that wide water, inescapable.
> Deer walk upon our mountains, and the quail
> Whistle about us their spontaneous cries;
> Sweet berries ripen in the wilderness;
> And, in the isolation of the sky,
> At evening, casual flocks of pigeons make
> Ambiguous undulations as they sink,
> Downward to darkness, on extended wings.

Harmonium reveals Stevens to be a poet of moral and humane temper, and the poems, disciplined and perfectly articulated, reflect a limited but significant picture of the twentieth century sensibility.

Bibliography:

Bloom, Harold. *Wallace Stevens: The Poems of Our Climate*. Ithaca, N.Y.: Cornell University Press, 1977. Places Stevens' work within the context of American poetry. Interprets Stevens in the light of Bloom's theory of literature, which has an Aristotelian slant. Three full chapters are devoted exclusively to *Harmonium*.

Litz, A. Walton. *Introspective Voyager: The Poetic Development of Wallace Stevens*. New York: Oxford University Press, 1972. One of the clearest and most enjoyable general studies. Shows stages of Stevens' development and provides lucid discussions of many *Harmonium* poems.

MacLeod, Glen G. *Wallace Stevens and Company: The Harmonium Years, 1913-1923*. Ann Arbor, Mich.: UMI Research Press, 1983. Examines Stevens' crucial involvement with major art and literary movements in the years up to *Harmonium* and shows how his perspective on art is a major element in the *Harmonium* poems. Looks at echoes of these movements in the poems.

Riddel, Joseph N. *The Clairvoyant Eye: The Poetry and Poetics of Wallace Stevens*. Baton Rouge: Louisiana State University Press, 1965. Solid, insightful close readings, covering many *Harmonium* poems. Examines Stevens' definitions of the imagined and the real in his work. This work continues to be among the most useful for beginning Wallace Stevens students.

Vendler, Helen. *On Extended Wings: Wallace Stevens' Longer Poems*. Cambridge, Mass.:

Harvard University Press, 1969. Classic study of Stevens' long poems. Provides excellent readings of the three long poems in *Harmonium*, "Sunday Morning," "Le Monocle de Mon Oncle," and "The Comedian as the Letter C." Most later critics cite this easily accessible, straightforward work; it is a fine place to begin research.

THE HARP-WEAVER AND OTHER POEMS

Type of work: Poetry
Author: Edna St. Vincent Millay (1892-1950)
First published: 1923

When Edna St. Vincent Millay won the Pulitzer Prize in 1923 for *The Harp-Weaver and Other Poems*, she was the first woman and only the second poet to win this award given annually since 1917 from an endowment created by the American newspaper publisher, Joseph Pulitzer. (Millay had been a finalist for the prize in 1922 but lost to the poet Edward Arlington Robinson, whose *Collected Poems* (1921) was chosen instead of her book of poetry, *Few Figs* (1920). When *The Harp-Weaver and Other Poems* was published in November, 1923, Millay was already well-known as the author of the groundbreaking *Renascence and Other Poems* (1917), as well as for stories written under the pseudonym Nancy Boyd, magazine articles, and five other poetry collections published in 1920 and 1921. In 1922, while writing for the American magazine *Vanity Fair*, she planned to write a novel, *Hardigut*, for which she even received an advance of $500. Finding herself ill and tired in Europe, where she had been assigned as a correspondent, Millay returned to the United States, however, and in July married Eugene Boissevan, whom she had met while attending Vassar College. They bought a farm in upstate New York, which they named Steepletop, where they remained until their deaths. As her career progressed, Millay, who liked to be called Vincent, wrote an opera libretto, *The King's Henchman* (1927), toured and read her poetry on the radio, recorded her poetry for RCA, translated Charles Baudelaire's controversial poetry collection *Flowers of Evil* (1857) with her friend George Dillon in 1936, and continued to publish poetry in books, magazines, and newspapers.

The poem "The Ballad of the Harp-Weaver" had been privately published before Millay collected it for the 1923 publication. Its placement as the last poem in part 2 of *The Harp-Weaver and Other Poems* marks the end of the first third of the book, as the publication itself marked the end of the first third of Millay's career. Divided into five sections and dedicated to her mother, Cora Buzzell Millay, the book includes a variety of lyric poems and forty sonnets on subjects ranging from the seasons and flora and fauna to reflections on love, friendship, and death. Unlike her contemporaries, Ezra Pound, T. S. Eliot, and William Carlos Williams, Millay eschewed experimentation and idiomatic American English, relying instead on the British poetical traditions of Robert Herrick, John Donne, William Shakespeare, William Wordsworth, and Alfred, Lord Tennyson.

Part 1 of *The Harp-Weaver and Other Poems* presents in ten rhyming lyric poems the themes of longing, frustration, and loneliness tempered with the poet's appreciation of nature's power and beauty. Each poem has a degree of tension in it as the speaker moves from a mood of restlessness in "My Heart, Being Hungry" to a spirit of action in "The Dragonfly," wherein Millay personifies the poet and the writing process in the metaphor of an insect breaking out of its cocoon and flying to freedom and life:

> Over the jewel-weed and pink marshmallows,
> Free of these and making song of them,
> I shall arise, and a song of the reedy shallows!

Part 2 of the collection begins with the *abab* rhyming stanzaic poem "Departure," hauntingly describing the speaker's mental flirtation with suicide and how she is abruptly brought back to reality by the steady voice of her mother asking, "Is there something the matter, / dear, she said/

That you sit at your work so silently?" The nine poems that follow profile the various ways in which love can be expressed.

The intensity of feeling created in the first ten poems of the book is sustained through the next ten as Millay introduces dialogue to broaden the perspectives and give depth. Her use of tetrameter, the ballad stanza, archaic expressions, and repetition give the poems timeless qualities. In "A Visit to the Asylum," for example, the speaker recollects a childhood memory of passing a mental institution as a child with hair "so red, you know." The "queer folk in the windows/ Would smile at me and call" and offer her flowers and fruits and other delicacies so that she would pass that way again. She would call to them as she passed, "You come see me!" The image the poem evokes of windows latticed "up and down" contrasts with the happiness of the people inside, who with "The merriest of eyes would follow me/ And make me compliments."

In other poems of part 2, the sea is an important symbol of nature's power, which Millay uses in a conventional manner. "The Curse" allows the poet to project herself as cremated ashes that are blown out to sea, then onto farmland, and finally into her mother's house, where no one recognizes her in this new form. The metaphysical quality of the poem and the speaker's symbolic homelessness create a tension in the poem about the theme of identity. In "Keen," Millay adopts the character of a woman whose lover has died at sea, who laments her loss but closes the meditation with pride that she loved a daring man rather than a timid one.

"The Betrothal" speaks of a loveless engagement and shows an effective use of irony. It complements the comic irony of "The Return to Town," the second poem in this section, just as "Humoresque" ironically parallels "A Visit to the Asylum." In "The Betrothal," the female speaker teases her fiancé for being unhappy that she loves another ("a dark head that never will be mine") and tells him with sensible resignation that if she weds him at least he will be happy, as "There's few enough as is." Love's sacrifice comes into clear focus in the last two poems of part 2, "The Pond" and "The Ballad of the Harp-Weaver."

"The Pond" tells the tale of past and present as the speaker passes a spot where a young girl drowned herself for a lost love. The speaker admires the girl's cleverness in looking as though she had been picking a flower on a busy road and just lost her balance. "The Ballad of the Harp-Weaver" demonstrates Millay's talent with the long narrative poem. The piece charts the growing intensity of a mother's love for her son and how she died on Christmas Day in the bitter cold. The boy, who must be about five, sees his mother get up in the night and go to her harp, where she weaves a wardrobe of finest threads until he awakes to find "Her hands in the harp-strings/ Frozen dead" surrounded by "The clothes of a king's son/ Just my size." The poem reflects precise word choice, use of the ballad form, and symbolism.

The third grouping of lyric poetry focuses on change and stability and combines several themes and imagistic patterns found in the previous two parts of the book. These eight free-verse and rhymed poems are a little less interconnected than the first twenty, but they have the same poignancy and relevance. "The Concert" recounts a leave-taking between two lovers as one plans to attend a concert alone and the other is insecure about staying home alone. Using allusions to battle, the speaker indicates how the spirit is renewed ("And over my head a flame") and perspective restored by a brief separation:

> You and I have nothing to do with music.
> We may not make of music a filigree frame,
> Within which you and I,
> Tenderly glad we came,
> Sit smiling, hand in hand.

In the last stanza, the speaker notes that no lasting harm can come from being apart for a few hours, "And you will know me still. I shall only be a little taller/ Than when I went" for having been independent of the clasp of love. "Spring Song" is an ironic poem with a two-line refrain about nature in conflict with an increasingly modern world. In the second stanza, the speaker announces that there will be no spring for anyone to enjoy because commerce and concrete have taken it away. Millay's speaker laments the paving over of gardens and chopping down of flowering trees and shrubs:

> Oh, well,—hell, it's all for the best.
> She certainly made a lot of clutter,
> Dropping petals under trees,
> Taking your mind off your bread and butter.

Yet, for all its apparent bitterness, the poem seems to celebrate the resilience of human nature in the closing couplet: "We shall hardly notice in a year or two./ You can get accustomed to anything."

Finally, "The Cairn" (a Celtic word for a stone mound erected as a memorial or a landmark) may be seen as the poem that captures Millay's central themes about education, emotion, knowledge, and imagination. As if in parallel to William Butler Yeats's poem "Among Schoolchildren," the speaker of Millay's "The Cairn" reflects on how learning facts is easy but learning to live is hard, and she challenges the passive person, whose description is punctuated with a period in one long opening sentence, to become actively alive through a series of exclamations that lead to the cautionary but insightful closing lines, "But the name of the mountain you climb all day,/ Ask not your teacher that." Learning life's lessons and defining an identity in the world should not be taught by someone else, but should be the result of the individual's struggle with experiences encountered in life.

Twenty-two numbered sonnets make up part 4 of Millay's book. She and her contemporary, Elinor Wylie, were the last American women poets consistently to model their sonnets on the work of the Elizabethan writers William Shakespeare, Michael Drayton, Samuel Daniel, and John Donne. Millay imitated the thought processes of these earlier poets and mirrored their syntactical and rhythmical patterns in her sonnets, as in number 17, "Loving you less than life," which reveals the use of irony and paradox reminiscent of the turns of images and phrases common to sixteenth century English sonnets. Number 18, "I, being born a woman and distressed," openly and candidly considers a female speaker's passion for her lover. After detailing how her lover excites her in his words, she closes the sonnet playfully, saying that when they meet again no words will be necessary. Sonnets 19, "What lips my lips have kissed," and 22, "Euclid alone has looked on Beauty bare," are often anthologized as representative of her style and capabilities in writing in this form.

Unlike the miscellaneous sonnets that characterize part 4, part 5, "Sonnets from an Ungrafted Tree," is a sequence that chronicles a woman's married life and closes in number 17 with her vigil before her husband's burial. The sequence progresses on two levels, the first the action that creates the plot and the second the revelation the unnamed woman has about each action she takes in preparation for her husband's death. The woman had returned unwillingly to tend her husband in his final illness after they had been separated for some time. Sonnets 1 to 3 set the scene of decay in richly imaged language and establish the essential differences between life and death, past and present, and duty and love. Clearly, the woman is motivated by a sense of duty. She begins her chores by collecting wood to build a fire (sonnet 4). In sonnet 5, a delivery man comes and in sonnet 8, neighbors come to leave food, but she avoids meeting anyone (sonnets 6 and 7), hiding in the cellar or behind the curtains and preferring to clean in solitude. Sonnets 9-11 depict the couple as they had been when young, and sonnet 12 illustrates his helplessness now. Sonnets 13-15 look at how she anticipates his death, first with dread and fear, then, in sonnet 16, with alarm as the public aspects of the funeral arise—"And crowds of people calling her name/ And questioning her, she'd never seen before." Finally, in sonnet 17, she is aware that what went before in her life would never be again. The sensory images and attention to detail combine with simple and direct language to give the sequence its common realism.

Edna St. Vincent Millay was a popular poet during her life. She was adept at depicting ordinary experiences, and she wrote verse that appealingly described love's vicissitudes, coping with frustration and solitude, and coming to terms with death. This universality and mastery of the common touch may in the long run keep her work available when the work of now popular poets, which offers a more partial view, has been relegated to obscurity.

Beverly E. Schneller

Bibliography:
Britten, Norman A. *Edna St. Vincent Millay.* Rev. ed. Boston: Twayne, 1982. Offers a solid overview of the poet's life and work. Britten's analysis of "Sonnets from an Ungrafted Tree" is particularly good.
Gould, Jean. *The Poet and Her Book: A Biography of Edna St. Vincent Millay.* New York: Dodd, Mead, 1969. Interprets the work through the lens of Millay's life. Illustrated.
Millay, Norma, ed. *Collected Poems: Edna St. Vincent Millay.* New York: Harper & Row, 1956. Edited by the poet's sister. Has no index, explanatory notes, or introductions, and poems are not left in their original sequences, but contains previously uncollected material.
Thesing, William B., ed. *Critical Essays on Edna St. Vincent Millay.* New York: G. K. Hall, 1993. Reprints reviews and early articles on Millay's work along with some newly commissioned critical essays.

HAVELOK THE DANE

Type of work: Poetry
Author: Unknown
Type of plot: Romance
Time of plot: Tenth century
Locale: England and Denmark
First published: c. 1350

> *Principal characters:*
> HAVELOK, a prince
> GODARD, his guardian
> GOLDEBORU, a princess
> GODRICH, her guardian
> GRIM, a fisherman
> UBBE, a Danish noble

The Story:

Athelwold was a good king. No one dared offer him a bribe, and throughout all England people were at peace. He was a particular guardian to widows, children, and innocent maidens. A messenger might go peacefully from town to town with a hundred pounds of gold in a sack. Athelwold's only heir was a young daughter, still a baby. When Athelwold knew that his death was upon him, he prayed for guidance and then summoned his earls and barons to his side. There was loud lamenting at the approaching end of their honored king. Athelwold's chief concern was for his daughter's care. It was decided that Godrich, Earl of Cornwall, would be the most trustworthy to bring up the princess. Godrich swore a great oath to safeguard the infant Goldeboru and to hold her lands in trust until she could reign.

Godrich watched the growing girl with envious eyes. She was fair to look upon, and Godrich could not bear to think of the day when she would be his sovereign. Acting then the part of a traitor, he took her secretly from Winchester to Dover and placed her in a remote castle. To guard the entrance he set his most trusted thanes with orders to let no one in to see the princess.

In Denmark, King Birkabeyn lay near death. He had reigned long and wisely, but he was leaving his son Havelok and his two little daughters without protection. He thought of his faithful friend, Godard, a rich man who was the most respected noble in the kingdom. Godard swore a great oath to guard the children well and to see that Havelok came into his inheritance when he became a man. After being shriven, Birkabeyn died content.

On the seashore Godard cruelly slit the throats of the two tiny girls and then seized Havelok. The boy, terrified at what he had been forced to witness, begged for mercy. Instead of killing Havelok straightway, Godard called for Grim, a fisherman, and commanded him to bind the prince and cast him into the sea with an anchor around his neck. Anxious to please his lord, Grim seized the boy and bound him tightly. Then he took him home to wait for night.

As Havelok dozed on the rude bed in the fisherman's hut, a great light shone from his mouth. Grim's wife was frightened and called her husband. Grim, awed, freed Havelok from his bonds. Bundling his wife, his five children, and Havelok aboard his fishing boat, he set sail for England. The group went up the Humber to land in a likely cove. After that the place was called Grimsby.

For twelve years Havelok grew rapidly. He was an active boy and a prodigious eater. Luckily,

Grim was a good fisherman, and he could trade his catches at the market in Lincoln. Corn and meat could be bought there, and ropes for the nets. Havelok, who helped Grim in all his labors, was especially good at peddling fish.

A great famine came upon the north of England. The crops withered and the fish fled English shores. Day after day Grim's family became poorer. Havelok, touched by the suffering of his foster family, resolved to seek his fortune in Lincoln. Although he could ill spare it, Grim cut a cloak from new sailcloth for Havelok and wished him well. The prince set out for town with his new cloak, but he had neither shoes nor hose. In the town, Havelok starved for three days. No one would hire him and he could find no food. At length he heard a cry for porters. Looking quickly around, he saw the earl's cook with a catch of fish to carry. In his eagerness Havelok knocked down eight or nine other porters to get to the cook first. Strong as a bull, the youth carried the fish to the castle. The next day the cook cried again for a porter, and this time Havelok carried a huge load of meat.

In the castle yard the cook greatly admired the strong fellow. He gave Havelok bread and meat, as much as he could hold, and engaged him as a steady helper. Eating regularly and working hard, Havelok became widely known for his strength. On a certain feast day the retainers held a stone-putting contest. A group of men brought in a stone so huge one man could barely lift it. Havelok easily heaved it many yards.

Godrich, hearing of Havelok's fame, decided to use the youth in his scheme to gain control of the kingdom. Thinking him only a churl, Godrich had Goldeboru brought from Dover and ordered Havelok to marry her. Both young people objected, but Godrich had his way. Havelok took his sorrowing bride back to Grim's cottage. That night the groom slept soundly but the bride stayed wakeful from shame at being mated to a churl. All at once a light issued from Havelok's mouth, and a voice told Goldeboru of her husband's birth and destiny. Awaking Havelok, she advised him to go at once to Denmark to claim his throne.

In the morning Havelok persuaded the three Grim brothers to go with him on the trip to Denmark. Arriving in that land, the impoverished group met Ubbe, a noble who bought a ring from Havelok. Ubbe, greatly taken with Havelok and his beautiful bride, offered them a cottage for the night. The couple accepted gratefully, and soon were asleep after their long voyage.

In the night a band of robbers tried to break in after overpowering the guard set by Ubbe. When Havelok awoke, he set about them valiantly. He seized the door bar and slew robbers right and left. This feat won him more admiration. Ubbe assigned the young couple to a rich bower for the rest of the night. When Ubbe stole in for a look at his guests, he was astonished to see a light streaming from Havelok's mouth and a cross marked on his shoulder. By these signs he knew that Havelok was Birkabeyn's son and heir to the Danish throne.

Calling all the barons of Denmark together, Ubbe dubbed Havelok a knight and proclaimed him king. The assembled nobles passed judgment on Godard, the traitor, who was brought before Havelok, flayed, and hanged on a gallows with a great nail through his feet.

Now master of Denmark, Havelok sailed with a strong force to England to seize that kingdom from Godrich. The battle was joined near Lincoln. Although Godrich fought valiantly and wounded Ubbe, he was finally captured by the wrathful Danes. The false Earl of Cornwall, bound hand and foot, was brought before Havelok for judgment. Godrich was put upon an ass and taken into Lincoln, where his crime was proclaimed. Then he was taken to a nearby green and burned to death. Havelok married one of Grim's daughters to the cook who had befriended him and made the man Earl of Cornwall. Grim's other daughter was married to the Earl of Chester. As for Havelok and Goldeboru, they lived together long and ruled wisely. Their union was blessed with fifteen children.

Critical Evaluation:

Havelok the Dane is one of the most interesting of the romances produced in medieval England. The customary patterns of romance are there: The hero is noble, brave, and pure. The heroine is noble, beautiful, and pure. The poem is given exceptional qualities by its rousing, energetic spirit of adventure. As one is carried along by the intricacy and suspense of the plot, one notices the unusually realistic detail that is the poem's most outstanding asset.

Havelok the Dane is not generally considered among the great works of Middle English literature, but this is as much the fault of critical neglect as it is of any weakness of the poem itself. *Havelok the Dane* may lack the literary polish of the works of, for example, Geoffrey Chaucer, but it should be appreciated on its own terms and enjoyed for what it has to offer. Along with *King Horn* (c. 1225)—often associated with *Havelok the Dane* in literary history because of common themes, though the two works are clearly by a different author—*Havelok the Dane* offers a compelling story of adventure, love, honor, and personal vindication.

Havelok the Dane is one of the most approachable of Middle English poems. The protagonist is likeable, and it is easy for the reader to understand his adventures on a human level. Unlike the idealized courtly romances that flourished on the continent, *Havelok the Dane* is among the most realistic of medieval poems. Although often conventional in its characters and plot, its sense of English geography and temperament makes it the link between the Anglo-Saxon period of centuries before and the great poems of the alliterative revival (such as *Pearl* [c. 1380] and *Piers Plowman* [c. 1362], both written by anonymous authors) that were to come in the second half of the fourteenth century, shortly thereafter.

Often, medieval romances appear to the modern reader as formulaic arrangements of conventional codes and manners. These poems, therefore, whatever their eloquence of composition, lack the emotional pulse to be found in modern novels. *Havelok the Dane* is an exception to this rule. Rather than being on the outside of a self-contained courtly ethic, the reader feels that the poem creates a world to which she or he can relate. Although the poem's action is fantastic (and delightfully and pleasingly so) it affirms the inner lives of its characters. One of the motifs in the poem that helps testify to its affirmation of the real and ordinary is the importance of food and cooking in the poem. The fact that Havelok's surrogate father is a cook enables the poet to use food as both symbol and reminder of the everyday in the midst of Havelok's heroic quest to regain his rightful inheritance. The detailed description of the various houses in the poem, from the fisherman's hut to the castle in which Goldeboru is imprisoned, also fortifies the poem's atmosphere of domesticity in the midst of derring-do. The houses in *Havelok the Dane* are not simply allegorical figures for states of mind or morality (as they are in the French poem of the thirteenth century, *The Romance of the Rose*); they are real places in real time where real people live (though, certainly, these realities are garbed within a wonderfully elaborate fictional and narrative texture).

There is realism also in how the poem depicts the lower classes and the harsh reality of poverty in medieval England. Although it is inconceivable that Havelok or any other protagonist of such a poem could be anything but an aristocrat, the fact that he relates empathetically to people below his station in life is a vital ingredient in the evolution of his character that psychologically prepares him to assume the kingship of Denmark. In many ways, this exemplifies the archetypal idea of the hero proving himself abroad before returning triumphantly home. The portrayal of Grim and his family, however, is far more than schematic.

The courtship of Havelok and Goldeboru is an especially winning feature of the book. Traditionally, courtly love is illicit and outside normal social channels. Havelok and Goldeboru, on the other hand, are matched up with each other by external forces. Their romance only begins when Havelok's true station in life is revealed. Yet the poem depicts their eventual relationship in strikingly sincere terms. Havelok and Goldeboru allow real-world contingencies to affect their feelings for each other, so the modern reader is able to recognize his or her own experience in their behavior to a far greater extent. *Havelok the Dane* departs from courtly conventions and achieves an often-underrated social and psychological realism. Havelok is not a particularly intellectual hero or a very passionate one, but he does come across as an attractive personality. Goldeboru's beauty and sympathetic nature are conveyed in a three-dimensional manner; she is not simply a stereotypical damsel in distress.

The realism of *Havelok the Dane* is geographical as well. *Havelok the Dane* was composed in the northern part of England (which was also to produce *Pearl* and *Piers Plowman*). Although all of England was ruled, in the fourteenth century, by a French-speaking Norman aristocracy, and had been since the victory of William the Conqueror at Hastings in 1066, the North was far less influenced by Norman manners and language. This regional quality resonates throughout *Havelok the Dane*. The character of Grim, for instance, is obviously intended to provide an explanation of cause or origin (what literary scholars terms an "etiological myth") for the English seaport of Grimsby. The name "Grimsby" is of Danish origin, and the entire region was occupied by Danes in the tenth century during the Viking raids. *Havelok the Dane* brings to mind the many cultural intertwinings between England and Scandinavia in the medieval era, and reminds readers that English national identity is not monolithic but composed of many different strands. The language of the poem itself contains many words of Danish or Scandinavian origin that have not made it into the modern English lexicon, which was far more influenced by the Norman-French dialects popular in the southern part of England. In its combination of the Danish theme with that of the protagonist's search for his own identity, *Havelok the Dane* is reminiscent of the anonymous Anglo-Saxon poem *Beowulf* (early eighth century) and of William Shakespeare's *Hamlet* (c. 1600-1601). Like Beowulf, Havelok leaves his native land and gains fame and fortune in another kingdom. Like Hamlet, Havelok struggles against a usurper who stands between him and the inheritance bequeathed him by his father and goes to England in order to clarify his political situation. Thus, *Havelok the Dane* can be seen as a bridge between two of the greatest works of English literature.

"Critical Evaluation" by Nicholas Birns

Bibliography:
Bradbury, Nancy Mason. "The Traditional Origins of *Havelok the Dane*." *Studies in Philology* 90 (Spring, 1993): 115-142. Looks at the layers of earlier myth, legend, and history that are preserved in the epic. Useful in separating the Danish, Continental, and insular English elements upon which the poem drew.
Gadomski, Kenneth H. "Narrative Style in *King Horn* and *Havelok the Dane*." *The Journal of Narrative Technique* 15 (Spring, 1985): 133-145. The most aesthetically sensitive of all recent critiques of the poem. Useful for the reader interested in a primarily literary and artistic approach to the work.
Levine, Robert. "Who Composed *Havelok* for Whom?" *Yearbook of English Studies* 22 (1992): 95-104. Speculates on the class, cultural, and social backgrounds of both the author and the audience of *Havelok the Dane*. The article is influenced by reception theory and sociohistorical criticism.
Smithers, G. V. "The Style of *Havelok*." *Medium Aevum*, 1988, 190-219. This formal and quantitative analysis looks not only at the literary but also the linguistic elements of the

poem's style. Some technical linguistic knowledge is required to fully appreciate the piece.

Wilson, R. M. *The Lost Literature of Medieval England*. New York: Methuen, 1952. Conveys a sense of the storehouse of native English myth and lore of which *Havelok the Dane* is one of the few extant examples. Provokes many speculations about the place of *Havelok the Dane* in the canon of English legend.

A HAZARD OF NEW FORTUNES

Type of work: Novel
Author: William Dean Howells (1837-1920)
Type of plot: Social realism
Time of plot: 1880's
Locale: New York City
First published: 1890

Principal characters:

BASIL MARCH, the editor of a literary magazine
MR. FULKERSON, the sponsor for the magazine
CONRAD DRYFOOS, the publisher of the magazine
MR. DRYFOOS, Conrad's father and a newly rich millionaire
CHRISTINE DRYFOOS, his daughter, in love with Angus Beaton
HENRY LINDAU, a socialist
ANGUS BEATON, the art director for the magazine, courting Christine
    Dryfoos, Margaret Vance, and Alma Leighton
MARGARET VANCE, a young woman involved in charity work
ALMA LEIGHTON, a young artist

The Story:

In his youth, Basil March had wished for a literary career. Family responsibilities turned him, however, to the insurance business, a field in which he proved to himself and his employers that he was only mediocre. After eighteen years with his firm, his employers decided to replace him and put him into a somewhat meaningless position. Rather than be so embarrassed, March resigned. Fortunately for him and his family's future, Mr. Fulkerson, a promoter of syndicated newspaper material, who had met the Marches years before, proposed that March take over the editorship of a new literary magazine that he was promoting. March at first demurred at Fulkerson's proposal, but the promoter, certain that March had the necessary taste and tact to be successful, finally persuaded him to take the position.

Mrs. March and the children had always lived in Boston, and so, when the prospect of moving to New York City appeared, even though it meant a career for her husband and their father, they needed considerable persuasion. At last, Mrs. March was convinced that the move to the larger city was imperative. She and her husband went to New York to find an apartment in which they could make themselves comfortable. After many days of searching, Mrs. March returned to Boston, leaving her husband to make a decision about the editorship. He did so a short time later.

March's problems in connection with the staff did not prove as difficult as he had imagined. Fulkerson, the promoter, had engaged an artist, Angus Beaton, to serve as art director, procured a cover sketch for the first issue, and made all the financial arrangements with the magazine's backer, Mr. Dryfoos, who had recently made a fortune for himself through the control of natural gas holdings. Mr. Dryfoos, who was trying to win his son Conrad away from a career as a minister, had undertaken to finance the magazine in order to give his Conrad a chance to enter business as the ostensible publisher of the periodical. Foreign articles and reviews were to be handled by an old German socialist, Henry Lindau, who had been March's tutor and whom the younger man had met accidentally in New York.

Despite March's fear and lack of confidence, the new magazine, *Every Other Week*, was a success from the very first issue; both the illustrations and the material caught the public's fancy. On the periphery of the activities concerning the magazine, however, there were many complications. The Dryfoos family, who had been simple farm folk, wanted to be taken into society; at least, the two daughters wanted to enter society. In addition, Christine, the older daughter, fell in love with Beaton, who was not in love with her. Instead, Beaton admired Margaret Vance, a young woman from a good family who was involved with charity work among the poor. Beaton also had an interest in Alma Leighton, the young artist from whom he had procured the cover sketch for the magazine. Fulkerson, the promoter, had also fallen in love. He was busy paying court to a Southern girl who boarded at the same house he did, and the girl's father, a Virginia colonel, was after Fulkerson to have the magazine print at least a portion of his work extolling the merits of slavery.

Because the magazine had been a success, Fulkerson suggested that, for publicity purposes, they should give a dinner party for members of the staff and the press. Mr. Dryfoos, who was asked to pay the bill for the proposed affair, vetoed the idea, but he agreed to have a small dinner party at his home for several of the men connected with the magazine. Among the guests was Henry Lindau, who had impressed the millionaire because he had lost a hand fighting in a war. Dryfoos did not realize that Mr. Lindau, who was doing the foreign-language work for the magazine, was a socialist. At the dinner party, the personalities and the principles of the men clashed openly. The next day, the millionaire bluntly told Basil March that the old man was to be fired. March wished to stick by the old German, but Mr. Lindau forced the issue by refusing to do any more work for the capitalistic owner of the magazine.

Another crisis occurred a short time later when Mr. Dryfoos and his son, who hated being a businessman rather than being a minister, had an open clash of wills. The situation became so acute that the father, calling one day when his son was alone in the office, struck the young man in the face. Outside the office, the father also had trouble with his daughter, Christine, for he had forbidden the art editor of the magazine, with whom she was in love, to visit her.

At that time, there was a streetcar strike in New York City. Young Conrad Dryfoos was very much in sympathy with the strikers, many of whom he knew as a result of his church work among the poor and sick of the city. At the instigation of Margaret Vance, the young woman whom he loved, he went out on the streets to try to bring peace among the rioting strikers and the police. He saw Mr. Lindau, the aged, one-armed socialist, being beaten by a policeman; when he ran to interfere, he was struck by a stray bullet and killed.

Mr. Dryfoos was heartbroken at the loss of his son, particularly because he felt that he had mistreated the young man. When he learned that his son had died trying to save Mr. Lindau from the policeman's club, he decided to accept the old man as a friend and to take care of him for the rest of his life. The decision came too late, however, for the old man died as a result of the beating he had received. In a last effort to show his change of heart, Mr. Dryfoos had Mr. Lindau's funeral conducted in his own home.

Still wishing to try to make his family happy, Mr. Dryfoos then swallowed his pride and went to see Angus Beaton, the artist. Confessing that he was sorry to have caused the young people unhappiness, he invited Beaton to resume his calls on Christine. The young man eventually pocketed his pride and called, but even her father's money could not make up for for his embarrassment over her lack of proper manners and decorum. Beaton later proposed to Alma, who rejected him in favor of pursuing her art career.

A few days later, Mr. Dryfoos resolved to take his wife and daughters to Europe. Before he left, he went to the offices of the magazine, where everyone had been wondering what the fate of the publication would be and whether Conrad Dryfoos' death had destroyed his father's interest in the periodical. Mr. Dryfoos magnanimously consented to sell the periodical to Fulkerson and March at a low figure and with very low interest on the money they needed in order to purchase it. Both March and Fulkerson were extremely happy about the turn of events. March saw his future secure at last, and he also saw that he would have a free hand in shaping the editorial policy. Fulkerson was happy because he, too, foresaw a prosperous future. As the result of his expectations, he was able to marry and settle down.

Some months afterward, they learned that the Dryfoos family had been taken up promptly by at least a portion of Parisian society. Christine Dryfoos had even become engaged to a penniless but proud French nobleman.

Critical Evaluation:

William Dean Howells is known as one of the principal proponents of the American school of realism in the late nineteenth century. Simply defined, "realism" refers to a narrative technique that values detailed description of everyday life and rejects improbable or extraordinary solutions to the problems of the novel's characters. The main goal of realism is to represent the world of the novel (usually a middle-class world, although occasionally a working-class world) as accurately as possible. Not only did Howells write many realist novels himself, but he also promoted other, younger realist writers such as Stephen Crane, Charles Chesnutt, and Frank Norris. In addition, Howells wrote one of the key defenses of realism with *Criticism and Fiction* (1891). In *Criticism and Fiction*, Howells urges, "Let [fiction] portray men and women as they are, actuated by the motives and the passions in the measure we all know; let it leave off painting dolls and working them by springs and wires."

A Hazard of New Fortunes came at a turning point in Howells' career. Previously, Howells was primarily concerned with reproducing middle-class manners and morals, as can be seen in his novel *The Rise of Silas Lapham* (1885). However, influenced by what he believed to be the unfair executions of activists following the Haymarket labor riot in Chicago in 1886, Howells began to examine issues of economic and class struggle. Once seen as a weak, flawed novel, *A Hazard of New Fortunes* is now seen as one of Howells' finest novels, in good part because of Howells' new focus. In the first half of the twentieth century, this novel was not valued by critics, largely because issues of class and economics were not considered worthy of serious study in literature. However, in the 1980's a new interest in social concerns led to a reevaluation of *A Hazard of New Fortunes*.

Another interesting feature of *A Hazard of New Fortunes* is that the main character and his wife, Mr. and Mrs. March, occupy prominent positions in several of Howells' other novels. Probably the best known of these is Howells' first novel, *Their Wedding Journey* (1872), which follows the Marches on their honeymoon. Howells revisits the Marches once again in *Their Silver Wedding Journey* (1899). Howells' technique of following a married couple over the course of their marriage is an innovative use of marriage in nineteenth century novels. Typically, novels of that time detailed the courtship of the couple and ended with the wedding. It was only in the latter half of the nineteenth century that writers such as Howells and his fellow novelist Henry James began to consider what occurs in a relationship after the wedding.

Traditionally, *A Hazard of New Fortunes* is seen as autobiographical due to the high level of similarities between Howells and his protagonist, Basil March. Just as the Marches' honeymoon in *Their Wedding Journey* mimics the tour that Howells and his wife took after their wedding, March's career move at the beginning of *A Hazard of New Fortunes* is similar to one that Howells had made. Howells also left his comfortable home in Boston for a job as an editor in New York City. March's triumph with his work mirrors Howells' successful leadership of *Harper's Magazine*. Because of these surface similarities, March's thoughts and feelings about his new life have often been attributed to Howells himself.

An extremely important aspect of *A Hazard of New Fortunes* is its setting: New York City. This urban setting allowed Howells to explore issues of class and ethnicity in a way that would not have been possible otherwise. The juxtaposition of people from vastly different backgrounds within a small geographical area is a feature of the city that enables Howells to examine more than just a middle-class existence. This is most prominently seen when the Marches are apartment hunting in New York and pass through various neighborhoods as they search for the one that would suit them best. The neighborhoods serve as physical markers of the divisions of class and ethnicity that exist in the city.

Although the main characters are solidly middle-class, class struggle can be powerfully felt in this novel. Both Conrad Dryfoos and Margaret Vance do charity work among the poor of the city, showing the other side of city life. Howells uses this contact not only to illustrate the differences between the classes but also to allow Conrad and Margaret to serve as the economic consciences of their respective families. Howells further shows that money is not the only determining factor of class. The situation of the Dryfoos sisters gives strong testimony to existence of prejudice against the nouveau riche. Although Mr. Dryfoos is able to negotiate successful business relationships, neither of the sisters is able to marry in New York City because their father's recent wealth has made them oblivious to the fact that they have neither the education nor the manners to fit in socially with the upper classes. These economic themes run throughout the novel until class tensions finally explode with the labor strike. Conrad's death shows that no one is safe from the random violence that these class divisions create. With this, Howells shows that even middle-class lives cannot escape being touched by the violence inherent in class struggle.

In this novel, Howells also exposes the economic underpinnings of the institution of marriage, primarily through the situation of Angus Beaton. Beaton's inability to find a suitable wife demonstrates Howells' awareness of this problem. Howells uses Beaton's courtships of Alma, Margaret, and Christine to illustrate the primary role economics plays within the dynamic of courtship and marriage. Finally, by allowing Alma to reject Beaton, Howells creates a respectable possibility for women other than marriage. Alma chooses her art over Beaton, making this character one of the first positive representations in American literature of a woman with a viable career.

"Critical Evaluation" by Jennifer Costello Brezina

Bibliography:

Cady, Edwin H. *The Realist at War: The Mature Years, 1885-1920*. New York: Syracuse University Press, 1958. An excellent source of autobiographical criticism. Traces parallels between Howells and Basil March. Uses events in Howells' life to explain his fictional choices in this period.

Crowley, John W. "Howells in the Eighties: A Review of Criticism." *Emerson Society Quarterly: A Journal of the American Renaissance* 32, no. 4 (1986): 253-277; 33, no. 1 (1987): 45-65. A fairly extensive annotated checklist of Howells' criticism published between 1979 and 1986.

Kaplan, Ann. *The Social Construction of American Realism*. Chicago: University of Chicago Press, 1988. An insightful study of representations of class within American realism. Includes a lengthy chapter about *A Hazard of New Fortunes* that examines the roles of the city and social difference in the novel.

Nettels, Elsa. *Language, Race, and Social Class in Howells' America.* Lexington: University Press of Kentucky, 1988. Examines Howells' use of dialect and vernacular as markers of class and ethnicity. Analysis of the speech patterns of Lindau, Madison Woodburn, and the Dryfoos family are included.

Taylor, Walter F. "William Dean Howells and the Economic Novel." In *Critics on William Dean Howells*, edited by Paul A. Eschholz. Coral Gables, Fla.: University of Miami Press, 1975. An early analysis of the novel and its economic implications. Contains a bibliography of other economic critiques.

HEADLONG HALL

Type of work: Novel
Author: Thomas Love Peacock (1785-1866)
Type of plot: Fiction of manners
Time of plot: Early nineteenth century
Locale: Wales
First published: 1816

> *Principal characters:*
> SQUIRE HEADLONG, the host
> MR. FOSTER, the optimist
> MR. ESCOT, the pessimist
> MR. JENKISON, a champion of the status quo

The Story:

Squire Harry Headlong differed from the usual Welsh squire in that he, by some means or other, had become interested in books, in addition to the common interests of hunting, racing, and drinking. He had journeyed to Oxford and then to London in order to find the philosophers and men of refined tastes introduced to him in the world of literature. Having rounded up a group of intellectuals, he invited them to Headlong Hall for the Christmas holidays.

Three of the men formed the nucleus of his house party. The first was Mr. Foster, an optimist. To him, everything was working toward a state of perfection, and each advancement in technology, in government, or in sociology was all for the good. He believed that humanity would ultimately achieve perfection as a result of its progress. Mr. Escot, on the other hand, saw nothing but deterioration in the world. The advances that Mr. Foster saw as improvement, Escot saw as evidences of corruption and evil that would soon reduce the whole human race to wretchedness and slavery. The third man of the trio was Mr. Jenkison, who took a position exactly in the middle. He believed that the amount of improvement and deterioration balanced each other perfectly and that good and evil would remain forever in status quo.

These philosophers, with a large company of other dilettantes, descended upon Headlong Hall. Among the lesser guests was a landscape gardener who made it his sole duty to persuade the Squire to have his estate changed from a wild tangle of trees and shrubs into a shaved and polished bed of green grass. Mr. Foster thought the grounds could be improved; Mr. Escot thought any change would be for the worse; and Mr. Jenkison thought the scenery perfect as it was.

There were ladies present, both young and old, but they did not join in the philosophical discussions. Many of the talks occurred after the ladies had left the dinner table and as the wine was being liberally poured, for Squire Headlong was aware that the mellowness produced by good burgundy was an incentive to conversation. The discussions took various turns, all of them dominated by the diametrically opposed views of Foster and Escot and soothed by the healing words of Jenkison. Escot harped constantly upon the happiness and moral virtue possessed by the savages of the past, virtue that lessened with each encroachment of civilization. As the savage began to build villages and cities and to develop luxuries, he also began to suffer disease, poverty, oppression, and loss of morality. Foster could not agree with this thesis. He pointed to the achievements of civilization in fields other than those of a materialistic nature. Shakespeare and Milton, for example, could not have achieved their genius in the primitive life Escot applauded. Escot, refusing to concede an inch, pointed to Milton's suffering, stating also that even if one person profited from the so-called advancements, fifty regressed because of them. Mr. Jenkison agreed that the subject left something to be said on either side.

Between these learned discussions, the gentlemen spent their time in attempts to fascinate the ladies. Escot had once been the suitor of one of the guests, but he had offended her father during an intellectual discussion and had fallen out of favor. He attempted now to regain his former place in her affection by humoring the father. During these periods of respite, the guests also entertained one another with singing and recitations, the selections being those they themselves had composed.

The Squire was planning a magnificent ball and had invited the whole neighborhood to be his guests. At the ball, the wine flowed freely, so that even Foster and Escot forgot some of their differences. Although he disapproved of any but aboriginal dances, Escot danced often with the lady of his choice. Foster, of course, thought the modern dance the utmost in refinement and an expression of the improved morality of humanity. Jenkison could see points both for and against the custom. During the evening, Squire Headlong was reminded by a maiden relative that should he not marry soon there would be no one to carry on the name that had been honored for many centuries. As his name implied, the Squire was not one to toy with an idea once it had entered his mind. Fixing on the lady of his choice in a matter of minutes, he proposed and was accepted. Then he arranged three other matches in an equally short time. Foster and Escot were aided in choosing brides and in getting permission from the father of Escot's beloved. Foster's bride was related to the Squire and presented no obstacle. Seizing on another man, the Squire told him of the plan and promptly chose a bride for the hapless individual.

Within a matter of days, the weddings took place. After promising to gather again in August, the guests then dispersed. Foster and Escot tried to the last to convince each other and the rest that only one philosophy was the true one, but Mr. Jenkison was not to fall into either of their traps. He would join them again in August, still convinced that there was merit in both of their arguments. Neither was right or wrong, but each balanced the other, leaving the world in its usual status quo.

Critical Evaluation:

Thomas Love Peacock's *Headlong Hall* is certainly prose fiction, but it is less than one hundred pages long and therefore much shorter than novels usually are. There is a plot of sorts, but not one to be taken seriously, and the course of events is clearly fortuitous rather than causal. No central character emerges other than the narrator, of whom readers know nothing. Of the other characters, four are perhaps more central than others, but none of them stands out and none shows any kind of development. Readers do not at any time enter into the private thinking of any character. Large portions of *Headlong Hall* consist only of labeled dialogue among the various speakers and are solely concerned with their conflicting ideas. If Peacock's book is to be called a novel at all, it should be specifically identified as a Romantic novel, so as not to confuse it with a Victorian or later one.

Another tradition of prose fiction influential in the early years of the nineteenth century was that of the romance, an originally poetic form dating from the Middle Ages and consisting mostly of chivalric tales, in which scene and incident are extravagantly imaginative and remote from those of everyday life. From this tradition arose Horace Walpole's *Castle of Otranto* (1764). Walpole's book, in turn, revived the long tradition of Gothic fiction, emphasizing fear and suspense. *Headlong Hall* does not fit into either of these traditions.

The two greatest novelists of Peacock's own time were Jane Austen (from whom he stole nothing) and Sir Walter Scott, who combined the romance and novel traditions to fictionalize real incidents in Scottish, English, and eventually French history from the Middle Ages to recent times. Peacock, like everyone else in his day, read Scott's novels and thought well of them. Peacock's lush treatment of natural scenery in *Headlong Hall* may have imitated Scott's descriptions, and the sensible opinions of Mr. Mac Laurel, a Scots-speaking poet and critic, may have been a more deliberate tribute. Known to be a successful poet, Scott had not, as of 1816, acknowledged his own authorship of his novels. Following Scott's example, Peacock also published his novels anonymously. *Headlong Hall* was the first, and the others were "by the author of *Headlong Hall*."

Peacock's, then, are in no sense conventional novels. They are akin to others written in his own times only in various inconsequential ways. Peacock looked beyond traditions of prose fiction to include drama and satire. Before writing *Headlong Hall* in 1815, Peacock had already written some not-very-successful longer poems and some dramas. Portions of the latter are reused in *Headlong Hall*, and the influence of the stage is evident throughout. In some cases, however, the drama imitated is Greek, for Peacock was particularly fond of classical Greek authors. He was also well read in the philosophical dialogues of Plato but found himself unable to accept their manipulative logic and facile conclusiveness. Unlike his friend Percy Bysshe Shelley, the great Romantic poet, Peacock was also unable to accept the idealism of the Greeks and their complacent reliance upon the sufficiency of human reason.

In reflection of its author's skepticism, *Headlong Hall* is above all else a satire. It documents the diversity (etymologically, the word "satire" refers to a "mixed plate") of opinions current in Peacock's time and assumes the reader's inability to resolve intellectual differences through any kind of rational procedure. These differences are inherent in human nature, and can never be resolved, Peacock implies. As Mac Laurel says at one point, "Noo, ye ken, sir, every mon is the centre of his ain system, an' endaivours as much as possible to adapt everything aroond him to his ain parteecular views."

The four principal viewpoints, as described in chapter one, are those of Mr. Foster, the perfectibilian, for whom the world and human society are inexorably improving; Mr. Escot, the deteriorationist, for whom the world and human society are inexorably worsening; Mr. Jenkison, for whom both are staying the same; and the Reverend Doctor Gaster, a comic clergyman intended to demonstrate the irrelevance of traditional Christianity to modern times. None of the speakers ever alludes to the just-concluded Napoleonic wars or to advancements in either science or medicine.

Each of these four has been identified with one or more actual persons. Foster, for example, sometimes echoes opinions very similar to Shelley's. Escot partially derives from the eighteenth century French writer Jean-Jacques Rousseau and his Scottish follower, James Burnett, Lord Monboddo. Jenkison has been identified with Peacock's friend Thomas Jefferson Hogg, but the opinion he expresses—that the world is basically unchanged throughout human existence—is also Peacock's, as is expressed in his preface to a reprinting of *Headlong Hall* in 1837. Peacock's conviction of the social world's essential stability led him to value Greek authors in particular as being among those who saw the foibles of humanity earliest and most clearly. For him, it was Christianity that fundamentally obscured the truth about humanity from itself and therefore required him to present Gaster as a comic figure. The plot (such as it is) of *Headlong Hall* revolves around a Christmas party, but there is never a meaningful religious observance of any kind within it. With all the eating and drinking that goes on, it is more like a Roman saturnalia than a serious Christian holiday.

Foster, Escot, Jenkison, and perhaps Gaster are perennial types to be found in any civilization at any time. The new characters introduced in chapter three are of a more specialized sort and will be meaningful primarily to those who have some prior familiarity with the literature of Peacock's time. They include Mr. Milestone, a famous landscape gardener utterly opposed to leaving the beauty of nature in its unaltered state and who seeks to replace it by manipulations or grotesques of various kinds. Mr. Cranium is a phrenologist, or one who believes that traits of human character are inherited and can be ascertained by examining the bumps on one's skull, these being supposedly indicative of specialized brain development beneath. Though entirely discredited now, phrenology was both popular and influential in Peacock's time, with implications for comparative anatomy, anthropology, and physical psychology—as well as literature. Among those who thought themselves well endowed with bumps of intelligence were the influential reviewers of books for widely read periodicals, of whom Mr. Gall and Mr. Treacle (bitter and sweet, respectively) are typical examples. Following them, there are two voluminous poets, a musician, a painter, a polymathic dilettante (Mr. Panscope, probably the poet Samuel Taylor Coleridge), and a group of young ladies, all of who prove irresistible to the learned gentlemen in the end. The world, it seems, will go on its biological way irrespective of philosophy.

"Critical Evaluation" by Dennis R. Dean

Bibliography:
Burns, Bryan. *The Novels of Thomas Love Peacock.* Totowa, N.J.: Barnes & Noble Books, 1985. Sound but not authoritative criticism, with unsurprising insights. Includes *Headlong Hall.*
Butler, Marilyn. *Peacock Displayed: A Satirist in His Context.* London: Routledge & Kegan Paul, 1979. The most influential book on Peacock in recent years, with acute critical discussions of the novels, including *Headlong Hall.*
Dawson, Carl. *His Fine Wit: A Study of Thomas Love Peacock.* Berkeley: University of California Press, 1970. A comprehensive survey, with sections devoted to his poetry, nonfictional prose, and novels. Good discussion of *Headlong Hall.*
Kjellin, Hakan. *Talkative Banquets: A Study in the Peacockian Novels of Talk.* Stockholm: Almqvist & Wiksell, 1974. Hard to find, but an interesting discussion of Peacock's use of dialogue.
McKay, Margaret. *Peacock's Progress: Aspects of Artistic Development in the Novels of Thomas Love Peacock.* Stockholm: Almqvist & Wiksell, 1992. The most recent book-length study of Peacock. Traces his growth as a novelist through all seven novels.
Mulvihill, James. *Thomas Love Peacock.* Boston: Twayne, 1987. A brief but up-to-date introduction to the man and his works. Includes discussion of *Headlong Hall.*

THE HEART IS A LONELY HUNTER

Type of work: Novel
Author: Carson McCullers (1917-1967)
Type of plot: Psychological realism
Type of plot: 1930's
Locale: A small Southern mill town
First published: 1940

> *Principal characters:*
> MR. SINGER, a mute man
> MICK KELLY, an adolescent girl
> BIFF BRANNON, a café proprietor
> JAKE BLOUNT, a frustrated, idealistic working man
> DR. COPELAND, an African American physician
> PORTIA, Dr. Copeland's daughter

The Story:

Two mutes, one a grossly overweight Greek man named Antonapoulos, the other, a tall, immaculate man named Mr. Singer, lived together for ten years in a small, Southern town; they had no other friends. After an illness, the Greek man changed. When he began to be obscene in public, the cousin for whom he worked sent him to the state insane asylum. Mr. Singer was despondent without his friend.

Mr. Singer started to eat all of his meals at the New York Café, owned by Biff Brannon. Biff felt a particular connection to people in need. When Jake Blount, a squat, powerful man, came to town, he went on a weeklong drinking spree at Biff's expense. One night, Jake found Mr. Singer eating at the café, and he decided that the mute man was the only person who could understand him and his message. Mr. Singer took the drunk Jake home, providing him a temporary place to stay. Only in the morning did Jake realize that Mr. Singer was mute. He still felt, however, that Mr. Singer could understand everything.

Mr. Singer had taken a room at the Kelly's boardinghouse, where he encountered Mick, one of the Kelly children. Just entering her teens, Mick was a gangly girl, always dressing in shorts, a shirt, and tennis shoes. She loved music and would go anywhere to hear it. Some nights, she went to a big house in town where she could hear symphonic music through the open windows while she crouched in the shrubbery. At home, Mick never shared her dreams or yearnings with anyone except Mr. Singer, who let her talk to him when she was lonely.

Mick decided, after entering high school, that she needed to make some friends. Planning a dance, she invited only high school students. Mick decorated the house with fall leaves and red crepe paper, and she borrowed an evening dress, high-heeled shoes, and a tiara from her sisters. On the night of the party, the guests arrived and separated into groups. When Mick handed out the promenade cards, the boys went to one side of the room, the girls to the other. Silence descended. A boy named Harry finally asked Mick to promenade around the block, but, while she and Harry walked, all of the neighborhood children joined the party. By the time Mick got back, the decorations were torn, the refreshments gone, and the invited and uninvited guests mixed up so badly that the party was in a state of bedlam. Everyone congregated in the street to run races and jump ditches, the partygoers forgetting their nearly adult state. Mick finally called off the party after she had been knocked breathless on a jump she could have made easily in her tennis shoes.

Portia worked for the Kellys. Her father, Dr. Copeland, was the only African American doctor in town. He was an idealistic man who had always struggled to help his people to raise themselves out of their poverty and ignorance. One night, Mr. Singer had stepped up and helped Dr. Copeland light a cigarette in the rain. It was the first time a white man had ever offered him help or smiled at him.

Jake, who had found a job as a carousel mechanic, tried to rouse the workers to revolt. He spent each Sunday with Mr. Singer, explaining that he had aspired to be an evangelist until he understood the inequality in the world. Jake had unintentionally insulted Dr. Copeland twice, but he was one of the first to talk about doing something about the injustice that had been done to Willie, Dr. Copeland's son. Willie had been sentenced to hard labor for knifing a man. After Willie and two others tried to run away from the prison camp, the guards put them in a cold shack for three days with their bare feet hoisted up by a looped rope. Doctors had had to amputate both of Willie's feet. Dr. Copeland, trying to see the judge about his son's case, was severely beaten and put in jail. Mr. Singer and Portia obtained his release on bail, and Jake went with Mr. Singer to Dr. Copeland's house. Jake and Dr. Copeland argued bitterly through the night, verbalizing their differing visions of how to advance justice in the world.

Attracted to Mr. Singer's peacefulness, Mick visited him whenever she could. He purchased a radio for his visitors' enjoyment, but, of them all, Mick was the most heartened by the music. Those were hours of deep pleasure for her. Beginning to record songs that existed in her imagination, Mick was certain that she would become a famous composer. She also fascinated Biff. After his wife died, he watched as Mick began to mature, but he seldom spoke to her. He was equally quiet with Mr. Singer when he visited at the Kelly's boardinghouse.

Mr. Singer did not know what to think of Dr. Copeland, Biff, Jake, and Mick, but they were always welcome to visit him. During his vacation, Mr. Singer traveled to see his Greek friend. Although Mr. Singer brought him beautiful presents, Antonapoulos rejected everything but food. Only in the presence of his friend did Mr. Singer take his hands out of his pockets. Then his hands flew as he tried to relate in sign language everything he had seen and thought since his friend had gone away. The man showed no interest, and Mr. Singer tried even harder to communicate. When he left, Antonapoulos was still impassive.

Mr. Singer's rent provided the Kelly family with some reliable income, but they were constantly plagued by financial problems. The situation worsened as the family was forced to pay hospital bills after one of the boys shot a neighbor child. When a sister became ill and could not work, the loss of her salary placed the whole family into a dilemma. They learned about a job opening at the local variety store, but they initially decided that Mick was too young to work. For the first time, they talked about her welfare, their concern prompting her to apply for the job. Mick got the position, but each night she was too tired for anything but sleep.

Mr. Singer again made the long trip to the asylum to see Antonapoulos. Again, he was laden with elaborate gifts. When he reached the asylum office, the clerk told him that his friend was dead. Stricken, he traveled back to town, went to his room, and shot himself. Mr. Singer's suicide left his four visitors alone and confused. Dr. Copeland, still sick, brooded over it. Jake Blount joined a deadly fight and, after hearing that the police were looking for him, left town. Mick did not sleep well for weeks after the funeral. All that she had left was Mr. Singer's radio. She felt cheated because she had no time, no money, no feeling anymore for music, but she had no one to blame for robbing her of her dreams. And Biff, who had watched Mr. Singer with Jake and Mick, still puzzled over the relationships he had observed. He wondered whether love might be the answer to human isolation and loneliness.

Critical Evaluation:

Carson McCullers' first novel, *The Heart Is a Lonely Hunter*, immediately received praise from many reviewers who commended her insights into the human condition. They lauded the work as one of a few truly distinguished first novels in American literature. Other critics have written of the text's failures, particularly focusing on weaknesses in plot and style. Despite these criticisms, the novel continues to receive a great deal of scholarly attention.

Some critics have focused on the allegorical qualities of *The Heart Is a Lonely Hunter*. They interpret the novel as a parable and the characters as abstractions of ideas more than as representations of real, complex individuals. The plot and characters, such scholars argue, dramatize McCullers' viewpoints about love and teach the audience how to avoid isolation.

In addition to these analyses, many scholarly commentaries have centered on *The Heart Is a Lonely Hunter* as an example of Southern gothic fiction. Critics have compared this and other texts by McCullers, such as *The Member of the Wedding* (1946) and *The Ballad of the Sad Cafe* (1943), to works by Eudora Welty, Flannery O'Connor, Katherine Anne Porter, and William Faulkner. Like these twentieth century writers, McCullers is praised for portraying the painful realities of Southern life. Realistically depicting small-town dullness and meanness, *The Heart Is a Lonely Hunter* highlights the social landscape of human desperation and separation. McCullers reflects the intolerance, poverty, and isolation of the South. Revealing the vast contrasts of the region, the novel exposes a cultural system that proliferates racial fear and hatred, rigid gender roles and expectations, and class division and conflict. McCullers also translates the general symptoms of this society into intersecting narratives of individual lives. The characters of the novel, with their peculiar incapacities and deformities, embody themes common to Southern grotesques: violence, disease, mutilation, and death. In *The Heart Is a Lonely Hunter*, Carson McCullers presents a harsh society in which oppression pervades human existence. Despite the actualities of Southern repression, McCullers also offers glimpses of the noble human struggle to create meaning and to connect.

The residents of the novel's small Southern town are engaged in a lonely search for love. They are frustrated by rigid gender roles, inequalities in race and class, failed personal relationships, and their inability to communicate with one another. Mick Kelly, Biff Brannon, Jake Blount, and Dr. Copeland are acutely aware of their isolation. These muted characters, in revolt against their loneliness, strive fruitlessly to share their dreams and desires. They fail in their attempts to express themselves.

At the center of the novel is a mute man, John Singer. He and his exceedingly overweight Greek friend, Antonapoulos, are cut off from everyone except each other. Although Singer was taught to speak in school, speech repulses him, and he rejects it as unnatural. After Antonapoulos is institutionalized, Singer keeps his hands trapped in his pockets. He becomes the most isolated character in town. The irony of his name apparent, he sings for no one. Although Singer meets other mutes, he is convinced that he can share his thoughts with Antonapoulos only. Singer continues his efforts to communicate with his friend, a grotesque man who remains uninterested in anything but his own physical pleasures. Despite Singer's desperate longing, he is unable to connect with the object of his adoration. Totally impassive, the Greek remains unresponsive to Singer's needs. He is unmoved by Singer's presence.

In ironic duplication of Singer's futile relationship with Antonapoulos, other principal characters of the novel attempt to communicate with Singer. Believing that they are abnormal because they do not adhere to the expectations of their society, they try to escape their isolation through Singer, but he remains closed to them. This does not matter, however, because Singer is less a person than a catalyst. They refer to him as Mr. Singer, a signal of their emotional distance from him. Unconcerned about Singer's unresponsiveness, his disciples see what they imagine him to be. Singer serves as a mirror of their own desires. His muteness makes him all the more appropriate for their projections. For these characters, love is not a selfless expression but a marred attempt to communicate their own needs and dreams.

Jake Blount is a frustrated social reformer, his aspirations of stirring the masses to revolt never realized. His powerful arms and nail-scarred hands reveal the potential violence that lies just beneath the surface of his character. Desperately searching the South for an audience to listen to his tirades about the plight of the working classes, Jake focuses on Singer. The mute man becomes Jake's audience.

Dr. Copeland, a black doctor who suffers from tuberculosis, is consumed by the desire to save his people from meekness and compliance. Stern and inflexible, he alienates himself from the people he seeks to help. Unlike her father and other characters in the novel, Portia connects with others. Despite her father's uncompromising nature, Portia loves and cares for him, and she mothers the Kelly children. Before Willie is sentenced to jail, Portia establishes a loving, interdependent relationship with her husband and her brother. Unable to join that family community, Dr. Copeland directs his attentions to Singer. The doctor reads far more into a simple gesture of kindness than is warranted, viewing the mute man as the only compassionate white man whom he has ever known. Convinced that Singer is a Jew, Dr. Copeland communicates with him as a member of another oppressed people.

Possibly the most richly developed character in the novel, Mick Kelly has a boy's name and measures herself against male role models. She struggles to find a voice in a society that maintains rigid gender expectations. She discovers an outlet in music. Certain that Singer hears music in his head, Mick allows only him into the inner room of her imagination, where she dreams of writing beautiful symphonies. When financial need requires her to surrender her autonomy for the sake of the family, Mick consults Singer. She feels that only he can understand her needs, and she requires his permission to quit school and take a job. Sacrificing her dreams of becoming a composer, Mick molds herself into acceptable gender expectations. She is cheated of her dreams and loses her vitality and hope.

The heavy-jawed Biff Brannon is trapped in a loveless marriage. Childless and alone after his wife's death, Biff feels a compelling need to connect with those around him. He is a participant and an observer of the lonely search for love and human connection. Biff offers selfless love in an attempt to eliminate his own isolation and the isolation of the other characters. Despite his sincere efforts, Mr. Singer, Jake Blount, Dr. Copeland, and Mick Kelly dismiss Biff or view him with suspicion. Ironically, they reject the only person who accepts them and attempts to connect with their humanity. Despite their rejection, Biff clings to his hopes for the possibility of human redemption and love.

Love is everything in *The Heart Is a Lonely Hunter*. Human communion is essential, yet McCullers demonstrates that it is also immensely complex, perhaps impossible. Most of McCullers' characters are driven to each other to satisfy selfish needs and desires, but she asserts that the most important love is unselfish. True human communion involves both give and take. The novel ends with an image of Biff waiting for the dawn, hoping that humans can someday share the rare and evanescent love that they so desperately need.

Donna J. Kessler

Bibliography:
Bloom, Harold, ed. *Modern Critical View: Carson McCullers*. New York: Chelsea House, 1986.

test

An introduction to McCullers' major works and a group of critical essays focused on various texts, including Lawrence Graves's "Penumbral Insistence: McCullers's Early Novels."

Carr, Virginia Spencer. *The Lonely Hunter: A Biography of Carson McCullers*. Garden City, N.Y.: Anchor Press, 1976. A biography, an important companion to McCullers' fictional works, demonstrating the connections between the author's life and experiences and her fictional themes and images.

_____. *Understanding Carson McCullers*. Columbia: University of South Carolina Press, 1990. A critical edition of Carson McCullers' major works, including a section devoted to *The Heart Is a Lonely Hunter*.

McDowell, Margaret B. *Carson McCullers*. Boston: Twayne, 1980. One of the important book-length critical examinations of McCullers' texts.

Westling, Louise. "Carson McCullers's Tomboys." *Southern Humanities Review* 4 (1982): 339-350. One of the several good analyses of McCullers' characterizations of adolescent girls.

HEART OF AZTLÁN

Type of work: Novel
Author: Rudolfo A. Anaya (1937-   )
Type of plot: Social realism
Time of plot: 1950's
Locale: The Southwest
First published: 1976

Principal characters:
    CLEMENTE CHÁVEZ, patriarch of the family
    ADELITA CHÁVEZ, his wife
    JASÓN and
    BENJIE, their sons
    JUANITA and
    ANA, their daughters
    CRISPÍN, the seer of the blue guitar
    SAPO, the neighborhood bully

The Story:

Clemente Chávez had been happy living in Guadalupe on his own land, but the lack of work had forced him to sell out and move his family to Albuquerque to be near his brother Roberto. Clemente and his family were welcomed to Barelas. Clemente and his son Jasón met many men from the barrio, including Crispín, the man with the blue guitar.

The next morning Roberto took Clemente with him to the railroad yard to find work. Adelita sent Jasón to the yard with a lunch for her husband. Jasón headed toward the water tank, which dominated the skyline. It read "Santa Fe" (which means "holy faith"). A stranger took the food from him, returning only what the stranger did not want. Still searching for his father, Jasón witnessed a man's death: A man named Sánchez was killed instantly when a huge railroad hook hit him in the head. The sound of the siren reminded Jasón of an Indian legend about the song of life and death. He remembered Crispín's blue guitar and rushed to him, asking him to play that song to save Sánchez, but it was impossible to save Sánchez. At the wake, Jasón first saw Sánchez's lovely eldest daughter, Cristina, and so the evening ended well.

Clemente found work immediately at the railroad yard, replacing the dead man. For a time life went well enough, but then Lalo tried to organize a wildcat strike to protest conditions at the railroad yard and the corrupt union shop. Though not involved, Clemente lost his job.

Soon after, the whole family went to a dance at the community center to celebrate the wedding of Mannie, El Super's daughter, to a wealthy gringo. Meanwhile, Benjie was in trouble outside. He had sold some drugs for a neighborhood gang and did not have the money he owed them. High on marijuana, he laughed at Frankie and Flaco's threats. Flaco pulled out a knife; Jasón wrested the knife away and punched him in the nose. Frankie came at Jasón, but Jasón was ready with a knee to the groin. Men rushed out from the dance and the fight was over.

Not long after, Jasón and his friends were invited to a party at Cindy's house while her parents were away. Cindy, the blonde daughter of a lawyer, lived at the country club and had a crush on Jasón. Jasón saw Cristina at the party, with her childhood friend Sapo, who had just been released after serving time for killing someone during a gang fight. Ignoring the concern

2782

of his friends, Jasón went to Cristina. She introduced him to her friend Lawrence (Sapo). Tensions rose, so Cristina asked Lawrence to take her home. The party over, Cindy tried to persuade Jasón to stay with her, but he refused.

It was the last Sunday of summer. Jasón wanted to play baseball, but Sapo, Frankie, and Flaco were looking for him. He and Willie were prepared to fight their three attackers, but when Sapo pulled a zip gun they knew they had to run. Jasón kicked Sapo's gun hand, breaking it, and they ran. Two shots were fired but no one was hit. Sapo turned his anger on Flaco, putting the gun to his head. He fired but the gun did not go off.

Meanwhile, the wildcat strikers searched for someone to lead them. They asked Crispín to play something to unite them. He played the story of Aztlán, the mythical land from which the people had come. Clemente was haunted by the story. Some of the men had looked at him when they called for a leader. He went to the *bruja* (witch) of *la piedra mala* (the evil stone) to find the truth. He was, he found, too weak.

Depressed over his lost job and lost authority, Clemente drank for weeks. He was returning home late one night, struggling against a winter storm, when he tripped and fell into the gutter. Too weak to get up, he determined to die, but Crispín found him. Crispín gave him new hope, telling him again the story of Aztlán, the place of origin of the people to which the people would one day return. With Crispín as guide and companion, Clemente returned to the *bruja*, this time with the strength to withstand the evil rock. There he saw a vision of the heart of Aztlán and his new path in life. He would lead his people.

He tried to enlist the aid of Father Cayo, the parish priest, but the priest stood with the powerful and not with the poor. Clemente then attended an organizational meeting at which his words were misunderstood. Lalo led a few men to burn the railroad yard, but they were quickly arrested. The police searched for Clemente, who moved from house to house in hiding. Needing medical care, he went to a hospital and was arrested.

Clemente was not yet his people's leader, but the shop bosses feared him and tried to buy him off. He refused. Meanwhile, Cindy had gotten pregnant and many in Barelas assumed Jasón was responsible. Jasón and some friends went to the church to help the girls with Christmas decorations, where a gossip told Cristina's mother that he had gotten Cindy pregnant. Jasón protested his innocence, but Cristina's mother refused to let her see Jasón anymore. The priest cursed him and demanded he leave the church.

Jasón tried to find Cindy to get her to tell Cristina the truth, but Cindy was gone. Cristina also wanted the truth. One afternoon she ran into Sapo, high on heroin. Sapo threatened to avenge himself against Jasón. Cristina pleaded that Jasón had only protected his brother Benjie, as a brother should. Sapo blurted out that Benjie was the one who had gotten Cindy pregnant, not Jasón, and demanded that Cristina go to the dance with him in payment for the information.

Jasón went to another dance at the community center. Cristina was there—with Sapo—and she looked scared. A rumble broke out and, in the confusion, Sapo ran off with Cristina. Jasón and his friend Chelo quickly searched for Cristina, first at her house then at the Red Ball café. Sapo, still high on heroin, had been at the café, looking for Benjie, but he had shot his friend Frankie instead. Jasón and Chelo went after Sapo, who had taken Benjie and Cristina to the water tank at the railroad yard. Sapo had threatened to kill Cristina unless Benjie climbed the ladder up the tank. Unable to fire at Jasón, Sapo fired at Benjie, hitting his hand. Benjie lost his grip and fell.

With Benjie in the hospital, the entire barrio came to hear the story of how Clemente had beaten the supports of the water tank with a sledge hammer until the hammer splintered and then continued beating them with his fists. A crowd gathered, waiting. Benjie would live, but he was paralyzed. Clemente finally rose up to lead his people; together they marched toward the railroad yard without fear.

Critical Evaluation:

Rudolfo A. Anaya may be the most acclaimed Chicano writer. Certainly his first novel, *Bless Me, Ultima* (1972), attracted a large, positive critical reception. It was the first Chicano novel to be a bestseller, and remains the most read and most studied of his works. *Bless Me, Ultima* was the first of a trilogy that includes *Heart of Aztlán* and *Tortuga* (1979). The first and third novels of the trilogy are narrated from a young boy's point of view; *Heart of Aztlán* has a more diffused narrative line. The three novels share the presence of a seer, or spiritual guide, whose influence is essential to the main characters, and they share mythic underpinnings as well.

Heart of Aztlán traces one year in the life of the Clemente Chávez family as they sell their land and head for the city. Family members react differently to the strange, often hostile urban setting. Clemente loses his job and heads down the path to self-destruction. His family seems to disintegrate around him. Juanita and Ana work to help support the family and quickly become much more independent than tradition allows. Clemente's wife, Adelita, seems to flourish while he withers. Benjie becomes a drug user and seller. Only Jasón seems relatively unaffected, but a local gang threatens him as well.

Intertwined in the family's struggle to understand and cope with an alien environment is the workers' struggle for fair labor practices by the Santa Fe railroad company, and for a fair union that will represent workers and not be bought by management. Clemente is the link between these two narrative strands.

Clemente has lost his way when Crispín saves him from the winter storm. It is not just Clemente who is lost, but the whole *raza*. The entire Chicano race (represented here by the barrio) has lost its bearings. Crispín explains the legend of Aztlán to Clemente: Aztlán is the holy land where *la raza* originated, a land they left but to which they must return. Aztlán is a kind of Aztec Garden of Eden. Clemente has a vision of Aztlán: He sees a river of people and touches the throbbing heart of Aztlán. He sees that the people have lost their spiritual bearings; they are no longer a community but rather have become self-interested individuals. He realizes that in order to defeat the railroad bosses—to defeat life's harsh realities—they must find again the heart of Aztlán, find their identity as a people and come together as a community.

In *Heart of Aztlán* Anaya attempts to use myth to tell the story of a people and relate it to the socioeconomic context. It is a larger task than the one he had set himself in his first novel. The size of the task, combined with the immense critical and popular success of *Bless Me, Ultima* make *Heart of Aztlán* suffer by comparison. *Heart of Aztlán* contains numerous subplots that often distract from the central narrative of Clemente's moral anguish and his development into a moral and social leader. *Heart of Aztlán* is nevertheless an important novel, one of the first to touch the theme of the Chicano movement.

Linda Ledford-Miller

Bibliography:

Alurista. "Myth, Identity and Struggle in Three Chicano Novels: Aztlán . . . Anaya, Méndez and Acosta." In *Aztlán: Essays on the Chicano Homeland*, edited by Rudolfo A. Anaya and Francisco A. Lomelí. Albuquerque: Academia/El Norte Publications, 1989. Sketches three versions of the myth of Aztlán. Demonstrates the influence of Mexican and Chicano versions of the myth on *Heart of Aztlán*.

Candelaria, Cordelia. "Rudolfo A. Anaya." In *Dictionary of Literary Biography*. Vol. 82. *Chicano Writers*. Edited by Francisco A. Lomelí and Carl R. Shirley. Detroit: Gale Research, 1982. A somewhat harsh survey of Anaya's works. Discusses oppressive nature of technology, religion, and capitalism on the Chicano community of *Heart of Aztlán*.

Lamadrid, Enrique. "The Dynamics of Myth in the Creative Vision of Rudolfo Anaya." In *Pasó por aquí: Critical Essays on the New Mexican Literary Tradition, 1542-1988*, edited by Erlinda Gonzales-Berry. Albuquerque: University of New Mexico Press, 1989. Compares myth in *Bless Me, Ultima* as a way of understanding the world versus myth in *Heart of Aztlán* as a way of changing the world.

Márquez, Antonio. "The Achievement of Rudolfo A. Anaya." In *The Magic of Words: Rudolfo A. Anaya and His Writings*, edited by Paul Vasallo. Albuquerque: University of New Mexico Press, 1982. Thorough discussion of the trilogy and its critical reception.

Pina, Michael. "The Archaic, Historical and Mythicized Dimensions of Aztlán." In *Aztlán: Essays on the Chicano Homeland*, edited by Rudolfo A. Anaya and Francisco A. Lomelí. Albuquerque: Academia/El Norte Publications, 1989. Excellent introduction to the history and meaning of the myth of Aztlán, its importance to Chicano nationalism, and its use in *Heart of Aztlán*.

HEART OF DARKNESS

Type of work: Novella
Author: Joseph Conrad (Jósef Teodor Konrad Nałęcz Korzeniowski, 1857-1924)
Type of plot: Psychological realism
Time of plot: Late nineteenth century
Locale: Belgian Congo
First published: serial, 1899; book, 1902

Principal characters:
MARLOW, the narrator
MR. KURTZ, the manager of the Inner Station, Belgian Congo
THE DISTRICT MANAGER
A RUSSIAN TRAVELER
KURTZ'S FIANCÉE

The Story:

A group of men were sitting on the deck of the cruising yawl, *The Nellie*, anchored one calm evening in the Thames estuary. One of the seamen, Marlow, began reflecting that the Thames area had been, at the time of the invading Romans, one of the dark and barbarous areas of the earth. Dwelling on this theme, he then began to tell a story of the most barbarous area of the earth that he had experienced.

Through his aunt's connections, Marlow had once secured a billet as commander of a river steamer for one of the trading companies with interests in the Belgian Congo. When he went to Belgium to learn more about the job, he found that few of the officials of the company expected him to return alive. In Brussels, he also heard of the distinguished Mr. Kurtz, the powerful and intelligent man who was educating the natives and at the same time sending back record shipments of ivory. The mysterious figure of Mr. Kurtz fascinated Marlow. In spite of the ominous hints that he gathered from various company officials, he became more and more curious about what awaited him in the Congo. During his journey, as he passed along the African coast, he reflected that the wilderness and the unknown seemed to seep right out to the sea. Many of the trading posts and stations the ship passed were dilapidated and looked barbaric. Finally, Marlow arrived at the seat of the government at the mouth of the river. Again, he heard of the great distinction and power of Mr. Kurtz, who had an enormous reputation because of his plans to enlighten the natives and his success in gaining their confidence. Marlow also saw natives working in the hot sun until they collapsed and died. Marlow had to wait impatiently for ten days at the government site because his work would not begin until he reached the district manager's station, two hundred miles up the river. At last, the expedition left for the district station.

Marlow arrived at the district station to find that the river steamer had sunk a few days earlier. He met the district manager, a man whose only ability seemed to be the ability to survive. The district manager, unconcerned with the fate of the natives, was interested only in getting out of the country; he felt that Mr. Kurtz's new methods were ruining the whole district. The district manager also reported that he had not heard from Kurtz for quite some time but had received disquieting rumors about his failing health.

Although he was impeded by a lack of rivets, Marlow spent months supervising repairs to the antiquated river steamer. He also overheard a conversation that revealed that the district manager was Kurtz's implacable enemy, who hoped that the climate would do away with his rival. The steamer was finally ready for use, and Marlow, along with the district manager, sailed to visit Kurtz at the inner station far up the river. The journey was difficult and perilous; the water was shallow; there were frequent fogs. Just as they arrived within a few miles of Kurtz's station, natives attacked the vessel with spears and arrows. Marlow's helmsman, a faithful native, was killed by a long spear when he leaned from his window to fire at the savages. Marlow finally blew the steamboat whistle, and the sound frightened the natives away. The district manager was sure that Kurtz had lost control over the natives. When they docked, they met an enthusiastic Russian traveler who told them that Kurtz was gravely ill.

While the district manager visited Kurtz, the Russian told Marlow that the sick man had become corrupted by the very natives he had hoped to enlighten. He still had power over the natives, but instead of his changing them, they had debased him into an atavistic savage. Kurtz attended native rituals, had killed frequently in order to get ivory, and had hung heads as decorations outside his hut. Later Marlow met Kurtz and found that the man had, indeed, been corrupted by the evil at the center of experience. Marlow learned from the Russian that Kurtz had ordered the natives to attack the steamer, thinking that, if they did so, the white men would run away and leave Kurtz to die among his fellow savages in the wilderness. Talking to Marlow, Kurtz showed his awareness of how uncivilized he had become and how his plans to educate the natives had been reversed. He gave Marlow a packet of letters for his fiancée in Belgium and the manuscript of an article, written sometime earlier, in which he urged efforts to educate the natives.

The district manager and Marlow took Kurtz, now on a stretcher, to the river steamer to take him back home. The district manager contended that the area was now ruined for collecting ivory. Full of despair and the realization that devouring evil was at the heart of everything, Kurtz died while the steamer was temporarily stopped for repairs.

Marlow returned to civilization. About a year later, he went to Belgium to see Kurtz's fiancée. She still thought of Kurtz as the splendid and powerful man who had gone to Africa with a mission, and she still believed in his goodness and power. When she asked Marlow what Kurtz's last words had been, Marlow lied and told her that Kurtz had asked for her at the end. In reality, Kurtz, who had seen all experience, had in his final words testified to the horror of it all. This horror was not something, Marlow felt, that civilized ladies could, or should, understand.

Critical Evaluation:

In one sense, *Heart of Darkness* is a compelling adventure tale of a journey into the heart of the Belgian Congo. The story presents attacks by the natives, descriptions of the jungle and the river, and characterizations of white men who, sometimes with ideals and sometimes simply for profit, invade the jungles to bring out ivory. The journey into the heart of the Congo, however, is also a symbolic journey into the darkness central to the heart and soul of humanity, a journey deep into primeval passion, superstition, and lust. Those who, like the district manager, undertake this journey simply to rob the natives of ivory, without any awareness of the importance of the central darkness, can survive. Similarly, Marlow, who is only an observer, never centrally involved, can survive to tell the tale; but those who, like Mr. Kurtz, are aware of the darkness, who hope with conscious intelligence and a humane concern for all humanity to bring light into the darkness, are doomed, are themselves swallowed up by the darkness and evil they had hoped to penetrate. Joseph Conrad manages to make his point, a realization of the evil at the center of human experience, without ever breaking the pattern of his narrative or losing the compelling atmospheric and psychological force of the tale. The wealth of natural symbols, the clear development of character, and the sheer fascination of the story make this a novella that has been frequently praised and frequently read ever since its publication in 1902. *Heart of Darkness* is, in style and insight, a masterpiece.

Christened Jósef Teodor Konrad Nałęcz Korzeniowski by his Polish parents, Joseph Conrad was able to write of the sea and sailing from firsthand knowledge. He left the cold climate of Poland early in his life to travel to the warmer regions of the Mediterranean, where he became a sailor. He began reading extensively and chose the sea as a central shaping metaphor for the ideas that were forming in his imagination. He traveled a great deal: to the West Indies, Latin America, Africa. Eventually, he settled in England and perfected (through the elaborate process of translating from Polish into French into English) a remarkably subtle yet powerful literary style.

Criticism of Conrad's work in general and *Heart of Darkness* in particular has been extensive and varied. Many critics concern themselves with Conrad's style; others focus on the biographical aspects of his fiction; some see the works as social commentaries; some are students of Conrad's explorations into human psychology; many are interested in the brooding, shadowy symbolism and philosophy that hovers over all the works. It is easy to see, therefore, that Conrad is a distinctively complex literary genius. E. M. Forster censured him as a vague and elusive writer who never quite clearly discloses the philosophy that lies behind his tales. Such a censure ignores Conrad's notion about the way some fiction can be handled. Partly as Conrad's mouthpiece, the narrator of *Heart of Darkness* states in the first few pages of the novel:

> The yarns of seamen have a direct simplicity, the whole meaning of which lies within the shell of a cracked nut. But Marlow was not typical (if his propensity to spin yarns be excepted), and to him the meaning of an episode was not inside like a kernel but outside, enveloping the tale which brought it out only as a glow brings out a haze, in the likeness of one of those misty halos that sometimes are made visible by the spectral illumination of moonshine.

The mention of the narrator brings up one of the most complex and intriguing features of *Heart of Darkness*: its carefully executed and elaborately conceived point of view. Readers can detect (if careful in their reading) that the novel is in truth two narratives, inexorably woven together by Conrad's masterful craftsmanship. The outer frame of the story—the immediate setting— involves the unnamed narrator who is apparently the only one on *The Nellie* who is profoundly affected by Marlow's tale, the inner story that is the bulk of the entire novella. Marlow narrates, and the others listen. The narrator's closing words show his feeling at the conclusion of Marlow's recounting of the events in the Congo:

> Marlow ceased, and sat apart, indistinct and silent, in the pose of a meditating Buddha. Nobody moved for a time. "We have lost the first of the ebb," said the Director suddenly. I raised my head. The offing was barred by a black bank of clouds, and the tranquil waterway leading to the uttermost ends of the earth flowed somber under an overcast sky—seemed to lead into the heart of an immense darkness.

Since Marlow's narrative is a tale devoted primarily to a journey to the mysterious "dark" continent (Africa), a superficial view of the tale is simply that it is essentially an elaborate story involving confrontation with exotic natives, treacherous dangers of the jungle, brutal savagery, and even cannibalism. Such a view, however, ignores larger meanings with which the work is implicitly concerned: namely, social and cultural implications; psychological workings of the cultivated European left to the uncivilized wilderness; and the richly colored fabric of symbolism that emerges slowly but inevitably from beneath the surface.

Heart of Darkness can also be examined for its social and cultural commentaries. It is fairly obvious that a perverted version of the "white man's burden" was the philosophy adopted by the ivory hunters at the Inner Station. Kurtz's "Exterminate the brutes!" shows the way a white man can exploit the helpless savage. The futile shelling from the gunboat into the jungle is also vividly portrayed as a useless, brutal, and absurd act perpetrated against a weaker culture than the one that nurtured Kurtz.

Here the psychological phenomena of Marlow's tale emerge. Kurtz, a man relieved of all social and civilized restraints, goes mad after committing himself to the total pursuit of evil and depravity. His observation "The horror! the horror!" suggests his final realization of the consequences of his life. Marlow also realizes this and is allowed (because he forces restraint upon himself) to draw back his foot from the precipice of madness. The experience leaves Marlow sober, disturbed, meditative, and obsessed with relating his story in much the same way Samuel Taylor Coleridge's Ancient Mariner must also relate his story.

On a symbolic level, the story is rich; a book could easily be written on this facet of the novel. An arbitrary mention of some of the major symbols must suffice here: the Congo River that reminded Marlow of a snake as it uncoiled into the darkness of Africa and furnished him with an uncontrollable "fascination of the abomination"; the symbolic journey into Marlow's own heart of darkness, revealing blindingly the evil of human nature and the human capacity for evil; the irony of the quest when the truth is revealed not in terms of light but in terms of darkness (the truth brings not light but rather total darkness). The entire symbolic character of the work is summarized at the end of Marlow's tale when he is forced to lie to Kurtz's intended spouse in order to preserve her illusion; the truth appears to Marlow as an inescapable darkness, and the novel ends with the narrator's own observation of darkness.

Heart of Darkness is one of literature's most somber fictions. It explores the fundamental questions about human nature: the capacity for ultimate evil; the necessity for restraint; the effect of isolation; and the necessity of relinquishing pride for one's own spiritual salvation. E. M. Forster's censure of Conrad may be correct in many ways, but it refuses to admit that through such philosophical ruminations Conrad allowed generations of readers to ponder humanity's heart of darkness.

"Critical Evaluation" by Wayne E. Haskin

Bibliography:

Beach, Joseph W. *The Twentieth-Century Novel: Studies in Technique.* New York: Century, 1932. Conrad's narrative style and his characterizations (especially of Kurtz) are discussed. How Conrad's life experiences are related to the plot is hypothesized.

Gillon, Adam. *Joseph Conrad.* Boston: Twayne, 1982. A book-length exploration of Conrad's style and how his technique evolved, especially regarding the narrator, Marlowe. There is also an analytical consideration of Kurtz.

Guerard, Albert J. *Conrad the Novelist.* New York: Atheneum, 1958. Examines some of the autobiographical elements of the work as well as Conrad's attitudes toward social and historical events of his time. Provides useful insights into Kurtz's character.

Hay, Eloise K. *The Political Novels of Joseph Conrad.* Chicago: University of Chicago Press, 1963. Presents the view that *Heart of Darkness* is not the masterpiece critical acclaim would suggest. Explores the social events and political climate of the time to show some of the influences on the plot and style.

Watt, Ian. "*Heart of Darkness.*" In *Conrad in the Nineteenth Century.* Berkeley: University of California Press, 1979. A discussion of sources and ideological perspectives relative to Kurtz and the Victorian era. A scholarly assessment in a readable style.

THE HEART OF MIDLOTHIAN

Type of work: Novel
Author: Sir Walter Scott (1771-1832)
Type of plot: Historical
Time of plot: Early eighteenth century
Locale: Scotland
First published: 1818

> *Principal characters:*
> DAVID DEANS, a dairyman
> JEANIE and
> EFFIE, his daughters
> REUBEN BUTLER, Jeanie's betrothed
> GEORDIE ROBERTSON (GEORGE STAUNTON), Effie's betrayer
> MEG MURDOCKSON, an evil woman
> THE DUKE OF ARGYLE, Jeanie's benefactor

The Story:

The first knowledge Jeanie Deans had that her sister Effie was in trouble came just a few moments before officers of justice arrived at the cottage to arrest Effie for child murder. They told Jeanie and her father, David Deans, that Effie had borne a male child illegitimately and had killed him or caused him to be killed soon after he was born. Effie admitted to the birth of the child but refused to name her seducer, and she denied that she had killed her baby, saying that she had fallen into a stupor and had recovered to find that the midwife who attended her had disposed of the child in some unknown fashion. In the face of the evidence, however, she was convicted of child murder and sentenced to be hanged. Jeanie might have saved her sister, for it was the law that if a prospective mother had told anyone of her condition she would not be responsible for her baby's death. Jeanie refused to lie, however, even to save her sister's life. Because Effie had not told anyone her terrible secret, there was no defense for her, and she was placed in the Tolbooth prison to await execution.

Another prisoner in the prison was Captain John Porteous, who was awaiting execution for firing into the crowd that was attending the hanging of a smuggler named Andrew Wilson. Wilson's accomplice, Geordie Robertson, had escaped, and the officers feared that Robertson might try to rescue Wilson. For that reason, Porteous and a company of soldiers had been sent to the scene of the execution to guard against a possible rescue. Porteous had fired into the crowd without provocation and had killed several people; when his execution was stayed for a few weeks, a mob headed by Robertson, who had disguised himself as a woman, broke into the prison, seized Porteous, and hanged him. Robertson thereupon became a hunted man.

Though she had refused to lie to save her sister, Jeanie Deans had not forsaken Effie. When she visited Effie in prison, she learned that Robertson was the father of her child. He had left her in the care of old Meg Murdockson, whom many considered to be a witch, and it must have been Meg who had killed or sold the baby. Meg's daughter Madge had long before been seduced by Robertson and had lost her mind for love of him; Meg had sworn revenge on any other woman Robertson might love. It was impossible, however, to prove the old woman's guilt or Effie's innocence, for Robertson had disappeared and Meg swore that she had seen Effie coming back from the river after drowning the baby.

Determined to save her sister, Jeanie decided to walk to London to seek a pardon from the king and queen. She told her plans to Reuben Butler, a minister to whom she had long been betrothed. Reuben was unable to marry her, for he had no position other than that of an assistant schoolmaster and his salary was too small to support a wife. Although he objected to Jeanie's plan, he helped her when he saw that she could not be swayed from her purpose. Reuben's grandfather had once given aid to an ancestor of the present duke of Argyle, and Reuben gave Jeanie a letter asking the duke's help in presenting Jeanie to the king and queen.

The journey to London was a long and dangerous one. Once Jeanie was captured by Meg Murdockson, who tried to kill her to prevent her saving Effie. Jeanie escaped from the old woman, however, and sought refuge in the home of the Reverend Mr. Staunton. There she met the minister's son, George Staunton, and learned from him that he was Geordie Robertson, her sister's betrayer. He admitted his responsibility to Effie, telling Jeanie that he had planned and executed the Porteous incident in order to rescue Effie from the prison, but that she had refused to leave with him. He had tried many other schemes to save her, including an attempt to force a confession from Meg that she had taken the baby, but everything had failed. He told Jeanie that he had been on his way to give himself up in exchange for Effie's release when he injured himself falling from his horse. He told Jeanie to bargain with the duke of Argyle, and as a last resort to offer to lead the authorities to Robertson in exchange for Effie's pardon. Geordie promised not to leave his father's house until Effie had been freed.

Jeanie at last reached London and presented herself to the duke of Argyle with Reuben's letter. The duke, impressed with Jeanie's sincerity and simplicity, arranged for an audience with the queen. She too believed Jeanie's story of Effie's misfortune. Through her efforts, the king pardoned Effie with the stipulation that she leave Scotland for fourteen years. Jeanie secured the pardon without revealing George Staunton's secret. The duke was so moved by Jeanie's goodness and honesty that he made her father the master of an experimental farm on one of his estates in Scotland, and he made Reuben the minister of the church. Jeanie's heart was overflowing with joy until she learned that Effie had eloped with her lover just three nights after her release from prison. No one knew where they were, as the outlaw's life was in constant danger because of his part in the Porteous hanging.

Reuben and Jeanie were married and were blessed with three fine children. They prospered in their new life, and Jeanie's only sorrow was her sister's marriage to George Staunton. She kept Effie's secret, however, telling no one that George was actually Robertson. After several years, George and Effie returned to London. George had inherited a title from his uncle, and as Sir George and Lady Staunton, they were received in court society. Effie wrote secretly to Jeanie and sent her large sums of money, which Jeanie put away without telling her husband about them. She could not reveal Effie's secret, even to him.

By chance, Jeanie found a paper containing the last confession of Meg Murdockson, who had been hanged as a witch. In it, Meg confessed that she had stolen Effie's baby and had given him to an outlaw. Jeanie sent this information to Effie in London, and before long Effie, as Lady Staunton, paid Jeanie a visit. Effie had used a pretext of ill health to go to Scotland while her husband, acting on the information in Meg's letter, tried to trace the whereabouts of their son. Although it was dangerous for George to be in Scotland where he might be recognized as Geordie Robertson, he followed every clue given in Meg's confession. In Edinburgh, he met Reuben Butler, who was there on business, and secured an invitation to accompany Reuben back to the manse. Unaware of George's real identity, Reuben was happy to receive the duke of Argyle's friend. Reuben did not know at the time that Effie was also a guest in his home.

As Reuben and George walked toward the manse, they passed through a thicket where they were attacked by outlaws. One, a young fellow, ran his sword through George and killed him. It was not until Reuben had heard the whole story of the Stauntons from Jeanie that he searched George's pockets and found information there that proved beyond doubt that the young outlaw who had killed George was his own son. Because Effie was grief-stricken by George's death, Jeanie and Reuben thought it useless to add to her sorrow by revealing the identity of his assailant. Reuben later traced the boy to America, where the young man continued his life of crime until he was captured and probably killed by Indians.

Effie stayed with Reuben and Jeanie for more than a year. Then she went back to London and the brilliant society she had known there. No one but Jeanie and Reuben ever knew the secret of Effie and George. After ten years, Effie retired to a convent on the Continent, where she spent her remaining years grieving for her husband and the son she had never known. Reuben and Jeanie Butler, who had been so unavoidably involved in sordidness and crime, lived out their lives happily and carried their secret with them to the grave.

Critical Evaluation:

Many critics have considered *The Heart of Midlothian* to be Sir Walter Scott's best novel. The reasons for its success are different from those of most of the Waverley series. The novel does not have the usual gothic props of ruined abbeys, specters, prophesying old hags, and lonely windswept castles. Only one scene, where Jeanie Deans meets George Staunton at moonrise in Nicol Muschat's cairn, is reminiscent of the wild, picturesque settings so frequent in Scott's fiction.

The plot of this novel is based on authentic historical events. The Porteous Riot of 1736 in Edinburgh's famous Old Tolbooth prison, which was commonly called "the heart of Midlothian," sets the action on its course. The story, however, is not one of social history or justice, nor is it a study of Scottish Presbyterianism. Long debates on both of these issues take up significant portions of the work, but Scott comes to no clear conclusions. It is not these issues that provide the unifying force that holds the story together.

The binding element is, instead, the novel's strong moral theme. Most of the main protagonists are caught in dilemmas of conscience. Jeanie Deans must decide between telling a lie to save her sister Effie's life or speaking the truth and thereby condemning her to execution. Effie herself has the choice of attempting to live virtuously as she was taught or being faithful to her dissipated, criminal lover. Their father, stern David Deans, must decide whether to adhere to his Presbyterian principles or to come to terms with the human condition and forgive Effie. George Staunton, alias Robertson, is forced either to follow his wild inclinations and stay with his desperate associates or to reform and assume responsibilities of position and inheritance; he must also confront his obligation to marry Effie, whom he has wronged. These varied dilemmas of conscience constitute the texture of the novel.

The heroine is the one strong character in the novel, but she differs strikingly from the usual Waverley heroine, who tends to be tall, beautiful, exceedingly well bred, romantic and, of course, wealthy. Jeanie Deans is unusual for being a peasant heroine, plain in appearance, not trained in social deportment, and lacking a romantic, gothic background. The moral seriousness of *The Heart of Midlothian* and the fact that Scott drew his heroine from the lower classes not only helped make the novel popular but also gave it a coherence and unity unusual in his fiction.

In most of Scott's novels, minor characters are largely drawn from Scottish rural life and humble occupations and are more real than upper-class figures. When dealing with them, Scott has a more energetic and colorful style. Critics often remark that the strength of his work lies in such characters as Caleb Balderstone of *The Bride of Lammermoor* (1819), Edie Ochiltree and Maggie Mucklebackit of *The Antiquary* (1816), and Callum Beg and Widow Flockhart of *Waverly* (1814). Scott reproduces their speech faithfully and with obvious relish.

In *The Heart of Midlothian*, however, although he still opposes the upper-class culture with that of the lower and exploits resulting tensions, he elevates a dairyman's daughter to the status of heroine. Furthermore, in spite of the unyielding virtue of her character and the contrived situation in which she becomes involved, he not only makes her believable but also enlists the sympathies of the reader on her side. She has common sense, and the rough, matter-of-fact elements in her daily life leave no doubt that she will conquer all adverse forces to triumph in Effie's cause. The law of retribution is at work here as in Scott's other novels, but Providence has a fresh, indefatigable agent in Jeanie. It is interesting that she was Scott's own favorite heroine.

Several scenes in *The Heart of Midlothian* are particularly believable, among them the Porteous Riot that opens the novel. Scott handles realistically the mob's capture of Tolbooth prison and the lynching of Captain Porteous. Another well-constructed, and for that reason moving, scene is that of Effie's trial. In such sections, Scott tightens his control over character interaction and uses great economy of language.

If some portions of the novel—Jennie's journey to London, for example, and the concluding section, which is almost an epilogue—seem protracted and rather unexciting, the story as a whole is well-knit and more logical than much of Scott's other fiction. Scott considered the function of the novel to furnish "solace from the toils of ordinary life by an excursion into the regions of imagination," and ordinarily he was indifferent to technique, concentrating, instead, on subject matter. He stressed factual accuracy but felt that too much care in composition might destroy what he termed "abundant spontaneity." Following his own dicta, he wrote rapidly with disregard for planning and revision. He improvised with careless haste, and his novels often suffer from poor style and construction. Critics have repeatedly faulted his work for improper motivation and lack of organic unity.

By contrast, *The Heart of Midlothian* does not give the impression that the author wrote at his usual breakneck speed, casually assembling scenes and characters together without fore-thought. Scott furnishes motivation more carefully, uses more consistent characterization, and logically carries through the dilemmas of conscience. Moreover, in dispensing with extraneous supernatural escapades, Scott concentrates on the sincerity and integrity of his lower-class protagonists to effect a democratic realism new in the historical English novel, a genre he himself had invented.

"Critical Evaluation" by Muriel B. Ingham

Bibliography:
Criscuola, Margaret M. "The Porteous Mob: Fact and Truth in *The Heart of Midlothian*." *English Language Notes* 22, no. 1 (September, 1984): 43-50. Concludes that the reality underlying this historical episode illuminates Scott's use of history and the ways in which he transformed fact into fiction.
Davis, Jana. "Sir Walter Scott's *The Heart of Midlothian* and Scottish Common-Sense Moral-ity." *Mosaic* 21 (Fall, 1988): 55-63. Common sense, morality, and Calvinism interact in the novel, as characters must choose between the law, their religion, and what their moral sense tells them is right.
Kerr, James. "Scott's Fable of Regeneration: *The Heart of Midlothian*." *English Literary History* 53, no. 4 (Winter, 1986): 801-820. Sees the novel as a political admonition, and

Jeanie Deans as a model of virtue. Deals more fully with the last quarter of the novel than many other commentaries do.

Millgate, Jane. "Scott and the Law: *The Heart of Midlothian.*" In *Rough Justice: Essays on Crime in Literature*, edited by M. L. Friedland. Toronto: University of Toronto Press, 1991. Investigates legal aspects of the plot. Scott was a lawyer, a sheriff, and sometimes a judge. Millgate asserts that no other novelist deals more often with the effects of law on human destiny than does Scott.

Thompson, Jon. "Sir Walter Scott and Madge Wildfire: Strategies of Containment in *The Heart of Midlothian.*" *Literature and History* 13 (Autumn, 1987): 188-199. Calls attention to the importance of a less obvious character and Scott's treatment of her. Madge is insane throughout but still affects the other characters.

THE HEART OF THE MATTER

Type of work: Novel
Author: Graham Greene (1904-1991)
Type of plot: Psychological realism
Time of plot: World War II
Locale: British West Africa
First published: 1948

Principal characters:
> MAJOR SCOBIE, a police chief in one of the colony's districts
> MRS. SCOBIE, his wife
> MRS. ROLT, a shipwreck victim and Scobie's mistress
> WILSON, a counterintelligence agent
> YUSEF, a Syrian merchant

The Story:

Major Scobie was chief of police in a British West African district. For fifteen years, he had built up a reputation for honesty. Then he learned that, in spite of his labors, he was to be passed over for the district commissionership in favor of a younger man. Those fifteen long years now seemed to him to have been too long and filled with too much work. Worse than his own disappointment was the disappointment of his wife. Mrs. Scobie needed the encouragement that a rise in official position would have given her to compensate for the loss of her only child some years before and her unpopularity among the official families of the district.

A love for literature, especially poetry, had set Mrs. Scobie apart from the other officials and their wives. Once the difference was discerned, the other Britishers distrusted and disliked her. They even pitied the man whom she had married. Nor were the Scobies much happier than people imagined them to be. Mrs. Scobie hated the life she led, and her husband disliked having to make her face it realistically; both drank. When she found he was not to be made district commissioner, she insisted that he send her to the Cape Colony for a holiday, even though German submarines were torpedoing many vessels at the time.

Scobie did not have the money to pay the expenses of the trip. For a previous excursion of hers from the colony, he had already given up part of his life insurance. After trying unsuccessfully to borrow the money from the banks, he went to Yusef, a Syrian merchant, who agreed to lend him the money at four percent interest. Scobie knew that any dealings he had with Yusef would place him under a cloud, for the British officials knew only too well that many of the Syrian's doings were illegal, including the shipment of industrial diamonds to the Nazis. Pressed by his wife's apparent need to escape the boredom of the rainy season in the coast colony, Scobie finally took the chance that he could keep clear of Yusef's entanglements, even though he knew that the Syrian hated him for the reputation of integrity he had built up during the past fifteen years.

To add to Scobie's difficulties, he learned that Wilson, a man supposedly sent out on a clerkship with a trading company, was actually an undercover agent working for the government on the problem of diamond smuggling. First, Scobie had no official information about Wilson's true activities; second, Wilson had fallen in love with Scobie's wife; and, third, Mrs. Scobie had bloodied Wilson's nose for him and permitted her husband to see her admirer crying. Any one of the counts would have made Scobie uneasy; all three in combination made him painfully aware that Wilson could only hate him, as Wilson actually did.

Shortly after his wife's departure, a series of events began to break down Major Scobie's trust in his own honesty and the reputation he had built up for himself. When a Portuguese liner was searched on its arrival in port, Scobie found a suspicious letter in the captain's cabin. Instead of turning in the letter, he burned it—after the captain had assured him that the letter was only a personal message to his daughter in Germany. A few weeks later, Yusef began to be very friendly toward Scobie. Gossip reported that Scobie had met and talked with the Syrian on several occasions, in addition to having borrowed money from the suspected smuggler.

One day, word came that the French had rescued the crew and passengers of a torpedoed British vessel. Scobie was with the party who met the rescued people at the border between the French and British colonies. Among the victims was a young bride of only a few months whose husband had been killed in the war. While she recuperated from her exposure in a lifeboat and then waited for a ship to return her to England, she and Scobie fell in love. For a time, they were extremely careful of their conduct, until one day Mrs. Rolt, the rescued woman, belittled Scobie because of his caution. To prove his daring as well as his love, Scobie sent her a letter that was intercepted by Yusef's agents. In payment for return of the letter, Scobie was forced to help Yusef smuggle some gems from the colony. Wilson, Scobie's enemy, suspected the smuggling done by Scobie, but he could prove nothing.

Mrs. Rolt pleaded with Scobie to show his love by divorcing his wife and marrying her. Scobie, a Roman Catholic, tried to convince her that his faith and his conscience would not permit him to do so. To complicate matters, Mrs. Scobie cabled that she was already on board ship on her way back home from Cape Town. Scobie did not know which way to turn. On her return, Mrs. Scobie nagged him to take communion with her. Unable to receive absolution because he refused to promise to give up adultery, Scobie took the sacrament of communion anyway, rather than admit to his wife what had happened. He realized that according to his faith he was damning his soul.

The worry over his sins, his uneasiness about his job, the problem of Yusef, a murder that Yusef had had committed for him, and the nagging of both his wife and Mrs. Rolt—all these made Scobie's mind a turmoil. He did not know which way to turn; for the church, a haven for many, was forbidden to him because of his sins and his temperament.

In searching for a way out of his predicament, Scobie remembered what he had been told by a doctor shortly after an official investigation of a suicide. The doctor had told Scobie that the best way to commit suicide was to feign angina and then take an overdose of evipan, a drug prescribed for angina. Scobie carefully made plans to take his life in that way because he wanted his wife to have his insurance money for her support after she returned to England. After studying the symptoms of angina, Scobie went to a doctor, who diagnosed Scobie's trouble from the symptoms he related. Scobie knew that his pretended heart condition would soon be common knowledge in the colony. Ironically, Scobie was told that he had been reconsidered for the commissionership of the colony but that he could not be given the post because of his illness. The news made little difference to Scobie, for he had already made up his mind to commit suicide.

To make his death appear convincing, he filled his diary with entries tracing the progress of his heart condition. One evening, he took his overdose of evipan, his only solution to difficulties that had become more than he could bear. He died, and only one or two people even suspected the truth. One of these was Mrs. Scobie, who complained to the priest after he had refused to give Scobie absolution. The priest, knowing of Scobie's virtues as well as his sins, cried out to her that no one could call Scobie wicked or damned, for no one knew God's mercy.

Critical Evaluation:

The fears and hopes, friendships and petty rivalries, loves and hates of Europeans immured in a colony on the African coast afforded Graham Greene, who actually worked in such a place during World War II, the material for this novel. The book continues the study of British people begun in earlier work by Greene. Major Scobie, like Arthur Rowe in *The Ministry of Fear* (1943), is a relatively friendless man—a type that seems to have fascination for the author. Like Rowe, in the earlier novel, Major Scobie is placed in a position where he can choose between life or death. The high point in both novels is that at which the choice is made. Beyond the immediate story, however, there are larger implications. *The Heart of the Matter*, written by one of the leading Catholic novelists of the day, is actually a religious story, a fable of the conflict between good and evil. It is a drama of the human soul in midpassage toward heaven or hell.

The Heart of the Matter is an intelligent, perceptive, and humane tour de force on the spiritual capacities and moral dilemmas of Henry Scobie, husband, chief of police, and Catholic. Each of these roles contributes something to the complications of Scobie's situation. While accepting a stern Roman Catholic framework, Greene challenges readers to find fault with a man who goes beyond dishonesty and infidelity to sacrilege and suicide. As Scobie degenerates, Greene dares readers, despite the evidence, to cast the first stone by involving their sympathies and appealing to a higher law of mercy that is beyond the human capacity to understand or forgive.

The hothouse setting in a British colony on the West African coast in the early 1940's is interesting in its own right. It affords opportunity for commentary on the uncertainties of the period and the limitations of the colonial mentality. Nevertheless, the setting is not the heart of the matter. Scobie's problems as a human being are always the central focus of the novel, and they spring from the confluence of his circumstances, his roles, and his character. Scobie is a perpetual outsider to the web of colonial life. Too self-contained, too reflective, too honest with himself and others, he is not able to assume the roles and act out the rituals that will bring him local success. Circumstances contribute to the evolution of the central conflict, but the maritime warfare and diamond smuggling are, for Scobie, rather occasions for sin than sin itself. They provide a context in which Scobie's character agonizes and falters as he takes on his major roles. In each of these roles, his character shines through, and it may be his ultimate transcendence that his strength of character maintains a stable core as its periphery comes into conflict with corrupting circumstances.

Scobie's first role is as husband to a wife who, to Scobie's credit, is far more irritating to readers than to him. It is through Scobie's patience and understanding that readers achieve any degree of sympathy for the human burden his wife bears. In the related role of father of a deceased daughter, readers see more of Scobie's, and his wife's, suffering. However, he understands her while she lacks the sensitivity, despite her love for poetry, to reciprocate. Paradoxically, Scobie's honesty about his own limitations and compassion for the plight of others leads to a kind of hubris, which manifests itself first in his attempts to make his wife happy. It is this same desire to fix up the world, to provide totally for another's security and happiness, that embroils him in his later relationship with the vulnerable Mrs. Rolt and occasions his infidelity.

In his role as chief of police, Scobie has the sort of reputation for impeccable honesty and fairness that, combined with a lack of ambition, is likely to stimulate the suspicion, gossip, and animosity of his small-minded peers. It is one of the novel's many fine ironies that Scobie's honesty is compromised by the compassion he feels for his wife's plight, for it is his perhaps excessive and blameworthy, even selfish, desire to free her that leads him to borrow money and put himself in the hands of Yusef. Indeed, it may ultimately be a desire to free himself, but it also lays him open to the less publicly dangerous but morally serious dishonesty with Mrs. Rolt. His desire, whether it is to please his wife or free himself, leads to a compromise of his office. His desire to provide insulation against suffering, whether it is compassionate or selfish, leads to a compromise of his marriage.

Scobie does not wish anything but to be at peace, and he hopes that if he can fix everything for his wife and thereby free himself of her, he can find peace. Subsequently, Scobie's compassion for Mrs. Rolt turns into a love that brings his desire to repair other lives to an impasse when he wins Mrs. Rolt and his wife decides to return. In the chain of consequences and of flawed moral decisions, his attempt to comfort Mrs. Rolt by a reckless declaration of love further leads to complicity in murder. Scobie's actions are, thus far, morally imperfect but entangled in mixed emotions and motives. It is in his role as Catholic that he commits the ultimate transgressions against God and the divine power of forgiveness.

Violation of public trust and infidelity can be pardoned or extenuated, but Scobie, as a Catholic, proceeds to the institutionally "unforgivable" sins. His love for Mrs. Rolt makes a valid confession impossible, because his selfishness and compassion make it impossible for him to promise to leave her. His concern for his wife forces him to receive Communion without absolution for his sin so that he will not betray himself to her and thus wound her. In so doing, he does violence to Christ in the Eucharist. Although well aware that Christ, for love of man, makes himself vulnerable to abuse by his availability in the sacrament, Scobie allows his human motives to lead him to desecrate that trust by receiving Christ while in a state of sin. Having sacrificed Christ to selfishness and human compassion, Scobie is left totally desolate; unable to live with these conflicts, he commits the sin that theoretically puts him beyond God's mercy: suicide.

Nevertheless, readers do not condemn Scobie. It is not that he is an automaton, a victim of circumstance. To excuse him on those grounds would trivialize the theology of the novel: "To understand all is to forgive all." Rather, readers clearly recognize his progressive sins but are led by Greene to participate in the mystery of divine mercy by extending compassion without selfishness. Raised to the divine level, the compassion that contributed to Scobie's corruption may also be his only hope of salvation.

"Critical Evaluation" by Edward E. Foster

Bibliography:
Bloom, Harold, ed. *Graham Greene*. New York: Chelsea House, 1987. In "The Trilogy," R. W. B. Lewis discusses the uneven development of style and vigor in Greene's early fiction, comparing *The Heart of the Matter* to *Brighton Rock* (1938) and *The Power and the Glory* (1940). *The Heart of the Matter* is the most traditional of the novels and the best example of Greene's blending of psychology and theology. Chronology and bibliography.
Boardman, Gwenn R. *Graham Greene: The Aesthetics of Exploration*. Gainesville: University of Florida Press, 1971. Chapter 4 discusses Greene's comments on the novel, its exploration of Catholicism, and its treatment of love. Bibliography.
DeVitis, A. A. *Graham Greene*. Boston: Twayne, 1986. Chapter 4 summarizes the critical controversy over the novel's religious issues, Greene's views of his fiction, the role of pride in the character of Scobie, the novel's setting, and Scobie's struggle with himself, with God, and with the Catholic church. Chronology, notes, and bibliography.
Evans, Robert O., ed. *Graham Greene: Some Critical Considerations*. Lexington: University of Kentucky Press, 1967. In "The Heart of the Novel: The Turning Point in *The Heart of the*

Matter," Kai Laitnen focuses on chapter 1 of book 2, where Scobie arrives to receive the shipwrecked people from the French colonial area, where the central threads of the novel intersect. Notes and bibliography.

O'Prey, Paul. *A Reader's Guide to Graham Greene*. New York: Thames and Hudson, 1988. Chapter 5 emphasizes the religious aspects of the novel, exploring the way that religion provides the framework for the characters and the author. Examines Greene's handling of the rigidity of Catholic doctrine, the novel's moral and dogmatic paradoxes, and its vision of God. Minor characters and the setting are also discussed. Bibliography.

HEARTBREAK HOUSE
A Fantasia in the Russian Manner on English Themes

Type of work: Drama
Author: George Bernard Shaw (1856-1950)
Type of plot: Play of ideas
Time of plot: 1913
Locale: Sussex, England
First published: 1919; first performed, 1920

> *Principal characters:*
> CAPTAIN SHOTOVER, an English eccentric and visionary
> LADY ARIADNE UTTERWORD and
> MRS. HESIONE HUSHABYE, his daughters
> HECTOR HUSHABYE, Hesione's husband
> ELLIE DUNN, a guest in Captain Shotover's house
> MAZZINI DUNN, her father
> BOSS MANGAN, an industrialist
> RANDALL UTTERWORD, Lady Ariadne's brother-in-law
> NURSE GUINNESS, a servant
> BILLY DUNN, an ex-pirate and burglar

The Story:

Young and pretty Ellie Dunn was the first of many guests to arrive at the home in Sussex, England, of Captain Shotover. Ellie, who had been invited by Mrs. Hushabye, Captain Shotover's eldest daughter, eventually renamed the home Heartbreak House because of all the disappointments she and others experienced there that day.

When Ellie arrived at the house, there was no one to greet her, and she sat reading William Shakespeare until she fell asleep. The elderly servant, Nurse Guinness, finally discovered Ellie just before the arrival of another visitor, Shotover's younger daughter, Lady Utterword, who was returning home after having been away from England for twenty-three years.

Mrs. Hushabye had invited Ellie, her father Mazzini Dunn, and Ellie's fiancée Boss Mangan to Captain Shotover's house because she wanted to persuade Ellie not to marry Mangan, a millionaire industrialist who had befriended Ellie's father. Mangan had given Dunn money to begin a business that failed after two years, after which Mangan bought the business, which then thrived, and gave Dunn a job managing it. Mrs. Hushabye wanted Ellie to marry someone she loved rather than someone to whom her father owed a debt.

In a conversation with Mrs. Hushabye, Ellie revealed that she had a secret passion for a mysterious man she had just met, a romantic adventurer named Marcus Darnley. When Mrs. Hushabye's husband, Hector, entered the room, Ellie discovered that Marcus Darnley was a name Hector had assumed as he told extravagant stories to impress her. Ellie was heartbroken and angry at her gullibility. Mrs. Hushabye told her that heartbreak was just life's way of educating her.

Boss Mangan finally made his appearance, and the process of his heartbreak began when Captain Shotover predicted that Mrs. Hushabye would see to it that Mangan did not marry Ellie. The next visitor to arrive was Randall Utterword, Lady Utterword's brother-in-law. Randall had invited himself after hearing from his brother that Lady Utterword was staying at Shotover's.

When Hector met Lady Utterword, he immediately fell in love with her, initiating the process of his heartbreak.

After dinner, in conversation with Ellie, Mangan revealed that he had ruined Ellie's father intentionally: He had given him money to start up a business, knowing Mazzini Dunn would fail and that this was a cost-efficient way to take over a new enterprise. Ellie declared that she was still willing to marry Mangan (even though Mangan was in love with Mrs. Hushabye and she herself was in love with Hector), because she would be marrying Mangan for his money. Ellie warned Mangan that if he backed out of their agreement, she would see to it that Mangan never saw Mrs. Hushabye again. Mangan collapsed into a chair and Ellie massaged his temples until Mangan fell into a deep, hypnotic sleep. While he rested in a trance, Mrs. Hushabye, Mazzini Dunn, and Ellie discussed Mangan, who heard every word of their conversations.

Suddenly, a pistol shot was heard upstairs, and Mazzini and Hector entered with a burglar who had been trying to steal Mrs. Hushabye's diamonds. Captain Shotover revealed that the burglar was a pirate named Billy Dunn, no relation to Mazzini and Ellie, who had once stolen ship's stores from Captain Shotover. Billy admitted that he only posed as a burglar in the houses of the wealthy, using his capture as a way of extorting money that the wealthy were willing to pay to avoid having their names dragged into the papers. It was revealed that Billy had formerly been married to Nurse Guinness. Ellie spoke privately with Captain Shotover, telling him that she would rather marry him. After Ellie and Shotover left for the kitchen, Hector and Randall talked of their passion for Lady Utterword, who then entered. Hector and Randall vied for her attention, and it was clear that she had broken both of their hearts.

That evening, everyone was relaxing in the garden when Lady Utterword offered the observation that what Shotover's house lacked was stables and horses. Stables, she claimed, were the real center of a proper household—"the people who hunt are the right people and the people who don't are the wrong ones." Then, in front of Mangan, the conversation turned to whether Ellie should marry him for his money. Mangan confessed that he actually had very little money, that he owned nothing and simply ran things for other investors. At that, Ellie announced that she would not marry Mangan and had never intended to marry him, that she had only wanted to feel her strength over him. She announced that she had that evening married Captain Shotover.

A distant explosion was heard and the house lights were put out. Nurse Guinness ran in to explain that the police had ordered the lights to be extinguished because planes were approaching in a bombing raid and that everyone was supposed to go down to the cellar. Most of them refused to take shelter, and Hector turned on all the lights in the house, making it a perfect target for the bombers. Billy Dunn and Mangan ran to a nearby gravel pit to hide in a cave as the planes drew closer, not knowing that Captain Shotover had stored dynamite there. Mrs. Hushabye and Ellie found the sound of the planes and the bombs as exciting as a Beethoven symphony, and Lady Utterword urged Randall to play his flute to show he was not afraid. It appeared that Mangan and Billy Dunn would survive the bombing raid and that the others would die because they had refused to go to the cellar, but when the final and most terrific explosion came it was a direct hit on the dynamite cache. Mangan and Billy Dunn were killed and everyone else survived. With that the planes disappeared and the danger was over. Ellie was disappointed and Hector disgusted because their world had become dull again. Mrs. Hushabye exclaimed that the experience had been glorious and expressed her hope that the planes would come again the following night. Ellie, radiant at the prospect, added her hope for more excitement.

"The Story" by Terry Nienhuis

Critical Evaluation:

Heartbreak House has always held an equivocal place in the Shavian canon. Its admirers—and they are many—bracket it with George Bernard Shaw's best, beside such acknowledged masterpieces as *Man and Superman* (1903) and *Saint Joan* (1923). Severer critics see it as an unsuccessful attempt to create a mood of Chekhovian melancholy and fatalism in a framework of political allegory and social satire, a mixture of comedy, tragedy, dialectic, and prophecy that never quite coalesces into unity of theme or structure.

Shaw himself was as much to blame as anyone for some of the misconceptions regarding this play. Always ready, even eager, to instruct his public, in this instance he maintained an attitude of reticence toward his work and appeared hesitant to let it pass out of his hands. Although part of it had been written as early as 1913, and it was in its final form by 1916, the play was not published until three years later and not performed until a year after that. Even then Shaw apparently preferred to let his work speak for itself and without his mediation, for when asked on one occasion to interpret some of the lines he answered brusquely that he was merely the author and therefore could not be expected to know. Perhaps he was still smarting from the abuse he had received following the publication of his pamphlet, *Common Sense About the War* (1915), which was read by the jingoistic wartime public as a piece of pacifist propaganda. This could explain his reluctance to present his most sweeping indictment of society as being unable and unwilling to bring its moral judgments and political convictions into balance with its potential of destruction. War, Shaw seems to say, is no longer the trade of the professional soldier or the recreation of the feudal elite; all of humankind is now involved in the common catastrophe, and society must perish if it cannot realize its possibilities for good as opposed to its capacities for destruction.

Heartbreak House presents almost the whole range of Shaw's thought, and few of his plays are more representative or more inclusive in the themes and motifs touched upon if not explored, which include war, love, society, education, religion, politics, and science. The only element lacking is the Shavian principle of the Life Force. A drama of ideas, the work looks back to the earlier plays and anticipates *Saint Joan* and *The Apple Cart* (1929). As comment on upper-class life it continues and brings to a climax the themes Shaw presents in *Getting Married* (1908) and *Misalliance* (1910). Shaw himself is present in his various manifestations, as the recorder of that verbal interplay which in the Shavian drama often takes the place of conflict, as the playwright of ideas, as the master of comedy, as the maker of epigrams, and as the teacher, the critic, the philosopher, the parodist, the fabulist, and the poet.

A clue to the meaning of the play is provided in the subtitle: "A Fantasia in the Russian Manner on English Themes." Shaw had been studying the work of Anton Chekhov and seeing productions of his plays in London. In at least three, *The Cherry Orchard* (1904), *The Seagull* (1896), and *Uncle Vanya* (1897), he saw exempla of the theme he himself had in mind: the disintegration of a society from within and its final collapse in the face of forces it had previously ignored or denied. Shaw may have begun his play with a similarity of tone in mind—the atmosphere, he said, was the initial impulse—but he ends with effects quite different from those we find in Chekhov. The difference is partly one of temperament, the Russian power of enclosing the poetry of all experience in the single instance, and it is partly the fact that the haunted landscapes of Chekhov's world have little in common with those aspects of British middle- and upper-class life that Shaw observed so shrewdly. Shaw's people exist only in the light of his ethical and political values; Chekhov's exist within the world of their own moral and spiritual blight. The sound of the axe echoing through the twilight at the end of *The Cherry Orchard* is more portentous than the bombs that rain fire and death from the sky at the close of *Heartbreak House*.

The essential differences between these two plays are not altogether to Shaw's disadvantage, for *Heartbreak House*, although it lacks the larger expressiveness of Chekhov's theater, exhibits all the intellectual vigor and wild poetry, the clash of ideas and personalities, of disquisitory drama at its best. A thesis play, it is admitted as such in Shaw's preface, where he states that Heartbreak House is more than a title: it is the Europe—or England—of culture and leisure in the period before World War I. As the alternative to Heartbreak House he sees only Horseback Hall, peopled by those who have made sport a cult. In either case, there is no true leadership in this world of cross-purposes, futile desires, and idle talk. The people have courage of a sort, but they are able to do little more than clench their fists in gestures of defiance as the bombs drop from the sky.

The setting of the play is the Sussex home, built like a ship, of Captain Shotover, an eighty-eight-year-old eccentric and retired sea captain credited by hearsay with selling his soul to the devil in Zanzibar and with marriage to a black witch in the West Indies. Cranky, realistic, fantastically wise, he drinks three bottles of rum a day, strives to attain the seventh degree of concentration, and spends his time tinkering with death-dealing inventions. To Ellie Dunn, a young singer arriving as the guest of the captain's daughter Mrs. Hesione Hushabye, the atmosphere of the house seems as puzzling and unpredictable as its owner. No one bothers to greet visitors; members of the family are treated like strangers; strangers are welcomed like old friends. An elderly servant calls everyone ducky. When Lady Ariadne Utterword returns for a visit after twenty-three years in the Colonies with Sir Hastings Utterword, her empire-building husband, neither her father nor her sister recognizes her. The captain persists in confusing Mazzini Dunn, Ellie's father, with a rascally ex-pirate who had robbed him many years before. Arriving unexpectedly, Boss Mangan, the millionaire industrialist whom Ellie is to marry, is put to work in the captain's garden.

From this opening scene of innocent, seemingly irresponsible, comedy the play proceeds to more serious business, and by the end of the first act the characters have assumed their allegorical identities. Lady Ariadne is Empire, the prestige of foreign rule. Hesione Hushabye is Domesticity, the power of woman's love and authority at home. Hector, her husband, is Heroism, a man capable of brave deeds but so tamed by feminine influence that his only escape is through romantic daydreams and Munchausen-like tales of derring-do. Mazzini Dunn is the nineteenth-century Liberal, a believer in progress but too sentimental to be an intellectual force. He has consequently become the tool of Boss Mangan, a figure of capitalistic Exploitation. Randall Utterword, Lady Ariadne's brother-in-law, is Pride, a Foreign Office official symbolically in love with his sister-in-law and filled with snobbish regard for caste. Looming over these figures is old Captain Shotover, the embodiment of Old England and its genius, no longer the captain of the great Ship of State but the half-cracked, drunken skipper of a house built like a ship, suggesting his own and his country's maritime history. Captain Shotover is the triumph of the play. In spite of his allegorical significance, he is always superbly himself, larger than life and yet lifelike, re-living his past and creating his future in terms of his own fantastic logic.

The people in the play come together in twos and threes to speak in their own as well as in their allegorical characters. Childlike resentments, old grievances, brooding frustrations, impossible dreams, and unexpected disillusionments break through their masks in the heavily charged atmosphere that the play generates, but all this sound and fury leads nowhere. *Heartbreak House* is idleness dramatized, impotence of mind and will translated into speech and gesture. Ultimately, all criticism of *Heartbreak House* reduces itself to a single issue: Can comedy, even brilliantly presented, sustain a theme of tragic significance? As Shaw himself declared, he was only the writer. It is the readers and the playgoers who must answer this question.

Bibliography:
Berst, Charles A. *"Heartbreak House:* Shavian Expressionism." In *Bernard Shaw and the Art of Drama.* Urbana: University of Illinois Press, 1973. An unusual but very convincing interpretation of the play, which emphasizes its dreamlike atmosphere. Concludes that Shaw owed more to August Strindberg and Luigi Pirandello than to Anton Chekhov.

Crompton, Louis. *"Heartbreak House."* In *Shaw the Dramatist.* Lincoln: University of Nebraska Press, 1969. Concludes that Shaw's play is simultaneously experimental and reactionary, experimental in its use of Chekhov a model and reactionary in its use of the ideas of the stern, English Victorian writer and social critic Thomas Carlyle.

Gibbs, A. M. *"Heartbreak House": Preludes of Apocalypse.* New York: Twayne, 1994. A book-length analysis of the play that includes literary, theatrical, historical, and biographical contexts for the play, as well as a sustained and focused interpretation of it. A number of very useful appendices. A perfect introduction for students.

McDowell, Frederick P. W. "Technique, Symbol, the Theme in *Heartbreak House."* *PMLA* 68, no. 3 (June, 1953): 335-356. After many years, still one of the most thorough and lucid short discussions of the play. McDowell shows how the characters are used as abstractions to create musical motifs.

Weintraub, Stanley. *Journey to Heartbreak: The Crucible Years of Bernard Shaw, 1914-1918.* New York: Weybright and Talley, 1971. A sophisticated approach that uses Shaw's life to show the genesis and development of the play. Weintraub places *Heartbreak House* in the context of World War I England, characterizing Shaw as an "embattled intellectual in wartime."

THE HEAT OF THE DAY

Type of work: Novel
Author: Elizabeth Bowen (1899-1973)
Type of plot: Psychological realism
Time of plot: 1942-1944
Locale: London
First published: 1949

> *Principal characters:*
> STELLA RODNEY, an attractive widow
> RODERICK RODNEY, her son
> ROBERT KELWAY, her lover
> HARRISON, a British Intelligence agent
> LOUIE LEWIS, the wife of a British soldier

The Story:

The afternoon of the first Sunday in September, 1942, found Harrison sitting at a band concert in Regent Park. He was not listening to the music but was, in fact, merely killing time until he could see Stella Rodney at eight o'clock. Thinking of Stella and the awkward subject he must discuss with her, he kept thrusting the fist of his right hand into the palm of his left. This unconscious motion, as well as his obvious indifference to the music, aroused the curiosity of an adjacent listener, Louie Lewis, a clumsy, cheaply clad young woman with an artless and somewhat bovine expression. Lonely without her soldier husband and entirely a creature of impulse, she offended Harrison by breaking into his reverie with naïve comments that he brusquely rebuffed. Unabashed, she trailed after him when he left the concert, giving up only when he abruptly left her to keep his engagement.

In her top-floor flat in Weymouth Street, Stella wondered rather idly why Harrison was late. Her attitude of waiting was more defiant than expectant, for she had no love for her visitor. She hardly knew how he had managed to insinuate himself into her life; first, he had turned up unaccountably at the funeral of Cousin Francis Morris, and since then, his attentions had steadily increased. There had been a subtle shade of menace in his demand that she see him that night, and a curious sense of apprehension had prompted her to consent. As she awaited his knock, her glance flickered impatiently about the charming flat, and she recalled the facts that gave shape to her existence: her young son, Roderick, now in the British army; her ex-husband, long divorced and dead; her own war work with Y.X.D.; and her lover, Robert Kelway, who was also in government service.

When Harrison arrived, he received a cool and perfunctory greeting. His first remarks were hesitant and enigmatic, but he soon launched into words that left Stella wide-eyed with shock and disbelief. He told her that her lover was a Nazi agent passing English secrets on to Germany. Harrison himself was connected with British Intelligence, and he had been assigned to cover Kelway's movements. There was just one way to save the traitor. Stella must give him up and switch her interest to Harrison. Then Kelway's fate might be averted or indefinitely postponed.

The blunt proposition unnerved Stella. She refused to believe in Kelway's guilt, for Harrison did not impress her as a trustworthy man. She played for time, winning a month's delay in which to make up her mind. Harrison sharply advised her not to warn Robert: The slightest change in his pattern of action would result in his immediate arrest. As the interview ended, the telephone rang. It was Roderick, announcing his arrival on leave in London. Upon Harrison's departure, Stella pulled herself together and made quick preparation to receive her son.

Roderick's arrival helped a little, temporarily depriving Stella of the time to worry. Roderick was young and vulnerable, and his father's early abdication had made Stella feel doubly responsible for her son. Roderick wanted to talk about his new interest in life, the run-down estate in Ireland recently bequeathed him by cousin Francis Morris. The boy was determined to keep his new property; but until the war was over, the task of looking after it would be largely Stella's responsibility.

The night after Roderick's leave expired, Robert Kelway came to Stella's flat. She gave no hint of her inward agitation, although she casually inquired if he knew Harrison. Gazing at her attractive, considerate lover, Stella silently marveled that he should be a suspect—he, a lamed veteran of Dunkirk. Because she knew nothing about his family, she renewed her request that they visit his mother and sister in the country. A subsequent Saturday afternoon at Holme Dene revealed nothing strange about Robert's background. On the night of her return from Robert's home, she found Harrison waiting at her apartment; he proved that he had been keeping watch by telling her where she had been and why.

Roderick's interests briefly summoned Stella to Ireland. Robert protested at losing her for even a few days, and they parted affectionately. In Ireland, Stella's distrust of Harrison received a jolt; he had been truthful, she learned, when he told her that he had been a friend of Cousin Francis Morris. She resolved that she would acquaint Robert with Harrison's accusation. When she returned to London, Robert met her at the station. Minutes later, in the taxi, she revealed what she had heard; Robert, deeply hurt, made a complete denial. Later that night, he begged her to marry him, but Stella, both surprised and disturbed, succeeded in parrying his proposal.

A few nights later, Harrison had dinner with Stella in a popular restaurant. She stiffened with apprehension when he told her that he knew she had disobeyed him by putting Robert on his guard. Before Stella could learn what Harrison intended to do, she was interrupted by the untimely intrusion of Louie Lewis, who crudely invited herself to their table after spotting Harrison in the crowd. Stella managed to intimate that she would meet Harrison's terms if he would save Robert from arrest. Angry at Louie, Harrison made no response; roughly dismissing the two women, he stalked off, leaving them to find their way home through blacked-out London. Louie was fascinated by Stella's superior charm and refinement and accompanied her to the doorway of her apartment.

Robert was at Holme Dene, so Stella did not have a chance to warn him of his danger until the next night. In the early morning darkness of Stella's bedroom, they pledged their love anew, sensing that it was to be their last meeting. When Robert finally revealed that he was an ardent Nazi, prizing power above freedom, Stella found no way to reconcile their views. Faint footsteps, as of outside watchers, were heard as Robert dressed and prepared to leave. He climbed up the rope ladder to the skylight in the roof and then came back down again to kiss Stella once more. He told her to take care of herself as he hurriedly disappeared through the skylight. The next morning, Robert's body was found lying in the street where he had leaped or fallen from the steeply slanting roof.

More than a year passed before Stella saw Harrison again. There had been Allied landings in Africa and the invasion of Italy, and there was the ever-growing prospect of a Second Front. In the beginning, Stella had had questions to ask Harrison about Robert, when he returned it seemed pointless to ask them. There was an air of constraint over their conversation and a feeling that Robert's death had removed any real link between their lives. Harrison made no romantic overtures; he even seemed faintly relieved when Stella told him that she was soon to be married.

Critical Evaluation:

The wartime setting of this book is no more than incidental, for the story, dealing with contrasting faiths and loyalties, is altogether timeless. Though the general atmosphere is electric with danger, Elizabeth Bowen muffles the sound of bombs and antiaircraft guns so that they only provide background for the drama of Stella Rodney, Robert Kelway, and the enigmatic Harrison. The problem of Stella Rodney is that of a woman asked to question her own judgment of the man she loves. Elizabeth Bowen is at her best in dealing with complex personal relationships, and here she inspects some barriers to emotional and intellectual harmony that are embodied in a conflict between patriotism and love. Like Henry James, she is interested in the collision of finely grained personalities, and the very nature of her subject matter demands a style that is sensitive and involved.

Bowen often expressed her concern for the disintegration of tradition and value in the twentieth century by depicting the discrepancy between modern woman's changing aspirations and her felt desire for the traditional roles. In *The House in Paris* (1936) and *The Death of the Heart* (1938), the heroines are restless and dissatisfied in the roles of wife or mother; in *The Heat of the Day*, Stella tests "free womanhood." This novel combines the portrayal of a woman's dilemma with two other representations of Bowen's concern—the neglected family estate and the events of World War II.

Stella Rodney is Bowen's "free woman." She is a professional working in military intelligence, a longtime divorcée, and the mother of a grown son. She has a lover whom she has known for two years, but she dates and knows other men. Still, the relationship with Robert is the most important. Stella is sensitive, strong, and articulate, not only about others but also about her own problems. She has let her son and others believe for years that she left her husband, that she was the femme fatale, the self-sufficient one. In fact, she was divorced by her husband, who left her for his nurse. Stella's son Roderick discovers this fact and confronts his mother, saying it puts "everything in a different light." She admits that it was a matter of saving face; when most people believed that she was the guilty party, she let the story go on. She says to Harrison that it is better to sound like "a monster than look a fool." That remark suggests the paradox in Stella's psyche: She craves to be identified as a free woman, *capable de tout*, but her inner self is not quite in concert with that image. Therefore, there is the divorce story, her relationship to Roderick (she takes pains to show that he is not tied to her, but she worries a great deal about him), and her attitude to Robert (their relationship is a stable one, but Stella refuses his marriage proposal).

Stella is not alone in her ambivalence about how to react to changes in society. Cousin Nettie Morris is driven to insanity by the difficulties of woman's "place" at the family estate, Mount Morris. It seems she takes refuge in madness. One of the novel's most memorable scenes is the nonconversation between Roderick and Nettie at Wisteria Lodge, the asylum. Nettie is not so mad as others would like to think. Visiting Mount Morris in Ireland, Stella understands how the lack of real choices for the traditional woman can drive her insane.

Stella's dividedness is expressed in her attitude toward Mount Morris. She had sold her own house, stored her furniture, and rented a furnished luxury flat in London, thus making herself more independent. Nothing in the flat reflected her personality. Stella finds herself again saddled with place, family, and tradition when Cousin Francis wills Mount Morris to her son—

whom he never met but who was conceived at Mount Morris when Stella and her husband spent their honeymoon there. Stella's ambivalence begins when she attends Cousin Francis' funeral; it grows when, after twenty-one years, she revisits Mount Morris, knowing that Roderick will carry on the tradition she had rejected. Bowen herself believed that the attitude of her time against family estates was erroneous and that it had even contributed to the general disintegration of society. She became the first female Bowen to inherit Bowen's Court near Dublin since its construction in 1776, but in 1960, she was forced by financial exigency to sell the house, and in 1963 it was torn down.

Stella is repeatedly characterized as typical of her generation, a generation often described as having "muffed" the century. She became an adult just after World War I, and now there is World War II. The specific details of the war years in London give concrete reality to Stella's own trauma and are skillfully interwoven in her involvement with Robert. "The heat of the day" is Stella's middle age, her "noon," and the agony of the decision to question Robert's loyalty. It is also, of course, the height of the war and a turning point in the century.

As both Bowen's structure and her symbols clearly suggest, the generation that follows Stella's, that of Roderick and Louie Lewis, represents at once a new integration and a rebirth. Stella's story—her "defeat" as a free woman—is framed and intersected by the story of the working-class Louie Lewis, whose vague desires for motherhood culminate in a triumphant pregnancy while her husband is fighting abroad. She is unaware of the identity of the child's father. The novel ends with the birth of her son just after D-Day and her return to the south coast of England where her parents had been killed by a bomb in the early days of the war. Roderick intends to reside at Mount Morris and has great plans about restoring it with modern farming methods. Both members of the next generation are able to resolve the dichotomies that so plagued their parents' generation—dichotomies about family, place, tradition, and role. The three white swans, a recurrent positive symbol in Bowen (they figure in *The Death of the Heart* as well) appear only at Mount Morris and at the end of the book as Louie wheels her new baby. Flying straight, the swans symbolize a positive rebirth and the resolution of the war in the "direction of the west." Bowen's symbols, however, are more suggestive than absolute. Louie's and Roderick's clear choices are more than enough direction for interpreting the novel. Stella's generation had "botched" it; the only hope is in the next.

"Critical Evaluation" by Margaret McFadden-Gerber

Bibliography:
Austin, Allen E. *Elizabeth Bowen*. Rev. ed. Boston: Twayne, 1989. Good introduction that discusses Bowen's style, syntax, use of narrator, and evocative settings. Provides a detailed analysis of the setting, theme, and character in *The Heat of the Day*, comparing Bowen's portrayal of three English classes with Forster's. Helpful annotated bibliography.
Heath, William. *Elizabeth Bowen: An Introduction to Her Novels*. Madison: University of Wisconsin Press, 1961. Good introductory source. Provides clear analysis of setting, character, and theme in *The Heat of the Day*, revealing the novel's use of the Faust motif and connecting private anguish and public disaster.
Jordan, Heather Bryant. *How Will the Heart Endure? Elizabeth Bowen and the Landscape of War*. Ann Arbor: University of Michigan Press, 1992. Discusses the importance of Bowen's uniquely Anglo-Irish background and the role of the Big House in the novel. Detailed discussion of theme, language, and style, which emphasize important moral distinctions between silence and speech, and between traitor and spy.

Kenney, Edwin, Jr. *Elizabeth Bowen*. Lewisburg, Pa: Bucknell University Press, 1974. Presents connections between the personal world of the Anglo-Irish country house and the larger world of international affairs and between public and privates concerns. Also stresses the importance of Bowen's setting during the bombing of London, which intensifies the feelings of her characters.

Lee, Hermione. *Elizabeth Bowen: An Estimation*. Totowa, N.J.: Barnes & Noble Books, 1981. Excellent introduction. Emphasizes the novel's use of structure, style, and syntactical mannerisms such as inversion, double negatives, and passive constructions, to reveal the emotional state of the characters' lives and the turmoil of wartime London.

HEDDA GABLER

Type of work: Drama
Author: Henrik Ibsen (1828-1906)
Type of plot: Social realism
Time of plot: Late nineteenth century
Locale: Norway
First published: 1890 (English translation, 1891); first performed, 1891

Principal characters:
GEORGE TESSMAN, a scholar
HEDDA TESSMAN, his wife
MISS JULIANA TESSMAN, his aunt
MRS. ELVSTED, Hedda's old schoolmate
JUDGE BRACK, a friend of the Tessmans
EILERT LOVBERG, Hedda's former suitor

The Story:

When aristocratic Hedda Gabler, daughter of the late General Gabler, consented to marry Doctor George Tessman, everyone in Hedda's set was surprised and a little shocked. Although George was a rising young scholar and would soon be a professor at the university, he was not considered to be the ideal mate for Hedda. He was dull and prosaic, absorbed almost exclusively in his books and manuscripts, whereas Hedda was the beautiful, spoiled darling of her father and all the young men who had flocked around her. Hedda was now twenty-nine, however, and George was the only one of her admirers to offer her marriage and a villa that had belonged to the widow of a cabinet minister.

The villa was somewhat beyond George's means, but it was what Hedda wanted, and with the prospect of a professorship and with his Aunt Juliana's help, he managed to secure it. He arranged a long wedding tour that lasted nearly six months, because Hedda wished that also. On their honeymoon, George spent much of his time searching libraries for material in his special field, the history of civilization. Hedda was bored, and by the time she returned to the villa she hated George. It began to look as if George might not get the professorship, which would mean that Hedda would have to forego her footman and saddlehorse and some of the other luxuries she craved. George's rival for the post was Eilert Lovberg, a brilliant but erratic genius who had written a book in George's own field that critics had acclaimed as a masterpiece. Hedda, completely bored and disgusted with her situation, found her only excitement in practicing with the brace of pistols that had belonged to her father, the general's only legacy to her.

George discovered that Eilert had written a second book that was even more brilliant and important than the first, a book written with the help and inspiration of a Mrs. Elvsted, whose devotion to the erratic genius had reformed him. Lovberg brought the manuscript of this book with him one evening to the Tessman villa. Hedda proceeded to make the most of this situation, for Thea Elvsted, whom she had despised when she was her schoolmate, was also her husband's former sweetheart. The fact that this mousy creature had been the inspiration for Eilert Lovberg's success and rehabilitation was more than Hedda could bear. Eilert Lovberg had once been in love with Hedda, and he had urged her to throw in her lot with his; at the time, she had been tempted to do so but had refused because his future was so uncertain. Now Hedda felt regret mingled with anger that another woman possessed what she had lacked the courage to hold for herself.

Her impulse was to destroy, and circumstances played into her hands. When Lovberg called at the Tessman villa with his manuscript, George was on the point of leaving with a friend, Judge Brack, for a bachelor party. They invited Lovberg to accompany them, but though he would have preferred to remain at the villa with Mrs. Elvsted and Hedda, Hedda, determined to destroy his handiwork, sent him off to the party. All night, Hedda and Mrs. Elvsted awaited the revelers' return.

George was the first to come back, and told them what had happened. The party had involved heavy drinking, and on the way home Lovberg had lost his manuscript. George had recovered it and brought it to the villa. In despair over the supposed loss of his manuscript, Lovberg had spent the remainder of the night at Mademoiselle Diana's establishment. By the time he returned to the villa, George had gone. Lovberg told Mrs. Elvsted that he had destroyed his manuscript, but to Hedda he confessed that he had lost it and that, as a consequence, he intended to take his own life. Without telling him that the manuscript was at that moment in the villa, Hedda urged him to do the deed beautifully, and she pressed into his hand a memento of their relationship, one of General Gabler's pistols with which she had once threatened Lovberg.

After his departure, Hedda coldly and deliberately thrust the manuscript into the fire. When George returned and heard from Hedda's own lips what had happened to Lovberg's manuscript, he was unspeakably shocked; half believing that she had burned it for his sake, he was also flattered. He resolved to keep silent and devote his life to reconstructing the book from Mrs. Elvsted's notes.

Hedda might have been safe but for the manner in which Lovberg met his death. He had returned to Mademoiselle Diana's establishment, where he became embroiled in a brawl in which he was accidentally killed. Judge Brack, a sophisticated man of the world who was as ruthless in his way as Hedda was in hers, became suspicious. He had long admired Hedda's cold, dispassionate beauty, and had wanted her as his mistress. The peculiar circumstances of Eilert Lovberg's death gave him his opportunity when he learned that the pistol with which Lovberg met his death was one of a pair belonging to Hedda. The judge threatened Hedda with an investigation. Hedda could not face a public scandal, but she refused to give in to the judge's proposal. While her husband and Mrs. Elvsted were beginning the long task of reconstructing the dead Lovberg's manuscript, Hedda calmly went to her boudoir and with the remaining pistol she died beautifully—as she had urged Lovberg to do—by putting a bullet through her head.

Critical Evaluation:

In *Hedda Gabler*, Henrik Ibsen constructed a complex play that caused considerable bewilderment among his contemporaries. Some found fault; some simply confessed puzzlement. One problem was that the play, one of Ibsen's later ones, was often judged in the context of his earlier work. When the broad social issues treated in earlier plays were found lacking or deficient, *Hedda Gabler* was pronounced inferior. The most common misperception of *Hedda Gabler* stemmed, however, from a tendency to interpret the play through its title and hence its protagonist, who was considered totally devoid of any redeeming virtues.

Later critical opinion focused more carefully on the structure of the play. One critic called attention to a typical Ibsen device that came to be characterized as "retrospective action." That term describes Ibsen's way of revealing the crucial events preceding the action of the play in the first few scenes of the exposition by reuniting characters after a long absence and allowing them to bring each other up to date on past events. In *Hedda Gabler*, the Tessmans, returning from their extended honeymoon, tell much of themselves in conversation with Juliana and others. Despite this sophisticated device for surmounting a theatrical obstacle, however, the play is not without structural weaknesses. Lovberg's apocalyptic attitude is unconvincing; Ibsen's view of scholarly enterprise as a batch of notes in someone's briefcase is ludicrous; and Hedda's lack of affiliation with the play poses a threat to dramatic unity. The play nevertheless holds up under critical review because the dialogue, characterization, and strong underlying theme carry it through.

Ibsen's method of playwrighting is largely responsible for the verbal polish and linguistic sensitivity of the dialogue. After completing a play, Ibsen habitually rested and let his mind lie fallow for a while, during which time he would allow ideas for his next work to begin incubating. When he did begin writing, he wrote quickly, and he usually completed a first draft in about two months. Next, he set the draft aside for another two months or so to "age," and only then did he begin the final process of refining each nuance to perfection. That stage usually took him two to three weeks, and the final version was usually ready for the printer within a month (by the following month, the play was off the press and ready for distribution). It was in that final process of refining *Hedda Gabler* that Ibsen added George Tessman's fussy expostulations, his characteristic, questioning "Hmm's?" and "Eh's"; Judge Brack's inquisitorial manner; as well as such fillips of imagery as "vine leaves in his hair." Out of these final revisions came the exquisitely fine-tuned dialogue of *Hedda Gabler*.

Because the character of Hedda Gabler stands out in bold relief by contrast with the other characters in the play, those others must be given serious consideration at least as the medium for Hedda's development. Hedda's three major counterfoils, George Tessman, Eilert Lovberg, and Brack, are all rather static characters. Although their personalities are revealed gradually as the play progresses, none undergoes any fundamental change. George Tessman begins and ends as a somewhat abstracted, woolly-headed personality; Lovberg is incurably incompetent; and Brack is a coldly calculating, manipulative type. In interaction with these men, Hedda dominates the scene: a self-centered creature of impulse and indulgence, she was her father's spoiled darling (significantly, the play is titled *Hedda Gabler*, not *Hedda Tessman*). Hedda's contempt for Tessman and her opportunism grow in inverse ratio to her husband's declining prospects, but when she is caught in the matrix of Lovberg's inelegant death, Tessman's ineffectuality, Brack's obscene proposition, and her unwanted pregnancy, Hedda prefers an efficient suicide to a messy life. Hedda's life does not meet her exacting standards, but her suicide fulfills her sense of style in a way that living could not. Ibsen's deep insight into one vivid personality thus constitutes the play *Hedda Gabler*.

"Critical Evaluation" by Joanne G. Kashdan

Bibliography:

Holtan, Orley I. *Mythic Patterns in Ibsen's Last Plays*. Minneapolis: University of Minnesota Press, 1970. An extended discussion of the mythic content in Ibsen's last seven plays, Holtan's book offers an interesting treatment of Hedda as an example of the archetype of the destructive female.

Meyer, Michael. *Ibsen: A Biography*. Garden City, N.Y.: Doubleday, 1971. A standard biography of Ibsen, it contains a good discussion of both the play itself and its place in Ibsen's oeuvre. Meyer stresses the complexity of the title character and suggests that Hedda may be a disguised self-portrait of the author.

Meyerson, Caroline W. "Thematic Symbols in *Hedda Gabler*." *Scandinavian Studies* 22, no. 4 (November, 1950); 151-160. Reprinted in *Ibsen: A Collection of Critical Essays*, edited by Rolf Fjelde. Englewood Cliffs, N.J.: Prentice-Hall, 1965. In this influential article, Meyerson explores the significance of such symbols as Hedda's pistols and Thea's hair, as well as the procreative imagery in regarding Lovberg's manuscript as a child.

Sandstroem, Yvonne. "Problems of Identity in *Hedda Gabler*." *Scandinavian Studies* 51, no. 4 (Autumn, 1979): 368-374. An article that presents an interesting close reading of a central aspect of the play, namely, Ibsen's use of such titles as "general" and "doctor" as a tool for characterization and as a means of illuminating the reasons behind Hedda's suicide.

Weigand, Herman J. *The Modern Ibsen: A Reconsideration.* New York: Holt, 1925. An excellent introduction to Ibsen's later plays, this volume contains an insightful analysis of *Hedda Gabler*, with appropriate attention devoted to the title character, her husband George Tessman, and the other characters.

THE HEIDI CHRONICLES

Type of work: Drama
Author: Wendy Wasserstein (1950-   )
Type of plot: Social morality
Time of plot: 1965-1989
Locale: New York and Chicago
First performed: 1988; first published, 1988

Principal characters:
HEIDI HOLLAND, art historian and feminist
PETER PATRONE, her friend
SCOOP ROSENBAUM, her friend and would-be lover
SUSAN JOHNSTON, her friend

The Story:

Heidi lectured on woman artists, then flashed back to a high school dance in 1965, where she and her friend Susan began their investigation of the opposite sex. At the next dance, at a McCarthy rally in 1968, Heidi met Scoop Rosenbaum, who seduced her. In 1970, Heidi and Susan joined a women's consciousness-raising group, where Heidi's inability to fit in became apparent. She was still seeing Scoop. At a Women in Art protest in front of the Chicago Art Institute in 1974, Heidi met Peter's new boyfriend, Mark. Heidi was engaged in the issues of her times, yet she was never entirely engrossed in issues. She remained an outsider, an individualist who observed the follies of others' commitments rather than committing to relationships herself.

Heidi told Peter that she was "not involved with" Scoop. "I just like sleeping with him," she said. Peter saw through Heidi's shell and responded ironically: "What a perky seventies kind of gal you are! You can separate sexual needs from emotional dependencies." Peter knew, however, that Heidi's emotional needs were not being fulfilled either professionally or socially.

In 1977, Heidi was at a wedding: Scoop was marrying Lisa. Despite the flippant air of cynicism at the wedding, especially as provided by the wit of Peter and the droll sarcasm of Susan, for Heidi the moment was painful. She was experiencing the consequences of her inability to connect with Scoop. Scoop introduced them to Lisa as "Peter Patrone and his fiancée, Heidi." In the ensuing conversation, Scoop and Heidi avoided discussing their relationship. Scoop and Heidi danced slowly to "You Send Me."

Heidi continued her art lecture at Columbia in 1989. Then, in 1980, Lisa was having a baby shower. She was very pregnant. The women there bonded. Heidi had progressed in her career and was writing books. The women exchanged gifts and gossip: Scoop was being unfaithful to Lisa, news that Heidi received with mixed emotions. In a television studio in 1982, the friends were together again to participate in a panel show on the baby boom generation. The friends mocked the hostess, April, with in-jokes and double entendres, and the show got out of hand. After the airing, Heidi assailed Peter and Scoop for not allowing her to speak for herself—their witty rejoinders prevented a serious discussion of Heidi's book, but more important, demonstrated that both men had automatically protected her and acted as her spokespersons, instead of letting her speak for herself. In the next scenes, Heidi's career moved forward, and she delivered a lecture as a distinguished alumna. Heidi revealed the real motivations in her life, as she related an incident in a women's locker room: "Suddenly I stop competing with all of them.

Suddenly I'm not even racing." Heidi's way was to stand back and watch while others raced past, for whatever goal they considered important. The price, however, was that "I'm just not happy. I'm afraid I haven't been happy for some time." Heidi felt stranded and alone, in a world that was supposed to unite women: "I thought the whole point was that we wouldn't feel stranded. I thought the point was that we were all in this together."

On Christmas Eve, 1987, Peter, who was a pediatrician and Heidi met at the children's hospital where he worked. She told Peter she was moving out of New York, to Northfield, Minnesota, to teach. Peter finally declared his need for Heidi's friendship, and she agreed to stay in New York. Scoop visited Heidi's apartment for a final farewell. She had adopted a baby, Judy, and Scoop had sold his magazine, intent on moving on with his creative life. Heidi held Judy and rocked her.

Critical Evaluation:

The story of Heidi Holland is told in a series of disconnected scenes in episodic fashion. It is the story of what happened to the young women of the feminist era beginning in the 1970's, when the hopes and expectations of the movement were high. Heidi moves through the New York and Chicago scene of art, magazine publishing, and television, without the true love that eludes her, possibly because she has never reconciled herself to the feminist rhetoric of her peers, or possibly because she is truly independent of male dominance, an emancipated woman who is paying the price for her independence.

Heidi is an art historian, and much of what the audience knows about her comes from the lectures she gives on women artists. The artists she lectures on are intentionally paired with famous male artists, so that the audience understands that the equality that women artists have deserved for so long has been denied them, not by considerations of talent, but by a chauvinistic, paternal social system that places women in very limited categories. According to Heidi's lectures, for example, Sofonisba Anguissola, a contemporary of the great male Renaissance painters such as Titian, is every bit as deserving of fame and admiration, but she and her six sisters were not recognized because of their sex. The same prejudice holds true through the Romantic era, right up to twentieth century American painters such as Lily Martin Spence and Judy Chicago.

The disrespect for women in history is a metaphor for the more complicated disrespect of modern men toward women. Heidi's story is the story of finding her own respect in writing and speaking and the story of her failure as a person because she cannot find someone to love. Her best friends are Peter, who sticks with her through her life, and Susan, who represents a "fallen" feminist, the alternative life Heidi could have had if she had not taken feminist rhetoric seriously.

Scoop represents the consummate male ego and an attractive and intelligent possibility for Heidi. The match is not be, despite Scoop's best efforts, because the very qualities that endear him to Heidi are those despised by the feminist movement: a desire to protect, a sense of play, a caring that borders on overprotection. Heidi in turn cannot let that part of herself free that Scoop finds attractive—intelligence with bitterness, and the equality of partnership that men find both enticing and threatening.

The play's plot is about the lives of the characters, as they cross paths, gathering for events such as weddings and gallery openings. Heidi becomes more and more aloof and unattainable; she feels betrayed by the promises of closeness that the feminist movement made in its infancy. Meanwhile, her friends go in and out of relationships, which she interprets either as weaknesses or the privileges of those less sensitive to gender inequalities. The play is by no means simplistic in its treatment of the relationship of the sexes. The drama is built on the complex exchanges women make for some sort of happy life.

There is no question that this work is, to a degree, autobiographical. Wasserstein's world is the theater, but the same prejudices and assumptions apply in theater as they do in art. The central questions of the play are what Wasserstein has spent her life asking in her work: Where is the camaraderie promised by the women's movement? Have women really made any progress in a man's world? Is there still a minimum requirement of sexual attractiveness for acceptance into the world of human relationships? Has the world changed at all from the time of Titian and Sofonisba Anguissola?

Stylistically, the play both gains and loses from its episodic form. Since the playwright can move quickly in the out of a scene and a period, there is not always a successful buildup of tension from scene to scene. The characters are not enclosed in the same space, which also lessens dramatic tension. On the other hand, the broken scenes reflect Heidi's sense of disconnectedness and incompleteness. Her friends move in and out of the scenes, coming from full, connected lives of their own, while Heidi seems to find no connection from one moment to the next, other than her growing erudition and articulation of women's art. The progress she makes in her career is not dramatized, but announced in dialogue; she seems to remain the same person, while her friends have all evolved into what they have "sold out" to become: a successful magazine publisher from an idealistic reporter, a table-hopping career woman from a fellow-feminist zealot, and a caring pediatrician from an acerbic, bitingly witty homosexual.

The real charm of the play lies not in its understanding of human folly, but in the expression of that folly in the wit of the characters. When the play turns serious, the moments are immediately undercut by humor and self-deprecating dismissal of emotions. Not one is allowed to feel deeply for any length of time without undercutting that emotion with wit. Heidi, by adopting a child, is the only character to adhere to the altruism and hope of the earlier decades; her friends have simply lived their lives without the liberal spirit that inspires feminism. They cling to each other and let each other go, as survival dictates. Heidi alone remembers the promise never to let her friends feel stranded. Ultimately, the play's value lies in its success at capturing the transition of American society from the idealistic 1960's to the indifferent 1990's.

Thomas J. Taylor

Bibliography:
Arthur, Helen. "Wendy Wasserstein's *The Heidi Chronicles*." Review of *The Heidi Chronicles*, by Wendy Wasserstein. *Nation* 261, no. 12 (October 16, 1995): 443-445. Discusses the play as adapted for television rather than the original play. Criticizes the drama's use of historical markers (events, songs) as ineffective.
Finn, William. "Sister Act." *Vogue* 182, no. 9 (September, 1992): 360. Summarizes Wasserstein's career and themes.
Shapiro, Walter. "Chronicler of Frayed Feminism." *Time*, March 27, 1989, 90-92. Describes *The Heidi Chronicles'* use of anger and jokes to diminish the pain of loneliness that is central to the play. Describes the playwright's family as the source for much of her bitter humor.

HEIMSKRINGLA

Type of work: Folklore
Author: Snorri Sturluson (1179-1241)
Type of plot: Saga
Time of plot: Legendary times to twelfth century
Locale: Norway
First transcribed: c. 1230-1235 (English translation, 1844)

Principal characters:
ODIN, ancestor of the Northmen
ON JORUNDSSON, of Sweden
HALFDAN THE BLACK, of Norway
HARALD THE FAIRHAIRED, his son
AETHELSTAN, of England
HAKON THE GOOD, Harald's son
ERIC BLOOD-AX, Hakon's brother
OLAF TRYGGVESSON, Christianizer of Norway
OLAF THE SAINT
MAGNUS THE GOOD, his stepson
HARALD SIGURDSSON THE STERN, Olaf the Saint's brother
OLAF THE QUIET, Harald's son
MAGNUS BAREFOOT, Olaf's son
EYSTEIN,
SIGURD, and
OLAF, Magnus' sons
MAGNUS SIGURDSSON
HARALD GILLE, Sigurd Magnusson's half brother
INGE,
SIGURD, and
EYSTEIN, Harald's sons
HAKON SIGURDSSON
ERLING SKAKKE, counselor to Inge
MAGNUS, his son

The Stories:
In Asaland in Asia near the Black Sea lived Odin, the conqueror of many nations, and a great traveler, whose people believed he would have success in every battle. When a neighboring people beheaded his friend Mime as a spy and sent the head to Odin, he smeared the head with herbs to keep it from rotting and sang incantations over it. Thereafter the head could speak to Odin and discover secrets for him. While the Romans were subduing the world, Odin learned that he was to rule the northern half. Traveling through Russia and northern Germany, he finally settled in the Scandinavian peninsula. There he appeared handsome to his friends and fiendish to his enemies. His foes were helpless in battle against him, for he could change his own shape and wish himself from place to place. He made laws for his people: that the dead should be burned, that blood-sacrifice be made for good harvests, and that taxes be paid yearly. When he was near death, Odin said that he would go to Valhalla and wait there for all good warriors. Then

he died quietly in his bed, and afterward the rulers of the northland claimed descent from him. The sacrifices his people made to Odin were sometimes great. When King On Jorundsson of Sweden was sixty years old, he made an oracular sacrifice of a son to Odin. His answer from Odin was that he would live sixty years longer if he sacrificed a son every ten years. He sacrificed as he was told until he had given up nine of his ten sons. By that time he was so old and weak that his people refused to let the tenth son be sacrificed, and so On died of extreme old age. After that people dying from weakness of age were said to have On's sickness.

After twenty generations of Yngling rulers in the Scandinavian countries came Halfdan the Black, born about 820, the king of Norway. In those days a king was an intermediary between the people and the supreme powers, whose favor he courted by sacrifices. Halfdan was considered a good king because the harvests were plentiful during his lifetime. He died young in a sleighing accident while crossing thin ice. His people begged so hard for his body to insure continued good seasons that finally the body was quartered, and each quarter and the head were sent to separate provinces to spread his good influence.

Harald the Fairhaired was Halfdan's son. He sent some of his henchmen to bring him a young woman to be his concubine, but she refused to bow to a king of such a small territory and sent word that she would consider him when he ruled all of Norway. His attendants thought her attitude warranted punishment; Harald considered it a challenge. Ten years later, after he had conquered all of Norway, he sent for the woman and married her. He had many children by her and other women. When he was fifty years old, he divided his kingdom among his sons and gave them half the revenues.

At that time Aethelstan, the king of England, sent Harald a sword. When Harald accepted it, however, Aethelstan's messengers claimed that he was then subject to their king. The following summer Harald sent his nine-year-old son Hakon to Aethelstan to foster, as a foster father was always subject to a real father. Each king tried to outdo the other, but each ruled in his own kingdom until his dying day. When he was seventy-nine years old Harald died in his bed.

Hakon went from England to Norway when he heard of his father's death. He was then fifteen years old. At the same time, the chief Norse king had sailed west to ravage England; he was Hakon's brother, Eric Blood-Ax, so called because he had slain at least four of his brothers. Eric was killed in England and Hakon subdued Norway. Hakon, who had been converted to Christianity while in England, began to practice Christian habits of fasting and prayer in Norway. Although he did not insist on forcing Christianity on his followers, many of them, out of friendship for him, allowed themselves to be baptized. Hakon wanted to forego sacrifices to the gods, but a counselor persuaded him to humor the people who still believed devoutly in blood sacrifice. Known to his country as Hakon the Good, he was killed in battle with Eric's sons, to whom he left the kingdom.

The years during which Eric's sons ruled Norway were so bad that there was a scarcity of both fish and corn, and the people went hungry. Among other petty kings, the sons killed Tryggve Olafsson, whose wife escaped to bring Olaf Tryggvesson to birth.

As a child, Olaf Tryggvesson spent six years in slavery before his uncle learned where marauding Vikings had sent him after capturing the boy and his mother as they were on their way to a place of safety in Russia. By the time he was twelve, Olaf himself was a Viking chieftain. After harrying various parts of England he made peace with Aethelred, the English king, and thereafter always kept the peace with England. By that time his aim was to be a crusader, for he had come under the influence of Christianity during his raids on England. Having been converted and baptized by the English priests, he wanted to Christianize his own land as well. He set sail for Norway in 995. Between that date and 1000, when he was decoyed into a one-sided battle with the kings of Denmark and Sweden and lost his life at Svolder, he converted all of Norway as well as many of the outlying islands, either by the force of his own personality, or, when that did not suffice, by force of arms. Norway was a Christian land by the time Olaf died, but there was no Norwegian king strong enough to rule its entirety while the Danes and Swedes laid claim to various parts of the country.

When he was very young, Olaf Haraldsson joined Viking expeditions to England, Jutland, Holland, France, and Spain. In England, where the Norwegians were fighting the Danes, who were then in power in England, he was present at the stoning to death of the archbishop who had confirmed Olaf Tryggvesson. It was said that in Spain Olaf Haraldsson dreamed of a fearful man who told him to give up further travel to the Holy Land and to go back to Norway. In 1015, he sailed for Norway to reestablish Christianity and to regain the throne once held by his ancestor, Harold the Fairhaired. Though he did not have the striking personality of Olaf Tryggvesson, Olaf Haraldsson had persistence enough to spread Christianity by his bands of missionaries, to win control over Norway, and to set up a central government. The latter was his hardest task, as it meant taking away some of the traditional powers of the chieftains. He created a form of justice that worked equally for the chieftains and the common people, and because of their resentment the chieftains rose against him at last. With a superior force they fought him at Stiklestad, and in 1030 he was cut down. His hope for national union and independence seemed doomed until suddenly rumors were spread that miracles had occurred where his body had fallen. People began to give Olaf Haraldsson a new name, Olaf the Saint, and the whole Norwegian people suddenly craved the independence for which he had fought.

Olaf the Saint's stepson, Magnus, obtained the title of King of Norway without much trouble. Afterward he made a treaty with King Hardacanute of Denmark to keep the peace as long as they both should live, the one surviving to become the ruler of the other's country. When Hardacanute died, Magnus thereupon became king of Denmark. Since Hardacanute had also become king of England after the death of his father, Magnus laid claim to England when Edward the Good became the English king; he was prevented from invading England, however, by trouble stirred up in Denmark by a false friend whom he had made earl there. Letters were exchanged between Magnus and Edward over Magnus' claim to England. Edward's reply was so sensible and courageous that Magnus was content to rule in his own land and to let Edward reign in England.

Greater troubles beset Magnus when his uncle, Harald Sigurdsson, returned north after many years in Russia, Constantinople, and the Holy Land. Harald had left Norway after the battle of Stiklestad, when his brother Olaf the Saint was killed. He plundered all through the south lands and at Constantinople joined the royal guard called the Vaeringer. Meanwhile he had collected much booty, which he sent to the Russian king for safekeeping until he should have finished his wanderings. When he tired of life in Constantinople, he traveled north to Russia. There he married Ellisiv, the king's daughter, and then traveled with her and his booty toward Norway. Eventually he made a deal with Magnus. He received half of Norway in return for half his booty. When Magnus, called the Good, died of illness, Harald, in contrast called the Stern, ruled alone. He was a harsh ruler and he met his death in England while trying to unthrone Harald Godwinsson, Edward's successor.

Through these times miracles continued to be credited to Olaf the Saint. Sometimes he appeared to people in dreams, as he did to Magnus the Good just before his death. Sometimes a pilgrimage to his shrine cured people who had been crippled from birth or who had been maimed in fighting. It was even said that Olaf could pull the root of a tongue so that a man whose tongue had been cut out could speak again. His shrine was in Nidaros.

After Harald the Stern, his sons Magnus and Olaf ruled Norway, but Magnus soon died of a sickness. Olaf, called the Quiet, reigned for twenty-six years. There was peace in Norway during that time, and the country gained in riches and cultivation.

Thereafter Olaf's son Magnus and his nephew, Hakon Magnusson, ruled Norway, but Hakon soon died of an illness. Magnus' reign was of ten years' time, most of which he spent in expeditions to reduce the island possessions to full submission to the central government in Norway. Under Magnus, for the first time, the government became a strong power. Because Magnus returned from one of his expeditions to Scotland wearing the Scottish national costume, his people called him Magnus Barefoot. On a foraging expedition, in 1103, Magnus was killed in Ireland before he was thirty years old.

From that time until 1130 peace reigned in Norway and the Church increased its powers. In the early days the Norwegian churches had been under the archbishopric of Bremen, but during that time they gained an archbishopric of their own at Lund in Skane. Magnus' sons, Eystein, Sigurd, and Olaf, ruled the country, but Olaf was only a small boy. Those years were also the period of the crusades. Sigurd took men and ships to the Holy Land while Eystein ruled at home. Sigurd was gone three years and gained much glory in England, Spain, Constantinople, and Palestine. He was afterward called the Crusader. When he came back to Norway, he and Eystein were jealous of each other's powers. Olaf died young and Eystein died before Sigurd. Sigurd had strange fancies before he himself died, but he had done much to improve the legal system of the country by increasing the powers of the Things. The congregation of people at the Things became the highest authority in the land, and even the kings argued their cases before those representative bodies.

Neither Olaf nor Eystein had sons. Magnus, Sigurd's son, became king, but his sole rule was threatened by Harald Gille, who came from Ireland and claimed to be Sigurd's half-brother. Harald passed an ordeal by hot iron to prove his paternity. After Sigurd's death, Harald was proclaimed king over part of Norway. It was said that Magnus was foolish, but Harald was cruel. A series of civil wars ensued, ending when Harald captured Magnus and had him blinded and otherwise mutilated. Thereafter Magnus was called the Blind. He retired to a monastery. Harald was killed by the order and treachery of Sigurd Slembedegn, a pretender to the throne.

In the days when Harald's sons reigned there were more civil wars. Crippled Inge was the most popular of Harald's three sons. Sigurd and Eystein led separate factions, and so there was always unrest in the country.

In 1152, Cardinal Nicholas came to Norway from Rome to establish an archbishopric at Nidaros, where King Olaf the Saint reposed. Cardinal Nicholas was well loved by the people and improved many of their customs. When the pope died suddenly, Nicholas became Pope Adrian IV. He was always friendly with the Norsemen.

After Sigurd and Eystein had been killed in different battles, Inge ruled alone. He was twenty-six when he was killed in battle with Hakon Sigurdsson, who had claimed Eystein's part of Norway. Hakon was little to be trusted. Erling Skakke, previously a power behind Inge's throne, then took it upon himself to create a strong party that could put upon the throne whomever it chose. None of his party favored Hakon, called the Broad-Shouldered, who was defeated in battle within a year, when he was only fifteen, in 1162.

Erling Skakke's party finally decided to put Erling Skakke's son Magnus on the throne. The child was five years old at the time. He was a legitimate candidate, however, for his mother was a daughter of Sigurd the Crusader. Erling Skakke was jealous of power, yet he gave much of the traditional authority of the throne to the bishops in exchange for their blessing on Magnus as king; he also made an agreement with King Valdemar of Denmark under which he gave

Valdemar a part of Norway as a fief under the Danish crown in exchange for peace. It had been a long time since a foreign king had claim to part of Norway. Erling Skakke spent much of his time wiping out the descendants of Harald Gille, and in time he became a tyrant in order to hold the throne safe for his child, Magnus Erlingsson.

Critical Evaluation:

Snorri Sturluson's *Heimskringla* can seem confusing to twentieth century readers. The work is obviously intended to be a history, but it also contains such mythical characters as gods, notably Odin, who was an early king. The saga concentrates on the personality and deeds of each successive king, and much of it was originally cast in the form of poetry.

Heimskringla originated in thirteenth century Iceland, which then had a total population of less than 100,000, most of whom were not literate. However, the outstanding landholders were well educated, and a few leading families sought power by any means. Such people were vitally interested in the history of their motherland, Norway.

Snorri was a leading figure in the political and artistic life of Iceland. Descended from wealthy and powerful families on both sides, his ancestors were important enough to have played major parts in Iceland's sagas, particularly *Egil's Saga*, which some critics believe Snorri himself wrote. Children from such families as his were usually sent away from home to be raised and educated. From the age of two on, Snorri lived at Oddi, which Jon Loptsson had made a center of culture and of political intrigue.

As an adult, Snorri threw himself into practical affairs, amassing estates all over the island by marriage and through political alliances. In 1218, he visited Norway and Sweden, making himself immensely popular at the court of Norway by his skill in writing in the complex court meters of contemporary poetry and by his charm. Returning home, he continued to write and to be politically active. The complex feuds between families and factions worsened under King Hakon of Norway, who wished to weaken Iceland until he could take over, as he eventually did in 1262. The king turned against Snorri after his second visit to Norway. In 1241, Gissur Thorvaldsson led seventy men to Snorri's home, where they hunted him down and murdered him in the cellar.

A man of such background would naturally have interested himself in history. For roughly a century, saga histories had been popular; they were often written by contemporaries who knew of the events firsthand. Snorri had access to these, both those that remain extant and some that have been lost. Just how much oral history had survived to his day without being written down is unknown, but Snorri was known to have collected such material. He also knew the rather uncritical stories of saints' lives, as well as old poems popular among the people, which in his introduction to *Heimskringla* he carefully distinguishes from the histories. He also considered the court poems of the previous four centuries factually reliable, as they were written for those who had taken part in the events depicted.

Just where Snorri got the legends concerning Odin and the other Aesir and Vanir gods has been a subject of contention among scholars. Of these, Eugen Mogk believes that Snorri had fewer sources available to him than were later available, whereas George Dumezil believed that Snorri relied heavily on oral tradition. The way Snorri used this material varies considerably between his *Prose Edda* and *Heimskringla*. In both, the Christian writer maintains that later people imagined powerful humans of earlier times to have been gods, yet in both works Odin and his contemporaries are shown using considerable magic. Snorri's *Prose Edda* contains much more of a supernatural element than does *Heimskringla*, however.

When assessing Snorri's methods of handling material, it is useful to compare him to the pioneer writers of Greek history, Herodotus and Thucydides. Herodotus reports legendary material and includes supernatural events uncritically, whereas Thucydides bases his work on what he knows firsthand or can check from several sources. Snorri uses legends when he is writing about the prehistory of his country, but he tones down the supernatural content. He may even have added false etymologies to substantiate his belief that the stories were based on history. In describing events of later centuries, Snorri uses more reliable sources. Yet he lacks what both Greek writers provide: analysis of the causes of events.

Instead, Snorri's interest focuses on the personalities of the powerful political players he depicts. This interest seems only natural in someone whose own life depended on his accurate reading of the powerful figures around him. He is a master at finding incidents to illuminate a character. There is, for example, the description of a two-year-old King Harald-to-be wishing when he grew up to have enough warriors to eat all the cows that his brother had wished for. He often seems to have chosen episodes to display personalities as much as for their historical importance. Thus a plot summary does little justice to the interest of the work. Yet at the conclusion of many of the lives, Snorri explains and evaluates the individual both morally and historically.

With the exception of a few specialists, most readers in later times, even in Norway or Iceland, have had to read *Heimskringla* in translation. Usually these translations are in prose, although in Snorri Sturluson's age poetry was used because it is easier to memorize material in meter and rhyme. Moreover, such tales were often recited on special occasions where poetry seemed more dignified than prose. By Snorri's day, court poetry had reached a state of high refinement, and he was a master of it. The enjoyment of reading Snorri's work is only an echo of what must have been the effect on those people for whom he wrote it, yet *Heimskringla* allows later readers a vivid glimpse into an earlier time.

"Critical Evaluation" by Edra C. Bogle

Bibliography:
Bagge, Sverre. *Society and Politics in Snorri Sturluson's "Heimskringla."* Berkeley: University of California Press, 1991. Using modern methods of historiography, Bagge concentrates on the work "as a description of society" in thirteenth century Norway and Iceland, dealing primarily with the political conflicts depicted. Examines similarities to the medieval history of other European countries.
Ciklamini, Marlene. *Snorri Sturluson.* Boston: Twayne, 1978. A useful introduction to the author, intended for the general reader as well as for the scholar. The slim book includes chapters on Snorri's life, "Snorri's Literary Heritage," the *Prose Edda*, and detailed summaries of and commentaries on *Heimskringla*.
Magnusson, Magnus, and Hermann Palsson, trans. *King Harald's Saga: Harald Hardradi of Norway, from Snorri Sturluson's "Heimskringla."* Harmondsworth, England: Penguin Books, 1966. An extremely readable introduction begins this translation of one section of *Heimskringla*. King Harald fought Harold of England just before Harold's defeat at the Battle of Hastings, and he may well have changed British history by preparing the way for William the Conqueror.
Parergon: Bulletin of the Australian and New Zealand Association for Medieval and Renaissance Studies 15 (1976): 3-54. Special Issue on Snorri Sturluson, edited by Hans Kuhn. Four scholarly articles that include examinations of literary and historical aspects of *Heimskringla*.

Sturluson, Snorri. *The Stories of the Kings of Norway Called the Round of the World*. Translated by William Morris and Eirikr Magnusson. London, Bernard Quaritch, 1905. Volume 4 contains a long historical and biographical introduction and three indexes, to persons, places, and subjects in the work.

HELEN

Type of work: Drama
Author: Euripides (c. 485-406 B.C.E.)
Type of plot: Love
Time of plot: Seven years after the sack of Troy
Locale: Egypt
First performed: Helenē, 412 B.C.E. (English translation, 1782)

Principal characters:
HELEN, wife of King Menelaus
MENELAUS, king of Sparta
THEOCLYMENUS, king of Egypt
THEONOE, a prophetess, sister of Theoclymenus

The Story:

Helen prayed before the tomb of Proteus, late king of Egypt, who had protected her from any dishonor while her husband Menelaus was leading the Greek hosts at the siege of Troy in the mistaken belief that the phantom Helen, carried off by Paris, son of the Trojan king, was really his wife. She recalled that when the three goddesses, Hera, Cypris (Aphrodite), and Athena had appeared before Paris and asked him to judge which was the fairest, Cypris had promised him Helen as a prize for choosing her. Hera, enraged at being rejected, had caused a phantom Helen to be carried off to Troy. In Egypt, the real Helen prayed for the safety of her husband and for protection against Theoclymenus, son of Proteus, who was determined to marry her.

She was accosted by Teucer, an exile from Achaea, who brought tidings of the end of the war—the ruin of the Greeks seeking their homelands, the disappearance of Menelaus and Helen, and the suicide of Leda, Helen's mother, who had killed herself because she could not endure her daughter's shame. The anguished Helen then warned Teucer not to seek out the prophetess Theonoe, as he intended, but to flee, for any Greek found in Egypt would be killed. The chorus grieved for Helen, who lamented her miserable fate and threatened suicide. In despair, she took the advice of the chorus and herself sought out Theonoe.

Menelaus, shipwrecked and in rags, appeared before the palace seeking aid, only to be berated and sent off by a portress who warned him that since Theoclymenus had Helen in his possession no Greeks were welcome in Egypt. Menelaus was astounded, for he had just left his Helen secure in a nearby cave. As he stood there in bewilderment, Helen emerged from her conference with Theonoe and confronted amazed Menelaus. Helen could not convince him that she was indeed his wife until a messenger brought word to Menelaus that the Helen he had left at the cave was gone, having soared away into the air. The long-separated lovers then embraced, rejoiced, and told each other of all the adventures that had befallen them. Their immense happiness was darkened by the realization of their present plight: Theoclymenus was determined to make Helen his own, and Menelaus was in danger of his life. The two resolved that if they could not concoct some scheme for escape, they would commit suicide rather than be separated again.

Theonoe, aware of the presence of Menelaus, appeared to inform him that although Hera had relented and was now willing to let him return to Sparta with Helen, Cypris was unwilling to have it revealed that she had bribed Paris to be chosen as the most beautiful of the goddesses. Therefore Theonoe, serving Cypris, felt obliged to expose Menelaus to her brother. Terrified, Helen fell to her knees in tears and supplication, and the enraged Menelaus threatened that they would die rather than submit. Theonoe relented, promised to keep silent, and urged them to devise some way of escape.

After rejecting several of Menelaus' desperate proposals, Helen hit upon a scheme which she put into operation as soon as Theoclymenus returned from a hunting trip. Appearing before him in mourning clothes and addressing him for the first time as her lord, Helen told him in a pitiful voice that a shipwrecked Greek warrior had just brought her word that Menelaus had drowned at sea. She was now ready, she added, to marry Theoclymenus if he would permit proper burial honors, in the Greek fashion, for her husband. Theoclymenus consented and turned to Menelaus, who was posing as the bearer of the sad tidings, for instructions concerning Greek burial rites for a king drowned at sea. He was told that there must be a blood-offering, an empty bier decked and carried in procession, bronze arms, a supply of the fruits of the earth, all to be taken out to sea in a large ship from which the widow must commit everything to the waters. The gullible Theoclymenus, anxious to foster piety in the woman who was about to become his wife, agreed to everything, and preparations were made for both a funeral and a royal wedding.

Later, a breathless messenger came running to Theoclymenus with the news that Helen had escaped with Menelaus. He described in detail how the Greek stranger commanding the ship had permitted a large number of shipwrecked sailors to come aboard and how, when the time came to slay the bull, the stranger, instead of uttering a funeral prayer, had called upon Poseidon to allow him and his wife to sail safely to Sparta. The aroused Egyptians sought to turn back the ship, but they were slaughtered by the Greek warriors whom Menelaus had smuggled aboard. Theoclymenus, enraged, realized that pursuit was hopeless but resolved to avenge himself on his treacherous sister, Theonoe. A servant from the palace tried in vain to convince him that he ought to accept events as they had happened. Both the servant and Theonoe were saved from death when the Dioscuri, the twin sons of Zeus, appeared from the sky to restrain Theoclymenus' rage and explain to him that Heaven had ordained the return of Helen and Menelaus to their homeland. Theoclymenus was chastened, and the chorus chanted familiar lines about the irony of Fate.

Critical Evaluation:

The story of *Helenē* is taken from a tradition established in the sixth century B.C.E. by the Greek poet Stesichorus, who believed that Paris had carried off to Troy only a phantom Helen fashioned by Hera, while the real Helen was taken to Egypt by Hermes. Some critics have praised this play, asserting that it has appropriate rhetoric throughout, consistent characterization, and a faultless plot. Perhaps the only exceptions to its evenness of tone are the first ode of the chorus and the murder of the fifty Egyptian galley-men. Others have been troubled with its melodrama and what they see as a contrived plot.

Only seven plays each survive by two of the acknowledged masters of Greek tragedy, Aeschylus and Sophocles, but nineteen are extant by the third, Euripides. He is thought to have written at least eighty. Of the three, Euripides is regarded as the dramatist most interested in psychology. In Medea (431 B.C.E.) and *Hippolytus* (428 B.C.E.) he portrays women whose passions lead them to horrible crimes. The witch Medea, wife of Jason, arranges the death of her husband's mistress and her father and kills her own two sons. Phaedra, wife of Theseus and stepmother and would-be lover of Hippolytus, arranges the death of her stepson when he spurns her advances. Most of Euripides' extant plays, in fact, concern women, and in *Helen* he offers one of his most engaging characters. As in *Alcestis* (438 B.C.E.), which also involves a rescue-escape plot and is the earliest of his plays that survives, the character of the woman is considerably stronger than those of the men around her.

Traditionally, from Homeric times, Helen was despised for being a willing hostage to the Trojan prince Paris and for being disloyal to her Spartan Greek husband, Menelaus (brother of the king, Agamemnon). In this version of the story, what Paris kidnapped from Menelaus was a phantom; the real Helen did not cause the Trojan War, and the Greek hatred of Helen is ungrounded. The play takes place in Egypt seventeen years after her supposed abduction.

In her opening speech Helen introduces the theme of the tension between appearance and reality. She is uncertain of the facts regarding her own birth; the entire world is in error about her identity. Tension would also have existed for an Athenian audience between the familiar world of Greece and mysterious one of Egypt.

Although the blame for the bloody, ten-year-long Trojan War belongs to Aphrodite, the goddess of love and lust, and to her phantom self, whom Paris abducted, Helen feels the guilt and disgrace that led to her mother's suicide; she understands why the Greek chieftain Teucer hates Helen. Their meeting is played out ironically: He leaves her saying she may look like Helen but her heart is not at all like hers. He goes so far as to wish that Helen die miserably, which reminds her, as she laments to the chorus of captive Greek women, that her life is monstrous, ironically because of her beauty. Confronted with the possibility of forced marriage to the barbarian (non-Greek) Theoclymenus, she insists she would prefer suicide.

In many of his plays Euripides' characters speak in sweeping terms of women's issues. The chorus, in this instance, advises Helen to consult the prophet Theonoe, sister of Theoclymenus, as "It is right for women to stand by a woman's cause." When she does consult Theonoe, the prophet proves to be strikingly reasonable and just, even compassionate, despite her supposed Egyptian barbarism. Another female character, the old portress at the palace gate, who figures briefly in the comic scene where Menelaus appears in rags, is also admirable and at least equal in wit to the Spartan hero.

Men do not come off well in this play at all. The unperceptive Teucer, for example, whose brother Ajax was fabled as a physical but not a mental giant, is easily deluded by Helen. When Menelaus is confronted with "the real" Helen, he seems utterly addled, and when the servant tells of the phantom Helen's disappearance, Helen must explain everything to Menelaus line by line. Moreover, the elaborate and successful ruse (another distortion of reality) concocted to effect their escape is all Helen's idea.

The first lustful and then vengeful Theoclymenus is the villain of the piece, first duped by Helen and then checked by her brothers, Castor and Pollux, in a contrived ending. The *deus ex machina* ending imposes further strain on the concept of reality. This device is anticipated at the start of the play; the phantom Helen is herself a sort of *deus ex machina*.

Among the male characters only the old servant, who recognizes the frustrating unpredictability of the gods and the unreliability of prophecy (a favorite theme in Euripides' plays), seems really sensible. The art of prophecy, he says "was invented as a bait for making money," and "The best prophet is common sense, our native wit."

Scholars have pointed to *Helen*'s historical context: the ruinous Athenian war with Sparta and to the disastrous naval expedition against Sicily that took place a year before the play was performed. Some critics insist the play should not be taken seriously, but others detect a serious antiwar message.

The haunting losses of the Trojan War are mentioned throughout, from Helen's opening speech and the meeting with Teucer to the choral lament for the dead in the latter half of the play. The supreme irony, of course, is that the ghastly war was fought over a phantom. This message is not lost on the servant, who says simply, "Yours was a story, but he [Menelaus] fought with the spear, and all/ his hard fighting was fought for nothing." Fearing their exposure to Theoclymenus, Menelaus contemplates suicide before Helen's appeal to Theonoe succeeds, and his response is that of the hero in time of battle: "I would rather die in action than die passively." Such a reaction, however, is ludicrous in a comic context. It is typical of the male, Euripides seems to say, that Menelaus can see only one way out, whereas the clever Helen not only wins over Theonoe by argument, but also deceives Theoclymenus with the supposed funeral ceremony at sea for Menelaus.

Athenian audiences suffering from the news of the defeat in Sicily and still struggling with the costs of the war with Sparta, which Athens was to lose, may have been distracted by the comic aspects of this escape story, but they must also have recognized the darker messages. The causes of war are illusory; heroism may be a delusion; the human costs of war are staggering; war, most notably as a solution to problems, is futile.

"Critical Evaluation" by Ron McFarland

Bibliography:
Austin, Norman. *Helen of Troy and Her Shameless Phantom.* Ithaca, N.Y.: Cornell University Press, 1994. The fullest account of the Helen story. Devotes nearly seventy pages to Euripides' play. Close reading, comment, bibliography.
Burnett, Anne Pippin. *Catastrophe Survived.* Oxford, England: Clarendon Press, 1971. Argues that Theonoe makes crucial decisions and saves the play from frivolity. Regards the play as a comedy of ideas.
Segal, Charles. "The Two Worlds of Euripides' *Helen.*" *Transactions of the American Philological Association* 102 (1971): 553-614. Surveys critical responses to the play and focuses on its serious philosophical aspects. Argues that it transcends its genre.
Taylor, Don. Introduction to *Euripides: The War Plays*, by Euripides. London: Methuen, 1990. Comments on *Helen* as a production, along with two other plays on the Trojan War; discussion concerns not only the war context but also the play's comic aspects.
Whitman, Cedric H. *Euripides and the Full Circle of Myth.* Cambridge, Mass.: Harvard University Press, 1974. Stresses the theme of appearance versus reality. Sees the play as a romance and as a drama of ideas.

HENDERSON THE RAIN KING

Type of work: Novel
Author: Saul Bellow (1915-   )
Type of plot: Mock-heroic
Time of plot: Late 1950's
Locale: Central East Africa
First published: 1959

Principal characters:

EUGENE HENDERSON, an American millionaire, a traveler in Africa, and a philosophical clown

ROMILAYU, his native guide and companion

WILLATALE, the queen of the Arnewi tribe

MTALBA, her sister

ITELO, the prince-champion of the Arnewi

DAHFU, the chief of the Wariri tribe

HORKO, the king's uncle

THE BUNAM, the chief priest of the Wariri

GMILO, a lion superstitiously believed to contain the spirit of Dahfu's father

ATTI, a lioness

DAHFU, her cub, as named by Henderson

The Story:

The seeker in Bellow's fiction is no Ulysses, Hamlet, Don Quixote, Gulliver, Huck Finn, or Ishmael. He is the philosophical clown, the innocent American, and adventurous discoverer of a spiritual quest that begins with the knowledge that "man's character is his fate" and ends with the realization that "man's fate is his character." Eugene Henderson is a tremendously comic figure, oversized in physique, great in his appetites, obsessed by the demands of an "I want, I want" that clamors without appeasement within him. He is fifty-five years old and has a violent temper; he has more money than even his eccentric needs demand, a second wife, and an assortment of children. He has turned his home into a pig farm, learned to play the violin, and acquired a reputation for drinking and crude manners. When he tries to sum up his life, it is, as he says, a mess, a fact he realizes without knowing the reasons for it. When he can no longer face himself, his family, or his past, he flees to Africa with dreams of becoming another Dr. Grenville or Albert Schweitzer. Africa, as Henderson sees it, is an empty and secret land, the last outpost of the prehuman past, a land unmarked by the footprints of history.

With a native guide, Romilayu, he arrives in the land of the Arnewi, where he engages in a ritual wrestling bout with Itelo, the champion of the tribe. Yet even in that remote place, he cannot escape his past; he remains a millionaire, a wanderer, a violent man looking for peace and happiness. The queen of these gentle people tells him that his malady is the grun-tumolani, the will to live instead of to die. Accepted by the Arnewi and courted by the queen's sister, Mtalba, Henderson plans to cleanse the tribe's sacred cistern, which is infested with frogs. His homemade bomb, however, blasts away the wall of the cistern, and the water seeps into the parched earth. Rather than face the consequences of this disaster, he runs away.

Henderson next turns up among the Wariri, a more warlike and savage tribe. The king is Dahfu, a ruler considerably more educated than his subjects, for he has studied in a missionary school and can speak to Henderson in English. While watching a tribal festival, Henderson is moved to lift the statue of Mummah, goddess of clouds, after several of the Wariri have failed to budge the massive idol. His act of strength, he soon discovers, is sacramental. When a sudden downpour follows, he is acclaimed as the new Sungo, or rain king, of the tribe, and he is compelled to put on the green silk drawers of his office. Henderson, elevated to a post in which he becomes a scapegoat for the capricious rain goddess, is no better off than he was before; he is as much governed by ritual as King Dahfu, who will rule only as long as his powers of procreation last. When those powers fail, he will be strangled and another ruler selected.

In the end, Dahfu is the means of Henderson's salvation. In an underground pit, he keeps a pet lion, Atti, a creature hated and feared by the Wariri because they believe the beast has bewitched their king. As Dahfu continues to postpone the ritual capture of the wild lion supposed to contain his father's spirit, the chief priest and the king's uncle plot against him. Under Dahfu's tutelage, meanwhile, Henderson learns to romp with the lion and imitate its roars. Dahfu tells him to act the lion's role and to be a beast; recovery of his humanity will come later.

Dahfu's lion cult impresses Henderson. His failure has been his bullish or piggish attempt to alter the world around him, to kick back when he felt that he had been kicked by fate. Instead he must alter himself; in particular, he must cure himself of fear by thinking like a lion, by imagining the lion at the cortex of his brain and making himself over as a lion. In spite of his crushing failure with the Arnewi, he has learned two things that help him in his daily lion lessons. First, although a man when struck is likely to strike out in revenge (as the Wariri but not the Arnewi do), pure virtue can break the chain of blows. The Arnewi, principally Mtalba, the aunt of Prince Itelo, who was once the companion of Dahfu, are virtuous but cowlike as a result of loving their cows; hence their virtue is not for Henderson. Second, he has been confirmed in a sense of his own worth by Mtalba, who oozed the odor of sanctity and was prepared to marry him. The demanding voice of the "I want, I want" within Henderson becomes the roar of the lion as Dahfu instructs him that man is still animal, but that it is possible for him to be a lion and not a pig.

The king's final lesson is that of courage in meeting death, which Henderson has always thought the biggest problem of all. When Dahfu is killed while trying to capture a wild lion, possibly through the chief priest's conniving, Henderson flees the Wariri to avoid becoming the next king, and he returns with a captured lion cub to America. The last glimpse of Henderson is at the airport in Newfoundland. He is playing with a little boy, the child of American parents, who speaks only Persian. Dahfu and his lion have done their work. Henderson's spirit is finally at home in the animal housing of his flesh.

Critical Evaluation:
Saul Bellow's novel *Henderson the Rain King* is a complex, richly comic novel of affirmation, at once serious, philosophical, and humorous. The hero, Eugene Henderson, undertakes a journey that parodies at the same that it reenacts the traditional heroic quest. In its interweaving of many thematic strands, this tightly knit work explores most of the major concerns of twentieth century American literature—self-definition, parents and children, death and life, good and evil, existential being and becoming, women and men—with humor and sympathy.

The narrative moves from sickness and sterility to health and fertility, from curse to blessing, from pointless materialism to spiritual direction, and from alienation to community. Henderson, through a comic heroic journey, overcomes his own sterility and fragmentation, brings water to the parched land of the Wariri tribe, and receives the blessing of wholeness himself. A boisterous, undisciplined giant, he learns the need for existential acceptance of his own limitations and of life's inevitable admixture of good and evil. By identifying with others in their affliction and by learning to accept responsibility for his own acts, he comes to a full realization of his own potential for both aggressive action and nurturance; he grows from incapacitating, though comic, self-hatred and self-doubt to wholeness and health. On his return to Connecticut he is ready to begin healing others, to attend medical school, and to become a doctor.

Henderson, the first-person narrator, tells his tale through parody and self-mockery. He is unsure how to begin because he cannot separate the tangled strands of his life. Trying to explain his trip to Africa, he makes several false starts and has unconnected flashbacks, which provide a context for his adventures. The Henderson of the pre-African section is described in self-mocking terms. It is only after his arrival in Africa, after he has shed his possessions and technology, that his genuine sympathy and motivation for his frequently bizarre acts become apparent.

In this novel, Bellow exploits literary and comic conventions to deflate his hero and at the same time to place him in a larger heroic context. Bellow gives form to the spiritual dimensions of his story through classical and biblical allusions and through the recurring motif of signs and portents. The outrageous Henderson is ironically juxtaposed with such figures as the English physician and missionary Sir Wilfred Grenfell, the legendary Greek questing heroes Ulysses and Oedipus, and the biblical figures Moses, Joseph, and Christ. By means of these references, the book is suffused with a sense of the sacredness and connectedness of life. Similarly, Bellow draws literary texts such as Jonathan Swift's satire *Gulliver's Travels* (1726), Herman Melville's epic novel *Moby Dick: Or, The Whale* (1851), and the essays of American transcendentalist Ralph Waldo Emerson and poetry of the English Romantics Percy Bysshe Shelley and William Wordsworth.

Henderson's mock-heroic journey recapitulates the stages of heroic development identified by Joseph Campbell in his 1949 study *The Hero with a Thousand Faces* as separation, initiation, and return. According to Campbell, the heroic journey is a rite of passage, a process of growth and self-knowledge attained by the death of an outmoded, ineffective pattern of behavior, and the rebirth of the self on a "higher spiritual dimension."

The components of Henderson's problematic life—potential sources of pride, pleasure, and meaningful identity such as his family, farm, animals, money and violin lessons—are unbearable burdens. He thinks of himself as a displaced person usurping the rightful place of a worthier one: "For who shall abide the day of His (the rightful one's) coming?" Although he is of monumental physical stature, he is incomplete, his face is "like an unfinished church." Enmeshed in a world of "swinish materialism," he has lost contact with the values of his ancestors and with his own inner being. Although his first name, Eugene, signifies that he is well-born, he must undergo a symbolic rebirth in order to attain spiritual wholeness. He must leave his suburban Connecticut life behind in order to regain his soul. This separation is the first stage of Henderson's heroic journey, and it is marked by comic self-importance and self-doubt, by improbable encounters with primitive African tribes, and by deeply philosophical discussions with their princes and with King Dahfu, ruler of the fierce Wariri tribe. On his return, Henderson, having learned to heal his troubled soul, is prepared to become a healer of the body, but he is not shown actually carrying out the routines of daily life with his family in Connecticut. Instead, the novel closes with his plane's stopover in Newfoundland (the name is symbolic) and with Henderson running in joyous circles in the snow. The novel's optimistic ending remains controversial, and some critics have questioned its appropriateness.

Henderson is in the tradition of the American hero who is determined to "do something about it" (whatever present crisis "it" may be at the moment) and moves toward ever new frontiers. For Henderson, as for his generation, the only remaining significant frontier is the encounter with death and with the self in the knowledge of that death.

Although *Henderson the Rain King* is clearly in the mainstream of the American literary tradition, the novel's brilliance derives from Bellow's life-affirming vision. In Henderson, he creates a hero who tackles his problems head-on, and who can laugh at both life and himself. Because Bellow's hero is able to bring a new self to birth, the novel unlike many contemporary novels such as Norman Mailer's *An American Dream* (1965) or Ralph Ellison's *Invisible Man* (1952), ends not in existential despair or in avoidance and isolation but rather in a triumphal return to society.

"Critical Evaluation" by Karen F. Stein

Bibliography:

Dutton, Robert R. *Saul Bellow*. Boston: Twayne, 1982. Focuses on the underlying philosophical theme of humans as "subangelic," situated between animals and divinity. *Henderson the Rain King*, with its biblical references and its menagerie of pigs, lions, cattle, and a bear, fits this theme easily.

Fuchs, Daniel. *Saul Bellow: Vision and Revision*. Durham, N.C.: Duke University Press, 1984. Traces the evolution of the novel from manuscript versions to the finished book.

Hyland, Peter. *Saul Bellow*. New York: St. Martin's Press, 1992. Starts with a brief overview of Bellow's life and career, then discusses the novels chronologically. The discussion of *Henderson the Rain King* focuses on its mixture of the comic and serious.

Malin, Irving. *Saul Bellow and the Critics*. New York: New York University Press, 1967. Twelve essays on Bellow's works. Most of the essays refer to *Henderson the Rain King* to some extent; David Hughes's essay, "Reality and the Hero," compares and contrasts the work to Vladimir Nabokov's *Lolita* (1955) to "illuminate the problems of the contemporary novelist."

Wilson, Jonathan. *On Bellow's Planet: Readings from the Dark Side*. Cranbury, N.J.: Fairleigh Dickinson University Press, 1985. Analyzes *Henderson the Rain King* in terms of anthropology, examining the relation between ritual and order in African societies and in twentieth century America. Includes a discussion of the novel's ending.

HENRY IV

Type of work: Drama
Author: Luigi Pirandello (1867-1936)
Type of plot: Psychological realism
Time of plot: 1922
Locale: A solitary villa in Italy
First performed: 1922; first published, 1922 as *Enrico IV* (English translation, 1922)

> *Principal characters:*
> HENRY IV, a man who believes he is Henry IV, Holy Roman emperor
> THE MARCHIONESS MATILDA SPINA, beloved of Henry before the
> accident
> BARON TITO BELCREDI, Matilda's lover
> FRIDA, her daughter, engaged to
> CHARLES DI NOLLI, a young count and nephew to Henry
> DOCTOR DIONYSIUS GENONI, a psychiatrist
> HAROLD,
> LANDOLPH,
> ORDULPH, and
> BERTHOLD, attendants who pretend to be Henry's secret counselors

The Story:

Henry IV thought that he was living during the eleventh century. Every effort was made to encourage his delusion. In fact, he lived in the present day.

The experienced valets introduced Berthold to his new position as a secret counselor at the court of Henry IV. Count Charles Di Nolli, nephew of Henry IV, hired these men to dress in eleventh century costumes and impersonate the participants in the historical debate between church and state that took place in Canossa in 1077. The valets complained that, though dressed and ready, they were idle until Henry IV supplied them with a cue to act. The men examined two portraits depicting a youthful Henry IV and his arch enemy, Matilda, marchioness of Tuscany, that were stylistically at odds with the medieval surroundings.

Charles, accompanied by the marchioness Dona Matilda Spina, and her daughter, Frida, who was engaged to Charles, brought Doctor Dionysius Genoni to observe and evaluate Henry IV's condition. Baron Tito Belcredi, Matilda's lover, completed the party. Matilda's likeness had served for that of the portrait of Matilda of Tuscany, so Charles ordered the valets to lock Henry IV's door to keep him away from her. The doctor expressed surprise that the surrounding illusion was so complete, while the others were surprised that Matilda's twenty-year-old portrait resembled Frida more than Matilda.

The portraits, souvenirs of a pageant twenty years earlier, reminded everyone of a tragic occurrence. No one remembered who had first proposed the pageant. Belcredi insisted that he had originated the idea, but Matilda thought not. She did reveal, however, that her choice to represent Matilda of Tuscany caused Henry to impersonate Henry IV, in order to be near her. She also confessed that he had been in love with her, which caused Belcredi to dispute the true character of Henry IV. He had been a superb actor, so was he really outgoing and humorous, or had he simulated it? Belcredi saw Henry IV as his rival for Matilda's affections and, though no one knew it, he had pricked Henry IV's horse during the pageant, causing Henry to fall and strike his head. When Henry regained consciousness, he thought he was the historical figure.

Berthold rushed in. He had unintentionally angered Henry IV and feared reprisal. His entry agitated and frightened the visitors. The valets explained that it was no longer possible to isolate Henry IV so the doctor, Belcredi, and Matilda decided to don costumes and interview him. Matilda chose to be the mother-in-law of Henry IV. The doctor chose to be a bishop. Belcredi chose to be a monk. It almost seemed that Henry IV penetrated their disguises because he accused Belcredi of being Peter Damiani, another archenemy of Henry IV. Henry IV's appearance, including dyed hair and makeup to retain the look of youth in the portrait, surprised the others. At the interview's conclusion, Henry IV bowed, left the room, and Matilda burst into tears.

Later, as the Doctor and Belcredi discussed Henry IV's condition, Matilda insisted that he was not insane. Matilda had sent for her old masquerade dress. The doctor planned to shock Henry IV into sanity by placing Frida, dressed as Matilda, and Charles, dressed as Henry, into the empty portrait frames. As they seemed to come alive, Matilda was to appear as herself to usher Henry IV into reality.

Frida entered wearing the costume, and they all experienced déjà vu. Landolph asked the doctor and Matilda to put their costumes on again and see Henry IV. The others left, and Matilda tried to convince Henry IV that Matilda of Tuscany was interceding with the pope in his behalf because of his love for her. Alone with his attendants, Henry IV, suddenly furious about his wasted years and Belcredi's liaison with Matilda, admitted that he had recovered his senses sometime earlier. The valets did not know whether to believe him, but he was able to convince them.

Henry IV said good night to his attendants. As he walked down the darkened hall, the doctor's plan was put into effect, and Henry was badly frightened as the images seemed to come to life. Frida, timid, was frightened in turn, and everyone rushed in from their hiding places. Matilda had heard of Henry IV's recovery from the valets. Everyone was angry at his ruse. Henry IV told of his gradual recovery and justified his deception by explaining that he had lost so many years of his life that he preferred to continue wearing the mask. He remembered Belcredi causing his accident and knew why he did it. In his mind, Frida was the Matilda he remembered. He terrified Frida when he took her in his arms.

When Belcredi rushed at him, Henry IV drew Landolph's sword and stabbed Belcredi. Seriously wounded, Belcredi was carried out, insisting that Henry IV was sane. A moment later, Matilda screamed her grief, and Henry IV realized that, by his rash action, he had condemned himself to a lifetime's impersonation of Henry IV.

Critical Evaluation:

By the 1950's some critics judged Sicilian-born Luigi Pirandello to be the most important playwright of his era. That estimation probably originated partly on the basis of his 1934 Nobel Prize in Literature and partly because of the psychological realism of his works, especially his dramas. Since the plays were marred by rather clumsy exposition, form was definitely not a factor in this choice.

Among Pirandello's best-known works are *Six Characters in Search of an Author* (1921), *Henry IV* (1922), and *Right You Are (If You Think So)* (1922). Even though the plots are widely different, all deal with the same theme: reality and identity.

Walter Starkie, whose 1926 study of Pirandello probably contains the most exhaustive and credible analysis of his work, points out that Pirandello represents the culmination of various Italian theatrical traditions. One tradition is that of the *commedia dell'arte*, a type of professional theater that developed in the sixteenth century and that utilized masks so extensively that the masks became synonymous with and inseparable from the characters they represented. Another tradition is that of the grotesqueries, dramatic pieces that are neither comedy nor tragedy and that intermingle reality and fantasy. Such works probably developed from the attempts to turn the improvisational *commedia* into a literary form. The third is the Futuristic movement, which was an outgrowth of expanding technology and depicted human beings as a small part of a vast machine. The movement reflected the dissatisfaction of a society that had lost not only the security of a sense of belonging but also the knowledge of who and what function it served.

Each of these theatrical influences seems to be incorporated in Pirandello's work, and each had its special place in the story of *Henry IV*. *Henry IV* is indisputably a story of many masks, both literal and figurative, as well as a story of dissociation. The man behind the mask of Henry is never identified to the audience. Throughout the play, he is simply referred to as Henry. That identity began with a literal mask: a costume and identity that he selected for a pageant. The audience learns how his choice of masks was influenced. The woman he loves chooses to be a certain historical character. He chooses Henry IV because of the historical connection between the two. During the pageant, he suffers a blow to his head, and when he regains consciousness, he believes himself to be Henry IV. He begins to inhabit fantasy created by his mask. Those around him have to wear masks to enter into his reality.

A major theme not only in *Henry IV* but also in Pirandello's other plays and novels is the question: What constitutes reality, and whose reality is correct? Each of the other characters, for example, has a totally different memory of Henry before his accident. Since memory betrays, the only memory available may be a delusional one. The characters assemble in a room dominated by two huge portraits; one is of the youthful Henry IV, in his pageant costume, painted as he was twenty years earlier. When Henry appears, his visitors are shocked to see that he wears yet another mask, the mask of youth. His hair is dyed and he wears heavy makeup to reproduce the youth of the man in the portrait. To Henry IV himself, he is twenty-six years old; that is his truth. Within his world and existence, it is only his reality that matters; to the others it might have been fantasy but to himself it was reality. There was no way to separate fantasy from truth.

Critics have theorized that Pirandello's relentless investigations into identity and reality resulted from the mental illness of his wife. The playwright was constantly confronted by a person whose reality was radically different from those about her. Somewhat insidiously, her perceptions forced realities and identities, like masks, onto those around her. For example, if she saw her husband as her betrayer, he was, in a very real sense, just that, and he had to deal with her in that role. It was such a dilemma that Pirandello translated into his plays, novels, and short stories. His dramatic legacy about perception and reality was passed on to theatrical movements such as absurdism.

H. Alan Pickrell

Bibliography:
Binion, Ralph. "The Play as Replay or the Key to Pirandello's *Six Characters in Search of an Author, Henry IV, and Clothe the Naked*." In *Soundings: Psychohistorical and Psycholiterary*. New York: Psychohistory Press, 1981. The only essay in Binion's collection that deals with theater. His expositions of Pirandello's themes, based on what he perceives as expressions of the author's psychological repressions, are both interesting and dangerous, because one is tempted to accept Binion's theories as facts.

Cambon, Glauco. *Pirandello: A Collection of Critical Essays*. Englewood Cliffs, N.J.: Prentice-Hall, 1967. Two essays deal peripherally with *Henry IV*, but the collection deals extensively with the thoughts and themes to be found in all of Pirandello's dramas.

Pirandello, Luigi. *Naked Masks: Five Plays*. Translated by Edward Storer, edited and with an introduction by Eric Bentley. New York: E. P. Dutton, 1952. Contains Pirandello's best known and most popular plays. Bentley, who was one of the major critics of twentieth century modernist dramas, offers excellent insights into *Henry IV*.

Starkie, Walter. *Luigi Pirandello*. New York: E. P. Dutton, 1926. A major book-length study on Pirandello. The starting point for all subsequent study. Not a biography but a work of meticulous scholarship about influences and themes.

HENRY IV, PART I

Type of work: Drama
Author: William Shakespeare (1564-1616)
Type of plot: Historical
Time of plot: 1403
Locale: England
First performed: 1592; first published, 1598

> *Principal characters:*
> HENRY IV, first Lancastrian English king
> PRINCE HAL, Henry's son and successor-to-be
> HENRY PERCY, SR.,
> HENRY PERCY, JR., or HOTSPUR,
> THOMAS PERCY,
> EDMUND MORTIMER, and
> OWEN GLENDOWER, noblemen and enemies of the king
> SIR JOHN FALSTAFF, friend of Prince Hal

The Story:

After he forced the anointed king, Richard II, to relinquish his crown, Henry Bullingbrook became King of England in 1399 as Henry IV. Within only a few years Henry IV himself began to face challenges to his kingship when the nobles who had supported him against Richard II began to defy the new king and aspire to the throne. Henry Percy, Jr., or Hotspur, defeated, on behalf of Henry IV, the invading army of Douglas of Scotland in northern England, but Hotspur then refused to subordinate himself to the king's authority and turn his Scottish prisoners over to the king. Realizing the threat of revolt by Hotspur and other nobles affiliated with him, Henry IV postponed his planned trip to the Holy Land and began to make preparations to confront the challenge of Hotspur and his allies. Among these were Owen Glendower, Welsh leader and alleged magician, who captured the Earl of March, and Edmund Mortimer, who had been sent by the king to defeat Glendower. Angry because he had been Richard II's chosen successor, Mortimer joined with Glendower, marrying his daughter and aligning himself with her father, Hotspur, and Hotspur's father, Henry Percy, Sr. Also allied with Hotspur were the Scotsmen under Douglas, whose defeat but retention by Hotspur had precipitated the conflict. Realizing the serious threat represented by such a powerful alliance, Henry IV began to gather his forces to protect his throne.

Notably absent from the king's supporters was his own son, Prince Hal, who was occupied with drunken revelry with the prankster Sir John Falstaff and Falstaff's thieving cohorts. Hal did not, however, join in the highway robbery performed by Falstaff and his friends, being content to play a joke on Falstaff by accosting the robbers, his friends, and frightening them away, and then returning the stolen money to its owners. Hal's enjoyable antics were terminated by a summons from his father, and upon being chastised for his waywardness, Prince Hal promised that he would atone for his inattention to matters of state by killing his father's most determined enemy, Hotspur.

At the same time that King Henry IV was developing a new alliance with his son and Falstaff, who was allowed to organize a troop of foot soldiers, the powerful alliance in opposition to the king was beginning to unravel. First, Hotspur's father, Henry Percy, Sr., sent notice that he could not bring his troops to Shrewsbury, the anticipated place of battle, because he was ill. Angry and undaunted as befitting his name, Hotspur insisted on continuing with the planned confrontation, stating his intention to kill Prince Hal personally. Next came the news that Owen Glendower was not going to help in the fight against the king because of supernatural premonitions of failure. Hotspur still persisted, despite Edmund Mortimer's also staying in Wales, in obedience to his father-in-law.

The day of battle arrived with appropriately tempestuous weather. Armed conflict became certain when Thomas Percy, Earl of Worcester, decided not to tell Hotspur of the king's final offer of amnesty if the nobles disbanded their troops, reaffirmed subordination and allegiance to Henry IV, and returned to their homes. Falstaff, meanwhile, asserted his belief (in no one's hearing) that honor was not worth fighting for and that he would avoid actual fighting if at all possible. The battle began, with Douglas killing Blount, one of the nobles supporting Henry IV. Falstaff arrived to denounce Blount's death as the predictable result of fighting for honor and, in his opinion, vanity. Hal then ran to Falstaff, to borrow Falstaff's sword for use in the battle, but found that Falstaff's scabbard contained only a bottle of wine. After rescuing his father from danger in a fight with Douglas by forcing Douglas to withdraw, Hal then met Hotspur.

In his prideful exuberance preceding the fight with Hal, Hotspur complained about Hal's nonexistent military record and bemoaned that killing Hal would not increase his own fame. Hal responded by promising to elevate his military reputation by killing Hotspur, and the battle began. While Hal and Hotspur were courageously struggling, Douglas encountered Falstaff, and rather than fight, Falstaff fell down and faked death, thus surviving Douglas' onslaught. Meanwhile, Hal defeated and killed Hotspur, and then saw Falstaff lying still and apparently dead. Hal bemoaned his old friend's death and departed, upon which Falstaff arose and proceeded to stab the dead Hotspur, in preparation for his planned contention that he killed the famous military leader. Hal then returned, listened to Falstaff's fabrication, and laughed and promised to lie to help his old friend conceal his cowardice if he could. Finally, Hal returned to his father and obtained the release of Douglas, the Scottish leader, because of Douglas' valor. The Shrewsbury battle solidified the reign of Henry IV as the first Lancastrian king of England; Prince Hal redeemed himself with his valor.

Critical Evaluation:

Widely recognized as the greatest English writer, William Shakespeare created plays that have provided the measure of dramatic excellence for centuries. *Henry IV, Part I* is a play that contributed considerably to Shakespeare's fame. It has been successful in production from the date of its first performance until the present. It is widely regarded as the best of Shakespeare's history plays. Essentially, Shakespeare created a new type of drama by his use of historical materials (such as Holinshed's *Chronicles of England, Scotland, and Ireland*, 1587). He used them to depict patriotically events of English history. Shakespeare helped to authenticate English historical and cultural tradition while at the same time altering and enhancing historical materials to create works of art. Shakespeare's histories are not factually precise; they are dramas.

Shakespeare's artistic embellishment is evident in the play in a number of ways. One of the most important is his creation of a structural symmetry lacking in the original, factual material that leaves the reader with a clear impression of the opposing forces involved in Henry's struggle to keep his crown. Shakespeare was also one of the first dramatists to integrate comic subplots into otherwise serious plays, as a way to entertain his heterogeneous audience and to unify his plays' themes. In *Henry IV, Part I*, the comic subplot of Falstaff and his cohorts (not really a part of English history) achieves all of these purposes. As humor, Falstaff's comments and actions enliven the play, such as his hacking and damaging his sword in order to support his preposterous story of valiant resistance to attack, when in fact he ran away at the very first sign of danger, as the audience is well aware. The Falstaff subplot serves to unify the play and elucidate its themes. Falstaff is the embodiment of misrule, cowardice, and fun. Shakespeare juxtaposes him and others who are his opposite, such as the valiant Hotspur and the serious, worried Henry IV. Falstaff is also parallel to Hotspur in their efforts to forcibly take that which others possess, in Falstaff's case the money of travelers on the highway and in Hotspur's case the kingship of Henry IV. On another level, however, Hotspur and Falstaff contrast; Falstaff is notoriously cowardly and is convinced that honor is only a word. Hotspur is the opposite, prone to anger and violence and so honor-crazed that he bemoans Prince Hal's lack of military reputation because he sees killing Hal as unlikely to sufficiently enhance his own status. This juxtaposition is astutely symbolized in Act V of the play, when Hotspur lies dead on stage because of excess interest in honor while Falstaff lies beside him, alive but exposed as equally excessive in cowardice. That juxtaposition of extremes also enables Shakespeare to convey a central theme of the play, the nature of true honor, represented by Hal, who embodies the happy medium between Falstaff and Hotspur. Hal, unlike Hotspur, enjoys diversions and humor, but not to the drunken, cowardly excess of his friend Falstaff. Hal is admirably courageous in defending his father and his kingdom from Hotspur, but unlike Hotspur is not in constant conflict with even allies as a result of excessive pride and militancy.

Shakespeare also creates structural parallels and contrasts in the plot as a way to delineate the qualities of his characters and as a way to integrate symbolism into the play. For example, important paralleling is done of King Henry IV and Prince Hal. Alike in their ultimate devotion to defense of their rule from rebellious nobles, they are opposites too. King Henry is reserved, in contact only with a chosen few in his aristocratic, military circle. Thus, he is not a well-loved king and must constantly fight to retain power. Hal, however, is regularly in enjoyable, intimate contact with all levels of English society, ranging from barmaids like Mistress Quickly (whose name speaks for itself) to the aristocratic, military group of his father. Thus, it seems clear, Hal will eventually be a popular king. King Henry decides to postpone his trip to the Holy Land in favor of military defense of his kingship, a clear hint that he is not a particularly peaceful ruler but rather one prone to respond violently to violent challenge, regardless of religious commitments. In contrast, Prince Hal engineers the release of Douglas, the Scottish leader who has fought vigorously against the king and Hal, preferring leniency to the fate his father imposes at the play's end upon Worcester and Vernon: death. In fact, one could say that Hal is forgiving of Douglas' transgressions, a clear indication of a subtle level of biblical symbolism in the play. Like the Old Testament God, Henry IV is wrathful and violent, leading by brute force, but like Christ, Hal is devoted to the commoners of the realm and is forgiving of those who oppose him (with the exception of Hotspur, who had to be dealt with by violence).

Thus, Shakespeare creates an artistic and structural symmetry in *Henry IV, Part I* via subplots, parallels, and contrasts that achieves interrelated purposes of audience entertainment, character clarification, symbolic integration, and thematic expression. Such complex compression gives the play a multiplicity in unity that has helped to generate its enduring appeal.

John L. Grigsby

Bibliography:
Baker, Herschel. Introduction to *Henry IV, Part I*, by William Shakespeare. In *The Riverside Shakespeare*, edited by G. Blakemore Evans. Boston: Houghton Miflin, 1974. Brief intro-

duction to the play, with explanation of Shakespeare's use of his sources, his different levels of plotting, and use of humor.

Bevington, David. Introduction to *Henry IV, Part I*, by William Shakespeare. New York: Oxford University Press, 1987. General introduction to the play. Discusses its performance history, its sources, its major characters, its structural unity, and its politics.

Cohen, Derek. "The Rite of Violence in *I Henry IV.*" *Shakespeare Survey* 38 (1985): 77-84. A detailed analysis of Hotspur as structural center of the play, explaining his evolution from comic to heroic and then to tragic figure.

Fehrenbach, Robert J. "The Characterization of the King in *I Henry IV.*" *Shakespeare Quarterly* 30 no. 1 (Winter, 1979): 42-50. Contends that a focus upon King Henry is crucial to comprehension of Shakespeare's use of indirect characterization.

Levin, Lawrence. "Hotspur, Falstaff and the Emblem of Wrath in *I Henry IV.*" *Shakespeare Studies* 10 (1977): 43-65. Analyzes the relationship between Hotspur and Falstaff, contending Falstaff is a visual representation of the wrath that controls Hotspur.

HENRY IV, PART II

Type of work: Drama
Author: William Shakespeare (1564-1616)
Type of plot: Historical
Time of plot: 1405-1413
Locale: England
First performed: 1597; first published, 1600

> *Principal characters:*
> KING HENRY IV
> HENRY or "HAL," Prince of Wales
> JOHN OF LANCASTER, another son of the king
> EARL OF WESTMORELAND, a member of the king's party
> EARL OF NORTHUMBERLAND, enemy of the king
> SIR JOHN FALSTAFF, a riotous old knight
> SHALLOW, a country justice
> THE LORD CHIEF JUSTICE, judge of the King's Bench
> MISTRESS QUICKLY, hostess of the Boar's Head Tavern in Eastcheap

The Story:

After the battle of Shrewsbury many false reports were circulated among the peasants. Northumberland believed for a time that the rebel forces had been victorious, but his retainers, fleeing from that stricken field, brought a true account of the death of Hotspur, Northumberland's valiant son, at the hands of Prince Henry, and of King Henry's avowal to put down rebellion by crushing those forces still opposing him. Northumberland, sorely grieved by news of his son's death, prepared to avenge that loss. Hope for his side lay in the fact that the archbishop of York had mustered an army, because soldiers so organized, being responsible to the church rather than to a military leader, would prove better fighters than those who had fled from Shrewsbury field. News that the king's forces of twenty-five thousand men had been divided into three units was encouraging to his enemies. In spite of Northumberland's grief for his slain son and his impassioned threat against the king and Prince Henry, he was easily persuaded by his wife and Hotspur's widow to flee to Scotland, there to await the success of his confederates before he would consent to join them with his army.

Meanwhile, Falstaff delayed in carrying out his orders to proceed north and recruit troops for the king. Deeply involved with Mistress Quickly, he used his royal commission to avoid being imprisoned for debt. With Prince Henry, who had paid little heed to the conduct of the war, he continued his riotous feasting and jesting until both were summoned to join the army marching against the rebels. King Henry, aging and weary, had been ill for two weeks. Sleepless nights had taken their toll on him, and in his restlessness he reviewed his ascent to the throne and denied, to his lords, the accusation of unscrupulousness brought against him by the rebels. He was somewhat heartened by the news of Glendower's death.

In Gloucestershire, recruiting troops at the house of Justice Shallow, Falstaff flagrantly accepted bribes and let able-bodied men buy themselves out of service. The soldiers he took to the war were a raggle-taggle lot. Prince John of Lancaster, taking the field against the rebels, sent word by Westmoreland to the archbishop that the king's forces were willing to make peace, and he asked that the rebel leaders make known their grievances so that they might be corrected.

When John and the archbishop met for a conference, John questioned and criticized the archbishop's dual role as churchman and warrior. The rebels announced their intention to fight until their wrongs were righted, so John promised redress for all. Then he suggested that the archbishop's troops be disbanded after a formal review; he wished to see the stalwart soldiers that his army would have fought if a truce had not been declared.

His request was granted, but the men, excited by the prospect of their release, scattered so rapidly that inspection was impossible. Westmoreland, sent to disband John's army, returned to report that the soldiers would take orders only from the prince. With his troops assembled and the enemy's disbanded, John ordered some of the opposing leaders arrested for high treason and others, including the archbishop, for capital treason. John explained that his action was in keeping with his promise to improve conditions and that to remove rebellious factions was the first step in his campaign. The enemy leaders were sentenced to death.

News of John's success was brought to King Henry as he lay dying, but the victory could not gladden the sad old king. His chief concern lay in advice and admonition to his younger sons, Gloucester and Clarence, regarding their future conduct, and he asked for unity among his sons. Spent by his long discourse, the king lapsed into unconsciousness.

Prince Henry, summoned to his dying father's bedside, found the king in a stupor, with the crown beside him. The prince, remorseful and compassionate, expressed regret that the king had lived such a tempestuous existence because of the crown and promised, in his turn, to wear the crown graciously. As he spoke, he placed the crown on his head and left the room. Awaking and learning that the prince had donned the crown, King Henry immediately assumed that his son wished him dead in order to inherit the kingdom. Consoled by the prince's strong denial of such wishful thinking, the king confessed his own unprincipled behavior in gaining the crown. Asking God's forgiveness, he repeated his plan to journey to the Holy Land to divert his subjects from revolt, and he advised the prince, when he should become king, to involve his powerful lords in wars with foreign powers, thereby relieving the country of internal strife.

The king's death caused great sorrow among those who loved him and to those who feared the prince, now Henry V. A short time before, the chief justice, acting on the command of Henry IV, had alienated the prince by banishing Falstaff and his band, but the newly crowned king accepted the chief justice's explanation for his treatment of Falstaff and restored his judicial powers.

Falstaff was rebuked for his conduct by Henry V, who stated that he was no longer the person Falstaff had known him to be. Until the old knight learned to correct his ways, the king banished him, on pain of death, to a distance ten miles away from Henry's person. He promised, however, that if amends were made Falstaff would return by degrees to the king's good graces. Undaunted by that reproof, Falstaff explained to his cronies that he yet would make them great, that the king's reprimand was only a front, and that the king would send for him and in the secrecy of the court chambers they would indulge in their old foolishness and plan the advancement of Falstaff's followers. Prince John, expressing his admiration for Henry's public display of his changed attitude, prophesied that England would be at war with France before a year had passed.

Critical Evaluation:

The third play in William Shakespeare's second tetralogy, *King Henry IV, Part II* is based on Raphael Holinshed's *Chronicles of England, Scotland, and Ireland* (1577) and on an anonymous Elizabethan drama, *The Famous Victories of Henry V*. It offers a collection of well-rounded characters for whose creation Shakespeare makes slender use of his sources. The drama resolves the conflict, carried over from *King Henry IV, Part I*, between the king and rebellious nobles. In its essence this conflict is one of local versus national rule. The second play also continues the character development of Prince Hal as an ideal future king. The denial of characters' expectations, marked by sudden dramatic reversals, represents a unifying motif of the drama.

Retaining the main plot of the rebellion and the subplot involving Falstaff and his companions from *Henry IV, Part I*, the drama limits action in favor of rhetoric. To the panoply of characters surrounding the king from *Henry IV, Part I*, Shakespeare adds the astute and farsighted Warwick as an adviser and the upright chief justice as another father figure for Prince Hal. Additions also enhance the subplot involving Falstaff. He is furnished, in *Henry IV, Part II*, with a spirited young boy as a page, with the histrionic, swaggering Pistol, and with the sharp-tongued Doll Tearsheet. In a further strand in the subplot, Justice Shallow, his cousin Silence, and Shallow's servants serve as humorous country bumpkins who willingly play into Falstaff's hands.

Rumors of battles linger through much of the drama, but they prove to be only rumors. As the rebels regroup under the able archbishop of York following their loss at Shrewsbury, the king's divided army prepares to move against the centers of rebel strength, Wales and York, arousing expectations of decisive battles. The threat of battle in Wales simply evaporates as the king learns the news that Glendower, the Welsh leader, has died. In the north, Prince John entices the rebels into a deceptive truce and sends their leaders to summary execution. The crushing of rebel power consolidates the king's rule, yet ironically he is too ill to enjoy the fruits of his victory. The action seems subdued and anticlimactic, the elimination of the rebel threat and the consolidation of regal power pave the way for an orderly succession.

Instead of vivid action, the play offers rhetorical confrontations to strengthen the dramatic conflict and to help resolve the two poles that influence Prince Hal—his father and Falstaff. In one of many indications that the fat knight will be rejected, Falstaff freely expresses his indiscreet opinions of other characters—Justice Shallow, Prince John, and Hal—in soliloquies. His comments on others are less extensive but no less indiscreet. In two early scenes, encounters between Falstaff and the chief justice foreshadow the major rhetorical confrontations involving Hal. Falstaff, who has escaped punishment for theft only because he holds a military commission, attempts to intimidate the chief justice, who has sought to admonish him about his thievery. To the chief justice, Falstaff pretends that he is deaf. This joke turns on Falstaff, who hears but fails to understand what others are saying. To the chief justice Falstaff intimates that the king is dying, that Hal will become king, and that as Hal's friend Falstaff will have important influence. Unmoved by any personal threat, the chief justice demonstrates his commitment of law as an ideal.

The scene foreshadows Hal's three great rhetorical confrontations in the drama: with the king, his real father; with the chief justice, a just and wise father figure; and with Falstaff, a parody of a father figure who must be rejected. In Act IV, scene iv, Hal is summoned to his dying father's bedside. The king's doubts about him are reinforced when Hal, thinking his father dead, removes the crown from a pillow to meditate on the pain and grief it has brought. Regaining consciousness, the king notices that the crown is missing and concludes that Hal has seized it prematurely. When the prince returns, the king denounces him for ingratitude, citing numerous examples from the past, but this sense of personal injury gives way to a more important concern—the future of the nation under Hal's rule. He fears that Hal will recklessly give power to Falstaff and others like him. As a consequence, the national unity that the king has achieved will degenerate into riot and anarchy. In an eloquent response, Hal convinces the king that he has been mistaken about Hal's intentions. He assures the king that he will follow the king's example, not Richard's. Following the speech, the king, now more confident, advises Hal to rely on the wise counselors who have served him and to involve the country in a foreign war in order to promote unity.

Following the king's death, his counselors and Hal's brothers fear impending chaos. In order to reassure them, Hal addresses the chief justice, who is convinced that he has the most to lose. Of his three confrontations, this is the only one that Hal deliberately manages; the other two are either unexpected or opportunistic. Assuming the role of an injured party, Hal demands that the chief justice explain his earlier decision to send Hal to prison. The chief justice recounts the episode in detail and argues that authority and justice demanded Hal's punishment. Pointedly, he asks Hal to explain how his sentence was unjust. The king's response, moving in its dignity, affirms to the chief justice that he had been correct, confirms him in his office, retains him as counselor, and assures those present that Hal will follow the example of his father.

The third confrontation is arranged by Falstaff, who has rushed from Gloucestershire to London after hearing of Hal's succession. Arriving in time for the coronation procession, Falstaff thrusts himself forward and addresses the king with impudent familiarity: "God save thee, my sweet boy!" Hal coldly turns aside and directs the chief justice to speak to Falstaff. The move astonishes Falstaff, who believes that the chief justice will be punished for his transgressions, and he again directs his speech to Hal. Speaking as king, Henry V denounces Falstaff as a misleader of youth and banishes him from the royal presence. Incredulous at this reversal and denial of his expectation, Falstaff thinks the king will send for him in private, but even Justice Shallow discerns the finality of the king's tone. By the play's end, Hal has convinced the skeptics of his ability to rule.

"Critical Evaluation" by Stanley Archer

Bibliography:

Ornstein, Robert. *A Kingdom for a Stage.* Cambridge, Mass.: Harvard University Press, 1972. In a critical study that includes all of Shakespeare's history plays, Ornstein devotes a chapter to *Henry IV, Part II.* He describes Hal's development and his rejection of Falstaff.

Pearlman, Elihu. *William Shakespeare: The History Plays.* Boston: Twayne, 1992. A valuable scholarly overview of the histories. The chapter on *Henry IV, Part II* is divided into numerous brief analyses of characters and themes.

Porter, Joseph A. *The Drama of Speech Acts.* Berkeley: University of California Press, 1979. Analyzes speech and oratory in the second tetralogy. A chapter on *Henry IV, Part II* explores the contrasts between Falstaff's speech and Hal's.

Tillyard, E. M. W. *Shakespeare's History Plays.* London: Chatto & Windus, 1944. Strong on historical interpretation, Tillyard's study explores the important themes of the second tetralogy. Traces the growth and development of Hal's character.

Traversi, Derek Antona. *Shakespeare: From "Richard II" to "Henry V."* Stanford, Calif.: Stanford University Press. A close reading of the second tetralogy includes a chapter on *Henry IV, Part II* that emphasizes character development and style.

HENRY V

Type of work: Drama
Author: William Shakespeare (1564-1616)
Type of plot: Historical
Time of plot: Early fifteenth century
Locale: England and France
First performed: c. 1598-1599; first published, 1600

Principal characters:
HENRY V, the king of England
CHARLES VI, the king of France
PRINCESS KATHARINE, his daughter
THE DAUPHIN, his son
MONTJOY, a French herald

The Story:

Once the toss-pot prince of Falstaff's tavern brawls, Henry V was now king at Westminster, a stern but just monarch concerned with his hereditary claim to the crown of France. Before the arrival of the French ambassadors, the young king asked for legal advice from the archbishop of Canterbury. The king thought he was the legal heir to the throne of France through Edward III, whose claim to the French throne was, at best, questionable. The archbishop assured Henry that he had as much right to the French throne as did the French king, and both he and the bishop of Ely urged Henry to press his demands against the French.

When the ambassadors from France arrived, they came not from Charles, the king, but from his arrogant eldest son, the Dauphin. According to the ambassadors, the Dauphin thought the English monarch to be the same hot-headed, irresponsible youth he had been before he ascended the throne. To show that he considered Henry an unfit ruler with ridiculous demands, the Dauphin presented Henry with tennis balls. Enraged by the insult, Henry told the French messengers to warn their master that the tennis balls would be turned into gun stones for use against the French.

The English prepared for war. The Dauphin remained contemptuous of Henry, but others, including the ambassadors who had seen Henry in his wrath, were not so confident. Henry's army landed to lay siege to Harfleur, and the king threatened to destroy the city and its inhabitants unless it surrendered. The French governor had to capitulate because help promised by the Dauphin never arrived. The French—with the exception of King Charles—were alarmed by the rapid progress of the English through France. King Charles, however, was so sure of victory that he sent his herald, Montjoy, to Henry to demand that the English king pay a ransom to the French, give himself up, and have his soldiers withdraw from France. Henry was not impressed by this bold gesture.

On the eve of the decisive battle of Agincourt, the English were outnumbered five to one. Henry's troops were on foreign soil and riddled with disease. To encourage them, and also to sound out their morale, the king borrowed a cloak and in this disguise walked out among his troops, from watch to watch and from tent to tent. As he talked with his men, he told them that a king is but a man like other men, and that if he were a king he would not want to be anywhere except where he was, in battle with his soldiers. To himself, Henry mused over the cares and responsibilities of kingship. He thought of himself simply as a man who differed from other men only in ceremony, itself an empty thing.

Henry's sober reflections on the eve of a great battle, in which he thought much English blood would be shed, were quite different from those of the French, who were exceedingly confident of their ability to defeat the enemy. Shortly before the conflict began, Montjoy again appeared to give the English one last chance to surrender. Henry, who was not discouraged by the numerical inferiority of his troops, again refused to be intimidated. As he reasoned in speaking with one of his officers, the fewer troops the English had, the greater would be the honor to them when they won.

The following day the battle began. Under Henry's leadership, the English held their own. When French reinforcements arrived at a crucial point in the battle, Henry ordered his men to kill all their prisoners so that their energies might be directed entirely against the enemy before them. Soon the tide turned. A much humbler Montjoy approached Henry to request a truce for burying the French dead. Henry granted the herald's request, and at the same time learned from him that the French had conceded defeat. Ten thousand French had been killed, and only twenty-nine English.

The battle over, nothing remained for Henry but to discuss with the French king terms of peace. Katharine, Charles' beautiful daughter, was Henry's chief demand, and while his lieutenants settled the details of surrender with the French, Henry made love to the princess and asked her to marry him. Though Katharine's knowledge of English was slight and Henry's knowledge of French little better, they were both acquainted with the universal language of love. French Katharine consented to become English Kate and Henry's bride.

"The Story" by James Marc Hovde

Critical Evaluation:

Henry V is the last play in the cycle in which William Shakespeare explores the nature of kingship and compares medieval and Renaissance ideal rulers. In *Henry IV, Part I*, Hal (the nickname by which Henry was known in his youth) soliloquizes that his roguish behavior, which so disturbs his father and the court, is policy—a temporary ploy soon to be discarded, after which he will astonish and delight his critics. True to that promise, Hal becomes the perfect English king, a true representative of all of his people, one who understands his own vices and virtues and those of his citizens. His youthful escapades have taught him a deep understanding of the human nature of the citizens he must rule, making him wise beyond his years.

Henry V, Shakespeare's summarizing portrait of what a good king should be, acts in the best Elizabethan tradition. The archbishop of Canterbury's description in Act I, scene i, confirms him as well rounded, a man of words and of action, a scholar, diplomat, poet, and soldier. He can "reason in divinity," "debate of commonwealth affairs," "discourse of war" or of music, and "unloose the Gordian knot of policy . . . in sweet and honeyed sentences." Unlike his father, who was tortured by self-recrimination, Henry V is sure of his authority, power, and ability. Proud of his country and followers, he attributes his successes to God's leadership. Unlike Richard II, Henry V keeps fears and worries private. He stays attuned to his subjects' undercurrents of feelings, as when he walks among them in disguise instead of relaying on censored reports. His effective spy system ferrets out traitors, whom he disposes of swiftly and violently. His earlier experiences help him to distinguish loyal subjects and good soldiers from the disloyal and incompetent; in Act IV, scene i, he rejects flattery but values blunt honesty. Moreover, he surrounds himself with good advisers whose advice he follows. He is generous to friends and supporters, rewards loyalty, and in his St. Crispin's speech he calls those who fight by his side "brothers" no matter what their rank or class. Above all, Henry V is flexible, able to be a king in war and a king in peace and capable of gentle mercy as well as harsh justice. His leniency to enemy villagers wins their hearts, but he is merciless to French captives who broke the rules of war, killing English baggage boys.

As a model king, Henry V is, above all else, politic, a follower of Niccolò Machiavelli's principles as enunciated in *The Prince* (1513) and able to manipulate language and people to attain his country's welfare. The opening action demonstrates Machiavellian policy consummately managed. As a new, untried king with a youthful reputation for riotous living, Henry V must secure his throne, extend his power, and improve his reputation while he still has youth, vigor, and political support. At the same time, he must take his subjects' minds off the internal conflicts, rebellions, and usurpations that had plagued his father's reign and he must unite diverse English factions. The quickest, most effective way to achieve these ends is to do as his father advised: "busy giddy minds with foreign quarrels." The French, by contemptuously dismissing Henry V as an effeminate wastrel fit only for the tennis courts, provide the perfect common enemy.

Henry's forceful yet poetic retorts to French insults couple powerful rhetoric with personal magnetism, and his threat to confiscate church property motivates its representatives to find religious and legal justifications for a foreign war. Thus England has not only "means and might" but a righteous "cause": ousting a usurper. The attack on France will be a holy war, fully backed by holy church and legal precedent: "God for Harry, England, and Saint George!" Extending England's legal claims in the tradition of Edward III reminds Henry's subjects and his European critics of his glorious ancestry and evokes English patriotism. Here, Henry V effectively employs Machiavellian strategies; his forceful rhetoric demonstrates good policy and good kingship. His warning to Harfleuer, for example, paints such a grim picture of death and destruction, of raped maidens and skewered infants, that fearful town officials surrender peacefully.

The victorious battle at Agincourt, the play's crux, proves Hal's right to rule England. Shakespeare carefully avoids mentioning the main historical reason for victory, the fact that the English battle methods of foot soldiers with long bows were superior to the medieval French methods of single armored knights waging hand-to-hand combat. He chooses instead to attribute the victory to a glorious English king whose rhetoric and personal valor was able to inspire common men to brave deeds against impossible odds. The French Dauphin and his nobles provide the antithesis to Hal's good English king, for they are vain, arrogant and overconfident, willing to leave the battle to servants and to flee at the first real opposition; they are disorganized and quarrelsome, whereas, thanks to Henry V's leadership, the English fight as an organized "band of brothers," their hearts "in the trim," "warriors for the working-day" ready for God to "dispose the day."

Act V shows Henry V as the complete hero king. The first four acts having demonstrated Henry's virtues in war, Act V shows a more casual Henry, commanding but at ease, a king for peace. It also demonstrates what a hero king can bring to England: a peace treaty with provisions for lands, power, title, and honor, as well as an attractive queen whose intelligence and proud spirit make her worthy to carry on both royal lines. A "conqu'ring Caesar," Hal tempers justice with mercy, restores order and harmony, and strengthens political bonds through a royal marriage that weds nations and provides a new garden, sullied but mendable, for England's royal gardener, the king, to cultivate and make profitable. Henry does not bargain away what was gained in the field but stays firm. He shows another facet of his rhetoric and understanding of psychology when he adopts the appealing role of a blunt solider, unused to wooing, to win a hesitant princess who does not wish to be forced into a loveless political marriage.

Henry V purposefully lends weight to the Tudor myth of divine right and reflects glory on Henry's descendant, Elizabeth I. Henry's victories confirm his (and by extension Elizabeth I's) God-given right to power. Elizabethan audiences were meant to understand that the qualities and blessings of Henry V had been passed on to Elizabeth by right of birth. Moreover, Henry V provides a model of good kingship: the harsh realities of political life demand both action and thought, mercy and justice, war and peace. A good king uses whatever tools available to attain order, harmony, peace and prosperity, for good ends justify the means.

"Critical Evaluation" by Gina Macdonald

Bibliography:
Berger, Thomas L. "Casting 'Henry V.'" *Shakespeare Studies: An Annual Gathering of Research, Criticism, and Reviews* 20 (1987): 89-104. Emphasizes that understanding the Elizabethan custom of multiple acting roles helps readers make thematic, ironic, comic, and aesthetic connections in the play.
Cook, Dorothy. "'Henry V': Maturing of Man and Majesty." *Studies in the Literary Imagination* 5, no. 1 (April, 1972): 111-128. Argues that the play demonstrates Henry's responsibility and personal maturity, his political and military virtues in Acts I and II and his private virtues in the final acts. The play's structural pattern alternates triumphs and reversals and uses a quickening pace, multiple plotting contrasts, and a psychologically effective dramatic balance.
Kernan, Alvin. "The Henriad: Shakespeare's Major History Plays." *The Yale Review* 59, no. 1 (October, 1969): 3-32. Concludes that the tetralogy records "the passage from the Middle Ages to the Renaissance and the modern world" and depicts Henry V as a consummate politician with a clear-cut public role that is necessitated by his desire to rule well.
Rabkin, Norman. "Rabbits, Ducks, and 'Henry V.'" *Shakespeare Quarterly* 28, no. 3 (Summer, 1977): 279-296. Rabkin argues the "fundamental ambiguity" of the play: Henry as both model Christian monarch and brutal Machiavel, a ruthless, expedient, manipulative ruler with spiritual and political virtues. This mature duality makes Henry V a good but inscrutable king.
Thayer, C. G. "The Mirror of All Christian Kings." In *Shakespearean Politics: Government and Misgovernment in the Great Histories.* Athens: Ohio University Press, 1983. Argues that the pragmatic, responsible Henry V is Shakespeare's model for a Renaissance monarch. Ruling more by personal achievement than by divine right, he reflects the kind of kingship considered ideal in 1599.

HENRY VI, PART I

Type of work: Drama
Author: William Shakespeare (1564-1616)
Type of plot: Historical
Time of plot: 1422-1444
Locale: England and France
First performed: c. 1592; first published, 1598

Principal characters:
KING HENRY VI
DUKE OF GLOSTER, uncle of the king and Protector of the Realm
DUKE OF BEDFORD, uncle of the king and Regent of France
HENRY BEAUFORT, bishop of Winchester, afterward cardinal
RICHARD PLANTAGENET, who becomes duke of York
JOHN BEAUFORT, earl of Somerset
EARL OF SUFFOLK
LORD TALBOT, a general, afterward earl of Shrewsbury
CHARLES, the Dauphin, afterward king of France
THE BASTARD OF ORLEANS, a French general
MARGARET OF ANJOU, afterward married to King Henry
JOAN LA PUCELLE, also known as Joan of Arc

The Story:

The great nobles and churchmen of England gathered in Westminster Abbey for the state funeral of King Henry V, hero of Agincourt and conqueror of France. The eulogies of Gloster, Bedford, Exeter, and the bishop of Winchester, profound and extensive, were broken off by messengers bringing reports of English defeat and failure in France, where the Dauphin, taking advantage of King Henry's illness, had raised a revolt. The gravest defeat reported was the imprisonment of Lord Talbot, general of the English armies. Bedford swore to avenge his loss. Gloster said that he would also hasten military preparations and proclaim young Prince Henry, nine months old, king of England. The bishop of Winchester, disgruntled because the royal dukes had asked neither his advice nor aid, planned to seize the king's person and ingratiate himself into royal favor.

In France, the Dauphin and his generals, discussing the conduct of the war, attempted to overwhelm the depleted English forces. Although outnumbered and without leaders, the English fought valiantly and tenaciously. Hope of victory came to the French, however, when the Bastard of Orleans brought to the Dauphin's camp a soldier-maid, Joan La Pucelle, described as a holy young girl with God-given visionary powers. The Dauphin's attempt to trick her was unsuccessful, for she recognized him although Reignier, duke of Anjou, stood in the Dauphin's place. Next she vanquished the prince in a duel to which he had challenged her in an attempt to test her fighting skill.

The followers of the duke of Gloster and the bishop of Winchester rioted in the London streets, as dissension between church and state grew because of Winchester's efforts to keep Gloster from seeing young Henry. The mayor of London declaimed the unseemly conduct of the rioters.

When the English and the French fought again, Lord Salisbury and Sir Thomas Gargrave, the English leaders, were killed by a gunner in ambush. Meanwhile Lord Talbot, greatly feared by the French, had been ransomed in time to take command of English forces in the siege of Orleans. Enraged by the death of Salisbury, Talbot fought heroically, on one occasion with La Pucelle herself. At last the English swarmed into the town and put the French to rout. Talbot ordered Salisbury's body to be carried into the public market place of Orleans as a token of his revenge for that lord's murder.

The countess of Auvergne invited Lord Talbot to visit her in her castle. Fearing chicanery, Bedford and Burgundy tried to keep him from going into an enemy stronghold, but Talbot, as strong-willed as he was brave, ignored their pleas. He whispered to his captain, however, certain instructions concerning his visit.

On his arrival at Auvergne Castle the countess announced that she was making him her prisoner in order to save France from further scourges. Talbot proved his wit by completely baffling the countess with double talk and by signaling his soldiers, who stormed the castle, ate the food and drank the wine, and then won the favor of the countess with their charming manners.

In addition to continued internal strife resulting from Gloster's and Winchester's personal ambitions, new dissension arose between Richard Plantagenet and the earl of Somerset. Plantagenet and his followers chose a white rose as their symbol, Somerset and his supporters a red rose, and in the quarrel of these two men the disastrous Wars of the Roses began. In the meantime Edmund Mortimer, the rightful heir to the throne, who had been imprisoned when King Henry IV usurped the crown some thirty years before, was released from confinement. He urged his nephew, Richard Plantagenet, to restore the family to the rightful position the Plantagenets deserved. Youthful King Henry VI, after making Plantagenet duke of York, much to the displeasure of Somerset, was taken to France by Gloster and other lords to be crowned king of France. In Paris, Talbot's chivalry and prowess were rewarded when he was made earl of Shrewsbury.

In preparation for the battle at Rouen, La Pucelle won Burgundy over to the cause of France by playing upon his vanity and appealing to what she termed his sense of justice. The immaturity of the king was revealed in his request that Talbot go to Burgundy and chastise him for his desertion. The duke of York and the earl of Somerset finally brought their quarrel to the king, who implored them to be friendly for England's sake. He pointed out that disunity among the English lords would only weaken their stand in France. To show how petty he considered their differences he casually put on a red rose, the symbol of Somerset's faction, and explained that it was merely a flower and that he loved one of his rival kinsmen as much as the other. He appointed York a regent of France and ordered both him and Somerset to supply Talbot with men and supplies for battle. Then the king and his party returned to London.

The king's last assignment to his lords in France was Talbot's death knell; Somerset, refusing to send horses with which York planned to supply Talbot, accused York of self-aggrandizement. York, in turn, blamed Somerset for negligence. As their feud continued, Talbot and his son were struggling valiantly against the better-equipped and larger French army at Bordeaux. After many skirmishes Talbot and his son were slain, and the English suffered tremendous losses. Flushed with the triumph of their great victory, the French leaders planned to march on to Paris.

In England, meanwhile, there was talk of a truce, and the king agreed, after a moment of embarrassment because of his youth, to Gloster's proposal that Henry accept in marriage the daughter of the earl of Armagnac, a man of affluence and influence in France. This alliance, designed to effect a friendly peace between the two countries, was to be announced in France by Cardinal Beaufort, former bishop of Winchester, who, in sending money to the pope to pay for his cardinalship, stated that his ecclesiastical position gave him status equal to that of the loftiest peer. He threatened mutiny if Gloster ever tried to dominate him again. The king sent a jewel to seal the contract of betrothal.

The fighting in France dwindled greatly, with the English forces converging for one last weak stand. La Pucelle cast a spell and conjured up fiends to bolster her morale and to assist her in battle, but her appeal was to no avail, and York took her prisoner. Berated as a harlot and condemned as a witch by the English, La Pucelle pleaded for her life. At first she contended that her virgin blood would cry for vengeance at the gates of heaven. When this appeal failed to move York and the earl of Warwick, she implored them to save her unborn child, fathered, she said variously, by the Dauphin, the duke of Alencon, and the duke of Anjou. She was condemned to be burned at the stake.

In another skirmish the earl of Suffolk had taken as his prisoner Margaret, daughter of the duke of Anjou. Enthralled by her loveliness, he was unable to claim her for himself because he was already married. He finally struck upon the notion of wooing Margaret for the king. After receiving her father's permission to present Margaret's name to Henry as a candidate for marriage, Suffolk went to London to petition the king. While Henry weighed the matter against the consequences of breaking his contract with the earl of Armagnac, Exeter and Gloster attempted to dissuade him from following Suffolk's suggestions. Their pleas were in vain. Margaret's great courage and spirit, as described by Suffolk, held promise of a great and invincible offspring.

Terms of peace having been arranged, Suffolk was ordered to conduct Margaret to England. Suffolk, because he had brought Margaret and Henry together, planned to take advantage of his opportune political position and, through Margaret, rule youthful Henry and his kingdom.

Critical Evaluation:

This play is the first in a trilogy of plays about the reign of King Henry VI of England, and the story is continued in a fourth play, *Richard III* (c. 1592-1593). The series of plays depicts the Wars of the Roses, which was civil warfare in England arising out of a dispute about the rightful succession to the throne. The theme of the series, an important and practical one to William Shakespeare's Elizabethan audience, is the necessity for a strong and secure monarchy to ensure the peace and prosperity of the realm. *Henry VI, Part I* deals with events leading up to the war.

The play can be confusing to read for a number of reasons, one of which is that it portrays disunity. The society it reflects is confused, inconsistent, and disorderly. In addition, the events shown in the play occurred over a period of many years, but in the play are telescoped down to fit into two or three hours. Consequently, the action tends to be fast-paced, unevenly developed, and sometimes disjointed. There are many short scenes and complete reversals of fortune in the war. The historical details are sometimes distorted and not always fully consistent. The cast of characters is very large, and several of them are central to the action of the play, but no single one of them dominates the play as a whole. Finally, a number of conflicts are presented, the causes of which are complex. An audience may be helped along by abridgment and stagecraft; audiences and readers alike benefit from an understanding of the play's historical background.

After the death of the strong and popular Henry V, the English face two problems: the resurgence of unity and fighting spirit among the French, who seek to reestablish France's sovereignty, and the disintegration of England, lacking an effective leader. The duke of Bedford makes a gloomy prophesy at the funeral of Henry V: "Posterity, await for wretched years," which is fulfilled during the course of the play in the emergence of a power struggle between the duke of Gloster and the bishop of Winchester and in the ultimately disastrous quarrel between Richard Plantagenet and the earl of Somerset.

Winchester is portrayed as a corrupt, power-hungry bishop who buys his elevation to cardinal and who seeks to overthrow the rightful, secular authority of the Protector. This can be seen as anti-Roman Catholic propaganda, a politically orthodox, patriotic bias widely shared by the Elizabethan audience. The dispute between Richard and Somerset is more complex. They are motivated by the desire for power and influence as well as by envy and mutual dislike. In Richard's case, he seems to be more than a mere opportunist. The dying Edmund Mortimer establishes his position, and right seems to be on Richard's side in his claim to the house of York, and perhaps the English throne. Richard is more developed and more ambiguous than most of the characters in the play. Audiences see in him not only imperative ambition but also a more thoughtful judgment, as in the scene in which Henry unwisely puts on a red rose and Richard chooses to hold his tongue.

The situation of the English armies fighting in France, poorly provisioned and equipped, lacking reinforcements, and close to mutiny, is a consequence of the dissension among the nobles at home, and to some extent a parallel to it. Leadership, values, and focus are generally absent, and replaced by uncertainty and self-interest.

Lord Talbot is an example of how an English leader should be. He is courageous and strong, loved by his own people and feared by his enemies. In the incident with the countess of Auvergne, audiences see he is charming but nobody's fool. He is loyal, optimistic and God-fearing. Talbot, like England, is betrayed and brought to ruin by the self-serving discord among the English nobility.

The portrayal of the French is unflattering. Their success in battle is the result of problems in the English ranks rather than to any virtue of their own, and the English blame it on French sorcery. Any pretensions the French have to valor are undercut. The Dauphin, Charles, for example, proclaims that he prefers to die rather than run; the next thing the audience sees him do is flee, complaining bitterly of the cowardice of his men. The scenes about the French are often comic, with Shakespeare mocking the French as effete blusterers whose main interest is making love.

Many critics have objected to the playwright's version of Joan of Arc, but in this play, with its clear anti-French, anti-Catholic bias, the portrayal is hardly surprising. Even the French characters undermine Joan's holiness with lust and wise-cracking innuendo. The play shows her to be whore, hypocrite, sorceress, and liar. All these attributes of a characterization were presumably popular with an Elizabethan audience.

In the final act, the alliance between Margaret of Anjou and the earl of Suffolk, the arrangements for the marriage between Henry and Margaret, and Suffolk's vow to use his influence with her to control the king and the realm form a strong link with the next play in the trilogy. *Henry VI, Part I*, written early in Shakespeare's career, lacks the stature of the later plays. Its structure is loose and episodic. The characters are generally impelled by one dominant characteristic and lack the subtlety of Shakespeare's later characterizations. The verse does not achieve the fluency and grandeur seen in the later plays. Critics have disputed whether the play was written by Shakespeare alone, or even whether Shakespeare wrote any of it at all. Modern scholarship tends to attribute the play entirely to Shakespeare, however, and to find in its vigor the greatness that the playwright would later show in abundance.

"Critical Evaluation" by Susan Henthorne

Bibliography:
Berry, Edward I. "*1 Henry VI:* Chivalry and Ceremony." In *Patterns of Decay: Shakespeare's Early Histories*. Charlottesville: University Press of Virginia, 1975. Addresses some of the issues raised by earlier critics. Concludes that the play needs to be read in sequence, not alone.
Bevington, David. "The First Part of King Henry the Sixth." In *William Shakespeare: The Complete Works*, edited by Alfred Harbage. Rev. ed. New York: Viking Press, 1969. Examines the functions of the characters. Considers multiple authorship theories and date of composition.
Blanpied, John W. *Time and the Artist in Shakespeare's English Histories*. Newark: University of Delaware Press, 1983. Examines how the playwright transforms historical material into drama. Contains a chapter on *Henry VI, Part I* that sees the play as flawed and immature, but one from which Shakespeare learned about his craft.
Saccio, Peter. *Shakespeare's English Kings: History, Chronicle, and Drama*. New York: Oxford University Press, 1977. Contains a section on the play recounting Shakespeare's sources. Includes genealogical charts and maps.
Tillyard, E. M. W. *Shakespeare's History Plays*. London: Chatto & Windus, 1944. Argues against multiple authorship theories, claiming the structure of the play shows clear signs of Shakespeare's style.

HENRY VI, PART II

Type of work: Drama
Author: William Shakespeare (1564-1616)
Type of plot: Historical
Time of plot: 1444-1455
Locale: England
First performed: c. 1590-1591; first published, 1594

Principal characters:
KING HENRY VI
DUKE OF GLOSTER, his uncle
CARDINAL BEAUFORT, great-uncle of the king
RICHARD PLANTAGENET, duke of York
EDWARD and
RICHARD, York's sons
DUKE OF SOMERSET, leader of the Lancaster faction
DUKE OF SUFFOLK, the king's favorite
EARL OF SALISBURY, a Yorkist
EARL OF WARWICK, a Yorkist
MARGARET, queen of England
ELEANOR, duchess of Gloster
JACK CADE, a rebel

The Story:

The earl of Suffolk, having arranged for the marriage of King Henry VI and Margaret of Anjou, brought the new queen to England. There was great indignation when the terms of the marriage treaty were revealed. The contract called for an eighteen-month truce between the two countries, the outright gift of the duchies of Anjou and Maine to Reignier, Margaret's father, and omission of her dowry. As had been predicted earlier, no good could come of this union, since Henry, at Suffolk's urging, had broken his betrothal to the daughter of the earl of Armagnac. However, Henry, pleased by his bride's beauty, gladly accepted the treaty and elevated Suffolk, the go-between, to a dukedom.

The voices were hardly still from the welcome of the new queen before the lords, earls, and dukes were expressing their ambitions to gain more control in affairs of state. The old dissension between the duke of Gloster and Cardinal Beaufort continued. The churchman tried to turn others against Gloster by saying that Gloster, next in line for the crown, needed watching. The duke of Somerset accused the cardinal of seeking Gloster's position for himself. These high ambitions were not exclusively the failing of the men. The duchess of Gloster showed great impatience with her husband when he said he wished only to serve as Protector of the Realm. When she saw that her husband was not going to help her ambitions to be queen, the duchess hired Hume, a priest, to traffic with witches and conjurers in her behalf. Hume accepted her money, but he had already been hired by Suffolk and the cardinal to work against the duchess.

Queen Margaret's unhappy life in England, her contempt for the king, and the people's dislike for her soon became apparent. The mutual hatred she and the duchess had for each other showed itself in tongue lashings and blows. The duchess, eager to take advantage of any turn

2853

of events, indulged in sorcery with Margery Jourdain and the notorious Bolingbroke. Her questions to them, all pertaining to the fate of the king and his advisers, and the answers which these sorcerers had received from the spirit world, were confiscated by Buckingham and York when they broke in upon a seance. For her part in the practice of sorcery the duchess was banished to the Isle of Man; Margery Jourdain and Bolingbroke were executed.

His wife's deeds brought new slanders upon Gloster. In answer to Queen Margaret's charge that he was a party to his wife's underhandedness, Gloster, a broken man, resigned his position as Protector of the Realm. Even after his resignation Margaret continued in her attempts to turn the king against Gloster. She was aided by the other lords, who accused Gloster of deceit and crimes against the state; but the king, steadfast in his loyalty to Gloster, described the former protector as virtuous and mild.

York, whose regency in France had been given to Somerset, enlisted the aid of Warwick and Salisbury in his fight for the crown, his claim being based on the fact that King Henry's grandfather, Henry IV, had usurped the throne from York's great-uncle. Suffolk and the cardinal, to rid themselves of a dangerous rival, sent York to quell an uprising in Ireland. Before departing for Ireland, York planned to incite rebellion among the English through one John Cade, a headstrong, warmongering Kentishman. Cade, under the name of John Mortimer, the name of York's uncle, paraded his riotous followers through the streets of London. The rebels, irresponsible and unthinking, went madly about the town wrecking buildings, killing noblemen who opposed them, and shouting that they were headed for the palace, where John Cade, the rightful heir to the throne, would avenge the injustices done his lineage. An aspect of the poorly organized rebellion was shown in the desertion of Cade's followers when they were appealed to by loyal old Lord Clifford. He admonished them to save England from needless destruction and to expend their military efforts against France. Cade, left alone, went wandering about the countryside as a fugitive and was killed by Alexander Iden, a squire who was knighted for his bravery.

Gloster, arrested by Suffolk on a charge of high treason, was promised a fair trial by the king. This was unwelcome news to the lords, and when Gloster was sent for to appear at the hearing, he was found in his bed, brutally murdered and mangled. Suffolk and the cardinal had hired the murderers. So was fulfilled the first prophecy of the sorcerers, that the king would depose and outlive a duke who would die a violent death.

Shortly after Gloster's death the king was called to the bedside of the cardinal, who had been stricken by a strange malady. There King Henry heard the cardinal confess his part in the murder of Gloster, the churchman's bitterest enemy. The cardinal died unrepentant. Queen Margaret became more outspoken concerning affairs of state, especially in those matters on behalf of Suffolk, and more openly contemptuous toward the king's indifferent attitude.

At the request of Commons, led by Warwick and Salisbury, Suffolk was banished from the country for his part in Gloster's murder. Saying their farewells, he and Margaret declared their love for each other. Suffolk, disguised, took ship to leave the country. Captured by pirates, he was beheaded for his treacheries and one of his gentlemen was instructed to return his body to the king.

In London, Queen Margaret mourned her loss in Suffolk's death as she caressed his severed head. The king, piqued by her demonstration, asked her how she would react to his own death. Evasive, she answered that she would not mourn his death; she would die for him. The witch had prophesied Suffolk's death: She had said that he would die by water.

Returning from Ireland, York planned to gather forces on his way to London and seize the crown for himself. He also stated his determination to remove Somerset, his adversary in court matters. The king reacted by trying to appease the rebel by committing Somerset to the Tower. Hearing that his enemy was in prison, York ordered his army to disband.

His rage was all the greater, therefore, when he learned that Somerset had been restored to favor. The armies of York and Lancaster prepared to battle at Saint Albans, where Somerset, after an attempt to arrest York for capital treason, was slain by crookbacked Richard Plantagenet, York's son. Somerset's death fulfilled the prophecies of the witch, who had also foretold that Somerset should shun castles, that he would be safer on sandy plains. With his death the king and queen fled. Salisbury, weary from battle but undaunted, and Warwick, proud of York's victory at Saint Albans, pledged their support to York in his drive for the crown, and York hastened to London to forestall the king's intention to summon Parliament into session.

Critical Evaluation:

Like the first play of the Henry VI trilogy, this play contains a large cast of characters. The time span covered in the second play is much shorter than that covered in the first, but the second play's action sprawls, covering a wide range of events. The depiction of a number of nobles, many of them hypocritical and self-serving, who group and regroup, deceive and dissemble, creates a potentially bewildering situation for the reader, requiring close attention. There are many threads of the narrative that are carried over from *Henry VI, Part I*, and a prior reading of that play enhances understanding of this one. More consistently than the preceding play, however, *Henry VI, Part II* explores its major thematic material: the consequences throughout the realm of an ineffectual monarch.

The animosity between the duke of Gloster and Cardinal Beaufort is one of the basic conflicts in the first part of the play. This conflict divides the other nobles into factions. Gloster, who has been the Protector of the Realm since the infant Henry became king, displays genuine concern for the welfare of the realm rather than self-interest. He refuses to join in his wife's ambitious hopes for his advancement. All he wants is to guide the young, unworldly king and protect him from harmful influences that would adversely affect England. Gloster's downfall lies in his assumption that he commands the loyalty of many of the other nobles, whom he believes share his own right-minded support of the king. Gloster, virtuous and loyal, is betrayed by everyone. Even those who have respect for him have their own agenda to pursue. His short-sightedness is a flaw, a failure in responsibility, because it has the tragic consequence of leaving the inadequate king and England itself vulnerable to the destructive effects of others' self-interest.

The duke of York is the contrast to Gloster. His fortunes wax as Gloster's wane. His cynicism is the opposite of Gloster's naïve goodness. York supports factions and chooses friends solely on consideration of who will serve his purpose best. York sides with Gloster against the cardinal at first because York believes it will help his cause, but later he allies himself with the cardinal and even his old enemies the dukes of Somerset and Suffolk in the plot to get rid of Gloster. He enjoins the support of the earls of Salisbury and Warwick because they will be useful to him when he makes his claim to the throne. The plot he hatches of using Jack Cade to foment rebellion against the king is based on the deception of the rebels. York is a Machiavellian villain, a character type that crops up frequently in drama of this period. For York, the end justifies the means. He is fully conscious of his own villainy, which he communicates to the audience, disclosing his plans and his motives.

King Henry is a virtuous man, pious and dutiful, but these virtues are not enough. He seems unable to understand that the terms of his marriage weaken his kingdom. He willingly surrenders hard-won territories in France. He remains blind to the true nature of his queen, who diminishes him personally with her scorn for his passive religiosity and with her relationship with Suffolk. Henry recognizes the cardinal's malice against Gloster and is not fooled by the queen, Suffolk, York, and the cardinal when they band together and declare Gloster to be personally ambitious to the point of treason, but he is quite helpless to save Gloster. He is unwilling or unable to exert his authority and impotently rails against what he rightly sees as a tragedy.

It is not only the nobility which is affected by the lack of a strong ruler. The populace is also in disorder. Saunder Simpcox, the imposter who falsely claims that his sight has been miraculously restored to him, shows that honesty and right values have become distorted. Although Gloster shrewdly sees the truth of the matter and deals with it swiftly, the king, as usual, is helpless.

The Jack Cade rebellion occurs after Gloster's death and the king is without genuine support. The whole episode is full of cynicism. The commoners lack faith in all leadership and authority. They have no illusions about Cade, seeing through his false claims to noble birth. Cade's ambitions are absurd, his logic clearly false, him promises beyond all that is possible. He is a caricature. Underlying this grotesque veneer is a more sinister truth. Cade and his rebels have might but no judgment, and they abuse whatever power they gain. Their rebellion violates the established political and moral orders. Ironically, it is a vision of an England that has vanished, the strong England of Henry V's time, that brings the rabble to its senses. Alexander Iden, who ultimately kills Cade, represents the right values. He lives a serene life, content with his lot. The Cade rebellion is a precursor of the civil war to come, and illustrates William Shakespeare's contention that society consists of interdependent strata arranged in a hierarchy. If the harmony of this structure is perverted at any level, all levels will suffer the consequences.

As a drama, *Henry VI, Part II* is superior to *Henry VI, Part I*. Its characterizations are more subtle. There are a number of well-executed comparisons and parallels. The self-serving rebellions of Cade and York help to provide a dramatic unity and coherence that do not occur in the linear, historical narrative. The verse is generally better both in terms of metrical fluency and imagery. There is some fine prose dialogue in the Jack Cade scenes, in which the abuse of language parallels the abuse of political power. This early play does not achieve the stature of Shakespeare's later history plays, but it is worthy of attention.

"Critical Evaluation" by Susan Henthorne

Bibliography:

Berry, Edward I. "*2 Henry VI:* Justice and Law." In *Patterns of Decay: Shakespeare's Early Histories*. Charlottesville: University Press of Virginia, 1975. Analyzes the play in the context of the whole of the trilogy. Addresses in the footnotes some of the negative criticism of earlier critics and recommends other critical analyses.

Blanpied, John W. *Time and the Artist in Shakespeare's English Histories*. Newark: University of Delaware Press, 1983. A chapter on *Henry VI, Part II* finds the play superior to *Henry VI, Part I*. Analyzes structure and characters.

Saccio, Peter. *Shakespeare's English Kings: History, Chronicle, and Drama*. New York: Oxford University Press, 1977. Contains a section on Henry VI discussing the history as recounted in Shakespeare's sources, as understood by twentieth century scholarship, and as it is dramatized in the plays. Includes genealogical charts and maps.

Tillyard, E. M. W. *Shakespeare's History Plays*. London: Chatto & Windus, 1944. Praises the structure of *Henry VI, Part II*, defending it against negative criticism.

Turner, Robert K., and George Walton Williams. "The Second and Third Parts of King Henry the Sixth." In *William Shakespeare: The Complete Works*, edited by Alfred Harbage. Rev. ed. New York: Viking Press, 1969. Useful introductory essay analyzes sources and style of the two plays, comparing them with Shakespeare's later history plays.

HENRY VI, PART III

Type of work: Drama
Author: William Shakespeare (1564-1616)
Type of plot: Historical
Time of plot: 1455-1471
Locale: England and France
First performed: c. 1590-1591; first published, 1595

Principal characters:
KING HENRY VI
EDWARD, the prince of Wales, his son
LOUIS XI, the king of France
RICHARD PLANTAGENET, the duke of York
EDWARD, York's son, afterward King Edward IV
EDMUND, York's son, the earl of Rutland
GEORGE, York's son, afterward the duke of Clarence
RICHARD, York's son, afterward the duke of Gloster
LORD HASTINGS, of the duke of York's party
THE EARL OF WARWICK, a king-maker
MARGARET, the queen of England
LORD CLIFFORD, Margaret's ally
LADY GREY, afterward Edward IV's queen
LADY BONA, the sister of the queen of France

The Story:

In the House of Parliament, the duke of York, his sons, and the earl of Warwick rejoiced over their success at Saint Albans. Riding hard, the Yorkists had arrived in London ahead of the routed king, and Henry, entering with his lords, was filled with consternation when he saw York already seated on the throne, to which Warwick had conducted him. Some of the king's followers were sympathetic toward York and others were fearful of his power; the two attitudes resulted in defection in the royal ranks. Seeing his stand weakened, the king attempted to avert disorder by disinheriting his own son and by pledging the crown to York and his sons, on the condition that York stop the civil war and remain loyal to the king during his lifetime.

Annoyed by the reconciliation and contemptuous toward the king because of her son's disinheritance, Queen Margaret deserted the king and raised her own army to protect her son's rights to the throne. The queen's army marched against York's castle as York was sending his sons to recruit forces for another rebellion. York's sons had persuaded their father that his oath to the king was not binding because his contract with the king had not been made in due course of law before a magistrate.

In a battle near Wakefield, Lord Clifford and his soldiers killed Rutland, York's young son, and soaked a handkerchief in his blood. Later, as he joined Margaret's victorious army, which outnumbered York's soldiers ten to one, Lord Clifford gave York the handkerchief to wipe away his tears as he wept for his son's death. York's sorrow was equaled by his humiliation at the hands of Margaret, who, after taking him prisoner, put a paper crown on his head that he might reign from the molehill where she had him placed to be jeered by the soldiers. Clifford and Margaret stabbed the duke of York and beheaded him. His head was set on the gates of York.

Hearing of the defeat of York's forces, Warwick, taking the king with him, set out from London to fight Queen Margaret at Saint Albans. Warwick's qualities as a general were totally offset by the presence of the king, who was unable to conceal his strong affection for Margaret, and Warwick was defeated. Edward and Richard, York's sons, joined Warwick in a march toward London.

King Henry, ever the righteous monarch, forswore any part in breaking his vow to York and declared that he preferred to leave his son only virtuous deeds, rather than an ill-gotten crown. At the insistence of Clifford and Margaret, however, the king knighted his son as the prince of Wales.

After a defiant parley, the forces met again between Towton and Saxton. The king, banned from battle by Clifford and Margaret because of his antipathy to war and his demoralizing influence on the soldiers, sat on a distant part of the field lamenting the course affairs had taken in this bloody business of murder and deceit. He saw the ravages of war when a father bearing the body of his dead son and a son with the body of his dead father passed by. They had unknowingly taken the lives of their loved ones in the fighting. As the rebel forces, led by Warwick, Richard, and Edward approached, the king, passive to danger and indifferent toward his own safety, was rescued by the prince of Wales and Margaret before the enemy could reach him. He was sent to Scotland for safety.

After a skirmish with Richard, Clifford fled to another part of the field, where, weary and worn, he fainted and died. His head, severed by Richard, replaced York's head on the gate. The Yorkists marched on to London. Edward was proclaimed King Edward IV; Richard was made duke of Gloster, and George, duke of Clarence.

King Edward, in audience, heard Lady Grey's case for the return of confiscated lands taken by Margaret's army at Saint Albans, where Lord Grey was killed fighting for the York cause. The hearing, marked by Richard's and George's dissatisfaction with their brother's position and Edward's lewdness directed at Lady Grey, ended with Lady Grey's betrothal to Edward. Richard, resentful of his humpback, aspired to the throne. His many deprivations resulting from his physical condition, he felt, justified his ambition; he would stop at no obstacle in achieving his ends.

Because of their great losses, Margaret and the prince went to France to appeal for aid from King Louis XI, who was kindly disposed toward helping them maintain the crown. The French monarch's decision was quickly changed at the appearance of Warwick, who had arrived from England to ask for the hand of Lady Bona for King Edward. Warwick's suit had been granted, and Margaret's request denied, when a messenger brought letters announcing King Edward's marriage to Lady Grey. King Louis and Lady Bona were insulted; Margaret was overjoyed. Warwick, chagrined, withdrew his allegiance to the House of York and offered to lead French troops against Edward. He promised his older daughter in marriage to Margaret's son as a pledge of his honor.

At the royal palace in London, family loyalty was broken by open dissent when King Edward informed his brothers that he would not be bound by their wishes. Told that the prince was to marry Warwick's older daughter, the duke of Clarence announced that he intended to marry the younger one. He left, taking Somerset, one of King Henry's faction, with him. Richard, seeing in an alliance with Edward an opportunity for his own advancement, remained; he, Montague, and Hastings pledged their support to King Edward.

When the French forces reached London, Warwick took Edward prisoner. The king-maker removed Edward's crown and took it to crown King Henry once again, who had, in the meantime, escaped from Scotland only to be delivered into Edward's hands and imprisoned in the Tower. Henry delegated his royal authority to Warwick and the duke of Clarence, in order that he might be free from the turmoil attendant upon his reign.

Richard and Hastings freed Edward from his imprisonment. They formed an army in York; while Warwick and Clarence, who had learned of Edward's release, were making preparations for defense, Edward, marching upon London, again seized King Henry and sent him to solitary confinement in the Tower.

Edward made a surprise attack on Warwick near Coventry, where Warwick's forces were soon increased by the appearance of Oxford, Montague, and Somerset. The fourth unit to join Warwick was led by Clarence, who took the red rose, the symbol of the House of Lancaster, from his hat and threw it into Warwick's face. Clarence accused Warwick of duplicity and announced that he would fight beside his brothers to preserve the House of York. Warwick, a valiant soldier to the end, was wounded by King Edward and died soon afterward. Montague was also killed.

When Queen Margaret and her son arrived from France, the prince won great acclaim from Margaret and the lords for his spirited vow to hold the kingdom against the Yorkists. Defeated at Tewkesbury, however, the prince was cruelly stabbed to death by King Edward and his brothers. Margaret pleaded with them to kill her too, but they chose to punish her with life. She was sent back to France, her original home. After the prince had been killed, Richard of Gloster stole off to London, where he assassinated King Henry in the Tower. Again he swore to get the crown for himself.

The Yorkists were at last supreme. Edward and Queen Elizabeth, with their infant son, regained the throne. Richard, still intending to seize the crown for himself, saluted the infant with a Judas kiss, while Edward stated that they were now to spend their time in stately triumphs, comic shows, and pleasures of the court.

Critical Evaluation:

In *Henry VI, Part III*, which belongs to William Shakespeare's tetralogy of history plays dealing with the political upheaval that followed Henry Bolingbroke's overthrow and murder of Richard II, England continues to suffer the evils of civil strife and social disorder arising from the war between the houses of York and Lancaster. Shakespeare's general purpose in this series of plays is to reassert the power of Providence, to glorify England, and to suggest the nature of her salvation; only with the restitution of the rightful heir to the throne at the end of *Richard III* will England be able to bind her wounds and enjoy peace once again.

Henry VI, Part III is a powerful study of disorder and chaos; the play interweaves a cohesive body of imagery and symbolism with the action of its plot to create a strong unity of impression centering on the theme of anarchy and disunity. Chaos prevails on all levels of society, from the state, to the family, to the individual. At the highest level of authority and social organization—the throne—anarchy has replaced traditional rule. The king, who must be the center of political strength and embody the sanctity of social duty, oath, and custom, is instead the essence of weakness; Henry not only yields the right of succession to York, but eventually abdicates in favor of Warwick and Clarence. Whenever he attempts to intervene in events, his weak voice is quickly silenced; finally he is silenced permanently, and his murder represents the ultimate overturning of political order and rejection of the divine right upon which his rule was founded. Contrasted to Henry, the representative of rightful power, is Richard, who in this play becomes the epitome of total anarchy. Richard murders the prince, the king, and his brother Clarence, boasting later, "Why, I can smile, and murder whiles I smile"; he scornfully disregards any form of moral obligation and eventually falls victim to unreasoning fears and nightmares.

The primary social bond, that of the family, is likewise in a state of dissolution. Again, the malady begins at the level of the king; Henry disinherits his own son, the rightful heir, thus causing his wife Margaret to cut herself off from him, sundering their marital bond. York's three sons become hopelessly divided by their conflicting ambitions. In Act II, scene v, Shakespeare shows, by means of the morality tableau, that the same family breakdown prevails among the common people as well. Simultaneously with its presentation of political and social chaos, the play dramatizes the disruption that is occurring in individuals' morality. Hatred, ambition, lust, and greed are the keynotes, while duty, trust, tradition, and self-restraint are increasingly rare.

Henry VI, Part III thus depicts a society in the throes of anarchy and war, a society where kings surrender their duties, fathers and sons murder each other, and brothers vie for power at any cost. Yet the play contains an occasional feeble ray of light, such as Henry's weak protests against the cruelty of the usurpers, his pleas for pity for the war's victims, and his ineffectual calls for an end to the conflict and a restoration of peace and order. These scattered flickers, dim as they are, along with several prophecies planted throughout the play, foreshadow the coming hope, the resolution of conflict, and the return of peace and rightful authority which will follow in *Richard III*.

Bibliography:
Evans, Gareth Lloyd. *The Upstart Crow: An Introduction to Shakespeare's Plays*. London: J. M. Dent and Sons, 1982. A comprehensive discussion of the dramatic works of William Shakespeare. While emphasis is on critical reviews of the plays, there are also discussions of sources, as well as material on the circumstances which surrounded the writing of the plays.
Leggatt, Alexander. *Shakespeare's Political Drama: The History Plays and the Roman Plays*. New York: Routledge, 1988. A discussion of Shakespeare's history plays, dealing with English history from the reign of King Henry II to that of Henry VIII, as well as three plays dealing with Roman history: *Julius Caesar* (1599-1600), *Antony and Cleopatra* (1606-1607), and *Coriolanus* (1607-1608).
Pierce, Robert B. *Shakespeare's History Plays: The Family and the State*. Columbus: University of Ohio Press, 1971. A general discussion of Shakespeare's history plays. The three plays on King Henry VI are discussed in a relatively positive way but are still generally treated as experimental.
Ribner, Irving. *The English History Play in the Age of Shakespeare*. London: Methuen, 1965. A revised edition of the 1957 work first published in the United States by Princeton University Press. A discussion of history plays in the Elizabethan era of English drama, including a discussion of Shakespeare's contributions in the field. The development of the form through the period is discussed, and its sources are considered.
Shakespeare, William. *The Third Part of King Henry VI*. Edited by Andrew S. Cairncross. Cambridge, Mass.: Harvard University Press, 1964. Part of the *Arden Shakespeare* series. This volume contains more than sixty pages' worth of introductory notes, including discussion of the various original texts, the sources of the play, and a critical evaluation of the work, as well as genealogical tables.

HENRY VIII

Type of work: Drama
Author: William Shakespeare (1564-1616) with John Fletcher (1579-1625)
Type of plot: Historical
Time of plot: 1520-1533
Locale: England
First performed: 1613; first published, 1623

Principal characters:
KING HENRY VIII
THOMAS WOLSEY, cardinal of York and lord chancellor of England
CARDINAL CAMPEIUS, papal legate
CRANMER, the archbishop of Canterbury
DUKE OF BUCKINGHAM
DUKE OF SUFFOLK
DUKE OF NORFOLK
GARDINER, the bishop of Winchester
THOMAS CROMWELL, Wolsey's servant
QUEEN KATHARINE, wife of Henry, later divorced
ANNE BOLEYN, maid of honor to Katharine, later queen

The Story:

Cardinal Wolsey, a powerful figure at court during the reigns of Henry VII and Henry VIII, was becoming too aggressive. Wolsey was of humble stock, which fact accentuated his personal qualities. He had lacked the advantages of family and ancestral office, and his political prominence was entirely the result of his own wisdom, manner, and persistence. Unscrupulous in seeking his own ends, he had ruthlessly removed obstacles in his climb to power.

One such hindrance to his ambitious designs was the duke of Buckingham, accused of high treason. When Buckingham was brought before the court for trial, Queen Katharine, speaking in his defense, protested against the cardinal's unjust taxes and informed the king of growing animosity among his people because he retained Wolsey as his adviser. Wolsey produced witnesses, among them Buckingham's discharged surveyor, who testified to Buckingham's disloyalty. The surveyor swore that, at the time of the king's journey to France, the duke had sought priestly confirmation for his belief that he could, by gaining favor with the common people, rise to govern England. In his long and persistent testimony the surveyor played upon earlier minor offenses Buckingham had committed, and he climaxed his accusation with an account of the duke's assertion that he would murder the king in order to gain the throne.

In spite of Katharine's forthright protestations against Wolsey in his presence, her repeated contention that the testimony against Buckingham was false, the accused man was found guilty and sentenced to be executed. The duke, forbearing toward his enemies, recalled the experience of his father, Henry of Buckingham, who had been betrayed by a servant. Henry VII had restored the honor of the family by elevating the present duke to favor. One difference prevailed between the two trials, the duke stated; his father had been unjustly dealt with, but he himself had had a noble trial.

Wolsey, fearing reprisal from Buckingham's son, sent him to Ireland as a deputy; then, incensed and uneasy because of Katharine's open accusations, he pricked the king's conscience with questions regarding his marriage to Katharine, who had been the widow of Henry's brother. Wolsey furthered his cause against Katharine by arousing Henry's interest in Anne Boleyn, whom the king met at a ball given by the cardinal.

The plan followed by Wolsey in securing a divorce for Henry was not a difficult one. In addition to his evident trust of Wolsey, the king felt keenly the fact that the male children born to him and Katharine in their twenty years of marriage had been stillborn or had died shortly after birth. Consequently, there was no male heir in direct succession.

The cardinal's final step to be rid of his chief adversary at court was to appeal to the pope for a royal divorce. When Cardinal Campeius arrived from Rome, Katharine appeared in her own defense. Wolsey once more resorted to perjured witnesses. Requesting counsel, Katharine was told by Wolsey that the honest and intelligent men gathered at the hearing were of her choosing. Cardinal Campeius supported Wolsey's stand.

In speeches of magnificent dignity and honesty, Katharine denounced the political treachery that had caused her so much unhappiness. Later, however, Katharine, expelled from the court and sequestered in Kimbolton, was able to feel compassion for Wolsey when informed that he had died in ill-repute; her undying devotion to Henry was indicated in her death note to him. Altruistic to the last, she made as her final request to the king the maintenance of the domestics who had served her so faithfully. Her strength to tolerate the injustices she had endured lay in her trust in a Power which, she said, could not be corrupted by a king.

Ambition overrode itself in Wolsey's designs for power. His great pride had caused him to accumulate greater wealth than the king had. The cardinal also used an inscription, *Ego et Rex meus*, which subordinated the king to the cardinal, and had a British coin stamped with a cardinal's hat. These, among many other offenses, were of little importance compared with Wolsey's double-dealing against the king in the divorce proceedings. Wolsey feared that Henry would marry Anne Boleyn instead of seeking a royal alliance in France, so Wolsey asked the pope to delay the divorce. When his letter was delivered by mistake to the king, Wolsey, confronted with the result of his own carelessness, showed the tenacious character of the ambitious climber. Although he realized that his error was his undoing, he attempted to ingratiate himself once more with the king.

He could not save himself. He could instigate the unseating and banishment of subordinates and he could maneuver to have the queen sequestered, but Henry wished no meddling with his marital affairs. Repentant that he had not served God with the effort and fervor with which he had served the king, Wolsey left the court, a broken man. He was later arrested in York, to be returned for arraignment before Henry. He was saved the humiliation of trial, however, because he died on the way to London.

Henry, shortly after the divorce, secretly married Anne Boleyn. After Wolsey's death she was crowned queen with great pomp. Cranmer, the new archbishop of Canterbury, became Henry's chief adviser. Jealousy and rivalry did not disappear from the court with the downfall of Wolsey. Charging heresy, Gardiner, bishop of Winchester, set out to undermine Cranmer's position with the king. Accused as a heretic, Cranmer was brought to trial. Henry, trusting his favorite, gave him the royal signet ring which he was to show to the council if his entreaties and reasoning failed with his accusers. Cranmer, overcome by the king's kindness, wept in gratitude.

As he stood behind a curtain near the council room, the king heard Gardiner's charges against Cranmer. When Gardiner ordered Cranmer to the Tower, stating that the council was acting on the pleasure of the king, the accused man produced the ring and insisted upon his right to appeal the case to the king. Realizing that they had been tricked by a ruse that Wolsey had used for many years, the nobles were penitent. Appearing before the council, Henry took his seat at the table to condemn the assemblage for their tactics in dealing with Cranmer. After giving his blessings to those present and imploring them to be motivated in the future by unity and love, he asked Cranmer to be godfather to the daughter recently born to Anne Boleyn.

At the christening Cranmer prophesied that the child, Elizabeth, would be wise and virtuous, that her life would be a pattern to all princes who knew her, and that she would be loved and feared because of her goodness and her strength. He said that she would rule long and every day of her reign would be blessed with good deeds.

Critical Evaluation:

Henry VIII is the last of William Shakespeare's histories, in terms of both time of composition and the date of its setting. It is very different from Shakespeare's earlier history plays such as *Henry V* or *Richard III*. First of all, the events of the play were much closer to those of Shakespeare's own time. Henry VIII had died only eighteen years before Shakespeare was born, and his daughter Elizabeth, whose birth is hailed at the end of the play, was herself Shakespeare's patron. Shakespeare had to treat certain political themes that might still have current relevance more gingerly than he would events that had occurred two or three centuries before. At the same time the playwright must have felt more emotion in writing about Henry VIII and his daughter than remote, long-dead kings; this emotion clearly shows through in the play's final scene.

Another difference between *Henry VIII* and the rest of the history plays is its genre. By the time of the play's composition, Shakespeare had written several of his most successful late romances, including *Cymbeline* (c. 1609-1610), *The Winter's Tale* (c. 1610-1611), and *The Tempest* (1611). The modes of treatment used by Shakespeare in these plays were also applied to *Henry VIII*. This is particularly demonstrated by the way the play does not end tragically, but amid joy and reconciliation. The way the overall pattern of the plot predominates over action and narrative is another marked differentiation between this history play and its predecessors.

King Henry himself displays this pattern in the play. He does not so much dominate the action as coordinate it. All the actions of the major characters are in reference to him. All the participants in political intrigue wish to gain his ear or influence. Although he is personally involved in the play's events, as is evidenced by his divorce from Katherine and remarriage to Anne spurring the drama's action, he is always somewhat above the fray, an image of the play's wish for harmony.

If there is tragedy in *Henry VIII*, it is not that of the king himself, but Cardinal Wolsey, much as it is Brutus, not the title character, who is the tragic figure in Shakespeare's *Julius Caesar* (c. 1599-1600). The audience sees Wolsey at the height of his power and intrigue as he successfully maneuvers against Buckingham, and suspects that the wheel of fate is about to turn against him. Unlike Shakespeare's earlier tragic protagonist Macbeth, Wolsey does not get to stir up serious trouble regarding the authority of his king; he is apprehended before his plans go too far. Even though Wolsey is sentenced to death, Shakespeare, with his characteristic late insights into the mixed nature of much human motivation, gives Wolsey's character a graceful and sympathetic turn as he goes to his end. In Wolsey's final speech, the audience can see inside his own thought processes, such that they do not necessarily think he has been well motivated from the beginning, but they do perceive that he has faced his demise in a spirit of Christian humility and self-knowledge.

Scholars have speculated that *Henry VIII* was influenced by the masques prominent in the Jacobean court of the early 1600's. These masques, which integrated music and ceremony into the pattern of drama, prized a kind of serenity and a pleasing overall composition. For all the historical material and political jostling of the play, there is also a stateliness and a gravity that raise the play above the level of chronicle and controversy.

There is controversy in abundance in the historical material of which the play is composed. The reign of Henry VIII was the most eventful period of English history. At the beginning of his reign, England was a minor country in an overwhelmingly Catholic Europe. At its end, England was a rising power of the North, a bulwark of Protestantism, and a pioneer in maritime exploring and trade. This development is shown in the play. At the beginning, Henry meets with the king of France at Field of Cloth of Gold. This lavish and splendid occasion, eloquently described in the opening dialogue between Norfolk and Buckingham, celebrates Henry's sovereignty. He is, however, one European crowned head in the company of another. At the end of the play, Henry, for better or for worse, has set England on its own course in control of its own destiny. His divorce from Katherine of Aragon, potentially the most pettily personal of issues, has been developed into a metaphor for wresting control of law and morality away from the Pope and into the power of the English crown. At the end of the play, when the prophecies are made concerning Elizabeth, it is mentioned that her successor shall "make new nations," a possible reference to the English colonization of Virginia which was occurring as Shakespeare was writing the play. The path of English history had been changed forever.

The English Reformation, that is to say England's religious changeover from Catholicism to Protestantism, is not at the center of Shakespeare's play. Neither a polemicist nor an ideologue, Shakespeare was concerned to honor the grandeur of the English royal family and the society for which it stood. Though Shakespeare's positive portraits of Cranmer, the archbishop of Canterbury, and the accused heretic Cromwell show that his sympathies lie with Protestantism, the play's spiritual heart is not sectarian. Cranmer's response of providential joy to the birth of Elizabeth is less political or religious than a kind of miraculous wonder reminiscent of the endings of Shakespeare's late romances. Elizabeth's birth, like Leontes' reunion with his daughter and heir Perdita in *The Winter's Tale*, signifies that there is a bright future ahead for the world of the play. The unusually auspicious portents that arrive with the birth of the child operate to soothe the tensions and rivalries that have just transpired and open the way for a calmer, more serene era. Shakespeare may have just been trying to flatter the royal family and Elizabeth's successor James. Most likely, however, Cranmer's speech represents the genuine praise of the playwright for the society that had fostered his talent.

"Critical Evaluation" by Nicholas Birns

Bibliography:
Donoghue, Denis. *The Sovereign Ghost: Studies in Imagination.* Berkeley: University of California Press, 1976. Emphasizes how Shakespeare portrays artistic as well as political order in *Henry VIII.*
Frye, Northop. *A Natural Perspective: The Development of Shakespearean Comedy and Romance.* Ithaca, N.Y.: Columbia University Press, 1965. Discusses the providential nature of Elizabeth's birth at the end of the play and the manner in which the prophecy at her birth causes the play to function as a romance as much as a history.
Hamilton, Donna B. *Shakespeare and the Politics of Protestant England.* Lexington: University Press of Kentucky, 1992. Argues that Shakespeare's presentation of Henry VIII is a reflection on the religious controversies of Shakespeare's day. Valuable in glimpsing the political issues behind Shakespeare's negative portrayal of Wolsey.

Kermode, Frank. "What There Is to Know About Henry VIII." In *Shakespeare: The Histories*, edited by Eugene M. Waith. Englewood Cliffs, N.J.: Prentice-Hall, 1965. Seizes on essential elements of *Henry VIII* for an understanding of the play's place in Shakespeare's canon. A good starting place.

Richmond, Hugh M. *King Henry VIII*. Manchester: Manchester University Press, 1994. An informative treatment of the relationship between the historical King Henry VIII and Shakespeare's character. Discusses the role of Protestantism and English nationalism in Shakespeare's portrait of the king.

THE HEPTAMERON

Type of work: Short fiction
Author: Marguerite de Navarre (Marguerite d'Angoulême, Queen of Navarre, 1492-1549)
First published: L'Heptaméron, 1559 (English translation, 1597)

Marguerite de Navarre, the sister of King Francis I of France, played an important role in the intellectual and spiritual life of France during the first half of the sixteenth century. She and her brother were both Catholic, but she was much more tolerant toward Protestants than was her brother. She befriended and protected such eminent French Protestant writers as Jean Calvin and Clément Marot. Although Marguerite de Navarre wrote numerous excellent poems on religious and philosophical topics, she has remained famous for her creative series of short stories that Claude Gruget called *The Heptameron* when he prepared her manuscript for publication in 1559, ten years after her death.

Italian culture was influential in France in the sixteenth century, and eminent Italian artists, including Leonardo da Vinci, had come to France and enriched the cultural life of France. Many French intellectuals, including Marguerite de Navarre herself, read Italian; the works of such important fourteenth century Italian writers as poet Francesco Petrarch and prose writer Giovanni Boccaccio were admired and frequently imitated by sixteenth century French writers.

Love was the principal theme in Petrarch's refined sonnets written for his beloved Laura and in Boccaccio's collection of one hundred short stories, *The Decameron* (1353), but Petrarch and Boccaccio wrote about love from different perspectives. Petrarch described love in an idealistic manner, and his love for Laura was based on true mutual respect and admiration. The tales in *The Decameron* often describe much less sympathetic characters, and love frequently is depicted in a violent and rather degrading manner. Boccaccio had written a treatise on the dignity of women, and the moral commentaries that follow each tale in *The Decameron* make it clear that he did not approve of the mistreatment of women by men. Although these tales are told from many different fictional perspectives, it is Boccaccio himself who proposed the moral lesson for each tale and his attitude toward the various characters is quite clear to his readers.

Marguerite de Navarre chose to imitate Boccaccio's masterpiece in a creative manner. The fictional framework of *The Heptameron* is deceptively simple. Ten well-educated French characters, five men and five women, are visiting an elegant spa at Cauterets in the Pyrenees, when flooding caused by heavy rains blocks the roads and forces them to stay in the mountain village. Once they realize that it will be impossible to leave Cauterets until the roads become passable, the travelers decide to pass the time by taking turns telling stories to one another for as many days as they are forced to stay in Cauterets. In her prologue to *The Heptameron*, Marguerite de Navarre explains that her imitation of Boccaccio will not be servile, because her characters promise to tell stories about actual events, not fictional events, as Boccaccio had done so masterfully in *The Decameron*. Although numerous references in *The Heptameron* are made to actual people, including Marguerite de Navarre and her brother King Francis I, it has never been determined with certainty the degree to which her tales are historically correct. Most critics prefer to treat her tales as fictional stories in which historical characters are mentioned.

A more significant difference between *The Heptameron* and *The Decameron* is that Marguerite de Navarre has her listeners comment on the tales that they have just heard. Thus, several different interpretations are proposed for each tale. The narrator presents a specific perspective for the events in each short story, but after the end of each tale, the listeners intervene and propose differing reactions to the same characters. Frequently, the comments of the listeners are longer than the tale itself, and the reader is in the intellectually stimulating position of either choosing from several proposed meanings for a specific tale or rejecting all these interpretations and selecting one more in keeping with his or her own moral and ethical beliefs.

A third difference between *The Decameron* and *The Heptameron* is in their length. Boccaccio's work includes ten full fictional days of storytelling, with ten tales told on each day. Boccaccio completed his *Decameron* in 1353, many years before his death in 1375. Marguerite de Navarre did not live long enough to complete her story collection as she had originally planned. The title comes from the Greek word "hepta," meaning seven, because her first editor, Claude Gruget, found only seventy-two complete tales, which he organized into seven full days of storytelling and two tales for the eighth day. Modern scholarship indicates that Marguerite de Navarre began composing these tales around 1543. Although she lived until 1549, her health during the last six years of her life was quite poor, which explains why she was unable to write one hundred tales for her characters.

Although many different topics are explored in the seventy-two extant tales that form *The Heptameron*, the most frequently treated theme is that of relationships between men and women and, more specifically, with the opposition between virtuous and immoral men and women. Marguerite de Navarre was an idealistic Christian who believed firmly both in the reality of God's love for human beings and in the very real possibility of mutual love between men and women. She understood, however, that many selfish people were unable to recognize that when physical love is not based on mutual respect and free consent, it is nothing more than sexual exploitation, if not rape. Many tales in *The Heptameron* deal directly with the exploitation of women by men. Among the forms of sexual exploitation denounced by Marguerite de Navarre's fictional narrators and commentators are rapes, attempted rapes, incest, adultery committed by clergymen, and the selling of sexual favors.

The first tale illustrates well how both the tale itself and the extended comments of the listeners help readers to arrive at their own moral interpretations. This story is told by Simontault, a married man who holds almost all women, except his wife, in low esteem. His lack of objectivity becomes clear both from the tales he tells and his remarks on other tales. Readers soon learn to be skeptical of whatever Simontault tells them. Although none of the four characters in the first tale is morally virtuous, Simontault singles out the one woman in this story for especially harsh criticism and is much more lenient in his comments on the three male characters.

In this tale, a prosecutor's wife is maintaining adulterous relationships with the local bishop, who buys her gifts with money that people have contributed to his diocese, and with a rich young man named Du Mesnil. The wife tries to ensure that the three men in her rather complicated life not discover the truth, but one evening the bishop stays beyond his assigned time and the impatient Du Mesnil sees him leave her house. When he rebukes her for sleeping with a bishop and not with him, she decides to get rid of Du Mesnil lest her husband learn of her double adultery. She tells her husband that Du Mesnil attempted to rape her, and the prosecutor hires a hit man who murders Du Mesnil. The prosecutor also has one of Du Mesnil's servants arrested in order to prevent her from revealing the truth about the murder, which she witnessed. All the prosecutor's efforts are in vain, and the king orders that the prosecutor and his wife be arrested for murder. They flee to England, but foolishly decide to return to France, where they are soon arrested. He is sentenced to life imprisonment as a galley slave; she becomes a prostitute after her release from prison.

It is clear to readers that none of these four characters is morally admirable. The bishop has violated his vow of chastity, committed adultery, and stolen money from his diocese. Du Mesnil is also an adulterer, who believes that his mistress should sleep only with him. The prosecutor and his wife have no redeeming moral qualities. The narrator does not express moral disapproval for all four characters, however. He states that the bishop, Du Mesnil, and the prosecutor were all victims of an evil woman, whom he compares to Eve. He then claims that all women since Eve have made a determined effort to torment, kill, and damn men. Simontault's misogyny and paranoia are painfully clear when he claims that unnamed women had mistreated him with similar cruelty. Simontault is also rather masochistic, because he adds that he prefers the suffering imposed on him by physically attractive women to idyllic treatment at the hands of less beautiful women who do not seek to dominate him sexually. Simontault is a psychologically unstable character who suffers from severe delusions.

Parlemente, whom most critics feel expresses the opinions of Marguerite de Navarre herself, ridicules Simontault by suggesting that because he enjoys being dominated by women, he should not criticize women at all. She then asks a sensible woman named Oisille to tell a tale about a virtuous woman in order to counterbalance Simontault's absurd conclusion that all women are like the murderous wife in the first tale.

In just the first few tales from *The Heptameron*, readers come to distrust both the various narrators and commentators, and Marguerite de Navarre helps her readers to arrive at their own moral interpretations of her tales. Throughout *The Heptameron*, there is an extraordinary thematic diversity. This short-story collection is a marvelously ambiguous work that has intrigued and challenged readers since its publication in 1559.

Edmund J. Campion

Bibliography:
Cholakian, Patricia. *Rape and Writing in "The Heptaméron" of Marguerite de Navarre*. Carbondale: Southern Illinois University Press, 1991. A fascinating feminist reading of *The Heptameron*. Examines many tales in which Marguerite de Navarre denounces rape and other acts of violence against women.
Davis, Betty J. *The Storytellers in Marguerite de Navarre's "Heptaméron."* Lexington, Ky.: French Forum, 1978. Explores the personality differences among the storytellers in *The Heptameron* and their relationships with one another.
Lyons, John D. *Exemplum: The Rhetoric of Example in Early Modern France and Italy*. Princeton, N.J.: Princeton University Press, 1989. Examines the narrative technique of using fictional examples in order to illustrate general psychological types. Contains an excellent analysis of Marguerite de Navarre's insights into the motivation for human behavior.
Lyons, John D., and Mary B. McKinley, eds. *Critical Tales: New Studies of "The Heptameron" and Early Modern Culture*. Philadelphia: University of Pennsylvania Press, 1993. Fifteen essays that examine narrative and rhetorical techniques, and the importance of gender and love in *The Heptameron*. Contains a bibliography of important critical studies on Marguerite de Navarre.
Tetel, Marcel. *Marguerite de Navarre's "The Heptameron": Themes, Language, and Structure*. Durham, N.C.: Duke University Press, 1973. Contains an excellent analysis of both positive and negative representations of love in *The Heptameron*.

HERCULES AND HIS TWELVE LABORS

Type of work: Folklore
Author: Unknown
Type of plot: Adventure
Time of plot: Antiquity
Locale: Mediterranean region
First published: Unknown

Principal characters:
HERCULES, a hero of virtue and strength
EURYSTHEUS, his cousin

The Story:

Hercules was the son of a mortal, Alcmena, and the god Jupiter. Because Juno was hostile to all children of her husband by mortal mothers, she decided to be revenged upon the child. She sent two snakes to kill Hercules in his crib, but the infant strangled the serpents with ease. Then Juno caused Hercules to be subject to the will of his cousin, Eurystheus.

As a child, Hercules was taught by Rhadamanthus, who one day punished the child for misdeeds. Hercules immediately killed his teacher. For this act, his foster father, Amphitryon, took Hercules away to the mountains to be reared by rude shepherds. Early in youth, Hercules began to attract attention for his great strength and courage. He killed a lion single-handedly and took heroic part in a war. When Juno, jealous of his growing success, called on Eurystheus to use his power over Hercules, Eurystheus demanded that Hercules carry out twelve labors. Juno and Eurystheus hoped that Hercules would perish in one of them.

The First Labor. Juno had sent a lion to eat the people of Nemea. The lion's hide was so protected that no arrow could pierce it. Knowing that he could not kill the animal with his bow, Hercules met the lion and strangled it with his bare hands. Thereafter he wore the lion's skin as a protection when he was fighting, for nothing could penetrate it.

The Second Labor. Hercules had to meet the Lernaean hydra. This creature lived in a swamp, and the odor of its body killed all who breathed the fetid fumes. Hercules began the battle but discovered that for every head he severed from the monster two more appeared. Finally he obtained a flaming brand from a friend and burned each stump as he severed each head. When he came to the ninth and invulnerable head, he cut it off and buried it under a rock. Then he dipped his arrows into the body of the hydra so that he would possess more deadly weapons for use in future conflicts.

The Third Labor. Hercules captured the Erymanthian boar and brought it back on his shoulders. The sight of the wild beast frightened Eurystheus so much that he hid in a large jar. With a fine sense of humor, the hero deposited the captured boar in the same jar. While on this trip, Hercules incurred the wrath of the centaurs by drinking wine they had claimed for their own. To escape from them, he had to kill most of the half-horse men.

The Fourth Labor. Hercules was ordered to capture a stag that had antlers of gold and hoofs of brass. To capture this creature, Hercules pursued it for a whole year.

The Fifth Labor. The Stymphalian birds were carnivorous. Hercules alarmed them with a bell, shot many of them with his arrows, and caused the rest to fly away.

The Sixth Labor. Augeas, the king of Elis, had a herd of three thousand oxen whose stables had not been cleaned for thirty years. Commanded to clean the stables, Hercules diverted the rivers Alpheus and Peneus through them and washed them clean in one day. Because Augeas refused to pay the agreed amount, Hercules later declared war on him.

The Seventh Labor. Neptune had given a sacred bull to Minos, the king of Crete. Minos' wife, Pasiphae, fell in love with the animal and pursued it around the island. Hercules overcame the bull and took it back to Eurystheus by making it swim the sea while he rode upon its back.

The Eighth Labor. Like the Stymphalian birds, the mares of Diomedes fed on human flesh. Usually Diomedes found food for them by feeding to them all travelers who landed on his shores. Diomedes tried to prevent Hercules from driving away his herd. He was killed and his body fed to his own beasts.

The Ninth Labor. Admeta, Eurystheus' daughter, persuaded her father to send Hercules for the girdle of Hippolyta, the queen of the Amazons. The Amazon queen was willing to give up her girdle, but Juno interfered by telling the other Amazons that Hercules planned to kidnap their queen. In the battle that followed, Hercules killed Hippolyta and took the girdle from her dead body.

The Tenth Labor. Geryoneus, a three-bodied, three-headed, six-legged, winged monster possessed a herd of oxen. Ordered to bring the animals to Eurystheus, Hercules traveled beyond the pillars of Hercules, now Gibraltar. He killed a two-headed shepherd dog and a giant herdsman and finally slew Geryoneus. He loaded the cattle on a boat and sent them to Eurystheus. Returning on foot across the Alps, he had many adventures on the way, including a fight with giants in the Phlegraean fields, near the present site of Naples.

The Eleventh Labor. His next labor was more difficult, for this task was to obtain the golden apples in the garden of the Hesperides. No one knew where the garden was, and Hercules set out to roam until he found it. In his travels, he killed a giant, a host of pygmies, and burned alive some of his captors in Egypt. In India, he set Prometheus free. At last, when he discovered Atlas holding up the sky, Hercules assumed this task, releasing Atlas to go after the apples. Atlas returned with the apples and reluctantly took up his burden again. Hercules brought the apples safely to Eurystheus.

The Twelfth Labor. This was the most difficult labor of all. After many adventures, he brought the three-headed dog Cerberus from the underworld. He was forced to carry the struggling animal in his arms because he had been forbidden to use weapons of any kind. Afterward, he took Cerberus back to the king of the underworld. So ended the labors of this mighty ancient hero.

Critical Evaluation:

Hercules—whose name came from the Latin form of the Greek word Herakles, meaning Hera's, or Juno's, fame—rightfully deserved to rule Mycenae and Tiryns. Because of Juno's machinations, however, his cousin Eurystheus had become his lord. Driven mad by Juno, Hercules killed his own wife and children and was required by the Delphic oracle to atone for his crime by becoming King Eurystheus' vassal. Eurystheus originally assigned ten *athloi*, ordeals for a prize, but he refused to count either the killing of the hydra (because Hercules had been assisted by his nephew Iolaus) or the cleansing of the Augean stables (because Hercules had demanded payment). The athloi required twelve years and are described according to Apollodorus, the first or second century mythographer; in that version, however, the third and fourth labors are reversed, as are the fifth and sixth. In some recountings, the last two labors are also reversed, which subtracts from the supreme accomplishment of conquering death, as it were, by returning from Hades. The same twelve exploits, nearly life-size, were sculpted on the metopes of the Temple of Zeus at Olympia in the mid-fifth century B.C.E.; four of those scenes have been reconstructed from the fragments. In his *Heracles* (c. 420 B.C.E.), Euripides perhaps reflects an earlier tradition, which begins with Homer, when he lists encounters with the Centaurs, with Cycnus the robber, and with pirates in place of the boar, the stables, and the bull.

The twelve labors are not the extent of Hercules' fame. Apollodorus, as well as Pausanias and Diodorus Siculus detail the "life" of this folk hero, and Ovid briefly recounts the labors and death of the hero in book 9 of his *Metamorphoses* (c. 8). From their accounts, and from other sources, there is an additional wealth of exploits accomplished before, during, and after the labors. Among those before is Hercules' fathering a child by each of the fifty daughters of King Thespius. During the labors, Hercules performed a number of well-known *parerga*, or "side deeds," such as joining Jason's Argonauts in quest of the Golden Fleece. He never completed that journey, however, since he was left at Mysia looking for his lost squire and boy-love Hylas. Among other *parerga* are his rescue of Alcestis from death after she had volunteered to die in place of her husband, King Admetus of Pherae. He also rescued Hesione, daughter of the king Laomedon of Troy, who was to have been sacrificed to Poseidon's sea monster. In Italy, he killed the fire-breathing Cacus who had stolen the cattle of Geryoneus that Hercules was driving back to Eurystheus. In Libya, he lifted the giant Antaeus from his mother Earth, from whom he derived his strength, and crushed him. He rescued Prometheus from the rock in the Caucasus and Theseus from the Underworld.

After the labors, Hercules sought to marry Iole, the daughter of Eurytus, the king of Oechalia and the man who had taught him archery. Eurytus refused, and Hercules killed the king's son, for which he was sold into slavery to Omphale, the queen of Lydia. There he performed numerous feats, including killing a great snake, fathering a child with Omphale, and burying the body of the fallen Icarus, who had flown too near the sun. Freed, Hercules went on to seek revenge on Laomedon and Augeas for their refusal to honor their debts for services rendered. He later married Deianira, whom he soon had to rescue from the lustful Nessus, who instructed Deianira to dip Hercules' tunic into the dying centaur's blood. The wearing of the tunic, he told her, would prevent Hercules, who was notorious for his amours, from loving another. Soon Hercules returned to Oechalia, where he murdered Eurytus and abducted Iole. In desperation and ignorance, Deianira sent him the tunic, and as soon as Hercules put it on it began to sear his flesh, for Nessus' blood had been poisoned by an arrow that long ago had been dipped in the Hydra's blood.

By the twelve labors, Hercules earned the immortality promised by the Delphic oracle, and so when Hercules died (having mounted his own funeral pyre), Jupiter persuaded all the gods, including Juno, to accept him into the pantheon. He took Hebe ("Youth") to wife and was thereafter universally honored. If Hercules' mythic origins are indeed solar, it is appropriate that he enjoyed apotheosis, or deification, and allegorical union with Youth, since the sun, having passed through the twelve zodiacal constellations, returns each year, renewed in strength. On the other hand, Hercules may well have been the original male consort to a pre-Greek mother goddess (Hera) as his name would imply. Whatever his origins, throughout the ancient world in religion and literature, he was welcomed as the ultimate folk hero, simple but not obtuse, powerful but humane, whose myths symbolized the pains and indignities that even great men, beloved of Jupiter, must undergo to attain undying glory. On him, the Athenians modeled their local hero, Theseus. Elsewhere he was variously worshiped as a hero, if not a god. The Cynics and Stoics, for example, admired his attention to duty and hardy self-reliance.

In art, Hercules is a favorite subject—his broad, muscled shoulders draped with the skin of a Nemean lion. Although he gained fame for his archery and physical strength, he is usually represented wielding a knotted club. In Roman art, representations of his brutality tend toward brutishness, so that he becomes more the gladiator than the noble demigod who courageously submitted to the will and whims of the lesser. More than any other figure, Hercules drew together the mythic experiences of Olympians and Titans, monsters and human beings, death and immortality.

"Critical Evaluation" by E. N. Genovese

Bibliography:
Bonnefoy, Yves, comp. *Mythologies*. Chicago: University of Chicago Press, 1991. An excellent reference source for the beginner. Includes a concise history and interpretation of the twelve labors of Hercules. An excellent companion to the study of mythology as well as source for bibliographic references to major criticism of myth.

Farnell, Lewis Richard. *Greek Hero Cults and Ideas of Immortality*. Oxford, England: Clarendon Press, 1970. Examines hero worship in Greece. Detailed discussion of the origin, function, and ritual of the cult of Hercules. An exceptional work for a serious study in the meanings and influences of this myth in the Greek culture.

Galinsky, G. Karl. *The Herakles Theme*. Totowa, N.J.: Rowman and Littlefield, 1972. Traces interpretations and characterizations of Hercules through a wide body of literature and art. Examines the twelve labors individually and explores the myth's influence in literature.

Kirk, G. S. *The Nature of Greek Myths*. Woodstock, N.Y.: Overlook Press, 1975. Traces Hercules' labors in classical literature. Analyzes the meaning of the myth and how it applies within the Greek culture. Excellent source for analyzing the structure and meaning of myth.

Schoo, Jan. *Hercules' Labors*. Chicago: Argonaut, 1969. Includes a detailed description and explanation of each of the twelve labors, as well as bibliographic information. Illustrations supplement discussion of the oral tradition of the Hercules myth. Excellent source.

HEREWARD THE WAKE
Last of the English

Type of work: Novel
Author: Charles Kingsley (1819-1875)
Type of plot: Historical
Time of plot: Eleventh century
Locale: England, Scotland, and Flanders
First published: 1866

> *Principal characters:*
> HEREWARD THE WAKE, a Saxon thane and outlaw
> LADY GODIVA, his mother
> TORFRIDA, his wife
> ALFTRUDA, his second wife
> MARTIN LIGHTFOOT, a companion in his wanderings
> WILLIAM THE CONQUEROR, Duke of Normandy and King of England

The Story:

Hereward was the son of the powerful Lord of Bourne, a Saxon nobleman of a family close to the throne. A high-spirited, rebellious youth, he was a source of constant worry to his mother, Lady Godiva. Hereward lacked a proper respect for the Church and its priests and lived a boisterous life with boon companions who gave him their unquestioning loyalty.

One day, a friar came to Lady Godiva and revealed that Hereward and his friends had attacked him and robbed him of what the priest insisted was money belonging to the Church. Lady Godiva was angry and hurt. When Hereward came in and admitted his crime, she said that there was no alternative. She maintained that for his own good, he should be declared a wake, or outlaw. Upon his promise not to molest her messenger, for Hereward really did not mind being outlawed as he wished to see more of the world, Lady Godiva sent Martin Lightfoot, a servant, to carry the news of Hereward's deed to his father and to the king. Hereward was then declared an outlaw subject to imprisonment or death.

Before he left his father's house, however, he released his friends from their oath of allegiance. Martin Lightfoot begged to be allowed to follow him, not as his servant but as his companion. Then Hereward set out to live among the rude and barbarous Scottish tribes of the north. His first adventure occurred when he killed a huge bear that threatened the life of Alftruda, ward of a knight named Gilbert of Ghent. He achieved much renown for his valorous deed. The knights of Gilbert's household, however, were jealous of Hereward's courage and his prowess, and they tried to kill him. Although he escaped the snares laid for him, he decided that it would be best for him to leave Scotland.

Accordingly, he went to Cornwall, where he was welcomed by the king. There the king's daughter was pledged in marriage to a prince of Waterford. A giant of the Cornish court, however, had become so powerful that he had forced the king's agreement to give his daughter in marriage to the ogre. With the help of the princess and a friar, Hereward slew the giant, whose death freed the princess to marry the prince whom she really loved.

After leaving Cornwall, Hereward and his companions were wrecked upon the Flemish coast. Hereward stayed there for a time in the service of Baldwin of Flanders and proved his valor by defeating the French in battle. There, too, Torfrida, a lady wrongly suspected of sorcery, schemed to win his love. They were wed after Hereward had fought in a successful campaign against the Hollanders, and a daughter was born of the marriage.

Meanwhile, King Edward had died, and Harold reigned in England. A messenger came to Hereward with the news that Duke William of Normandy had defeated the English at the battle of Hastings and that King Harold had been killed. Hereward then decided to return to Bourne, his old home. There, accompanied by Martin Lightfoot, he found the Norman raiders encamped. He found too that his family had been despoiled of all of its property and that his mother had been sent away. Without revealing their identity, he and Martin secretly went out and annihilated all the Normans in the area. Hereward swore that he would return with an army that would push the Norman invaders into the sea.

Hereward then went to his mother, who received him happily. Lady Godiva accused herself of having wronged her son and lamented the day she had proclaimed him an outlaw. He took her to a place of refuge in Croyland Abbey. Later, he went to the monastery where his aged, infirm uncle, Abbot Brand, was spending his last days on earth. There Hereward was knighted by the monks, after the English fashion. Hereward went secretly to Bourne and recruited a rebel army to fight against Duke William.

Although there were many men eager to fight the Normans, the English forces were disunited. Another king, an untried young man, had been proclaimed; but because of his youth, he did not have the support of all the English factions. Hereward had been promised help from Denmark, but the Danish king sent a poor leader through whose stupidity the Danes were inveigled into positions where they were easily defeated by the Normans at Dover and Norwich. Instead of coming to Hereward's aid, the Danes then fled. Hereward was forced to confess the failure of his allies to his men, but they renewed their pledge to him and promised to continue fighting. The situation seemed hopeless when Hereward and his men took refuge on the island of Ely. There, with Torfrida's wise advice, Hereward defeated Duke William's attack upon the beleaguered island. Hereward and his men retreated to another camp of refuge.

Shortly afterward, Torfrida learned of Hereward's infidelity with Alftruda, the ward of Gilbert of Ghent. She left Hereward and went to Croyland Abbey, where she proposed to spend the last of her days ministering to the poor and to Hereward's mother. Hereward went to Duke William and submitted to him. The conqueror declared that he had selected a husband for Hereward's daughter. In order to free herself from Hereward, Torfrida falsely confessed that she was a sorceress, and her marriage to Hereward was annulled by the Church. Hereward then married Alftruda and became Lord of Bourne under Duke William. His daughter, despite her entreaties, was married to a Norman knight.

Hereward, the last of the English, had many enemies among the French, who continually intrigued against him for the favor of Duke William. As a result, Hereward was imprisoned. The jailer was a good man who treated his noble prisoner as kindly as he could, although he was forced to chain Hereward.

One day, while Hereward was being transported from one prison to another, he was rescued by his friends. Freed, he went back to Alftruda at Bourne, but his life was not a happy one. His enemies plotted to kill him. Taking advantage of a day when his retainers were escorting Alftruda on a journey, a group of Norman knights broke into Bourne castle. Although Hereward fought valiantly, he was outnumbered. He was killed, and his head was exhibited in victory over the door of his own hall.

When she heard of his death, Torfrida came from Croyland Abbey and demanded Hereward's body. All were so frightened, especially Alftruda, by Torfrida's wild appearance and her reputation as a witch that Hereward's first wife got her way and the body was delivered to her.

She carried it away to Croyland for burial. Therefore, Hereward, the last of the English, died, and William of Normandy became William the Conqueror and King of England.

Critical Evaluation:

Charles Kingsley was a Church of England clergyman who spent his life as the priest in an English village. He was also one of the best-known public figures between 1850 and his death in 1875. He came to public attention as a writer of political tracts calling for social reform on behalf of the poor. His deep interest in history brought him appointments as chaplain to Queen Victoria, Regius Professor of Modern History at Cambridge, and tutor to the Prince of Wales. These appointments required him to give public lectures and to preach sermons, all of which were published and reached a wide audience. It is as a novelist, however, and as an exponent of what was called Muscular Christianity, that he was remembered.

Kingsley's first novels, *Yeast* (1848) and *Alton Locke* (1850), were social problem novels, set in contemporary England and addressing the economic and social conditions of the working classes. His interests then shifted to the historical novel and to primarily religious themes. *Hypatia* (1853) is set in the Roman Empire, *Westward Ho!* (1855) in the sixteenth century, and *Hereward the Wake* (1866), his last novel, in the eleventh century. This shift represents his withdrawal from his previous democratic sentiment as a Christian Socialist. The three historical novels dwell on the themes of Muscular Christianity, the hero as servant of God, and the conflict between Germanic and Latin cultures. The two other novels that he wrote during this period, *Two Years Ago* (1857) and *Water-Babies* (1862), also deal with religious themes.

Kingsley preached the virtues of what came to be called Muscular Christianity. True Christianity, he argued, emphasized masculine values rather than feminine ones. It stressed athleticism over the intellect, valued aggressiveness, and believed that real men keep a stiff upper lip and march on despite adversity. The Muscular Christian is the stuff of which heroes were made. Kingsley believed that the course of history was determined by the actions of a few great men of genius. As a Christian, Kingsley wanted the hero to be the servant of God and took the Old Testament figures Joshua and David as his models. In *Hereward the Wake* the protagonist is a model of the Muscular Christian hero. Kingsley draws the young man Hereward as at first little more than a loutish delinquent who enjoys violence. Later, after his exile, the character matures into a chivalric Christian knight who protects the weak and fights for justice. Chivalry, which Kingsley defined as struggle in the service of justice, was the difference between the merely muscular and the Muscular Christian.

The theme of the conflict between Germanic and Latin culture is at the forefront in all three of Kingsley's historical novels. In *Hypatia*, the conflict takes the form of the contrast between vigorous Goths and decadent Egyptians. In *Westward Ho!*, the conflict is between English seadogs and Spaniards. Kingsley believed that Latin culture was decadent and effeminate, while Germanic culture, once Christianized, was redemptive and manly. He argued that divine Providence, the guiding hand for human history, had set up the conflict and had called forth the Germans to lay the groundwork for the Protestant Reformation, English liberties, and the spread of Germanic civilization throughout the world by means of the British Empire. Having developed his ideas in the earlier novels, he gave utterance to them in a series of lectures at Cambridge, published under the title *The Roman and the Teuton* (1864), which remains the most systematic exposition of his historical interpretation. In *Hereward the Wake*, the conflict is rather less clear cut. The Saxons are Germanic, but as the descendants of Scandinavians, so are their enemies the Normans. The novel suggests that the Normans' Germanness has been contaminated or weakened by French influences. This is especially the case with respect to religion. Kingsley sees the Saxon church as more Germanic and therefore purer than the continental church. He has the Normans import the worst sort of scheming, malevolent, ascetic monks into England, while the Saxon monks are honest, forthright, and truly devout.

As befits a Muscular Christian, Kingsley never was a clear or systematic thinker, but in *Hereward the Wake* his thinking is especially muddled. He wants his readers to be on the side of Hereward and of William the Conqueror, for both men are examples of Christian heroes. Hence Kingsley had to turn elsewhere for a villain. While William is praised for his chivalric Christian knighthood, the minor character Ivo Taillebois, one of William's ambitious and unscrupulous henchman, fills the role of villain. This is not artistically satisfactory, for Hereward is left without an enemy worthy of his efforts. Another example of Kingsley's muddled thinking is his attitude toward the Normans. He stresses repeatedly that the Normans, descendants of Viking Germanic heroes, are to be admired despite their French culture. Moreover, because Kingsley believed that God guided history, and because as a Muscular Christian he did not like losers, he approved of the Norman Conquest. Hence, although he tells the story of a patriotic guerrilla struggle for national independence, he is unable to write convincingly about Hereward's goals and achievements.

Kingsley writes good descriptive passages that vividly describe the marshy fenland region around Cambridge, where most of the novel's action takes place. An enthusiastic walker, Kingsley had observed the countryside and reproduced well what he had seen. His descriptions of siege and battle scenes, most notably the defense of Ely and the defeat of William's invading troops, are controlled and effective. He was unable, however, to write effectively about the interior lives of his characters. This failure is especially marked in Kingsley's attempt to capture Hereward's interior motivations for his love for Torfrida and for his submission to William. In the final analysis, Kingsley was reluctant to explore his Muscular Christian hero's psychological flaws, for to admit that Muscular Christian heroes could be flawed undercut Kingsley's idea of heroism.

"Critical Evaluation" by D. G. Paz

Bibliography:
Chitty, Susan. *The Beast and the Monk: A Life of Charles Kingsley.* London: Hodder and Stoughton, 1974. This biography, using correspondence previously closed to researchers, is the best available analysis of Kingsley's personality, and especially of his relationship with his wife. A chapter is devoted to the writing of *Hereward the Wake.*
Collums, Brenda. *Charles Kingsley: The Lion of Eversley.* New York: Barnes & Noble Books, 1975. This good biography is a useful introduction to Kingsley's public life. It includes an analysis of *Hereward the Wake.*
Sanders, Andrew. *The Victorian Historical Novel, 1840-1880.* New York: St. Martin's Press, 1979. Provides essential background to the Victorians' interest in historical fiction. A chapter is devoted to *Hereward the Wake,* comparing the novel's view of history with the views that Kingsley expressed in *The Roman and the Teuton.*
Uffelman, Larry K. *Charles Kingsley.* Boston: Twayne, 1979. A general survey of Kingsley's literary reputation and an analysis of his works. It is the best beginning point for study of Kingsley.
Vance, Norman. *The Sinews of the Spirit: The Ideal of Christian Manliness in Victorian Literature and Religious Thought.* New York: Cambridge University Press, 1985. A comprehensive survey of Victorian attitudes toward Christian manliness, using Hereward as an example.

HERLAND

Type of work: Novel
Author: Charlotte Perkins Gilman (1860-1935)
Type of plot: Social realism
Time of plot: Early twentieth century
Locale: Utopia in South America
First published: serial, 1915; book, 1979

Principal characters:
> TERRY NICHOLSON, a misogynist explorer who exploits women
> JEFF MARGRAVE, a chivalric doctor who idolizes women
> VANDYCK JENNINGS, a sociologist whose reason bifurcates his comrades' extremities
> ELLADOR,
> CELIS, and
> ALIMA, citizens of Herland

The Story:

Three American male explorers, Terry Nicholson, Jeff Margrave, and Vandyck Jennings, were intrigued when they heard rumors of a land inhabited entirely by women. It was whispered that no man had ever returned from this strange place. Fascinated, the men employed a native guide to lead them to view the isolated "Herland," as Terry derisively termed it. Upon arriving, the explorers were instantly greeted by young Ellador, Celis, and Alima. When the men attempted to catch them, they were surprised to discover that the women's quick, easy strides surpassed their own. Curious, the explorers made their way to the village, convinced that such a civilization of beauty and efficiency must surely be the result of a male-dominated population. Reaching the town, the invaders were met by a multitude of women. Because they refused to cooperate with Herland's citizens the men were seized, born aloft, anesthetized, and comfortably confined.

While the men were imprisoned, assigned tutors taught them the national language, culture, and history; the prisoners were also instructed about the behavior expected of them as guests of Herland. The Americans learned that Herland was once a slaveholding civilization inhabited by both men and women. Constant warfare with the native populations in the region had killed almost all the men. When the few remaining slaveholders and all the older women were killed by male slaves who intended to control the fortressed country and its young female inhabitants, the women were forced to defend themselves and they vanquished their conquerors. After that, no man had existed in Herland for two thousand years. The women maintained their species through a miraculous development of parthenogenesis, an inherited power of a few that had become a characteristic of the entire race of women. This amazing capability of self-fertilization not only enabled the women to bear only female children, but it became the religious focus of the country. Herlanders believed not in a personalized god but in a maternal pantheism. The country collectively recognized that its life force and driving salvation were derived from its children. All the inhabitants collaborated and pooled their resources to ensure that Herland's collective citizenry became what they called Conscious Makers of People. Selective motherhood, communal nurturing, and equitable education eliminated the destructive behaviors of the former civilization, and collaboration replaced aggression.

Vandyck and Jeff studiously applied themselves to their lessons. With their newly discovered knowledge, they were able to adapt to their surroundings. Terry, however, remained angry and anxious in his captivity, and he struggled to regain control according to his old notions. He never missed an opportunity to deride his captors and never stopped referring to the women in derogatory or patronizing terms. Yet he could neither outwit nor charm his guardians.

During the educational process, the tutors innocently engaged their students with questions about American societal practices. Herland's enforced isolation left its citizens hungry for knowledge of other cultures. Often the women were surprised by the explorers' descriptions, which unconsciously depicted primitive crudities inherent in American culture, which apparently affected all realms of society including the family, economics, division of labor, education, and religion. The novel's narrator, Vandyck, revealed a growing awareness that some aspects of American culture were patriarchal and barbaric when contrasted with Herland's superior and egalitarian system.

Once the men had mastered the rudimentary aspects of Herland's culture, history, and language, they were freed from bodily restraint but still not allowed to leave the country. Soon after, they fell in love with the young women they had first encountered. Eventually, the three foreigners married the three Herland women in a triple ceremony sanctioned by the entire community. The men were dismayed, however, to discover that the collective Herlandic ideology resisted Western notions of relationships based on physical possession. The marriages were to be based on Herlandic ideals of communal platonic love, not on a patriarchal belief in individualized possession. Initially, none of the three women could see any point to sexual intercourse, nor could any of them be persuaded to add her husband's surname to her given name. The new wives also resisted establishing private marital residences with their new husbands, and they continued their beloved work as foresters.

Ellador and Vandyck nevertheless reached great emotional depths in a marriage based on reason and equality. Even Jeff, whose assimilation had occurred too readily and with little thought, was thoroughly content in the life he shared with Celis. Only Terry, the most misogynistic of the three, refused to give up what he perceived to be his rights as a man and husband. When he unsuccessfully attempted to rape his wife, Alima in self-defense thwarted his assault. Terry was thereupon imprisoned, tried for his crime, and banished from the country. Vandyck and Ellador decided to accompany him, since Ellador wished to learn more about Western society for Herlandic purposes. Jeff refused to leave the civilization and chose to remain with Celis, who was carrying a child, the first in two thousand years of Herlandic history to be produced by the union of a woman and a man.

Critical Evaluation:

In her autobiography, *The Living of Charlotte Perkins Gilman* (1935), Gilman wrote: "In my judgment it is a pretty poor thing to write, to talk, without a purpose." Charlotte Perkins Gilman undoubtedly dedicated her life to the purpose of women's rights for the sake of all. Describing herself as a humanist, Gilman spent her life writing and lecturing with the goal that women attain the right to share in the totality of social order.

A prolific writer, Gilman published 2,173 works in her lifetime. These texts encompassed varying genres in the disciplines of sociology, political science, economics, literature, and women's studies. In her attempt to address women's relations to patriarchal society, she juxtaposed ideologies of utopianism, such as those espoused by her contemporary Edward Bellamy, with the evolutionary thought of another contemporary, Lester Frank Ward. In her three utopian works, *Moving the Mountain* (1911), *Herland*, and its sequel, *With Her in Ourland* (1916), Gilman dramatized the theories she espoused in her critical works.

In her critical masterwork, *Women and Economics* (1898), Gilman addressed her recurring theme of gynocentrism, a theory that dominated the fictionalized country of Herland. A central position in Gilman's work is given to the gynocentric theory, in which women are promoted as the primary and dominant form of the species while men are viewed simply as assistants to the reproductive process. Gilman believed that the displacement of gynocentric thought by what she termed androcentric practices of male domination had forced women into the confining roles that thwarted their development as human beings. Gilman noted that "women are not underdeveloped men, but the feminine half of humanity is underdeveloped humans."

Gilman believed that widely held societal conventions enforced the patrifocal status and that these conventions were all the more insidious because they encouraged women to accept their subordination. Men, too, suffered from being taught to dominate. Such conventions dehumanize both women and men, Gilman argued, and limit the potential of human societies. Only by exposing such limiting ideologies could women recognize their subjugation, reach autonomy, and participate in collective political action to reform a limited society into a fully actualized, humanized one.

Gilman's fictional Herland is a playful dramatization of such beliefs. In the book, Gilman skillfully employs satire to parody late nineteenth century and early twentieth century patriarchy and the confining conventions embedded within its social order. Her work is not only one of the first utopian novels written by a woman about women but also a work whose progressive message resolutely dismantled widely accepted patriarchal beliefs of the time. In Herland, the focus of society is not male-dominated but guided by birth-centered, womanized New Motherhood. A genuine community is depicted operating collectively to nurture, rear, and educate its children. Such communal motherhood eliminates the need for family as agency. Specialists care for the children, creating a new society that shares no remnants of destruction, hierarchy, or aggression. Instead, social consciousness, collective democracy, and the nurturing of citizens and environment becomes the national priority. In Herland, the society's children are its most important and precious production; the creating of Herlandic children, from self-conception to citizenship, encompasses not only the country's industry but its theological and national ideology as well.

Employing wit and humor, Gilman uses the principle of negativity to illustrate the nonsensical nature of patriarchal conventions. She denounces what Western society is by illustrating through the example of Herland what it is not. Much of the fiction revolves around displaying the paradox of patrifocal thought and convention. The questions the Herlanders ask, which make up much of the twelve chapters, are innocent enough on the surface, but what the citizens expose by applying logic and reason to the unknown is inescapable. They ask: Why should there be surnames? Why should a woman lose her name and identity after marriage? Why is long hair considered feminine by men when only male lions in the animal kingdom have manes and only men in China wear queues? What, they ask, do women in the other world do all day if they do not work outside of the domestic sphere? Why should the women who have the least amount of children have the most servants? Why should an omnipotent, loving god have left a legacy of hellfire and perdition? Why should that god be personalized as a manlike figure?

Not only are the visiting men at first puzzled by such questions but they are also disgruntled to discover that the women are indifferent to their charms as men. These women do not display the traditional feminine "graces" of passivity, helplessness, and renunciation that the men were accustomed to in their world. They slowly come to the realization that such accepted behavior in the women they have known in American society is not inherent, biological behavior but a conditioned response to masculine expectations. If Herlandic women are different, they differ only because they have been free to pursue autonomy. In the absence of men, these women established through collective efforts a utopic nation; they provided for others a model for the origin of a peaceful civilization. The inclusion of men as equals in their vision is emphasized by the appearance of Celis as the New Mother and her readiness to bring about a rebirth of Herland into a land for them all. That world is Gilman's dream, that utopian fiction her wish for human reality.

Michele Mock Murton

Bibliography:
Allen, Polly Wynn. *Building Domestic Liberty: Charlotte Perkins Gilman's Architectural Feminism*. Amherst: University of Massachusetts Press, 1988. Analyzes Gilman's theories about transforming domesticity to liberate women.

Gubar, Susan. "*She* in *Herland:* Feminism as Fantasy." In *Coordinates: Placing Science Fiction and Fantasy*, edited by George E. Slusser, Eric S. Rabkin, and Robert Scholes. Carbondale: Southern Illinois University Press, 1983. Asserts that women's abusive reality within the patriarchy enables a visionary revolution. Argues that Gilman's utopic work serves as a rejection of the patriarchy.

Keyser, Elizabeth. "Looking Backward: From *Herland* to *Gulliver's Travels*." In *Critical Essays on Charlotte Perkins Gilman*, edited by Joanne B. Karpinski. New York: G. K. Hall, 1992. Discusses Gilman's utopia as a transcendent reinterpretation of Jonathan Swift's satire on male pride in *Gulliver's Travels*.

Lane, Ann J. Introduction to *Herland*, by Charlotte Perkins Gilman. New York: Pantheon Books, 1979. Provides a new introduction to the book, which had long been out of print. Argues that Gilman's use of humor originates from a personal and political praxis to promote a transformative, socialized world.

_____. *To Herland and Beyond: The Life and Work of Charlotte Perkins Gilman*. New York: Pantheon Books, 1990. Discusses Gilman's life and its impact on her work. Examines relationships that influenced Gilman as well as Gilman's significant influence on others as a theorist, social critic, lecturer, essayist, and creative writer.

A HERO OF OUR TIME

Type of work: Novel
Author: Mikhail Lermontov (1814-1841)
Type of plot: Psychological realism
Time of plot: 1830-1838
Locale: The Russian Caucasus
First published: Geroy nashego vremeni, serial, 1839; book, 1840 (English translation, 1854)

Principal characters:
"I," supposedly Lermontov, Narrator One
MAKSIM MAKSIMICH, Narrator Two
GRIGORIY ALEKSANDROVICH PECHORIN, Narrator Three, the
"Hero of Our Time"
BELA, a young princess
KAZBICH, a bandit
AZAMAT, Bela's young brother
YANKO, a smuggler
PRINCESS MARY, the daughter of Princess Ligovskoy
GRUSHNITSKI, a cadet and suitor to Princess Mary
VERA, the former sweetheart of Pechorin
LIEUTENANT VULICH, a Cossack officer and a Serbian

The Story:
The Narrator met Maksim Maksimich while on a return trip from Tiflis, the capital of Georgia, to Russia. The season was autumn, and in that mountainous region snow was already falling. The two men continued their acquaintance at the inn where they were forced to take refuge for the night. When the Narrator asked Maksim Maksimich about his experiences, the old man told of his friendship with Grigoriy Pechorin, a Serbian who had come from Russia about five years before to join a company of cavalry in the Caucasus.

To relieve their boredom on that frontier post, the soldiers played with Azamat, the young son of a neighboring prince. As a result of this friendship, the prince invited Maksimich and Pechorin to a family wedding. At that celebration, Pechorin and Kazbich, a bandit, met and were equally attracted to Bela, the beautiful young daughter of the prince. Azamat, observing this development, later offered to give Bela to Kazbich in exchange for the bandit's horse. Kazbich laughed at the boy and rode away.

Four days later, Azamat was back at the camp and visiting with Pechorin, who promised to get Kazbich's horse for the boy in exchange for Bela. The promise was fulfilled. Insane with rage at his loss, Kazbich tried to kill Azamat but failed. Suspecting that Azamat's father had been responsible for the theft, Kazbich killed the prince and stole his horse in revenge for the loss of his own animal.

Weeks passed, and Pechorin became less attentive to Bela. One day she and Maksimich were walking on the ramparts when Bela recognized Kazbich on her father's horse some distance away. An orderly's attempt to shoot Kazbich failed, and he escaped. Kazbich, however, had recognized Bela, too, and a few days later, when the men were away from camp, he kidnaped her. As Pechorin and Maksimich were returning to camp, they saw Kazbich riding away with Bela. They pursued the bandit, but as they were about to overtake him, he thrust his knife into

Bela and escaped. Although Pechorin seemed to be deeply grieved by Bela's death, he laughed when Maksimich tried to comfort him.

The Narrator, having parted from Maksim Maksimich, stopped at an inn in Vladikavkaz, where he found life very dull until, on the second day, Maksimich arrived unexpectedly. Before long, there was a great stir and bustle in preparation for the arrival of an important guest. The travelers learned that Pechorin was the expected guest. Happy in the thought of seeing Pechorin again, Maksimich instructed a servant to carry his regards to his former friend, who had stopped off to visit a Colonel N——. Day turned to night, but still Pechorin did not come to return the greeting. Dawn found Maksimich waiting at the gate again. When Pechorin finally arrived, he prevented Maksimich's intended embrace by coolly offering his hand.

Maksimich had anticipated warmth and a long visit, but Pechorin left immediately. Neither Maksimich's plea of friendship nor his mention of Bela served to detain Pechorin. Thus Maksimich bade his friend good-bye. The Narrator attempted to cheer him, but the old man remarked only that Pechorin had become too rich and spoiled to bother about old friendships. In fact, he would throw away Pechorin's journal that he had been saving. The Narrator was so pleased to be the recipient of the papers that he grabbed them from the old man and rushed to his room. The Narrator left the next day, saddened by the reflection that when one has reached Maksim Maksimich's age, scorn from a friend causes the heart to harden and the soul to fold up. Later, having learned that Pechorin was dead, the Narrator published three tales from the dead man's journal, as Pechorin himself had written them.

First Pechorin wrote that Taman, a little town on the seacoast of Russia, was the worst town Pechorin had ever visited. For want of better lodging, he was forced to stay in a little cottage that he immediately disliked. Greeted at the door by a blind, crippled boy, Pechorin admitted to a prejudice against people with physical infirmities. To him, a crippled body held a crippled soul. His displeasure was enhanced when he learned there was no icon in the house—an evil sign.

In the night, Pechorin followed the blind boy to the shore, where he witnessed a rendezvous that he did not comprehend. The next morning a young woman appeared at the cottage, and he accused her of having been on the beach the night before. Later, the young woman returned, kissed him, and arranged to meet him on the shore.

Pechorin kept the appointment. As he and the young woman sailed in a boat, she tried to drown him; he, in turn, thrust her into the swirling, foaming water and brought the boat to shore. He was stunned to find that she had swum to safety and was talking to a man on shore. Pechorin learned that the man was a smuggler. The blind boy appeared, carrying a heavy sack which he delivered to the woman and the smuggler. They sailed away in a boat. Pechorin returned to the cottage to find that his sword and all of his valuables had been stolen.

Quite a different atmosphere pervaded Pechorin's next experience, as described in his journal. While stopping at Pyatigorsk, a fashionable spa, he met Grushnitski, a wounded cadet whom he had known previously. The two men were attracted to Princess Mary, and Pechorin was angry—though he pretended indifference—because Princess Mary paid more attention to Grushnitski, a mere cadet, than she did to him, an officer. The men agreed that young society women looked upon soldiers as savages and upon any young man with contempt.

Pechorin opened a campaign of revenge against Princess Mary. On one occasion he distracted an audience of her admirers; again, he outbid her for a Persian rug and then disparaged her sense of values by putting it on his horse. Her fury at these and other offenses gave Pechorin the satisfaction of revenge for her favor of Grushnitski.

Grushnitski wanted Pechorin to be friendly toward Princess Mary so that the cadet might be accepted socially through his association with her. Having seen Vera, a former lover of his but now married, Pechorin decided to court Princess Mary as a cover for his illicit affair with Vera.

As excitement mounted in anticipation of the ball, the major social event of the season, antagonism between Pechorin and Grushnitski and Pechorin and Princess Mary grew. Grushnitski's excitement and pride were the result of his promotion; Princess Mary would see him in his officer's uniform.

Succumbing to Pechorin's attitude of indifference, Princess Mary consented to dance the mazurka with him. Pechorin, wishing Grushnitski to suffer a nasty surprise, did not divulge this news when Grushnitski later boasted that he intended to have this honored dance with the princess.

After the ball, it was rumored that Princess Mary would marry Pechorin, and so he fled to Kislovodsk to be with Vera. Grushnitski followed, but not to continue his association with Pechorin, whom he deliberately ignored. A short time later, the princess and her party arrived in Kislovodsk to continue their holiday.

Still furious at the affront which had caused his disappointment at the ball, Grushnitski enlisted the aid of some dragoons in an attempt to catch Pechorin in Princess Mary's room. When this effort failed, Grushnitski challenged Pechorin to a duel. According to the plan, Pechorin would have an empty pistol. Having discovered the plot, Pechorin compelled Grushnitski to stand at the edge of an abyss during the duel. Then he coolly shot the young officer, who tumbled into the depths below. Grushnitski's death was reported an accident. Later, Princess Mary's mother asked Pechorin to marry Princess Mary. He refused and wrote in his journal that a soft, protected life was not his way.

On another occasion, Pechorin and a group of Cossack officers were ridiculing the fatalism of the Moslems. Lieutenant Vulich, a renowned gambler, offered to prove his own faith in fatalism. While Pechorin and the Cossacks watched aghast, Vulich aimed a pistol at his head and pulled the trigger. No shot was fired. He then aimed at a cap hanging on the wall; it was blown to pieces. Pechorin was amazed that the pistol had misfired on Vulich's first attempt. He was sure he had seen what he called the look of death on Vulich's face. Within a half hour after that demonstration, Vulich was killed in the street by a drunken Cossack.

The next day Pechorin decided to test his own fate by offering to take the maddened Cossack alive, after an entire detachment had not dared the feat. He was successful. Later, when Pechorin discussed the incident with Maksim Maksimich, the old man observed that Circassian pistols of the type which Vulich used for his demonstration were not really reliable. He added philosophically that it was unfortunate that Vulich had stopped a drunk at night. Such a fate must have been assigned to Vulich at his birth.

Critical Evaluation:

Although Mikhail Lermontov is better known as a poet than as a novelist in his native Russia, *A Hero of Our Time*, his only completed novel, is widely considered to be one of Russia's greatest novels. In Pechorin, the novel's hero, Lermontov gives the first psychological portrait of the Russian literary type, the superfluous man. The superfluous man was to become a major figure in the novels and stories of Russian writers such as Alexander Herzen, Ivan Turgenev, and Ivan Gonchorov. Superfluous men, set apart from society by their superior talents or perceptions, are doomed to waste their lives, partly because of lack of opportunity to fulfill themselves but also because they lack any sense of purpose.

Lermontov is not the inventor of the superfluous man: The Russian poet Alexander Pushkin created the superfluous hero Eugene Onegin in the 1833 poem of that name. In creating

Pechorin, Lermontov draws both on Pushkin and on the life and works of the English poet George Gordon, Lord Byron. The cult of Byronism, which romanticized the stance of the cynical yet passionately rebellious outsider, was sweeping through Russia, along with the cult of Napoleon as the supposed liberator of the oppressed masses.

Lermontov looks into the concept of superfluity more deeply than Pushkin does, probing into its psychological and social origins and suggesting that it was the logical endpoint of many of the typical vices of his age. Hence the ironic label for Pechorin, "hero of our time." Like the so-called lost generation of disillusioned idealists of the 1830's following the abortive Decembrist Revolt against Czar Nicholas I's oppressive regime, Pechorin's creative genius finds no legitimate channel for expression and then thus turns in on itself and grows destructive. He wreaks destruction on all around him: He kills Grushnitski in a duel, reopens an old wound for Vera, and breaks Princess Mary's heart.

In analyzing Pechorin, Lermontov analyzed the *mal du siècle*—the sickness of the age. Lermontov's techniques of analysis are innovatory and worthy of note. The first two of the five narratives, "Bela" and "Maksim Maksimich," show Pechorin through the eyes of others. "Princess Mary" is in the form of Pechorin's diary, providing a format that allows the character to reveal his complex inner life. "Taman" and "The Fatalist" are first-person narratives in which Pechorin records his adventures in the Crimea and the Caucasus.

In a moving passage, Pechorin wonders why he refused to tread on the road of gentle pleasures and peace of mind. He compares himself to a seaman born and bred on the deck of a pirate ship, so accustomed to storms and battles that on land he feels bored. Pechorin's actions—couched in an engaging black humor—are shown with unerring psychological truth. He is a self-confessed emotional vampire, feeding off the suffering and joys of others. Unable to embrace any purpose, and dependent on others to provide his entertainment, he is doomed to be a social parasite, an analytical observer, and a mischief-maker.

The structure of the five stories of *A Hero of Our Time* was innovative in its time. The three sections of Pechorin's journal, "Taman," "Princess Mary," and "The Fatalist" are arranged in chronological order. They are preceded in the novel by "Bela" and "Maksim Maksimich," although the events narrated in those sections occur after the events of the journal. Such deliberate manipulation of time sequences is now commonplace in fiction and film, in devices such as flashbacks, but in Lermontov's time, this approach was experimental.

The unorthodox time sequence enables the author to arouse the reader's curiosity and then satisfy it. It also allows the reader to move from an external evaluation of Pechorin to an internal self-revelation. Pechorin is first seen at one remove, through the eyes of Maksim Maksimich, before he is seen in person. Finally the reader is taken directly to the source, hearing Pechorin's voice through his journal.

The time sequence is also psychologically revealing in terms of Pechorin's character development. "Taman" shows Pechorin as a naïve young officer, barely in control of events. The gender roles of "Bela" are reversed, with the girl as aggressor and Pechorin as near-victim. By the time of Bela, Pechorin has developed a more demoniac personality, and Bela's life falls victim to it. In "Princess Mary," which takes place before "Bela" but is narrated after it, Pechorin's attitudes have already hardened, although Princess Mary, more fortunate than Bela, escapes with only a broken heart. Grushnitski, however, crosses Pechorin and pays with his life. Pechorin's cynical comment after he kills Grushnitski in a duel is significant: "*Finita la commedia*" (the comedy is over). Pechorin has reached such a distance from the tragic events he orchestrates that he sees them as a humorous entertainment for himself.

The position of "The Fatalist" at the novel's end suggests that it is of significance to the whole. The words "fate" and "will" are used frequently, most often by Pechorin. He exercises his free will when it suits him, then takes refuge in the concept of fate to avoid taking responsibility for his actions.

Pechorin uses both terms to blur the distinction between good and evil, a typically romantic and potentially destructive tendency remarked upon by French writer Albert Camus in his study *The Rebel* (1951), in which he attempts to trace the origins of state terrorism such as that exhibited by Nazi Germany. Camus traces what he terms the religious confusion between good and evil back to John Milton's Satan in *Paradise Lost* (1665), and forward to the romantic period and the Byronic hero. Significantly, Camus quotes Lermontov rather than Byron to illustrate his point. He comments that in order to combat evil, the rebel, because he judges himself innocent, renounces good and creates evil again. The romantic hero, Camus says, feels compelled to do evil by his nostalgia for an unrealizable good. His excuse is sorrow. Camus' comment reveals much about Pechorin and his dual nature as both hero and villain, as well as his paradoxical effect on the reader.

"Critical Evaluation" by Claire J. Robinson

Bibliography:
Eikhenbaum, B. M. *Lermontov*. Translated by Ray Parrott and Harry Weber. Ann Arbor, Mich.: Ardis, 1981. First published in Russia in 1924, this literary and historical evaluation of Lermontov's works is still much admired for its role in placing them in Russian literary context.
Garrard, John. *Mikhail Lermontov*. Boston: Twayne, 1982. Arguably the best overview for the general reader of Lermontov's life and works. The section on *A Hero of Our Time* focuses on its literary background and on Pechorin as hero, including a psychological analysis and pointed insights into the extent of the author's identification with Pechorin.
Kelly, Laurence. *Lermontov*. New York: George Braziller, 1977. Entertaining biography does not deal directly with Lermontov's works, but enriches the perceptive reader's appreciation of their autobiographical aspects. Parallels between the lives and personalities of Lermontov and Pechorin are striking.
Lavrin, Janko. *Lermontov*. New York: Hillary House, 1959. Short, lucid, intelligent summary of Lermontov's life, major works, and recurrent themes.
Mersereau, John, Jr. *Mikhail Lermontov*. Carbondale: Southern Illinois University Press, 1962. This revised doctoral dissertation provides a useful and readable critical analysis of Lermontov's works. Contains a valuable discussion of Lermontov's romanticism and a detailed treatment of *A Hero of Our Time*.

THE HEROES OF ROMANCES

Type of work: Fiction
Author: Nicolas Boileau-Despréaux (1636-1711)
Type of plot: Satire
Time of plot: 1660's
Locale: Hades
First published: Dialogue des héros de roman, 1688 (English translation, 1713)

Principal characters:
PLUTO, the Greek god of the underworld
MINOS, a judge in Hades
RHADAMANTHUS, another judge in Hades
DIOGENES, a Greek philosopher
CYRUS, a Persian king
HORATIUS COCLES, a Roman military hero
CLELIA, a Roman noblewoman
JOAN OF ARC, a French military heroine

The Story:

Pluto received the dead after they had been judged by Minos and Rhadamanthus. Minos expressed his surprise that recent arrivals from Europe were speaking in an extremely artificial and sentimental manner. Pluto attributed this odd style to the pernicious effect of the excessive gallantry in seventeenth century French works written by popular novelists and poets such as Madeleine de Scudéry, Marin Le Roy de Gomberville, La Calprenède, and Jean Chapelain. He assured the incredulous Minos that French writers had transformed famous military heroes and heroines such as Alexander the Great, King Cyrus of Persia, and even Joan of Arc into little more than sentimental lovers. Minos refused to believe that intelligent readers would accept such grotesque distortions of historical reality. Rhadamanthus and Pluto tried to prove to him that it was, unfortunately, true. Rhadamanthus then stated that even longtime residents of Hades, including Sisyphus, Ixion, and Prometheus, had complained bitterly about the inane prattle of these new arrivals from France. Minos, Rhadamanthus, and Pluto asked Diogenes to persuade some of these French fictional characters to speak with them.

The first person who came to see them was King Cyrus. Pluto knew a great deal about this historical figure because he had read Herodotus. Pluto had heard that classical learning was greatly admired in seventeenth century France, and he could not believe that French writers would ignore such an eminent authority as Herodotus. This fictional Cyrus, however, had changed his name to Artamenes, and his main goal was not to conquer large areas in the Middle East but rather to find his beloved Mandana, who was abducted eight times in Madeleine de Scudéry's very popular ten-volume romance, titled *Artamenes: Or, The Grand Cyrus* (1649-1653). When Cyrus informed Pluto of his complete lack of interest in anything other than his love for Mandana, Pluto reached the conclusion that this eminent military conqueror had become little more than a sentimental and foolish lover who wept and whined incessantly about his failure to win the hand of Mandana in marriage.

After the departure of Cyrus, two famous Roman historical figures appeared and Diogenes informed Pluto, Minos, and Rhadamanthus that they were Horatius Cocles and Clelia. Pluto had read about their exploits in Titus Livy's *The History of Rome* (c. 26 B.C.E.-15 C.E.). He remembered that Clelia had swum across the Tiber River in order to escape from the soldiers of Porsena, and Horatius Cocles had defended a bridge all by himself against a horde of soldiers. Pluto firmly expected Horatius Cocles and Clelia to be much more sensible than the sentimental Cyrus, but he was badly mistaken. His knowledge of the lives of Horatius Cocles and Clelia was based on a careful reading of a trustworthy and respected Roman historian and not on Madeleine de Scudéry's immensely popular but highly imaginative ten-volume novel *Clelia* (1654-1660). Like Cyrus, Horatius Cocles lamented his inability to win the love of his beloved, who preferred another man to him. He kept repeating two verses about the exquisite beauty of Clelia, and Pluto compared this foolish character to the mythological nymph Echo who spoke endlessly of her love for Narcissus. When Clelia came to see them, both Pluto and Diogenes hoped that this illustrious and brave Roman noblewoman would not be as superficial as Cyrus and Horatius Cocles, but, unfortunately, she also behaved in a very odd manner. In the first volume of her novel *Clelia*, Madeleine de Scudéry had included a map of the Kingdom of Tender Love. Clelia believed that she now lived in the Kingdom of Tender Love and not in the Elysian Fields, and she asked them for directions to the Country of Gallantry. Pluto suggested that she should seek admission to an insane asylum instead of visiting the Country of Gallantry.

After conversations with equally superficial lovers from other contemporary novels and also characters from plays by Philippe Quinault, Pluto despaired of encountering a sensible person among the new arrivals in Hades. Diogenes, however, held out some hope for sanity because the valiant French national heroine and martyr Joan of Arc had agreed to speak with them. Pluto could not believe that any French writer would dare portray such a heroine in other than reverential terms. Pluto, who knew a great deal about ancient and modern history, realized that Joan of Arc had lost her life as a result of her courageous efforts to free her homeland from English occupation. Pluto had once again made the mistake of relying on objective histories, and he had failed to read Jean Chapelain's epic poem *The Maid* (1655). The main interest of Chapelain's Joan of Arc was not to raise the siege of Orleans and to restore freedom to France but rather to be loved by a fellow warrior named Dunois. The Maid of Orleans, who liberated France from English domination, became in Chapelain's turgid verse a sentimental lover indistinguishable from any other character in numerous French plays and novels from the seventeenth century. Near the end of this dialogue, an unnamed Frenchman appeared and told Pluto that these alleged heroes and heroines were, in fact, his neighbors. At the end of this satiric dialogue, Pluto recommended that they all be encouraged to drink from Lethe, a river in Hades whose water caused forgetfulness. This was, in Pluto's opinion, the only possible cure for their foolishness.

Critical Evaluation:

Although Nicolas Boileau-Despréaux composed his *The Heroes of Romances* in 1666 and revised it just four years later, he never authorized the publication of this work during his lifetime, although it was published without his permission first in 1688 and then in 1693. Such unauthorized publications occurred frequently in seventeenth century France because the concepts of intellectual property and copyright did not yet exist and, as a result, a French writer did not then possess the legal right to prevent the publication of his or her works, if a manuscript happened to fall into the hands of an unscrupulous publisher. In the preface to this dialogue, which he wrote shortly before his own death, Boileau-Despréaux claimed that he opposed publishing this work while Madeleine de Scudéry was still alive because he did not want to hurt her feelings. Madeleine de Scudéry had come to be admired for the sincerity of her commitment to high moral standards and to deep spirituality. Even after her death in 1707 at the advanced age of ninety-nine, Boileau-Despréaux would not authorize the publication of *The Heroes of Romances*, even though all the writers whom he had criticized in this satiric dialogue were by then deceased. He sensed perhaps that the exceedingly nasty and condescending opinions expressed in this work would provoke very unfavorable reactions from readers, who might then think poorly of the works of Boileau-Despréaux himself.

Although Boileau-Despréaux clearly amused his readers by contrasting the true historical figures of King Cyrus, Alexander the Great, Horatius Cocles, Clelia, and Joan of Arc with their representations in certain French plays, poems, and novels of the seventeenth century, the basic premise for Boileau-Despréaux's aesthetic assessment of these works is highly questionable. Boileau-Despréaux assumes that fidelity to historical truth should be the criterion for judging the value of a literary work based on people who actually existed. This is, of course, a perfectly valid standard to use in assessing the objectivity of a biography or a historical study, but it is not at all certain that this is a reliable criterion to be used in evaluating epic poetry, plays, or novels. Like the very popular Scottish historical novelist Sir Walter Scott, Madeleine de Scudéry never claimed that her historical fictions should be considered reliable from the point of view of historical fact. Such was not the concern of Madeleine de Scudéry. Twentieth century scholars interested in French novels of the seventeenth century have argued persuasively that Madeleine de Scudéry was a gifted and creative writer whose well-structured novels reveal profound insights into the very different perceptions of love by men and women and into the nature of heroism and self-sacrifice. Contrary to Boileau-Despréaux's affirmations in his *The Heroes of Romances*, Madeleine de Scudéry knew very well the historical facts as presented by such eminent classical historians as Herodotus and Livy, but she believed that a creative writer should adapt classical sources to satisfy the expectations and sensitivities of his or her contemporaries.

The very harsh criticism that Boileau-Despréaux levels against Madeleine de Scudéry, Chapelian, Quinault, Gomberville, and La Calprenède had the unfortunate effect of persuading generations of French readers that the works of these prolific writers merited the oblivion into which they had fallen even before Boileau-Despréaux's death in 1711. It has only been since the 1960's that scholars have come to question seriously the validity of Boileau-Despréaux's evaluations of these writers. Madeleine de Scudéry, for example, has been viewed by many late twentieth century scholars as an extraordinarily original novelist who wrote persuasively both on the importance of equality between men and women and on the central role of spiritual and moral values in people's daily lives. By an extraordinary turn of fate, the writers whom Boileau-Despréaux dismisses as incompetent in his *The Heroes of Romances* came, in the last third of the twentieth century, to be considered as highly creative novelists, poets, and playwrights whereas the critical reception of Boileau-Despréaux's own works has become less and less enthusiastic with the passage of time.

Edmund J. Campion

Bibliography:
Borgerhoff, Elbert B. O. *The Freedom of French Classicism.* Princeton, N.J.: Princeton University Press, 1950. Contains a solid assessment of Boileau-Despréaux's central importance. Describes the numerous connections between originality and imitation in French classicism.
Brody, Jules. *Boileau and Longinus.* Geneva: Droz, 1958. A thoughtful study of Boileau-Despréaux's aesthetic theory. Describes the originality and the limits of Boileau-Despréaux's approach to literature.

France, Peter. *Rhetoric and Truth in France: Descartes to Diderot*. Oxford, England: Clarendon Press, 1972. Describes the central role of classical rhetoric in major French literary works during the classical era and during the Enlightenment. Explains why Boileau-Despréaux and many other eminent French writers from his era were uncomfortable with those writers who imitated classical sources freely.

Pocock, Gordon. *Boileau and the Nature of Neo-Classicism*. Cambridge, England: Cambridge University Press, 1980. Explains Boileau-Despréaux's reasoning for modern writers' close imitation of ancient works. Develops an original reading of Boileau-Despréaux's influential *Art of Poetry* (1674).

White, Julian Eugene. *Nicolas Boileau*. New York: Twayne, 1969. A lucid introduction in English to the life and times of Nicolas Boileau-Despréaux. Annotated bibliography.

HEROIDES

Type of work: Poetry
Author: Ovid (Publius Ovidius Naso, 43 B.C.E.-17 C.E.)
First transcribed: Before 8 C.E. (English translation, 1567)

In the *Heroides* or *Letters of the Heroines*, the Roman poet Ovid composed a series of dramatic letters in elegiac verse, alternating lines of dactylic hexameter and dactylic pentameter. "Elegy," writes one of Ovid's heroines, "is the weeping strain," and indeed the mood of most of these letters is that of sadness. Most of the heroines have been rejected by famous heroes, Dido by Aeneas, Ariadne by Theseus, Hypsipyle by Jason, Oenone by Paris. Some are apprehensive of coming death either for themselves or for their lovers; Canace, Dejanira, Sappho, and Dido are about to commit suicide. Medea is about to kill the new wife of Jason and her own two children.

Almost all of the heroines are in hopeless, pitiful situations, caught at a turning point in their lives. Yet in these turning points there is conflict, both internal and between several people, a reminder that Ovid was also a dramatist, though his play *Medea* is no longer extant. The letters are the ancestors of the familiar dramatic monologues of Robert Browning and also of the interior monologue as it was used by James Joyce and Fyodor Dostoevski, for in their writing the heroines reveal their inmost thoughts. Moreover, what the heroine says usually sets the scene for the reader: Through reminiscence, she tells the events of the past that led up to her present woe. Sometimes Ovid transports the reader directly into the mind of the heroine, as she shifts rapidly from one association to another, or from a past memory to the present. In telling the different stories dramatically, Ovid remains in the background, almost out of sight.

The *Heroides* have inspired different generations of English poets, from Geoffrey Chaucer, who felt deep sympathy for Canace, and his contemporary John Gower to John Donne, who imitated several of the letters in his own poetry, and Alexander Pope, who wrote one of his finest poems, "Eloisa to Abelard," in imitation of the verse epistles.

Ovid's "Canace to Macareus" is one of the finest short dramatic poems in classic literature. As it opens, Canace is telling her brother and lover Macareus that she has been ordered by their father, Aeolus, to kill herself as punishment for having had a child by her brother. She tells in close detail how she had become pregnant by Macareus, how her sympathetic nurse had tried unsuccessfully to induce an abortion, and finally how the newborn baby had betrayed itself by crying as the nurse was trying to carry it past Aeolus, wrapped in a bundle of sticks. Aeolus, the household tyrant, paradoxically able to control the four winds but not his own passion, is the inflexible villain of Canace's letter. Ovid succeeds in getting his readers to sympathize with the incestuous couple and to question any sort of inflexible legal or moral code.

A poet can, however, say only so much on the theme of rejected love. Ovid sometimes seems bored with his subject matter, especially when he takes his material from another poet. When he borrows Dido from Vergil, for example, his poem becomes only a good, but obvious, imitation; and Ovid's "Dido to Aeneas" adds almost no new detail to Vergil's story in the *Aeneid* (c. 29-19 B.C.E.).

Although many of the letters seem sentimental or mawkish to later perception, Ovid's power as a storyteller and dramatist is obvious, and many of the characters he depicts seem "true" or "real." Some of the unforgettable scenes and figures in the *Heroides* include the indulgent nurse and the petty tyrant Aeolus in "Canace to Macareus"; Ariadne lying on the rocks of her island watching Theseus' sails disappear in the distance; and Paris flirting with Helen at the table of her husband, Menelaus. The realism in the *Heroides* is psychological: What Ovid's characters think and do seems natural even in later times. Ovid also writes sympathetically about the social outcast and the mentally sick; he shows understanding for Dido and Medea, both close to insane, and for the incestuous Canace and Phaedra.

Ovid's verse is artificial, and he makes no effort to give his heroines an individual style or poetic voice; all sound similar. Yet they retain their psychological individuality, which Ovid shows through their actions and their thoughts. Despite the fact that the poet relies on his readers' acquaintance with the stories—he often builds his poems dramatically on allusions that have in later times become obscure and puzzling—Ovid presents the physical and psychological details of his stories with vigorous and compelling power.

Bibliography:
Mack, Sara. *Ovid: The Grammarian and Society in Late Antiquity.* Translated by Janet Lloyd. New Haven, Conn.: Yale University Press, 1988. An elegant introduction to the poet that will persuade even the general reader to explore Ovid further. Presents often subtle analysis of individual passages. An intelligent, often original, and always firmly grounded study. Includes a useful bibliography.
Martindale, Charles, ed. *Ovid Renewed: Ovidian Influences on Literature and Art from the Middle Ages to the Twentieth Century.* Cambridge, England: Cambridge University Press, 1988. Discusses the extent to which Ovid's work permeated the European tradition of literature and the visual arts. Includes essays that trace Ovid's influence in writers ranging from Chaucer to T. S. Eliot's *The Waste Land* (1922).
Williams, Gareth. "Ovid's Canace: Dramatic Irony in *Heroides.*" *Classical Quarterly* 42, no. 1 (January-July, 1992): 201-210. Analyzes the literary background of the story of Canace's death as told by Ovid. Concludes that Ovid probably drew on Euripedes' "Aeolus."

HERZOG

Type of work: Novel
Author: Saul Bellow (1915-   )
Type of plot: Psychological realism
Time of plot: 1960's
Locale: New York City, Chicago, Ludeyville, the Berkshires
First published: 1964

Principal characters:

MOSES ELKANAH HERZOG, the protagonist
MADELEINE PONTRITTER HERZOG, his former wife
JUNE, his and Madeleine's daughter
VALENTINE GERSBACH, his best friend and Madeleine's lover
RAMONA DONSELL, his girlfriend
WILLIAM HERZOG, his brother
LUCAS ASPHALTER, his friend, a zoologist

The Story:

Herzog went through a difficult time. While living in New York City, in June, he spent most of his time writing letters. Sometimes he wrote them on paper, sometimes only in his mind. He wrote to people he knew, people he had never met, and people who had died long before he was born. He wrote to Dwight David Eisenhower, thirty-fourth president of the United States; Friedrich Wilhelm Nietzsche, who died in 1900; his dead mother; some of his intellectual rivals; even God. In the letters, he argued about intellectual things the people had said or written; sometimes he argued about things he himself had said or written, or had failed to say or write.

When his girlfriend, Ramona, told him he should rest at her place on the shore, he instead left New York by train to visit a friend on Martha's Vineyard in Massachusetts. While traveling, he continued writing letters. At Martha's Vineyard, he went to the room his host and hostess had prepared for him. Then, leaving a letter explaining his actions, he immediately sneaked out of the house and returned by air to New York. Back in his apartment, he started writing letters again.

During most of the next day, he wrote letters. He went to dinner at Ramona's apartment, where he spent the night. The next morning, he called his lawyer, Harvey Simkin, to discuss the possibility of getting custody of his daughter, June; he had heard that Madeleine, Herzog's former wife, and Valentine Gersbach, her lover, had locked June in a car when they wanted to talk. Simkin had to go to court that morning but agreed to leave a message at the courthouse for Herzog. While waiting for Simkin's message, Herzog attended several trials, including one involving an unmarried couple accused of beating the woman's son to death. Herzog left the courtroom and later that day flew to Chicago. There, he went to his father's old house, now inhabited by his aging stepmother, and got a pistol his father owned. It had two bullets in it. Herzog intended to use one on Madeleine and the other on Gersbach. By now it was dark. He went to the house where he, Madeleine, and June had lived. Through the kitchen window, he saw Madeleine doing the dishes. Walking around the house, he looked through the bathroom window and saw Gersbach giving June a bath. Gersbach bathed June with obvious love, and June enjoyed being bathed. The sight made Herzog realize that he could not kill anyone.

Herzog drove to the house of Phoebe and Valentine Gersbach. Phoebe would not admit that

Gersbach and Madeleine were having an affair, and Herzog was unsuccessful when he asked her to help him get custody of June. He left and spent the night with his old friend Lucas Asphalter, who had recently been in the newspapers for giving mouth-to-mouth respiration to his tubercular pet monkey. The monkey died anyway. Asphalter arranged for Herzog to see June the next day.

The next afternoon, he was driving with June in his rented car when a truck collided with them. June was not hurt, but Herzog was knocked unconscious. The policemen who investigated recognized that Herzog was not at fault in the accident, but they arrested him for possessing a loaded revolver. He and June were taken to the police station. When Madeleine came to get June, she made it clear that she hated Herzog.

Herzog's brother, William, paid his bail and agreed to visit Herzog's house in Ludeyville, Massachusetts. Herzog had used money he had inherited from his father to buy the house as a home for Madeleine, who at that time wanted to live in the country. Herzog had spent his entire inheritance buying the house and improving it. He had loved living there and working on it, but when Madeleine tired of the country they had moved to Chicago. The house had been deserted a long time.

Herzog went from Chicago to "his country place." Mice ran through the house, and birds roosted in the rooms. Lovers used it as a meeting place. Nevertheless, Herzog felt "joy" and peace in Ludeyville for the first time in a long time. There, he "began his final week of letters."

When William came to the house, he saw that it was well built and beautifully situated. He told his brother that he could probably sell it as a summer place but that Herzog would never get back the money he had put into it because it was not close enough to the usual tourist haunts.

William drove Herzog into town, where Herzog arranged to have the electricity turned on and to have a woman come out to clean the house. Herzog learned that Ramona, who was visiting friends in Barrington, Massachusetts, a few minutes' drive away, had been trying to telephone him. Herzog called her and had William drive him to Barrington, where he invited Ramona to dinner at his house that evening. She accepted, and William drove Herzog back to Ludeyville. Herzog picked up the cleaning woman, who started work on the kitchen. He decided to stop writing letters. He also decided to stay in Ludeyville for a while, and to bring Marco, his son by his first wife, there for a visit after Marco's summer camp ended.

Throughout these experiences, Herzog recalled events from his childhood, including his father's repeated failures, especially at bootlegging during the time the family lived in Montreal; the family's suffering in Canada and later in Chicago; his failed first marriage; his terrible marriage to Madeleine and the way in which she and Gersbach, whom Herzog had considered his best friend, had fooled him entirely; and his love for his children and his two brothers and one sister. He especially thought about his relationship with Madeleine and wondered why she hated him so much.

Critical Evaluation:

Critics generally recognize *Herzog* as a masterpiece and call it one of the most significant works by Saul Bellow, who was awarded the Nobel Prize in Literature in 1976. The novel's narrative, which switches from limited third person to first person, affords insights into the intellectual mind of Moses Herzog as he works his way through a very disturbed period. Toward the end of the novel, at his home in the country, Herzog starts to regain his composure. He experiences joy for the first time when he communes with nature and finally prepares to stop writing letters. A summary of the plot cannot, however, give a comprehensive impression of the novel's shifts from past to present, which depict Herzog's tortured attempts to explain the world and control his life rationally. In the process, he ends up seeing a world in fragments and feeling that his life is disintegrating. Nor can a summary do justice to Bellow's depiction of Herzog's capacity for love, his naïve innocence, and the pain he suffers.

The novel captures the texture of the places where Herzog lives. Bellow uses concrete details to create the hectic, indeed frantic life that Herzog lives in New York City and Chicago, as well as the peace he finds in Ludeyville. Like Herzog, the reader becomes immersed in the different sights, sounds, and smells.

Bellow allows the reader inside Herzog's mind, a mind in chaos and near collapse. The first words of the novel, "If I am out of my mind, it's all right with me, thought Moses Herzog," are echoed again toward the novel's end. Herzog first thinks these words after most of the adventures in the book are past, that is, after he has returned to Ludeyville and begun to achieve peace. Throughout most of the narrative, however, Herzog does not recognize how disturbed he is. There is no indication that he sees anything absurd in his letter writing, and he fully intends to kill Madeleine and Gersbach. Ultimately, he does recognize how close to total insanity he had come.

When his brother, William, suggests that he enter a hospital for a while, Herzog finds the idea of rest tempting, but he refuses. Yet toward the end of the novel he begins to regain his psychological balance. Some critics claim that Bellow is implying that the self-analysis Herzog undergoes in the telling of his story is what makes hospitalization unnecessary. At any rate, Herzog accepts the possibility that he and the rest of the world will never be completely sane, and this acceptance seems a necessary part of his return to a kind of sanity. He recognizes that he cannot control all things intellectually and that he must even let his daughter June go, trusting her to the care of Madeleine and Gersbach. Although both have betrayed Herzog and Madeleine hates him, he recognizes that they treat June with love.

The most obvious symptom of Herzog's insanity is his letter writing. Toward the end of the book, he recognizes that words alone are often inadequate for understanding and explaining many problems and that he must accept that inadequacy. He learns to accept his imperfections and absurdities, and those of others, and to recognize the absurdity of writing letters that he never mails. He learns that he need not justify all his actions and right every wrong and that an imperfect Herzog in an imperfect world can experience a kind of joy that has nothing to do with words and very little to do with the intellect.

Toward the end of the novel, Herzog finds joy and peace communing with nature and God. He also awaits the coming of Ramona, indicating that he will begin communing directly with his fellow human beings instead of writing them letters. The narrative becomes much less digressive and much easier to follow toward the end, reflecting Herzog's return to sanity. Bellow thus structures the novel to show a mind coming to grips with reality and moving toward peace and stability. With the message that life despite its pain and absurdities is worth living, *Herzog* is ultimately a profoundly optimistic, life-affirming novel.

Richard Tuerk

Bibliography:
Clayton, John Jacob. *Saul Bellow: In Defense of Man.* Bloomington: Indiana University Press, 1968. One of the pioneering studies on Bellow. Interprets the changes the protagonist in *Herzog* undergoes in the course of his narrative as symbolizing hope for humanity.
Cohen, Sarah Blacher. *Saul Bellow's Enigmatic Laughter.* Urbana: University of Illinois Press, 1974. Includes a discussion of *Herzog* that contrasts the protagonist's experience in his house

in Ludeyville, where he lives in a kind of "Eden communing only with God and nature," with the novel's end, where he awaits the coming of another human being, a sign of his return to sanity.

Dutton, Robert R. *Saul Bellow*. Rev. ed. Boston: Twayne, 1982. Points out that Saul Bellow in *Herzog* is showing how one man's earthly salvation lies "in learning to live with himself."

Pifer, Ellen. *Saul Bellow Against the Grain*. Philadelphia: University of Pennsylvania Press, 1990. Discusses Herzog's growing awareness of his relationship with God.

Wilson, Jonathan. *On Bellow's Planet: Readings from the Dark Side*. Rutherford, N.J.: Fairleigh Dickinson University Press, 1985. Sees *Herzog* as a novel about the protagonist's release from his obsession with Madeleine and consequently from his need to write letters that involve intellectual conflicts with others.

HESPERIDES
Or, The Works Both Humane and Divine
of Robert Herrick, Esq.

Type of work: Poetry
Author: Robert Herrick (1591-1674)
First published: 1648

"As thou deserv'st, be proud; then gladly let/ The Muse give thee the Delphick Coronet." This brief epigram, one of hundreds Robert Herrick included in his collection of twelve hundred poems, best describes the pride with which he presented his *Hesperides* and the recognition he received after years of neglect. His subtitle indicates the inclusion in one volume of his *Hesperides* and his *Noble Numbers,* a group of ecclesiastical poems, prayers, hymns, and apothegms dated 1647. This collection, together with fifteen or so poems discovered by nineteenth century scholars and about twice the number recovered later in manuscript, constitute the literary remains of one of the finest lyricists in the English language.

The arrangement of the poems in *Hesperides* (the name itself is a conceit based on the legend of nymphs who guarded with a fierce serpent the golden apples of the goddess Hera) is whimsical. Most of the lyrics were composed in Devonshire, where Herrick was vicar of Dean Prior from 1629 until the Puritan victories caused his removal from his parish in 1647. Restored to his living in 1662, he lived until his death in the West Country which had inspired his pagan-spirited, rustic verse.

The great Herrick scholar, L. C. Martin, has discovered a chronology, from the collation of many manuscripts, which indicates the four general periods in which these poems were composed, carefully rewritten, and then painstakingly published. From the time of his apprenticeship to his goldsmith uncle at least one poem remains, "A Country Life," which may have been one of the reasons why the youthful poet was allowed to terminate his service and go to Cambridge. Though Herrick's activities during his university period are remembered chiefly for the letters he wrote asking his uncle for money, he also composed a variety of commendatory poems and memory verses. One, the longest poem he wrote, is addressed to a fellow student who was ordained in 1623.

The second period, and perhaps the most important, was from 1617 to 1627, when he became the favorite of the "sons" of Ben Jonson. Herrick's famous poem, "His Fare-well to Sack," epitomizes these formative years of good talk, wide reading, witty writing, and good fellowship. In this poem too are the names of the poets who most influenced him—Anacreon, Horace, and by implication, Catullus and Theocritus. The well-known "The Argument of His Book" echoes the pastoral strain in the poet's declaration of his literary interests:

> I sing of *Brooks,* of *Blossomes, Birds,* and *Bowers*:
> Of *April, May,* of *June,* and *July-Flowers.*
> I sing of *May-poles, Hock-carts, Wassails, Wakes,*
> Of *Bride-grooms, Brides,* and of their *Bridall-cakes.*
> I write of *Youth,* of *Love,* and have Accesse
> *By* these, to sing of cleanly-*Wantonnesse.*
> I sing of *Dewes,* of *Raines,* and piece by piece
> Of *Balme,* of *Oyle,* of *Spice,* and *Amber-Greece.*
> I sing of *Times trans-shifting*; and I write
> How *Roses* first came *Red,* and *Lillies White.*

I write of *Groves*, of *Twilights*, and I sing
The Court of *Mab*, and of the *Fairie-King*.
I write of *Hell*; I sing (and ever shall)
Of *Heaven*, and hope to have it after all.

The Dean Prior vicar's hope for heaven seems to be based on his "cleanly-Wantonnesse," even if one considers his many mistresses—Corinna, stately Julia, smooth Anthea, and sweet Electra—as imaginary, the idealized woman of poetic tradition. Herrick's philosophy is Anacreontic, taking the *carpe diem* attitude of the Cavalier poets. The best-known example from his work, in his own time as well as currently, is "To the Virgins, to Make Much of Time," which begins: "Gather ye Rosebuds while ye may."

That Herrick was a man of his time may be ascertained by a glance at the rich variety of his poetic subjects. Set in the form of the madrigal, "Corinna's going a Maying," catches all the excitement of the festival in the most intricate of singing forms. A ballad in the manner of Campion is "Cherrie-ripe," one which deserves to be better known:

Cherrie-Ripe, Ripe, Ripe, I cry
Full and faire ones; come and buy:
If so be, you ask me where
They doe grow? I answer, There,
Where my *Julia's* lips doe smile
There's the Land, or Cherry-Ile:
Whose Plantations fully show
All the yeere, where Cherries grow.

In the manner of William Shakespeare he composed "The mad Maids Song," with the same "Good Morrows" and the strewing of flowers for the tomb, but in this instance the lament is for a lover killed by a bee sting. In the style of Christopher Marlowe and then Sir Walter Raleigh, Herrick continues the Elizabethan shepherd-maiden debate in "To Phillis to love, and live with him":

Thou shalt have Ribbands, Roses, Rings,
Gloves, Garters, Stockings, Shoes, and Strings
Of winning Colours, that shall move
Others to Lust, but me to Love.
These (nay) and more, thine own shall be,
If thou wilt love, and live with me.

With a master of arts degree (1620), and a disciple of Jonson, Herrick never forgot his classical background. As an epigrammatist he was without peer, especially since he injected strong originality into a conventional and satiric form. He often made his parishioners models for these satiric verses, as in this comment on one man's discomfiture:

Urles had the Gout so, that he co'd not stand;
Then from his Feet, it shifted to his Hand:
When 'twas in's Feet, his Charity was small;
Now 'tis in's Hand, he gives no Almes at all.

Nor does he spare himself and his friends: "Wantons we are; and though our words be such,/ Our Lives do differ from our Lines by much."

An extension of this mode is Herrick's Anacreontic verse. In "To Bacchus, a *Canticle*" he begs the god of revelry and reproduction to show him the way to have more than one mistress. Somewhat more restrained and in the vein of Catullus are his lyrics to Lesbia and the epithalamia with which he greeted his many friends and relatives who, despite all his verses, insisted on getting married. In "The cruell Maid" he echoes, or is echoed by, his contemporary, Andrew Marvell:

> Give my cold lips a kisse at last:
> If twice you kisse, you need not feare
> That I shall stir, or live more here.
> Next, hollow out a Tombe to cover
> Me; me, the most despised Lover:
> And write thereon, *This Reader, know,*
> *Love kill'd this man*. No more but so.

The more humble and bucolic songs of Horace, however, were the poet's abiding love. While he may have wished for the court rather than the parish, his best work was composed amid peaceful surroundings on pleasant rural subjects. His "To Daffadills" is a more delicate and subtle poem than the well-known lyric by Wordsworth:

> Faire Daffadills, we weep to see
> You haste away so soone:
> As yet the early-rising Sun
> Has not attain'd his Noone.
> Stay, stay,
> Untill the hasting day
> Has run
> But to the Even-song;
> And, having pray'd together, we
> Will goe with you along.

In the final period represented in *Hesperides*, "His returne to London" is a significant poem illustrating the sophisticated side of his genius, the pomp and circumstance which made a lasting poetry for this faithful royalist. He sings here "O Place! O *People!* Manners! fram'd to please/ *All Nations, Customes, Kindreds, Languages!*" as he links himself with his Elizabethan patron saints, the Renaissance man who took all life and all things for their province.

"And here my ship rides having Anchor cast," he writes in his concluding poems of the book which he sent forth to find "a kinsman or a friend." He honestly thought and in fact knew "The Muses will weare blackes, when I am dead." Ironically, his death went almost unnoticed, though his verses were recalled in oral tradition for many years before the recovery of his work by modern scholarship—a most appropriate tribute to the man who gives such a vivid picture of the folk and their wassails, harvests, wakes, and loves.

Bibliography:
Coiro, Ann Baynes. "Herrick's *Hesperides*: The Name and the Frame." *Journal of English Language History* 52, no. 2 (Summer, 1985): 311-336. Deals with the political and social conflicts that affected *Hesperides* and questions Herrick's apparent royalism, seeing ambiguity in his poetry praising the political establishment of his time.
Deming, Robert H. *Ceremony and Art: Robert Herrick's Poetry*. The Hague: Mouton, 1974.

Stresses the ceremonial and liturgical aspects of Herrick's poetry, emphasizing the influence of Anglican theological precepts upon his approaches to artistic endeavor.

Moorman, F. W. *Robert Herrick: A Biographical and Critical Study.* London: John Lane, 1910. One of the first extended studies of *Hesperides* and of Herrick's other poetry. Useful biographical information. Still the foundation to an understanding of Herrick's poetry.

Rollin, Roger B. *Robert Herrick.* Boston: Twayne, 1966. Comprehensive study of *Hesperides*, providing analysis of the major thematic elements, expositions of individual poems, biographical and historical data.

Rollin, Roger B., and J. Max Patrick, eds. *"Trust to Good Verses": Herrick Tercentenary Essays.* Pittsburgh: University of Pittsburgh Press, 1978. A series of essays covering a variety of subjects on Herrick, including the areas of love poetry, mysticism, and historical sources. Bibliography.

A HIGH WIND IN JAMAICA

Type of work: Novel
Author: Richard Hughes (1900-1976)
Type of plot: Psychological realism
Time of plot: Early nineteenth century
Locale: Jamaica, the high seas, and England
First published: 1929

> *Principal characters:*
> MR. BAS-THORNTON, a plantation owner in Jamaica
> MRS. BAS-THORNTON, his wife
> JOHN,
> EMILY,
> EDWARD,
> RACHAEL, and
> LAURA, their children
> MARGARET FERNANDEZ, Emily's friend
> HARRY FERNANDEZ, Margaret's brother
> CAPTAIN JONSEN, the captain of a pirate ship
> A DUTCH SEA CAPTAIN, a captain murdered by Emily

The Story:

Five young Bas-Thorntons lived on the family's run-down sugar plantation in Jamaica. On the day after Emily's tenth birthday, they were allowed to make their first visit away from home. They went to meet Margaret and Harry Fernandez, children of creole neighbors, on a nearby plantation. The Fernandez children often ran around barefoot, like blacks; Emily thought it quite wonderful. During their visit, the region was shaken by a slight earthquake. Emily was wildly excited and galloped her pony into the sea. For the first time she realized that there were forces in the world over which neither she nor adults had any control.

If the earthquake was the most thrilling event of Emily's life, the death of a pet cat was soon to be the most terrible. The next evening, back home, a hurricane struck the island. While the house shook under the force of wind and rain, Tabby streaked through the house and dashed out into the storm pursued by a pack of wild jungle cats. That night, the house and the surrounding countryside were blown flat, but to the children the destruction was nothing compared with the mystery of Tabby's horrible fate.

Mr. and Mrs. Bas-Thornton had no way of knowing what was passing through the children's minds. Fearing that the hurricane must have been a shock to them, the parents reluctantly decided to send them back to England to school. They and the Fernandez children were shortly put aboard the *Clorinda*, in care of Captain James Marpole.

Pirates boarded the vessel off the Cuban coast. The *Clorinda*'s stores and valuables were seized, and the children removed to the marauder for their supper. Captain Marpole, mistaking efforts to return the children for the splash of bodies thrown overboard, left the scene under full sail. Later, he wrote the Bas-Thorntons that the pirates had callously murdered the children. Actually, Captain Jonsen, leader of the pirate crew, was surprised to find himself the custodian of seven young travelers.

The pirate ship went to Santa Lucia, Cuba, where the *Clorinda*'s cargo was auctioned off. While playing there, Emily's older brother John fell forty feet to his death from a warehouse doorway. The pirate ship presently put to sea with the surviving children.

For weeks, the pirate ship sailed aimlessly over the ocean in search of booty. The children were allowed to do much as they pleased and to amuse themselves with two pigs and a monkey that the vessel carried. Emily began to be aware of her identity as a separate personality; the shipboard life that she had accepted unquestioningly at first began to disturb her. One night, Captain Jonsen came into the children's quarters in a drunken state. When he tried to stroke Emily's hair, she bit his thumb. Margaret, more mature, was sick after the incident, but a few days later, she went to the captain's cabin to live. From that time on, she avoided the other children.

Emily and the captain avoided each other after the drunken incident, until a thigh wound Emily received from a marlin spike dropped by Rachael brought about a reconciliation. Captain Jonsen carried her to his cabin, dressed the gash, and gave her his bunk.

Emily was still confined to bed, her wound healing, when the pirates captured a Dutch steamer carrying a cargo of wild animals. The ship's captain was bound and left tied on the floor of Emily's cabin while Captain Jonsen and his crew amused themselves with the animals aboard their prize. While Emily screamed futilely, the Dutch captain managed to roll toward a knife lying in a corner. He was not a handsome man. He seemed to have no neck, and he reeked of cigar smoke; the fact that he was tied up like an animal added to Emily's terror. His fingers were groping for the blade when she threw herself out of her bunk. Seizing the knife, she slashed at him until he was covered with wounds. Leaving him to bleed to death, she then hurled the weapon toward the door and dragged herself back to the bunk.

Margaret was the first to enter the cabin, so the first boatload of pirates to return from the captured steamer thought she had committed the crime. Horrified, they dropped her overboard to drown. The freebooters in the second boat, assuming that she had accidentally fallen in, picked her up. In the excitement caused by the murder, no one noticed her come aboard, and she was not disturbed when she rejoined the younger children in the hold.

With the captain's death hanging over their heads, intimacy between children and pirates came to an end. Realizing the wantonness of her deed, Emily had to bear the double burden of her conscience and the fear that Margaret would identify the real culprit.

The sight of a man-of-war on the horizon finally brought Captain Jonsen to a decision; it was time he and the children parted company. With his ship disguised as a shabby cargo vessel, the *Lizzie Green*, he persuaded the captain of a passing steamship to relieve him of his young passengers. The children were laying their own plans for capturing another prize—the steamship—when the mate called Emily aside to coach her in what he hoped would be the children's story. Emily willingly promised to say that the captain of the *Lizzie Green* had rescued them from pirates. It was she, however, who, in a childish burst of confidence to the stewardess aboard the steamer, told the secret of the pirate vessel. On that information, a gunboat apprehended Captain Jonsen and his men; they were imprisoned in Newgate. The young Bas-Thorntons were reunited with their parents, who had sold the plantation and moved to England. Margaret and Harry Fernandez went to stay with relatives.

Although Emily had revealed their captors' identities readily enough, the prosecuting attorney had good reason for doubting his ability to obtain a conviction. The children told about the pirates' monkey and some turtles the *Clorinda* had carried, but they had little to say about life aboard the pirate ship. All memory of John seemed obliterated from their minds. It was accepted by the grown-ups, and gradually by the children, that he had died trying to protect the girls. This conclusion was substantiated by Margaret's condition of shock and loss of memory. Emily became the chief witness for the Crown. Asked about the Dutch captain and the possibility that he had been murdered, she became hysterical but managed to say she had seen him lying in a pool of blood. Her statement was enough for a conviction. As she left the courtroom, she saw in Captain Jonsen's eyes the same despairing look she had seen in Tabby's the night of the hurricane. Captain Jonsen was condemned to be hanged.

A few days later, Emily was taken to her new school by her parents. The headmistress spoke feelingly of the experiences Emily had undergone, but anyone else, looking at her, would have found that Emily's innocent young face blended perfectly with the others as she stood chattering with the quiet-mannered young ladies who were to be her new friends.

Critical Evaluation:

Richard Hughes's fame has rested on just a handful of novels, each one quite different and quite remarkable in itself. *A High Wind in Jamaica*, originally published as *The Innocent Voyage* in the United States, was the first of these. It has been claimed, wrongly, that the novel is without ancestors. It is based on an actual event narrated to Hughes by an old woman who had been one of the children, and Joseph Conrad used the same story for his *Romance* (1903).

The novel can be placed within a tradition of prose fiction that deals thematically with children, or, more precisely, with the interplay of the world of childhood and the adult world. Hughes's contribution to this has been crucial, marking the demise of certain Victorian attitudes about children, and the emergence of modernist attitudes based on the work of Sigmund Freud and his associates.

The nineteenth century had begun, at least in children's literature, by stressing the fallen nature of children and the need for strict discipline to counteract the effects of a child's natural tendency to wilfulness and rebellion. In adult literature, such a view had not taken such deep root, partly because of a residual Lockean view of childhood as a regrettable stage of life to be completed as quickly as possible; this view was displaced by Romanticism's celebrations of the innocence of childhood.

As the Victorian novel developed, the notion of the 'innocent' child, exploited and mistreated by the adult world, emerged. Writers used this figure to criticize society. Another version of this emerged in Americans Mark Twain's and Henry James's works, in which the naïveté of the child unmasks the hypocrisies of the adult world. Toward the end of the century, the fallen child finally disappeared in children's literature, to be replaced by a sentimentalized version of the innocent child, or, more significantly, by a depiction of the childhood world as basically separate from the adult.

In *A High Wind in Jamaica*, Richard Hughes is one of the first writers to suggest that this separate world is, in fact, much more strange, much less innocent, than the late Victorians had supposed. Children left to themselves largely unsupervised can let loose, or find let loose within themselves, primitive forces and drives—something with which the earlier Calvinist writers would have agreed. Hughes also makes important use of the theories of the infant sexuality and developing sexuality proposed by Freud and others between the end of the Victorian era and the writing of this book. Emily's latent awareness of the Captain's sexuality, and the implied sexual behavior of Margaret illustrate this. Hughes also takes as a central theme Freud's opposition of libido and civilization. Unfettered by the constraints of society, the primitive drives, fears, and egocentrisms of the children's libido are allowed full play, with devastating results.

As in William Golding's *Lord of the Flies* (1954), Hughes, by setting his background in jungle conditions, shows just how quickly the lawlessness and ferocity of untamed nature lets loose the lawlessness and ferocity of the children. Furthermore, Hughes removes his children from civilization by placing them in a self-enclosed world of lawlessness, the pirate ship, which becomes a powerful symbol of its adult paradigm. The central irony of the novel is that it is the pirates who appear innocent and naïve; the children seem fierce.

The children's amorality is as shocking as in Golding's depiction, done thirty years and a world war later. Hughes, however, depicts more forcefully than Golding the strangeness of such violence, whether libidinal or learned. Readers are shocked, for example, not just by Emily's act of murder, but by her strange ability to forget about it; readers are also shocked in the matter of John's death.

The story is told mainly through Emily's eyes, but sympathetic narrative insights into the connection, or lack of connection, that she makes are withheld. Hughes maintains himself as the clinical observer, and readers are made to feel as spectators of an alien world where normative human relationships and sensitivities appear only fleetingly, to be marginalized by the ineffective gesturings of the adults.

Tabby's nightmarish death hangs uneasily over the consciousness of the children. The wild animals captured by the pirates are a mock adult equivalent of the jungle wildcats that have torn their pet to pieces. The children know more about the savagery of the natural world than the adults do. Similarly, the intensities of the children's play on board ship mock the ineptness and half-heartedness of the adult pirates. The adults play at life; the children are totally involved in their own version of it. Hughes's ability to depict such intensities in economical, understated language is one of the main ways the sense of alienation is achieved.

Hughes's symbols and plot motifs are also bizarre and unpredictable. The parents' state of mind mirrors Captain Marpole's; it is their fear that produces the initial unpredictability. The children try to make sense of it according to the logic of their world; for adult readers, however, their logic creates a second level of the bizarre. The final symbol of the adult world, the court of law, is the crowning irony of society's perception of childhood innocence, the final act of the bizarre. It is also an excellent example of Hughes's use of plot episodes as extended metaphor. Dramatic irony underlines the book's thematic ironies. Readers are left to wonder whether they, too, have blotted out their own childhoods. If "the child is father to the man," as William Wordsworth proclaimed, then what are people? Hughes's novel is black comedy, a grim reminder of civilization as a game, with people as mere players. It is the children who are the experts—because they make their own rules.

"Critical Evaluation" by David Barratt

Bibliography:
Henighan, T. J. "Nature and Convention in *A High Wind in Jamaica*." *Critique* 9, no. 1 (1967): 5-18. One of the few literary discussions of the novel. Relevant and useful.
Hughes, Penelope. *Richard Hughes: Author, Father*. Gloucester, N.H.: Alan Sutton, 1984. Memories of her father, quoting extensively from letters and anecdotes. Includes photos and some of Hughes's drawings.
Poole, Richard. *Richard Hughes: Novelist*. Bridgend, Mid Glamorgan, Wales: Poetry Wales Press, 1986. A full-length study of Hughes as novelist. Includes sections on biography, Hughes's novels (including a chapter on *A High Wind in Jamaica*), and his theoretical thinking. Poole concentrates on Hughes's narrative voice and stance. A full bibliography of Hughes's own writing and an index are included.

Savage, D. S. "Richard Hughes, Solipsist." *Sewanee Review* 94, no. 4 (Fall, 1986): 602-613. Substantial essay. Discusses the painful awareness Hughes had of the isolation of the ego and the illusory nature of human experience, with the consequent emptiness of accepted moral standards.

Thomas, Peter. *Richard Hughes*. Cardiff, Wales: University of Wales Press, 1973. Discusses the ways in which the novels have explored the areas where instinct and need become rationalized into principle. Emphasizes Hughes's ability to go against accepted opinion and fashion—and often to invert them. Index included.

HIPPOLYTUS

Type of work: Drama
Author: Euripides (c. 485-406 B.C.E.)
Type of plot: Tragedy
Time of plot: Antiquity
Locale: Troezen in Argolis
First performed: Hippolytos, 428 B.C.E. (English translation, 1781)

Principal characters:

THESEUS, the king of Athens
HIPPOLYTUS, the son of Theseus and Hippolyta, the queen of the Amazons
PHAEDRA, Theseus' wife
APHRODITE, goddess of physical love
ARTEMIS, goddess of spiritual love

The Story:

Aphrodite became angry because Hippolytus, the offspring of an illicit union between Theseus and Hippolyta, alone among the citizens of Troezen refused to do her homage. Instead, the youth, who had been tutored by the holy Pittheus, honored Artemis, goddess of the chase and of spiritual love. Aphrodite, jealous of Artemis and incensed at his neglect of her altars, vowed revenge: She would reveal to Theseus the love his wife, Phaedra, had for her stepson.

Some time before, Hippolytus had gone to the country of Pandion to be initiated into the holy mysteries. Phaedra, seeing the handsome youth, had fallen in love with him, and because her heart was filled with longing she had dedicated a temple to the Cyprian goddess. Poseidon, ruler of the sea, had once promised Theseus that three of his prayers to the sea god would be answered. Aphrodite planned to use that promise to accomplish her revenge.

Now it happened that Theseus had killed a kinsman, and as punishment for his crime he had been exiled for a year in Troezen. Hippolytus, returning from the chase, paid his respects with song and garlands before the altar of Artemis. Reminded by a servant that an image of Aphrodite stood nearby, he answered impatiently that he acknowledged the power of the Cyprian goddess, but from afar. He was dedicated to chastity and had no desire to become her devotee. After Hippolytus had left the shrine, the attendant asked Aphrodite to indulge the young man's foolish pride.

Phaedra, who had accompanied her husband when he left Athens, moped in her hopeless passion for the young prince, so much so that her servants expressed deep concern over her illness and wondered what strange malady affected her. A nurse, alarmed at Phaedra's restiveness and petulance, was the most concerned of all. When her mistress expressed a desire to hunt wild beasts in the hills and to gallop horses on the sands, the nurse decided that Phaedra was light-headed because she had not eaten food for three days. The nurse swore by the Amazon queen who had borne Theseus a son that Phaedra would be a traitor to her own children if she let herself sicken and die. At the mention of Hippolytus' name Phaedra started; then she moaned pitifully. Thinking how horrible it was that she had been stricken with love for her husband's son, she bewailed the unnatural passions of her Cretan house. Urged by the nurse, she finally confessed her true feelings for her stepson. The nurse was horrified at the thought of the possible consequences of such a sinful passion, and the attendants mourned at what the future seemed to hold for all concerned. Phaedra told them that she was determined to take her own life in order to preserve her virtue and to save Theseus from shame.

The nurse reconsidered, however, and advised her mistress to let matters take a natural course; she would offend Aphrodite if she were to resist her love for Hippolytus. Phaedra was quite scandalized when the nurse suggested that she see Hippolytus. The nurse said that she had a love charm that would end Phaedra's malady, but that the potion was ineffectual without a word from Hippolytus' mouth or an item of his clothing or personal belongings.

Phaedra's attendants melodically invoked Aphrodite not to look askance upon them in their concern for their mistress. The nurse, eager to aid the lovesick woman, went to Hippolytus and told him of Phaedra's love. The young huntsman was shocked, and he rebuked the nurse for a bawd and expressed his dislike for all mortal womankind. Phaedra, having overheard her stepson's angry reproaches and his condemnation of all women, feared that her secret would be revealed. To make Hippolytus suffer remorse for her death, she hanged herself.

Theseus, who had been away on a journey, was grief-stricken to discover that Phaedra had taken her life. His grief turned to rage, however, when he read a letter clenched in his dead wife's hand, which claimed that Hippolytus had caused her death by his attempts to ravish her. Wild with sorrow and rage, Theseus called on Poseidon to grant the first of his requests: that the god destroy Hippolytus that very day. His attendants implored him to be calm, to consider the welfare of his house, and to withdraw his request.

Hippolytus, returning at that moment, encountered his father and was mystified by Theseus' passionate words. Standing over the body of his dead wife, the king reviled his bastard son and showed him the letter Phaedra had written. Hippolytus proudly defended his innocence, saying that he had never looked with carnal desire upon any woman. Theseus, refusing to believe his son's protestations, banished the young man from his sight. Hippolytus departed, still insisting to his friends that he was innocent.

Going down to the seashore, Hippolytus entered his chariot after invoking Zeus to strike him dead if he had sinned. As he drove along the strand on the road leading to Argos, an enormous wave rose out of the sea and from the whirling waters emerged a savage, monstrous bull, whose bellowing echoed along the shore. The horses drawing Hippolytus' chariot panicked and ran away, the bull in pursuit. Suddenly, one of the chariot wheels struck a rock and the car overturned. Hippolytus was dragged across the rocks and mortally injured.

When Theseus learned that his son still lived, he was indifferent but consented to have him brought back to the palace. While he waited, Artemis appeared and told him of his son's innocence and of Phaedra's guilty passion for Hippolytus. Aphrodite, she declared, had contrived the young hunter's death to satisfy her anger at his neglect of her shrines.

Hippolytus, his body maimed and broken, was carried on a litter into his father's presence. Still maintaining his innocence, he moaned with shameless self-pity and lamented that one so pure and chaste should meet death because of his frightened horses. They were, he said, the principal means by which he had always honored Artemis, goddess of the hunt. When she told him that Aphrodite had caused his death, he declared that he, his father, and Artemis were all victims of the Cyprian's evil designs.

Knowing the truth at last, Hippolytus took pity on the broken-hearted Theseus and forgave his father for his misunderstanding and rage. Theseus arose from the side of the dead prince. Miserably he faced the prospect of living on after having caused the destruction of his innocent, beloved son.

Critical Evaluation:

Hippolytus is an intriguing play from both a religious and a psychological standpoint. Euripides dramatizes the traditional rivalry in Greek religion between Aphrodite, the goddess of love, and Artemis, the goddess of chastity. The three major characters—Phaedra, Hippolytus, and Theseus—are caught in that antagonism and must suffer for it. Just as a statue of each goddess frames the stage, so the dramatic action is set between the appearance of Aphrodite in the prologue and the appearance of Artemis at the end. The contrast between these two, as Euripides shows it, however, is not between carnal love and spiritual love, but between uncontrolled passion and artificial restraint.

Aphrodite is an intense, volatile goddess who does not hesitate to destroy her own devotee, Phaedra, in order to wreak vengeance on Hippolytus, who, she believes, has deeply offended her by his conduct and attitude. Artemis appears as the revealer of truth and the calm reconciler of father and son. Once passion is spent, there remains a clear-eyed, sobering, and immeasurably sad view of things.

The goddess of passion works her will through two violently emotional people, Phaedra and Theseus. Although perhaps not technically incestuous, Phaedra's love for the young man is clearly immoral and wrong. However, the intensity of her feelings, which are obviously beyond her control, and the sincerity of her guilt and anguish make her the most sympathetic and moving figure in the play. Hippolytus is innocent of any actual wrongdoing, but his self-righteous moralism and abnormally rigid sexual behavior not only render him personally unsympathetic but, more important, are major stimulants to the sequence of actions that leads to the final catastrophe. Theseus' impulsive vengeance adds the third element to the drama. Uncontrollable passion, arrogant self-righteousness, and mindless revenge combine to create a multiple tragedy.

From a dramatic standpoint, there is one problem in that Phaedra, the most important character in the play, dies when the plot is little more than half over. With her death, the intensity of the play flags. The debate between Theseus and Hippolytus over the causes of her death and Theseus' subsequent condemnation of Hippolytus lack the feelings that make Phaedra's scenes so vital, although they do resolve the action and grant to the father and son a measure of sympathy and tragic stature they had previously lacked. It is, however, the vividness, intensity, and tragic ambiguity of Phaedra's character that makes *Hippolytus* one of Euripides' greatest and most provocative plays.

Bibliography:
Euripides. *Hippolytus*. Translated by Robert Bagg. New York: Oxford University Press, 1973. In his translator's introduction, Bagg claims that Hippolytus' possession by Artemis can be explained by the concept of *sophrosyne*, a strength of character so free of guilt and clear of mind that the individual is not even tempted to commit a wrong, weak, or greedy action.
_____. *Hippolytus*. Edited by W. S. Barret. Oxford, England: Clarendon Press, 1964. Scholarly edition of the play, which includes a discussion of the legend and cult of Hippolytus, evidence for lost plays on the subject, the history of the text in antiquity and the middle ages, and a commentary on the play.
_____. *Hippolytus*. In *Three Plays by Euripedes*, translated by Philip Vellacott. 1953. Reprint. Baltimore, Md.: Penguin Books, 1974. In his introduction, Vellacott points out two major themes in *Hippolytus*, that of *syngnome*, or pardon, which differs from forgiveness in its emotional detachment and lack of religious implications, and that of the deep gulf of misunderstanding between men and women.
Kitto, H. D. F. "Euripidean Tragedy: The *Hippolytus*." In *Greek Tragedy: A Literary Study*. 1939. Reprint. London: Methuen, 1978. Focuses on such issues as the contrast in character development in Phaedra and Hippolytus; the seeming lack of unity in the play; and the role of the goddesses, especially Aphrodite.

Lattimore, Richard. Introduction to *Hippolytus*, by Euripides, edited by David Grene and Richard Lattimore. 1955. Reprint. Chicago: University of Chicago Press, 1975. Explains the interest Greek audiences had in women and their place in society. Discusses how the play hinges on the monstrousness of the relationship Phaedra desires and points out the weakness of the somewhat mechanical denouement.

HIROSHIMA

Type of work: New journalism
Author: John Hersey (1914-1993)
First published: 1946

Principal personages:
KIYOSHI TANIMOTO, a Methodist minister
TERUFUMI SASAKI, a Red Cross surgeon
TOSHINKI SASAKI, a personnel clerk
MASAKAZU FUJII, a doctor in private practice
HATSUYO NAKAMURA, the widow of a soldier and mother of
    two daughters and a son
WILHELM KLEINSORGE, a German Jesuit priest

The Story:

Six people began their day routinely on August 6, 1945. Dr. Fujii sat on his porch in his underwear, reading the newspaper. Dr. Sasaki arrived at Red Cross Hospital a little earlier than usual and began treating patients. The Reverend Tanimoto helped a parishioner move belongings from a house in the suburbs. Father Kleinsorge lay down on his cot to read after morning mass. Mrs. Nakamura gave her three children some peanuts to eat while they rested on their mats. Miss Sasaki sat down at her desk to begin work. Each of these people survived the explosion of an atomic bomb dropped on Hiroshima at 8:15 that morning.

Immediately following the explosion, Mr. Tanimoto began to help others, often feeling ashamed that he himself had not been injured. He accompanied many of the members of his neighborhood association to Asano Park, a designated gathering place for the group. Father Kleinsorge and his fellow Jesuits also went to Asano Park because their designated "safe area" was afire. Mrs. Nakamura took her children to Asano Park where they waited with others for food and help.

Miss Sasaki spent the hours after the explosion caught under bookcases and building beams that had twisted and broken her left leg under her; the rubble and her injuries prevented her from pulling herself out of the ruins of her office. After several men extricated her and propped her up under a metal lean-to, she waited with two other badly wounded survivors.

Dr. Sasaki and Dr. Fujii were among the few physicians who survived the bombing. Dr. Sasaki, having taken a pair of glasses from an injured nurse to replace his broken ones, treated the wounded and dying. Dr. Fujii had to extricate himself from the crossed beams of his ruined home and private hospital. With a broken collarbone and many lesser injuries, he was not able to care for other wounded people. He walked to his family's house on the outskirts of town to spend the first night after the bombing.

Until the surrender of Japan on August 15, Mr. Tanimoto continued to help others, procuring rice from an army aid station and taking water to survivors in Asano Park. Dr. Sasaki treated the wounded at the hospital for three days after the bombing, working with almost no sleep. He went to his mother's house to rest for a day, then returned to the hospital. Father Kleinsorge also helped and comforted the wounded in Asano Park and helped take survivors to the Novitiate in the hills beyond the edge of the city.

Miss Sasaki was moved from a military hospital to a school that had quickly been converted to a hospital. Mrs. Nakamura and her children, who also suffered from the effects of the bomb, left the city to stay with family. During the year after the war ended, Mrs. Nakamura managed to rent a small wooden shack and send her children back to school. She spent all of her savings. Miss Sasaki, now crippled and no longer engaged to be married, left the hospital nine months after the explosion. She converted to Catholicism under the instruction of Father Kleinsorge. Mr. Tanimoto continued to minister to parishioners' needs despite having lost his church building. Dr. Fujii lost another home, this time to a flood, but bought a clinic in a suburb of Hiroshima, where he resumed practicing medicine. Dr. Sasaki continued as a physician at Red Cross Hospital and married in March, 1946. All six people suffered in varying degrees from symptoms of radiation poisoning ranging from energy loss to hair loss and blood disorders.

Over the next forty years, Mrs. Nakamura brought up her children and supported them and herself in a series of jobs she worked whenever she had sufficient energy. She retired at the age of fifty-five from a job with a chemical plant. She joined a folk music group and enjoyed enough financial security to be able to travel, among other places to a shrine to soldiers in Tokyo.

For five years after the bombing, Dr. Sasaki continued to practice at Red Cross Hospital, often doing surgery (with mixed success) to remove extensive scarring from radiation burns. In 1951, he went into private practice and from that point on he prospered. He never investigated medical effects of the bombing, concentrating instead on expanding his practice. In 1963, he underwent surgery for lung cancer, which brought him near death, an experience that changed his approach to practicing medicine from interest in the financial rewards to a new focus on its inherent satisfactions. He eventually established a home for elderly patients. Although he dwelt little on the bombing, Dr. Sasaki expressed one regret, that in the first days after the bombing, he had been unable to keep good records of deaths or to store the ashes appropriately.

Father Kleinsorge, in the forty years after the explosion, was repeatedly hospitalized for treatment of radiation sickness, but he continued to proselytize tirelessly for his faith. He became a Japanese citizen and took a new name, Father Makoto Takakura. Father Takakura was especially effective working with other atomic bomb survivors, with whom he felt a strong kinship and an understanding unmatched in other relationships. He died in 1977 after a long illness and was buried on a hill above the Nagatsuke Novitiate; his grave was almost continually decorated with fresh flowers.

One of Father Takakura's converts to Catholicism, Miss Sasaki, spent years helping to support her younger siblings. Then, at the suggestion of Father Takakura, she entered the convent, taking her vows in 1957 as Sister Dominique Sasaki. She cared for orphans as well as retirees and found her greatest strength in helping people feel less lonely while they died.

Dr. Fujii returned to medical practice in Hiroshima and built a new clinic in 1948 on the site of the old one. His recommended treatments to fellow survivors included techniques for relaxing; he also recommended having an alcoholic drink at regular intervals. He eventually built an American-style house and continued to enjoy the better things in life. By early 1964, however, Dr. Fujii's health had deteriorated, and his last eleven years were spent in limited awareness.

The Reverend Tanimoto continued to preach and minister to the citizens of Hiroshima in the years after the bombing, despite a lack of funds and his own lessened energies. He traveled to the United States several times to raise money for the peace movement and for American plastic surgery on young women badly scarred by the bomb. He also gave lectures on his experiences. On one trip, his life was featured on a popular television show, *This Is Your Life.* His work in the United States distanced him from the Japanese peace movement, however, for many perceived him to be seeking personal recognition. Tanimoto developed relationships with both Norman Cousins, an American evangelist and motivational speaker, and the American novelist Pearl S. Buck. After retiring in 1982, Mr. Tanimoto lived comfortably in Hiroshima.

Critical Evaluation:

In 1945, John Hersey was awarded the Pulitzer Prize for *A Bell for Adano* (1944), a novel based on his observations as a reporter in Italy and characterized by attention to realistic detail and psychological insight. (The novel led to a lawsuit filed against the author by an Army officer who felt that his experiences to some extent paralleled those of a character in the book.) Hersey demonstrated anew his powers as a reporter and a writer when he documented the experiences of survivors of the atomic bomb in his nonfiction account, *Hiroshima*. Hersey's interest in the Far East, which is evident both in *Hiroshima* and his novel *The White Lotus* (1965), probably stemmed from his having spent his childhood in China, where his parents were missionaries. In his years as a professor of literature at Yale University, Hersey wrote fiction as well as nonfiction works, including *The Writer's Craft* (1974).

Hersey's account of six survivors of the atomic bombing of Hiroshima was initially written as a three-part series for *The New Yorker*, but the editors of the magazine instead decided to print the entire text in the issue dated August 31, 1946. The first edition and its subsequent printings presented four sections: "A Noiseless Flash," "The Fire," "Details Are Being Investigated," and "Panic Grass and Feverfew." Each section dramatically presented the experiences of the six survivors in a chronology, respectively, of moments, hours, days, and months. A fifth section, "The Aftermath," which marked the fortieth anniversary of the bombing, detailed the biographies of the six survivors during the years following the war.

Although it is nonfiction, Hersey's account uses such structures and devices common to fiction as scene-by-scene construction, dialogue that reveals character, third-person point of view, symbolic detail, and theme. Although time determines the five major divisions of the book, each scene is recounted from the perspective of one of the survivors. Hersey describes, for example, Mr. Tanimoto's feelings as he attempts to swim across the river, praying the while for God to help him and thinking "It would be nonsense for me to be drowned when I am the only uninjured one." Hersey thus establishes Tanimoto's sense of purpose and his expectation of God's order.

Symbolic details fill the book. When the atomic bomb destroys Miss Sasaki's office building, Hersey concludes his description with the comment "There, in the tin factory, in the first moment of the atomic age, a human being was crushed by books." The books symbolize the scientific knowledge that killed thousands of people in an instant, whose deaths were the cost of having eaten of the fruit of the tree.

Another important literary device in *Hiroshima* is Hersey's fine irony. When Mr. Tanimoto describes the morning of the bombing as "perfectly clear and so warm that the day promised to be uncomfortable," the understated "uncomfortable" capitalizes on the readers' knowledge of the horrors to follow. In another ironic passage, Hersey notes that after the bombing, Father Kleinsorge "had to leave the buried ones to die," shockingly reversing the expected pattern. Irony also underscores Hersey's description of the plants that grew in the weeks following the bombing: "Over everything . . . was a blanket of fresh, vivid, lush, optimistic green; the verdancy rose even from the foundations of ruined houses." This scene "horrifie[s] and amazes[s]" Miss Sasaki as she is carried through the city on her way to Red Cross Hospital. The "optimistic green" contrasts starkly with the outlook of Miss Sasaki, crippled and alone.

Another pattern that emerges in the book is a fairy-tale language and mode of description that suggests the powerlessness of small figures in a global script. When the bomb exploded, two descriptions in particular reinforce the childlike status of the survivors. When Mrs. Nakamura, "seemed to fly into the next room over the raised sleeping platform, pursued by parts of her house," Hersey describes the parts of the house pursuing her as in a fairy-tale transformation of an inanimate object. He describes Dr. Fujii pinned under crossbeams "like a morsel suspended between two huge chopsticks," again employing a description of vulnerability suited to a child's tale.

Hersey fits many of his survivors into the thematic pattern of the journey of a hero who undergoes trials and hardships that lead to rebirth and transformation in a new community. Miss Sasaki, for instance, who is in the months following the bombing described as a passive sufferer, develops into an adult with a sense of purpose in her community. Her transformation through faith leads to her rebirth as Sister Dominique, a nun competent in institutional management but strongest in sustaining others through fatal illness and comforting them when they are dying. Dr. Sasaki experiences a rebirth after nearly dying from his surgery: "Haunted by the loneliness he had felt when he thought he was dying, he now did his best to move closer to his wife and his children." A hero's truth contained in Dr. Sasaki's experience can be explained as the necessity of participation. Although his efforts to help the wounded after the bombing had certainly fit the term "heroic," Dr. Sasaki experiences his own transformation only after he feels the presence of death within himself.

Perhaps the most important theme of *Hiroshima* is memory. The recollected lives of six people call upon every reader to remember. In a compelling spur to recollection, Hersey reports at regular intervals and in italics the dates of nations' first test explosions of new nuclear weapons, brief reminders that compose an inescapable knocking on the readers' collective conscience. In the final description of arguably the most dynamic of the six survivors, Mr. Tanimoto, Hersey concludes by noting that Mr. Tanimoto's "memory, like the world's, was getting spotty." The book stands as Hersey's goad to memory and conscience.

Janet Taylor Palmer

Bibliography:
Huse, Nancy Lyman. *John Hersey and James Agee: A Reference Guide.* Boston: G. K. Hall, 1978. A comprehensive listing of articles and books about Hersey's work. The introduction provides a useful critical context.
_____. *The Survival Tales of John Hersey.* Troy, N.Y.: Whitston Publishing, 1983. The first chapter includes an analysis of the first four segments of *Hiroshima* and discusses Hersey's intention to win the reader's sympathy for the six survivors.
Mannix, Patrick. *The Rhetoric of Antinuclear Fiction: Persuasive Strategies in Novels and Films.* Lewisburg, Pa.: Bucknell University Press, 1992. Brief treatment of *Hiroshima* within a broader discussion of the dynamic of emotional appeal.
Sanders, David. *John Hersey Revisited.* Boston: Twayne, 1991. Chapter 1 includes a significant discussion of *Hiroshima*. Also provides a strong analysis of "The Aftermath" and Hersey's assessment of the impact of the atomic bomb.
Yavenditti, Michael. "John Hersey and the American Conscience." *Pacific Historical Review* 43 (February, 1974): 24-49. Thorough study of the reception of *Hiroshima*. Concludes that the book did not lead its American readers to reconsider the legitimacy of the decision to drop the bomb.

THE HISTORY OF ENGLAND

Type of work: History
Author: Thomas Babington Macaulay (1800-1859)
Time covered: 56 B.C.E.-1702 C.E.
First published: The History of England from the Accession of James II, books 1 and 2,
1849; books 3 and 4, 1855; book 5, unfinished, 1861

> *Principal personages:*
> CHARLES II
> JAMES II
> WILLIAM III
> MARY, William's wife
> JOHN CHURCHILL, the duke of Marlborough
> WILLIAM PENN

Thomas Macaulay knew little about English history before the seventeenth century. He knew almost nothing about foreign history. He was not interested in art, science, philosophy, or religion. As a Whig, he had no sympathy with the Tories and little understanding of James II. He overlooked many of the authoritative books covering the period about which he was writing. Therefore, in *The History of England* he is sometimes unfair to certain figures or mistaken in facts and interpretations. Overall, however, he has created an eminently readable history with vivid pictures of the actors and the social and cultural background against which they performed.

Macaulay was a child prodigy who started writing early. Before he was eight years of age, this future historian, poet, and essayist had completed an outline of history and a poem in three cantos modeled after the poetry of Sir Walter Scott. He went to Trinity College, Cambridge, intending to enter law. Before he passed his bar examinations in 1826, he had attracted attention by a critical essay on John Milton, the first of many he contributed to the influential *Edinburgh Review*. His essays about the Indian question earned him an appointment on a commission to India.

While in India, he wrote in his diary his intention to compile a five-volume history, the first part to cover the thirty years from the revolution of 1688 to the beginning of Walpole's administration. It would end with the death of George IV and achieve unity by covering "the Revolution that brought the crown into harmony with the Parliament and the Revolution which brought the Parliament into harmony with the nation." Further planning convinced him of the need to precede his account of the revolution by the story of the reign of James II.

When he returned to England, he had barely begun his project before he was named secretary of war. This post gave him no time for literary work, until the elections of 1841 turned him out of office and into his study. He progressed slowly on his history until the return of his party to power in 1846, when he was appointed paymaster general. In spite of public demands on his time, the first two volumes of *The History of England* appeared within three years of this appointment.

The ten chapters begin with an account of Roman times and bring the story of England down to the crowning of William and Mary on February 13, 1689. Diary entries reveal Macaulay's worry about how to begin. He had to start somewhere and so, in the first paragraph, he bravely announces his purpose to "offer a slight sketch of my country from the earliest times." Romans,

Saxons, and Danes move through the first chapter, bringing the reader up to the general elections of 1660 and the return of Charles II to England. In the next chapter, Macaulay follows the career of Charles II until his death in 1685. At this point, the historian is ready to begin his task in earnest. His announced purpose in the third chapter is to "give a description of the state in which England was at the time when the crown passed from Charles II to his brother, James."

First, Macaulay stresses the small population of the British Isles in 1685, perhaps five million, with half living in England. Then he discusses the revenue available. Excise taxes, taxes on chimneys, and the rest brought in hardly a fifth as much to the crown as France was collecting. Then follows a study of the army and the navy, on which the money was largely spent. A discussion of agriculture and mineral wealth introduces the country gentlemen and the yeomanry, with a glance at the clergy. Next, the historian's attention fixes on the towns and their growth, following the expansion of trade and manufacturing, with special attention to London. Discussion of communication with London leads to a section on the postal system, inns, and highwaymen. A study of England's cultural status, both literary and scientific, precedes the final section on the terrible condition of the very poor.

The description of the death of Charles II, in chapter 4, is a sample of Macaulay's style. The ten pages read like a historical novel, except that the historian has footnotes available for the details of the palace room, the visitors at the bedside, and such bits as the king's dying comment about winding the clock at his bedside. The surreptitious visit of the priest, John Huddleston, and the reaction of the crowd outside the palace bring vividness to the event.

The succession of James II to the throne is the theme of the other six chapters of the first two volumes. The new monarch lacked the political acumen and the general knowledge of the world possessed by Charles II; otherwise, he might not have been so easily duped by his Jesuit adviser, for he did possess administrative ability, more, perhaps, than Macaulay grants him.

The exciting part of this section tells of James's following the invasion of England by William of Orange and of his capture by "rude fishermen of the Kentish coast," who mistook the royal party for Jesuits and the monarch for his hated adviser, Father Petre. Then came his flight to France, the convention that formulated the Declaration of Rights, and the coronation of William and Mary. Because of this stirring material, excitingly told, thirteen thousand copies of the history were sold in four months.

Such success worried Macaulay. Attempting to make the other volumes dealing with William as colorful, he provided himself with a timetable: two book pages a day, two years to finish the first draft, and another year for revision and polishing. He felt the need for making every sentence clear and precise, for seeing that his paragraphs had continuity. Such labor took longer than he had planned. It was nearly seven years before he had the manuscript of volumes 3 and 4 ready for the printer. Their twelve chapters brought England's story to the end of the war with France in 1697. The public acceptance justified the time taken in its composition. Within two months, 26,500 copies were sold, and Macaulay's royalties amounted to twenty thousand pounds.

Macaulay's diary frequently voiced his desire for fame and immortality. "I think posterity will not let my book die," he wrote in 1838. In addition to the wealth it brought, the success of the work replaced the Tory view of English history, as voiced by David Hume in his *History of England* (1754-1761), with the Victorian concept originated with Macaulay.

In the new volumes, Macaulay showed himself kindly disposed toward Mary in her trying position between her Catholic father and her Protestant husband, William of Orange, who divided his attention between her and Elizabeth Villiers. William did love Mary, however. The last lines of Macaulay's history tell about "a small piece of black silk ribbon," found next to

William's skin when his remains were being laid out. "The lords in waiting ordered it to be taken off. It contained a gold ring and a lock of the hair of Mary."

Macaulay admired William. The Dutch king had an enormous task, organizing England, reconquering Ireland, and subduing rebellious Scotland, all the while carrying on a war in France. Macaulay does seem to overestimate William's political genius, and his account of the king's yearning to return to Holland and leave England for Mary to rule is considered by some scholars an exaggeration of William's basic disillusionment with English life. With a rosy picture of the prosperity amid which William rode into London on Thanksgiving Day in November, 1697, and with the promise of a happier age, the volumes published during the writer's lifetime come to an end.

When Macaulay died, he had completed only three chapters of the concluding volume, bringing the story up to the prorogation of Parliament, April 11, 1700. His sister, Lady Trevelyan, prepared this material for publication exactly as Macaulay had left it, with "no references verified, no authority sought for or examined," but she did include several fragments, among them six pages describing the death of William with which Macaulay had probably intended to conclude his work. She also compiled a fifty-page, double-column index of the five books.

In his presentation of his characters, Macaulay is often biased. As one who did not accept doubt, who decided on one of two conflicting stories and frequently did not mention the existence of the other, he saw a person as good or bad. Historians have pointed out his failure to do justice to William Penn. Being a Whig, Macaulay used more severe criteria toward Tories, as is evident in his discussions of James's relations with Catherine Sedley, and William's with Elizabeth Villiers. What was lamentable in William was a crime in James, whom he portrayed as a libertine and black monster.

His villains are sometimes caricatures. The crafty Robert Ferguson and Titus Oates, whose perjury about the Popish Plot brought death to the innocent, are made physically hideous. In chapter 4, Macaulay writes of Oates's "short neck, his forehead low as that of a baboon, his purple cheeks, and his monstrous length of chin" and features "in which villainy seemed to be written by the hand of God." For Marlborough, even when he was plain John Churchill, Macaulay turned to lampoons for details, although he must have known they were biased. Perhaps his dislike was based on the unproved accusation that Marlborough had tried to overthrow William.

In a work of such magnitude, errors of fact and interpretation are bound to creep in, but even some that were pointed out to Macaulay during his lifetime remained uncorrected. In other cases, he did not have access to the journals and scholarly research now available. Another source of error arose from Macaulay's attitude toward everything outside the British Isles. Except for India, where he had lived for four years, he practically ignored the colonies. American history is brought in chiefly in connection with happenings in England. Captain Kidd and the piratical activities of New England and New York appear to explain the fate of an English ministry, while the Jamaica earthquake of 1692 serves only as one more reason for the unpopularity of William's reign.

Macaulay's style has also come in for some criticism. His efforts toward clearness lead at times to verbosity, and his attempts to emphasize sometimes create a paragraph where a sentence would serve. Its basic flaw is that Macaulay thought as an orator. His history is more impressive when read aloud than when read silently; it is more rhetorical than literary.

No book lacking in inherent worth can outlast its century, and *The History of England* has remained a landmark of its kind. As long as people are moved by an exciting story, interestingly told, they will continue to read Macaulay's history with both enjoyment and profit.

Bibliography:
Burrow, J. W. *A Liberal Descent: Victorian Historians and the English Past.* Cambridge, England: Cambridge University Press, 1983. Defends Macaulay, who, as the most important historian of his day, reflected the historical ethos of the Victorians. Asserts that Macaulay's work is largely unintelligible to modern readers.

Edwards, Owen Dudley. "*The History of England.*" In *Macaulay.* New York: St. Martin's Press, 1988. Thorough analysis of *The History of England*, particularly in relation to Macaulay's Whig principles and his conception of the need for a work to refute Tory historians such as Hume, John Lingard, and Archibald Alison. Good introduction for the nonspecialist.

Hamburger, Joseph. *Macaulay and the Whig Tradition.* Chicago: University of Chicago Press, 1976. Suggests that scholars have stereotyped Macaulay as a Whig or liberal Whig, ignoring his position as a classicist, whose highest priority was the reduction of the danger of civil war.

Himmelfarb, Gertrude. "Who Now Reads Macaulay?" In *The New History and the Old.* Cambridge, Mass.: The Belknap Press of Harvard University Press, 1987. Good general introduction that places *The History of England* in its contemporary context as a best-seller. Defends its continuing importance as a liberal examination of the political life of England.

Madden, William. "Macaulay's Literary Style." In *The Art of Victorian Prose*, edited by George Levine and William Madden. New York: Oxford University Press, 1968. Observes that Macaulay's need to find the meaning and pleasure lost to him in private life led him to create a comprehensive public myth in *The History of England*.

THE HISTORY OF HENRY ESMOND, ESQUIRE
A Colonel in the Service of Her Majesty Q. Anne

Type of work: Novel
Author: William Makepeace Thackeray (1811-1863)
Type of plot: Bildungsroman
Time of plot: Late seventeenth and early eighteenth centuries
Locale: England and the Low Countries
First published: 1852

> *Principal characters:*
> HENRY ESMOND, a Castlewood ward
> FRANCIS ESMOND, Viscount Castlewood
> RACHEL ESMOND, his wife
> BEATRIX, their daughter
> FRANK, their son
> LORD MOHUN, a London rake
> FATHER HOLT, a Jacobite spy
> JAMES STUART, the exiled pretender

The Story:

Henry Esmond grew up at Castlewood. He knew there was some mystery about his birth, and he dimly remembered that long ago he had lived with weavers who spoke a foreign tongue. Thomas Esmond, Viscount Castlewood, had brought him to England and turned him over to Father Holt, the chaplain, to be educated. That much he learned as he grew older.

All was not peace and quiet at Castlewood in those years; Thomas Esmond and Father Holt had been involved in a plot for the restoration of the exiled Stuart king, James II. When James attempted to recover Ireland for the Stuarts, Thomas Esmond rode off to his death at the Battle of the Boyne. His widow fled to her dower house at Chelsea. Father Holt disappeared. Henry, a large-eyed, grave-faced twelve-year-old boy, was left alone with servants in the gloomy old house.

There his new guardians and distant cousins, Francis and Rachel Esmond, found him when they arrived to take possession of Castlewood. The new Viscount Castlewood, a bluff, loud-voiced man, greeted the boy kindly enough. His wife was like a girl herself—she was only eight years older than Henry—and Henry thought her the loveliest lady he had ever seen. With them were a little daughter, Beatrix, and a baby in arms, Frank.

As Henry grew older, he became increasingly concerned over the rift he saw developing between Rachel and her husband, both of whom he loved because they treated him as one of the immediate family. It was plain that the hard-drinking, hard-gambling nobleman was wearying of his quiet country life. After Rachel's face was disfigured by smallpox, her altered appearance led her husband to neglect her even more. Young Beatrix also felt that relations between her parents were strained.

When Henry was old enough, he was sent to Cambridge on money left to Rachel by a deceased relative. Later, when he returned to Castlewood on a vacation, he realized for the first time that Beatrix was extremely pretty. Rachel had great regard for her young kinsman. Before his return from Cambridge, Rachel, according to Beatrix, went to Henry's room ten times to see that it was ready.

Relations between Rachel and the Viscount were all but severed when the notorious Lord Mohun visited Castlewood. Rachel knew her husband had been losing heavily to Mohun at cards, but when she spoke to the Viscount about the bad company he was keeping, he flew into a rage. He was by no means calmed when Beatrix innocently blurted out to her father, in the company of Mohun, that the gentleman was interested in Rachel. Jealous of another man's attentions to the wife he himself neglected, the Viscount determined to seek satisfaction in a duel.

The two men fought in London, where the Viscount had gone on the pretext of seeing a doctor. Henry suspected the real reason for the trip and went along, for he hoped to engage Mohun in a duel himself and thus save the life of his beloved guardian. The Viscount, however, was in no mood to be cheated out of a quarrel. He was heavily in debt to Mohun and thought a fight was the only honorable way out of his difficulties. Moreover, he knew Mohun had written letters to Rachel, although, as the villain explained, she had never answered them. They fought, and Mohun fatally wounded the Viscount. On his deathbed, the Viscount confessed to Henry that he was not an illegitimate child but the son of Thomas, Lord Castlewood, by an early marriage and thus the true heir to the Castlewood title. Henry Esmond generously burned the dying man's confession and resolved never to divulge the secret.

For his part in the duel, Henry Esmond was sent to prison. When Rachel visited Henry in prison, she was enraged because he had not stopped the duel and because he had allowed Mohun to go unpunished. She rebuked Henry and forbade him to return to Castlewood. When Henry left prison, he decided to join the army. For that purpose, he visited the old dowager Viscountess, his stepmother, who bought him a commission.

Henry's military ventures were highly successful and won for him his share of wounds and glory. He fought in the campaign of the Duke of Marlborough against Spain and France in 1702 and in the campaign of Blenheim in 1704. Between the two campaigns, he returned to Castlewood, where he was reconciled with Rachel. There he saw Frank, now Lord Castlewood, and Beatrix, who was cordial toward him. Rachel cautioned Henry that Beatrix was selfish and temperamental and would make no man happy who loved her.

After the campaign of 1704, Henry returned to his cousins, who were living in London. To Henry, Beatrix was more beautiful than ever and even more the coquette; but he found himself unable to make up his mind whether he loved her or Rachel. Later, during the campaign of 1706, he learned from Frank that Beatrix was engaged to an earl. The news put Henry in low spirits because he now felt she would never marry a poor captain like himself.

Henry's affairs of the heart were put temporarily into the background when he came upon Father Holt in Brussels. The priest told Henry that while on an expedition in the Low Countries, Thomas Esmond, his father, had seduced the young woman who was Henry's mother. A few weeks before his child was born, Thomas Esmond was injured in a duel. Thinking he would die, he married the woman so that her child would be born with an untainted name. Thomas Esmond, however, did not die, and when he recovered from his wounds, he deserted his wife and married a distant kinswoman, the dowager Viscountess, Henry's stepmother.

When Henry returned to Castlewood, Rachel informed him that she had learned his secret from the old Viscountess and consequently knew that he, not Frank, was the true heir. For the second time, Henry refused to accept the title belonging to him.

Beatrix's interest in Henry grew after she became engaged to the Duke of Hamilton and learned that Henry was not illegitimate in birth but the bearer of the title her brother was using. Henry wanted to give Beatrix a diamond necklace for a wedding present, but the Duke would not permit his fiancée to receive a gift from one of illegitimate birth. Rachel came to the young man's defense and declared before the Duke, her daughter, and Henry the secret of his birth and title. Later, the Duke was killed in a duel with Lord Mohun, who also met his death at the same time. The killing of Rachel's husband was avenged.

The Duke of Hamilton's death gave Henry one more chance to win Beatrix's heart. He threw himself into a plot to put the young Stuart pretender on the throne when old Queen Anne died. To this end, he went to France and helped smuggle into England the young chevalier whom the Jacobites called James III, the king over the water. The two came secretly to the Castlewood home in London, the prince passing as Frank, the young Viscount, and there the royal exile saw and fell in love with Beatrix.

Fearing the results of this infatuation, Lady Castlewood and Henry sent Beatrix to Castlewood against her will. When a report that the queen was dying swept through London, the prince was nowhere to be found. Henry and Frank made a night ride to Castlewood. Finding the pretender there in the room used by Father Holt in the old days, they renounced him and the Jacobite cause. Henry realized his love for Beatrix was dead at last. He felt no regrets for her or for the prince as he rode back to London and heard the heralds proclaiming George I the new king.

The prince made his way secretly back to France, where Beatrix joined him in his exile. At last, Henry felt free to declare himself to Rachel, who had grown very dear to him. Leaving Frank in possession of the title and the Castlewood estates, Henry and his wife went to America. In Virginia, he and Rachel built a new Castlewood, reared a family, and found happiness in their old age.

Critical Evaluation:

Critical reaction to *The History of Henry Esmond, Esquire: A Colonel in the Service of Her Majesty Q. Anne* has been as varied as reader reactions have been to the characters themselves. William Makepeace Thackeray had attempted to offset contemporary charges of "diffuseness" by providing a well-integrated novel; he sacrificed profitable serial publication to do so, and concluded that the book was "the very best" he could do. Many critics have agreed with him. Others, however, remain loyal to the panoramic social vision and ironic authorial commentary of the earlier *Vanity Fair* (1847-1848).

Thackeray cast *The History of Henry Esmond, Esquire* in the form of a reminiscential memoir: An old man recounts his earlier life, describing it from the vantage point of a later time and distancing it further with third-person narration. The occasional use of "I" suggests the involved narrator, either at emotional high points or moments of personal reflection. The distancing in time is increased by Esmond's daughter's preface, wherein Rachel Esmond Warrington not only "completes" certain details of the plot but also suggests ambiguities in the characterization of her own mother, Rachel, and of her stepsister, Beatrix. Readers of later times reacted favorably to this early use of a central intelligence whose point of view, limited and not omniscient, can suggest the disparities between appearance and reality. The readers' interpretations of the narrator's "reliability" can also shift. The question arises whether Esmond is providing a framework within which to reveal only the exemplary and to vindicate himself, or whether he is recollecting as honestly as the self can permit, with the reader knowing more at many points than he.

Thackeray set the novel in the early eighteenth century and attempted to catch the flavor of the Augustan Age, with its military conflicts, its waverings between Church of England and Catholicism, and the problems of its monarchs, William, Queen Anne, George II, and the Stuart Pretender. Thackeray was lauded for his adeptness in suggesting the language and manners of that earlier time without sending readers to glossaries or lapsing into linguistic archness. The novel, therefore, is praised by many critics as a polished example of the historical tale. In this novel as in *Vanity Fair*, he is primarily concerned with portraying the social class of masters—primarily the newly arrived and still aspiring scions of society. Their foibles were his special target.

For some readers, the novel's fascination lies in its domestic realism. Commentators find much to explore in the rendering of the marriage conventions. Lord and Lady Castlewood, new heirs to Castlewood, befriend the supposedly illegitimate Henry Esmond and gradually reveal the strained bonds that hold their marriage together. The narrator, Esmond sides with Rachel, seeing that the husband is carousing, unfaithful, and not too intelligent. Henry Esmond may lament the fate of such a fine woman, but Thackeray also shows in the dramatic scenes that Rachel, who began by worshiping her husband, is also quite capable of both restrictive possessiveness and emotional repression.

A historical tale and a novel of domestic manners, *The History of Henry Esmond, Esquire* is also an example of that favorite nineteenth century form, the *Bildungsroman*, or novel of development and education, which is also represented in such popular contemporary examples as *David Copperfield* (1849-1850) and *Great Expectations* (1860-1861). Henry Esmond remembers his childhood vaguely, a time spent with poor weavers. Brought to Castlewood, he is treated with favor by Lord Castlewood but kept in place as a page. It is only with the death of Lord Castlewood that Henry begins to receive any emotional support, when the new heirs arrive. Thackeray carefully distances Esmond to be eight years younger than Rachel and eight years older than her daughter Beatrix. Esmond's growth is the principal subject, but Thackeray also depicts the growth of Frank and Beatrix, children who are alternately spoiled by and emotionally isolated from Rachel. The much sought-after but loveless Beatrix reveals how isolated she was made to feel by the possessive nets her mother cast over the father and then over the seemingly favored brother. When she temporarily consoles Esmond, Beatrix reveals motivation for her romantic conquests. Although Esmond in the end turns away from her, Thackeray portrays her as a complex personality.

Esmond's progress takes him through Cambridge, imprisonment, and military campaigns; he experiences the loss of one idol after another and gradually acquires knowledge of the ways of the world. The reader watches for his insight to develop, for memory and maturity to coincide. Whether or not Esmond achieves that wholeness is yet another point for critics and readers to ponder.

Esmond has virtuously denied himself his birthright as legitimate heir to Castlewood so that young Frank may assume the title and Rachel and Beatrix can stay ensconced in society, but some might think Henry revels in the self-sacrifice. He has also chosen to believe that Beatrix will admire him for military daring and political plotting. Therefore, when the Stuart Pretender misses a chance for the throne in order to secure an amorous chance with Beatrix, Esmond loses two idols at once. "Good" Henry Esmond is settled at the end of the novel on a Virginia plantation in the New World, and his marriage to the widowed Rachel is compressed into two pages. All ends happily, except for those strange overtones and even stranger suggestions in the preface by the daughter of this autumnal marriage. She reminds readers that Esmond was writing for a family audience, that his role had been carefully established, and that she, Rachel Esmond Warrington, like Beatrix, had also suffered from her mother's possessiveness and jealousy.

Ultimately, what readers may enjoy most in the novel is the psychological penetration into love bonds that Thackeray provides through the "unreliable" narrator. Dramatic irony permits the reader more knowledge than Esmond permits himself. As readers circle back in their own memories to the daughter's preface, the whole range of interrelationships and ambivalences of human affairs unfolds. The characters remain fascinating puzzles long after the historical details fade. Emotional life, the subtleties of rejection and acceptance, time rendered both precisely and in psychological duration—these are the elements that continue to tantalize readers of *The History of Henry Esmond, Esquire.*

"Critical Evaluation" by Eileen Lothamer

Bibliography:
Ferris, Ina. "The Uses of History: *The History of Henry Esmond.*" In *William Makepeace Thackeray*, edited by Herbert Sussman. Boston: Twayne, 1983. Focuses on Thackeray's self-conscious realism and analyzes the complex question of how fiction can respond to and reflect reality. Begins with a brief contemporary reaction to the novel, as well as Thackeray's own statements about the work.
Hardy, Barbara. *The Exposure of Luxury: Radical Themes in Thackeray.* Pittsburgh: University of Pittsburgh Press, 1972. Discusses aspects of Thackeray's social criticism and shows his preoccupation with the surface manners of his society. Examines Thackeray's self-consciousness and lack of moral optimism as elements of his radical thinking and caring about humanity.
Loofbourow, John. *Thackeray and the Form of Fiction.* Princeton, N.J.: Princeton University Press, 1964. An excellent starting point for serious study. Discusses the interrelationship of form and content in four novels: *The History of Henry Esmond, Esquire: A Colonel in the Service of Her Majesty Q. Anne, The History of Pendennis* (1848-1850), *The Newcomes* (1953-1855), and *Vanity Fair.*
Lukacs, George. "*Henry Esmond* as an Historical Novel." In *Thackeray: A Collection of Critical Essays*, edited by Alexander Welsh. Englewood Cliffs, N.J.: Prentice-Hall, 1968. Examines the ways in which Thackeray uses history as the framework within which to construct his novel.
Peters, Catherine. *Thackeray's Universe: Shifting Worlds of Imagination and Reality.* Boston: Faber & Faber, 1987. Readable and well balanced. Relates Thackeray's fiction to his life, in particular stressing his challenge to his society. Includes a selected bibliography.
Tilford, John E., Jr. "The Love Theme of *Henry Esmond.*" In *Thackeray: A Collection of Critical Essays*, edited by Alexander Welsh. Englewood Cliffs, N.J.: Prentice-Hall, 1968. Discusses love as the theme of the novel and as it related to Thackeray's own life.

THE HISTORY OF HERODOTUS

Type of work: History
Author: Herodotus (c. 484-c. 424 B.C.E.)
Locale: Greece, Egypt, and Asia Minor
First transcribed: Historiai Herodotou, c. 425 B.C.E. (English translation, 1709)

Principal personages:
CROESUS, the king of Lydia
SOLON, an Athenian statesman
CYRUS THE GREAT, the king of Persia
DARIUS, Cyrus' cousin
XERXES, Darius' son and successor
LEONIDAS, the king of Sparta

Herodotus wrote and compiled a history of the wars of the Grecians and Persians of the fifth century B.C.E. The famous first sentence of the work reads:

> I, Herodotus of Helicarnassus, am here setting forth my history, that time may not draw the color from what man has brought into being, nor those great and wonderful deeds, manifested by both Greeks and barbarians, fail of their report, and, together with all this, the reason why they fought one another.

As the first to use the word "history," Herodotus deserves Cicero's title, "father of history." To be sure, this son of wealthy upper-class parents did not have the critical attitude toward his sources that would be the hallmark of the later historian. Interesting anecdotes of the wars between the Greeks and the Persians found their way into his pages whether he could verify them or not, but he does sometimes hedge and tag certain items as hearsay. Judging from his quotations, he must have read widely. From the details in his descriptions and the comments such as "this I saw," he must have visited most of the places he mentions. The true greatness of Herodotus lies in the fact that he was the first important writer to depart from the verse of Homer and others, to produce Europe's first prose literature. Some predecessors chronicled the beginnings of their small communities or states, but the writings of Herodotus embrace a vaster panorama: not only Greece, but also Egypt, Sardis, and Babylon as well. He looked for the reasons for the events. His aim was to trace the early rivalries between Greek and barbarian; in the process he recounted the story of many tribes, described the lands they inhabited, and reported many of their interesting customs. Those who want greater accuracy can consult Thucydides (c.455-c. 400 B.C.E.), who wrote more than a generation later. His work is more objective, but it lacks the color of Herodotus' account.

The Persians maintained that the Phoenicians originally started the quarrel by kidnapping women from Argos. Later the Hellenes raided the port of Tyre and abducted Europa, the king's daughter. The wars actually started, however, when Croesus, whose magnificent court was visited by Solon, desired to enlarge his empire by conquering some of the Ionian cities of Asia Minor. When he consulted the oracles, he was persuaded at Delphi to gather his allies for an attack on the mainland. The invasion resulted in a stalemate, however, and Croesus returned to Lydia, where his capital, Sardis, was surprised and captured by the Persians. Only a rainstorm, sent by the gods, saved him as he was being burned to death. The same miracle persuaded Cyrus to free his captive after taking possession of some of his vassal states. With them, Cyrus went on to capture Babylon. However, the Massagetae, under Queen Tomyris, were too strong in their resistance and strategy. Book 1 ends with the death of Cyrus.

Book 2 tells how Cambyses, the son of Cyrus, became king and planned to march against Egypt. The rest of the book is a tourist's guide and history of Egypt from its beginnings to the coronation of Amasis.

Book 3 tells how Cambyses marched against Amasis. The Egyptian king having died in the meantime, the mercenary army of his son was no match for the Persian, who then gave an indication of his incipient insanity by dishonoring his slain enemies.

Book 4 introduces Darius, cousin of and successor to Cambyses, who let the barbarous Scythians outwit him into making peace with them. The next volume begins with a plan that failed. Two Paeonian nobles, wishing to be named rulers over their people, brought their beautiful sister to Sardis, where Darius saw her, carrying water on her head, leading a horse, and spinning. Anxious to spread such industry throughout his empire, he had the Paeonians sent throughout Asia Minor. The book deals largely with the revolt in Ionia, the growth of Athens, and its expedition, encouraged by Aristagoras, against Sardis. Although the capital was captured and burned, Darius rallied and defeated the invaders at Salamis, in Cyprus.

Book 4 tells of a battle fought between 353 Ionian triremes (galleys) and six hundred Babylonian ships. By dissension among the enemy rather than by his strength, Darius defeated them and went on to besiege and conquer Miletus. Again Greek bickering helped him during his march to Athens, but the Athenians, rallying and with a few Plataeans, successfully engaged the forces of Darius at Marathon, on September 14, 450 B.C.E. The Persians were driven back with a loss of 6,400 dead. The Athenians lost only 192 in the battle.

Book 7 tells in considerable detail how Darius prepared to revenge his defeat. Fate delayed him, rebellious Egypt sidetracked him, and death ended his plans. The uncertain Xerxes, succeeding his father to the throne, undertook the Egyptian campaign. After a quick victory, at the head of twenty thousand soldiers, he marched on Athens. It took seven days for his army to cross the Hellespont bridge, erected by his engineers, and he, reviewing them, lamented that none would be alive a hundred years hence.

Many Greek cities were quick to surrender. Only Athens, as Herodotus boasts, dared confront the host of Xerxes. Themistocles interpreted the oracle's counsel to defend the city with "wooden walls" as advice to use the two hundred warships originally built for an attack on Egypt. Nature, however, provided a better defense in an east wind that wrecked four hundred Persian galleys along with uncounted transports and provision carriers. Neither armed forces nor natural obstacles, however, halted Xerxes' army until it reached the Pass of Thermopylae. There, for a day, the Athenians and Spartans checked the Persian host until a traitor revealed another path to the invader. The next day the Persians were again on the march, leaving all the defenders and many thousands of their own troops dead behind them.

In book 8, there is an account of Xerxes' march into Athens and setting fire to the Acropolis. The "wooden walls" of the Athenian fleet, however, were victorious at Salamis on September 20, 480 B.C.E. Winner of the greatest glory was the Persian queen Artemis, who used the confusion of battle to get revenge on another Persian by ramming and sinking his ship. Xerxes thought she was attacking an enemy and the Athenians believed she had changed loyalties, so both sides lauded her.

Fearing that the Greeks might sail on to destroy his bridge, Xerxes ordered a retreat. From the Asian mainland he sent demands for a peace treaty, promptly refused by both Athens and Sparta.

Book 9 tells how Mardonios renewed the attack against the Greeks in the hope of sending word of victory back to Xerxes in Sardis. Although temporarily checked by the Thebans, he again entered Athens, whose citizens had fled to Salamis to assemble their allies. When they marched back, Mardonios burned what was left of Athens and retreated.

Except for cavalry skirmishes, neither side wanted to engage in battle until the sacrifices were propitious, but Mardonios' patience broke first, and he fell into a trap at Plataea, where he was killed and his army routed; there were twenty thousand Persian and Boeotian casualties against ninety-one Spartans and fifty-two Athenians killed.

At Thermopylae, Leonidas, the Spartan king, had been crucified and beheaded by the Persians. Certain Greeks wanted to dishonor Mardonios in the same way, but they were told that dishonoring a dead enemy was worthy only of barbarians. Some of the fleeing Persians were pursued and killed at Mycale. Their defeat ended Xerxes' ambitious plan to crush the Hellenes.

Modern historians have honored Herodotus by translating his history into English. Littlebury's version (1709) is outstanding in style, but reveals the writer's imperfect knowledge of Greek. George Rawlinson translated the work in 1858. The most satisfactory translation is the two-volume work published by G. C. Macaulay in 1890.

Bibliography:

Evans, J. A. S. *Herodotus.* Boston: Twayne, 1982. Includes a survey of Herodotus and his interest in the Persian Wars, the background for his work, and a chronology of the events covered in his account of those wars. Discusses the events and the accuracy of Herodotus' accounts.

Glover, Terrot Reaveley. *Herodotus.* Freeport, N.Y.: Books for Libraries Press, 1969. Places Herodotus in the context of his account of the Persian Wars. Relates how Herodotus proceeded with his work. Includes contributions of Herodotus.

Hartog, François. *The Mirror of Herodotus.* Berkeley: University of California Press, 1988. Emphasizes how Herodotus presents groups such as the Egyptians and the Scythians. Analyzes the accuracy of that representation. Excellent concluding chapter.

Lister, R. P. *The Travels of Herodotus.* London: Gordon and Cremonesi, 1979. An account of the travels in which Herodotus gathered the information used in his history. Maps and illustrations. Discusses Herodotus' way of integrating fact and myth into his work.

Myres, John. *Herodotus, Father of History.* Oxford, England: Clarendon Press, 1953. Supports the claim that Herodotus is the father of history. Discusses the criticisms of Herodotus in light of the lack of precedents for Herodotus' writing. Excellent historical notes.

A HISTORY OF NEW YORK
By Diedrich Knickerbocker

Type of work: Novel
Author: Washington Irving (1783-1859)
Type of plot: Satire
First published: 1809

Principal personages:
HENDRICK HUDSON, the Dutch explorer
WOUTER VAN TWILLER, the first governor of New Amsterdam
WILHELMUS KIEFT, the second governor of New Amsterdam
PETER STUYVESANT, the last governor of New Amsterdam
GENERAL VON POFFENBURGH, the commander of Fort Casimir
JAN RISINGH, the governor of the province of New Sweden

The fun of reading a parody is heightened by acquaintance with the material being bur-lesqued. Although Washington Irving confessed, in the "Author's Apology" added to the edition of 1848, that his idea had been to parody Samuel L. Mitchell's *A Picture of New York* (1807), a knowledge of Mitchell's book is not necessary to the enjoyment of Irving's work. The parody is only part of the humor of *A History of New York, By Diedrich Knickerbocker*, which was originally begun as a collaboration between Washington Irving and his older brother Peter and had the original title *A History of New York from the Beginning of the World to the End of the Dutch Dynasty*.

The work reveals the interest of its twenty-five-year-old author in history, customs, and etymology; the burlesquing of several literary styles—his notebook supplies the names of some of the authors parodied, names now largely forgotten—reveals Irving as a literary critic. Irving was in the process of finishing the book when his fiancée, Matilda Hoffman, died suddenly. At first he was too stunned to continue working, then he returned to the manuscript as an anodyne for his grief and finished it quickly. About the same time, he conceived the idea of ascribing the authorship to an imaginary and eccentric Dutchman. The hoax was elaborately contrived and began when the public press printed a story about the disappearance of a man named Diedrich Knickerbocker. A short time later, an advertisement appeared, supposedly signed by the owner of the boardinghouse where Knickerbocker had lived, offering for sale "a very curious kind of written book," which the landlord ostensibly had printed to reimburse himself for the old gentleman's unpaid rent.

On December 6, 1809, *A History of New York*, in seven parts and 130,000 words, was first offered for sale. Legends about its reception spread rapidly. A Dutch woman in Albany threatened to horsewhip the author for his slanderous account of an ancestor. A number of famous New York families reportedly prepared to sue the publisher. On the other hand, Sir Walter Scott was reported to have complained of sore ribs from laughing so hard over the book.

Irving's style ranges from playful to erudite. Evidence of his wide reading appears on almost every page, and voluminous footnotes clothe it with pseudo-scholarship. At first, readers thought these references were part of the humor; later scholars began tracing them to actual, though minor, Roman and Greek writers. The author's pleasantries are apparent from the be-ginning. Book 1, according to him, was "learned, sagacious, and nothing at all to the purpose," and he suggested that the idle reader skip it. When Irving embarks on a study of cosmogony or creation of the world, he advises the reader to "take fast hold of his skirt or take a short cut and wait for him at the beginning of some smoother chapter."

The first books contain more chatter than matter, the humor waggish. Noah is mentioned in connection with travel by sea, so as to get the reader to America. In one place, the author defends the killing of the American Indians because, not having used European procedure to improve ground, they demonstrably had not used the talents bestowed on them, had proved careless stewards, and therefore had no right to the soil. Biblical authority was claimed for their extermination.

In book 2, the author proceeds to the settlement of the province of Nieuw Nederlandts. He confessed that this was the procedure of Hans von Dunderbottom, who took a running start of three miles to jump over a hill and arrived at it out of breath. So he "sat down to blow and then walked over it at his leisure."

One source of the book's humor lies in the derivation of names. The four explorers who pass through Hell Gate and reach the Island of Manna-hata ("The Island of Manna") were named Van Kortlandt (Lack-land), Van Zandt (Earth-born), Harden Broeck (Tough Breeches), and Ten Broeck (Ten Breeches or Thin Breeches). Irving usually refers to the governors by his translation of their names. Wouter van Twiller, for example, becomes "Walter the Doubter," who lives up to his name by smoking his pipe and maintaining silence in every crisis. According to Irving, this man of wisdom, five feet, six inches in height and six feet, five inches in circumference, settled a disagreement between a debtor and creditor by weighing the papers containing their claims, finding them equally weighty, and decreeing that the accounts were balanced. After he made the constable pay the fees, he had no further law trials.

His successor, Wilhelmus Kieft or "William the Testy," defies the Yanokies ("Silent Men") from Mais-Tchusaeg and Connecticut by bombarding them with proclamations and by building a fortress with a lusty bugler, a flag pole, Quaker guns, and a windmill. One of the most amusing scenes in the book is the description of the Yankees marching to war at Oyster Bay, where they were defeated by the doughty burghers, who thereupon celebrated on oysters and wine. Later, this governor disappeared; either he was lost in the smoke of his pipe or carried away like King Arthur. Peter Stuyvesant "the Headstrong" then became the governor.

Stuyvesant is the favorite of Diedrich Knickerbocker, who devotes three volumes to him. It was he who built the battery to hold off the Yankee invasion, though actually their own witch hunting diverted them from their proposed expedition. Then he declared war on Governor Risingh of the colony of New Sweden, across the Delaware, who had captured Fort Casimir by treachery. (The writer who supplied Irving's model for the flowery description of that campaign is unknown.) When the Dutch fighters paused at noon to eat, the author advised his readers to do the same. Then the battle was resumed, the only casualty being a flock of geese killed by a wild Swedish volley.

Stuyvesant had other troubles, first the Yankees from Connecticut and later the "roaring boys of Merryland"—King Charles I of England who gave New World territory to his brother, the Duke of York, and lent him a fleet to conquer it. Against the arrival of the British ships, the Dutch "fortified themselves—with resolution" and burned everything in the colony of British origin. Their defense was futile, however. With melancholy, the white-haired Knickerbocker narrates the end of his "beloved Island of Manna-hata" on August 27, 1664. In the 1812 edition of the history, Irving presents an additional account of his imaginary author and tells of his return to New York, now a British colony, and of his death. He was buried, "say the old records," in St. Mark's Cemetery beside his hero, Peter Stuyvesant.

In the revised 1848 edition, Irving added an "apology" and an explanation. In setting down the amusing legends of New York, he declared, he had not intended offense to living descendants of any of the old families. His purpose had been to present the history of that remote and almost forgotten age in the spirit of imaginative fancy and legend. It is this happy blend that constitutes the most important contribution of *A History of New York*.

Bibliography:
Black, Michael L. "Political Satire in Knickerbocker's *History*." In *The Knickerbocker Tradition: Washington Irving's New York*, edited by Andrew B. Myers. Tarrytown, N.Y.: Sleepy Hollow Restorations, 1974. Black identifies the historical figures who are the primary targets of Irving's satire but also argues for the universal quality of Irving's caricatures. Black also explains the pre- and postpublication hoaxes surrounding the work.
Bowden, Mary Weatherspoon. *Washington Irving*. Boston: Twayne, 1981. An excellent basic introduction to *A History of New York*. Emphasizes Irving's combination of accurate New York history and satire on contemporary political issues.
Ferguson, Robert A. "'Hunting Down a Nation': Irving's *A History of New York*." In *Washington Irving: The Critical Reaction*, edited by James W. Tuttleton. New York: AMS Press, 1993. An introduction to Irving's life, work, and criticism. Ferguson believes that *The History of New York* represents harder-edged humor than does Irving's later work, and that Irving questions the vision of the Founding Fathers in a combination of "light burlesque comedy" and "acerbic satire."
Hedges, William L. *Washington Irving: An American Study, 1802-1832*. Baltimore, Md.: The Johns Hopkins University Press, 1965. Through analysis of the literary motifs of Irving's work from 1802-1832, Hedges provides a picture of the its complexity.
Williams, Stanley T. *The Life of Washington Irving*. 2 vols. New York: Oxford University Press, 1935. The first and possibly most definitive literary biography of Irving. Williams provides an analysis of the work, a chronicle of its creation, a history of its reception and popularity, and a bibliography.

THE HISTORY OF PENDENNIS
His Fortunes and Misfortunes, His Friends, and His Greatest Enemy

Type of work: Novel
Author: William Makepeace Thackeray (1811-1863)
Type of plot: Bildungsroman
Time of plot: Mid-nineteenth century
Locale: England
First published: serial, 1848-1850; book, 1849-1850

Principal characters:
ARTHUR PENDENNIS (PEN), a young snob
HELEN PENDENNIS, his mother
MAJOR ARTHUR PENDENNIS, his uncle
LAURA BELL, Mrs. Pendennis' ward
EMILY COSTIGAN, an actress
BLANCHE AMORY, an heiress
HENRY FOKER, Pen's friend

The Story:

Major Arthur Pendennis, a retired army officer, impeccably dressed, dignified, yet affable, sat in his London club looking over his mail and considering which of several invitations would be most advantageous to accept. He left until last a letter from his sister-in-law, which begged him to come to Fairoaks because her son Arthur, who was known to the family as Pen, had become infatuated with an actress twelve years older than himself and insisted on marrying the woman. Helen Pendennis implored the major, who was young Pen's guardian, to use his influence with the sixteen-year-old boy.

Although of an old family, Pen's father, John Pendennis, had been forced to earn his living as an apothecary and surgeon. He prospered financially, and at the age of forty-three he married Helen Thistlewood, a distant relative of one of his aristocratic patrons. His life's aim was to be a gentleman, and by fortunate transactions he was able to buy the small estate of Fairoaks. He acquired family portraits and was henceforth known as Squire Pendennis. He referred proudly to his brother the major, who associated with well-known aristocrats. John Pendennis had died while his son was still a schoolboy. After that melancholy event, Pen took first place in the family, and his mother was solicitous for his welfare and happiness. She had already planned that he should marry Laura Bell, his adopted sister and the orphan of the Reverend Francis Bell, whom she herself had loved years before.

Helen Pendennis was horrified at Pen's infatuation with an actress, but Pen, blind with youthful romance, saw Emily Costigan as the ideal of all womanhood. Although she was beautiful and her reputation was unquestioned, she was crude and unintelligent. Pen was introduced to her father, Captain Costigan, by Henry Foker, a dashing, wealthy young schoolmate. The captain was a shabby, rakish Irishman who was constantly finding his daughter's income insufficient for the drinks he required. He assumed that Pen was a wealthy young aristocrat and urged Emily to accept his proposal of marriage. Emily regarded Pen as a child, but at the same time she was flattered by the serious attentions of a landed young gentleman.

When the major arrived at Fairoaks, Pen had almost won his indulgent mother's consent. The major handled the situation adroitly. Using many references to his aristocratic friends, he hinted that Pen, too, could be received in their homes if only he made a brilliant marriage. Then he called on Captain Costigan and informed him that Pen was dependent on his mother and that his prospects were only five hundred pounds a year. The captain wept over the deceitfulness of man and gave up Pen's letters and verses in return for a small loan. Emily wrote Pen a short note that Pen thought would drive him to distraction; but it did not. Meanwhile, the major arranged through his aristocratic and influential friends to give Emily an opportunity to play an engagement in London. Suffering over his broken love affair, Pen was so restless and moody it seemed wise for him to join his friend, Henry Foker, and attend the University of Oxbridge.

He entered the university posing as a moneyed aristocrat. By herself practicing rigid economies, his mother gave him an adequate allowance, and Pen entered enthusiastically into all sorts of activities. His refined and diversified tastes led him into expenditures far beyond his means. As a result, he ended his third year deeply in debt. He was made still more miserable when he failed an important examination. Overcome by remorse at his reckless spending and his thoughtlessness, he went to London. There Major Pendennis treated his nephew with cold disapproval and ignored him. His mother, however, welcomed him home with affection and forgiveness. Laura Bell offered a solution by suggesting that the money left her by her father be turned over to Pen to clear his debts. Laura also induced him to return to the university. When he received his degree, he came back to Fairoaks, still restless and depressed, until an event of local interest aroused him.

Clavering Park, the mansion owned by Sir Francis Clavering, was reopened. Sir Francis was a worthless spendthrift whose title was his only claim to respect. After living many years abroad, he had advantageously married Jemima Amory, a widow recently returned from India. She had been left a large fortune, and, although uneducated, she was well liked because of her generosity and good nature. In addition to the Claverings' young son, the heir to the now great Clavering fortune, Lady Clavering had a daughter named Blanche by a previous marriage. Although extremely pretty, Blanche was a superficial, self-centered girl whose demure appearance disguised a hard and cruel disposition. Pen and Laura soon became friendly with their new neighbors, and Pen imagined himself in love with Blanche. Helen confided to Pen her dearest wish that he should marry Laura. Pen, conscious of the sacrifices his mother had made for him and of Laura's generosity, made a grudging offer of marriage, which Laura spiritedly refused.

His dignity was hurt, and he decided he would make a place for himself in the world; he went to London to read for the law. Despite his good resolutions, he was unable to settle down to serious study. He became a young man about town who took pride in the variety of his acquaintances. He shared rooms with George Warrington, a philosophic man whom Pen came to respect and love. Through Warrington's influence, Pen at last began to earn his own living by writing. Eventually, he published a successful novel. Pen read law, wrote for a living, and spent his evenings at dinners and balls.

His disordered life finally resulted in a serious illness, and his mother and Laura went to London to care for him. Accompanied by George Warrington, Pen later went abroad. There Helen Pendennis, worn out with worry over Pen, became ill and died, and the party returned to Fairoaks for her burial. The estate was rented. Pen was now heir to the small fortune his mother had left, and he returned to London. During his residence in London, his uncle had again become actively interested in him. Feeling that Pen should improve his station in life, the shrewd major had decided the Claverings could be useful to Pen, and he had encouraged his nephew to cultivate the family once more.

One night, Pen and the major were invited to a dinner given by the Claverings. While the men were sitting over cigars and wine, Colonel Altamont appeared. He was drunk. It was known that for some mysterious reason Sir Francis Clavering had given this man large sums of money. Major Pendennis, who during his career in the army had been stationed in India, immediately recognized Altamont as Mr. Amory, Lady Clavering's first husband. The major did not divulge his knowledge to anyone but Sir Francis, to whom he issued the ultimatum that Sir Francis must go to live abroad and that he must give his place in Parliament to Pen. If he refused, the major threatened to expose the fact that Amory was still alive and that the marriage of Sir Francis and Lady Clavering was illegal. Another point the major made was that Clavering Park should be left to Blanche Amory. Sir Francis had no choice but to agree.

Major Pendennis continued his intrigue by urging Pen to marry Blanche. Pen uneasily fell in with his uncle's plans. He did not know how his place in Parliament had been secured, but he did know that he was not in love with Blanche. He became engaged to her, however, and began to campaign for his seat in Parliament. Laura, who had been abroad as companion to Lady Rockminster, returned to the area. When Pen saw her again, he began to regret his plan to marry Blanche.

The major's valet, Morgan, had learned of the Claverings' complicated marriage situation and planned blackmail on his own account. After a violent quarrel with the major, Morgan told Pen how Major Pendennis had forced Sir Francis to give up his seat in Parliament in favor of Pen. Pen was shocked by this news and by his uncle's unethical methods. He and Laura agreed that he should give up his candidacy for the district, but that he must, although he loved Laura, go on with his plans to marry Blanche, after having proposed to her. This sacrifice to honor, however, proved unnecessary, for Pen discovered that Blanche had forsaken him for his old friend Henry Foker, who had just inherited a large fortune. Their marriage left Pen free to marry Laura. Because Lady Rockminster held Laura in great affection, the marriage was approved even by the class-conscious major.

The simple wedding of Pen and Laura replaced the fashionable one that had been planned for Clavering Church. Blanche did not marry Foker. When Foker learned by chance that her father was still alive and that Blanche had kept the knowledge from him, he dropped his plans to marry her. Blanche became the wife of a French count. Lady Clavering, who had truly believed her husband dead, was horrified to learn that Amory was still alive, but the legality of her marriage to Sir Francis was established when it was learned that Amory had contracted several marriages before the one with her.

Pen and Laura lived happily. Laura had expectations from her friend and patroness, Lady Rockminster, and Fairoaks had increased in value because the new railroad bought rights through it. Later, when Sir Francis died, Pen was elected to Parliament. He had almost forgotten how to be a snob.

Critical Evaluation:

As is demonstrated by its subtitle, *The History of Pendennis: His Fortunes and Misfortunes, His Friends, and His Greatest Enemy* is a *Bildungsroman*, the story of the coming of age of Arthur Pendennis, the devoted son of a devoted and unworldly mother. It is likewise a *Künstlerroman*, a tale about the development of a young artist. The novel is the most autobiographical of William Makepeace Thackeray's works, detailing some of the ways in which he learned about himself and the world in which he lived to become a writer of "good books." *The History of Pendennis* is also a study of Thackeray's technique and provides background for the persona who goes on to narrate *The Newcomes* (1853-1855) as well as exemplifying Thackeray's struggles with Victorian prudery.

Thackeray modeled *The History of Pendennis* upon Henry Fielding's *Tom Jones* (1749), hoping to capture some of that eighteenth century author's frankness, which had become unfashionable in Thackeray's time. Thackeray reinvented Fielding's frankness in terms of a modern morality. The wrapper of *The History of Pendennis*, which was published in monthly numbers from 1848 to 1850, presents a young man torn between the forces of good and evil—a youthful figure clasped on one side by a woman who represents marital duty and on the other side by imps and a mermaid who represents the siren lure of worldly temptations. More than halfway into the novel, the author defines his purpose: "Our endeavor is merely to follow out, in its progress, the development of the mind of a worldly and selfish, but not ungenerous or unkind or truth-avoiding man." *The History of Pendennis* is arranged in blocks of action that are connected only by the fact that Pen participates in them all. The novel's plot is loose, working in scenes. In its characterizations *The History of Pendennis* is a masterpiece. The characterization of Pen's uncle, Major Pendennis, is full and complex, making the major one of the most famous snobs in English fiction. Thackeray draws the major as a complete human being, neither abating his snobbery nor denying him the possession of good and admirable qualities. The major's kindness toward Pen is admirable, and his skill at extracting Pen from many difficult situations is unfailing. At the novel's end, when the major triumphs over Morgan, he seems almost heroic.

Critics have pointed out that Thackeray anticipates modern psychoanalytical theory in Pen's relationship with his mother, Helen. Thackeray writes of Helen's supervision of her son's loves, "I have no doubt there is a sexual jealousy on the mother's part, and a secret pang." There is much in the novel that suggests an Oedipal relationship between son and mother. In all of Pen's relationships with women, Helen is seen as the jealous rival; the only woman she is willing to see Pen marry is Laura. This is possibly because by marrying Laura Bell, a domestic who is Helen's ward, Pen will be marrying a woman who is an extension of his mother's personality. Major Pendennis, on the other hand, wants Pen to marry Blanche Clavering. The major is willing to blackmail an acquaintance, Sir Francis Clavering, to procure Pen a seat in Parliament and Blanche's hand in marriage. Pen must choose between two very different women—Blanche or Laura Bell—and the conflicting advice of his interfering elders, to find his own reality, balancing his uncle's "keen perception without the withering selfishness" and his mother's world of emotions without the romantic illusion.

The women in the novel are set against one another as the antitheses of good and evil. Blanche Clavering represents the evil side of women because she is a contemptible cheat. The good women are Helen and Laura Bell, whose hand Pen captures after being purged of his worst faults. Although the reader is set up by Thackeray to admire Helen, the character strains sympathy in her cruel treatment of Fanny Bolton, the servant who nurses Pen through an illness. Here the Oedipal complex again comes into play. Laura often seems too certain of her own virtue and too sure of the correctness of her own opinion, which makes her—like Helen—less than entirely admirable, entirely good.

Although Pen's education progresses primarily through his loves, it is through his choice of career that he truly matures. To become a writer means to be able to determine the relationship between fact and fiction. Pen's involvement with Emily Costigan, an Irish actress older than he, is allegorical in its depiction of Pen's serene unconsciousness of the philosophical implications of his actions. After Pen determines to study law at Oxbridge and becomes a writer, he engages in an affair with Fanny Bolton, his landlady's daughter. Attracted by her adorable simplicity, he is extricated from this affair by an illness, which serves as a sort of purgation. In his affair with Blanche Clavering, Pen acts out the role of world-weary lover, and he believes he has matured when he comes to accept disillusionment; however, his real discovery of maturity comes when he realizes that he cannot abide his uncle's worldliness.

When Blanche rejects Pen for a more suitable match, he is free to marry Laura, whose honest devotion represents the alternative to living with Blanche and her deceptiveness. Laura becomes Pen's muse, his living "laurel wreath." It is through Laura Bell that Pen is able to face himself and free himself from the romantic illusions of his mother (only to some extent, because Laura Bell is an extension of Helen) and the worldly disillusionment he learned from his uncle. His experiences on Grub Street as he develops as a writer complete his maturation.

In *The History of Pendennis*, Thackeray attempts to make his readers see through the social and literary hypocrisy that characterized the Victorian era. In this long, sustained work, Thackeray leaves his readers with a panoramic view of humankind under the guidance of a witty persona. Following in the footsteps of Fielding (especially in *Tom Jones*), he laid the groundwork for the novel of psychological realism. Most of all, Thackeray is noteworthy for his charitable renderings of all individuals in all walks of life.

"Critical Evaluation" by Thomas D. Petitjean, Jr.

Bibliography:
Betsky, Seymour. "Society in Thackeray and Trollope." In *From Dickens to Hardy*, edited by Boris Ford. New York: Penguin Books, 1982. Suggests that Thackeray writes of his own social milieu, which includes the evils of self-interest and snobbery, and that he observes with a cool, detached eye.
Lester, John A., Jr. "Thackeray's Narrative Technique." *PMLA* 69 (1954): 392-409. Discusses Thackeray's doublings backward and forward in time as he reveals the story, and his variation of telling the story in his own words and then presenting it in dramatic scenes.
Loofbourow, John. "Neoclassical Conventions: *Vanity Fair, Pendennis, The Newcomes*." In *Thackeray and the Form of Fiction*. Princeton, N.J.: Princeton University Press, 1964. Asserts that Thackeray experimented with hybridizations of neoclassical conventions where chivalry is combined with mock-epic, pastoral with romance, and sentimentality with satire as part of *The History of Pendennis*' sustained narrative.
Ray, Gordon Norton. *The Buried Life: A Study of the Relation Between Thackeray and His Personal History*. Cambridge, Mass.: Harvard University Press, 1952. Suggests the original persons upon whom Thackeray modeled his fictitious characters. Especially relevant for *The History of Pendennis*, Thackeray's most autobiographical novel.
Wagenknecht, Edward. "Counter-blast: W. M. Thackeray." In *Cavalcade of the English Novel*. 1943. Reprint. New York: Holt, Rinehart and Winston, 1965. Discusses the parallels in the works of Charles Dickens and Thackeray. Also analyzes Thackeray's career, his technique and point of view, and his shortcomings as a novelist.

HISTORY OF PLYMOUTH PLANTATION

Type of work: History
Author: William Bradford (1590-1657)
First published: 1856

William Bradford's *History of Plymouth Plantation* is generally felt by both U.S. and English historians to be one of the most important volumes of the Colonial period in America. The work survived apparently only by the rarest of chances. It was begun in 1630 by Bradford, who was one of the hardy band who came to Plymouth on the *Mayflower* and who served as governor of that colony for thirty-three years; he completed chapter 10 that same year. Most of the remainder he wrote in pieces through 1646; later, he entered a few items up to 1650.

The manuscript remained in the family, passing first to the governor's oldest son, Major William Bradford; subsequently to his son, Major John Bradford; and then to his son, Samuel. Meanwhile, it was being borrowed and mined for various other histories of Colonial America. While borrowed by Increase Mather, it narrowly escaped being burned when Mather's house was destroyed in 1676. After numerous uses by other historians, it eventually came to rest in the bishop of London's library in Fulham Palace, probably taken there by a soldier during the Revolutionary War. There it was found and the first complete edition of the manuscript was published in 1856.

Long before it was published, much of its contents had passed into U.S. history and myth. Factually, Bradford's account of the trials and misadventures of the settlers at Plymouth is the fullest and best available. It begins with the unfolding of the "occasion and inducements thereunto" of the Plymouth Plantation, the author professing that he will write "in a plain style, with singular regard unto the simple truth in all things," as far as his "slender judgment" will allow. Chapter 1 begins with the background of the trip—the years 1550 to 1607 and the origin of the Pilgrim Church in England.

Bradford gives a telling account of how the Pilgrims were forced to flee to Holland in 1608, the immense suffering they underwent while there, their manner of living in that alien land, and their eventual determination to sail to the New World. Eventually, all preparations were made for this mighty undertaking. At first, they were to sail in two ships, but one, because of the fear and duplicity of the captain, was finally abandoned, and the trip made in only one, the *Mayflower*, of which Christopher Jones was master.

The Pilgrims arrived at Cape Cod on November 11, 1620. Their consternation upon arriving on the foreign shore is graphically described by Bradford. He stood "half amazed" at the people's condition upon arrival. They could see nothing but "a hideous and desolate wilderness, full of wild beasts and wild men," with "savage barbarians," who were "readier to fill" the sides of the Pilgrims "full of arrows than otherwise."

The first section, or book, ends with the account of the Pilgrims' choice of Plymouth as their mainland home, after some days of searching. This particular spot was chosen for two reasons: The harbor was deep enough to accommodate shipping, and the settlers had found, back from the coast, "divers cornfields and little running brooks," a place "just as they supposed fit for situation." On December 25, they began to "erect the first house for common use" at Plymouth.

The account of the landing at the spot that has later become associated with Plymouth Rock is interesting for its nondramatic quality. Bradford's is the only contemporary account of that landing, and it is notable in its differing from the account that popular lore has come to associate with the landing. There was no rock; this was the later invention of Elder John Faunce who, in

1741, at the age of ninety-five, identified a certain rock as the "place where the forefathers landed." Contrary to the widely held mental image of the Pilgrims' arrival, the landing was made from a shallop, not the *Mayflower*; there were no women present; and no Indians appeared with hands outstretched in greeting.

Bradford's second book is handled, for the sake of brevity, "by way of annals, noting only the heads of principal things, and passages as they fell in order of time, and may seem to be profitable to know or to make use of." It begins with the famous Mayflower Compact, which was "Occasioned partly by the discontented and mutinous speeches that some of the strangers," that is, non-Separatists, voiced about their future: "That when they came ashore they would use their own liberty, for none had power to command them, the patent they had being for Virginia and not for New England."

Next comes the account of the starving days, when more than half of the original passengers on the Mayflower died, "especially during January and February, two or three a day," of hunger or of scurvy and other diseases. At times, there were only "six or seven sound persons" to tend the numerous sick and dying.

The account of the first Thanksgiving is given with Bradford's simplicity and restraint, with hints of the joy showing through. All things were had "in good plenty," and all colonists were "recovered in health and strength." Fish and fowl were plentiful. Besides numerous fowl, "there was great store of wild turkeys, of which they took many, besides venison, etc." All the great provisions "made many afterwards write so largely of their plenty here to their friends in England, which were not faind but true reports." Thus Bradford gives the account of the origins of one of the United States' great institutions.

After the first rich harvest, however, lean days returned. Bradford records these days faithfully and fully. He records also the numerous other occurrences: the arrival of new ships with additions to the colony, accounts of numerous encounters with the Indians, associations with the surrounding colonies. One interesting section is that concerning the organization of the Undertakers, the people combining their talent and energy in a herculean effort to lift the debt imposed by the London Adventurers, the people in England who had financed the flight of the Pilgrims in the first place and who continued to exact payment from the Pilgrims for a debt that never grew smaller, no matter how much New England material was returned in payment.

There is an interesting and derogatory account of the notorious settlement at Merrymount, founded by Captain Wollaston and two or three other persons who brought numerous servants with them from England. After Wollaston departed for Virginia, Merrymount was taken over by a Mr. Morton, a man "having more craft than honesty," who led the Merrymounters in "a dissolute life, pouring out themselves into all profaneness. And Morton became Lord of Misrule," and continued as such until John Endicott came from England, caused the maypole to be cut down, "rebuked them for their profaneness and admonished them to look there should be better walking." This event has been beautifully written up by Nathaniel Hawthorne in "The Maypole of Merrymount."

Another interesting account is that of Roger Williams, whom Bradford calls "a man godly and zealous, having many precious parts but very unsettled in judgment." Bradford tells how Williams, viewed by many twentieth century commentators as perhaps the first American democrat, fell "into some strange opinions, and from opinion to practice," which eventually caused his exile and his founding of Providence, Rhode Island, a haven for persons interested in freedom of conscience.

The essentially gentle and Christian character of the chronicler is revealed in his final comment on Williams. "He is to be pitied and prayed for; and so I shall leave the matter and desire the Lord to show him his errors and reduce him into the way of truth." From beginning to end, such is the tone of this great account of the forefathers of the United States, without which U.S. histories would be incomplete.

Bibliography:
Daly, Robert. "William Bradford's Vision of History." *American Literature* 44 (January, 1973): 557-569. Analyzes events narrated in *Of Plimouth Plantation* to show that at first Bradford noted God's cooperation in the colony's survival and prosperity; after 1638, or perhaps as early as 1632, however, internal threats demonstrated God's withholding of aid. Accordingly, the history changes from a public report of divine aid to a more private lament.
Garbo, Norman S. "William Bradford: *Of Plymouth Plantation*." In *Landmarks of American Writing*, edited by Hennig Cohen. New York: Basic Books, 1969. Theorizes that Bradford was the first to express the American trait of feeling committed to a predestined, historical mission.
McIntyre, Ruth A. *Debts Hopeful and Desperate: Financing the Plymouth Colony.* Plymouth, Mass.: Plimouth Plantation, 1963. In discussing the business side of the colonists' undertaking, makes use of Bradford's many passages devoted to his support from English merchant adventurers, commercial affairs, troubles, debts and repayments, and final solvency.
Scheick, William J. "The Theme of Necessity in Bradford's *Of Plymouth Plantation*." *Seventeenth-Century News* 32 (Winter, 1974): 88-90. Argues that Bradford at first ascribed to God's providence human actions that in reality proceeded from the postlapsarian, corrupt "necessity" of depraved human hearts. Awareness of this resulted in diminished faith and confidence, and loss of the communal ideal.
Westbrook, Perry D. *William Bradford.* Boston: Twayne, 1978. Discusses the major themes of Bradford's history, comments on the artistry of its prose, its early impact, and responses of modern historians to it.

THE HISTORY OF ROME

Type of work: History
Author: Livy (Titus Livius, 59 B.C.E.-17 C.E.)
First published: Ab urbe condita libri, c. 26 B.C.E.-15 C.E. (English translation, 1600)

Titus Livius Patavinus (named for his birthplace, Padua) was originally a teacher of rhetoric and apparently, from casual references in his writing, a friend of the Emperor Augustus. Perhaps the emperor, as part of his program to glorify Rome, suggested that Livy stop teaching and write a history of the city. The project represented a challenge. His only sources were traditions, the official temple annals listing the consuls and the chief events of each year, and personal records, frequently exaggerated, kept by the famous families. In *The History of Rome*, Livy attempts to narrate the history of nearly eight centuries, from the time of Romulus and Remus to the reign of Tiberius. The work comprised 142 books, of which barely a quarter have been preserved: books 1-10 and 21-45, along with some fragments of several others. Even so, this material is enough to fill six volumes in one English translation and thirteen in another.

Like Herodotus, Livy was always attracted to a colorful story. Thomas Macaulay declared in disgust: "No historian with whom we are acquainted has shown so complete indifference to the truth." Probably a truthful chronicle was not what Livy set out to produce. In addition to his patriotic duty, he wanted by his dramatic power and the charm of his style to impress the sophisticated readers of Rome. Accuracy came second. He was no soldier in his battles, no statesman in recording the problems of government; even as a geographer he was most hazy. In an epoch when research was unknown, he was no critical historian. When he found two conflicting accounts, he was likely to choose the more colorful, or include both and let the reader be the judge.

The History of Rome was issued in decades, or units of ten, a volume at a time, the first between 27 and 25 B.C.E., at the time Vergil was writing his *Aeneid.* The work did what the author intended: painted vividly the grandeur of Rome, even though, like an artist, he sometimes changed details for better composition. Whatever his faults as a historian, Livy the novelist, the dramatist, and the orator left unforgettable pages for readers of later generations.

It is a wonder that so much of Livy's work has come down to the present; he had many enemies. Pope Gregory I, for example, ordered all available copies burned because of the superstitions they contained, and other Church fathers were also to blame for the hundred books that have disappeared, including those about Livy's own times. More than one modern historian has wished he could exchange the first ten books available for those in which Livy set down what he had witnessed, rather than heard or read. Few, however, would willingly give up the books dealing with the sixteen years of the Punic Wars, the story of the life and death struggle between Rome and Carthage.

"It would be a satisfaction to me," declares Livy in the preface to the first decade of his history, "that I have contributed my share to perpetuate the achievements of a people, the lords of the world." He determines "neither to affirm nor refute" the traditions antedating the founding of Rome, even though they were "more suited to the fiction of poetry than to the genuine record of history." In writing them down, however, his aim is to acquaint the Romans of his day with the lives and customs of ancestors who might serve as examples in the present low moral status of Rome, "when we can neither endure our vices nor their remedies."

He begins by repeating the legend of Aeneas, who led the Trojans to Latium and married Lavinia. He lists the petty chiefs who followed, making no changes in the story of Romulus and

Remus and their wolf nurse. He relates briefly the account of the founding of Rome, April 21, 753 B.C.E., when the ceremonies ended with the quarrel between the brothers and the death of Remus. Inviting in the discontented from the neighboring tribes, Romulus populated the city, then provided wives by kidnaping the Sabine women who came as guests to a feast.

In the remaining books of the first decade, which carries the story through 460 years, Livy pays special attention to Rome's virtuous and exemplary citizens: Cincinnatus, summoned from his plow to drive back the Aequians; Virginius, protecting his daughter Virginia from lustful decemvir Appius Claudius; Camillus, returning from exile to fight the Gauls; Manlius, defending the capitol; and the patriotic Curtius, riding his horse into a chasm in the Forum to preserve his city. The decade ends when the defeat of the Samnites leaves Rome the master of Italy.

The next ten books have been lost. Only because they were summarized in an epitome does the world know Livy's account of what happened between 294 and 219 B.C.E.

At the beginning of the next decade, books 21-30, Livy declares: "I am about to relate the most memorable of all wars that were ever waged, the war which the Carthaginians under Hannibal maintained against the Roman people." As far as ancient history goes, he was undoubtedly right. It was a war between the Indo-Germanic and the Semitic races for world dominion. The two were not only equally matched but also familiar with the enemy's war tactics and potential power, and their hatred for each other, as the historian pointed out, was as strong as their armies.

Livy never minimized the exploits of twenty-six-year-old Hannibal, who became the outstanding figure in his book. What details he could not find recorded of the crossing of the Alps by ninety thousand infantry, twelve thousand cavalry, and thirty-seven elephants, he made up from his imagination. Scipio the father, having failed to stop the Carthaginians in Gaul, tried again on the plains of Italy, but one defeat after another brought terror to the imperial city. After Trebia and Lake Trasimene, the delaying tactics of Fabius Maximus succeeded in holding back the invaders for a time, but the impatience of another consul, Varro, resulted in the culminating Roman disaster at Cannae (216 B.C.E.). Had Hannibal taken advantage of his victory, he could easily have entered Rome.

Book 25 deals with another phase of the struggle. Marcellus, besieging Syracuse, was held at bay for three years by the craft of a seventy-four-year-old mathematician, Archimedes, with his invention of the catapult and the grappling hooks that lifted the prows of Roman ships trying to attack the breakwater, and sank them. Ultimately, however, the Romans found the weak spot in the defenses and captured the island.

On another battlefront, a second Scipio, later to be called Africanus, was trying to keep Spain from being used as the Carthaginians' European headquarters. A comparison of the version by Livy with another by Polybius shows the superiority of Livy's technique. Though Scipio could not immobilize Hasdrubal entirely or prevent his departure with reinforcements for his brother in Italy, the delay did contribute to the Carthaginian defeat on the Metaurus River, a Roman victory that was quickly neutralized by the death of Marcellus in a clash with Hannibal. Eventually, however, Roman might prevailed when Scipio carried the war into Africa. Although Hannibal was recalled for the defense of Carthage, his veterans were no match for the Roman legionaries at the Battle of Zama (202 B.C.E.), and defeated Carthage was wiped from the map.

An additional fifteen books of Livy's history survive, dealing with Roman expansion in Greece and Asia and ending when Macedonia became a Roman province. This story is an anticlimax. No longer were the soldiers fighting for the life of Rome, but the plunder they hoped to acquire, so that the reader does not follow the story with the same interest. Even in these pages, however, the storytelling ability of Livy is still apparent. It is easy to understand why he was called the greatest prose writer of the Age of Augustus.

Bibliography:

Dorey, T. A., ed. *Livy*. London: Routledge & Kegan Paul, 1971. Covers the various extant sections of Livy's history of Rome, as well as essays of his influence on later European historians and thinkers such as Montesquieu. Good on Livy's coverage of the Second Punic War.

Levene, D. S. *Religion in Livy*. Leiden, The Netherlands: E. J. Brill, 1993. Analyzes Livy's history as a vehicle intended to revive the traditional Roman religion, augmenting the national pride and confidence of the Augustan Rome of Livy's time.

Momigliano, Arnaldo. *The Classical Foundations of Modern Historiography*. Berkeley: University of California Press, 1990. Traces Livy's influence on later historians and defends Livy against the charge that, although a great stylist, he is practically useless as a historian.

Moore, Timothy J. *Artistry and Ideology: Livy's Vocabulary of Virtue*. Frankfurt, Germany: Atheneum, 1989. A closely argued literary and linguistic analysis of Livy's prose style. Shows Livy as a conscious artist making similar rhetorical and linguistic choices to orators such as Cicero and poets such as Vergil. Knowledge of Latin is helpful with this book.

Woodman, A. J. *Rhetoric in Classical Historiography: Four Studies*. London: Croom Helm, 1988. Compares Livy's style and discourse to those of other Greek and Latin historians. Shows how Livy's rhetoric is deployed to further his political and moral allegiances and to ingratiate the author's presentation to the reader.

THE HISTORY OF THE DECLINE AND FALL
OF THE ROMAN EMPIRE

Type of work: History
Author: Edward Gibbon (1737-1794)
First published: 1776-1788

Edward Gibbon's *The History of the Decline and Fall of the Roman Empire* is the definitive history of the Roman empire from the end of its golden age to its final political and physical disintegration. The massive character of the work, testifying to the years devoted to its composition by its scholar-author, is the first, but most superficial sign, of its greatness. The style—urbane, dramatic, polished—assures its eminent place in literature. Finally, as history, the work stands or falls on the accuracy and depth of its report of events covering more than twelve centuries, and in this respect *The History of the Decline and Fall of the Roman Empire* continues to prevail as the most authoritative study on this theme ever written. Later scholars have challenged minor points or added to the material of the history, but Gibbon's work stands as the source of all that is most relevant in the story of Rome's declining years.

The account begins with a critical description of the age of the Antonines. Gibbon concentrates on the period from 96 to 180 C.E., a time that he describes as "a happy period," during the reigns of Nerva, Trajan, Hadrian, and the two Antonines. The first three chapters are prefatory to the body of the work; they establish the claim that Rome was then at the height of its glory as an Empire—it was strong, prosperous, active, with world-wide influence. After the death of Marcus Aurelius, and with the ascent of Commodus (180-192), the Empire began its long and gradual decline. The body of Gibbon's work is devoted to a careful recital of the events that followed.

Gibbon was more interested in recounting the principal events of the Empire's history than he was in analyzing events in an effort to account for the downfall of Rome. He did not, however, entirely ignore the question of causes. At the close of his monumental history he reports four principal causes of Rome's decline and fall: "I. The injuries of time and nature. II. The hostile attacks of the barbarians and Christians. III. The use and abuse of the materials. And, IV. The domestic quarrels of the Romans."

It is customary for commentators on Gibbon to emphasize the reference to the opposing influences of Christianity and barbarism; in particular, some critics have been inclined to charge Gibbon with a lack of sympathetic understanding of the early Christian church. It is clear from Gibbon's narrative and summary statement, however, that the Christian contribution to the eventual downfall of Rome was only part of a complex of causes, and it seems unlikely that the Christian effort would have succeeded if the Roman Empire had not already been in decline.

In any case, it is not so much what Gibbon says as his way of saying it that has proved irritating. In the first place, Gibbon writes as if he were located in Rome; his view of events is from the Roman perspective, although it does not always exhibit a Roman bias. Second, his objectivity, when it is achieved, has been offensive to some who so cherish the Christian church that they cannot tolerate any discussion of its faults; it is as if such critics were demanding that Gibbon maintain historical impartiality about the Romans but not about the Christians.

When the *The History of the Decline and Fall of the Roman Empire* first appeared, the chapters on Christianity—15 and 16—immediately became the objects of critical attack. Gibbon seems to have anticipated this response, for he wrote, "The great law of impartiality too often obliges us to reveal the imperfections of the uninspired teachers and believers of the

Gospel; and, to a careless observer, their faults may seem to cast a shade on the faith which they professed." Perhaps this word of caution would have pacified the critics had not Gibbon immediately brought into play his urbane sarcasm, so distasteful to the insistently pious: "The theologian may indulge the pleasing task of describing Religion as she descended from Heaven, arrayed in her native purity. A more melancholy duty is imposed on the historian. He must discover the inevitable mixture of error and corruption which she contracted in a long residence upon earth, among a weak and degenerate race of beings."

Obviously, there is no truly impartial judge. Gibbon's tone is acceptable, even proper, to those who share his skepticism, but to others more emotionally involved in the Christian faith Gibbon seems cynical to the point of gross distortion.

Gibbon asks how the Christian faith came to achieve its victory over Rome. He rejects as unsatisfactory an answer which attributes Christianity's force to the truth of its doctrine and the providence of God. Five causes of the rapid growth of the Christian church are then advanced: "I. The inflexible, and, if we may use the expression, the intolerant zeal of the Christians. . . . II. The doctrine of a future life. . . . III. The miraculous powers ascribed to the primitive church. IV. The pure and austere morals of the Christians. V. The union and discipline of the Christian republic, which gradually formed an independent and increasing state in the heart of the Roman empire."

In his comments on these five causes Gibbon discusses Jewish influences on the Christian faith and explains how the Roman religion had failed to be convincing in its mythology and doctrine of a future life; although he admits the persuasive power of the Christian use of the claim of immortality, he speaks with skeptical condescension of the efforts of philosophers to support the doctrine of a future life, and he is sarcastic when he mentions "the mysterious dispensations of Providence" which withheld the doctrine from the Jews only to give it to the Christians. When he speaks of the miracles, Gibbon leaves the impression that the pagans failed to be convinced because no such events actually took place. "The lame walked, the blind saw, the sick were healed, the dead were raised," he writes, but he adds that "the laws of Nature were frequently suspended for the benefit of the church."

Gibbon argues that the emperors were not as criminal in their treatments of the Christians as some Christian apologists have argued. He maintains that the Romans acted only with caution and reluctance after a considerable amount of time and provocation, and that they were moderate in their use of punishments. He offers evidence in support of his claim that the stories of martyrdom were often exaggerated or wholly false, and that in many cases the Christians sought martyrdom by provoking the Romans to violence. Gibbon concludes by casting doubt on the numbers of those punished by death, and he insists that the Christians have inflicted more punishments on one another than they received from the Romans.

Discussion of Gibbon's chapters on Christianity sometimes tends to turn attention away from the historian's virtues: the inclusiveness of his survey, the liveliness of his account, and his careful documentation of historical claims. Gibbon did not pretend that he was without moral bias, but his judgments of the tyrannical emperors are defended by references to their acts. It was not enough for Gibbon to discover, for example, that Septimus Severus was false and insincere, particularly in the making of treaties; the question was whether Severus was forced, by the imperious demands of politics, to be deceitful. Gibbon's conclusion was that there was no need for Severus to be as false in his promises as he was; consequently, he condemns him for his acts. In similar fashion he reviews the tyrannical behavior of Caracalla, Maximin, and other emperors before the barbarian invasion of the Germans.

Gibbon names the Franks, the Alemanni, the Goths, and the Persians as the enemies of the

Romans during the reigns of Valerian and Gallienus, when a weakened Empire was vulnerable to attack from both within and without. Perhaps the Empire would have wholly disintegrated at that time had not Valerian and Gallienus been succeeded by Claudius, Aurelian, Probus, and Diocletian, described as "great princes" by Gibbon and as "Restorers of the Roman world."

Several chapters of this massive work are devoted to a recital and discussion of the acts and influence of Constantine I, who reunited the Empire which had been divided under Diocletian and, as a consequence of his conversion to the Christian faith, granted tolerance to the Christians by the Edict of Milan. One result of the consequent growth of Christianity was a growing emphasis upon the distinction between temporal and spiritual powers; the result was not that Church and state remained apart from each other, but that the bishops of the Church came to have more and more influence on matters of state. The date 476 is significant as marking the end of the West Roman Empire with the ascent to power of Odoacer, the barbarian chieftain.

The remainder of Gibbon's classic story of Rome's decline is the story of the increase of papal influence, the commencement of Byzantine rule, the reign of Charlemagne as emperor of the West, the sacking of Rome by the Arabs, the retirement of the popes to Avignon, the abortive efforts of Rienzi to restore the government of Rome, the return of the popes and the great schism, and the final settlement of the ecclesiastical state.

Bibliography:

Gibbon, Edward. *The History of the Decline and Fall of the Roman Empire.* Edited by H. H. Milman. Boston: Phillips, Sampson, and Company, 1850. Excellent chronological table of contents for each chapter is extremely helpful. Also includes the first complete index to the entire work of Gibbon.

_____. *Memoirs of My Life, Edited from the Manuscripts by Georges A. Bonnard.* New York: Funk & Wagnalls, 1969. Accepted as the definitive critical edition of Gibbon's memoirs. Chapter 7 gives Gibbon's account of his writing on the Roman Empire. Extensive notes.

Grant, Michael. *The Fall of the Roman Empire: A Reappraisal.* Radnor, Pa.: Annenberg School Press, 1976. A reappraisal written as a tribute to Gibbon. Historical survey of the Roman Empire up to 476 C.E. Analysis of Gibbon's coverage. Gives a twentieth century perspective to Gibbon's work.

Jordan, David P. *Gibbon and His Roman Empire.* Champaign: University of Illinois Press, 1971. A critical analysis of Gibbon. Discusses Gibbon's claiming that he was "the historian of the Roman Empire." The last chapters reconstruct *The Decline and Fall* from Jordan's perspective. Concludes that Gibbon created his own Roman Empire, then described its decline and fall.

Morison, James Cotter. *Gibbon.* London: Macmillan, 1904. A biography that emphasizes Gibbon's work as a historian on Rome, as well as his talents in picturing the Roman Empire. Questions the accuracy of some of Gibbon's material.

HISTORY OF THE KINGS OF BRITAIN

Type of work: History
Author: Geoffrey of Monmouth (c. 1100-1154)
First published: Historia regum Britanniae, c. 1136 (English translation, 1718)

Geoffrey of Monmouth, a scholarly clergyman who was to become bishop of St. Asaph's in Wales, undertook to write a national history of Britain from its origin through the seventh century, some nineteen centuries of history by his reckoning. Arranged in twelve books, on the pattern of Vergil's *Aeneid* (29-19 B.C.E.), Geoffrey's account traces the reigns of nearly a hundred British kings, beginning with the nation's mythical founder Brutus. As in the *Aeneid*, there is an important contrast between the first six and the final six books. The first part narrates events that took place over approximately ten centuries, while the latter six books, concerned primarily with the age of King Arthur, are limited to less than two centuries.

To a striking degree, the history is Welsh-centered, with most of the action occurring in Wales and the English counties that border it. It is reasonable to infer that in his writing Geoffrey was influenced by an intent to endow his native Wales and western Britain with a glorious past. For example, the river Severn, which flows through southwestern England, is the stream most often mentioned in Geoffrey's account, though to history the Thames has greater importance. The original Trojans, Celts, and other tribes living in the land before the Roman conquest in the first century, as well as some Roman settlers, are all collectively labeled Britons. In Geoffrey's account, they are arrayed against the Saxons, a collective name for the Germanic tribes that began invading the land in the fifth century.

Geoffrey purports to be translating a book by Archdeacon Walter of Oxford, a man about whom little is known beyond Geoffrey's references; even the book's existence is in doubt. The Archdeacon, though, may have been known to Geoffrey, since he lived at Oxford during years when both were alive. The primary sources appear to have been the histories of Bede and Nennius, the *Aeneid*, and traditional Welsh stories and myths. In the early books, Geoffrey makes cross-references to events from the Bible and from Greek and Roman history in an effort to establish parallel chronologies. Yet in spite of references to actual rulers from the past like the Roman leaders Julius Caesar and Claudius, what Geoffrey produced was a highly readable mythic history, whose protagonists are essentially fictional characters. The Roman and Saxon invasions were historical events, but in his account Geoffrey mingles fact with extraordinary fiction.

Like many other medieval historians, he begins his narrative with the Trojan War, since he believed that the country was founded by a descendant of the Trojan princes who dispersed after the fall of Troy. Brutus, the mythic founder of Britain, is a great-grandson of the Trojan prince Aeneas, the legendary founder of Rome. Setting out from Rome in his odyssey, Brutus travels to Greece, where he joins other Trojan exiles. In armed struggle against the Greeks, they conquer a third of the country, but, in the interests of avoiding further strife, they decide to embark for Britain after a prophecy of Diana directs them to do so. By sea, they make their way to the island, defeat the giants who dominate the land, and found a kingdom. They then proceed to establish cities, including the capital Trinovant, later London.

A long series of kings who descended from Brutus are briefly mentioned, including Bladud, founder of Bath. More attention is devoted to the story of King Leir, who parcels out his kingdom among his daughters. For Leir, the folly of disinheriting his youngest daughter ends with good fortune. After he has been exiled to France, she aids him in removing her two sisters from power and reclaiming his throne.

Following another long list of kings, the story of King Belinus, still a pre-Roman monarch, is narrated. Belinus unites with his brother Brennius, and the two conquer first Gaul and later Rome. In the first century B.C.E., Julius Caesar arrives with a large Roman force but is driven back to France by heroic Britons. Later, the Emperor Claudius returns and establishes Roman rule over England. Roman rule is highly disordered because of rebellions and incursions by Picts and other tribes living in remote areas. Further, the Romans are unwilling to provide sufficient garrisons and after a time grow reluctant to bring reinforcements from Gaul.

After the Romans cease military operations in the land, the Saxons begin their depredations. Following the departure of the Romans, efforts to unite the kingdom prove unsuccessful. The story of Vortigern, Hengest, and Horsa, taken primarily from Bede, is narrated as a tale of violence and revenge that continues through generations of monarchs. Vortigern, an ambitious Briton, betrays King Constantine and his son Constans. With the help of Saxon allies, whom he has invited to England as allies against the Picts and other rebellious Britons, Vortigern seizes the throne for himself. Constantine's two younger sons, Aurelius Ambrosius and Uther Pendragon, flee to Europe. An interest in prophecy leads Vortigern to locate the youthful magician Merlin to seek his guidance.

By the beginning of book 7, halfway through the narrative, the groundwork is laid for the final portion. The last books introduce the reign of Arthur, portrayed as a Briton champion against the Saxons. Book 7 is entirely devoted to the "Prophecy of Merlin," a piece written by Geoffrey before he began the *Historia regum Britanniae* and incorporated into the narrative. The prophecy offers a mystical vision of the future that features symbolic dragons, animal imagery, and strange transformations. Taken as a whole, it is a troubling anticipation of chaos, without any clear resolution, though it is intended to foreshadow national history.

Following the prophecy, the narrative resumes with an account of the two remaining sons of Constantine, who return from exile, defeat Vortigern, and restore their line with Aurelius Ambrosius as king. Uther Pendragon leads armies against enemies who are still in rebellion and becomes king after his brother is treacherously slain. Through the trickery of Merlin, Uther begets Arthur with Igerne, wife of Gorlois, Duke of Cornwall, and, after Gorlois dies in battle, marries Igerne.

Books 9-11 are wholly concerned with the exploits of Arthur. A Briton leader against the Saxons, he becomes king while still a boy, unites his nation, and gathers chiefs and kings from outlying and remote areas to his thriving court at Caerleon, later Camelot, on the Usk River. Having united his own nation, he ventures abroad to conquer Gaul and Norway, and, after refusing demanded tribute from Rome, leads an English army to the continent in battle with the Romans. The Romans summon monarchs from their eastern provinces to their aid, but to no avail. In a decisive battle, Lucius, the Roman emperor, is killed, though losses are heavy on both sides. Arthur loses two of his best knights, Kay and Bedivere. Later, he moves his army to the gates of Rome, before being called back to Britain by a treasonous rebellion fomented by his nephew Mordred.

Mordred raises an immense army of 800,000, but Arthur's war-hardened veterans prevail against the huge force. A final great battle, alleged to have occurred in the year 542 by Geoffrey, leads to the deaths of the mythic monarch and of Mordred. The queen has entered a convent, and the Briton crown goes to Constantine, son of the Duke of Cornwall.

Following Arthur's death, other kings, notably Constantine, Cadwallo, and Cadwallader, continue the struggle against the Saxons, until a dire famine in the seventh century forces all but a few native Britons to abandon their native land. In 689, King Cadwallader, the last of the Briton line, dies in exile in Rome. The Saxons gain dominance over the kingdom by returning and resettling before the native Britons. The narrative ends with prophecies that suggest the Britons will someday reclaim their land.

Critics of Geoffrey's narrative sometimes label it folklore, for, despite authentic portions, the work reveals many historical defects. On a grand scale, Geoffrey reveals a flaw that besets many later histories as well: the inclination to project realities of the present onto the past. Thus he writes of ranks of nobility in pre-Roman Britain that did not exist until after the Norman conquest. He assumes at least a partially unified kingdom in Celtic times, when in reality nothing resembling national unity was achieved before the tenth century. Even more extraordinary, he believes that in a prehistoric era, British kings led a military expedition against Rome. This account and that of Arthur's similar adventures abroad serve to create the illusion of Britons aspiring to empire from the remote past.

The narrative introduces scores of monarchs who were previously unknown and for whom no other historical record exists, and it is apparent that Geoffrey is filling out his story with fictional characters. Like other early historians, he provides long, often eloquent, speeches, furnished verbatim, that were uttered in a preliterate time. Finally, his numerical estimates exceed the credible, even for his own day. Although it was possible to raise large armies of hundreds of thousands in the ancient world, such occurrences were highly unusual. Mordred's combined force of 800,000 exceeds anything ever known in early British history. Equally incredible is the force of 300,000 Northmen who supposedly made a coordinated invasion of the island by ship; such an expedition would have required more than eight thousand Viking ships.

It is in the treatment of the supernatural, though, that the qualities of mythic history are most apparent. Obvious elements include the frequent references to battles against giants, incredible transformations, the influence of magic, numerous prophecies, and abundant dragon and animal imagery.

Geoffrey's most significant achievements were not historical but literary. His book served as a source for characters and plots in both English and European literatures. He first created Sabrina, the nymph transformed into a river goddess, who becomes a symbol of Christian grace in Edmund Spenser's *Faerie Queene* (1590-1596) and John Milton's *Comus* (1634). He narrated for the first time the story of King Leir and his three daughters, a tale which William Shakespeare turned into the greatest of English tragedies. He also organized the scattered fragments of the Arthurian story into a coherent whole. In doing so, he gave the story a cyclic form, with mythic beginnings and endings. As in the story of Belinus, Arthur attempts to expand his rule from kingdom to empire, an objective perhaps attributable to the example of Rome and the precedent of Vergil's *Aeneid*.

Stanley Archer

Bibliography:

Ashe, Geoffrey. *The Discovery of King Arthur.* Garden City, N.Y.: Anchor Press/Doubleday, 1985. Ashe surveys available historical sources, including the *Historia regum Britanniae*, to assess Arthur's impact on history. He offers an exhaustive account of Arthurian settings and locales.

Barber, Richard. *Arthur of Albion.* New York: Barnes & Noble, 1961. Barber traces Arthur's origin in the *Historia regum Britanniae* and other early texts. He further chronicles the great flowering of Arthurian literature during the late Middle Ages.

Brengle, Richard L., ed. *Arthur, King of Britain.* New York: Appleton-Century-Crofts, 1964.

Brengle reprints Geoffrey's chapters on Arthur in his collections of sources. Among the secondary sources republished, the book includes useful critical essays on Geoffrey's history.

Cummins, W. A. *King Arthur's Place in Prehistory.* Wolfeboro Falls, N.H.: Alan Sutton, 1992. Cummins undertakes a thorough analysis of the *Historia regum Britanniae* and provides a valuable bibliography. His book supports the highly speculative thesis that Stonehenge played an important part in the line of Briton kings that included Arthur.

Tatlock, J. S. P. *The Legendary History of Britain: Geoffrey of Monmouth's "Historia regum Britanniae" and Its Early Vernacular Versions.* Berkeley: University of California Press, 1950. Tatlock provides a careful account of the structure of Geoffrey's history. In his analysis of it, he treats Geoffrey's work as primarily imaginative.

HISTORY OF THE PELOPONNESIAN WAR

Type of work: History
Author: Thucydides (c. 459-c. 402 B.C.E.)
Time of plot: 431-411 B.C.E.
Locale: Greece and the Mediterranean
First transcribed: Historia tou Peloponnesiacou polemou, 431-404 B.C.E. (English translation, 1550)

Principal personages:
PERICLES, the founder of Athenian democracy
THUCYDIDES, an Athenian general and historian
DEMOSTHENES, the famous orator
ALCIBIADES, an Athenian general and turncoat
NICIAS, an Athenian general
ARCHIDAMUS, the king of Sparta
BRASIDAS, a Spartan general

In writing his *History of the Peloponnesian War*, Thucydides looked for human causes behind results and refused to credit the gods with responsibility for the acts of human beings. Impartially he chronicled the clash of a military and a commercial imperialism: the land empire of the Spartans confronting the Athenian maritime league. Some have attributed to him an attitude of moral indifference, such as is revealed in his report of the debate between Athenian and Melian ambassadors, but he wrote with no intention of either moralizing or producing a cultural history. He was a military man interested in the vastly different political and economic patterns of Athens and Sparta. Writing for intelligent readers rather than for the ignorant masses, he saw in the modes and ideals of their cultures an explanation of their ways of warfare.

The eight books of Thucydides' history, divided into short paragraph-chapters, provide a few facts about their author. In book 4, for example, he refers to himself as "Thucydides, son of Olorus, who wrote this history." He must have been wealthy, for, discussing Brasidas' attack on Amphipolis, he states that the Spartan "heard that Thucydides had the right of working gold mines in the neighboring district of Thrace and was consequently one of the leading men of the city." He also tells frankly of his failure as the commander of a relief expedition to that city and of his twenty years' exile from Athens as punishment. Apparently he spent the years of his exile in travel among the sites of the battles he describes, thereby increasing the accuracy of his details. Students of warfare find that he gives descriptions of the tricks and stratagems of both siege and defense. Not until 404, after the war had ended, did he return to Athens. He seems to have been killed about 400 B.C.E., either in Thrace for the gold he carried, or in Athens for publicly writing his opinions.

In his masterpiece of Greek history, the Athenian Thucydides wrote of the war between the Peloponnesians and the Athenians from the time it began, "believing it would be great and memorable above all previous wars." Thucydides explains the rivalry of Athens and Sparta, the two great states of Hellas then at the height of their power. He was proud of the advances made by his native Athens over the ways of the barbarians. "In ancient times the Hellenes carried weapons because their homes were undefended and intercourse unsafe." Swords, however, like the old-fashioned linen undergarments and the custom of binding the hair in knots, had gone out of style by his time.

Rivalry between the two cities had a long tradition. It had kept Spartans from fighting beside Athenians at Marathon, but it took a commercial form when the Lacedaemonians demanded that their allies, the Megarians, be allowed to market their products in Athens. Pericles, the orator, statesman, and patron of the arts, took the first step toward breaking his own Thirty Years' Truce, agreed upon in 445 B.C.E. In a fiery oration, he declared that to yield to the Spartans would reduce the Athenians to vassals.

The final break, according to Thucydides, came later. He dates the year, 431, according to the calendars of the three leading states: Chrysis had been high priestess of Argos for forty-eight years; Aenesias was ephor of Sparta; and Pythodorus was concluding his archonship in Athens. In that year Thebes, at the invitation of disgruntled Plataean citizens, made a surprise attack on Plataea, a Boeotian ally of Athens.

To understand the situation fully, it is necessary to keep in mind a clash of political concepts that the historian does not mention. In 445 B.C.E., under Pericles, Athens had become a radical democracy whose policy was to send help to any democratically inclined community. Sparta and its allies were just as eager to promote their conservative oligarchy. To both, self-interest was paramount.

Violation of the truce by Thebes, says Thucydides, gave Athens an excuse to prepare for war. Its walled city could be defeated only by a fleet, and Sparta had no fleet. On the other hand, landlocked Sparta could withstand everything except a full-scale land invasion, and Athens had no army. The Lacedaemonians begged their friends in Italy and Sicily to collect and build ships, and Athens sent ambassadors to raise armies and completely surround Sparta. Thucydides was honest enough to admit that public opinion largely favored the Spartans, who posed as the liberators of Hellas.

Sparta moved first by invading the Isthmus of Corinth in 431 B.C.E. Strife during the winter and summer of the first year (as the historian divided his time) consisted largely of laying waste the fields around the fortified cities. Like many primitive peoples, the Greeks stopped fighting during planting and harvesting (the entries frequently begin with: "The following summer, when the corn was coming into ear . . ."). The war was also halted for games, not only the Olympic games of 428, but the Delian, Pythian, and Isthmian games as well.

In the summer of the next year, a plague broke out in Athens and raged intermittently for three years. Seven chapters of book 2 provide a vivid description, "for I myself was attacked and witnessed the suffering of others." The seriousness of the plague protected Athens because enemy troops were afraid to approach its walls.

The most vivid part of Thucydides' history deals with the Syracuse campaign of 416. An embassy from Egesta, Sicily, sought Athenian help against its rival city of Selinus. The ambitious Alcibiades thought this would be a good excuse for Athens to annex Syracuse. With Alcibiades, Nicias, and Lamachus sharing the command, the best-equipped expeditionary force ever sent from a Greek city sailed for Sicily with 134 triremes, 5,100 hoplites or heavy-armed infantry, 480 archers, and 820 slingers.

Alcibiades had left behind bitter enemies who accused him of defacing sacred statues on the day the fleet sailed. Though there was no evidence against him, he was ordered home to defend himself. Fearing treachery, he fled to Sparta, where he was warmly welcomed. Informed of the Athenian expedition, the Lacedaemonians sent a military adviser to Syracuse. The Persians offered to outfit a fleet for Alcibiades to lead against Athens. His patriotism outweighed his injured pride, however, and eventually he returned to Athens and won several victories for the city before another defeat sent him again into exile. This occurred, however, after the period covered by Thucydides' history.

In the campaign before Syracuse, Nicias disregarded the advice of Demosthenes and was defeated on both land and sea. "Of all the Hellenic actions on record," writes Thucydides, "this was the greatest, the most glorious to the victor, and the most ruinous to the vanquished. Fleet and army vanished from the face of the earth; nothing was saved, and out of the many who went forth, few returned home. This ended the Sicilian expedition."

The account of the expedition practically ends Thucydides' history. There is another book, but it does not rise to the dramatic pitch of book 7. Though he lived eleven years after these events and four years after the end of the war, Thucydides did not chronicle its last stages, perhaps because they were too painful. After Alcibiades had been exiled a second time, Sparta starved the Athenians into surrender, and with this defeat their glory faded. For the next thirty years Sparta was the supreme power in Hellas.

As Thomas Macaulay wrote, Thucydides surpassed all his rivals as the historian of the ancient world. Perhaps not as colorful as Herodotus, "the Father of History," he was certainly more accurate; and although the annals of Tacitus contain excellent character delineation, his pages, by contrast, are cold. Thucydides may be superficial in his observations and shallow in his interpretation of events, but he accumulated facts and dates and presented them in a three-dimensional picture of people and places. For this reason his work has survived for more than twenty-three hundred years.

Bibliography:
Hildebrand, Alice von, ed. *Greek Culture: The Adventure of the Human Spirit.* New York: Braziller, 1966. Insightful discussion of two texts from Thucydides' *History of the Peloponnesian War* concludes that the work illuminates the glory of the Greek spirit and civilization. Illustrations, preface, and introduction.

Kennedy, George. *The Art of Persuasion in Greece.* London: Routledge & Kegan Paul, 1963. Points out Thucydides' rhetorical strategy in writing the *History of the Peloponnesian War* and the ways in which it differs from that of his predecessor, Herodotus. Analyzes Thucydides' narrative power.

Livingstone, R. W., ed. *The Pageant of Greece.* Oxford, England: Clarendon, 1953. A collection of works from antiquity. Concludes that Thucydides' narrative power is rooted in his personal struggle to understand the "true picture of the events of the war" by recording only a first-hand account of what he saw. A helpful source for beginning researchers of Thucydides and his principal literary work. Illustrated.

Smith, Charles Forster. Introduction to *Thucydides: History of the Peloponnesian War, Books I and II.* Rev. ed. New York: Putnam's, 1928. Gleans biographical information about the book's author from Thucydides' *History of the Peloponnesian War,* lamenting the lack of valid biographies on the writer, whom Smith calls the greatest historian who ever lived.

Strauss, Leo. *The City and Man.* Chicago: Rand McNally, 1964. Notes the need to review the history of classical antiquity. Text addresses Thucydides as a "scientific historian" who wrote for all ages.

THE HIVE

Type of work: Novel
Author: Camilo José Cela (1916-   )
Type of plot: Social realism
Time of plot: December, 1943
Locale: Madrid
First published: La colmena, 1951 (English translation, 1953)

Principal characters:

MARTÍN MARCO, a down-and-out writer
FILO, Martín's kindhearted sister
ROBERTO GONZÁLEZ, Filo's accountant husband
DOÑA ROSA, a stern café owner
SEÑORITA ELVIRA, a fallen woman
DOÑA RAMONA BRAGADO, a dairy owner and procuress

The Story:
   One cold December afternoon in 1943, four years after the end of the Spanish Civil War, the waiter in Doña Rosa's café, La Delicia, threw out a pale, feeble, poorly dressed man who was unable to pay his tab. The waiter disobeyed Doña Rosa's orders, however, to beat the man as a lesson for his impudence. The wretch was Martín Marco, a freelance writer down on his luck. After having offered to leave a book in payment, Martín continued on his customary nightly wandering though Madrid. Everyday existence had been hardscrabble and bleak for the people of Spain ever since the Fascist dictator, Generalísimo Francisco Franco, assumed power after a bloody three-year conflict that had ravaged the country and left its citizenry deeply divided. Stopping before a show window of toilet fittings, Martín reflected on the gross class disparities of his day. He idealistically pondered the unlikely possibility of a socialist Utopia. Tired, cold, and hungry, and with his brain in turmoil, Martín purchased a few chestnuts with his remaining pocket money. He proceeded to the apartment of his poor but sympathetic sister, Filo. Since her husband, Roberto González, had yet to arrive, Martín was sure to be able to eat at least one fried egg that she would lovingly prepare for him. The two discussed Martín's good fortune in arriving while González was still at work, for the brothers-in-law had long disliked each other. Hurrying out to avoid encountering the man he always referred to as "that beast," Martín met his friend Paco, and they exchanged reading material.
   Later that night, Martín bumped into an old acquaintance, La Uruguaya, a prostitute in the company of a free-spending client. He accepted their invitation to have a drink reluctantly, for he found the woman vaguely repugnant. Subsequently, he continued on his way through Madrid. Passing through one of the city's red-light districts, Martín met police patrolling the area. He appeared disoriented when they demanded that he produce his papers. Fearful without exactly knowing why, Martín, now rambling and barely coherent, identified himself as a sometime author of newspaper articles; the authorities were satisfied. He ended up spending the night in a brothel run by Doña Jesusa, a friend of his deceased mother. He spent the night with the prostitute Purita, who kindly offered to buy him breakfast the following morning.
   The next afternoon, Martín, broke as usual, encountered another friend, Ventura Aguado, from whom he sheepishly borrowed money so that he could treat Ventura to a coffee. Leaving

the café, Martín met a former schoolmate and girlfriend, who was, like him, a Republican sympathizer. Nati Robles had once thought that the study of politics and the philosophy of law would be all she needed to be happy. Martín noted how much better dressed Nati appeared than she had been as a university suffragist. He somewhat nervously accepted her invitation to a drink. In a serendipitous gesture, Nati presented Martín with fifty pesetas so that he could treat her as well as buy her a gift. On his way to a secondhand bookshop where he intended to purchase a print for Nati, Martín stopped for a drink at Doña Rosa's café, from which he had been unceremoniously removed the previous day. There, Martín paid his outstanding debt and tipped the waiter generously before commenting insultingly on the poor quality of the establishment. When he finally reached the shop, he was chagrined to discover that his only remaining twenty-five pesetas had fallen out of his pocket when he used the café's lavatory.

A few days later, Martín borrowed a black tie from Pablo Alonso, a friend who was good-heartedly providing him with free lodging. Martín then set off to visit his mother's grave, again making little sense and muttering vague pronouncements about the means of production and distribution. An unspecified something that had appeared in that day's newspaper—either an article Martín had written or a belated denunciation of his political sympathies—frightened his friends, and they organized an all-out search for Martín before the authorities should find him. While they discussed plans for hiding the unbalanced Martín or packing him off to Barcelona long enough for the affair to blow over, Martín remained oblivious to his troubles. Trying to save the very same newspaper that threatened to be his undoing, he vowed to read the want ads and find himself a respectable job working for the government or in a bank.

Critical Evaluation:

To a certain extent, it is misleading to claim Martín Marco as the novel's principal protagonist, for *The Hive* contains nearly three hundred fictional characters. Camilo José Cela's unflattering, but clear-eyed, depiction of Madrid as a stagnant hive of listless, desperate, immoral activity in the years immediately following the victory of Franco's Fascist forces in the Spanish Civil War (1936-1939) garnered him no end of trouble with the official censors. As a result, the book's publication was delayed by five years (it was first published in Argentina). Four decades later, this work, along with such other important Cela novels as *The Family of Pascual Duarte* (1942), *Mrs. Caldwell Speaks to Her Son* (1953), and *San Camilo, 1936* (1969), contributed to his election as the 1989 winner of the Nobel Prize in Literature and his reputation as one of Spain's most influential postwar authors.

By turn vulgar and comic, somber and hopeful, *The Hive* exhibits little respect for conventional narrative sequence. Instead, it consists of more than two hundred short vignettes that leap from setting to setting and from character to character over a five- or six-day period. The non-chronological flow of the six chapters and short final section, as well as the considerable repetition and overlapping of episodes, reinforces the sense of inertia, both spiritual and economic, that plagues the residents of the city. With a cessation of the hostilities that had so brutalized the soul of their nation only a few years earlier, they had hoped for a better life. Heat and food were, however, in short supply in the winter of 1943, and nearly all the major characters in the novel suffer from poverty, hunger, and cold.

These physical deprivations have their counterpart in the sluggish intellectual climate of the capital, where promising university graduates are reduced to scribbling fragments of poems during their hours of idleness or to working at unchallenging jobs. The onerous pressures of political conformity also weigh heavily on the watchful and wary citizenry, who dare not trespass against the Fascist policies or traditional Catholic sympathies of the state. *The Hive* is replete with moral guardians—night watchmen intent on keeping order and Fascist supporters like the café owners Doña Rosa and Celestino Ortiz (the latter an adherent of Friedrich Nietzsche), who are ready to denounce their fellows on the slightest suspicion of complicity with the losing side in the war.

The merciless realities of Spain's social, cultural, and economic isolation made day-to-day survival particularly difficult for women, many of whom had to turn to a life of prostitution to stay alive. *The Hive* depicts figures such as Doña Jesusa, who runs a thriving brothel; Doña Ramona Bragado, who supplements the income from her dairy by acting as a procuress who supplies destitute young women to gentlemen who are eager to pay for their services; and Doña Celia Vecino, a "respectable" widow who rents rooms in her home to couples seeking beds for illicit trysts. For every impoverished woman in need of quick money—like the selfless Victorita, who plans to use her gains to buy food for her tubercular boyfriend—there seems to be at least one financially secure man desirous of the pleasure of her company.

Martín Marco emerges as the thread linking the dispersed locales of the capital and many of its downtrodden survivors. He therefore provides an essential element of narrative continuity in what would otherwise be an extremely fragmented novel. Martín merits consideration as the work's principal protagonist because he so completely embodies the suppressed spirit and lifeblood of the nation. He therefore comes to represent the unjustifiable squandering of Spanish potential under Franco's punishing dictatorship. That a university-educated writer and intellectual should feel compelled to write such pandering articles as "Reasons for the Spiritual Permanence of Isabella the Catholic" is a telling indication of the extent to which the nation's productive heart and soul were being suppressed in the name of an extreme right-wing vision of law and order. Martín's apparent mental unbalance symbolizes the profound disorientation and alienation of his time, and prefigures the harsh effects of the sustained repression that countless Spanish citizens suffered for almost four decades until Franco's death in 1975. The last sentence of *The Hive* shows Martín laughing uncontrollably at the notion of the suburban sprawl surrounding Madrid (the city's outer belt), as if liberation or escape from this stifling milieu were forever to remain unattainable for himself and those like him.

Gregory J. Racz

Bibliography:
Foster, David W. *Forms of the Novel in the Work of Camilo José Cela.* Columbia: University of Missouri Press, 1967. Contains a helpful chapter analyzing the unique "slice of life" structure and imbricated patterning of *The Hive* in contrast to the widely varying compositional designs of the rest of the author's novelistic oeuvre.
Henn, David. *C. J. Cela: "La Colmena."* London: Grant & Cutler, 1974. The most comprehensive study of Cela's novel. Provides a concise biographical sketch of the author and a useful historical backdrop to the action of the work. Includes extended sections on theme, style, and structure, as well as a detailed chapter on the symbolic importance of the figure of Martín Marco.
Ilie, Paul. *Literature and Inner Exile: Authoritarian Spain, 1939-1975.* Baltimore, Md.: The Johns Hopkins University Press, 1980. Considers a definition of inner exile as the deepseated alienation from the dominant values of a society in which one is constrained to remain a participating member. Though not a study of Cela or his works, this in-depth critical analysis of the sociopolitical consequences of Franco's unforgiving rule captures the estrangement of protagonists such as Martín Marco.

McPheeters, D. W. *Camilo José Cela*. New York: Twayne, 1969. An excellent starting place for any investigation into Cela's life and work. The author's literary output is considered within the historical and aesthetic context of his day. The chapter dedicated to *The Hive* is an excellent introduction to the novel.

Roy, Joaquín, ed. *Camilo José Cela: Homage to a Nobel Prize*. Coral Gables, Fla: University of Miami Press, 1991. Specialized essays commemorating Cela's 1989 Nobel Prize in Literature. Contains three pieces on *The Hive*: Thomas Deveny's "Cela on Screen: *La colmena*"; Bernardo Antonio González's "Reading *La colmena* Through the Lens: From Mario Camus to Camilo José Cela"; and William M. Sherzer's "The Role of Urban Icons in Cela's *La colmena*." Also includes essays on two other influential Cela works: *The Family of Pascual Duarte* and *San Camilo, 1936*.

HIZAKURIGE

Type of work: Novel
Author: Jippensha Ikku (1765-1831)
Type of plot: Farce
Time of plot: Early nineteenth century
Locale: Japan's Tokaido highway
First published: Tōkaidōchū hizakurige, 1802-1822 (English translation, 1929)

Principal characters:
YAJIROBEI, a middle-aged ne'er-do-well
KITAHACHI or KITA, Yajirobei's companion

The Story:

Yajirobei inherited money at his home in Fuchu, and he came to Edo with his companion Kita to spend it. The money was soon wasted in riotous entertainment, and they lived in poverty. Yaji married and Kita went to work as an apprentice. Yaji's wife died, and he was left with bills to pay, particularly to the rice dealer, bills he could not meet. Meanwhile, Kita was turned out of the shop where he had been apprenticed for embezzling money. With trouble on every side and nothing to tie them down, the pair decided to skip town and make a trip to the sacred shrine at Ise.

Along the way they had many adventures and met all sorts of people. At Odawara they ate *uiro*—a bean confection that is a specialty of the place. They also had to deal with a unique type of bath called *goemonburo.* Unlike an ordinary Japanese bath, which is made of wood, this was a metal pot with a fire built directly beneath it. Bathers stood on a wooden platform to keep from burning their feet. Unfamiliar with this type of bath, the city slickers removed the wooden board and put on clogs to protect their feet. Kita, as a result, kicked a hole in the bottom of the tub and ruined it.

Yaji thought he had arranged with the maid at the inn that she would sleep with him that night, but while he was going to the bathroom, Kita told the maid that Yaji was sick, covered with boils, foul smelling, and disgusting. The maid kept the money Yaji had paid her, but never showed up for the rendezvous.

At a river crossing they encountered a pair of blind travelers. When one blind man offered to carry the other across the river, Yaji got on his back instead. When the blind man went back to pick up his companion, Kita tried the same trick only to get dumped into the river. That evening at an inn at Kakegawa they encountered the same pair of blind men drinking sake. To get even for having been dumped in the river, Kita drained their cups for them and ended up drinking the whole jug of sake, making the blind men think they had spilled it. In the end Kita's ruse was exposed.

As they approached Akasaka, Yaji grew weary, so Kita offered to go on ahead and find an inn for the night. A short time later Yaji stopped at a tea house for some refreshment and was warned that the road ahead was dangerous because it was haunted by a fox. He nevertheless walked on in the darkness until he came across Kita sitting beside the road enjoying a whiff of tobacco. Yaji assumed that this was not Kita at all, but the fox who had simply changed his appearance to look like Kita. Consequently, Yaji beat his friend with a stick and tied him up, groping around under his clothes trying to find his tail to prove he was a fox. Finally when a village dog ignored Kita, Yaji decided that perhaps Kita was not a fox in disguise after all.

At Iga Ueno they encountered a man who asked if they were from Edo. Yaji said they were and claimed to be none other than Jippensha Ikku and went on to tell this man that he was writing *Hizakurige* as they traveled. Eventually this charade was discovered. When they were served *konnyaku*, a local delicacy, they failed to realize that it was supposed to be cooked on the hot rocks provided. Kita and Yaji thought the rocks were some sort of food that was supposed to be eaten. They pretended to know what they were doing, but as usual their ignorance was revealed.

More trouble awaited them when, at last, they reached Ise and there encountered none other than Tarobei, the rice dealer from Edo whose bill they had left unpaid. From Ise they continued on to Kyoto and Osaka to see the sights in those great cities. On the way they had more farcical experiences. On a boat down the Yodo River, Yaji tried to do an imitation of a famous Edo actor, but even the people from the west of the country knew more about the actor than he did. They met a man carrying an urn containing his late wife's ashes and mistakenly ate the ashes thinking it was some sort of local dish. Having reached Osaka at last, their journey ended.

Critical Evaluation:

Travel books were popular in Japan during the Edo period (1603-1867). During this time common people lived very restricted lives, and one of the few forms of entertainment that allowed any sort of freedom was travel. Additionally, all people were expected to make the pilgrimage to Ise at least once in their lifetime, and therefore they had a pious excuse for enjoying the freedom of travel and release from their daily routines. As a consequence, guidebooks were numerous. Such guidebooks commonly provided travelers with directions for travel, but also included information on local history. They informed the traveler of local craft products and food specialties at every stop along the way. Unusual local customs were also explained.

Jippensha Ikku adds to this guidebook format by adding the element of farcical humor. He does this in several ways. In *Hizakurige*, which has also been translated as *Shanks' Mare*, his most common technique is the device of having the supposedly sophisticated Edoites traveling through the countryside, showing they know nothing of the local customs. Never willing to admit their ignorance, they always end up making a mess of things and embarrassing themselves.

An example of this ignorance of local customs is found in the bath scene at Odawara. Seeing the wooden board floating on top of the bath, Yaji supposes this is a lid to keep the water warm. He does not realize he is supposed to stand on it to protect his feet from the hot bottom of the tub. Instead he finds a pair of toilet clogs to wear into the bath. That he would wear such filthy clogs in water people will bathe in is revolting. When Kita, wearing the clogs, breaks the bottom out of the bath, everyone realizes what a disgusting thing he has done, and he ends up having to pay for the ruined bathtub.

Sometimes it is not ignorance that leads them into embarrassing situations, but foolishness. At one point when Yaji is spending the night with a geisha, he is embarrassed by the fact that he is wearing soiled underwear. Not wanting her to see this, he secretly tosses his underwear out the window into the darkness. The next morning as they leave the geisha house, there is his soiled loincloth hanging from a tree in the garden for everyone to see. Not willing to ignore this, the geisha makes the gardener retrieve the item and return it to Yaji.

Some readers used to the more formal traditions of Japanese literature may be surprised at the scatological obsessions Ikku displays in this work, but there is a long and rich tradition of such humor in Japanese folk literature and art. For the reader who tires of the coarse and ribald humor of the situations in which the travelers find themselves, the author also provides a demonstration of his excellent ear and his flair for capturing colloquial language. Not only do Yaji and Kita carry on a continuous humorous dialogue laced with puns, word plays, and literary allusions, the author also contrasts their colloquial language, typical of Edo, with that of rustics from the provinces and with that of the people from the west of the country. He includes the spoken language of all classes of people.

The novel is also an encyclopedia of customs, beliefs, lore, and history of the areas visited. The material may be presented humorously and irreverently, but it is nonetheless informative. Readers laugh when Yaji buys a wooden box at Hakone Pass and pays more than it is worth simply because a pretty young woman is selling it, but those boxes of inlaid wood are still the traditional specialty product of that area.

Structurally, *Hizakurige* is episodic and picaresque. Each episode and encounter is essentially independent of the others. There is very little attempt to use one episode to build on another. For its humor, informativeness, and its witty banter, however, *Hizakurige* was an enormously popular work. Between 1802 and 1809 the author wrote the parts dealing with the trip from Edo through Ise to Kyoto and Osaka. At first he took the travelers only as far as Hakone, but readers demanded more so he continued to write about the entire length of the Tokaido highway. In 1810 he took them on a further journey to make a pilgrimage to the island of Shikoku, and in 1811 they travelled to Miyajima. Between 1812 and 1822 they traveled along the Kisokaido, another major highway that passes through the mountains of central Japan. In 1814 he added an introduction to the whole which provides some background about his heroes.

Stephen W. Kohl

Bibliography:
Aston, W. G. *A History of Japanese Literature*. Rutland, Vt.: Charles E. Tuttle, 1972. Pages 369 to 375 present biographical information on Ikku and offer two evaluations of *Hizakurige*, "the most humorous and entertaining book in the Japanese language," which "people of nice taste had better not read."
Kato, Shuichi. *The Modern Years*. Vol. 3 in *A History of Japanese Literature*. Translated by David Chibbett. New York: Kodansha International, 1983. Sets Ikku in the context of Edo culture and identifies several important features of his writing.
Keene, Donald. *World Within Walls: Japanese Literature of the Pre-Modern Era, 1600-1867*. New York: Holt, Rinehart and Winston, 1976. Provides a brief discussion of the author and his story and situates it within the context of its time and culture.
Satchell, Thomas, trans. *Shanks' Mare: Being a Translation of the Tokaido Volumes of Hizakurige, Japan's Great Comic Novel of Travel and Ribaldry*, by Jippensha Ikku. Rutland, Vt.: Charles E. Tuttle, 1960. Provides biographical information about the author.

H.M.S. PINAFORE
Or, The Lass That Loved a Sailor

Type of work: Drama
Author: W. S. Gilbert (1836-1911)
Type of plot: Operetta
Time of plot: Second half of the nineteenth century
Locale: Portsmouth harbor, England
First performed: 1878; first published, 1878

Principal characters:

JOSEPHINE, the Captain's daughter
RALPH, the lowly sailor who loves Josephine
SIR JOSEPH PORTER, First Lord of the Admiralty, and Josephine's suitor
CAPTAIN CORCORAN, Josephine's father
LITTLE BUTTERCUP, who loves the Captain

The Story:

Lying at anchor in Portsmouth harbor, the *Pinafore* was the scene of hectic activity. Sir Joseph Porter, K.C.B., First Lord of the Admiralty, had announced his intention to visit the ship. The sailors swabbed the decks and were inspected by the captain, who was as content with them as they were with him. One member of the crew, however, was far from happy. Ralph, the lowly foremast hand, was sunk in gloom and despair. He loved Josephine, the captain's daughter, but because of his low rank she repulsed his advances and rejected his love.

Before Sir Joseph's arrival, Little Buttercup came on board, plying her trade as a seller of ribbons and laces, scissors and knives, treacle and toffee. In a conversation with the captain she hinted that appearances are often deceiving. The captain noticed that Little Buttercup had physical charms not displeasing to him. Sir Joseph's barge approached, and the First Lord was soon on board, accompanied by his sisters, his cousins, and his aunts. After inspecting the crew, he gave them instructions for success. His own formula had been simple enough. He had polished door handles, stuck close to his desk, and never gone to sea. Sir Joseph then proceeded to the purpose of his visit. He had come to ask Josephine to marry him.

Josephine had no intention of marrying Sir Joseph, whom she disliked. Not able to give an outright refusal, she informed him that marriage with such a high-ranking officer was impossible because she was only a captain's daughter. Sir Joseph admired her modesty, but brushed the objection aside. Rank, he assured her, was absolutely no barrier, for love leveled all rank. Josephine hastened to agree with him, and everyone immediately assumed that a marriage would soon take place.

Giving up all hope of winning Josephine, Ralph put a pistol to his head and prepared to pull the trigger. At that moment Josephine rushed in, told him not to destroy himself, and proclaimed her undying love for him. At this turn of events there was general rejoicing among Ralph's messmates, with the exception of an unsavory character by the name of Dick Dead-eye.

The couple laid plans to steal ashore the next evening to be married. Once the ceremony was performed, they reasoned, nobody could do anything about it. Dick Dead-eye went to the captain and warned him of the plan. Accordingly, just as the lovers and their accomplices were quietly tiptoeing away, the captain entered, enraged at Ralph's presumption and at the low company in which he found his daughter. Ralph was thrown into the brig.

Attracted by the captain's swearing, Sir Joseph came rushing up in time to hear what had happened. The sisters, the cousins, and the aunts were horribly shocked. Sir Joseph was equally shocked, so shocked that he administered a very severe rebuke to the captain. In the midst of the argument, Little Buttercup appeared. To the astonishment of everyone, she announced that many years ago she had been a baby-sitter. Two infants had been put into her care, one of lowly birth, the other of high position. She was very fond of one of them, so she had changed them around. The captain was really of low birth, and Ralph was the patrician.

This astounding announcement resulted in a very odd situation which was quickly and amicably arranged. The captain changed places with Ralph, who became captain instead. Sir Joseph announced that he could not marry Josephine since she was only the daughter of a common sailor. Accordingly, Josephine married Ralph; the captain married Little Buttercup, and Sir Joseph married a well-born cousin.

Critical Evaluation:

In December, 1877, after the moderately successful production of *The Sorcerer* had begun, William Schwenck Gilbert offered his musical collaborator, Arthur Seymour Sullivan, a libretto for a new comic opera, with a note appended: "I have very little doubt whatever but that you will be pleased with it." Sullivan was indeed pleased, and although he was suffering intense pain from a kidney disorder, he composed the music rapidly. On the evening of May 25, 1878, three nights after *The Sorcerer* completed its run, the Comedy Opera Company presented *H.M.S. Pinafore*, which was to become one of the great triumphs of the musical theater.

The opening performance of *H.M.S. Pinafore* was nearly a failure. Some scandal attached to the character of Sir Joseph, who was clearly a satirical portrait of Sir William H. Smith, a publisher appointed by Queen Victoria as First Lord of the Admiralty. The first season of the production languished during the June heat. Most affluent Londoners vacationed outside the city, and the cast and chorus, threatened with cancellation of the whole production, agreed to accept a cut of one-third of their salaries. Eventually, however, *H.M.S. Pinafore* began to attract a following. The Savoy Company, under D'Oyly Carte, performing at such theaters as the (English) Opéra Comique, the Imperial, and the Olympic, enjoyed a London run of two years.

Almost concurrently, *H.M.S. Pinafore* was performed in pirated and often poorly staged versions in America. To secure American royalty rights and correct misconceptions about the quality of the work, Gilbert, Sullivan, Alfred Cellier (another composer for the Carte company), and selected members of the original cast mounted an impressive production of the comic opera at the Fifth Avenue Theater in New York City, starting December 1, 1879. The authorized version of *H.M.S. Pinafore* was widely hailed, and touring companies performed it throughout the United States as well as England.

Reasons for the popularity of Gilbert's comedy are not difficult to identify. Apart from Sullivan's tuneful score, the book is delightfully arch, bubbling over with high spirits and clever invention. Gilbert satirizes, with wit but little malice, pretensions of social superiority in class-conscious Victorian England. In the pecking order of rank, Sir Joseph Porter is superior to Captain Corcoran, and the captain in turn lords it over his crew. Even the lowly British tar is snobbish about his rank. After all, every sailor on the *Pinafore* is an Englishman, and his national pride, for which he feels superior to seamen of other nations, makes him better than "a Roosian, a French or Turk or Proosian." Even the revelation by Buttercup that the captain is of lowly birth and Ralph Rackstraw is of high birth scarcely disturbs the Victorian audience's sense of social justice. Sir Joseph, who likes to think of himself as democratic but who is really a snob, has to marry his cousin Hebe instead of Josephine, who has fallen in class, finding herself the daughter of a humble sailor. At the same time the former Ralph, elevated in rank to the captain of H.M.S. *Pinafore*, can claim Josephine. As for the onetime captain, he is free to marry at his own social level, and wisely chooses the buxom Little Buttercup.

Buttercup was slightly addled when she was "young and charming." She mixed up the infant Ralph and the infant captain, a worrisome mistake perhaps, but no serious harm was done. No matter what his social caste, each Englishman (and Englishwoman too, including sisters, cousins, and aunts) knows what is the proper duty and decorum for his prescribed caste. Gilbert's satire does not bite too deep: It ultimately affirms the existing order.

Bibliography:
Bailey, Leslie. *Gilbert and Sullivan and Their World*. New York: Thames and Hudson, 1973. Examines the original production of *H.M.S. Pinafore* and its antecedents in *The Bab Ballads* (1869). Photographs and sketches of early productions of the operetta.
Cellier, François, and Cunningham Bridgeman. *Gilbert and Sullivan and Their Operas*. New York: Benjamin Blom, 1970. Considers the original production of *H.M.S. Pinafore*. Explores Gilbert's role as stage manager and traces improvisations and changes in the script. Examines the history of the operetta in England and the United States.
Dunn, George E. *A Gilbert & Sullivan Directory*. New York: Da Capo Press, 1971. A comprehensive dictionary that includes references to Gilbert's many allusions. Shows correlations among various Gilbert and Sullivan works.
Heylar, James, ed. *Gilbert and Sullivan: Papers Presented at the International Conference Held at the University of Kansas in May, 1970*. Lawrence: University of Kansas Library, 1971. Contains a study of rank and station in *H.M.S. Pinafore*, a consideration of the American reception of the work, and the connections between French theater and the operetta.
Moore, Frank Ledlie. *Handbook of Gilbert and Sullivan*. New York: Schocken Books, 1975. Gives an overview of *H.M.S. Pinafore* and examines the role of Richard D'Oyle Carte in the success of the operetta.

HOLY SONNETS

Type of work: Poetry
Author: John Donne (1572-1631)
First published: 1633, 1635, and 1899

It is generally agreed that the nineteen "Holy Sonnets" were written over a period of several years in John Donne's life, the first of them as early as 1609 and some after the death of Donne's wife in 1617. The poems fall into various groups according to the way they are read. One authority sees them as disconnected pieces; another sees four distinct groups, two of six poems each, one group of four, and one of three. Other readers find a unifying principle that makes all nineteen poems a sequence. The fact that at their first appearance they were given the title "Divine Meditations" suggests that early editors saw in them a common thread, that of a liturgical exercise, which borrowed heavily from the Scriptures, especially the Book of Lamentations and the Psalms.

The power and intensity of the sonnets derive from the way Donne yokes together into one brief exercise an abundance of wit and many traditions, allusions, and emotional states. The poems are at once very formal and very private as they depict the drama of a religious individual working through a formal exercise in very personal ways. The poems are a record of a soul's quest to demonstrate and experience faith, and the language and imagery convey a struggle to resolve deep conflicts. The struggle is marked by anguish and, at times, despair.

One of the thematic strains evident in the sonnets is the effort to subdue natural feelings by binding them with doctrinal imperatives and to place reason and wit at the service of religious faith. By nature irreverent, Donne persistently views the sacred through profane eyes and the profane through the eyes of a devout Christian. As a result, the sonnets have the unpredictability and individuality that is characteristic of Donne's secular poetry. Donne is undaunted by the sanctity of his religious feelings and the holiness of his enterprise. Christ is shown to be jealous, God is called upon to "ravish" the supplicant poet, and Christ's "Spouse" is most pleasing and true when embraced and "open to most men."

This mingling of the sacred and profane is strikingly evident in the poetic form Donne chose to achieve his artistic and emotional aims, the sonnet, for that form represents the interplay of individual expression and formal restrictions. He says in one of the sonnets, "I am a little world made cunningly/ Of Elements . . ." and he shapes his thoughts and emotions according to the demands of the sonnet form. Although the above line reflects the notion that humans are microcosms and that God made humans in his image, it also shows Donne's awareness of the relation of his art to his religion. To become a fully realized Christian, he must, as it were, become a fully realized sonnet.

To get to that point, Donne chose a structure that divides into distinct parts. The first eight lines of the sonnet, the octave, are patterned after the Italian sonnet, which rhymes *abbaabba*. The final six lines divide into four lines that rhyme *cddc* or *cdcd* and are followed by a concluding couplet. This structure allows for a dramatic shift in tone and argument as the poet passes from the octave to the sestet, and for a strong closure of two lines. Donne's image of the "little world" aptly describes the nature of the sonnet wrought by a mind struggling with fear and doubt, for the sonnet "contains" in two ways: It holds the poet's thoughts and feelings and holds them in by giving them form. Each sonnet is held together by the tension between the poet's impulse to overflow the boundaries of his form, which symbolizes doctrinal restrictions, and the need to conform to the demands of the sonnet.

The impulse to go beyond what is permitted or wise is evident in the first sonnet of the sequence, in which the poet exclaims that he runs toward Death. The sonnet sustains the image of the Christian soul trying to outrun Despair. The poem's tension derives in part from conflicting images. On the one hand, the individual runs, yet he "dare not move." He is tempted by the devil and looks to God for rescue. He is pulled toward hell by his sinful nature and by the weight of his past sins, yet he is drawn toward heaven by his desire for redemption. He is active in sin yet passive in his relation to God, his heart of iron attracted to God's magnetic presence. The symbolic nature of the sonnet contributes to the tension as well, representing the poet in the act of creating—seeking—though his redemption requires only that he be drawn to God like iron to a magnet.

Contrary states at war within the Christian's soul find abundant expression throughout the sonnets. While the poet is helpless and dependent on God's mercy for redemption, he has long been active in the life of sin that made him unworthy. The poet's anguish is in no little part the result of the dilemma he expresses in the second sonnet: He is pursued by the Satan who hates him, and he fears he is rejected by the God who loves him.

The dilemma extends to the nature of his own sins, as the third sonnet shows. Whereas drunkards, thieves, and lechers can remember their past joys and thereby gain relief in their future punishment, he has no such relief, for his profane love was itself filled with grief and therefore was at once the effect of sin and its cause. In the next sonnet, the poet's dilemma is that of the thief who wishes to be freed from prison, yet, because he is under a sentence of execution, wishes to remain imprisoned. Rescue from these dilemmas is possible through repentance, but that may not be enough or it may be out of reach, for, he asks, who can help him begin? In sonnet 8, he pleads to be taught how to repent. Time and again he finds himself at God's mercy, for he can do little more than pray and hope, ever conscious that sin has betrayed both his body and his soul.

The poet's sense of hopelessness is lightened somewhat by the mood of the most famous of the "Holy Sonnets," which begins, "Death be not proud. . . ." The poet's fear and doubt are momentarily suspended as he contemplates the awful image of Death reduced to a short sleep, after which he shall wake eternally and find that Death itself has died. This positive mood reappears in sonnet 17, where the poet seems assured of ultimate redemption, for God not only woos the poet's soul and offers all his Love but even fears the poet will give his love to saints and angels or that the seductions of Satan and this world will drive him out. This more optimistic mood is rare, however. The dominant note of the sonnets is fear and trembling, born of the poet's full and painful awareness of his own sinfulness, which causes him to doubt that his soul will ever attain heaven.

At times, the poet's self-loathing is so intense that the imagery becomes violent, as in sonnet 11: "Spit in my face you Jewes, and pierce my side,/ . . . crucifie mee,/ For I have sinn'd, and sinn'd." The repetition of "and sinn'd" reinforces the poet's sense of being damned, separated from God, and unworthy of God's grace. In sonnet 14, images of violence take on sexual overtones as well: Only in being ravished will the poet become chaste. The entire sequence of sonnets ends, fittingly, with a sonnet that begins with the poet confessing that contrary mental states meet in him; he alternately suffers cold faithlessness, hot remorse, and fits of devout faith. His best days are those in which he shakes with fear, as with a fever.

While the Christian soul is expressing his sense of unworthiness and depicting the nature of his dilemma, another conflict is taking place between the poet's faith and reason. Sonnet 9 suggests that reason is partly to blame for the poet's predicament, for it seems to make his sins worse in the eyes of God. Why, he asks, is he punished for sins that result from the use of reason, which God gave man and which sets man above animals? Sonnet 14 answers this question: Human reason is God's viceroy; as such, it should protect man against sin, but it is the slave to sin and proves weak and faithless. Reason and its companions, wit and logic, cannot penetrate God's mysteries, yet reason's very nature, at least in Donne, is to question and probe.

The "Holy Sonnets" represent not only the poet's sense of his unworthiness and the uncertain nature of his redemption but his attempt to mitigate his sins and demonstrate the earnestness and sincerity of his faith. His demonstration takes many forms, not the least of which is to confess his sins and his contrition. At the same time, the sonnet offers God further proof of the poet's earnestness. Those elements that jar and jibe in the poet's little world include the logic that subverts logic and brings the sonnet and the poet to the paradox that reason can only accept, not unravel. Faith, not reason, will get the poet to heaven, and faith makes reason not only useless but ridiculous.

The best way to demonstrate the point, Donne seems to be saying, is to subvert reason by reasoning oneself into a paradox. The poet does so repeatedly, ending sonnet after sonnet at the point where he has reasoned himself into a logical knot: Satan hates him but does not want to lose him; his sins have caused grief, yet he is punished for them; Christ's red blood cleanses his soul and makes it white; Death shall die; he will never be chaste until God ravishes him; and his best days are those filled with fearful trembling. Ironically, reason is the principal instrument of his damnation and the principal cause of his dilemma, yet it is also the principal instrument of his salvation. It resolves the poet's moral dilemma by defeating itself, opening the way for faith to make the leap and for God's grace to shine down on him.

Bernard E. Morris

Bibliography:

Archer, Stanley. "The Archetypal Journey Motif in Donne's *Divine Poems*." In *New Essays on Donne*, edited by Gary A. Stringer. Salzburg, Austria: Institut für Englische Sprache und Literatur Universität Salzburg, 1977. Argues that the image of the journey as a motif runs through most of the divine poems and gives them a thematic unity that has been neglected by earlier critical analyses of Donne's religious poetry.

Donne, John. *The Complete English Poems*. New York: Alfred A. Knopf, 1991. This attractive volume in the Everyman's Library series offers an introduction and ample textual glosses by C. A. Patrides, a noted authority on Donne. The book's substantial bibliography lists important sources on Donne's poetry.

_____. *The Divine Poems*. Edited by Helen Gardner. London: Oxford University Press, 1959. Gardner's long introduction includes a critical reading of the "Holy Sonnets" and a discussion of the dates of their composition. Her essay-length commentaries provide further help in understanding Donne's divine poems.

Grenander, M. E. "Holy Sonnets VII and XVII: John Donne." In *Essential Articles for the Study of John Donne's Poetry*, edited by John R. Roberts. Hamden, Conn.: Archon Books, 1975. A close study of two sonnets that focuses on the emotional development in the poems and its relation to their structure. Grenander's approach offers a guide to those wishing to study other sonnets in this group.

Peterson, Douglas L. "John Donne's *Holy Sonnets* and the Anglican Doctrine of Contrition." In *Essential Articles for the Study of John Donne's Poetry*, edited by John R. Roberts. Hamden, Conn.: Archon Books, 1975. Peterson argues that the "Holy Sonnets" are a sequence that is unified by Donne's attempt to express and realize contrition.

HOMAGE TO MISTRESS BRADSTREET

Type of work: Poetry
Author: John Berryman (1914-1972)
First published: 1956

Anne Dudley was born in 1612, presumably in Northampton, England, of a well-read and intelligent Nonconformist father. In 1628, at the age of sixteen, she married twenty-five-year-old Simon Bradstreet, a graduate of Cambridge University. They sailed to America on the *Arabella* in 1631. Anne herself was a Puritan of profound religious conviction, but she was intelligent and well educated, and with her natural inclinations strengthened by her surroundings in the New World she became capable of strong-willed behavior, even to the point of rebellion. She could not unquestioningly accept the tenets of American Calvinism and energetically stood up to the demands of her father and her husband, both of whom became governors of Massachusetts Colony. At the same time, she became the mother of eight children, overcame illnesses, was a loving daughter and wife, and wrote enough poetry to fill a thick volume. She died in 1672.

In *Homage to Mistress Bradstreet*, John Berryman's response to Anne Bradstreet is one of total approbation. He warms to her with a fervor that at times approaches adulation. The poem covers her whole life, yet it is not a biography and merely provides an account of the external aspects of her life. More important, the poem is an attempt to give a spiritual biography of the woman and of Colonial Massachusetts. Berryman's success in this attempt is notable because of the power of his language and style.

Berryman catches the essence of his subject's conflicting characteristics, the power of her personality, in the first stanza. She is restless but patient. She was a loving mother but also a scholar of both literature and the Lord. As the stanzas develop, so does her character. She realizes that in the alien New World she and her husband must love each other. They must recognize worldly love and its importance because time is transitory. The years rot away.

In the fourth stanza, the poem's art and power become apparent. The first three and a half stanzas are spoken by the poet about his subject. Then the poet's voice blends with that of Mistress Bradstreet, who continues the poem with only occasional interruptions by the poet and occasional dialogues between her and someone else. This stylistic technique, which pushes back the limitations of poetry—a technique begun by the great innovator Ezra Pound and carried on by various followers—was highly praised. By telescoping statements and feelings and by omitting transitions, the poet can reach more deeply into the very essence of poetry.

The fifth stanza, spoken by Mistress Bradstreet, continues the catalog of happenings in her world. She recounts the voyage on the *Arabella* and the death of the woman for whom the ship was named. The poet touches on her hopes and aspirations and fears, and on the Puritans' troubles in the New World. All recountings are energized by the subject's strong character and brightened by her personality. She breathes poetry and revels in life. She deftly switches from present to past, effectively overlaying one time with another. She goes back to her youth when smallpox blasted the beauty from her face but when romance and mystery came to her in the person of Simon, her husband to be.

Her memory is agonized by memory of her revulsion at the Calvinism of John Cotton and her attraction, despite being a good Calvinist, to Catholicism; she recognized that she must be disciplined against the easier attraction. The uncertain journey of her life is reemphasized time and again as she remembers that her patience is short and that she rebels against the life around her. The conflict between body and soul—the weakness of the flesh and the hoped-for strength of the spirit—are especially powerful in her memory. Sex pulls her like a magnet, floods her very being, and rises to a crescendo of glory in the accomplishment of having children, especially her first, born when she was twenty-one. Perhaps no lines in the whole poem are superior to the statement of the joy of this accomplishment.

The iron bands of her environment are revealed in her reaction to the trial of Anne Hutchinson for "Antinomianism" and "traducing the ministers and their ministry" and to Hutchinson's consequent excommunication and banishment by the synod of churches and by Governor Winthrop. Mistress Bradstreet's reaction was ambivalent. She despised the mistreatment of Anne Hutchinson for her dissenting views, but she burned inwardly more than outwardly.

As she reveals herself in her examinations of herself, Mistress Bradstreet is of the earth and of the spirit, but it is a balance never firmly and indisputably established. She is also Mother Earth and encompasses the whole of life. Like Walt Whitman at a later period, she is large enough to include all. She renounces nothing, however petty and repulsive. The poem's ending is a great affirmation.

In the style and technique of the poem lies both its glory and its occasional lapse into weakness. The language is compact, muscular, and powerful, the words are simple, direct, earthy, slangy, idiomatic, and effective. The art of telescoping and compacting sometimes vitiates the poem's own strength, as when a fifty-two-word, eight-line parenthesis separates, for no logical or aesthetic reason, the subject from its verb. Such technical weaknesses are few, however.

In outline, this curious but somberly moving poem of fifty-seven eight-line stanzas is effectively organized as the spiritual autobiography of a complex personality who lived with physical hardship and spiritual travail the double life of a woman and an artist. Despite the rough intellectuality of the verse and the elliptical intimacy of the material, a careful reading shows how apt the writer's form and diction are for his task. In this work Berryman shows that the American past may be employed as a subject for serious poetry without reshaping it to the wonder of legend or exploiting it for sentimentality.

Bibliography:

Halliday, E. M. *John Berryman and the Thirties: A Memoir.* Amherst: University of Massachusetts Press, 1987. Provides an analysis of the thinking and writing that went into John Berryman's first important poem, the book-length *Homage to Mistress Bradstreet.* It is the nature of confessional poetry that it can hardly be understood without an understanding of the poet.

Kelly, Richard J., and Alan K. Lathrop, eds. *Recovering Berryman: Essays on a Poet.* Ann Arbor: University of Michigan Press, 1993. The discussion goes beyond Berryman's *Homage to Mistress Bradstreet* period, covering the whole of Berryman's career. Focuses on his writing and only tangentially on his life; the title is a pun on Berryman's excessive drinking at the end of his life.

Mancini, Joseph, Jr. *The Berryman Gestalt: Therapeutic Strategies in the Poetry of John Berryman.* New York: Garland, 1987. Includes valuable discussions of the significance of *Homage to Mistress Bradstreet* and why it was an eye-opening adventure for a poet to undertake.

Matterson, Stephen. *Berryman and Lowell: The Art of Losing.* Totowa, N.J.: Barnes and Noble Books, 1988. Though this volume treats two confessional poets equally, Berryman is shown to be more important. Matterson's discussion of Berryman's early poetry reveals an understanding and important revelations about *Homage to Mistress Bradstreet.*

Thomas, Harry, ed. *Berryman's Understanding: Reflections on the Poetry of John Berryman.* Boston: Northeastern University Press, 1988. An excellent introduction to Berryman's poetry, especially *Homage to Mistress Bradstreet.* The book shows some of the convolutions of poetry until 1970, when Berryman killed himself, and beyond. Also discusses the revival of interest in the poetry of Anne Bradstreet.

HOMEWARD
Songs By the Way

Type of work: Poetry
Author: Æ (George William Russell, 1867-1935)
First published: 1894

George William Russell's pen name was Æ. His first volume of poems appeared during a turbulent moment of Irish history when political turmoil was bound together with religious and cultural strife. In *Homeward*, Æ attempted, through awakening his readers' spiritual insights, to bring balm to his strife-torn country.

Throughout the nineteenth century, many in Ireland had been trying to change the political status of their country from colony of England to independent nation. Irish representatives argued in the British parliament, and there were mass protests and armed revolts. By the 1890's, neither political nor military struggles had borne much fruit but they had helped stimulate a strong national cultural current. Writers touched by this current contended that the authentic Celtic roots of Irish life were being buried under superficial British traditions.

At the same time, some proposed religious innovations. In Ireland, religion could not be separated from politics. The British colonists were Protestant and earlier on had disestablished and, for a period, banned the practice of Catholicism, the religion of the Irish masses. Religious hatreds compounded nationalist fervor to cause occasional fanatical outbreaks of unproductive violence. Writers such as William Butler Yeats and Æ were so put off by this sectarianism that they turned away from Christianity altogether and became attracted to esoteric, Orientally influenced faiths.

Æ embraced the new "religion" of theosophy and, in 1891, moved into a communal household with other converts. He was living in this house when he wrote the poems for his first collection of verse, in which he strove to put his spiritual beliefs into poetic form.

Guided by Indian philosophy, theosophy involved a belief in the reincarnation of souls. It was thought that in sleep or meditation, each person's soul could remember former lives or, diving deeper, link up with the grand soul of the universe. Æ is a shortened version of Aeon, the gnostic name for the first men on earth, whose pristine experience, according to theosophical belief, could be recaptured through proper spiritual exercise and attentiveness. In writing poems about these subjects, Æ was not trying simply to explain the basic doctrines of theosophy, but, as an Irish nationalist, to show that the primary ideas of the philosophy were contained in ancient Celtic lore. Whereas in prose works such as *The Candle of Vision* (1918), he worked out connections in a scholarly way, in *Homeward* he suggested them by showing how mystical epiphanies arose naturally from contact with the Irish countryside.

Far from presenting metaphysics in meter, however, Æ tries in each poem to re-create a moment of vision in which the speaker, through his communing with nature, rises to glimpse a higher realm. The seventy-five-page book contains sixty-seven short lyrics, few more than a page in length. Employing the ballad form, usually with four-line stanzas and rhyme schemes of *aabb*, *abab*, or *abac*, Æ lightly and naturally expounds on a theosophical concept. The single-mindedness of his endeavor is, in fact, the chief complaint made against his poetry, which, for all its graceful music, is often said to lack variety and contrast. If form and thought throughout the book tend to be monotonous, there is nevertheless a traceable progress in the collection, which charts the history of a speaker who begins mired in Earth's miseries, moves to a fuller appreciation of the mysteries of nature, and finally finds a metaphysical guide in his own soul.

The first movement places the speaker's spiritual development within the poverty and unhappy history of Ireland. This situating of Æ's thought provides a valuable ballast for his higher flights, making it clear that his writing is an attempt to come to grips with, not escape from his condition. In the volume's second poem, "Recognition," he imagines a farmer who, "Over fields a slave at morning/ bowed him to the sod." This man, who, because of his intimacy with nature, should have been most in tune with deeper, spiritual levels, is blind to them most of the time because of the weight of his toil. Æ reveals that it is his own overburdened heart that is driving him to search for a meaning to life. In "The Place of Rest," for example, he writes that only the sea knows of the wounds that have lacerated his feelings.

The second grouping of poems is especially concerned with elucidating theosophical doctrines. The sequence of poems: "Dusk," "Night," "Dawn," and "Day," is an interesting and ironic example of his expositions. The irony resides in the way the contents of the poems reverse what would be expected from a casual perusal of the titles. Common sense would indicate that the sequence represents an upward movement, climaxing with "Day," when a man or woman's full powers would be on display.

According to theosophical premises, however, which hold that the hidden soul speaks with clearest accents in dreams, it is "Night" that forms the apex of the twenty-four-hour round. Then an individual is in contact with other souls and the universe. As Æ puts it, in dreams: "The olden Beauty shines: each thought of me/ Is veined through with its fire." It is heartbreaking to wake up from such heavenly communion. In "Dawn," Æ explains, one is "thrown downward" from the happy unconscious watches of the night. In "Day," the poet evokes images of prisons and darkness to indicate the sense of entrapment that comes when an individual is no longer synchronized with true being. In the sequence's closing irony, though, Æ mentions the one remaining joy that makes the day livable, that is, the chance that when awake one will remember a fragment of the previous night's dream.

These four poems are not representative of other poems in this section, which more typically begin with a picture of the Irish countryside. This reflects Æ's belief that, second to dreams, concourse with nature offered the surest way to rise to theosophical understanding. In "The Singing Silences," the poet begins by picturing a still night, with barely visible flowers, more visible constellations, and a thick, soporific mix of perfumes and natural sounds. Relaxed and drowsy, the speaker feels his life running in harmony with nature, but then his thought branches out and he speculates that, perhaps, analogously, the earth and the material universe are harmonized with another, less distinct realm of souls.

In the final set of poems, a spiritual guide often appears, either from without or within the speaker. This guide does not so much offer counsel as become an accompanying presence. In "Three Counsellors," for example, after the speaker receives instruction from people telling him to retire from life or, alternately, become an activist, he hears from one with a superior recommendation. This "all-seeing" adviser tells him: "Only be thou thyself." Such an admonition fits the tenor of theosophical thought, which holds that every person's soul contains all knowledge. Therefore, it would be more productive for individuals to plumb their own inner depths than to listen to teachers.

Whereas "Three Counsellors" states this message in an uncharacteristically didactic manner, it is presented in a more dramatic form in "The Hermit." Here, the speaker retires from city life and forms a relation with a mysterious old enchanter, who "Smiles and waves and beckons me." Although depicted as another person, this enchanter may best be viewed as the spokesman for the speaker's inner soul. "Alter Ego," the poem that immediately follows, makes this connection explicit. The piece begins by describing how the narrator is chasing a fairy lover through the forest. Unsuccessful by day, he is able to approach this being in his dreams, thus indicating that the entity is an integral part of himself. It is the anthropomorphic embodiment of the theosophical self. For the spiritual seeker, being allowed to catch a glimpse of the soul so personified is a step beyond the bare apprehension of principles into the ability to conduct an internal dialogue that will lead to new stages of enlightenment.

The danger with poetry that seeks to teach abstract theories is that it may become stilted and removed from the warmth of communication about more concrete human concerns. Æ largely avoids these dangers. Each of his poems is set up as a single moment of apprehension, and the moment is usually one triggered by an experience of nature or other everyday incident. In "Pity," for example, the speaker is sitting with a friend looking down at a town, and from this situation is generated his reflections. Grounding spiritual meditations in average occurrences gives them a homely concreteness. Moreover, by restricting himself to writing short poems, he is not tempted to treat the intricacies of theosophical dogma but uses each poem to lay open a single thought. Concerned above all to lead readers to see the naturalness of his convictions, Æ chooses simple words and a verse form that avoids intrusive rhymes. However, this verse form, although it flows with a soft rhythm, often reads as if it were transcriptions of a man talking to himself.

Æ cannot be placed in the front rank of poets because his writing is restricted to one subject, which is itself limited. His Irish contemporary and friend William Butler Yeats, a poet of the first rank, wrote poems that, like Æ's, were brief explications of his esoteric philosophy. Yeats, however, also wrote poems on Irish current events and encounters with people from different backgrounds, poems that retold old fables, and ambitious longer works such as "The Tower" (1928), which integrated aesthetic and political discourse. Æ lacked Yeats's range, and the specialized field he did explore, that of a rarefied philosophy, is of small scope. It is the poets who are concerned with the tragedies and comedies of normal women and men that usually have the broadest array of topics at their command. Within his limits, however, Æ produced a body of work of high quality. With consummate skill, he conveyed a feeling for both the beauty and power of nature and for the underlying depths of being that seem to exist behind life's veil.

James Feast

Bibliography:

Davis, Robert Bernard. *George William Russell ("Æ")*. Boston: Twayne, 1977. Brings out the predominant themes of Æ's verse, while pointing to such effects as the use of color words and occasional archaic diction.

Figis, Darrell. *Æ (George W. Russell): A Study of a Man and a Nation*. Dublin: Maunsel, 1916. Explains how important Æ was as a leader of a philosophical coterie that read his poetry as revelation more than as art. Figis argues that the writing suffered because this reverence made Æ unwilling to probe his doctrines sufficiently.

Kain, Richard M., and James H. O'Brien. *George Russell (Æ)*. Lewisburg, Pa.: Bucknell University Press, 1976. Provides background to link Æ's study of Indian thought to his writings. The authors examine "Three Counsellors," for example, as understandable in relation to his reading of the Indian religious epic *The Bhagavad Gītā* (about 400 C.E.).

Russell, George W. *Letters from Æ*. Edited by Alan Denson. London: Abelard-Schuman, 1961. Includes a reply from Æ to a reviewer of *Homeward*, in which he takes the critic to task for dismissing the book's Indian influence. He argues that the spiritual wealth of the East should not be overlooked.

Summerfield, Henry. *The Myriad-Minded Man: A Biography of George William Russell, "Æ" 1867-1935*. Totowa, N.J.: Rowman and Littlefield, 1975. Useful to supplement the poems insofar as it provides a detailed summary of the theosophical beliefs that influenced Æ. Also notes where he differed from the traditional interpretations of this thought.

THE HOMEWOOD TRILOGY

Type of work: Novel
Author: John Edgar Wideman (1941-   )
Type of plot: Psychological realism
Time of plot: Mid-nineteenth century to the 1980's
Locale: Homewood area of Pittsburgh, Pennsylvania
First published: 1985: *Damballah*, 1981; *Hiding Place*, 1981; *Sent for You Yesterday*, 1983

Principal characters:

> JOHN FRENCH, a wallpaper hanger
> FREEDA HOLLINGER FRENCH, his wife
> LIZABETH FRENCH LAWSON, their daughter
> JOHN (DOOT) LAWSON, her son, a writer and a college professor
> TOMMY LAWSON, another son of Lizabeth
> MOTHER BESS SIMPKINS, an old woman who befriends Tommy
> CARL FRENCH, a son of John and Freeda
> BROTHER TATE, Carl's best friend, an albino
> LUCY TATE, Brother's sister and Carl's lover

The Story:

Damballah. A young slave saw his fellow slave Orion, who refused to disavow his god Damballah or to obey his white master, dragged into the barn to be killed. Later, the boy listened as the ghost of Orion retold his stories, then threw Orion's head into the river.

Many years later, John French and his wife, Freeda Hollinger French, were living in Homewood. When his dog found a dead black baby in the garbage, Lemuel Strayhorn got John to help him bury it. On one occasion, Freeda stuck her hand through a window to keep her husband out of trouble. On another, after his little daughter Lizabeth ate a caterpillar, John ate one too, so that if it was poisonous, they would die together.

When she was a child, Hazel, a relative of the Frenches, was pushed too hard by her brother Faun, fell down the rickety stairs, and was crippled for life. Then her mother's hair caught fire and she, too, fell down the stairs and died. A year later, Hazel died. As Faun was dying, Lizabeth heard his final words, in which he expressed his regret.

When Freeda was near death, she began mumbling about a "Chinaman." Then she saw an Asian American in her doorway. She died the next morning.

Two watermelon stories were told. One concerned a drunk who was sitting on a stack of watermelons, fell through a plate glass window, and severed his arm. The other story, from slavery days, was about a barren woman named Rebecca, whose husband Isaac found the baby they had prayed for in a watermelon.

The radio singer Reba Love Jackson dedicated her first song to her own dead mother and her second to a man who had just lost his mother. Other songs were for a blind blues singer, for preaching, for a man she loved, for her fans, for her birthday, and finally, for Homewood.

John Lawson was remembering a happy day during his childhood, when he met his father for lunch. John suddenly realized that instead of entertaining a visiting poet, he should have gone to hear his own son perform at school.

When Rashad was in Vietnam, he sent his mother-in-law in Homewood a banner with a picture of her granddaughter on it. On his return home, Rashad became a drug dealer, living high but certain to get jailed or killed. Sadly, his mother-in-law took down the banner and put it away.

John Lawson's brother Tommy and his friends decided to rob a fence named Indovina, but their plan went wrong, and a black man was killed. Tommy told John that he would rather die than go back to prison. He was going to make a run for it. While Tommy was in prison, his mother Lizabeth went regularly to see him, even though it nearly broke her heart. One day, on her way home, she stopped to visit with her brother Carl and confided her fear of losing her faith in God.

Before the Civil War, the slave Sybela Owens and Charlie Bell, the white man who loved her, fled to the North and settled in Homewood. Sybela and Charlie were the progenitors of the French family. May, who told their story, bemoaned the fact that so many of their male descendants ended up dead or in prison. In conclusion, the author said that these stories constituted a letter to his own brother, who was in prison, and urged him not to give up hope.

Hiding Place. Clement, a black man who often ran errands for the elderly "Mother" Bess Simpkins, went up Bruston Hill to see her, but she acted peculiar. Tommy Lawson was there, hiding from the police. At first, Bess just fed Tommy and told him to leave, but then she took pity on him and let him remain with her. Bess began telling Tommy his family history. Meanwhile, Clement brought up whatever the two of them needed and kept quiet about where Tommy was. Someone found out, but when the police came after him, Tommy had disappeared. Though Bess had never meant to leave Bruston Hill alive, she decided to go down and plead Tommy's case with the law.

Sent for You Yesterday. In the prologue, the albino Brother Tate recounted his nightmare about a train, based on a childhood game. When they were boys, Carl French and he used to dare each other to remain on the track as a train came closer and closer. During that same period, the charismatic, piano-playing Albert Wilkes returned to Homewood after a long absence. Because she knew that someone would kill Albert, Freeda French tried to keep John at home and away from his friend. One night, she succeeded. That was the night Albert died.

Several years later, Brother Tate began to play the piano. After his little son Junebug was killed by his own siblings, who hated him because he was white in color like his father, Brother stopped playing. He also stopped talking, and Junebug's mother, Samantha, whom he loved dearly, went insane. One night, Brother Tate remained on the track and let the train hit him.

Carl had always loved Lucy. She let him make love to her when they were both thirteen, but after that Carl had to wait years between encounters. Long afterward, Lucy explained in Doot's presence that she could not marry Carl because he lacked the strength of the older generation, people like John and Freeda and even Albert. Doot had been learning from these stories, however. Finally he saw Brother Tate and Albert Wilkes, and it was then he found himself dancing.

Critical Evaluation:

Often called the greatest African American writer of the late twentieth century, John Edgar Wideman explores the issue of black identity from the vantage point of a boy from Homewood, the son of a waiter, who achieved great success in the white community. Attending the University of Pennsylvania on a scholarship, Wideman was a fine student, popular with his classmates, and a star basketball player. He was elected to Phi Beta Kappa and selected as a Rhodes Scholar, only the second African American in history to win that high honor. Returning to the United States, he became a professor at the University of Pennsylvania, where he was involved in starting a black studies program and began writing fiction. In his early works, Wideman remained in the mainstream of American literature. Even though he experimented in form, he was never far from James Joyce or from his own contemporaries. It was not until the 1970's, when he moved to Wyoming to concentrate on his writing, that Wideman broke free of tradition. During the eight years between the publication of *The Lynchers* (1973) and that of *Damballah*, the first volume in *The Homewood Trilogy*, Wideman evidently found both his own voice and his own identity.

Wideman's voice is in fact the blending of the many voices of his characters. Although the author's persona, John Lawson, appears frequently, he is usually doing the listening and the questioning, rather than the talking. For a time, he may serve as a narrator, if only to repeat what he hears, but then he tends to disappear, and other characters will report their thoughts, their memories, or their dreams.

Because Wideman sees the swirling internal lives of his characters, which are by nature baroque, as at least as important as their external lives, there is nothing minimalistic about his writing. Yet despite his wealth of material, his multitude of voices, and the drifts through time that are inevitable when the mind is unmoored from its anchor in the present, Wideman never abandons his readers, never leaves them in confusion. He possesses a sixth sense for where the boundaries are and when to return to previously introduced facts and previously established motifs. As a result, the extremely complex books of *The Homewood Trilogy* are also extremely readable.

The themes that unify the trilogy all appear at the beginning of *Damballah*, which opens with a letter to the author's brother in prison. Later, other doomed characters appear, including Tommy Lawson, who has been involved in a robbery and a killing, and John's brother-in-law Rashad, whose fancy clothes and showy car are sure evidence of illegal activity. There are also junkies, like Tommy's friend who shoots the crippled storekeeper because there are only thirteen dollars in his cash register. What these individuals do to the community is symbolized by their smashing of the old records that were so precious to John French. They are destroying not only their own lives but the heritage and the identity of their people.

Not only the criminals and the junkies are destroying Homewood. One of Wideman's women narrators mentions the young boys who show pride in the fact of having fathered infants but have no interest in providing a home for them. In contrast, though from time to time he might wander off, John French always returns to his family. He has a sense of responsibility toward his wife and the children who bear his name.

Not everything that is wrong with Homewood is the fault of its residents. Wideman speaks with scorn of the white people who own the community and mercilessly squeeze their profits out of its hardest-working residents. However, as Mother Bess tells Tommy, life has always been hard. It was not easy for Sybela to escape from slavery, but she did it, and Mother Bess expects Tommy, Sybela's descendant, to show the same courage.

Wideman does not imply that he knows answers to the problems in Homewood, but he does believe that when African Americans reject their identity and their heritage, they lose their most important source of strength. The comments Wideman makes to his brother about the meaning of home, the invocation to Damballah, and the inclusion of the family tree and the "begats" all indicate the most important theme in the trilogy: not merely the presence of the past, but the necessity of the past. Whereas the second novel of the trilogy ends with the initiation of Tommy, the fugitive from the law, the final book concludes with the redemption of John Lawson, who, like Wideman himself, though highly successful in the outside world, knows that he must look to Homewood for his full identity.

Rosemary M. Canfield Reisman

Bibliography:

Berben, Jacqueline. "Beyond Discourse: The Unspoken Versus Words in the Fiction of John Edgar Wideman." *Callaloo* 8 (Fall, 1985): 525-534. Looks at the differences between the deliberately misleading dialogue in *Hiding Place* and the truer expressions of feeling in the characters' nonverbal communications, dreams, and fantasies. An excellent analysis of Wideman's technique.

Birkerts, Sven. "The Art of Memory." *The New Republic* 207 (July 13, 1992): 42-49. Argues that Wideman, on the basis of his short fiction and *The Homewood Trilogy*, is the preeminent male African American writer of his generation. Praises his skill in moving through time and in and out of memory, in order to chronicle the history of a family, a place, and a people.

Coleman, James W. *Blackness and Modernism: The Literary Career of John Edgar Wideman.* Jackson: University Press of Mississippi, 1989. A major book-length study that includes three chapters on *The Homewood Trilogy*, a good summary of Wideman's literary career, a 1988 interview with the author, and a helpful bibliography.

Rowell, Charles H. "An Interview with John Edgar Wideman." *Callaloo* 13 (Winter, 1990): 47-61. Focuses on Wideman's perception of the influences that have shaped his literary development. Also contains revealing information about Wideman's themes and about the central importance of the South in African American culture.

Saunders, James Robert. "Exorcising the Demons: John Edgar Wideman's Literary Response." *The Hollins Critic* 29 (December, 1992): 1-10. Contends that Wideman's fiction reveals his growing understanding that, however fully he is accepted in the white world, a black intellectual must maintain his connection with his own people. Also comments sympathetically on how violence has affected Wideman's life and influenced his thinking.

THE HONORARY CONSUL

Type of work: Novel
Author: Graham Greene (1904-1991)
Type of plot: Psychological realism
Time of plot: Early to mid-1970's
Locale: Argentina
First published: 1973

Principal characters:
  EDUARDO PLARR, a middle-aged doctor
  CHARLEY FORTNUM, a British honorary consul
  CLARA FORTNUM, his wife and Plarr's mistress
  LEON RIVAS, a revolutionary priest
  COLONEL PEREZ, a policeman
  AQUINO, a kidnapper

The Story:
  Dr. Eduardo Plarr, a man incapable of making emotional commitments, had returned to the provincial town of Corrientes, Argentina, on the border between Argentina and Paraguay, after completing medical school in Buenos Aires, in order to be of use to the poor. He was also drawn back to the place by memories of his father, an Englishman who had sent his wife and young son to safety in Argentina many years before and who had remained behind in Paraguay.
  Plarr, clinging to the mistaken belief that his father was still alive, came into contact with a band of Paraguayan guerrillas led by Plarr's boyhood friend, Father Leon Rivas. Rivas, who had intended to be lawyer, was now a priest. His faith had failed him, however, and, feeling he could no longer quote the Bible to the poor to comfort them in their poverty, he decided the time had come to take some action. He and the mysterious revolutionary figure El Tigre came up with their plan to kidnap an American ambassador who was to visit the Corrientes area, in order to exchange him for political prisoners in Paraguay.
  Because Plarr through his relationship with Clara Fortnum, wife of the English honorary consul, would be able to discover the plans for the visit and the routes the car would take, Rivas included Plarr's father on the list of prisoners to be released. Plarr did not know that the old man had been shot during the escape of Aquino, another member of the band of kidnappers. In the hope that he might be able to save his father, Plarr agreed to help.
  Rivas and the kidnappers, acting on the information Plarr had provided them, were waiting at the designated point when Charley Fortnum, the honorary consul, unexpectedly passed them in his car. Fortnum had been anxious to return home to his pregnant wife and had left the ambassador early, thus disrupting the plans of the kidnappers. Expecting only the car of the American ambassador, the kidnappers abducted Fortnum and took him to a remote mud hut in the "barrio popular," where they kept him sedated with drugs obtained from Dr. Plarr. When Fortnum's life appeared to be in danger because of the effect of the drugs on a system ravaged by alcoholism, the kidnappers sent for Dr. Plarr, who was reluctantly drawn deeper into the affair.
  Plarr, who recognized Fortnum, informed the kidnappers of their mistake and of the un-likelihood that Fortnum would be worth anything as a bargaining tool, since he was only an

"honorary" consul. He hoped to take Fortnum home and pass off the whole affair to him as a drunken hallucination, but Rivas and the others refused to believe him and decided to continue with their plans. Plarr returned to the city and comforted Clara, who suspected that he knew more about Charley's disappearance than he was letting on. Colonel Perez of the local police, a friend of Plarr, also suspected that Plarr knew something about the situation, partly because his father's name was on the list of prisoners to be released.

Fortnum attempted to befriend his captors, thinking that this might facilitate his escape. The kidnappers supplied him with whiskey, which he shared with Aquino, who became slightly drunk. Fortnum thereupon attempted to escape, but Aquino shot him in the ankle. Plarr traveled to Buenos Aires to visit his mother and to find out what the British embassy there was doing about Fortnum's abduction. An official at the embassy suggested that he send word to the newspapers in Great Britain to prod the diplomatic service to take action in the case. It was apparent that the home office would be only too happy to sacrifice Charley Fortnum to make a statement to the guerrillas. Plarr attempted to organize an Anglo-Latin club to protest the inaction of the diplomatic service but without much success. Time seemed to be rapidly running out for Fortnum.

Plarr was contacted again by the kidnappers to treat Fortnum's injury. This time, Charley recognized him and realized his part in the conspiracy. Plarr treated his injury, but the kidnappers refused to let him return to the city. When it became apparent that the law was closing in, Marta, Rivas' wife, asked him to perform a final mass before shooting Fortnum, which he had promised to do if their demands were not met. The ceremony was interrupted by the voice of the policeman, Perez, speaking through a bullhorn, informing the kidnappers that the hut was surrounded by armed paratroopers and that they must free Fortnum and come out, one by one, by morning.

Miguel, one of the kidnappers who had been on watch outside the hut, was killed when he attempted to run back inside. Plarr convinced the kidnappers to vote on what to do about Fortnum, but they remained committed to their course of action, largely because of Aquino's influence. They passed the night in uneasy silence, waiting for the hour of Perez's ultimatum. Plarr decided that perhaps he could still do something to save those in the hut. He hoped to appeal to his friendship with Perez, but when he left the hut, he was shot and wounded. Father Rivas, who came out of the hut to aid his friend, was shot in the stomach. As the two old friends lay side by side, Plarr jokingly absolved Rivas, who then died. The paratroopers closed in.

Fortnum survived and became aware of Plarr's affair with Clara and of the fact that the unborn child was not his. He watched her at Plarr's funeral, appalled by her apparent lack of feeling for Plarr, who at the end had come to love her. He also thought with some fondness of his kidnappers, who were not necessarily "bad" men. Fortnum was informed of the official version of events, according to which Rivas had killed Plarr. He determined to confront Crichton, a representative of the English ambassador, with the truth: that Plarr had only been wounded by the first shot and was subsequently killed in cold blood. When he and Clara returned home, she began to show her true feelings about Plarr's death. Fortnum agreed that if the child was a boy, they would name him Eduardo.

Critical Evaluation:

Despite his difficulties in writing *The Honorary Consul*, Graham Greene considered it his favorite novel, partly because of the success he felt he had achieved in showing a believable change in Dr. Plarr's character. One of the more important themes treated in the novel is the idea of commitments, both personal and political. Dr. Plarr is presented early on as a man incapable of forming a commitment. His relationship with Clara, the wife of the honorary consul, Charley Fortnum, is only one in a long line of affairs. He does feel a strange attraction to her, finding it difficult to get her out of his thoughts, but it is not until the novel's end that he acknowledges any deeper feeling for her. His jealousy when he realizes how Fortnum loves his wife indicates that he, too, has begun to love her.

Plarr admires Rivas for his political commitment and his willingness to go to such extremes as political kidnapping to achieve his goals. Like several of Greene's other protagonists, Plarr is reluctant to help the kidnappers, but he does act, largely because he is interested in the fate of his father, whose freedom is part of the exchange deal the guerrillas hope to arrange. By the time he learns about his father's death, Plarr has other reasons for aiding the kidnappers: He wants to make Fortnum as comfortable in his captivity as possible (perhaps out of a sense of guilt he feels for his affair with Clara) and he wants to see his friend Father Rivas and the other kidnappers survive the experience.

Another important theme in the novel is fatherhood. Plarr is motivated to become involved with the kidnappers because of a commitment to a father he has never met and can scarcely remember. Unable after so long to picture his father, Plarr finds himself borrowing the features of Charley Fortnum in his imaginings. This is fitting, since at the end of the novel, Fortnum confesses to a feeling for Plarr that borders on the fatherly. The term "father" is also continually applied to the failed priest, Rivas. At first, Charley calls him "father," thinking to remind him that a father does not usually kill his son; later, he uses the title out of respect for Rivas' genuine priestly calling. Rivas cannot completely rid himself of his priesthood in his new role as revolutionary champion of the poor; even a blind man who comes to the hut senses that Rivas is a priest. As Colonel Perez's deadline draws nearer, the Catholic kidnappers begin to look more to Rivas the "father" than to Rivas the leader.

The theme of fatherhood is further developed in the situation at the novel's end. Fortnum, an Englishman married to the Paraguayan Clara, who is pregnant, agrees to name the child, if it is a boy, Eduardo. This family unit is an ironic mirror of Plarr's own. In a sense, Fortnum is more than a mere father figure to Plarr: He becomes Plarr's father, since it is through him that Plarr learns to love and become capable of commitment.

Despite its unhappy plot and tragic ending, *The Honorary Consul* is also a very humorous, comic novel. The initial situation—a bumbling group of kidnappers mistakenly kidnap a lowly British honorary consul in place of an American ambassador—certainly has its share of comic implications. The various characters have their measure of comic traits. Aquino, for example, goes out of his way to return Charley's change after buying him a bottle of liquor—but the comedy does not demean them. At the end, Fortnum is able to look back almost fondly on his captivity and remember the kidnappers with some respect.

A sense of the absurd permeates the novel and gives it much of its meaning. Father Rivas comes to the conclusion that God is "a great joker somewhere who likes to give a twist to things." Greene combines this sense of absurdity with a sense of hope. As Plarr says, "Nothing is ineluctable. Life has surprises. Life is absurd. Because it's absurd there is always hope."

Craig A. Larson

Bibliography:
Couto, Maria. *Graham Greene: On the Frontier.* New York: St. Martin's Press, 1988. Sees the novel as an exploration of social change among the liberation movements in Latin America. Excellent discussion of the role of personal faith in the struggle for dignity and freedom.

De Vitis, A. A. *Graham Greene*. Rev. ed. Boston: Twayne, 1986. An excellent starting point for a consideration of Greene's work. Analyzes structures and repeated themes throughout Greene's canon. Updated to include Greene's later novels.

Miller, R. H. *Understanding Graham Greene*. Columbia: South Carolina University Press, 1990. An excellent introduction to themes in the novel. Treats the realism of the work at some length.

Sharrock, Roger. *Saints, Sinners and Comedians: The Novels of Graham Greene*. Notre Dame, Ind.: Notre Dame University Press, 1984. Excellent treatment of the novel and its themes, particularly the theme of political commitment—"the political duty of a Christian in an unjust society."

Thomas, Brian. *An Underground Fate: The Idiom of Romance in the Later Novels of Graham Greene*. Athens: Georgia University Press, 1988. Insightful treatment of the romantic aspects of *The Honorary Consul*. Thomas shows how Greene deals with contemporary political problems that are intricately bound in Christian symbolism.

HOPSCOTCH

Type of work: Novel
Author: Julio Cortázar (1914-1984)
Type of plot: Parable
Time of plot: 1950's
Locale: Paris and Buenos Aires
First published: Rayuela, 1963 (English translation, 1966)

Principal characters:
 HORACIO OLIVEIRA, an unemployed Argentine intellectual
 LA MAGA, Horacio's lover
 MORELLI, a famous author

The Story:

The novel begins with a "Table of Instructions" for reading *Hopscotch,* which consists of two main books. The reader is given a choice between reading chapters 1 through 56 (the first two sections) and a more unconventional reading beginning with chapter 73 and proceeding in hopscotch fashion through all 153 chapters.

From the Other Side. Horacio Oliveira was an unemployed Argentine intellectual in his forties, living first in Paris and then, around 1950, in Buenos Aires. He searched day and night for some unknown element that he sensed was missing from his life. Adrift in Paris, he spent much of his time listening to jazz and classical records, smoking, drinking, wandering the streets, and playing intellectual mind games with a small group of his bohemian friends, a Russian, a North American couple, two Frenchmen, an Asian, and a Spaniard, who form a group, called the Serpent Club. His female companion, La Maga, was perceived by herself and by the others as their intellectual inferior, although she was much more attuned to her surroundings and to life. She was intuitive and straightforward, with neither the need nor a capacity for intellectualizing. La Maga was devoted to Oliveira, but he, despite having relationships with other women, was wildly jealous and eventually abandoned her because he suspected that she had or would in the future have an affair with Osip Gregorovius, the Russian in the group.

Oliveira left La Maga shortly after the death of her infant son, Rocamodour. Although he repented shortly thereafter and searched the streets of Paris for her, he never found her again. Friends suggested that she had gone to nurse Pola, a former lover of Oliveira who suffered from breast cancer. Later, Oliveira looked for her in her native Uruguay; occasionally he feared that she might have committed suicide by drowning.

From This Side. Oliveira had returned to Buenos Aires and was living with a former girlfriend, Gekrepten, across a narrow street from one of his oldest friends, Traveler, and his wife, Talita. Oliveira's search for La Maga had become more desperate, since his need to rationalize and intellectualize his entire existence had cost him what could have brought him happiness. Traveler arranged a job for Oliveira at the circus where he and Talita worked, but Oliveira's presence was a strain on his friends' marriage, since Oliveira began to see in Talita a replacement for, perhaps even a reincarnation of, La Maga. When the circus owner sold out and purchased an asylum for the insane, the three friends became caretakers there and left Gekrepten behind, much to her distress. Oliveira confused Talita with La Maga more often, but he recognized that he was infringing on Traveler's life. This led him to fear that Traveler might kill him. Eventually, he barricaded himself in his room and filled it with traps made of yarn, basins of water, and other objects placed strategically on the floor to warn him of Traveler's approach. Traveler nevertheless forced his way into the room, where Oliveira was precariously perched on the window sill. After doing all he could to calm his friend and keep him from jumping from the window, Traveler retreated to the courtyard below. Here, he joined Talita, who stood on a hopscotch drawing, and looked up at Oliveira, who still stood at the window.

From Diverse Sides. In the more unconventional, hopscotchlike reading of the novel, the "Table of Instructions" guides the reader through all but one of the fifty-six chapters of the first two sections and all of the chapters in the third section. In this reading, the "expendable" chapters are interspersed randomly within the chronological sequence of the first part of the book. The reader pieces together the collage of chapters, aided by the author's introductory instructions and numbers at the end of each chapter. This second reading constructs a novel that ends in a perpetual open-ended deadlock, alternating between chapters 58 and 131. In this reading, it becomes clear that Oliveira was recuperating and being cared for by Gekrepten, Traveler, and Talita. Whether he was recovering from his madness, a fall from the window, or some other accident or illness is never made clear.

Critical Evaluation:

Julio Cortázar was a major figure in what became known as the "boom" period in Latin American literature. A small group of writers, among them Jorge Luis Borges from Argentina, Alejo Carpentier from Cuba, Mario Vargas Llosa from Peru, José Donoso from Chile, Gabriel García Marquez from Colombia, and Carlos Fuentes from Mexico brought Latin American literature to international prominence within a span of less than thirty years in a literary flowering that had not been matched in Spanish literature since the "Siglo de Oro," the golden seventeenth century.

Hopscotch, Cortázar's second and most influential, best-known work, may well have had more of an impact on Latin American literary history than any other novel of the "boom" period because of its revolutionary and iconoclastic structure. It quickly became a best-seller in many languages, and it received more critical attention than any of Cortázar's other works.

Cortázar's work is a product of the two schools of writing that dominated Buenos Aires during the period between 1920 and 1940: the Florida group, with its European type of intellectualism, polished style, and universal themes; and the Boedo group, with its realistic scenes, urban themes, and unkempt style. Yet Cortázar's fiction remains universal, dealing with the search for self-identity, the fantastic that lurks beyond everyday reality, and the relationship between human beings and society. For Cortázar, the fantastic represents an alteration in the laws that govern an ordered reality according to the Western notion of logic and reason. Cortázar initially creates realistic settings and conventional characters in familiar situations, but he soon traps the reader by strange, even nightmarish, events that threaten the established order.

In *Hopscotch*, the author revolutionizes the conventional modes of novelistic expression and strives for a new mode of consciousness. That is the real subject of the book. Cortázar demonstrates that the so-called real, concrete world is only one side of a coin whose opposing side is the fantastic, the repressed, the hidden, the taboo. Like the surrealists, Cortázar ventures on the darker, ignored, and repressed side of human nature: obsessions, desires, and states between dream and wakefulness. He did not consider those darker dimensions to be pathological or abnormal; rather, he considered them to be pathways to a dimension of existence it is necessary to confront in order to appreciate life fully and in all its complexity.

In *Hopscotch*, Cortázar articulates his theory of the antinovel. Morelli, an old man, is a famous author, one read by the bohemians; his manuscript notes on the antinovel are discovered while he is in the hospital recovering from a car accident. It is Morelli who proposes to make the reader an accomplice in the creative process.

Cortázar not only challenges the traditional novelistic structure but also revolutionizes language. His aim is to destroy literary rhetoric and false, hollow, and outmoded forms. His use of imagery is richly varied. His characters play with words, engage in word games, and invent languages. Cortázar also makes unusual orthographic changes based on phonetics, joining words in strings to emphasize their vulgarity.

The author used structural and stylistic playfulness in his fiction as a means of saving himself from the crushing seriousness of the world he tried to influence through his writings. What is most striking about this novel's form are the "expendable chapters" and the "table of instructions," which tell the reader in what order to integrate the "expendable chapters" between those of the first two parts. The "expendable chapters" serve various functions. They form a running commentary on the construction of the novel and on the difficulties and contradictions inherent in it. They display the raw cultural material of the novel. Sometimes they suggest the frame of mind in which the novel might be read, at others they intentionally catch the readers off guard, jolting them out of their inertia. Cortázar often suggests inserting them contrapuntally, either to subvert the causality of the main narrative or to multiply its resonances.

The several, seemingly contradictory, endings to the novel (in some, Oliveira commits suicide, in others he does not) draw the reader into a bewildered but deep and critical commitment to the reading and involvement in the novel. Cortázar stresses that the reader is the most important character in the novel because without the reader there would be no novel. Since the reader is the re-creator of the action, Cortázar's understanding of the relationship between character and action differs from the traditional view. In *Hopscotch*, the parts and whole are inseparable; not only are characters agents who help build the story, that story is also a part of their identity and only in their being does it become meaningful. The readers must assimilate the text and reconstruct a story on the basis of the author's clues and their own sensitivity and knowledge. The story becomes meaningful only when it becomes part of the reader's experience and understanding.

The readers are assisted in interpreting the novel by the characters who discuss Morelli's aesthetics and thereby reveal the organizational principles of the novel. The novel is a variation on a number of experiences; the characters' world shapes the reader's larger world through the act of reading, and the characters function as guides to the reader. Cortázar demonstrates that an objective reality can be known to people only through their experience of it. The initial step in the process of understanding is the emotional and intuitive response; the reader completes the process by intellectually understanding the emotional effect. Cortázar's aim is not merely to create interesting characters but to design a novel in which characters and action build each other. In this process, the reader becomes the central organizing factor.

Genevieve Slomski

Bibliography:
Alazraki, Jaime, and Ivar Ivask, eds. *The Final Island: The Fiction of Julio Cortázar.* Norman: University of Oklahoma Press, 1978. Insightful reading of Cortázar's novels and short stories in the context of the "boom" period in Latin American literature. Contains a bibliography.

Boldy, Steven. *The Novels of Julio Cortázar*. Cambridge, England: Cambridge University Press, 1980. Offers an in-depth reading of Cortázar's major novels, examining the author's stylistic experimentation as a living process. Contains a bibliography.

Garfield, Evelyn Picon. *Julio Cortázar*. New York: Frederick Ungar, 1975. An excellent introduction to the major works of Cortázar. Contains biographical information on the author as well as a discussion of parody in his work.

Peavler, Terry J. *Julio Cortázar*. Boston: Twayne, 1990. In this thought-provoking overview and comprehensive treatment of Cortázar's short stories and novels, the author places Cortázar's work in a literary and historical context. Contains a chronology and bibliography.

Yovanovich, Gordana. *Julio Cortázar's Character Mosaic*. Toronto, Canada: University of Toronto Press, 1991. Excellent study of characterization in Cortázar's longer fiction. Discusses the lack of traditional treatment of character in *Hopscotch*. Also includes a bibliography.

HORACE

Type of work: Drama
Author: Pierre Corneille (1606-1684)
Type of plot: Tragedy
Time of plot: Antiquity
Locale: Rome
First performed: 1640; first published, 1641 (English translation, 1656)

> *Principal characters:*
> HORACE, the most courageous of the Roman soldiers
> SABINE, his Alban wife
> OLD HORACE, his father, formerly a soldier
> CAMILLE, Horace's sister
> CURIACE, Sabine's brother, in love with Camille
> VALERE, a Roman soldier in love with Camille
> JULIE, the confidante of both Sabine and Camille
> TULLE, the ruler of Rome

The Story:

The cities of Rome and Alba were at war, although they had been united by ties of patriotism and blood, for Alba was the birthplace of the founders of Rome, Romulus and Remus. Sabine, the wife of Horace, was divided in her loyalties between the city of her birth, where her brothers still lived, and the city of her famous warrior-husband. The battle was to be decided by armed combat between three heroes from each side. Sabine drew little comfort from that resolution, for it meant the defeat either of her kinsman or of her husband. Camille, the betrothed of Curiace, the Alban warrior-brother of Sabine, felt her loyalties divided between her beloved and her brother Horace. Even though the oracles had been favorable toward her coming marriage, she envisioned the imminent horror in her dreams.

Before the battle took place, Curiace visited Camille at the home of her father, Old Horace. He declared his abiding love for her, though as an Alban patriot he remained loyal to his city. They commented on the oracles and wished for a lasting peace. When the two warriors met, however, Horace was insistent on the outcome of the trial by combat. Curiace, who stressed the need for peaceful understanding, was dismayed to hear that his prospective brothers-in-law were to represent the Romans. He was even more oppressed in spirit when a messenger announced that he and his two brothers were to defend the honor of Alba. Horace wanted no sympathy from Curiace, though he bore him no personal ill will, but Curiace saw love of wife and family as superior to Horace's kind of patriotism.

Horace allowed the lovers a moment together before the battle. Camille, mindful of the fact that she was the daughter and sister of famous warriors, denounced the patriotism that could make her choose between love of family and of her future husband. She begged Curiace to avoid a battle that could only end in tragedy. His first duty, however, was to his country, as he told her brutally. Sabine and Camille then begged for the cause of love of home and family, while Horace and Curiace defended honor and patriotism. The women were unsuccessful in their suit, and as the young men went off to prepare for the combat, Old Horace comforted them. Young Horace, loving to his sister and kind to his aged parent, sought glory in battle; Curiace, no less patriotic, felt that he had lost wife, brothers, and brothers-in-law by a grim turn of fate.

Sabine, given at first to confusion and later to bitterness, lamented her sad position as the sister of the Alban warriors and the wife of their adversary. When she inquired of her friend Julie whether her husband or her brothers had been vanquished, she was told that no resolution had been reached; the king had only just arranged the combatants and charged them to fight to the death, that the fate of the two principalities might be determined. Camille, wearied by her solitary wonderings and fears, joined the discussion. She renounced the deceptive oracle, and neither the wife nor the prospective bride could find solace for their anxiety and grief. Sabine declared that a wife was the most bereaved, to which Camille replied that her sister-in-law had never been in love. For the moment the controversy was resolved by Old Horace, who declared that Rome suffered most; all else was in the hands of the gods.

Julie brought word that the Alban brothers had been victorious, that two of Old Horace's sons were dead, and that Horace had fled the battlefield. The old man was appalled that his son could see his brothers die without drawing new courage from such defeat and either go down to death or glory. Camille felt some relief that both her lover and brother were for the moment spared, and Sabine was content that her husband was alive. Old Horace could share in none of these sentiments, for he was concerned above all for honor, country, manliness.

Valere, dispatched by Tulle to bring comfort to Old Horace, told of the outcome of the battle. He said that Horace had retreated as a ruse in order to attack the Albans at a disadvantage and that he had killed all three. The old man, his family honor vindicated, rejoiced in the face of Camille's great sorrow. Left alone, she lamented the death of her two brothers and her lover and reviled Rome as the symbol of patriotic infamy.

Into this scene of unrestrained grief came the victorious warrior accompanied by his faithful soldier-in-arms bearing the swords of the vanquished brothers. Displaying the arms, now the spoils of war, that had killed their brothers, he taunted Camille with the glory of Rome, but she responded that his deed was murder. When he accused her of disloyalty, her replies inflamed him to murder, and with the sword of Curiace he killed his sister, a deed he defended as an act of justice. Sabine was shocked by her husband's bloody deed, and he crudely tried to comfort her, feeling that he had performed an act of patriotism justified by the insult to his country. The deeds of heroism he recounted only heightened the despair of his wife, who declared that her only wish was to die.

Old Horace, proud of his son's achievements but saddened by his vindictiveness, was distressed over the turn of events, which might now deprive him of his last offspring. The fate of his son he must now leave to his king. Tulle, in response to the eloquent plea by Valere, allowed Horace to speak for himself. The hero and murderer wanted most to die, knowing that his past glory had been dimmed by the murder of his own sister. Sabine begged the king to kill her that her husband might live; Old Horace wished the king to save the last of his sons. Tulle, after he had heard all the pleas, felt that Horace's fate rested with the gods, that a king could only pardon that which he could not condone.

Critical Evaluation:

Horace is typical of Pierre Corneille's tragedies for presenting a tragic hero caught in a dilemma, in this case having to choose between the exigencies of patriotism and those of familial affection. In this respect, the play belongs to a long classical tradition, and in its construction *Horace* adheres to the dramatic principles generally followed by Corneille and his great younger contemporary, Jean Racine. The plot develops rapidly, with considerable suspense. After a brief expository opening, setting the stage for the war between Rome and Alba, there is the first surprise, or *coup de théâtre*: War as such will be averted and the outcome will be decided by three warriors on each side. That leads to the crisis: The three Horace and the three Curiace brothers have been chosen to represent their respective states. The first news of the struggle indicates that the Curiace brothers have triumphed. Then the truth, the second *coup de théâtre*, is revealed: Horace ran away merely as a ruse to enable him to eliminate the Curiace brothers one at a time. The struggle has been resolved in favor of Rome. A second crisis now arises, for which Corneille was much criticized by his contemporaries because with it he appeared to violate the law of the unity of action. Horace's sister Camille bitterly condemns the harsh Roman ethic that has caused her the loss of Curiace. The third surprise is Horace's unexpected murder of Camille.

Horace is a singularly unattractive hero. One can hardly sympathize with his single-minded approach to glory, which ignores all human sentiment. A hero who murders his own sister inevitably strikes the spectator as an impossible extremist who cannot inspire any feelings other than disgust. The circumstances of his struggle with the Curiaces hardly give him pause, and he never expresses any sense of revulsion at what lies ahead, as does Curiace. Horace seems to suppress whatever normal human feelings he has in favor of his patriotism. One may point out that although the conflict in Horace's soul is not apparent in the words, it can be revealed by the actor who plays the role. This is undoubtedly the locus of difficulty in accepting *Horace* as tragedy, for the tragic hero should evince a capacity for suffering. Most critics who have written on the nature of tragedy would agree with the famous critic Cleanth Brooks's assertion that tragedy deals "with the meaning of suffering" and that in no tragedy "does the hero merely passively endure."

The only defense of Horace seems to lie in the fact that, after his orgy of blood-letting, he seems momentarily pervaded by a feeling of despair. To the accusations of Valere, a disappointed suitor of Camille, he responds by agreeing that he deserves death. Yet it soon becomes clear that the real reason behind Horace's desire for death is his conviction that anything he does henceforth is bound to be anticlimactic. He has attained the apogee of glory, from which the only path open to him leads downhill, to mediocrity.

Frustration with Horace can lead the reader to seek the real tragic hero elsewhere. Curiace, for instance, suffers deeply because of the dilemma in which he is caught. Of the range of attitudes toward duty that are explored in the play, his is the most human. He is not, however, the kind of active character that Horace is, and he does nothing to shape his destiny.

Besides Horace, the only active character is Camille, who resembles the heroines of Racine in that her inability to control her passion results in her destruction. Hers is indeed a tragic role, though she cannot be considered the central character. In reality, the fate of all the characters in *Horace* is essentially tragic, but there is no escaping the conclusion that Horace is the central character and that, if this play is tragic, Horace must be considered a tragic hero, in spite of his apparent insensibility. Lockert's view that Horace has been forcing himself to appear inhuman is helpful here: Horace has had to do violence to his gentler feelings, and as a result he cannot entertain any doubt that he is right. Hence the appearance of insensibility. The very fact that he must rationalize his position to himself makes him highly vulnerable to any allegation that his ideal is unworthy. When Camille attacks his patriotism, he reacts violently as a man who will stop at nothing to prevent his painfully acquired position from being destroyed.

Horace can be compared to Lady Macbeth, who calls upon the spirits of night to dry up her human feelings, thus revealing that the heartlessness she displays is not natural to her. This is made manifest in her sleepwalking scene, in which we see the terrible guilt that weighs on her conscience. It was not Corneille's intention to show such a development in his tragic hero, nor could he have done so in the limits prescribed by the unities, especially of time. Nevertheless, the last scene presents a Horace who has been disillusioned and is doomed to an existence devoted primarily to justifying, at least to himself, what he did.

"Critical Evaluation" by Robert A. Eisner

Bibliography:
Abraham, Claude. *Pierre Corneille*. New York: Twayne, 1972. An excellent introduction to Pierre Corneille's plays. Thoughtful analysis of the ethical and moral conflicts in *Horace*, a tragedy in which characters must choose between their loyalty to the state and their love for family members.

Brereton, Geoffrey. *French Tragic Drama in the Sixteenth and Seventeenth Centuries*. London: Methuen, 1973. A general introduction to French tragedies of the sixteenth and seventeenth centuries. Also contains two long, lucid chapters on Corneille. Brereton analyzes Corneille's skill in using historical sources to create powerful conflicts among his characters.

Harwood-Gordon, Sharon. *Rhetoric in the Tragedies of Corneille*. New Orleans: Tulane University, 1977. Very clear rhetorical analyses of Corneille's major tragedies. In her discussion of *Horace*,. Harwood-Gordon effectively contrasts the passionate speeches of Sabine with the insensitive arguments of the two Horaces.

Muratore, Mary Jo. *The Evolution of the Cornelian Heroine*. Potomac, Md.: Studia Humanitatis, 1982. Explores the evolution in Corneille's representations of heroines in the tragedies he wrote between the 1630's and his retirement in 1674. Muratore contrasts Sabine and Camille, the leading female characters in *Horace*.

Nelson, Robert J. *Corneille, His Heroes and Their Worlds*. Philadelphia: University of Pennsylvania Press, 1963. Examines the changing meaning of heroism and the conflicts between love and duty that Corneille's male characters face. Discusses the ethical and moral dimensions in *Horace*.

THE HORSE'S MOUTH

Type of work: Novel
Author: Joyce Cary (1888-1957)
Type of plot: Picaresque
Time of plot: Late 1930's
Locale: London
First published: 1944

> *Principal characters:*
> GULLEY JIMSON, an unconventional artist
> SARA MONDAY, his onetime model and "wife"
> D. B. COKER, a barmaid
> HARRY "NOSY" BARBON, an aspiring artist
> GEORGE HICKSON, an art collector and Jimson's sometime patron
> A. W. ALABASTER, a critic
> SIR WILLIAM BEEDER, a rich collector
> C. PLANT, Jimson's closest friend

The Story:

Just out of prison, Gulley Jimson looked up his old friend Coker, the plain barmaid at the Eagle. Coker wanted him to press a lawsuit over some of his paintings; if Gulley collected, Coker would collect from him. At last, Gulley managed to get away from her and return to his studio in an old boat shed. The shack roof leaked, and the walls sagged. His paints and brushes had either been stolen or ruined by rain and rats, but the Fall, although damaged, was there. The Fall, depicting Adam and Eve in their fall from grace, would be his masterpiece.

Gulley had a questionable reputation as an artist. Several years back, he had painted some nudes of Sara Monday, startling portraits in the Impressionist style of a lovely woman in her bath. Sara had lived with Gulley as his wife. When the breakup came, she had kept the pictures and sold most of them to a collector named Hickson. She kept one or two for herself. Gulley, past sixty years old now, had done nothing since the Sara nudes to enhance his reputation, but he still had faithful followers of eccentric outcasts and young Nosy. Nosy, wanting to be an artist, worshiped art and Gulley Jimson.

To complete the Fall, Gulley needed paints and brushes. In order to get Gulley to see Sara Monday and secure evidence for a lawsuit to compel Hickson to return the Sara nudes, Coker bought him some paints and brushes. Gulley periodically worked on the Fall, driven primarily by a compulsion to paint, sometimes by desire for a beer or some food.

When Coker pinned him down and took him to see Sara, Gulley was stunned to find her an aging woman to whom he felt drawn even while he pitied her. Sara willingly signed a statement that she had given the pictures to Hickson; then she tried to renew her affair with Gulley, who responded with his old ardor. Sara had been badly treated by a succession of men, but, like Gulley, she had few complaints. Both felt that the short-lived prosperity and good times they had enjoyed were worth the pain they currently were suffering.

Working intermittently on the Fall, Gulley frequently had to trick Coker into buying him paints. Once she persuaded him to go with her to Hickson to try to get the pictures or a settlement for them. When Hickson seemed ready to settle a small sum on Gulley, even though

Hickson had legally taken the pictures in return for a debt, Gulley slipped some valuable snuffboxes in his pocket and was caught by Hickson and the police. Although this bit of foolishness cost him six months in jail, he maintained a bemused tolerance for Hickson.

In jail, Gulley received a letter from the self-styled Professor Alabaster, who planned to write a life history of the painter of the Sara Monday pictures. Gulley thought the idea ridiculous until he decided there might be money in it. He was energized with an idea for another masterpiece, and after his release, he hurried back to the boat shed to finish the Fall and get started on his new work. He found Coker pregnant and in possession of the shed. Betrayed by her lover and her job at the pub lost, she had moved to the shed with her mother. Gulley had to find some way to get the Fall out. Before he had made any plans, he met "Professor" Alabaster. Alabaster not only wanted to write Gulley's life history but also hoped to sell some of Gulley's work to Sir William Beeder, a collector who admired the paintings possessed by Hickson. Gulley tried to interest Alabaster and Sir William in one of the new masterpieces he was going to paint, but Sir William had a great desire for one of the Sara nudes or something similar.

Gulley still hoped to interest Sir William in the Fall, but when he went again to the boat shed, he found that Coker's mother had cut it up to mend the roof. Gulley decided there was no use in losing his temper again and doing something foolish; then he would land back in jail before he could do another masterpiece or make a sale to Sir William. Besides, he suddenly realized that he was tired of the Fall.

In the meantime, if Sir William wanted a Sara nude, perhaps Gulley could persuade old Sara to give him one of the small ones she had kept; but Sara, understandably nostalgic, loved to take out the portraits of her lovely youth and dream over them. Gulley tried various schemes without success.

When Sir William left London, Gulley persuaded Alabaster into giving him the key to Sir William's apartment. He pawned the furniture and art collections to buy paints and reluctantly let a sculptor rent one end of the drawing room to work on a piece of marble. Gulley, in what he considered proof of his honesty, kept the pawn tickets so that Sir William could redeem his possessions. He used one wall for a typically epic painting, on which he could not stop working, that he was sure would please Sir William. When the owner returned unexpectedly, however, Gulley decided to talk to him from a distance and ducked out.

With faithful Nosy, Gulley went to the country for a time. There he devised a new scheme to obtain money, but a thug beat him up and sent him to the hospital. While recuperating, Gulley had another vision for a masterpiece and wrote Sir William about his idea. Alabaster replied for Sir William, who still insisted on a simple, non-epic, not-painted-on-my-wall nude and thanked Gulley for "caring" for the furniture.

By the time Gulley got back to the boat shed, Coker had had her baby and was firmly installed there. Gulley was welcome but did not feel at ease. Gulley moved into another empty building and set about preparing the wall for a painting of the Creation. He was aided by Nosy and several young art students he had charmed. He tried repeatedly to get a nude from Sara. When Hickson died and gave the Sara pictures to the nation, Gulley was famous. Alabaster found a backer for the life history, and distinguished citizens called on Gulley to see about buying more pictures from him. In the meantime, Gulley copied one of his old pictures of Sara from the original in the Tate Gallery and had sold it as a study to Sir William for an advance payment of fifty pounds.

He made one last try to get a picture from Sara. When she refused, he inadvertently pushed her down the cellar stairs and broke her back. Realizing that he was running out of time, he raced back to the Creation and painted like a madman, trying to finish the picture. He never completed the painting; his landlord tore the building down over his head. Thrown from his scaffold, he regained consciousness in a police ambulance and learned that he had suffered a stroke. He did not grieve. Drawing on the wisdom of a lifetime of resistance to conventional thinking, he told a nun who said he should pray instead of laughing, "same thing, mother."

Critical Evaluation:

The painter Gulley Jimson, the protagonist of Joyce Cary's *The Horse's Mouth*, is a man nearing seventy who, despite physical infirmities and nearly total poverty, remains undiminished in his maverick resistance to all social systems, which he regards as lethal to the development of an individual's imaginative freedom. Cary describes Jimson in a preface as "an original artist . . . always going over the top into No Man's Land." Jimson is an aging iconoclast whose intelligence, education, and incisive understanding of human behavior had not prevented him from living beyond the pale of respectable society amid a loose grouping of bohemians, eccentric thinkers, and working-class individualists. Jimson's choice to reject the rewards available to a man of his talent who accepts the standards of the academy is strongly supported by Cary's depiction of the artistic establishment as a clique of snobs and poseurs. Jimson's choice is ultimately inevitable as a result of Jimson's complete commitment to an artistic vision of existence. As he puts it, he did not plan to start being an artist: "It starts on you. Why I had a real job once, a job of work. But art got me and look at me now."

From the moment he saw a painting by Edouard Manet, the French Impressionist master, which "gave me the shock of my life," Jimson has been subordinating every claim on his attention that is not art. With something like religious zeal, he tries to capture the wonder of the universe with brush and pigment. For him, the moment when he confronts a clean surface and makes his first stroke is like "a miracle," an instant of exultation surpassing any other sensual or intellectual act, transforming an object or space "into a spiritual fact, an eternal beauty," which momentarily makes the artist feel "I am God." Jimson understands this attraction and has ordered his life accordingly. He has been "married" several times, suffered many financial tribulations, lost friends and family, spent time in jail and in the hospital, been insulted by collectors and critics (whom he calls "crickets" and discusses in intricate analogies involving the game of cricket) and is worse off in his seventh decade than at any other point in his life. He is also as happy as he has ever been, still excited by the images of light and color he sees in the infinitely varied landscape of London and still able to confront the disappointments and rebuffs of the world with an antic humor that Cary makes one of the defining elements of Jimson's character.

Drawing on his own experiences as an art student in Paris and Edinburgh and a life-long fascination with painting, Cary produced a picture of the art scene that remains accurate. Cary renders the life of Jimson, friends, and the streets of London in the 1930's with a sense of detail and dialogue that rivals Charles Dickens. This is an aspect of his skill in the traditionally narrated novel and serves as a ground for the novel's major achievement—the continuous revelation of character through the flow of first-person narration. Jimson's sensibility is thus effectively established, as are his volatile moods.

The novel is conceived as a kind of memoir dictated to "my honorary secretary" from the hospital where Jimson is confined after a stroke. This framing device enables Cary to let Jimson speak, rather than write, in a combination of a recollective past and an immediate present, with the narrative recording actions as they occur. This method conveys the spontaneity and impulsiveness of Jimson's responses to the world and captures the excitement that inspires his artistic vision. It is also more logical for the character; Jimson is not the type to write a book.

Clearly influenced by James Joyce's *Portrait of the Artist as a Young Man* (1916) and *Ulysses* (1922), Cary has located the essential action of the novel in Jimson's mind, and has given him a voice that reflects the precept of Jimson's spiritual guide, William Blake (called "Old Bill," "Billy," or "Old Randipole" in affectionate but awestruck familiarity), that "Energy is Eternal Delight." From the opening passage, which records Jimson's rhapsodic responses to the light on the Thames, to his evocation of sensual ecstasy with his truest love Sara Monday, to his almost delirious exuberance as a new picture begins to take shape, Cary has devised a vocabulary and syntax which expresses the psychological condition of an artist's elevated consciousness.

In addition to the intricate, poetic rhythms of the descriptive passages, which echo the patterns of Jimson's thoughts as he assimilates color and light and gathers these fragments of perception into a vision of human existence, the structural arrangements of the narration are purposely paralleled to the shape and form of the painting. The syntax duplicates the manner in which Jimson puts the parts of the painting together as Cary works toward as lucid and incisive an examination of the creative process as might be found in modern literature. Although he is concentrating on the efforts of a visual artist, the dexterity with which Jimson handles a traditional vocabulary suited to a discussion of aesthetic issues effectively makes *The Horse's Mouth* as much about the writer's life as the painter's.

Gulley Jimson is Cary's portrait—in the manner of Joyce's conception of Stephen Dedalus—of the artist as a street-smart, wary, aging enthusiast whose often sardonic humor and self-protective outlaw antics are a cover for his wounded romanticism and fragile idealism. Jimson calls the artist "A son of Los," the figure in Blake's mythic pantheon who is the Prophet of the Lord. Jimson still believes that "the world of imagination is the world of eternity" and has tried to conduct his life accordingly.

"Critical Evaluation" by Leon Lewis

Bibliography:
Adams, Hazard. *Joyce Cary's Trilogies: Pursuit of the Particular Real*. Gainesville: University Presses of Florida, 1983. Discusses Cary's philosophical and political ideas in *The Horse's Mouth*. Particularly good on Cary's uses of William Blake's poetry.
Bloom, Robert. *The Indeterminate World: A Study of the Novels of Joyce Cary*. Philadelphia: University of Pennsylvania Press, 1962. Considers Cary's attempt to combine the serious and the comic in a single novel; includes a useful list of Cary's other publications.
Cook, Cornelia. *Joyce Cary: Liberal Principles*. New York: Barnes & Noble Books, 1981. An incisive overview of the themes, motifs, and intellectual backgrounds of *The Horse's Mouth* from a social perspective.
Echeruo, Michael J. C. *Joyce Cary and the Dimensions of Order*. New York: Harper & Row, 1979. Examines *The Horse's Mouth* as an expression of an existential impulse toward human freedom and artistic expression.
Wolkenfeld, Jack. *Joyce Cary: The Developing Style*. New York: New York University Press, 1968. Emphasizes the use of poetic language in the depiction of the protagonist's artistic vision and his personal psychology.

THE HOUND OF THE BASKERVILLES

Type of work: Novel
Author: Sir Arthur Conan Doyle (1859-1930)
Type of plot: Detective and mystery
Time of plot: Late nineteenth century
Locale: London and Devon, England
First published: serial, 1901-1902; book, 1902

> *Principal characters:*
> SHERLOCK HOLMES, the world's greatest detective
> DR. WATSON, his friend and chronicler
> SIR HENRY BASKERVILLE, the Canadian heir of Sir Charles Baskerville
> BARRYMORE, an old family servant of the Baskervilles
> MRS. BARRYMORE, his wife, also a servant at Baskerville Hall
> DR. MORTIMER, a concerned neighbor of Sir Henry Baskerville
> MR. STAPLETON, a naturalist
> MISS STAPLETON, a woman posing as Mr. Stapleton's sister
> MR. FRANKLAND, a neighbor
> SELDEN, an escaped murderer

The Story:

When Dr. Mortimer visited Holmes and Watson in their rooms in Baker Street, he brought a centuries-old account of the death of the debauched and ruthless Sir Hugo Baskerville, allegedly killed by a diabolical hound. Mortimer's friend and neighbor, Sir Charles Baskerville, had recently died under circumstances which suggested that this ancient curse on the family persisted. Mortimer was concerned for the safety of the Canadian heir, Sir Henry Baskerville, who was to arrive in London the next day en route to the Baskerville estate in Devon. Mortimer also described the few neighbors on the moor, a group consisting of Mr. Stapleton, Miss Stapleton, Mr. Frankland, and Mr. Frankland's daughter.

Arriving with Mortimer the next day, Sir Henry showed Holmes a note warning him to stay away from Baskerville Hall, and Holmes discovered evidence that his visitors had been followed. Although Holmes was intrigued by the problem, he said that he had other obligations to honor first, so it was agreed that Watson should go to Baskerville Hall as companion, observer, and protector. From the Hall, Watson wrote Holmes regularly and in detail about everything he learned and observed.

The moor, already forbidding at night, was now terrorized by Selden, the notorious murderer, who had escaped from Princetown prison. Added to the presence of Selden and the possibility that the diabolical, night-stalking Hound of the Baskervilles had returned was the peculiar behavior of Barrymore and his wife. On the first night, Sir Henry and Watson heard a woman's loud sobs. Later, Watson observed Barrymore stealthily placing a candle in a second floor window. By catching him in the act, Watson and Sir Henry forced Barrymore and his wife to admit that he was signaling Selden, the murderer, who was Mrs. Barrymore's younger brother. Sir Henry and Watson tried unsuccessfully to catch Selden by following his answering light. In the process, Watson noticed a tall, thin figure on a hill and deduced that this might be the person who had warned Sir Henry against coming to Dartmoor. He determined to find this man and discover his intentions. Miss Stapleton, mistaking Watson for Sir Henry, urgently warned him to leave Devon. Sir Henry, meeting her later, was overwhelmed by her beauty and character and was on the point of declaring his love for her when Stapleton suddenly appeared on the moor and castigated Sir Henry for daring to declare his affections. Stapleton followed this odd action by a visit during which he begged Sir Henry's pardon and explained how accustomed he had become to his sister's company. He invited Sir Henry to dinner and Sir Henry happily accepted.

During this time, Watson had discovered that a young woman had written a letter to Sir Charles asking him to meet her at the spot where the ghostly hound later chased him and frightened him to death. After speaking with her, he found that she had written the note at Stapleton's urging. On his return to Baskerville Hall, Watson observed through Frankland's telescope a boy running across the moor toward the remains of the Neolithic stone huts on the hillside. Since Barrymore and his wife had been supplying Selden, the supplies carried by this boy must be for the mysterious stranger Watson had seen on the moor. Watson examined a number of stone ruins until he found one containing evidence of habitation. There he sat and waited. At nightfall, he heard footsteps and a familiar voice. It was Holmes, who had been keeping watch on the moor while reading Watson's reports. Scanning them for clues, he had investigated Stapleton's background, finding that he was in fact another heir to the Baskerville fortune and that the young woman living with him was his wife. As Holmes and Watson spoke, a terrible scream announced the death of Selden, who had been wearing Sir Henry's cast-off clothes and had fallen fatally while pursued by the spectral hound. Laying a trap that night, Holmes, Watson, and Inspector Lestrade—just arrived from Scotland Yard—ambushed and killed the hound as it stalked Sir Henry. Stapleton escaped into the Grimpen Mire, where he apparently took a wrong step and sank into the bog. Stapleton, it transpired, had been the spy in London, and it had been the woman posing as his sister who had sent the warning note.

Critical Evaluation:

Because the Sherlock Holmes tales are one of the first instances of a magazine series based on one character, Sir Arthur Conan Doyle may be considered, in a limited sense, a literary innovator. As a writer of detective stories, he made no secret of his admiration for Edgar Allan Poe and Poe's creation, the French detective, Dupin. His admiration for Poe's plots was nearly matched by the impression made upon him by the American author's ability to create gloomy ambience. Building on the work of predecessors like Poe and Wilkie Collins, Doyle created two characters whose popularity was unrivaled until the advent of Agatha Christie's characters, Hercule Poirot and Captain Hastings.

It is ironic that Doyle, who did not consider the Holmes stories to be serious literary efforts and, in fact, tried to kill the Holmes character in his story, "The Final Problem," in *The Memoirs of Sherlock Holmes* (1894), is immortalized as the creator of one of the most famous figures in detective fiction. Despite his own disinclination to continue the Holmes stories after he had established himself as the author of such novels as *The White Company* (1891), Doyle nevertheless began again. The expenses of his home and family after success had been achieved continued to increase beyond even his expanded earning power, and the public refused to believe that Holmes was dead. Some, believing implicitly in Holmes's existence, were convinced either that Watson had made an error or that the stupid intermediary, Doyle, had garbled the information. When Doyle needed money again, the public was waiting for this particular product.

The series of tales in *The Return of Sherlock Holmes* (1905) is the answer to Doyle's need and to the demands of the public. However, this series of stories was preceded by *The Hound of the Baskervilles*, a novel-length story that Doyle wrote after an acquaintance told him a similar tale one day on Dartmoor, when damp and dismal weather made playing golf impossible. Doyle's fascination with the subject persuaded his friend to take Doyle on a small walking tour of the area. In this case, the plot came to him before he began to consider the character he would use to unify it. He decided to use a well-known character who would need no introduction. In this way, *The Hound of the Baskervilles* became a Holmes story, some would say the best known of all the Holmes stories. Still not committed to the idea of reviving Holmes, Doyle used the simple expedient of setting the tale in the time before Holmes's apparent death at the Reichenbach Falls.

The Hound of the Baskervilles is Doyle's tour de force in this genre. The barren and forbidding moor of Devon, the Grimpen Mire, the spectral hound, dark and old Baskerville Hall, all create an atmosphere that is both more exotic and more gothic than any possible venue in London. Doyle's descriptive powers are given full reign by the stratagem of absenting Holmes from the body of the story, leaving the narration to the letters and diary of the far more credulous and impressionable Watson. Through Watson's observing but undiscerning eye and ear, the reader senses the implied threat of the moor and is witness to the animal-like visage of Selden, the mysterious actions of the Barrymores, the contradictory and alarming behavior of the Stapletons, the horrifying sounds of the unseen hound, even the sinister presence of the mysterious stranger who is actually Holmes.

The disappearance and surprising reappearance of Holmes is a stock-in-trade used before by Doyle to mask the solution to a riddle and, ostensibly, by Holmes in order to lull a villain into a false sense of security. It is clear from Holmes's summing up at the end of the tale that the rational detective was at no point impressed by claims of supernatural forces stalking the Baskerville family. One critic notes that the references to "light" and "darkness" in this tale represent, as in previous stories, Holmes as the light of reason opposed to the darkness of both evil and ignorance. Holmes's appearance in the story with his lucid, analytical approach would prematurely debunk the legend and dissipate the gothic atmosphere. It would also make withholding the solution much more difficult, for it is his appearance that brings the answer to some of the most vexing questions in the mystery. Holmes's absence also accentuates his mental acuity, since he is not present to be misled by false evidence. The Barrymores' actions are not pertinent to the solution of the problem. The Stapletons' actions are puzzling only if one does not know that Sir Charles's brother had a son—Stapleton. Holmes is free of the confusing influences of the other characters and is therefore able to see more clearly into the heart of the mystery.

The villain is described by Holmes quite early in the story as being "worthy of our steel." Stapleton, alias Baskerville, is an unusual entomologist who thinks nothing of dashing into the dreaded Grimpen Mire in pursuit of a butterfly for his extensive collection. He is, in fact, the only person who is determined enough to mark a safe passage through the treacherous bog which has swallowed up so many creatures. However, when he and Watson witness the agonizing end of a small moor pony as it sinks into the ooze, Stapleton is notable for his cold-blooded lack of concern, thus demonstrating that, despite his determination, he lacks compassion for living beings. Until Holmes unravels the mystery and kills the great hound, it is as if Stapleton is in league with the great bog and the moor. Even the fog rolls in at precisely the wrong moment and forces Watson, Holmes, and Lestrade to retreat during their ambush. He is very much a part of the gothic horror of the story.

Thus, *The Hound of the Baskervilles* is a compilation of the narrative and plot techniques that made the Holmes stories so popular. Further, it is a novel-length tale that is as cohesive as any short story, with all the action concentrated in one locale. Its combination of mystery and gothic techniques, as well as its length, make it a standard by which Doyle's and other writers' efforts are measured.

James L. Hodge

Bibliography:

Carr, John Dickson. *The Life of Sir Arthur Conan Doyle*. New York: Harper, 1949. Includes a chapter that examines the genesis of the idea for *The Hound of the Baskervilles*.

Ferguson, Paul F. "Narrative Vision in *The Hound of the Baskervilles*." *Clues* 1, no. 2 (Fall/Winter, 1980): 24-30. Explores the contrast between Watson's "artistic imagination" and Holmes's "scientific imagination."

Hall, Trevor H. *Sherlock Holmes and His Creator*. London: Gerald Duckworth, 1978. Examines Holmes as he relates to Doyle's life and era. The comments on *The Hound of the Baskervilles* are more descriptive and appreciative than critical.

Jaffe, Jacqueline A. *Arthur Conan Doyle*. Boston: Twayne, 1987. Examines Doyle as a literary figure, considering his oeuvre as a whole and exploring it from within the context of his biography. The comments on *The Hound of the Baskervilles*, as on the other Holmes stories, are the best available for a serious student of the subject.

Pearsall, Ronald. *Conan Doyle: A Biographical Solution*. New York: St. Martin's Press, 1977. Provides a useful discussion of *The Hound of the Baskervilles* from the point of view of a Holmes enthusiast and student of the mystery story.

THE HOUSE BY THE CHURCHYARD

Type of work: Novel
Author: Joseph Sheridan Le Fanu (1814-1873)
Type of plot: Horror
Time of plot: Late eighteenth century
Locale: Chapelizod, a suburb of Dublin
First published: 1863

Principal characters:

MR. MERVYN, the son of Lord Dunoran

LORD DUNORAN, an Irish peer convicted of murdering Mr. Beauclerc

PAUL DANGERFIELD, the real murderer of Mr. Beauclerc

ZEKIEL IRONS, Dangerfield's accomplice in the murder

DR. BARNABY STURK, a witness to the murder

The Story:

Lord Dunoran, an Irish peer, had been executed after being convicted of murdering a man named Beauclerc in London. His estates had been declared forfeit to the crown, and his family was left under a shadow. Eighteen years after his death, his son, who had assumed the name Mr. Mervyn, took his father's body back to Ireland and buried it in the family vault in the Anglican church in Chapelizod, a suburb of Dublin. After the burial, Mervyn moved into an old house that was reputed to be haunted; several families had moved out of it after having seen strange apparitions and heard noises at night. Mervyn hoped that he might pick up some clues in the neighborhood that would lead him to the true murderer of Beauclerc, for the young man still believed his father innocent of the crime for which he had paid with his life.

About the same time that young Mervyn took up residence in the haunted house, another stranger came to Chapelizod, a man named Paul Dangerfield, who was looking after the affairs of a local nobleman. Dangerfield, a very rich man, had soon ingratiated himself with the local people by his apparent good sense and liberality. The villagers were very suspicious of young Mervyn, however, for he kept to himself and only a few people knew his real identity.

The appearance of Paul Dangerfield aroused apprehension in the minds of two men in Chapelizod, Zekiel Irons, the clerk at the Anglican church, and Dr. Barnaby Sturk, a surgeon at the garrison of the Royal Irish Artillery. They both recognized Paul Dangerfield to be Charles Archer, the man who had actually committed the murder of which Lord Dunoran had been convicted. Irons had been the murderer's accomplice, and Dr. Sturk had been a witness to the murder.

Zekiel Irons resolved to help young Mervyn discover the guilt of Archer-Dangerfield, for he knew he could never live securely until the murderer was in prison or dead. Irons had been present when Dangerfield had killed his other accomplice when that man had tried to blackmail him. On two occasions, Irons visited Mervyn and told him some of what he knew; on both occasions, he warned Mervyn not to tell anyone about it, lest the information get back to Dangerfield, who would then kill Irons.

Dr. Sturk, who was pressed for money, was trying to become an agent for Lord Castlemallard, who was represented by Dangerfield. Sturk made the mistake of threatening Dangerfield with exposure if the agency were not forthcoming, and shortly after he was found one night, terribly beaten. Since he was in a deep coma, no one knew who had tried to kill him. Suspicion pointed to Charles Nutter, the man Sturk was trying to replace as the nobleman's agent in

Chapelizod, for Nutter had disappeared on the same night that Sturk was attacked. No one suspected that Dangerfield might have been the attacker, for he was known to have been helpful to Sturk.

Dr. Sturk lingered on, and for a time it even seemed as if he might recover. Dangerfield convinced Mrs. Sturk that an operation was the only chance her husband had, and he arranged for a surgeon, for a high fee, to operate on the doctor. Dangerfield actually hoped the operation would be a failure and that Sturk would die without revealing the identity of his attacker. The operation was a partial success, for Sturk regained consciousness and lived for several days, during which time he made depositions to the magistrates about the identity of his attacker and the fact that Dangerfield had murdered Beauclerc years before. At this point, Zekiel Irons, too, went to the magistrates and told what he knew about the identity of Paul Dangerfield and the part he himself had played in the murder. Even in the face of that evidence, the magistrates found it difficult to believe Dangerfield guilty because, apart from the fact that Dangerfield had paid for the operation and had lent money to Mrs. Sturk, Charles Nutter's disappearance was cause for doubt.

Charles Nutter was apprehended in Dublin within one day of Dangerfield's arrest and was able to prove that he had been away on other business at the time of the attack on Dr. Sturk. It was when he had passed close to the scene of the crime that he had frightened off Dangerfield and prevented his being able to finish the deed. Nutter had not run away; he had simply been to England and Scotland trying to straighten out his domestic affairs. A woman had attempted to prove that he was a bigamist because he had married her several years before his marriage to the woman the people in Chapelizod knew as his wife. He had married the first woman, but she herself was a bigamist, so Nutter had tried to find her first husband so as to prove that he had never been legally married to the woman. He had left secretly so as not to be arrested as a bigamist before he could gather evidence to clear his name.

In another quarter of the village, the apprehension of Dangerfield had great implications. He had been engaged to the daughter of the commanding general of the Royal Irish Artillery, although he was many years older than the girl. General Chattesworth had been quite anxious to have his daughter, Gertrude, marry Dangerfield because of his wealth. The girl, however, was in love with Mervyn and secretly engaged to him. Dangerfield's arrest put a stop to the general's plan to marry his daughter to a man she did not love.

The apprehension of Dangerfield, however, did more than open the way for Mervyn's marriage to the general's daughter. The information that Dr. Sturk and Zekiel Irons gave concerning the murder of Beauclerc cleared Mervyn's father, Lord Dunoran. When Parliament met again, it returned to Mervyn his good name, his title, and the estates forfeited at the time of his father's conviction.

Paul Dangerfield, alias Charles Archer, was never convicted, nor was he tried by a court. He died mysteriously in his cell in the county gaol in Dublin while awaiting trial. Not long afterward, the new Lord Dunoran and Gertrude Chattesworth were married in a great ceremony at Chapelizod.

Critical Evaluation:
Although Joseph Sheridan Le Fanu is best remembered as a master of the psychological horror story, his first literary efforts were in the field of the Irish historical romance. These early works were ignored by critics and readers, and Le Fanu abandoned the novel and turned to writing short fiction and editing. It was not until after the death of his wife in 1858 and the long seclusion that followed that he returned to long fiction and produced the major novels of his

last years, the first of which was *The House by the Churchyard*. The major topics of the work, violent murder and retribution, are characteristic of his late novels, but the novel also reflects Le Fanu's earlier interest in historical and social subjects and can be seen as a transition between the two phases of his career.

All of Le Fanu's novels are depictions of lush life—and something more. Death, mystery, and the supernatural are the grim twilight materials of his fiction. Constant speculation on death and the supernatural enabled him to communicate a spectral atmosphere to his novels. A master of terror, Le Fanu has been favorably compared with such other great writers of the supernatural as Wilkie Collins and Edgar Allan Poe. This novel is generally regarded as his masterpiece, although *Uncle Silas* (1864) was the most popular during Le Fanu's lifetime.

The setting of *The House by the Churchyard*, the Dublin suburb of Chapelizod, was an area Le Fanu knew and loved in his youth. This becomes clear in the warmth and humor with which he captures the atmosphere and character of small-town Irish life in the late eighteenth century. Some critics have faulted the novel as too diffuse and fragmentary, but, in fact, Le Fanu carefully balances the activities of the various social and economic groups as he gradually brings the different plot lines together. The serious courtship of Mr. Mervyn and Gertrude Chattesworth and the doomed love between Captain "Gipsy" Devereux and the rector's daughter, Lilias Walsingham, are carefully juxtaposed against the farcical romantic entanglements of the clownish members of the Royal Irish Artillery and their equally comic lady friends. Even the central villainy, Paul Dangerfield's murder of Dr. Sturk, is set opposite Mary Matchwell's absurd attempt to defraud Charles Nutter's widow of her inheritance. Coupled with Le Fanu's acute social observations, it is this balance between the comic and the horrific that gives *The House by the Churchyard* its unique place in the Le Fanu canon.

This is not to minimize the element of sensation in the novel but to put it into proportion. Murder and violence dominate the second half of the book, although the comic is never completely subdued; but after Sturk's beating, there is a definite acceleration in the pace and intensification of the suspense. Whereas the focus of the novel is constantly shifting in the early sections of the book, the action in the second half concentrates on the activities of fewer characters, notably Mervyn's efforts to vindicate his father's name, Zekiel Irons' sinister partial confession and bizarre actions, Paul Dangerfield's ambiguous machinations, and, most vivid of all, the suffering of the mute, zombielike victim, Barnaby Sturk.

Since Sturk alone can unravel the mystery, the question whether he will recover or at least speak, comes to dominate the novel. The climax of the book is the "trepanning" scene that gives Sturk the strength and stimulus to expose Dangerfield (trepanning is the archaic medical practice of drilling a small hole in the skull to relieve pressure). The detective writer and historian Dorothy Sayers has rightly stated: "For sheer grimness and power, there is little in the literature of horror to compare with the trepanning scene in Le Fanu's *The House by the Churchyard*. . . . That chapter itself would entitle Le Fanu to be called a master of murder and horror."

Once the aristocratic Paul Dangerfield is revealed to be the nefarious Charles Archer, he assumes a kind of evil grandeur that makes him almost the equal of Le Fanu's gothic archvillain, Silas Ruthyn. Trapped and condemned, Dangerfield-Archer confesses and rationalizes his crime with a cool, stylish audacity that places him in the best tradition of the gothic hero-villain. "I assure you," he tells Mervyn, "I never yet bore any man the least ill-will. I've had to remove two or three—not because I hated them—I did not care a button for any—but because their existence was incompatible with my safety which, Sir, is the first thing to me, as yours is to you." Then he casually commits suicide.

Although *The House by the Churchyard* may not possess the sustained, mounting terror and the continuing dramatic intensity of Le Fanu's gothic masterpiece *Uncle Silas*, it has a breadth, scope, humor, and social realism that the later novel lacks. For this reason, in spite of the greater popularity of *Uncle Silas*, many critics and readers consider *The House by the Churchyard* to be the crowning achievement of Le Fanu's career.

Bibliography:

Browne, Nelson. *Sheridan Le Fanu.* London: Arthur Barker, 1951. A brief overview of Le Fanu's life and work. Contains an introductory survey of his fiction, with particular emphasis on the atmospheric effects in his works. Brief, illuminating comments on *The House by the Churchyard.*

Gates, David. "'A Dish of Village Chat': Narrative Technique in Sheridan Le Fanu's *The House by the Churchyard.*" *Canadian Journal of Irish Studies* 10, no. 1 (June, 1984): 63-69. Discusses speech, dialogue, and narrative voice in the novel, as well as the interaction between these and various other techniques. Also discusses Le Fanu's debt to earlier novelists.

McCormack, W. J. *Dissolute Characters: Irish Literary History Through Balzac, Sheridan Le Fanu, Yeats, and Bowen.* Manchester, England: Manchester University Press, 1993. Substantial critical commentary on Le Fanu, a section of which is devoted to *The House by the Churchyard.* Discusses various aspects of the novel, including its cultural context. Further illumination of both the novel and Le Fanu's career is provided by the study's complex overall focus.

_____. *Sheridan Le Fanu and Victorian Ireland.* Oxford, England: Clarendon Press, 1980. The definitive study of Le Fanu and the Ireland of his time. Uses a substantial amount of primary source material and a sophisticated critical methodology to create a comprehensive picture of Le Fanu's cultural background and intellectual interests. Discussion of *The House by the Churchyard* focuses on the presence and significance of the past.

Sullivan, Kevin. "*The House by the Churchyard*: James Joyce and Sheridan Le Fanu." In *Modern Irish Literature: Essays in Honor of William York Tindall,* edited by Raymond J. Porter and James D. Brophy. New Rochelle, N.Y.: Iona College Press, 1972. Links Le Fanu's work with later developments in Irish writing. Among the more explicit connections is the one made by the common setting of *The House by the Churchyard* and James Joyce's *Finnegans Wake* (1939).

THE HOUSE BY THE MEDLAR TREE

Type of work: Novel
Author: Giovanni Verga (1840-1922)
Type of plot: Impressionistic realism
Time of plot: Mid-nineteenth century
Locale: Sicily
First published: I Malavoglia, 1881 (partial English translation, 1890, 1953; complete translation, 1964)

Principal characters:
PADRON 'NTONI, the head of the Malavoglia family
BASTIANAZZO, his son
LA LONGA, Bastianazzo's wife
'NTONI, their oldest son
LUCA, their second son
MENA, their oldest daughter
ALESSIO, their youngest son
LIA, their youngest daughter
UNCLE CRUCIFIX DUMBBELL, a local usurer
GOOSEFOOT, his assistant
DON MICHELE, a brigadier of the coast guard

The Story:

In the village of Trezza, on the island of Sicily, the Malavoglia family had once been great. Now the only Malavoglia left were Padron 'Ntoni and his little brood in the house by the medlar tree. Nevertheless, they were happy and prosperous, living well on the income brought in by their boat, the *Provvidenza.*

When the oldest grandson, 'Ntoni, was conscripted, the first sadness fell on the household. In that same year, other things went badly, and the market for fish was poor. With 'Ntoni gone, the money that came in had to be divided with extra help that Padron was forced to hire. Eventually, Padron 'Ntoni had to arrange a loan with Uncle Crucifix Dumbbell to buy a shipment of coarse black beans on credit from him. The beans were to be resold at Riposto by Padron's son, Bastianazzo. Although La Longa, Bastianazzo's wife, was skeptical of this deal, she kept quiet, as she was expected to do. Soon afterward, Bastianazzo sailed away on the *Provvidenza* with the cargo of beans aboard. All the villagers whispered that the beans were spoiled, and that Uncle Crucifix had cheated the Malavoglia family. It was well known that Uncle Crucifix was an old fox in all money matters.

If the beans were sold, Padron 'Ntoni's family would be well off. The man whose son was to marry Mena Malavoglia eagerly anticipated his boy's good fortune. The women of the village, and others too, agreed that Mena was everything a woman should be, but luck went against the Malavoglia family. In the early evening, a huge storm came up. Down at the tavern, Don Michele, the brigadier of the coast guard, predicted the doom of the *Provvidenza.* When word came that the boat had been lost, and Bastianazzo with her, grief engulfed the Malavoglia family. To add to their troubles, Uncle Crucifix began to demand his money. All the neighbors who brought gifts of condolence to the house by the medlar tree looked about the premises as if they saw Uncle Crucifix already in possession.

2998

Padron 'Ntoni and his family stubbornly set to work to repay the loan. It was decided to have Mena married as soon as possible. Alfio Mosca, who drove a donkey cart and often lingered to talk with the young woman, was grieved at the news. One day, the *Provvidenza*, battered but still usable, was towed into port. The Malavoglia rejoiced. At the same time, 'Ntoni arrived home. Luca, the second son, was drafted. Each member of the family slaved to make enough money to repay the debt.

Uncle Crucifix was fiercely repeating his demands. At last, he decided to pretend to sell his debt to his assistant, Goosefoot; then, when officers were sent to Padron 'Ntoni's house, people could not say that a usurer or the devil's money had been involved in their troubles. A short time later, a stamped paper was served on the Malavoglia family. Frightened, they went to a city lawyer, who told them that Uncle Crucifix could do nothing to them because the house was in the name of the daughter-in-law, and she had not signed the papers in the deal of beans. Padron 'Ntoni felt guilty, however; he had borrowed the money and it must be paid back. When he asked advice from the communal secretary, the official told him that the daughter-in-law must give dower rights on the house to Goosefoot, who was now the legal owner of the note. Although Goosefoot protested that he wanted his money, he nevertheless accepted a mortgage.

As the family began to gather money to repay the loan, luck again went against them. New taxes were put on pitch and salt, two necessary commodities, and personal relations between Goosefoot and the family were strained when he and young 'Ntoni came to blows over a woman. In the village, there was talk of smugglers, and the rumors involved two of 'Ntoni's close friends. Goosefoot enlisted the aid of Don Michele to watch 'Ntoni closely.

When Mena's betrothal was announced, Alfio Mosca sadly left town. Padron 'Ntoni, happy over the approaching marriage of his granddaughter, offered Goosefoot part of the money on the loan. Goosefoot, however, demanded all of it and refused to be moved by the fact that Mena needed a dowry. To add to these troubles, the Malavoglia family learned that Luca had been killed in the war. Goosefoot began again to send stamped papers. When Padron 'Ntoni appealed to the lawyer, he was told that he had been a fool to let La Longa give up her dower rights in the house, but that nothing could be done about the matter now. The family had to leave the house by the medlar tree and move into a rented hovel.

Somewhat repaired and on a fishing excursion, the *Provvidenza* ran into a storm. When Padron 'Ntoni was injured by a blow from the falling mast, young 'Ntoni had to bring the boat in alone. After the old man had recovered, 'Ntoni announced his decision to leave home; he could no longer stand the backbreaking, dull work of his debt-ridden family. His mother, grief-stricken by his departure, contracted cholera and soon died. Meanwhile, Mena's engagement had been called off by her betrothed's father. Everything was against the Malavoglia. Goosefoot and Uncle Crucifix gave the family no rest, but insisted that they too were poor and needed their money.

When young 'Ntoni returned to his home with no fortune and clothing more ragged than ever, the villagers laughed with derision. Alessio, the youngest son, now began to help with the work, and he and 'Ntoni were able to earn a little money to apply on the family debt. 'Ntoni, still discontented, was often drunk coming home from the tavern.

Don Michele told the boy's young sister Lia, whom he secretly admired, that she and Mena must keep their eyes on 'Ntoni, because he was involved with the smugglers. Although the frightened women pleaded with their brother, he refused to listen to them. One night, Don Michele knocked at Lia's door and told her that she must find her brother, for the police were planning to ambush the smugglers. His warning came too late for the sisters to act, and 'Ntoni was caught after he had stabbed Don Michele in a scuffle during the raid.

Padron 'Ntoni spent all of his savings in an attempt to rescue his grandson. Then he was told a false version of the incident, that 'Ntoni had stabbed Don Michele because he had learned of an affair between the soldier and Lia. The old man was so horrified by this news that he suffered a stroke, from which he never completely recovered. Lia left home immediately, without attempting to make known the true facts of the case, and young 'Ntoni was sent to the galleys for five years.

Under the direction of the youngest son, Alessio, the affairs of the family gradually began to mend. Uncle Crucifix and Goosefoot finally got their money, and Alessio and his bride regained possession of the house by the medlar tree.

Critical Evaluation:

The House by the Medlar Tree was planned by Giovanni Verga to be the first of five novels dealing, each in its turn, with the economic, social, and ethical aspirations of the five principal social classes in nineteenth century Italy. It is generally agreed that Verga drew the inspiration for this literary structure from the cyclical works of Honoré de Balzac and Émile Zola. Only two of Verga's five novels were finished: *The House by the Medlar Tree* and *Mastro-don Gesualdo* (1889; English translation, 1893). The former is striking for its choral presentation of human relationships, its success in achieving a poetic, eternalizing tone to realistic investigation, and its astounding objectivity. The latter makes near-perfect use of classical novel structure by depicting, in a linear manner, the inner life of one man through his outward existence.

The House by the Medlar Tree, while complete in itself, must also be considered as but one level of interest in Verga's vast design. Despite the author's objectivity, the central theme common to this design is that humans, no matter what their discomforts and tragedies, are ultimately better off in the position in which they are born. Portrayal of a static world, however, is not the result of such an assumption. Verga's characters fight desperately and in infinitely different ways against the cruelty of their condition. Verga does not pronounce judgment upon their reactions: The heroic, the pathetic, and the cruel all are portrayed realistically.

The mainstream of criticism on *The House by the Medlar Tree* views the disintegration of the Malavoglia family somewhat in the terms of Greek tragedy. The family, headed by paterfamilias Padron 'Ntoni, who unquestioningly guides their moral, social, and economic life with ancient Sicilian proverbs, begins the novel in a state of relative success on all three levels. A familiar theme of Padron 'Ntoni's proverbs is that prosperity is possible only when the family works completely together, at all times, and does not try for more than its due share. Strangely enough, it is he who arranges to buy the black beans on credit. Although La Longa is afraid, almost the entire family is enthusiastic about the possibility of sudden profit; they commit what may be considered an act of collective hubris by trying to gain what is beyond their proper realm. The ensuing shipwreck, in which Bastianazzo dies and the family is torn asunder, may be seen as the resultant nemesis. It is only in their working together, unquestioningly, that the family is able to survive economically and retain a portion of their former prestige and dignity in the eyes of their fellow villagers.

The struggle is long, however—too long for some of the family to bear. Young 'Ntoni is the first family member to question the struggle, and the only one to question it on a rational level. Having been conscripted, he has seen other social environments and other values while in service, and soon refutes his grandfather's principle that only total loyalty will bring the meager success so long accepted in Trezza as the maximum hope. He abandons the family when they need him most in order to find his fortune in the world outside, thus proving himself un-

Christian in the eyes of the village and committing hubris on a personal level. When he returns home in failure, he is greeted with ridicule from Trezza and openly displays antisocial behavior.

Lia likewise commits individual hubris when she acknowledges Don Michele's attentions. He is of a superior class, so the relationship is doomed and can only end in destroying her reputation and that of her family. Her desperation and her attraction to his material gifts, however, are overwhelming. Although she is rebelling on an emotional rather than a rational level, the result is the same as it was for young 'Ntoni—her reputation is ruined, her family is dragged further down in the eyes of Trezza, and her moral decline begins. Thus, by a family member again acting as an individual bent on individual survival, the total family unit sinks deeper into poverty and debasement.

In the end, the united efforts of the least questioning—La Longa, Mena, Luca, Alessio, and Padron 'Ntoni—reverse the trend. Lines of good and evil, reward and punishment, however, cannot be clearly drawn. La Longa dies from suffering and exhaustion. Gentle, virtuous Mena cannot marry because of her sister's reputation. Luca is drafted and killed in a war no one in the village really knows about. Padron 'Ntoni is sent to the poorhouse in his last illness. Alessio inherits the family's somewhat reversed fortunes, and young 'Ntoni, after serving a prison term, sets out for the world again, partly because of village ostracism and partly because he is determined again not to be strangled by life. There is no comment by Verga on his rightness or wrongness or on his chances of failure or success.

In 1881, the author wrote:

> [*The House by the Medlar Tree*] is the sincere and impartial study of how most probably the first inquietudes for well-being must be born and develop in the humblest of conditions; and what confusion and disturbance the ill-defined desire for the unknown and the realization that one is not well-off, or could at least be better off, must bring into a family which has lived until now in a relatively happy state.

Interpretation and conclusion are the right of the reader, but in *The House by the Medlar Tree*, Giovanni Verga's contrary purpose of almost scientific objectivity as an author must be kept continuously in mind.

"Critical Evaluation" by Roberta L. Payne

Bibliography:
Alexander, Alfred. *Giovanni Verga: A Great Writer and His World*. London: Grant & Cutler, 1972. Critical study aimed at providing English-speaking readers an introduction to Verga's ideology and the background of his fiction. Pays special attention to the development of *The House by the Medlar Tree*.

Alexander, Foscarina. *The Aspiration Toward a Lost Natural Harmony in the Work of Three Italian Writers: Leopardi, Verga, and Moravia*. Lewiston, N.J.: Edwin Mellen Press, 1990. Analyzes the family in *The House by the Medlar Tree* as the social group that stabilizes society. Demonstrates how the breakdown of family ties leads to social disintegration.

Bergin, Thomas G. *Giovanni Verga*. Westport, Conn.: Greenwood Press, 1969. Critical study of Verga's canon, demonstrating the novelist's development of his craft. A chapter on *The House by the Medlar Tree* explicates the novel and explores Verga's debt to French naturalist writers.

Cecchetti, Giovanni. *Giovanni Verga*. Boston: Twayne, 1978. Introductory study of the writer's career. Excellent, detailed analysis of *The House by the Medlar Tree*, establishing its place in Verga's canon and commenting on structure, plotting, and style.

Pacifici, Sergio. *The Modern Italian Novel from Manzoni to Svevo.* Carbondale: Southern Illinois University Press, 1967. Asserts that Verga intended *The House by the Medlar Tree* as a realistic assessment of human existence and human passion. Discusses several important themes, including generational conflict and the disillusionment of youth with political and social systems.

THE HOUSE IN PARIS

Type of work: Novel
Author: Elizabeth Bowen (1899-1973)
Type of plot: Psychological realism
Time of plot: Post-World War I
Locale: France and England
First published: 1935

> *Principal characters:*
> HENRIETTA MOUNTJOY, a brief visitor in Paris, eleven years of age
> LEOPOLD MOODY, another visitor, nine years of age
> MISS NAOMI FISHER, their hostess for a day
> MADAME FISHER, Naomi's invalid mother
> KAREN MICHAELIS, a friend of Naomi and former pupil of her mother
> MAX EBHART, a young, attractive, and intellectual Parisian

The Story:

Eleven-year-old Henrietta arrived at the Gare du Nord uncomfortably early in the morning. She had never been in Paris before, but she was to be there for one day only, between two night trains. By a previous arrangement, the girl was met at the station by Miss Naomi Fisher, an acquaintance of Henrietta's grandmother, who would look after her during her day in Paris.

Clutching her plush toy monkey while the taxi bumped through gray Paris streets, Henrietta drowsily absorbed Miss Fisher's nervous chatter. The flow of comments, however, was not entirely pointless: Henrietta was presently made to comprehend that her stopover would be affected by rather unusual developments at Miss Fisher's house. Miss Fisher's mother was ill, although today she was feeling better, and Miss Fisher could still hope to take Henrietta out for a short sight-seeing expedition after lunch. A more important complication seemed to be the presence of Leopold.

Miss Fisher explained with obvious agitation that Leopold was an added responsibility, which she had not foreseen when she agreed to meet Henrietta. He was nine years old, and he had come from Italy to see his mother, who was a very dear friend of Miss Fisher. Apparently, Henrietta gathered, he had never seen his mother before, a fact that struck the little girl as being odd and mysterious. Miss Fisher agreed that the circumstances were rather unusual, but she evaded a more direct explanation. She was careful to tell her that Leopold was naturally excited and anxious; Henrietta might play with him, if she liked, but she must not question him about his mother.

Upon arriving at the house in Paris, Henrietta had breakfast and a nap on the sofa before she awoke to find Leopold standing across the salon and gazing at her curiously. The children made wary approaches to acquaintanceship and tentatively compared notes on their respective journeys. In spite of Miss Fisher's injunction, Henrietta managed to learn that Leopold lived at Spezia with his foster parents. Before she could find out more about him, she was summoned upstairs to meet Madame Fisher. She seemed a queer person to Henrietta; her manner was ironic and penetrating, and, to her daughter's distress, she insisted on discussing Leopold's father. Once, Madame Fisher intimated, he had broken her daughter's heart. Now he was dead.

Left alone below, Leopold rummaged through Miss Fisher's purse in a vain search for information about his mother. After Henrietta rejoined him, the children had lunch and played aimlessly at cards. While they were occupied, the doorbell rang, and Miss Fisher was heard to go to the door. A few minutes later, she entered the room, her face suffused with regret and pity. Leopold struggled to affect nonchalance when she told him that his mother was not coming, after all.

Leopold had no way of knowing that his mother was the Englishwoman Karen Michaelis, who was now married to Ray Forrestier. She had become engaged to Ray more than ten years earlier, and their friends had rejoiced in what seemed an ideal match. They had planned to delay their marriage, however, until Ray completed a diplomatic mission in the East. Shortly after his departure from England, Karen had visited her aunt in Ireland. Upon returning home, she had found a pleasant surprise awaiting her, her friend Naomi Fisher, who was spending a few days in London.

Karen and Naomi had been intimate ever since Karen as a schoolgirl had spent a year under the roof of Madame Fisher in Paris. There she had perfected her French and lived under Madame's keen-eyed supervision, along with other English and American girls who were accepted into the establishment from time to time. There, too, she had first become acquainted with Max Ebhart, a dark, taut, brilliant young man whose conversation and intellect Madame Fisher found stimulating. Rather unaccountably, Max had become engaged to the unassuming Naomi and had accompanied her to England to aid in the settlement of an aunt's estate. Karen welcomed the opportunity to see Naomi, but she expressed reluctance to encounter Max, whose strong self-possession and penetrating mind had always affected her strangely.

Naomi's persistence prevailed, however, and on the final day of her stay in London, she succeeded in arranging a meeting between the three of them. While Naomi prepared tea inside the almost empty house of her dead aunt, Max and Karen sat outside on the lawn. Little was said, but both were conscious of the tension that always existed between them. That night, as Karen said good-bye at the station, she looked at Max, and when their eyes met it was with the mutual admission that they were in love.

One month later, Max telephoned from Paris, asking Karen to meet him in Boulogne the following Sunday. There they walked and talked, the thought of Naomi shadowing their conversation. Before they parted, they arranged to meet again at Hythe on the next Saturday. They spent the night together and decided that they must marry, in spite of their unwillingness to hurt Naomi. Max went back to Paris to impart the difficult news to his fiancée.

Karen never saw Max again; word of his suicide came in a telegram from Naomi. Weeks later, Naomi herself crossed the channel to tell Karen how Max had slashed his wrists after a trying interview with Madame Fisher. When Karen confessed that she was going to bear Max's child, the two girls considered the plans she must make. Karen had already tried to break off her engagement with Ray Forrestier, but he had written that he would never give her up. Nevertheless, she intended to be gone when he returned to London; she would travel to Paris with Naomi and then go on to Germany for perhaps a year. She and Naomi would find a good home for the child. Meanwhile, no one—except possibly Karen's mother—should ever know.

These were the facts about his parents that Leopold had never learned. Now, when his mother had failed him by not coming to get him at the house in Paris, he stood, for a moment, immovable, steeped in misery. His air of resolution and determined indifference gave way and, crossing to the mantelpiece and pressing himself against it, he burst into sobs. Henrietta tried to comfort him, but he ignored her. Recovering from his spasm of grief, he was sent upstairs to endure Madame Fisher's careful scrutiny. He found her surprisingly sympathetic. She told him something of his mother's marriage to Ray Forrestier, and he confided his determination not to return to his foster parents in Italy. Some inner force in the elderly invalid seemed to stiffen and encourage him.

Downstairs the doorbell rang once more, and Miss Fisher came running swiftly up the steps. She directed Leopold to the salon where he found a tall, pleasant-looking Englishman. It was Ray Forrestier; overruling Karen's doubts, he had come to accept Leopold as his own son and to restore him to his mother.

Critical Evaluation:

Elizabeth Bowen's ability to create suspense would have stood her in good stead had she chosen to write detective novels. *The House in Paris* gradually unravels a human secret that not only the characters of the novel but also the readers find both absorbing and oppressive. The author's method is not to emphasize physical action but to unfold complex relationships between people, driving a story slowly to a conclusion that is logical but necessarily incomplete. There are no formulaic endings in Bowen's novels, no dovetailing of desire and fulfillment; as long as people live, she convincingly and calmly implies, there are questions that will be only partially answered, wishes that will be only partially granted. In *The House in Paris*, she presents the situation that a child has created merely by existing: an inadvertent love and an inadvertent begetting become a problem to several people. Rarely has the problem of an illegitimate boy been traced with more keenness and candor.

Bowen uses the figures of an unwed mother and illegitimate child—traditional social pariahs—to express the child's perspective of adult society, the changing role of women, and the importance of accepting the past. Although Henrietta and Leopold at first seem to be the most important characters in *The House in Paris*, they are not. Bowen uses their perception of reality, however, in portraying the adults' stories. Bowen's main concern is with the adults, but she is very much aware of the connection between the adult reality and the child's world. The structure of *The House in Paris* suggests both the connection between the two realities and the absolute gulf separating them. The first and last sections of the book, both entitled "The Present," frame the longer middle section, "The Past." Henrietta's and Leopold's consciousness dominate "The Present," whereas those of their parents' generation dominate "The Past." The character Naomi Fisher, for example, who appears in both parts, is viewed by the children as "Miss Fisher" and by her mother and her contemporaries as "Naomi."

A child's loneliness is often Bowen's metaphor for that deep human loneliness brought about by fate or misfortune. Leopold—abandoned as an infant by his mother, his father dead—sees himself as utterly alone and bereft of identity. He is a stranger to the values of his biological family and to the community of the "house in Paris." At nine years of age, he expects to be initiated into those mysteries, accepted by his mother, and made a part of the community. Instead, he must cope anew with his mother's rejection; he weeps because this is the end of his hopes and plans. Much of the material devoted to Leopold is narrated through the consciousness of the observing child, Henrietta, whose perception helps to balance Leopold's solipsistic self-analysis.

Bowen often uses the discrepancy between women's changing aspirations and the traditional roles assigned by society as metaphor for the disintegration of society as a whole. Karen is ambivalent about the roles of wife and mother. Maturing in an upper-class environment free of anxieties about family or money, she nevertheless feels unfulfilled. Even after she becomes engaged to the man she is expected to marry, she keeps asking, "What next? What next?" She wants to escape from the too-secure future that is held out to her, and she complains bitterly to her Aunt Violet that she will be too "safe" with Ray as a husband. Karen rebels by taking her best friend's fiancé as lover and canceling her own engagement. Ironically, Karen regretted that no one would ever know of her action, believing that her "revolution" had changed nothing. Yet there were serious consequences. Max commits suicide when he learns that Madame Fisher had planned that he break with Naomi; his rebellion had therefore been useless. Karen becomes pregnant and gives Leopold away to be adopted by foster parents. She cannot rid herself of ambivalent feelings toward her son and her past, and when she makes an attempt to see him on that day in the house in Paris, she lacks the courage to take the final step.

In *The House in Paris*, Bowen uses structure, symbol, and plot to achieve a clear statement about the value and organic character of the past. In the book's structure, the past is bounded by the present, showing the essential interpenetration of the two. Leopold personifies the past's ongoing character; in him the others are embodied. The house itself is a symbol of the past's inserting itself into the present, for the events of the present had their origin when the characters first met there when Karen was a schoolgirl.

In her use of enclosed spaces to give meaning to her characters, Bowen reminds the reader of Jane Austen and George Eliot. Not only in "the house in Paris" but also at 2 Windsor Terrace in *The Death of the Heart* (1938), in Stella's apartment and at Mount Morris in *The Heat of the Day* (1949), and in her early works *The Hotel* (1927) and *The Last September* (1929), Bowen places her female and adolescent characters within architectural structures. Rooms, houses, apartments, mansions—these are the spaces where the drama of female lives takes place. Employing little natural description, Bowen fills her works with depictions of interiors.

In *The House in Paris*, the house belongs to Madame Fisher, the strongest personality in the book. Both Karen and Max come to realize that if they fail to assert their wills, she will dominate them. Ray also senses this and takes the courageous step Karen could not: He decides to accept Leopold (and Karen's past). Ray's gesture is not totally romantic; he understands the difficulties involved. It may now be hoped that Karen can reintegrate past and present and break through to the future. Unwed mother and illegitimate son have been accepted and taken into society, but Bowen leaves open the question whether there will be a change now that Karen's personal revolution has taken place. Possibly Karen will continue to wonder, "What next? What next?" Bowen does not seem to hold out much hope, merely implying that a beginning, an attempt at reintegration, has been made.

"Critical Evaluation" by Margaret McFadden-Gerber

Bibliography:

Austin, Allan E. *Elizabeth Bowen*. Rev. ed. Boston: Twayne, 1989. Good introduction that discusses Bowen's style, syntax, use of narrative voice, and evocative settings. Analyzes the theme, character, and setting of *The House in Paris* and argues that Ray is the novel's value center. Helpful annotated bibliography.

Jordan, Heather Bryant. *How Will the Heart Endure?: Elizabeth Bowen and the Landscape of War*. Ann Arbor: University of Michigan Press, 1992. Discusses the importance of Bowen's uniquely Anglo-Irish background and its influence on her writing, examining her use of the term race to describe national or cultural characteristics, among them the ideal of the Big House in Anglo-Ireland and the provincialism of the English middle class, which is represented by the Michealises.

Kenney, Edwin, Jr. *Elizabeth Bowen*. Lewisburg, Pa.: Bucknell University Press, 1974. Good introduction to *The House in Paris* that discusses Bowen's use of structure to express the theme of separation between child and adult. Also provides detailed analysis of setting and character.

Lassner, Phyllis. *Elizabeth Bowen*. Basingstoke, England: Macmillan, 1990. Excellent introduction to *The House in Paris*, providing interesting critical evaluation from a feminist perspective. Discusses narrative structure, character, setting, and theme, noting Karen's ambivalence toward traditional home and family values.

Lee, Hermione. *Elizabeth Bowen: An Estimation*. Totowa, N.J.: Barnes & Noble Books, 1981. Asserts that the journeys that structure *The House in Paris* also reveal theme, subject, and character development. Analyzes the relationship between identity and time, noting contrasting speeds and pace of time in the novel's three sections. Discusses Bowen's blending of gothic suspense, melodrama, comedy, and documentary realism.

HOUSE MADE OF DAWN

Type of work: Novel
Author: N. Scott Momaday (1934-   )
Type of plot: Psychological realism
Time of plot: 1945-1952
Locale: New Mexico and Los Angeles
First published: 1968

Principal characters:
ABEL, a young Pueblo Indian
FRANCISCO, his grandfather
BEN BENALLY, Abel's best friend
ANGELA, a rich white woman
MILLY, a white social worker
JOHN TOSAMAH, an Indian "preacher" in Los Angeles
FATHER OLGUIN, a Hispanic village priest
JUAN REYES, an albino Indian and a witch

The Story:

Abel, a young Jemez Pueblo Indian, returned to his New Mexico village in 1945 after fighting in the Pacific theater during World War II. The war left him emotionally devastated and unable to participate in the world he had left behind, the world of his grandfather, Francisco. Now an old man with a lame leg, Francisco in his youth had been a respected hunter and participant in the village's religious ceremonies. He had raised Abel from a young age, after the death of Abel's mother and older brother, Vidal (Abel did not know who his father was). Francisco had instilled in Abel a sense of native traditions and values, but the war and other events had severed Abel's connections to that world of spiritual and physical wholeness and connectedness to the land and its people, a world known as a "house made of dawn."

At about the same time Abel returned to his village, Angela St. John, a rich, unhappy white woman, arrived to indulge in the area's mineral baths. Through Father Olguin, the village's well-meaning but isolated and ineffective Catholic priest, she hired Abel to chop the wood at the house she had rented. Disenchanted with her own life and ambivalent about her new pregnancy, she was instantly attracted to Abel and soon seduced him. Angela sensed an animal-like quality in Abel that she hoped would revive her flagging emotional health. She also sensed Abel's sadness and promised to help Abel find a good job and get off the New Mexico reservation.

One rainy night, Abel had a fight with a sinister and mysterious albino man, Juan Reyes, described almost exclusively as "the white man." Abel had surmised that Juan was a witch; outside a bar, in the rain, he stabbed Juan to death. At his trial, Abel told the lawyers that Juan was a "snake" and that any man would have done the same thing. Father Olguin tried unsuccessfully to convince the lawyers and the judge that this was a sensible conclusion in Abel's world. Abel was sent to jail.

Upon his release, Abel was relocated to Los Angeles, where he became friends with Ben Benally, another Indian from New Mexico, who was the lover of Milly, a white social worker. Ben and Abel talked of their lives in New Mexico, and Ben kept Abel in touch with the faith that Abel could no longer express. Ben sang the songs of the Navajo Nightway and Beautyway ceremonies for Abel during their many visits. But Abel did not fit well in Los Angeles. In particular, he had troubles with John Tosamah, a storefront preacher for his own "Holiness Pan-Indian Rescue Mission." Tosamah's message was a mixture of wisdom and articulate trickery, and he teased Abel as a "longhair" unable to adapt to the demands of a modern, urban world. Abel also had a confrontation with a sadistic, corrupt police officer whose nickname was "culebra" (snake). When Abel went to avenge a humiliation by the policeman, he was beaten nearly to death. Angela had not seen Abel for several years, but she lived in Los Angeles and came to visit him in the hospital after Ben called her. She was happy and healthy when she came to see Abel, and her visits revived Abel's spirits, just as he had helped revive hers years ago.

Having failed in Los Angeles, Abel returned to New Mexico, where his grandfather was dying. Abel took care of Francisco for seven days during which the old man drifted in and out of consciousness. During this time, Francisco again told Abel all the stories of his youth and reminded him of the importance of being a good man and maintaining the right connections with the world around him. When Francisco died, Abel prepared him according to his people's traditions. He then smeared his own body with ashes and began to run as the sun rose. He was participating in the same ritual that his grandfather had described to him, running a "race for the dead." As he ran, Abel began to sing for himself and for his grandfather, regaining his place in the world where he belonged.

Critical Evaluation:

N. Scott Momaday, who was born in 1934 in Oklahoma of Kiowa, Cherokee, and white heritage, grew up in New Mexico, where his father was a school principal. There, Momaday had intimate contact with Navajo and Jemez Pueblo people and cultures. His familiarity with those two worlds, along with his formal training in creative writing at Stanford University, shaped the writing of his first novel, *House Made of Dawn*, which was published in 1968 and won the Pulitzer Prize the next year. Momaday's novel is credited with beginning a period of renewed interest in and activity by American Indian writers. After its publication, a rich stream of fiction and poetry began issuing from a varied field of American Indian tribes and experiences.

House Made of Dawn is written in a style that frequently echoes the language of William Faulkner, Ernest Hemingway, and others. In the story's narrative structure, the plot is revealed out of chronological order and from multiple points of view. Several elements of the story remain unnarrated, leaving occurrences and motivations open for the reader's speculation.

Although the style of *House Made of Dawn* reflects twentieth century practices, the novel adheres to the symbolic universes of the Jemez Pueblo and Navajo Indians. Abel is, for example, frequently associated with bears, which hold great healing powers and are to be both respected and feared. Elements of the Nightway, a lengthy Navajo healing ceremony, also are important to the novel. In that ceremony, which lasts for seven days and ends at dawn (the time when the novel begins and ends), a person sings over another who seeks healing. Ben Benally does exactly this for his good friend Abel in the third section of the novel, which is entitled "The Night Chanter." Part of the Nightway appears in this section as Ben sings it, and the novel takes its title from a line in the ceremony. Jemez Pueblo and Navajo traditions also have stories about heroic twins who are dependent upon each other to accomplish their tasks: the Stricken Twins, and Monster-Slayer and Born-of-Water. Some critics have seen Ben and Abel as representations of those twins.

The novel's dependence on symbolic traditions outside Western civilization creates some obstacles to Western understanding that parallel Abel's frustrations at trying to understand the world he encounters in the army and in Los Angeles. Some critics have viewed this aspect of the novel as a nice literary revenge, since Western civilization has appeared bewildering (sometimes fatally so) to many American Indians since first contact, and since the West's definition of good literature often has excluded the works of American Indians from publication and the classroom.

House Made of Dawn is a classic example of what William Bevis has termed the "homing in" plot found among many works by American Indian writers. Bevis contrasts this plot with the Western plot tradition, in which the hero leaves home to grow up and seek his fortune and independence elsewhere. The homing-in plot involves an Indian protagonist returning to his or her roots, which frequently are found on a reservation. The protagonist is assisted in this return by an older tribal member, often an older relative. The homing-in plot firmly establishes a character's identity in a particular, natural landscape and within a set of reciprocal relationships to a particular people. By contrast, the Western paradigm often values the interests of the individual over those of the community; in fact, society is often seen as a threat to the individual.

The themes in *House Made of Dawn* include the struggle of American Indians to balance their often-threatened cultural and religious identities with, or against, the modern, urban, Anglo world. Abel is representative of this struggle, especially of the generation that came of age during World War II. Momaday has said that Abel's experience is a "dislocation of the psyche," a dislocation caused by "having to deal immediately . . . not only with the traditional world but with the other world which was placed over the traditional world so abruptly and with great violence." It would, however, be simplistic to assume that the novel argues for an Indian identity that excludes all elements of Western civilization. Francisco, for example, has happily integrated two religions and participates in Jemez Pueblo and Catholic rituals throughout the book.

Another theme is the concept of *hozho*, a Navajo word meaning wholeness and beauty in the relationships of an individual to the people and the natural world. When one of these relationships falls out of balance, physical and spiritual illness can follow. The novel is the story of Abel's healing and of how he regains his balance with his world and the people important to him. Perhaps the most essential theme of the book is the regenerative power of words. Characters are healed by the sharing of stories and songs, and the native heritage that is threatened by the modern world is preserved through the words handed from one generation to the next. In many ways, the novel depicts and participates in the oral tradition characteristic of American Indian tribal cultures. In the oral tradition, words are more than representations of things or ideas; a word and its subject are equals, the word containing the power of the subject it refers to. In this way, songs and stories invoke the events they describe. A song of healing can enact an actual healing, as it does for Abel in *House Made of Dawn*.

Scott Andrews

Bibliography:
Bevis, William. "American Indian Novels: Homing In." In *Recovering the Word: Essays on Native American Literature*, edited by Brian Swann and Arnold Krupat. Berkeley: University of California Press, 1987. Discusses *House Made of Dawn* alongside other important American Indian texts.
Coltelli, Laura. *Winged Words: American Indian Writers Speak*. Lincoln: University of Nebraska Press, 1990. An interview with Momaday concerning his fiction and the issues informing it. Especially useful in understanding the ideas at work in *House Made of Dawn*.

Owens, Louis. *Other Destinies: Understanding the American Indian Novel.* Norman: University of Oklahoma Press, 1992. Places *House Made of Dawn* in relation to other novels by American Indians. Provides an insightful reading of the novel and its characters.

Scarberry-Garcia, Susan. *Landmarks of Healing: A Study of "House Made of Dawn."* Albuquerque: University of New Mexico Press, 1990. A book-length study of the Navajo and Jemez Pueblo religious and cultural symbols that shape the novel. Important for understanding the novel's cultural context and its subtle allusions.

Schubnell, Matthias. *N. Scott Momaday: The Cultural and Literary Background.* Norman: University of Oklahoma Press, 1985. Contains a biographical sketch and chapters that discuss the roles of nature and of language in Momaday's work. One chapter, "The Crisis of Identity," examines *House Made of Dawn* in particular. Also includes a history of the novel's reception and an extensive critical bibliography (up to 1985).

THE HOUSE OF BLUE LEAVES

Type of work: Drama
Author: John Guare (1938-   )
Type of plot: Absurdist
Time of plot: October 4, 1965
Locale: Sunnyside, Queens, New York City
First performed: 1971; first published, 1971

Principal characters:
ARTIE SHAUGHNESSY, a zookeeper and would-be songwriter
BANANAS, his wife
RONNIE, their son
BUNNY FLINGUS, their neighbor
BILLY EINHORN, a Hollywood director
CORINNA STROLLER, a Hollywood starlet

The Story:

Zookeeper and would-be songwriter Artie Shaughnessy played and sang to unreceptive, jeering patrons of El Dorado Bar on amateur night. Afterward, in his cluttered apartment in Sunnyside, Queens, he slept on the living-room couch, dreaming aloud that his son Ronnie had come to New York as pope. Meanwhile, Ronnie, dressed in Army fatigues, had surreptitiously climbed through the unlocked window into his old bedroom. Artie's dream was interrupted by the arrival of his neighbor and lover, Bunny Flingus, who excitedly admonished him to get dressed so they could attend the pope's motorcade outside and secure the pope's blessing on their union and on Artie's music, which would ensure their marriage and a Hollywood songwriting career. Artie agreed to get dressed on the condition that Bunny cook for him, but she refused, denying him her cuisine (although not her bed) until their wedding.

As they talked, Artie's sickly wife, Bananas, entered in nightclothes; she, remaining unnoticed, then returned to her room and cried out. She returned to the room, hysterical, but became calmer after Artie forced sedatives down her, while Bunny hid in the kitchen. Artie then fed Bananas, who behaved like a puppy. Bunny emerged from the kitchen and confronted Artie about divorce. Artie told Bananas that he had found for her a sanatorium. He described a lovely tree there, with blue leaves, leaves that had blown away in the form of a flock of bluebirds to canopy another tree, leaving the first one bare.

Sensing Artie's indecision, Bunny insisted that he call his old friend Billy Einhorn, the famous Hollywood moviemaker. Challenged, Artie telephoned Billy to tell him that he would be going to Hollywood with Bunny, a woman he had first met in a steam bath. As a cheerful Bunny left to pack for Hollywood, a depressed Bananas was persuaded by Artie to go with him to see the pope for healing. They left, taking Artie's sheet music to be blessed as well.

Ronnie, left alone, sneaked out of his room, cradling a large box that contained a homemade bomb. He delivered a monologue about the ways his father and others had disparaged him, citing an instance when Billy Einhorn had been in town looking for the ideal American boy for a *Huckleberry Finn* movie and Ronnie had humiliated himself auditioning for Billy, who deemed him retarded. Then Ronnie again secluded himself in his room.

Artie returned with Bananas and Bunny and was greeted by the arrival of Corinna Stroller, a beautiful starlet whose only film had been directed by Billy Einhorn, her fiancé. Corinna, who tried not to reveal that she was deaf, wore a transistorized hearing aid that malfunctioned, so she disconnected it. When Artie insisted that she listen to his songs, his audition was futile. Furthermore, it was interrupted by three shivering nuns who had been locked out on the roof while hoping to see the pope and now appeared at the window, asking to watch His Holiness on Artie's television. A startled Corinna dropped her transistors and could not find them. Artie herded the nuns into Ronnie's room, where Ronnie was discovered dressed as an altar boy. Artie concluded that his son had been chosen to be an attendant to the pope.

Artie resumed auditioning. At Banana's sly request, Artie played his first composed song and then "White Christmas," which brought to his attention that both songs had the same tune. Angry with Bananas for this exposure, Artie called the sanatorium and asked an attendant to come for her. Corinna announced that she and Billy planned marriage and a two-year stay in Australia, which would leave Artie without a Hollywood connection. Dismayed, Artie remained deaf to Ronnie's announced intention to blow up the pope. A struggle between Ronnie and the nuns ensued when Corrina, in departing, offered two tickets to the mass at Yankee Stadium. Also pursuing Ronnie was an officer who had arrived to arrest him for being absent without leave from his unit, which was destined for Vietnam. Just as a sanatorium attendant arrived to pick up a Mrs. Arthur Shaughnessy, Bunny entered and answered to the name, thus being mistakenly straitjacketed and dragged away. Striving to elude the MP, Ronnie tossed the packaged bomb to an unsuspecting Corinna as she left. It exploded in the hallway, killing her and two of the nuns.

Billy Einhorn arrived from Hollywood to mourn his beloved as Artie, amidst feigned consolation, tried to persuade Billy to take him to Hollywood. Bananas appeared and demanded that Billy rescue Ronnie, whereupon Billy called the Pentagon and got Ronnie assigned to Rome, to be near the pope. Bunny brought in a meal for Billy that caused him to ask her to accompany him to Australia. He advised Artie to stay in Queens, where he could remain Billy's ideal audience and could care for Bananas. His dreams shattered, Artie was left alone with his wife. As he kissed her tenderly, he gently strangled her in despairing love. As her body became lifeless, blue leaves began to fall and Artie went into his act for the Eldorado, singing "I'm Here with Bells On."

Critical Evaluation:

John Guare's *The House of Blue Leaves* won the five drama awards of the 1970-1971 season, including the Obie and the New York Drama Critics Circle Award as the Best American Play. In 1986, it was well received in a New York revival that garnered four Tony awards and an effective PBS production. Preceded by twelve produced one-act plays, Guare's first full-length play was followed by others, including the award-winning collaborative musical adaptation of Shakespeare's *Two Gentlemen of Verona* (1971) and *Six Degrees of Separation* (1990). However, *The House of Blue Leaves* is critically considered his most important work, most clearly revealing his characteristic ability to blend tragedy and farce.

Guare uses the comic chaos of the Shaughnessy household to call attention to the American obsession with facile success and with a value system in which the pope and movie stars are indistinguishable media gods, television is a shrine, and assassins are glorified in headlines. Middle-aged Artie, with his small talent but big dreams of writing hit songs, represents the little people who have succumbed to the materialistic, celebrity-worshipping American ethos and yet are trapped by the inescapable economic and domestic problems of their actual lives. Encouraged to revere surface fame rather than to develop inner resources, people are lured by the outwardly apparent beauty, fame, money, power of a celebrity's success, and these qualities become the basis of their value structure. Such people are bitterly disappointed when their pursuit of a better life proves unattainable. A native of New York City's Queens, Guare was aware of the problems of urban folk who dream of escaping their unalluring middle-class environment.

Guare employs farcical and absurdist action against a realistic background and a linear plot to set up a counterpoint with the desperation and unrealistic dreams of the characters' lives. Supported by Bunny, Artie believes that the pope's blessing and his moviemaker friend Billy will allow him to escape a long marriage with a troubled wife to find salvation through success in Hollywood as a songwriter. His dreams explode when Billy steals Bunny away and leaves Artie behind in Queens with his wife, whom Artie then strangles as his only way to escape reality. By the play's conclusion, friendship, marriage, and extramarital affairs have all proved hollow, and religious beliefs have proved to be driven by false secular values.

In his foreword to the play, Guare attributes his mixture of genres to seeing tragic drama by August Strindberg and a farce by Georges Feydeau on two successive nights and determining that if these disparate authors had been conjoined, their offspring could be *The House of Blue Leaves*. Guare combines tragedy and comedy, and farce, satire, and absurdist comedy with social criticism. Cartoonist characterizations are juxtaposed with such realistic elements as the nonfarcical character of Bananas, a shabby Queens apartment, and actual historical events. On twelve occasions, the characters directly address the audience, an important device in reinforcing the play's mixture of styles: Artie addresses the audience as bar patrons at both the start and end of the play; Bananas notices the audience and welcomes them into her home; and Bunny addresses many observations directly to the theater, as does the bomb-making Ronnie in his long monologue. In addition to bridging the gulf between audience and stage and creating a sense of comic detachment, the device heightens the blurring between fantasy and reality that is embodied by Artie and Bunny.

Guare's use of farcical devices, irony, and black humor, achieved through juxtaposition of the fantastic with the realistic and of the ridiculous with the painful, is apparent in several of the author's other plays, which also show the author attacking the false value systems of American culture. *Marco Polo Sings a Solo* (1973) highlights a famous astronaut attempting to live up to his heroic media image while isolated from his normal world. In *Rich and Famous* (1974), a protagonist stops at nothing, including the staging of his own suicide, to become a famous playwright. In *Six Degrees of Separation* (1990), a young African American hustler lives out his own fantasy to be an accepted member of high society by posing as a college-educated son of Sidney Poitier.

Critics have been divided on the artistic success of *The House of Blue Leaves*. For some, the juxtaposition of absurdist comedy with realistic pathos represents the plays's distinctive strength, and they find an inner coherence of vision and incident within the play's apparent formlessness. For other critics, such a mixture hinders the comedy by encouraging laughter at the essentially tragic. However, even reviewers objecting to the mixture of forms agree that *The House of Blue Leaves* is a powerful play of its day.

Guare sees a dichotomy in American society and relies on nonconventional devices to express his insights. Yet beneath the play's irony and mordantly humorous attacks, there lies a belief in humanity and an intuitive feeling for the mystery of life's purposes. These qualities, concluded the English critic John Harrop, render Guare more quintessentially American than those contemporaries who glibly speak of American virtues. Guare's vision—and the means he uses to project that vision—sets him apart and render his play and his work distinctive.

Christian H. Moe

Bibliography:

Bernstein, Samuel J. *The Strands Entwined: A New Direction in American Drama.* Boston: Northeastern University Press, 1980. Contains a twenty-page chapter on *The House of Blue Leaves,* which reviews the 1971 production criticism and provides insightful analysis of the play. In Bernstein's view, Guare effectively uses comic techniques obliquely to attack questionable values of American culture.

Guare, John. Foreword to *The House of Blue Leaves.* New York: New American Library, 1987. Guare briefly discusses play-related autobiographical events, including witnessing juxtaposed productions of a Strindberg drama and a Feydeau farce and conceiving the tragic comic structure of *The House of Blue Leaves.* In a preceding preface he compares the play's decade-separated openings.

Harrop, John. "Ibsen Translated by Lewis Carroll: The Theatre of John Guare." *New Theatre Quarterly* 3, no. 10 (May, 1987): 150-154. An overview of Guare's plays perceives *The House of Blue Leaves* as an exploration of the national obsession with facile success. Immediately following Harrop's interview with Guare (155-159) is an extensive checklist including chronology, succinct synopses, and bibliography (160-177).

Kolin, Philip, ed. *American Playwrights Since 1945: A Guide to Scholarship, Criticism, and Performance.* New York: Greenwood Press, 1989. Includes Don B. Wilmeth's helpfully detailed chapter on Guare, which includes a production history and criticism of *The House of Blue Leaves.* An extensive bibliography of secondary sources includes published reviews of the play.

Marranca, Bonnie, and Gautam Dasgupta. *American Playwrights: A Critical Survey.* Vol. 1. New York: Drama Book Specialists, 1981. Guare and his major work are thoughtfully discussed in an eleven-page chapter. *The House of Blue Leaves* is viewed as a play as much about human failure as about the ironies of fate.

A HOUSE OF GENTLEFOLK

Type of work: Novel
Author: Ivan Turgenev (1818-1883)
Type of plot: Psychological realism
Time of plot: Nineteenth century
Locale: Russia
First published: Dvoryanskoye gnezdo, 1859 (English translation, 1869)

Principal characters:
MARYA DMITRIEVNA, a widow
LAVRETZKY, her cousin
LIZA, her daughter
VARVARA, Lavretzky's wife
PANSHIN, an official

The Story:

Marya, since the death of her husband, had become a social leader in her small provincial town. Her daughter Liza spoke French quite well and played the piano. Her other children had the best tutors available. She took great delight in receiving guests, especially Panshin, who had an important position in Moscow. Her evening gatherings were always entertaining when Panshin was there to quote his own poetry.

It was rumored that Lavretzky was returning to the district. Although he was a cousin of the house, Marya scarcely knew how to treat him, for Lavretzky had made an unfortunate marriage. He was now separated from his pretty wife, who was reputed to be fast and flighty. Lavretzky's visit created no difficulties, however. He was a rather silent, affable man, and he noticed Liza with interest. Liza was a religious-minded and beautiful girl of nineteen. It was very evident that the brilliant Panshin was courting her with the full approval of her mother. On the evening of his visit, Lavretzky was not impressed with Panshin's rendition of his musical romance, but the ladies were ecstatic.

The following day Lavretzky went on to his small country estate. The place was run-down because it had been uninhabited since his sister's death. Lavretzky, content to sink into a quiet country life, ordered the gardens cleaned up, moved in some newer furniture, and began to take an interest in the crops. He seemed suspended in a real Russian atmosphere, close to the land. His new life was particularly pleasing after his residence in France and the painful separation from his wife.

Lavretzky had had an unusual upbringing. His father, disappointed by his failure to inherit an aunt's fortune, had decided to make his son a strong man, even a Spartan. At twelve years of age, Lavretzky was dressed in Highland kilts and trained in gymnastics and horsemanship. He was given only one meal a day, and he took cold showers at four in the morning. Along with the physical culture intended to produce a natural man according to Rousseau's doctrines, the father indoctrinated his son with Voltaire's philosophy.

Lavretzky's father died after enduring great pain for two years. During this time, he lost his bravery and atheistic independence, and at the end, he was a sniveling wreck. His death was a release to Lavretzky, then twenty-three years old, who immediately enrolled in a university in Moscow. At the opera one night, he met Varvara, the beautiful daughter of a retired general who lived mostly by his wits. At first, Varvara's parents had little use for Lavretzky, whom they took to be an unimportant student. When they learned that he came of a good family and was a landed proprietor, they favored an early marriage. Because Varvara wanted to travel, Lavretzky wound up his affairs and installed his new father-in-law as overseer of his properties.

In Paris, Varvara began a dizzy social whirl. Her adoring husband was content merely to be at her side, and he let her indulge her whims freely. She soon had a reputation as a brilliant hostess, but her guests thought her husband a nonentity. Lavretzky had no suspicion that his wife was anything but a devoted wife and mother to their daughter until a letter accidentally came into his hands, from which he learned of her lover and of their furtive meetings. Lavretzky left home immediately and took up separate residence. When he wrote to Varvara, telling her of the reason for the separation, she did not deny her guilt but only asked for consideration. After settling an income on his wife, Lavretzky had returned to Russia.

At first, Lavretzky stayed on his estate; later, he began to ride into town occasionally to call on Marya and her family. After he became better acquainted with Liza, the young girl scolded him for being so hardhearted toward his wife. According to Liza's religious beliefs, Lavretzky should have pardoned Varvara for her sins and continued the marriage. Lavretzky warned Liza that the carefree young diplomat Panshin was all surface and no substance and that he was not the man for her. Lavretzky had an ally in Marfa, the old aunt, who also saw through Panshin's fine manners and clever speeches. When Panshin proposed to Liza by letter, she put off making a decision.

Liza's music teacher was an old, broken German named Lemm. Although Lavretzky had little ear for music, he had a deep appreciation for Lemm's talent. He invited the old man to his farm. During the visit, the two men found that they had much in common. Lavretzky was saddened to see that the old music teacher was hopelessly in love with Liza.

One night, Panshin brilliantly held forth in Marya's drawing room on the inadequacies of Russia. He asserted that the country was far behind the rest of Europe in agriculture and politics. The English were superior in manufacture and merchandising, the French in social life and the arts, the Germans in philosophy and science. His views were those of the aristocratic detractors of Russia. The usually silent Lavretzky finally took issue with Panshin and skillfully demolished his every argument. Liza listened with approval.

Lavretzky came upon a brief notice in the society section of a French paper, which informed him that his wife was dead. For a while he could not think clearly, but as the import of the news came home to him he realized that he was in love with Liza. Riding into town, he gave the paper quietly to Liza. As soon as he could be alone with her, he declared his love. The young girl received his declaration soberly, almost seeming to regard their love as a punishment. Although troubled at first by her attitude, Lavretzky soon achieved a happiness he had never expected to find.

His happiness was short-lived, however. One day, his servant announced that Varvara had returned with their daughter. She told him she had been very ill and had not bothered to correct the rumor of her death. Now she asked only to be allowed to live somewhere near him. Suspecting that her meekness was only assumed, Lavretzky arranged for her to live on a distant estate, far from his own house.

Liza was controlled when he told her the news. She seemed almost to have expected the punishment, for she was convinced that sorrow was the lot of all Russians. Varvara brazenly called on Marya and completely captivated her with her beauty, her French manners, and her accomplished playing and singing. Liza met Lavretzky's wife with grave composure. For a time, Varvara complied with her promise to stay isolated on the distant estate, where she frequently entertained Panshin. In the winter, when she moved to Moscow, Panshin was her devoted follower. At last, she went back to Paris.

Liza entered a convent. Lavretzky saw her once from a distance as she scurried timidly to a prayer service. Taking what strength he could from the soil, he remained on his farm. When he was forty-five years old, he visited the house where Liza had lived. Marya and everyone else he had known in the household had died. He felt ill at ease among the younger, laughing generation.

Critical Evaluation:

The publication of *A House of Gentlefolk* established Ivan Turgenev as a great novelist. Although critical opinion generally awarded *Fathers and Sons* (1867) the honor of being Turgenev's masterpiece, this earlier novel was for more than half a century his most universally acclaimed work. *A House of Gentlefolk* is to be appreciated on two separate yet interlocking and organically unified levels: the social-historical and the artistic. Although in the novel as a work of art these two aspects are inextricably fused, they may nevertheless be studied individually to illuminate more clearly some of the work's underlying themes and to gain deeper insight into the characters.

Any discussion of Turgenev is enriched by an understanding of social movements in Russia in the mid-nineteenth century. A cultural controversy had arisen during the author's lifetime centering on the question of the relative worth of foreign (that is, Western European) versus exclusively Russian ideals. The so-called Westerners were a group of Russians who believed that democracy could cure the ills of society; these individuals repudiated Russia's autocratic government as well as her Greek Orthodox religion as outmoded and repressive institutions. They viewed their homeland as morally, intellectually, and politically primitive by comparison with England, France, and Germany, which had, either through philosophical soul-searching or actual practical experimentation, advanced toward increasingly democratic institutions.

In bitter opposition to the Westerners, there arose a group known as the Slavophiles, composed of many of Russia's finest poets and novelists, philosophers and scholars. These men viewed Western European culture as decadent, corrupt, and morally rotten; they looked to a new and pure Slavic society, headed by Russia, to rejuvenate Western philosophy. In their enthusiasm over slavonic culture, the early Slavophiles often lived among the Russian peasant population to study their way of life, art and music, social customs, and legal arrangements. Ironically, rather than leading them to a seemingly obvious condemnation of the tyranny under which the bulk of the Russian population suffered, their experiences and worship of all things slavonic led them instead to condone autocracy and Orthodoxy simply because the masses accepted them unquestioningly.

Although Turgenev is classified as a Westerner in this debate, such classification is misleading in that it does not account for his clear thinking on the issue. With his brilliant insight and objectivity, he saw the pitfalls of both camps and avoided their excesses. He was, like the Westerners, a passionate believer in democracy for the people, but he understood from his heart the deep and powerful force of the Slavophile argument. Nowhere is Turgenev's lucidity and freedom of spirit more evident than in *A House of Gentlefolk*, where, in the character of Lavretzky, he has embodied all the emotional and psychological richness of Slavophilism with none of its rigidness or excess. In a lengthy digression about Lavretzky's lineage, which precedes his appearance in the novel, the author is careful to stress his hero's dual background: His mother was a peasant, whereas his father belonged to the landed aristocracy and had become totally cut off from his people because of his extended residence in Europe. Lavretzky himself enters the story just returned from a stay in Paris with his shallow and unfaithful wife; he is coming home to his neglected ancestral estate in order to reestablish closeness to the land.

In the sole political scene in the novel, it is Lavretzky who eloquently summarizes Slavophile doctrine, insisting that the essential life and spirit of Russia resides in the common folk; he completely annihilates the feeble platitudes of the unhealthy, superficial, and egotistical bureaucrat Panshin. It is crucially important, however, that Lavretzky, unlike his real-life counterparts, is a democratic revolutionary spirit in the truest sense of the word, as witnessed in his freedom and individuality and in his love for the land and its people.

The woman who grows to love and be loved by Lavretzky is Liza, the heroine of *A House of Gentlefolk*. Turgenev has endowed her character with all the attributes shared by generations of Russian women, thus giving her a universal quality. Liza's personality, since it represents the spirit at the heart of the novel, is of central importance. She is a religious girl, beautiful in her moral strength and purity rather than physical attractiveness, and impressive in her calm passivity, her endurance, and her single-minded devotion. She is never revealed directly to the reader by the author but rather develops as a character through her reflection in the people around her; readers learn most about Liza through the eyes and heart of Lavretzky, but in the last analysis, she remains an elusive, if entrancing, figure.

Artistically, *A House of Gentlefolk* is more like an extended short story than a novel. The plot is slight: In a time span of only two months (not counting the brief epilogue), Lavretzky returns home and falls in love with Liza; his wife returns after she was believed dead; Liza enters a convent; and Lavretzky goes to his estate brokenhearted. The central theme is embodied in the love story, around which all the elements in the novel revolve; setting, atmosphere, and minor characterizations all combine to produce the single effect of the love sequence. This powerful singleness of effect gives the novel an extraordinary cohesiveness and perfection of structure.

This cohesiveness is perhaps best seen in Turgenev's evocation of a summer atmosphere, which coincides throughout the story with the emotions of the hero and heroine. The spirit of summer pervades the scene of Liza meeting Lavretzky in the garden, for example, imbuing the passage with an unsurpassed lyrical beauty. Likewise, the minor personages in the story, while being among Turgenev's most brilliant sketches of character, owe their primary importance to their relationship to the hero or heroine. The odious Panshin; the passionate old German, Lemm; Liza's mother and her crusty, wise old aunt, Marfa Timofyevna; Lavretzky's worthless and malicious wife, Varvara: All these unforgettable figures serve to reveal something about the two central characters. Along with the summer atmosphere and country landscape, of which they almost seem a part, they set the stage for the love story long before its participants make their entrance. The reader is given detailed portraits of a collection of minor characters before receiving any more description of Liza than that she is "a slender, tall, dark-haired girl of nineteen"; Lavretzky's belated appearance is preceded by a nine-chapter digression on his genealogy.

In his usual fashion, Turgenev uses his characters' love affairs to test their strength and worth. When in the epilogue Lavretzky returns after eight years to visit the house where Liza used to live, readers find that, despite his shattering loss of happiness, he has not only survived but emerged from the ordeal a better and kinder man. On one level, Turgenev has produced in his hero a symbol of the indomitable strength of the Russian soul; on another, he has shown the capacity inherent in all people for transcendence of pain and growth through suffering. *A House of Gentlefolk* is an elevating tale of melancholy but not defeat, and of sadness mingled with hope.

"Critical Evaluation" by Nancy G. Ballard

Bibliography:

Costlow, Jane T. *Worlds Within Worlds: The Novels of Ivan Turgenev*. Princeton, N.J.: Princeton University Press, 1990. Costlow examines *A House of Gentlefolk* as Turgenev's vision of Russian history and of individuals within that history.

Knowles, A. V. *Ivan Turgenev*. Boston: Twayne, 1988. In a brief discussion (pp. 55-60), of the novel, also known as *Home of the Gentry*, Knowles notes that the novel is the least often read of Turgenev's novels despite its many excellent features that show Turgenev at his most characteristic.

Seeley, Frank Friedeberg. "The 'Turgenev heroine': *A Nest of Gentry*." In *Turgenev: A Reading of His Fiction*. New York: Cambridge University Press, 1991. Seeley focuses (pp. 183-198) on Turgenev's romantic and idealistic female characters, seeing Liza as the prototype of the author's ideal, who compensates through poetry and music for the lack of love and understanding in her life.

Woodward, James B. *Metaphysical Conflict: A Study of the Major Novels of Ivan Turgenev*. Munich: Otto Sagner, 1990. Woodward probes (pp. 41-78) the personal relationships between characters in *A House of Gentlefolk* and traces the debate and conflict between Slavophiles and Westernists in Russia in the mid-nineteenth century. Adds to the understanding of social and cultural problems of the period.

Yarmolinsky, Avrahm. *Turgenev: The Man, His Art, and His Age*. New York: Collier Books, 1961. Yarmolinsky identifies the time, place, and conditions of Turgenev's writing of *A House of Gentlefolk*. Notes that the author wanted to show the vulgar side of Westernism and to have the Slavophile Lavretzky triumph over his opponent.

THE HOUSE OF LIFE
A Sonnet Sequence

Type of work: Poetry
Author: Dante Gabriel Rossetti (1828-1882)
First published: 1869; expanded editions, 1870, 1881; final version, 1894

If the sonnet is, as Dante Gabriel Rossetti claimed, "a moment's monument," then *The House of Life* is the record of a lifetime. In this continually growing and changing sequence of poems, Rossetti recorded the subtlest shifts in a life torn between two great doomed passions: his love for his wife, Elizabeth Siddal, whom he married in 1860 but who died only two years later; and his love for his mistress, Jane Morris, who was married to his friend, colleague, and business partner William Morris.

Sixteen sonnets were first published, not in book form, in 1869. In 1870, Rossetti published his first book of poetry, entitled simply *Poems*. The longest section of the volume was a collection of fifty sonnets and ten songs "Towards a work to be called 'The House of Life.'" Rossetti continued to write poetry throughout the next decade. The bulk of his literary composition occurred in 1870-1872 and 1879-1881, and in 1881 Rossetti published his last book of poetry, entitled *Ballads and Sonnets*. The longest section of that volume, too, was *The House of Life*, which had now grown to 102 sonnets. The cumulative effect of adding, rearranging, and, in one case, deleting verses was to change radically the reading experience of *The House of Life*; therefore, a full analysis must cover both the 1870 and the 1881 versions of the sonnet sequence.

The 1870 *House of Life* is a set of poems tracing the emotional effects of a brief, but intense, relationship that is predominantly sexual in nature. It arises directly out of Rossetti's relationship with Elizabeth Siddal. It begins with the birth of Love, which the poet adores in near-sacrilegious fashion: "Unto my lips . . . present/ The body and blood of Love in sacrament" (Sonnet 2). The lovers meet, kiss, marry, and reach the "Supreme Surrender" in the space of four sonnets, and spend day after day with each other: "The hours of Love fill full the echoing space" (Sonnet 12). These hours are doomed to be short; in sonnet 15, Rossetti already foresees the passing of their "Winged Hours," and by the next sonnet he has seen his beloved's "golden hair undimmed in death."

The poet falls into tearful grief; symbolically, the images in his verses change from birds and flowers to fire, tempests, and, most memorably, the terrible "Willowwood" (sonnets 24 to 27). The rhyme words in these four sonnets encompass the full range of despair: "drouth," "sterility," "abyss," "widowhood," and, of course, "death." At the end of the "Willowwood" sequence, new rhyme words appear: "soul . . . face . . . grace . . . aureole" (Sonnet 27). It is the turning point of the 1870 *House of Life*, signaling Rossetti's acceptance of his fate and his departure on a journey toward hope. His grief has given way to a meditation on death itself, rather than the death of his beloved; successive sonnets focus on couples, on parents and children, even on those who have never met ("Known in Vain"). That is not to say that there are not moments of despair; for example, when spring returns, it "earns/ No answering smile from me" (Sonnet 34). Yet, as the succeeding sequence entitled "The Choice" reveals, such emotions are held within a frame of faith in "God's word" and "God's breath." Thoughts of lost opportunities haunt him still, like "virgins, whom death's timely knell/ Might once have sainted" but who have been left "half entered in the book of Life" (Sonnet 39). He proclaims, "Retro Me, Sathana!"— "Get thee behind me, Satan"—and resumes his passage along the "narrow ways" of single life

(Sonnet 42). He recognizes that the "Vase of Life" is empty for him now: "My name is Might-have-been" (Sonnet 46). He also recognizes that he can smile again, that a new self has been created to mourn in the poet's place; thus he can reduce death to the status of "an infant child"—the only child of his marriage. It is not joy, but through the "written spell" of his sonnets he has come to a sense of hope, with which he can bring *The House of Life* (1870) to a close.

Between 1870 and 1881, much happened to Rossetti, which profoundly influenced *The House of Life*. He managed to spend much of 1870 and 1871 at his mistress Jane Morris' home, and composed as many as thirty additional sonnets during those happy months. Then came the events that dramatically changed Rossetti's life. Late in 1871, a journalist, Robert Buchanan, attacked the sexuality of Rossetti's verses in an article, "The Fleshly School of Poetry." Although Rossetti fought back, Buchanan's mudslinging fatally injured the poet's reputation; in 1872, Rossetti attempted suicide. Then, after two relatively quiet years, William Morris finally broke off most relations with Rossetti; never again would the poet's relationship with Jane Morris reach the absolute peace he described in "Silent Noon" (Sonnet 19, 1881).

The 1881 version of *The House of Life*, therefore, follows a dramatically different course than the 1870 version. Part 1, "Youth and Change," traces a relationship that is both less abrupt and less explicit in its passion. Reflecting Rossetti's fear that renewed charges of fleshliness might be brought against this new volume, the poet's beloved now does not yield until the seventh sonnet, and one of the most physical verses of the 1870 sequence, "Nuptial Sleep," is deleted. From there, passion quickly gives way to fulfilled pleasure; as the relationship develops, he learns to appreciate his beloved's beauty and love in various settings (sonnets 19 and 20 move from "Noon" to "Moonlight"). Not until Sonnet 24 does the first note of warning intrude; the poet here distinguishes himself from the youth who loves blindly, not seeing that change rules every relationship. In Sonnet 30 he notes that Summer is giving way to Winter, but then concludes with an affirmation of love's "imperishable core." Thus the poet does not have to face the reality of separation until Sonnet 45. Although he feels the separation to be deathlike, and is plunged into the depths of despair in "Willowwood," he wins through to acceptance by the end of the section.

In part 2, "Change and Fate," the poet is unable to maintain his hard-won hope. He seeks for grace, imagined as a soul-nourishing rain. Although he can create a "song-cloud," his spirit remains dry; the only water that appears is the infinite sea, which in Sonnet 62 threatens the poet with drowning and in Sonnet 73 appears to drown even the hopes of men and women. Looking back at the course of his love, he knows the relationship has ended its course. He can even, as the sonnet entitled "The Landmark" makes plain, recognize the point where his love affair started to fracture; he yearns to retrace his steps, but his more rational part knows that such a course leads only to the grave. In what is perhaps the darkest moment of the sequence, he envisions his beloved as Lilith, who "subtly of herself contemplative,/ Draws men [in] . . . Till heart and body and life are in [her] hold" (Sonnet 78). This sonnet, originally written to accompany a picture, Rossetti imported into *The House of Life* specifically to create a low point. In the next sonnet, these two strains, of deadly love and frightful sea, are brought together in an achieved moment of stasis Rossetti calls "The Monochord," which brings to the poet a sense of "regenerate rapture."

This is the turning point of the 1881 *House of Life*. Although he may never again feel the fever of youthful love, with its short-lived but infinite pleasures matched only by its long-lived and equally infinite pains, he has gained the ability to "see life steadily and see it whole," in the motto for Rossetti proclaimed by his contemporary Matthew Arnold. Rossetti has lost the material form of his beloved, but he has succeeded in transferring his love to a series of material substitutes: "Old and New Art" in sonnets 74-76, "Memorial Thresholds" in Sonnet 81, "Hero's Lamp" in Sonnet 88, a "Vase of Life" in Sonnet 95. All of these are images of that aesthetic impulse that led Rossetti to compose his 102 sonnets in the first place. Through the process of aesthetic composition, Rossetti has created a persona to grieve for him, and has thus restored himself to life in Sonnet 96:

> So Life herself, they spirit's friend and love,
> Even still as Spring's authentic harbinger
> Glows with fresh hours for hope to glorify.

The water that the grieving youth desperately longs for is found, in the "tears unseal'd" of a "new Self"—the self created by the poet in his expanded sonnet sequence. With his destructive grief contained safely within the persona of the poem, Rossetti can envision "the spray of some sweet life-fountain" (Sonnet 101) one day sacramentally bathing his spirit in its life-bearing dew. That would truly be a baptism to a new life, bringing Rossetti full circle to the *Vita Nuova* of Dante Alighieri, the fourteenth century Italian poet, which Rossetti had translated for his first publication, *The Early Italian Poets*, in 1861.

Dante Gabriel Rossetti's sonnet sequence *The House of Life* stakes a claim to greatness on three different grounds. It is the finest example of technical mastery over the sonnet form in Victorian literature; its complex variations in rhyme scheme and meter anticipate the outright shattering of poetic constraints in the twentieth century. It is also a stunning addition to that essential Victorian form that includes such disparate examples as Alfred, Lord Tennyson's *In Memoriam A. H. H.* (1850) and George Meredith's *Modern Love* (1862), the extended verse consolation. Rossetti manages to fuse Tennyson's success at presenting the long agony of recovering from the death of a beloved with Meredith's success at capturing in sensuous form those far more subtle emotions that are experienced during the collapse of a relationship. Finally, *The House of Life* stands as the poetic autobiography of one of Victorian England's most tormented souls, a man for whom happiness was an ideal to be pursued, but never an emotion to be achieved—one who went through his life carrying only "the bliss of being sad" (Sonnet 84, 1881).

Hartley S. Spatt

Bibliography:
Boos, Florence S. "Style in *The House of Life*." In *The Poetry of Dante G. Rossetti*. The Hague: Mouton, 1976. Covers a wide range of topics, including influences on Rossetti, the development of the mannered style, and the way in which his style reflects guilt over his unlawful affair with Jane Morris.
Gates, Barbara. "Revising *The House of Life*." *Victorian Poetry* 21, no. 1 (Spring, 1983): 65-78. Using sonnets that remained unpublished in either the 1870 or 1881 edition, Gates attempts to define Rossetti's principles of revision and selection.
The Journal of Pre-Raphaelite Studies 2, no. 2 (March, 1982). A special edition dedicated to the work of Dante Gabriel Rossetti. Includes essays on imagery, the use of time, and philosophical issues raised in *The House of Life*.
Riede, David G. *Dante Gabriel Rossetti and the Limits of Victorian Vision*. Ithaca, N.Y.: Cornell University Press, 1983. Discusses Rossetti's ornate style, claiming that it represents a way of dealing with the tension between Rossetti's desire to express his personal experience

and his equal desire to conceal the morbid nature of his grief for his dead wife and the adulterous nature of his love for Jane Morris.

Victorian Poetry 20, nos. 3-4 (Autumn/Winter, 1982). A special double issue devoted to the works of Dante Gabriel Rossetti. Offers several articles on *The House of Life*, including an important essay detailing the work put into the composition of the 1881 volume, a study of individual sonnets, and an analysis of the Christian aesthetic of the sonnet sequence.

THE HOUSE OF MIRTH

Type of work: Novel
Author: Edith Wharton (1862-1937)
Type of plot: Naturalism
Time of plot: Early twentieth century
Locale: New York
First published: 1905

Principal characters:
> LILY BART, a young woman
> LAWRENCE SELDEN, her friend
> SIMON ROSEDALE, a financier
> PERCY GRYCE, an eligible young man
> GUS TRENOR, a wealthy socialite
> JUDY TRENOR, his wife
> BERTHA DORSET, a woman who hated Lily
> GEORGE DORSET, her husband

The Story:

Lawrence Selden enjoyed watching Lily Bart put a new plan into operation. She was a very beautiful and clever young lady, and no matter how impromptu any action of hers appeared, Selden knew that she never made an unplanned move. Lily had almost no money of her own; her beauty and her good family background were her only assets. Her father had died soon after a reversal of his financial affairs, and her mother had drilled into her the idea that a wealthy marriage was her only salvation. After her mother's death, Lily was taken in by her aunt, Mrs. Peniston, who supplied her with a good home. However, Lily needed jewels, gowns, and cash to play bridge if she were to move in a social circle of wealthy and eligible men.

Simon Rosedale, a Jewish financier, would gladly have married Lily and provided her with a huge fortune, for he wanted to be accepted into the society in which Lily moved. Lily, however, thought that she still had better prospects, the most likely one being Percy Gryce, who lived with his watchful widowed mother.

Lily used her knowledge of his quiet life to her advantage. Selden, Lily, and Gryce were all houseguests at the home of Gus and Judy Trenor, an ideal opportunity for Lily, who assumed the part of a shy, demure young girl. Yet when Gryce was ready to propose, she let the chance slip away, for Lily abhorred the kind of scheming, manipulative person she had become. Even more important, perhaps, she was attracted to Selden, who truly understood her, even though he was poor and could offer her no escape from her own poverty.

Gus Trenor offered to invest some of Lily's small income, and over a period of time, he gave her more than eight thousand dollars, which he assured her was profit on the transaction. With that amount, she was able to pay most of her creditors and reopen her charge accounts. Gus seemed to think, however, that his wise investment on her account should make them better friends than Lily felt was desirable.

Lily unexpectedly came into possession of letters that Bertha Dorset had written to Selden, whom she had once loved. She had preferred to marry George Dorset's fortune, but she continued to write to Selden after her marriage.

3025

When Gus Trenor began to get more insistent in his demands for Lily's companionship, she became really worried. She knew that people were talking about her and that her position in society was precarious. She turned to Selden for advice. He told her that he loved her for what she could be, but that he could give her nothing now. He had no money, and he would not even offer her his love because he could not love her as the scheming, ruthless fortune hunter she was.

One night, Lily received a message that Judy Trenor wanted her to call. When she arrived at the Trenor home, Lily found Gus there alone; he had sent the message. Gus told her then that the money had not been profit on her investment but a gift from him. When he intimated that she had always known the money was from him personally, Lily was terrified, but at last she managed to get out of the house. She knew then that there was only one thing for her to do. She must accept Rosedale's offer of marriage. She put off writing to him, though, and accepted the Dorsets' invitation to accompany them on a Mediterranean cruise on their yacht.

Selden also left New York. Unbeknownst to Lily, he had seen her leave the Trenor house on the night Gus had tricked her into thinking Judy wanted her to call. Selden had always refused to believe the unsavory stories circulating about Lily, but the evidence of his own eyes, he thought, was too plain to be ignored. When he met Lily abroad, he treated her with cool courtesy.

Lily returned to New York when her aunt, Mrs. Peniston, died, who left Lily ten thousand dollars. Lily planned to repay Gus Trenor with her inheritance, and she found the delay in settling her aunt's estate intolerable. Meanwhile, Bertha Dorset's insinuations about Lily's conduct abroad, coupled with the talk about Lily and Gus Trenor, finished Lily's reputation. She took various positions, until at last she was reduced to working in the factory of a milliner. She had first offered to accept Rosedale's former proposal of marriage, but since her fall she was no longer useful to Rosedale, and he now refused to marry her. He knew that Lily had the letters Bertha had written Selden, and he also knew that George Dorset no longer loved his wife and would gladly marry Lily. It seemed to Rosedale that Lily had only two alternatives, either to take George Dorset away from Bertha or to go to Bertha with the letters and force her once again to receive her.

At first, Lily's feeling for Selden made her shrink from doing anything that would harm him. Then she lost even her menial job. Without money to buy food or to pay for her room in a dingy boardinghouse, she reluctantly took the letters and started to the Dorset home. On the way, she stopped to see Selden. When he again told her that he loved her, or rather that he could love her if she were to give up her greed for wealth and position, she gave up her plan and, unseen by him, dropped the letters into the fireplace. She thanked him for the kindness he, and he alone, had given her, and walked out into the night.

When she returned to her room, she found the check for the ten thousand dollars of her inheritance. She sat down at once and wrote a check to Gus Trenor for the amount she owed him and put it in an envelope. In another envelope, she placed the ten-thousand-dollar check and addressed the envelope to her bank. She put the two envelopes side by side on her desk before she lay down to sleep; but sleep would not come. At last, she took from her bureau a bottle of chloral. She poured the contents of the bottle into a glass and drank it all, then lay down again.

The next morning, feeling a sudden need to see Lily at once, Selden went early to her rooming house. There he found a doctor already in attendance and Lily dead from an overdose of chloral. On her desk, he saw the two envelopes. The stub of the open checkbook beside them told the story of Lily's last effort to square her accounts. He knew then that his love for her had been justified, but the words he spoke as he knelt by her bed came too late.

Critical Evaluation:

Edith Wharton's *The House of Mirth* dramatizes the decline and death of Lily Bart, a young woman who is doomed by her own virtue in a materialistic society that either debases or destroys its members. Viewed from this point of view, the novel can be considered an example of American naturalism, a term applied to literature to indicate the author's reliance on a governing determinism in which the protagonist's career is dictated by hereditary or environmental forces. Caught up in a matrix of forces, naturalistic protagonists cannot be held responsible for their actions because they possess little or no freedom of will. Consequently, the naturalistic novel manifests an ethical orientation that is neither moral nor immoral but amoral. This is but one of the features that distinguish naturalism from realism; others include a focus on the lower classes, an attack on false values, a reformist agenda, imagery that is animalistic or mechanistic, and a plot of decline that leads to catastrophic closure for the protagonist through a deterministic sequence of causes and effects.

In *The House of Mirth*, Lily's nature is characterized by a duality that is the result of irreconcilable hereditary traits. From her mother, she inherited a calculating impulse and her attractive appearance, which she uses to maintain her social status. From her father, Lily inherited a contradictory impulse to revolt, an aesthetic sensitivity, and the desire to write poetry and to profit from the experience of her father, who was forced to abandon his artistic inclinations to support his wife's lavish habits. Lily also inherited her father's scruples, idealism, and sentimentality—all virtues without survival value in the moral wasteland of the nouveau riche. The moral imperatives that perished in her father for lack of reinforcement are resurrected in Lily as a monument to his memory and to her own ruin. What leads to her doom above all else is Lily's fatal vacillation between the moral and the material. She revolts against the materialistic values of her mansion-dwelling friends but lacks the moral training to adapt to life outside that milieu. Lacking the ability to survive either inside or outside her society, Lily's death becomes inevitable.

In her imagery, Wharton reinforces the determinism at work in the novel. As the title suggests, the dominant metaphor Wharton deploys is that of the house, which serves as a springboard for her attack on false values. The "house of mirth" becomes an emblem for the moral wasteland contained within the pleasure palaces of the old and newly rich. Those who live in these mansions are materially wealthy but spiritually bankrupt. Love is the only luxury they cannot afford, and it has been replaced by a mere love of objects.

Wharton sets up the contrast between the Trenors' drawing room and Nellie Struther's kitchen. Unlike the pleasure palaces of Lily's wealthy friends, Nellie's kitchen is physically small but spiritually vast. Here the family and love for one another are more important than material possessions. The spiritual contentment is contrasted with Lily's restlessness and with the void within her. The attraction Lily feels for that spiritual world is indicated by the nest on the cliff and the baby that Lily cradles in her lap, even as her ascent of the stairs leading to Nellie's kitchen underscores her moral incline.

The metaphor of the stairwell has broader significance, for the plot structure of *The House of Mirth* may be likened to a descending stairwell that represents Lily's decline, which is effected by a series of social descents. She is abandoned by the Trenors, who occupy the highest rung of the social ladder, because her principles are at odds with their amorality. Landing with the Dorsets, who occupy a slightly lower social rung, Lily is alienated by Bertha's ruthlessness and finally abandoned by them as well. Her social decline continues in her association with the Brys and Rosedale, the embodiment of the new rich. Revolted by their rampant greed, Lily takes up with the hedonistic, pleasure-seeking Gormons, who occupy an even lower social level. Lily is cast out from this circle as a consequence of Bertha's insinuations about her reputation, and she herself cannot tolerate the improprieties of Norma Hatch, a wealthy, indolent divorcée. Lily's final refusal to accept money from Gus Trenor seals her fate and plunges her into real poverty—a realm in which she is ill-equipped to survive because of her refined tastes, vacillating nature, and lack of moral training.

Wharton's attack on false values in *The House of Mirth* is yet another trait of the naturalistic novel. As she shows in the career of Lily Bart, inhabitants of the house of mirth are doomed by their virtues and rewarded by their vices. Had Lily lacked her moral impulse she would have become a successful New York socialite. Had she, on the other hand, received strong moral training at home, she could have adapted to life outside the ornamental realm of high society, where personal relations cannot survive. Lily's inability to survive in either world symbolizes the price paid for the pursuit of the American materialistic dream, which debases and detroys what is best in the individual.

Stephen G. Brown

Bibliography:
Bendixen, Alfred, and Annette Zilversmit, eds. *Edith Wharton: New Critical Essays.* New York: Garland, 1992. Essays on various aspects of Wharton's art. In "Reading Mrs. Lloyd," Judith Fryer analyzes the cultural significance of the tableaux vivants with illustrations of the paintings that Lily Bart enacted. Elaine Showalter, a feminist critic, in "The Death of the Lady (Novelist)" sees the death of the "lady" necessary for the birth of the woman artist.
Howe, Irving, ed. *Edith Wharton: A Collection of Critical Essays.* Englewood Cliffs, N.J.: Prentice-Hall, 1962. A collection of some of the pioneering essays on Edith Wharton. Irving Howe's essay, "A Reading of *The House of Mirth*," praises Wharton's style though he regrets her somewhat overcharged rhetoric. Diane Trilling in "*The House of Mirth* Revisited" stresses the heroine's moral ambiguity.
Lawson, Richard H. *Edith Wharton.* New York: Frederick Ungar, 1977. Discusses the ways in which *The House of Mirth* was a turning point in the development of Wharton's professional writing skills.
McDowell, Margaret B. *Edith Wharton.* Boston: Twayne, 1976. In chapter 2, the author draws a parallel between Lily Bart's gradual destruction by a hostile society and her growing aspiration to become independent and responsible. Also contains an excellent annotated bibliography and chronology.
Wharton, Edith. *The House of Mirth.* Edited by Shari Benstock. Case Studies in Contemporary Criticism. Boston: Bedford Books of St. Martin's Press, 1994. Contains the complete, authoritative text, as well as a brief biography and historical context, critical history, and essays from cultural, Marxist, feminist, deconstructive, and psychoanalytic perspectives.

THE HOUSE OF THE SEVEN GABLES
A Romance

Type of work: Novel
Author: Nathaniel Hawthorne (1804-1864)
Type of plot: Gothic
Time of plot: 1850
Locale: Salem, Massachusetts
First published: 1851

Principal characters:
MISS HEPZIBAH PYNCHEON, a spinster
CLIFFORD PYNCHEON, her brother
JUDGE JAFFREY PYNCHEON, a kinsman
PHOEBE PYNCHEON, a distant cousin
MR. HOLGRAVE, Miss Hepzibah's lodger

The Story:

The House of the Seven Gables was a colonial house built in the English style of half-timber and half-plaster. It stood on Pyncheon Street in quiet Salem. The house had been built by Colonel Pyncheon, who had wrested the desirable site from Matthew Maule, a poor man executed as a wizard. Colonel Pyncheon was responsible for the execution, and he was taking the doomed man's land, so Maule, at the moment of his execution, declared that God would give the Pyncheons blood to drink. Despite this grim prophecy, the colonel had his house, and its builder was Thomas Maule, son of the old wizard.

Colonel Pyncheon, dying in his great oak chair just after the house had been completed, choked with blood so that his shirtfront was stained scarlet. Although doctors explained the cause of his death as apoplexy, the townsfolk had not forgotten old Maule's prophecy. The time of the colonel's death was inauspicious. It was said that he had just completed a treaty by which he had bought huge tracts of land from the Indians, but this deed had not been confirmed by the general court and was never discovered by any of his heirs. Rumor also had it that a man was seen leaving the house about the time Colonel Pyncheon died.

More recently, another startling event had occurred at the House of the Seven Gables. Jaffrey Pyncheon, a bachelor, had been found dead in the colonel's great oaken armchair, and his nephew, Clifford Pyncheon, had been sentenced to imprisonment after being found guilty of the murder of his uncle.

These events were in the unhappy past, however, and in 1850, the House of the Seven Gables was the home of Miss Hepzibah Pyncheon, an elderly, single woman, who let one wing of the old house to a young man of radical tendencies, a maker of daguerreotypes, whose name was Mr. Holgrave.

Miss Hepzibah was about to open a shop in one of the rooms of her house. Her brother Clifford was coming home from the state prison after thirty years, and she had to earn money in some way to support him. On the first day of her venture as a storekeeper, Miss Hepzibah proved to be a failure. The situation was saved, however, by the arrival of young Phoebe Pyncheon from the country. Soon she was operating the shop at a profit.

Clifford arrived from the prison a broken man of childish, querulous ways. Once he tried to throw himself from a big arched window which afforded him almost his only contact with the outside world. He was fond of Phoebe, but Miss Hepzibah irritated him with her sullen scowling. For acquaintances, Clifford had Uncle Venner, a handyman who did odd jobs for the neighborhood, and the tenant of the house, Mr. Holgrave, the daguerreotypist.

The only other relative living in town was the highly respected Judge Pyncheon, another nephew of old Jaffrey Pyncheon, for whose murder Clifford had spent thirty years in prison. He was, in fact, the heir of the murdered man, and he had been somehow involved with Clifford's arrest and imprisonment. For these reasons, Clifford refused to see him when the Judge offered to give Clifford and Hepzibah a home at his country seat.

Meanwhile, Phoebe had become friendly with Mr. Holgrave. In turn, he thought that she brought light and hope into the gloomy old house, and he missed her greatly when she returned to her home in the country. Her visit was to be a brief one, however, for she had gone only to make some preparations before coming to live permanently with Miss Hepzibah and Clifford.

Before Phoebe returned from the country, Judge Pyncheon visited the House of the Seven Gables and, over Miss Hepzibah's protest, insisted on seeing Clifford, who, he said, knew a family secret which meant great wealth for the judge. When at last she went out of the room to summon her brother, Judge Pyncheon sat down in the old chair by the fireplace, over which hung the portrait of the Colonel Pyncheon who had built the house. As the judge sat in the old chair, his ticking watch in his hand, an unusually strong family likeness could be noted between the stern judge and his Puritan ancestor in the portrait. Unable to find Clifford to deliver the Judge's message, Miss Hepzibah returned. As she approached the door, Clifford appeared from within, laughing and pointing to the chair where the judge sat dead of apoplexy under the portrait of the old colonel: His shirtfront was stained with blood. The wizard's curse had been fulfilled once more; God had given him blood to drink.

The two helpless old people were so distressed by the sight of the dead man that they crept away from the house without notifying anyone and departed on the train. The dead body of the judge remained seated in the chair.

It was some time before the body was discovered by Holgrave. When Phoebe returned to the house, he admitted her. He had not yet summoned the police because he wished to protect the old couple as long as possible. While he and Phoebe were alone in the house, Holgrave declared his love for her. They were interrupted by the return of Miss Hepzibah and the now-calm Clifford. They had decided that to run away would not solve their problem.

The police attributed the judge's death to natural causes, and Clifford, Miss Hepzibah, and Phoebe became the heirs to his great fortune. It now seemed certain that Jaffrey Pyncheon had also died of natural causes, not by Clifford's hand, and that the judge had so arranged the evidence to make Clifford appear a murderer.

In a short time, all the occupants of the House of the Seven Gables were ready to move to the judge's country estate which they had inherited. They gathered for the last time in the old room under the dingy portrait of Colonel Pyncheon. Clifford said he had a vague memory of something mysterious connected with the picture. Holgrave offered to explain the mystery and pressed a secret spring near the picture. When he did so, the portrait fell to the floor, disclosing a recess in the wall. From this niche, Holgrave drew out the ancient Indian deed to the lands which the Pyncheons had claimed. Clifford then remembered he had once found the secret spring. It was this secret that Judge Pyncheon had hoped to learn from Clifford.

Phoebe asked how Holgrave happened to know these facts. The young man explained his name was not Holgrave, but Maule. He was, he said, a descendant of the wizard, Matthew Maule, and of Thomas Maule, who built the House of the Seven Gables. The knowledge of the hidden Indian deed had been handed down to the descendants of Thomas Maule, who built the compartment behind the portrait and secreted the deed there after the colonel's death. Holgrave was the last of the Maules, and Phoebe, the last of the Pyncheons, would bear his name. Matthew Maule's curse had been expiated.

Critical Evaluation:

In reputation, *The House of the Seven Gables* usually stands in the shadow of its predecessor, *The Scarlet Letter* (1850). It is, however, a rich and solid achievement. Its characters are among Nathaniel Hawthorne's most complex. The author himself thought it, in comparison with the earlier work, "more characteristic of my mind, and more proper and natural for me to write." In his preface, Hawthorne explicitly states his moral: "the truth, namely that the wrong-doing of one generation lives into the successive ones, and, divesting itself of every temporary advantage, becomes a pure and uncontrollable mischief." This sentiment echoes the biblical adage that "The fathers have eaten sour grapes, and the children's teeth are set on edge." Hawthorne's interest in the heritage of sin was probably whetted by the history of his own family. His first American ancestor, William Hathorne (Nathaniel himself added the *w* to the family name), was a soldier and magistrate who once had a Quaker woman publicly whipped through the streets. William's son John, having, as Nathaniel said, "inherited the persecuting spirit," was a judge at the infamous Salem witch trials, during which a defendant cursed another of the three judges with the cry, "God will give you blood to drink!" Thenceforth, as Hawthorne noted, although the family remained decent, respectable folk, their fortunes began to decline.

The fate of the Pyncheon family of the novel is considerably more dramatic. Matthew Maule's curse on Colonel Pyncheon, who has persecuted him for witchcraft and wrested from him the land on which the seven-gabled house is to be built, is precisely that which Judge John Hathorne had heard in a similar trial. It is apparently fulfilled on the day of the housewarming, when Colonel Pyncheon dies of apoplexy, the hemorrhage rising through his throat to stain his white shirt. Hawthorne would have readers believe, however, that such sins as Pyncheon's are not so easily paid for. The family occupies the mansion, but misfortune is their constant lot. There are repeated apoplectic deaths, sometimes heralded by an ominous gurgling in the throat; greed leads Judge Jaffrey Pyncheon, like his ancestor, to participate in a trumped-up trial, this time against his own cousin; and years of pride and isolation have thinned the family blood so that, like the scrawny chickens that peck in the Pyncheon garden, they are an unattractive, ineffectual lot. Judge Pyncheon is a monster who hides his avarice and callousness behind a facade of philanthropy and civic service. Clifford, like Hawthorne's Young Goodman Brown, is a sensitive soul who is unmanned by his confrontation with evil; after years of imprisonment, he is poised on the brink of madness. Hepzibah, a spinster who has spent most of her life waiting for her brother's release, is virtually helpless either to resolve her precarious financial situation or to deal with her malevolent cousin.

Only young Phoebe possesses both goodness and energy. It is significant that she is the "country cousin" whose father married beneath his rank and that Hepzibah observes that the girl's self-reliance must have come from her mother's blood. Thus Hawthorne casts his vote for the energizing effects of a democratic, as opposed to an aristocratic, social system; he has Holgrave, the daguerreotypist, support this view with the comment that families should continually merge into the great mass of humanity, without regard to ancestry.

The other fully vital character in the novel is Holgrave, the young daguerreotypist. He is one of Hawthorne's most charming creations: a perceptive, adventurous man who has been, it seems, almost everywhere, and done almost everything. His conversations with Phoebe reveal him as a radical who believes that the past "lies upon the Present like a giant's dead body," preventing any generation's true fulfillment—a thesis frequently expressed by Hawthorne's contemporary, Ralph Waldo Emerson. Holgrave goes so far as to suggest that institutional buildings should "crumble to ruin once in twenty years, or thereabouts, as a hint to the people to examine into and reform the institutions which they symbolize." He is also a psychologist; his daguerreotypes, which inevitably go beyond mere pictorial likeness to expose personality, symbolize his own insight into human nature.

At the end of the novel, readers are led to believe that the curse is broken as Phoebe, the last of the Pyncheons, plans to marry Holgrave, who turns out to be a descendant of old Matthew Maule. The curse's effects can all be explained naturally: Holgrave observes that perhaps old Maule's prophecy was founded on knowledge that apoplectic death had been a Pyncheon trait for generations. Avarice and cruelty can certainly be passed on by example, and pride, isolation, and inbreeding can account for the "thin-bloodedness" of the once-aristocratic family. Now, as Phoebe, whose blood has already been enriched by plebeian stock, and Holgrave, who has escaped the stifling influence of his own declining family by traveling widely, replace a tradition of hatred with that of love, it seems plausible that the curse may indeed have run its course. Perhaps the chain of ugly events—what Chillingworth of *The Scarlet Letter* termed "dark necessity"—can be terminated by positive acts of goodwill.

The novel is replete with gothic characteristics: mystery, violence, a curse, gloomy atmosphere, archaic diction, and visits from the spirit world. The novel is not realistic, but it demonstrates what Henry James called Hawthorne's "high sense of reality," in describing how the sins of fathers are felt by children for generations to come. The ending, however, discloses that, although Hawthorne recognized the deterministic effects of heredity, environment, and the human predisposition to evil, he was essentially a hopeful man who believed that the individual possesses a residuum of will that can cope with and perhaps change "dark necessity."

"Critical Evaluation" by Sally Buckner

Bibliography:
Abel, Darrel. *The Moral Picturesque: Studies in Hawthorne's Fiction.* West Lafayette, Ind.: Purdue University Press, 1988. Sees the novel as an allegory about love versus self-love, tradition versus ambition and pride, and imagination versus preoccupation with the present fact.
Donohue, Agnes McNeill. *Hawthorne: Calvin's Ironic Stepchild.* Kent, Ohio: Kent State University Press, 1985. Calls the novel Hawthorne's attempt to "gloss over" his basically tragic view that the parents' sins are visited upon the children. Argues that its dominant symbol, after the house itself, is the garden of Eden, which in turn is connected to the idea of the Fall. Claims the book's ending indicates that Phoebe and Holgrave will be tempted into another Fall.
Male, Roy R. *Hawthorne's Tragic Vision.* Austin: University of Texas Press, 1957. Argues that the book's theme is the interpenetration of past and present. Breaks new ground in the critical understanding of Hawthorne.
Martin, Terrence. *Nathaniel Hawthorne.* Boston: Twayne, 1983. Focuses on ways in which Hawthorne and his characters view the effects of the past on the present. Also investigates the novel's treatment of Hawthorne's theme of the relationship between head (Holgrave) and heart (Phoebe).
Waggoner, Hyatt H. *The Presence of Hawthorne.* Baton Rouge: Louisiana State University Press, 1979. Originally an introduction to an edition of the novel, the chapter "From Darkness to Light" argues that the book expresses Hawthorne's "greatly desired belief in the possibility of redemption from evil." Also shows that the book is "radically democratic."

THE HOUSE OF THE SPIRITS

Type of work: Novel
Author: Isabel Allende (1942-   )
Type of plot: Magical Realism
Time of plot: 1920's-1970's
Locale: Unnamed South American country
First published: La casa de los espíritus, 1982 (English translation, 1985)

> *Principal characters:*
> ESTEBAN TRUEBA, the patriarch of the Trueba family
> CLARA, his wife
> BLANCA, their daughter
> JAIME and
> NICOLÁS, their twin sons
> ALBA, Blanca's daughter

The Story:

At the turn of the century, the eccentric family of a feminist named Nívea and an ambitious politician named Severo del Valle had a prominent place in society. The beauty of their green-haired daughter Rosa and the supernatural powers of her clairvoyant younger sister Clara were legendary. Their Uncle Marcos was a carefree explorer. Rosa the Beautiful was engaged to Esteban Trueba, who went to work in the mines hoping to strike gold; she died after accidentally sipping poisoned brandy.

After Rosa's death, Esteban moved to his family's ruined country estate, Tres Marías; he rebuilt it with the money he had saved to marry Rosa and became a rich man. Esteban abused young peasant girls in the area. He refused to acknowledge Esteban García, his first child, born to his servant Pancha García, and he fathered many other illegitimate children. He returned to the city when his mother, Ester Trueba, was dying; her inheritance had been squandered by her husband, and she lived in poverty, overwhelming her children with her fears and her illnesses.

Clara had remained silent for nine years after Rosa's death. When she spoke again, it was to predict that she would marry Esteban at the age of nineteen. When he married her, his efforts to please her proved to be disastrous when he gave her a rug made out of the hide of her beloved dead dog, Barrabás. Esteban built an extravagant house for Clara, which was soon populated by her spiritualist friends. His unmarried sister, the tormented Férula, went to live with them at Clara's request.

The Truebas named their first-born Blanca. When the family moved to Tres Marías, the girl met the peasant Pedro Tercero García, the foreman's grandson, and started a romantic liaison with him. The rebellious Blanca showed no inclination for her mother's spiritualism or her father's fits of rage. Esteban established a lifelong friendship with Tránsito Soto at a brothel called Red Lantern, and he gave her money to set up her own business in the city.

Férula, who pampered Clara because she showed her affection, caused Esteban to become jealous of her relationship with his wife and was told to leave; Nana, the old nanny, was happy at her departure. When Férula died, her ghost appeared to the family. Clara's parents died in an automobile accident before the birth of her twin sons, Jaime and Nicolás; Clara placed her mother's decapitated head in a hat box. While Blanca attended a convent school, the boys went to a British institution. Jaime later became a generous doctor to the poor; he performed an abortion when Nicolás, a playboy interested in mystical experiences, was responsible for his girlfriend Amanda's becoming pregnant.

Clara predicted the earthquake that destroyed Tres Marías. Esteban spent four months recuperating from his broken bones while Clara and Pedro Segundo García, the father of Blanca's lover, rebuilt the estate. The French count Jean de Satigny told Esteban about the young lovers' secret meetings. Esteban, enraged, hit his daughter and also Clara, who would not speak to him again after that. Pancha García's grandson, Esteban García, helped him to find and punish Pedro Tercero, who lost three fingers.

Esteban told Blanca that he had killed her lover, and when he found out about her pregnancy he forced Jean de Satigny to marry her and gave them money to go away. Clara told her daughter that the baby's father, Pedro Tercero, was alive. Blanca left her husband when she discovered his illicit affairs. When Blanca's green-haired daughter Alba was born in "the big house on the corner," it brought happiness to Esteban. Clara died on Alba's seventh birthday, changing Esteban's life; with his love gone forever, he concentrated on Alba's upbringing and his political endeavors as senator. Blanca was in charge of the house, but she could not stop its decline.

The strong-willed Blanca resumed meeting Pedro Tercero, who had become a Socialist revolutionary and political singer. At the age of eighteen, Alba met Miguel, Amanda's brother, and became involved in student demonstrations. Esteban, taken hostage by the peasants, was saved by Pedro Tercero, and Alba found out that he was her father. The conspiracy to eliminate the Socialist government led to political turmoil and the president's death. Jaime, who refused to accept the demands of the military leading the coup, was tortured and killed.

Esteban, a witness to the horrors of the new political repression, decided to help Blanca and Pedro Tercero leave the country. Clara's spirit protected Alba when she was arrested and tortured by Esteban García, who had become a policeman and a colonel. Clara told her granddaughter to create stories in her mind to forget the pain and suffering inflicted upon her and the others. At Esteban's request, Tránsito Soto, who represented the chance of social mobility, was able to free Alba from jail through her political contacts.

Alba, pregnant with a child whose father was either Miguel or Esteban García, did not stop hoping for a better future. She thought of Miguel, who was still in hiding. She and her grandfather, inspired by Clara's and Blanca's writings and their own memories, decided to write down the family's story. Esteban died in Alba's arms, murmuring Clara's name. The rage of his earlier years had changed into tenderness.

Critical Evaluation:

Born in Peru, the Chilean writer Isabel Allende became the most widely read woman writer in Latin America after the publication of her first novel, *The House of the Spirits*, and foreign-language versions of the book established her international critical success and led to a major motion picture in 1994. After having worked as a journalist in Chile, Allende started writing fiction in Venezuela, where she lived in exile after the assassination of her uncle, President Salvador Allende. In 1988, she moved to the United States. Her first novel was followed by *Of Love and Shadows* (1984), *Eva Luna* (1987), *Stories of Eva Luna* (1990), *The Infinite Plan* (1991), and *Paula* (1994).

In *The House of the Spirits*, Allende traces the lives of the del Valle and the Trueba families, their relations with one another, and their participation in the history of their times. The half-century historical span encompasses four generations chronologically and includes flashbacks and foreshadowing. The past is reclaimed by the use of Clara's notebooks "that bore witness to life," Blanca's letters, and the memories of the first-person narrators Alba and her grandfather, who reconstitute the saga together. Narrative circularity is achieved in the epilogue, written by Alba, and the novel ends, as it had begun, with Clara's words, "Barrabás came to us by sea."

The book, a testimonial text inscribing a period in the history of Chile and Allende's family, started as a letter to the author's dying grandfather in Chile, in which she declared that all memories would be saved through her writing. The country is unnamed and characters often function on a symbolic level, but they are manifestly Chilean: The candidate, later called the president, is Salvador Allende, the poet is the late Nobel laureate Pablo Neruda; and Allende's eccentric relatives serve as models for a number of the other characters.

Allende dedicated the work to her mother, her grandmother, and "all the other extraordinary women of the story." There is emphasis on the female characters, and the female perspective is evident in the presentation of the effects of political activity on family life and personal relationships. Yet the perspective is not exclusively female, for Esteban collaborates with Alba in the writing of the story and the author includes diverse points of view from a broad social spectrum.

Written in the tradition of Latin America's Magical Realism, a synthesis of realism and the supernatural, the novel presents characters caught between fact and fantasy. Diaries and testimonies as well as dreams, the irrational, and the fantastic serve as sources for the narrative. Clara's clairvoyance, her Uncle Marcos' magic books, Pedro García's special powers, Nicolás' attempted clairvoyance, and ghostly happenings constitute a world in which the line between imagination and reality merges.

Magical Realism blends with politics, giving the novel a romantic tone. When the Truebas are drawn into the violent confrontations between oligarchs and socialists, magic subsides and realism takes over, with a grim depiction of political brutality and its power to disintegrate families. The terror after the military coup hits all the members of the Trueba family, regardless of the politics they had represented. Victims such as Alba and her friend Ana Díaz in the concentration camp articulate the voice of the oppressed. Blanca, Alba, and other women are shown as they become involved politically in acts of solidarity and resistance against the powers that victimize.

The story moves the reader to reject dictatorship and abuses of power at all levels. Machismo, related to the abuse of power by men, is represented by Esteban. Blanca is entrapped in her father's plot to hide Alba's illegitimacy, although he himself procreates many children out of wedlock. Pancha's grandson, Esteban García, a monster created by the tyrannical patriarchal system embodied in Esteban Trueba, revenges himself on Alba and, ironically, brings a kind of poetic justice when Esteban's tyranny turns against him. Allende gives concrete forms to her belief that conflicts of race, class, gender, and ethnicity perpetuate hate and violence and turn victims into aggressors.

Alba's unborn daughter embodies the hope for a future of reconciliation and love, just as writing is also an act of hope. Words and language have the power to recover what is lost and to re-create lives and stories, real or invented. Isabel Allende transcends national boundaries with her lyrical and imaginative story set against a turbulent political background. Her novel represents a complex but universal world of love, death, eternity, and time.

Ludmila Kapschutschenko-Schmitt

Bibliography:
Allende, Isabel. *Paula.* Translated by Margaret Sayers Peden. 1st ed. New York: HarperCollins,

1995. A personal memoir that provides autobiographical details about the author's life and works. Blends real and magical worlds as in *The House of the Spirits*.

Earle, Peter G. "Literature as Survival: Allende's *The House of the Spirits*." *Comparative Literature* 28 (1987): 543-554. Discusses the novel as a female saga in which Nívea, Clara, Blanca, and Alba represent stages of women's sociopolitical awareness. Notes the significance of the names, which refer to degrees of luminosity and symbolize light and hope.

Gazarian-Gautier, Marie-Lise. *Interviews with Latin American Writers*. Normal, Ill.: Dalkey Archive Press, 1992. Allende discusses her first three novels and the influence of women's storytelling in her family. She explains that the loss of her roots and her longing for Chile while in exile led her to write the first book.

Hart, Patricia. *Narrative Magic in the Fiction of Isabel Allende*. Rutherford, N.J.: Fairleigh Dickinson University Press, 1989. Examines how magic functions in Allende's fiction in a spectrum that includes social and political comment. Includes a comparative analysis of Allende's novel and Gabriel García Márquez's *One Hundred Years of Solitude* (1967), which concludes that Allende forges the use of a unique "magical feminism."

Riquelme Rojas, Sonia, and Edna Aguirre Rehbein, eds. *Critical Approaches to Isabel Allende's Novels*. New York: Peter Lang, 1991. A collection of essays that explores Allende's three novels from several perspectives, including a study of the connection with the picaresque tradition and parodic writing in the contemporary literature of Latin America. Also includes an interview with Allende in 1989.

THE HOUSE ON MANGO STREET

Type of work: Novel
Author: Sandra Cisneros (1954-   )
Type of plot: Bildungsroman
Time of plot: Mid-1960's
Locale: Latino neighborhood in Chicago
First published: 1984

Principal characters:

ESPERANZA CORDERO, a young girl growing up in a Latino quarter of
  Chicago
ALICIA, her friend and a struggling college student
SALLY, a beautiful neighborhood girl
MAGDELENA (NENNY), Esperanza's younger sister
LUCY, Esperanza's quiet friend from Texas
RACHEL, Lucy's little sister

The Story:

Esperanza Cordero and her family had not always lived on Mango Street. The family of six had lived in a series of run-down apartments before finally buying a small house with crumbling brick. Esperanza was disappointed. It was not a real house, not the house she had imagined they would someday live in. They said this house was only temporary, but Esperanza knew better.

Esperanza loved her family but resented having to look after her little sister, Nenny. She hoped someday to have a best friend to play with instead. She also wanted a new name, because her Spanish name meant "sadness" to her. She made up Zeze the X. She met Cathy, who gossiped about the neighbors and said that her father wanted to move because people like the Corderos kept moving in. Esperanza and Nenny met Lucy and Rachel, newly arrived from Texas. They pooled their savings to buy a bike for ten dollars and took turns riding it. They visited the black man's junk store and heard his music box play. Esperanza knew that some people were afraid of her neighborhood and called them "Those Who Don't." She explained, "They think we're dangerous." She herself felt safe and secure in her neighborhood of brown-skinned people.

Esperanza's friend Alicia, the college student, got up one morning and saw a mouse behind the sink. Her father said there was no mouse. Alicia was afraid of two things in life, her father and mice. She studied at night and, ever since her mother had died, got up with the "tortilla star" every morning to make the lunches for her brothers and sisters.

Esperanza passed the days out in the street playing jump rope with Nenny, Lucy, and Rachel and singing rhymes about their neighbors. One day, the woman in the family of little feet gave them some old high heels, and they wore them through the neighborhood. The grocery man said they were too young to be wearing such shoes, but they did not take them off until a whiskey bum offered Rachel a dollar for a kiss. Then they all ran away and hid the shoes under a bushel basket on Lucy's back porch.

Esperanza often thought she did not fit in. She would have liked to eat in the school's canteen with the kids who bring lunch instead of walking home for lunch, but the Mother Superior yelled at her. She was also embarrassed about her rice sandwich. At her little cousin's baptism, she hated wearing scuffed brown shoes with her pretty new dress, but her Uncle Nacho made her feel great by saying she was the prettiest girl there and dancing with her until everyone clapped.

Esperanza was growing up. The girls gossiped about becoming physically mature. Esperanza got her first job. It did not go well because an Oriental man tricked her by pretending to be friendly in the lunchroom, then grabbing and kissing her hard. Her *abuelito* (grandfather) died, and she felt sorrow for her grieving father. Her Aunt Lupe was dying from an incurable bone disease. The girls made fun of Lupe one day, but Esperanza felt so bad she began to bring her aunt books and poems, which she read to her. Aunt Lupe was the first person to hear Esperanza recite one of her own poems. She was also the first to encourage Esperanza to be a writer. Soon after she died.

Esperanza went to see Elenita, the witch woman, to have her future read in the cards. She was disappointed because Elenita told her she would have "a home in the heart" when what she wanted was a real house of her own. She learned stories about her neighbors and friends. Geraldo had just arrived from Mexico when he was killed in a hit-and-run accident. No one was notified. Edna's grown daughter Ruthie kept saying her husband would come to take her home, but he never did. Earl, the jukebox repairman who lived in Edna's basement, brought his wife home occasionally, but no one could agree about what she looked like. Sire, the boy Esperanza fell in love with, was older than she was; she spied on him and Lois walking together and dreamed of feeling the weight of a boy's arm around her.

Sally was the girl the schoolboys called beautiful. Her father beat her for going with boys, but Esperanza did not believe the stories the boys told about Sally. Another girl, Minerva, already had two children although she was not much older than Esperanza. She read her sad poems to Esperanza.

Esperanza continued to daydream about the house she would own one day, in which she would let bums live in the attic. She believed she was the ugly daughter in which no man would be interested. Her mother, on the other hand, was beautiful and smart, and could have been somebody.

Esperanza and the girls had a secret place they called The Monkey Garden, where they went to escape their mothers. One day Esperanza found Sally there with Tito and his friends, holding Sally's keys in exchange for a kiss. Esperanza told on them, but neither Sally nor Tito's mother cared, so Esperanza felt stupid to have tried to rescue her. One night, Sally lied to Esperanza and left her alone at the circus with a boy who then raped her. Sally later got married to a door-to-door salesman.

The three sisters convinced Esperanza that if she ever left Mango Street, as she threatened to, she must promise to come back. Alicia told her "you are Mango Street." Esperanza compared her very own imagined house to a space "quiet as snow" and clean as paper. She called Mango the house to which she both belonged and did not belong. She promised herself that one day she would pack her books and papers and go away, but that she would come back for the ones she left behind.

Critical Evaluation:

The House on Mango Street, published in 1984, was Sandra Cisneros' first work of fiction. With its appearance she became recognized as the most powerful writer of a group of emerging Chicana writers that included Ana Castillo, Denise Chávez, and Gloria Anzaldua. This group was the second big wave of Latin American writers to emerge in late twentieth century American fiction, following the successes of a number of Latin American male writers in the 1970's.

Cisneros' training as a poet is evident in her fiction. The author has described the forty-six short vignettes that make up the novel as combining aspects of poems and short stories. The tiny chapters are intensely lyrical, written in a prose highly charged with metaphor. Each section has a title, and each could stand alone as an autonomous piece, like a prose poem. Esperanza's voice unifies the pieces, however, and creates a continuing narrative. Her quest for identity shapes the otherwise loose plot. The nonlinear narrative moves from one event to another, often revisiting settings and characters in much the same way a young girl's conversation or inner thoughts might skip from one story to another.

Based on Cisneros' experiences growing up in a Latino neighborhood in Chicago, *The House on Mango Street* is the story of a girl's search for identity as she comes of age. The narrative covers one crucial year in the life of Esperanza, a Chicana, who is ethnically Mexican and culturally Mexican American. Cisneros has suggested that her book, though written in English, employs Latina syntax and sensibility. For effect and mood she sometimes uses Spanish phrases that an English-only reader must comprehend from context.

Esperanza describes her world with a child's innocence that is beginning to fade. Despite approaching puberty, with its longings and confusion, she is an astute observer of the world around her, especially of the adults and their actions. She intuitively seems to understand the emotions of her friends, family, and neighbors.

She begins to reject traditional roles and to seek out those who can give her support as a fledgling writer. "Bums in the Attic," "The Three Sisters," and "A House of My Own" are significant pieces in the narrative, marking stages in the development of Esperanza's sense of identity, which she knows is linked to her need to write.

The world of Mango Street is filtered through Esperanza's sensibility. Each event or person she describes has affected her in an essential way. Her youth makes her a reliable narrator; her observations are honest and unexaggerated, without guile. She actually narrates a story with a dual plot: One is the story of her own search for identity, about creativity and becoming an artist; the other is the story of her Latino neighborhood, the individuals the reader comes to know in her neighborhood. She alludes to racism and classism, although her child's voice suggests that her awareness of these social problems has only just begun. The humor, joys, frustrations, and desperation she describes in the women's stories create a mosaic of Latina life.

Esperanza's descriptions focus on the women she knows, and her portraits reveal how women's lives are made difficult by the men who dominate them. Her perspective often points to the ways society at large oppresses Latin Americans, which impose a double yoke on the Latina women. Living in a strongly patriarchal society, often in fear of violence, they find their choices for survival and self-expression limited. It is their fate the narrator wants to escape.

Esperanza insists that she must have a house of her own to support her intent to be a writer. The need for a house and that to be a writer are actually inseparable. The house she imagines and describes becomes her symbol for freedom and artistic expression. It also ties her to her community and is the source of her identity and her stories. How artistic creation strengthens identity and provides dignity is an important theme of the novel.

In subsequent works—including the collection of stories *Woman Hollering Creek* (1991) and the volumes of poetry *My Wicked, Wicked Ways* (1987) and *Loose Woman* (1994)—Cisneros continued to explore feminism, biculturalism, family violence, artistic creativity, and personal identity. Her work offers insights into what it means to be a Mexican American living in the United States.

JoAnn Balingit

Bibliography:

Cisneros, Sandra. Interview by Reed Way Dasenbrock. In *Interviews with Writers of the Post-Colonial World*, edited by Feroza Jussawalla and Dasenbrock. Jackson: University Press of Mississippi, 1992. Cisneros discusses the genesis of her first novel, her use of voices, the effect of bilingualism on her writing, her life in Texas, her parents' lives, feminism, her favorite writers, and her novel then in progress.

De Valdés, Maria Elena. "In Search of Identity in Cisneros' *The House on Mango Street*." *Canadian Review of American Studies* 23, no. 1 (Fall, 1992): 55-72. De Valdés systematically charts the stages of Esperanza's search for identity, which is complicated by her "double marginalization" in being both a Chicana and a woman. Reviews key chapters to suggest what ideas they contribute to major themes in the novel.

Ganz, Robin. "Sandra Cisneros: Border Crossings and Beyond." *Melus* 19, no. 1 (Spring, 1994): 19-29. Ganz uses biographical information drawn from many sources to show how Cisneros' stories successfully cross borders of gender and ethnicity.

McCracken, Ellen. "Sandra Cisneros' *The House on Mango Street:* Community-Oriented Introspection and the Demystification of Patriarchal Violence." In *Breaking Boundaries: Latina Writing and Critical Readings*, edited by Asunción Horno-Delgado et al. Amherst: University of Massachusetts Press, 1989. McCracken considers the novel from a feminist perspective, finding that it criticizes capitalistic and patriarchal social structures that oppress Latin women.

Olivares, Julián. "Sandra Cisneros' *The House on Mango Street* and the Poetics of Space." In *Chicana Creativity and Criticism: Charting New Frontiers in American Literature*, edited by Maria Herrera-Sobek and Helena María Viramontes. Houston, Tex.: Arte Público Press, 1988. Olivares argues that the house motif represents Cisneros' "house of story-telling"; the narrative charts a young writer coming into her own. Whereas her real house represents confinement, the imaginary one represents her ability to transcend the conditions of her life by writing stories about them.

THE HOUSE ON THE HILL

Type of work: Novel
Author: Cesare Pavese (1908-1950)
Type of plot: Psychological realism
Time of plot: 1943-1945
Locale: Northern Italy
First published: La casa in collina, 1949 (English translation, 1956)

> *Principal characters:*
> CORRADO, a schoolteacher, about forty years old
> ELVIRA, the daughter of Corrado's landlady
> CATE, a woman with whom Corrado had a love affair
> DINO, Cate's son, and possibly Corrado's as well
> FONSO, a passionate young partisan

The Story:

Corrado was a teacher in Turin, Italy. A man alone, whose parents lived in their distant village in the northern Italian countryside, he stayed in a rented room in a house owned by an aged woman and her middle-aged, unmarried daughter. Corrado had no friends and his only honest confidant was his dog, Belbo. As World War II continued into its fourth year, Allied air attacks increased in frequency and intensity, and during the night raids Corrado left his rented room in the city to find refuge in the hills outside Turin. It was during one of these air raids that Corrado by seeming accident stumbled upon an inn, Le Fontane, the house on the hill, where a convivial band of fellow refugees amused one another with songs and stories. In the nights that followed, and soon after during the days, Corrado returned often to Le Fontane, finally making it his real residence, returning to Turin only to teach at his school and to stop by his rented room for necessities. It was also at Le Fontane that Corrado discovered Cate, a former lover. He learned that she had a son, and that Cate's son Dino was also named Corrado; however, the woman stubbornly refused to reveal if the boy was indeed Corrado's son.

Although it displeased his Turin landlady and her middle-aged, unmarried daughter Elvira, Corrado continued to spend more and more time at the inn, discussing politics and the war with the young and passionate Fonso, who supported the anti-Fascist partisans, conversing with Cate, and roaming the hills with Dino. It seemed to Corrado as if his life had begun again, but while the others, especially Fonso, became active in the partisan movement, Corrado remained unconnected and essentially uncommitted, a talker rather than a participant. One day the Germans arrived, arresting everyone except Corrado and Dino, who were away. In panic, Corrado left Dino with Elvira and found refuge in a neighboring monastery, a cloistered school. When, after a time, Elvira brought Dino to the cloister, Corrado and the boy pretended not to know each other; their only interactions were brief, whispered conversations snatched in odd moments.

At the monastery, Corrado reverted to his role of teacher and took over a study hall of students. He read from the breviary of Father Felice and learned that human suffering and sorrow seemed to be an eternal cycle, and that no terrors or tortures by the Nazis or their Fascist allies were new to the world, just as the retaliations of the partisans were set into an endless, recurring pattern. However, while Corrado could accept intellectually such thoughts, when his own safety was threatened, he reacted from his instincts rather than his philosophy.

An alarm spread through the monastery that the Germans and the pro-Fascist Italians were coming, so Corrado fled. When he learned that it had been a false alarm, he returned to find that Dino had also gone, most likely to join Fonso and the other partisans. Corrado left the cloister, making his way at night through the war-torn countryside to his parent's house in the small village of Belbo in northern Italy. Once there, safely away from the war but also removed from contact with Dino, Cate, and the others, Corrado reflected upon what had happened and wrote his story.

Critical Evaluation:

Recognized by his contemporaries as one of the most talented and passionate of Italian writers of his generation, Cesare Pavese wrote novels which were shaped by three major influences: existential philosophy, classical culture and mythology, and American literature. In *The House on the Hill* he combines all three to create a powerfully told, emotionally moving story that skirts around the edges of actions, hinting at, rather than engaging, in the violence of war and in the emotional struggle that are its central themes. Just as its narrator and central character, Corrado, avoids full participation in the violent events of his day, so the novel unfolds a story set against the backdrop of world war and civil war without any actual scenes of battle or combat.

From existentialism, Pavese took the theme of the importance of engagement in the world and the need for the fearless, active role intellectuals should play in the social and moral issues of the day. Pavese clearly believed that an intellectual who did not become positively engaged in the world, in particular through political or other practical action, has committed an act of betrayal; thus, Corrado's stance of speaking against the Fascist regime and its Nazi supporters but not acting upon his words is a betrayal. The extent of that intellectual and moral dishonesty is highlighted in the novel by Corrado's other betrayals. He has earlier renounced his lover, Cate, and he later abandons Dino, her son (and quite probably his as well), when threatened by arrest by the Germans. Ironically, the threat of arrest is only a rumor, so that Corrado's desertion of Dino is caused by only the illusion of danger, not its reality. Although physical cowardice is part of Corrado's makeup, his true fault, at least in existentialist terms, is his moral and intellectual refusal to take a stand and become truly involved with life around him. It is not merely the struggle against Fascism and Nazism that he avoids, but also real relationships with other human beings, most notably his lover and the boy who is likely his own child.

Pavese often sought to combine elements of Greek and Roman mythology and culture into his works, especially in his evocations of the Mediterranean landscape, with its resonances and allusions to the classical past of the region. Critics have noted his drive to fuse the myths and geography of classical literature with modern obsessions and problems, and *The House on the Hill* clearly follows this pattern, although its references and allusions are often subtle and unobtrusively woven into the text. The novel has carefully detailed descriptions of the northern Italian hills, scenes of a world at war, with cities and villages burning and pillaged, and a central character, Corrado, who suffers through an odyssey of pain and suffering. In Pavese's modern, ironic, and perhaps even at times cynical story, the wanderer returns home to find he has lost everything he held dear and has gained only a bitterly won and painful knowledge of the true extent of his loss.

The style of *The House on the Hill* owes a great deal to Pavese's close study of American literature. Known as one of the leading Americanists of his generation, Pavese was an enthusiastic and perceptive reader, translator, and critic of United States authors. His university thesis in 1930 was on Walt Whitman, and that same year he began contributing a series of enthusiastic and perceptive essays on American culture to the Italian intellectual journal *La Cultura*. He translated American authors such as Sinclair Lewis, Sherwood Anderson, and Herman Melville, including a version of Melville's uniquely American novel, *Moby Dick* (1851). Pavese was especially influenced by F. Scott Fitzgerald and Ernest Hemingway, and touches reminiscent of Hemingway, especially that American writer's own antiwar novel, *A Farewell to Arms* (1929), are particularly notable in Pavese's prose style in *The House on the Hill*.

Another feature of American literature that Pavese noted in his studies was its unique tendency to make an intensely local landscape into a universal setting for stories that address the general human condition. William Faulkner's Yoknapatawpha County, Mississippi, while remaining the particular "postage stamp of soil" of the American South as described by its author, could still resonate with archetypes and universal patterns. Hemingway's use of the Michigan landscape in stories such as "Big Two-Hearted River" was, in a fashion, much the same. Pavese's evocations of the northern Italian landscape, with his deliberate if subtle allusions to classical and mythical motifs, performs a similar function and achieves a similar effect: The reader follows a story that is set in a specific time and place but that transcends the immediate and limited to become universal to all of human experience.

It is difficult and perhaps ultimately unimportant to place *The House on the Hill* into any single genre of fiction. It could be cataloged equally as well as a war novel, an existential work, a psychological study, or a thinly disguised personal confession. It has a very definite location and time for its action—northern Italy on the brink of invasion and civil war during World War II—its themes of suffering, loss, and betrayal are universal and timeless. There is a sense that all of human history, and the tragedy which is attendant upon it, is present in the events of *The House on the Hill*. Pavese's novel manages to rise above the restrictions of its particular place and time, while remaining vivid and immediate in a recognizable reality.

Michael Witkoski

Bibliography:
Biasin, Gian-Paolo. *The Smile of the Gods: A Thematic Study of Cesare Pavese's Works.* Translated by Yvonne Freccero. Ithaca, N.Y.: Cornell University Press, 1968. Reviews the author's career and accomplishments. Examines Pavese's techniques of linking classical themes with modern persons and events.
Bondanella, Peter, and Julia Conaway Bondanella, eds. *Dictionary of Italian Literature.* Westport, Conn.: Greenwood Press, 1979. Provides the background material needed to begin a study of Pavese and his novels. Provides a brief but perceptive study of *The House on the Hill*, especially in relationship to Pavese and existentialism.
Flint, R. W. Introduction to *Selected Works*, by Cesare Pavese. Translated by R. W. Flint. New York: Farrar, Straus & Giroux, 1968. The introduction to a standard edition of Pavese's works in English, helps to establish the parameters for judging the writer's works.
Lajolo, Davide. *An Absurd Vice: A Biography of Cesare Pavese.* Translated and edited by Mario and Mark Pietralunga. New York: New Directions, 1983. An intensely personal view of Pavese's life and career. Despite its prejudices, it provides some interesting insights into *The House on the Hill*.
O'Healy, Aine. *Cesare Pavese.* Boston: Twayne, 1988. An excellent introduction to Pavese's works. Places *The House on the Hill* into its proper place within his career. For an introductory volume, it is remarkably complete.

Thompson, Doug. *Cesare Pavese: A Study of the Major Novels and Poems*. New York: Cambridge University Press, 1982. Examines *The House on the Hill* in the light of Pavese's ambivalent relationship with the Italian Communist Party, and his refusal, or perhaps inability, to translate his own anti-Fascist views into action.

HOW GREEN WAS MY VALLEY

Type of work: Novel
Author: Richard Llewellyn (Richard Dafydd Vivian Llewellyn Lloyd, 1906-1983)
Type of plot: Regional
Time of plot: Early twentieth century
Locale: Wales
First published: 1939

> *Principal characters:*
> GWILYM MORGAN, a Welsh miner
> BETH MORGAN, his wife
> HUW MORGAN, their son and the narrator
> IVOR,
> DAVY,
> OWEN,
> IANTO, and
> GWILYM, other sons
> ANGHARAD, their daughter
> BRONWEN, Ivor's wife
> MARGED, Gwilym's wife
> IESTYN EVANS, Angharad's husband
> MR. GRUFFYDD, the minister

The Story:

How beautiful and peaceful the valley looked to Huw Morgan when he was ready to leave it. All the memories of a long lifetime came back to him. Huw's earliest memories were of his father and brothers when they came home from the mines on Saturday night. There was trouble brewing at the mines. The men talked of unions and organizing, and the owners were angry.

Huw loved his family very much. When he learned that his brother Ivor was to marry, he was sorry to lose his brother; but from the first moment Huw saw Ivor's Bronwen, he loved her, and that love for his sister-in-law stayed with him all of his life. Another brother, Ianto, married soon afterward. His wife was a woman from the village, where Ianto went to live.

Trouble came at last to the mines. The men in the pits went on strike for twenty-two weeks, but the owners were the stronger because they were not watching their families starve. The men finally went back to work for less money than before. After the first strike, Huw's father would never again join the men trying to form a union, for he could not bring himself to lead men out of work. Davy and the other boys, however, were more bitter than ever. When their father ordered his sons never to attend another meeting, Davy, Owen, and Gwilym left home and took a room in a lodging house. Their mother cried all night, but their father would not change his mind. It was a miserable time for six-year-old Huw. When his sister, Angharad, found that the three boys were living in filth, she went to the rooming house to take care of them. Their father then relented and allowed the boys to come home, but he said that they would be lodgers only, not sons.

After his father became superintendent at the mine, Huw heard some of the miners say that his father and Ivor, who agreed with him, might be beaten or even killed by some of the more violent miners. Frightened, he told his mother what he had heard. One winter night, she and Huw went to the mountain where the miners were meeting, and she told the men there that she would kill anyone who harmed her husband. On the way home, his mother slipped on the bank of a little river. Huw, standing in the icy water, supported his mother on the bank until help came. After that, he knew nothing until he awoke in his bed, and his father told him that he had saved his mother's life and the life of his new baby sister. Huw had fever in his legs for almost five years and never left his bed during that time.

During his sickness, Bronwen nursed him, and his brothers read to him until he was far beyond his years in learning. While he was in bed, he first met the new minister, Mr. Gruffydd, who was to become his best friend. Huw's brother Owen fell in love with Marged Evans. When Marged's father found Owen kissing Marged, he said terrible things to the boy, so that Owen would have nothing more to do with Marged. Gwilym married her, for he had always loved her.

Ianto's wife died, and he came home to live. By this time, Huw was in good health once more. He went to the National School over the mountain but had many fights before he was accepted by the other boys.

Angharad and Iestyn Evans, the son of the mine owner, began to keep company, but Angharad did not seem to be happy. It was some time before Huw learned that Angharad loved Mr. Gruffydd, but that he could not take a wife because he was poor. Huw began to think love caused heartache instead of happiness.

One day, he took a basket of food to Gwilym's house, and there he found Marged completely mad. Thinking he was Owen, she told him she could not live without him. Huw ran to find Gwilym. Before he returned with his brother, Marged had thrown herself into the fire and burned to death. Afterward, Gwilym and Owen went away together, but no one knew where.

Iestyn Evans' father died. Soon after, Iestyn and Angharad were married in London. Davy was married before they came home; for the wedding, Huw had his first long trousers. Bronwen told him that he was now a man. Shortly afterward, Huw was put out of school for beating the teacher, who had made a small child wear around her neck a sign announcing that she was Welsh. Huw went to work in the pits with his brothers. Owen and Gwilym had returned home, and all the boys lived again in the valley. Owen soon received a telegram from London about an engine he was trying to perfect, and he and Gwilym left again. From London, they went to the United States. Soon afterward, Davy went to London on mine union business.

Iestyn had gone to Cape Town on business, and Angharad came home from London alone. Soon gossip started because Mr. Gruffydd and Angharad often took carriage rides together. Finally, Angharad left the valley and went to Cape Town. Mr. Gruffydd also left the valley.

When Ivor was killed in a cave-in at the mine, Huw's mother sent Huw to live with Bronwen in her loneliness. Discharged from the mines for striking one of the workmen who made a slurring remark about Angharad and Mr. Gruffydd, Huw became a carpenter. Ianto had already left the pits, and only his father and Davy were left in the mines. Davy decided to go to New Zealand. Ianto went to Germany, where he thought he could do better in his trade. The family was now scattered.

One day, the workers flooded the mines, and Huw's father was crushed by a cave-in. Huw crawled to his father and stayed with him until he died. Huw's heart was as empty as his mother's when he told her the terrible news. Everyone of whom Huw had thought during this reverie was now dead. He walked slowly away from his valley and from his memories.

Critical Evaluation:

A major issue for critical readers of *How Green Was My Valley* is determining if the novel belongs to the tradition of realism, as some critics have stated, or romance, as others believe. In fact, the novel is the rare combination of the two. This nostalgic and sentimental novel honors the traditions of the past, but the romance is overlaid with a fineness of detail that conjures the particular feeling of life in a Welsh coal-mining town.

How Green Was My Valley can be thought of as belonging to the tradition of the Adamic myth, in which a character falls from his blissful innocence into uncertainty. The setting of the novel, identified only as "the Valley," lends credibility to this analysis. A reader will be hard put to identify the exact setting. The events occur in a Welsh coal-mining community, but historical events of the world outside the Valley never intrude on the lives of the characters. The story seems to take place in a gauzy, timeless era when life was less complicated, and better. Only scant references to Winston Churchill, the home secretary of Great Britain, and a slight allusion to the Boer Wars identify the time of the novel as the beginning of the twentieth century. The Valley is a world unto itself, and all that one needs to live a good and proper life can be found there.

The narrator, Huw Morgan, tells the story of his growing up, and his story, moving from innocence to experience, corresponds to the history of the Valley. It too is moving from a past grounded in tradition to an uncertain future. While Huw is as much a product of the Valley as his coal-mining neighbors, he is detached somewhat in his role of observer. His education, first obtained as a bookish child confined to a bed for a long period and later augmented at a National School outside the Valley, sets him apart from rustic folk of the Valley.

Huw declines to take the examination for entrance to the university and decides to become a miner like his brothers. Huw's entrance into the mine marks the point between boyhood and manhood. It is no accident that Huw fails as a coal miner and instead becomes a skilled carpenter, a trade he learns at the side of Mr. Gruffydd, the minister. This trade is appropriate for "Christlike" Huw, a human of great kindness. Huw's compassionate point of view serves as a striking foil to the dominating patriarchal culture of the Valley. One scene that particularly illustrates this tension occurs in church when Huw publicly questions the deacons' decision to banish an unwed pregnant woman from the congregation.

While Huw may stand for New Testament values, the traditional patriarchal culture of the Valley has more in common with Old Testament values, and those who violate those values will be outcast. Mr. Gruffydd, at the beginning of the novel, represents Old Testament values. He approves of training Huw to fight in order to teach wrongdoers a lesson. Gruffydd also approves the execution, without a trial, of the alleged murderer of a little girl. Justice in the novel is always quick and forceful. Huw's father Gwilym, the living embodiment of patriarchy, declines to involve police when Elias steals his turkeys. The law of the Valley sanctions his taking matters into his own hands, although it could lead to violence. Even Huw is quick with his fists to protect the Valley's law, which advocates personal integrity, kindness to others, and loyalty to family and community.

The patriarchy of the Valley dictates that men and women play distinctly separate roles. Men are to work, provide needed income for the family, serve the community, and honor their women. Women are to marry, have children, and provide food and clothing for the family. Despite relegating women to the domestic sphere, Richard Llewellyn creates two strong female characters: Huw's mother, Beth, and his sister-in-law Bronwen. These women correspond to the archetypes of mother and wife. Beth's devotion to her family is admirable, as shown when she makes a public speech to the union men who, she suspects, are plotting to attack her husband for not supporting their efforts. Beth has no interest in the union dealings, however; she speaks out only in her husband's defense. Bronwen is not outwardly as strong, yet she survives the early death in the mine of her husband with grace and composure. She is the embodiment of feminine sensuality, beauty, patience, kindness, and long-suffering.

Bronwen exhibits these traditional positive traits in contrast to Huw's sister, Angharad. Bronwen marries Ivor for love; Angharad disregards her love for Gruffydd and instead marries the son of a mine owner. Bronwen lives in relative poverty, working hard and sacrificing quietly for her children. On the other hand, Angharad, although she lives in relative comfort, is estranged from her husband, has no joy from children, and has a look of starvation in her eyes.

Mr. Gruffydd, who felt his pittance of a salary made him unworthy to marry Angharad, suffers also from unrequited love. Gruffydd's aging and growing sense of ennui correspond to the waning traditional culture of the Valley. In his youth, Gruffydd, a spirited, powerful preacher motivating the miners to stand up for themselves and God, was a strong supporter and vital member of the community. As he ages, especially without the love of Angharad, he is diminished, losing his spiritual efficacy and his prominence in the community. Ultimately, he is banished from the Valley by the deacons for breaking the conventions of the Valley's patriarchy: He has become too intimate with Angharad, a married woman estranged from her husband.

Throughout the novel, the struggle between the union men and the mine owners provides a background to the more detailed brush strokes that depict the daily events of the Morgan family. The rioting incited by the coming of the unions, ironically aided by several of the Morgan brothers, brings events to a close. Finally and dramatically, the death of Gwilym Morgan and the breakup of his family signal the radical changes coming to the Valley. His sons, barred from working the mines because of their involvement with the unions, scatter from the Valley. Those who do stay suffer diminution, as does Mr. Gruffydd, or death, as Gwilym does. The sixty-year-old Huw Morgan is the last to leave, long after all the others have gone. The novel ends sadly where it began, with Huw reflecting on the dramatic changes that have turned his "Eden" into a slag heap.

"Critical Evaluation" by Chris Benson

Bibliography:
Felton, Mick. "Richard Llewellyn." In *British Novelists, 1930-1959*. Vol. 5. Detroit: Gale Research, 1983. Describes *How Green Was My Valley* as an iconoclastic literary achievement of detailed characterization and realism. Finds that the novel accurately portrays the Welsh community, lifestyle, and dialect.
Lindberg, Laurie. "Llewellyn and Giardina, Two Novels About Coal Mining." *Journal of the Appalachian Studies Association* 1 (1989): 133-140. Identifies *How Green Was My Valley* as a regional novel that presents what is universal about the human character and its condition. Ideas explored include growth from innocence to experience, the individual exploited by industrial power, and loss of "Eden."
Price, Derrick. "*How Green Was My Valley*: A Romance of Wales." In *The Progress of Romance: The Politics of Popular Fiction*, edited by Jean Radford. London: Routledge & Kegan Paul, 1986. Maintains *How Green Was My Valley* is more than a close view of a working-class Welsh community. Analyzes elements of romance in the story, including rural patriarchy, male-female relationships, replacement of the pastoral with the industrial, and the passing of old ways and beginning of new ways.
Woods, Katherine. "The Sound of Music on the Green Hills of Wales." *The New York Times Book Review*, February 11, 1940, 3, 19. Asserts that the novel strongly follows the Romantic tradition, while incorporating elements of realism and local color in depicting Welsh independence, pride, courage, and love. Slightly critical of the novel's nostalgic sentimentality.

HOWARDS END

Type of work: Novel
Author: E. M. Forster (1879-1970)
Type of plot: Domestic realism
Time of plot: Early twentieth century
Locale: England
First published: 1910

Principal characters:
HENRY WILCOX, a British businessman
RUTH, his first wife
CHARLES, his older son
PAUL, his younger son
MARGARET SCHLEGEL, Henry Wilcox's second wife
HELEN, Margaret's sister
THEOBALD, Margaret's brother
LEONARD BAST, a poor young man
JACKY, Leonard's wife

The Story:

The Wilcox family met Margaret Schlegel and her sister Helen while both families were vacationing in Germany. Neither group expected the chance acquaintance to amount to anything more, but later, after all had returned to England, Helen Schlegel was invited to visit the Wilcox family at Howards End, their country home near London. While there, Helen fell in love with Paul Wilcox. The Wilcox family disapproved of the match and Paul backed off. With that, the acquaintance ended. Several months later, however, the Wilcoxes rented a house across the street from the Schlegel home. Both of the young people were out of the country, and when Mrs. Wilcox and Margaret Schlegel met again, they became friends.

Also acquainted with the Schlegels was a young man named Leonard Bast, whose umbrella had been accidentally taken by Helen at a concert. The young man interested the girls and their brother by his conversation when he had called to reclaim his umbrella. They did not know that he had a vulgar wife, a woman some years older than he who had trapped him into a distasteful marriage.

Some months after the acquaintance between Mrs. Wilcox and Margaret Schlegel had ripened into friendship, Mrs. Wilcox became ill and died. Much to the surprise of her husband and sons, she left, in addition to her will, a note leaving Howards End to Margaret. Deeply upset at the idea of losing the house, the Wilcoxes decided to disregard the note, since it was not a part of the official will.

Margaret Schlegel, who knew nothing of the bequest, was glad that the tie between herself and the Wilcox family had been broken. She suspected that her sister might still be in love with Paul Wilcox and feared that Helen suffered when she came into contact with other members of the family.

Long after Mrs. Wilcox's death, Margaret and her sister were sitting in the park one evening when they met Mr. Wilcox. He told them that the firm for which Leonard Bast worked was unreliable. Acting on that information, the girls advised the young man to change jobs, and he did so. A few weeks later, the long-term lease on the Schlegels' home was due to expire. Although they searched diligently, they found nothing suitable. Hearing of their predicament,

Mr. Wilcox sent a letter to Margaret offering to lease them his house in London. Margaret went with him to look at the house. While they were there, Mr. Wilcox declared himself. Margaret, who was well into her thirties, was surprised but not embarrassed or shocked. She asked only for some time to think over both the rental of the house and the proposal of marriage, and a few days later she agreed to marry Mr. Wilcox.

Before Margaret's marriage, Mr. Wilcox's daughter was married at a house owned by the Wilcoxes near Wales. Helen Schlegel, who disapproved of Margaret's approaching marriage, appeared at the wedding celebration with Leonard Bast and his wife. Helen had learned that through their bad advice Bast had lost everything he had, including his job. Helen thought that Mr. Wilcox ought to recompense the young man. Mrs. Bast was discovered in a tipsy condition on the lawn. There, she revealed to Mr. Wilcox and Margaret that she had been Mr. Wilcox's mistress many years before. Margaret was willing to forgive Mr. Wilcox but resolved not to help the Basts, which she felt in the circumstances would be unnecessary and in poor taste.

Helen felt sorry for Bast and spent part of one night with him, then remorsefully left England. She tried to give Bast five thousand pounds, most of her fortune, but he refused to accept her aid. The relationship between Helen and Bast was unknown to Margaret, who went ahead with plans for her marriage to Mr. Wilcox despite the fact that his sons did not approve of their father's second marriage. Helen's refusal to return for the ceremony did not surprise her sister, but when eight months had gone by without her return, Margaret began to worry about her.

Helen finally came back to England and sent word that she wanted some books stored in the house at Howards End. She acted so mysteriously, however, refusing to meet with them directly, that Margaret became seriously worried. When Margaret saw Helen, however, the reason became clear, for Helen was pregnant. When Helen asked to be permitted to spend one night with her sister in the unoccupied house at Howards End, Mr. Wilcox refused to give his permission.

The two sisters stayed in the house nevertheless. The following morning, Mr. Wilcox's older son, Charles, came to force them to leave. Directly after his arrival, Leonard Bast came to the house in search of Margaret, from whom he hoped to get a loan. When Charles saw him, he seized a saber that hung on the wall and struck Bast on the shoulders with the flat of the weapon several times. The shock of seeing Helen and the beating were too much for Bast's weak heart, and he died suddenly.

Charles was tried for manslaughter and sentenced to three years in prison. The disgrace was too great for his father, who became an invalid. Margaret saw no alternative to the situation than to move her husband and her sister into the house at Howards End, where Helen's child was born. Mr. Wilcox came to love the baby during his illness and convalescence, and Helen and the child, much to the displeasure of the other Wilcoxes, were permitted to remain. A few months before Charles's release from prison, Mr. Wilcox called a family conference. He had made a new will giving all of his money to the children by his first marriage, but the house at Howards End was to go to Margaret and after her death to Helen's illegitimate child. The mansion that had played so great a part in all of their lives thus eventually came to Margaret Schlegel, just as the first Mrs. Wilcox had wished before her death.

Critical Evaluation:

E. M. Forster was not a prolific author. He is well known to students of fiction, however, as a thorough critic, as well as an important novelist in his own right, and his *Aspects of the Novel* is a major contribution to study in that field. Prior to his best work of fiction, *A Passage to India* (1924), *Howards End* was ranked as his most mature novel. Particularly important in Forster's fiction are his subtle and complete characterization, his deft use of irony, the careful plotting of action, and the eternal contrast between illusion and reality. *Howards End* is second only to *A Passage to India* in illustrating these characteristics.

The country house has long been an important image and symbol in English literature. From its appearance in such an early seventeenth century poem as Ben Jonson's "To Penshurst," to its celebration by Alexander Pope in the eighteenth century, to its centrality in the nineteenth century fiction of Jane Austen, Anthony Trollope, and Henry James, to its prominence in the modern works of E. M. Forster and Evelyn Waugh, the manor house has provided not only a dramatic setting but also an embodiment of certain social, moral, and spiritual values. Despite its various literary manifestations, the apotheosis of the country estate is in essence a reaction against the introduction of the mercantile ethic, its manifestation in the phenomenon of industrialism, and the consequent growth of large cities. It is, in brief, a nostalgic image for a way of life, based on the land, that possessed a definite social hierarchy and took its rhythms from nature. While it pays special homage to individuality, intellect, and imagination, its chief virtues are the classical ones of restraint and moderation. The country house, therefore, is a correlative for a human ideal that found its first flowering in the Renaissance.

In addition to these attributes, the house in Forster's novel *Howards End* represents an image of cultural unity. The book's epigraph, "Only connect . . . ," suggests the major theme and describes the prescription required to bring about moral health to Edwardian England. To Forster this society, on the verge of becoming completely urbanized and industrialized, is fractured, lacking order and direction. He looks toward the traditional values embodied in Howards End for a solution to this dilemma.

Three principal forces are at work in *Howards End*. The first is embodied in the Schlegel family, which stands for the past, art, imagination, and culture; second, there are the Wilcoxes, representing the present, practical intelligence, and business acumen. The third force points to the future and is found in the parvenu, Leonard Bast. The drama of the novel resides primarily in the conflict between the Schlegels and the Wilcoxes, both solid middle-class families, for the right to direct England's future—or at least to determine its dominant values. Leonard Bast, a member of the working class and always on the periphery, is seemingly lost in the shuffle. He is without manners, culture, or any business sense, yet he aspires to the center of power, held jointly by the Schlegels and the Wilcoxes. After his ignominious death "resolves" the conflict between the two families, it is, ironically, his illegitimate child, conceived by Helen Schlegel in an act of moral protest against the establishment, who will inherit Howards End and—readers may infer—the spoils of the battlefield, the future of England.

From the beginning, it appears that these three forces have nothing in common. Margaret, Helen, and their brother celebrate the "poetic" inner self, the passion of existence, while despising the world of telegrams, profit and loss, and machines. That world, peopled and directed by their rivals, Henry Wilcox and his son, Charles, dedicates itself to practicality, to the "prose" of life, as Forster phrases it. Although he is not fully a part of either, Leonard does have one foot in each; he is a small-business clerk, yet he ravenously and superficially fills his life with cultural items, books, concerts, and intelligent conversations.

Nevertheless, the deep connections among these three forces begin to appear as the novel unfolds: In a private will, Ruth Wilcox leaves Howards End to Margaret in recognition of their mutual identities, and Jacky, Leonard's wife, is revealed to have been Henry's mistress. These connections are further strengthened by the real attractions that grow up among them. Initially, Paul Wilcox and Helen fall in love; the engagement, however, is broken off as unseemly. Later, Henry and Margaret discover in each other a passionate need—a fact apparently recognized by the late and mysterious Mrs. Wilcox—and eventually marry. Last, there is the fruitful if misdirected union of Helen and Leonard. *Howards End*, therefore, describes a society that on the surface seems fractured and disjointed, but as it is gradually revealed, one which is fundamentally joined by needs and desires of love and fellowship. All that is required to cement the connection is human will and a place to validate the union.

Under the influence of Ruth Wilcox, Margaret provides the will that is constantly directed to the acquisition of Howards End, her rightful legacy; but it finally takes the tragic-comic death of Leonard at the hands of Charles Wilcox to force the principal characters into making all the "connections." With Charles imprisoned and the Wilcox clan disgraced, Henry Wilcox, the practical man-of-action, is thoroughly deflated, and it remains for the "poetic" Margaret to assume the leadership and direction of the family.

In the denouement, Forster gathers all of his principal characters at Howards End for one last conversation. The atmosphere is of peace and joy, not unlike the aftermath of a wedding in which all tensions are abated and passion, fruitfulness, and unity are celebrated. The house itself, cut off from the asseverations of culture and the workday, allows its inhabitants to feel the rhythms of nature and the ties that bind them. It is autumn, and around them a bountiful harvest proceeds; it is a time of expectations, further attested by the health of Helen and Leonard's child. Nevertheless, Forster is too much of a realist to conclude on a note of simple optimism. He sees, like Helen and Margaret, that the smog of London is encroaching on the house. It is a complete moment, to be sure, but one stolen from the past. At last, Forster knew that it was also the autumn of the country house as well as of the Renaissance and that it was the spring of the modern world.

"Critical Evaluation" by David L. Kubal

Bibliography:
Duckworth, Alistair M. *"Howards End": E. M. Forster's House of Fiction.* New York: Twayne, 1992. Excellent overview of the novel's literary and historical contexts. Chapter analyzing the problems of narrative voice and authorial intrusion.
Furbank, P. N. *E. M. Forster: A Life.* New York: Harcourt Brace Jovanovich, 1978. Definitive biography: detailed and well written; copiously illustrated. Demonstrates how Forster incorporated into *Howards End*, through the characters of Margaret Schlegel and Leonard Bast, his concerns about culture and society.
Godfrey, Denis. *E. M. Forster's Other Kingdom.* New York: Barnes & Noble Books, 1968. Focuses on the mystical qualities of *Howards End.* Good analysis of each of the characters.
Trilling, Lionel. *E. M. Forster.* New York: New Directions, 1943. Classic study of Forster's fiction; credited with focusing attention on *Howards End* as a masterpiece of humanist literature.
Widdowson, Peter. *E. M. Forster's "Howards End": Fiction as History.* London: Chatto & Windus for Sussex University Press, 1977. Cultural critique of Forster's liberalism that compares the novel to C. F. G. Masterman's *The Condition of England* (1900).

HOWL

Type of work: Poetry
Author: Allen Ginsberg (1926-   )
First published: 1956

When read as a social commentary and revolutionary manifesto, Allen Ginsberg's "Howl" certainly merits special consideration. This is especially true of its remarkable tone, perverse romanticism, and impassioned indictment of society, and the numbing effects of materialism and mechanization. Ginsberg reveals a deep concern with the damnation and corruption of his contemporaries, and he criticizes the constrictive social focus of the late 1940's and early 1950's. Indeed, much of the poem appears to reflect elements of the darker side of existential pessimism, in which cynicism is founded in self-obsession, psychosis, and fear. The poem also reveals a primitivist impulse, itself generated and propelled by what Ginsberg called "neural impulses and writing impulses." The poet claimed that such impulses were a consequence of "physiological movements" that created an organic "pattern."

The poem is liberally seasoned with bombast and subscribes to the illusion that obscenity is sacramental and cathartic; that creativity involves a venal perspective that is perversely original; and that a spiritual war against "mass homogenization" is a necessary prerequisite to artistic integrity. As the work develops, Ginsberg provides a helter-skelter tour-de-force through horrendous volumes of alcohol and drugs, and the reader is carried through an urban maze of slums, poverty, and unspeakable dissipation—all, as Ginsberg has declared, in the interest of a "fresh" image and a medium of expression intended to convey a feeling of doom and terror. Early in the poem, he writes:

> I saw the best minds of my generation destroyed by madness, starving hysterical naked, dragging
>   themselves through the negro streets at dawn looking for an angry fix,
> angelheaded hipsters burning for the ancient heavenly connection to the starry dynamo in the
>   machinery of night, . . .

Ginsberg goes on to claim that in his youth he saw poets and scholars who cowered and burned in horror; who got busted, ate fire, and drank turpentine; who purgatoried themselves night after night with dreams, drugs, and waking nightmares. He describes "mind leaping" hallucinatory illuminations, a "motionless world of Time" that was crowded with "Peyote soldiers," vegetable "vibrations," and rantings in unrestrained confession. In Ginsberg's writing, disembodied rage and paranoia descend to new depths of horror, and social protest is transformed into a fanciful embroidery of artistry, pathological withdrawal, and self-mutilation.

After its initial publication, some came to regard the poem as a latent manifesto for the Beat generation; others saw it as a spiritual and political declaration of righteous indignation; still others condemned the poem as little more than obscene drivel. The legal proceedings that accompanied the poem's reception were sensational and far-reaching, involving the U.S. Customs, the American Civil Liberties Union, the San Francisco *Chronicle*, the juvenile department of the San Francisco police department, and a host of reputable critics and writers.

The poem was first published in England by Villiers. It then passed through U.S. Customs and on to San Francisco where it was published by Lawrence Ferlinghetti's City Lights Books in the fall of 1956. Although charged with being obscene, the poem was found to have some redeeming social importance and was therefore not ruled censorable by the courts.

"Howl" most certainly fueled a controversy about the value and focus of contemporary literature. Harvey Cox, a theologian, did not especially like the poem but was prompted on the strength of it to regard Ginsberg as the "elder statesman" of a "significant subculture of American society." Others felt that the work was too insignificant to warrant such praise. The poet James Dickey felt that it was a typical "our-love-against-their-madness-and-money" diatribe. Most readers, however, probably regard the poem as a generic manifesto of protest that focuses on a select grouping of destructive societal elements, which serve as a catalyst for the poet's feelings of spiritual frustration.

"Howl" is revolutionary and Whitmanesque at the same time. The poem relies on linguistic grandeur, operatic catalogs, obscene references, and rambling digressions. Much of the imagery is primal and cannibalistic, and it is presented with a vigor and energy that is as honest and as direct as it is shocking. For Ginsberg, the contemporary scene is "desanctified" and desolate; as a consequence, his humanity is sacrificed in a fire of modernity that has sacramental proportions. Fear and its usual corollary, anger, propel the reader through a series of images that suggest an obsessive preoccupation with unrestrained sexuality (a common enough medium of rebellion, regardless of the generation being described) and drunkenness.

The poem is divided into three sections. The longest, part 1, is, in Ginsberg's words, a "lament for the Lamb in America." Here, time is perceived as the opposite of holiness, even as holiness itself can only be manifested in love. Ginsberg argues that the individual is compelled to fabricate a pseudoreality through consciousness of the holy and eternal that is itself timeless and placeless. Part 2, which was written under the influence of peyote, displaces the focus on the protagonist narrator by presenting the antagonist, Moloch, the Old Testament deity who demanded human sacrifices and here represents the ills of society. This section ends with an apocalyptic description of the insanity of Ginsberg's generation. In the penultimate line, the poet exclaims:

> Breakthroughs! over the river! flips and crucifixions! gone down the flood!
> Highs! Epiphanies! Despairs! Ten years' animal screams and suicides!
> Minds! New loves! Mad generation! down on the rocks of Time!

Part 3 was addressed specifically to Carl Solomon, a "lunatic saint" and fellow inmate when Ginsberg was in Rockland Hospital's psychiatric ward in 1948 ("Howl" was dedicated to Solomon). This section was meant to incite the reader and serves as an affirmation of the glory of the Lamb. The poet claims to be with his friend in catatonic madness, murder, shock therapy, and psychotic sexuality. The conclusion is a crescendo of zealous anger:

> I'm with you in Rockland
> where we wake up electrified out of the coma by our own souls' airplanes roaring over the roof
>   they've come to drop angelic bombs the hospital illuminates itself imaginary walls collapse O
>   skinny legions run outside O starry spangled shock of mercy the eternal war is here O victory
>   forget your underwear we're free
> I'm with you in Rockland
> in my dreams you walk dripping from a sea-journey on the highway across America in tears to the
>   door of my cottage in the Western night

In presenting Solomon as the symbolic victim and redeemer of his generation, Ginsberg tries to acknowledge the full discordance of modern life, the deterioration of self, and the ambiguity and complexity of feeling.

Part 4, "Footnote to Howl," which was originally left out on the advice of noted poet Kenneth Rexroth, argues that if people pay attention and observe carefully, they will realize the holiness of all things and come to understand that perception is reciprocal. In other words, Ginsberg claims here that what we see will be what we are.

Ginsberg felt that his metrics were heavily influenced by his friend Jack Kerouac and by his reading of Walt Whitman, the Bible, and William Blake. In fact, the poet saw himself as a "divine Blakean angel" who was creating a poetry of vision. In "Howl," protest is a spiritual imperative patterned in a series of frames, snapshots, and catalogs. These frames serve as a "single breath unit" based on free association and at once sensational and personal. Part 1, a seventy-eight-line sentence, defines humanity's "mode" of "consciousness" through what the poet calls "density"; in clustering an associative and connotative wealth of imagery into that single line, Ginsberg creates a mix of bop and vernacular prosody.

For Ginsberg, as for his select group of Beats, the peculiar dementia inherent in their bleak moods of social hatred and self-pity was oddly gratifying. In their fear of life's unmanageability and in their need to exceed the bounds of normalcy where they could inflate the poetic into a vision of hypermagical proportions, Ginsberg's disenfranchised hipsters became obsessed with reinventing themselves in fictional contexts that complied with their escapist perceptions. In "Howl," the poet nags at circumstance, and he yearns for salvation through some kind of psychiatric and political nirvana. Here, fictional insanity and real insanity may be indistinguishable, and certain perceptions may conform only to an incoherent prescription embodying a set of power-driven illusions and agonizing self-hate. In speaking of his generation, Ginsberg is apostolic and romantic in the extreme, reflecting an untempered preoccupation with self-indulgences that are themselves rhapsodized as the anguished response to society's betrayals, atrocities, horrible abuses, and irregularities.

In "Howl," Ginsberg managed to catalog the excesses of the Beat generation with a rhetorical flair that was vigorous, insistently reductive, and censorious. Yet one senses that his invective cannot assuage his purist intentions. He hungers to preach and prophesy and reform according to the dictates of his own insufferable ethic of self-sufficiency and self-interest. However, the events and memories he describes—including the intemperate machinations and the talking, babbling, drinking, doping, sweating, withdrawing, and vomiting—accumulate in a litany of "disgorging," infantile self-destruction. In "Howl," Ginsberg presents a hip, generic Everyman who feels compelled to witness the self-destruction, anguish, and anger that served as a foundation for so much of the thinking that underlay the perspective of the Beat generation.

Matts Djos

Bibliography:

Ginsberg, Allen. *Howl: Original Draft Facsimile, Transcript & Variant Version, Fully Annotated by Author, with Contemporaneous Correspondence, Account of First Public Reading, Legal Skirmishes, Precursor Texts & Bibliography.* Edited by Barry Miles. New York: Harper & Row, 1986. An impressive study of the annotations, allusions, inspirations, revisions, and original typescripts of the poem. The book also presents contemporaneous correspondence from a range of poets and critics who were involved with the poem.

Hyde, Lewis, ed. *On the Poetry of Allen Ginsberg.* Ann Arbor: University of Michigan Press, 1984. An excellent collection of essays, reviews, and biographical materials. Gregory Stephenson's explication of "Howl" is especially comprehensive and helpful. The discussion of "Howl" in the 1950's and James Breslin's essay on the poem's genesis provide interesting information on the circumstances leading up to the original publication.

Merrill, Thomas F. *Allen Ginsberg.* Boston: Twayne, 1969. Provides a good overview of the publication history, structure, and theme of "Howl." Also includes a useful chronology.

Ostriker, Alicia. "Blake, Ginsberg, Madness, and the Prophet as Shaman." In *William Blake and the Moderns*, edited by Robert J. Bertholf and Annette S. Levitt. Albany: State University of New York Press, 1982. Explains how Ginsberg's reading of Blake inspired a series of religious visions that led him to believe that the poet is a prophet of madness who must "illuminate mankind."

Portuges, Paul. *The Visionary Poetics of Allen Ginsberg*. Santa Barbara, Calif.: Ross-Erickson, 1978. Portuges writes about Ginsberg's quest for a transcendent, mystical vision. He describes the poet's fascination with the poetry of William Blake and his interest in jazz, drugs, mantras, and Tibetan Buddhism.

HUDIBRAS

Type of work: Poetry
Author: Samuel Butler (1612-1680)
Type of plot: Satire
Time of plot: 1640-1660
Locale: England
First published: part 1, 1663; part 2, 1664; part 3, 1678

Principal characters:
SIR HUDIBRAS, a Presbyterian knight
RALPHO, Sir Hudibras' squire, a religious Independent
THE WIDOW, a wealthy woman, friend of Sir Hudibras
SIDROPHEL, an astrologer
CROWDERO, a fiddler

The Story:

Sir Hudibras, a Presbyterian knight, was one of those who had ridden out against the monarchy during England's Civil War. He was a proud man, one who bent his knee to nothing but chivalry and suffered no blow but that which had been given when he was dubbed a knight. Although he had some wit, he was very shy of displaying it. He knew Latin, Greek, and Hebrew; indeed, his talk was a kind of piebald dialect, so heavily was it larded with Greek and Latin words and tags. He was learned in rhetoric, logic, and mathematics, and he frequently spoke in a manner demonstrating his learning. His notions fitted things so well that he was often puzzled to decide what his notions were and what was reality.

In figure he was thick and stout, both before and behind, and he always carried extra victuals in his hose. He rode a mealy-mouthed, walleyed, skinny old nag whose tail dragged in the dust, and he encouraged his horse with a single old spur. Sir Hudibras had a squire named Ralpho, who was an Independent in religion—a fact that accounted for his partisanship and dogmatic approach to the many discussions and arguments that he had with his master on matters of faith. Ralpho was a tailor by trade, but his belief in the efficacy of divine revelation to the individual had made him something of a religious oracle, at least in his own opinion.

Sir Hudibras and Ralpho rode forth from the knight's home to reform what they called sins and what the rest of the world regarded as mild amusement. After they had gone a few miles on their journey they came to a town where the people danced to a fiddle and, even worse in Sir Hudibras' eyes, indulged themselves in the sport of bearbaiting. To the knight's resolve to end these activities Ralpho added his agreement that they were certainly unchristian. When the knight advanced, however, he was met by an unsympathetic crowd. Among the rabble were several leaders. One was Crowdero, a fiddler with one wooden leg, who played his instrument for the mob in the absence of more martial fifes and drums. Another leader was Orsin, the bear keeper, who led his charge at the end of a rope fastened to the creature's nose. Talgol, a butcher, was also in the van, as was a woman named Trulla, an amazon of a damsel. When Sir Hudibras called upon the people to disperse and return quietly to their homes, leaving Crowdero a prisoner, a fight began.

Ralpho was soon bucked off his horse when someone put a burr under the animal's tail. Sir Hudibras, pulled from his steed, fell on the bear, who became enraged and escaped from his keeper. The bear's escape scattered the crowd and Crowdero was left behind, the prisoner of

Sir Hudibras and Ralpho, because the fiddler's wooden leg had been broken in the melee. Having swooned from fear, Hudibras also lay helpless for a time, but he was soon revived by Ralpho. The pair took their prisoner to the end of the town and placed his good leg in the stocks. They hung his fiddle, bow, and case above the stocks as a trophy of victory.

The people who had been dispersed by the enraged bear, overcoming their fright, planned to attack the knight and release his victim. Hudibras and Ralpho sallied out of their quarters to the attack. A blow on Ralpho's horse caused the animal to unhorse his rider. Hudibras, at first frightened, summoned his courage and charged. The crowd dispersed once again, and Hudibras went to the aid of his squire. When the knight's back was turned, Trulla attacked him from behind and quickly overpowered him. Rejoined by her friends, the woman marched Hudibras to the stocks to take the place of Crowdero. Placed in the stocks, Hudibras and Ralpho discussed and argued their situation and what had occasioned it. Then a widow who had heard of the knight's plight came to see him in the stocks. After much discussion, she agreed to have Hudibras set free if he would consent to a whipping. He agreed to the condition and was released.

Sir Hudibras, once out of the stocks, was reluctant to keep the bargain he had made. He was anxious for the widow's hand too, but for her money rather than her love. Hudibras and Ralpho argued long about flagellation. Hudibras suggested that the whipping be administered to Ralpho, as a proxy for the knight. Ralpho refused and an argument ensued. When the two were almost at swords' points, they heard a terrible din. They looked about and saw coming down the road a party of people making a noisy to-do over a poor man who had let his wife take over his authority. Sir Hudibras tried to break up the crowd, but a volley of rotten eggs and other filth defeated him and cooled his ardor for reform. The knight, going to clean himself after his most recent encounter with sin, decided to lie to the widow about having received a whipping.

Before approaching the widow's house, Sir Hudibras went to consult Sidrophel, an astrologer. Hudibras and Ralpho agreed that a godly man might reasonably consult with such a man if the godly man were on a Christian errand. Hudibras, soon convinced that Sidrophel and his apprentice, Whachum, were frauds, perhaps dabblers with the devil, sent Ralpho off to find a constable. Meanwhile, Hudibras overcame the pair and went through the astrologer's belongings. Instead of going for a constable, however, Ralpho decided to go to the widow. He was afraid that the authorities might think Hudibras was involved in black magic.

Ralpho, telling all to the widow, revealed that Hudibras was going to lie about having received a whipping and that he was only after the widow's money. When Hudibras arrived a short time later, the widow hid Ralpho and let the knight tell his long string of half-truths and lies. The widow, knowing the truth, treated him to a somewhat frightening masquerade, with Ralpho as the chief sprite. Hudibras and the squire decided to escape before worse could happen to them. They went through a window and escaped on their saddleless horses.

The poet then turned in the last part of the poem to talk directly about the religious groups for which Ralpho and Hudibras stood—the Independents and the Presbyterians—and how they had fallen out with one another after the end of the civil war and had eventually, in their weakness, paved the way for the Restoration of the Stuart line in the person of Charles II.

Critical Evaluation:

Samuel Butler's *Hudibras* ridicules the Presbyterians, Dissenters, and others who fought against the crown in the conflict between Charles I and Oliver Cromwell. Published shortly after the Restoration of Charles II, the poem had immense popularity for a time. The king himself carried a copy in his pocket and quoted from it. *Hudibras* uses burlesque with telling effect. Mean and low persons, things, and situations are described in lofty language. The contrast between the poem's lofty language and its grubby subject matter exists to highlight the hypocrisy and absurdity of Dissenting reformers in seventeenth century England. Butler makes no pretence of impartiality. The poem shows the Dissenters as ridiculous, odious, and obnoxious. Butler also wanted to draw attention to the false learning rampant in England at the time. Astrology, fortune-telling, alchemy, sympathetic medicine, and other pseudosciences are presented in the poem in such a way as to show the readers of his time the absurdity of such practices and their practitioners.

The word "satire" comes from a Latin word for a mixed plate, and *Hudibras* is a somewhat disorganized mix of various objects of ridicule. More specifically, *Hudibras* is a travesty or burlesque. Such satire depends on form. Understanding Butler's poem is considerably a matter of what he manages to do with form. A central technique of *Hudibras* is Butler's deliberately creating a mismatch between his heroic language and ridiculous hero. One goal of satire is to call attention to the discrepancies between the ideal and the actual, between the world as people say it is and the world as it is. The implicit message of much satire is that, compared to the inappropriate behavior of people and the absurdity of life, the inappropriate and silly writings of an obscure scrivener is a small thing.

The self-absorbed zeal of Sir Hudibras and Ralpho is an example of the distance between human pretence and human reality. A brief quotation from the beginning of the poem illustrates how, when describing Hudibras, verse that should be gallant and romantic begins to sound like a bad jingle:

> Sir Hudibras, his passing worth,
> The manner how he sallied forth,
> His arms and equipage are shown,
> His horse's virtues and his own;
> The adventures of the Bear and Fiddle
> Is sung, but breaks off in the middle.

This is how travesty (the word, etymologically, relates to clothing) works. *Hudibras* begins with a tune that breaks off in the middle. The hero's horse's virtues come before those of the hero. The language, meter, and tone of the beginning of the poem make clear that what is to follow is not heroic but comic. The whole serious business of the Puritan revolution in England in the seventeenth century is treated as something trivial. The satire intends, by belittling the Dissenters, to cut them down to a more realistic size. An implicit point is that where common sense, good humor, and restraint are lacking, the silly and the irrelevant are to be found in abundance.

Samuel Butler was so successful in making fun of the Puritans in *Hudibras* that the poem became a model of verse form. "Hudibrastic verse" is deliberately bad poetry, with jingle-jangle lines of iambic tetrameter, rhymed in couplets. Tone and diction are purposefully scrambled, mixing the serious with the silly, in order to show that those who are foolish should not undertake something serious. Butler's verse form was imitated for more than a century after *Hudibras*. Jonathan Swift used the form extensively in the eighteenth century, for example.

The hero of Butler's satire, Hudibras, is named after a character in Edmund Spenser's *The Faerie Queene* (1590). Butler's Hudibras is, like Spenser's, intolerant, intemperate, and something of a troublemaker. A clearly intended parallel also exists between Hudibras and Ralpho and Don Quixote and Sancho Panza. This parallel is, implicitly, an ironic attack on Hudibras, Ralpho, and whom they represent because Don Quixote and Sancho Panza are sympathetic characters and Hudibras and Ralpho are not. Not only do Hudibras and Ralpho not measure up to the heroes of classical literature, they also fail to measure up to their silly but likable Spanish counterparts. They represent everything that was not likable about the era of Puritan ascendancy in England. They are zealous crusaders, quite satisfied about their certainty that the world is in need of reform and that they are the ones suited to bring about that reform. They do have certain small differences of opinion, however, about some of the details.

Hudibras is Butler's idea of certain Presbyterians of his time. In a mechanical way Hudibras has acquired some wide learning, which he uses without judgment or restraint and with a large helping of intellectual pride. Ralpho, in turn, represents an Independent of Butler's time. Ralpho has no need for the structures of Hudibras' learning or for Hudibras' church. Ralpho believes himself mystically illuminated from within. The inner light that he thinks guides him is supposedly a superior agency, more directly connected to God than anything that Hudibras can parade from his store of knowledge.

Samuel Butler did not trust either the man who would believe his book before he would his senses or the man who thought his intuition was infallible. Butler, who was skeptical and conservative, was himself a person of learning, who had in addition the understanding that allowed him to see the pretensions of the learned. In the Puritans' government Butler saw ill-considered reform, ideology rising above fact, and violent intolerance for other points of view. The reformers, in his estimation, needed reforming.

Butler doubted that sudden, radical, and violent change in English life, custom, and government could be justified by claims to a spiritual enlightenment that had not been available before in history. He set out to skewer the people who claimed to have a greater understanding of the will of God. His method of attacking them was to mock them. His attack on pretence is not a fire-and-brimstone sermon but rather a giggle during prayer. His is a cunning, if ephemeral, way of deflating pretence. Deliberately writing silly verse, after all, is less silly than taking oneself very seriously.

"Critical Evaluation" by John Higby

Bibliography:
Bond, Richmond P. *English Burlesque Poetry, 1700-1750.* New York: Russell & Russell, 1964. This classic study places *Hudibras* in the burlesque tradition. Argues that the poem is not, on the other hand, a travesty.
Butler, Samuel. *Hudibras.* Edited by John Wilders. Oxford, England: Clarendon Press, 1967. This edition provides much useful information. Copious notes.
Jack, Ian. *Augustan Satire: Intention and Idiom in English Poetry, 1660-1750.* Oxford, England: Clarendon Press, 1957. Calls *Hudibras* a "low satire" and places the poem in the context of other major satiric poems through most of a century.
Richards, Edward Ames. *Hudibras in the Burlesque Tradition.* New York: Columbia University Press, 1937. Gives an account of the influence of Butler's poem in colonial America. Places the poem in the context of the burlesque tradition.
Wasserman, George. *Samuel "Hudibras" Butler.* Rev. ed. Boston: Twayne, 1989. A chapter on Butler's thought is followed by two chapters on *Hudibras.* Bibliography.

HUGH SELWYN MAUBERLEY

Type of work: Poetry
Author: Ezra Pound (1885-1972)
First published: 1920

The young American poet Ezra Pound had been living in Europe for more than a decade when he published his first major work, *Hugh Selwyn Mauberley*. In London, Pound had become professionally acquainted with many of the leading artists and intellectuals, including the novelists Wyndham Lewis and Ford Madox Ford; the critic T. E. Hulme; poets T. S. Eliot, Hilda Doolittle, Amy Lowell, and John Gould Fletcher; and the sculptor Henri Gaudier-Brzeska. Pound also met Henry James and helped the Anglo-Irish poet W. B. Yeats hone a new style for what many saw to be the new age of literature. In addition to writing poetry, Pound was active as an editor for such innovative literary magazines as *Poetry*, *Egoist*, and *Blast*. Among his lasting contributions are Imagism and the experimentation with free verse.

Pound was in a unique position to bear painful witness to two equally devastating phenomena. The first was the utter indifference with which society at large greeted the efforts of young people to improve human values and perceptions through their art. The second phenomenon was World War I. *Hugh Selwyn Mauberley* is a double-edged indictment of that war, which changed everything, and of the poets and artists who had failed to change anything. Yet *Hugh Selwyn Mauberley* is also that very thing whose absence the poet mourns—a poetry that has the courage to present a true report without forsaking beauty.

The first three sections of the poem rely heavily on allusions to the classical age of Homeric Greece to establish a stark contrast between past and contemporary expectations of art and the artist. Pound emphasizes this point further through the dashed expectations of his alter ego, Mauberley. Pound later told a correspondent, "I am no more Mauberley than Eliot is Prufrock. . . . Mauberley is a mere surface." Still, Pound's dedication to the poem tells us it is "an ode for the choice of his [own] tomb," and like Pound, who was born in Idaho, Mauberley is an American "born/ in a half savage country." As an alter ego, Mauberley most likely represents a former self who failed by setting himself the unachievable goal "to resuscitate the dead art/ Of poetry."

Mauberley was not wrong to aim so high, the poet tells us, but he compares it to trying to wring "lilies from the acorn." Thus, he eventually became lost, and forgotten, in his own aesthetic subtleties, just as Homer's Odysseus got wrapped up in the "elegance of Circe's hair." In any case, the "age demanded" other things from its artists, "an image/ Of its accelerated grimace/ / . . . a mould in plaster,/ Made with no loss of time." While artists labored fruitlessly away at what the age regarded as meaningless nothings, "a tawdry cheapness" set the standard for public taste and the classical vitality of Sappho, Dionysus, and the Faun was replaced by "a knave or an eunuch" hypocritically mouthing Christian pieties until, instead of the crowning laurel for the heroes and gods of old, there was but a "tin wreath."

All of this would be nothing more than the commonplaces of social criticism that poets have, since time immemorial, leveled at their ages were it not for the witheringly real intervention of World War I. It is to the bitter ironies of that event that the poet directs his attention in parts 4 and 5. "These fought in any case," he tells us in stark terms, and yet for what did they fight and die. Amid the melodrama of Mauberley's failures and of the age's cheapness of mind and values there was only "wastage as never before," and now when the poet quotes from the classics it is to remind his readers that to die for one's country is neither fitting nor sweet if that nation is the contemporary England (or France, Germany, or the United States) that had been described in parts 2 and 3.

In *Hugh Selwyn Mauberley*, Pound discarded the free verse techniques he had developed in the preceding decade, returning in parts 1 through 3 to the traditional quatrain. In parts 4 and 5, though, as if to underscore the failure of poetry to prevent the war and at the same time to display poetry's ability to mirror the war's catastrophe, Pound resorts to free verse and to the compression of Imagism in describing such sights as the bodies left to rot in the no-man's-lands of trench warfare: "laughter out of dead bellies."

Ironically, then, the very poem that laments Mauberley's failure to resuscitate the dead art of poetry brings that art back to life as a tool for commenting on a "botched" civilization's failure to live up to its own ideals: "There died a myriad,/ / For two gross of broken statues,/ For a few thousand battered books." The relationship between this climax and the remainder of the poem, which continues for another eight sections, is simply that they repeat parts 1 through 3 by reviewing the circumstances by which a civilization betrayed its artists, and the artists betrayed the service of conscience they owed their civilization.

The Pre-Raphaelite movement sought intentionally to outrage middle-class tastes and conventions while calling for a poetry and painting divorced from social concerns. The public moralists won by default, however, since the artists became increasingly self-absorbed and self-destructive. The result outlined in *Hugh Selwyn Mauberley* is that the poets and artists of his generation became either totally ineffectual but affected aesthetes like Brennbaum of the "sky-like limpid eyes" and impeccable dress or highly paid literary hacks like Mr. Nixon, who learned how to tailor their work to the taste of editors and reviewers and who caution the young Mauberley to "give up verse, my boy,/ There's nothing in it." Part 10, meanwhile, bewails the fate of "the stylist" (thought to be the novelist Ford Madox Ford) who takes refining his art seriously but lives in unrefined squalor and can barely make ends meet. For potential benefactors, the wealthy, represented by the Lady Valentine, poetry has become a "border of ideas" rather than any center to their lives, values, or interests.

The ironic conclusion, "Envoi," which mimicks a seventeenth century poetic style, suggests that Mauberley has learned nothing from his own frustrations or the war's destructiveness. Yet there is that gentle touch in the aestheticism of wishing that his beloved's graces might live as "roses might, in magic amber laid,/ . . . / Braving time." This otherwise age-old wish that beauty might yet survive its own undoing by being preserved in and through art is more genuine and vigorous than the claim that only by being unforgiving of personal failures and of those of others can anyone earn the right to consider and comment on the proper place of beauty.

Shortly after the publication of *Hugh Selwyn Mauberley*, Pound published *Mauberley*, which is both a commentary on and an extension of the original sequence. As if Pound felt that he had not sufficiently crucified the errant Mauberley in the first work, where his worst offense was that he had been "unaffected by 'The march of events,'" now his art is judged to be "but an art/ In profile" and he has become "incapable of the least utterance or composition." Another explanation of Pound's intentions, however, can be found in the short "Medallion" with which *Mauberley* ends. It is a masterful description of a soprano in concert, a word painting worthy of the High Renaissance, which is alluded to in the reference to Bernardino Luini, a contemporary of Leonardo da Vinci. The medallion also calls to mind Henry James's metaphor for the structure of his novel *The Ambassadors* (1903), whose tone and style Pound confessed to having attempted to duplicate in verse. Finally, the readers are told that the "honey-red" of her hair seemed spun of "intractable amber," reminding us of the image of rose preserved from the ravages of time by amber in Mauberley's earlier "Envoi"; thus the third "artist" to share the spotlight with Luini and James in Pound's closing paean to servers of the Beautiful is none other than his own fictive creation, Hugh Selwyn Mauberley. This is not unworthy company, nor does it make Mauberley's "art in profile" an inferior art, especially since Pound, in drawing his portrait of Mauberley, seems to be practicing the same technique by asking us to imagine what the poet is gazing on rather than to gaze at the poet.

Hugh Selwyn Mauberley, through the very process of its concealments and confusions, forces us to focus sharply and clearly on issues that might seem to transcend the aesthetic—issues such as war, public morality, and literary politics—but that are, in Pound's view, inextricably intertwined with the aesthetic. In severely criticizing one kind of aestheticism, the poem manages only to create another, but that is the poem's theme—that there is not a separation but a very vital and nurturing link not only between art and life but between the artist and society.

Hugh Selwyn Mauberley's critical reputation has seldom wavered. Virtually from the time of its publication, it has been recognized as an important statement by a major poetic voice. The greater critical acclaim for T. S. Eliot's poem *The Waste Land* (1922), which shows some similarity of technique, serves to overshadow Pound's achievement somewhat (the irony is that Pound had played a crucial editorial role in giving Eliot's poem its form). While Pound's *Cantos* (1930-1966), to which the poet devoted most of the rest of his creative life, has also kept *Hugh Selwyn Mauberley* from receiving the full critical attention it deserves, there is little denying that the earlier work was the proving ground for both the techniques and the ideas that created the *Cantos*.

Russell Elliott Murphy

Bibliography:

Espey, John. *Ezra Pound's Mauberley*. Berkeley: University of California Press, 1974. In this major full-length study devoted exclusively to Mauberley, Espey focuses on the Mauberley persona, Pound's sources, and the poem's overall structure. Concludes that *Hugh Selwyn Mauberley* is a summing up of all Pound had achieved up to that point and prefigures the *Cantos*.

Hoffmann, Frederick J. *The 20's: American Writing in the Post-War Decade*. New York: Macmillan, 1962. The definitive treatment on that rich literary decade, Hoffmann's study discusses *Hugh Selwyn Mauberley* in its social, literary, and intellectual context.

Kenner, Hugh. *The Pound Era*. Berkeley: University of California Press, 1971. A critical overview of Pound's achievement and of his place in and impact on twentieth century literature and culture. A highly engaging text for the more ambitious student who wishes to understand *Hugh Selwyn Mauberley* in the context of Pound's career.

Leavis, F. R. *New Bearings in English Poetry: A Study of the Contemporary Situation*. 1932. Reprint. Ann Arbor: University of Michigan Press, 1960. Leavis' chapter on Pound set the tone and direction for much subsequent criticism and remains an important source for the discussion of *Hugh Selwyn Mauberley*.

Witemeyer, Hugh. *The Poetry of Ezra Pound: Forms and Renewal, 1908-1920*. Berkeley: University of California Press, 1981. This thoroughgoing analysis of Pound's early poetry and poetic theories culminates in an extended treatment of *Hugh Selwyn Mauberley*. The poem is a critique of a failed impressionist aesthetic rendered in the emerging terms of the modernist aesthetic Pound was to perfect in the *Cantos*.

THE HUMAN COMEDY

Type of work: Novel
Author: William Saroyan (1908-1981)
Type of plot: Sentimental
Time of plot: Twentieth century
Locale: Ithaca, California
First published: 1943

> *Principal characters:*
> KATEY MACAULEY, a widow
> HOMER,
> ULYSSES, and
> MARCUS, her sons
> BESS, her daughter
> MARY ARENA, Marcus' sweetheart
> THOMAS SPANGLER, the manager of a telegraph office
> MR. GROGAN, the assistant in the telegraph office
> TOBEY GEORGE, Marcus' friend from the army
> LIONEL, Ulysses' friend

The Story:

Mr. Macauley was dead, and his wife and children had to take care of themselves. When Marcus went into the army, Homer, the next oldest, obtained a job on the night shift in the telegraph office in Ithaca, California. He worked at night because he was still attending school during the day. Little Ulysses watched his family and wondered what was going on, because his baby's mind could not comprehend all the changes that had taken place in his home.

Every morning Homer arose early and exercised in his room so that he would be physically fit to run the 220-yard low hurdles at high school. After he and Bess had eaten their breakfast, Mary Arena, who was in love with Marcus, came from next door, and she and Bess walked to school together.

In the ancient-history class, taught by Miss Hicks, Homer and Hubert Ackley the Third insulted each other. Miss Hicks kept the boys after school, but Coach Byfield had picked Hubert to run the 220-yard low hurdles that afternoon, and Hubert told Miss Hicks that the principal had asked that he be excused. Indignant at the deceit, Miss Hicks also sent Homer to run the race. Although Hubert was the winner, Homer felt that justice had been done.

Thomas Spangler was in charge of the telegraph office, and Mr. Grogan, an old man with a weak heart, was his assistant. Mr. Grogan got drunk every night, and one of Homer's duties was to see to it that Mr. Grogan stayed awake to perform his duties. A problem that weighed on Homer's mind ever since he had taken his new job and had grown up overnight was whether the war would change anything for people. Mr. Grogan and Homer often talked about the world, Homer declaring that he did not like things as they were. Seeing everyone in the world mixed up and lonely, Homer said, he felt that he had to say and do things to make people laugh.

Mrs. Macauley was happy that her children were so human. Since her husband had died, Katey Macauley had pretended to see him and discuss with him problems that arose concerning the rearing of her family. She felt that the father was not dead if he lived again in the lives of his children. One afternoon, she had a premonition of Marcus' death, for she imagined that her husband came to her and told her he was going to bring Marcus with him.

Little Ulysses had a friend, Lionel, who was three years older than Ulysses. The older boys chased Lionel away from their games because they said that he was dumb. When Lionel came to Mrs. Macauley to ask whether he was stupid, the kind woman assured him that he was as good as everyone else. Lionel took Ulysses to the library with him to look at all the many-colored books on the shelves. Ulysses, who spent his time wandering around and watching everything, was pleased with the new experience.

Marcus wrote to Homer from an army camp somewhere in the South, and Homer took the letter back to the telegraph office with him. The letter told about Marcus' friend, an orphan named Tobey George. Marcus had described his family, Homer, Ulysses, Bess, his mother, and his sweetheart, Mary, to Tobey. Tobey had no family of his own, so he was grateful to Marcus for telling him about the Macauley family. Marcus had told Tobey that, after the war, he wanted Tobey to go to Ithaca and marry Bess. Tobey was not so certain that Bess would want to marry him, but he felt for the first time in his life that he had a family that was almost his own. Marcus had written to Homer, as the new head of the family, to tell him about Tobey George and to ask him to look after his mother and Bess.

Homer was moved by his brother's letter. When he had finished reading it, he told Mr. Grogan that if Marcus should be killed, he would spit at the world. Homer could express his love for Marcus in no other way.

The same events repeated themselves many times in Ithaca. Ulysses continued to watch everything with increasing interest. Mary and Bess sang their songs and went for their evening walks. Telegrams came, and Homer delivered them. Soldiers began coming home to Ithaca, to their mothers, and to their families. Homer had been working at the telegraph office for six months. One Sunday night, while he was walking downtown with Lionel and Ulysses, he saw through the window of the telegraph office that Mr. Grogan was working alone. He sent the two small boys home and went in to see if Mr. Grogan needed him. The old man had suffered one of his heart attacks, and Homer ran to the drugstore to get some medicine for him. Mr. Grogan attempted to type out one more telegram, a message for Katey Macauley telling her that her son Marcus had been killed in action. When Homer returned with the medicine, he found Mr. Grogan slumped over the typed-out message. He was dead. Homer went home with the message that Marcus had been killed.

That night, a soldier got off the train at Ithaca. He was Tobey George. He walked around for a time before he went to see Marcus' family. When he came to the Macauley porch, he stood and listened to Bess and Mary singing inside the house. Bess came outside and sat next to him while he told her that Marcus had sent him to be a member of the family. When Homer came to the porch with the telegram, Tobey called him aside and told him to tear up the message. Tobey assured him that Marcus was not dead; Marcus could never die. Mrs. Macauley came onto the porch, and Ulysses ran to Tobey and took his hand. For a while, the mother looked at her two remaining sons. Then she smiled at her new son as the family walked into the house.

Critical Evaluation:
The Human Comedy was first written by William Saroyan as a screenplay. The film appeared in February, 1942, with Mickey Rooney as the leading actor. By May, 1943, Saroyan had revised the screenplay into his first novel. This process of development helps explain the organization of chapters as vignettes that jump quickly from scene to scene without clear transitions. Such a quick pace may have been unusual for the era in which the book was written, but this rapid movement had been used earlier in William Faulkner's *The Sound and the Fury* (1929). In retrospect, Saroyan's method of rapid movement is not distracting.

Some criticize *The Human Comedy* for its seemingly naïve, sentimental treatment of life in small-town America. Some see this work as a form of propaganda used to support the war effort during World War II. The novel admittedly suffers from overly simplistic presentations of United States soldiers as being noble, even when drunk, and of would-be criminals as being essentially good at heart. This seeming naïveté is precisely the strength of the novel. In an era when faith in human character and the destiny of humanity was in question, Saroyan returns to the values of people in the small towns of the United States as a way of affirming the humanity and dignity of people around the world. This novel is set in Ithaca, but one can readily see that Saroyan is writing about his own hometown, Fresno, California, which he loved deeply and portrayed in nostalgic terms. Furthermore, in this novel Saroyan is writing about his own childhood, during which he struggled as a fatherless Armenian child who delivered telegrams to help with his family's expenses.

The Human Comedy may be seen as an illustration of several major themes, such as the unity of humanity in spite of war, the struggles of growing up in a small town, and the essential goodness of people. Several times the philosophical Katey Macauley tells her son Homer how the war is a product of loneliness and the lack of God's grace in the world, or how each individual has the potential to re-create the world as a place filled with people to be loved. This positive interpretation of humanity is reiterated by others such as Thomas Spangler, who offers to help an armed robber named John by giving him money and a second chance to make a new start in life. According to Spangler, the penitentiaries and graveyards are full of good Americans who are not criminals, but mere victims of bad luck and hard times. This same positive view is applied to people around the world on both sides of the war.

The Human Comedy seems to present the world in terms too easy to accept, but the novel also probes aspects of the human condition that are not easy to explain. For example, the Armenian grocery store owner, Ara, gives his son John whatever he desires from the grocery store, but still the son is not happy. The melancholy of this little life is difficult to fathom. Food, clothing, and human love do not take away the feelings of grief in the soul. This truth is explored throughout the novel in the life of the leading character, Homer Macauley, as he experiences defeat in a hurdles race at school, or feels the pain of others to whom he delivers announcements from the U.S. War Department about recent deaths, or encounters the evils of a local house of prostitution. In part, Homer's pain is that of a boy growing up to see that the world is not as sweet and innocent as it seems. The death of Homer's older brother, Marcus, near the end of the novel combined with Mr. Grogan's death at the telegraph key desk make Homer at least temporarily bitter so that he wants to spit at the world. Spangler tries to comfort Homer by assuring him that Marcus, like all good people, will never die, but can be remembered in all things thriving with life and love. This is the same message that Homer's mother gives him earlier in the novel concerning how she would feel if news came of Marcus' death.

Although such insights belong to the sentimental, other aspects of the novel introduce beliefs that some would find surprising in a largely naturalistic novel. For example, Mrs. Macauley sees her deceased husband at the dinner table after the others have gone and holds conversations with him. In one of these conversations her former husband informs her about Marcus' impending death, which comes to pass. On a more positive note, Tobey George, an orphaned friend of Marcus, senses a strong identity with Ithaca as his future home and, as the conclusion of the novel suggests, he will eventually realize this dream by marrying Bess Macauley, Marcus' sister. While few of the characters in this novel are overtly Christian, many of them embody spiritual values which serve as major guiding forces in their lives. The qualities of generosity, compassion, love, and trust are portrayed repeatedly in the major and minor characters.

Some critics may fault *The Human Comedy* for being less than realistic about the painful dimensions of life, but the novel offers a humane and hopeful approach to surviving the challenges of growing up and facing the atrocities of war. In practice, often the best way to deal with the death of a loved one is to focus on good memories of the loved one. Similarly, one of the best ways to deal with the problem of aging is to keep contributing to society until one's dying day, as Mr. Grogan does. Such advice is finally very practical and affirming, not just sentimental. As the title of the novel suggests, this work is a comedy, which typically ends with a resolution of conflict or at least a harmonizing of events. As the name of the leading character also suggests, this is a story about overcoming great odds, and, after a journey (spiritual or otherwise), finding a home.

"Critical Evaluation" by Daven M. Kari

Bibliography:
Calonne, David Stephen. *William Saroyan: My Real Work Is Being.* Chapel Hill: University of North Carolina Press, 1983. The first major study after William Saroyan's death in 1981. Treats *The Human Comedy* as a discussion of the family of humanity, as a portrayal of the journey from boyhood to manhood, and as an illustration of the triumph of love over death.
Floan, Howard R. *William Saroyan.* New York: Twayne, 1966. Traces William Saroyan's literary career from 1934 to 1964 in four phases, the third phase being started by *The Human Comedy.* Still useful as an introduction to Saroyan's works. Chronology and annotated bibliography.
Hamalian, Leo, ed. *William Saroyan: The Man and the Writer Remembered.* Madison, N.J.: Fairleigh Dickinson University Press, 1987. Articles by acquaintances and friends of William Saroyan. Largely anecdotal and sometimes poorly written, the accounts nevertheless give glimpses of the author's daily life.
Lee, Lawrence, and Barry Gifford. *Saroyan: A Biography.* New York: Harper & Row, 1984. Reveals William Saroyan's achievements and failures as a writer and as a person. Useful for placing *The Human Comedy* in its historical and cultural context.
Saroyan, Aram. *William Saroyan.* San Diego: Harcourt Brace Jovanovich, 1983. A review of William Saroyan's life by his son, himself a poet, essayist, and novelist. Well illustrated with photographs and includes a bibliography of works by William Saroyan. Especially useful for exploring the autobiographical elements in *The Human Comedy.*

THE HUMAN FACTOR

Type of work: Novel
Author: Graham Greene (1904-1991)
Type of plot: Spy
Time of plot: Late Cold War era
Locale: Suburban Berkhamsted and London
First published: 1978

Principal characters:
   MAURICE CASTLE, British Intelligence officer
   SARAH, his wife
   SAM, Sarah's son
   ARTHUR DAVIS, Castle's coworker
   COLONEL DAINTRY, the new head of security
   SIR JOHN HARGREAVES, Daintry's superior
   DOCTOR EMMANUEL PERCIVAL, also of British Intelligence
   CORNELIUS MULLER, a representative of apartheid

The Story:

Maurice Castle, sixty-two years old, worked a desk job in a two-man subsection of British Intelligence. Castle's duties and those of his younger office mate Arthur Davis involved receiving and sending information to and from South Africa, where Castle had previously worked as a field agent. One day on his way to lunch, Castle met the new head of security, Colonel Daintry. Though polite, Daintry asked Castle to open his briefcase and show that he was not removing any classified papers.

Later, Castle rode the train to his home in Berkhamsted, where he sensed something amiss. His wife Sarah told him that their young son Sam had measles. Castle's anxiety subsided somewhat. What he valued most in life was Sarah, a black woman he had met in South Africa, and her son Sam. That weekend, Daintry and others from security met at the country house of Sir John Hargreaves, Daintry's superior, for a pheasant shoot and a discussion of the security leak that had been traced to Castle's office. Over whiskey and cigars, Sir John decided that once the culprit was identified he would have to be eliminated to spare British Intelligence the embarrassment of a public treason trial. To facilitate that end, he had invited Doctor Percival to join them in case they should need suggestions for an undetectable poison.

One morning, Castle bought two copies of *War and Peace* from Halliday, the bookseller he visited. Sir John Hargreaves later reported that in a few weeks Castle would confer with Cornelius Muller, a leader of the South African apartheid group called BOSS. Seven years ago Muller had been one of Castle's adversaries when Castle's love for Sarah had led him to break the race laws in South Africa. Hargreaves also informed Castle of Uncle Remus, a White House position paper that would unite Britain, the United States, and the apartheid government to protect their shared financial concerns if a race war should close South African gold and diamond mines. Hargreaves ordered Castle to set aside past differences and work with Muller.

About three weeks later, Doctor Percival accompanied Davis to a strip club under the excuse of wanting an evening's relaxation. Davis told Castle that Percival had mentioned Uncle Remus and the British establishment at Porton. Castle found this odd. He wondered if Percival suspected a leak and was planting a false rumor. When Percival later lunched with Hargreaves at his club, the doctor named Davis as the leak. He had uncovered discrepancies in Davis' behavior that he connected with the heavy drinking and emotional strain he had observed in Davis at the strip club. Though he lacked the hard evidence of guilt that Daintry wanted, Percival recommended that they proceed by using a poisonous mold from decaying peanuts to make Davis' eventual death look like liver failure.

Castle's first meeting with Cornelius Muller seven years after South Africa left him uneasy, although Muller was polite and apologetic. Castle later delivered a report of this meeting to Boris, his communist contact. Castle also verified from Boris that Carson, the Marxist who had helped Sarah escape from South Africa, was really dead as Muller had claimed. Castle's motive for being the double agent was simple gratitude rather than shared ideology: Carson had freed Sarah, and Castle expressed his gratefulness by sending secrets to this friend. Now, on seeing that Operation Uncle Remus supported apartheid, Castle wanted to retire.

Castle heard of Davis' death at the wedding reception of Daintry's daughter. Daintry and Castle went immediately to Davis' apartment, where Castle noticed men from the special branch. He began to doubt the findings of natural causes. Castle drafted another report for Boris. The notes Muller left with Castle about blacks in South Africa had used the frightening phrase the "final solution." Although Castle communicated with the Russians through a book code based on *War and Peace*, for the first time he linked himself in his report with Carson. Knowing he was going too far, he began using an emergency telephone code to signal for a safe passage out of England.

Castle took the transcribed copy of Muller's notes to Halliday, for Halliday to give to his son, whom Castle suspected was his intermediary with the Russians. Castle later told Sarah that he was the double agent. She backed him, but Castle insisted that Sarah take Sam to his mother's house and tell her that they had quarreled. Castle became anxious over news reports of the arrest of Halliday's son, another bookseller, who was picked up on the charge of selling pornography. If he had had Castle's report on him, Castle would be exposed as the double agent.

Meanwhile, Muller contacted Sir John Hargreaves with a troubling intuition about Castle. Muller said that he had left some inconsequential notes with Castle but that he did not trust him. Sir John knew firsthand the importance of intuition. He reluctantly met with Doctor Percival and raised the possibility that they had killed the wrong man. Percival reminded Sir John that the false information he had given Davis about Porton had later surfaced, a confirmation, Percival thought, of Davis' guilt. Hargreaves nevertheless sent Daintry to Castle's house to question him.

Castle's need to talk led him to tell Daintry that Davis had not been the leak. When Daintry asked Castle if he was the double agent, Castle equivocated. Daintry later reported to Percival that Davis' murder had been a mistake. Hours later, Castle was surprised when Halliday senior arrived at his home and admitted that he and not his son was Castle's intermediary. Castle realized that his ignorance of his contact revealed how little even the communists had trusted him. Halliday had mapped an escape. Castle traveled in disguise to Moscow by way of the Caribbean.

Once there, he reminded the Russians that they had agreed to bring Sarah and Sam. Sam lacked a passport, however, and the British stalled them with bureaucratic delays. Finally, Castle made telephone contact with Sarah in England. Sarah told him she could not leave without Sam, and Castle said he understood. She urged him to go on hoping, but the silence made her realize that the line was dead.

Critical Evaluation:

In *The Human Factor* Graham Greene develops an idea he mentioned in an essay on the adventure novels of John Buchan. Greene credited Buchan with being "the first to realize the enormous dramatic value of adventure in familiar surroundings happening to unadventurous men." Some of Greene's early novels illustrate Buchan's premise—*A Gun for Sale: An Entertainment* (1936), *The Confidential Agent* (1939), and *The Ministry of Fear: An Entertainment* (1943)—but *The Human Factor* is his most thoughtful treatment of this idea. Greene elaborates movingly on the costs and value of human compassion by placing unadventurous characters like Castle and Davis in the setting of modern espionage. The novel's epigraph, a quote by Joseph Conrad, also helps to identify this focus on humanity: "I only know that he who forms a tie is lost. The germ of corruption has entered into his soul."

This germ of corruption in *The Human Factor* is openheartedness, a quality that outweighs commitment to an ideology. Castle's betrayal of his government is motivated solely by a personal kindness by Carson, the Marxist who arranged Sarah's escape from a South African prison. At one point Castle's mother reminds him of a childhood insecurity: "You always had an exaggerated sense of gratitude for the least kindness." In one of Greene's most unsettling ironies, Castle's human ties thus become both his greatest strength and greatest vulnerability.

For example, to shield Sarah from any repercussions, Castle has sent his secrets to Russia in complete secrecy. This display of love, however, only increases his precariousness by increasing his loneliness. Castle prowls streets carrying the self-incriminating report about Muller and seeking the therapy of someone in whom to confide. Even a priest, on hearing Castle admit that he is not Catholic, slams the confessional door in his face. Castle describes himself to Sarah as someone born to be a half-believer. When a human face like Carson's is attached to Marxism or those of the humble priests he met in Africa are attached to Christianity, he feels inner stirrings of commitment. What he wants most, however, is "not the City of God or Marx but the city called Peace of Mind." This he is denied.

Castle learns "the age-old lesson that fear and love are indivisible"; others are defined by a crippling emotional aridity. Away from apartheid, Cornelius Muller adapts like a chameleon to attitudes in England, and his hollow apologies to Castle and Sarah indicate his complete lack of convictions. Muller's later intuition about Castle's disloyalty arises from his recollection that Castle offered friendship to Carson. To Muller, such benevolence corrupts. Muller describes an agent years ago in Africa who leaked secrets: "He too cultivated friendships—and the friendships took over."

Doctor Percival is Greene's most inhuman character. His interest in fishing supplants an interest in his fellow man. Percival expounds on the varieties of fish even as the naked women contort before him at the strip club. Percival dehumanizes the murder plot against Davis by rendering it in comfortable metaphors ("we seem to have a fish on the line"). Like the sterile boxes in the abstract art he notices at Hargreaves' country house, Percival's chilling inhumanity rationalizes killing the wrong man, thereby thwarting all remorse. He even tells Sarah that blocking her passage to Russia is "nothing personal." As with Muller, this cold-as-fish politeness affronts more than open hostility does; hostility would at least imply some human emotion.

Daintry's plight may be the saddest. Realizing that "they killed my marriage with their secrets" and hating the subsequent loneliness imposed on him, Daintry remains an outsider at his own daughter's wedding. At the reception he accidentally smashes one of his former wife's ornamental owls, one of a hundred such pieces of bric-a-brac. This human blunder reminds Castle of Daintry's smashed marriage and stirs his sympathy. In Daintry's final visit, Castle finds his longed-for chance to talk. Daintry ultimately does his duty, but he realizes that he must resign, a decision that only intensifies his solitude. Greene's unsparing emotional realism thus makes *The Human Factor* important not only among his own works but also in the growth of the spy novel from the uncomplicated politics and morality of John Buchan to the richer ambiguities of modern fiction.

Glenn Hopp

Bibliography:
DeVitis, A. A. "The Later Greene." In *Essays in Graham Greene.* Vol. 1, edited by Peter Wolfe. Greenwood, Fla.: Penkevill, 1987. This essay and the revised edition of DeVitis' book *Graham Greene* (Boston: Twayne, 1986) offer a number of insights on *The Human Factor*, in particular on Greene's use of chess metaphors and his novel's debt to the moral ambiguities of Joseph Conrad's 1907 novel *The Secret Agent.*
O'Prey, Paul. *A Reader's Guide to Graham Greene.* New York: Thames and Hudson, 1988. Comments (pages 135-140) usefully on *The Human Factor* and draws on Greene's own remarks.
Shapiro, Henry L. "Morality and Ambivalence in *The Human Factor.*" In *Essays in Graham Greene.* Vol. 2, edited by Peter Wolfe. Greenwood, Fla.: Penkevill, 1990. Explores one of Greene's recurrent concerns and discusses the link between religion and espionage.
Wolfe, Peter, ed. *Essays in Graham Greene.* Vol. 3. St. Louis: Lucas Hall Press, 1992. Introduces and reprints three important early essays on Greene.
_____. *Graham Greene the Entertainer.* Carbondale: Southern Illinois University Press, 1972. The best book on Greene's early novels that prepared for *The Human Factor*, Wolfe's study is also one of the most perceptive books on the thriller as an art form.

HUMBOLDT'S GIFT

Type of work: Novel
Author: Saul Bellow (1915-   )
Type of plot: Psychological realism
Time of plot: 1970's
Locale: Chicago, New York City, Corpus Christi, Houston, Madrid, Paris
First published: 1975

> *Principal characters:*
> CHARLIE CITRINE, the narrator and protagonist, a respected author and
>   historian
> DENISE, his former wife
> VON HUMBOLDT FLEISHER, a poet and Charlie's friend
> WALDEMAR WALD, Humboldt's uncle
> KATHLEEN, Humboldt's former wife
> GEORGE SWIEBEL, Charlie's friend
> PIERRE THAXTER, Charlie's friend
> RENATA KOFFRITZ, Charlie's girlfriend
> ROGER KOFFRITZ, her son
> THE SEÑORA, her mother
> RINALDO CANTABILE, a minor Chicago gangster

The Story:

By the 1970's, Charles Citrine, a respected author in his mid-fifties, had won two Pulitzer Prizes, one for his book on Woodrow Wilson, twenty-eighth president of the United States, and one for his Broadway play, *Von Trenck.* Charlie's former wife, Denise, demanded higher support payments. His twenty-nine-year-old girlfriend, Renata Koffritz, wanted to marry him. During a poker game, Charlie gave Rinaldo Cantabile a check for $450. At the insistence of his friend, George Swiebel, who had seen Cantabile cheat, Charlie stopped payment on the check. Insulted, Cantabile battered Charlie's Mercedes-Benz with a baseball bat and forced Charlie to pay the debt in front of several people. Then Cantabile took Charlie up to an unfinished skyscraper and dropped all the money except two $50 bills that he used to buy dinner. At dinner, Cantabile asked Charlie to help his wife with a Ph.D. dissertation on Charlie's dead friend, the poet Von Humboldt Fleisher, but Charlie refused.

The next day, Charlie meditated while waiting for a court hearing about his payments to Denise. Cantabile entered Charlie's apartment and Charlie told him about a movie scenario he and Humboldt had written in 1952. In court, the judge, hearing that Charlie was going to Europe, threatened him with bond and then set a payment sum of $200,000 for Denise. Denise gave him a letter from Kathleen, Humboldt's former wife, which informed him that Humboldt had left him something. Charlie was surprised because they had been estranged and because he had not thought that Humboldt, who died destitute, had anything to leave.

That afternoon, Charlie met his friend Pierre Thaxter, with whom he was hoping to publish a journal. Cantabile found Charlie and Thaxter, forced them into his car, and took them to the office of a businessman who had been caught cheating the Mafia. Pretending that Charlie was a Mafia gunman, Cantabile threatened the man. A police detective arrested Charlie and Cantabile but let Thaxter go. Instead of trying to get Charlie released from jail, Thaxter went to the movies. Charlie was released when the secretary of the threatened man talked her employer into dropping charges against Charlie.

Several days later, instead of going directly to Milan, as planned, Charlie and Renata flew to New York to find out about Charlie's legacy from Humboldt. They went to Coney Island, where Waldemar Wald, Humboldt's uncle, lived in a nursing home. There, Waldemar gave Charlie a large envelope with a letter Humboldt had written Charlie shortly before his death. Although Humboldt had been suffering from manic-depressive disorder and paranoia for years, the letter indicated that he had regained his sanity shortly before his death. The envelope also contained a movie scenario Humboldt had written and a copy of the 1952 scenario. Humboldt had sealed and registered the envelope containing the 1952 scenario and mailed it to himself in 1960, thus establishing copyright to it. Humboldt wrote in his letter that another copy of the 1952 scenario existed but that its location was unknown. Charlie considered the legacy worthless, but he was moved that Humboldt had thought of him just before his death.

In New York, Thaxter told Charlie that his publisher would pay Charlie's expenses in Europe if Charlie would collaborate with Thaxter on what Thaxter called a cultural Baedeker or travel guide. The first city they would treat was Madrid. Thaxter said that he was on his way to Paris to begin writing a book on dictators, and he suggested meeting Charlie there. Kathleen also saw Charlie. After her second husband had died, she worked for a movie company, and she was going to Spain to work on a film. Charlie discovered that Humboldt had left Kathleen the same scenario he had left Charlie. She offered it to a movie company that took an option on it for $3000. Charlie told Kathleen to keep all the money, but she insisted on splitting any proceeds from the scenario with him.

In New York, Charlie learned that his brother Julius, who lived in Texas, was going to have open-heart surgery. Since Charlie refused to marry her, Renata refused to go to Texas with Charlie. So Charlie sent her ahead to Milan and went to Texas, planning to meet her later. After Julius' successful surgery, Charlie called Renata and made plans to meet her in Madrid instead of Milan, because Thaxter told him that his publisher had agreed to cover Charlie's expenses there.

Renata had not arrived by the time Charlie arrived in Madrid. The next morning, Renata's mother, the Señora, came to Charlie's hotel room to tell him that Renata had told her to fly to Madrid with Renata's son, Roger, and to charge the tickets to Charlie. Still having heard nothing from Renata, Charlie sent her a cable proposing marriage. He received no reply. The Señora left Madrid, not telling Charlie where she was going and leaving Roger with Charlie, who was running out of money. Charlie then learned that Thaxter was not in Paris. Calling Thaxter's publisher, he heard that Thaxter was in Argentina and had never spoken to the publisher about the cultural Baedeker or about paying Charlie's expenses in Madrid. Charlie discovered that Renata had left Milan. Later, she sent him a letter telling him she had married someone else.

Charlie and Roger moved into the Pensión La Roca, which was much cheaper than the hotel. After spending January and February in Madrid, Cantabile found Charlie and told him that the 1952 scenario had been made into a successful movie. Initially, Charlie did not believe him, but he finally accompanied Cantabile to Paris, saw the movie, and met with Cantabile, two lawyers, and two representatives of the movie company. In front of these five men, Charlie opened the sealed envelope Humboldt had registered and mailed to himself, produced the scenario, and proved that he owned the rights to the scenario. The lawyers Cantabile had hired started negotiating with the movie producers and they settled on $80,000. Charlie asked the representatives of the producers if they were interested in another scenario from the same source. They said yes and took an option on Humboldt's scenario for $5,000. Charlie insisted that

Cantabile had nothing to do with the new scenario and that he would get only 10 percent of whatever figure was agreed on for the scenario that had been made into a movie, called *Caldofreddo*. Eventually, Charlie told his lawyer to pay Cantabile $8,000 and send him away.

Earlier, Cantabile had told Charlie that Thaxter had been kidnapped in Argentina. Thaxter wrote an open letter from Argentina, appealing to Charlie for help in paying his ransom. Charlie contacted Thaxter's publisher and offered to pay $25,000 ransom if the publisher would put up the money and repay himself from what Thaxter would earn from writing about his experiences in captivity.

Back in Spain, the Señora picked up Roger. Kathleen came to Madrid and told Charlie that the people to whom she had offered an option on Humboldt's scenario had declined. Charlie admitted to having forgotten the earlier option but told Kathleen about his offering an option to the producers of *Caldofreddo*. He also admitted that he was broke. Kathleen suggested that he come to Almería, Spain, where she was working on a film. Before Charlie could leave, a letter from Thaxter's publisher arrived, saying that Thaxter's kidnapping might be a hoax; Thaxter had an article published in *The New York Times*, in which he asked for ransom funds. People from all over the world sent money, so Charlie did not need to pay the ransom.

Later, Charlie returned to New York, where he had moved Waldemar from the nursing home to an apartment on the Upper West Side. Charlie, Waldemar, and Waldemar's friend, Menasha, reburied Humboldt and Humboldt's mother. At the cemetery, Menasha, who had wanted to be an opera singer but had a terrible voice, sang several songs. As Menasha walked away from the graves, he uncovered some sprouts. Charlie thought they were crocuses.

Critical Evaluation:

A plot summary of *Humboldt's Gift* hardly does justice to the novel. In 1976, the year after its publication, Saul Bellow received the Nobel Prize in Literature. Although the prize is given for the complete body of an author's works, many critics insist that *Humboldt's Gift* won Bellow the prize.

Like most of Bellow's novels, *Humboldt's Gift* is highly intellectual and digressive. Critics have noted that, as of *Herzog* (1964), Bellow's novels begin to resemble philosophical essays. Charlie Citrine ponders at length abstract topics like death, reincarnation, friendship, love, and memory. Often he meditates or launches into monologues containing philosophical and theological speculations. These digressions occur so often that at times the readers may have trouble following the narrative thread and distinguishing between the narrative's past and present.

Some critics interpret the novel as having two protagonists, Charlie and Humboldt. Humboldt, incidentally, is modeled in part on the poet Delmore Schwartz, whose first work, *In Dreams Begin Responsibility* (1938), was called the decade's most promising book but whose reputation quickly faded when his later works were not perceived to live up to the early promise. Most critics agree, however, that Charlie, the first-person narrator, is the main protagonist and that as Humboldt's fame fades, Charlie's begins to shine. Charlie's narrative weaves present and past events, and while most of them involve Humboldt, Charlie's point of view predominates.

Charlie can, with some justification, be accused of being foolish. He finds himself attracted to people like Cantabile and his former wife Denise, who bully and use him, and until near the end of the book, he lets them have their way. His association with Renata is self-destructive. While claiming to be interested in philosophical matters, Charlie views Renata primarily as a source of sexual gratification. She in turn treats him mainly as a source of money and, through the marriage she hopes for, prestige. When she believes that he probably will never marry her, she ruthlessly uses his money to meet and marry in Milan an extremely wealthy man with whom she had an affair while she was still involved with Charlie. She even manages to leave her son with Charlie while she is on her honeymoon.

Charlie's friend Thaxter also uses him. Thaxter lies to Charlie and leads a life of luxury even after Charlie, largely because of Thaxter's extravagance, loses most of his money. Charlie finally asserts himself, in effect cutting himself off from Thaxter and refusing to be used by Cantabile, the producers of *Caldofreddo*, and others.

The crocuses sprouting at the novel's end, and the reburial of Humboldt, symbolize Charlie's beginning to grow. The money from Humboldt's gift has freed him from Denise's demands. Once Renata, Cantabile, and Thaxter are no longer part of his life, Charlie may begin to find happiness. More important even than the money he gets as a result of Humboldt's legacy is the lesson he draws from Humboldt's example. By the end of the novel, Charlie, with all his intellectual pretensions, has recognized that love and poetry are more important than sex and money.

Richard Tuerk

Bibliography:

Chavkin, Allan. "Humboldt's Gift and the Romantic Imagination." *Philological Quarterly* 62 (1983): 1-19. Discusses the novel as reflecting Bellow's "essential romantic humanism" and interprets the flower symbolism at the end as "the possibility of spiritual rebirth."

Dutton, Robert R. *Saul Bellow*. Rev. ed. Boston: Twayne, 1982. Includes a detailed discussion of *Humboldt's Gift* and concludes that Charlie needed to break with Cantabile, Denise, and Renata to achieve peace.

Newman, Judie. "Bellow's 'Indian Givers': Humboldt's Gift." *Journal of American Studies* 15 (1981): 231-238. Discusses Bellow's message in the novel that the artist must give "of himself, freely and without condescension."

Pifer, Ellen. *Saul Bellow Against the Grain*. Philadelphia: University of Pennsylvania Press, 1990. In her discussion of *Humboldt's Gift*, the author interprets the crocuses at the end of the novel as symbols of "the 'unseen' processes of rejuvenation ceaselessly at work in the world" and of Citrine's own determination "to find a 'personal connection' to creation."

Wilson, Jonathan. *On Bellow's Planet: Readings from the Dark Side*. Madison, N.J.: Fairleigh Dickinson University Press, 1985. Argues that Charlie Citrine, not Humboldt, is the central figure in the novel and that Citrine is Bellow's "avatar."

THE HUNCHBACK OF NOTRE DAME

Type of work: Novel
Author: Victor Hugo (1802-1885)
Type of plot: Historical
Time of plot: Fifteenth century
Locale: France
First published: Notre-Dame de Paris, 1831 (English translation, 1833)

Principal characters:
> QUASIMODO, the hunchback of Notre Dame
> ESMERALDA, a Gypsy dancer
> CLAUDE FROLLO, the archdeacon of Notre Dame
> PHOEBUS DE CHATEAUPERS, Esmeralda's sweetheart
> GRINGOIRE, a stupid and poverty-stricken poet

The Story:

Louis XI, King of France, was to marry his oldest son to Margaret of Flanders, and in early January, 1482, the king was expecting Flemish ambassadors to his court. The great day arrived, coinciding both with Epiphany and with the secular celebration of the Festival of Fools. All day long, raucous Parisians had assembled at the great Palace of Justice to see a morality play and to choose a Prince of Fools. The throng was supposed to await the arrival of the Flemish guests, but when the emissaries were late, Gringoire, a penniless and oafish poet, ordered the play to begin. In the middle of the prologue, however, the play came to a standstill as the royal procession passed into the huge palace. After the procession passed, the play was forgotten, and the crowd shouted for the Prince of Fools to be chosen.

The Prince of Fools had to be a man of remarkable physical ugliness. One by one the candidates, eager for this one glory of their disreputable lives, showed their faces in front of a glass window, but the crowd shouted and jeered until a face of such extraordinary hideousness appeared that the people acclaimed this candidate at once as the Prince of Fools. It was Quasimodo, the hunchback bell ringer of Notre Dame. Nowhere on earth was there a more grotesque creature. One of his eyes was buried under an enormous wen. His teeth hung over his protruding lower lip like tusks. His eyebrows were red bristles, and his gigantic nose curved over his upper lip like a snout. His long arms protruded from his shoulders, dangling like an ape's. Though he was deaf from long years of ringing Notre Dame's thunderous bells, his eyesight was acute.

Quasimodo sensed that he had been chosen by popular acclaim, and he was at once proud and suspicious of his honor as he allowed the crowd to dress him in ridiculous robes and hoist him above their heads. From this vantage point, he maintained a dignified silence while the parade went through the streets of Paris, stopping only to watch the enchanting dance of a Gypsy girl, Esmeralda, whose grace and charm held her audience spellbound. She had a little trained goat with her that danced to her tambourine. The pair were celebrated throughout Paris, though there were some who thought the girl a witch, so great was her power in captivating her audience.

Late that night the poet Gringoire walked the streets of Paris. He had no shelter, owed money, and was in desperate straits. As the cold night came on, he saw Esmeralda hurrying ahead of him. Then a black-hooded man came out of the shadows and seized the Gypsy. At the same time, Gringoire caught sight of the hooded man's partner, Quasimodo, who struck Gringoire a terrible blow. The following moment a horseman came riding from the next street. Catching sight of Esmeralda in the arms of the black-hooded man, the rider demanded that he free the girl or pay with his life. The attackers fled. Esmeralda asked the name of her rescuer. It was Captain Phoebus de Chateaupers. From that moment Esmeralda was hopelessly in love with Phoebus.

Gringoire did not bother to discover the plot behind the frustrated kidnapping, but had he known the truth he might have been more frightened than he was. Quasimodo's hooded companion had been Claude Frollo, archdeacon of Notre Dame, a man who had once been a pillar of righteousness, but who now, because of loneliness and an insatiable thirst for knowledge and experience, had succumbed to the temptations of necromancy and alchemy.

Frollo had befriended Quasimodo when the hunchback had been left at the gates of Notre Dame as an unwanted baby; Quasimodo was slavishly loyal to him. He acted without question when Frollo asked his aid in kidnapping the beautiful Gypsy. Frollo, having admired Esmeralda from a distance, planned to carry her off to his small cell in the cathedral, where he could enjoy her charms at his leisure.

As Quasimodo and Frollo hurried back to the cathedral, Gringoire continued on his way and found himself in a disreputable quarter of Paris. Captured by thugs, he was threatened with death if none of the women in the thieves' den would marry him. When no one wanted the pale, thin poet, a noose was lowered about his neck. Suddenly Esmeralda appeared and volunteered to take him, but Gringoire enjoyed no wedding night. Esmeralda's heart belonged to Phoebus; she had rescued the poet only out of pity.

In those days the courts of Paris often picked innocent people from the streets, tried them, and convicted them with little regard for justice. Quasimodo had been seen in his role as the Prince of Fools and had been watched as he stood before the Gypsy girl while she danced. There was a rumor that Esmeralda was a witch, and most of Paris suspected that Frollo, Quasimodo's only associate, was a sorcerer. Consequently, Quasimodo was brought into a court, accused of keeping questionable company, and sentenced to a severe flogging and exposure on the pillory. Quasimodo endured his disgrace stoically, but after his misshapen back had been torn by the lash, he was overcome with a terrible thirst. The crowd jeered and threw stones. They hated and feared Quasimodo because of his ugliness.

Presently Esmeralda mounted the scaffold and put her flask to Quasimodo's blackened lips. This act of kindness moved him deeply and he wept. At that same time Frollo had happened upon the scene, caught sight of Quasimodo, and departed quickly. Later Quasimodo was to remember this betrayal. One day Phoebus was entertaining a lady in a building overlooking the square where Esmeralda was dancing. The Gypsy was so smitten with Phoebus that she had taught her goat to spell out his name with alphabet blocks. When she had the animal perform this trick, the lady called her a witch and a sorceress. Phoebus, however, followed the Gypsy and arranged for a rendezvous with her for the following night.

Meanwhile, Gringoire happened to meet Frollo, who was jealous of the poet because he was rumored to be Esmeralda's husband. Gringoire, however, explained that Esmeralda did not love him; she had eyes and heart only for Phoebus. Desperate to preserve Esmeralda for himself, Frollo trailed the young gallant and asked him where he was going. Phoebus said that he had a rendezvous with Esmeralda. The priest offered him money in exchange for an opportunity to conceal himself in the room where this rendezvous was to take place, ostensibly to discover whether Esmeralda was really the girl whose name Phoebus had mentioned. It was a poor ruse at best, but Phoebus was not shy at lovemaking and agreed to the bargain. When he learned that the girl was really Esmeralda, Frollo leaped from concealment and wounded Phoebus with a dagger. Esmeralda could not see her lover's assailant in the darkness, and when she fainted, Frollo escaped. A crowd gathered, murmuring that the sorceress had slain Phoebus. They took the Gypsy off to prison.

Now tales of Esmeralda's sorcery began to circulate. At her trial, she was convicted of witchcraft, sentenced to do penance on the great porch of Notre Dame and from there to be taken to a scaffold in the Place de la Greve and publicly hanged. Phoebus was not dead; he had escaped the night of the attack and had kept silent rather than implicate himself in a case of witchcraft. When Esmeralda was on her way to Notre Dame, she caught sight of him riding on his beautiful horse and called out to him, but he ignored her completely. She then felt that she was doomed.

When she came before Frollo to do penance, he offered to save her if she would be his, but she refused. Quasimodo suddenly appeared on the porch, took the girl in his arms, and carried her to sanctuary within the church. Esmeralda was safe as long as she remained within the cathedral walls.

Quasimodo hid her in his own cell, where there was a mattress and water, and brought her food. He kept the cell door locked so that if her pursuers did break the sanctuary, they could not reach her. Aware that she would be terrified of him if he stayed with her, he entered her cell only to bring her his own dinner.

Frollo, knowing that the Gypsy was near him in the cathedral, secured a key to the chamber and stole in to see Esmeralda one night. She struggled hopelessly, until suddenly Quasimodo entered and dragged the priest from the cell. With smothered rage, he freed the trembling archdeacon and allowed him to run away. One day a mob gathered and demanded that the sorceress be turned from the cathedral. Frollo was jubilant. Quasimodo, however, barred and bolted the great doors. When the crowd charged the cathedral with a battering ram, Quasimodo threw stones from a tower where builders had been working. When the mob persisted, he poured melted lead upon the crowd below. Then the mob secured ladders and began to mount the facade, but Quasimodo seized the ladders and pushed them from the wall. Hundreds of dead and wounded lay below him.

The king's guards joined the fray. Looking down, Quasimodo thought that the soldiers had arrived to protect Esmeralda. He went to her cell, but to his amazement, he found the door open and Esmeralda gone.

Frollo had given Gringoire the key to her chamber and had led the poet through the cathedral to her cell. Frollo convinced her that she must fly, since the church was under siege. She followed him trustingly, and he led her to a boat where Frollo was already waiting. Frightened by the violence of the priest, Gringoire fled. Once more, Frollo offered to save Esmeralda if she would be his, but she refused him. Fleeing, she sought refuge in a cell belonging to a madwoman. There the soldiers found her and dragged her away for her execution the next morning at dawn.

Meanwhile, Quasimodo roamed the cathedral searching for Esmeralda. Making his way to the tower which looked down upon the bridge of Notre Dame, Quasimodo came upon Frollo, who stood shaking with laughter as he watched a scene far below. Following the direction of the priest's gaze, Quasimodo saw a gibbet erected in the Place de la Greve and on the platform a woman in white. It was Esmeralda. Quasimodo saw the noose lowered over the girl's head and the platform released. The body swayed in the morning breeze. Then Quasimodo picked up Frollo and thrust him over the wall on which he had been leaning. At that moment, Quasimodo understood everything that the priest had done to ensure the death of Esmeralda.

He looked at the crushed body at the foot of the tower and then at the figure in white upon the gallows. He wept.

After the deaths of Esmeralda and Claude Frollo, Quasimodo was not to be found. Then in the reign of Charles VIII, the vault of Montfaucon, in which the bodies of criminals were interred, was opened to locate the remains of a famous prisoner who had been buried there. Among the skeletons were those of a woman who had been clad in white and of a man whose bony arms were wrapped tightly around the woman's body. His spine was crooked, one leg was shorter than the other, and it was evident that he had not been hanged, for his neck was unbroken. When those who discovered these singular remains tried to separate the two bodies, they crumbled into dust.

Critical Evaluation:

Victor Hugo, leader of the French Romantic movement, not only could tell a gripping story but also could endow his essentially Romantic characters with a realism so powerful that they have become monumental literary figures. *The Hunchback of Notre Dame* has every quality of a good novel: an exciting story, a magnificent setting, and deep, lasting characterizations. Perhaps the compelling truth of this novel lies in the idea that God has created in the human form an imperfect image of God, an image fettered by society, by the body, and by temptation, but one which, in the last analysis, has the freedom to transcend these limitations and achieve spiritual greatness.

Hugo was inspired to write *The Hunchback of Notre Dame* when he accidentally discovered the Greek word for "fate" carved into an obscure wall of one of the Notre Dame Cathedral's towers. Each personality in the novel is built around a "fixed idea": Claude Frollo embodies the consuming, destructive passion of lust; Esmeralda, virgin beauty and purity; Quasimodo, devotion and loyalty. Hugo's characters do not develop but simply play out their given natures to their conclusions. In analyzing the character of archdeacon Claude Frollo, it is helpful to understand Hugo's theory that the advent of Christianity in Western Europe marked a new era in literature and art. Christianity views the individual as a creature half animal and half spirit—the link between beast and angel. Working with this interpretation, writers could present people as ugly and lowly as well as beautiful and sublime. Christian writers could, in Hugo's view, attain a new synthesis in the understanding of human character, more meaningful because realistic, not achieved by writers of antiquity, who only depicted idealized, larger-than-life subjects on the grounds that "art should correct nature." Claude Frollo excludes all human contact from his life and locks himself up with his books; when he has mastered all the legitimate branches of knowledge, he has nowhere to turn in his obsession but to the realm of alchemy and the occult. He is ultimately destroyed, along with those around him, because in denying his animal nature and shutting off all avenues for the release of his natural drives and affections, he falls into the depths of a lustful passion that amounts to madness.

As the novel develops, Quasimodo, the hunchback of the novel's title, is increasingly trapped between his love for the Gypsy Esmeralda and his love for the archdeacon, his master and protector. These two loyalties finally create an irreconcilable conflict; a choice must be made. When the priest destroys the Gypsy, the bell ringer hurls his master from the heights of Notre Dame: a fitting death for Frollo, symbolic of his descent from the sublime to the bestial. In Quasimodo, Hugo dramatizes his belief that the grotesque and the sublime must coexist in art and literature, as they do in life. The writer, Hugo pointed out, "will realize that everything in creation is not humanly beautiful, that the ugly exists beside the beautiful, the unshapely beside the graceful . . . and [he] will ask . . . if a mutilated nature will be the more beautiful for the mutilation." Esmeralda is the embodiment of innocence and beauty. She is held in reverence even by the criminal population of Paris, who vaguely equate her in their minds with the Virgin Mary. Her beauty, however, is too innocent and pure to exist amid the brutality and sinfulness of her world. Of all the men in the book, only one is worthy of Esmeralda: the hunchbacked Quasimodo, who loves her so totally and unselfishly that he would rather die than go on living after she is executed. Appropriately, it is Esmeralda and Quasimodo who are finally "married" in the charnel house at Montfaucon; theirs is the perfect union of physical and spiritual beauty.

Almost more than by any of the human characters, the novel is dominated by the presence of the cathedral itself. The hero, Quasimodo, understands Notre Dame: He is in tune with its "life." Like its deformed bell ringer, Notre Dame is ugly and beautiful, strong and vulnerable, destructive and life-giving. Quasimodo's monstrous face hides a loving, faithful spirit, and his twisted body conceals a superhuman strength; Notre Dame's beautiful sanctuary is enclosed by an exterior encrusted with gargoyles. Her treasures are guarded by doors that six thousand maddened vagrants cannot batter down. The cathedral and the ringer work together, almost as one entity, to protect Esmeralda in her room hundreds of feet above the city.

Setting was all-important to Hugo. As the foremost French Romanticist of the nineteenth century, he was fascinated by the medieval period and strove to reconstruct it in such a way that it would live again in his novel. Hugo believed that a description built on exact, localized details would recapture the mood of a historical period; he also believed that setting was as crucial as characterization in engraving a "faithful representation of the facts" on the minds of his readers. Early in the novel, therefore, Hugo devotes an entire section to a description of the cathedral and the city of Paris, and throughout the book, he offers brief passages of historical background that add verisimilitude to his narrative.

In the preface to his play *Cromwell* (1827), Hugo wrote, "The place where this or that catastrophe took place becomes a terrible and inseparable witness thereof; and the absence of silent characters of this sort would make the greatest scenes in history incomplete in the drama." Thus, in *The Hunchback of Notre Dame*, not only does the cathedral live almost as a personality, but so also does the Place de la Greve spread its influence over the lives of all the characters. The cathedral and the square are the two focal points not only of the setting but also of the plot and the theme of the novel; the former embodies the spiritual and beautiful, the latter the lowly and cruel. It is the cathedral that enfolds the humble and loyal Quasimodo and the compassionate Esmeralda, while the square, the scene of poverty, suffering, and grisly death, with its Rat-Hole and its gibbet, claims Esmeralda, her lunatic mother, and Claude Frollo as its victims.

"Critical Evaluation" by Nancy G. Ballard

Bibliography:
Brombert, Victor. *Victor Hugo and the Visionary Novel.* Cambridge, Mass.: Harvard University Press, 1984. An insightful analysis of the visionary qualities in Victor Hugo's major novels. Examines Hugo's artistry in describing events from several different perspectives in *The Hunchback of Notre Dame.*
Grant, Richard B. *The Perilous Quest: Image, Myth, and Prophecy in the Narratives of Victor Hugo.* Durham, N.C.: Duke University Press, 1968. Examines Hugo's creative use of myths and religious images in his novels. Discusses the importance of medieval legends to *The Hunchback of Notre Dame.*
Grossman, Kathryn M. *The Early Novels of Victor Hugo: Towards a Poetics of Harmony.* Geneva: Droz, 1986. Contains a thoughtful study of Hugo's first four novels. The chapter on

The Hunchback of Notre Dame explores images of women and family relationships in the novel.

Houston, John Porter. *Victor Hugo*. Boston: Twayne, 1988. Contains an excellent general introduction to Hugo's works and an annotated bibliography of important critical studies on Hugo. Discusses images of Paris and the importance of medievalism in *The Hunchback of Notre Dame*.

Maurois, André. *Olympio: The Life of Victor Hugo*. Translated by Gerard Hopkins. New York: Harper, 1956. A well-documented biography of Hugo. Describes well the role of fate and images of Christianity in *The Hunchback of Notre Dame*.

HUNGER

Type of work: Novel
Author: Knut Hamsun (Knut Pedersen, 1859-1952)
Type of plot: Impressionistic realism
Time of plot: Late nineteenth century
Locale: Norway
First published: Sult, 1890 (English translation, 1899)

> *Principal character:*
> THE NARRATOR, a young writer

The Story:

The narrator lived in Kristiania, the capital city of Norway, where he suffered greatly from hunger. When he woke in the morning, he looked around his spartan, drafty room for something to eat but as usual found nothing. He knew that his condition was becoming desperate. He had looked in vain for work, and he had had to take most of his belongings to the pawnshop. His only other source of income was the occasional sale of a story or article to one of the local newspapers.

After getting out of bed, the narrator started walking the streets of the city. He felt bad because old friends seemed to shun him, thinking that he was going to ask them for money. He was embarrassed because he was unable to give even the smallest coin to a beggar. His sense of shame led him to take his vest to a pawnshop that he had not visited before, after which he gave most of the money from the vest to the beggar.

While thinking about his writing projects, the narrator behaved erratically. He told gratuitous lies to strangers and accosted two unfamiliar women, one of whom took note of him. After a fruitless day, he returned home to find a letter from his landlady, in which she demanded the next month's rent. When the narrator awoke the next morning, he could feel the influence of artistic inspiration. While still in the grip of this emotion, he managed to write down a lengthy and, to his mind, promising sketch. Since he had no money left, he decided to move out of his room. Carrying his few belongings, he went to a newspaper editor to sell his story. The editor was unable to find time to read the piece, however, so the narrator spent the night in the nearby woods.

The next day he was even hungrier. He tried to borrow money for food from friends, and he applied for work, but without success. He planned to spend the night on a bench. When he was interrupted by a policeman, he walked back to his old lodgings, where he found a letter waiting for him from the newspaper editor, who praised his manuscript and informed him that he would pay ten crowns for it. This gave the narrator money for food and other necessities for a while.

Two weeks later the money was used up, and the narrator was starving again. He was hallucinating about finding money in the streets, about his current writing project, which seemed extremely promising to him, and about the young woman with whom he had spoken two weeks earlier. The lack of food had made him ill. He looked emaciated and was shivering with fever. In this condition he was found by a police officer and taken to the station, where he was put in jail for the night.

By the time he was released the following morning, the narrator had had nothing to eat for three days. He started walking the streets again and became more and more disoriented. Having tried to borrow money for food from several acquaintances, he tried unsuccessfully to sell another article. He finally found an old friend who took pity on him by pawning his watch so that the narrator could have something on which to live.

A week passed, and the narrator no longer had any money. His health was very poor, as he had lost much of his hair, was troubled by headaches, and had become very nervous. A week with nourishing food had, however, given him the strength to start several essays, on which he worked feverishly. When he tried to sell one of them, however, he was told that it was too complex to appeal to a newspaper's audience.

The following day, the narrator went to a store in order to buy a candle on credit. Through a mistake of the clerk, he was given almost five crowns. He immediately went to a café where he ordered a large steak, which he consumed greedily. In his starved condition, however, he was unable to keep the food down and vomited repeatedly on his way back to his lodgings.

Close to his quarters he came across a woman who appeared to be waiting for him next to a street lamp. After a little while, he noticed that she was one of the two women he had accosted earlier, the woman to whom he had privately given the name Ylajali. They spent a pleasant time together as he escorted her home. As she left him, she hurriedly pulled her veil aside and kissed him.

The following day, as he was walking the streets of the city, the narrator met an old friend and was invited to share some beer with him. Because of his prolonged starvation, he became intoxicated after drinking only a small amount and began to do odd things. He ordered a wagon and went to the homes of strangers, asking for fictitious people. He went back to the store where he had earlier been given the money and yelled at the clerk. Toward evening, he met the editor to whom he had earlier sold his work, who give him an advance of ten crowns. The next day, he again met Ylajali and spent some time with her at her home. What he had hoped would be a romantic encounter turned out to be a disappointment, however, and he soon left.

As winter came, the narrator was living in extremely demeaning circumstances in the poorest part of town. He was trying to write, but without success, as his health had taken a turn for the worse. When he lost his place to live, he saw no alternative than to find work on board a ship bound for England.

"The Story" by Jan Sjåvik

Critical Evaluation:

Knut Hamsun's *Hunger* is part of the late nineteenth century literary tradition of impressionistic realism and was conceived in the same philosophical and aesthetic environment that led to the works of Sigmund Freud. Hamsun delves into the subconscious of his protagonist and creates a depiction of madness seen from inside the mind of the madman. The fact that this madness derives from hunger is significant, because this story of a young journalist literally starving to death is autobiographical to some extent. When Hamsun first presented the manuscript of his work for publication, the editor was so struck by his emaciation that he paid Hamsun an advance on the work before he had even read the title.

On one level, this is a madman's story of a madman, but on another, it is an account of life in a large city of the industrial age. The city where the action takes place, Kristiania, is like any city in which individuals try to sell their art, literature, or journalism and discover that there is no market for the best they can produce. Kristiania is presented as a city full of people seeking fame and fortune but forced instead to discover that they will not be able to reach their goals. Such people often become discouraged and are obliged to seek employment in a field far removed from their original ambition. The protagonist of *Hunger* finds himself in precisely this situation.

What lifts this novel from being merely a story about a poor boy doing poorly in the big city is Hamsun's description of the internal workings of this particular mind. He demonstrates the foolish pride and motiveless behavior that come from a tenuous existence such as that led by the protagonist. The starving man lies, as the saying goes, even when it is not necessary. He has no regular habits and is at the mercy of his own strange whims. The incident when he persists in telling a strange woman on the street that she has lost her nonexistent book is a case in point. Time and again, even when facing starvation, he lies to save his pride. Hamsun explains that at the stage when the body is starving, the mind falters and mistakes inconsequential things for life's necessities. Hamsun terrifyingly depicts the odd sort of seemingly lucid logic that is to an impartial observer nothing but nonsense.

While Hamsun is able to depict the workings of such a mind broken by the stress of hunger, he does not present a full picture of the book's protagonist. Yet because of this omission, his study of psychological pressure is all the more vivid and effective. The reader does not know much about the young man in the novel, only that he is starving and periodically reduced to chewing on wood shavings or bits of cloth. Hamsun focuses the reader's full attention on the issue of the mind, and he does so in a masterful fashion.

On yet another level, *Hunger* is a portrait of failure. The book is a collection of episodes divided into four sections and united only by underlying themes. Each section describes the thoughts and actions of the protagonist at different times. There is, strictly speaking, no beginning or end to the novel. At the end of each section there is a stroke of good luck. The protagonist sells a story or gets a loan. Then the novel immediately jumps to the next episode in his life when he is starving, and the cycle begins anew.

At the end of the book, the young writer joins the crew of a steamship bound for England. The effect of this conclusion is not, however, that of escape but that of pessimism. There is a flaw in this man's character, one that Hamsun only hints at, that damns him to a continuing cycle of luck and hunger. It is a cycle that the reader at the end of the novel feels can lead eventually only to death.

"Critical Evaluation" by Glenn M. Edwards

Bibliography:
Ferguson, Robert. *Enigma: The Life of Knut Hamsun.* New York: Farrar, Straus & Giroux, 1987. An excellent biography of Hamsun. Presents a balanced and detailed overview of Hamsun's life and places *Hunger* in the context of the author's life and works.
Kittang, Atle. "Knut Hamsun's *Sult:* Psychological Deep Structures and Metapoetic Plot." In *Facets of European Modernism: Essays in Honour of James McFarlane,* edited by Janet Garton. Norwich, England: University of East Anglia, 1985. In a complex and resourceful reading of *Hunger,* Kittang stresses the development of consciousness and its relationship to language.
McFarlane, J. W. "The Whisper of the Blood: A Study of Knut Hamsun's Early Novels." *PMLA* 71, no. 4 (September, 1956): 563-594. In this immensely influential discussion of Hamsun's early novels, McFarlane devotes considerable attention to *Hunger.* Shows that Hamsun's interest in the unconscious life of the mind was actually a tool for reaching a higher degree of verisimilitude.
Næss, Harald. *Knut Hamsun.* Boston: Twayne, 1984. A general survey of Hamsun's works.

Includes a section devoted to *Hunger*, as well as additional references throughout the text. Næss discusses the narrator-protagonist's experiments with his own mind as a focus of narration.

_____. "Who Was Hamsun's Hero?" In *The Hero in Scandinavian Literature: From Peer Gynt to the Present*. Austin: University of Texas Press, 1975. Discusses the protagonist in *Hunger* in the context of the heroes of other Hamsun novels. Næss stresses the sadomasochistic aspects of the *Hunger* narrator's behavior.

HUON OF BORDEAUX

Type of work: Poetry
Author: Unknown
Type of plot: Epic
Time of plot: Ninth century
Locale: Paris, Jerusalem, Rome, and the fairy kingdom of Mommur
First published: First half of the thirteenth century (English translation, c. 1534)

Principal characters:
>HUON OF BORDEAUX, the older son of the dead duke of Guienne
>GERARD, his younger brother
>CHARLEMAGNE, the king of France
>CHARLOT, his older son
>EARL AMAURY, Charlot's evil adviser
>DUKE NAYMES, Charlemagne's adviser
>THE ABBOT OF CLUNY, the uncle to Huon and Gerard
>GERAMES, a loyal hermit
>OBERON, the king of fairyland
>GAWDIS, the amir of Babylon
>CLARAMOND, his daughter

The Story:

King Charlemagne, grown old and wishing to relinquish the burden of government, summoned his court and consulted with his nobles to determine the succession to his throne. His plan was to abdicate in favor of his two sons, but the nobles of France were not willing to accept his favorite, Charlot, partly because of the young prince's association with Earl Amaury, kinsman of the infamous Ganelon, who had betrayed Roland to his death. The earl, Charlot's partisan, took the occasion to revenge himself on the noble house of Guienne. His suggestion was that Charlot be given a province to govern before he took over the responsibilities of a state. When it came to Charlemagne's attention that the two sons of the dead duke had not yet come to Paris to pay their respects and render homage, Earl Amaury hoped that the king—who had become violent and unreasonable in his judgments and punishments—would dispossess them and give their lands to Charlot.

Sent to conduct the heirs of the dead duke to Charlemagne's court, messengers discovered that what the king's wise adviser, Duke Naymes, had stated was indeed the case: The brothers, Huon and Gerard, had been too young to come to court before. The messengers, pleased with their reception by the duchess, the boys' mother, and with the manly bearing of young Huon of Bordeaux, the older son, returned with word that the young noblemen would soon follow them to swear fealty to the king. Huon and Gerard set out on their journey to Paris, stopping on the way at the monastery of Cluny, where their uncle was abbot. The noble churchman decided to accompany his nephews to Charlemagne's court.

Earl Amaury had, in the meantime, persuaded Charlot to ambush the boys and kill them, a plan to which the prince agreed because the boys' lands were extensive. In the fray, Charlot was killed when Huon struck him with his sword and severed his helmet. In spite of the abbot's testimony, however, Charlemagne refused to believe that Huon had acted in self-defense and without knowledge of his assailant's identity. In a trial by combat with Earl Amaury, Huon killed that knight, who died before he could give a true account of his villainy. Still unenlightened, the angry king sent Huon on a pilgrimage to Jerusalem and ordered him to kiss three times the beautiful Claramond, the daughter of Gawdis, amir of Babylon, and to return with white hairs from the amir's beard and teeth from his mouth.

Obedient to Charlemagne's command, Huon parted company with his brother Gerard, in whose care he left his lands. Although there had been love between the brothers in the past, Gerard eventually became false to his trust and plotted great evil against his brother, for Huon's return was greatly delayed. Though fortune often favored him and provided him with kinsmen in odd corners of the world, the wicked paynims abused him, imprisoned him, and on many occasions carried him far from his destination. Gerames, a hermit, became his loyal follower after chance threw them together, and he was close at Huon's heels when the Christian knight kissed Claramond and got the teeth and the hair from the severed head of the amir after that ruler had received the bowstring from the dread caliph of Arabia. Huon gave the teeth and hair to the hermit for safekeeping.

Huon was aided in his adventures by two gifts from Oberon, the dwarf king of the Otherworld, born of an ancient union between Julius Caesar and Morgan le Fay. Gerames, the wise hermit, had warned Huon not to speak to Oberon, but Huon, ignoring his advice, spoke to the dwarf and so won the protection of the white magic of that strange little creature. Huon was able to carry with him the gifts from Oberon. One was a cup that filled up at the sign of the cross and emptied when it was held in the hand of a wicked person. The other was a horn that Huon was to blow to summon Oberon's help when grave danger threatened. Like the boy who cried wolf in Aesop's fable, Huon blew the horn too frequently, and Oberon was sometimes tempted not to respond. Moreover, Huon's dignity and prudence sometimes left him. Despite warnings, he embraced the lovely Claramond before they were married and so brought about an interminable separation; and he once imprudently allowed a giant to arm himself before a contest. At last, however, with the combined help of the hermit and the fairy king, Huon and Claramond reached Rome, where their marriage was blessed by the Pope himself, who was Huon's uncle.

On his return to France with his bride, Huon found that his brother was now his foe and that well-wishers like Duke Naymes could not protect him from the anger and dotage of Charlemagne. Oberon, however, could. The fairy king made his appearance, humbled Charlemagne, and saw to it that Huon and Claramond were secure in all of their rights. Though Huon interceded for his brother's life and made the court weep by his display of generosity, Oberon was obdurate, and Gerard and his fellow conspirators were hanged. As a final favor, Huon was promised that he would someday inherit Oberon's kingdom.

Critical Evaluation:

Huon of Bordeaux is a French epic poem or *chanson de geste*, written in the first quarter of the thirteenth century. As the term *chanson de geste* indicates, this type of composition was intended to be chanted, most likely to a simple melody played on a zither or lutelike instrument, called the *vielle*. The poem is composed in assonanced decasyllabic verse arranged in stanzas of irregular length. Each stanza is separated from the next by a short pause that lends itself to a brief musical interlude, which in turn would have provided the storyteller with an opportunity to recall and organize the next stanza. The term *chanson de geste* further points out that the song's subject matter relates to *geste*, that is, to exploits and deeds.

Huon of Bordeaux is an original and successful composition of approximately 10,553 verses. Despite its considerable size, the unknown author succeeds in steadily advancing the complex plot while maintaining a cohesiveness that is crucial to an audience's understanding of a text this long. Although the author respects the conventions of the epic genre in plot and setting, he also introduces elements borrowed from other literary traditions, in particular the Arthurian romance. *Huon of Bordeaux* is undeniably a *chanson de geste*, but it also has definite characteristics of the verse romance. This form of experimentation within a literary genre has been the focus of a number of interesting critical studies that have led to a better understanding of the process of generic transformation and renewal and to a renewed appreciation of these types of texts.

The poet's use of the fantastic or *merveilleux* is especially striking in *Huon of Bordeaux*, for it transforms a potentially wearisome account of heroic deeds and travel afar into a spellbinding adventure filled with marvel and wonder. It is interesting to note that it is from this work that William Shakespeare later drew inspiration for the green dwarf Oberon in his *Midsummer Night's Dream* (1595-1596). Subsequently, in the eighteenth century, the German author Christoph Wieland, a translator of several of Shakespeare's works, reintroduces the character of Huon of Bordeaux in his verse romance *Oberon* (1780). Wieland's work in turn led to the Romantic opera of the same title by Carl Maria von Weber (1826). The infectious nature of the material of *Huon of Bordeaux* ensured the poem lasting popularity. A cycle was developed around it in the second half of the thirteenth century. In the fifteenth century, the poem was rewritten in both Alexandrine verse and prose. It was translated into English in 1530 by the English diplomat John Bourchier, Lord Berners, who had previously undertaken the translation of Jean Froissart's *Chronique de France, d'Angleterre, d'Écosse et d'Espagne* (1360-1400). It must have been Lord Berners' translation of *Huon of Bordeaux* that Shakespeare knew. The original poem itself was regularly reprinted, at times even in popular series, right up to the nineteenth century.

"Critical Evaluation" by Geert S. Pallemans

Bibliography:
Rossi, Marguerite. *"Huon de Bordeaux" et l'évolution du genre épique au XIIIe siècle.* Paris: Champion, 1975. The only detailed book-length literary study of the poem. Excellent for the serious student interested in the evolution of the epic genre. Contains a thorough study of the epic technique and the way it has been used in *Huon of Bordeaux*. Analyzes sources, themes, and characters. Also includes an exhaustive bibliography and index.
Ruelle, Pierre, ed. *Huon de Bordeaux.* Bruxelles: Presses Universitaires de Bruxelles, 1960. A critical edition of the original poem that discusses the extant manuscripts and a previous edition. Contains a detailed linguistic study of the text, as well as a complete summary of the poem. Traces the literary sources of the text and establishes a date. Includes notes, glossary, index of proper names, and five facsimile pages.
Steele, Robert. *Huon of Bordeaux, Done into English by Sir John Bourchier, Lord Berners: And Now Retold by Robert Steele.* London: Allen, 1895. A modernized version of the sixteenth century translation by John Bourchier. The language of Steele's version, though updated, manages to retain much of the charm of Bourchier's original translation.
Suard, François. "Le Cycle en vers de Huon de Bordeaux." In *La Chanson de geste et le mythe carolingien: Mélanges René Louis.* Vol. 2. Saint-Père-Sous-Vézelay: Musée Archéologique Régionale, 1982. A study of the continuations and reworkings of the original *Huon de Bordeaux*. Analyzes key episodes in order to place the respective continuations in relationship to the others.

HYDE PARK

Type of work: Drama
Author: James Shirley (1596-1666)
Type of plot: Comedy of manners
Time of plot: Early seventeenth century
Locale: London
First performed: 1632; first published, 1637

Principal characters:
LORD BONVILE, a sporting peer
TRIER, his friend, betrothed to Julietta
FAIRFIELD, favored suitor to Mistress Carol
RIDER and
VENTURE, her rejected suitors
BONAVENT, a merchant returned after seven years' absence
MISTRESS BONAVENT, his wife, who thinks herself a widow
LACY, Mistress Bonavent's suitor
JULIETTA, Fairfield's sister, pursued by Lord Bonvile
MISTRESS CAROL, Mistress Bonavent's cousin and companion

The Story:

Mistress Bonavent's husband, a merchant, had been missing for seven years, and she had for some time considered a second marriage to Lacy, her persistent suitor. Mistress Carol, her cousin and companion, urged her not to give away so lightly the independence she had won. Mistress Carol herself swore never to marry, even though she carried on flirtations with Rider, Venture, and Fairfield. Rider and Venture, vying with each other for the lady's favor, had each given her a gift which she in turn presented to his rival. Comparing notes, they concluded that Fairfield must be the favored suitor.

Lacy, summoned by Mistress Bonavent's servant, felt certain that his suit was successful. Into this confused arena of love arrived Lord Bonvile, a sportsman who admired both horses and women, and Bonavent, disguised in order to find out what had happened during his absence.

Fairfield's overtures to Mistress Carol were rejected, but Lacy's to Mistress Bonavent were accepted, and the wedding was set for that very morning. Mistress Carol told her cousin that she was acting rashly, no man being worth the candle. Bonavent soon learned that the sound of merriment in his own house augured no good for that returned merchant who, held captive by a Turkish pirate, had only recently been ransomed. Lacy, perhaps too merry with wine and anticipation, bade the stranger welcome and asked, then demanded, that he dance with and, finally, for them. Bonavent's dancing was ridiculed, especially by sharp-tongued Mistress Carol. Lacy tried to make amends by inviting him to join additional revels in Hyde Park that very day.

In the meantime Fairfield, despairing because of his love for Mistress Carol, said farewell to his sister Julietta and wished her well in her coming marriage to Jack Trier. It soon became apparent to the young woman that her suitor was not in earnest in his avowals of love, for he introduced her to his friend Lord Bonvile and then left them. Before his departure Trier had whispered in the lord's ear that he was in a sporting house and the lady was a person of easy virtue. As a woman of good breeding, and aware only that her fiancé had shown poor manners, Julietta invited Lord Bonvile to accompany her to the park, an invitation which provided her betrothed with an opportunity to try her chastity.

When the two aggrieved lovers, Rider and Venture, appealed to Mistress Carol not to make sport of them by passing their gifts on to their rival, she declared that she had no interest in them and had always told them so; in their persistence, however, they had paid little attention to her. Fairfield, coming to say good-bye, first asked her to swear to one agreement without knowing what it was. Convinced at last that the agreement would not commit her to love, marry, or go to bed with him, she agreed; at his request she then swore never to desire his company again or to love him. The oath sealed with a kiss, he departed, leaving her in a state of consternation.

Julietta, courted by a baffled lord whose very propositions were turned into pleasantries, remained aloof from her still more baffled suitor, who could not determine how far the flirtation had gone in Hyde Park. Still in disguise, Bonavent learned that Lacy and his wife were indeed married but that the marriage had not yet been consummated—to the pleasure of his informant, Mistress Carol, who by now was distressed by affection for the previously spurned Fairfield. She sent a message by Trier asking Fairfield to come to see her, but on his arrival she denied that she had sent for him. Fairfield, in turn, offered to release her from her oath if she would have him, but she turned coquette and rejected his proposal. Consequently, he refused to believe her when she protested that she now loved him.

Lord Bonvile, torn between his desire to play what he thought was a sure thing and to play the horses, which were a gamble, pushed his suit too far, and for his brashness received a lecture on titles and good breeding, a remonstrance that he took to heart.

The disconsolate Mistress Carol met Julietta, who informed the spurned one that Fairfield was as disconsolate as she. Mistress Carol then concocted a stratagem at the expense of Venture, a poet, horseman, and singer. She goaded him into writing a poem on the lengths to which he would go for her love, and to this effusion she later affixed the name of Fairfield. Meanwhile, in Hyde Park, Bonavent hired a bagpipe and made the bridegroom dance to the tune of a sword at his legs, a return for the courtesy extended at the wedding festivities. In a note to his wife, the merchant informed her of his return but urged her to secrecy for the time being.

Mistress Carol, who now pretended to believe that Venture's hyperbole was a suicide note from Fairfield, summoned her recalcitrant suitor. Thinking that she was still making fun of him, he denied any intention of doing away with himself and in turn accused her of duplicity. He added that he would make himself a gelding so that women would no longer concern him— a threat more real to Mistress Carol than that of suicide. On the spot she abandoned all pride and proposed marriage to him. He immediately accepted.

Lord Bonvile, having learned too late from Trier that he was the victim of a jealous lover, was accepted by Julietta as a worthy suitor, now that his thoughts were as lofty as his position in society. Bonavent, to show himself unresentful, proposed a merry celebration and placed willow garlands on the heads of the disappointed lovers: Trier, Lacy, Rider, and Venture. He received the good wishes of Lacy and pledged himself to entertain the whole party at supper with tales of his captivity.

All this, however, had been prophesied earlier in Hyde Park, when Lord Bonvile and his Julietta, Fairfield and Mistress Carol, and Mr. and Mistress Bonavent had heard the song of Philomel, the nightingale. The others had heard only the cuckoo.

Critical Evaluation:

The career of James Shirley, a prolific playwright, began in 1625, when King Charles I ascended the throne, and ended in 1642, when the outbreak of civil war led to the closing of the theaters. The dominant dramatist of his era, Shirley wrote most of his approximately thirty plays for Christopher Beeton's company, Queen Henrietta's Men, at the Phoenix Theatre (also called the Cockpit), an indoor private playhouse, and when Philip Massinger died in 1640, Shirley became the principal playwright for the King's Men. The closing of the theaters two years later ended his career as dramatist, but he had the rare satisfaction of seeing his works revived successfully in the 1660's.

Shirley cannot be credited with landmark innovations or significant lasting influence, but he did produce a steady stream of popular plays in which he exploited the themes, devices, and character types of others while creating works uniquely his own, and he was in large measure responsible for the continued vitality of Renaissance drama into the 1640's. Whereas his tragedies are derivative and suggest the decadence of the serious drama of the period, the comedies not only recall those of his excellent predecessors, but also look forward to the comedies of the Restoration.

An antilicentiousness links Shirley to the Elizabethans more closely than to the Restoration playwrights. Whatever his genre—comedy, tragedy, or tragicomedy—virtue is rewarded, and although sexual wrongdoing is not condoned, reformation is accepted. His plays are not homiletic but are entertainments in the mainstream of earlier Elizabethan practice. Therefore, plot development and pacing are primary, sometimes to the detriment of characterization. In the comedies, this does not lessen the realism, for the characters are recognizable types, and the action is set in a realistically portrayed London. Shirley's London is not the city of Thomas Dekker, Ben Jonson, or Thomas Middleton (merchants and apprentices are rare in Shirley's comedies); it is closer to the Restoration London of George Etherege, William Wycherley, and William Congreve. Like those of these later playwrights, Shirley's plays are urbane comedies of manners that dramatize the often contrasting values of town, country, and court through skillfully developed plots that intermingle different comic modes: intellectual, sentimental, and situational.

The Master of the Revels licensed *Hyde Park* on April 20, 1632, and it probably was first presented at the Phoenix soon after to coincide with the seasonal opening of Hyde Park, a favorite London gathering place and sporting center which recently had become a public facility. Popular when premiered, the play was regularly performed prior to the closing of the theaters and was revived in 1668, when (according to diarist Samuel Pepys) actual horses were brought onstage for the racing scenes.

Hyde Park shares traits with earlier Elizabethan comedies: clever servants, letters that advance plots, disguise, and multiple plots. In addition, the romance between Carol and Fairfield recalls that of Beatrice and Benedick in William Shakespeare's *Much Ado About Nothing* (c. 1598-1599), whose ambience resembles that of *Hyde Park*, although Shakespeare's Italian milieu has become London's fashionable world of gentry and nobility. Carol also is descended from Kate of *The Taming of the Shrew* (c. 1593-1594); both are termagants who mock suitors and obscure their true feelings with biting wit. Francis Beaumont and John Fletcher's scornful lady character is another ancestor of Carol. Other links in characterization and in theme with earlier themes may also be rather easily traced. Despite these echoes of past practice, *Hyde Park* presents a realistic portrait of social habits in London at the height of the Caroline period. Further, although Carol and Fairfield recall Elizabethan predecessors, they also are forerunners of Millamant and Mirabell, bickering lovers in Congreve's *The Way of the World* (1700), their verbal sparring paralleling the proviso scene and marital conditions agreement in Congreve's play.

3091

In each of the three plots of *Hyde Park*, the action of which occurs on a single day, a woman is pursued by two rivals for her hand. During the play, the woman's position in each triangle changes unexpectedly. Mistress Bonavent's marriage to Lacy ends before it is consummated when her merchant husband surprisingly returns after a seven-year absence. Julietta, whom Lord Bonvile attempts to seduce, becomes instead his prospective wife. Carol, who earlier entered into an antimarriage pact with Fairfield, does a turnabout and proposes to him—allegedly to save the seemingly distraught man's life. Carol is important in the scheme of the play because she represents feminism, which questions enforced or arranged marriages and argues for greater freedom for women to make their own choices, including not to marry at all. Shirley balances the Carol-Fairfield story with the Bonavent plot, which stresses the importance of marriage as a social institution. Typical of comedies, the play ends on a conciliatory and celebratory note, with a couple reunited and marriages in prospect. Atypically, most of the suitors are unsuccessful (Lacy, Rider, Trier, and Venture), although they seem unaffected by their failure.

Its title notwithstanding, only the third and fourth acts of *Hyde Park* take place in the London park, where the suitor plots converge against a background of foot and horse racing, events that are metaphors for the main actions. Just as there are unexpected victors in the races, so are there surprise winners and losers in the suitors' pursuit of the women. The anticipated winners do not always prevail, with dark horses sometimes suddenly overtaking them. The racing motif strengthens the unity of the romantic story lines and focuses attention upon the theme of unpredictability in the course of love. More important, and the thematic core of the play, is Lord Bonvile's attempted seduction of Julietta. When she reacts to him with a lengthy and eloquent paean to chastity, he is repentant and asks for her hand in marriage. His reformation, the conversion of a lecher by dint of a woman's virtue, distinguishes him from the rake of Restoration drama and highlights a primary difference between this play and the licentious comedies of manners of the age that followed.

"Critical Evaluation" by Gerald H. Strauss

Bibliography:
Levin, Richard. "The Triple Plot of *Hyde Park*." *Modern Language Review* 62, no. 1 (January, 1967): 17-27. Demonstrates that Shirley achieves thematic unity and maintains continuity in his play through three analogous plots. Shows how the Hyde Park setting functions figuratively as well as dramatically.
Lucow, Ben. *James Shirley*. Boston: Twayne, 1981. An overview of Shirley's varied and prolific career. Starts with a brief biographical section and turns to a chronological analysis of Shirley's works. An authoritative introduction that reflects mainstream critical judgments.
Nason, Arthur Huntington. *James Shirley, Dramatist*. New York: Benjamin Blom, 1967. Includes extensive summaries of the plays. There is a minimum of critical analysis, but the brief comments are illuminating and not at all dated.
Shirley, James. *Hyde Park*. New York: Methuen, 1987. Includes the text of the play and commentary by Thomas Trussler that covers stage history, structure, and thematic matters.
Wertheim, Albert. "Games and Courtship in James Shirley's *Hyde Park*." *Anglia* 90 (1972): 71-91. Focuses upon the plot elements (primarily games, trials, and tricks) that unify the play. Shows how language and imagery not only reinforce the three plots but also tighten the overall structure.

HYDRIOTAPHIA, URN-BURIAL
Or, A Discourse of the Sepulchral Urns
Lately Found in Norfolk

Type of work: Philosophy
Author: Sir Thomas Browne (1605-1682)
First published: 1658

Hydriotaphia, Urn-Burial is one of the great glories of Renaissance scholarship and without doubt one of the greatest essays in English literature. The work is ostensibly a study on some forty or fifty Roman funeral urns that had been recently discovered near Norfolk. The wonderfully associative mind of the author immediately reads philosophical implications out of, and rich analogues into, the urns.

Regarded as one of the finest specimens of baroque prose of the seventeenth century, *Hydriotaphia, Urn-Burial* is also a superb example of the occasional essay. It is distinguished for a number of reasons. Like all of Sir Thomas Browne's works, it displays a combination of education and sensibility characteristic of the writers of the seventeenth century, for whom science was an equal partner with classical learning. *Hydriotaphia, Urn-Burial* is a demonstration of Browne's enormous reading, enviable memory, and intense interest in humanity's beliefs, habits, and hopes.

Browne uses the incidence of the discovery of these burial urns as a prompt for philosophical speculations about humankind, specifically the concepts of mutability and impermanence. The first chapters, largely descriptive of burial customs and living habits of past civilizations, are merely prelude to the more significant topic toward which the author is aiming in his thoughtful and provocative conclusion. The thrust of Browne's method becomes clear at the end of the fourth chapter, when he begins the process of reexamining various burial customs in the light of theological, and specifically Christian, concerns.

The final chapter of *Hydriotaphia, Urn-Burial* takes readers beyond the immediate subject of burial customs to contemplate the nature of death, life, and afterlife. In a poignant meditation on the inevitability of death and the vanity of human aspirations to overcome it, Browne muses in his conclusion on the implications of his findings. His vision, however, is not ultimately pessimistic. Paradoxically, the inability of people to guarantee immortality by their own efforts is balanced by the great comfort the author finds in his Christian faith. The promises of Christ provide him assurance that all people—even those whose deaths are marked by no monuments, whose remains are not preserved in funeral urns—may find true immortality in a realm where time and change have no meaning.

In the "Epistle Dedicatory," addressed to "My worthy and Honoured Friend, Thomas Le Gros, of Crostwick, Esquire," Browne sets his tone. He broods on the common fate of all people, asking who can know the fate of one's own bones or how often one is to be disinterred and scattered, as the bones in these Roman urns are now being brought again from their private seclusion. The uncertainty of one's ashes depresses his enthusiasm for earthly affairs at the same time that it excites his curiosity. He feels that it is his right and duty as physician, and man, to read the bones of our ancestors and learn from them, to make the living profit from the dead and to keep the living alive as long as possible.

Browne begins with a study of burial customs of ancient times, touching first on biblical Abraham and the patriarchs, and Adam, then proceeds whimsically to the assertion that God interred but one body, that of Moses. Browne next takes up the subject of the burning of corpses, which he asserts was widespread in ancient times. He begins with Homer's account of Patroclus and Achilles, discusses the older tradition in Thebes, and then ranges to Israel, to the Amazons, and even to the Americas.

Next Browne says he will not discuss the ceremonies and rites of cremation or interment that are generally touched on by authors, but will talk only on the collected bones and ashes of the Romans discovered recently in England. He then moves from this narrower subject to a learned discussion of the burial customs of the peoples loosely associated with, or suggested by, the predecessors of seventeenth century Englishmen—the Romans, Druids, Danes, and others.

He points out that Caesar expressly says that the priests of the Druids used to burn and bury. History is silent on whether this custom held in the land of the early Britons, but since history speaks out clearly that the Romans distinctly influenced these early natives of Britain in many ways—for example, in getting them to build temples and wear gowns and study Roman law with the intention of following it—probably, Browne feels, these people also followed their religious rites and customs in burial.

Browne further reminds his readers that in Norway and Denmark numerous burial urns obviously not of Roman origin in design are found containing not only bones but numerous other substances such as knives, pieces of iron, brass and wood, and, in Norway, one containing a "brass gilded Jewes-harp."

In the next chapter Browne continues with an inquiry into the various ways people have decorated the insides of sepulchres and tombs. He observes that people have not been so much concerned with how great they have been in life if they can be richly memorialized in death. He observes that the great affect great tombs, and large urns contain no mean ashes. He observes also the changing customs about the artifacts that have been placed in tombs, from the earliest customs when want dictated that only the most meager items be included to more opulent times when objects of much value were buried with the remains of the great people.

Browne also discusses the inscriptions that have headed graves, what kinds of bones make the best skeletons, the various positions in which peoples have placed their dead, and the time allowed between death and interment.

From the physical facts of life and death Browne rises to the spiritual. In these flights of fancy he, as a Christian, reaches his greatest heights of philosophy and poetry. He realizes that life is transitory, of short duration, and life after death should be of greater importance than life on earth. He believes, however, that many people, perhaps most people, throughout the ages have failed to anticipate the wonders of the next world because of eagerness to exhaust the pleasures of this world. His feelings on the subject are at the same time an affirmation of faith in religion, which is characteristic of his general attitude, and a horror at those people who are shortsighted in their overall view.

The full value of this magnificent work can be appreciated only by actual reading of some of the great organ-music lines, of which the following are typical:

> Were the happiness of the next world as closely apprehended as the felicities of this, it were a martyrdome to live; and unto such as consider none hereafter, it must be more than death to dye, which makes us amazed at those audacities, that durst be nothing, and return into their *Chaos* again.

> But to subsist in bones, and be but Pyramidally extant, is a fallacy in duration.

One of Browne's most eloquent meditations deserves a long quotation:

> But the iniquity of oblivion blindely scattereth her poppy, and deals with the memory of men without distinction to merit of perpetuity. Who can but pity the founder of the Pyramids? Herostratus lives

that burnt the Temple of Diana, he is almost lost that built it; Time hath spared the Epitaph of Adrian's horse, confounded that of himself. In vain we compute our felicities by the advantage of our good names, since bad have equall durations; and Thersites is like to live as long as Agamemnon. Who knows whether the best of men be known? or whether there be not more remarkable persons forgot, then any that stand remembered in the known account of time? Without the favour of the everlasting register, the first man had been as unknown as the last, and Methuselahs long life had been his only Chronicle.

Oblivion is not to be hired: The greater part must be content to be as though they had not been, to be found in the Register of God, not in the record of man. Twenty-seven Names make up the first story before the flood, and the recorded names ever since contain not one living Century. The number of the dead long exceedeth all that shall live. The night of time far surpasseth the day, and who knows when was the Aequinox? Every hour adds unto that current Arithmetique which scarce stands one moment.

In many ways the most philosophically incontrovertible and stylistically memorable of Browne's statements in this work is the oceanlike roll of "Grave-stones tell truth scarce fourty years. Generations passe while some trees stand, and old families last not three oaks." As these examples demonstrate, Browne's prose stands at a summit of the English language. It represents the achievement of an especially rich period in the history of the literature, and study of his vocabulary, rhetoric, and style continues to reveal not only the achievement of the Renaissance but also many truths that have not changed.

One of the curiosities associated with Browne is the fact that the author of *Hydriotaphia, Urn-Burial* became a victim of persons interested in burial places. His coffin was invaded in 1840 and his skull was stolen and subsequently sold by the sexton of the church in which he was interred.

Bibliography:
Bennett, Joan. *Sir Thomas Browne: A Man of Achievement in Literature*. Cambridge, England: Cambridge University Press, 1962. A chapter on *Hydriotaphia, Urn-Burial* examines Browne's thought and how the prose style reflects Browne's character and temperament.
Davis, Walter R. "*Urne Buriall*: A Descent into the Underworld." *Studies in the Literary Imagination* 10, no. 2 (Fall, 1977): 73-87. Sees *Hydriotaphia, Urn Burial* as a metaphorical journey of Browne's mind through various stages of faith and compares the book to similar works of exploration and meditation.
Donovan, Dennis G., Magaretha G. Hartley Herman, and Ann E. Imbrie. *Sir Thomas Browne and Robert Burton: A Reference Guide*. Boston: G. K. Hall, 1981. A very useful list of publications from 1643 to 1977 emphasizes criticism and interpretation of Browne and his work. Augments previous bibliographies of Browne; many annotations are extensive.
Fish, Stanley E., ed. *Seventeenth-Century Prose: Modern Essays in Criticism*. New York: Oxford University Press, 1971. A compendium of useful essays on the various prose styles in Browne's era. Of particular interest are "The Styles of Sir Thomas Browne," by Austin Warren; "Sir Thomas Browne: The Relationship of *Hydriotaphia, Urn Burial* and *The Garden of Cyprus*," by Frank L. Huntley; and "*Hydriotaphia, Urn Burial*: The Ethics of Mortality," by Leonard Nathanson.
Nathanson, Leonard. *The Strategy of Truth: A Study of Sir Thomas Browne*. Chicago: University of Chicago Press, 1967. Analysis and interpretation of *Hydriotaphia, Urn Burial* occupy a whole chapter, placing it in the larger framework of Browne's work.

HYMNS

Type of work: Poetry
Author: Callimachus (c. 303-c. 240 B.C.E.)
First published: Hymni, third century B.C.E. (English translation, 1755)

Callimachus' *Hymns* are an important contribution to the body of literature produced in the Egyptian city of Alexandria during the period following the death of Alexander the Great. The classical era of Athens had long passed, and under Ptolemy I Soter, Alexander's general who established Egypt as an independent kingdom in 305 B.C.E., literary and intellectual influence had shifted to Alexandria and its famous library.

Callimachus was born in Cyrene, a Greek city (modern Shahat) in Libya. He was trained in Athens, taught at Eleusis, and was eventually invited to Alexandria by King Ptolemy II Philadelphus, the youngest son of Ptolemy I Soter. Under the patronage of the Ptolemies, Callimachus served as librarian for about twenty years, during which he composed the catalog (*Pinakes*) of the library. This opportunity provided Callimachus a solid educational foundation and fostered the erudition for which his poetry is known.

Callimachus' *Hymns* are difficult to date. Although it is likely that they were written for religious occasions, it is not known for which ceremonies each was composed, nor whether they were for public or private celebrations. Their style—and in some cases, their content—display Callimachus' assertion that the age of the epic had long passed and that short and polished poems were best. It was this attitude that led to a dispute between Callimachus and his pupil Apollonius of Rhodes, who challenged Alexandrian standards and continued the Homeric epic tradition in his *Argonautica* (third century B.C.E.). The argument is reflected within the hymns themselves.

The first hymn, the shortest of the six with its ninety-five lines, addresses the birth and youth of Zeus, the most important of the Greek gods, and his subsequent rise to supremacy. This hymn exemplifies Callimachus' erudition, his delight in witty play with local geography and customs and, finally, his interest in competing traditions. Callimachus immediately introduces the contention between the island of Crete and the Peloponnesian region of Arcadia as the location of Zeus's birthplace. According to most traditions, Zeus's father, Cronus, fearing his children would one day overthrow him, threatened to devour them. Cronus' wife Rhea therefore fled from him when she was pregnant with Zeus. Tradition tends to favor Crete as the place where Rhea secretly gave birth to Zeus. Callimachus, however, elects Arcadia and cites a proverb of the Cretan poet Epimenides, "Cretans are liars, always," to justify his reasoning. He further accuses the Cretans of mere foolishness for having constructed a tomb for Zeus, who as a divinity is obviously immortal. To support Arcadia's claim, Callimachus notes a region there called "Rhea's primal childbed."

After he was born in Arcadia, Zeus was turned over to the nymph Neda and brought to Crete; en route to Knossos the navel falls at the town Thenae, nearby which was a place the locals called the Plain of the Navel. Callimachus decides another argument, that between Mount Dicte and Mount Ida as the Cretan mountain where Zeus was reared, in support of the former. On Mount Dicte, Zeus is protected by the Curetes, fostered by the nymph Adrasteia, and nourished by the milk of the she-goat Amaltheia and the honeycombs of the mountain's bees. Callimachus also addresses an alternative explanation of Zeus's ascent to superiority. Whereas many previous poets had attributed Zeus's rule to his luck when drawing lots with his brothers Poseidon and Hades, Callimachus ascribes Zeus's power rather to his ability to devise and execute perfect plans while young. Here the poet is likely alluding to Ptolemy II Philadelphus' rise to power over his elder brothers.

By all the means at his disposal, Callimachus removes Zeus's right to supremacy from mere acts of chance to his meritable power and might. The poet also addresses the symbols of Zeus, notably the eagle and mortal kings who rule all aspects of life (for which he cites the poet Hesiod), and connects Zeus's selection and favor of them as proof of his all-encompassing supremacy. The hymn closes on a prayer that petitions Zeus for prosperity.

The second hymn presents the joyful worship at Cyrene and the expectations of Apollo's epiphany on the Carneia, one of his feast days. Apollo, the multifaceted and beneficent god, will appear only to the good, among whom the poet numbers himself. Certain natural phenomena signal Apollo's approach to his followers. All the world is subsumed by Apollo's enchanting music, for he sits to the right of his father Zeus. Callimachus systematically celebrates the plethora of images connected to Apollo: his golden dress (symbolizing his wealth), his lyre, his bow, his beauty. He hails Apollo as the lord of archery, music, and prophecy, and as the founder of cities (Apollo was four years old when he founded his first) and altars.

Callimachus describes Apollo's visit to Battus, the founder of Cyrene, but he is not satisfied to end with a discussion of his hometown. He recalls that the celebratory cry "Hie! Hie! Paieon!" was invented at Delphi when Apollo slew the Pythian serpent. Earlier, Callimachus noted a palm from Delos, the island where Apollo's mother Leto gave birth to him. Callimachus thus brings together the global aspects of the god and in so doing emphasizes the majestic power he may bestow on his followers.

The second hymn closes with a story regarding Apollo and the goddess Envy, which seems to mask the tension between Callimachus and Apollonius of Rhodes. Callimachus' Apollo argues that whereas the sea may be vast (as is Apollonius' poem) it often carries much trash and worthless bunk. In this way, the hymn responds to its own beginning: Apollo not only visits the worthy but ruins the unworthy and inane. Callimachus concludes his hymn by imploring Apollo to relieve all places where the goddess Envy abides.

The third hymn, which is quite long, continues Callimachus' retelling of the origin of divine beings, a typical subject for hymns. Addressed to Artemis, the goddess of the hunt and moon and sister of Apollo, the hymn celebrates her decision to remain a virgin and turn to a life that stays away from the domestic affairs typical to women of ancient Greek society. This hymn, which shows Callimachus at his most playful and witty, commences by recanting Artemis' petition of her father, Zeus. This affords Callimachus the opportunity humorously to imagine a sibling rivalry between Artemis and Apollo. With Zeus's consent, Artemis assembles her entourage of nymphs and journeys with them to the smith of the cyclopes. Callimachus' wit shines in this comic episode, contrasting the concern of the maidenly nymphs with the brutishness of the cyclopes, and heightens Artemis' pivotal role between these two extremes. Callimachus further cites the interesting tradition of Hermes playing the bogeyman to anxious children.

Furnished with a bow and arrows and provided with hunting dogs by the god Pan, Artemis then turns to her first hunt. As with the hymn to Apollo, Callimachus provides a list of Artemis' attributes and symbols, ranging from her ability to ease the pains of childbirth to her deliverance of prosperity to her favorites. The poet reverently offers his own talents to Artemis and pledges to compose a song for her and her mother, Leto. In the remainder of the hymn, the poet discusses Artemis' attributes, highlights localities sacred to her, and names her favorites. This often humorous hymn closes with a more serious admonition to avoid her scorn.

The fourth hymn is the longest, extending to 326 lines, and celebrates the island Delos, where

Leto gave birth to Apollo. Skillfully, Callimachus recounts the boldness of the island (originally called Asteria) that offered asylum to Leto from Hera's anger when no other location on earth dared do so, and he decorates Delos' bravery with the well-polished story of the river god Peneius and his conversion to aid Leto. Callimachus thereby paints an interesting image of the internal tensions between Hera and the children of Zeus by another consort. The pace of the action before Apollo's birth allows him to tell an entertaining story, but the hymn is more than that, and it concludes with a discussion of the victorious perseverance of Apollo, Leto, and Delos itself. The hymn draws a direct correlation between Apollo and Ptolemy II Philadelphus.

The fifth hymn celebrates the ritual washing of a statue of Pallas Athene in the sea, as happened during the Plynteria festival in Athens. This ceremony, located in the town of Argos, provides the opportunity for the poet to tell the story of Athene's bath in the spring Hippocrene on Mount Helicon and to offer an alternative version of the blinding of Teiresias, the sage who was of fundamental importance to Oedipus and Odysseus in the revelation of their destinies. The hymn's speaker seems to be a priestess of the goddess, who tells the story and delivers admonitions to the followers while they wait in the procession.

Teiresias' mother is the nymph Chariclo, who is favored by Athene. One day, the unfortunate youth Teiresias sought to quench his thirst and found his way up Mount Helicon to the very spring where Athene had stopped to bathe. Having become a witness to the goddess naked, Teiresias was punished and his sight stolen from him. In response to the complaints of his mother, however, Athene consented to giving Teiresias second sight (the gift of prophecy), ability to understand the language of birds, long life, a useful walking staff, and a unique consciousness among the shades in the Underworld, the region of the dead. This story differs greatly from the other popular version, which is represented in Ovid's *Metamorphoses* (c. 8 C.E.).

The sixth hymn celebrates the earth mother Demeter. It was apparently composed for a feast (that of the Thesmophoria, most likely) at Alexandria. Although he cites the well-known story of Demeter's search and seasonal grief for her daughter Persephone, the poet decides to put aside the sorrowful story and celebrate Demeter's attributes and gifts. He offers a myth about the indigenous inhabitants of Greece and of Demeter's curse on the impious Erysichthon, who is driven mad with hunger for having offended the goddess who makes the earth abundant with food. Callimachus does not mention the traditionally gruesome ending of the tale in self-cannibalism but returns rather to an aspect of the feast, the procession of the Basket. He concludes the hymn with a prayer proper and a petition for prosperity.

The six hymns and other poems of Callimachus played an important role in the literary life of Alexandria and influenced later writers, among them the Roman poets Ovid, Catullus, and Propertius, who all recognized their debt to him.

Stephen C. Olbrys

Bibliography:

Bundy, Elroy L. "The Quarrel Between Kallimachos and Apollonios, Part I: The Epilogue of Kallimachos's Hymn to Apollo." *California Studies in Classical Antiquity* 5 (1972): 39-94. An interesting discussion regarding the debate of Alexandrian standards of poetry and its influence on the second hymn.

Ferguson, John. *Callimachus*. Boston: Twayne, 1980. An extremely useful and accessible overview of Callimachus' life and works. Chapter 7 offers a superior examination of important themes in the *Hymns* and a detailed discussion of the literary style, political ramifications, historical context, and composition of each hymn. An excellent source for beginners. Includes a concise bibliography on all aspects of Callimachus' work, notes, a chronology, and an index.

McKay, K. J. *Erysichthon: A Callimachean Comedy* (*Mnemosyne* Supplementum 7). Leiden, The Netherlands: E. J. Brill, 1962. Examines the style and meaning of the sixth hymn and its reflection of Callimachus' wit.

Pfeiffer, Rudolfus, ed. *Callimachus*. 2 vols. Oxford, England: Clarendon Press, 1949-1953. The standard commentary on the structure and meaning of Callimachus' texts. Technical and advanced.

Webster, T. B. L. *Hellenistic Poetry and Art*. London: Methuen, 1964. The chapter on Callimachus provides a solid and rewarding discussion of the poet in relation to the literary and historical context of his time.

HYPATIA
Or, New Foes with an Old Face

Type of work: Novel
Author: Charles Kingsley (1819-1875)
Type of plot: Historical
Time of plot: Fifth century
Locale: Egypt and Italy
First published: 1853

Principal characters:
PHILAMMON, a young monk
HYPATIA, a female Greek philosopher and teacher
RAPHAEL ABEN-EZRA, a young Jew and Hypatia's pupil
MIRIAM, an old Jewish crone
AMAL, a young Gothic chief
PELAGIA, Amal's mistress
ORESTES, Roman prefect of Alexandria

The Story:

Philammon might never have left the little colony of monks three hundred miles above Alexandria if he had not strayed into an ancient temple in search of kindling. There, on the temple walls, he saw paintings of a life unknown to him in his monastic retreat, and he longed to visit the greater outside world. That very day, against the advice of the abbot and Aufugus, a monk whom he highly respected, he started out in a small boat and traveled down the river toward Alexandria.

In that splendid city at the mouth of the Nile lived Hypatia, the beautiful philosopher and teacher, one of the last to champion the ancient Greek gods. As she sat with her books one day, she was visited by the Roman prefect, Orestes, with the news that Pelagia, a beautiful courtesan who was Hypatia's rival for the hearts and souls of men, had left the city. Pelagia had transferred her affections to Amal, a Goth chieftain, and had joined him on a trip up the Nile in search of Asgard, home of the old Gothic gods.

Cyril, the patriarch of Alexandria, had reported to Orestes that the Jews of the city were about to rise and slaughter the Christians, but Orestes chose to ignore the matter and let events take their course. Hypatia, who also had reason to oppose the Christian patriarch, suggested that Cyril make his charges before the Roman tribunal, which would, of course, postpone action against the Jews.

On his way to the palace, Orestes met a wealthy young Jew, Raphael Aben-Ezra. Raphael suggested that the prefect plead ignorance of any plot in his reply to Cyril. Raphael also disclosed to the Roman that Heraclian, a Roman leader, had recently sailed for Italy, where he planned to destroy the Gothic conquerors of Rome and make himself emperor. His news led Orestes to think of the power he might hold south of the Mediterranean if the expedition succeeded.

Sailing down the Nile, Philammon met Pelagia and the party of Goths traveling in the opposite direction. He helped the men kill a hippopotamus. When he warned them that they could never cross the cataracts to the south, the Goths decided to turn back. Philammon was given a place in their boat.

Orestes sent Hypatia a letter delivered by the old Jewish crone Miriam. It contained Raphael's news and a proposal that Hypatia marry the prefect and share the throne he was planning to create for himself in Egypt. Hypatia's reply was that she would accept the offer if Orestes would renounce his Christian faith and aid her in restoring the Greek gods. Having no desire to face excommunication, Orestes was disturbed by her answer. At Raphael's suggestion, he decided to wait for a month in the hope that Hypatia's desire to marry a future emperor would overcome her religious zeal.

When they arrived in Alexandria, Philammon left the Goths and went to deliver to the patriarch Cyril the letters of introduction he carried. While waiting to see the patriarch, Philammon overheard a plot to raid the Jewish quarter the next day.

That night as he lay in bed in the patriarch's house, Philammon heard cries that the Jews were burning Alexander's Church. Joining a crowd of monks hurrying toward the edifice, he was attacked by a band of Hebrew marauders. The report of the conflagration, however, was false; it had been a trick of the Jews to lure the Christians into ambush. During the street fighting, the Roman constabulary, which was supposed to keep order, remained aloof.

Miriam had taken a mysterious interest in Raphael's welfare. The next morning, she hastened to his quarters to warn him to flee. Christians were attacking the Jewish quarter and were pillaging the houses and expelling their inhabitants. To Miriam's exasperation, Raphael showed no interest in the fate of his wealth. Calmly exchanging his rich robes for a Christian's tattered rags, he prepared to leave the city. Miriam was left to save what she could of his possessions.

Philammon was one of the Christians who aided in despoiling the Jews. During the rioting, he began to compare the conduct of the monks of Alexandria with the principles of charity and good works he had been taught. Hearing of Hypatia and her teachings, he naïvely went to the museum where she lectured, in the hope of converting her to Christianity by his arguments. Nearly put out of the building by her pupils when he rose to dispute with her, he was spared at Hypatia's request. After the lecture, she invited him to visit her the following day.

The Alexandrian monks were incensed when they learned that Philammon had been to listen to the discourse of a pagan. When he visited Hypatia again, they accused him of being a heretic, and the young monk barely escaped being murdered. Charmed by Hypatia's beauty and purity, Philammon begged to become her pupil.

Raphael had fled to Italy and found himself in a devastated Rome. Heraclian, after his defeat by the Goths, was preparing to reembark for Africa. After Raphael had saved one member of the ill-fated expedition and his daughter, Victoria, from two barbarian soldiers, he sailed with them from Ostia to Berenice, a port on the coast of Africa.

Meanwhile, in Alexandria, Philammon had become Hypatia's favorite pupil. Learning that the youth had deserted his Christian brethren, Aufugus went to the city to find him. One day, the two men met in the street. Aufugus, seeing that Philammon was determined to remain with his mentor, declared that the young monk was actually his slave and appealed to Orestes, who was passing by, to force Philammon to go with him. Philammon fled to take temporary refuge with the Goths in Pelagia's house.

After Philammon had returned to his own rooms, he received a summons from Miriam. She confirmed the fact that he was Aufugus' slave, for she had seen Philammon bought in Athens fifteen years before. Although Miriam had received the report of Heraclian's defeat by fast messenger, she wrote a letter which declared that Heraclian had been the victor. She sent Philammon to deliver the letter to Orestes.

The prefect immediately planned a great celebration, in which the beautiful Pelagia should dance as Venus Anadyomene. Philammon hotly objected to the plan, for when Miriam told him he was a slave she had implied also that Pelagia was his sister. Orestes was annoyed and ordered the monk to be thrown into jail. There, Philammon was held prisoner until the day of the celebration. Released, he hurried to the arena in time to witness the slaughter of some Libyan slaves by professional gladiators. Orestes, with Hypatia beside him, watched from his box.

When Pelagia was carried into the amphitheater by an elephant and introduced as Venus, Orestes' hirelings tried to raise a cry to proclaim him Emperor of Africa. No one responded. Pelagia danced before her audience until Philammon, overcome by shame, could bear the sight no longer. Running to stop her shameful dance, he was caught up by the elephant's trunk and would have been dashed to death if Pelagia had not persuaded the animal to put him down. Pelagia left the amphitheater. Philammon was hustled away by the guards.

Orestes, however, was determined that his plan should succeed. When the uproar caused by Philammon began to die down, he stepped forward and offered himself as emperor. As had been prearranged, the city authorities began a clamor for him; but hardly had they started their outcry when a monk in the topmost tiers shouted that Heraclian had been defeated. Orestes and Hypatia fled.

When he returned home, Philammon found Pelagia in his quarters. He begged his sister, as he now called her, to leave the Goth, Amal, and repent her ways, but the courtesan refused. Instead, she entreated him to ask Hypatia to accept her as a pupil, so that Amal, whose affection for her was failing, would love and respect her as the Greek woman was respected. Hypatia, however, had no pity for her hated rival. Philammon, carrying the news of her refusal to his sister, could not help thinking fondly of his own religion with its offer of pity to all transgressors.

Hypatia knew the populace would soon be clamoring for her blood and that she would be forced to flee. In one last desperate effort to hold to her creed, she forced herself into a trance that she might have a visitation from the gods. The only face she saw, however, was Pelagia's.

When Miriam visited Hypatia the same day with the promise that she should see Apollo that night if she would visit the house of the Jewish woman, the distraught philosopher agreed; but the Apollo the crone showed her was Philammon, stupefied by drugged wine. As Miriam had foreseen, Hypatia realized at last that the only gods she would ever see were those that existed in her own mind. Shamed and angered, she went away. The final blow to fall on Hypatia was the news Raphael brought her on his return to Alexandria the next day. Under the persuasion of Augustine, the famous philosopher-monk, he had become a converted Catholic before leaving Berenice and had married Victoria. That afternoon, as she started for the museum to give her farewell lecture, Hypatia was torn to pieces by some of Cyril's monks.

When he learned of Hypatia's fate, Philammon visited Pelagia and pleaded with her to flee with him. He then met Amal by chance. In a struggle that ensued, they fell from a tower together, and the Goth was killed. After Amal's death, Pelagia was willing to leave the city. Together they returned to the desert, where Pelagia lived in solitary penitence and Philammon became abbot, eventually, of the community he had left. Brother and sister died at the same time and were buried in a common grave.

Before he departed from Alexandria forever, Raphael learned from Miriam that she was his mother. Jewish by birth, she had been converted to Christianity and had lived in a convent until it was sacked by heathens. Afterward, she had renounced her faith and had sworn the destruction of everyone not of her own race. Raphael had been given to a rich Jewish woman, who had represented him to her husband as her own child. After confessing her relationship to her son, Miriam died on his shoulder. She had been mortally wounded by the Goths after the death of their leader.

The victory that the patriarch Cyril gained by Hypatia's death was only temporary. Although it marked the end of her creed in Egypt, it also signified the decline of the Egyptian church; for the Christians, splitting into many factions, did not hesitate to use on one another the same violence they had once displayed toward the Greek philosopher.

Critical Evaluation:

Charles Kingsley, the son of a clergyman of the Church of England and himself a clergyman, studied at Cambridge University and was the parish priest for the Anglican parish in Eversley, Hampshire, from 1842 until his death. He read widely, especially on historical subjects, and was Regius Professor of Modern History at Cambridge University from 1860 to 1869. He wrote pamphlets in support of progressive reforms and was known as a Christian Socialist because of his interest in improving the social and economic life of the working classes. He also wrote poetry, and some of his novels were best-sellers. His first two novels, *Yeast* (1848) and *Alton Locke* (1850), dealt with contemporary social problems; *Hypatia* represented a shift in his literary interests away from social problems and toward more specifically religious themes.

Kingsley was concerned about two major cultural trends that were strong during the 1840's and 1850's: the spread of rationalist and Transcendentalist ideas, especially through the works of Edward Gibbon and the American philosopher Ralph Waldo Emerson, and the growing strength of Catholicism, in the forms of both Roman Catholicism and the Oxford Movement, which sought to increase the ceremonial aspects of worship in the Church of England. Gibbon, the historian of *The History of the Decline and Fall of the Roman Empire* (1776-1788), had challenged Christianity by arguing that the new religion was partially responsible for weakening the bonds of the Roman Empire. Emerson taught that humans possessed the innate and intuitive capacity to know the truth; social customs, organized religion, and orthodox doctrines interfered with the search for truth and the relationship between individuals and God. Simultaneously, Catholicism was growing strong. The Roman Catholic church itself was increasing in numbers, in part due to the conversions of several prominent Anglicans, most notably John Henry Newman. These conversions, along with the church's confident assertions of papal authority, seemed to foreshadow the reconversion of England itself. Within the Church of England, the Oxford Movement, or Anglo-Catholicism—which denied that Anglicanism was Protestant—was making headway; it emphasized the medieval elements in Anglican doctrine and worship. By the middle of the century, many Anglicans were afraid that English Protestantism was about to be overwhelmed from the left by rationalism and from the right by Catholicism.

Hypatia is part of a four-way debate in fictional form on these religious issues. In 1847, Elizabeth Harris published a novel, *From Oxford to Rome, and How It Fared with Some Who Lately Made the Journey*, which told the story of a fictional character who had been raised a Protestant, became an Emersonian Transcendentalist, then an Anglo-Catholic, and then a Roman Catholic, but who regretted ever having left his original church. John Henry Newman read this work and was stimulated to write one of his own, *Loss and Gain* (1848), an autobiographical piece that satirized the various religious currents of the day, described how conversion to Roman Catholicism brought the gain of religious certitude, and emphasized the virtues of celibacy. Kingsley, who had already published two novels, wrote *Hypatia: Or, New Foes with an Old Face* in response to Newman. The subtitle that Kingsley gave his novel indicates the topical nature of his themes; it alerted his readers to expect rebuttals of both agnostic rationalism and the authority of tradition. Angered by Kingsley's depiction of the patristic church, Nicholas Cardinal Wiseman, the leader of Roman Catholicism in England, published a novel of his own, *Fabiola* (1854), and Newman published *Callista* (1856) to defend the ancient church against Kingsley's attack.

Hypatia rejected the ideology of Transcendentalism by stressing the road to salvation offered by orthodox Christianity. Kingsley made Hypatia, ostensibly the novel's central character, a sympathetic figure. Committed to reason, she wants to revive the pagan idea of Nature's life force in the from of Neoplatonic philosophy. (Neoplatonism teaches that knowledge comes from recognizing a thing's essential form, rather than from observing its many incidental qualities.) At the end of the novel, however, she comes to learn that paganism is dead. In a dramatic scene, she is stripped naked and murdered by a mob of fanatical monks, just as she is about to realize the truth of the pure, simple Christianity of the Protestant Reformation. Kingsley's message here is to warn of both the inadequacy of rationalism and the dangers of superstition.

The novel's main theme, however, is the rejection of Catholic themes. Hatred of celibacy pervades the story. The monks whom Philammon meets in Alexandria are a violent, ignorant, and intriguing lot led by the Patriarch Cyril of Alexandria, whose fundamental Christian commitment is obscured by fanaticism and lack of scruples. For Kingsley, love reaches full perfection in the love between man and woman, and celibate monks therefore lack a central Christian virtue. The story challenges Roman Catholicism's valuation of the authority of the fourth and fifth century church fathers by describing a church that has become obsessed with jealousy, petty rivalries, and vicious theological quarrels. Although Kingsley gives some credit to Cyril and Augustine, he clearly denies that the nineteenth century church should appeal to the patristic age for its justification. Finally, the story hints at the corruption caused by the connection between church and state forged during the fourth century. Emperors had ceased to persecute the church; they bribed it instead.

Kingsley adds several positive messages, however, to his tale. He praises marriage; Raphael Aben-Ezra, one of the novel's few fully admirable characters, becomes a Christian only after Bishop Synesius of Cyrene shows him that apostolic Christianity values marriage and that celibacy is a sign of the church's decay. Marriage, the highest form of love, thus even has the power to save souls. Kingsley also used the novel to voice his belief in what was called "Muscular Christianity." Synesius, a man of vigor who loved hunting, riding, good deeds, and hymn-writing, is a caricature of the bluff Victorian parson and squire. Amal and the Goths, filled with barbaric vitality and violence, point to a future when the masculine, Protestant, Germanic peoples of northern Europe will overshadow and purify the effeminate, Catholic peoples of the Mediterranean. Hence, the novel ends with hope. Although Philammon returns to his little colony of monks, he does so only because the world is not ready for the purified Christianity that is to come.

"Critical Evaluation" by D. G. Paz

Bibliography:

Chapman, Raymond. *Faith and Revolt: Studies in the Literary Influence of the Oxford Movement.* London: Weidenfeld and Nicolson, 1970. This book explores the traces that the Oxford Movement left on nineteenth century literature. Three chapters compare and contrast Kingsley's and John Henry Newman's religious views.

Martin, Robert Bernard. *The Dust of Combat: A Life of Charles Kingsley.* New York: W. W. Norton, 1960. The best biography of the man. A chapter is devoted to Kingsley's relationship with his publishers, the genesis of *Hypatia*, and his efforts to publish it in serial and book forms.

Sanders, Andrew. *The Victorian Historical Novel, 1840-1880*. New York: St. Martin's Press, 1979. A critical examination of a select group of novels written under the influence of Sir Walter Scott, focusing on works by the great midcentury writers. A chapter discusses *Hypatia* and the rejoinders to it, *Fabiola* and *Callista*.

Vance, Norman. *The Sinews of the Spirit: The Ideal of Christian Manliness in Victorian Literature and Religious Thought*. Cambridge, England: Cambridge University Press, 1985. Covering the period from the early 1830's to the late 1860's, this is an important study of the ways that Victorians attempted to combine various meanings of "Christian" and "manliness." A chapter compares the attitudes toward celibacy of Kingsley and Newman.

Wolff, Robert Lee. *Gains and Losses: Novels of Faith and Doubt in Victorian England*. New York: Garland, 1977. This is a comprehensive critical discussion of several hundred novels with religious themes. It has an extensive analysis of *Hypatia*, and it explores the relationships between that novel and the earlier works by Elizabeth Harris and John Henry Newman.

THE HYPOCHONDRIAC

Type of work: Drama
Author: Molière (Jean-Baptiste Poquelin, 1622-1673)
Type of plot: Comedy
Time of plot: Seventeenth century
Locale: Paris
First performed: 1673; first published, 1674 as *Le Malade imaginaire* (English translation, 1732)

Principal characters:
    ARGAN, an imaginary invalid
    BÉLINE, his second wife
    ANGÉLIQUE, Argan's daughter
    CLÉANTE, her lover
    BÉRALDE, Argan's brother
    THOMAS DIAFOIRUS, the doctor's son
    TOINETTE, Argan's maidservant

The Story:

Argan was the worst sort of hypochondriac. Each day saw him trying some sort of new drug, and as a result the doctor and the apothecary could exist almost exclusively on their profits from Argan. Toinette, his maidservant, was certain that there was absolutely nothing the matter with her master, but she tried in vain to persuade him not to worry about his health. He refused to listen to her, determined to be an invalid.

He was encouraged in his supposed illness by his doctor and by Béline, his second wife, who used his weakness to further her schemes to get his money. Because the law said that a second wife could not inherit, it was essential to Béline that Argan make a settlement on her while he still lived. To that end also she tried to get him to place his two daughters in a convent, so that they could not interfere or claim money for themselves.

Argan had plans for his older daughter, Angélique. He was intending to force her betrothal to his doctor's son in order to have a doctor in the family. He told the girl that a dutiful daughter would take a husband useful to her father, but Angélique, who loved a young man named Cléante, begged her father not to force her to marry Thomas Diafoirus, the doctor's son. Argan was firm, however, because the young man would also inherit a large sum of money from his father and another from his uncle, the apothecary. If Angélique would not obey his wishes, he threatened to place her in a convent, as her stepmother wished him to do. Toinette scolded him severely for trying to force his daughter to marry against her wishes, but he would not be moved. Toinette, wishing to help Angélique, got word to Cléante that his beloved was to be married off to someone else.

Cléante disguised himself as the friend of Angélique's singing master and told Argan that he had been sent to give her a lesson. Toinette pretended to change her mind and sympathize with Argan's position regarding the marriage. In that way she could offer to guard Angélique, while in reality giving the young lovers an opportunity to be alone together.

While pretending to be the teacher, Cléante had to witness the meeting between Thomas and Angélique. Thomas was a great boob of a boy who quoted memorized speeches to Argan, Angélique, and Béline. His father, the doctor, was quite proud that Thomas had always been a little slow in learning and that he followed blindly the opinions of the ancients, not accepting such new medical discoveries, for example, as the thesis that blood circulated through the system.

Poor Angélique knew that she could never marry such a stupid oaf. She begged her father at least to give her time to become acquainted with Thomas, but the most he would give her was four days. At the end of that period, she must either marry Thomas or go into a convent. In order to be assured of Argan's money, Béline continued to plead with him to choose the convent for his daughter.

Argan's brother, Béralde, called on him and also pleaded Angélique's cause. He thought it wicked to force her to marry against her wishes, and he knew that Argan was not really ill and did not need a doctor in the family. In fact, he knew that the doctor would soon cause his brother's death by the constant "drenching" of his abdomen. Béralde sent the medicines away, whereupon the doctor renounced his patient and predicted his death within four days. The apothecary canceled his contract to give his nephew a marriage settlement, and neither of the professionals would be soothed by Argan's protestations that it was his brother and not he who had denounced them and their treatments. Argan believed that he would surely die without their attention.

Toinette and Béralde decided to trick the hypochondriac. Toinette disguised herself as a physician and told Argan that his former doctor had been entirely mistaken in his diagnosis of Argan's illness. His liver and bowels were not ailing, but his lungs were; he must cut off his arm and pluck out his eye because they were drawing off all his strength. Even Argan would not agree to such a drastic remedy. The poor man felt he was doomed.

Nevertheless, he would not relent concerning Angélique. Since the doctor and the apothecary had broken the marriage contract, Angélique must go to a convent and become a nun. When Béralde accused him of being influenced by his wife, Argan agreed to Toinette's suggestion that he allow his wife to prove her love for him. Because Toinette knew Béline's greed, she suggested that Argan act dead so as to see from her response that it was him she loved and not his money.

The plan was carried out. When Toinette cried to Béline that Argan was dead, the wife praised heaven that she was rid of her dirty, disgusting husband, and she tried to bribe Toinette to help her keep Argan's death a secret until she could get certain papers and money into her possession. At that, Argan rose from his supposed deathbed to confront his wife, who fled in terror.

Toinette persuaded Argan to try the same plan with his daughter, and when Angélique was told that her father was dead, she wept for him. Cléante came into the room and Angélique told him that now she could not marry him. Her father was dead, and she could make amends for her previous refusals to obey him only by carrying out his wishes now. Argan again rose from his deathbed, this time to bless his daughter for her faithfulness. Toinette and Béralde reminded him of his daughter's love and of his duty to reward her by allowing her to marry the man of her choice. Argan agreed that she could marry Cléante if he would become a doctor and minister to Argan's needs. Cléante was willing, but Béralde had a better idea. Argan should become a doctor himself; then he could give himself constant attention. All that was needed was that he don cap and gown. He could then spout gibberish and make it sound learned. So the matter was settled, and the old hypochondriac gave his blessing to the young lovers.

Critical Evaluation:

On February 17, 1673, the fourth performance of *The Hypochondriac* was staged with Molière playing the role of the hypochondriac Argan. Toward the end of the final scene, Molière was seized with a fit of choking brought on by a hemorrhage of the lungs. However, such was his dedication and strength of will, that he managed to finish the scene and take his bows without his fellow actors even realizing his condition. He collapsed immediately after the final curtain call, was carried home, and died within a few hours. It was one of the most dramatic deaths in literary history. Aside from its poignancy, the incident reflected the most crucial aspect of Molière's genius: his ability to convert painful realities into joyous farce, to defy the limitations of human life through comedy of the most superb and transcendent quality.

The Hypochondriac (also translated as *The Imaginary Invalid*) is the last of Molière's plays and the culmination of an art that had its roots both in the traditions of old French farce and in the Italian *commedia dell'arte* form. Features of the former can be detected in the play's irrepressible high spirits, its uproarious slapstick, and its hilarious and rollicking episodes. The influence of *commedia dell'arte* shows in Molière's use of masks, a device with which he never ceased to experiment. After initially using masks the French neoclassicists had adopted from the Italian theater, he soon modified and expanded their function until they became a device perfectly suited to the expression of his comic genius. In *The Hypochondriac*, masks are employed with particular effectiveness in the characterization of the various doctors.

Molière would not have become the great writer that he was if he had not transcended his artistic origins and transformed his raw materials with the spark of genius. As it was, that spark kindled comedies with unforgettable characters and universal themes, and it produced plays of unsurpassed comedy, rich in passion, meaning, and implication.

The Hypochondriac contains some of Molière's most memorable characters; Argan in particular is one of his finest creations. Like all of Molière's comic heroes, Argan has fallen prey to an obsession that dominates his every thought and action. He is a domestic tyrant whose entire household revolves around treatment of his imagined illness, and whose selfishness extends to the point that he attempts to force his daughter into marriage with a witless doctor, so that he can profit from free medical attention. He is opposed every step of the way and eventually duped by the bold, clever, and inventive maidservant, Toinette. Surrounding these two central figures are a cluster of minor characters including Argan's lovely and generous daughter Angélique; his scheming and greedy second wife Béline; his practical, sensible brother Béralde; his daughter's suitor, the automaton Thomas Diafoirus; and a motley assortment of doctors and apothecaries, among them Monsieur Purgon, Monsieur Fleurant, and Monsieur Diafoirus the elder. In all of these characterizations, Molière presents universal types rather than unique individuals; he concentrates on the character's dominant traits, simplifying so as to create a single powerful dramatic effect. As in all his comedies, Molière subordinates plot to characterization in *The Hypochondriac*; he created the roles to fit the actors who were to perform them, supplying them with a plot just sufficient to allow them room to develop those roles. Above all, the plays were written to be performed rather than read; and the plots are marked by a blissful disregard of probability and a constant intrusion of musical interludes, song, and dance.

The Hypochondriac is a play of considerable thematic complexity. On the surface it is an attack on incompetent doctors and unscrupulous quacks, but many critics have seen deeper parallels between the open satire on medicine and a disguised attack on religion that they perceive in the play. Whether or not the author consciously intended those parallels, there are certainly many analogies between the doctors in *The Hypochondriac* and priests and theologians. Like Argan's doctors, churchmen of Molière's time preached with unbending dogmatism, summarily condemned anyone who questioned their authority, and propagated more of their kind through obscure and inaccessible initiation rites. Just as Monsieur Purgon and

Monsieur Fleurant dispense their drugs, priests dispense blessings, and Argan is as dependent on his apothecary as a religious fanatic on his confessor.

Beneath this parallel between medicine and religion lies the crucial theme in the play, that blind obedience to a fallible authority is dangerous. This theme is conveyed in a number of ways, primarily through the characterization of Argan, the extreme example of a man who has totally surrendered his free will to others and thereby lost his ability to reason clearly. He is so at the mercy of the doctors that he accepts without question the curse that Monsieur Purgon delivers as punishment when his patient delays taking his enema by several minutes: "I will that before four days are up you get into an incurable state." This central theme is also reflected in several minor relationships: Monsieur Fleurant, the apothecary, takes orders blindly from his superior in the medical hierarchy, Monsieur Purgon, and Thomas Diafoirus worships the ancients and follows his father's commands as a puppet obeys a puppeteer.

The dialogue also conveys this theme and stresses the parallel between medical and theological dogmatism. The biblical echo is unmistakable, for example, when Toinette, disguised as a doctor, advises Argan to cut off one arm and gouge out one eye; one hears behind the line the admonition to sinners in Mark, 9:43-47, "And if thy hand offend thee, cut it off. . . . And if thine eye offend thee, pluck it out." The implications are provocative. At least one viable interpretation is that Molière is objecting to the abuse of the body and denial of its natural needs, and consequent warping of the spirit, occasioned both by absurd medical practice and the excesses of Christianity. Also fascinating is Molière's constant use of numbers, suggestive both of meaningless medical jargon and religious superstition. Argan in the opening scene equates the quantity of medicines consumed and enemas administered in a month to the quality of his health, much as a scrupulous devotee might worry that he or she had recited too few rosaries or lit too few votive candles during the week. Likewise, Monsieur Purgon's absurd formula for the proper number of grains of salt to put on an egg ("Six, eight, ten, using even numbers; just as in drugs you use uneven numbers") may be Molière's way of satirizing not only contemporary medical gimmicks but also such Church practices as indulgences sold to cut down the length of one's stay in purgatory.

It is above all Molière's unsurpassed comedy, however, that an audience remembers, and that ensures the ongoing popularity of *The Hypochondriac*. Scenes of sheer fun, such as Argan's tabulation of his monthly medical expenses, or Thomas Diafoirus' bungled attempt to recite his memorized declaration of love, are unforgettable, as is the moment when the invalid flies out of his chair, brandishing a stick, to chase a maidservant around the table before he suddenly realizes he cannot walk. Now, as in 1673, audiences roar with laughter.

"Critical Evaluation" by Nancy G. Ballard

Bibliography:

Hubert, Judd D. *Molière and the Comedy of Intellect*. Berkeley: University of California Press, 1962. In the penultimate chapter, Hubert explores comic uses of language in *The Hypochondriac* and discusses the irony that Molière, who was then dying, played the role of an imaginary invalid in the first performances of his last comedy.

Johnson, Roger, Jr., Editha S. Neumann, and Guy T. Trail, eds. *Molière and the Commonwealth of Letters: Patrimony and Posterity*. Jackson: University Press of Mississippi, 1975. Contains many essays on the critical reception of Molière's comedies after his death in 1673, as well as an excellent bibliography and a survey of criticism on Molière.

Knutson, Harold C. *The Triumph of Wit: Molière and Restoration Comedy*. Columbus: Ohio

State University Press, 1988. Discusses such important English Restoration playwrights as John Dryden and William Wycherley, who imitated plays by Molière. Interprets engravings by Molière's contemporaries to show that Argan differed both in style of clothing and in behavior from more sympathetic characters.

Moore, Will G. *Molière: A New Criticism*. Oxford, England: Clarendon Press, 1949. An excellent introduction to Molière's comedies. Stresses that Molière was not just a playwright but also an actor and the head of a theatrical troupe. Examines the role of mime and nonverbal gestures in Molière's plays.

Walker, Hallam. *Molière*. Rev. ed. Boston: Twayne, 1990. Contains an annotated bibliography of critical studies on Molière and discusses the importance of music and dance in *The Hypochondriac*, which was created by Molière in collaboration with the composer Charpentier and the choreographer Beauchamp.